Trademark and Unfair Competition Conflicts

With the rise of internet marketing and e-commerce around the world, international and cross-border conflicts in trademark and unfair competition law have become increasingly important. In this groundbreaking work, Tim Dornis—who, in addition to his scholarly pursuits, has worked as an attorney, a public prosecutor, and a judge, giving him experience in both civil and common law jurisdictions—presents the historical-comparative, doctrinal, and economic aspects of trademark and unfair competition conflicts law. This book should be read by any scholar or practitioner interested in the international aspects of intellectual property generally, and trademark and unfair competition law specifically. This title is also available as Open Access on Cambridge Core at http://dx.doi.org/10.1017/9781316651285.

Tim W. Dornis holds the Chair in Private Law, International Private and Economic Law, and Comparative Law at Leuphana Law School, Germany. He studied law and economics in Germany (Eberhard Karls Universität Tübingen) and in the United States (Columbia University, LL.M. (James Kent Scholar), and Stanford Law School, J.S.M.). Before his appointment, Professor Dornis spent several years practicing in an international law firm and as a civil law judge. His scholarship has been awarded a number of prizes and he frequently publishes in international law reviews and journals.

Cambridge Intellectual Property and Information Law

As its economic potential has rapidly expanded, intellectual property has become a subject of front-rank legal importance. *Cambridge Intellectual Property and Information Law* is a series of monograph studies of major current issues in intellectual property. Each volume contains a mix of international, European, comparative and national law, making this a highly significant series for practitioners, judges and academic researchers in many countries.

A list of books in the series can be found at the end of this volume.

Trademark and Unfair Competition Conflicts

Historical-Comparative, Doctrinal, and Economic Perspectives

Tim W. Dornis

Leuphana University (Germany)

CAMBRIDGE
UNIVERSITY PRESS

CAMBRIDGE
UNIVERSITY PRESS

University Printing House, Cambridge CB2 8BS, United Kingdom

One Liberty Plaza, 20th Floor, New York, NY 10006, USA

477 Williamstown Road, Port Melbourne, VIC 3207, Australia

4843/24, 2nd Floor, Ansari Road, Daryaganj, Delhi – 110002, India

79 Anson Road, #06–04/06, Singapore 079906

Cambridge University Press is part of the University of Cambridge.

It furthers the University's mission by disseminating knowledge in the pursuit of education, learning, and research at the highest international levels of excellence.

www.cambridge.org
Information on this title: www.cambridge.org/9781107155060
10.1017/9781316651285

First published 2017

A catalogue record for this publication is available from the British Library.

Library of Congress Cataloging-in-Publication Data
Names: Dornis, Tim W., author.
Title: Trademark and unfair competition conflicts : historical-comparative, doctrinal, and economic perspectives / Tim W. Dornis.
Description: Cambridge, United Kingdom; New York : Cambridge University Press, 2017. | Series: Cambridge intellectual property and information law; 34
Identifiers: LCCN 2016031771 | ISBN 9781107155060 (hardback)
Subjects: LCSH: Conflict of laws – Trademarks. | Conflict of laws – Competition, Unfair. | Trademark – Law and legislation. | Competition, Unfair. | Antitrust law.
Classification: LCC K7571 .D67 2017 | DDC 346.04/88–dc23
LC record available at https://lccn.loc.gov/2016031771

ISBN 978-1-107-15506-0 Hardback

This book is dedicated to my mother,

Ursula Dornis-Briem (1944–2014).

Contents

Acknowledgments

My work in this field commenced almost ten years ago. At that time, I was sitting on the bench as a judge at the Regional Court of Stuttgart in Germany. In the beginning, it was little more than curiosity about the vexing problems in international trademark and unfair competition conflicts. However, it quickly became obvious that the complexity of the topic invited—indeed, required—an extensive scholarly endeavor and that my fascination (not to say obsession) strongly suggested a return to full-time academia. This is the path I took when I decided to transform my ideas into a book. In 2014, the manuscript was approved by the Faculty of Law at the University of Zurich (Switzerland) as a postdoctoral habilitation thesis. The text that was submitted for print is current as of December 2015.

I have presented ideas, concepts, and excerpts from this book at a number of conferences and other academic fora, including the 2008 and 2009 fellows' sessions at the Stanford Program in International Legal Studies, the 2009 Stanford JSD colloquium, the 2009 Bay Area Fellows' Intellectual Property and Technology Law Workshop at Berkeley University School of Law, the 2011 Habilitationskolloquium at the Max Planck Institute for Comparative and International Private Law, and the 2011 Global Fellow Forum sessions that I attended as a Global Fellow from Practice and Government at New York University School of Law. I am grateful for all the helpful comments I received on these and other occasions. In addition, I am indebted to my many colleagues and friends for enduring the discussions that I forced on them in recent years. I have benefited immensely from your collegiality, patience, and ideas.

My research abroad, notably as a fellow at the Stanford Program in International Legal Studies, was funded by the Deutsche Forschungsgemeinschaft with a full research scholarship. The Swiss National Science Foundation has generously supported an open-access publication of this book with a grant for the promotion of scholarly research.

In addition to these institutions, I owe particular thanks to my habilitation adviser, Andreas Heinemann (University of Zurich). First of all,

I must thank him for giving me the chance to embark on such an ambitious project at a time when expectations were rather humble. He also served as an excellent mentor while providing me with the academic freedom necessary to develop my own ideas. Furthermore, I wish to thank Wolfgang Ernst (Oxford University), Franco Ferrari (New York University), and Beate Gsell (Ludwig-Maximilians-Universität of Munich) not only for being my role models from the time I was a young scholar but also for granting me valuable advice and words of encouragement along the way. Two other individuals who made an iconic imprint on me when I was their student are Barton Beebe (New York University) and Mark A. Lemley (Stanford University). They played a tremendous role in fostering and enhancing my modest understanding of intellectual property law in all its beauty.

I would also like to thank Matt Gallaway (Cambridge University Press) for his swift and professional handling of my manuscript submission, several anonymous peers for their helpful remarks during the review process, and the editors for accepting my book into the *Cambridge Intellectual Property and Information Law Series*. Furthermore, without Morgan Stoffregen's editing and her most professional support throughout all stages of writing, this book would not have been possible. It goes without saying that any mistakes or oversights that remain are mine alone.

Finally, more than I can say, I am grateful to my wife, Christina, and our children, Josephine, Frederick, and Benedikt. Your love, patience, and understanding during the many times that I was away in the library (or present but still absent-minded) have been a miracle and the greatest gift of all.

Abbreviations

A.B.A.J.	American Bar Association Journal
A.C.	The Law Reports, Appeal Cases
AcP	Archiv für die civilistische Praxis
ADHGB	Allgemeines Deutsches Handelsgesetzbuch
AfP	Archiv für Presserecht
AG	Aktiengesellschaft or Amtsgericht
AIDA	Annali italiani de diritto d'autore, della cultura e dello spettaculo
AIPLA Q.J.	AIPLA Quarterly Journal
AIPPI	Association Internationale pour la Protection de la Propriété Intellectuelle/ International Association for the Protection of Intellectual Property
ALI	American Law Institute
All ER	The All England Law Reports
Am. Econ. Rev.	American Economic Review
Am. J.Comp. L.	American Journal of Comparative Law
Am. J.Int'l L.	American Journal of International Law
Am. J.Leg. Hist.	American Journal of Legal History
Am. L.Reg.	American Law Register
Am. U.L.Rev.	American University Law Review
Ann. Inst. Dr.Int.	Annuaire de L'Institut de Droit International
Antitrust L.J.	Antitrust Law Journal
AnwBl	Anwaltsblatt
AöR	Archiv des öffentlichen Rechts
ArchVölkR	Archiv des Völkerrechts
art.	Article
ASCAP	American Society of Composers, Authors and Publishers
ass'n	Association
ATS	Alien Tort Statute

AWD	Außenwirtschaftsdienst des Betriebsberaters
BB	Betriebs-Berater
BerDGesVölkR	Berichte der Deutschen Gesellschaft für Völkerrecht
Berkeley J.Int'l L.	Berkeley Journal of International Law
Berkeley Tech. L.J.	Berkeley Technology Law Journal
BG	Schweizer Bundesgericht
BGB	Bürgerliches Gesetzbuch
BGBl.	Bundesgesetzblatt
BGE	Entscheidungen des Schweizerischen Bundesgerichts—Amtliche Sammlung
BGH	Bundesgerichtshof
BGHZ	Amtliche Sammlung der Entscheidungen des Bundesgerichtshofs in Zivilsachen
BIRPI	United International Bureaux for the Protection of Intellectual Property
Bl.	Blatt
BlPMZ	Blatt für Patent-, Muster- und Zeichenwesen
BR-Drs.	Deutscher Bundesrat—Drucksachen
Brit. Y.B. Int'l L.	British Yearbook of International Law
Brook. J. Int'l L.	Brooklyn Journal of International Law
Brook. L. Rev.	Brooklyn Law Review
BT-Drs.	Deutscher Bundestag—Drucksachen
Buff. L. Rev.	Buffalo Law Review
B.U. L. Rev.	Boston University Law Review
Bus. Hist.	Business History
BVerfG	Bundesverfassungsgericht
BVerfGE	Amtliche Sammlung der Entscheidungen des Bundesverfassungsgerichts
BVerwG	Bundesverwaltungsgericht
Cal. L. Rev.	California Law Review
Cambridge L.J.	Cambridge Law Journal
Cambridge Yb. Eur. L.	Cambridge Yearbook of European Law
Cardozo Arts & Ent. L.J.	Cardozo Arts & Entertainment Law Journal
Cardozo L. Rev.	Cardozo Law Review
Cf.	Confer
Ch.	Chapter
Ch. D.	Chancery Division
Chi. J. Int'l L.	Chicago Journal of International Law
Chi.-Kent L. Rev.	Chicago-Kent Law Review

Cir.	Circuit
CISG	United Nations Convention on the International Sale of Goods
C.J.	Chief Justice
cl.	Clause
CLIP	Principles on Conflict of Laws in Intellectual Property
Clunet	Journal du droit international, fondée par E. Clunet
C.M.L. Rev.	Common Market Law Review
Co.	Company
Colum. J. Eur. L.	Columbia Journal of European Law
Colum. J.L. & Arts	Columbia Journal of Law & the Arts
Colum. J. Transnat'l L.	Columbia Journal of Transnational Law
Colum. L. Rev.	Columbia Law Review
Colum. Sci. & Tech. L. Rev.	Columbia Science and Technology Law Review
Colum.-VLA J. L. & Arts	The Columbia Journal of Law & the Arts
COM	Document of the European Commission
Conn. L. Rev.	Connecticut Law Review
Copyright L. Symp.	Copyright Law Symposium
Cornell L.Q.	Cornell Law Quarterly
Cornell L. Rev.	Cornell Law Review
CR	Computer und Recht
CRi	Computer und Recht international
Ct.	Court
Duke J. Comp. & Int'l L.	Duke Journal of Comparative and International Law
Duke L.J.	Duke Law Journal
DZWir	Deutsche Zeitschrift für Wirtschafts- und Insolvenzrecht
EC	European Community
ed.	Edition or editor
eds.	Editors
EG	Europäische Gemeinschaft/European Community
EGBGB	Einführungsgesetz zum Bürgerlichen Gesetzbuch
EIPR	European Intellectual Property Review
Emory Int'l L. Rev.	Emory International Law Review
Emory L.J.	Emory Law Journal
ERCL	European Review of Contract Law

ERPL	European Review of Private Law
et al.	et alii
et seq.	et sequens
EU	European Union
EuGH	Europäischer Gerichtshof
EuGVÜ	Brussels Convention
EuLF	European Legal Forum
EuZW	Europäische Zeitschrift für Wirtschaftsrecht
e.V.	Eingetragener Verein
EWG	Europäische Wirtschaftsgemeinschaft
EWiR	Entscheidungen zum Wirtschaftsrecht
FG	Festgabe
Fla. J. Int'l L.	Florida Journal of International Law
Fla. L. Rev.	Florida Law Review
fn.	Footnote
Fordham Intell. Prop. Media & Ent. L.J.	Fordham Intellectual Property, Media & Entertainment Law Journal
Fordham Int'l L.J.	Fordham International Law Journal
Fordham L. Rev.	Fordham Law Review
FS	Festschrift
F.S.R.	Fleet Street Reports
Ga. J. Int'l & Comp. L.	Georgia Journal of International and Comparative Law
GATS	General Agreement on Trade in Services
GemS-OGB	Gemeinsamer Senat der Obersten Gerichtshöfe des Bundes
Geo. J. Int'l L.	Georgetown Journal of International Law
Geo. L.J.	Georgetown Law Journal
Geo. Wash. L. Rev.	George Washington Law Review
German Y.B. Int'l L.	German Yearbook of International Law
GmbH	Gesellschaft mit beschränkter Haftung
GPR	Zeitschrift für Gemeinschaftsprivatrecht
GRUR	Gewerblicher Rechtsschutz und Urheberrecht
GRUR Ausl.	Gewerblicher Rechtsschutz und Urheberrecht, Auslands- und internationaler Teil
GRUR Int.	Gewerblicher Rechtsschutz und Urheberrecht, Internationaler Teil
GRUR-RR	Gewerblicher Rechtsschutz und Urheberrecht, Rechtsprechungs-Report

GS	Gedächtnisschrift
GWB	Gesetz gegen Wettbewerbsbeschränkungen
Harv. Int'l L.J.	Harvard International Law Journal
Harv. J. L. & Pub. Pol'y	Harvard Journal of Law & Public Policy
Harv. L. Rev.	Harvard Law Review
Harv. L. Rev. F.	Harvard Law Review Forum
Hastings Int'l & Comp. L. Rev.	Hastings International & Comparative Law Review
Hastings L.J.	Hastings Law Journal
HG	Handelsgericht
HGB	Handelsgesetzbuch
H.L.	House of Lords
Hofstra L. Rev.	Hofstra Law Review
Hous. L. Rev.	Houston Law Review
HWR	Handel, Wirtschaft, Recht
ibid.	Ibidem
I.C.J.	International Court of Justice
I.C.L.Q.	International and Comparative Law Quarterly
id.	Idem
Idaho L.J.	Idaho Law Journal
IHR	Internationales Handelsrecht
IIC	International Review of Industrial Property and Copyright Law
ILM	International Legal Materials
Inc.	Incorporated
Ind. J. Glob. Leg. Stud.	Indiana Journal of Global Legal Studies
Ind. L.J.	Indiana Law Journal
Ind. L. Rev.	Indiana Law Review
IJGLS	Indiana Journal of Global Legal Studies
Ill. L. Rev.	University of Illinois Law Review
Int. & Comp. L.Q.	International & Comparative Law Quarterly
Int. J. L. & Info. Tech.	International Journal of Law and Information Technology
Int'l Bus. Law.	The International Business Lawyer
Int'l Soc.	International Sociology
Iowa L. Rev.	Iowa Law Review
IP	Intellectual property
IPJ	Intellectual Property Journal
I.P.Q.	Intellectual Property Quarterly

IPR	Internationales Privatrecht
IPRax	Praxis des Internationalen Privat- und Verfahrensrechts
IPRG	Bundesgesetz über das Internationale Privatrecht (Schweiz)
IPRspr.	Deutsche Rechtsprechung auf dem Gebiete des Internationalen Privatrechts
JBL	Journal of Business Law
JBl	Juristische Blätter
JBNSt	Jahrbücher für Nationalökonomie und Statistik
J. Copyright Soc'y U.S.A.	Journal of the Copyright Society of the U.S.A.
JherJB	Jherings Jahrbücher
J. Intell. Prop. L.	Journal of International Property Law
J. Intell. Prop. L. & Pract.	Journal of International Property Law & Practice
J. Int'l Econ. L.	Journal of International Economic Law
J. L. & Com.	Journal of Law and Commerce
J. L. & Econ.	Journal of Law and Economics
J. L., Econ. & Org.	Journal of Law, Economics, and Organization
J. Legal Stud.	Journal of Legal Studies
J. Libertarian Stud.	Journal of Libertarian Studies
J. Pat. Off. Soc'y	Journal of the Patent and Trademark Office Society
J. Pol. Econ.	Journal of Political Economy
J. Priv. Int'l L.	Journal of Private International Law
J. Publ. L.	Journal of Public Law
JR	Juristische Rundschau
Jurid. Rev.	Juridical Review
JuS	Juristische Schulung
JW	Juristische Wochenschrift
JZ	Juristenzeitung
KantonsG	Kantonsgericht
KartellR	Kartellrecht
KG	Kammergericht
K&R	Kommunikation und Recht
Law & Contemp. Probs.	Law & Contemporary Problems
Law & Pol'y Int'l Bus.	Law and Policy in International Business
Law & Society Rev.	Law & Society Review

Law & Soc. Inquiry	Law & Social Inquiry: Journal of the American Bar Foundation
LG	Landgericht
lit.	Littera
L.J.	Lord Justice
Lloyd's Rep.	Lloyd's Law Reports
LLP	Limited Liability Partnership
LMCLQ	Lloyd's Maritime and Commercial Law Quarterly
loc. cit.	loco citato
Loy. Consumer L. Rev.	Loyola Consumer Law Review
L. Q. Rev.	Law Quarterly Review
Ltd.	Limited
MarkenR	Markenrecht
Marq. Intell. Prop. L. Rev.	Marquette Intellectual Property Law Review
Md. J. Int'l L.	Maryland Journal of International Law
Md. L. Rev.	Maryland Law Review
MDR	Monatsschrift für deutsches Recht
Mem. St. U. L. Rev.	Memphis State University Law Review
Mercer L. Rev.	Mercer Law Review
MMR	Multimedia und Recht
mn.	margin number
Mich. J. Int'l L.	Michigan Journal of International Law
Mich. L. Rev.	Michigan Law Review
Minn. L. Rev.	Minnesota Law Review
MittPat	Mitteilungen der Deutschen Patentanwälte
MMR	Multimedia und Recht
Mod. L. Rev.	Modern Law Review
Mo. L. Rev.	Missouri Law Review
M.R.	Master of the Rolls
MuW	Markenschutz und Wettbewerb
N.C. L. Rev.	North Carolina Law Review
Nebr. L. Rev.	Nebraska Law Review
NILR	Netherlands International Law Review
NIPR	Nederlands Internationaal Privaatrecht
NJW	Neue Juristische Wochenschrift
NJW-RR	NJW-Rechtsprechungsreport Zivilrecht
no.	Number or numéro
nos	Numbers or numéros
Notre Dame L. Rev.	Notre Dame Law Review
n. r.	not reported

Nr.	Nummer
NTIR	Nordisk Tidskrift for International Ret
Nw. U. L. Rev.	Northwestern University Law Review
n. y. r.	not yet reported
N.Y.U. J. Int'l L. & Pol.	New York University Journal of International Law and Politics
N.Y.U. L. Rev.	New York University Law Review
ObG	Obergericht
ÖBA	Österreichisches Bank-Archiv
ÖBl	Österreichische Blätter für gewerblichen Rechtsschutz und Urheberrecht
ÖJZ	Österreichische Juristenzeitung
OGH	Österreichischer Oberster Gerichtshof
O.J. EU	Official Journal of the European Community (or, since 2003, European Union)
OLG	Oberlandesgericht
op. cit.	opere citato
ORDO	Jahrbuch für die Ordnung von Wirtschaft und Gesellschaft
Or. L. Rev.	Oregon Law Review
Ox. J. Leg. Stud.	Oxford Journal of Legal Studies
p.	Page
Pac. L.J.	Pacific Law Journal
PAngV	Preisangabenverordnung
para.	Paragraph
paras.	Paragraphs
PatentR	Patentrecht
Pat. & Trademark Off. Soc'y	Patent & Trademark Office Society
P.C.I.J.	Permanent Court of International Justice
Penn. St. Int'l L. Rev.	Penn State International Law Review
PIL	Private International Law
Quarterly J. Econ.	Quarterly Journal of Economics
Q.B.	The Law Reports, Queen's Bench Division
Q.C.	Queen's Counsel
RabelsZ	Rabels Zeitschrift für ausländisches und internationales Privatrecht
RCDIP	Revue critique de droit international privé
RDIPP	Rivista di diritto internazionale privato e processuale
RdW	Recht der Wirtschaft (Austria)

Recueil des Cours	Recueil des Cours de l'Académie de Droit International de La Haye
Rev. crit. dr. int. priv.	Revue critique de droit international privé
Rev. dr. int. comp.	Revue de droit international et de droit comparé
Rev. Econ. & Stat.	Review of Economics and Statistics
Rev. Econ. Stud.	Review of Economic Studies
RG	Reichsgericht
RGBl.	Reichsgesetzblatt
RGSt	Amtliche Sammlung der Entscheidungen des Reichsgerichts in Strafsachen
RGZ	Amtliche Sammlung der Entscheidungen des Reichsgerichts in Zivilsachen
Riv. dir. int. priv. proc.	Rivista di diritto internazionale privato e processuale
RIW	Recht der Internationalen Wirtschaft
Rome I Regulation	Regulation 593/2008/EC on the Law Applicable to Contractual Obligations
Rome II Regulation	Regulation 846/2007/EC on the Law Applicable to Non-Contractual Obligations
Rutgers L.J.	Rutgers Law Journal
Rutgers L. Rev.	Rutgers Law Review
s.	section (in a paragraph)
Santa Clara Computer & High Tech. L.J.	Santa Clara Computer & High Technology Law Journal
S. Cal. L. Rev.	Southern California Law Review
SchwJbIntR	Schweizerisches Jahrbuch für Internationales Recht
S.C. L. Rev.	South Carolina Law Review
sec.	Section
seq.	Sequens (or sequentes)
sess.	Session
SeuffArch	J.A. Seuffert's Archiv für Entscheidungen der obersten Gerichte in den Deutschen Staaten
sic!	Zeitschrift für Immaterialgüter-, Informations- und Wettbewerbsrecht/ Revue du droit de la propriété intellectuelle, de l'information et de la concurrence
SJZ	Schweizerische Juristen-Zeitung
SMU L. Rev.	SMU Law Review
Stan. J. Int'l L.	Stanford Journal of International Law
Stan. L. Rev.	Stanford Law Review

St. Thomas L. Rev.	St. Thomas Law Review
Suffolk Transnat'l L. Rev.	Suffolk Transnational Law Review
Sup. Ct.	Supreme Court (USA)
Sup. Ct. Rev.	Supreme Court Review
Sw. L. Rev.	Southwestern Law Review
SZIER	Schweizerische Zeitschrift für internationales und europäisches Recht
Tex. Int'l L.J.	Texas International Law Journal
Tex. L. Rev.	Texas Law Review
Theoretical Inq. L.	Theoretical Inquiries in Law
Trademark Rep.	Trademark Reporter
Transnat'l L. & Contemp. Probs.	Transnational Law & Contemporary Problems
TRIPS	Agreement on Trade-Related Aspects of Intellectual Property Rights
Tul. L. Rev.	Tulane Law Review
U. C. Davis L. Rev.	U. C. Davis Law Review
U. Chi. L. Rev.	University of Chicago Law Review
U. Cin. L. Rev.	University of Cincinnati Law Review
UCLA L. Rev.	UCLA Law Review
UFITA	Archiv für Urheber- und Medienrecht
UGP	Unlautere Geschäftspraktiken (Richtlinie)
U. Miami L. Rev.	University of Miami Law Review
UMKC L. Rev.	University of Missouri at Kansas City Law Review
UN	United Nations
UNIDROIT	International Institute for the Unification of Private Law
U. Pa. L. Rev.	University of Pennsylvania Law Review
U. Pitt. L. Rev.	University of Pittsburgh Law Review
UrheberR	Urheberrecht
U.S./US/USA	United States of America
Utah L. Rev.	Utah Law Review
UWG	Gesetz gegen den unlauteren Wettbewerb
v.	versus
Va. J. Int'l L.	Virginia Journal of International Law
Va. L. Rev.	Virginia Law Review
Val. U. L. Rev.	Valparaiso University Law Review
Vand. J. Transnat'l L.	Vanderbilt Journal of Transnational Law
Vand. L. Rev.	Vanderbilt Law Review
VersR	Versicherungsrecht
VO	Verordnung

vol.	volume
Wake Forest L. Rev.	Wake Forest Law Review
Wash. L. Rev.	Washington Law Review
Willamette L. Rev.	Willamette Law Review
WIPO	World Intellectual Property Organization
Wis. L. Rev.	Wisconsin Law Review
WM	Wertpapier-Mitteilungen
Wm. & Mary L. Rev.	William & Mary Law Review
W. New Eng. L. Rev.	Western New England Law Review
WRP	Wettbewerb in Recht und Praxis
WTO	World Trade Organization
WuB	Entscheidungen zum Wirtschafts- und Bankrecht
WuW	Wirtschaft und Wettbewerb
WZG	Warenzeichengesetz
Yale Hum. Rts. & Dev. L.J.	Yale Human Rights and Development Law Journal
Yale J. Int'l L.	Yale Journal of International Law
Yale L.J.	Yale Law Journal
Yearb. P.I.L.	Yearbook of Private International Law
ZaöRV	Zeitschrift für ausländisches öffentliches Recht und Völkerrecht
ZBJV	Zeitschrift des Bernischen Juristenvereins
ZEuP	Zeitschrift für Europäisches Privatrecht
ZfGewRS	Zeitschrift für gewerblichen Rechtsschutz
ZfPW	Zeitschrift für die gesamte Privatrechtswissenschaft
ZfRV	Zeitschrift für Rechtsvergleichung
ZfSchwR	Zeitschrift für Schweizerisches Recht
ZGE	Zeitschrift für Geistiges Eigentum
ZHR	Zeitschrift für das gesamte Handels- und Wirtschaftsrecht
ZIP	Zeitschrift für Wirtschaftsrecht und Insolvenzpraxis
ZPO	Zivilprozessordnung
ZR	Blätter für Zürcherische Rechtsprechung
ZUM	Zeitschrift für Urheber- und Medienrecht
ZVglRWiss	Zeitschrift für vergleichende Rechtswissenschaft

Table of Cases

I International Courts

Barcelona Traction, Light and Power Company, Limited (Belgium v. Spain), Judgment of 5 February 1970, I.C.J. Reports 1970, 3 – p. 436.

Nottebohm Case (Liechtenstein v. Guatemala), Judgment of 6 April 1955, I.C.J. Reports 1955, 4 – p. 436.

The Case of the S.S. "Lotus" (France v. Turkey), Judgment of 7 September 1927, P.C.I.J. Series A.—No. 10 – pp. 434–435, 479.

II Court of Justice of the European Union

Ahlström Osakeyhtiö et al. v. Commission, C-89/85 (27 September 1988), [1988] E.C.R. 5193 – p. 448.

Arsenal Football Club plc v. Matthew Reed, C-206/01 (12 November 2002), [2002] E.C.R. I-10273 – pp. 48, 353.

BergSpechte, C-278/08 (25 March 2010), [2010] E.C.R. I-2517 – p. 332.

Centrafarm BV and Others v. Sterling Drug, C-15/74 (31 October 1974), [1974] E.C.R. 1147 – p. 322.

CNL-SUCAL v. HAG ("HAG II"), C-10/89 (17 October 1990), [1990] E.C.R. I-3711 – pp. 320, 345.

Consorzio del Prosciutto di Parma and Salumificio S. Rita, C-108/01 (20 May 2003), [2003] E.C.R. I-5121 – p. 377.

III National Courts

1 Austria

(a) Oberster Gerichtshof (OGH)

(b) Appellate Courts (OLG)

2 Germany

(a) Bundesverfassungsgericht (BVerfG)

(b) Gemeinsamer Senat der Obersten Gerichtshöfe des Bundes (GemS-OGB)

GemS-OGB 2013 GRUR 417—*Medikamentenkauf im Versandhandel* (22 August 2012) – pp. 204, 208, 216.

(c) Bundesverwaltungsgericht (BVerwG)

BVerwG 1984 GRUR 350—*Esslinger Neckarhalde* (9 August 1983) – p. 47.

(d) Bundesgerichtshof (BGH)

BGHZ vol. 11, 214—*KfA* (8 December 1953) – p. 552.
BGHZ vol. 13, 244—*Cupresa-Seide* (11 May 1954) – p. 282.
BGH 1955 GRUR 150—*Farina* (13 July 1954) – p. 68.
BGH 1955 GRUR 411—*Zahl 55* (11 January 1955) – pp. 64, 68.
BGH 1955 GRUR 541—*Bestattungswerbung* (8 July 1955) – pp. 361, 366.
BGHZ vol. 19, 392—*Freiburger Wochenbericht* (27 January 1956) – p. 281.
BGHZ vol. 21, 266—*Uhrenrohwerke* (13 July 1956) – pp. 68, 69.
BGHZ vol. 22, 1—*Flava Erdgold* (2 October 1956) – pp. 68, 196, 485.
BGH 1957 GRUR 231—*Taeschner* (15 January 1957) – pp. 68–69.
BGH 1957 GRUR 358—*Kölnisch Eis* (8 February 1957) – p. 47.
BGHZ vol. 23, 365—*SUWA* (22 February 1957) – p. 281.
BGH 1957 GRUR 499—*Wipp* (10 May 1957) – p. 48.
BGH 1958 GRUR 189—*Zeiß* (24 July 1957) – p. 69.
BGH 1958 GRUR 444—*Emaillelack* (28 February 1958) – p. 335.
BGH 1959 GRUR 277—*Künstlerpostkarten* (11 November 1958) – p. 367.
BGH 1959 GRUR 143—*Blindenseife* (14 November 1958) – p. 367.
BGH 1959 GRUR 285—*Bienenhonig* (23 January 1959) – p. 361.
BGH 1960 GRUR 372—*Kodak* (18 December 1959) – p. 69.
BGHZ vol. 32, 133—*Dreitannen* (29 March 1960) – p. 44.
BGHZ vol. 34, 169 (21 December 1960) – p. 416.
BGH 1962 GRUR 243—*Kindersaugflaschen* (30 June 1961) – pp. 68–71, 203, 207, 216, 543, 561–562.
BGH 1963 GRUR 36—*Fichtennadelextrakt* (13 July 1962) – p. 335.
BGHZ vol. 40, 391—*Stahlexport* (20 December 1963) – pp. 70–71, 482, 540.
BGHZ vol. 41, 84—*Maja* (22 January 1964) – pp. 48, 196, 485.
BGH 1965 GRUR 315—*Werbewagen* (4 December 1964) – p. 361.
BGH 1968 GRUR 591—*Pulverbehälter* (3 May 1968) – p. 372.

BGHZ vol. 51, 236—*Stuttgarter Wochenblatt I* (18 December 1968) – p. 281.
BGH 1970 GRUR 523—*Telefonwerbung I* (19 June 1970) – pp. 361, 367.
BGH 1971 GRUR 153—*Tampax* (23 October 1970) – pp. 210, 506–507.
BGH 1972 GRUR 367—*Besichtigungsreisen* (3 December 1971) – pp. 208, 540.
BGHZ vol. 59, 82 (22 June 1972) – p. 416.
BGH 1973 GRUR 81—*Gewinnübermittlung* (22 September 1972) – p. 367.
BGH 1973 WM 1070—*Ölfeldrohre* (12 July 1973) – p. 447.
BGHZ vol. 64, 183—*August Vierzehn* (16 April 1975) – p. 416.
BGH 1976 GRUR 316—*Besichtigungsreisen II* (7 November 1975) – p. 208.
BGH 1977 GRUR 672—*Weltweit-Club* (13 May 1977) – pp. 208, 216, 541.
BGHZ vol. 69, 295 (29 September 1977) – p. 416.
BGH 1979 GRUR 790—*Organische Pigmente* (29 May 1979) – p. 224.
BGH 1980 GRUR 797—*Topfit Boonekamp* (27 February 1980) – p. 9.
BGH 1980 GRUR 858—*Asbestimporte* (9 May 1980) – p. 566.
BGHZ vol. 81, 291—*Bäckerfachzeitschrift* (3 July 1981) – p. 298.
BGH 1985 GRUR 876—*Tchibo/Rolex* (8 November 1984) – pp. 356, 372, 563.
BGH 1985 GRUR 550—*DIMPLE* (29 November 1984) – p. 49.
BGHZ vol. 94, 268 (8 May 1985) – p. 416.
BGH 1987 GRUR 172—*Unternehmensberatungsgesellschaft I* (9 October 1986) – p. 566.
BGH 1987 GRUR 520—*Chanel No. 5 (I)* (18 December 1986) – p. 306.
BGH 1988 GRUR 453—*Ein Champagner unter den Mineralwässern* (4 June 1987) – p. 377.
BGH 1988 GRUR 916—*PKW-Schleichbezug* (14 July 1988) – p. 71.
BGH 1990 GRUR 221—*Forschungskosten* (9 March 1989) – p. 307.
BGH 1991 GRUR 463—*Kauf im Ausland* (15 November 1990) – pp. 208, 216, 292, 539–547, 566.
BGH 1991 GRUR 914—*Kastanienmuster* (23 May 1991) – p. 307.
BGH 1993 GRUR 55—*Tchibo/Rolex II* (17 June 1992) – pp. 354, 356, 372.
BGH 1998 GRUR 419—*Gewinnspiel im Ausland* (26 November 1997) – pp. 208, 292, 540, 541.
BGH 1999 GRUR 161—*MAC Dog* (30 April 1998) – p. 328.
BGH 1999 GRUR 252—*Warsteiner II* (2 July 1998) – pp. 328, 376.
BGH 1999 GRUR 1128—*Hormonpräparate* (3 December 1998) – p. 375.

(e) Reichsgericht in Zivilsachen und Strafsachen (RGSt & RGZ)

RGZ vol. 58, 281—*Leinen garantiert vierfach* (17 June 1904) – p. 282.
RGZ vol. 66, 236—*Sansibar* (21 June 1907) – p. 40.
RGZ vol. 88, 183—*Sackpflüge* (31 March 1916) – p. 54.
RG 1917 GRUR 125—*Unkosten* (30 March 1917) – p. 282.
RGZ vol. 95, 164 (11 March 1919) – p. 386.
RGZ vol. 97, 90—*Pecose* (4 November 1919) – pp. 40–41.
RGZ vol. 99, 23—*Treuhänder* (23 April 1920) – p. 282.
RGZ vol. 108, 8—*Saccharin* (19 June 1923) – pp. 55, 58, 65.
RGZ vol. 108, 241 (3 October 1923) – p. 416.
RGZ vol. 108, 272—*Merx* (27 May 1924) – p. 298.
RGSt vol. 58, 429 (1 December 1924) – p. 280.
RGZ vol. 117, 318—*Kruschensalz* (24 June 1927) – p. 234.
RGZ vol. 118, 76—*Springendes Pferd/Hengstenberg* (20 September 1927) – pp. 58, 59, 196, 509.
RGZ vol. 120, 47—*Markenschutzverband* (24 January 1928) – pp. 298, 308.
RGZ vol. 120, 325—*Sonnengold* (30 April 1928) – pp. 9, 41.
RG 1931 JW 1906—*Supra* (14 April 1931) – p. 67.
RGZ vol. 134, 342—*Benrather Tankstelle* (18 December 1931) – p. 280.
RGZ vol. 135, 385—*Künstliche Blumen* (19 March 1932) – p. 370.
RGZ vol. 140, 25—*Hohner Mundharmonika* (17 February 1933) – pp. 53, 64–66.
RGZ vol. 141, 110—*The White Spot* (26 May 1933) – p. 46.
RGZ vol. 145, 396—*Bestattungsunternehmen I* (9 November 1934) – p. 366.
RGZ vol. 149, 102 (19 October 1935) – p. 485.
RG 1936 GRUR 670—*Primeros* (10 January 1936) – p. 507.
RGZ vol. 150, 265—*Stecknadeln* (14 February 1936) – p. 65.
RG 1937 GRUR 466—*Mulla 500* (12 March 1937) – p. 65.

(f) Obergerichte (OLG)

Badisches Appellationsgericht, 3 Zeitschrift für französisches Civilrecht (1873) 670 (9 April 1873) – p. 28.
Obergericht Mainz, 9 Zeitschrift für französisches Civilrecht (1878) 444 (19 January 1878) – p. 28.
OLG Karlsruhe 38 SeuffArch Nr. 258 (27 February 1882) – p. 28.
OLG Koblenz 1968 GRUR Int. 164—*Liebeshändel in Chioggia* (14 July 1967) – p. 194.
OLG Hamburg 1987 GRUR Int. 105—*IR/UV-Kombinationstrockner* (15 May 1986) – p. 507.
OLG Stuttgart 1987 GRUR 925—*expo data* (22 August 1986) – p. 507.

OLG Koblenz 1993 GRUR 763—*Kfz-Reinigungsmittel* (25 February 1993) – p. 562.
OLG Karlsruhe 2002 MMR 814—*Intel* (10 July 2002) – p. 199.
OLG Hamm 2004 MMR 177—*nobia.se* (31 July 2003) – p. 199.
OLG München 2005 MMR 608—*800-FLOWERS* (16 June 2005) – p. 199.
OLG München 2006 GRUR-RR 130—*UltraMind* (12 January 2006) – p. 199.
OLG München 2009 IPRax 256 (6 December 2007) – p. 212.

(g) Landgerichte (LG)

LG Hamburg 1999 MMR 612—*Animal Planet* (5 May 1999) – p. 199.
LG Stuttgart 2007 MMR 668—*Marktortprinzip bei E-Mail-Werbung* (15 May 2007) – p. 555.

3 Switzerland

(a) Bundesgericht (BG)

BGE vol. 21 I 1181 (23 November 1895) – p. 307.
BGE vol. 22 I 155 (27 March 1896) – p. 307.
BGE vol. 26 II 644 (8 December 1900) – p. 57.
BGE vol. 36 II 255 (22 April 1910) – p. 57.
BGE vol. 39 II 264 (13 June 1913) – p. 307.
BGE vol. 39 II 640 (11 July 1913) – p. 57.
BGE vol. 39 I 633 (12 November 1913) – p. 194.
BGE vol. 43 II 98 (16 February 1917) – p. 57.
BGE vol. 47 II 354 (13 June 1921) – p. 57.
BGE vol. 52 II 444 (15 November 1926) – p. 307.
BGE vol. 71 I 344 (15 October 1945) – p. 57.
BG 1961 GRUR Int. 544 (9 May 1961) – p. 216.
BGE vol. 91 II 117 (30 March 1965) – pp. 205, 222.
BG 1967 GRUR Int. 364—*Sihl/Silbond* (15 November 1966) – pp. 216, 506.
BGE vol. 116 II 365—*Nivea* (12 July 1990) – p. 333.
BG 1997 GRUR Int. 167—*item communication* (9 August 1995) – p. 222.
BG 2000 GRUR Int. 639—*Kodak II* (7 December 1999) – p. 196.
BGE vol. 129 III 353—*Puls-Tip* (17 March 2003) – p. 329.

(b) Handelsgerichte

Handelsgericht Zürich, 1985 GRUR Int. 411 (9 January 1984) – p. 196.

4 United Kingdom

A.G. Spalding & Bros. v. A.W. Gamage [1913] 30 R.P.C. 388 – p. 83.
Arsenal Football Club Plc. v. Reed [2003] EWCA Civ 696 – p. 364.
Barnsley Brewery Company Ltd. v. RBNB [1997] F.S.R. 462 – p. 365.
Blanchard v. Hill [1742] 2 Atk. 484, 26 E.R. 692 – p. 80.
Blofeld v. Payne [1833] 4 B. & Ad. 410, 110 E.R. 509 – p. 80.
Burgess v. Burgess [1853] 3 De G.M. & G. 896, 43 E.R. 351 – p. 90.
Churton v. Douglas [1859] 28 L.J. Ch. 841 – p. 98.
Collins Co. v. Brown [1857] 3 Kay & J. 423, 69 E.R. 1174 – p. 83.
Commissioners of Inland Revenue v. Muller & Co.'s Margarine, Ltd. [1901] A.C. 217 – pp. 97, 130, 158.
Croft v. Day [1843] 7 Beav. 84, 49 E.R. 994 – p. 90.
Cruttwell v. Lye [1810] 17 Ves. Jr. 335, 34 E.R. 129 – p. 96.
Cutler v. Wandsworth Stadium Ltd [1949] A.C. 398 – p. 374.
De Wut v. Hendricks [1824] 2 Bing. 314, 130 E.R. 326 – p. 417.
Edelsten v. Edelsten [1863] 1 De G.J. & S. 185, 46 E.R. 72 – pp. 80–81.
Euromarket Designs Inc. v. Peters and Crate & Barrel Ltd. [2001] F.S.R. 20 – p. 518.
Foster v. Driscoll and Others [1929] 1 K.B. 470 – p. 417.
Gee v. Pritchard [1818] 2 Swans. 402, 36 E.R. 670 – p. 80.
Hall v. Barrows [1863] 4 De G.J. & S. 150, 46 E.R. 873 – p. 81.
Hodgkinson Corby Ltd. and Another v. Wards Mobility Services Ltd. [1995] F.S.R. 169 – pp. 364, 365.
Jamieson & Co. v. Jamieson [1898] 15 R.P.C. 169 – p. 83.
John Walker & Sons Ltd. and Others v. Henry Ost & Co. Ltd. and Another [1970] 1 W.L.R. 917 – p. 241.
Leather Cloth Co. Ltd. v. American Leather Cloth Co. Ltd. [1863] 4 De G.J. & S. 137, 46 E.R. 868 – pp. 82, 99.
Levy v. Walker [1879] 10 Ch. D. 436, All E.R. 1173 – p. 82.
Lonrho Ltd v. Shell Petroleum Co Ltd (No.2) [1982] A.C. 173 – p. 374.
McCall v. Abelesz and Another [1976] Q.B. 585 – p. 374.
Mecklermedia Corporation and Another v. D.C. Congress GmbH [1998] Ch. 40 – p. 241.
Millington v. Fox [1838] 3 My. & C. 338, 40 E.R. 956 – p. 81.
Perry v. Truefitt [1842] 6 Beav. 66, 49 E.R. 749 – p. 90.
Phones 4u Ltd. v. Phone4u.co.uk. Internet Ltd. [2006] EWCA Civ 244, [2007] R.P.C. 5 – pp. 358, 365.
R. Johnston & Co. v. Archibald Orr Ewing & Co. [1882] 7 App. Cas. 219 – p. 169.
Reddaway v. Banham [1896] A.C. 199 – p. 83.
Regazzoni v. KC Sethia (1944) Ltd. [1958] A.C. 301 – p. 417.

Singer Mfg. Co. v. Loog [1882] 8 App. Cas. 15 – p. 82.
Sykes v. Sykes [1824] 3 B. & C. 541, 107 E.R. 834 – pp. 80–81.
The Mogul Steamship Company, Ltd. v. McGregor, Gow, & Co., and Others [1889] 23 Q.B.D. 598 – p. 364.
Whiteman Smith Motor Co., Limited v. Chaplin [1934] 2 K.B. 35 – p. 98.
William Crawshay v. William Thompson and Others [1842] 4 Man. & G. 357, 134 E.R. 146 – p. 81.

5 *United States*

A. Bourjois & Co. v. Katzel, 260 U.S. 689, 43 S.Ct. 244, 67 L.Ed. 464 (1923) – pp. 116, 128.
A. L. A. Schechter Poultry Corp. v. United States, 295 U.S. 495, 55 S.Ct. 837, 79 L.Ed. 1570 (1935) – p. 85.
A.T. Cross Co. v. Sunil Trading Corp., 467 F.Supp. 47 (S.D.N.Y. 1979) – pp. 176, 527.
A.V. by Versace, Inc. v. Gianni Versace, S.p.A., 87 F.Supp.2d 281 (S.D.N.Y. 2000) – p. 574.
A.V. by Versace, Inc. v. Gianni Versace, S.p.A., 126 F.Supp.2d 328 (S.D.N.Y. 2001) – p. 527.
ACG Products, Ltd. v. Gu, No. 10-cv-716-wmc, 2011 WL 7748354 (W.D. Wisc., 4 November 2011) – p. 176.
Adam Hat Stores v. Scherper, 45 F.Supp. 804 (E.D. Wis. 1942) – p. 109.
Addressograph-Multigraph Corp. v. American Expansion Bolt & Mfg. Co., 124 F.2d 706 (7th Cir. 1941) – p. 139.
Aerogroup International, Inc. v. Marlboro Footworks, Ltd., 955 F.Supp. 220 (S.D.N.Y. 1997) – pp. 174, 528.
Air Turbine Technology, Inc. v. Atlas Copco AB, 295 F.Supp.2d 1334 (S.D. Fla. 2003) – pp. 175, 523.
Alcoa. See *U.S. v. Aluminum Co. of America*, 148 F.2d 416 (2nd Cir. 1945).
America Online, Inc. v. Aol.Org, 259 F.Supp.2d 449 (E.D.Va. 2003) – p. 574.
American Auto. Ass'n v. Spiegel, 205 F.2d 771 (2nd Cir. 1953) – p. 149.
American Banana Co. v. United Fruit Co., 213 U.S. 347, 29 S.Ct. 511, 53 L.Ed. 826 (1909) – pp. 170, 225, 449, 485.
American Photographic Pub. Co. v. Ziff-Davis Pub. Co., 135 F.2d 569 (7th Cir. 1943) – p. 140.
American Rice, Inc. v. Arkansas Rice Growers Co-op. Ass'n, 701 F.2d 408 (5th Cir. 1983) – pp. 67, 161, 164, 176, 182–183, 522–525, 529.
American Rice, Inc. v. Arkansas Rice Growers Co-op. Ass'n, 532 F.Supp. 1376 (D.C. Tex. 1982) – p. 176.

Curb v. MCA Records, Inc., 898 F.Supp. 586 (M.D. Tenn. 1995) – p. 239–240.
Dastar Corp. v. Twentieth Century Fox Film Corp., 539 U.S. 23, 123 S.Ct. 2041, 156 L.Ed.2d 18 (2003) – pp. 252, 323.
Dawn Donut Company v. Hart's Food Stores, Inc., 267 F.2d 358 (2nd Cir. 1959) – pp. 145, 147.
Deepsouth Packing Co. v. Laitram Corp., 406 U.S. 518, 92 S.Ct. 1700, 32 L.Ed.2d 273 (1972) – pp. 129, 238.
Del Monte Fresh Produce Co. v. Dole Food Co., Inc., 136 F.Supp.2d 1271 (S.D. Fla. 2001) – p. 574.
Dennison Mfg. Co. v. Thomas Mfg. Co., 94 F. 651 (C.C.D. Del. 1899) – pp. 85, 89.
Derringer v. Plate, 29 Cal. 292, 87 Am. Dec. 170 (1865) – pp. 24, 28, 92–95, 104, 127, 130, 159.
Dodge Stationery Co. v. Dodge, 145 Cal. 380, 78 P. 879 (1904) – p. 98.
Dorr-Oliver, Inc. v. Fluid-Quip, Inc., 94 F.3d 376 (7th Cir. 1996) – p. 357.
Draper v. Skerrett, 116 F. 206 (C.C.E.D. Pa. 1902) – p. 101.
Dunkin' Donuts, Inc. v. Mercantile Ventures, No. EP-91-CA-154-B, 1992 WL 156566 (W.D. Tex., 8 January 1992) – pp. 175, 184.
Durable Toy & Novelty Corp. v. J. Chein & Co., 133 F.2d 853 (2nd Cir. 1943) – p. 115.
Dwinell-Wright Co. v. National Fruit Product Co., 129 F.2d 848, 54 U.S.P.Q. 149 (1st Cir. 1942) – p. 144.
Dwyer Instruments, Inc. v. Sensocon, Inc., No. 3:09-CV-10 TLS, 2009 WL 8705579 (N.D. Indiana, 20 November 2009) – p. 175.
E. Leitz, Inc. v. Watson, 152 F.Supp. 631 (D.D.C. 1957) – p. 158.
E.E.O.C. v. Arabian American Oil Co., 499 U.S. 244, 111 S.Ct. 1227, 113 L.Ed.2d 274 (1991) – p. 244.
E.I. Du Pont De Nemours Powder Co. v. Masland, 244 U.S. 100, 37 S.Ct. 575, 61 L.Ed. 1016 (1917) – pp. 116, 303.
Eastern Wine Corp. v. Winslow-Warren, Ltd., 137 F.2d 955 (2nd Cir. 1943) – p. 122.
Elgin National Watch Co. v. Illinois Watch Case Co., 179 U.S. 665, 21 S.Ct. 270, 45 L.Ed. 365 (1901) – pp. 83, 89.
Eli Lilly & Co. v. Natural Answers, Inc., 233 F.3d 456 (7th Cir. 2000) – p. 357.
Ely-Norris Safe Co. v. Mosler Safe Co., 7 F.2d 603 (2nd Cir. 1925) – pp. 330, 337.
Erie R. Co. v. Tompkins, 304 U.S. 64, 58 S.Ct. 817, 82 L.Ed. 1188 (1938) – pp. 138, 468.
Estate of P.D. Beckwith v. Commissioner of Patents, 252 U.S. 538, 40 S.Ct. 414, 64 L.Ed. 705 (1920) – p. 144.

Hanover Star Milling Co. v. Allen & Wheeler Co., 208 F. 513 (7th Cir. 1913) – p. 103.
Hanover Star Milling Co. v. Metcalf, 240 U.S. 403, 36 S.Ct. 357, 60 L.Ed. 713 (1916) – pp. 39, 76, 83, 89–90, 93, 99, 102–105, 130–135, 184, 247–248, 255.
Harrods Ltd. v. Sixty Internet Domain Names, 302 F.3d 214 (4th Cir. 2002) – p. 574.
Hartford Fire Ins. Co. v. California, 509 U.S. 764, 113 S.Ct. 2891, 125 L.Ed.2d 612 (1993) – pp. 170, 225, 390–391, 451–454, 531–532.
Hecker H-O Co. v. Holland Food Corp., 36 F.2d 767 (2nd Cir. 1929) – p. 165.
Hilson Co. v. Foster, 80 F. 896 (C.C.S.D.N.Y. 1897) – pp. 99, 108–109.
Hilton v. Guyot, 159 U.S. 113, 16 S.Ct. 139, 40 L.Ed. 95 (1895) – p. 399.
Hong Leong Finance Ltd. (Singapore) v. Pinnacle Performance Ltd., No. 12 Civ. 6010(JMF), 2013 WL 5746126 (S.D.N.Y., 23 October 2013) – p. 176.
Hormel Foods Corp. v. Jim Henson Productions, Inc., 73 F.3d 497 (2nd Cir. 1996) – p. 351.
Houbigant, Inc. v. Development Specialists, Inc., 229 F.Supp.2d 208 (S.D.N.Y. 2002) – pp. 175, 527.
Humble Oil & Refining Co. v. American Oil Co., 405 F.2d 803, 160 U.S.P.Q. 289 (8th Cir. 1969) – p. 133.
IIT v. Vencap, Ltd., 519 F.2d 1001 (2nd Cir. 1975) – p. 464.
In re Agent Orange Product Liability Litigation, 580 F.Supp. 690 (E.D.N.Y. 1984) – p. 258.
In re Maxwell Communication Corp. plc, 186 B.R. 807 (S.D.N.Y. 1995) – p. 573.
In re Trade-Mark Cases, 100 U.S. 82, 10 Otto 82, 25 L.Ed. 550 (1879) – pp. 83, 99, 107, 142, 252, 322.
Industrial Rayon Corporation v. Dutchess Underwear Corporation, 92 F.2d 33 (2nd Cir. 1937) – p. 115.
Ingenohl v. Walter E. Olsen & Co., 273 U.S. 541, 47 S.Ct. 451, 71 L.Ed. 762 (1927) – pp. 134, 157, 169.
Int'l Bancorp, LLC v. Societe des Bains de Mer et du Cercle des Etrangers a Monaco, 329 F.3d 359 (4th Cir. 2003) – pp. 154, 574.
Interboro Brewing Co. v. Standard Brewing Co. of Baltimore, 246 U.S. 677, 38 S.Ct. 315, 62 L.Ed. 934 (1918) – p. 143.
International Academy of Business and Financial Management, Ltd. v. Mentz, No. 12-cv-00463-CMA-BNB, 2013 WL 212640 (D. Colo., 18 January 2013) – p. 176.
International Business Machines Corp. v. Comdisco, Inc., No. 91 C 6777, 1993 WL 155511 (N.D. Ill., 10 May 1993) – p. 175.

L'Aiglon Apparel v. Lana Lobell, Inc., 214 F.2d 649 (3rd Cir. 1954) – p. 149.
Laker Airways Ltd. v. Sabena, Belgian World Airlines, 731 F.2d 909 (D.C.C., 1984) – pp. 401, 434, 438, 450–451.
Lauritzen v. Larsen, 345 U.S. 571, 73 S.Ct. 921, 97 L.Ed. 1254 (1953) – pp. 411–412, 453.
Lawrence Mfg. Co. v. Tennessee Mfg. Co., 138 U.S. 537, 11 S.Ct. 396, 34 L.Ed. 997 (1891) – pp. 85, 107.
Leatherman Tool Group, Inc. v. Cooper Industries, Inc., 47 U.S.P.Q.2d 1045 (D. Or. 1997) – pp. 184, 529.
Les Ballets Trockadero de Monte Carlo, Inc. v. Trevino, 945 F.Supp. 563 (S.D.N.Y. 1996) – pp. 183, 528.
Levi Strauss & Co. v. Sunrise Intern. Trading Inc., 51 F.3d 982 (11th Cir. 1995) – p. 527.
Libbey Glass, Inc. v. Oneida Ltd., 61 F.Supp.2d 720 (N.D. Ohio 1999) – pp. 174, 528.
Liberty Toy Co. v. Fred Silber Co., 149 F.3d 1183 (6th Cir. 1998) – p. 574.
Litecubes, LLC v. Northern Light Products, Inc., 523 F.3d 1353 (Fed. Cir. 2008) – p. 573.
Lithuanian Commerce Corporation, Ltd. v. Sara Lee Hosiery, 47 F.Supp.2d 523 (D.N.J. 1999) – pp. 176, 523.
Lois Sportswear, U.S.A., Inc. v. Levi Strauss & Co., 799 F.2d 867 (2nd Cir. 1986) – p. 354.
London Film Productions Ltd. v. Intercontinental Communications, Inc., 580 F.Supp. 47 (S.D.N.Y. 1984) – p. 242.
Los Angeles News Service v. Reuters Television Intern. Ltd., 149 F.3d 987 (9th Cir. 1998) – p. 239.
Loucks v. Standard Oil Co., 120 N.E. 198, 224 N.Y. 99 (N.Y. 1918) – p. 399.
Louis Vuitton Malletier, S.A. v. Akanoc Solutions, Inc., No. C 07-03952 JW, 2010 WL 5598337 (N.D. Ca., 19 March 2010) – pp. 175, 529.
Love v. Associated Newspapers, Ltd., 611 F.3d 601 (9th Cir. 2010) – p. 176.
M/S Bremen v. Zapata Off-Shore Co., 407 U.S. 1, 92 S.Ct. 1907, 32 L.Ed.2d 513 (1972) – pp. 412–413.
Maison Lazard et Compagnie v. Manfra, Tordella & Brooks, Inc., 585 F.Supp. 1286 (S.D.N.Y. 1984) – p. 149.
Maison Prunier v. Prunier's Rest. & Cafe, 159 Misc. 551, 288 N.Y.S. 529 (Sup. Ct. 1936) – pp. 152–153.
Mannington Mills, Inc. v. Congoleum Corp., 595 F.2d 1287 (3rd Cir. 1979) – pp. 440–441, 450.

Sterling Drug, Inc. v. Bayer AG, 792 F.Supp. 1357 (S.D.N.Y. 1992) – pp. 516, 572.
Stevo Design, Inc. v. SBR Marketing Ltd., 919 F.Supp.2d 1112 (D. Nev. 2013) – p. 176.
Stork Restaurant, Inc. v. Sahati, 166 F.2d 348 (9th Cir. 1948) – p. 153.
Subafilms, Ltd. v. MGM-Pathe Communications Co., 24 F.3d 1088 (9th Cir. 1994), cert. denied, 513 U.S. 1001 (1994) – pp. 129, 238–239, 253.
Sundor Brands, Inc. v. Borden, Inc., 653 F.Supp. 86 (M.D. Fla. 1986) – p. 327.
Swift v. Tyson, 41 U.S. 1, 16 Pet. 1, 10 L.Ed. 865 (1842) – pp. 135, 468.
Talbot v. Seeman, 1 Cranch 1, 5 U.S. 1, 2 L.Ed. 15 (1801) – p. 399.
Tel-Oren v. Libyan Arab Republic, 726 F.2d 774 (D.C. Cir. 1984) – p. 470.
The Name LLC v. Arias, No. 10 Civ. 3212(RMB), 2010 WL 4642456 (S.D.N.Y., 16 November 2010) – p. 176.
The Paquete Habana, 175 U.S. 677, 20 S.Ct. 290, 44 L.Ed. 320 (1900) – p. 465.
Theodore Rectanus Co. v. United States Co., 226 Fed. 545 (6th Cir. 1915) – p. 93.
Thomas & Betts Corp. v. Panduit Corp., 71 F.Supp.2d 838 (N.D. Ill. 1999) – p. 523.
Thomsen v. Cayser, 243 U.S. 66, 37 S.Ct. 353, 61 L.Ed. 597 (1917) – p. 449.
Three Degrees Enterprises, Inc. v. Three Degrees Worldwide, Inc., 22 U.S.P.Q.2d 1357 (3rd Cir. 1991) – pp. 175, 184.
Tiffany & Co. v. Tiffany Productions, 147 Misc. 679, 264 N.Y.S. 459 (Sup. Ct. 1932) – p. 120.
Timberlane Lumber Co. v. Bank of America N.T. & S.A., 549 F.2d 597 (9th Cir. 1976) – pp. 161–163, 172–174, 438, 440–442, 450, 523, 526.
Tire Engineering and Distribution, LLC v. Shandong Linglong Rubber Co., Ltd., 682 F.3d 292 (4th Cir. 2012) – p. 176.
TNT USA, Inc. v. TrafiExpress, S.A. de C.V., 434 F.Supp.2d 1322 (S.D. Fla. 2006) – pp. 175, 527.
Tommy Hilfiger Licensing, Inc. v. Costco Companies, Inc., No. 99 Civ. 3894 (LMM), 2001 WL 55735 (S.D.N.Y., 23 January 2001) – pp. 173, 181.
Tommy Hilfiger Licensing, Inc. v. Costco Companies, Inc., No. 99 Civ. 3894 (LMM), 2001 WL 262590 (S.D.N.Y., 14 March 2001) – p. 574.
Torah Soft Ltd. v. Drosnin, 136 F.Supp.2d 276 (S.D.N.Y. 2001) – p. 521.
Totalplan Corp. of America v. Lure Camera Ltd., Nos. 82-CV-0698E(M) thru 82-CV-0701E(M), 1993 WL 117504 (W.D.N.Y., 12 April 1993) – p. 176.

Totalplan Corporation of America v. Colborne, 14 F.3d 824 (2nd Cir. 1994) – pp. 183–184.
Toys "R" Us, Inc. v. Abir, No. 97 Civ. 8673 (JGK), 1997 WL 857229 (S.D.N.Y., 19 December 1997) – p. 574.
Trader Joe's Co. v. Hallatt, 981 F.Supp.2d 972 (W.D. Wash. 2013) – p. 173.
Triangle Publications, Inc. v. Rohrlich, 167 F.2d 969 (2nd Cir. 1948) – p. 122.
Ty Inc. v. Perryman, 306 F.3d 509 (7th Cir. 2002) – pp. 124, 341, 351.
U.S. Printing & Lithograph Co. v. Griggs-Cooper & Co., 119 Ohio St. 151, 162 N.E. 425 (1928) – p. 143.
U.S. Printing & Lithograph Co. v. Griggs, Cooper & Co., 279 U.S. 156, 49 S.Ct. 267, 73 L.Ed. 650 (1929) – p. 143.
U.S. v. International Broth. of Teamsters, 945 F.Supp. 609 (S.D.N.Y. 1996) – p. 573.
U.S. v. Pacific & Arctic Railway & Navigation Co., 228 U.S. 87, 33 S.Ct. 443, 57 L.Ed. 742 (1913) – p. 449.
U.S. v. Sisal Sales Corp., 274 U.S. 268, 47 S.Ct. 592, 71 L.Ed. 1042 (1927) – p. 449.
U.S. v. the La Jeune Eugenie, 26 F. Cas. 832 (C.C.D. Mass. 1822) – p. 400.
Ubiquiti Networks, Inc. v. Kozumi USA Corp., No. C 12-2582 CW, 2012 WL 1901264 (N.D. Ca., 25 May 2012) – p. 175.
Underhill v. Hernandez, 168 U.S. 250, 18 S.Ct. 83, 42 L.Ed. 456 (1897) – p. 242.
United Air Lines, Inc. v. United Airways, Ltd., No. 09-CV-4743 (KAM) (JMA), 2013 WL 1290930 (E.D.N.Y., 4 March 2013) – p. 173.
United Drug Co. v. Theodore Rectanus Co., 248 U.S. 90, 39 S.Ct. 48, 63 L.Ed. 141 (1918) – pp. 77, 90, 95, 102, 104, 106, 108–109, 127, 129–130, 132, 134–135, 142–143, 145, 148–150, 153, 159, 167, 169, 171, 177, 184, 188, 202, 247, 249, 251, 271, 325, 334.
United States v. Aluminum Co. of America, 148 F.2d 416 (2nd Cir. 1945) – pp. 390, 443, 448–450, 506.
Update Art, Inc. v. Modiin Pub., Ltd., 843 F.2d 67 (2nd Cir. 1988) – p. 239.
V'Soske, Inc. v. Vsoske.com, No. 00 Civ. 6099(DV), 2003 WL 1747144 (S.D.N.Y., 1 April 2003) – p. 175.
V'Soske, Inc. v. Vsoske.com, No. 00 CIV 6099 DC, 2002 WL 230848 (S.D.N.Y., 15 February 2002) – p. 175.
Vacuum Oil Co. v. Eagle Oil Co. of New York, 154 F. 867 (C.C. N.J. 1907) – pp. 63, 165–167, 169, 257.

Introduction

We all know the story. Since the second half of the last century, the globalization of communication and transacting has gained enormous momentum. Global trade and commerce have multiplied. Most importantly, the rise of the internet has made cross-border marketing an everyday phenomenon. Today, one can buy virtually anything from anywhere in the world. Of course, this phenomenon has also brought a number of downsides. With respect to intellectual property—specifically, trademark and unfair competition law—the extension of marketplaces seems to have led to a rise in collisions between different countries' trademarks, trade names, and similar designations, as well as to conflicts between different policies of unfair competition prevention. Most concretely, the fact that the use of a trademark on a website or any other commercial online communication can be accessed from anywhere on the planet also means that, at least in theory, infringement claims can emanate from anywhere on the planet. A recent American case is illustrative:

> Cecil McBee, an American jazz icon with a more than fifty-year career, was appalled when he learned that Delica Co., a Japanese clothing retailer, had adopted the trademark Cecil McBee—his name—for a line of whimsical and arguably immodest fashion for young women. Delica had retail shops only in Japan and did not sell outside of the country. It did, however, operate the website cecilmcbee.net, which contained information on its products. After McBee unsuccessfully sued in Japanese courts to have the company's trademark cancelled, he sought relief in a US federal court, where he claimed false endorsement and dilution under the Lanham Act.[1]

One may find it arguable that an individual should have a right to protect his branded personality against someone who has taken great efforts to limit the reach of her activities. At the same time, these doubts may dissolve if the scenario is concerned not with a good-faith trademark user but with an actor intentionally seeking to extend international market shares—or even with the proverbial "trademark pirate." While exact

[1] *McBee v. Delica Co., Ltd.*, 417 F.3d 107 (1st Cir. 2005).

figures on injuries are hard to find, estimates run high. In Cecil McBee's case, the judge shed light on what she considered the detriment to be:

> One can easily imagine a variety of harms to American commerce arising from wholly foreign activities by foreign defendants. There could be harm caused by false endorsements, passing off, or product disparagement, or confusion over sponsorship affecting American commerce and causing loss of American sales. Further, global piracy of American goods is a major problem for American companies: annual losses from unauthorized use of United States trademarks, according to one commentator, now amount to $200 billion annually. . . . In both the antitrust and the Lanham Act areas, there is a risk that absent a certain degree of extraterritorial enforcement, violators will either take advantage of international coordination problems or hide in countries without efficacious antitrust or trademark laws, thereby avoiding legal authority.[2]

Whether or not we accept the judge's pessimistic perspective, her words demonstrate that international trademark and unfair competition disputes are not limited to cases of individual misery. The issue is actually more wide reaching and often becomes a question of public interest. Lawmakers and courts thus find themselves confronted with the basic conundrum arising from disputes over international commercial activities—the conflict between economics and politics. In a globalized world, marketplaces and territories no longer correspond to the same geographic area. The "market," it seems, has acquired an existence of its own—one that is largely beyond the state and its territorial regulatory order. As a consequence, policy makers must choose between two opposing paradigms. The first is to go with tradition and rely on the territoriality of rights and laws. This option, however, inevitably leads to underprotection in many cases, a result barely palatable for activist judges and lawmakers, among others. The second option is to embrace transnational marketplace regulation by extraterritorially extending nation-states' legislative domain. Understandably, this choice not only suits individual plaintiffs but often also has more appeal for courts and regulators because it, at least prima facie, protects the interests of national right owners and, accordingly, of the national economy as a whole. The problem, however, is that neither of these two roads is very promising. While the first tries to move backwards in time toward nationally cabined rights and policies, the second bears a risk of chaos and confusion, for if all nation-states insisted on extraterritorial rights protection, we would ultimately find ourselves in a Hobbesian *bellum omnium contra omnes*.

It is therefore no surprise that trademark and unfair competition conflicts law, like many sectors of international economic law, has arrived at

[2] *Id.* at 119.

a crossroad that requires a reconceptualization of structure and technique. This is the point where we must ask whether and to what extent scholarship and practice have dealt with the relevant issues and have asked the right questions. Even though problems of this kind have been debated for a long time (far before the advent of digital communications and expedited international trade), our understanding of the fundaments is still woefully incomplete. Of course, interest in intellectual property and unfair competition law, as well as conflicts law (also known as private international law or choice of law), has grown and is constantly increasing. Nonetheless, issues of *international* intellectual property and *international* unfair competition conflicts still seem to be situated in a legal "no man's land." Indeed, numerous scholarly desiderata exist. An especially problematic void in current scholarship is its blind spot with respect to the interrelation between substantive law policies and conflicts law. The fact that peculiarities of conflicts doctrine can be traced to substantive law structures is far from new wisdom. For example, the iconic Franz Kahn, one of Europe's most influential nineteenth-century conflicts scholars, explained in 1898 that

> [s]ubstantive law is both the origin and the terminus of private international law analysis. This is the natural cycle, not the all-too-often vicious circle. All conflicts norms have been developed—and will be developed anew every day—based on substantive law norms. Constructing a private international law regime without such a substantive law foundation would be akin to setting a spire into the vacuous air.[3]

Yet quite often the analysis of international trademark and unfair competition conflicts law remains limited to formal and technical issues of traditional conflicts law doctrine. In addition, questions of public international law and international comity have been, so far, a neglected aspect of international trademark and unfair competition law. Finally, the field's history, particularly how it has played out in common law versus civil law regimes, has received insufficient attention. Even though singular forays into history and specific jurisdictions' laws have been attempted in scholarly articles and sometimes even court decisions, a detailed historical-comparative account of common law and civil law doctrine is still missing.

My inquiry seeks to fill all these gaps. I will start with a historical-comparative account in chapters 1 and 2. Even though it is always tempting

[3] Franz Kahn, *Über Inhalt, Natur und Methode des internationalen Privatrechts*, 40 JherJB 1, 56 (1898) ("Das materielle Recht bildet sowohl Ausgangspunkt, wie Endpunkt der privatinternationalen Untersuchung. Das ist der natürliche Kreislauf, nicht etwa der so oft auf diesem Gebiete uns erschreckende circulus vitiosus. Aus der Sachnorm heraus hat man jede Kollisionsnorm entwickelt, und entwickelt man sie täglich neu. Ohne diese materielle Unterlage ein internationales Privatrecht konstruiren zu wollen, hieße einen Kirchturm in die leere Luft stellen." (author's translation)).

for a comparativist to follow Ernst Rabel's advice to undertake a comparison of the "law of the whole world,"[4] my focus will be on American and European law—not just for reasons of time and space but also because these legal systems lend themselves well to an illustrative analysis. The United States is the world's largest common law jurisdiction. Its trademark and unfair competition doctrine and conflicts law is representative of other common law systems in many respects. In addition, the long-time American penchant—not to say passion—for international market regulation through the extension of domestic rights and policies further makes it an apt object of investigation. The laws of the European Union and Germany (as Europe's largest civil law jurisdiction) present themselves as logical counterparts. An incidental look at other civil law jurisdictions—namely, France, Austria, and Switzerland—rounds out the picture. My portrayal of these legal systems' history will be complemented in chapter 3 by an analysis of the most influential theoretical and scholarly contributions to the field. Then, in chapter 4, in order to provide the groundwork for a more policy-oriented conflicts system, I will use a functionalist-comparative lens to analyze the underlying policies of trademark protection and unfair competition prevention. Finally, in chapter 5, I will look at the limitations of public international law and the principles of international comity with the aim of providing guidance for a modernized concept of jurisdictional self-restraint. These five chapters will bring out the optimal result that can be hoped for from such a comparative analysis—the building of a functionally coherent system that provides the context within which to contrast the nationally varying solutions.[5] It is on this basis that I will present, in chapter 6, a reconceptualization of conflicts doctrine, notably a typology of international trademark conflicts and unfair competition violations. In this regard, the last part of chapter 6 will be particularly interesting for those who are open to what Konrad Zweigert and Hein Kötz have described as an "applied" version of comparative law—an approach suggesting the application of national (or supranational) rules in light of a larger international universe.[6]

In a broader context, my inquiry will show that trademark and unfair competition law, both in substance and with regard to conflicts law, is representative of a phenomenon that is often evoked in many sectors of the law but that is nowhere near as advanced and so emblematically evolved as here—the functional convergence of legal orders toward a truly

[4] Ernst Rabel, *Aufgabe und Notwendigkeit der Rechtsvergleichung* (1924), reprinted in *Gesammelte Aufsätze, vol. III* (Hans G. Leser ed., 1967), 1, 5 („Der Stoff des Nachdenkens über die Probleme des Rechts muß das Recht der gesamten Erde sein . . . .").

[5] Konrad Zweigert & Hein Kötz, *Introduction to Comparative Law* 45 (3rd edn., 1998).

[6] *Id.* at 11 and 18.

transnational law. This convergence is most striking at the level of substantive law. Under modern regimes of trademark protection and unfair competition prevention, market information infrastructure can be described as the most basic and important subject matter of protection. Unmanipulated information transmission and consumer decision making are paramount for the functioning of competition mechanics in free marketplaces. Accordingly, the fields' core policies aim at protecting market information with regard to content, transmission, and processing—all with a focus on the consumer's ultimate transacting (or nontransacting). This orientation toward the quintessence of competition has also been laid out rudimentarily in public international law instruments on trademark protection and unfair competition prevention, notably the Paris Convention and the Agreement on Trade-Related Aspects of Intellectual Property Rights. Ultimately, as we will see, it is this infrastructure of market information regulation that also provides the foundation for a reconceptualized trademark and unfair competition conflicts doctrine. By this means, as Franz Kahn prophesied, conflicts law will be built on a transnationally uniform architecture of substantive law functions.

Before I start my inquiry, however, two terminological caveats are in order. First, with regard to substantive law, I will regularly need to refer to the purposes of a norm. Simply put, the "purpose" is what lawmakers intended to achieve by implementing a certain rule. I will call this aspect of normativity the "policy" of the law. While it may be familiar to common law jurists, readers with a civil law background should note that the issue is akin to an analysis of the so-called *Gesetzeszweck*, or *ratio*, of a law. Second, with respect to conflicts law, terminological affairs are more complicated. As Friedrich K. Juenger pointed out some decades ago, no name had ever been universally accepted for the discipline dedicated to determining the applicable law in cases with international elements.[7] This situation has not changed. Today, the terms "private international law," "conflict of laws," and "choice of law" may be used to refer to this discipline. I will not tilt at windmills and shall thus also use "choice of law" and "conflict of laws" (or simply "conflicts law" or "conflicts") interchangeably throughout the book. Worth pointing out, however, is the fact that my inquiry concerns issues of choice as such and of the territorial scope of the applicable law which is also debated under the doctrine of subject-matter jurisdiction. With this in mind, the reader should not stumble over an occasional recurrence to terminological subtleties.

[7] Friedrich K. Juenger, *Choice of Law and Multistate Justice* 4 (1993).

1 Civil Law History
Germany and Europe

> The personality right, in principle, extends across the whole world: for the personality can exert its power over all mankind. . . . Since, however, full trademark protection will not be granted on the basis of the owner's personality alone, but usually also requires owner activity and a contribution by public authorities, an indirect localization exists. The same personality that is protected worldwide with respect to unfair competition enjoys trademark protection in one state where a trademark is registered, but not in another where no such registration exists. . . . If it is correct that the trademark right is a universal right of its owner's personality, but as an enhancement of such a right localized in and valid only in the territories of single countries, a domestic trademark can be infringed on only inside the national territory, a foreign trademark only abroad.
>
> Author's translation from Josef Kohler, *Warenzeichenrecht* 206–207 and 246 (2nd edn., 1910)

Introduction

Both in Europe and the United States, a socioeconomic cataclysm of industrialization and market liberalization—including the invention of branding, mass advertising, and marketing psychology—was the driving force behind the construction of modern trademark and unfair competition laws. During the last two centuries, legal doctrine accordingly underwent partly groundbreaking transformations. Many of these account for today's transatlantic dichotomy, particularly in the field of trademark and unfair competition choice of law, or conflicts law. My analysis will focus on the most relevant characteristics of legal doctrine between the eighteenth and twenty-first centuries.[1] I argue that a closer look at conceptual and

[1] The history of German, European, and US trademark and unfair competition law has been ably documented and explained many times. I do not intend to plow on the same ground. For Germany and Europe, *see, e.g.*, Elmar Wadle, *Fabrikzeichenschutz und Markenrecht—Geschichte und Gestalt des deutschen Markenschutzes im 19. Jahrhundert, Erster Teil: Entfaltung* (1977); Elmar Wadle, *Entwicklungslinien des deutschen Markenschutzes im 19. Jahrhundert*, 1979 GRUR 383; Jürgen Simon, *Das allgemeine Persönlichkeitsrecht und seine gewerblichen Erscheinungsformen* (1981); Elmar Wadle,

structural differences, as well as commonalities between European and US law, provides the basis for a reconceptualization of the field.

With regard to commonalities, there is one aspect that has always, albeit mostly subconsciously, dominated the field across jurisdictions: cases of alleged trademark infringement are considered an issue of individual property rights protection. It is usually the plaintiff-as-right-owner who asks the court to protect a hard-earned reputation, goodwill, or business position against the defendant-as-villain trying to ride on her coattails. Indeed, it is the subjectivism of right owners' and courts' perspectives that has driven trademark doctrine toward a system of propertization, the extension of trademark rights as domains of economic power, and protection against competition in the marketplace. By the 1800s, this extension of private rights had already become the order of the day in private law in general—both in Germany (as in other European jurisdictions) and in the United States. Trademark law was no exception from this trend. In fact, a closer look at German and US doctrines reveals that the propertization of trademark rights started around the same time and has grown continuously since.

Yet the methods used to extend property in trademarks have varied widely between the two countries' systems. Roughly summarized, German trademark propertization can be understood as an evolution of formalistic rights protection. The subject matter of statutory and court-made rules was a state-granted privilege. The US equivalent, by contrast, can be seen as founded on a nonformal concept of goodwill protection. Trademarks were considered market-based entitlements rather than state-granted monopolies. These divergent conceptions necessarily led to distinctly different approaches to conflicts law, as reflected in current practice. In Germany, the idea of formal property in trademarks and an adherence to the traditional conception of state-granted rights have led to a rule of strict territoriality. Under the dominant *lex loci protectionis* rule, trademark rights are, in principle, protected only against infringing conduct *within* the granting state's territory; foreign-based activities or commercial effects are, at best, of secondary concern. Quite differently,

Fabrikzeichenschutz und Markenrecht—Geschichte und Gestalt des deutschen Markenschutzes im 19. Jahrhundert, Zweiter Teil: Historisch-dogmatische Grundlinien (1983); Friedrich-Karl Beier & Annette Kur, *Das Verhältnis von Markenrecht und Recht des unlauteren Wettbewerbs im Wandel der Zeiten*, 477, in *Festschrift für Wolfgang Fikentscher zum 70. Geburtstag* (Bernhard Großfeld et al. eds., 1998); Elmar Wadle, *Werden und Wandel des deutschen Markenrechts*, 337, in *Geistiges Eigentum—Bausteine zur Rechtsgeschichte, vol. II* (Elmar Wadle ed., 2003); Sonja Martina Baehr, *Die historische Entwicklung des Markenrechts in Deutschland* (2008). My inquiry has widely benefited from and is significantly based on Elmar Wadle's authoritative illustration of German trademark law history. For the United States, *see infra* chapter 2 (p. 76 *et seq.*), notably the references in fn. 1.

US practice, from the beginning, built on a concept of virtually borderless and liquid market extensions. Accordingly, it considers commercial effects to be of ultimate importance in conflicts determination.

While both systems appear to have perpetuated the dichotomy, a new trend has recently begun. On the one hand, US courts are becoming more cautious in applying domestic law to foreign-based conduct. Indeed, the "*Bulova* test" for Lanham Act subject-matter jurisdiction, established in the 1950s, has increasingly come under critique. German courts, on the other hand, have gone in the opposite direction. Most recently, in an internet trademark conflict, the Bundesgerichtshof required "commercial effects" within the country, disregarding the once ironclad rule that territorial conduct was required. Notwithstanding these moderate beginnings of approximation, however, legal doctrine everywhere is far from having established a consistent or feasible solution for the difficult balancing between the universality of trademark rights and their underprotection. In this regard, the situation still resembles what Frank I. Schechter, in a slightly different context, described almost a century ago as an attainment of "forward strides ... by appeals to 'good conscience' and 'judicial sensibilities' rather than to strictly legal principles derived from a critical analysis."[2] The first two chapters—which examine distinct elements of the history of German, European, and US law—will be my starting point for such a critical analysis. In the following chapters, I will analyze the scholarly debate taking place around the world, the structure of substantive law conceptions and its thus-far unexplained convergence, and the doctrine of international comity. On this basis, in the last chapter, I will attempt to suggest a reconceptualization of trademark and unfair competition conflicts law.

For this chapter, which looks at German and European civil law, several aspects are of particular interest; these themes will guide the order of my exploration. In German trademark law, the dichotomy between registered rights as formal state grants and nonregistered entitlements as informal rights, especially under the rules against unfair competition, has become so deeply ingrained that a reconceptualization has become virtually impossible. Not surprisingly, the strict distinction between formal trademark "property" and "nonproperty" unfair competition prevention still dominates modern doctrine (*see infra* p. 9 *et seq.*). At the conflicts level, this separation of fields has had a significant impact. Trademark conflicts law has transformed from an initial idea of the universality of rights under Josef Kohler's 1880s theory of personality

[2] Frank I. Schechter, *The Rational Basis of Trademark Protection*, 40 Harv. L. Rev. 813, 813 (1927).

protection into a rule of strict territoriality that limits the application of domestic law to territorial conduct only (*lex loci protectionis*). Unfair competition conflicts doctrine, by contrast, has embraced a marketplace effects principle similar to the approach in international antitrust law from the 1960s (*see infra* p. 53 *et seq.*). It is only recently that the effects principle has also surfaced in German trademark conflicts, notably in the Bundesgerichtshof's 2004 *HOTEL MARITIME* decision and its recourse to a testing of "commercial effects." While this represents a first step toward modernization, the replacement of the formalist *lex loci protectionis* with a balancing-of-interests and commercial-effects testing hardly offers a consistent or workable standard for conflicts resolution (*see infra* p. 74–75).

Section 1 Substantive Trademark and Unfair Competition Law

Even though today the protection of trademark rights is universally acknowledged as part of the larger field of unfair competition prevention,[3] a dichotomy has strictly divided the two sectors. Trademark law has been and continues to be dominated by the idea that trademarks are state-granted monopoly rights and privileges. This is due in part to the fact that protection was initially an issue of state-backed enforcement, largely through administrative and criminal law sanctions. Even though a system of private enforcement gained ground over time, remnants of privilege theory have survived—and it is this foundation of privilege theory that also governs in conflicts law.

I Structure: State Regulation and Formal Privileges

Throughout the nineteenth and most of the twentieth century, the doctrinal characterization of what constituted a "trademark," "unfair competition," and protectable subject matter was heterogeneous. Most importantly (and as a caveat), the issue was often not the protection of "trademarks" in a modern sense but the protection of personal names, firm or corporate names, and other indicators of source or origin. In particular, criminal law sanctions were first applied with regard to the protection of names and firm names, not of

[3] *See, e.g.*, RGZ vol. 120, 325, 328—*Sonnengold* (30 April 1928); BGH 1980 GRUR, 797, 799—*Topfit Boonekamp* (27 February 1980); Alfons Kraft, *Die Entwicklung des Warenzeichenrechts als Teil des allgemeinen Wettbewerbsrechts*, 729, 729, in *Gewerblicher Rechtsschutz und Urheberrecht in Deutschland, Festschrift zum hundertjährigen Bestehen der Deutschen Vereinigung für gewerblichen Rechtsschutz und Urheberrecht und ihrer Zeitschrift, vol. II* (Friedrich-Karl Beier et al. eds., 1991) (with further references).

trademarks.[4] While these doctrinal intricacies are important to keep in mind, they must not fog our more specific view: substantive law doctrine in the field began as a system of preventing fraud and deception, but over time its strict and exclusive public policy impetus was lost, giving way to a structure oriented toward the protection of individual rights. What remained unchanged was the understanding of trademarks as state-granted privileges.

A The Criminal Law Beginnings

Early nineteenth-century Germany and Western Europe witnessed a fundamental alteration of social and economic conditions. Legal approaches to trademark protection changed accordingly. Prior to the nineteenth century, the guild system (*System der Zünfte*) had governed, whereby market competition was regulated on the basis of producer self-administration.[5] On the macrolevel, of course, absolutistic lawmakers in Germany's states regulated trade and commerce through tariffs, certain prohibitions on production and trade, and the granting of privileges (for instance, for industrial inventions or book reprints). Yet on the microlevel—notably with respect to individual transacting—they intervened only sporadically.[6] One example was the control of product quality.[7] With respect to trademark or trade-name use

[4] *See, e.g.*, Elmar Wadle, *Entwicklungslinien des deutschen Markenschutzes im 19. Jahrhundert*, 1979 GRUR 383, 383 *et seq.*; Diethelm Klippel, *Die Bedeutung des Rheinischen Rechts für die Entwicklung des Namens- und Firmenschutzes in Deutschland*, 123, 133–134, in *Revolution, Reform, Restauration: Formen der Veränderung von Recht und Gesellschaft* (Heinz Mohnhaupt ed., 1988); Elmar Wadle, *Der Weg zum gesetzlichen Schutz des geistigen und gewerblichen Schaffens—Die deutsche Entwicklung im 19. Jahrhundert*, 93, 147–148, in *Gewerblicher Rechtsschutz und Urheberrecht in Deutschland, Festschrift zum hundertjährigen Bestehen der Deutschen Vereinigung für gewerblichen Rechtsschutz und Urheberrecht und ihrer Zeitschrift, vol. I* (Friedrich-Karl Beier et al. eds., 1991).

[5] For a historical overview, *see, e.g.*, Joseph Ludwig Brunstein, *Studien im österreichischen Markenrecht—Ausschliessliches Gebrauchsrecht, Markendelict, Processhindernde Vorfragen* 1 *et seq.* (1895); Arnold Seligsohn, *Gesetz zum Schutz der Warenbezeichnungen* 17 *et seq.* (2nd edn., 1905); Adolf Lobe, *Die Bekämpfung des unlauteren Wettbewerbs, vol. I: Der unlautere Wettbewerb als Rechtsverletzung nach dem Bürgerlichen Gesetzbuch und den Nebengesetzen* 72 *et seq.*, 115 *et seq.* (1907); Frank I. Schechter, *The Historical Foundations of the Law Relating to Trade-Marks* 19 *et seq.* (1925); Johannes Andreas Bolle, *Entwicklungslinien und systematische Stellung der Regeln über den unlauteren Wettbewerb im deutschen und englischen Recht* 9 *et seq.*, 35–36 (1928); Jürgen Simon, *Das allgemeine Persönlichkeitsrecht und seine gewerblichen Erscheinungsformen* 117 (1981).

[6] *See also* Henning von Stechow, *Das Gesetz zur Bekämpfung des unlauteren Wettbewerbs vom 27. Mai 1896—Entstehungsgeschichte und Wirkung* 23 *et seq.* (2002) (with further references).

[7] *See, e.g.*, Wolfgang Schuhmacher, *Verbraucher und Recht in historischer Sicht* 25–26 (1981); *see also* Elmar Wadle, *Fabrikzeichenschutz und Markenrecht—Geschichte und Gestalt des deutschen Markenschutzes im 19. Jahrhundert, Erster Teil: Entfaltung* 20 *et seq.* (1977); Elmar Wadle, *Fabrikzeichenschutz und Markenrecht—Geschichte und Gestalt des deutschen Markenschutzes im 19. Jahrhundert, Zweiter Teil: Historisch-dogmatische Grundlinien* 332 *et seq.* (1983).

beyond this modest domain, however, there was no regulation, nor was there a general system of unfair competition prevention.[8] In other words, since there was no freedom of competition, no regulation was necessary.

This situation would change in the early nineteenth century. From then on, the increasing incorporation of freedom of economic activity and freedom of trade (*Gewerbefreiheit*) into German states' legal systems set the stage for a growing use of trade names and trademarks in daily commerce. The guild system was first deprived of its powers, and then completely disintegrated. One example is Prussia, where the introduction of freedom of economic competition was combined with an abolition of the guilds in 1810 and 1811.[9] Furthermore, innovations in production methods and an extension of trade infrastructure brought further momentum to the economic transformation in state and society. In addition to the shift toward market liberalism in economic and legal thought, the advent of mass production and consumption accelerated the development of competition.[10] Starting around 1840, transportation infrastructure was modernized, and the existing economy of handcraft and small-business manufacturing was superseded by methods of industrialized and standardized production.[11] This stimulated a need for more expandable instruments of market communication. Production and consumption no longer coincided temporally and geographically. The growing distance between producer and consumer resulted in anonymity and alienation.[12] While product features, notably source

[8] *See* Wolfgang Schuhmacher, *Verbraucher und Recht in historischer Sicht* 11–33 (1981).

[9] Henning von Stechow, *Das Gesetz zur Bekämpfung des unlauteren Wettbewerbs vom 27. Mai 1896—Entstehungsgeschichte und Wirkung* 27 (2002).

[10] Elmar Wadle, *Fabrikzeichenschutz und Markenrecht—Geschichte und Gestalt des deutschen Markenschutzes im 19. Jahrhundert, Erster Teil: Entfaltung* 32 *et seq.* (1977); Elmar Wadle, *Entwicklungslinien des deutschen Markenschutzes im 19. Jahrhundert*, 1979 GRUR 383, 383; Friedrich-Karl Beier & Annette Kur, *Das Verhältnis von Markenrecht und Recht des unlauteren Wettbewerbs im Wandel der Zeiten*, 477, 477–478, in *Festschrift für Wolfgang Fikentscher zum 70. Geburtstag* (Bernhard Großfeld et al. eds., 1998); Elmar Wadle, *Werden und Wandel des deutschen Markenrechts*, 337, 342 *et seq.*, in *Geistiges Eigentum—Bausteine zur Rechtsgeschichte, vol. II* (Elmar Wadle ed., 2003).

[11] *See, e.g.*, Elmar Wadle, *Der Weg zum gesetzlichen Schutz des geistigen und gewerblichen Schaffens—Die deutsche Entwicklung im 19. Jahrhundert*, 93, 105, 139 *et seq.*, in *Gewerblicher Rechtsschutz und Urheberrecht in Deutschland, Festschrift zum hundertjährigen Bestehen der Deutschen Vereinigung für gewerblichen Rechtsschutz und Urheberrecht und ihrer Zeitschrift, vol. I* (Friedrich-Karl Beier et al. eds., 1991); Wolfgang Schuhmacher, *Verbraucher und Recht in historischer Sicht* 37 (1981) (comparing mid-nineteenth-century industrialization in Germany with that in Austria); *see also* Elmar Wadle, *Fabrikzeichenschutz und Markenrecht—Geschichte und Gestalt des deutschen Markenschutzes im 19. Jahrhundert, Erster Teil: Entfaltung* 32–33 (1977).

[12] For an extensive account of this development, *see* Heinrich Bechtel, *Wirtschaftsgeschichte Deutschlands—Vom Beginn des 16. bis zum Ende des 18. Jahrhunderts, vol. II* 258 *et seq.* (1952); for the development of trade name and trademark use, *see, e.g.*, Erwin Dichtl,

and origin, had been an issue of local information for centuries, extended marketplaces could no longer offer a reliable face-to-face trust mechanism. This bore a risk of deterioration in quality.[13] And, in fact, unfair competition became widespread.[14] Legal doctrine was forced to follow suit and accept the challenge of regulation.

Yet, under the influence of liberalist thought, the idea had come to govern that the state should largely abstain from regulation in areas that had been taken over by individual freedom and private activity.[15] In other

Grundidee, Entwicklungsepochen und heutige wirtschaftliche Bedeutung des Markenartikels, 17, 18–19, in *Markenartikel heute: Marke, Markt und Marketing* (Clemens-August Andreae et al. eds., 1978); Elmar Wadle, *Der Weg zum gesetzlichen Schutz des geistigen und gewerblichen Schaffens—Die deutsche Entwicklung im 19. Jahrhundert*, 93, 105, 139 *et seq.*, in *Gewerblicher Rechtsschutz und Urheberrecht in Deutschland, Festschrift zum hundertjährigen Bestehen der Deutschen Vereinigung für gewerblichen Rechtsschutz und Urheberrecht und ihrer Zeitschrift, vol. I* (Friedrich-Karl Beier et al. eds., 1991); Elmar Wadle, *Werden und Wandel des deutschen Markenrechts*, 337, 342 *et seq.*, in *Geistiges Eigentum—Bausteine zur Rechtsgeschichte, vol. II* (Elmar Wadle ed., 2003).

[13] For a lucid illustration, *see, e.g.*, Otto Mayer, *Die concurrence déloyale—Ein Beitrag aus dem französischen Rechte zur Lehre vom geistigen Eigenthum*, 26 Zeitschrift für das Gesammte Handelsrecht 363, 394–395 (1881) ("Im Strome des Verkehres tritt die Person häufig ganz zurück. Man kennt schließlich nur den Ort, den Laden, die Werkstätte, woraus man seine Waaren bezieht; oder gar es verschwindet auch dieses aus der Beachtung. Die Waaren werden ja meist nicht vom Ursprungsorte unmittelbar entnommen; sie gehen durch so und so viele Hände, bevor sie den endgültigen Abnehmer d.h. den Verbraucher finden. . . . Hier aber reicht der Name nicht mehr aus. Je weiter er sich von der Person entfernt, desto mehr wird er zum Abstraktum."); *see also* R. Klostermann, *Das geistige Eigenthum an Schriften, Kunstwerken und Erfindungen, nach Preussischem und internationalem Rechte, vol. I (Allgemeiner Theil—Verlagsrecht und Nachdruck)* 216–217 (1867). For the problem of alienation as such, *see, e.g.*, E.P. Harris, *Random Thoughts on Trade and Advertising*, 8 Inland Printer 202–203 (December 1890) ("The manufacturer once made everything in one shop, and sold to everybody near him. Now he only makes one or a few things, and must supply more customers, who are widely scattered. The consumer, who once looked to the comparatively local jack-at-all-trades producer to supply all his wants, must now use the products of numerous and remote manufacturers. Thus there is an ever-widening distance between the producer and the consumer. But the producer and consumer should know each other . . . . The railroad only allows producer and consumer to drift farther and farther from an acquaintance with each other. Only the printer's ink can bridge the distance, and bring the producer and consumer into relations of intimacy. The locomotive and printing press must go hand in hand.").

[14] As a scholar put it in 1870: "Der rechte Spekulant geht aus von dem Grundsatz: mundus vult decipi, ergo decipiatur. Die glänzende Außenseite der Produkte ist ihm die Hauptsache, viel weniger die Haltbarkeit, die Solidität. . . . Alle erlaubten und unerlaubten Mittel der Täuschung und der Reklame werden von gewissenlosen Menschen in Szene gesetzt; und, was das schlimme ist, der eine kann nicht hinter dem andern zurückbleiben, so häuft sich Täuschung auf Täuschung, Betrug auf Betrug. Sind wir von amerikanischem, englischem und französischem Humbug noch weit entfernt, so sind diese Dinge bei uns doch auch schon so entwickelt wie irgend wünschenswerth." *See* Gustav Schmoller, *Zur Geschichte der deutschen Kleingewerbe im 19. Jahrhundert—Statistische und nationalökonomische Untersuchungen* 230–231 (1870).

[15] *See, e.g.*, Hans Schuler, *Die Concurrence déloyale und ihre Beziehungen zu Name, Firma, Marke, Fabrik- und Geschäftsgeheimnis im französischen, schweizerischen und deutschen Recht*

words, state intervention had to have a relevant and necessary purpose in order to be justified. With respect to trademark and trade-name protection, such justification was considered to exist when protection of the consuming public against fraud and deception or with regard to public health was at stake. This, however, was not an issue of private rights enforcement.[16] The panacea instead was seen in criminal law sanctions.[17] Beyond this narrow sector, as was further contended, no regulation was indicated. The 1871 Criminal Code of the German Reich was paradigmatic for this era.[18] Section 287 of the code penalized the false use of personal and trade names in the branding or trading of goods or packaging.[19] This provision was actually based on the 1851 Prussian Criminal Code, which, in turn, had implemented the Dresden

45 (1895) ("Der tiefere Grund, welcher die deutsche Rechtsprechung in diesem Sinne geleitet hat, ist wohl der, die einmal anerkannte Freiheit in Handel und Verkehr sich auch uneingeschränkt entwickeln zu lassen, die Furcht, es möchte Willkür des Richters hemmend eingreifen, so dass man lieber die Auswüchse dieser missbrauchten Freiheit dulden als dem Missbrauch entgegentreten wollte."); Josef Kohler, *Der unlautere Wettbewerb—Darstellung des Wettbewerbsrechts* 58 (1914). For the French law, *see also* Francis Déak, *Contracts and Combinations in Restraint of Trade in French Law—A Comparative Study*, 21 Iowa L. Rev. 397 (1936); Walter J. Derenberg, *The Influence of the French Code Civil on the Modern Law of Unfair Competition*, 4 Am. J. Comp. L. 1, 2 (1955).

16 *See, e.g.*, Otto Mayer, *Die concurrence déloyale—Ein Beitrag aus dem französischen Rechte zur Lehre vom geistigen Eigenthum*, 26 Zeitschrift für das Gesammte Handelsrecht 363, 434 *et seq.* (1881); for Switzerland, *see, e.g.*, F. Meili, *Das Markenstrafrecht auf Grund des eidgenössischen Markenschutzgesetzes sowie der von der Schweiz abgeschlossenen Staatsverträge und der internationalen Konvention von 1883* 10 *et seq.* (1888); for an overview, *see* Elmar Wadle, *Fabrikzeichenschutz und Markenrecht—Geschichte und Gestalt des deutschen Markenschutzes im 19. Jahrhundert, Zweiter Teil: Historisch-dogmatische Grundlinien* 280 *et seq.*, 337 *et seq.* (1983); Siegbert Lammel, *Recht zur Ordnung des Wettbewerbs: Deutschland*, 3806, 3807, in *Handbuch der Quellen und Literatur der neueren europäischen Privatrechtsgeschichte, vol. III: Das 19. Jahrhundert, 3rd part: Gesetzgebung zu den privatrechtlichen Sondergebieten* (Helmut Coing ed., 1986).

17 For the early nineteenth-century landscape, *see, e.g.*, Philipp Allfeld, *Grundriss des gewerblichen Rechtsschutzes* 99 (1910) (featuring an overview of Prussia, Bavaria, and other German states). *See also* Elmar Wadle, *Der Weg zum gesetzlichen Schutz des geistigen und gewerblichen Schaffens—Die deutsche Entwicklung im 19. Jahrhundert*, 93, 142 *et seq.*, in *Gewerblicher Rechtsschutz und Urheberrecht in Deutschland, Festschrift zum hundertjährigen Bestehen der Deutschen Vereinigung für gewerblichen Rechtsschutz und Urheberrecht und ihrer Zeitschrift, vol. I* (Friedrich-Karl Beier et al. eds., 1991).

18 Gesetz, betreffend die Redaktion des Strafgesetzbuches für den Norddeutschen Bund als Strafgesetzbuch für das Deutsche Reich of 15 May 1871, Deutsches Reichsgesetzblatt 1871, Nr. 24, 127–205.

19 Section 287 stated: "Wer Waaren oder deren Verpackung fälschlich mit dem Namen oder der Firma eines inländischen Fabrikunternehmers, Produzenten oder Kaufmanns bezeichnet oder wissentlich dergleichen fälschlich bezeichnete Waaren in Verkehr bringt, wird mit Geldstrafe von funfzig bis zu Eintausend Thalern oder mit Gefängniß bis zu sechs Monaten bestraft." For the perceived deficiencies of the provision for want of a concurrent civil law protection, *see* Wilhelm Endemann, *Der Markenschutz nach dem Reichsgesetz vom 30. November 1874*, 32 Archiv für Theorie und Praxis des Allgemeinen Deutschen Handels- und Wechselrechts 1, 3–4 (1875).

Agreement reached by member states of the German Customs Union (*Zollverein*) in 1838.[20] At the Custom Union's conference, member-state delegates had agreed on two basic premises. First, they had established a uniform standard of enforcement for all member states and their subjects. Second, they had identified criminal law sanctions as the preferred instrument of regulation.[21] But this approach was soon to be superseded by alternative conceptions of trademark and name protection.

B From State Regulation to Individual Rights Protection

Over time, a broader understanding of trademark and unfair competition policies—particularly the regulatory aspect of market information correctness—gained ground. This also brought ideas of private individual rights protection to the fore. In an 1839 treatise on political economy, for instance, self-evaluation and marketing of the quality of products (as well as the use of a personal name or mark) was described as having both "the purpose to protect purchasers from fraud and the economic purpose to promote sale of those wares in the quality of which the purchasers can trust."[22] Indeed, by the early nineteenth century, ideas of consumer trust and quality preservation had become part of the theoretical debate. As one scholar posited in 1827:

[20] Section 269 of the Prussian Criminal Code stated: "Wer Waaren oder deren Verpackung fälschlich mit dem Namen oder der Firma und mit dem Wohn- oder Fabrikorte eines inländischen Fabrik-Unternehmers, Produzenten oder Kaufmanns bezeichnet, oder wissentlich dergleichen fälschlich bezeichnete Waaren in Verkehr bringt, soll mit Geldbuße von funfzig bis zu Eintausend Thalern, und im Rückfalle zugleich mit Gefängniß bis zu sechs Monaten bestraft werden." For the original text, *see, e.g.*, Georg Beseler, *Kommentar über das Strafgesetzbuch für die Preußischen Staaten und das Einführungsgesetz vom 14. April 1851* (1851).

[21] Member states agreed that "es hierbei in der Hauptsache nur auf eine Gleichstellung der vereinsländischen Handelsleute oder Fabrikanten mit den eigenen Unterthanen ankomme, und daß ... im Allgemeinen auf Einführung einer, jedoch nur auf Antrag der Betheiligten zu handhabenden Strafbestimmung über den Mißbrauch fremder Waarenbezeichnungen in denjenigen Vereinsstaaten, wo eine solche noch gar nicht, oder wenigstens nicht in Bezug auf die Waaren- oder Fabrikzeichen anderer vereinsländischer Unterthanen, bestehe, Bedacht zu nehmen seyn werde, ohne auf Gleichstellung des Strafmaaßes zu bestehen, indem die Bestimmung des letzteren jeder einzelnen Regierung zu überlassen sey." (Hauptprotokoll über die zweite Generalkonferenz der Bevollmächtigten der Zollvereinsstaaten, 56–59 (cited after Elmar Wadle, *Fabrikzeichenschutz und Markenrecht—Geschichte und Gestalt des deutschen Markenschutzes im 19. Jahrhundert, Erster Teil: Entfaltung* 74 (1977))).

[22] Karl Heinrich Rau, *Lehrbuch der politischen Oekonomie, vol. II–Grundsätze der Volkswirthschaftspolitik* § 219, 350 (2nd edn., 1839) ("[D]en polizeilichen Zweck, um die Käufer vor Betrug zu schützen, als [auch] den volkswirthschaftlichen, den Absatz solcher Gewerkswaaren vermöge des größeren Zutrauens, welches die Käufer in sie setzen können, zu befördern." (author's translation)).

Trademarks are a kind of a substitute for public expert control since anyone must take care to maintain the good reputation of his mark by upholding the quality of his ware. At the same time, a well-reputed mark is the foundation for extensive sales and can be the basis of a useful monopoly, which in turn further spurs better-quality fabrication.[23]

This modernization of policies not only suggested a stronger emphasis on the private rights aspect of trademark protection but also included a distinctive flavor of personality rights protection. In 1844, for instance, Robert von Mohl, in a leading treatise on administrative and police law, explained that the deceptive use of another's trade name was an invasion of personality rights.[24] Even though von Mohl did not conclude that the private right element of name protection ultimately also required establishing a civil law remedy,[25] his reference to the owner's individual rights was a predecessor to Josef Kohler's later iconic personality rights theory.[26]

Under a different lens, von Mohl's explanation reflects a more general and trans-European debate on trademark protection, particularly with respect to the character of trademark rights as private entitlements. This is illustrated by the development of French doctrine, which at times also influenced German law. Interest in foreign trademark and unfair competition regimes was common in nineteenth-century scholarship. Not only had inter-European trade increased, but in Germany, the French *code civil* was

[23] Johann Carl Leuchs, *Gewerb- und Handelsfreiheit; oder über die Mittel das Glük der Völker, den Reichthum und die Macht der Staaten zu begründen* 178 (1827) ("Fabrikzeichen ersezen in gewisser Hinsicht die Schauanstalten, indem jeder durch gute Waare dafür sorgen muß, daß sein Zeichen sich in gutem Ruf erhält. Zugleich begründet ein solches in gutem Ruf befindliches Zeichen einen ausgebreiteten Absaz und begründet dadurch ein nüzliches Monopol, das um so mehr zu besserer Fabrikation auffordert." (author's translation)).

[24] Robert von Mohl, *Die Polizei-Wissenschaft nach den Grundsätzen des Rechtsstaates, vol. III* § 29, at 301 (2nd edn., 1845) ("Nicht selten kömmt es im Gewerbsleben vor, daß von einem in keiner Weise dazu Befugten auf einer von ihm verfertigten Waare der Name oder das unterscheidende Verfertigungszeichen eines anderen Gewerbenden angebracht wird. Diese Handlung enthält nun aber nicht nur eine Täuschung des Käufers, welcher absichtlich über die Person des Verfertigers irre geführt wird; sondern sie ist auch ein entschiedenes Unrecht gegen Denjenigen, dessen Name fälschlich gebraucht wird. Einmal ist es eine Verletzung seiner Persönlichkeit, indem ein Anderer sich ohne sein Wissen und gegen seinen Willen für ihn ausgiebt, wenigstens bei bestimmter Gelegenheit. Zweitens wird es in der Regel eine Verläumdung gegen ihn seyn, indem wohl gewöhnlich eine schlechtere Waare, als er sie zu verfertigen pflegt, lügenhaft für die seinige ausgegeben wird. Endlich wird ihm in doppelter Beziehung in seinem Gewerbe geschadet. Einmal durch Verlockung eines Theiles seiner Abnehmer, welche sein Erzeugniß zu kaufen beabsichtigten und nun durch die falsche Ausschrift zu einem Fremden geführt werden; zweitens, und häufig noch weit bedeutender, durch die Verderbung seines Rufes, welcher unter der schlechtern auf seinen Namen gestellten Waare leidet.").

[25] He found penal sanctions sufficient. [26] *See infra* p. 21–27.

governing law in numerous areas of the Reich due to the Napoleonic annexations in the early nineteenth century.[27] French law, however, differed significantly from the German states' common law (*gemeines Recht*) and their statutory trademark laws. Postrevolutionary France had implemented numerous laws protecting intellectual property. Protection was granted to *propriété littéraire et artistique*. In patent law, for instance, the invention as such was deemed a *propriété de son auteur*. While trademark protection was initially also founded on a concept of criminal law protection against *contrefaçon*, it soon also became a question of protecting the owner's individual *propriété industrielle*.[28] Under a genuine natural law perspective, trademark rights were characterized as sacred rights of production and labor (*droits sacrés de la production et du travail*).[29] Remarkably, however, and in line with post-revolutionary France's aversion to privileges, there were no state-administered rights in trade names or marks.[30] Furthermore, during the second half of the nineteenth century, the scope of protection was extended to cover instances of improper conduct, even absent the infringement of formal property rights. Establishing fairness in commerce became the chief concern.[31] In French trademark doctrine, the subject matter was amended from the protection of property to the prevention of unfair competition (*concurrence déloyale*).[32] The legal basis was found in article 1382 of

[27] *See, e.g.*, Otto Mayer, *Die concurrence déloyale—Ein Beitrag aus dem französischen Rechte zur Lehre vom geistigen Eigenthum*, 26 Zeitschrift für das Gesammte Handelsrecht 363 (1881); *see also* Elmar Wadle, *Das rheinisch-französische Deliktsrecht und die Judikatur des Reichsgerichts zum unlauteren Wettbewerb*, 365, 365–366, in *Geistiges Eigentum—Bausteine zur Rechtsgeschichte, vol. II* (Elmar Wadle ed., 2003).

[28] For an extensive illustration, *see, e.g.*, Adrien Gastambide, *Traité théorique et pratique des contrefaçons en tous genres* 410 *et seq.* (1837); Étienne Blanc, *Traité de la contrefaçon et de sa poursuite en justice* 145 *et seq.* (1838); Eugène Pouillet, *Traité des marques de fabrique et de la concurrence déloyale en tous genres* 942 *et seq.* (5th edn., 1906); for a summary, *see* Walter Bühler, *Die zivilrechtliche Bekämpfung des unlauteren Wettbewerbs in der Praxis des schweizerischen Bundesgerichts* 90 *et seq.* (1930).

[29] *See, e.g.*, Adrien Gastambide, *Traité théorique et pratique des contrefaçons en tous genres* 1 (1837); Friedrich-Karl Beier, *Grundfragen des französischen Markenrechts* 31 *et seq.* (1962); *see also* Elmar Wadle, *Fabrikzeichenschutz und Markenrecht—Geschichte und Gestalt des deutschen Markenschutzes im 19. Jahrhundert, Erster Teil: Entfaltung* 50–51 (1977); Elmar Wadle, *Entwicklungslinien des deutschen Markenschutzes im 19. Jahrhundert*, 1979 GRUR 383, 387.

[30] For the early abolition of privileges in France, *see* notably the French Constitution of 3 September 1791 and its prologue: "Il n'y a plus, pour aucune partie de la Nation, ni pour aucun individu, aucun privilège, ni exception au droit commun de tous les Français."

[31] Rudolf Krasser, *Die Entwicklung der Ordnung des Wettbewerbsrechts in der französischen und deutschen Rechtsprechung des 19. Jahrhunderts*, 145, 152, in *Wissenschaft und Kodifikation des Privatrechts im 19. Jahrhundert, vol. IV* (Helmut Coing & Walter Wilhelm eds., 1979).

[32] Elmar Wadle, *Das rheinisch-französische Deliktsrecht und die Judikatur des Reichsgerichts zum unlauteren Wettbewerb*, 365, 374, in *Geistiges Eigentum—Bausteine zur Rechtsgeschichte, vol. II* (Elmar Wadle ed., 2003).

the *code civil.*[33] In the end, civil law remedies prevailed in both trademark and unfair competition law. Indeed, private rights enforcement upon the individual's initiative had become the guiding paradigm in practice. Although criminal sanctions still existed, they were of only secondary concern.[34] By the end of the century, French law had abandoned the concept of state-administered and state-enforced monopolies and privileges.[35]

C The Positivist Concept of Privilege Grants

While countries such as Austria followed the French lead,[36] and several Italian states acknowledged the concept of private trademark property,[37] German lawmakers were more hesitant. They refused to acknowledge name and trademark rights as preexisting or natural entitlements.[38] German

[33] Rudolf Krasser, *Die Entwicklung der Ordnung des Wettbewerbsrechts in der französischen und deutschen Rechtsprechung des 19. Jahrhunderts*, 145, 158, in *Wissenschaft und Kodifikation des Privatrechts im 19. Jahrhundert, vol. IV* (Helmut Coing & Walter Wilhelm eds., 1979).

[34] *See, e.g.*, Adrien Gastambide, *Traité théorique et pratique des contrefaçons en tous genres* 427 (1837) ("Les cas sont rares, il faut le dire, où cette juridiction a été saisie. La gravité de la peine a été et serait encore trop souvent une cause d'acquittement. L'usage est de poursuivre ces affaires par la voie civile.").

[35] Otto Mayer, *Die concurrence déloyale—Ein Beitrag aus dem französischen Rechte zur Lehre vom geistigen Eigenthum*, 26 Zeitschrift für das Gesammte Handelsrecht 363, 367 (1881) ("Der Rechtsschutz, der gewährt wird, ohne besonderes Gesetz, auf Grund des allgemeinen Rechtes, stützt sich sicherlich nicht mehr auf ein Privilegium oder Monopol mit außerprivatrechtlicher Begründung. ... Wir werden also untersuchen, wie jener Rechtsschutz auf den gemeinen Deliktsbegriff sich gründet und wie hieraus die Idee einer propriété immatérielle erwächst."). *See also* Adriano Vanzetti, *Funktion und Rechtsnatur der Marke (2. Teil)*, 1965 GRUR Ausl. 185, 186 ("So verstanden, stellte der Begriff des Eigentums eine politische Bekräftigung des liberalen Individualismus und eine Absage an das Privilegienwesen dar. ... wurde dem Begriff ... ein viel weiterer Sinn beigelegt als man das heute tut, indem man praktisch das Eigentum der Inhaberschaft an einem absoluten subjektiven Recht gleichsetzte, gerade weil der Begriff Eigentum nur dazu diente, die Existenz eines individuellen Rechtes anstatt eines gnadenweise erteilten Privilegs herauszustellen.").

[36] *See, e.g.*, in the Austrian Trademark Act of 7 December 1858. *See also, e.g.*, Moriz von Stubenrauch, *Das österreichische Marken- und Musterschutzgesetz* 1 *et seq.*, 11, and 19 (1859); Joseph Ludwig Brunstein, *Studien im österreichischen Markenrecht—Ausschliessliches Gebrauchsrecht, Markendelict, Processhindernde Vorfragen* 7 (1895); *see also* Siegbert Lammel, *Recht zur Ordnung des Wettbewerbs: Österreich*, 3821, 3822, in *Handbuch der Quellen und Literatur der neueren europäischen Privatrechtsgeschichte, vol. III: Das 19. Jahrhundert, 3rd part: Gesetzgebung zu den privatrechtlichen Sondergebieten* (Helmut Coing ed., 1986); for Switzerland, *see, e.g.*, F. Meili, *Das Markenstrafrecht auf Grund des eidgenössischen Markenschutzgesetzes sowie der von der Schweiz abgeschlossenen Staatsverträge und der internationalen Konvention von 1883* 23 *et seq.* (1888).

[37] *See, e.g.*, Adriano Vanzetti, *Funktion und Rechtsnatur der Marke (2. Teil)*, 1965 GRUR Ausl. 185, 186.

[38] This also seemed to be the case in Switzerland. *See, e.g.*, Hans Schuler, *Die Concurrence déloyale und ihre Beziehungen zu Name, Firma, Marke, Fabrik- und Geschäftsgeheimnis im französischen, schweizerischen und deutschen Recht* 69–70 (1895). For contemporary German

scholarly commentary, by contrast, exhibited a natural rights conception of intellectual property quite similar to and influenced by French doctrine. In 1843, for instance, a leading treatise described a natural rights concept of industrial property (*industrielles Eigenthumsrecht*) that was intended to provide owners with absolute and exclusive rights of use.[39] Despite a natural rights foundation, however, positive law still provided for utilitarian confines to individual "property":

> The concept of this property right develops from natural law. The positive right under natural law, however, . . . must be brought in conformity with the interest in progress of the state's welfare. If the latter prevails, the former must be cut back. In the end, the natural-law concept of property in ideas must be modified.[40]

As the author continued:

doctrine, *see, e.g.*, Elmar Wadle, *Entwicklungslinien des deutschen Markenschutzes im 19. Jahrhundert*, 1979 GRUR 383, 387; Elmar Wadle, *Fabrikzeichenschutz und Markenrecht—Geschichte und Gestalt des deutschen Markenschutzes im 19. Jahrhundert, Zweiter Teil: Historisch-dogmatische Grundlinien* 24 *et seq.* (1983); Horst-Peter Götting, *Gewerblicher Rechtsschutz—Patent-, Gebrauchsmuster-, Design- und Markenrecht* § 2 para. 29 (10th edn., 2014).

39 Other theorists agreed with this perspective, equating all kinds of intellectual property. *See, e.g.*, Heinrich August Meissner, *Die Fabrikgerichte in Frankreich* 104 (1846) ("Das Eigenthum an allen Geistesproducten beruht auf dem ausschließlichen Rechte des Menschen auf die noch in seinem Geiste verschlossenen Ideen und Gedanken. Man trägt dieses, sei es auf das Civilrecht, sei es nur auf Billigkeit gegen Einzelne oder aus Rücksichten der Staatsverwaltung sich stützend, . . . auf das Product solchen Gedankens über . . . ."). Similarly, the later theory of natural rights protection also paralleled concepts of trademark and copyright protection. *See, e.g.*, Arnold Seligsohn, *Gesetz zum Schutz der Warenbezeichnungen* 15 (2nd edn., 1905) ("Zeichenschutz und Urheberrecht dienen aber demselben Zweck. Beide wollen verhindern, daß sich jemand die Früchte der geistigen Arbeit oder der geschäftlichen Tätigkeit eines anderen aneignet."); Alexander Elster, *Gewerblicher Rechtsschutz umfassend Urheber- und Verlagsrecht, Patent- und Musterschutz, Warenzeichenrecht und Wettbewerbsrecht* 207 (1921) ("Das Zeichenrecht dient dem Zweck, dem alle gewerblichen Schutzrechte dienen, daß nämlich niemand zu eigenem Nutzen die Früchte der geistig-gewerblichen Arbeit ernte, die ein anderer gesät hat.").

40 Stuve, *Das industrielle Eigenthum und die Nachbildung* 7 (1843) ("So entwickelt sich der Begriff dieses Eigenthumsrechtes aus dem Naturrechte. Das positive Recht aber, welchem höhere Rücksichten gebieten, die Bestimmungen des Naturrechts mit den Anforderungen, welche die Sorge für den Fortschritt der allgemeinen Staatswohlfahrt mit sich führt, in Einklang zu bringen und, wenn diese überwiegend sind, jene zu beschränken, sieht sich auch hier durch solche Rücksichten genöthigt, den naturrechtlichen Begriff des Eigenthumsrechts an Ideen zu modifiziren." (author's translation)). For the later theory of natural rights protection, *see, e.g.*, Arnold Seligsohn, *Gesetz zum Schutz der Warenbezeichnungen* 15 (2nd edn., 1905) ("Zeichenschutz und Urheberschutz dienen aber fast demselben Zweck. Beide wollen verhindern, daß sich jemand die Früchte der geistigen Arbeit oder der geschäftlichen Tätigkeit eines anderen aneignet."); Alexander Elster, *Gewerblicher Rechtsschutz umfassend Urheber- und Verlagsrecht, Patent- und Musterschutz, Warenzeichenrecht und Wettbewerbsrecht* 207 (1921) ("Das Zeichenrecht dient dem Zweck, dem alle gewerblichen Schutzrechte dienen, daß nämlich niemand zu eigenem Nutzen die Früchte der geistig-gewerblichen Arbeit ernte, die ein anderer gesät hat.").

The individual's property right must yield to the requirements that the public's welfare has. And even if the positive law would go so far as to include the natural-law concept of property in ideas to its full extent, one would need to establish an accompanying principle to expropriate the individual in the interest of the public welfare.[41]

Finally, with regard to the nature and scope of trademark property,[42] he went on to explain that

> [e]ach manufacturer has the legal right to designate his wares in a way that allows them to be distinguished from those of his competitors with little effort and attention. In order to provide to the manufacturer with this right to distinguish his wares from those of others, the law grants an exclusive property right in the designation he chooses.[43]

This express reference to the legal granting of a property right is representative of the positivist doctrine that dominated the scholarly discussion in Germany.[44] And this doctrine had another important characteristic: it established a formal foundation for trademark rights. This foundation was not the French notion of preexisting property in names and

[41] Stuve, *Das industrielle Eigenthum und die Nachbildung* 8–9 (1843) ("Das Eigenthumsrecht des Einzelnen muß den Anforderungen, welche die Wohlfahrt der Gesammtheit an dasselbe macht, weichen und jedenfalls wäre, wenn das positive Recht den naturrechtlichen Begriff des Eigenthums an Ideen in seiner ganzen Ausdehnung in sich aufnähme, die Nothwendigkeit vorhanden, demselben ein Expropriationsrecht zum Behufe des allgemeinen Nutzens an die Seite zu setzen." (author's translation)).

[42] *Id.* at 58 and 75 ("Von dem Eigenthume an Waarenbezeichnungen").

[43] *Id.* at 75–76 ("Jedem Fabrikanten gesteht das Gesetz die Befugniß zu, seine Fabrikate auf eine Art und Weise zu bezeichnen, daß dieselben von den Erzeugnissen seiner Concurrenten mit Anwendung geringer Aufmerksamkeit unterschieden werden können. Um dem Fabrikanten dieses Mittel, seine Fabrikate vor anderen gleichartigen kenntlich zu machen, zu sichern, gewährt ihm das Gesetz ein ausschließliches Eigenthumsrecht an dem von ihm gewählten Zeichen." (author's translation)). *See also* C. J. A. Mittermaier, *Grundsätze des gemeinen deutschen Privatrechts mit Einschluß des Handels-, Wechsel- und Seerechts, Erste Abtheilung* 945 (4th edn., 1830) ("Jeder Fabrikant kann ein Fabrikzeichen bei dem Handelsgericht angeben, und damit seine Produkte bezeichnen, und so jedem Andern den Gebrauch des nämlichen oder eines ähnlichen Zeichens, das sich nicht unzweifelhaft von dem Seinigen unterscheidet, untersagen.").

[44] *See, e.g.*, C. Th. Kleinschrod, *Beiträge zu einer deutschen Gewerbeordnung mit Rücksicht auf die bayerische Gewerbsgesetzgebung* 176 (1840); for a later position, *see* Otto Mayer, *Die concurrence déloyale—Ein Beitrag aus dem französischen Rechte zur Lehre vom geistigen Eigenthum*, 26 Zeitschrift für das Gesammte Handelsrecht 363, 437 (1881) ("Ganz richtig bezeichnet L. v. Stein literarisches Eigenthum, Patente, Muster- und Markenschutz in diesem Sinne als Stücke des Verwaltungsrechts. Das sind sie bei uns durch und durch."); for further doctrinal attempts at private rights and property characterization of marks and trade names in the early 1800s, *see* Elmar Wadle, *Fabrikzeichenschutz und Markenrecht—Geschichte und Gestalt des deutschen Markenschutzes im 19. Jahrhundert, Zweiter Teil: Historisch-dogmatische Grundlinien* 344 *et seq.* (1983).

trademarks but rather the idea of state-granted rights. As a scholarly treatise on trade and business theory explained in 1841:

> Simply putting an arbitrarily adopted designation on one's products does not give one the right to enjoin others from using the same designation; such a right can be granted only by the state's power, and only within its dominion.[45]

Just as drastically, another scholar stated in 1866:

> I only claim that, under our German legal system, an exclusive right of the manufacturer or merchant in his fabrication and trade symbols cannot be acknowledged absent a special legal writ granting the right.[46]

In the end, the foundation on formal state grants had become a determinative characteristic of trademark rights. Private rights would never come into existence without the sovereign's permission.[47] Under trademark law, finding an infringement was equated with the violation of a legal monopoly:

> One acknowledges the order of morals and equity, demanding protection of the product of one's mind. And instead of providing each single owner with a special monopoly, one generalizes the prohibition for anybody by establishing a legal command. . . . [T]he legal protection of the manufacturer and merchant for their designations can also be explained as a monopolization for the exclusive use for

[45] J. G. Hoffmann, *Die Befugniss zum Gewerbebetriebe. Zur Berichtigung der Urtheile über Gewerbefreiheit und Gewerbezwang, mit besonderer Rücksicht auf den Preussischen Staat dargestellt* 440 (1841) ("Daraus, daß Jemand ein willkürlich angenommenes Zeichen auf seine Fabrikate setzt, folgt noch keineswegs ein Recht, Andern den Gebrauch desselben zu verwehren; dieses Recht kann nur die Staatsgewalt, und auch diese nur im Bereiche ihres Machtgebiets verleihen." (author's translation)).

[46] G. Krug, *Ueber den Schutz der Fabrik- und Waarenzeichen nebst den einschlagenden Gesetzen sämmtlicher deutscher Staaten* 8 (1866) ("Ich behaupte nur, daß nach unserem in Deutschland herrschenden Rechtssystem ein ausschließliches Recht des Fabrikanten und Kaufmanns auf seine Fabrik- und Handelszeichen ohne besonderen, ein solches gewährenden, gesetzlichen Erlaß nicht anzuerkennen ist." (author's translation)); *see also id.* at 27 ("Ein ausschließliches Recht . . . auf . . . Fabrikzeichen und Waarenstempel ist nach den Grundsätzen des in Deutschland herrschenden Rechtssystems nicht anzuerkennen. Es wird erst durch besondere gesetzliche Verleihung begründet . . . ."). *See also* Friedrich Hack, *Die Aufgabe des Staats in Beziehung auf das gewerbliche Leben mit Rücksichtnahme auf die bestehenden Staats-Einrichtungen*, 23 Zeitschrift für die gesammte Staatswissenschaft 39, 87–88 (1867).

[47] For copyrights and commercial rights as monopolies, *see, e.g.*, Otto von Gierke, *Deutsches Privatrecht, vol. I: Allgemeiner Teil und Personenrecht* § 85 III 2, at 757, § 82 V, at 714–715 (1895); Martin Wolff, *Das Internationale Privatrecht Deutschlands* 157 (2nd edn., 1949); Elmar Wadle, *Der Weg zum gesetzlichen Schutz des geistigen und gewerblichen Schaffens—Die deutsche Entwicklung im 19. Jahrhundert*, 93, 148, in *Gewerblicher Rechtsschutz und Urheberrecht in Deutschland, Festschrift zum hundertjährigen Bestehen der Deutschen Vereinigung für gewerblichen Rechtsschutz und Urheberrecht und ihrer Zeitschrift, vol. I* (Friedrich-Karl Beier et al. eds., 1991).

their wares and makes. Infringement of this monopoly will, under the general legal rules establishing the monopoly, be characterized as a delict per se.[48]

In sum, even though there was a general conception that personal and firm names, as well as trademarks, could be understood as individual entitlements, the idea of a natural law foundation did not leave a permanent mark in German doctrine. On the contrary, trademarks remained state-granted rights and privileges.

II Substance: Personality Rights and Private Property

Ever since, the formal structure of state-granted privileges has dominated in German doctrine. With respect to substance, two additional aspects are important. First, as alluded to above, by the nineteenth century, an idea of competitor personality protection had taken over in scholarship. This concept was perfected by Josef Kohler in his theory of personality rights protection. Second, the development on the theoretical plane was accompanied by a shift in statutory law. The German Trademark Acts of 1874 and 1894 ultimately established a private rights concept of protection.

A Josef Kohler's Personality Rights Theory

As we have seen, personality rights protection was not a new concept at the end of the nineteenth century. In fact, it had existed prior to Kohler's famous groundwork. An early explanation can be found in R. Klostermann's 1869 treatise on intellectual property law:

> The law of firm and trade marks is founded on a ground quite different from the intellectual property in inventions and trade samples. It is not a product of intellectual labor, through which the firm sign or the trademark is brought into existence, but an emanation of the personality, as the expression of which it represents itself.[49]

[48] G. Krug, *Ueber den Schutz der Fabrik- und Waarenzeichen nebst den einschlagenden Gesetzen sämmtlicher deutscher Staaten* 12 (1866) ("Man erkennt das Gebot der Moral und Billigkeit an, das geistige Product zu schützen und statt jedem Einzelnen diesen Schutz durch besonderes Monopol zu verleihen, generalisirt man dieses Verbot für alle Fälle durch Aufstellung eines Rechtssatzes. ... [K]ann auch ... der gesetzliche Schutz des Fabrikanten und Kaufmanns für seine Zeichen als die Monopolisirung im ausschließlichen Gebrauch derselben für ihre eigenen Waaren und Fabrikate bezeichnet werden, wogegen alsdann die Verletzung dieses Monopols, nach einmal gegebener genereller gesetzlicher Begründung derselben, sich von selbst als ein Delict charakterisirt." (author's translation)); for the later concept of state-granted trademark monopoly rights, *see, e.g.*, Alfred Hagens, *Warenzeichenrecht* 33 (1927).

[49] R. Klostermann, *Das geistige Eigenthum an Schriften, Kunstwerken und Erfindungen, nach Preussischem und internationalem Rechte, vol. I (Allgemeiner Theil—Verlagsrecht und Nachdruck)* 214 (1867) ("Dagegen beruht das Recht der Firmen und Fabrikzeichen

Later scholars, such as Carl Gareis, extended this conception. According to Gareis, trademark rights were individual entitlements intended to spur ambition and motivation:

> In order to accommodate the higher human desire not only to live on the basis of making use of one's powers and abilities, but also to be respected as an individual, the legal order acknowledges and protects a certain name that identifies the individual (especially for commercial transactions, by acknowledging firm name and trademark protection) and by protecting the honor of the individual's (good) name and reputation.[50]

Notwithstanding these preceding foundations of trademark-as-personality protection, Kohler's concept has so significantly dominated and predetermined German practice and scholarship that it requires a literal citation at length.[51] In his 1884 treatise on trademark law, he elaborated on the idea that individuality should be guaranteed and protected:

auf einem wesentlich anderen Grunde als das geistige Eigenthum an Erfindungen und Waarenmustern, es ist nicht ein Product der geistigen Arbeit, durch welche die Firma oder das Waarenzeichen hervorgebracht wird, sondern ein Ausfluß der Persönlichkeit, als deren Ausdruck sich die Firma und das Waarenzeichen darstellt." (author's translation)) and also in R. Klostermann, *Das geistige Eigenthum an Schriften, Kunstwerken und Erfindungen, nach Preussischem und internationalem Rechte, vol. II (Patentgesetzgebung—Musterschutz—Waarenbezeichnungen)* 389–390 (1869) ("Das Recht zum ausschliesslichen Gebrauche solcher Waarenbezeichnungen ist ein Vermögensrecht, welches seine Grundlage in dem Rechte der Persönlichkeit hat und am nächsten dem Rechte der kaufmännischen Firma verwandt ist. . . . Auch in Bezug auf die Waarenbezeichnungen besteht ein solches Vermögensrecht nur kraft besonderer gesetzlicher Bestimmung. Nach den Grundsätzen des Gemeinen Rechts ist die unbefugte Anmassung fremder Waarenbezeichnungen und selbst der unbefugte Gebrauch einer fremden Firma nicht strafbar. Allein dieser Eingriff ist nunmehr durch die Gesetzgebung fast sämmtlicher Staaten unter Strafe gestellt worden und es ist dringend zu wünschen, dass die noch vorhandenen wenigen Ausnahmen bald verschwinden und dass der Schutz der Waarenbezeichnungen in der weitesten Ausdehnung zum allgemeinen und internationalen Rechte erhoben werde.").

[50] Carl Gareis, *Das juristische Wesen der Autorrechte, sowie des Firmen- und Markenschutzes*, 35 Archiv für Theorie und Praxis des Allgemeinen Deutschen Handels- und Wechselrechts 185, 197 (1877) ("Dem höher stehenden Triebe der Menschen, nicht bloß im Gebrauch der individuellen Kräfte individuell möglichst gut zu leben, sondern sich dabei auch als Individuum anerkannt zu sehen, entspricht die Rechtsordnung durch rechtliche Anerkennung und Schutz eines bestimmten, das Individuum kenntlich machenden Namens (speciell für den Handelsverkehr durch Anerkennung der Firma und des Markenschutzes), sowie durch Schutz der mit jener Individualisierung durch Namen normal verbundenen Ehrenachtung (des guten Namens)." (author's translation)).

[51] Kohler himself duly credited the work of Carl Gareis, Otto von Gierke, and others. He referred in particular to the Swiss Bundesgericht's nineteenth-century case law and its foundation of personality rights doctrine. *See, e.g.*, Josef Kohler, *Der unlautere Wettbewerb—Darstellung des Wettbewerbsrechts* 21–22 (1914). For a comparison of the developments in US and German universality theory in the 1870s and after, *see* Timothy H. Hiebert, *Parallel Importation in U.S. Trademark Law* 29 *et seq.* (1994).

> The relations between the person and the thing, which is expressed by the mark as a sign of origin, is of an individual rights nature: it is the manifestation of the creator, the expression of the producer's activity. The right of the producer, however, to be recognized as such, and the right to demand that he will not be foisted on a product that is not of his produce, is among the most important emanations of, one of the most important manifestations of, the individual right.[52]

Trademark protection was not necessarily a consequence of labor and investment—it was a genuine emanation of the owner's personality.[53] Also, according to Kohler, protection was not founded primarily on legislative acts, as trademarks were more than state-granted benefits. As he posited, contemporary German common law (*gemeines Recht*) was capable of providing protection in addition to statutory trademark law:

> Even though statutory law does not provide special rules on the right in marks, a certain kind of right already exists on the basis of acknowledging the individual right as such. Since the right to demand that nobody impute another's work result for his own wares, that nobody be entitled to "put off his goods for sale as the goods of a rival trader," that is the direct emanation of the individual right as the right to exclusive use of one's own personal capacities and

[52] Josef Kohler, *Das Recht des Markenschutzes mit Berücksichtigung ausländischer Gesetzgebungen und mit besonderer Rücksicht auf die englische, anglo-amerikanische, französische, belgische und italienische Jurisprudenz* 73 (1884) ("Die Beziehung der Person zur Sache, welche durch die Marke als Ursprungszeichen ausgedrückt wird, ist eine individualrechtliche: sie ist die Manifestirung des Schöpfers, der Ausdruck der Produktionsthätigkeit des Erzeugers. Das Recht des Erzeugers aber, als solcher anerkannt zu werden, und das Recht zu verlangen, dass dem Erzeuger kein ihm nicht zugehörendes Produkt untergeschoben wird, ist einer der wichtigsten Ausflüsse, eine der wichtigsten Manifestationen des Individualrechts." (author's translation)); *see also* Josef Kohler, *Warenzeichenrecht—Zugleich zweite Auflage des Rechts des Markenschutzes mit Berücksichtigung ausländischer Gesetzgebungen (1884)* 62 (2nd edn., 1910). For Kohler's critique of Gareis and von Gierke, *see* Josef Kohler, *Der unlautere Wettbewerb—Darstellung des Wettbewerbsrechts* 21 (1914); *see also* Paul Kent, *Das Reichsgesetz zum Schutz der Waarenbezeichnungen vom 12. Mai 1894—Unter Berücksichtigung in- und ausländischer Literatur und Rechtsprechung sowie der Praxis des Patentamts* 12–13 (1897); Arnold Seligsohn, *Gesetz zum Schutz der Warenbezeichnungen* 14 (2nd edn., 1905). For a general critique of the theory (particularly Swiss case law), *see* Karl Martin Sandreuter, *Rechtliche Natur, Entstehung und Endigung des Markenrechts* 23 *et seq.* (1932).

[53] For commentary on the theory of personality rights protection, *see, e.g.*, Otto von Gierke, *Deutsches Privatrecht, vol. I: Allgemeiner Teil und Personenrecht* § 84 IV 1, 736 *et seq.* (1895); Otto von Gierke, *Der Rechtsgrund des Schutzes gegen unlauteren Wettbewerb*, 1895 GRUR (ZfGewRS) 109; Paul Kent, *Das Reichsgesetz zum Schutz der Waarenbezeichnungen vom 12. Mai 1894—Unter Berücksichtigung in- und ausländischer Literatur und Rechtsprechung sowie der Praxis des Patentamts* 12 (1897); Marcus, *Ist die Unterlassungsklage nach dem Wettbewerbsgesetz noch statthaft, wenn die Handlung vor Klageerhebung seitens des Täters rückgängig gemacht war?*, 1903 JZ 172, 172; Adolf Lobe, *Die Bekämpfung des unlauteren Wettbewerbs, vol. I: Der unlautere Wettbewerb als Rechtsverletzung* 183 *et seq.* and 211 (1907) (with a detailed summary of contemporary opinions in "Anhang I").

dispositions. That this individual right, however, is not only a postulate directed at lawmakers, but already acknowledged under the law as it stands now, should not be in doubt.[54]

This last point in Kohler's conception seems to contradict the contemporary paradigm of state-granted privileges. Indeed, the protection of personality rights could have been interpreted as a distinctly antiformalist model of rights acquisition and protection. But this is not what resulted from Kohler's theory. He never rejected lawmakers' independent and genuine power to create rights. The acquisition of rights by state grant was never seen as a mere declaratory matter. Kohler's dichotomy—which allowed for both state-backed and personality-founded rights acquisition and protection—ultimately led to a determinative peculiarity of German trademark law in both substantive and conflicts doctrines. Before I address this point in more detail, however, I will take a closer look at the second aspect of trademark propertization: the statutory implementation of the private rights protection paradigm.

B The Statutory Introduction of Private Rights Protection

Beginning mid-century, the statutory landscape of intellectual property protection had begun to change. The protection of corporate names was statutorily implemented throughout the German Reich in 1862. Copyrights also became an issue of uniform statutory protection in 1870.[55] The 1874 Trademark Act[56] absorbed protection that had formerly been granted under the Criminal Code (*Reichsstrafgesetzbuch*), and it enhanced the protection of personal and firm names. From then on,

[54] Josef Kohler, *Das Recht des Markenschutzes mit Berücksichtigung ausländischer Gesetzgebungen und mit besonderer Rücksicht auf die englische, anglo-amerikanische, französische, belgische und italienische Jurisprudenz* 77–78 (1884) ("Auch wenn und soweit die Gesetzgebung keine besonderen Bestimmungen über Zeichenrecht gibt, ist eine Art Zeichenrecht bereits mit der Anerkennung des Individualrechts als solchen [*sic*] gegeben. Denn das Recht zu verlangen . . ., dass Niemand sich ein fremdes Arbeitsverdienst für seine Waaren imputieren dürfe, dass Niemand berechtigt sei, to put off his goods for sale as the goods of a rival trader [*sic*], das ist ja der unmittelbare Ausfluss des Individualrechts als des Rechts der eigenen ausschließlichen Bethätigung der persönlichen Kräfte und Anlagen. Dass aber dieses Individualrecht nicht bloss ein Postulat an die Gesetzgebung ist, dass es bereits die Anerkennung des geltenden Rechtes geniesst, darüber sollte kein Zweifel sein . . . ." (author's translation)). In this regard, he also referred to American law and the doctrine in *Derringer v. Plate*. *See also infra* p. 27 *et seq.* and p. 90 *et seq.*

[55] Protection of firm names was established by article 27 of the 1861 ADHGB (Allgemeines Deutsches Handelsgesetzbuch). Copyrights became an issue of uniform protection throughout the German Reich in the Copyright Act. *See, e.g.*, Elmar Wadle, *Entwicklungslinien des deutschen Markenschutzes im 19. Jahrhundert*, 1979 GRUR 383, 387–388.

[56] Gesetz über den Markenschutz of 30 November 1874, Deutsches Reichsgesetzblatt 1874, Nr. 28, 143–146.

right owners were entitled to civil law sanctions.[57] Toward the end of the century, the prevalence of fraud prevention had lost its once dominant position.

A prominent illustration of the new mind-set was Wilhelm Endemann's 1875 commentary on the Trademark Act, in which he described protection as fostering a dual policy—protecting both the public and the individual right owner. Interestingly, as Endemann further pointed out, the act's emphasis was now on individual rights protection. Protection of the public was a mere reflex:

> The draft Act's motives, at some points, also give regard to a concern of protecting the public. And it cannot be denied that what the Act prescribes does, at the same time, provide some aspects of general security in commercial transacting. Yet, it will become evident that this is not too much, and that what can be observed is only an unplanned consequence of this other concern, not a voluntary main purpose. The governing principle of the Act is protection of business persons in using their trademarks. . . .
>
> What is acknowledged is due ownership of the trademark, and this ownership is supported by sharp-edged weapons of civil and criminal law, protecting against unauthorized use of the same mark. The ensuing benefit for the public interest must be accepted; it is, however, in the lawmakers' sense, an actual side benefit only. We have to make clear from the beginning that the whole Act concerns only the relations between members of the business community acting as manufacturers or merchants, but that a direct protection of consumers or purchasers against improper designations is not sought after.[58]

[57] In addition, criminal law protection continued to exist. For an illustration, *see, e.g.*, Elmar Wadle, *Der Weg zum gesetzlichen Schutz des geistigen und gewerblichen Schaffens—Die deutsche Entwicklung im 19. Jahrhundert*, 93, 166, in *Gewerblicher Rechtsschutz und Urheberrecht in Deutschland, Festschrift zum hundertjährigen Bestehen der Deutschen Vereinigung für gewerblichen Rechtsschutz und Urheberrecht und ihrer Zeitschrift, vol. I* (Friedrich-Karl Beier et al. eds., 1991). For contemporary Swiss law, *see, e.g.*, F. Meili, *Das Markenstrafrecht auf Grund des eidgenössischen Markenschutzgesetzes sowie der von der Schweiz abgeschlossenen Staatsverträge und der internationalen Konvention von 1883* 16 (1888).

[58] Wilhelm Endemann, *Der Markenschutz nach dem Reichsgesetz vom 30. November 1874*, 32 Archiv für Theorie und Praxis des Allgemeinen Deutschen Handels- und Wechselrechts 1, 2 (1875) ("Die Motive des Regierungsentwurfs gedenken allerdings auch hie und da des Schutzes des Publikums. Auch läßt sich nicht leugnen, daß, was das Gesetz verfügt, zugleich für die allgemeine Sicherheit des Verkehrs in Betreff seiner Objekte Einiges leistet. Allein es wird sich zeigen, daß dies doch nicht allzuviel ist, und daß, was davon zu bemerken, nur die unwillkürliche Folge jener andern Richtung darstellt, nicht bewußter Verfolgung als Hauptzweck seine Entstehung verdankt. Der leitende Gedanke des Gesetzes ist Schutz der bei Führung der Waarenzeichen interessirten Geschäftsleute. . . . Es wird eine berechtigte Inhaberschaft des Waarenzeichens anerkannt und dieser gegen unberechtigten Gebrauch desselben Zeichens eine scharfe Waffe civil- und strafrechtlicher Art in die Hand gegeben. Was dabei für das öffentliche Interesse herausspringt, erscheint als ein Vortheil, der gewiß mitzunehmen ist, der aber im Sinne der Gesetzgebung doch nur einen thatsächlichen Nebengewinn bildet. Wir haben von

And while such a "privatized" understanding of trademark policy was still an issue of debate under the 1874 act,[59] it came to dominate under the 1894 act.[60] Indeed, the idea that protection of the public is secondary to private rights enforcement has governed trademark law ever since. Over time, the policy of trademark protection was transformed from its initially communitarian focus into an individualist orientation toward private property. Not surprisingly, administrative and criminal law sanctions lost their importance as the main tools of regulation.[61] Despite this shift toward

vornherein festzustellen, daß sich das ganze Gesetz lediglich in den Rechtsbeziehungen zwischen den als Producenten oder Händler am Verkehr betheiligten Geschäftsleuten bewegt, während ein direkter Schutz der Konsumenten oder Abnehmer gegen unwahre Bezeichnung nicht gesucht wird." (author's translation)). For the parliamentary debate, *see* Deutscher Reichstag, *Stenographische Berichte der Verhandlungen des Deutschen Reichstages (stenographic reports)*, vol. 34, 1874/75, 32 *et seq.* (4th session, 4 November 1874), 79 *et seq.* (7th session, 10 November 1874), 98 *et seq.* (8th session, 11 November 1874), 127 *et seq.* (10th session, 14 November 1874), and 175 (12th session, 17 November 1874).

59 For the heated parliamentary debate, *see* Deutscher Reichstag, *Stenographische Berichte der Verhandlungen des Deutschen Reichstages (stenographic reports)*, vol. 34, 1874/75, 33 (4th session, 4 November 1874), representative Dr. Reichensperger ("Auch ich bin der Ansicht . . ., daß das Gesetz mehr auf das Interesse des großen Publikums berechnet werden muß, als auf das Interesse der Geschäftswelt, daß vor Allem die Konsumenten gegen die Verfälschungen zu schützen sind . . . ."), 104 (8th session, 11 November 1874), respresentative Ackermann ("Im vorliegenden Falle handelt es sich nicht blos um das Interesse des zunächst an seiner Marke, seinem Namen, seiner Firma Geschädigten, sondern in ganz eminenter Weise ist auch das Interesse des großen Publikums, der Gesammtheit bei der Sache engagirt."), 106 (8th session, 11 November 1874), representative Dr. Braun ("[E]s ist also ein reines Privatinteresse."), 134 (10th session, 14 November 1874), representatives Dr. Reichensperger, Dr. Eberty, and Dr. Braun.

60 Gesetz zum Schutz der Waarenbezeichnungen of 12 May 1894, Deutsches Reichsgesetzblatt 1894, Nr. 22, 441–448. *See, e.g.*, Paul Kent, *Das Reichsgesetz zum Schutz der Waarenbezeichnungen vom 12. Mai 1894—Unter Berücksichtigung in- und ausländischer Literatur und Rechtsprechung sowie der Praxis des Patentamts* 12–13 (Berlin 1897) (with further references). For an excellent explanation of the reorientation in trademark doctrine from the 1870/71 Criminal Code to the 1874/1894 acts, *see* Elmar Wadle, *Entwicklungslinien des deutschen Markenschutzes im 19. Jahrhundert*, 1979 GRUR 383 *et seq. See also*—again (*supra* fn. 59)—the debate in the German Reichstag preceding the enactment of the 1874 act where the national-liberal representative (and professor of law) Georg Beseler correctly prophesized that the act would implement "ein ganz neues Rechtsprincip, ja eine neue Rechtsinstitution" (Deutscher Reichstag, *Stenographische Berichte der Verhandlungen des Deutschen Reichstages (stenographic reports)*, vol. 34, 1874/75, 101 (8th session, 11 November 1874)).

61 *See, e.g.*, Paul Kent, *Das Reichsgesetz zum Schutz der Waarenbezeichnungen vom 12. Mai 1894—Unter Berücksichtigung in- und ausländischer Literatur und Rechtsprechung sowie der Praxis des Patentamts* 16–17 (1897) (characterizing criminal sanctions in the 1894 act as mere amendments ("Ergänzungen") to private rights protection); for a characterization of trademarks as both private and public legal constructs, *see*, however, Arnold Seligsohn, *Gesetz zum Schutz der Warenbezeichnungen* 15–16 (2nd edn., 1905) ("Das Zeichenrecht ist aber nicht bloß privatrechtlicher Natur, es hat auch einen öffentlichrechtlichen Charakter. Die Allgemeinheit ist zunächst insofern an diesem Recht interessiert, als jede Nachahmung eines Zeichens das große Publikum irreführt und die Sicherheit des Verkehrs beeinträchtigt.").

private rights protection, however, the idea of trademarks as state-granted privileges remained the major structural underpinning of trademark-as-property protection under the 1874 and 1894 Trademark Acts.[62] It was this idea that gave German trademark doctrine its formalist character.

III Consequences: The Field's Dichotomies

Despite a formal shift to trademark-as-property protection, neither of the two nineteenth-century Trademark Acts established a uniform system of private property rights protection in trademarks. This is not surprising given that neither of the acts covered the entire range of trade symbols and indications. The dichotomy between registered or state-granted rights and other entitlements therefore did not disappear. To the contrary, as we will see, statutory trademark law provided the foundation for an advancement of Kohler's theory of personality rights protection, thereby contributing to an even deeper consolidation of formalist structures. In the end, the formalist concept of trademark property not only established a separation between trademark protection and unfair competition prevention but also led to a stringent stratification within the field, with registered rights taking precedence over nonregistered positions.

A The Trademark/Unfair Competition Dichotomy

A striking characteristic of trademark and unfair competition law—one that remains alive and well today—was its bifurcation, with the protection of trademark "property" on the one hand and the prevention of unfair "conduct" on the other. Kohler's 1884 critique is enlightening for the still existent conflict between the two concurrent regimes:

> If the individual right is fully sufficient—why, then, should we have a special law on trademarks? Is not the existence of such a law the most eloquent proof for the fact that individual rights protection alone is not enough to completely cover the field? And should not the trademark legislation be conceived of as the best and as a sufficient legal instrument to govern the field, from now on dominating solely and without concurrent legal devices? . . . Should it not lead into confusion if, next to the new order, the ruins of the old law persist? This question is paramount; and the whole scholarly understanding of our field depends on a correct answer to it.[63]

[62] For the 1874 act's reporter's formalist understanding, *see* Elmar Wadle, *Der Weg zum gesetzlichen Schutz des geistigen und gewerblichen Schaffens—Die deutsche Entwicklung im 19. Jahrhundert*, 93, 167, in *Gewerblicher Rechtsschutz und Urheberrecht in Deutschland, Festschrift zum hundertjährigen Bestehen der Deutschen Vereinigung für gewerblichen Rechtsschutz und Urheberrecht und ihrer Zeitschrift, vol. I* (Friedrich-Karl Beier et al. eds., 1991).

[63] Josef Kohler, *Das Recht des Markenschutzes mit Berücksichtigung ausländischer Gesetzgebungen und mit besonderer Rücksicht auf die englische, anglo-amerikanische, französische, belgische und*

Answers to Kohler's questions differed widely in the years following their publication. Since the next chapter will address US doctrine on this issue in more detail, a deep analysis is not required at the moment. A brief discussion, however, is helpful and necessary.

In 1865, the Supreme Court of California was faced with a similar issue in *Derringer v. Plate.*[64] The court had to clarify the relation between common law rights acquisition and protection under an 1863 Californian trademark statute. The question was whether the statute constituted a " 'complete scheme' for the acquisition and protection of property in trademarks." The court's answer to this question was no.[65] As it explained, lawmakers had not attempted to "divest persons of existing rights of property, nor ... to preclude them from acquiring title as they had formerly done, by adoption and use."[66] As a result, common law rights and statutory rights alike would be protected. Both systems would allow for rights acquisition and protection. German law took a different route at this point. Initially, courts adjudicating on the basis of French law were willing to extend protection against unfair competition (*concurrence déloyale*) beyond statutory black letters.[67] Early case law actually mirrored *Derringer*: Courts agreed on the fact that the special protection of trademarks under the French Republic's or the German Reich's federal legislation would not overrule preexisting structures of unfair competition prevention on the basis of the German states' statutory or common law regimes (*gemeines Recht*).[68] But this understanding soon vanished.

italienische Jurisprudenz 83 (1884) ("Wenn das Individualrecht völlig ausreicht, warum ein besonderes Markengesetz? Ist nicht das Vorhandensein eines solchen Gesetzes das beredteste Zeugniss dafür, dass der Individualschutz dieses Gebiet nicht deckt? Und sollte nicht diese Markengesetzgebung als bestes und ausreichendes juristisches Hülfsmittel erdacht sein und nunmehr dieses Gebiet allein und concurrenzlos beherrschen und jede sonstige Regelung ausschließen? ... [S]ollte es nicht zur Verwirrung führen, wenn neben dieser Neuordnung die Trümmer des alten Rechtszustandes fortbestehen? Diese Frage ist kapital, von ihrer richtigen Beantwortung hängt das ganze wissenschaftliche Verständniss [u]nserer Materie ab." (author's translation)).

64 *Derringer v. Plate*, 29 Cal. 292, 87 Am. Dec. 170 (1865).

65 *Id.* at 296.

66 *Id.* at 297.

67 Several decisions had found actionable cases under article 1382 of the *code civil* and the concept of *concurrence déloyale. See, e.g.*, Badisches Appellationsgericht, 3 Zeitschrift für französisches Civilrecht (1873) 670, 673 (9 April 1873); Obergericht Mainz, 9 Zeitschrift für französisches Civilrecht (1878) 444, 447 *et seq.* (19 January 1878); OLG Karlsruhe 38 SeuffArch Nr. 258, at 331, 332 (27 February 1882); for an explanation of French doctrine holding both statutory trademark law and articles 1382 and 1383 of the *code civil* applicable, *see* Otto Mayer, *Die concurrence déloyale—Ein Beitrag aus dem französischen Rechte zur Lehre vom geistigen Eigenthum*, 26 Zeitschrift für das Gesammte Handelsrecht 363, 419–420 (1881); *see also* Josef Kohler, *Der unlautere Wettbewerb—Darstellung des Wettbewerbsrechts* 36 *et seq.* (1914).

68 For a modern summary, *see, e.g.*, Elmar Wadle, *Das rheinisch-französische Deliktsrecht und die Judikatur des Reichsgerichts zum unlauteren Wettbewerb*, 365, 375, in *Geistiges Eigentum—Bausteine zur Rechtsgeschichte, vol. II* (Elmar Wadle ed., 2003).

In fact, even earlier, Germany's statutory system of rights acquisition had been destined to favor registration, when the 1874 and 1894 acts detached the acquisition of rights from a requirement of prior use in commerce. And a trademark's actual use was also irrelevant beyond the domain of formal rights. Neither the 1874 nor the 1894 act allowed rights to be acquired on the basis of use alone.[69] Under the 1874 act, acquisition required application for registration; under the 1894 act, registration only created the right.[70] This positivistic shift toward registered rights protection was completed by the Reichsgericht's 1880 *Apollinarisbrunnen* decision, the high-water mark of trademark rights' formality.

The plaintiff, a corporation selling mineral water under the firm name "Apollinarisbrunnen, vormals Kreuzberg," based its suit on an alleged violation of the 1874 act's anticonfusion provisions[71] and on a claim of unfair competition under articles 1382 and 1383 of the French *code civil.* The argument was that the defendant's use of the mark "Apollinarisbrunnen" for mineral water was deceptive. In principle,

[69] Edwin Katz, *Gesetz zum Schutz der Waarenbezeichnungen und unlauterer Wettbewerb, Vortrag gehalten vor der Juristischen Gesellschaft von Berlin und im Berliner Anwaltsverein, Veröffentlichungen des Berliner Anwalt-Vereins, Heft 4*, 3, 22 (1894) (including a critical reference to the different situation in the United States and the Netherlands); for an overview, *see* Friedrich-Karl Beier, *Gedanken zum Verhältnis von Warenzeichen- und Ausstattungsschutz im künftigen deutschen Markenrecht* 1967 GRUR 628, 629.

[70] *See, e.g.*, W. Rhenius, *Gesetz zum Schutz der Waarenbezeichnungen vom 12. Mai 1894* § 12 comment 1 (1897) ("Rechtskraft der Eintragung. Das Zeichenrecht ... hat die Eintragung in die Zeichenrolle zur nothwendigen Voraussetzung. Die Eintragung wirkt, solange sie besteht, unabhängig von ihren materiellen Voraussetzungen, mit formaler Rechtskraft."); Paul Kent, *Das Reichsgesetz zum Schutz der Waarenbezeichnungen vom 12. Mai 1894—Unter Berücksichtigung in- und ausländischer Literatur und Rechtsprechung sowie der Praxis des Patentamts* 240 (1897); Chr. Finger, *Das Reichsgesetz zum Schutz der Warenbezeichnungen vom 12. Mai 1894* 230 (2nd edn., 1906); Josef Kohler, *Warenzeichenrecht—Zugleich zweite Auflage des Rechts des Markenschutzes mit Berücksichtigung ausländischer Gesetzgebungen (1884)* 125–128 (2nd edn., 1910); Friedrich Jüngel & Julius Magnus, *Das deutsche Warenzeichenrecht* 464 (6th edn., 1933). For Austria as well, acquisition only by registration was acknowledged. *See, e.g.*, Joseph Ludwig Brunstein, *Studien im österreichischen Markenrecht—Ausschliessliches Gebrauchsrecht, Markendelict, Processhindernde Vorfragen* 25 *et seq.* (1895). For the legal fortification of formal application to the register, *see* W. Rhenius, *Gesetz zum Schutz der Waarenbezeichnungen vom 12. Mai 1894* § 7 comment 1 (1897) ("Vor der Eintragung ... entsteht durch die Anmeldung bereits ein Recht, und zwar ein öffentlich-rechtlicher Anspruch auf Eintragung .... Die Freiheit, ein Zeichen zu benutzen, soweit dadurch nicht in Rechte Dritter eingegriffen wird, erhält durch die Anmeldung eine rechtliche Seite ...."). For the different nature of Swiss law, *see, e.g.*, Hans Mertzlufft, *Markenschutz und unlauterer Wettbewerb* 26–27 and 30 (1936) (with references to case law); Rudolf Pfister, *Untersuchungen über das Verhältnis der Grundsätze über den unlauteren Wettbewerb zu den Bestimmungen der gewerblichen Spezialgesetze* 47 (1936); Walter R. Schluep, *Das Markenrecht als subjektives Recht* 170 *et seq.* (1964).

[71] §§ 13 para. 1 and 18 of the 1874 Act. *See* RGZ vol. 3, 67, 67–*Apollinarisbrunnen* (30 November 1880).

the *code civil* was applicable at the defendant's place of business. But the court had doubts whether the code's general principles could apply concurrently to the German Reich's uniform trademark act. Ultimately, the Reichsgericht denied the subsidiary application of general principles:

> What remains to be explored is whether the plaintiff can refer to article 1382 of the Code civil insofar as she claims ... that the defendant, ... apart from the provisions of the Trademark Act, has committed a wrongful act. However, application of article 1382 of the Code civil cannot be conceded in this regard. The Trademark Act, as is evident from the introductory motives of the draft act, ... aims to regulate civil-law protection of trademarks for the whole German Reich uniformly and exhaustively; it would, hence, be incompatible to qualify an act deemed admissible under the Trademark Act as wrongful and leading to a claim for damages within the domain of article 1382 Code civil.[72]

At its core, the Reichsgericht's formalistic positivism disregarded the protections provided by natural and individual private rights. Use-based rights were considered inexistent, and there was no concurrent protection against unfair competition beyond the trademark act. In essence, the idea of an absolute and exclusive system of state-granted statutory privileges prevailed.

A few years later, in its *Reiner Kakao* decision, the Reichsgericht further explained that "the Act considers trademarks as formal rights,

[72] RGZ vol. 3, 67, 69—*Apollinarisbrunnen* (30 November 1880) ("Hiernach bleibt nur noch zu untersuchen, ob die Klägerin die Bestimmung des Art. 1382 Code civil insoweit für sich anrufen kann, als sie behauptet, ... daß der Beklagte ... abgesehen von den Bestimmungen des Markenschutzgesetzes sich hierdurch einer widerrechtlichen Handlung schuldig mache. Indessen kann eine Anwendbarkeit des Art. 1382 Code civil in dieser Hinsicht nicht zugestanden werden. Das Markenschutzgesetz hat sich, wie schon die Einleitung zu den Motiven des Entwurfs deutlich ergiebt ..., zur Aufgabe gestellt, den Schutz der Warenbezeichnungen ... auch civilrechtlich für das Deutsche Reich einheitlich und erschöpfend zu regeln; damit wäre es aber unvereinbar, eine Handlung, welche nach dem Markenschutzgesetz erlaubt ist, im Geltungsgebiete des Art. 1382 Code civil als eine widerrechtliche, welche zum Schadensersatz verpflichten würde, anzusehen." (author's translation)); for an illustrative critique, *see* Josef Kohler, *Der unlautere Wettbewerb—Darstellung des Wettbewerbsrechts* 43–44 (1914); for the general impact of the decision, *see* Friedrich-Karl Beier & Annette Kur, *Das Verhältnis von Markenrecht und Recht des unlauteren Wettbewerbs im Wandel der Zeiten*, 477, 479, in *Festschrift für Wolfgang Fikentscher zum 70. Geburtstag* (Bernhard Großfeld et al. eds., 1998). The court had decided in a similar manner before. *See, e.g.*, RGZ vol. 1, 26, 27–28 (19 December 1879); RGZ vol. 2, 140, 141 (10 November 1880). For the development of case law prior to and after *Apollinarisbrunnen, see, e.g.*, Diethelm Klippel, *Die Bedeutung des Rheinischen Rechts für die Entwicklung des Namens- und Firmenschutzes in Deutschland*, 123, 139 *et seq.*, in *Revolution, Reform, Restauration: Formen der Veränderung von Recht und Gesellschaft* (Heinz Mohnhaupt ed., 1988); Elmar Wadle, *Das rheinisch-französische Deliktsrecht und die Judikatur des Reichsgerichts zum unlauteren Wettbewerb*, 365, 368 *et seq.*, in *Geistiges Eigentum—Bausteine zur Rechtsgeschichte, vol. II* (Elmar Wadle ed., 2003).

to be created only by the formal act of application and registration."[73] Referring to *Apollinarisbrunnen*, the court continued:

> The argument that . . . protection of registered marks, if applied for with the intent of usurpation of another's symbol and in order to create the possibility of confusion, must be denied on the basis of the underlying dolus [i.e., bad faith] brings back the aspect that has just been excluded in the course of the Trademark Act's introduction, notably the elimination of unfair competition principles by imposition of a formal regime of trademark protection.[74]

According to the court, ignoring infringing activities or unfair competition whenever the alleged invader could claim to have acquired a formally valid registration was far from exceptional:

> In large parts of Germany, lawmakers [when conceiving of the Trademark Act] were confronted with a legal situation under which attachment of [confusing] trademarks, despite their effects on the public, was deemed to be something legally indifferent. They were thus not prevented from founding their newly created law on a purely formal principle with the advantage of highest precision and certainty.[75]

This positioning led to a lock-in: beyond the trademark act's black-letter rules, no other regime of rights protection or unfair competition prevention would apply. In essence, the general rules of private law rights protection had become inoperable with respect to the informal regulation of fairness in competition.[76]

[73] RGZ vol. 18, 93, 95—*Reiner Kakao* (13 November 1886) ("Das Reichsgesetz betrachtet das Warenzeichen als ein lediglich durch den formalen Akt der Anmeldung zur Eintragung zu erzeugendes Recht."). For Kohler's critique, *see* Josef Kohler, *Der unlautere Wettbewerb—Darstellung des Wettbewerbsrechts* 57 (1914).

[74] RGZ vol. 18, 93, 100—*Reiner Kakao* (13 November 1886) ("Die Ansicht, welche bei Anerkennung, daß der Schutz aus dem Gesichtspunkte einer Verantwortlichkeit für unehrlichen Wettbewerb durch das Markenschutzgesetz mit seiner formalen Rechtsordnung beseitigt ist, doch wieder dem eingetragenen Zeichen, wenn es in vorsätzlicher Usurpierung des von einem Anderen geführten Zeichens zum Zwecke der Möglichkeit einer Verwechslung im Verkehre angemeldet ist, wegen des darin liegenden Dolus die Wirksamkeit versagen will [citation to Josef Kohler, Das Recht des Markenschutzes] bringt den Gesichtspunkt, den sie eben noch als infolge der Einführung des Markenschutzgesetzes aufgegeben anerkannt, wieder in die Sache hinein." (author's translation)).

[75] *Id.* at 101 ("Da . . . der Gesetzgeber sich einem Rechtszustande in großen Teilen Deutschlands gegenüber fand, nach welchem die Anbringung solcher Kennzeichen trotz ihrer Wirkung auf das Publikum als etwas rechtlich durchaus Indifferentes galt, war er eben nicht gehindert, das von ihm erst zu schaffende Recht von einem rein formalen Prinzipe aus mit den Vorzügen größter Präzision und Sicherheit zu begründen." (author's translation)). *See also* Arnold Seligsohn, *Gesetz zum Schutz der Warenbezeichnungen* 148 (2nd edn., 1905) (with further explanation and reference to contemporary case law).

[76] For a cynical critique of the Reichsgericht's "naivety," *see* Josef Kohler, *Warenzeichenrecht—Zugleich zweite Auflage des Rechts des Markenschutzes mit Berücksichtigung ausländischer Gesetzgebungen (1884)* 69 (2nd edn., 1910) ("Die

B The Privilege/Personality Right Dichotomy

Even though the 1894 act, for the first time, offered protection against the unauthorized use of another's trade dress, as well as indications of origin,[77] this protection was still qualitatively inferior to a registered trademark. The extension of protectable subject matter was primarily due to the contemporary lack of a functional system of unfair competition prevention.[78] Accordingly, it did not attain the same strength or dignity as a registered—and thereby expressly state-granted—entitlement. Unlike the scope of protection granted to registered trademark owners, for instance, there was no cause of action to enjoin an infringer with respect to the violation of a nonregistered entitlement; the only option besides criminal law sanctions was a claim for damages. In addition, in a dispute between a registered right and a nonregistered entitlement, the registered right would always prevail—even if the later registration had been applied

frühere deutsche Rechtsprechung befolgte hier ein ganz formales System: da man von dem Persönlichkeitsrecht noch keinen Begriff hatte und der naiven Ansicht war, als ob das Markenrecht etwas vom Himmel Herabgebrachtes wäre, was sich gar nicht in das System eingliedert .... Diese Rechtsprechung zeigte eben die Unvollkommenheit der damaligen deutschen Rechtspflege, den völligen Niedergang unseres Rechtes gegenüber früheren Zeiten, die Folgen einer Rechtsbehandlung, welche sich in veraltete unpraktische Kleinlichkeiten verlor und für die Bedürfnisse unserer Tage gar keinen Sinn hatte, und endlich jene Landrechts-Jurisprudenz, welche sich an den Buchstaben heftete .... "). For a more recent evaluation of the *Apollinarisbrunnen* doctrine, *see, e.g.*, Wolfgang Hefermehl & Adolf Baumbach, *Wettbewerbsrecht*, UWG Einl para. 16 (18th edn., 1995) ("Gelangten die angelsächsischen und französischen Gerichte durch eine kluge Fortbildung des bürgerlichen Rechts zu einer den unerlaubten Wettbewerb vorbildlich bekämpfenden zivilen Rechtsprechung, so entwi[c]kelten sich die Zustände in Deutschland umso nachteiliger. Die Proklamierung des Grundsatzes der Gewerbefreiheit durch die Gew[erbeordnung] von 1869 ... hemmte die [Rechtsprechung] ideologisch, ohne eine klare gesetzliche Grundlage ... zu entwickeln. Die Instanzgerichte des französischen Rechtsgebiets, des Rheinlands, machten verheißungsvolle Ansätze. Diese knickte RG 3, 68 durch einen ungeheuerlichen Gegenteilsschluß: Weil der Gesetzgeber ein Markenschutz[gesetz] geschaffen habe ..., sei alles erlaubt, was dort nicht verboten sei. Die Gerichte wurden damit zum Hüter der Unlauterkeit.").

[77] *See* §§ 15, 16 Trademark Act 1894 (prohibiting the production and marketing of "Waaren oder deren Verpackung oder Umhüllung, oder Ankündigungen, Preislisten, Geschäftsbriefe, Empfehlungen, Rechnungen oder dergleichen mit einer Ausstattung, welche innerhalb betheiligter Verkehrskreise als Kennzeichen gleichartiger Waaren eines Anderen gilt" as well as of similar wares, trade dress, or other kind of indication that had been "fälschlich mit einem Staatswappen oder mit dem Namen oder Wappen eines Ortes, eines Gemeinde- oder weiteren Kommunalverbandes zu dem Zweck vers[ehen], über Beschaffenheit und Werth der Waaren einen Irrthum zu erregen."). For an illustration, *see, e.g.*, Henning von Stechow, *Das Gesetz zur Bekämpfung des unlauteren Wettbewerbs vom 27. Mai 1896—Entstehungsgeschichte und Wirkung* 137 *et seq.* (2002).

[78] Horst-Peter Götting, *Länderteil Deutschland*, 199, 217, in *Handbuch des Ausstattungsrechts—Der Schutz der nichteingetragenen Marke und Ausstattung im In- und Ausland, Festgabe für Friedrich-Karl Beier zum 60. Geburtstag* (Gerhard Schricker & Dieter Stauder eds., 1986).

for in knowledge of the preexisting nonregistered right and of the confusion that might ensue.[79] This difference is reflective of the doctrinal foundations: registered trademarks were seen only as constructs of state authority, granted at the individual's request and therefore the unconditioned property of their owners.[80]

Kohler's theory of personality rights protection did not alter this stratification. While his concept may have been understood as establishing a new basis for the acquisition and protection of rights, the persisting duality of rights springing from the owner's "personality" and her "trademark" ultimately only deepened the dichotomy. For this understanding of personality rights theory, Hoffmann may again serve as an early example. As discussed above, Hoffmann was a prominent advocate of privilege theory in trademark law.[81] In addition, he distinguished between different categories of formal and informal rights. While trade-name and trademark rights were founded on state grants, the deceptive use of a person's signature was *contra bones mores*. The abuse of signatures was an offense universally deemed improper:

> There is only one category of manufacturer's marks where it must be acknowledged unconditionally that their imitation is improper: it is designation with the full name of a manufacturer by a seal, representing his handwriting. Without regard to status or trade, good morals and custom prevent in all countries, where education and culture are guaranteed, imitation of an individual's signature. This

[79] *See, e.g.*, RG 1899 BlPMZ 19, 21—*Export Spaten Bier I* (22 January 1898); RG 1900 BlPMZ 216, 217—*Export Spaten Bier II* (2 March 1900). Another difference to registered rights protection was the requirement of *intent* for a claim to exist with respect to the infringement of a nonregistered right. For further details, *see, e.g.*, Andreas Sattler, *Emanzipation und Expansion des Markenrechts—Die Entstehungsgeschichte des Markengesetzes von 1995* 73 *et seq.*, 103 *et seq.* (2015).

[80] *See, e.g.*, Philipp Allfeld, *Kommentar zu den Reichsgesetzen über das Gewerbliche Urheberrecht* § 15 note 2, at 614 (1904) ("Der Ausstattungsschutz ist ein viel weniger wirksamer, als der Schutz des Zeichenrechts . . . Hieraus ergibt sich, daß ein selbständiges Ausstattungsrecht vom Gesetze nicht anerkannt ist; nur gegen unredlichen Konkurrenzbetrieb soll der Ausstattungsbesitzer geschützt sein."); Chr. Finger, *Das Reichsgesetz zum Schutz der Warenbezeichnungen vom 12. Mai 1894 nebst den Ausführungsbestimmungen und dem internationalen Warenbezeichnungsrecht* § 15, at 348 (2nd edn., 1906) ("Es liegt jedoch in der Sache begründet, daß die Warenausstattung nicht in demselben Umfange Schutz erhalten kann, wie die Warenzeichen. . . . [Warenzeichen] werden nur durch die Willkür des Verkäufers bestimmt und können daher bedingungslos als sein Eigentum betrachtet werden . . . ."); Walther Oppenheim, *Die Verwirkung im gewerblichen Rechtsschutz* 5 (1932) ("Die Ausstattung war vom Gesetzgeber ursprünglich als Warenkennzeichnung, die nicht eintragungsfähig ist, gedacht; sie steht nach der Absicht des Gesetzgebers als geringeres Recht dem eingetragenen Warenzeichenrecht gegenüber und genießt daher nach dem Wortlaut des § 15 WzG. nur in geringerem Umfange Schutz, insbesondere keinen negatorischen Schutz gegen objektiv rechtswidrige Verletzungen.").

[81] *See supra* p. 17–21.

custom thereby significantly facilitates transacting and commerce; hence, there is no written law necessary to provide for universal respect for this rule.[82]

Morals and custom (*Sitte*) was an internationally uniform concept. While trademark protection regimes varied across borders, honesty in trade was considered transnational.[83] By mid-century, a dichotomy between rights protection and unfair competition prevention had developed—a bifurcation to be perfected with Kohler's personality rights theory.

Kohler rejected *Apollinarisbrunnen*'s formalist limitation of trademark protection.[84] He understood the 1874 act to have substituted preexisting state statutes but not the general principles, particularly the so-called *actio doli* of the German *gemeines Recht*, which was designed, among other things, to cover unfair competitive conduct.[85] As he believed, statutory and nonstatutory law would continue to govern the field concurrently. He characterized all rights as emanations of their owner's personality:

The personality right as such does not need a special act of acquisition; it comes into existence with the personality itself: it can only develop and unfold into

[82] J. G. Hoffmann, *Die Befugniss zum Gewerbebetriebe. Zur Berichtigung der Urtheile über Gewerbefreiheit und Gewerbezwang, mit besonderer Rücksicht auf den Preussischen Staat dargestellt* 440 (1841) ("Nur in Bezug auf eine Art der Fabrikzeichen scheint unbedingt anerkannt werden zu müssen, daß ihre Nachahmung durchaus unanständig sei: das ist nämlich die Bezeichnung mit dem vollen Namen des Fabrikanten mittelst eines Stempels, der seine eigene Handschrift darstellt. Die Sitte verpönt in allen Ländern, worin auf Bildung Anspruch gemacht wird, das Nachahmen der eigenen Namensunterschrift eines jeden Menschen ohne Standes- und Gewerbsunterschied. Diese Sitte dient so wesentlich zur Erleichterung des Verkehrs, daß es keines geschriebenen Gesetzes der einzelnen Staaten bedarf, um derselben überall Achtung zu verschaffen." (author's translation)).

[83] This distinction, as Elmar Wadle has shown, reappears in later illustrations of personality rights protection, such as those by J. K. Bluntschli and Rudolf Klostermann. *See* Elmar Wadle, *Fabrikzeichenschutz und Markenrecht—Geschichte und Gestalt des deutschen Markenschutzes im 19. Jahrhundert, Erster Teil: Entfaltung* 293 (1977); *see also* R. Klostermann, *Das geistige Eigenthum an Schriften, Kunstwerken und Erfindungen, nach Preussischem und internationalem Rechte, vol. I (Allgemeiner Theil—Verlagsrecht und Nachdruck)* 213–214 (1867) and R. Klostermann, *Das geistige Eigenthum an Schriften, Kunstwerken und Erfindungen, nach Preussischem und internationalem Rechte, vol. II (Patentgesetzgebung—Musterschutz—Waarenbezeichnungen)* 389–390 (1869); J. K. Bluntschli, *Deutsches Privatrecht* § 50 end note (3rd edn., 1864).

[84] *See* his critique of the *Apollinaris* decision in Josef Kohler, *Warenzeichenrecht—Zugleich zweite Auflage des Rechts des Markenschutzes mit Berücksichtigung ausländischer Gesetzgebungen (1884)* 69 (2nd edn., 1910) (cited literally in fn. 76 *supra*); Josef Kohler, *Der unlautere Wettbewerb—Darstellung des Wettbewerbsrechts* 57 (1914) ("Das Jahrzehnt der Jurisprudenz von 1880 bis 1890 gehört nicht zu den Glanzzeiten der deutschen Rechtsgeschichte: es bewies ein merkwürdiges Ungeschick in der Handhabung des Rechts, einen öden Formalismus . . . .").

[85] Josef Kohler, *Das Recht des Markenschutzes mit Berücksichtigung ausländischer Gesetzgebungen und mit besonderer Rücksicht auf die englische, anglo-amerikanische, französische, belgische und italienische Jurisprudenz* 83 *et seq.*, 89 *et seq.* (1884); Josef Kohler, *Der unlautere Wettbewerb—Darstellung des Wettbewerbsrechts* 43–44 (1914).

different directions, with the single aspects of the personality more or less stepping into the light.[86]

Yet formal trademark rights had to be chosen. They came into existence by application or registration, not by use in commerce.[87] Protection under the *actio doli*, by contrast, depended on trademark use alone.[88] Hence, Kohler, too, distinguished different sectors of rights protection:

86 Josef Kohler, *Warenzeichenrecht—Zugleich zweite Auflage des Rechts des Markenschutzes mit Berücksichtigung ausländischer Gesetzgebungen (1884)* 119 (2nd edn., 1910) ("Das Persönlichkeitsrecht an sich bedarf keines besonderen Erwerbsaktes; es ist bereits mit dem Bestehen der Persönlichkeit gegeben: es kann sich nur nach verschiedenen Seiten hin entwickeln und entfalten, wenn die einzelnen Persönlichkeitsgüter mehr oder weniger ans Licht treten." (author's translation)).

87 For the 1894 Trademark Act, it was registration. *See* Josef Kohler, *Warenzeichenrecht—Zugleich zweite Auflage des Rechts des Markenschutzes mit Berücksichtigung ausländischer Gesetzgebungen (1884)* 127–128 (2nd edn., 1910) ("[D]ass bei uns der Eintrag der Marke nicht bloss deklarativer, d.h. erklärender Art ist, wie man es im französischen Rechte behauptet, sondern dass durch die Eintragung eben erst das volle Markenrecht geschaffen wird; dadurch wird nicht in Abrede gestellt, dass möglicherweise der Berechtigte bereits kraft allgemeinen Persönlichkeitsrechts geschützt ist, so dass die Marke nur eine Verstärkung des Persönlichkeitsrechtes enthält. In einem solchen Falle sind die vor der Eintragung erfolgten Zuwiderhandlungen zwar verfolgbar, aber nur kraft allgemeinen Persönlichkeitsrechts, nicht kraft Markenrechtes, so dass regelmäßig nur eine zivilrechtliche, keine strafrechtliche Gegenwirkung eintritt."); Otto von Gierke, *Deutsches Privatrecht, vol. I: Allgemeiner Teil und Personenrecht* § 84 IV 1c, at 737 (1895); Arnold Seligsohn, *Gesetz zum Schutz der Warenbezeichnungen* 148 (2nd edn., 1905). For Austria, *see, e.g.*, Joseph Ludwig Brunstein, *Studien im österreichischen Markenrecht—Ausschliessliches Gebrauchsrecht, Markendelict, Processhindernde Vorfragen* 25 *et seq.* (1895). Similarly, with regard to criminal law sanctions, Kohler extended the distinction. By adherence to the principle of *nulla crimen sine lege*, he rejected penal sanctions absent statutory foundation; criminal law had to be positive law. *See* Josef Kohler, *Das Recht des Markenschutzes mit Berücksichtigung ausländischer Gesetzgebungen und mit besonderer Rücksicht auf die englische, anglo-amerikanische, französische, belgische und italienische Jurisprudenz* 84 (1884) ("Jede Strafgesetzgebung aber ist eine positive; während der Civilschutz sich aus dem Bestehen des Civilrechts von selbst ergibt, bedarf der Strafschutz seiner besonderen Sanktion, er darf nicht aus dem Rechte und der Rechtsverletzung heraus abgeleitet werden: nicht in allen Fällen der Rechtsverletzung ist das Bedürfniss einer strafrechtlichen Sanction gegeben, und ob ein solches gegeben ist, hat nur die positive Gesetzgebung zu entscheiden; wie denn auch kraft des legalpolitischen Grundsatzes: ‚nulla poena sine lege' ...."); Josef Kohler, *Warenzeichenrecht—Zugleich zweite Auflage des Rechts des Markenschutzes mit Berücksichtigung ausländischer Gesetzgebungen (1884)* 127–128 (2nd edn., 1910); *see also* Paul Kent, *Das Reichsgesetz zum Schutz der Waarenbezeichnungen vom 12. Mai 1894—Unter Berücksichtigung in- und ausländischer Literatur und Rechtsprechung sowie der Praxis des Patentamts* 245 (1897).

88 For the acquisition of trademark rights by use, *see* Josef Kohler, *Das Recht des Markenschutzes mit Berücksichtigung ausländischer Gesetzgebungen und mit besonderer Rücksicht auf die englische, anglo-amerikanische, französische, belgische und italienische Jurisprudenz* 84–85 (1884) ("[S]etzt ein solches pseudonymes Erkennungszeichen nicht nur voraus, dass der Gewerbetreibende sich desselben continuell und consequent bedient hat, sondern es kann erst dann als die Domäne des Gewerbetreibenden betrachtet werden, wenn der Verkehr die Beziehung zur Person verstanden hat, erst dann, wenn das Zeichen als Bezeichnungsmittel des betreffenden Verkehrstreibenden, als das Emblem seiner Waare, als die Flagge erkannt wird, unter welcher seine Waare im

By this means, the system of the registered mark gives the transacting person the eminent advantage that the mark he has chosen will immediately be associated with his person, that it will immediately be an unmistakable signal of the origin of his wares, without first having to make use of the medium of traffic and transacting in order to bring out such a connection and characterization. . . .[89]

The trademark is nothing else than an individual right consolidated, secured, and reinforced by state regulation. . . . Hence, the state-regulated trademark right is the augmentation of the pure individual right: this is the true relation, the correct characterization of the thing.[90]

In essence, Kohler conceived of a two-layered structure: commercial activity was protected as an emanation of the personality per se. In addition, a higher level of protection, beyond mere personality rights, could be achieved by trademark registration. It was then an enhanced or upgraded right that constituted the subject matter of protection. As we will see in the following, this reinforcement of personality rights by registration[91] should prove significant for subsequent ideas in international trademark and unfair competition doctrine.[92]

One aspect in particular is intimately related to this idea of upgraded rights. While the dual structure of trademark and personality rights protection (or unfair competition prevention) had been a source of debate

Strome des Verkehrs cursirt: denn vorher fehlt es an der Verbindung zwischen Person und Zeichen . . . .").

89 Josef Kohler, *Das Recht des Markenschutzes mit Berücksichtigung ausländischer Gesetzgebungen und mit besonderer Rücksicht auf die englische, anglo-amerikanische, französische, belgische und italienische Jurisprudenz* 86–87 (1884) ("[S]o gibt das System der einregistrirten Marke dem Verkehrstreibenden den eminenten Vortheil, dass die von ihm gewählte Marke sofort mit seiner Person in Verbindung tritt, dass sie sofort zum untrüglichen Kennzeichen der Herkunft seiner Waare erhoben wird, ohne dass es erst des Mediums des Verkehrs bedarf, um diese Verbindung, diese Charakterisirung zu vollziehen . . . ." (author's translation)).

90 Josef Kohler, *Das Recht des Markenschutzes mit Berücksichtigung ausländischer Gesetzgebungen und mit besonderer Rücksicht auf die englische, anglo-amerikanische, französische, belgische und italienische Jurisprudenz* 88 (1884) ("[D]as Markenrecht ist nichts anderes, als ein durch staatliche Regulative gefestigtes, gesichertes und gesteigertes Individualrecht. . . . So ist denn das staatlich regulirte Markenrecht der Comparativ des puren Individualrechts: das ist das wahre Verhältniss, das die die richtige Charakteristik der Sache." (author's translation)).

91 *See* again Josef Kohler, *Warenzeichenrecht—Zugleich zweite Auflage des Rechts des Markenschutzes mit Berücksichtigung ausländischer Gesetzgebungen (1884)* 127–128 (2nd edn., 1910); and also Alexander Elster, *Gewerblicher Rechtsschutz umfassend Urheber- und Verlagsrecht, Patent- und Musterschutz, Warenzeichenrecht und Wettbewerbsrecht* 208 (1921) ("Öffentliches und privates Recht treffen sich auf dem Gebiet des Zeichenrechts und schützen das persönliche und vermögensrechtliche Gut nicht nur um seiner selbst willen, sondern auch im Interesse des Verkehrs und des Staates. Dies drückt sich in der Verstärkung des materiellen Rechts durch formale Vorschriften aus.").

92 *See infra* p. 53 *et seq.*

ever since *Apollinarisbrunnen*, courts and legal scholars accorded scarce attention to defining protectable subject matter. Rights in a trademark were never deemed to be directly connected to or intertwined with the tangible assets or premises of their owner's business. To the contrary, rights in trade symbols and in production and business equipment or real estate were deemed to be distinctly separate and independent from one another.[93] Yet Kohler's understanding of an upgrading of rights made the trademark an asset of the owner's business.[94] Rights in the trademark were thus detachable from the owner's personality. And detachment led to an amalgamation with the business.[95] In more general terms, with regard to the correlation between "personality" and "business," Kohler elaborated in 1914:

> It is due to a superficiality of analysis ... if it is overlooked that the person's activities and their automatic outcome will—in certain directions—be dissociated from the person and take on an independent nature within the commercial enterprise. ... The enterprise as such can be sold and transferred; thereby a part of the person is peeled off, similar to organic life where fission and pullulation can create a new entity or, at least, make elements of an existing entity the part of a different creation.[96]

[93] *See, e.g.*, Josef Kohler, *Warenzeichenrecht—Zugleich zweite Auflage des Rechts des Markenschutzes mit Berücksichtigung ausländischer Gesetzgebungen (1884)* 63 (2nd edn., 1910) ("Ebensowenig ist das Zeichen mit dem Eigentum an einem bestimmten Unternehmensgebäude verknüpft; es ist nicht an einen bestimmten Ort gebunden.").

[94] *See, e.g.*, the Reichsgericht on an international trademark dispute, arguing on the basis of personality rights protection in RGZ vol. 18, 28, 31—*Hoff* (2 October 1886) ("Nun müssen Warenzeichen, Namen und Firmen des Handeltreibenden und Produzenten als unkörperliche Güter für ihre rechtliche Behandlung an einen bestimmten Raum als ihren Sitz geknüpft werden. Dies ist wegen ihrer hier allein in Betracht kommenden Bedeutung als Figuren- oder Namenmarken für Waren der Ort des Handelsunternehmens oder der Niederlassung des Produzenten. Von dieser Stelle aus äußert die betreffende Individualitätsbethätigung ihre Wirkung.").

[95] *See* Josef Kohler, *Warenzeichenrecht—Zugleich zweite Auflage des Rechts des Markenschutzes mit Berücksichtigung ausländischer Gesetzgebungen (1884)* 64 (2nd edn., 1910) ("Das Zeichenrecht ist ein Persönlichkeitsrecht ...; allein dieses Persönlichkeitsmittel gehört zu den eben genannten, welche sich von der Persönlichkeit ablösen und dem Unternehmen einfügen können, sodass das Ganze mit dem Unternehmen verwächst und dadurch von der Persönlichkeit unabhängig wird.").

[96] Josef Kohler, *Der unlautere Wettbewerb—Darstellung des Wettbewerbsrechts* 23 (1914) ("Es ist ... eine oberflächliche Behandlungsweise, zu verkennen, daß das von der Person eingeleitete automatische Wirken sich nach gewissen Richtungen von der Person ablösen und in dem gewerblichen Unternehmen eine selbständige Natur annehmen kann. ... Das Unternehmen ist also einer Veräußerung fähig; damit geht ein Stück der Person von der Person ab, ähnlich wie im organischen Leben eine Knospung und Spaltung eintreten kann, welche ein neues Wesen erzeugt oder mindestens einen Teil des bisherigen Wesens zum Bestandteil eines anderen Wesens macht." (author's translation)); *see also* Otto von Gierke, *Deutsches Privatrecht, vol. I: Allgemeiner Teil und Personenrecht* § 84 I, at 728 (1895) ("Das Recht an der Marke war als ein besonderes Privatrecht anerkannt und geschützt. ... Von Hause aus war es an die Person

Over time, the trademark was conceived of as protecting the owner's business as such. It became an asset of the going concern. Friedrich Jüngel and Julius Magnus explained this dominant position in 1933:

> [The trademark right] has, over time, gained an economically and legally different shape: the mark has become a property asset that is dissociated from the holder's personality .... The purpose and the subject matter of mark protection is not the person of the holder, but his business. ... The right in the sign is a property right; an absolute right, that has, however, no self-contained legal existence; it is only the accessory to a certain business concern.[97]

As a result, the owner's place of business would determine the location of what had to be protected.[98] Interestingly, the value to be protected was thus clearly detached from actual market conditions. No matter how far the trademark owner's commercial activity extended, the place of business was the cynosure of its legal protection. As we will see in the following, German conflicts doctrine did not consider the trademark owner's

gebunden. ... War das Recht an der Marke Zubehör eines Grundstückes, einer Gerechtigkeit oder eines Gewerbebetriebes geworden, so gieng es mit der Hauptsache auf Erben und sonstige Rechtsnachfolger über. Zum Theil wurde das Markenrecht zu einem selbständig vererblichen und veräu[ß]erlichen Vermögensrechte."; *see also id.* at 738 ("Zubehör des Geschäftsbetriebes")).

97 *See, e.g.*, Friedrich Jüngel & Julius Magnus, *Das deutsche Warenzeichenrecht* 214 (6th edn., 1933) ("[Das Markenrecht hat] im Laufe der Zeiten volkswirtschaftlich wie rechtlich eine andere Gestaltung gewonnen: die Marke ist zu einem von der Persönlichkeit des Trägers losgelösten Vermögenswert geworden .... Ziel und Gegenstand des Z[eichen]schutzes ist nicht die Person des Z[eichen]inhabers, sondern sein Geschäftsbetrieb .... Das Z[eichen]recht ist ein Vermögensrecht, und zwar ein absolutes, das allerdings keinen selbständigen rechtlichen Bestand hat, sondern nur als Zubehör zu einem bestimmten Geschäftsbetrieb ...." (author's translation)) (with further references); Reinhold Richter, *Studie über die Lehre vom akzessorischen Charakter des dem Ausländer gewährten Markenrechts*, 1926 GRUR 100, 101–102; Alfred Hagens, *Warenzeichenrecht* 32–33 (1927); Ernst A. F. Warnecke, *Warenzeichenschutz und unlauterer Wettbewerb unter besonderer Berücksichtigung des Verhältnisses der §§ 12 und 14 WZG und 1 und 16 UWG untereinander und zu anderen Gesetzen* 7 (1928). This aspect had been illustrated around the same time by Fritz Ostertag in economic terms for the Swiss regime of trademark protection. Not only was the trademark inseparably connected to the owner's business, but it was an asset of the business: "[D]as Markenrecht ist daher ein Vermögensrecht, ein Immaterialgüterrecht. Die Marke wird auch vom Kaufmann als wichtiges Aktivum seines Unternehmens behandelt." *See* Fritz Ostertag, *Territorialität oder Universalität im Markenrecht*, 212, 216, in *Festgabe Fritz Goetzinger* (Universität Basel ed., 1935); for Austria, *see, e.g.*, Leo Geller, *Österreichisches Markenschutzgesetz* 14 (4th edn., 1906) ("Das Markenrecht klebt an dem Unternehmen, für welches die Marke bestimmt ist, erlischt mit demselben und übergeht im Falle des Besitzwechsels an den neuen Besitzer.").

98 *See, e.g.*, Martin Wolff, *Private International Law* 292 (2nd edn., 1950) ("The question whether a person has acquired ... a trade mark should be answered, not by the law of the domicile of the merchant, but by the law of the place of business. The reason is that all these rules are mainly concerned, not with his personality, but with the enterprise as such; the enterprise often becomes independent of the trader's person ....").

information capital in the trade symbol or her goodwill as being spread across the market and across the customer base. This characteristic is what largely distinguishes German trademark conflicts doctrine from its American counterpart.[99]

At this point, we can conclude that the German practice of trademark and unfair competition law did not manage to fill the void that had developed after the decline of the guild system. While courts in other European jurisdictions did find and provide for sufficient grounds, the German courts failed to implement remedial schemes beyond the codified regime. As a result, a coherent system of unfair competition prevention did not develop until the German Civil Code and the Unfair Competition Act came into force around the turn of the century.[100] Further, a more specific consequence of the doctrinal struggle is the deep divergence between trademark protection and unfair competition prevention that developed during the nineteenth century. With the dichotomy came a bifurcation of the field. For this book, the latter aspect is particularly relevant. While it seemed as if the field's bifurcation might be overcome in early twentieth-century theory, the division has survived all attempts at reconciliation and, ultimately, has been implemented in modern European doctrine.

IV The Twentieth Century: A Triumph of Separatism

The interrelation of trademark protection and unfair competition prevention has been a problematic issue not only in Germany but in the United States as well. US doctrine has long struggled with the question of whether trademark protection has a place within the field of or in proximity to unfair competition repression. Early twentieth-century practice appeared to have brought at least a formal clarification for the United States when the Supreme Court declared in *Hanover Star* that "the common law of trademarks is but a part of the broader law of unfair competition."[101] I will address this issue in more detail in my discussion of US law in the next chapter. In the meantime, it is worth mentioning that US doctrine ultimately adopted a rather homogeneous and comprehensive concept of trademark and unfair competition law. Today, the two

[99] For US doctrine, *see infra* p. 94 *et seq.*

[100] *See, e.g.*, Siegbert Lammel, *Recht zur Ordnung des Wettbewerbs: Deutschland*, 3806, 3808, in *Handbuch der Quellen und Literatur der neueren europäischen Privatrechtsgeschichte, vol. III: Das 19. Jahrhundert, 3rd part: Gesetzgebung zu den privatrechtlichen Sondergebieten* (Helmut Coing ed., 1986); Henning von Stechow, *Das Gesetz zur Bekämpfung des unlauteren Wettbewerbs vom 27. Mai 1896—Entstehungsgeschichte und Wirkung* 35 *et seq.* (2002).

[101] *Hanover Star Milling Co. v. Metcalf*, 240 U.S. 403, 413 (1916).

areas are rarely distinguished with regard to their doctrinal foundations. This has not been the case in Germany—not just as a consequence of nineteenth-century formalism but also due to subsequent developments.

A Reichsgericht *Sansibar* and *Pecose*: A Shaky Hierarchy of Policies

One may be tempted to conclude that German formalism lost its dominance at the beginning of the twentieth century. After all, the 1894 act implemented a rule against the unauthorized use of another's trade dress (*Ausstattung*), absent formal registration.[102] With the 1896 Unfair Competition Act,[103] lawmakers had added a number of gap-filling provisions on the prevention of unfair competition in addition to formal trademark rights protection, and the courts had extended the 1900 German Civil Code's defense of unfairness[104] to the trademark regime, which allowed for fending off bad-faith registrations or other kinds of improper attack on a competitor.[105] Indeed, the most prominent incipiency of such deformalization can be found in the 1907 *Sansibar* decision, in which the German Reichsgericht—quite different from its prior formalism—found preexisting and use-based entitlements to ultimately prevail over a bad-faith registration. In *Sansibar*, the defendant argued that the plaintiff had intentionally chosen the defendant's unregistered right for registration in order to oust her from the established market position. The court succinctly jettisoned the once ironclad rule of positivism:

> The Trademark Act, even though intended to exclusively regulate the field of trademarks as the sole legal instrument, still remains the law for a special regime and thus does not preclude application of general principles of the Civil Code that provide protection against unfair acts in commerce.[106]

[102] *See supra* p. 32 *et seq.*
[103] Gesetz zur Bekämpfung des unlauteren Wettbewerbes of 27 May 1896, Deutsches Reichsgesetzblatt 1896, Nr. 13, 145–149.
[104] In particular, sections 826 and 229 German Civil Code (BGB).
[105] *See, e.g.*, Arnold Seligsohn, *Gesetz zum Schutz der Warenbezeichnungen* 29 (2nd edn., 1905); Chr. Finger, *Das Reichsgesetz zum Schutz der Warenbezeichnungen vom 12. Mai 1894 nebst den Ausführungsbestimmungen und dem internationalen Warenbezeichnungsrecht* 234 *et seq.* (2nd edn., 1906); for an overview, *see, e.g.*, Wolfgang Gloy, *Die Entwicklung des Wettbewerbsrechts und seiner Nebengebiete*, 855, 858 *et seq.*, in *Gewerblicher Rechtsschutz und Urheberrecht in Deutschland, Festschrift zum hundertjährigen Bestehen der Deutschen Vereinigung für gewerblichen Rechtsschutz und Urheberrecht und ihrer Zeitschrift, vol. II* (Friedrich-Karl Beier et al. eds., 1991).
[106] *See, e.g.*, RGZ vol. 66, 236, 240—*Sansibar* (21 June 1907) ("Allein das Warenzeichengesetz ist, wenn es auch das ihm zugewiesene Gebiet ausschließlich regelt, immerhin ein Sondergesetz und will den Grundsätzen des Bürgerlichen Gesetzbuchs, welche Schutz gegen illoyale Handlungen im Verkehrsleben bezwecken, den Eingang nicht verschließen . . . ." (author's translation)).

As it seemed, the strict registration theorem from the dark *Apollinarisbrunnen* era had been replaced by a reasonable substantive-balancing analysis.[107] But the issue remained contested.

Even though the dissolution of formalism as such was well received, some feared that the courts might overshoot the mark. In particular, one of the court's statements in the 1919 *Pecose* decision, describing the law of unfair competition as a regime of higher order and hierarchy (*Recht höherer Ordnung*[108]), provoked heavy critique. A dominance of unfair competition principles over trademark law was perceived as a threat to the system of state-granted registered rights.[109] Evidently, the trademark register had attained utmost practical relevance for the nationwide acquisition of rights by the second half of the nineteenth century. At the same time, however, the extension of formal rights to markets that a right holder only planned to explore—hence, in advance of actual marketing activity—was still seen skeptically. At issue were the potentially anticompetitive effects of such advance performance in the sense of right ownership before market activity. The question in practice was how to limit windfall profits for early registrants, particularly those lacking genuinely *bona fide* motives.

Seen in this light, the Reichsgericht's concept of a hierarchy of orders was the reflection of an ongoing conflict between the sphere of strictly formal trademark rights protection and that of more flexible unfair competition prevention. While the former illustrated a basically liberalist conception of an optimally extended sphere of freedom of competition,

[107] *See, e.g.*, Josef Kohler, *Warenzeichenrecht—Zugleich zweite Auflage des Rechts des Markenschutzes mit Berücksichtigung ausländischer Gesetzgebungen (1884)* 69 *et seq.* (2nd edn., 1910); Alfred Hagens, *Warenzeichenrecht* 31 (1927); *see also* Friedrich-Karl Beier & Annette Kur, *Das Verhältnis von Markenrecht und Recht des unlauteren Wettbewerbs im Wandel der Zeiten*, 477, 479 n. 10, in *Festschrift für Wolfgang Fikentscher zum 70. Geburtstag* (Bernhard Großfeld et al. eds., 1998) (with numerous references to case law).

[108] *See* RGZ vol. 97, 90, 93–94–*Pecose* (4 November 1919); and also later RGZ vol. 120, 325, 328 *et seq.—Sonnengold* (30 April 1928).

[109] *See, e.g.*, Hermann Isay, *Die Gefährdung des gewerblichen Rechtsschutzes durch die Anwendung des § 1 UWG*, 1928 GRUR 71, 78–79; Landenberger, *Anmerkungen auf der Versammlung des Deutschen Vereins für den Schutz des gewerblichen Eigentums vom 19. Januar 1928*, 1928 GRUR 206, 208 ("Wenn das Warenzeichenrecht ein Recht minderer Ordnung ist, wie dies von manchen Schriftstellern vertreten wird, so möge es abgeschafft werden. … [M]an muß in diesem Zusammenhang vielmehr von einem ‚Recht höherer Unordnung' als von einem ‚Recht höherer Ordnung' sprechen."). Ulmer criticized the Reichsgericht with particular clarity when he explained: "Eine solche Auffassung [i.e., the Reichsgericht formula] ist aber nur solange tunlich, als die Anwendung der Grundsätze aus dem allgemeineren Rechtsgebiet nur eine ausnahmsweise ist und noch als Durchbrechung empfunden werden kann. Sie ist—rechtsgeschichtlich betrachtet—die ständige Wurzel der Rechtsfortbildung gegenüber vorwiegend formal geregeltem Recht." *See* Eugen Ulmer, *Warenzeichen und unlauterer Wettbewerb in ihrer Fortbildung durch die Rechtsprechung* 68 (1929).

the latter expressed a concern for a more "socialized" and "politicized" regulation of the marketplace.[110] Since the two fields' doctrinal and structural interrelation had never been fully clarified, it had become a constant source of practical dispute and theoretical confusion. Not surprisingly, in the years to come, the challenge remained: how to determine the exact boundaries between the extension of absolute and exclusive rights and the principles of free and unhindered competition in light of varying conceptions of the economic policies at work when "fairness" was at issue.

B Eugen Ulmer: An Almost Reconciliation

Ironically, it was the *maître penseur* of twentieth-century German intellectual property law who further contributed to the consolidation of registration formalism. Even though he provided for more clarity, his influential concept of the two fields' interrelation did not overcome the dichotomy.

Indeed, in 1929, Eugen Ulmer seemed to present a final solution to the problem in his habilitation thesis.[111] And, ever after, he has actually been praised for having successfully reconciled trademark and unfair competition policies.[112] As we have seen, unfair competition prevention was deemed to regulate commerce and competition in general, whereas trademark law was designed to protect individual rights. Ulmer rejected this separation. Yet with respect to the subject matter that should be protected, his theory was still based on the primacy of individual rights protection.

He considered both trademark and unfair competition law to be part of commercial tort doctrine. This concept was not new—after all, both sectors had already been characterized as interrelated.[113] Ulmer,

[110] A quite illustrative example among the proponents of a more socialized trademark/unfair competition regime was Alfred Rosenthal, who explained (with a kind of realist indignation) in *Die geistige Einstellung des Richters zu Prozessen betr. Nachahmung von Firmen- und Warenbezeichnungen*, 1923 MuW 145, 148: „Wenn das Leben stärker ist, als die von der Doktrin errichteten Grenzlinien zulassen, dann sollte man die Grenzlinien verschieben. . . . Unser Bestreben, alles zu reglementieren, einzuteilen und abzugrenzen, führt zur Scholastik."

[111] Eugen Ulmer, *Warenzeichen und unlauterer Wettbewerb in ihrer Fortbildung durch die Rechtsprechung* (1929).

[112] *See, e.g.*, Friedrich-Karl Beier & Annette Kur, *Das Verhältnis von Markenrecht und Recht des unlauteren Wettbewerbs im Wandel der Zeiten*, 477, 480–481, in *Festschrift für Wolfgang Fikentscher zum 70. Geburtstag* (Bernhard Großfeld et al. eds., 1998).

[113] *See, e.g.*, Alexander Elster, *Gewerblicher Rechtsschutz umfassend Urheber- und Verlagsrecht, Patent- und Musterschutz, Warenzeichenrecht und Wettbewerbsrecht* 8 (1921) ("Daher berührt sich der Markenschutz . . . aufs engste [mit dem allgemeinen Wettbewerbsschutz], wenn er auch im übrigen patentähnlich aufgezogen ist. Hier ist von irgendeinem, geistigen Eigentum' unmittelbar nicht die Rede."); for a comparative perspective, *see also* Edwin Katz, *Weltmarkenrecht* 7 (1926).

however, gave the idea a richer foundation. A comparative analysis of different national laws served as a blueprint for what could be characterized as an early transnational theory of core policies:

> The value to be legally protected on the field of trademarks and firm names is to be found in the business enterprise. It is a part of those intangible business assets that are incapable of a self-contained protected existence, and that we—in order to find a concept for their legal protection—can position as an immaterial good next to the holder's other legal entitlements. This value is part of the area that Pisko ... has explained as "secured sales option." English legal terminology provides the term "goodwill" ..., French [terminology] summarizes it in "la clientèle et l'achandalage" ...; we will ... speak of the advertising capacity ... of the business.[114]

The value embodied in what he called "advertising capacity" (*Werbekraft*) was represented by the entrepreneurial use of trademarks and trade or firm names, and by the indication of source or origin in commercial advertising.[115] Since all jurisdictions alike protected advertising capacity, he found the goodwill that was incorporated into consumers' minds to be the universal and only relevant subject matter. Accordingly, preventing

[114] Eugen Ulmer, *Warenzeichen und unlauterer Wettbewerb in ihrer Fortbildung durch die Rechtsprechung* 3–4 (1929) ("Der Wert, der auf dem Gebiet der Waren- und Unternehmenskennzeichnung rechtlich zu schützen ist, ruht in dem Unternehmen. Er ist ein Teil jener zu rechtlich geschützter Eigenexistenz unfähigen, unkörperlichen Unternehmenswerte, die wir, um die Denkformen für den Rechtsschutz zu gewinnen, in ihrer Zusammenfassung als Immaterialgut anderen Rechtsgütern zur Seite stellen können. Er gehört demjenigen Gebiet an, das Pisko ... mit 'gesicherter Absatzgelegenheit' bezeichnet. Die englische Rechtssprache hat dafür den Ausdruck 'goodwill' ..., die französische sieht es in 'la clientèle et l'achalandage' ..., zusammengefaßt, wir werden, wo wir es im Auge haben, von der Werbekraft ... des Unternehmens sprechen." (author's translation)). In a footnote, Ulmer further defined advertising capacity (Werbekraft) as the business's relationship to its present and future customer base: "Darunter soll nicht nur die Fähigkeit, neue Kunden zu werben, sondern auch die Beziehung zum alten Kundenkreis verstanden werden." *Id.* at 4 n. 4.

[115] A similar concept had been developed by Schechter under the rubric of protecting trademark distinctiveness. Instead of "advertising capacity," he spoke of "selling power." *See* Frank I. Schechter, *The Rational Basis of Trademark Protection*, 40 Harv. L. Rev. 813, 818 (1927) ("The true functions of the trademark are, then, to identify a product as satisfactory and thereby to stimulate further purchases by the consuming public.... To describe a trademark merely as a symbol of good will, without recognizing in it an agency for the actual creation and perpetuation of good will, ignores the most potent aspect of the nature of a trademark and that phase most in need of protection.... [T]oday the trademark is not merely the symbol of good will but often the most effective agent for the creation of good will, imprinting upon the public mind an anonymous and impersonal guaranty of satisfaction, creating a desire for further satisfactions. The mark actually sells the goods. And, self-evidently, the more distinctive the mark, the more effective is its selling power."). For an overview and explanation of European terminology regarding the same phenomenon, particularly the German *Kundschaft* (customer base) and the Italian *avviamento* (business value) or *collettore di clientela* (customer collector), *see* Walter R. Schluep, *Das Markenrecht als subjektives Recht* 330–332 (1964).

consumer confusion (*konfundierender unlauterer Wettbewerb*) had to be seen as the most basic tenet of both trademark protection and unfair competition repression.[116]

In addition to this overarching policy, however, Ulmer still adhered to the idea that the register's genuine function required an exceptional treatment of registered rights. The law of unfair competition allowed for rights to be acquired naturally—that is, by making use of a trademark in the course of trade or commerce. Registration and the granting of rights in advance of actual use in the marketplace, by contrast, provided for trademark rights to develop within an artificially created sphere of individual freedom.[117] This geographic area covered the full national territory. This function became known as the principle of trademark promotion and fostering (*Prinzip der Entwicklungsbegünstigung*).[118] As Ulmer understood, promoting and fostering the development of nascent trademarks were of ultimate import. The registrant needed security to plan and invest in her marketing activities—in particular, in building the goodwill of her trademark. Without a wide-reaching guarantee of right protection, incentives to create and establish new trademarks would be limited. Seen in this light, no alternative to the register existed, and concerns for potentially anticompetitive effects had to stand back.[119]

Accordingly, depending on the stage of development, either the policy of trademark promotion or that of confusion prevention governed. In *statu nascendi*, registration was the instrument for fostering the

[116] Eugen Ulmer, *Warenzeichen und unlauterer Wettbewerb in ihrer Fortbildung durch die Rechtsprechung* 58 (1929) ("Eine Zusammenfassung der verschiedenen Systeme wird heute am besten in der folgenden Betrachtungsweise durchgeführt werden können: Grundlage ist die Norm vom konfundierenden unlauteren Wettbewerb in der Ausprägung, die sie im deutschen und englischen Recht gefunden hat.").

[117] For a similar explanation of US trademark registration under the Lanham Act, *see, e.g.*, William Jay Gross, *The Territorial Scope of Trademark Rights*, 44 U. Miami L. Rev. 1075, 1090 *et seq.* (1990); Graeme B. Dinwoodie, *Trademarks and Territory: Detaching Trademark Law from the Nation-State*, 41 Hous. L. Rev. 885, 898–899 n. 44 (2004).

[118] Eugen Ulmer, *Warenzeichen und unlauterer Wettbewerb in ihrer Fortbildung durch die Rechtsprechung* 58–59 and 63–66 (1929). For contemporary commentary, *see, e.g.*, Carl Becher, *Warenzeichengesetz und Internationale Registrierung* § 15 note 5 Ia, at 118 (1931) ("Anwartschaftsrecht"). For a practical implementation, *see, e.g.*, BGHZ vol. 32, 133, 142—*Dreitannen* (29 March 1960).

[119] Eugen Ulmer, *Warenzeichen und unlauterer Wettbewerb in ihrer Fortbildung durch die Rechtsprechung* 65 (1929) ("Die Betonung des Gedankens der Entwicklungsbegünstigung auf Kosten der Interessen der freien Konkurrenz, die durch die Vielfalt der zugeteilten Monopole belastet wird, ist eine feststehende Wertung des deutschen Rechts, an der de lege lata grundsätzlich nichts zu ändern sein wird."). This also is the modern perspective. *See, e.g.*, Horst-Peter Götting, *Gewerblicher Rechtsschutz—Patent-, Gebrauchsmuster-, Design- und Markenrecht* § 5 para. 22 (10th edn., 2014). For the identical concern in Swiss and US law, *see, e.g.*, Marco Hauser, *Die Inzidenz der Publikumsinteressen auf Wesen und Umfang des Markenrechts* 95 (1966); Stephen L. Carter, *The Trouble with Trademark*, 99 Yale L. J. 759, 777 (1990).

development of trademark rights. Registered rights would then prevail over a competitor's nonregistered entitlement or a pre-acquired position. But registration was limited to fostering legal certainty. It played only a servant function to the rules of unfair competition prevention.[120] In the later stages of a trademark's life, upon acquisition of marketplace goodwill, the idea of developing nascent trademarks would yield to the principles of preventing confusion. In this last stage, the protection of existing rights and acquired positions on the market (*Besitzstandswahrung*)—not trademark promotion—governed.[121] This concept overthrew the previously dominant idea of a so-called self-sufficiency of the trademark register (*Selbstgenügsamkeit*); the register was a mere facet of the overall system of trademark/goodwill protection, not the ultimate denominator of rights creation and enforcement.[122]

Even though Ulmer brought the two concurrent protection systems in harmony with each other, he did not do away with the dichotomy. This is mostly due to the fact that he defined trademark rights as immaterial property. Unfair competition prevention, however, remained a category of commercial torts.[123] Accordingly, consumer protection was still of secondary concern. Consumer interests and their protection were a mere reflex of individual-competitor protection. Competitors' interests

[120] Eugen Ulmer, *Warenzeichen und unlauterer Wettbewerb in ihrer Fortbildung durch die Rechtsprechung* 70 (1929) ("Im Zeichen der Reife hilft uns das Bild des Verkehrslebens weiter: die entwickelten Kräfte sind gegeben und ihrer Stärke entsprechend durch das Wettbewerbsrecht betont; für das Registerrecht bleibt hier die wesentlich polizeiliche Aufgabe, den lebendigen Impulsen gesicherte Bahnen zu weisen. … Wir bleiben im Rahmen beider Bilder, wenn wir die rechtlichen Wirkungen des Registers von seiten seiner Funktionen her sehen: es sind Funktionen der Förderung, die es in dem Prozesse der Zeichenbildung wahrzunehmen hat, und wesentlich Funktionen der Sicherung und Ordnung, die ihm im fortgeschrittenen Stadium der Entwicklung zukommen. Gleichzeitig ist mit dieser funktionellen Anschauung des Registers, mit der Auffassung, daß das Register (sowohl im Stadium der Entwicklung wie in dem der fertigen Ausbildung) ein dienendes Glied im Rahmen des Ganzen ist, der Gegensatz zu dem ursprünglich unserem Rechte zugrunde liegenden Selbstgenügsamkeitsprinzip des Registers am schärfsten formuliert und der Vorstellungskreis, in dem auch das RG. noch befangen ist, wenn es von einem Gegensatz des Rechts höherer und niederer Ordnung spricht, verlassen.").

[121] Eugen Ulmer, *Warenzeichen und unlauterer Wettbewerb in ihrer Fortbildung durch die Rechtsprechung* 69–70 (1929).

[122] *See* fn. 120 (with a literal citation of Ulmer's explanation). For the traditional view on register "Selbstgenügsamkeit," *see, e.g.*, Walther Oppenheim, *Die Verwirkung im gewerblichen Rechtsschutz* 4–5 (1932).

[123] *See* Eugen Ulmer, *Warenzeichen und unlauterer Wettbewerb in ihrer Fortbildung durch die Rechtsprechung* 9 (1929) ("Die Vorstellung vom Markenrecht als Immaterialgüterrecht is fruchtbar."); and also Arthur Nussbaum, *Deutsches internationales Privatrecht—Unter besonderer Berücksichtigung des österreichischen und schweizerischen Rechts* 339 (1932) ("Der unlautere Wettbewerb ist nicht, oder zum mindesten nicht notwendig, Verletzung eines Immaterialgüterrechts, sondern er ist ein Delikt, das üblicherweise dem Bereich des 'gewerblichen Rechtsschutzes' hinzugerechnet wird.").

were what mattered.[124] By this means, Ulmer ultimately further extended Kohler's concept of upgrading personality rights. In addition to the idea of trademark and unfair competition law being part of the larger fields of economic and commercial torts, the focus on individual rights protection remained formative throughout the century.

C Europe: Rights Formalism and Individualization

In the following decades, German doctrine further extended the protection of nonregistered entitlements. Ultimately, full-fledged trademark rights could be acquired either by registration or by the use of symbols having earned a sufficient level of recognition among the consuming public (*Verkehrsgeltung*).[125] In this regard, the 1936 Trademark Act[126] became an additional pillar of full-fledged rights acquisition. The act's provision on the protection of trade dress in section 25 (*Ausstattung*) was widely understood to have established a valid domain of use-based rights.[127] Ever after, both categories—registered and use-based rights—seemed to be equivalent with regard to the extent and intensity of protection.[128] It was even posited that German trademark law had changed its paradigm of protection from registration to use.[129] Other European countries faced a similar situation. In Switzerland, for example, the equivalence of registered and use-based rights had been

124 Eugen Ulmer, *Warenzeichen und unlauterer Wettbewerb in ihrer Fortbildung durch die Rechtsprechung* 75–76 (1929) ("D[as] Interesse der Allgemeinheit mag für die Betrachtung im Hintergrund bleiben: der Unternehmer, der den Gedanken des konfundierenden unlauteren Wettbewerbs für sich ins Feld führt, steht im Vordergrund der Rechtsverteidigung. Immerhin bedeutet das Interesse der Allgemeinheit eine Stärkung seiner Position, die in der Wertung ihren Ausdruck finden mag.").

125 For the debate, *see, e.g.*, Andreas Sattler, *Emanzipation und Expansion des Markenrechts—Die Entstehungsgeschichte des Markengesetzes von 1995* 119 *et seq.*, 144 *et seq.* (2015).

126 Warenzeichengesetz of 5 May 1936, Reichsgesetzblatt II, 134.

127 The equality of registration and use had been expressly acknowledged earlier already by the Reichsgericht. *See, e.g.*, RGZ vol. 141, 110, 119—*The White Spot* (26 May 1933) ("Da somit die Ausstattung nach § 15 WZG. und das Warenzeichen an sich als gleichwertige Rechte einander gegenüberstehen und die Bestimmungen des Warenzeichengesetzes sinngemäß auf den Ausstattungsschutz anzuwenden sind . . . ."); *see also* Friedrich Jüngel & Julius Magnus, *Das deutsche Warenzeichenrecht* 466 (6th edn., 1933).

128 *See, e.g.*, Horst-Peter Götting, *Länderteil Deutschland*, 199, 215–216, in *Handbuch des Ausstattungsrechts—Der Schutz der nichteingetragenen Marke und Ausstattung im In- und Ausland, Festgabe für Friedrich-Karl Beier zum 60. Geburtstag* (Gerhard Schricker & Dieter Stauder eds., 1986); Friedrich-Karl Beier & Annette Kur, *Das Verhältnis von Markenrecht und Recht des unlauteren Wettbewerbs im Wandel der Zeiten*, 477, 486, in *Festschrift für Wolfgang Fikentscher zum 70. Geburtstag* (Bernhard Großfeld et al. eds., 1998); Elmar Wadle, *Werden und Wandel des deutschen Markenrechts*, 337, 354, in *Geistiges Eigentum—Bausteine zur Rechtsgeschichte, vol. II* (Elmar Wadle ed., 2003).

129 Ludwig Heydt, *Zum Begriff der Weltmarke*, 1952 GRUR 321, 323; Friedrich-Karl Beier, *Gedanken zum Verhältnis von Warenzeichen- und Ausstattungsschutz im künftigen deutschen Markenrecht*, 1967 GRUR 628, 630.

acknowledged even earlier, at the beginning of the century.[130] For a moment, it appeared as if the pendulum had swung back.

Yet, even though the categories' equivalence with respect to the protection of "property rights" was acknowledged, the two categories remained separate concepts: propertization via registration, on the one hand, and the gradual development of possessive rights in an intangible goodwill within the marketplace, on the other.[131] The latter was still considered more "fleeting" in character.[132] Hence, even proponents of equality continued to adhere to the doctrinal dichotomy: registered rights would be protected by trademark law, and use-based rights would remain largely an issue of unfair competition prevention.[133] Moreover, the equality of use-based and registered rights was never fully integrated into other European countries' national laws. On the contrary, the second half of the twentieth century witnessed another swing of the pendulum. A number of national laws changed their protection principles from "use" to "registration."[134] The main reason for this countermovement was industry lobbying.[135] The ideas brought forward in this regard had already influenced Ulmer's theses on the register's functions: in essence, registration systems were

[130] *See, e.g.*, Fritz Ostertag, *Territorialität oder Universalität im Markenrecht*, 212, 212, in *Festgabe Fritz Goetzinger* (Universität Basel ed., 1935).

[131] *See, e.g.*, the courts' language with respect to registered and use-based rights categorization in BGH 1957 GRUR 358, 359 *et seq.—Kölnisch Eis* (8 February 1957); BVerwG 1984 GRUR 350, 351—*Esslinger Neckarhalde* (9 August 1983); and also on the level of constitutional law: BVerfGE vol. 51, 193, 216 *et seq.—Weinbergsrolle* (22 May 1979); BVerfG 1988 GRUR 610, 612—*Esslinger Neckarhalde II* (8 March 1988).

[132] *See, e.g.*, Fritz Ossenbühl, *Anmerkung zu Bundesverwaltungsgericht, 1. Senat, 09.08.1983, 1 C 142/80—Esslinger Neckarhalde*, 1984 GRUR 351, 352 ("Auch beim Ausstattungsschutz handelt es sich um ein 'von der Rechtsordnung anerkanntes Vermögensrecht', das lediglich wegen seiner andersartigen Entstehungsvoraussetzungen und seiner an den Fortbestand der Verkehrsgeltung geknüpften Existenz einen 'flüchtigeren' Charakter als das Recht am eingetragenen Warenzeichen aufweist."); *see also* Albrecht Krieger, *Das Warenzeichen als Eigentumsrecht im Sinne des Artikels 14 des Grundgesetzes*, 1980 GRUR 335, 341 *et seq.*

[133] *See, e.g.*, Horst-Peter Götting, *Länderteil Deutschland*, 199, 215, in *Handbuch des Ausstattungsrechts—Der Schutz der nichteingetragenen Marke und Ausstattung im In- und Ausland, Festgabe für Friedrich-Karl Beier zum 60. Geburtstag* (Gerhard Schricker & Dieter Stauder eds., 1986).

[134] For the Benelux Convention on Intellectual Property (Trademarks and Designs), *see, e.g.*, Cohen Jehoram & van Nispen & Huydecoper, *European Trademark Law—Community Trademark Law and Harmonized National Trademark Law* 343 *et seq.* (2010). Switzerland had a similar tendency. *See* Friedrich-Karl Beier, *Warenzeichenrecht—Rückkehr zum Eintragungsprinzip? Überlegungen zur Reform des Markenrechts*, 1973 GRUR Int. 407, 409. For an overview on the Scandinavian systems, *see* Friedrich-Karl Beier, *Gedanken zum Verhältnis von Warenzeichen- und Ausstattungsschutz im künftigen deutschen Markenrecht*, 1967 GRUR 628, 633.

[135] *See, e.g.*, Martin Röttger, *Gedanken zur Schaffung einer EWG-Marke*, 1959 GRUR Ausl. 329, 331–332; Ludwig Heydt, *Wege zur Vereinheitlichung des europäischen Markenrechts*, 1960 GRUR Ausl. 348, 354–355; Rudolf Callmann, *Vorschläge für eine EWG-Marke unter Berücksichtigung der Markenprobleme in USA*, 1960 GRUR 514, 516.

deemed to establish transparency; only by prioritizing registered rights, it was contended, could trademark conflicts with prior users' unregistered rights be prevented, thereby avoiding costly and ultimately useless trademark registration, promotion, and advertising efforts.[136] In this light, one can understand why European Union law—under the Trademark Directive and the Trademark Regulation—does not provide for equivalence, either.[137] As the directive's preamble explains, trademarks "acquired through use" are taken into account "only in regard to the relationship between them and trade marks acquired by registration."[138] Hence, despite the fact that national regimes may and actually do provide for the protection of use-based trademark rights, acquisition and protection at the community level is an issue of registration formalities.[139]

Finally, formalism of this registration preference has been accompanied by a more general, increasingly property-oriented perspective in modern European trademark doctrine. Both the directive and the regulation employ the terms "property" and trademark "proprietor."[140] In this light, it is little surprise that scholarly commentary and the European Court of Justice have succumbed to a doctrine of protecting owner investment under a specifically property-oriented perspective. Traditionally, the primary function of a trademark was its capacity to distinguish between competitors' products and to indicate product origin. In particular, the Court of Justice used to emphasize the guarantee of origin as the "essential function of the trade mark."[141] Other trademark

[136] For an example of sunken investments by a junior industry user, *see* BGH 1957 GRUR 499—*Wipp* (10 May 1957); *see also* Friedrich-Karl Beier, *Warenzeichenrecht—Rückkehr zum Eintragungsprinzip? Überlegungen zur Reform des Markenrechts*, 1973 GRUR Int. 407, 409 (with further references).

[137] *See, e.g.*, art. 1 and art. 4 para. 4b of the Directive 2008/95/EC of the European Parliament and of the Council of 22 October 2008 to approximate the laws of the Member States relating to trade marks (codified version), O.J. EU (8 November 2008), L 299/25; and also art. 1, art. 6, and art. 8 para. 4 of the Council Regulation (EC) No 207/2009 of 26 February 2009 on the Community Trade Mark (codified version), O.J. EU (24 March 2009), L 78/1.

[138] Recital 5 of the Directive 2008/95/EC of the European Parliament and of the Council of 22 October 2008 to approximate the laws of the Member States relating to trade marks (codified version), O.J. EU (8 November 2008), L 299/25.

[139] *See, e.g.*, Günther Eisenführ & Detlef Schennen, *Kommentar zur Gemeinschaftsmarkenverordnung*, Art. 6 para. 3 (4th edn., 2014). For a wise prophecy, *see* Friedrich-Karl Beier, *Warenzeichenrecht—Rückkehr zum Eintragungsprinzip? Überlegungen zur Reform des Markenrechts*, 1973 GRUR Int. 407, 410.

[140] *See, e.g.*, articles 5, 6, and 7 of the directive and articles 16 *et seq.* of the regulation ("Community Trade Marks as Objects of Property").

[141] More recently, *e.g.*, *Google France and Google*, C-236/08, 237/08, and 238/08, para. 77 (23 March 2010), [2010] E.C.R. I-2417; *L'Oréal and Others*, C 487/07, para. 58 (18 June 2009), [2009] E.C.R. I-5185. *See also*, *e.g.*, *Arsenal Football Club plc v. Matthew Reed*, C-206/01, para. 51 (12 November 2002), [2002] E.C.R. I-10273; for Germany, *see, e.g.*, BGHZ vol. 41, 84, 91—*Maja* (22 January 1964); *see also* Walter

functions—such as quality control and advertising functions—were initially considered less dominant and protectable only within the scope of protecting the trademark's indication-of-origin function.[142] Indeed, prior to the European harmonization of trademark law, many aspects of modern trademark goodwill were protected by unfair competition law only, and not trademark doctrine. One example is the protection of famous marks against their use for dissimilar products.[143] While trademark law was protecting the symbol as an indication of origin, unfair competition law was protecting its value as an advertising tool and the underlying entrepreneurial performance.[144] This rather narrow scope of trademark functions, however, was early on contested in scholarly commentary, which argued that the economic multifunctionality of trademarks should be supplemented by the recognition of more than one legal purpose, thereby giving particular regard to the right owner's interests in protection of her investment.[145] European and national lawmakers responded to this concern. Today, article 5(2) of the directive offers member states the opportunity to protect well-known trademarks against use that takes unfair advantage of or is detrimental to a trademark's distinctive character or reputation. Article 9(1)(c) of the regulation contains a similar provision. And the Court of Justice has recently extended its perspective on

R. Schluep, *Das Markenrecht als subjektives Recht* 68 *et seq.*, 265 *et seq.* (1964); Alois Troller, *Immaterialgüterrecht, vol. I*, 205 *et seq.* (3rd edn., 1983); Karl-Heinz Fezer, *Markenrecht*, Einl D para. 1 and 21 *et seq.* (4th edn., 2009); Cohen Jehoram & van Nispen & Huydecoper, *European Trademark Law—Community Trademark Law and Harmonized National Trademark Law* 9 (2010).

142 *See, e.g.*, Friedrich-Karl Beier, *Die Funktionen der Marke*, 225, 228 *et seq.*, in *Markenrechtliche Abhandlungen: Beiträge zur neueren Entwicklung des Warenzeichen-, Aussattungs- und Herkunftsschutzes, 1956–1986* (Friedrich-Karl Beier, 1986); more recently, *see* Franz Hacker, in *Kommentar zum Markengesetz* Einl. para. 32 (Paul Ströbele & Franz Hacker eds., 11th edn., 2015); Cohen Jehoram & van Nispen & Huydecoper, *European Trademark Law—Community Trademark Law and Harmonized National Trademark Law* 9–10 (2010).

143 *See, e.g.*, BGH 1985 GRUR 550, 552—*DIMPLE* (29 November 1984); for further examples and illustration, *see* Friedrich-Karl Beier & Annette Kur, *Das Verhältnis von Markenrecht und Recht des unlauteren Wettbewerbs im Wandel der Zeiten*, 477, 486 *et seq.*, in *Festschrift für Wolfgang Fikentscher zum 70. Geburtstag* (Bernhard Großfeld et al. eds., 1998).

144 Karl-Heinz Fezer, *Markenrecht*, Einl C MarkenG para. 14 (4th edn., 2009).

145 *See* Hermann Isay, *Die Selbständigkeit des Rechts an der Marke*, 1929 GRUR 23, 26; for the later debate, *see, e.g.*, Walter R. Schluep, *Das Markenrecht als subjektives Recht* 67 *et seq.* (1964); Friedrich-Karl Beier & Ulrich Krieger, *Wirtschaftliche Bedeutung, Funktionen und Zweck der Marke (68), Bericht erstattet im Namen der Landesgruppe der Bundesrepublik Deutschland*, 1976 GRUR Int. 125; Ulrich Loewenheim, *Warenzeichen, freier Warenverkehr, Kartellrecht*, 1051, 1055–1056, in *Gewerblicher Rechtsschutz und Urheberrecht in Deutschland, Festschrift zum hundertjährigen Bestehen der Deutschen Vereinigung für gewerblichen Rechtsschutz und Urheberrecht und ihrer Zeitschrift, vol. II* (Friedrich-Karl Beier et al. eds., 1991).

trademark functions. Its 2009 *L'Oréal* opinion, even though still emphasizing product origin as essential, lists further examples:

> [Trademark] functions include not only the essential function of the trade mark, which is to guarantee to consumers the origin of the goods or services, but also its other functions, in particular that of guaranteeing the quality of the goods or services in question and those of communication, investment or advertising.[146]

Hence, mere confusion prevention no longer appears to be the primary policy.[147] The extension of trademark functions and owners' rights under European Community law and within national regimes has moved doctrine toward an implementation of the trademark-as-property protection paradigm.[148] I will analyze substantive law in more detail in chapter 4. At the moment, it suffices to conclude that the legal entitlement granted to a trademark owner is no longer only an exclusive right; it has achieved a position of almost absolute dominion.[149]

D The Final Blow: Propertization vs. Socialization

Finally, despite Ulmer's resourceful explanation of the structural overlap between trademark and unfair competition law, his theory and its implementation did not do away with the second dichotomy in German doctrine—the distinction between registered and use-based rights. Ulmer may have paved the way for the recognition of use-based rights.[150] Nevertheless, he largely adhered to the distinction between two spheres:

[146] *Google France and Google*, C-236/08, 237/08, and 238/08, para. 58 (23 March 2010), [2010] E.C.R. I-2417.

[147] For further discussion, *see, e.g.*, Vito Mangini, *Die Marke: Niedergang der Herkunftsfunktion?*, 1996 GRUR Int. 462, 466; Adriano Vanzetti, *Die Funktion der Marke in einem System der freien Übertragbarkeit*, 1999 GRUR Int. 205, 205 *et seq.*; Claudius Marx, *Deutsches, europäisches und internationales Markenrecht* para. 65 *et seq.* (2nd edn., 2007); Karl-Heinz Fezer, *Markenrecht*, Einl D MarkenG para. 20 and 27 *et seq.* (4th edn., 2009).

[148] *See* Frauke Henning-Bodewig, *Marke und Verbraucher*, 176, 184, in *Die Neuordnung des Markenrechts in Europa—10. Ringberg-Symposium des Max-Planck-Instituts für ausländisches und internationales Patent-, Urheber- und Wettbewerbsrecht* (Gerhard Schricker & Friedrich-Karl Beier eds., 1996); Louis Pahlow, *Das Recht an der Marke als Benutzungsrecht des Markeninhabers*, 2006 WRP 97, 100. *See also, e.g.*, Catherine Seville, *EU Intellectual Property Law and Policy* 288–289 (2009); Karl-Heinz Fezer, *Markenrecht*, Einl C MarkenG para. 8 (4th edn., 2009); Horst-Peter Götting, *Gewerblicher Rechtsschutz—Patent-, Gebrauchsmuster-, Design- und Markenrecht* § 5 para. 30 *et seq.* (10th edn., 2014); Cohen Jehoram & van Nispen & Huydecoper, *European Trademark Law—Community Trademark Law and Harmonized National Trademark Law* 6–7, 241, and 533 (2010).

[149] *See, e.g.*, Cohen Jehoram & van Nispen & Huydecoper, *European Trademark Law—Community Trademark Law and Harmonized National Trademark Law* 241 (2010) ("The trademark right is an exclusive right and an absolute, subjective right.").

[150] *See* Friedrich-Karl Beier, *Warenzeichenrecht—Rückkehr zum Eintragungsprinzip? Überlegungen zur Reform des Markenrechts*, 1973 GRUR Int. 407, 408–409 (arguing

registration was a domain qualitatively different and separate from the use of a trademark on the market. Not only were the two areas distinguished according to their temporally different relevance for rights acquisition; in addition, registration rights remained an *aliud* to use-based positions.[151] And even though it was confusion prevention that was paramount to Ulmer's theory, the ultimate distinction came to be explained by a different aspect of consumer concerns. In this regard, the final decades of the twentieth century witnessed a further step toward separation, notably also in European trademark and unfair competition doctrine.

While both trademark and unfair competition law initially focused on protecting individual entitlements, the two sectors moved in different directions. Trademark law continues to protect individual rights; unfair competition law has evolved toward a so-called social or institutional model of protecting consumer interests and the public's interest in unhindered competition. The individualization of trademark protection is reflected, for instance, in the Misleading and Comparative Advertising Directive, which speaks of "exclusive rights o[f] the proprietor of a registered trade mark."[152] The concept of an institutional model of unfair competition prevention is most prominently expressed in the Unfair Commercial Practices Directive's article 1, which explains that the directive's purpose is "to contribute to the proper functioning of the internal market and [to] achieve a high level of consumer protection."[153] It was this concurrent evolution—propertization in trademark law and socialization in unfair competition law—that let the two areas drift even farther apart.

that Ulmer's analysis contributed to the equivalence of registered and nonregistered rights).

151 This distinction is still alive in modern commentary. *See, e.g.*, Horst-Peter Götting, *Gewerblicher Rechtsschutz—Patent-, Gebrauchsmuster-, Design- und Markenrecht* § 5 para. 31 (10th edn., 2014) ("Das Markenrecht entsteht entweder durch Eintragung . . . oder durch Benutzung im geschäftlichen Verkehr und Erwerb der Verkehrsgeltung . . .. Es kann sich bei der Marke also um ein formelles oder ein materielles Recht handeln.").

152 *See* recital 13 Directive 2006/114/EC of the European Parliament and of the Council of 12 December 2006 Concerning Misleading and Comparative Advertising (codified version), O.J. EU (8 November2008), L 299/25.

153 Directive 2005/29/EC of the European Parliament and of the Council of 11 May 2005 concerning unfair business-to-consumer commercial practices in the internal market and amending Council Directive 84/450/EEC, Directives 97/7/EC, 98/27/EC and 2002/65/EC of the European Parliament and of the Council and Regulation (EC) No 2006/2004 of the European Parliament and of the Council ("Unfair Commercial Practices Directive"), O.J. EU (11 June 2005), L 149/22. *See also, e.g.*, Pedro A. De Miguel Asensio, *The Private International Law of Intellectual Property and of Unfair Commercial Practices: Convergence or Divergence?*, 137, 153, in *Intellectual Property and Private International Law* (Stefan Leible & Ansgar Ohly eds., 2009); for European and German doctrines, *see also* Franz Hacker, in *Kommentar zum Markengesetz* § 2 para. 6 (Paul Ströbele & Franz Hacker eds., 11th edn., 2015).

Of course, both sectors are still connected. Trademark law has left space for additional protection by unfair competition law—in principle, unfair competition law provides protection wherever trademark law has left gaps.[154] Similarly, modern trademark doctrine has been supplemented by protection against conduct formerly categorized as unfair competition; anti-dilution protection is one example. However, close interrelations at the fringes do not overcome the fundamental dichotomy. Trademark law is a domain of private rights and investment protection. Unfair competition law seeks to regulate the market and competitors' conduct. Right owners' interests dominate on one side, while public policy concerns govern on the other.[155] In the words of one modern leading scholar in the field:

> The sector of unfair competition rules is concerned if the issue is protection of the functioning of the market with respect to marketplace effects. Yet, if the focus is on the protection of legal rights, the issue is under the umbrella of intellectual property.[156]

In essence, the perspective has not changed much from what Alfred Hagens wrote almost a century ago:

> While the law of preventing unfair competition, in a narrow sense, regulates—as a kind of civil police law—the order of competition on the basis of the public's economic and moral interest, the law of trademark protection pursues its purpose by granting individual rights to the business owners.[157]

[154] *See, e.g.*, Joachim Starck, *Die Auswirkungen des Markengesetzes auf das Gesetz gegen unlauteren Wettbewerb*, 1996 DZWir 313; Paul Katzenberger, *Kollisionsrecht des unlauteren Wettbewerbs*, 218, 220–221, in *Neuordnung des Wettbewerbsrechts, 11. Ringberg-Symposium des Max-Planck-Instituts für ausländisches und internationales Patent-, Urheber- und Wettbewerbsrecht* (Gerhard Schricker & Frauke Henning-Bodewig eds., 1998); for an overview, *see, e.g.*, Franz Hacker, in *Kommentar zum Markengesetz* § 2 para. 40 *et seq.* (Paul Ströbele & Franz Hacker eds., 11th edn., 2015).

[155] *See, e.g.*, Frauke Henning-Bodewig, *Marke und Verbraucher*, 176, 176–177 and 184–185, in *Die Neuordnung des Markenrechts in Europa—10. Ringberg-Symposium des Max-Planck-Instituts für ausländisches und internationales Patent-, Urheber- und Wettbewerbsrecht* (Gerhard Schricker & Friedrich-Karl Beier eds., 1996); Paul Katzenberger, *Kollisionsrecht des unlauteren Wettbewerbs*, 218, 220–221, in *Neuordnung des Wettbewerbsrechts, 11. Ringberg-Symposium des Max-Planck-Instituts für ausländisches und internationales Patent-, Urheber- und Wettbewerbsrecht* (Gerhard Schricker & Frauke Henning-Bodewig eds., 1998); Louis Pahlow, *Das Recht an der Marke als Benutzungsrecht des Markeninhabers*, 2006 WRP 97, 101; Franz Hacker, in *Kommentar zum Markengesetz* § 2 para. 24 (Paul Ströbele & Franz Hacker eds., 11th edn., 2015).

[156] Josef Drexl, in *Münchener Kommentar zum Bürgerlichen Gesetzbuch, vol. XI*, IntImmGR para. 163 (Franz Jürgen Säcker et al. eds., 6th edn., 2015) ("Geht es um den Schutz der Funktionsfähigkeit des Marktes unter Berücksichtigung der Marktauswirkungen, befindet man sich im Bereich der lauterkeitsrechtlichen Regelung. Steht dagegen der Rechtsgüterschutz im Mittelpunkt, handelt es sich um immaterialgüterrechtlichen Schutz." (author's translation)).

[157] Alfred Hagens, *Warenzeichenrecht* 31 (1927) ("Während aber das Wettbewerbsrecht im engeren Sinne als eine Art Zivilpolizeirecht die Ordnung des geschäftlichen Wettbewerbs auf Grund des volkswirtschaftlichen und sittlichen Interesses der

Section 2 Trademark and Unfair Competition Choice of Law

In Germany, international trademark and unfair competition disputes are governed by the system of trademark and unfair competition conflicts law, or choice of law. This field has traditionally been characterized as a subcategory of international tort law, which is part of the larger field of private international law.[158] While critics have called for this area to be characterized as a field of international economic law,[159] its traditional classification has prevailed (at least formally) at the European level. The Rome II Regulation encases intellectual property and unfair competition law (along with antitrust law) within the larger context of "non-contractual obligations."[160] In this regard, its historical foundation in tort conflicts appears to persist. While I will address doctrinal intricacies of such a retrograde perspective in more detail in chapter 3, a closer look at German and European choice-of-law doctrine under a historical-comparative perspective helps reveal and explain the most fundamental issues that currently stand in the way of a consistent reconceptualization of the field.

I From Universality to Territoriality

A The Worldwide Scope of Personality Rights

As described above, Kohler was the most noticeable voice in German scholarship to formulate a theory of trademark personality rights.[161] From the concept of personality rights ensued the idea of universal protection in international conflicts:

> The trademark right is not a locally restricted entitlement; it cannot be locally segmented in the sense that a locally confined acquisition would be possible like it is with tangible property situated in different countries or with rights in immaterial goods that manifest themselves economically in locally different acts.

Gesamtheit regelt, verfolgt das [Warenzeichen]-Recht seinen Zweck durch Ausbildung von Individualrechten einzelner Geschäftsinhaber." (author's translation)). For an instructive critique, *see* Manfred Balz, *Paradigmenwechsel im Warenzeichenrecht?—Zu einigen Grundsatzproblemen der Europamarke*, 45 RabelsZ 317, 319, 326 *et seq.* (1981).

158 *See, e.g.*, RGZ vol. 140, 25, 29—*Hohner Mundharmonika* (17 February 1933); BGH 2002 GRUR 618, 619—*Meißner Dekor* (18 October 2001); among scholarly commentary, *see* Eugen Ulmer, *Commentary to Reichsgericht, decision of 14 April 1931 (421/30 II)—Supra*, 1931 JW 1906, 1907; more recently, *e.g.*, Helmut Köhler, in Helmut Köhler & Joachim Bornkamm, *Gesetz gegen den unlauteren Wettbewerb*, Einl UWG para. 5.4 (33rd edn., 2015).

159 *See, e.g.*, Karl-Heinz Fezer, *Markenrecht*, Einl H para. 1 (4th edn., 2009).

160 *See* Regulation (EC) No. 864/2007 of the European Parliament and of the Council of 11 July 2007 on the law applicable to non-contractual obligations (Rome II), O.J. EU (31 July 2007), L 199/40.

161 *See supra* p. 21 *et seq.*

> The trademark right is different: the trademark right, as the personality's right to validity and manifestation is, like all personality rights, not bound to any local restriction. ... From this principle, it follows automatically that the trademark right ... with respect to its foundation and formation is to be governed by only one legal regime—the law of its home country. Protection in foreign countries, hence, is just a locally extended home-country right protection; the right in a foreign country is an extension of the domestic right only.[162]

Early on, German courts adopted Kohler's concept of virtually unlimited rights. The application of domestic law in international trademark and unfair competition conflicts was an issue of protecting the right owner's comprehensive and globally valid right of personality.[163] In favor of domestic parties, the scope of protection for their trademark rights and for national competitors' interests was territorially unlimited.

The seminal Reichsgericht case in this regard, *Hoff*, was decided in 1886. The case centered on the legality of the defendant's exportation of beer in barrels from Germany to the United States and her subsequent bottling and branding of the beer with the plaintiff's German trademark, "Hoff," in the United States. In principle, the court's argument was based on the concept of the 1874 Trademark Act's exclusivity:

[162] Josef Kohler, *Das Recht des Markenschutzes mit Berücksichtigung ausländischer Gesetzgebungen und mit besonderer Rücksicht auf die englische, anglo-amerikanische, französische, belgische und italienische Jurisprudenz* 412–413 (1884) ("Das Markenrecht hat kein lokal beschränktes, lokal abtheilbares Rechtsgut, so dass ein localer beschränkter Erwerb in dem Sinne möglich wäre, wie bei dem Eigenthumsgute, das in verschiedenen Staaten liegt, oder wie bei den Immaterialgüterrechten, welche sich wirthschaftlich in local getrennten Akten manifestiren—ganz anders das Markenrecht: das Markenrecht als das Recht der Persönlichkeit auf ihre Geltung und Manifestirung ist, wie alle Persönlichkeitsrechte, an keine localen Schranken gebunden .... Aus diesem Princip folgt von selbst der Satz, dass das Markenrecht ... bezüglich seiner Begründung und Entstehung nur nach einem Rechte, nach dem Rechte des Heimathlandes, zu beurtheilen ist, so dass der Schutz in fremden Ländern nur eben ein local erweiterter Schutz des im Heimathlande entstandenen Rechts, das Recht im fremden Lande nur eine Erstreckung des heimischen Rechtes ist." (author's translation)).

[163] *See, e.g.*, RGZ vol. 18, 28, 32—*Hoff* (2 October 1886); RGZ vol. 51, 263, 267—*Mariani* (2 May 1902) ("Das Zeichenrecht dagegen ist kein örtlich beschränktes, örtlich abteilbares Rechtsgut; es ist an sich an keine örtlichen Schranken gebunden. ... Deshalb ist das in verschiedenen Staaten anerkannte Zeichenrecht für ein und dasselbe Zeichen einer und derselben Person, die nur in einem der Staaten eine Niederlassung hat, nicht für den einzelnen Staat ein schlechthin selbständiges und unabhängiges Zeichenrecht; es enthält vielmehr nur die rechtliche Erstreckung des Zeichenrechtes des Niederlassungsstaates auch auf andere Staaten. Daraus ergiebt sich einmal der Rechtsgrundsatz der Einheit und Einheitlichkeit des in verschiedenen Staaten anerkannten subjektiven Zeichenrechtes ...."); RGZ vol. 88, 183, 184—*Sackpflüge* (31 March 1916); for commentary, *see also* Paul Kent, *Das Reichsgesetz zum Schutz der Waarenbezeichnungen vom 12. Mai 1894—Unter Berücksichtigung in- und ausländischer Literatur und Rechtsprechung sowie der Praxis des Patentamts* 245 (1897).

> The Trademark Act intends to exhaustively regulate protection [for registered trademarks]. As far as protection for trademarks does not ensue from the act itself, there is no protection with respect to the German Reich's territory. And as far as the act restricts protection to domestic infringements, the respective rights or entitlements are without protection against infringements undertaken abroad. Application of a foreign law in order to attain inland protection for the rights covered by the act is excluded by the existence and the tendencies of the [Trademark Act].[164]

Yet, since no protection would ensue without the application of federal statutory law, the court extended the argument. In this regard, personality right protection became a convenient instrument to cater for domestic right owners' concerns—what a difference to the formalistic minimalism in *Apollinarisbrunnen*:[165]

> But we fail to see why the [Trademark Act]—if the right at issue, due to its nature, is geographically unlimited and if it can also suffer injury abroad—should not have extended protection for domestic rights so far as the country's actual powers can reach, notably with respect to court jurisdiction and access to assets within its territory.[166]

In the decision's wake, late nineteenth-century Reichsgericht practice applied domestic trademark law to virtually all allegedly infringing activities, regardless of whether a defendant's conduct had occurred in Germany or abroad. All owners of German trademarks could therefore sue for any alleged infringement abroad—as long as only personal jurisdiction existed.[167]

164 RGZ vol. 18, 28, 30—*Hoff* (2 October 1886) ("Den [dem eingetragenen Warenzeichen] zu gewährenden Schutz will das Reichsgesetz erschöpfend regeln. Soweit der Schutz nicht in dem Gesetze selbst zu finden ist, giebt es keinen im Gebiete des Deutschen Reiches für diese Güter geltend zu machenden Schutz. Beschränkt das Gesetz seinen Schutz auf im Inlande vorgenommene Verletzungen, so sind die betreffenden Güter gegen im Auslande vorgenommene hier überhaupt schutzlos. Die Anwendung eines ausländischen Schutzgesetzes zur Erreichung eines Schutzes im Inlande für die im Gesetze behandelten Rechtsgüter ist durch die Existenz und die Tendenz des Reichsgesetzes ausgeschlossen." (author's translation)).

165 *See supra* p. 27 *et seq.*

166 RGZ vol. 18, 28, 33—*Hoff* (2 October 1886) ("Allein es ist gar nicht einzusehen, weshalb das Gesetz, wenn die Berechtigung ihrer Natur nach räumlich unbeschränkt ist und das anerkannte Rechtsgut auch im Auslande Schaden leiden kann, nicht in seinem Schutze so weit hätte gehen sollen, als die Machtmittel des Staates vermöge der Zuständigkeit seiner Gerichte und der Fähigkeit des Zugriffes auf das in seinem Bereiche befindliche Vermögen reichen ...." (author's translation)).

167 *See, e.g.*, RGZ vol. 18, 28, 32—*Hoff* (2 October 1886); RGZ vol. 51, 263, 267—*Mariani* (2 May 1902); RGZ vol. 108, 8, 9—*Saccharin* (19 June 1923); Paul Kent, *Das Reichsgesetz zum Schutz der Waarenbezeichnungen vom 12. Mai 1894—Unter Berücksichtigung in- und ausländischer Literatur und Rechtsprechung sowie der Praxis des Patentamts* 245 (1897); Arnold Seligsohn, *Gesetz zum Schutz der Warenbezeichnungen* 151 (2nd edn., 1905).

Some years later, in the Reichsgericht's *Gratisschnittmuster* decision, this concept of borderless personality rights was extended to cases of international unfair competition infringements.[168] Like trademark infringement, acts of unfair competition were deemed violations of personality rights.[169] Over time, the idea of universal protection governed both trademark and unfair competition law in theory and practice. Adolf Lobe's 1907 explanation of unfair competition law illustrates the principle:

> It further is irrelevant for the question of civil law liability whether the conduct at issue, causing a violation of the victim's right to commercial activity, has occurred on domestic territory or abroad. Protection for certain immaterial goods is not geographically limited; even less can it be limited with respect to protection of the personality and of personality rights. Commercial activity reaches beyond the home country and, from there, can take effect in all parts of the world. It, then, is always the personality protected in Germany that is infringed upon by restrictions to its freedom of activity—no matter whether this happens in Germany or abroad.[170]

Contrasting trademarks to patents, Lobe went on to explain:

> With respect to the protection of those commercial instruments that also constitute an immaterial good, and where the instrument's use is, due to its nature, not limited to the domestic territory, like personal name, trade name, trademark, trade dress, the same principle applies. But this is not the case for the patent right, because it is a state-granted privilege that is valid within the granting country's borders only.[171]

168 RG 1901 JW 851, 852—*Gratisschnittmuster* (22 October 1901). The court's (brief) reasoning in *Gratisschnittmuster* did not explicitly refer to a personality right in terms of unfair competition prevention. The case concerned an allegedly improper offer in a fashion magazine, which was published in Germany and sold in both Germany and Austria. The court referred only to the *Hoff* decision (concerning trademark universality) to justify upholding the lower instance's decision enjoining the defendant from selling the magazine in Germany *and* Austria.

169 *See, e.g.*, Adolf Lobe, *Die Bekämpfung des unlauteren Wettbewerbs, vol. I: Der unlautere Wettbewerb als Rechtsverletzung* 398–399 (1907); Josef Kohler, *Der unlautere Wettbewerb—Darstellung des Wettbewerbsrechts* 22 *et seq.* (1914).

170 Adolf Lobe, *Die Bekämpfung des unlauteren Wettbewerbs, vol. I: Der unlautere Wettbewerb als Rechtsverletzung* 398–399 (1907) ("Es ist weiter aber auch gleichgültig für die zivilrechtliche Haftung, ob die Handlung, die die Verletzung des gewerblichen Betätigungsrechts bewirkt, im Inlande oder im Auslande erfolgt ist. Wie schon der Schutz für manche immaterielle [*sic*] Güter nicht räumlich beschränkt ist, so erst recht nicht der Schutz für die Persönlichkeit und die Persönlichkeitsrechte. Vollends die gewerbliche Tätigkeit greift über den Heimatstaat hinaus und kann vom Heimatort aus in alle Weltteile wirken. Stets ist es dann die in Deutschland unter Schutz stehende Persönlichkeit, die verletzt wird, wenn ihre Betätigungsfreiheit beschränkt wird, gleichgültig, ob dies in Deutschland oder im Ausland geschieht." (author's translation)).

171 Adolf Lobe, *Die Bekämpfung des unlauteren Wettbewerbs, vol. I: Der unlautere Wettbewerb als Rechtsverletzung* 399–400 (1907) ("Für den Schutz derjenigen Erwerbsmittel, die ebenfalls ein immaterielles Rechtsgut bilden, dessen Gebrauch und Verwendung seiner

Other jurisdictions followed a similar directive. For example, Swiss courts and scholars also considered their domestic trademark rights to be universally valid and protectable on the basis of trademarks being personality rights.[172]

B Alfred Hagens and the Territoriality of Trademarks

Even though Kohler himself, in the second edition (1910) of his trademark treatise, attempted to backpedal from his initial position on trademark universality, his original concept remained the governing approach during the first decades of the twentieth century.[173] Prima facie, Kohler's revised explanation did not have a significant impact on legal practice. Yet his corrected model of trademark territoriality, which highlights the aspect of "upgrading" and the corresponding materialization of personal entitlements through state grants, would prove determinative. As Kohler explained:

Natur nach nicht auf das Inland beschränkt bleibt, wie Name, Firma, Warenzeichen, Ausstattung gilt das gleiche. Das ist jedoch beim Patent nicht der Fall, weil dieses nur ein innerhalb der Grenzen des Staats, in dem es erteilt ist, verliehenes Privilegium ist." (author's translation)). *See also* Philipp Allfeld, *Gesetz zum Schutz der Warenbezeichnungen vom 12. Mai 1894* § 21 comment 4, at 110–111 (1894) ("Der civilrechtliche Schutz des [Warenzeichen-]Gesetzes ist auf die im Inlande begangenen Störungen des Rechts nicht beschränkt; denn auch wenn die Handlung im Auslande begangen wurde, richtet sich ihre Spitze gegen ein inländisches Rechtsgut; das inländische Recht muß aber die inländischen Rechtsgüter schützen, wo immer der Angriff dagegen erfolgt; hier ist nicht das Territorialprinzip, sondern das Schutz- oder Realprinzip am Platze.").

172 *See, e.g.*, BGE vol. 26 II 644, 650–651 (8 December 1900); BGE vol. 36 II 255, 257 (22 April 1910); BGE vol. 39 II 640, 650 (11 July 1913); BGE vol. 43 II 98, 102–103 (16 February 1917); BGE vol. 47 II 354, 356 (13 June 1921). For an extensive discussion, *see* Ed. v. Waldkirch, *Der Gebrauch der Marke nach schweizerischem Recht*, 50 ZfSchwR 127, 133 (1931) ("Als solches sei [das Markenrecht] seiner Natur nach nicht national, sondern universal. Nur der spezielle Markenschutz, dessen Vorbedingung die Erfüllung der Förmlichkeiten des Staates, in dem der Schutz nachgesucht wird, ist, sei national oder territorial. Es müsste daher eine territoriale Einschränkung des Individualrechtes besonders ausgesprochen sein, was nach schweizerischem Recht nicht der Fall ist."); *but see also* Karl Martin Sandreuter, *Rechtliche Natur, Entstehung und Endigung des Markenrechts* 23 *et seq.*, 55 *et seq.* (1932). Indeed, it was not until 1945 that the Swiss Bundesgericht changed horses and founded protection on a theory of trademarks as immaterial property. *See* BGE vol. 71 I 344, 346 (15 October 1945); *see also* Alois Troller, *Immaterialgüterrecht, vol. 1* 134 *et seq.* (3rd edn., 1983); Alois Troller, *Die territoriale Unabhängigkeit der Markenrechte im Warenverkehr*, 1960 GRUR Ausl. 244, 245–246; Hans Trüeb, *Markenschutz beim Import von Konzernware—Bemerkungen zur Rechtsprechung des Schweizerischen Bundesgerichts*, 1962 GRUR Ausl. 10, 10; Jürgen Hoth, *Territoriale Grenzen des Schutzbereichs von Warenbezeichnungen*, 1968 GRUR 64, 64–65.

173 *See, e.g.*, Werner Pinzger & Felix Heinemann, *Das deutsche Warenzeichenrecht—Kommentar des Reichsgesetzes zum Schutz der Warenbezeichnungen nebst den internationalen Verträgen* § 12 note 19, at 217–218 (1926); for a summary of the existing positions, *see, e.g.*, Alfred Hagens, *Warenzeichenrecht* 188–189 (1927); Friedrich Jüngel & Julius Magnus, *Das deutsche Warenzeichenrecht* 464–465 (6th edn., 1933).

> The personality right, in principle, extends across the whole world: for the personality can exert its power over all mankind. ... Since, however, full trademark protection will not be granted on the basis of the owner's personality alone, but usually also requires owner activity and a contribution by public authorities, an indirect localization exists. The same personality that is protected worldwide with respect to unfair competition enjoys trademark protection in one state where a trademark is registered, but not in another where no such registration exists.[174]

Other scholars, too, attempted to put forward restrictions on personality rights protection. Their suggestions were founded on the idea that trademarks, as immaterial rights or goods, could and should be detached from their owner's personality.[175] But adherence to universality did not disappear immediately.

The ultimate change in direction occurred with the Reichsgericht's 1927 *Hengstenberg* decision.[176] In this case, the issue at hand was whether a foreign right owner's foreign-based conduct could affect a domestic plaintiff trademark owner's national rights. The parties used quite similar trademarks. The domestic plaintiff had German registrations; the Italian defendant's trademark was an international registration. The court rejected the contemporary theory of universality:[177]

> There is an opinion that German trademark rights are not territorially limited but rather protected beyond the Reich's borders. Hence, the right owner is thought to be able to pursue and enjoin infringements that have occurred abroad even if he

[174] Josef Kohler, *Warenzeichenrecht—Zugleich zweite Auflage des Rechts des Markenschutzes mit Berücksichtigung ausländischer Gesetzgebungen (1884)* 206–207 (2nd edn., 1910) ("[S]o erstreckt sich das Persönlichkeitsrecht prinzipiell über die ganze Erde: denn die Persönlichkeit kann über die ganze Menschheit ihre Macht entfalten. ... Da nun aber zum vollen Schutz der Marke nicht das Vorhandensein der Persönlichkeit genügt, sondern meist zu gleicher Zeit eine Betätigung der Person unter Mitwirkung der öffentlichen freiwilligen Gerichtsbarkeit erforderlich ist, so tritt dadurch eine mittelbare Verörtlichung ein. Dieselbe Persönlichkeit, welche bezüglich des unlauteren Wettbewerbs auf der ganzen Erde geschützt wird, geniesst in dem einen Staate, in welchem ihre Marke eingetragen ist, markenrechtlichen Schutz, während sie im andern ihn nicht geniesst." (author's translation)). *See also id.*, at 246–247 ("Ist es richtig, dass das Zeichenrecht zwar ein universelles Persönlichkeitsrecht darstellt, aber als Markensteigerung in den einzelnen Ländern verörtlicht ist und nur bezüglich dieser Gebiete gilt, so kann eine inländische Marke nur im Inland, eine ausländische nur im Auslande verletzt werden ...."); *see also* Carl Ludwig von Bar, *Theorie und Praxis des Internationalen Privatrechts, vol. II*, comment 357 and 358, at 273–274 (2nd edn., 1889).

[175] *See, e.g.*, Richard Alexander-Katz, *Die rechtliche Natur des Markenrechts sowie des Rechts an Waarenausstattungen*, 1901 GRUR 102, 104 and 105–106; Julius Magnus, *Warenzeichenrecht (Bericht)*, 1923 GRUR 162, 163; for an overview, *see also* Jürgen Hoth, *Territoriale Grenzen des Schutzbereichs von Warenbezeichnungen*, 1968 GRUR 64, 64.

[176] *See* RGZ vol. 118, 76, 81–82—*Springendes Pferd/Hengstenberg* (20 September 1927).

[177] For existing precedents, *see, e.g.*, RGZ vol. 18, 28—*Hoff* (2 October 1886); RGZ vol. 45, 143—*Schlüssel-Marke* (7 November 1899); RGZ vol. 51, 263, 267—*Mariani* (2 May 1902); RGZ vol. 108, 8, 9—*Saccharin* (19 June 1923).

has no protection there. The only precondition is that German courts have jurisdiction. This opinion, which has also found followers among scholarly commentators, cannot . . . be upheld.[178]

The court's decision to restrict the universality of protection was based on a perceived similarity between trademark and patent rights with regard to their national restrictedness, as well as the international trademark system's foundation on territorially limited rights.[179] Early on, international patent doctrine had laid out a strictly territorial limitation of rights. This restriction was due mainly to two factors. First, patent law was always perceived as firmly founded on state grants alone. Second, patent right enforcement was largely devoid of personality protection purposes.[180] Interestingly, the Second Civil Senate in *Hengstenberg* explicitly referred to a critique of Hagens, its former presiding justice,[181] who had been an opponent of trademark universality. In his rejection of unlimited rights protection, he provided the court's arguments concerning both the trademark's patent-like territoriality and the international system of trademark protection. Formally, Hagens described trademark rights as state-granted monopolies. Accordingly, it was unthinkable to extend them to foreign sovereigns' territories.[182]

In substance, his critique expressed that the time for the territoriality of trademark rights had come; universality was no longer necessary or legitimate. Trademark universality in *Hoff* had reflected a basic mistrust of foreign regimes' protection standards for domestic exporters. After all, the worldwide codification of trademark law had begun only at the end of

[178] *See* RGZ vol. 118, 76, 80–81—*Springendes Pferd/Hengstenberg* (20 September 1927) ("[Es w]ird der Standpunkt vertreten, daß das deutsche Warenzeichenrecht nicht territorial beschränkt, sondern über die Grenzen des Reichs hinaus geschützt sei, so daß der Zeicheninhaber auch dessen Verletzung im Ausland, ohne daß er dort einen Zeichenschutz besitze, verbieten und im Inland gerichtlich verfolgen könne, sofern nur ein inländischer Gerichtsstand gegeben sei. Diese Auffassung, die auch im Schrifttum Anhänger gefunden hat, . . . läßt sich . . . nicht aufrechterhalten." (author's translation)).

[179] *See id.* at 81–82.

[180] For the Reichsgericht's treatment of patent right territoriality, *see, e.g.*, RG 1890 JW 280, 281; RGZ vol. 30, 52, 55—*Congorot* (15 October 1892); *see also* Frank Peter Regelin, *Das Kollisionsrecht der Immaterialgüterrechte an der Schwelle zum 21. Jahrhundert* 52 (2000) (with further references).

[181] The Second Civil Senate of the Reichsgericht was competent to hear trademark cases. Hagens had left the Senate a few years before the *Hengstenberg* case was decided. In addition, the *Hengstenberg* reasons made reference to Seligsohn's commentary arguing against trademark universality. *See* RGZ vol. 118, 76, 81—*Springendes Pferd/Hengstenberg* (20 September 1927).

[182] For the Reichsgericht's reference to Hagens, *see* RGZ vol. 118, 76, 81—*Springendes Pferd/Hengstenberg* (20 September 1927). *See also* Alfred Hagens, *Warenzeichenrecht* 188–190 (1927); Friedrich Jüngel & Julius Magnus, *Das deutsche Warenzeichenrecht* 464–465 (6th edn., 1933).

the nineteenth century.[183] In the 1880s, the United States in particular was seen as a territory of trademark insecurity. After the Supreme Court had struck down the federal statute in 1879, concerns about the protection of foreigners were commonplace.[184] It is therefore not surprising that the *Hoff* court extended protection for German trademark owners into the United States. But an increase in national codifications around the world and the creation of an international system of intellectual property protection beginning in the 1880s provided the foundation for more trust in and acceptance of foreign regimes' trademark laws.[185] This was also reflected in the German Reich's accession to the Paris Convention (1903), the Madrid Agreement Concerning the International Registration of Marks (1922), and the Madrid Agreement for the Repression of False or Deceptive Indications of Source on Goods (1925).[186] Apparently, the era of intellectual property territoriality had arrived.

C Under the Surface: Fairness-Standard Universality

But Hagens's elaboration on trademark nationality also provides an additional—and quite different—insight into the interplay of trademark and

[183] Christian von Bar, *Territorialität des Warenzeichens und Erschöpfung des Verbreitungsrechts im Gemeinsamen Markt* 24–25 (1977); for a detailed overview, *see* Edwin Katz, *Weltmarkenrecht* 111 *et seq.* (1926).

[184] *See, e.g.*, Josef Kohler's insightful illustration and analysis of the *Trademark Cases* (1879) in Josef Kohler, *Das Recht des Markenschutzes mit Berücksichtigung ausländischer Gesetzgebungen und mit besonderer Rücksicht auf die englische, anglo-amerikanische, französische, belgische und italienische Jurisprudenz* 69 (1884) ("Diese Entscheidungen haben das ganze federale Markenwesen umgestossen, da nach der englischen Anschauung von der Bedeutung der Präjudizien solche Aussprüche des höchsten Gerichtshofes die Rechtssprechung und Rechtsübung unverweigerlich binden. Doch war der Schrecken eigentlich grösser im Auslande, als in den Vereinigten Staaten selbst; denn hier war es sichere und unbezweifelte Jurisprudenz, dass die Marke auch ohne Eintrag und ohne Bundesgesetz ihren Schutz geniessen müsse jure communi, so dass man das jus singulare füglich entbehren könne .... Im Auslande aber fürchtete man insbesondere für die Gültigkeit der internationalen Verträge und Regulirungen, und es wurde eifrig debattirt, welches nun die Stellung der Ausländer sei, die mit Rücksicht auf internationale Verträge in Amerika ihre Marken zum Eintrage gebracht hatten .... ").

[185] *See, e.g.*, Martin Seligsohn, *Die örtlichen Grenzen des Zeichenrechts*, 193, 198, in *Abhandlungen zum Arbeitsgebiet des Reichspatentamts—Festgabe zur Feier des 50jährigen Bestehens des Reichspatentamts* (Hermann Isay ed., 1927).

[186] *See* Christian von Bar, *Territorialität des Warenzeichens und Erschöpfung des Verbreitungsrechts im Gemeinsamen Markt* 25 (1977). Of course, this must not neglect that accession to international conventions occurred relatively late due to German industries' fears of too much protection for competitors from abroad. *See* Elmar Wadle, *Der Weg zum gesetzlichen Schutz des geistigen und gewerblichen Schaffens—Die deutsche Entwicklung im 19. Jahrhundert*, 93, 109, in *Gewerblicher Rechtsschutz und Urheberrecht in Deutschland, Festschrift zum hundertjährigen Bestehen der Deutschen Vereinigung für gewerblichen Rechtsschutz und Urheberrecht und ihrer Zeitschrift, vol. I* (Friedrich-Karl Beier et al. eds., 1991).

unfair competition protection in the international arena. In *Gratisschnittmuster*, as we have seen, the Reichsgericht had extended the paradigm of personality rights protection to unfair competition conflicts. A bit more than two decades later, of course, the curtain had fallen again on trademark universality with *Hengstenberg*. But domestic parties' interests could still be protected, even without the extraterritorial protection of national "rights." After all, the effectuation of domestic interests was possible by means of international unfair competition prevention.[187] A part of Hagens's illustration on industrial property protection reflects the other side of the coin with respect to the universality of personality rights—necessarily, universal protection had to be accompanied by an assumption of transnationally uniform fairness standards for competition. Trademark rights may have been subject to different nations' legal rules, but unfair competition seemed to be prevented under virtually identical standards everywhere:

> The [Reichsgericht] has expressly extended this principle . . . to the field of unfair competition. The violation committed abroad affects the competitor's commercial relations, having their center in the inland seat of his business, in the same way as if it had occurred domestically; it has been undertaken in competition and can injure the competitor's business or creditworthiness. . . . With respect to unfair competition, however, the situation is quite different from trademark infringement where violation of an absolute right is at issue, a right that exists only under the conditions of a single country's legislation. In unfair competition, what is at issue is conduct deemed improper under the general and uniform perspective of culture states.[188]

This last aspect may explain why choice of law in unfair competition did not also succumb to an argument of territoriality—at least not immediately. In fact, looking at the subject matter that was considered protectable, the difference to trademark "rights" may not have been overly

[187] *See also* Christian Joerges, *Die klassische Konzeption des internationalen Privatrechts und das Recht des unlauteren Wettbewerbs*, 36 RabelsZ 421, 446 (1972).

[188] Alfred Hagens, *Warenzeichenrecht* 189 (1927) ("Das [Reichsgericht] hat diesen Grundsatz . . . ausdrücklich auf das Gebiet des unlauteren Wettbewerbs erstreckt. Denn auch die im Auslande geschehene Zuwiderhandlung wirkt auf die geschäftlichen Beziehungen des Konkurrenten, die ihren Mittelpunkt in dessen geschäftlicher Niederlassung im Inlande haben, gerade so zurück, als wenn sie im Inlande selbst geschehen wäre, da sie zu Zwecken des Wettbewerbs ausgeübt und geeignet ist, dessen Geschäftsbetrieb oder Kredit zu schädigen . . . In der Tat liegt aber beim unlauteren Wettbewerb die Sache wesentlich anders wie beim [Warenzeichen], wo es sich um die Verletzung eines absoluten, nur nach den Bedingungen einer einzelstaatlichen Gesetzgebung bestehenden Rechts, nicht um eine nach allgemeiner Kulturanschauung als sittenwidrig geltenden und daher einzelstaatlich für unerlaubt erklärten Handlung handelt." (author's translation)).

significant. In essence, agreement existed that the distinction was to be made between "property" protected by trademark law and "possession" of a market position protected by unfair competition norms. As Ulmer explained in 1931:

> The trademark right founds on the monopoly granted to the owners by means of registration; it enjoys artificially created legal protection, where it is justified to limit the owner's entitlement to the Reich's territory, notably since other countries have established equivalent means of according protection for their territories. With respect to unfair competition prevention, where protection of self-acquired consumer recognition for a designation is at issue and where the legal order acknowledges the natural possession in a competitive position, this aspect does not matter.[189]

With respect to the protection of "self-acquired consumer recognition,"[190] a more territorial perspective would have suggested itself quite casually. After all, consumer recognition was an issue of geographical extension and, accordingly, quite apt to be territorially segmented.

[189] Eugen Ulmer, *Commentary to Reichsgericht, decision of 14 April 1931 (421/30 II)—Supra*, 1931 JW 1906, 1907 ("[D]as Warenzeichenrecht beruht auf dem den Berechtigten im Wege des Eintragungsverfahrens zugestandenen Monopol; es genießt künstlich geschaffenen Rechtsschutz, bei dem es sich rechtfertigen läßt, die Berechtigung auf das Reichsgebiet zu beschränken, zumal die anderen Staaten einen entsprechenden Weg zur Verleihung des Schutzes für ihr Gebiet zur Verfügung stellen. Bei dem Wettbewerbsrecht, bei dem es sich um den Schutz selbsterrungener Verkehrsbekanntheit einer Bezeichnung handelt und die Rechtsordnung den natürlich gewordenen wettbewerbsrechtlichen Besitzstand anerkennt, fällt der entsprechende Gesichtspunkt weg." (author's translation)).

[190] For earlier scholarship explaining the same conception, *see, e.g.*, Edwin Katz, *Gesetz zum Schutz der Waarenbezeichnungen und unlauterer Wettbewerb, Vortrag gehalten vor der Juristischen Gesellschaft von Berlin und im Berliner Anwaltsverein, Veröffentlichungen des Berliner Anwalt-Vereins, Heft 4*, 3, 14, and 17 (1894) (qualifying registration of a trademark as the creation of property ("wohlerworbenes Privatrecht") and unfair competition prevention as protecting a competitor's possessory status within the marketplace ("redlicher Besitz")). Literally (*id* at 17), he explained: "[S]oweit nun Zeichen dieser Art bis jetzt von bestimmten Gewerbetreibenden bereits in einem solchen Umfange gebraucht worden sind, daß dieselben innerhalb der betheiligten Verkehrskreise als Kennzeichen der Waaren eines bestimmten Geschäftsbetriebes gelten, soll der Gefahr vorgebeugt werden, daß ein Dritter die Erweiterung des neuen Gesetzes benutzend, das werthvoll gewordene Zeichen sich aneignet, eintragen läßt und den bisherigen Besitzer außer Besitz setzt. Tritt ein solcher Fall ein, so darf der bisherige Besitzer die Löschung des Zeichens gegen den Occupanten beantragen, und das Zeichen für sich eintragen lassen. Das Gesetz will hier den redlichen Besitz schützen." *See also* Philipp Allfeld, *Gesetz zum Schutz der Warenbezeichnungen vom 12. Mai 1894* § 9 comment 3, at 53–54 (1894) (comparing factual possession ("faktischer Besitz") with formal entitlement ("formelle Berechtigung") of nonregistered and registered rights); and, later, Hans Freiherr von Godin, *Wettbewerbsrecht, Kommentar zum Gesetz gegen den unlauteren Wettbewerb nebst Warenzeichenverletzungen, Zugabeverordnung und Rabattgesetz* U § 1 para. 37 (2nd edn., 1974) (with respect to nonregistered rights: "Ihr Kennzeichenschutz beruht auf dank intensiver Arbeit gewohnheitsrechtlich anzuerkennendem erworbenen Besitzstand.").

A territorial restriction of domestic unfair competition law may thus have been manifest. Yet, despite the fact that, over time, the paradigm of personality rights protection also became questionable in international unfair competition disputes, a connection between the parties' "market capital" or "customer base" and their respective political-national territories was not established. Such a more tangible localization of the subject matter could have provided (and, in the United States, actually did provide[191]) a convenient point of attachment. But it did not.

In this regard, Hagens's understanding displays the major defects of contemporary doctrine. He combined universal personality rights protection under unfair competition standards with the idea of a transnational consensus on fairness, at least among civilized nations and cultures. The concept subsequently reappeared. Courts and legal scholars often found the application of domestic fairness rules admissible on the grounds that other nations' legal regimes would have decided the same way.[192] Since these foreign jurisdictions were not in a "state of barbarism,"[193] the application of domestic standards, the argument went, violated neither public international law nor individual rights. Trademarks had become territorially confined. Fairness standards, however, underwent a subtle transformation toward universal validity and effectuation.

191 See *infra* p. 76 *et seq.*

192 *See, e.g.*, Jack J. Rappeport, *Trade-Mark and Unfair Competition in International Conflict of Laws: An Analysis of the Choice of Law Problem*, 20 U. Pitt. L. Rev. 1, 22 (1958) ("[I]n each of these cases, one gets the feeling that even though the harm is not a basis of liability in the countries where the parties are competing, yet it is inconceivable that there can be a strong policy promoting this kind of shabby conduct in those countries. The courts apparently did not know what the foreign law was, and also did not care, and it would seem proper for them not to care and to assume that there could not be a policy in those countries favoring fraud and basic dishonesty.").

193 For an earlier example from US case law, *see, e.g.*, *Vacuum Oil Co. v. Eagle Oil Co. of New York*, 154 F. 867, 875 (C.C. N.J. 1907) ("The presumption is that the law in the foreign countries where any part of the fraudulent business was carried on is the same as our own, and that fraudulent acts are unlawful there as here. . . . It is apparent that an act that violates the law of fair dealing and good conscience must be of universal recognition. To assume the contrary is to suppose the foreign countries in question to be in a state of barbarism, and that is to assume a state of affairs that justify this court in applying the law of the forum. . . . But while the action is founded upon fraud, it is also of a transitory character, and the fact that some of the fraudulent acts were committed outside the jurisdiction of this court and outside of the United States will not avail the defendants."). For a critique, *see, e.g.*, Robert Alpert, *The Export of Trademarked Goods from the United States: The Extraterritorial Reach of the Lanham Act*, 81 Trademark Rep. 125, 143 (1991).

II From International Torts to International Economic Law?

Against this backdrop, it comes as no surprise that the shift toward territoriality occurred later and more subtly for international unfair competition doctrine. Unfair competition choice of law has a troubled history of meandering[194] and, upon a closer look, stands in stark contrast to trademark conflicts law.

A From *Lex Loci Delicti Commissi* to Nussbaum's Rule

As in trademark doctrine, over time, universality in unfair competition conflicts law was modified and eventually replaced. Structurally, however, the jettisoning occurred differently. It was not territoriality (or nationalization) of the protectable subject matter that led to the alteration but a return to the *lex loci delicti commissi* rule.[195] In tort conflicts, the place where a competitive act was deemed to occur could be either the place of the alleged infringer's conduct or the place where the victim had suffered detrimental effects.[196] For international unfair competition, this provided a simple rule. Since victims would suffer loss and damage generally at their place of business, courts could virtually always find national law applicable if the plaintiff was German. As the Reichsgericht stated in 1903:

> The violation committed abroad affects the competitor's commercial relations, having their center in the inland main establishment of his business, in the same way as if it had occurred domestically; it has been undertaken in competition and can injure the competitor's business or creditworthiness.[197]

[194] For an insightful analysis of case law from late nineteenth until mid-twentieth century, *see* Christian Joerges, *Die klassische Konzeption des internationalen Privatrechts und das Recht des unlauteren Wettbewerbs*, 36 RabelsZ 421, 439 et seq. (1972).

[195] *See, e.g.*, RGZ vol. 140, 25, 29—*Hohner Mundharmonika* (17 February 1933); BGH 1955 GRUR 411, 413—*Zahl 55* (11 January 1955). For a contemporary account of case law and scholarly commentary, *see, e.g.*, Eugen Ulmer, *Commentary to Reichsgericht, decision of 14 April 1931 (421/30 II)—Supra*, 1931 JW 1906, 1907 ("Sehen wir uns in der modernen Literatur um, so finden wir im ganzen gegenüber der älteren Auffassung, die vom Persönlichkeitsrecht ausgehend zu der umfassenden Anwendung deutschen Wettbewerbsrechts für den deutschen Gewerbetreibenden auch bei ausländischen Konkurrenzhandlungen kommt . . ., eine Wendung zum Grundsatz der lex loci delicti commissi. Die unlauteren Wettbewerbshandlungen werden in den größeren Zusammenhang der unerlaubten Handlungen gestellt . . ..").

[196] *See, e.g.*, RGZ vol. 55, 199, 200 (16 June 1903).

[197] *Id.* ("[D]enn auch die im Auslande geschehene Zuwiderhandlung wirkt auf die geschäftlichen Beziehungen des Konkurrenten, die ihren Mittelpunkt in dessen geschäftlicher Hauptniederlassung im Inlande haben, gerade so zurück, als wenn sie im Inlande selbst geschehen wäre, da sie zu Zwecken des Wettbewerbes ausgeübt und geeignet ist, dessen Geschäftsbetrieb oder Kredit zu schädigen." (author's translation)); *see also* Arthur Nussbaum, *Deutsches internationales Privatrecht—Unter besonderer*

Over time, this place-of-business rule was complemented by an extended place-of-conduct approach. As the Reichsgericht explained in 1923, for instance, the defendant's dispatch of a letter with allegedly infringing content in Germany already sufficed to fulfill the requirement of territorial conduct.[198] Subsequent case law extended both the place-of-conduct and the direct-impact rule.[199] On this basis, with an extensive degree of discretion for the interpretation of what constituted relevant domestic conduct or impact, a judge could always generously determine infringing activities that were at least partly based on German territory.[200] Ultimately, therefore, nothing had changed. Under both personality rights protection and tort conflicts law, a virtually genuine effects principle (*Auswirkungsprinzip*) governed in international unfair competition disputes.[201] Still, the only precondition that had to be fulfilled by a German competitor in order to attain the application of national law was establishing personal jurisdiction over the defendant.[202]

In addition, a second instrument provided for the application of German law, even in cases where neither domestic injury nor conduct could be found. The so-called Nussbaum rule required the application of German law among German competitors.[203] The Reichsgericht's 1933 *Hohner Mundharmonika* opinion illustrates the rule in operation.

Berücksichtigung des österreichischen und schweizerischen Rechts 340 (1932) (with further explanation and citations to case law from the Reichsgericht and appellate courts).

198 *See also* RGZ vol. 108, 8, 9—*Saccharin* (19 June 1923).

199 *See, e.g.*, Christian Joerges, *Die klassische Konzeption des internationalen Privatrechts und das Recht des unlauteren Wettbewerbs*, 36 RabelsZ 421, 446 *et seq.* (1972) (with further references to post-1920s case law).

200 *See, e.g.*, RGZ vol. 150, 265, 269–271—*Stecknadeln* (14 February 1936); RG 1937 GRUR 466, 470—*Mulla 500* (12 March 1937). *See also* Rainer Hausmann & Inés Obergfell, in *Lauterkeitsrecht: Kommentar zum Gesetz gegen den unlauteren Wettbewerb (UWG), vol. I*, Einleitung I para. 184 (Karl-Heinz Fezer ed., 2nd edn., 2010); for a critique of this "path of least resistance," *see* Kamen Troller, *Das internationale Privatrecht des unlauteren Wettbewerbs in vergleichender Darstellung der Rechte Deutschlands, Englands, Frankreichs, Italiens, der Schweiz und der USA* 117 (1962).

201 *See also* Christian Joerges, *Die klassische Konzeption des internationalen Privatrechts und das Recht des unlauteren Wettbewerbs*, 36 RabelsZ 421, 457 *et seq.* (1972); Anton K. Schnyder, *Wirtschaftskollisionsrecht—Sonderanknüpfung und extraterritoriale Anwendung wirtschaftsrechtlicher Normen unter besonderer Berücksichtigung von Marktrecht* § 18 para. 503 (1990) (with references to Swiss and German case law); Rainer Hausmann & Inés Obergfell, in *Lauterkeitsrecht: Kommentar zum Gesetz gegen den unlauteren Wettbewerb (UWG), vol. I*, Einleitung I para. 183 (Karl-Heinz Fezer ed., 2nd edn., 2010).

202 *See* RGZ vol. 108, 8, 9—*Saccharin* (19 June 1923); Eugen Ulmer, *Commentary to Reichsgericht, decision of 14 April 1931 (421/30 II)—Supra*, 1931 JW 1906, 1906, 1908; Adolf Lobe, *Die Bekämpfung des unlauteren Wettbewerbs, vol. I: Der unlautere Wettbewerb als Rechtsverletzung* 398–399 (1907).

203 For Arthur Nussbaum's conflicts analysis of intellectual and industrial property, *see* Arthur Nussbaum, *Deutsches internationales Privatrecht—Unter besonderer Berücksichtigung des österreichischen und schweizerischen Rechts* 336–346 (1932).

The court, while generally refusing to find domestic injuries as a result of the foreign-based conduct at issue,[204] still applied German unfair competition law on the basis of the parties' common place of business. The plaintiff, a producer of harmonicas sold under the trademark "Hohner's Nr. 13," contested the defendant's production and exportation of harmonicas to India under the brand "Mouth Organ No. 2113." In particular, the plaintiff argued that the defendant's use of "13" was a violation of German trademark and unfair competition law.[205] The court denied an infringement of the plaintiff's German trademark. At that time, as we have seen, territoriality no longer allowed for the extension of domestic trademark rights. In addition, the court explained that a violation of German unfair competition principles might also lie in the defendant's conduct if at least some of the relevant activities had occurred on domestic territory.[206] Since the deception of customers had occurred in India, however, German law was inapplicable under the place-of-conduct rule:

> The possibility of an "inland impact of the unfair competition on the commercial relations" of the victim-competitor, hence, the possibility of domestic injury at the victim-competitor's business seat ensuing from the act exclusively committed abroad, is irrelevant for the issue at bar. Commission of a tort requires conduct and injury, not the indirect consequences of the tortious act that are not an element of the tort.[207]

Despite this restrictive approach, the court ultimately turned to a policy that became known as the Nussbaum rule.[208] In cases where two parties shared a common residence or place of business, this rule allowed for the application of domestic law to all competition among German actors, even if the places of conduct and injury were located abroad. Conceiving this rule, Arthur Nussbaum had started from an assumption that trademark rights were immaterial property and that unfair competition prevention was a tort.[209] Yet he disagreed with contemporary case law that

[204] RGZ vol. 140, 25, 29—*Hohner Mundharmonika* (17 February 1933). [205] *Id.* at 26.
[206] *Id.* at 29.
[207] *Id.* at 29—rejecting the holding in RGZ vol. 55, 199 ("Die Möglichkeit einer 'Zurückwirkung des Wettbewerbsverstoßes auf die geschäftlichen Beziehungen' des Verletzten, also die Möglichkeit des Eintritts eines Schadens infolge der allein im Ausland begangenen Handlung im Inland, wo das Geschäftsunternehmen des Verletzten seinen Sitz hat, ist rechtlich für die hier zu entscheidende Frage des anzuwendenden Rechts ohne Bedeutung. Zum Begehen gehören Handlung und Verletzung, nicht die Schadensfolge, die kein Tatbestandsmerkmal ist." (author's translation)).
[208] *See* RGZ vol. 140, 25, 29—*Hohner Mundharmonika* (17 February 1933); for the rule, *see* Arthur Nussbaum, *Deutsches internationales Privatrecht—Unter besonderer Berücksichtigung des österreichischen und schweizerischen Rechts* 339–340 (1932).
[209] *Id.* at 339.

unfair competition should always affect the victim at her place of business and that, accordingly, domestic law had to govern all incidents of unfair competition among nationals in foreign markets.[210] Instead, he posited a much narrower concept of "competitive damage": the place where the damage occurred in cases of unfair competition (if analyzed under tort principles) would not be the victim's place of business but the *consumer's* residence or place of transacting.[211] In this regard, Nussbaum was far more insightful than contemporary doctrine since he actually duly qualified the subject matter of protection in unfair competition cases. But this did not alter courts' practice. To the contrary and quite paradoxically, his elaboration ultimately became the basis for a new extension of the national unfair competition rules. As he explained:

> The current practice should be justifiable on the ground that all commercial actors that have their seat inside this country have to accommodate their competitive activities with respect to each other, even if undertaken abroad, to the domestic rules against unfair competition. Thereby, acts committed abroad will be covered by domestic law. This somewhat appears as a condition attached to the operation of an inland business establishment.[212]

The application of German standards of fairness and honesty was deemed a necessary and inevitable condition for domestic businesses.[213] By this means, since it was usually German parties litigating in German fora, the

[210] *See, e.g.*, RGZ vol. 55, 199 (16 June 1903); RG 1931 JW 1906 *et seq.—Supra* (14 April 1931); for Nussbaum's critique, *see* Arthur Nussbaum, *Deutsches internationales Privatrecht—Unter besonderer Berücksichtigung des österreichischen und schweizerischen Rechts* 340 (1932).

[211] Arthur Nussbaum, *Deutsches internationales Privatrecht—Unter besonderer Berücksichtigung des österreichischen und schweizerischen Rechts* 340 (1932).

[212] *Id.* at 340. ("[D]ürfte sich die bisherige Praxis aus der Erwägung rechtfertigen lassen, daß alle im Inlande niedergelassenen Gewerbetreibenden untereinander ihren gesamten Wettbewerb auch für das Ausland nach den inländischen Vorschriften gegen den unlauteren Wettbewerb einrichten müssen, so daß in diesem Rahmen die im Auslande begangenen Handlungen von dem inländischen Gesetz erfaßt werden. Letzteres erscheint gewissermaßen als eine Auflage, welche an die Ausübung des inländischen Gewerbebetriebes geknüpft wird; ...." (author's translation)). *See also* Eugen Ulmer, *Commentary to Reichsgericht, decision of 14 April 1931 (421/30 II)—Supra*, 1931 JW 1906, 1908.

[213] For a similar interpretation of the US Fifth Circuit's 1983 *American Rice* case, *see, e.g.*, Sarah Thomas-Gonzalez, *Extraterritorial Jurisdiction of the Lanham Act: American Rice, Inc. v. Arkansas Ricegrowers Cooperative Ass'n*, 11 Brook. J. Int'l L. 411, 435 (1985) ("The Fifth Circuit's decision that infringing goods sold abroad need not return to this country before jurisdiction may be granted will keep United States businesses aware of their obligation to avoid unfair trade practices, even when operating abroad."). For subject-matter jurisdiction under the US Supreme Court's *Steele* progeny, in particular the *American Rice* doctrine, *see infra* p. 159 *et seq.*

former universality of personality rights was actually succeeded by an inter-litigant extraterritoriality of domestic fairness standards. German law governed competition among Germans everywhere. And even though this may have seemed a reasonable rule to guarantee honesty in trade at first sight, it was soon criticized for its detrimental effects. The extensive application of German fairness standards to foreign competition was quickly exposed as an unfair burden to German competitors in foreign markets.[214] Nonetheless, the Nussbaum rule—albeit ultimately jettisoned in German and European doctrines—is still alive in other jurisdictions' modern scholarship and practice.[215]

B A Silver Lining: The *Kindersaugflaschen* Doctrine

Notwithstanding the critique, the Bundesgerichtshof initially also adhered to the Nussbaum rule, as well as the other detours that had been established, in order to provide for the application of domestic law in international unfair competition cases. On the basis of tort conflicts doctrine, the *lex loci delicti commissi* was determined by reference to the place of conduct, which, in turn (as the Reichsgericht had done before), was determined with remarkable leeway. Almost any contribution to foreign-based infringing conduct was sufficient to trigger the application of German law.[216] For example, the Bundesgerichtshof's 1956 *Uhrenrohwerke* decision found the domestic production of replica watch

[214] *See, e.g.*, Walter Köhler, *Verwechselungsgefahr im Ausland*, 1933 MuW 332, 334; Eduard Reimer, *Wettbewerbs- und Warenzeichenrecht, vol. II: Kommentar zum Gesetz gegen den unlauteren Wettbewerb, zum Zugabe- und Rabattrecht und zu den einschlägigen Bestimmungen des Gesetzes über Wirtschaftswerbung*, ch. 123, at 610 (1935); Leo Raape, *Internationales Privatrecht* 367 (3rd edn., 1950); Wilhelm Wengler, *Die Gesetze über unlauteren Wettbewerb und das internationale Privatrecht*, 19 RabelsZ 401, 413–414 (1954); Wilhelm Wengler, *Laws Concerning Unfair Competition and the Conflict of Laws*, 4 Am. J. Comp. L. 167, 177–178 (1955); Kamen Troller, *Das internationale Privatrecht des unlauteren Wettbewerbs in vergleichender Darstellung der Rechte Deutschlands, Englands, Frankreichs, Italiens, der Schweiz und der USA* 71 and 121 (1962); Jürgen F. Baur, *Zum Namensschutz im deutschen internationalen Privatrecht unter besonderer Berücksichtigung des Schutzes der Handelsnamen*, 167 AcP 535, 543 (1967); Gerhard Schricker, *Die Durchsetzbarkeit deutscher Werberegelungen bei grenzüberschreitender Rundfunkwerbung*, 1982 GRUR Int. 720, 722 ("[Deutsche Gewerbetreibende] schleppten das strenge UWG als Handicap im Wettbewerb mit sich."). For an example of support for the rule (for obvious contemporary political reasons), *see, e.g.*, Danielcik, *Ist unlauterer Wettbewerb im Ausland vor deutschen Gerichten und nach deutschem Recht verfolgbar?*, 1936 JW 2613, 2614 (application of German law would always be required "wenn es sich um volkswirtschaftlich bedeutsame Verstöße handelt. Dies folgt aus der volksgenössischen Treuepflicht, die überhaupt die Grundlage jenes vom RG. aufgestellten Rechtssatzes bildet.").

[215] *See infra* p. 159 *et seq.* and p. 171 *et seq.*, as well as *infra* p. 481–483.

[216] *See, e.g.*, BGH 1955 GRUR 150, 151—*Farina* (13 July 1954); BGHZ vol. 21, 266, 270—*Uhrenrohwerke* (13 July 1956); BGHZ vol. 22, 1, 18—*Flava/Erdgold* (2 October 1956); BGH 1955 GRUR 411, 413—*Zahl 55* (11 January 1955); BGH 1957 GRUR 231, 235—

parts, even though produced solely for export, to suffice.[217] And even though occasional attempts to limit the scope of German law were undertaken, the established doctrine of virtual universality remained largely unchanged. One example is the Bundesgerichtshof's 1957 *Zeiß* decision, where the court explained that allegedly unfair competitive activities occurring abroad should not be governed by the stricter standards of domestic law if the conduct at issue was considered legitimate under the foreign state's regime.[218] But this only changed the concrete outcome in *Zeiß*. In essence, the conflicts technique remained unaltered: the places of conduct and impact were still broadly defined, thereby principally preserving the reign of German law.[219]

The first and most dramatic shift away from the predominance of domestic law occurred in 1961 with the *Kindersaugflaschen* case. The competing parties were concurrently marketing similar baby bottles on different continents and in several countries around the world. Competition in Germany did not exist, though: the plaintiffs' sales in Germany were small, and the German defendant only produced, but did not sell, its bottles in Germany. The plaintiff asserted a violation of German unfair competition law by, inter alia, the defendant's allegedly slavish imitation of the plaintiff's bottles. But the Bundesgerichtshof did not abide by its former willingness to widely extend German law to international and cross-border disputes. Instead, it introduced a new conflicts approach that, among other things, defined the place where the competitive interests of parties collide:

Taeschner (15 January 1957); BGH 1958 GRUR 189, 197—*Zeiß* (24 July 1957); for an overview, *see* Benedict Czempiel, *Das bestimmbare Deliktsstatut—Zur Zurechnung im internationalen Deliktsrecht* 75–76 (1991); Karl-Heinz Fezer & Stefan Koos, in *Staudingers Kommentar zum Bürgerlichen Gesetzbuch: Internationales Wirtschaftsrecht*, Internationales Wettbewerbsprivatrecht para. 445 (15th edn., 2010).

217 BGHZ vol. 21, 266, 270—*Uhrenrohwerke* (13 July 1956).

218 BGH 1958 GRUR 189, 197—*Zeiß* (24 July 1957) ("Wird in einem ausländischen Staat eine Handlungsweise, die nach deutschem Recht an und für sich wettbewerbswidrig wäre, als zulässig angesehen, so muß gefragt werden, ob sie bei dieser Sachlage, also unter Berücksichtigung des Umstands, daß die ausländische Verkehrsauffassung sie billigt, mit den Anschauungen des anständigen deutschen Kaufmanns zu vereinbaren ist und deshalb nicht gegen § 1 UWG verstößt. Die Beurteilung kann daher auch bei Anwendung deutschen Rechts je nach dem Land, in dem die Wettbewerbshandlung begangen worden ist, durchaus verschieden ausfallen."); *see also* BGH 1960 GRUR 372, 377—*Kodak* (18 December 1959).

219 *See also, e.g.*, Heinz Binder, *Zur Auflockerung des Deliktsstatuts*, 20 RabelsZ 401, 413 *et seq.* (1955); Wilhelm Wengler, *Die Gesetze über unlauteren Wettbewerb und das internationale Privatrecht*, 19 RabelsZ 401, 413–414 (1954); Günther Beitzke, *Auslandswettbewerb unter Inländern—BGHZ 40, 391*, 1966 JuS 139, 147; Rainer Hausmann & Inés Obergfell, in *Lauterkeitsrecht: Kommentar zum Gesetz gegen den unlauteren Wettbewerb (UWG), vol. I*, Einleitung I para. 185 (Karl-Heinz Fezer ed., 2nd edn., 2010).

> Unfair competition can ... usually be committed only where the competitors' competitive interests collide; for only at the place of competitive interests' intersection does the concern for avoiding unfair competitive conduct exist.[220]

This approach to unfair competition choice of law has come to be characterized as the so-called marketplace principle or rule.[221] In light of this analysis, the defendant's activities in Germany—where the baby bottles were produced, not marketed—did not suffice to establish a sufficiently marketplace-related connex. In short, mere preparatory activity prior to the market entry could not qualify as a connecting factor.[222] The relevant point of attachment in the case, as the court went on to explain, was to be found abroad:

> The element of unfairness in such a case must be seen in the use of an imitated product in the battle for customers, notably, e.g., if such use can evoke an incorrect belief in the product's origin or quality on side of the buyers. This can, however, usually only occur in market areas where the competing products at issue come across each other.[223]

Interestingly, the court also questioned—albeit hesitantly—the application of the Nussbaum rule more generally. As it explained, the application of German law to domestic defendants' foreign-based conduct in cases where the plaintiff was a foreign party was inadequate: binding domestic competitors alone to stricter national standards would distort competition between the parties in foreign markets.[224] As we will see, even though this argumentation is principally correct, it still does not cut through the thicket.[225] Yet, with *Kindersaugflaschen*, German practice had made a big leap toward a less individualized perspective and a more economic approach to resolving international unfair competition disputes.

The Nussbaum rule suffered another blow in 1963, with the Bundesgerichtshof's *Stahlexport* opinion.[226] As the court explained, the application of German law to German competitors' activities in foreign

[220] BGH 1962 GRUR 243, 245—*Kindersaugflaschen* (30 June 1961) ("Unlauterer Wettbewerb kann ... in der Regel nur dort begangen werden, wo wettbewerbliche Interessen der Mitbewerber aufeinanderstoßen; denn nur an dem Ort wettbewerblicher Interessenüberschneidung wird das Anliegen der Verhinderung unlauterer Wettbewerbshandlungen berührt." (author's translation)).

[221] For an extensive discussion, *see infra* p. 203 *et seq.*

[222] BGH 1962 GRUR 243, 245–246—*Kindersaugflaschen* (30 June 1961).

[223] *Id.* at 245 ("Das Unlautere liegt in solchem Fall vielmehr in der Verwendung des nachgeahmten Erzeugnisses im Kampf um den Kunden, so wenn z. B. diese Verwendung geeignet ist, irrige Herkunfts- oder Gütevorstellungen bei den Abnehmern hervorzurufen. Dies aber kann in der Regel nur auf Marktgebieten der Fall sein, auf denen die fraglichen Konkurrenzerzeugnisse einander begegnen." (author's translation)).

[224] *Id.* at 245. [225] *See infra* p. 480 *et seq.*

[226] BGHZ vol. 40, 391, 395 *et seq.*—*Stahlexport* (20 December 1963).

markets was to be considered an exception to a general application of the marketplace rule. In addition to the first step in *Kindersaugflaschen*, the *Stahlexport* holding further perfected conflicts doctrine in light of a necessity to avoid anticompetitive distortion. The court stated that the marketplace rule was the general approach, even for conflicts between domestic parties competing in foreign markets.[227] The *lex domicilii communis* should apply only under exceptional circumstances. For instance, German law might apply (even absent the defendant's domestic activity) in cases where competition in a foreign market occurs exclusively between German parties. In addition, all conduct intentionally and purposefully directed toward a German competitor in foreign markets was considered eligible for the application of German law.[228]

This last stand of Nussbaum was finally abolished in 2010. In *Ausschreibung in Bulgarien*,[229] the Bundesgerichtshof decided that the *Stahlexport* exceptions to the universal application of the marketplace principle would no longer be accepted. The parties in this case were German competitors in the Bulgarian market for industrial heating and burner equipment. In the course of a tendering procedure, the defendant had allegedly sent a telefax containing defamatory statements about the plaintiff to a potential customer. As the court explained, all relevant interests in the case were to be found at the place where the customer's decision making was to be affected: Bulgaria. Hence, unlike how the *Stahlexport* doctrine would have required, the parties' common domicile or place of business was irrelevant.[230] Ultimately, it is the marketplace alone that determines choice of law in unfair competition conflicts.

C Twenty-First Century: A Merger of Conflict Rules?

The advent of the marketplace rule has not remained the only element of economization in European choice of law. I will address the current

[227] *Id.*

[228] *Id.; see also* BGH 1988 GRUR 916, 917—*PKW-Schleichbezug* (14 July 1988); Karl F. Kreuzer, *Wettbewerbsverstöße und Beeinträchtigung geschäftlicher Interessen (einschl. der Verletzung kartellrechtlicher Vorschriften)*, 232, 245, in *Vorschläge und Gutachten zur Reform des deutschen internationalen Privatrechts der außervertraglichen Schuldverhältnisse, vorgelegt im Auftrag der Zweiten Kommission des Deutschen Rates für internationales Privatrecht* (Ernst von Caemmerer ed., 1983); *but see also, e.g.*, Günther Beitzke, *Auslandswettbewerb unter Inländern—BGHZ 40, 391*, 1966 JuS 139 *et seq.*; Andreas Höder, *Die kollisionsrechtliche Behandlung unteilbarer Multistate-Verstöße—Das Internationale Wettbewerbsrecht im Spannungsfeld von Marktort-, Auswirkungs- und Herkunftslandprinzip* 37 (2002).

[229] BGH 2010 GRUR 847—*Ausschreibung in Bulgarien* (11 February 2010).

[230] *Id.* at 848. The court still applied German conflicts law under article 40 of the EGBGB (Introductory Act to the Civil Code). For the decision and its conformity with Rome II, *see* Jochen Glöckner, *Der grenzüberschreitende Lauterkeitsprozess nach BGH v. 11.2.2010—Ausschreibung in Bulgarien*, 2011 WRP 137.

landscape of theories later, in chapter 3. For now, one aspect of the history of European trademark and unfair competition choice of law must be mentioned as the final step in the development of legal doctrine. Notwithstanding the still existing dichotomy between substantive trademark and unfair competition doctrine, as well as the differences in choice of law, it appears as if trademark and unfair competition choice of law have recently begun to move toward a common core.

For quite some time now, unfair competition choice of law has been founded on effects testing. It is not a perfectly dematerialized rule, but it has overcome the doctrine's initial foundations on defendant conduct and injury at the plaintiff's place of business. The rule is different, though, in trademark conflicts. The principle of trademark territoriality, as we have seen, still establishes a requirement of domestic conduct in order for an infringement of national rights to be found. Conduct abroad will not suffice for the infringement of a domestic trademark. The opposite is also true: domestic activity cannot impinge on foreign rights.[231] Hence, under the *lex loci protectionis* rule, actual conduct has usually been the ultimate parameter of conflicts determination. But this has changed.

Persuaded by rules in the WIPO Joint Recommendation Concerning Provisions on the Protection of Marks, and Other Industrial Property Rights in Signs, on the Internet,[232] the Bundesgerichtshof broadened the principle of territoriality in its 2004 *HOTEL MARITIME* decision.[233] I will analyze the decision in detail in chapter 6, focusing here on its most significant aspect: for an application of domestic trademark law, it no longer appears to be indispensable that the defendant actually acted domestically. More generally, it seems as if conduct is no longer a prime factor of conflicts determination at all. In *HOTEL MARITIME*, the owner of the German trademark registration "MARITIM," a large hotel chain, contested the defendant's use of "Hotel Maritime" for its Danish hotel and for advertising under a website with the domain "hotel-maritime.dk." The defendant owned a Danish trademark registration and was soliciting guests from Germany both by direct mail advertising and by providing significant parts of its website in German. The court agreed with the appellate decision that there was no actual activity in

[231] For an extensive analysis—and references to current theory and practice—*see infra* p. 193 *et seq.*

[232] WIPO, *Joint Recommendation Concerning Provisions on the Protection of Marks, and Other Industrial Property Rights in Signs, on the Internet (with Explanatory Notes), adopted by the Assembly of the Paris Union for the Protection of Industrial Property and the General Assembly of the World Intellectual Property Organization (WIPO) at the Thirty-Sixth Series of Meetings of the Assemblies of the Member States of WIPO September 24 to October 3, 2001* (WIPO Pub. No. 845(E)). For an extensive analysis, *see infra* p. 225 *et seq.*

[233] BGH 2005 GRUR 431—*HOTEL MARITIME* (13 October 2004).

Germany.[234] But this did not end the analysis. Instead, the Bundesgerichtshof went on to discuss "domestic effects" as an alternative criterion for conflicts attachment:

> Not any use of a mark on the internet is subject to the national legal order's protection of marks against confusion. Otherwise, protection of national rights would be extended shorelessly and would—contrary to the European freedom to provide services . . .—inadequately restrict self-expression of foreign enterprises. This would involve a significant limitation of opportunities to make use of rights on the internet since owners of confusingly similar marks, protected in different countries, could—irrespective of the priority of the conflicting marks—reciprocally demand forbearance of use from the other side. . . . What is required instead is that the offer exert sufficient economically relevant inland effect (defined as "commercial effect" by the WIPO).[235]

Ultimately, the plaintiff's claim failed as a result of the court's concrete balancing of the interests involved. The Bundesgerichtshof did not find "sufficient economically relevant inland effect." This outcome, as well as the details of this approach, may be questioned; the doctrine surely must evolve even further.[236] But its defects aside, the decision introduced a new and valid aspect: *HOTEL MARITIME* did not concern an instance of territorial conduct—it was the accessibility of the defendant's website in Germany that qualified as a substitute. In essence, this is an effects test. With this step toward dephysicalization, trademark conflicts doctrine has moved closer to international unfair competition theory. Territorial conduct or activity is no longer required; commercial effects may suffice to trigger the application of the legal regime where these effects have

[234] *Id.* at 432–433. ("Das Ber[ufungsgericht] hat zu Recht Unterlassungsansprüche der Kl[ägerin] aus ihren Marken . . . und ihrem Unternehmenskennzeichen . . . gegen den Auftritt der Bekl[agten] unter der Internet-Domain . . . und gegen die Verwendung der Bezeichnung . . . verneint, weil es an einer relevanten Verletzungshandlung im Inland fehle. Dagegen wendet sich die Revision ohne Erfolg mit der Begründung, das Ber[ufungsgericht] habe zu hohe Anforderungen an den Inlandsbezug gestellt.").

[235] *Id.* ("Nicht jede Kennzeichenbenutzung im Internet ist jedoch dem Schutz von Kennzeichen gegen Verwechslungen nach der nationalen Rechtsordnung unterworfen. Ansonsten würde dies zu einer uferlosen Ausdehnung des Schutzes nationaler Kennzeichenrechte und—im Widerspruch zur [europäischen] Dienstleistungsfreiheit . . .—zu einer unangemessenen Beschränkung der Selbstdarstellung ausländischer Unternehmen führen. Damit einhergehen würde eine erhebliche Beschränkung der Nutzungsmöglichkeiten von Kennzeichenrechten im Internet, weil die Inhaber verwechslungsfähiger Kennzeichenrechte, die in verschiedenen Ländern geschützt sind, unabhängig von der Prioritätslage wechselseitig beanspruchen könnten, dass die Benutzung des Kollisionszeichens unterbleibt. . . . Erforderlich ist vielmehr, dass das Angebot einen hinreichenden wirtschaftlich relevanten Inlandsbezug (von der WIPO als „commercial effect" bezeichnet) aufweist." (author's translation)).

[236] *See infra* p. 491 *et seq.*

occurred. As it may seem, the trademark conflicts rule under the *lex loci protectionis* and the unfair competition choice-of-law marketplace rule have begun to merge.

Conclusions

The development of trademark and unfair competition doctrine throughout the last two centuries has been dominated by a fundamental dichotomy: since trademark rights were deemed state-granted privileges and monopolies from the beginning, their existence—and, accordingly, their scope of protection—was considered to be inseparably tied to the granting state's political boundaries. Only in hindsight can it be said that this tradition of strictly formal rights territoriality has suffocated the evolution of a structured and comprehensive "effects" approach for international trademark disputes.[237] Unfair competition choice of law, by contrast, has undergone a much deeper scholarly debate with regard to the relevance of different aspects, including, inter alia, defendant conduct, impact on competitors, and effects on the marketplace. While a comprehensive and consistent approach may have yet to be developed, the so-called marketplace rule seems to be most apt for conflicts analysis under modern socioeconomic circumstances. In a sense, unfair competition choice of law—its historical detours and defects aside—has been emancipated from the spell of legal formalism.

Not only is this divergence between trademark and unfair competition law at the conflicts level problematic with respect to the impracticalities of decision making and with regard to its potential economic distortions, but it also suffers from a severe doctrinal inconsistency by overlooking the fact that, with regard to substantive law policies, both sectors have recently converged. This will be the subject of chapter 4. Yet this historical overview has already illustrated an intense entanglement—both trademark and unfair competition law are designed to provide for an optimal level of market information in favor of the consumer's decision making. If such a convergence has finally arrived at the level of substantive law, however, why then should choice of law still be handled so differently? Although attempts to explain the difference abound, none has managed to overcome the basic deficit of the traditional formalist myopia. An illustrative example that somewhat "translates" the substantive law dichotomy to the international arena is Gerhard Schricker's distinction, which is founded

[237] It will become visible in the next chapter that the United States provides a distinctly different picture.

on an assumption that "interests" might be unbounded or bounded, depending on the respective interest's upgrading "by state grant":

> Spheres of interest can transgress the national borders without further ado; tort protection does not stop in front of a border. Unlike trademark law, there is no segmentation in territorial protection zones, in which formal requirements for protection exist. The issue is not state-granted positions.[238]

What such a perspective fails to explain is that if unfair competition law is eligible to protect extraterritorially due to the fact that individual "spheres of interest" protected by tort principles may easily transcend national borders, why should trademark protection stop at political frontiers? Interests exist in both areas. In fact, those interests (not only on the side of the competing parties but also on the side of the regulating states) will be identical in most cases. Trademark rights do not simply establish monopolies of trade. The aim of preventing consumer confusion over the source of a branded product, a specific version of unfair competition protection, is what governs both trademark and unfair competition law. Furthermore, as developments in Germany and Europe have illustrated, whether a national regime grants formal "rights" or whether the interests involved are reconciled on the basis of "conduct rules" is often the result of historical happenstance rather than doctrinal consistency or economic necessity. A formalistic approach, therefore, necessarily disregards and inevitably misinterprets the interests involved in multijurisdictional conflicts.

Chapter 4 will provide the groundwork for a new concept of conflicts resolution in both trademark and unfair competition doctrines. At the moment, it suffices to conclude that whether information infrastructure and consumer decision making within the marketplace fall under the protection of trademark rights or under the enforcement of unfair competition rules of conduct should not make a difference regarding the resolution of cross-border disputes. What is sorely needed is a theory of reconciliation—a reconceptualization of both fields' choice of law fundament.

[238] Gerhard Schricker, *Territoriale Probleme und Klagerecht bei unlauterem Wettbewerb*, 1973 GRUR Int. 453, 457 ("Interessenbereiche [können] die Landesgrenzen ohne weiteres überschreiten; der Deliktsschutz macht vor ihnen nicht halt. Eine Aufteilung in territoriale Schutzzonen, in denen jeweils formale Schutzvoraussetzungen zu erfüllen wären, wird im Unterschied zum Markenrecht nicht gemacht. Es geht nicht um staatlich verliehene Positionen." (author's translation)).

2 Common Law History
United States

> We agree with the court below . . . that "since it is the trade, and not the mark, that is to be protected, a trademark acknowledges no territorial boundaries of municipalities or states or nations, but extends to every market where the trader's goods have become known and identified by his use of the mark. But the mark, of itself, cannot travel to markets where there is no article to wear the badge and no trader to offer the article."
>
> Hanover Star Milling Co. v. Metcalf, 240 U.S. 403, 415–416 (1916)

Introduction

Comparing the development of German and European law with American doctrine reveals a number of critical structural differences.[1] Unlike German doctrine, which has always been founded on formalist privilege theory, US law is distinctively nonformal. The concept of goodwill has governed both trademark protection and unfair competition prevention since the 1800s. While substantive trademark law has been wrought with debate on the extension of goodwill protection ever since, neither the realist attack of the 1900s nor the enactment of federal trademark law in 1946 nor the law and economics movement of the 1980s led to a jettisoning of goodwill as the central concept; not surprisingly,

[1] The history of US trademark and unfair competition law has been ably documented and explained. *See* Frank I. Schechter, *The Historical Foundations of the Law Relating to Trade-Marks* (1925); more recently, *see, e.g.*, Benjamin G. Paster, *Trademarks—Their Early History*, 59 Trademark Rep. 551 (1969); Sidney A. Diamond, *The Historical Development of Trademarks*, 65 Trademark Rep. 265 (1975); Daniel M. McClure, *Trademarks and Unfair Competition: A Critical History of Legal Thought*, 69 Trademark Rep. 305 (1979); Kenneth J. Vandevelde, *The New Property of the Nineteenth Century: The Development of the Modern Concept of Property*, 29 Buff. L. Rev. 325 (1980); Thomas D. Drescher, *The Transformation and Evolution of Trademarks—From Signals to Symbols to Myth*, 82 Trademark Rep. 301 (1992); Mira Wilkins, *The Neglected Intangible Asset: The Influence of the Trade Mark on the Rise of the Modern Corporation*, 34 Bus. Hist. 66 (1992); Keith M. Stolte, *How Early Did Anglo-American Trademark Law Begin? An Answer to Schechter's Conundrum*, 88 Trademark Rep. 564 (1998); Robert G. Bone, *Hunting Goodwill: A History of the Concept of Goodwill in Trademark Law*, 86 B. U. L. Rev. 547 (2006); Mark P. McKenna, *The Normative Foundations of Trademark Law*, 82 Notre Dame L. Rev. 1839 (2007).

trademark-as-property protection remains the order of the day (*see infra* p. 77 *et seq.*). Nonetheless, what has remained widely unexplored to date is the relevance of the goodwill concept for trademark and unfair competition conflicts law. A historical perspective reveals several stages of development, including the establishment of equity jurisdiction over cases of trespass on trademark property, a model of virtually unlimited common law rights, and the Supreme Court's *Tea Rose/Rectanus* doctrine. In the course of this evolution, trademark and unfair competition law transformed from a domain of absolute and universal rights into a system of market-related goodwill protection. This also laid the foundation for the extension of international goodwill. Another facet unexplored to date is the US federal legal system and its contribution to the "unboundedness" of market rights. While a matter of course for US theorists, the intricacies of *Swift* and *Erie* are a maze to civil lawyers. Here, the understanding of "federal common law" under *Swift* has been particularly important. An inherent tendency to disregard interstate variations of the common law under the pre-*Erie* system contributed to a general neglect of state sovereignty concerning issues of trademark rights extension. Quite surprisingly, the federalization of US trademark law under the 1946 Lanham Act and preceding statutory trademark laws also failed to substitute the common law foundation of rights acquisition and extension (*see infra* p. 127 *et seq.*). Hence, today, it is still *Tea Rose/Rectanus* that provides for a genuinely market-oriented theory of rights and a general disregard for political boundaries. This is lucidly revealed by a look at the Supreme Court's 1952 decision in *Steele v. Bulova Watch Co.*, the court's only precedent on the issue. As revealed by a critical historical analysis of the *Steele* reasoning and a closer look at its progeny, the tendency of US trademark and unfair competition conflicts law to overextend the protection of domestic rights and competitors is due to its common law foundations and its borrowing of "effects on US commerce" testing from international antitrust doctrine (*see infra* p. 151 *et seq.*).

Section 1 Substantive Trademark and Unfair Competition Law

Several aspects are important for this chapter's historical account. First, the roots of US trademark propertization must be traced to their beginnings—found in eighteenth-century England—in order to understand how substantive law came to be what it is. Second, within the paradigm of trademark-as-property protection, "goodwill" has become the most determinative element. At the same time, trade diversion has been the mirror image of goodwill protection. Indeed, US law has always been a system of trade-diversion prevention. Over time, the system of goodwill-as-property protection that had developed throughout the nineteenth century came into conflict with the structures of a modern society and economy. With the burgeoning of transcontinental trade and business activities at the beginning of the twentieth century, the idea of trademark property became less suitable. As a result, the property paradigm of US trademark and unfair competition law was modernized toward a market-oriented perspective.

I *The Early Straightjacket: Equity, Passing Off, and Universality*

The historical development of American society and economy differed from that of Europe in a number of respects. Yet, as in Europe, the United States witnessed a dramatic shift in its socioeconomic conditions in the nineteenth century. After the Civil War, a delocalization of trade and an extension of business activity commenced throughout the country. Prior to the 1860s, production and trade had been local, and the need for and use of identifying symbols in trade had been small. The subsequent expansion in territory, population, wealth, and income, however, soon led to a drastic proliferation and extension of marketplaces.[2] Production and distribution became more sophisticated due to technological innovation and enhanced infrastructural conditions.[3] With the concomitant increase in consumers' per capita income, the diversification of products and a multiplication of intranational and international trade ensued. Intensified competition was the result. Both marketplace expansion and intensified competition, in turn, led to the emergence of new advertising methods—notably, brand-name marketing. In essence, the replacement of direct transactions between producers and consumers by anonymous sales through retailers and middlemen made trademarks an important marketing tool.[4] The legal arena reflected this development: while

[2] Pamela Walker Laird, *Advertising Progress: American Business and the Rise of Consumer Marketing* 15 (1998); Sara Stadler Nelson, *The Wages of Ubiquity in Trademark Law*, 88 Iowa L. Rev. 731, 776–777 (2003); Robert G. Bone, *Hunting Goodwill: A History of the Concept of Goodwill in Trademark Law*, 86 B. U. L. Rev. 547, 575 (2006). For an overview of early twentieth-century developments (and the historical literature in the field), *see* Steven Wilf, *The Making of the Post-War Paradigm in American Intellectual Property Law*, 31 Colum. J. L. & Arts 139, 145 and 160 *et seq.* (2008).

[3] Robert P. Merges, *One Hundred Years of Solicitude: Intellectual Property Law, 1900–2000*, 88 Cal. L. Rev. 2187, 2207 *et seq.* (2000); Steven Wilf, *The Making of the Post-War Paradigm in American Intellectual Property Law*, 31 Colum. J. L. & Arts 139, 160 *et seq.* (2008).

[4] Frank I. Schechter deftly explained one facet of this development: "[D]ecisions ... based upon an antiquated neighborhood theory of trade, fail to recognize the fact that through the existence of the telephone, the automobile, the motor bus, the high-speed interurban trolley, and the railroad, the consumer now projects his shopping far from home and comes to rely more and more upon trademarks and tradenames as symbols of quality

disputes over trademark and unfair competition conflicts rarely occupied US courtrooms during the first half of the century,[5] they assumed a more conspicuous presence after the Civil War.[6] With this rise in case numbers, US law embarked on an adventurous journey toward a modern trademark and unfair competition regime.

A Trademark Protection in the Distorting Mirror of Law and Equity

The first obstacle in the way of a modern law was a remnant of medieval times. The demarcation between law and equity proved particularly burdensome with respect to a growing demand for judge-made redress among traders and merchants. Of course, after the merger of law and equity in the nineteenth century, common law courts no longer inquired about a special jurisdictional basis for ordering injunctive relief when a trademark infringement was at stake.[7] But the road that had brought doctrine this far was a winding one. A right owner's position had been significantly different in the eighteenth and early nineteenth centuries. At that time, trademark protection was based on the concept of fraud. No property right in the trademark was recognized.[8] It was thus questionable whether a court of equity would grant injunctive relief; after all, this

and guaranties of satisfaction." (Frank I. Schechter, *The Rational Basis of Trademark Protection*, 40 Harv. L. Rev. 813, 824 (1927)). For a general overview, *see, e.g.*, Pamela Walker Laird, *Advertising Progress: American Business and the Rise of Consumer Marketing* 31–32 and 185 (1998); Robert G. Bone, *Hunting Goodwill: A History of the Concept of Goodwill in Trademark Law*, 86 B. U. L. Rev. 547, 576 (2006); Robert G. Bone, *Schechter's Ideas in Historical Context and Dilution's Rocky Road*, 24 Santa Clara Computer & High Tech. L.J. 469, 477 *et seq.* (2008). For a perspective on how trademarks have fostered the development of modern corporate enterprises, *see* Mira Wilkins, *The Neglected Intangible Asset: The Influence of the Trade Mark on the Rise of the Modern Corporation*, 34 Bus. Hist. 66 (1992).

[5] *See, e.g.*, Edward S. Rogers, *Some Historical Matter Concerning Trade-Marks*, 9 Mich. L. Rev. 29, 42 (1910) (listing reported trademark decisions by year from 1837 to 1870 (total of 62)); Lawrence M. Friedman, *A History of American Law* 328 (3rd edn., 2005).

[6] Beverly W. Pattishall, *Two Hundred Years of American Trademark Law*, 68 Trademark Rep. 121, 133 (1978); Pamela Walker Laird, *Advertising Progress: American Business and the Rise of Consumer Marketing* 189–190 (1998); Edward S. Rogers, *Some Historical Matter Concerning Trade-Marks*, 9 Mich. L. Rev. 29, 42 (1910); Frank I. Schechter, *The Historical Foundations of the Law Relating to Trade-Marks* 134 (1925). The number of registered trademarks remained small compared to unregistered marks in use after the turn of the century. For the later development, *see, e.g.*, Wallace H. Martin, *Incentives to Register Given by the New Trade-Mark Act, Part I*, 36 Trademark Rep. 213, 214 (1946).

[7] Frank I. Schechter, *The Historical Foundations of the Law Relating to Trade-Marks* 145 (1925); *see also* Milton Handler & Charles Pickett, *Trade-Marks and Trade Names—An Analysis and Synthesis: II*, 30 Colum. L. Rev. 759, 769 (1930) ("The action at law is now mainly of historical interest, since trademark litigation is generally confined to equity.").

[8] Milton Handler & Charles Pickett, *Trade-Marks and Trade Names—An Analysis and Synthesis: II*, 30 Colum. L. Rev. 759, 769 (1930); Daniel M. McClure, *Trademarks and Unfair Competition: A Critical History of Legal Thought*, 69 Trademark Rep. 305, 311–312 (1979); Adair Dyer, *Unfair Competition in Private International Law*, 211 Recueil des Cours

always required the infringement of a subjective right, and not just fraudulent activity by the defendant. Accordingly, alleged infringers would often successfully object to bills in equity and assert that the suit should be brought in a court of law.[9] There, proof of the defendant's fraudulent intent was required—and this was not always easy to establish.

A prominent example of the courts' hesitation to enforce individual trademark rights is the 1742 English case *Blanchard v. Hill*,[10] in which the court denied relief against the defendant's use of the plaintiff's stamp on playing cards. The court was eager to explain that the royal charter entitling the plaintiff to the exclusive use of certain stamps on playing cards amounted to a "plain monopoly" and was therefore "illegal." Indeed, the anticompetitive nature of the charter as such appears to have been the main reason for the court's refusal to grant trademark protection.[11] But the overall climate at the time was not beneficial for an extension of subjective rights to trade names and marks, either. In particular, the general condemnation of trademark rights as anticompetitive disfavored protection. Upholding a strict requirement of fraudulent intent was one way to keep perceived detriments within narrow confines.

Yet, over time, cases of successful trademark infringement suits became more common. This was often due to a more generous handling of the fraud requirement. A famous example where the plaintiff managed to overcome the obstacles of contemporary law and equity doctrine is the 1824 case *Sykes v. Sykes*.[12] The defendant had marketed shot-belts and powder-flasks with imitations of the plaintiff's mark. The court found an infringement, noting that the plaintiff's sales had decreased after the defendant had started marketing identically labeled goods. What still seemed

373, 395–396 (1988–IV); Christopher Wadlow, *The Law of Passing-Off—Unfair Competition by Misrepresentation* para. 1–024 *et seq.* (4th edn., 2011).

9 *See, e.g., Gee v. Pritchard* [1818] 2 Swans. 402, 412–414, 36 E.R. 670, 674; *see also* Kenneth J. Vandevelde, *The New Property of the Nineteenth Century: The Development of the Modern Concept of Property*, 29 Buff. L. Rev. 325, 333 *et seq.* (1980); Robert G. Bone, *Hunting Goodwill: A History of the Concept of Goodwill in Trademark Law*, 86 B. U. L. Rev. 547, 561 (2006).

10 *Blanchard v. Hill* [1742] 2 Atk. 484, 26 E.R. 692, 693.

11 *See, e.g.*, Frank I. Schechter, *The Historical Foundations of the Law Relating to Trade-Marks* 136 (1925) ("[N]ot only was the thought of monopoly at that time still abhorrent to English law and business, but . . . a monopoly on playing cards was the classic example of a monopoly."); *see also* Eugen Ulmer, *Warenzeichen und unlauterer Wettbewerb in ihrer Fortbildung durch die Rechtsprechung* 47 (1929); Daniel M. McClure, *Trademarks and Unfair Competition: A Critical History of Legal Thought*, 69 Trademark Rep. 305, 312 (1979); Christopher Wadlow, *The Law of Passing-Off—Unfair Competition by Misrepresentation* para. 1–028 (4th edn., 2011); Mark P. McKenna, *The Normative Foundations of Trademark Law*, 82 Notre Dame L. Rev. 1839, 1852 (2007).

12 *Sykes v. Sykes* [1824] 3 B. & C. 541, 107 E.R. 834, 835; *see also Blofeld v. Payne* [1833] 4 B. & Ad. 410, 411–412, 110 E.R. 509, 510; *Edelsten v. Edelsten* [1863] 1 De G.J. & S. 185, 199, 46 E.R. 72.

to be important for the court, however, was that the defendant had marked his wares "in order to denote that they were of the genuine manufacture of the plaintiff."[13]

Soon after, the courts' rejection of a subjective rights theory in trademark protection started to falter. Indeed, the 1838 case *Millington v. Fox* seems to mark the first time that a court recognized a right to the exclusive use of marks.[14] This reflected a dramatic change of direction, particularly since it did not require fraud on the side of the defendant. The case, which appeared before an English court of equity, centered on an allegation that the defendants had marked steel with the plaintiffs' names and symbols. Lord Chancellor Cottenham, while not using express property terminology, declared that equity could be invoked even absent evidence of fraudulent intent on the side of the defendant:

> I see no reason to believe that there has, in this case, been a fraudulent use of the Plaintiffs' marks. ... That circumstance, however, does not deprive the Plaintiffs of their right to the exclusive use of those names; and, therefore, I stated that the case is so made out as to entitle the Plaintiffs to have the injunction made perpetual.[15]

By 1863, the courts' adoption of property terminology had become evident. In *Edelsten v. Edelsten*, Lord Chancellor Westbury stated:

> At law the proper remedy is by an action on the case for deceit: and proof of fraud on the part of the defendant is of the essence of the action: but this Court will act on the principle of protecting property alone, and it is not necessary for the injunction to prove fraud in the Defendant, or that the credit of the Plaintiff is injured by the sale of an inferior article. The injury done to the Plaintiff in his trade by loss of custom is sufficient to support his title to relief.[16]

[13] *Sykes v. Sykes* [1824] 3 B. & C. 541, 107 E.R. 834, 835. Concerning the decrease in the plaintiff's sales, the court noted, "It further appeared, that the plaintiff's sale had decreased since the defendants commenced this business." (*Id.*).

[14] *Millington v. Fox* [1838] 3 My. & C. 338, 352, 40 E.R. 956. *See also* Rudolf Callmann, *Unfair Competition Without Competition?—The Importance of the Property Concept in the Law of Trade-Marks*, 95 U. Pa. L. Rev. 443, 454 (1947); Daniel M. McClure, *Trademarks and Unfair Competition: A Critical History of Legal Thought*, 69 Trademark Rep. 305, 313 (1979); Kenneth J. Vandevelde, *The New Property of the Nineteenth Century: The Development of the Modern Concept of Property*, 29 Buff. L. Rev. 325, 342 (1980).

[15] *Millington v. Fox* [1838] 3 My. & C. 338, 352, 40 E.R. 956; for an interesting comparison with contemporary case law still insisting on the requirement of fraud, *see* Christopher Wadlow, *The Law of Passing-Off—Unfair Competition by Misrepresentation* para. 1–033 (4th edn., 2011) (referring to *William Crawshay v. William Thompson and Others* [1842] 4 Man. & G. 357, 134 E.R. 146).

[16] *Edelsten v. Edelsten* [1863] 46 E.R. 72, 1 De G.J. & S. 185, 199–200. *See also Hall v. Barrows* [1863] 4 De G.J. & S. 150, 156, 46 E.R. 873, 876 ("The case not only sh[o]ws how the name of the first maker may become a mere sign of quality, but it is very important as establishing the principle that the jurisdiction of the Court in the protection

In the same year, Westbury further explained in *Leather Cloth Co. v. American Leather Cloth Co.*:

> It is correct to say that there is no exclusive ownership of the symbols which constitute a trade mark apart from the use or application of them; but the word "trade mark" is the designation of these marks or symbols as and when applied to a vendible commodity, and the exclusive right to make such use[] or application is rightly called property. The true principle therefore would seem to be, that the jurisdiction of the Court in the protection given to trade marks rests upon property, and that the Court interferes by injunction, because that is the only mode by which property of this description can be effectually protected.[17]

Ultimately, trademark infringement had evolved from fraudulent passing off to trespass on property.[18] In prominently cited terms, the Supreme Court's 1879 *Trade-Mark Cases* illustrate what has been regarded by later courts and legal scholars as the final stage of the development of a "whole system of trademark property":

> The right to adopt and use a symbol or a device to distinguish the goods or property made or sold by the person whose mark it is, to the exclusion of use by all other persons, has been long recognized by the common law and the chancery courts of England and of this country, and by the statutes of some of the States. It is a property right for the violation of which damages may be recovered in an action at law, and the

of trade marks rests upon property, and that fraud in the Defendant is not necessary for the exercise of that jurisdiction.").

[17] *Leather Cloth Co. Ltd. v. American Leather Cloth Co. Ltd.* [1863] 4 De G.J. & S. 137, 46 E. R. 868, 870; *see also Levy v. Walker* [1879] 10 Ch. D. 436, 448, All E.R. 1173 ("The Court interferes solely for the purpose of protecting the owner of a trade or business from a fraudulent invasion of that business by somebody else. It does not interfere to prevent the world outside from being misled into anything."); *Singer Mfg. Co. v. Loog* [1882] 8 App. Cas. 15, 33 ("And I think it settled by a series of cases . . . that both trade-marks and trade names are in a certain sense property.").

[18] *See also Avery & Sons v. Meikle & Co.*, 81 Ky. 73, 90–91 (1883) ("The property really consists in the exclusive right of a manufacturer or owner to sell his products or goods as his own, and in being protected in the exercise of that right by the exclusion of all others from its enjoyment, either by selling theirs for his or causing others to do so. It is not necessary to a recovery in equity, where the trade-mark itself, in whole or in part, has been appropriated, to prove fraud or an inferiority of quality of the article of the defendant. This principle is based on the ground that a trade-mark, when in use, is property itself."); *Schneider et al. v. Williams*, 14 A. 812, 814 (N.J. Ch. 1888) ("The rule, as thus stated, I understand to be the established doctrine, now in force, on this subject, both in this country and England. The question to be considered is, does the bill show a property right in the complainants and their fellow-members in the trade-mark in question?"); Oliver R. Mitchell, *Unfair Competition*, 10 Harv. L. Rev. 275, 281 (1896); Kenneth J. Vandevelde, *The New Property of the Nineteenth Century: The Development of the Modern Concept of Property*, 29 Buff. L. Rev. 325, 341 *et seq.* (1980); Daniel M. McClure, *Trademarks and Unfair Competition: A Critical History of Legal Thought*, 69 Trademark Rep. 305, 313 (1979).

continued violation of it will be enjoined by a court of equity, with compensation for past infringement.[19]

When other courts added that trademark property conferred "an exclusive right good 'as against all the world,'"[20] the concept of trademark-as-property protection seemed to have gained universal hold.

One caveat is worth mentioning, though. Mark McKenna has recently raised doubts as to whether the distinction between actions at law and actions in equity is as clear-cut as it appears.[21] Nineteenth-century courts often used concepts of law and equity interchangeably, discussed the same precedents for different concepts, and spoke in the same terms regardless of the form of action. A distinction was—and is—therefore difficult to draw.[22] McKenna is right, and there is additional indicia suggesting that the terminology of "trademark property" was not as widely established throughout legal practice as has sometimes been posited. In 1857, for instance, the court in *Collins Co. v. Brown* insisted that it was "now settled law that there is no property whatever in a trademark."[23] Similar doubts can be found in other decisions.[24] Adoption of

[19] *In re Trade-Mark Cases*, 100 U.S. 82, 92 (1879). *See also Hanover Star Milling Co. v. Metcalf*, 240 U.S. 403, 413 (1916) ("Common-law trademarks, and the right to their exclusive use, are, of course, to be classed among property rights.").

[20] *See, e.g., John T. Dyer Quarry Co. v. Schuylkill Stone Co.*, 185 F. 557, 567 (C.C.D.N.J. 1911); *Elgin National Watch Co. v. Illinois Watch Case Co.*, 179 U.S. 665, 677 (1901). *See also* Grafton Dulany Cushing, *On Certain Cases Analogous to Trade-Marks*, 4 Harv. L. Rev. 321, 322 (1890) ("A trade-mark has become an absolute right. It is ... an exclusive right to that sign in connection with goods of a certain kind,—a right as against all the world."); Melville Madison Bigelow, *The Law of Torts* para. 171 *et seq.*, para. 559–560 (7th edn., 1901); John Henry Wigmore, *Select Cases on the Law of Torts—with Notes, and a Summary of Principles,* vol. I nos. 179, 184 *et seq.* (1912).

[21] *See* Mark P. McKenna, *The Normative Foundations of Trademark Law*, 82 Notre Dame L. Rev. 1839, 1855 *et seq.* (2007).

[22] *Id.* at 1856. *See also* Christopher Wadlow, *The Law of Passing-Off—Unfair Competition by Misrepresentation* para. 1–024 *et seq.* (4th edn., 2011).

[23] *Collins Co. v. Brown* [1857] 3 Kay. & J. 423, 426–427, 69 E.R. 1174, 1176 ("It is now settled law that there is no property whatever in a trade mark, but that a person may acquire a right of using a particular mark for articles which he has manufactured, so that he may be able to prevent any other person from using it, because the mark denotes that articles so marked were manufactured by a certain person; and no one else can have a right to put the same mark on his goods ... That would be a fraud upon the person who first used the mark in the market where his goods are sold.").

[24] *See, e.g., Reddaway v. Banham* [1896] A.C. 199, 209–210 ("The word 'property' has been sometimes applied to what has been termed a trade mark at common law. I doubt myself whether it is accurate to speak of there being property in such a trade mark, though, no doubt some of the rights which are incident to property may attach to it."); *Jamieson & Co. v. Jamieson* [1898] 15 R.P.C. 169, 191; *A.G. Spalding & Bros. v. A.W. Gamage* [1913] 30 R.P.C. 388. For a further illustration of the courts' "waver[ing] between the two horns of a dilemma," *see* Frank I. Schechter, *The Historical Foundations of the Law Relating to Trade-Marks* 151–153 (1925).

the property paradigm was often more a result of common sense and concrete case facts than of doctrinal necessity and reason.

Nevertheless, one thing remains for us to conclude. We can state indisputably that what had started as legal action on the basis of fraud gradually grew into a system of subjective rights protection. At the end of the nineteenth century, trademark law was on its way toward recognizing the individual rights character of trade names and marks.

B Passing Off: "The Whole Law and the Prophets on the Subject"

At first glance, the areas of trademark protection and unfair competition prevention—like the domains of law and equity—seem to have been clearly separated. However, the dichotomy between the protection of trademark "property" and the prevention of unfair competition "conduct" was superficial. Unlike German law, US doctrine was never strictly divided into two distinct sectors. Goodwill protection was and remains the common denominator.

As in European doctrine, the earlier development of trademark protection in the United States had led to an initial dichotomy within the field.[25] Formally, the distinction between technical trademarks and trade names (or "rights analogous to trademarks") was what drew the line. There was a general agreement in early doctrine that some indicia would always be considered common property. In the 1883 case *Avery & Sons v. Meikle & Co.*, the court expressed this understanding:

> The alphabet, English vocabulary, and Arabic numerals, are to man, in conveying his thoughts, feelings, and the truth, what air, light, and water are to him in the enjoyment of his physical being. Neither can be taken from him. They are the common property of mankind, in which all have an equal share and character of interest. From these fountains whosoever will may drink, but an exclusive right to do so cannot be acquired by any.[26]

Accordingly, while everyday words and symbols were considered off-limits for private appropriation, words and symbols that were of a new and unknown structure or usage were not. This category of technical trademarks—or trademarks proper, as it evolved during the nineteenth

[25] *See, e.g.*, Oliver R. Mitchell, *Unfair Competition*, 10 Harv. L. Rev. 275, 275–276 (1896) ("Logically speaking, the fact is that Unfair Competition is properly a generic title, of which trade mark is a specific division. Practically, however, the earlier development of the law of trade marks has fixed a different arrangement and has established trade marks as an independent title in the law. The scope of the generic name must therefore be correspondingly restricted."); *see* Walter J. Derenberg, *Trade-Mark Protection and Unfair Trading* 39 *et seq.* (1936).

[26] *Avery & Sons v. Meikle & Co.*, 81 Ky. 73, 90 (1883).

century—was capable of private appropriation.[27] Under today's trademark doctrine, this category comprises arbitrary, fanciful, invented, distinctive, and nondescriptive trademarks. Their illegitimate appropriation was a tort, and injunctive relief was available upon showing that the defendant had made use of an identical or similar trademark for the same product.[28] Quite differently, the protection of designations other than technical trademarks—namely, trade names; personal, corporate, and firm names; and geographical and descriptive terms—was not founded on a theory of formal property rights. These designations were deemed nonprotectable within the category of technical trademarks.[29] Yet protection was possible under a doctrine of unfair competition prevention, notably as "cases analogous to trademarks."[30] Over time, state and federal courts extended this doctrine of unfair competition to comprise ever more instances of unfairness. Ultimately, a wide range of unfair competitive conduct was covered.[31]

[27] *See, e.g.*, Grafton Dulany Cushing, *On Certain Cases Analogous to Trade-Marks*, 4 Harv. L. Rev. 321, 322 (1890); Amasa C. Paul, *The Law of Trade-Marks, Including Trade-Names and Unfair Competition* § 22, at 35 (1903); James Love Hopkins, *The Law of Trademarks, Tradenames, and Unfair Competition* § 3, at 11 (2nd edn., 1905); *see also* E.R. Coffin, *Fraud as an Element of Unfair Competition*, 16 Harv. L. Rev. 272, 274 *et seq.* (1903); Milton Handler & Charles Pickett, *Trade-Marks and Trade Names—An Analysis and Synthesis: I*, 30 Colum. L. Rev. 168, 168–169 (1930).

[28] *See, e.g., Lawrence Mfg. Co. v. Tennessee Mfg. Co.*, 138 U.S. 537, 548 *et seq.* (1891); Amasa C. Paul, *The Law of Trade-Marks, Including Trade-Names and Unfair Competition* § 19 (1903).

[29] *See, e.g., Avery & Sons v. Meikle & Co.*, 81 Ky. 73, 85–86 (1883); *Dennison Mfg. Co. v. Thomas Mfg. Co.*, 94 F. 651, 657 (C.C.D. Del. 1899); *Italian Swiss Colony v. Italian Vineyard Co.*, 158 Cal. 252, 256, 110 P. 913, 914 (1910); Sara Stadler Nelson, *The Wages of Ubiquity in Trademark Law*, 88 Iowa L. Rev. 731, 739 *et seq.* (2003); Robert G. Bone, *Hunting Goodwill: A History of the Concept of Goodwill in Trademark Law*, 86 B. U. L. Rev. 547, 564 (2006).

[30] *See, e.g., Shaver v. Heller & Merz Co.*, 108 F. 821, 826, 48 C.C.A. 48 (8th Cir. 1901); *Dennison Mfg. Co. v. Thomas Mfg. Co.*, 94 F. 651, 658 (C.C.D. Del. 1899); Grafton Dulany Cushing, *On Certain Cases Analogous to Trade-Marks*, 4 Harv. L. Rev. 321, 323 and 332 (1890); for later commentary, *see, e.g.*, Zechariah Chafee, Jr., *Unfair Competition*, 53 Harv. L. Rev. 1289, 1294–1295 (1940); Rudolf Callmann, *Unfair Competition Without Competition?—The Importance of the Property Concept in the Law of Trade-Marks*, 95 U. Pa. L. Rev. 443, 444 (1947).

[31] *See, e.g., International News Service v. Associated Press*, 248 U.S. 215 (1918); *A. L. A. Schechter Poultry Corp. v. United States*, 295 U.S. 495 (1935); for more on the doctrine's extension, *see* Charles Grove Haines, *Efforts to Define Unfair Competition*, 29 Yale L.J. 1 (1919); Walter J. Derenberg, *Trade-Mark Protection and Unfair Trading* 79 *et seq.* (1936); Frank S. Moore, *Legal Protection of Goodwill—Trade-Marks, Trade Emblems, Advertising, Unfair Competition* 46 (1936); Zechariah Chafee, Jr., *Unfair Competition*, 53 Harv. L. Rev. 1289, 1302 *et seq.* (1940); Harry D. Nims, *The Law of Unfair Competition and Trade-Marks, with Chapters on Good-Will, Trade Secrets, Defamation of Competitors and Their Goods, Registration of Trade-Marks, Interference with Competitors' Business, etc.*, vol. I § 1, at 36 *et seq.* (4th edn., 1947).

Even though, at that time, it seemed as if a line had been drawn between property and fairness protection, we must question whether this dichotomy ever actually existed. Despite the lack of formal property in unfair competition doctrine, protectable rights could be acquired by showing that the plaintiff had established secondary meaning.[32] In this regard, although property doctrine had not absorbed nontechnical trademarks, the general distinction between technical trademark property and unfair competition prevention was not well defined—and, in fact, was widely ineffective. Some courts were even willing to also find property rights in trade names and other nontechnical trademarks. One example is the 1904 case *Sartor v. Schaden*, in which the Supreme Court of Iowa started with a general recognition that "[t]here is a well-marked distinction between what is known as the 'infringement of a trade-mark' and 'unfair competition.' " The court explained that a trademark would be the "exclusive right of its proprietor." With regard to nontechnical trademarks, it stated:

> [A]side from the law of trade-marks, courts will protect trade-names or reputations, although not registered or properly selected as trademarks, on the broad ground of enforcing justice and protecting one in the fruits of his toil. This is all bottomed on the principle of common business integrity, and proceeds on the theory that, while the primary and common use of a word or phrase may not be exclusively appropriated, there may be a secondary meaning or construction which will belong to the person who has developed it. In this secondary meaning there may be a property right.[33]

The last part of this illustration, a concept of secondary-meaning-as-property protection, would later return in other court decisions and scholarly commentary.[34] Without belaboring the point, a basic fact is

[32] *See, e.g.*, *American Waltham Watch Co. v. United States Watch Co.*, 173 Mass. 85, 87, 53 N.E. 141, 142 (1899). *See also* E.R. Coffin, *Fraud as an Element of Unfair Competition*, 16 Harv. L. Rev. 272, 274 (1903); James Love Hopkins, *The Law of Trademarks, Tradenames, and Unfair Competition* § 15, at 28–29 (2nd edn., 1905); Milton Handler & Charles Pickett, *Trade-Marks and Trade Names—An Analysis and Synthesis: I*, 30 Colum. L. Rev. 168, 168–169 (1930).

[33] *Sartor v. Schaden*, 125 Iowa 696, 101 N.W. 511, 513 (1904).

[34] *See, e.g.*, *Weinstock, Lubin & Co. v. Marks*, 109 Cal. 529, 539, 42 P. 142 (1895) ("By device defendant is defrauding plaintiff of its business. He is stealing its goodwill, a most valuable property, only secured after years of honest dealing and large expenditures of money; and equity would be impotent, indeed, if it could contrive no remedy for such a wrong."); *Hainque v. Cyclops Iron Works*, 136 Cal. 351, 352, 68 P. 1014, 1015 (1902) ("If it be conceded that the word 'Cyclops' in this particular instance is the trade-name of plaintiffs rather than their trade-mark, that fact is not material. By a long-continued, exclusive use, plaintiffs and their predecessors in interest have acquired property rights in the use of the word which defendant is bound to respect."); *Clark Thread Co. v. Armitage*, 67 F. 896, 904 (C.C.S.D.N.Y. 1895) ("The broad principle … is that property shall be protected from unlawful assaults. That where a party has for long years advertised his

eye-catching: both sectors were founded on the principle that no competitor had a right to pass off her goods as those of another.[35] The prevention of passing off was designed to protect against the improper invasion of goodwill.[36] And impropriety was found in consumer confusion. James Love Hopkins described this in 1905:

goods by a certain name so that they are distinguished in the market by that name the court will not permit a newcomer, by assuming that name, to destroy or impair an established business."); Wallace R. Lane, *Development of Secondary Rights in Trade Mark Cases*, 18 Yale L.J. 571, 574 (1909) ("[W]ords in common use, geographical terms or proper names, while they may not be appropriated exclusively in their primary meaning, may come to have a secondary meaning which legitimately belongs exclusively to the person who has created and developed that meaning. In such meaning of such term, there is held to be a property right."). More generally, *see also* Oliver R. Mitchell, *Unfair Competition*, 10 Harv. L. Rev. 275, 280–281 (1896) ("Included in and making up the good will, and passing with it upon a sale of the business, is the business name, the trade marks, the trade names, and the trade secrets of the business . . .. And as the good will itself is property, the parts of which it is made up are, separately considered, property."); John Lewis, in Thomas M. Cooley, *A Treatise on the Law of Torts or the Wrongs which Arise Independently of Contract, vol. II* 736–737 (3rd edn., 1906) ("The good will of a business is often very valuable property." (with further references to case law)). For a 1930s summary of the debate, *see, e.g.*, Irvin H. Fathchild, *Statutory Unfair Competition*, 1 Mo. L. Rev. 20, 23 (1936) ("But is this stated difference between the law of trade-marks and the general law of unfair competition fundamental? Does not this statement reflect only a stage in the development of a fundamental rather than a fundamental itself? If the courts ... may evolve the proposition that the user of a particular trade-mark, trade-name, or label, acquires an exclusive property right therein, even as against an innocent adoption or use by others, may they not evolve also the proposition that the originator of a particular trade dress, not a technical trade-mark, acquires an exclusive property right therein, whether the later competitor acts fraudulently or innocently?"). And, finally, Frank S. Moore, *Legal Protection of Goodwill—Trade-Marks, Trade Emblems, Advertising, Unfair Competition* 26 (1936) ("Although a true or technical trade-mark is never property in the absolute sense, it is property in the qualified sense indicated."); Harry D. Nims, *The Law of Unfair Competition and Trade-Marks, with Chapters on Good-Will, Trade Secrets, Defamation of Competitors and Their Goods, Registration of Trade-Marks, Interference with Competitors' Business, etc., vol. I* § 1, at 66–67 (4th edn., 1947) (with further references to contemporary case law).

35 *See, e.g.*, Milton Handler & Charles Pickett, *Trade-Marks and Trade Names—An Analysis and Synthesis: I*, 30 Colum. L. Rev. 168, 181 (1930); William D. Shoemaker, *Trade-Marks—A Treatise on the subject of Trade-Marks with particular reference to the laws relating to registration thereof, vol. I* 9 (1931); Walter J. Derenberg, *Trade-Mark Protection and Unfair Trading* 42 (1936); Frank S. Moore, *Legal Protection of Goodwill—Trade-Marks, Trade Emblems, Advertising, Unfair Competition* 46 (1936); Zechariah Chafee, Jr., *Unfair Competition*, 53 Harv. L. Rev. 1289, 1296 (1940) ("In both [trademark infringement and unfair competition], the defendant is passing off his goods as the plaintiff's goods by the use of a visible symbol.").

36 *See, e.g.*, Oliver R. Mitchell, *Unfair Competition*, 10 Harv. L. Rev. 275, 284 (1896) ("[T]he common link binding all these branches being the good will of which each branch is a part. In every unfair competition case the defendant's attempt is to appropriate to himself some part of the good will, or the entire good will, of the plaintiff's business. It will be obvious, therefore, that any given rule of law applicable in trade mark cases, so far as it arises out of the nature of trade marks as a part of good will, is equally applicable to the other parts of good will, not by analogy, but because the cases are for the purpose of that particular rule identical."); Harry D. Nims, *The Law of Unfair Competition and Trade-*

> Unfair competition consists in passing off one's goods as the goods of another, or in otherwise securing patronage that should go to another, by false representations that lead the patron to believe that he is patronizing the other person.[37]

As he went on, "The principles involved in trademark cases and trade-name cases have been substantially identical."[38] Even though the facts that a plaintiff had to prove may have been different, the common foundation of all cases was the diversion of trade by misinformation. This has remained the touchstone of both fields in the United States ever since.[39] As Judge Learned Hand famously stated in his 1928 *Yale Elec. Corp. v. Robertson* opinion:

> The law of unfair trade comes down very nearly to this—as judges have repeated again and again—that one merchant shall not divert customers from another by representing what he sells as emanating from the second. This has been, and perhaps even more now is, the whole Law and the Prophets on the subject, though it assumes many guises.[40]

Marks, with Chapters on Good-Will, Trade Secrets, Defamation of Competitors and Their Goods, Registration of Trade-Marks, Interference with Competitors' Business, etc., vol. I § 10, 70 (4th edn., 1947) ("The distinction between trade-mark infringement and unfair competition usually is not a matter of controlling importance. In either case the marks involved are symbols of good-will. Good-will is property and the common purpose of suits for trade-mark infringement and for unfair competition is the protection of good-will." (with further references to case law in n. 10 and 11)).

[37] James Love Hopkins, *The Law of Trademarks, Tradenames and Unfair Competition* § 1, at 1 (2nd edn., 1905).

[38] *Id.* at § 3, at 9; Zechariah Chafee, Jr., *Unfair Competition*, 53 Harv. L. Rev. 1289, 1296–1297 (1940) ("[T]he falsehood is the same and the instinctive response of the customer is the same."). *See also* Judge Loring's concurring opinion in *Cohen v. Nagle*, 190 Mass. 4, 15, 76 N.E. 276, 281 (1906) ("The right of action in all cases is the same, namely: A defendant has no right to sell his goods as the goods of the plaintiff. The right of action is the same, whether the plaintiff complains that the defendant has used his (the plaintiff's) trade-mark, or that he has used a trade-name unfortunately so called, or that he has imitated his packages, or that he has in terms represented that his goods are the goods of the plaintiff's manufacture.").

[39] *See* United States Senate, Committee on Patents, Senate Report No. 1333, 79th Congr., 2nd Sess. (14 May 1946), repr. in 1946 U.S. Code Cong. Service, 1274, 1275 ("There is no essential difference between trade-mark infringement and what is loosely called unfair competition. Unfair competition is the genus of which trade-mark infringement is one of the species; 'the law of trade-marks is but a part of the broader law of unfair competition' [United Drug]. All trade-mark cases are cases of unfair competition and involve the same legal wrong."); *see also, e.g.*, Harry D. Nims, *The Law of Unfair Competition and Trade-Marks, with Chapters on Good-Will, Trade Secrets, Defamation of Competitors and Their Goods, Registration of Trade-Marks, Interference with Competitors' Business, etc., vol. I* § 1, 10, 36 *et seq.* (4th edn., 1947); Stephen L. Carter, *The Trouble with Trademark*, 99 Yale L. J. 759, 764 (1990); Robert N. Klieger, *Trademark Dilution: The Whittling Away of the Rational Basis for Trademark Protection*, 58 U. Pitt. L. Rev. 789, 795 (1997).

[40] *Yale Elec. Corp. v. Robertson*, 26 F.2d 972, 973 (2nd Cir. 1928). *See also* Ralph S. Brown, Jr.'s avowal in *Advertising and the Public Interest: Legal Protection of Trade Symbols*, 57 Yale L.J. 1165, 1169, 1206 (1948) ("These views are conservative also in that they would preserve the basis for judicial action in this area pretty much as it stands. Its historical

This common foundation of trademark and unfair competition law also surfaces with regard to the debate on the fields' interrelation. For quite some time, it was unclear whether trademark law was part of the domain of unfair competition prevention, or vice versa. One reason the issue was so vexing was that, on the basis of the fields' common principle, either trademark or unfair competition law could be duly characterized as the fundament.[41] And even though the question was formally answered by the Supreme Court in *Hanover Star Milling Co. v. Metcalf* in 1916, the homogeneity of policies has remained a critical point until today. As the Supreme Court majority explained, "the common law of trademarks is but a part of the broader law of unfair competition."[42] Repeating what

foundation, that 'the wrong involved is diverting trade from the first user by misleading customers who mean to deal with him' may be a narrow one, but its limitations serve as a barrier to powerful pressures.").

[41] *See, e.g.*, Oliver Mitchell's 1896 characterization of the field: "Unfair competition, as the designation of a legal wrong which the law will undertake to redress or prevent, has only of late years begun to make its appearance in the books. To most lawyers, it is safe to say, the title carries no very definite meaning .... This method of treatment regards as unimportant whatever variation may exist among the so called 'analogous' cases *inter se*, and is content to regard this law as a mere parasite upon the trade mark branch." (Oliver R. Mitchell, *Unfair Competition*, 10 Harv. L. Rev. 275, 275 (1896)).

[42] *Hanover Star Milling Co. v. Metcalf*, 240 U.S. 403, 413 (1916); more recently, *see, e.g.*, *Moseley v. V. Secret Catalogue, Inc.*, 537 U.S. 418, 428 (2003). For an earlier illustration of the hierarchy between trademark and unfair competition law in scholarly commentary, *see, e.g.*, Oliver R. Mitchell, *Unfair Competition*, 10 Harv. L. Rev. 275, 275 (1896) ("Logically speaking, the fact is that Unfair Competition is properly a generic title, of which trade mark is a specific division."); E.R. Coffin, *Fraud as an Element of Unfair Competition*, 16 Harv. L. Rev. 272, 272 n. 1 (1903); Charles Grove Haines, *Efforts to Define Unfair Competition*, 29 Yale L.J. 1, 9–10 (1919); Milton Handler & Charles Pickett, *Trade-Marks and Trade Names—An Analysis and Synthesis: I*, 30 Colum. L. Rev. 168, 200 (1930) ("Trade-mark law is not merely one branch of the law of unfair competition—it is the law of unfair competition."); Rudolf Callmann, *Unfair Competition Without Competition?—The Importance of the Property Concept in the Law of Trade-Marks*, 95 U. Pa. L. Rev. 443, 453 (1947) ("It is a commonplace for which no authorities need be cited that the law of trade-marks is but a part or secluded corner of the more inclusive law of unfair competition."). For an earlier understanding of trademark specialty in case law, *see, e.g.*, *G. & C. Merriam Co. v. Saalfield*, 198 F. 369, 373 (6th Cir. 1912); *Dennison Mfg. Co. v. Thomas Mfg. Co.*, 94 F. 651, 659 (C.C.D. Del. 1899); less clear still *Elgin National Watch Co. v. Illinois Watch Case Co.*, 179 U.S. 665, 674 (1901) ("In other words, the manufacturer of particular goods in entitled to the reputation they have acquired, and the public is entitled to the means of distinguishing between those and other goods; and protection is accorded against unfair dealing, whether there be a technical trademark or not. The essence of the wrong consists in the sale of the goods of one manufacturer or vendor for those of another."). Even after *Hanover Star*, courts and scholars struggled with a classification. *See, e.g., Coty, Inc. v. Parfums De Grande Luxe*, 298 F. 865, 878 (2nd Cir. 1924) ("And as this court said in Hercules Powder Co. v. Newton ..., the law of unfair competition is the natural evolution of the law of the trade-mark, out of which it has grown. ... Protection against unfair competition is afforded upon the same general principles upon which technical trade-marks are protected."). *See also* Frank I. Schechter's illustration of the issue in his 1925 *Historical Foundations*: "When we consider how great a factor trade-marks and good-will represent in commercial life today and

had been established under nineteenth-century English precedent, the court emphasized that "[the] essential element is the same in trademark cases as in cases of unfair competition." In particular, the court observed:

> Courts afford redress of relief upon the ground that a party has a valuable interest in the good will of his trade or business, and in the trademarks adopted to maintain and extend it. The essence of the wrong consists in the sale of the goods of one manufacturer or vendor for those of another.[43]

C *Kidd/Derringer*: Trademark Universality "US Style"

As illustrated in chapter 1, German law in the nineteenth century widely adhered to the idea of international trademark universality.[44] A look at what the US courts did at that time—notably how they interpreted the geographical scope of trademark rights protection and what they understood as rights universality—sheds a very different light on the issue. Curtis A. Bradley has argued that the universality theory was never "embraced wholesale" by US courts. Since the Supreme Court, under its *Tea Rose/Rectanus* doctrine,[45] had early on limited a trademark's scope of protection to the territory of its use, European-style universality never came into existence.[46] However, case law prior to *Tea Rose/Rectanus* suggests a different picture—one of virtually unlimited rights extension and trademark universality. Here, as in Germany, the boundlessness of nineteenth-century property doctrine actually did account for an interim peak in trademark extension.

Essentially, nineteenth-century trademark protection is part of contemporary legal doctrine on the creation of rights in nonphysical values.[47] As with other kinds of intangible value protection under the guise of formal "property" rights, trademark policy was designed to

when we remember that out of the so-called law of technical trade-marks has grown the law of unfair competition or *concurrence déloyale*, circumscribing at a hundred different points the predatory and overreaching instincts of the mercantile mind, the comparative brevity of the history of that law in the royal courts is remarkable indeed[.]" (Frank I. Schechter, *The Historical Foundations of the Law Relating to Trade-Marks* 4 (1925)).

[43] *Hanover Star Milling Co. v. Metcalf*, 240 U.S. 403, 412–413 (1916); *see also Croft v. Day* [1843] 7 Beav. 84, 88, 49 E.R. 994, 996; *Perry v. Truefitt* [1842] 6 Beav. 66, 49 E.R. 749; *Burgess v. Burgess* [1853] 3 De G.M. & G. 896, 902, 43 E.R. 351, 354. *See also* Frank I. Schechter's summary of what he deemed the "general principles" found in both English and US case law in Frank I. Schechter, *The Historical Foundations of the Law Relating to Trade-Marks* 146 (1925).

[44] *See supra* p. 53–57.

[45] For the doctrine of *Tea Rose/Rectanus, see infra* p. 102–110 and p. 129–134.

[46] Curtis A. Bradley, *Territorial Intellectual Property Rights in an Age of Globalism*, 37 Va. J. Int'l L. 505, 542 (1997).

[47] *See* Kenneth J. Vandevelde, *The New Property of the Nineteenth Century: The Development of the Modern Concept of Property*, 29 Buff. L. Rev. 325, 333 *et seq.* (1980).

accommodate pressing socioeconomic interests in a preindustrialized country. Both scholarship and practice agreed that valuable interests had to be protected, regardless of whether the form of wealth was tangible or intangible.[48] Political consensus was that the protection of investment had priority within a society and economy faced with the challenges of industrializing a scarcely populated continent. In this regard, it was contended, legal certainty and predictability were necessary to encourage economic activity.[49] In many cases, such an extension of investment protection could be achieved only by jettisoning the Blackstonian conception of property as overly physicalist. If no physical or material thing to be protected existed, the interest or value at issue would have to be fictionalized as a position of "property." Such an extended conception of intangible values, of course, confronted the most basic problem of property theory: the unrestricted protection of an individual's property was impossible without a correspondingly absolute limitation of other individuals' freedom of activity.[50] This absolute doctrine was impractical at best—and detrimental and immoral at worst. Over time, therefore, any and all positions of property had to be limited. For fictionalized matter, the restrictions were "invisible," and, hence, there was endless matter for dispute. Accordingly, legal practice was often based on a trial-and-error approach rather than a structured and consistent system of property rights and limitations.

With respect to trademarks, legal practice reflects the judiciary's struggle in a number of different ways. One example is the dichotomy between technical trademarks and nontechnical rights. What had begun as a quasi absolute concept of trademark-as-property protection was gradually downsized on a sliding scale of protection. In the end, as we have seen,[51] courts distinguished between a highly competition-sensitive area of nontechnical trademarks (e.g., descriptive or geographic indications), where market competition depended on maximum availability, and the area of technical trademarks, where the risk

[48] *See, e.g., Partridge v. Menck*, 2 Barb. Ch. 101, 103 (N.Y. Ch. 1847) (finding a "valuable interest" as sufficient to warrant property protection); Comment, *The Nature of Business Goodwill*, 16 Harv. L. Rev. 135, 136 (1902) (finding "great pecuniary value" and assignability as the two characteristics sufficient to allow for a qualification of goodwill as property); Francis J. Swayze, *The Growing Law*, 25 Yale L.J. 1, 10–11 (1915). For an extensive analysis, *see* Kenneth J. Vandevelde, *The New Property of the Nineteenth Century: The Development of the Modern Concept of Property*, 29 Buff. L. Rev. 325, 333 *et seq.* (1980).

[49] Morton J. Horwitz, *The Transformation of American Law, 1780–1860* 111 (1977).

[50] Kenneth J. Vandevelde, *The New Property of the Nineteenth Century: The Development of the Modern Concept of Property*, 29 Buff. L. Rev. 325, 329 (1980).

[51] *See supra* p. 84 *et seq.*

of monopolization if a trademark was appropriated was not deemed too pressing.[52] With respect to the interstate economy and its marketplaces, another modification was required regarding the geographic extension of rights. Here, too, an initially absolute dominion of rights protection had to be broken down over time. The California Supreme Court's 1865 *Derringer v. Plate*[53] case and the US Supreme Court's 1879 *Kidd v. Johnson*[54] decision illustrate the difficult correlation between absolute rights and an unrestricted geographical protection.

Kidd centered on a trademark for whiskey. The dispute arose over concurrent trademark use in the owner's initial place of business in Cincinnati (by his distillery's purchasers) and in New York (by his removed business). The Supreme Court's characterization of trademark rights, though deftly short, expresses the contemporary concept of absolute and exclusive trademark rights:

> The right to use the trade-mark is not limited to any place, city, or State, and, therefore, must be deemed to extend everywhere. Such is the uniform construction of licenses to use patented inventions. If the owner imposes no limitation of place or time, the right to use is deemed coextensive with the whole country, and perpetual.[55]

The *Derringer*[56] decision of the California Supreme Court was similarly unrestricted in its approach to the geographical scope of protection. The plaintiff, a resident of Philadelphia, sold pistols under his trademark, "Derringer, Philadel." The defendant manufactured similar pistols in San Francisco, and he employed the plaintiff's trademark. Under the heading "Right to a trade mark at common law," the California Supreme Court explained:

> [The] right to the trade mark accrues to [the trademark owner] from its adoption and use for the purpose of designating the particular goods he manufactures or sells, and although it has no value except when so employed, and indeed has no separate abstract existence, but is appurtenant to the goods designated, yet the trade mark is property, and the owner's right of property in it is as complete as that which he possesses in the goods to which he attaches it .... [D]octrine has been uniform for many years, that the manufacturer or merchant does possess an exclusive property in the trade mark adopted and used by him. ... [L]ike the title to the good will of a trade, which it in some respects resembles, the right of property in a trade mark accrues without the aid of the statute. The right is not limited in its enjoyment by

[52] For a discussion of the sliding-scale nature of the dichotomy, *see, e.g.*, Daniel M. McClure, *Trademarks and Unfair Competition: A Critical History of Legal Thought*, 69 Trademark Rep. 305, 318 (1979).

[53] *Derringer v. Plate*, 29 Cal. 292, 87 Am. Dec. 170 (1865).

[54] *Kidd v. Johnson*, 100 U.S. 617 (1879). [55] *Id.* at 619.

[56] *Derringer v. Plate*, 29 Cal. 292, 87 Am. Dec. 170 (1865).

territorial bounds, but subject only to such statutory regulations as may be properly made concerning the use and enjoyment of other property, or the evidences of title to the same; the proprietor may assert and maintain his property right wherever the common law affords remedies for wrongs. The manufacturer at Philadelphia who has adopted and uses a trade mark, has the same right of property in it at New York or San Francisco that he has at his place of manufacture.[57]

The last part of the court's argument in particular provided room for divergent interpretation. While it was widely acknowledged that common law trademark protection extended beyond areas of trading activity, it was not clear how far such protection would reach. A broad interpretation projected trademark rights beyond state and even national borders. As long as the jurisdiction at issue granted trademark protection under a common law system, trademark rights detached from their origin jurisdiction could be protected.[58]

What ultimately has proven more important, however, is something else. The concept of unlimited trademark rights was difficult to uphold in a world of expanding marketplaces. As had become increasingly evident, the overextension of property rights affected the public good. With the advent of transcontinental trade and commerce, the issue of protecting good-faith market investment progressively acted as a counterbalance to formal trademark property. Consequently, the principle of strict priority combined with potentially unlimited trademark protection was no longer adequate.[59]

[57] *Id.* at 294–296.

[58] This argument (based on both *Kidd* and *Derringer*) has apparently been brought forward in *Hanover Star Milling Co. v. Metcalf*, 240 U.S. 403, 416–418 (1916). One of the appellate decisions also appears to lean in this direction; *see Theodore Rectanus Co. v. United States Co.*, 226 Fed. 545, 550 (6th Cir. 1915) ("[I]f we concede to the first appropriator of the mark the prima facie right exclusive against all others and everywhere, courts of equity will not enforce it where the rules of laches or estoppel make such enforcement unjust, and that in such case the original owner does not lose his general right, but only the power of enforcing it, in a particular territory."); for a closer analysis of the appellate court's decision, *see* Walter J. Derenberg, *Trade-Mark Protection and Unfair Trading* 454–455 (1936). A similar understanding of a formalist theory of *in rem* rights has been contended in scholarly commentary. *See, e.g.*, Harry D. Nims, *The Law of Unfair Competition and Trade-Marks, with Chapters on Good-Will, Trade Secrets, Defamation of Competitors and Their Goods, Registration of Trade-Marks, Interference with Competitors' Business, etc., vol. I* § 218b, at 641 (4th edn., 1947); Beverly W. Pattishall, *Two Hundred Years of American Trademark Law*, 68 Trademark Rep. 121, 125–126 (1978); Kenneth J. Vandevelde, *The New Property of the Nineteenth Century: The Development of the Modern Concept of Property*, 29 Buff. L. Rev. 325, 343 and 346 (1980); Robert G. Bone, *Hunting Goodwill: A History of the Concept of Goodwill in Trademark Law*, 86 B. U. L. Rev. 547, 567 (2006).

[59] In California, an 1872 statutory change apparently transformed the requirements for trademark acquisition from use to recording. *See Whittier v. Dietz*, 66 Cal. 78, 4 P. 986 (1884) ("No one, since the codes went into operation, can acquire the exclusive use of a name or trade mark in this State, except by filing it for record with secretary of state."). In

II The Right/Markets Connex: Materialization, Goodwill, and Trade Diversion

At first glance, it may appear that German and US trademark and unfair competition doctrine underwent similar processes of de-ideologization. Indeed, Josef Kohler, in a comparative account of US and European law, actually described the United States' property paradigm as equivalent to his theory of personality rights protection. With only a trace of arrogance, he explained:

> In France, England, and America [reference to Derringer case], protection of the individual right of product designations is considered an emanation of general principles; and the merit of this perspective is not lessened by the fact that these regimes often operate with the category of property rather than with the category of individual right, for construction—as is well-known—is not the most valuable asset of these regimes. As with Roman law, their major aplomb is the secure manner in which their jurisprudence finds its way through all troubles, regardless of the momentary system and the possibilities of rational-juridical reason—and a good jurisprudence with wrong arguments is still ten times better than a bad jurisprudence with good arguments.[60]

In this light, one might have expected the *Kidd/Derringer* doctrine to be jettisoned in the same way that personality rights universality was rejected in Germany. After all, in both countries, unlimited geographical trademark protection had become increasingly inapt at regulating expanding marketplaces. But US law took a different turn. Unlike German doctrine, American legal thought did not shrink rights

later years, lawmakers changed statutory law several times. For an illustration of the trouble and confusion resulting from the meandering, *see, e.g.*, Walter J. Derenberg, *Warenzeichen und Wettbewerb in den Vereinigten Staaten von Amerika* 23 (1931).

[60] Josef Kohler, *Das Recht des Markenschutzes mit Berücksichtigung ausländischer Gesetzgebungen und mit besonderer Rücksicht auf die englische, anglo-amerikanische, französische, belgische und italienische Jurisprudenz* 78 (1884) ("Daher wird denn auch in Frankreich, England und Amerika [reference to Derringer] der Schutz dieses individuellen Rechts der Waarenbezeichnungen als Ausfluss allgemeiner Principien betrachtet; und dieses Verdienst wird nicht dadurch geschmälert, dass hier vielfach mit der Kategorie des Eigenthums statt mit der Kategorie des Individualrechts operirt wird, denn Constructionen sind bekanntlich nicht die starke Seite dieser Rechtsgebiete; ebenso wie beim römischen Rechte, beruht ihr Hauptaplomb in der sicheren Art, wie sich die Jurisprudenz durch alle Schwierigkeiten hindurch ihren Weg bahnt, ohne Rücksicht auf das augenblickliche System und auf die Möglichkeit rationell-juridischer Begründung—und eine gute Jurisprudenz mit falschen Gründen ist immer noch zehnfach besser, als eine schlechte Jurisprudenz mit guten Gründen." (author's translation)). Kohler slightly modified his arguments in *Warenzeichenrecht—Zugleich zweite Auflage des Rechts des Markenschutzes mit Berücksichtigung ausländischer Gesetzgebungen (1884)* 65–66 (2nd edn., 1910), and in *Der unlautere Wettbewerb—Darstellung des Wettbewerbsrechts* 18–19 (1914).

geographically to the owner's place of business.[61] Instead, the subject matter of protection was transformed. Goodwill remained the foundational concept, and the diversion of trade became its practical metric. The Supreme Court's *Tea Rose/Rectanus* doctrine established protection against goodwill invasion in accordance with the parties' marketplace activities and investment. Trademark and unfair competition doctrine thereby first became detached from the competitor's place of business or residence, and then from the state's territory.

A The Materialization of Trademark Rights

The detachment of trademark rights from both their owner's personality and from the place of business is characteristic of US law. While in Germany a trademark remained connected to its owner's business and state territory, US doctrine established a model of market-related rights; neither personality nor business place determined a right's location. This attachment of trademark goodwill to the marketplace has proven significant for conflicts law.

As *Kidd* and *Derringer* illustrate, nineteenth-century doctrine conceived of trademark rights as providing protection against the entire world.[62] Over time, the subject matter of protection was shrunk. The emphasis shifted to actual commercial activity. This development, however—from personal rights and rights attached to a place of business into a scheme of marketplace rights—did not occur instantaneously. Early definitions of goodwill in scholarship still focused on a localization of values in at least some tangible element of the business.[63] This corresponded to an environment of local communities and local trade where goodwill was attached to individuals or small businesses.[64] Joseph Story's mid-nineteenth-century definition of goodwill (frequently referred to in later trademark treatises and commentaries) specified the establishment of a business as a determinative factor. He defined goodwill as

> the advantage or benefit, which is acquired by an establishment, beyond the mere value of the capital, stock, funds, or property employed therein, in consequence of the general public patronage and encouragement, which it receives from constant or habitual customers, on account of its local position, or common celebrity, or

[61] *See supra* p. 32–39. [62] *See supra* p. 90–93.

[63] *See, e.g.*, C.J. Foreman, *Conflicting Theories of Good Will*, 22 Colum. L. Rev. 638, 639 *et seq.* (1922) (with numerous references to nineteenth-century case law); *see also* Mark P. McKenna, *The Normative Foundations of Trademark Law*, 82 Notre Dame L. Rev. 1839, 1843, 1885–1886 (2007).

[64] Robert G. Bone, *Hunting Goodwill: A History of the Concept of Goodwill in Trademark Law*, 86 B. U. L. Rev. 547, 575–576 (2006).

reputation for skill or affluence, or punctuality, or from other accidental circumstances or necessities or even from ancient partialities, or prejudices.[65]

Later scholars, building on this definition, referred to business-owner personality as the foundation of goodwill value. A. S. Biddle, for instance, posited in 1875 that goodwill was "a species of incorporeal personalty, . . . subject with but few exceptions to the general laws which regulate that kind of property."[66] In this regard, scholarly opinion in the United States still resembled the contemporary German doctrine of personality rights protection. Yet the foundation on personality rights never completely took hold in the United States, to the contrary. By 1883, for instance, Adelbert Hamilton had explained the concept of goodwill as being founded on the business as such: "Good-will denotes a relation existing between a man or firm and the public with reference to a particular business. It is the good-will of the public to the man or firm."[67]

This early separation of goodwill value from an owner's personality and a business's physical existence was implemented in practice as well. Over time, courts shifted the focus of protectable subject matter to all instances where a plaintiff's investment in general was at issue. As a result, the need for a tangible thing to support or to connect to the intangible interest or value was gradually abandoned.[68] At the beginning, English courts still interpreted goodwill as being founded on incidents of real property. One example is Lord Eldon's definition of "goodwill" in the 1810 case *Cruttwell v. Lye*, where he explained that "good-will . . . is nothing more than the probability, that the old customers will resort to the old place."[69]

[65] Joseph Story, *Commentaries on the Law of Partnership, as a Branch of Commercial and Maritime Jurisprudence, with Occasional Illustration from the Civil and Foreign Law* § 99 (4th edn., 1855).

[66] A.S. Biddle, *Good-Will (Part 1)*, 23 Am. L. Reg. 1, 8 (1875). Biddle also explained that "when you are parting with the good-will of a business, you mean to part with all that good disposition which customers entertain towards the house of business identified by the particular name or firm, and which may induce them to continue giving their custom to it." (*Id.* at 4).

[67] Adelbert Hamilton, *Note, Good-Will*, 15 Fed. Rep. 315, 316 (1883).

[68] Kenneth J. Vandevelde, *The New Property of the Nineteenth Century: The Development of the Modern Concept of Property*, 29 Buff. L. Rev. 325, 335 (1980). This issue must be distinguished from the question whether a trademark could be transferred by itself or only incidental to the business or property with which it had been used. For an overview of contemporary doctrine on this issue, *see, e.g.*, Wallace R. Lane, *The Transfer of Trademarks and Trade Names*, 6 Ill. L. Rev. 46 (1911); William D. Shoemaker, *Trade-Marks—A Treatise on the subject of Trade-Marks with particular reference to the laws relating to registration thereof, vol. I* 537 *et seq.*, 547 *et seq.* (1931); Harry D. Nims, *The Law of Unfair Competition and Trade-Marks, with Chapters on Good-Will, Trade Secrets, Defamation of Competitors and Their Goods, Registration of Trade-Marks, Interference with Competitors' Business, etc., vol. I* § 17, at 85 *et seq.* (4th edn., 1947).

[69] *Cruttwell v. Lye* [1810] 17 Ves. Jr. 335, 346, 34 E.R. 129.

Indeed, courts in both England and the United States went on for some time to describe goodwill as an appendage of real property, particularly the place of business.[70] This tangibility, however, faded toward the end of the century. The Supreme Court's 1893 decision in *Metropolitan Bank v. St. Louis Dispatch Co.* illustrates the shift. Starting with the general position that goodwill "is tangible only as an incident, as connected with a going concern or business having locality or name," the court went on to describe the goodwill of a newspaper company:

> As applied to a newspaper, the good will usually at[t]aches to its name, rather than to the place of publication. The probability of the title continuing to attract custom in the way of circulation and advertising patronage gives a value which may be protected and disposed of, and constitutes property.[71]

The US Court of Appeals for the Second Circuit added in 1897:

> Nor is [goodwill] indissolubly connected with any particular locality, or any specific tangible property. ... If good will be a "parasite," it is a "parasite" of the business from which it sprung, not of the mere machinery by which that business was conducted.[72]

These and similar cases[73] marked the end of a line of decisions that led trademark and unfair competition doctrine to radically detach value

[70] *See, e.g., Appeal of Elliot*, 60 Pa. 161 (1869) ("The good-will of an inn or tavern is local, and does not exist independent of the house in which it is kept."); *Rawson v. Pratt*, 91 Ind. 9, 16 (1883) (" 'Good-will' as property, is intangible, and merely an incident of other property. ... As a rule, it may be said that 'good-will' is never an incident of a stock of merchandise; but, generally speaking, it is an incident of locality or place, of the store-room or place of business."). In addition, *see* the famous debate on the connex between goodwill and business premises in *Commissioners of Inland Revenue v. Muller & Co.'s Margarine, Ltd.* [1901] A.C. 217. For a particularly bloomy (and late) definition, *see Smith v. Davidson*, 198 Ga. 231, 235–236, 31 S.E.2d 477, 479–480 (Ga. 1944) ("It is difficult to conceive of the good will of a business apart from the tangible properties used in such business, or as a thing of form and substance. It is more like a spirit that hovers over the physical, a sort of atmosphere that surrounds the whole; the aroma that springs from the conduct of the business; the favorable hue or reflection which the trade has become accustomed to associate with a particular location or under a certain name. As fragrance may add loveliness to the flower from which it emanates, so good will may add value to the physical from which it springs.").

[71] *Metropolitan Nat. Bank v. St. Louis Dispatch Co.*, 149 U.S. 436, 446 (1893).

[72] *Washburn v. National Wall-Paper Co.*, 81 F. 17, 20 (2nd Cir. 1897). For an approving analysis, *see, e.g.*, Harry D. Nims, *The Law of Unfair Competition and Trade-Marks, with Chapters on Good-Will, Trade Secrets, Defamation of Competitors and Their Goods, Registration of Trade-Marks, Interference with Competitors' Business, etc., vol. I* § 13, at 77 (4th edn., 1947).

[73] *See also Brett v. Ebel*, 29 A.D. 256, 51 N.Y.S. 573 (App. Div. 1898) (sale of goodwill without business); *Woodward v. Lazar*, 21 Cal. 448, 82 Am.Dec. 751 (1863). *See also* Comment, *The Nature of Business Goodwill*, 16 Harv. L. Rev. 135, 135 (1902) ("Thus the goodwill of a public house, instead of being incident to the premises alone, attaches to the name by which they are known."). More generally, and with numerous references to case

protection from both tangible business assets and personality. In this regard, the US conception of business goodwill (unlike the static understanding in contemporary German doctrine) evidenced a genuinely economic analysis. Goodwill was, as J. Roberton Christie explained in 1896, "the aggregate advantages arising from the business connection, reputation, and favourable situation of an established trading concern."[74] Customer relations and the public's favorable regard became the central aspect.[75] More concretely, it was the likelihood that customers would repeatedly return to a business or product that was seen as determinative.[76] English doctrine later came to characterize this phenomenon as "dog" goodwill, because dogs (unlike cats) are loyal to their owners.[77] In the United States, the same was expressed by reference to a "probable expectancy" of attracting the consuming public.[78] Ultimately, it was the information capital accumulated by performance and advertising investment in the marketplace that accounted for the scope of goodwill.[79]

law, *see* Harry D. Nims, *The Law of Unfair Competition and Trade-Marks, with Chapters on Good-Will, Trade Secrets, Defamation of Competitors and Their Goods, Registration of Trade-Marks, Interference with Competitors' Business, etc., vol. I* § 13, at 74 (4th edn., 1947) ("These [older] definitions seem to confine good-will to a locality. As early as 1859, however, the courts began to make it clear that good-will as they conceived it did not necessarily involve locality." (reference to *Churton v. Douglas* [1859] 28 L.J. Ch. 841–845)).

74 J. Roberton Christie, *Goodwill in Business*, 8 Jurid. Rev. 71, 71 (1896).

75 *See, e.g.*, C. J. Foreman, *Conflicting Theories of Good Will*, 22 Colum. L. Rev. 638, 638 (1922) ("To orthodox economists, consumers' good will is the favorable attitude of the persons with whom the entrepreneur has trade relations. It is above all a state of mind which is, indeed, frequently a direct result of these relations."). *See also* Thorstein Veblen, *The Theory of Business Enterprise* 126, 169 *et seq.* (1904); John A. Hobson, *The Evolution of Modern Capitalism—A Study of Machine Production* 246 (1913); John R. Commons, *Industrial Goodwill* 17 *et seq.* (1919).

76 *See, e.g., Dodge Stationery Co. v. Dodge*, 145 Cal. 380, 388, 78 P. 879, 882 (1904), and Norman F. Hesseltine, *A Digest of the Law of Trade-Marks and Unfair Trade* 90 *et seq.* (1906) (with further references).

77 *See Whiteman Smith Motor Co., Limited v. Chaplin* [1934] 2 K.B. 35, 42 ("The cat represents that part of the customers who continue to go to the old shop, though the old shopkeeper has gone; .... The dog represents that part of the customers who follow the person rather than the place; these the tenant may take away with him if he does not go too far."). *See also* Christopher Wadlow, *The Law of Passing-Off—Unfair Competition by Misrepresentation* para. 3–016 (4th edn., 2011).

78 *See* Frank I. Schechter, *The Historical Foundations of the Law Relating to Trade-Marks* 157 (1925) ("A trade-mark is a most important creative and also sustaining factor of that 'probable expectancy'."); *see also* Frank I. Schechter, *The Rational Basis of Trademark Protection*, 40 Harv. L. Rev. 813, 822 (1927) ("[C]reation and retention of custom, rather than the designation of source, is the primary purpose of the trademark today."); Edward S. Rogers, *The Lanham Act and the Social Function of Trade-Marks*, 14 Law & Contemp. Probs. 173, 176 (1949) ("Good will is trade expectancy. It is what makes tomorrow's business more than an accident.").

79 Frank S. Moore put this eloquently in *Legal Protection of Goodwill—Trade-Marks, Trade Emblems, Advertising, Unfair Competition* 7 (1936) ("Courtesy, care, service, honesty, fair

We can thus conclude that, over time, the American conception of trademark goodwill grew less attached to productive resources and more attached to the marketplace. The customer became the ultimate reference point. Quite differently, German legal doctrine at the time still adhered to a static concept of owner-centered rights protection. There, neither trademark nor unfair competition law were ever fully emancipated from personality rights protection.[80] Part of this distinction between German and US trademark doctrine has endured until today. As we will see in the following, it was the peculiar transformation of goodwill into a subject matter of market relations that particularly influenced the formation of US conflicts law.[81]

B The Reverse Picture: Trade-Diversion Prevention

While, formally speaking, the trademark right was always at the center of the plaintiff's claim, the real object of protection was the business's goodwill against invasion. The trademark as such was rarely characterized as the property right itself; indeed, in 1879, the Supreme Court clarified that words or symbols could not be the object of protection.[82] As

dealing, merit of goods create good reports which travel far and wide and continually tend to draw new customers to their source."). This understanding of goodwill has also gained hold in modern doctrine. *See, e.g.*, Frederick W. Mostert, *Well-Known and Famous Marks: Is Harmony Possible in the Global Village?*, 86 Trademark Rep. 103, 140 (1996) ("No longer can physical locality be considered as one of the most important and visible factors to establish good will. Contemporary consumers do not concern themselves with the site of the manufacturing plant or the actual location of the headquarters of the trademark owner. They are more interested in the continuous level of quality symbolized by internationally well-known or famous marks.").

80 *See supra* p. 27 *et seq.* 81 *See infra* p. 129 *et seq.* and p. 164 *et seq.*

82 *See In re Trade-Mark Cases*, 100 U.S. 82, 94 (1879) ("The trade-mark may be, and generally is, the adoption of something already in existence as the distinctive symbol of the party using it. At common law the exclusive right to it grows out of its use, and not its mere adoption. By the act of Congress this exclusive right attaches upon registration. But in neither case does it depend upon novelty, invention, discovery, or any work of the brain. It requires no fancy or imagination, no genius, no laborious thought. It is simply founded on priority of appropriation. ... If the symbol, however plain, simple, old, or well-known, has been first appropriated by the claimant as his distinctive trade-mark, he may by registration secure the right to its exclusive use."). For earlier case law, *see Leather Cloth Co. Ltd. v. American Leather Cloth Co. Ltd.* [1863] 4 De G.J. & S. 137, 46 E.R. 868, 870 ("It is correct to say that there is no exclusive ownership of the symbols which constitute a trade mark apart from the use or application of them; but the word 'trade mark' is the designation of these marks or symbols as and when applied to a vendible commodity, and the exclusive right to make such user [*sic*] or application is rightly called property."); *see also Hilson Co. v. Foster*, 80 F. 896, 897 (C.C.S.D.N.Y. 1897); *Hanover Star Milling Co. v. Metcalf*, 240 U.S. 403, 412—413 (1916); *Rosenberg Bros. & Co. v. Elliott*, 7 F.2d 962, 965 (3rd Cir. 1925). For scholarly commentary, *see* Edward S. Rogers, *Comments on the Modern Law of Unfair Trade*, 3 Ill. L. Rev. 551, 555 (1909); Frank S. Moore, *Legal Protection of Goodwill—Trade-Marks, Trade Emblems, Advertising, Unfair Competition* 9 (1936) ("It is his goodwill, and not his trade-marks, trade-names, or

Edward S. Rogers explained in 1909, "Each [tort] is a trespass upon business goodwill,"[83] and "every trader has a property in the good will of his business, that he has the right to the exclusive benefit of this good will."[84] At stake in both trademark and unfair competition disputes, therefore, was an injury to the plaintiff's business relations. In practice, actionable goodwill invasion was most conveniently found in cases of stealing customers, attracting patronage, or diverting trade. Indeed, court rulings regularly indicated that even the potential to divert trade was sufficient. For instance, in the 1845 case *Coats v. Holbrook, Nelson & Co.*, the New York Court of Chancery enjoined product imitation by a competitor, providing the following explanation:

> A man . . . has no right, and he will not be allowed, to use the names, letters, marks, or other symbols, by which he may palm off upon buyers as the manufactures of another the articles he is selling, and thereby attract to himself the patronage that without such deception, use of such names, &c., would have enured to the benefit of that other person who first got up, or was alone accustomed to use such names, marks, letters or symbols.[85]

Around the same time, in the 1849 case *Amoskeag Manufacturing Co. v. Spear*, another New York court said:

> He who affixes to his own goods an imitation of an original trade-mark, by which those of another are distinguished and known, seeks, by deceiving the public, to divert and appropriate to his own use the profits to which the superior skill and enterprise of the other had given him a prior and exclusive title. . . . [T]he owner is robbed of the fruits of the reputation that he had successfully labored to earn.[86]

other identifying devices associated with it standing by themselves, which is property recognized by law."); Harry D. Nims, *The Law of Unfair Competition and Trade-Marks, with Chapters on Good-Will, Trade Secrets, Defamation of Competitors and Their Goods, Registration of Trade-Marks, Interference with Competitors' Business, etc., vol. I* § 198a, at 530 *et seq.* (4th edn., 1947).

83 *See, e.g.*, Edward S. Rogers, *Comments on the Modern Law of Unfair Trade*, 3 Ill. L. Rev. 551, 553 (1909).

84 *Id.* at 555–556.

85 *Coats v. Holbrook, Nelson & Co.*, 3 N.Y. Leg. Obs. 404, 405, 2 Sandf. Ch. 586, 594, 7 N. Y. Ch. Ann. 713 (N.Y. Ch. 1845). Two years later, in *Partridge v. Menck*, the same court explained the diversion of trade through the use of a foreign trademark as "attempts to pirate upon the good will of the complainant's friends, or customers, or of the patrons of his trade or business" (*Partridge v. Menck*, 5 N.Y. Leg. Obs. 94, 2 Barb. Ch.101, 5 N.Y. Ch. Ann. 572 (N.Y. Ch. 1847)). *See also Cohen v. Nagle*, 190 Mass. 4, 8–9, 76 N.E. 276, 278 (1906).

86 *Amoskeag Mfg. Co. v. Spear*, 2 Sandf. 599, 605–606 (N.Y. Sup. Ct. 1849). Similarly, in 1868, the court in *Boardman v. Meriden Britannia Co.* explained that "the violation of property in trade-marks works a two fold injury; the appropriator suffers, in failing to receive that remuneration for his labors to which he is justly entitled, and the public in being deceived, and induced to purchase articles manufactured by one man, under the belief that they are the production of another" (*Boardman v. Meriden Britannia Co.*, 35 Conn. 402, 414 (1868)).

Numerous examples can be found in subsequent case law.[87] In addition, scholarly commentaries identified trade diversion as an indicator of illegitimately caused injury or harm. A particularly instructive explanation can be found in Hopkins's 1905 edition of *The Law of Trademarks, Tradenames, and Unfair Competition*:

> Unfair competition consists in passing off one's goods as the goods of another, or in otherwise securing patronage that should go to another, by false representations that lead the patron to believe that he is patronizing the other person. ... It is apparent that the simplest means of depriving another of the trade he has built up is to copy the marks he places on his merchandise. This is the easiest method of stealing his trade, and most universal because of the general use of marks or brands upon personal property. The use of such marks runs far back into the shadows of history .... It is only natural that these marks used in trade, or trademarks, should have first become the subjects of judicial consideration, and that the law concerning them should have reached a state of comparatively complete development before infringers began to employ other and more obscure means to divert trade.[88]

Among the most prominent twentieth-century decisions concerning the question of whether early trademark doctrine sought to protect consumers against fraud and deception is the Seventh Circuit's 1912 case *Borden Ice Cream Co. v. Borden's Condensed Milk Co.* As is commonly known, the court rejected a theory of consumer protection. Its reasoning, however, also illustrates the dominant perception of trade diversion at the time:

> It has been said that the universal test question in cases of this class is whether the public is likely to be deceived as to the maker or seller of the goods. This, in our opinion, is not the fundamental question. The deception of the public naturally tends to injure the proprietor of a business by diverting his customers and depriving him of sales which otherwise he might have made. This, rather than the protection of the public against imposition, is the sound and true basis for the private remedy.[89]

[87] *See, e.g., American Waltham Watch Co. v. United States Watch Co.*, 173 Mass. 85, 87, 53 N.E. 141, 142 (1899) ("It is desirable that the plaintiff should not lose custom by reason of the public mistaking another manufacturer for it. ... [T]he plaintiff, merely on the strength of having been first in the field, may put later comers to the trouble of taking such reasonable precautions as are commercially practicable to prevent their lawful names and advertisements from deceitfully diverting the plaintiff's custom."); *Draper v. Skerrett*, 116 F. 206, 209 (C.C.E.D. Pa. 1902) ("But it is nevertheless true that even without any strict proprietary interest, as a trade-mark, in the terms employed, a party is entitled to protection against the unfair use of them by another in the effort to take away the trade or custom which he has built up.").

[88] James Love Hopkins, *The Law of Trademarks, Tradenames and Unfair Competition* § 1, at 1–2 (2nd edn., 1905).

[89] *Borden Ice Cream Co v. Borden's Condensed Milk Co*, 201 F. 510, 513 (7th Cir. 1912). For a critical analysis, *see* Walter J. Derenberg, *The Influence of the French Code Civil on the Modern Law of Unfair Competition*, 4 Am. J. Comp. L. 1, 18 *et seq.* (1955).

Frank I. Schechter summarized the relevance of trade diversion in his 1927 analysis of English and US unfair competition and trademark law: "'The diversion of custom' is the gravamen of the action in either 'passing off' or 'unfair competition.'"[90]

As this summary reveals, trade diversion constituted an essential element of common law doctrine—and it became particularly determinative with regard to the localization of infringements in conflicts law. This is another striking difference from German doctrine, in which the place of conduct or the victim-competitor's place of business determined the applicable law.[91] Seen in this light, it becomes evident that German doctrine prior to the 1960s was virtually devoid of the considerations that American courts and scholars had undertaken much earlier. Localization of the customer base and the place where "lost transactions" would occur were of secondary concern at best. In the United States, by contrast, the marketplace became the governing paradigm in 1916, with the Supreme Court's introduction of a new doctrine on the geographical scope of trademark rights.

C *Tea Rose/Rectanus*: The Doctrine of Market-Based Rights

Indeed, the Supreme Court's *Tea Rose/Rectanus* doctrine marked the turning point for common law trademark rights' geographical protection. With a doctrinal shift, the court (in two decisions of 1916 and 1918[92]) ultimately curbed the extension of trademark rights, which had for a long time been interpreted as virtually unlimited. *Tea Rose/Rectanus*, though not inventing a completely new rule, provided the foundation for the modern concept of immediately market-based rights. The Supreme Court's majority opinion pointed out the "fundamental error of supposing that a trade-mark right is a right in gross or at large" and stated that "[t]here is no such thing as property in a trade-mark except as a right appurtenant to an established business or trade in connection with which the mark is employed."[93] The following discussion illustrates how the court deconstructed contemporary substantive law. The international effects of *Tea Rose/Rectanus* will be addressed later.[94]

Hanover Star centered on a dispute over the "Tea Rose" trademark. This trademark had been used by three parties, each of which claimed

[90] Frank I. Schechter, *The Rational Basis of Trademark Protection*, 40 Harv. L. Rev. 813, 820–821 (1927).

[91] *See supra* p. 32 *et seq.*

[92] *Hanover Star Milling Co. v. Metcalf*, 240 U.S. 403 (1916); *United Drug Co. v. Theodore Rectanus Co.*, 248 U.S. 90 (1918). For an explanation of how the term "Tea Rose/ Rectanus" came to denote the doctrine, *see, e.g.*, William Jay Gross, *The Territorial Scope of Trademark Rights*, 44 U. Miami L. Rev. 1075, 1083 (1990).

[93] *United Drug Co. v. Theodore Rectanus Co.*, 248 U.S. 90, 98 (1918).

[94] *See infra* p. 159 *et seq.*

exclusive rights. The dispute resulted in two lawsuits, one in Alabama and one in Illinois.[95] The facts of the case are complex, but a short illustration suffices here. Essential to note is the fact that the parties' areas of trademark use never overlapped geographically. In addition, the second-comer's use of the trademark was coincidental, not in bad faith.[96] The first party, Allen & Wheeler Co., had started manufacturing flour under the "Tea Rose" trademark in Ohio in 1872. The company was able to demonstrate significant sales under this trademark only north of the Ohio River, not in the southern states of Georgia, Florida, Alabama, or Mississippi. The second party, Hanover Star Milling, had adopted a similar trademark—"Tea Rose"—in good faith in 1885 and was extensively advertising and marketing its flour under this trademark in Alabama and other southern states, particularly Florida and Georgia. The third party, Metcalf, was a retail seller of flour in Alabama that was produced by another party, yet also marketed under an identical "Tea Rose" trademark. Allen & Wheeler alleged trademark infringement against Hanover. The latter sued Metcalf for trademark infringement and unfair competition. Metcalf, inter alia, contested Hanover's allegedly exclusive rights by reference to a prior use by Allen & Wheeler. The Supreme Court granted *certiorari*, and Hanover prevailed in both disputes.

The majority opinion, which began with the finding that neither party had a registered trademark, started its analysis on the basis of general common law: "Nor does it appear that in any of the states in question there exists any peculiar local rule, arising from statute or decision. Hence, the cases must be decided according to common law principles of general application."[97] Under the principles of federal common law, the court repeated its prior characterization of trademarks as property rights.[98] At the same time, it limited the scope of protection by reference to the trade and market relevance of trademark functions:

> [I]t is plain that in denying the right of property in a trademark it was intended only to deny such property right except as appurtenant to an established business or trade in connection with which the mark is used. ... In short, the trademark is treated as merely a protection for the good will, and not the subject of property except in connection with an existing business. ...[99]

[95] *Metcalf v. Hanover Star Milling Co.*, 204 F. 211 (5th Cir. 1913); *Hanover Star Milling Co. v. Allen & Wheeler Co.*, 208 F. 513 (7th Cir. 1913).

[96] For a concise summary and a map illustration on the case, *see* 5 J. Thomas McCarthy, *McCarthy on Trademarks and Unfair Competition* § 26:2 (4th edn., 2016).

[97] *Hanover Star Milling Co. v. Metcalf*, 240 U.S. 403, 411 (1916).

[98] For a discussion of *Erie*'s incorporation into trademark and unfair competition doctrine, *see infra* p. 134 *et seq*.

[99] *Hanover Star Milling Co. v. Metcalf*, 240 U.S. 403, 414 (1916).

> That property in a trademark is not limited in its enjoyment by territorial bounds, but may be asserted and protected wherever the law affords a remedy for wrongs, is true in a limited sense. Into whatever markets the use of a trademark has extended, or its meaning has become known, there will the manufacturer or trader whose trade is pirated by an infringing use be entitled to protection and redress. But this is not to say that the proprietor of a trademark, good in the markets where it has been employed, can monopolize markets that his trade has never reached, and where the mark signifies not his goods, but those of another. We agree with the court below ... that "since it is the trade, and not the mark, that is to be protected, a trademark acknowledges no territorial boundaries of municipalities or states or nations, but extends to every market where the trader's goods have become known and identified by his use of the mark. But the mark, of itself, cannot travel to markets where there is no article to wear the badge and no trader to offer the article."[100]

In the end, the majority rejected the interpretation that territorially unlimited trademark protection had been established under *Kidd v. Johnson* and *Derringer v. Plate.*[101] The geographical area of a trademark's protection could never exceed the reach of the trade in which the mark was used.[102] At this point, I will not address the question of whether the majority denied the relevance of political borders.[103] Important here is that the new doctrine was tangibly market oriented. Trade and commerce were to determine the scope of the market—goodwill would be deemed to extend only so far.

In *United Drug Co. v. Theodore Rectanus Co.*,[104] the other half of the *Tea Rose/Rectanus* doctrine, the trademark "Rex" was used by Ellen Regis, a Massachusetts resident, for medicine starting in 1877. The business was continued locally as a partnership with her son, and the trademark was recorded. In 1911, United Drug purchased the company with all trademark rights. Meanwhile, around 1883, Kentucky druggist Theodore Rectanus started using, in good faith, the same trademark for medicinal preparations. His use was limited to the city of Louisville and its vicinity; the same was true for the respondent purchaser who later acquired Rectanus's business in 1906. United Drug did not sell the first "Rex" products in Louisville until 1912. In its decision, the Supreme Court rejected a theory of trademark infringement, particularly the contention that a business owner having started trademark use in one place would be

[100] *Id.* at 415–416.
[101] *Id.* at 416–417 and 418. For the *Kidd/Derringer* doctrine, *see supra* p. 90 *et seq.*
[102] *Hanover Star Milling Co. v. Metcalf*, 240 U.S. 403, 417 (1916).
[103] *See infra* p. 129 *et seq.*
[104] *United Drug Co. v. Theodore Rectanus Co.*, 248 U.S. 90 (1918).

protected against second-comers if she subsequently decided to extend her trade:

> The asserted doctrine is based upon the fundamental error of supposing that a trade-mark right is a right in gross or at large, like a statutory copyright or a patent for an invention, to either of which, in truth, it has little or no analogy. . . . There is no such thing as property in a trade-mark except as a right appurtenant to an established business or trade in connection with which the mark is employed. The law of trade-marks is but a part of the broader law of unfair competition; the right to a particular mark grows out of its use, not its mere adoption; its function is simply to designate the goods as the product of a particular trader and to protect his good will against the sale of another's product as his; and it is not the subject of property except in connection with an existing business.[105]

The court—once again—rejected the idea of trademark rights' extension beyond the actual marketplace:

> It results that the adoption of a trade-mark does not, at least in the absence of some valid legislation enacted for the purpose, project the right of protection in advance of the extension of the trade, or operate as a claim of territorial rights over areas into which it thereafter may be deemed desirable to extend the trade. And the expression, sometimes met with, that a trade-mark right is not limited in its enjoyment by territorial bounds, is true only in the sense that wherever the trade goes, attended by the use of the mark, the right of the trader to be protected against the sale by others of their wares in the place of his wares will be sustained.[106]

Of course, the Supreme Court did not completely jettison the paradigm of absolute property rights in trademarks. As Kenneth J. Vandevelde has pointed out, the *Hanover Star* majority still preserved a potentially absolute and unlimited concept through a flexible application of the estoppel doctrine: a first user could not claim trademark rights in a geographical area where she had failed to extend her commercial activity; the formal ground for rights limitation here was abandonment.[107] This juggling with formal doctrine, however, did not mean that the conception of rights' extension and scope of protection had remained unaltered. Even though the Supreme Court literally upheld the idea of trademark property, the paradigm had gained a qualitatively different foundation. The court rejected the absolute extension of trademark rights as an end in itself.

[105] *Id.* at 101. [106] *Id.* at 98.

[107] *See* Kenneth J. Vandevelde, *The New Property of the Nineteenth Century: The Development of the Modern Concept of Property*, 29 Buff. L. Rev. 325, 346–347 (1980). For the court's argument, *see Hanover Star Milling Co. v. Metcalf*, 240 U.S. 403, 419 (1916) ("[N]o clearer evidence of abandonment by nonuser of trademark rights in the latter field could reasonably be asked for."). For a discussion of the estoppel doctrine in *United Drug*, *see* Walter J. Derenberg, *Warenzeichen und Wettbewerb in den Vereinigten Staaten von Amerika* 209 (1931).

Protectable subject matter was limited to what could be found within the marketplace; protection was "coterminous with the market actually covered."[108] In the wake of the *Tea Rose* and *Rectanus* judgments, courts no longer adjudicated on conflicts between abstract rights but instead began to separate different markets.[109]

The paradigm of a market/rights correlation is part of a bigger picture. A similar trend has actually been identified regarding the contemporary extension of rights into markets for unrelated goods. Shortly after the turn of the century, courts had also begun to extend trademark protection to separate product markets under a theory that would become known as the *Aunt Jemima* doctrine.[110] In short, this doctrine provided that if there was a likelihood that consumers might be confused about the source of a product, a trademark owner could protect even unexplored markets. As Steven Wilf has pointed out, both *Aunt Jemima* and *Tea Rose/Rectanus* reflect the conquest for consumers' minds.[111] Under both doctrines, the consumer is the cynosure of market allocation and the delimitation of rights.

Under this perspective, it also becomes clear that *Tea Rose/Rectanus* reflects a natural law approach. Earlier common law trademark doctrine had regularly made reference to a theory of natural rights protection, similar to the creation of copyrighted works. As *Blackstone's Commentaries* stated in 1884, the "right to the exclusive use of distinctive trade marks" was "somewhat analogous to literary copyright" for one

108 John P. Bullington, *Trade-Names and Trade-Marks—Territorial Extent of the Right Acquired*, 3 Tex. L. Rev. 300, 301 (1924) (with further references to state and federal court decisions); Irvin H. Fathchild, *Territoriality of Registered Trade-Marks*, 3 Idaho L.J. 193, 193 (1933).

109 For a list of cases (by circuit) following the *Tea Rose/Rectanus* rule, *see* 5 J. Thomas McCarthy, *McCarthy on Trademarks and Unfair Competition* § 26:4 (4th edn., 2016); *see also* Restatement (Third) of Unfair Competition § 19 (1995), comment.

110 *See Aunt Jemima Mills Co. v. Rigney & Co.*, 247 F. 407 (2nd Cir. 1917). For an analysis of the courts' shift from a concept of trademark conflicts within abstract markets to a conquest of the consumers' minds, *see* Steven Wilf, *The Making of the Post-War Paradigm in American Intellectual Property Law*, 31 Colum. J. L. & Arts 139, 157–158 (2008). For a discussion of the *Aunt Jemima* doctrine's extension into statutory and common law, *see, e.g.*, Robert N. Klieger, *Trademark Dilution: The Whittling Away of the Rational Basis for Trademark Protection*, 58 U. Pitt. L. Rev. 789, 797, 807 *et seq.* (1997).

111 *See* Steven Wilf, *The Making of the Post-War Paradigm in American Intellectual Property Law*, 31 Colum. J.L. & Arts 139, 156–158 (2008); Frank S. Moore, *Legal Protection of Goodwill—Trade-Marks, Trade Emblems, Advertising, Unfair Competition* 7 (1936) ("Goodwill can only exist as a result of impressions made upon the brains of customers and possible customers, and such impressions can be made only through the senses of sight, hearing, smell, taste, and touch."). For a discussion of the consumers' minds' occupation by brands and a terminology of "neural territory," *see* Rebecca Tushnet, *Gone in Sixty Milliseconds: Trademark Law and Cognitive Science*, 86 Tex. L. Rev. 507, 516–517 (2008).

reason: similar to literary property, the right to the exclusive use of a trademark was deemed to flow from a natural right to appropriate the fruits of one's own labor.[112] But it was not an act of creation per se that would promulgate the protectable *res*. Copyrights and patents were (and still are) protected as products of the mind. Common law trademarks, by contrast, were and are protected for their distinguishing function alone, a value that must flow and result from their actual use in the marketplace.[113] Therefore, the creation of trademark rights in a Lockean sense was not a singular act but rather the constant flow of marketing activities. Accordingly, the relevant "fruit of labor" in trademark terms was market investment (under the shorthand of "goodwill").[114] The trademark had become an instrument for securing its owner the benefit of her efforts within the marketplace.[115]

[112] *See* William Blackstone & Thomas M. Cooley, *Commentaries of the Laws of England in Four Books, vol. I* 404 n.7 (3rd edn., 1884); *see also* Grafton Dulany Cushing, *On Certain Cases Analogous to Trade-Marks*, 4 Harv. L. Rev. 321, 322–323 (1890) ("What it is important to recognize is this: That the foundation of the law of trade-marks is natural justice, or, as it is called, the principles of equity"); on the occupancy doctrine, *see also* Stephen L. Carter, *The Trouble with Trademark*, 99 Yale L.J. 759, 762 n. 9 (1990).

[113] For more on the distinction, *see, e.g., In re Trade-Mark Cases*, 100 U.S. 82, 94 (1879) ("The ordinary trade-mark has no necessary relation to invention or discovery. The trade-mark recognized by the common law is generally the growth of a considerable period of use, rather than a sudden invention. It is often the result of accident rather than design, and when under the act of Congress it is sought to establish it by registration, neither originality, invention, discovery, science, nor art is in any way essential to the right conferred by that act."); *see also* Stephen L. Carter, *Does It Matter Whether Intellectual Property Is Property?*, 68 Chi.-Kent L. Rev. 715, 720 (1993).

[114] *See, e.g., Avery & Sons v. Meikle & Co.*, 81 Ky. 73, 86–87 (1883) ("When a workman or manufacturer has, by skill, care, and fidelity, manufactured a good article, it becomes of the utmost importance to him that its origin and ownership should be known, and the law points out to him what means and how he may appropriate them to indicate this important fact, and when he adopts and uses [a mark to indicate origin], and his reputation is thereby built up, it is to him the most valuable of property rights. Sound policy, which dictates the protection of the public from imposition, the security of the fruits of labor to the laborer, the encouragement of skillful industry, and, above everything, the inculcation of truth and honor in the conduct of trade and commerce … demands that such a reputation so gained should be free from the grasp of piracy."). *See also Wolfe v. Barnett & Lion*, 24 La. Ann. 97, 99, 13 Am. Rep. 111 (1872) (referring to *Upton* on Trade Marks and his formulation as "the true rule" to be "[t]hat the honest, skillful and industrious manufacturer or enterprising merchant who has produced or brought into the market an article of use or consumption, that has found favor with the public, and who, by affixing to it some name, mark, device, or symbol, … shall receive the first reward of his honesty, skill, industry or enterprise; and shall in no manner and to no extent be deprived of the same by another."); *Lawrence Mfg. Co. v. Tennessee Mfg. Co.*, 138 U.S. 537, 546 (1891) (explaining a "just right" in the "custom and advantages" for the first appropriator due to her "enterprise and skill").

[115] *Boardman v. Meriden Britannia Co.*, 35 Conn. 402, 413–414 (1868) ("The object or purpose of the law in protecting trade-marks as property, is two fold; first, to secure to him who has been instrumental in bringing into market a superior article of merchandise, the fruit of his industry and skill; second, to protect the community from imposition, and furnish some guaranty that an article, purchased as the manufacture of one

Finally, under this perspective, it is also clear that the Supreme Court's doctrine of marketplace/rights correlation reflects the Lockean no-harm principle. By definition, the principle contradicted unlimited rights extension. When an individual had appropriated an object from the public domain through labor, it was clear that she was not to be deprived of it.[116] Anyone could acquire property through labor, but acquisition was limited by the public's claims in the commons—in other words, property could be acquired only as long as there was "enough, and as good left in common for others."[117] In this regard, the universal acquisition of trademark rights by simple use in one part of the state or national territory was questionable. *Tea Rose/Rectanus* implemented this concept of not taking more than necessary. According to Locke, "God [had given] the world ... to the use of the industrious and rational ...; not to the fancy or covetousness of the quarrelsome and contentious."[118] But even the industrious and rational had to respect some limitations:

> For as a man had a right to all he could employ his labour upon, so he had no temptation to labour for more than he could make use of. ... What portion a man carved to himself was easily seen; and it was useless, as well as dishonest, to carve himself too much, or take more than he needed.[119]

This last point is also important with regard to the question of how goodwill could be created and accumulated. By the late nineteenth century, advertising had become a progressively important marketing tool.[120] Theory and practice subsequently came to recognize the connection between goodwill and advertising efforts. Courts and scholars alike agreed that advertising investment, in addition to actual trading in the marketplace, generated goodwill.[121] The New York circuit court's 1897 case *Hilson Co. v. Foster* illustrated this point:

who has appropriated to his own use a certain name, symbol or device as a trade-mark, is genuine.").

116 *See, e.g.*, John Locke, *Two Treatises of Government, vol. V* ch. II, § 6, at 107 (1823); for a general analysis of natural law theory (use and abuse) in intellectual property law, *see* Wendy J. Gordon, *A Property Right in Self-Expression: Equality and Individualism in the Natural Law of Intellectual Property*, 102 Yale L.J. 1533, 1544–1545 (1993).

117 John Locke, *Two Treatises of Government, vol. V* ch. V, § 26, at 116 (1823) ("For this 'labour' being the unquestionable property of the labourer, no man but he can have a right to what that is once joined to, at least where there is enough, and as good left in common for others.").

118 *Id.* at § 34, at 118. 119 *Id.* at § 51, at 126.

120 *See, e.g.*, Steven Wilf, *The Making of the Post-War Paradigm in American Intellectual Property Law*, 31 Colum. J. L. & Arts 139, 160 *et seq.* (2008); *see also* Alfred D. Chandler, Jr., *Scale and Scope—The Dynamics of Industrial Capitalism* 65 (1990).

121 *See, e.g.*, *Chapman v. L.E. Waterman Co.*, 176 A.D. 697, 711, 163 N.Y.S. 1059 (App. Div. 1917) ("A demand created by advertisement belongs to the advertiser."); Frank S.

> Where the goods of a manufacturer have become popular not only because of their intrinsic worth, but also by reason of the ingenious, attractive and persistent manner in which they have been advertised, the good will thus created is entitled to protection. The money invested in advertising is as much a part of the business as if invested in buildings, or machinery, and a rival in business has no more right to use the one than the other.[122]

Mere advertising of a brand—without actual sales—might not have been enough to generate goodwill. But the use requirement for rights acquisition was still low. The branded product only had to be offered with an intention of continued marketing.[123] Hence, advertising could span geographical areas in advance of actual commerce.[124] Even though this model came under pressure with the advent of radio and television advertising, it would coin the doctrine of common law trademark acquisition for decades to come.[125] In particular, conflicts resolution was to be

Moore, *Legal Protection of Goodwill—Trade-Marks, Trade Emblems, Advertising, Unfair Competition* 52 (1936) ("Not only is advertising without doubt one of the most efficient instruments for the building up of commercial goodwill by creating a desire for goods and a belief in the minds of buyers that it will be beneficial to purchase them, but it also may be used as one of the most efficient means for the protection of goodwill.").

122 *Hilson Co. v. Foster*, 80 F. 896, 897 (C.C.S.D.N.Y. 1897). For an approving analysis and further references to contemporary case law, *see* Frank I. Schechter, *The Historical Foundations of the Law Relating to Trade-Marks* 167–168 (1925) (*see* in particular *id.* at 171 (conclusion #4): "The owner of a trade-mark who expends large sums of money in making his mark known to the public as a symbol and guarantee of the excellence of the quality of his product should receive the same protection from the courts for his investment in advertising his trade-mark that he would undoubtedly be entitled to receive for investment in plant or materials."). *See also* Edward S. Rogers, *Some Historical Matter Concerning Trade-Marks*, 9 Mich. L. Rev. 29, 43 (1910) (tracing increasing litigation towards the end of the nineteenth century to the "extended distribution of products [which] in turn is either the cause or the effect of modern advertising," and qualifying the interests involved as "more and more valuable," because "[a] well-known brand, trade mark or label is now-a-days the most valuable asset that a trader can possess"); for a modern analysis, *see, e.g.*, Pamela Walker Laird, *Advertising Progress: American Business and the Rise of Consumer Marketing* 191–196 (1998).

123 *See, e.g.*, William D. Shoemaker, *Trade-Marks—A Treatise on the subject of Trade-Marks with particular reference to the laws relating to registration thereof, vol. I* 114 *et seq.* (1931) (with further references to case law). Notably, use of the trademark on so-called advertising commodities, such as on a trading stamp or in catalogues, would qualify as "merchandise" within the meaning of statutory registration requirements. *See id.* at 123–125.

124 *See, e.g.*, Harry D. Nims, *The Law of Unfair Competition and Trade-Marks, with Chapters on Good-Will, Trade Secrets, Defamation of Competitors and Their Goods, Registration of Trade-Marks, Interference with Competitors' Business, etc., vol. I* § 35a, at 148 *et seq.* (4th edn., 1947).

125 *See, e.g.*, *Adam Hat Stores v. Scherper*, 45 F.Supp. 804, 806 (E.D. Wis. 1942) (challenging *Tea Rose/Rectanus* by reference to the fact that "[t]his rule of law was adopted before the days of extensive national advertising, especially by means of radio."); Harry D. Nims, *The Law of Unfair Competition and Trade-Marks, with Chapters on Good-Will, Trade Secrets, Defamation of Competitors and Their Goods, Registration of Trade-Marks,*

significantly influenced by the idea that goodwill transcended national borders upon advertising.[126]

III The Realist Attack: Much Ado about . . . Quite Little

The end of the nineteenth century was an era of formalism, a time of "mechanical" jurisprudence. In academic fora and courtrooms alike, legal reasoning and decision making were often reduced to a process of deducing mechanical rules from broader principles. The language of the law was paramount, and cases were decided by a rigid adherence to existing precedents—often, as perceived by critics, in the interest of business corporations in their struggle with workers, consumers, or other opposing parties in the market.[127] The theory and practice of trademark-as-property protection provides one example of such formalism. The doctrinal countermovement to formalism was so-called legal realism—or, more figuratively, the "realist attack."[128] Notwithstanding its overall groundbreaking impact on modern legal thought, the realist attack's practical consequences on trademark doctrine were humble. Property terminology may have been rethought. Yet neither the concept of goodwill nor the idea of private rights protection was replaced or reconceptualized. In fact, one might even conclude that some proponents of realism set the stage for a modern repropertization of trademarks.

A The Turn-of-the-Century Crisis

An oft-enunciated example of the formalist/realist debate was the 1918 Supreme Court case *International News Service v. Associated Press.*[129] Daniel M. McClure has aptly characterized the majority's opinion as a "high water mark of formalist conceptualism in trademark-unfair competition law."[130] The court granted the plaintiff a quasi property right to news stories that the plaintiff had written and published and that had been, according to the majority, misappropriated by the defendant, who had rewritten and published the news stories as its own. Particularly famous is their characterization of the defendant's activities as a "reap[ing] where it has not sown, and . . . appropriating to itself the harvest of those who

Interference with Competitors' Business, etc., vol. I § 218b, at 648 *et seq.* (4th edn., 1947) ("Many localities once 'remote' are remote no longer.").

126 *See infra* p. 164 *et seq.*

127 *See, e.g.*, William W. Fisher III, Morton J. Horwitz & Thomas A. Reed, *Introduction*, xi, in *American Legal Realism* (William W. Fisher III et al. eds., 1993).

128 *Id.* at xiii *et seq.*

129 *International News Service v. Associated Press*, 248 U.S. 215, 246 *et seq.* (1918).

130 Daniel M. McClure, *Trademarks and Unfair Competition: A Critical History of Legal Thought*, 69 Trademark Rep. 305, 324 (1979).

have sown."[131] Justices Holmes and Brandeis each wrote dissenting opinions. Holmes's critique has been recited ever since:

> Property, a creation of law, does not arise from value, although exchangeable—a matter of fact. Many exchangeable values may be destroyed intentionally without compensation. Property depends upon exclusion by law from interference.[132]

The open conflict between formalist and realist ideas of "property" in *International News Service* laid the foundation for a modern critique of the classic unfair competition doctrine.[133] It is actually not surprising that the realist attack, among other things, targeted the concept of trademark-as-property protection and the various ideas of what competitor goodwill protection should include. Not only had legal scholars been unable to agree on a uniform, consistent, and comprehensive definition of "trademark property" and "goodwill,"[134] but courts had also been unable to provide for workable standards—and they openly expressed their discontent with the void of theoretical insight and instruction. Indeed, legal thought had not managed to provide a theoretical structure or a practically workable model. An explanation for why certain conduct should be deemed admissible while other instances of business activity should be enjoined was amiss. Not surprisingly, practical outcomes were often unsatisfactorily diverse and imbalanced—while the idea of property rights seemed to overextend protection in some instances, it prevented adequate relief in other cases, even where commercial dishonesty was evident.[135] One example of the courts' self-acknowledged desperation is the 1935 case *Premier-Pabst Corp. v. Elm City Brewing Co.*:

> [S]ome have vaguely suggested that a right to a name may be a part of one's "good will" which is a subject-matter of property from which all others may be excluded. But such an assertion gets us nowhere. For "good will" itself is too loose and uncertain a quantity for aid in definition. As commonly conceived, it is a compound of many factors, and those factors chiefly associated with the concept seem

[131] *International News Service v. Associated Press*, 248 U.S. 215, 239–240 (1918).

[132] *Id.* at 246. For Justice Brandeis's dissenting opinion, *see id.* at 248 *et seq.*

[133] *See* Daniel M. McClure, *Trademarks and Unfair Competition: A Critical History of Legal Thought*, 69 Trademark Rep. 305, 325–326 (1979).

[134] *See* A.S. Biddle, *Good-Will (Part 1)*, 23 Am. L. Reg. 1, 1 (1875) ("There are few subjects in the law which seem to be less thoroughly understood and which have in consequence given rise to more conflicting decisions than that which stands at the head of this article."); Milton Handler & Charles Pickett, *Trade-Marks and Trade Names—An Analysis and Synthesis: II*, 30 Colum. L. Rev. 759, 776 n. 81 (1930). For a general critique, *see, e.g.*, Duncan Kennedy, *Form and Substance in Private Law Adjudication*, 89 Harv. L. Rev. 1685, 1732, 1748 (1976).

[135] *See, e.g.*, Edward S. Rogers, *New Concepts of Unfair Competition Under the Lanham Act*, 38 Trademark Rep. 259, 260 (1948); Daniel M. McClure, *Trademarks and Unfair Competition: A Critical History of Legal Thought*, 69 Trademark Rep. 305, 327 (1979); Doris E. Long, *Unfair Competition and the Lanham Act* 4 (1993).

to have little association with rights in a name. Thus value "as a going concern" is frequently considered as a part of "good will." But such value seems quite distinct from the value attributable to the right to a name. And again, good will is somewhat vaguely considered as the favorable regard of the purchasing public for a particular person, or for goods or services known to the public to emanate from a particular source; a regard founded (usually) on past dealings or reputation and of value in so far as it may be expected to produce further dealings. But good will so construed certainly is not property in any technical sense; for no man can have, either by prescription or contract, such a proprietary right to the favorable regard of the public that he may exclude others therefrom.[136]

Apart from the critique that contemporary formalism was biased toward protecting the corporate haves and disfavoring have-not newcomer and weaker parties, the debate was also seen as illustrating the disciplinary limitations of jurisprudence. With respect to goodwill in particular, the problem was how to "translate" genuinely economic concepts into policies of trademark and unfair competition law. In light of the complexity of real-world market transactions and inter-competitor and consumer-competitor relations, however, the goodwill paradigm was increasingly unmasked as being too unstructured and indeterminate. In other words, the spheres of marketplace economics and of legal doctrine were too far apart to allow for a smooth osmosis of ideas and concepts. As Christie's 1896 critique of "goodwill" highlighted, "The term was originally one of the market-place rather than of the law courts."[137] Accordingly, it seemed that the concept's time had expired. Indeed, during the first decades of the twentieth century, the classic doctrine of unfair competition had evolved into one of the realist's favorite *bête noires*.

B Courts' Adherence to "Transcendental Nonsense"

Arguably, the most prominent critique of formalism came from Felix S. Cohen. His iconic 1935 *Columbia Law Review* article, "Transcendental Nonsense and the Functional Approach,"[138] became world-famous for its cynical account of legal doctrine at the time. Mocking legal formalism and categorization as transcendental nonsense, Cohen described such

[136] *Premier-Pabst Corp. v. Elm City Brewing Co.*, 9 F.Supp. 754, 757 (D.C. Conn. 1935).

[137] J. Roberton Christie, *Goodwill in Business*, 8 Jurid. Rev. 71, 71 (1896). *See also* C. J. Foreman, *Conflicting Theories of Good Will*, 22 Colum. L. Rev. 638, 638 (1922) ("[T]he usual definitions of good will given in the textbooks on economics are almost entirely out of harmony with those contained in the law."). For a discussion of the lack of "official declarations of policy," *see, e.g.*, Bartholomew Diggins, *Federal and State Regulation of Trade-Marks*, 14 Law & Contemp. Probs. 200, 200 (1949). *See also* Frank I. Schechter, *The Historical Foundations of the Law Relating to Trade-Marks* 160 (1925).

[138] Felix S. Cohen, *Transcendental Nonsense and the Functional Approach*, 35 Colum. L. Rev. 809 (1935).

legal reasoning—especially that regarding trade-name protection—as devoid of a true policy foundation.

His critique started with an explanation of common myths and metaphors employed in traditional jurisprudence in order to masquerade the social forces that were actually molding the law and shaping the outcome of interest conflicts.[139] As he pointed out, contemporary doctrine's foundation on self-contained definitions and rules created a system of adjudication isolated from social reality. Per se, the justification and critique of legal rules in purely legal terms meant arguing in a vicious circle.[140] As he further illustrated, again referring to the historical development of trademark-as-property protection, courts and scholarship focused on the protection of intangible values, which ultimately resulted in a "divorce of legal reasoning from questions of social fact and ethical value."[141] In particular, he attacked the shift from passing-off theory and from the concept of preventing deception to a system of property protection. In this regard, he specified the "thingification" of property as the primary evil that circular reasoning had created.[142] In the end, the propertization of consumer responsiveness had become an instrument for creating and distributing a "new source of economic wealth or power." In short, property had become a perverted function of inequality.[143]

Cohen's critique not only alluded to the general "monopoly phobia" of the 1930s[144] but also demanded a new understanding of policies concerning marketplace and competition regulation. Clearly, a simple balancing of interests was inadequate. Cases of trade diversion by confusion and the large array of other scenarios of improper misappropriation would no longer fit under the same umbrella of property protection, prevention of unfairness, and trespass. The maze of "economic prejudice masquerading in the cloak of legal logic," as Cohen suggested, could be lifted only by a clear analysis of socioeconomic factors. The long-perceived homogeneity of policies—traditionally pushed into the catch-all concept of goodwill—was gone:

> The prejudice that identifies the interests of the plaintiff in unfair competition cases with the interests of business and identifies the interests of business with the interests of society, will not be critically examined by courts and legal scholars until it is recognized and formulated.[145]

Yet, as seen above, despite the fact that this realist critique was compelling and pointed, it did not lead to a sustainable modification of trademark

[139] *Id.* at 812. [140] *Id.* at 814. [141] *Id.* at 814. [142] *Id.* at 815. [143] *Id.* at 816.
[144] More on the monopoly phobia, *see infra* p. 121–123.
[145] Felix S. Cohen, *Transcendental Nonsense and the Functional Approach*, 35 Colum. L. Rev. 809, 817 (1935).

doctrine. By contrast, it appears as if realism ultimately contributed to an ever-deeper implementation of propertization tendencies. A look at case law from the beginning of the nineteenth century sheds some light on this development.

Notwithstanding the growing distrust of formalities, and regardless of the realist acid, courts and scholars continued to rely on the concept of goodwill and property rights protection. The eradication of meaningless concepts that Cohen strived for was never achieved.[146] Thus, even today, the concept of goodwill protection remains central to trademark and unfair competition doctrine, and a clear definition of confusion prevention is rarely sought after. Even though critical scholarship identified policies that courts should take into account, legal practice continued to adjudicate on the basis of traditional structures. A look at part of what became known as the so-called Holmes/Hand doctrine of the qualified nature of trademarks illustrates the meandering between modern policy analysis and traditional goodwill protection.[147]

Until the 1930s, decisions authored by Justice Holmes and Learned Hand served as major precedents for federal and state courts throughout the United States.[148] I have already alluded to Learned Hand's famous allegory of "the whole Law and the Prophets on the subject" in *Yale Elec. Corp. v. Robertson.*[149] As he explained, "The law of unfair trade comes down . . . to . . . that one merchant shall not divert customers from another by representing what he sells as emanating from the second."[150] Hand never accorded significant weight to an understanding of trademark or unfair competition law in terms of property protection. On the contrary, in subsequent cases, he stated that a trademark "never really gives any property in the words themselves" and that "[a] trade-mark is not property in the ordinary sense but only a word or symbol indicating the origin

[146] Daniel M. McClure, *Trademarks and Unfair Competition: A Critical History of Legal Thought*, 69 Trademark Rep. 305, 329 (1979). For the jettisoning of critical concepts of formalism, *see* Felix S. Cohen, *Transcendental Nonsense and the Functional Approach*, 35 Colum. L. Rev. 809, 823 (1935) ("Any word that cannot pay up in the currency of fact, upon demand, is to be declared bankrupt, and we are to have no further dealings with it.").

[147] For details, *see* Rudolf Callmann, *Unfair Competition Without Competition?—The Importance of the Property Concept in the Law of Trade-Marks*, 95 U. Pa. L. Rev. 443, 458 (1947).

[148] *See, e.g.*, Zechariah Chafee, Jr., *Unfair Competition*, 53 Harv. L. Rev. 1289, 1299 (1940); Edward S. Rogers, *New Directions in the Law of Unfair Competition*, 74 N.Y. L. Rev. 317, 320 (1940). For a discussion of the state of federal and state trademark doctrine pre- and post-*Erie*, *see infra* p. 134 *et seq.*

[149] *See supra* p. 84–90.

[150] *Yale Elec. Corp. v. Robertson*, 26 F.2d 972, 973 (2nd Cir. 1928).

of a commercial product."[151] Nonetheless, his conception of the field still situated individual goodwill at the center of infringement analysis. Revealingly, he amended his explanation in *Yale Elec. Corp.* by an open individual rights focus—one not too different from the Kohlerian conception of personality rights protection in nineteenth-century German doctrine:[152]

However, it has of recent years been recognized that a merchant may have a sufficient economic interest in the use of his mark outside the field of his own exploitation to justify interposition by a court. His mark is his authentic seal; by it he vouches for the goods which bear it; it carries his name for good or ill. If another uses it, he borrows the owner's reputation, whose quality no longer lies within his own control. This is an injury, even though the borrower does not tarnish it, or divert any sales by its use; for a reputation, like a face, is the symbol of its possessor and creator, and another can use it only as a mask. And so it has come to be recognized that, unless the borrower's use is so foreign to the owner's as to insure against any identification of the two, it is unlawful.[153]

A similar focus on right owners' concerns coined Justice Holmes's trademark jurisprudence. Since Holmes was much more of a realist, one could have expected him to be clearer about the fact that trademark protection was an issue of public policy, not of private property. However, his use of terminology also illustrates the entrapment in traditional goodwill terminology and doctrine.[154] Indeed, a look at some of his decisions reveals an inconclusiveness that Frank I. Schechter characterized as an "indication of the shifts and shadings of judicial thought" on the issue of trademark property.[155] Early, when Holmes was on the bench of the Massachusetts Supreme Judicial Court, he explained in *Chadwick v. Covell*:

When the common law developed the doctrine of trade-marks and trade-names, it was not creating a property in advertisements more absolute than it would have allowed the author of Paradise Lost, but the meaning was to prevent one man from palming off his goods as another's, from getting another's business or injuring his reputation by unfair means, and, perhaps, from defrauding the public.[156]

[151] *Durable Toy & Novelty Corp. v. J. Chein & Co.*, 133 F.2d 853 (2nd Cir. 1943) (L. Hand, J.); *Industrial Rayon Corporation v. Dutchess Underwear Corporation*, 92 F.2d 33, 35 (2nd Cir. 1937) (L. Hand, J.).

[152] *See supra* p. 21 *et seq.*

[153] *Yale Elec. Corp. v. Robertson*, 26 F.2d 972, 974 (2nd Cir. 1928).

[154] For an extensive critique, *see* Rudolf Callmann, *Unfair Competition Withouth Competition?—The Importance of the Property Concept in the Law of Trade-Marks*, 95 U. Pa. L. Rev. 443, 456–458 (1947).

[155] Frank I. Schechter, *The Historical Foundations of the Law Relating to Trade-Marks* 154–155 (1925).

[156] *Chadwick v. Covell*, 151 Mass. 190, 193, 23 N.E. 1068, 1069 (1890).

Here, though Holmes did not completely reject a property right, the prevention of palming off (in the sense of injury to reputation and business) was the policy behind trademark protection. This understanding also looms in Holmes's famous good-faith analogy in the Supreme Court's 1917 decision in *E.I. Du Pont De Nemours Powder Co. v. Masland*:

> The word "property" as applied to trademarks and trade secrets is an unanalyzed expression of certain secondary consequences of the primary fact that the law makes some rudimentary requirements of good faith.[157]

But this critical stance seems to have taken a back seat some years later in the 1927 case *Beech-Nut Packing Co. v. P. Lorillard Co.*, when Holmes again made use of "qualified" trademark-as-property and goodwill protection language:

> A trade-mark is not only the symbol of an existing good will although it commonly is thought of only as that. Primarily it is a distinguishable token devised or picked out with the intent to appropriate it to a particular class of goods and with the hope that it will come to symbolize good will. Apart from nice and exceptional cases and within the limits of our jurisdiction a trade-mark and a business may start together, and in a qualified sense the mark is property, protected and alienable, although as with other property its outline is shown only by the law of torts, of which the right is a prophetic summary.[158]

While it might be overly critical to imply that Holmes's arguments were vague or meandering with regard to the property concept of trademarks,[159] one thing is evident: his use of terminology never said farewell to the notion of trademark "property." Most notably, however, the individualistic concept of goodwill protection—which served the interests of right owners

[157] *E.I. Du Pont De Nemours Powder Co. v. Masland*, 244 U.S. 100, 102 (1917). For a similar rejection of "property" (albeit under concurrent recognition of "goodwill"), *see* his reasons in *Prestonettes, Inc. v. Coty*, 264 U.S. 359, 368 (1924) ("Then what new rights does the trade-mark confer? It does not confer a right to prohibit the use of the word or words. It is not a copyright. The argument drawn from the language of the Trade-Mark Act does not seem to us to need discussion. A trade-mark only gives the right to prohibit the use of it so far as to protect the owner's good will against the sale of another's product as his.").

[158] *Beech-Nut Packing Co. v. P. Lorillard Co.*, 273 U.S. 629, 632 (1927). In fact, his decision in *A. Bourjois & Co. v. Katzel*, 260 U.S. 689 (1923) had already been interpreted as "plac[ing] protection of the plaintiff's property right above the protection of the buying public." *See* Walter J. Derenberg, *Trade-Mark Protection and Unfair Trading* 61 (1936). Yet, it is important to mention that Holmes did not use property language in *A. Bourjois & Co.*

[159] *But see, e.g.*, Rudolf Callmann, *Unfair Competition Withouth Competition?— The Importance of the Property Concept in the Law of Trade-Marks*, 95 U. Pa. L. Rev. 443, 456–458 (1947).

above all—was evident in both Learned Hand's and Holmes's understandings of trademark protection and unfair competition prevention. This concept dominated trademark doctrine at the time and continues to do so today. Hence, given that even the most prominent critics of legal formalism adhered to traditional terminology, it is not surprising that the realist attack was no true purgatory for trademark and unfair competition doctrine.

C Frank I. Schechter: The Victory of Goodwill

Trademark-as-property and goodwill-as-property terminology was not the only thing that survived. Another aspect is still characteristic of modern law. In fact, the foundation for a shift toward even further goodwill extension was laid by Frank I. Schechter in 1927. Schechter's article "The Rational Basis of Trademark Protection"[160] is one of the twentieth century's most influential contributions to trademark doctrine.[161] Read together with his doctoral thesis at Columbia Law School, *The Historical Foundations of the Law Related to Trade-Marks*,[162] published two years earlier, this article laid the foundation for modern antidilution doctrine. Generally, Schechter rejected the concepts of trademark property and goodwill protection. With regard to the protection of trademark property, his 1925 critique stated authoritatively, "To say that a trade-mark is property and therefore should be protected clarifies the situation no more than to say that a trade-mark is protected and is therefore property."[163] Similarly, he deconstructed contemporary understanding of trademark goodwill. In "Rational Basis," he explained:

160 Frank I. Schechter, *The Rational Basis of Trademark Protection*, 40 Harv. L. Rev. 813 (1927).

161 *See, e.g.*, Sara Stadler Nelson, *The Wages of Ubiquity in Trademark Law*, 88 Iowa L. Rev. 731, 736 (2003).

162 Frank I. Schechter, *The Historical Foundations of the Law Relating to Trade-Marks* (1925). For an illustration of Schechter's doctoral thesis and both his works' impact on legal scholarship, *see, e.g.*, Sara Stadler Nelson, *The Wages of Ubiquity in Trademark Law*, 88 Iowa L. Rev. 731, 746 *et seq.* (2003); Robert G. Bone, *Schechter's Ideas in Historical Context and Dilution's Rocky Road*, 24 Santa Clara Computer & High Tech. L.J. 469, 474 *et seq.* (2008).

163 Frank I. Schechter, *The Historical Foundations of the Law Relating to Trade-Marks* 160 (1925); *see also* Frank I. Schechter, *Fog and Fiction in Trade-Mark Protection*, 36 Colum. L. Rev. 60, 65 (1936) ("Nothing is to be gained, in determining the nature of a trade-mark and the basis of its protection by describing the trade-mark as 'property.' "). *See also* Judge Loring's concurring opinion in *Cohen v. Nagle*, 190 Mass. 4, 18, 76 N.E. 276, 282 (1906): "Whether it is proper to say that the plaintiff in such a case as the case at bar has a right of property in such words as 'Keystone Cigars' is a point on which there is a difference of opinion. ... But whether it is or is not correct to say that such a plaintiff has property in such a word is not of consequence. If he has a right of property in such a word, this right of property results from his right to prevent others from using it. His right to prevent others from using it does not result from his property in it."

The true functions of the trademark are, then, to identify a product as satisfactory and thereby to stimulate further purchases by the consuming public. The fact that through his trademark the manufacturer or importer may "reach over the shoulder of the retailer" and across the latter's counter straight to the consumer cannot be over-emphasized, for therein lies the key to any effective scheme of trademark protection. To describe a trademark merely as a symbol of good will, without recognizing in it an agency for the actual creation and perpetuation of good will, ignores the most potent aspect of the nature of a trademark and that phase most in need of protection. To say that a trademark "is merely the visible manifestation of the more important business goodwill, which is the 'property' to be protected against invasion" or that "the good will is the substance, the trademark merely the shadow," does not accurately state the function of a trademark today and obscures the problem of its adequate protection. ... [T]oday the trademark is not merely the symbol of good will but often the most effective agent for the creation of good will, imprinting upon the public mind an anonymous and impersonal guaranty of satisfaction, creating a desire for further satisfactions. The mark actually *sells* the goods. And, self-evidently, the more distinctive the mark, the more effective is its selling power.[164]

Schechter called for a functional understanding of trademark protection. It was the mark's selling power, which he later also described as "drawing power" or "magnetism,"[165] that formed the subject matter of protection.[166] In his appeal for a new and unmasked look at trademark functions, Schechter found legal practice to be on the right path in extending doctrine beyond the traditional confines of unfair competition. Yet, as he posited, "the process ha[d] been one of making exceptions rather than of frank recognition of the true basis of trademark protection."[167] It was no longer

[164] Frank I. Schechter, *The Rational Basis of Trademark Protection*, 40 Harv. L. Rev. 813, 818–819 (1927).

[165] *See, e.g.*, Justice Frankfurter's famous explanation of the trademark's function in *Mishawaka Rubber & Woolen Mfg. Co. v. S.S. Kresge Co.*, 316 U.S. 203, 205 (1942) ("The protection of trade-marks is the law's recognition of the psychological function of symbols. If it is true that we live by symbols, it is no less true that we purchase goods by them. A trade-mark is a merchandising short-cut which induces a purchaser to select what he wants, or what he has been led to believe he wants. The owner of a mark exploits this human propensity by making every effort to impregnate the atmosphere of the market with the drawing power of a congenial symbol. Whatever the means employed, the aim is the same—to convey through the mark, in the minds of potential customers, the desirability of the commodity upon which it appears. Once this is attained, the trade-mark owner has something of value. If another poaches upon the commercial magnetism of the symbol he has created, the owner can obtain legal redress.").

[166] Earlier foundations for the selling-power theory of trademark protection can be found in Schechter's doctoral thesis. *See* Frank I. Schechter, *The Historical Foundations of the Law Relating to Trade-Marks* 150 (1925) ("The mark 'sells the goods.' "). At this point, Eugen Ulmer's concept of the trademark's advertising capacity (*Werbekraft*), formulated only a few years later, comes to mind. *See supra* p. 42–46.

[167] Frank I. Schechter, *The Rational Basis of Trademark Protection*, 40 Harv. L. Rev. 813, 821 (1927).

trade diversion founded on misleading or deceptive conduct that accounted for a doctrine of trademark infringement. He defined a new metric for assessing remediable damage to trademark owners:

> The real injury in all such cases can only be gauged in the light of what has been said concerning the function of a trademark. It is the gradual whittling away or dispersion of the identity and hold upon the public mind of the mark or name by its use upon non-competing goods.[168]

Against this backdrop, Schechter's theory of dilution may be duly characterized as an example of contemporary legal realism. His arguments in "Rational Basis" display, as Robert Bone has explained, "all the elements of a typical realist project."[169] Schechter's attack on the concept of trademark protection, his critique of property formalism, and his ultimate suggestion for a reconstruction of trademark law expressed a "common impatience with old theories," mirroring a similar pattern of realist critique in other sectors of the law.[170] His rejection of formal property rights in particular suggests that he was influenced by the realist critique.[171]

Nevertheless, Schechter did not fully demolish the cathedral of trademark protection—in fact, the opposite is true. Even though Schechter's invention of trademark uniqueness had made symbols part of the branded "'goods' themselves,"[172] he had not broken with traditional goodwill protection doctrine as fundamentally as it appeared.[173] Indeed, he added yet another facet of goodwill value to the trademark. Under his guidance, trademark law evolved from a tort model to a proprietary model

168 *Id.* at 825.

169 *See* Robert G. Bone, *Schechter's Ideas in Historical Context and Dilution's Rocky Road*, 24 Santa Clara Computer & High Tech. L.J. 469, 484–485 (2008).

170 *See* Frank I. Schechter, *The Rational Basis of Trademark Protection*, 40 Harv. L. Rev. 813, 813 (1927).

171 For an illustration of Schechter's entanglement with prominent realist thought within the Columbia Law School faculty during the 1920s and 1930s, *see, e.g.*, Steven Wilf, *The Making of the Post-War Paradigm in American Intellectual Property Law*, 31 Colum. J. L. & Arts 139, 168–169 (2008); Robert G. Bone, *Schechter's Ideas in Historical Context and Dilution's Rocky Road*, 24 Santa Clara Computer & High Tech. L.J. 469, 483 n. 83 (2008).

172 Sara Stadler Nelson, *The Wages of Ubiquity in Trademark Law*, 88 Iowa L. Rev. 731, 746 (2003).

173 *But see, e.g.*, John Wolff, *Non-Competing Goods in Trademark Law*, 37 Colum. L. Rev. 582, 602 *et seq.* (1937) ("The very incongruousness of Schechter's theory with the tradition and the fundamental principles of the common law forms the chief obstacle to its general acceptance in this country."); *see also* Robert N. Klieger, *Trademark Dilution: The Whittling Away of the Rational Basis for Trademark Protection*, 58 U. Pitt. L. Rev. 789, 797, 802, 804–805 (1997); Robert G. Bone, *Schechter's Ideas in Historical Context and Dilution's Rocky Road*, 24 Santa Clara Computer & High Tech. L.J. 469, 493 (2008).

of protection.[174] In the end, his ideas laid the ground for an even wider extension of goodwill protection. Regarding the practical implementation of his ideas, by 1932, New York courts had already begun to refer to Schechter's ideas,[175] thus providing relief to trademark owners. Furthermore, starting in the 1940s, state legislators had begun enacting antidilution statutes, and by 1995, a federal law on dilution prevention had been enacted.[176]

Here, it is not necessary to explore the practical impact of antidilution doctrine on US (or other jurisdictions') trademark law.[177] For the purpose of this inquiry, however, one aspect is particularly important: Schechter's theoretical achievement not only helped lift doctrine to a higher level of sophistication[178] but also led to a significant extension of goodwill protection. He extended the value basis of trademark protection. While his approach might appear to have been influenced by the realist critique, his advocation of broad property rights contradicts an interpretation as purely realist. This is the reason why he, even though having pointed out the circularity of contemporary property doctrine, ultimately became a target of Cohen's critique some years later:

> In practice, injunctive relief is being extended today to realms where no actual danger of confusion to the consumer is present, and this extension has been vigorously supported and encouraged by leading writers in the field.[179]

Schechter was one of these "leading writers,"[180] along with Harry D. Nims, Milton Handler, and Charles Pickett. Even though he had actually started on the realists' plane of restricting trademark-as-property theory,

[174] Steven Wilf, *The Making of the Post-War Paradigm in American Intellectual Property Law*, 31 Colum. J. L. & Arts 139, 171 (2008).

[175] *See Tiffany & Co. v. Tiffany Productions*, 147 Misc. 679, 264 N.Y.S. 459, 462 (Sup. Ct. 1932). *See also* Sara Stadler Nelson, *The Wages of Ubiquity in Trademark Law*, 88 Iowa L. Rev. 731, 759 *et seq.* (2003) (illustrating early case law on the issue).

[176] For a discussion of the development of statutory law, *see, e.g.*, Sara Stadler Nelson, *The Wages of Ubiquity in Trademark Law*, 88 Iowa L. Rev. 731, 760 *et seq.* (2003); Robert G. Bone, *Schechter's Ideas in Historical Context and Dilution's Rocky Road*, 24 Santa Clara Computer & High Tech. L.J. 469, 489 *et seq.* (2008).

[177] For an illustrative account, *see, e.g.*, Robert N. Klieger, *Trademark Dilution: The Whittling Away of the Rational Basis for Trademark Protection*, 58 U. Pitt. L. Rev. 789, 810 *et seq.* (1997); regarding the practical impact of dilution theory in US law, *see, e.g.*, Clarisa Long, *Dilution*, 106 Colum. L. Rev. 1029 (2006).

[178] For a modern illustration of Schechter's contribution to trademark doctrine, *see* Barton Beebe, *Intellectual Property Law and the Sumptuary Code*, 123 Harv. L. Rev. 809, 845–847 (2010).

[179] Felix S. Cohen, *Transcendental Nonsense and the Functional Approach*, 35 Colum. L. Rev. 809, 814 (1935).

[180] *See id.* at 814 n. 17 (reference to the "Rational Basis" article). *See also* Steven Wilf, *The Making of the Post-War Paradigm in American Intellectual Property Law*, 31 Colum. J. L. & Arts 139, 153 (2008).

his foundation for modern trademark law unhooked protection from the requirement of actual or potential trade diversion by consumer confusion. In the end, his theory is emblematic of the realists' failure. The relevant conclusion here is as simple as it is sobering: while a formal concept of property protection had already become obsolete by the pre-realist era, the concept of goodwill has resisted all attempts at politicization and functionalization. It is still central to modern doctrine.

IV Modern Theory and Practice: Economic Analysis and Repropertization

Post-realist reconceptualizations could not change the picture, either. After the Second World War, US trademark law underwent a significant transformation. Both court practice and scholarly analyses have become increasingly "economized." Yet even though these developments actually shed more light on the underlying policies and thus should have restricted the trademark-as-property and goodwill overgrowth, the opposite is true. US trademark law in the twenty-first century has actually attained a level of almost unlimited private property/goodwill dominance.

A The 1946 Lanham Act: Monopoly Phobia Well Cured

Of course, the realist attack was not limited to the language of the law. It also provided the groundwork for a more wide-reaching and fundamental interdisciplinary critique. In trademark law, it was economic theory that seemed to challenge the age-old concepts of trademark-as-property and goodwill protection. Indeed, early on, economists had uttered doubts with respect to trademark protection as such. By 1933, Edward Chamberlin's *Theory of Monopolistic Competition* had already formulated a powerful argument against product differentiation through brand loyalty. As he argued, trademarks could be used not only to insulate market shares from price competition but also to create undue barriers to entry for other branded products. Since the trademark owner could differentiate products from competitor products by mere advertising, consumer loyalty would, over time, lead to an isolation from competition.[181] As Ralph S. Brown, Jr., explained, advertising would do more than simply inform the consumer—it would "persuade and influence," creating fake perceptions of product differences and

[181] *See* Edward Hastings Chamberlin, *The Theory of Monopolistic Competition—A Re-Orientation of the Theory of Value* 61 (5th edn., 1947) ("[I]f a trademark distinguishes, that is, marks off one product as different from another, it gives the seller of that product a monopoly, from which we might argue . . . that there is no competition.").

ultimately a "waste of resources."[182] Consumers would no longer base their decisions on quality and price but on a misguided perception of the brand as distinct from alternative products. In essence, Brown, Chamberlin, and contemporary critics found trademark and unfair competition protection to create monopoly rights, leading to higher prices to the detriment of the consumer.[183] They advocated for a reduction of protection in order to eliminate monopolistic elements.[184] This approach, adopted sporadically in practice,[185] never fully took hold.[186] Courts acknowledged the general problems of monopolistic trademark rights but did not implement the theory beyond incidents of an occasionally narrower interpretation of the scope of trademark protection in single cases.[187]

A deepening of the debate on monopoly phobia[188] is not necessary here. It suffices to state that the Lanham Act's drafting (even though

[182] *See* Ralph S. Brown, Jr., *Advertising and the Public Interest: Legal Protection of Trade Symbols*, 57 Yale L.J. 1165, 1169 (1948). *See also* Kurt Borchardt, *Are Trademarks an Antitrust Problem? Part I*, 33 Trademark Rep. 49, 50 (1943). For the same critique in case law, *see, e.g., Triangle Publications, Inc. v. Rohrlich*, 167 F.2d 969, 980 n. 13 (2nd Cir. 1948) (Frank, J., dissenting) ("[T]rade-name doctrine ... enables one to acquire a vested interest in a demand 'spuriously' stimulated through 'the art of advertising' by 'the power of reiterated suggestion' which creates stubborn habits. ... This poses an important policy question: Should the courts actively lend their aid to the making of profits derived from the building of such habits, if and whenever those stubborn habits so dominate buyers that they pay more for a product than for an equally good competing product?").

[183] Edward Hastings Chamberlin, *The Theory of Monopolistic Competition—A Re-Orientation of the Theory of Value* 61–63 (5th edn., 1947); Ralph S. Brown, Jr., *Advertising and the Public Interest: Legal Protection of Trade Symbols*, 57 Yale L.J. 1165, 1183 (1948); A.G. Papandreou, *The Economic Effect of Trademarks*, 44 Cal. L. Rev. 503, 506 *et seq.* (1956); Charles E. Mueller, *Sources of Monopoly Power: A Phenomenon Called "Product Differentiation,"* 18 Am. U. L. Rev. 1, 2 *et seq.* (1968).

[184] Edward Hastings Chamberlin, *The Theory of Monopolistic Competition—A Re-Orientation of the Theory of Value* 191 *et seq.* (5th edn., 1947).

[185] For an example of critical monopoly terminology, *see, e.g., Eastern Wine Corp. v. Winslow-Warren, Ltd.*, 137 F.2d 955, 957 (2nd Cir. 1943) (Frank, J.: "[T]he legal protection of trade-names does not engender competition; on the contrary, it creates lawful monopolies, immunities from competition. And the legally forbidden invasions of those monopolies might often benefit consumers. Thus, ... the consuming public would be better off financially; nevertheless such competition would, of course, be enjoined."); *S.C. Johnson & Son v. Johnson*, 116 F.2d 427, 429 (2nd Cir. 1940) (L. Hand, J.).

[186] For counterarguments to the monopoly theory, *see, e.g.*, Edward S. Rogers, *The Lanham Act and the Social Function of Trade-Marks*, 14 Law & Contemp. Probs. 173, 176–177 (1949); Beverly W. Pattishall, *Trade-Marks and the Monopoly Phobia*, 50 Mich. L. Rev. 967 (1952); William M. Landes & Richard A. Posner, *Trademark Law: An Economic Perspective*, 30 J. L. & Econ. 265 (1987).

[187] *See, e.g.*, Sigmund Timberg, *Trade-Marks, Monopoly, and the Restraint of Competition*, 14 Law & Contemp. Probs. 323, 327 (1949).

[188] For use of the term "monopoly phobia"—likely first employed by Judge Frank—*see* his opinion in *Eastern Wine Corp. v. Winslow-Warren, Ltd.*, 137 F.2d 955, 958–959 (2nd Cir. 1943) ("There are some persons, infected with monopoly-phobia, who shudder in

debated during an era of antitrust critique) was not noticeably influenced by fears of monopoly enlargement. On the contrary, as the Senate Committee Report remarked, "Trade-marks, indeed, are the essence of competition, because they make possible a choice between competing articles by enabling the buyer to distinguish one from the other."[189] In addition, the concept of investment protection was considered a part of the modern act's purpose:

> To protect trade-marks ... is to protect the public from deceit, to foster fair competition, and to secure to the business community the advantages of reputation and good will by preventing their diversion from those who have created them to those who have not.[190]

In other words, the Lanham Act did not alter the existing design of common law rights protection at the interstate level. On the contrary, the goodwill paradigm even became ennobled by its inclusion into lawmakers' statutory policies.[191]

B The Economization of US Trademark Law

Notwithstanding legislators' optimism, from the beginning, courts and academics struggled to reconcile the Lanham Act's rationale with the field's common law foundations. This was especially due to the divergence between traditional protection patterns and modern concepts of information economics. In fact, Brown's aforementioned 1948 critique of trademark rights extension was based on an early economic analysis.[192] And it was not long until law and economics theory took over completely. Toward the end of the twentieth century, a wide array of scholarship became dominated by the Chicago school of economics. For modern trademark law, there is little doubt that an economic rationale, most prominently explained by William M. Landes and Richard A. Posner,[193] has become the most influential theory. One can agree with

the presence of any monopoly. But the common law has never suffered from such a neurosis. There has seldom been a society in which there have not been some monopolies, i.e., special privileges.").

189 United States Senate, Committee on Patents, Senate Rep. No. 1333, 79th Congr., 2nd Sess. (14 May 1946), repr. in 1946 U.S. Code Cong. Service, 1274, 1275.

190 *Id.*

191 For the conclusion that the Lanham Act was therefore more reactionary than progressive, *see, e.g.*, Daniel M. McClure, *Trademarks and Unfair Competition: A Critical History of Legal Thought*, 69 Trademark Rep. 305, 334 (1979).

192 *See* Ralph S. Brown, Jr., *Advertising and the Public Interest: Legal Protection of Trade Symbols*, 57 Yale L.J. 1165, 1185 *et seq.* (1948); for a deeper analysis, *see also* Mark A. Lemley, *The Modern Lanham Act and the Death of Common Sense*, 108 Yale L.J. 1687, 1688 *et seq.* (1999).

193 *See, e.g.*, William M. Landes & Richard A. Posner, *Trademark Law: An Economic Perspective*, 30 J. L. & Econ. 265 (1987).

Barton Beebe that in the United States "[n]o alternative account of trademark doctrine currently exists."[194]

Under the economists' credo, the function of trademark law is to reduce consumer search costs. Trademark and unfair competition doctrine is part of the law of torts, whose overall purpose is to promote economic efficiency.[195] Each trademark communicates a particular set of information that the consumer does not need to gather herself every time she considers a purchase.[196] By preventing the improper use of trademarks by nonproprietors, the system ensures that consumer reliance on a product's source is correct. The law thereby fosters the flow of true information in the marketplace. As Stacey L. Dogan and Mark A. Lemley posit, trademarks have "the potential to lead to better-informed customers and more competitive markets."[197] The reverse side of this protection of information infrastructure is the creation of incentives for producers to maintain or improve quality.[198] In this regard, trademark protection confers a benefit that all property rights provide: a right owner will invest in the creation or improvement of a resource only if she is certain that no one else can appropriate the fruit of her efforts.[199] Suppose that a trademark owner could not be assured that her use of the trademark is exclusive. In this case, she would have to expect dishonest competitors to apply her trademark to lower-quality products. These competitors might charge less and divert patronage from the trademark owner. Such a system would arguably produce no incentives for trademark owners to invest in the quality of their products.[200] To avoid misunderstanding, this incentive must be distinguished from the incentive referred to in the field of copyrights and patents. Trademark law

194 Barton Beebe, *The Semiotic Analysis of Trademark Law*, 51 UCLA L. Rev. 621, 623–624 (2004).

195 *See, e.g., Ty Inc. v. Perryman*, 306 F.3d 509, 510 (7th Cir. 2002) (Posner, J.: "The fundamental purpose of a trademark is to reduce consumer search costs by providing a concise and unequivocal identifier of the particular source of particular goods."); *Qualitex Co. v. Jacobson Products Co., Inc.*, 514 U.S. 159, 163–164 (1995); William M. Landes & Richard A. Posner, *Trademark Law: An Economic Perspective*, 30 J. L. & Econ. 265, 266, 268 *et seq.* (1987).

196 William M. Landes & Richard A. Posner, *Trademark Law: An Economic Perspective*, 30 J. L. & Econ. 265, 269 (1987).

197 Stacey L. Dogan & Mark A. Lemley, *Trademark and Consumer Search Costs on the Internet*, 41 Hous. L. Rev. 777, 778 (2004).

198 *See, e.g., Qualitex Co. v. Jacobson Products Co., Inc.*, 514 U.S. 159, 164 (1995); William M. Landes & Richard A. Posner, *The Economic Structure of Intellectual Property Law* 168 (2003).

199 *See* Robert B. Cooter Jr. & Thomas Ulen, *Law and Economics* 127 *et seq.* (6th edn., 2014); for trademarks, William M. Landes & Richard A. Posner, *Trademark Law: An Economic Perspective*, 30 J. L. & Econ. 265, 266 (1987).

200 William M. Landes & Richard A. Posner, *Trademark Law: An Economic Perspective*, 30 J. L. & Econ. 265, 270 (1987).

provides a strictly limited—one could say conditional—incentive only. Without ongoing investment and marketplace activity, trademark protection will cease to exist. There is no value in the creation of the trademark as such. It is only consumers' expected behavior within a functioning system of use and protection that opens an opportunity for trademark owners to reap the benefits of investing in quality and reputation. The premium that a right owner can charge for her products is thus not the result of the initial creation or invention of a trademark; it flows from the constant upholding of a certain quality standard and its communication to the public.[201] By and large, therefore, trademarks are instruments of market information. They are a part of the information infrastructure that connects producer and purchaser and channels the flow of communication in the marketplace.[202] Ideally, the protection of transmission structures for correct and true market information is to be understood as the dominant policy of any trademark protection system.[203]

[201] *See also* already Francis H. Upton, *A Treatise on the Law of Trade Marks with a Digest and Review on the English and American Authorities* 14 (1860) ("The right of property in trade marks does not partake in any degree of the nature and character of a patent or copyright, to which it has sometimes been referred—nor is it safe to reason from any supposed analogies existing between them.").

[202] For more on the terminology of "market language," which firms employ to communicate to consumers, *see* Stephen L. Carter, *The Trouble with Trademark*, 99 Yale L.J. 759, 763 (1990); on consumer search costs and advertising, *see* George J. Stigler, *The Economics of Information*, 69 J. Pol. Econ. 213, 216, 220 (1961). This is discussed extensively *infra* in chapter 4.

[203] For an illustration of the information-transmission model, *see, e.g.*, Robert G. Bone, *Hunting Goodwill: A History of the Concept of Goodwill in Trademark Law*, 86 B. U. L. Rev. 547, 549 *et seq.* (2006). Among the praise for this economic theory of trademark law and protection, the fact that this allegedly "modern" model is no recent invention or discovery has usually been overlooked. The most basic economic purposes of trademark protection (i.e., providing an efficient system of consumer information and the incentive for constant quality enhancement by right owners) were explained long before the economic model of trademark protection took the lead. One early voice of consumer-search-cost reasoning was German attorney Otto Hahn, in his commentary on the 1874 trademark act. *See* Otto Hahn, *Das deutsche Markenschutzgesetz sowie Vorschläge zur Aenderung desselben auf Grund der bisherigen Erfahrungen* 3–4 (1887) ("Allein wer die Bedürfnisse des Verkehrs, des Geschäfts genau kennt, der weiß, von welch unendlichem Wert es ist, eine Ware zu erkennen, eine bestimmte Ware und keine andere zu bekommen. … Man denke sich nun z.B.: ich kaufe für 5 Pfennige Nadeln. Es ist fast unmöglich, den Stahl zu prüfen. Das Geschäft des Verfertigers aber ist mir Bürge, daß ich welche von ausgezeichnetem Stahl kaufe. Den Verfertiger erkenne ich sofort an dem Warenzeichen und so ist mir eine große Mühe und Zeit in der Prüfung der Ware erspart. Ich habe eine Art Nadeln, von welchen ich gewiß weiß, daß sie von den besten sind. Daß der Produzent einer durch die Art der Erzeugung individuellen Sache diese als solche kenntlicher macht, ist das über alle Zweifel erhabene Recht jedes … Produzenten. Es ist bloß ein Mittel und zwar ein ganz erlaubtes, den Liebhaber seiner Ware schneller zur Gewißheit zu bringen, daß er eben das habe, was er sucht.").

C Modern Propertization and Repropertization

Notwithstanding its recent economization, trademark doctrine still contains numerous policies that defy a justification under economic theory. This is due largely to an adherence to traditional patterns of the common law—notably the unimpaired implementation of goodwill protection structures in both common law and modern statutory trademark law. In fact, the Lanham Act drafters did not intend to change the principal doctrinal foundation of use-based rights as developed under the reign of common law. As a result, federal law is still based on common law principles.[204] It is thus not much of a surprise that late twentieth-century law brought forward a number of peculiarities that go beyond concerns for consumer protection and information economization, and that these peculiarities found shelter in the paradigm of goodwill protection. In the end, this traditionalist character of federal statutory law may have been a determinative factor for the reinvigoration of property-based trademark doctrine.[205]

Scholarly commentary has particularly criticized the shift toward an extension of protection beyond the core of immediate trade-diversion-by-consumer-confusion. Under this extended doctrine, for noncompetitive or not directly competitive uses, protecting goodwill no longer needs to be connected to an attempted or actual diversion of trade. In essence, the actionable invasion of trademark rights has become an issue of goodwill misappropriation rather than of the prevention of confusion-caused trade diversion.[206] One example of the extension is so-called initial interest confusion. It applies when a second-comer uses a competitor's trademark to attract the attention of consumers who would not have purchased her product otherwise. Accordingly, the policy of prevention aims at

[204] *See, e.g., Inwood Laboratories, Inc. v. Ives Laboratories, Inc.*, 456 U.S. 844, 861 n. 2 (1982) (White, J., concurring) ("[T]he purpose of the Lanham Act was to codify and unify the common law of unfair competition and trademark protection."); Restatement of the Law—Unfair Competition (Third), introductory note to chapter 3 (1995) ("The statutory protection of trademarks is largely a codification of the common law."); *see also* Sara Stadler Nelson, *The Wages of Ubiquity in Trademark Law*, 88 Iowa L. Rev. 731, 738 n. 39 (2003).

[205] *See, e.g.*, Daniel M. McClure, *Trademarks and Competition: The Recent History*, 59 Law & Contemp. Probs. 13, 38–40 (1996); Mark A. Lemley, *Romantic Authorship and the Rhetoric of Property*, 75 Tex. L. Rev. 873, 900 (1997); Glynn S. Lunney, Jr., *Trademark Monopolies*, 48 Emory L.J. 367, 371–372 (1999); *see also* Mark A. Lemley, *The Modern Lanham Act and the Death of Common Sense*, 108 Yale L.J. 1687, 1688 (1999) ("Unfortunately, the changes in trademark doctrine over the last fifty years are not supported by the new economic learning. Rather, these changes have loosed trademark law from its traditional economic moorings and have offered little of substance to replace them.").

[206] Glynn S. Lunney, Jr., *Trademark Monoplies*, 48 Emory L.J. 367, 371–372 (1999); Robert G. Bone, *Hunting Goodwill: A History of the Concept of Goodwill in Trademark Law*, 86 B. U. L. Rev. 547, 574 and 592 *et seq.* (2006).

consumer protection in a presale setting—notably at saving the costs of having to search again for the product the consumer had been seeking prior to coming across the confusing information.[207] The issue of "confusion" has, however, been detached from the point of sale or transaction and thus also from the consumer's *actual* decision making. Therefore, in general, the subject matter of protection is goodwill beyond the search-cost rationale of the economic trademark protection model.[208] Similarly, the doctrine of so-called postsale confusion has projected traditional infringement theory away from the point of sale. In postsale confusion cases, the defendant's product creates a risk of confusion only *after* the point of sale or transaction. The actionable wrong appears to lie in the confusion of consumers regarding their postsale interaction with a competitor. In these cases as well, goodwill misappropriation theory, not genuine confusion prevention, governs.[209] Finally, the protection of merchandising rights and modern antidilution doctrine are further examples where protection has been extended beyond the core of efficiency-based confusion prevention policies.[210]

As all these examples illustrate, twentieth-century trademark law has extended the right owner's exclusive domain into numerous dimensions far beyond former protection levels. It is no longer market information transmission prior to the consumer's decision making that determines whether an infringement exists. Traditional confusion theory has lost its once governing status as basic trademark doctrine. Even economic theory, as the dominant approach in modern US law, has ultimately failed to delimit the scope of private rights protection. As it appears, the paradigm of trademark goodwill has reconquered the field and arrived at a stage of almost maximum propertization again.

Section 2 Interstate Trademark and Unfair Competition Law

Early twentieth-century trademark law did more than change the *Kidd/Derringer* paradigm of rights protection from universality to market-based rights. As a closer look at interstate trademark and unfair competition law of that time illustrates, the Supreme Court's *Tea Rose/Rectanus* doctrine reflects a second characteristic that would prove determinative for the development of conflicts law: under *Tea Rose/Rectanus*, trademark rights were distinctively apolitical. Like mushrooms growing in a forest, common law rights would cross state borders following any market extension

[207] *See* Stacey L. Dogan & Mark A. Lemley, *Trademark and Consumer Search Costs on the Internet*, 41 Hous. L. Rev. 777, 814–815 (2004).
[208] *See infra* p. 357–358. [209] *See infra* p. 353–356. [210] *See infra* p. 350–353.

initiated by their owner. The perceived interstate universality and homogeneity of the states' common law provided the ground for the non-territoriality of rights. Initially, this non-territoriality was further solidified under the *Swift* lens of a federal common law. Even the *Erie* shift in directions did not do away with a general common law of trademark protection and unfair competition prevention. Ultimately, the conception of virtually borderless, organic market rights had become so deeply implemented in the fundamentals of American trademark and unfair competition law that it would not change colors even by statutory federalization of this law under the 1946 Lanham Act.

I *The "Market Universality" of Trademark Rights*

As we have seen, similar to Germany's embrace of trademark and personality rights universality, the United States witnessed an era of absolute protection for trademarks. Unlike German doctrine, however, US trademark law remained an issue of local law for a long time. It took more than seventy years before a uniform federal statute came into place. Yet, even today, one could still claim that US trademark law is a domain of common law rights. This localization of rights has influenced the concept of rights territoriality in particular and, thus, necessarily also trademark conflicts law.

A *A. Bourjois & Co. v. Katzel*: The One-Way Street of Trademark Extension

Prima facie, the rejection of universal trademark validity was implemented by the Supreme Court's 1923 decision *A. Bourjois & Co. v. Katzel*,[211] a case concerning parallel imports. The issue at hand was the reach of foreign trademark rights into the United States, not the extension of domestic trademark rights to foreign territories. The plaintiff held domestic trademark rights, and the defendant had imported branded goods from France. In France, these goods were legitimately sold under the French trademark. Nonetheless, the Supreme Court found the defendant liable for trademark infringement. As the court explained, trademarks were of an explicitly territorial character. A domestic trademark right would reach only as far as the national boundaries, never beyond.[212]

[211] *A. Bourjois & Co. v. Katzel*, 260 U.S. 689 (1923).

[212] *Id.* at 691–692 (Holmes, J.) ("Ownership of the goods does not carry the right to sell them with a specific mark. It does not necessarily carry the right to sell them at all in a given place. If the goods were patented in the United States a dealer who lawfully bought similar goods abroad from one who had a right to make and sell them there could not sell them in the United States. … The monopoly in that case is more extensive, but we see no sufficient reason for holding that the monopoly of a trade-mark, so far as it goes, is less

Courts and legal scholars agree that *Katzel* marks the end of universality theory in US trademark law and that this rejection established acceptance of the territoriality principle.[213] However, the picture is more complex for two reasons. First, strictly speaking, the case concerned only the issue of parallel importation and the validity of foreign trademarks in the United States; it did not consider whether an extraterritorial extension of domestic rights was possible. The situation thus differed significantly from the facts that the Supreme Court had to decide on thirty years later in *Steele v. Bulova Watch Co.*[214] At best, therefore, *Katzel* marks an end to foreign rights' extraterritorial extension into the United States. It had no impact, however, on the issue of domestic rights' extraterritorial extension. The restriction of universality was unidimensional. Second, a closer look at the development of trademark conflicts at the interstate level reveals that even though US courts generally adhere to the principle of territoriality in intellectual property conflicts,[215] what they say and do differs in international trademark law. Here, as we will see, the doctrine of goodwill extension in *Tea Rose/Rectanus* is critical for international trademark conflicts.

B *Tea Rose/Rectanus*: The Doctrine of Nonterritorial Rights

As this inquiry has revealed, *Tea Rose/Rectanus* established a concept of rights acquisition through market occupation and investment.[216] But this is just one aspect of the doctrine. A second characteristic can be explained as a peculiarity of interstate trademark adjudication and is particularly important for the genesis of conflicts law with respect to international trademark disputes.

Let us recapitulate the Supreme Court's approach. Concerning the emphasis on market activities, the majority explained that a trademark "extends to every market where the trader's goods have become known

complete. It deals with a delicate matter that may be of great value but that easily is destroyed, and therefore should be protected with corresponding care. It is said that the trade-mark here is that of the French house and truly indicates the origin of the goods. But that is not accurate. It is the trade-mark of the plaintiff only in the United States and indicates in law, and, it is found, by public understanding, that the goods come from the plaintiff although not made by it. … It stakes the reputation of the plaintiff upon the character of the goods.").

213 *See, e.g., Société des Produits Nestlé, S.A. v. Casa Helvetia, Inc.*, 982 F.2d 633, 636–637 (1st Cir. 1992); *Roger & Gallet v. Janmarie, Inc.*, 245 F.2d 505, 511 (C.C.P.A. 1957); Restatement (Third) of Unfair Competition, § 24 comment f (1995); Curtis A. Bradley, *Territorial Intellectual Property Rights in an Age of Globalism*, 37 Va. J. Int'l L. 505, 543–544, 545 (1997).

214 *See infra* p. 159–161.

215 *See, e.g., Deepsouth Packing Co. v. Laitram Corp.*, 406 U.S. 518, 531 (1972) ("Our patent system makes no claim to extraterritorial effect …."); *Subafilms, Ltd. v. MGM-Pathe Communications Co.*, 24 F.3d 1088, 1093 (9th Cir. 1994) (copyright territoriality).

216 *See supra* p. 102–110.

and identified by his use of the mark. But the mark, of itself, cannot travel to markets where there is no article to wear the badge and no trader to offer the article."[217] The area of protection could never exceed the reach of the trade.[218] As we have seen, the understanding of *Kidd* and *Derringer*, as it had developed in the meantime, was practically invalidated.[219] There was no longer any immediate or automatic extension of use-based trademark rights under common law doctrine, and the possibility of universality and extraterritoriality appeared to be spellbound. Yet *Hanover Star* still offered a new and different version of extraterritoriality. As the majority, agreeing with the court below, explained:

> [S]ince it is the trade, and not the mark, that is to be protected, a trademark acknowledges no territorial boundaries of municipalities or states or nations, but extends to every market where the trader's goods have become known and identified by his use of the mark.[220]

This "no territorial boundaries" formulation by Justice Pitney, pitting market foundation against territoriality, can be characterized as *Hanover Star*'s most significant influence on conflicts doctrine. From this moment on, the concept of market rights would prevail over the idea of territorially limited entitlements. Ultimately, the factual dissolution of political boundaries would prove to have far more drastic consequences in the inter-nation context than at the interstate level.

Hanover Star's nonterritorial obliviousness is further reflected in the conception of different geographical zones of trademark protection that have been distinguished ever since by reference to the decision.[221] In the

[217] *Hanover Star Milling Co. v. Metcalf*, 240 U.S. 403, 416 (1916).

[218] *United Drug Co. v. Theodore Rectanus Co.*, 248 U.S. 90, 97 (1918) ("There is no such thing as property in a trade-mark except as a right appurtenant to an established business or trade in connection with which the mark is employed. ... [T]he right to a particular mark grows out of its use, ... its function is simply to designate the goods as the product of a particular trader and to protect his good will against the sale of another's product as his; and it is not the subject of property except in connection with an existing business."). In this regard, *United Drug* reflects what the House of Lords had already stated in 1901 in *Commissioners of Inland Revenue v. Muller & Co.'s Margarine, Ltd.* [1901] A.C. 217, 235 ("Goodwill regarded as property has no meaning except in connection with some trade, business, or calling. ... In this wide sense, goodwill is inseparable from the business to which it adds value, and, in my opinion, exists where the business is carried on. Such business may be carried on in one place or country or in several, and if in several there may be several businesses, each having a goodwill of its own." (per Lord Lindley)); for modern English doctrine *see* still: James J. Fawcett & Paul Torremans, *Intellectual Property and Private International Law* para. 13.128 (2nd edn., 2011).

[219] *See supra* p. 90 *et seq.*

[220] *Hanover Star Milling Co. v. Metcalf*, 240 U.S. 403, 416 (1916).

[221] *See, e.g.*, Julius R. Lunsford, Jr., *Geographical Scope of Registered Rights—Then and Now*, 61 Trademark Rep. 411, 414 (1971); *but see also* William Jay Gross, *The Territorial Scope of Trademark Rights*, 44 U. Miami L. Rev. 1075, 1078 and 1084 (1990) (pointing out

first zone, the "zone of actual market penetration," a trademark user has sold goods or rendered services with such intensity that a second-comer's use of the same mark would create a likelihood of confusion. This zone comprises all areas inhabited by consumers who customarily purchase the goods or services.[222] In the second zone, the "zone of reputation," a trademark may be so well known among consumers that the use of the mark by more than one party would also create a likelihood of confusion.[223] Finally, the "zone of natural expansion"[224] covers areas into which the trademark owner has the potential to expand.[225] The zone of actual market penetration and the zone of reputation are based on the concept of preventing consumer confusion.[226] By contrast, the zone of expansion is not so evidently justified by reference to information-economization concerns. Rights of this kind are not genuinely use based. Instead, scholarly analyses have referred to more individualistic and property-based ideas of "room to grow"[227] and "breathing space" for right owners.[228] The last zone in particular reflects the organic nature of goodwill and the inherent unboundedness of rights extension. Not only will local confusion

that Justice Holmes suggested a fourth zone delimited by state boundaries); Graeme B. Dinwoodie, *Trademarks and Territory: Detaching Trademark Law from the Nation-State*, 41 Hous. L. Rev. 885, 895 *et seq.* (2004).

222 For an instructive illustration of the different zones, *see* James M. Treece, *Security for Federally Registered Mark Owners Against Subsequent Users*, 39 Geo. Wash. L. Rev. 1008, 1020 (1971); Comment, *The Scope of Territorial Protection of Trademarks*, 65 Nw. U. L. Rev. 781, 787 *et seq.* (1970); Miles J. Alexander & James H. Coil, *Geographic Rights in Trademarks and Service Marks*, 68 Trademark Rep. 101, 102 *et seq.* (1978).

223 *See, e.g.*, William Jay Gross, *The Territorial Scope of Trademark Rights*, 44 U. Miami L. Rev. 1075, 1085–1086 (1990). Strictly speaking, under the common law doctrine of acquisition by use, the zone of reputation would not provide for trademark rights. After all, mere reputation does not fulfill the requirement of selling or offering a product. Yet, in *Hanover Star*, the Supreme Court acknowledged that fame and reputation may suffice to provide trademark rights, and that protection might extend beyond the limits of actual sales or rendering of services: "Into whatever markets the use of a trademark has extended, or its meaning has become known, there will the manufacturer or trader whose trade is pirated by an infringing use be entitled to protection and redress" (*Hanover Star Milling Co. v. Metcalf*, 240 U.S. 403, 415–416 (1916)).

224 *Hanover Star Milling Co. v. Metcalf*, 240 U.S. 403, 420 (1916).

225 *See, e.g.*, Miles J. Alexander & James H. Coil, *Geographic Rights in Trademarks and Service Marks*, 68 Trademark Rep. 101, 105–106 (1978); for a list of cases (by circuit), *see* 5 J. Thomas McCarthy, *McCarthy on Trademarks and Unfair Competition* § 26:20 (4th edn., 2016).

226 William Jay Gross, *The Territorial Scope of Trademark Rights*, 44 U. Miami L. Rev. 1075, 1110–1112 (1990). The consumer protection policy of trademark law applies to both the doctrine of actual market penetration and that of reputation. In both areas, the use of confusingly similar trademarks would disable the information function of the mark and hamper the efficient and competitive functioning of the market. *See id.* at 1113.

227 *See id.* at 1115.

228 *See, e.g.*, Miles J. Alexander & James H. Coil, *Geographic Rights in Trademarks and Service Marks*, 68 Trademark Rep. 101, 106 (1978); William Jay Gross, *The Territorial Scope of Trademark Rights*, 44 U. Miami L. Rev. 1075, 1087 (1990).

prevention policies prevail beyond political boundaries, but, as the third zone implies, there also is a quasi natural right of goodwill growth and projection.

Hence, under *Tea Rose/Rectanus*, the legitimacy of rights acquisition and protection is an issue of market dynamics, not of interstate or international politics and sovereignty. For almost a century, infringement analysis in US trademark law—at the local, interstate, and, ultimately, international level—has been an issue of market invasion.

C Holmes Concurring: A "Passive Figurehead" of State Sovereignty

Since legal analysis of this kind requires an economic rather than a political perspective, it is evident that a divergence of markets and political boundaries will rarely be a problem. In particular, such a divergence will not stand in the way of an extension of rights. Indeed, in an interstate setting, the unitary concept of goodwill under *Tea Rose/Rectanus* may be adequate, particularly if conflicts occur between common law jurisdictions where substantive law is nonstatutory. However, such an understanding of organic goodwill growth had a fundamental flaw from the beginning—a flaw that was foreshadowed by Justice Holmes in his concurring opinion in *Hanover Star*.[229]

Holmes agreed with the majority that trademark rights might extend within a zone of probable expansion. In addition, he further pushed the geographical scope of protection to state boundaries. Yet Holmes's concept of territorial rights also gave regard to state sovereignty, which had been neglected by the majority. As he explained:

> The question before us . . . is a question of state law, since the rights that we are considering are conferred by the sovereignty of the state in which they are acquired. This seems to be too obvious to need the citation of authority, but it is a necessary corollary of the Trade-Mark Cases . . .. Those cases decided that Congress cannot deal with trademarks as used in commerce wholly between citizens of the same state. It follows that the states can deal with them, as in fact they sometimes do by statute . . ., and when not by statute by their common law.
>
> As the common law of the several states has the same origin for the most part, and as their law concerning trademarks and unfair competition is the same in its general features, it is natural and very generally correct to say that trademarks acknowledge no territorial limits. But it never should be forgotten, and in this case it is important to remember, that when a trademark started in one state is recognized in another it is by the authority of a new sovereignty that gives its sanction to the right. The new sovereignty is not a passive figurehead. It creates

[229] *Hanover Star Milling Co. v. Metcalf*, 240 U.S. 403 (1916).

the right within its jurisdiction, and what it creates it may condition, as by requiring the mark to be recorded, or it may deny.[230]

Holmes's theory of territoriality never gained a foothold in case law or commentary. Courts notably rejected it on the grounds that since markets are not necessarily circumscribed by state boundaries, the extension of rights cannot follow political limitations.[231] This critique was no doubt justified with regard to the lack of a solid policy foundation. The mere extension of rights within a granting sovereign's boundaries without concurrent use of the trademark within the whole territory, as we have seen, defies the market information rationale underlying modern trademark policy.[232] Holmes's theory was thus subject to the same critique that was to be launched much later against the Lanham Act.[233]

A close reading of the concurrence, however, reveals that his theory is more than a "good in one part of the state, good in all" concept. Holmes's argument also is one of political segmentation for trademark extension. Whenever the trademark owner's business crosses state lines, protection will be granted under a different legal regime. Accordingly, the owner's

[230] *Id.* at 425–426 (Holmes, J., concurring). At this point, Holmes went on: "I think state lines, speaking always of matters outside the authority of Congress, are important in another way. I do not believe that a trademark established in Chicago could be used by a competitor in some other part of Illinois on the ground that it was not known there. I think that if it is good in one part of the state, it is good in all. But when it seeks to pass state lines, it may find itself limited by what has been done under the sanction of a power co-ordinate with that of Illinois and paramount over the territory concerned. If this view be adopted we get rid of all questions of penumbra, of shadowy marches where it is difficult to decide whether the business extends to them. We have sharp lines drawn upon the fundamental consideration of the jurisdiction originating the right. In most cases the change of jurisdiction will not be important because the new law will take up and apply the same principles as the old; but when, as here, justice to its own people requires a state to set a limit, it may do so, and this court cannot pronounce its action wrong."

[231] *See, e.g., Katz Drug Co. v. Katz*, 188 F.2d 696, 700 (8th Cir. 1951); *Humble Oil & Refining Co. v. American Oil Co.*, 405 F.2d 803, 160 U.S.P.Q. 289 (8th Cir. 1969); *but see Federal Glass Co. v. Loshin*, 224 F.2d 100, 102 (2nd Cir. 1955); *see also* Frank S. Moore, *Legal Protection of Goodwill* 162 *et seq.* (1936); Harry D. Nims, *The Law of Unfair Competition and Trade-Marks, with Chapters on Good-Will, Trade Secrets, Defamation of Competitors and Their Goods, Registration of Trade-Marks, Interference with Competitors' Business, etc., vol. I* § 218b, at 653 (4th edn., 1947). For case law rejecting and acknowledging the Holmesian state line dictum, *see* 5 J. Thomas McCarthy, *McCarthy on Trademarks and Unfair Competition* § 26:28 n. 3 and n. 4 (4th edn., 2016); for a contemporary approval in scholarly commentary, *see, e.g.*, John P. Bullington, *Trade-Names and Trade-Marks—Territorial Extent of the Right Acquired*, 3 Tex. L. Rev. 300, 310–311 (1924).

[232] *See supra* p. 123 *et seq.* For a concurrent policy of promoting and fostering trademarks by registration, *see* the discussion on Eugen Ulmer's reconciliation of policies in the 1920s German doctrine *supra* p. 42 *et seq.*

[233] For an economic critique of federal rights extension upon registration (or application) only, *see, e.g.*, Stephen L. Carter, *The Trouble with Trademark*, 99 Yale L.J. 759 (1990).

goodwill and its corresponding trademark protection consist of a bundle of different states' common law or statutory trademark rights.[234] Goodwill, as Holmes correctly understood, is not a uniform or homogeneous subject matter—it is a patchwork of different goodwill segments. In 1927, Holmes extended this conception of political rights to *international* trademark law. In *Ingenohl v. Walter E. Olsen & Co.*,[235] he explained—by reference to *Tea Rose/Rectanus*—that "[a] trade-mark started elsewhere would depend for its protection in Hongkong upon the law prevailing in Hongkong and would confer no rights except by the consent of that law."[236]

In the interstate context, two years later, Justice Pitney casually put forth an apparently similar understanding. In *United Drug*, he stated that "[p]roperty in trade-marks and the right to their exclusive use rest upon the laws of the several states, and depend upon them for security and protection."[237] But this apparent wisdom on the divergence of markets and political territories was never implemented in practice. As Holmes had pointed out, there was no practical necessity to give regard to sovereignty in the interstate context since "[i]n most cases the change of jurisdiction will not be important because the new law will take up and apply the same principles as the old."[238] Accordingly, the actual consequences of interstate political segmentation of trademark rights and goodwill portions were never drawn. Yet the fact that political boundaries were irrelevant under common law doctrine and at the interstate level did not make it a negligible factor for the international arena. We will see in the following how the concept of common law uniformity contributed to modern international trademark extraterritoriality—notably how the Supreme Court neglected Justice Holmes's early wisdom on political rights.[239] But first I must illustrate another prominent characteristic of the US state/federal system that has proven critical for trademark conflicts doctrine.

II *The Federal Common Law of Trademarks and the* Erie *Doctrine*

As the debate on Holmes's concurrence unveils, the development of *Tea Rose/Rectanus*, particularly its virtually apolitical extension of goodwill

[234] *See also* Graeme W. Austin, *The Story of Steele v. Bulova: Trademarks on the Line*, 395, 414, in *Intellectual Property Stories* (Jane C. Ginsburg & Rochelle Cooper Dreyfuss eds., 2006) (contrasting the existence of a single nonterritorial goodwill with an "orthodox legal theory" of different rights in different jurisdictions).

[235] *Ingenohl v. Walter E. Olsen & Co.*, 273 U.S. 541 (1927).

[236] *Id.* at 544.

[237] *United Drug Co. v. Theodore Rectanus Co.*, 248 U.S. 90, 98 (1918).

[238] *Hanover Star Milling Co. v. Metcalf*, 240 U.S. 403, 426 (1916) (Holmes, J., concurring).

[239] *See infra* p. 164 *et seq.*

and trademark rights, has its roots in a distinctive feature of the common law. Just as the distinction between law and equity led to an early propertization of trademark protection, the federal system of the common law under *Swift v. Tyson* accounts for the development of a widely homogeneous body of trademark cases and a corresponding disregard for states' substantive law policies.

A The Traditional Hodgepodge of State and Federal Common Law

Prior to the Lanham Act's enactment in 1946, US trademark and unfair competition law was a conglomerate of federal and state rules.[240] Under the doctrine of *Swift v. Tyson*,[241] each court had to apply either the law of the respective state (if a state court) or federal law (if a federal court). Accordingly, two separate bodies of case law evolved. While state courts promulgated principles of state common law, federal courts adjudicated on the basis of substantive federal common law.[242] Even though federal courts formally acknowledged that substantive rights in trademarks rested on the laws of the states,[243] federal common law was applied in infringement disputes before federal courts.[244] Not surprisingly, a consistent and uniform treatment of trademark and unfair competition cases was far from guaranteed. In light of the clutter of state and federal precedents, the resolution of a conflict depended on the forum in which the case landed.[245] In

[240] Bartholomew Diggins, *Federal and State Regulation of Trade-Marks*, 14 Law & Contemp. Probs. 200, 200 (1949); *see also* Edward S. Rogers, Statement, at 11 *et seq.*, in United States House of Representatives, *Hearings Before the Committee on Patents, Subcommittee on Trade-Marks*, 75th Congress, 3rd Session on H.R. 9041 (15–18 March 1938).

[241] *Swift v. Tyson*, 41 U.S. 1 (1842).

[242] Bartholomew Diggins, *Federal and State Regulation of Trade-Marks*, 14 Law & Contemp. Probs. 200, 202 (1949).

[243] *See, e.g.*, *United Drug Co. v. Theodore Rectanus Co.*, 248 U.S. 90, 98 (1918) ("Property in trade-marks and the right to their exclusive use rest upon the laws of the several states, and depend upon them for security and protection; the power of Congress to legislate on the subject being only such as arises from the authority to regulate commerce with foreign nations and among the several states and with the Indian tribes.").

[244] *Hanover Star Milling Co. v. Metcalf*, 240 U.S. 403, 410–411 (1916) ("It should be added that, so far as appears, none of the parties here concerned has registered the trademark under any act of Congress or under the law of any state. Nor does it appear that in any of the states in question there exists any peculiar local rule, arising from statute or decision. Hence, the cases must be decided according to common-law principles of general application.").

[245] Bartholomew Diggins, *Federal and State Regulation of Trade-Marks*, 14 Law & Contemp. Probs. 200, 200 (1949); *see also* Edward S. Rogers, Statement, at 39, in United States House of Representatives, *Hearings Before the Committee on Patents, Trade-Marks*, 72nd Congress, 1st Session (8 and 9 February 1932) ("The Chairman. Is there any unanimity or uniformity in the decisions of State courts and Federal courts on this subject of trademarks or is there great conflict? Mr. Rogers. Not very much conflict. The law is surprisingly uniform, and the law of infringement has been crystallized into a sentence. It

addition, early federal statutory trademark law was limited to procedural rules. The 1905 act,[246] for instance, provided for federal courts' jurisdiction in cases involving registered trademarks but left the nature and scope of trademark rights under the domain of the common law.[247] As commerce expanded across state lines, diversity-of-citizenship jurisdiction brought more and more cases involving disputes over unregistered trademarks and unfair competition into federal courts. Consequently, cases were increasingly decided by federal courts under rules of federal common law and without regard to state precedents.[248] As a result, in the cross-border regime of trademark and unfair competition law, state sovereignty was a matter of negligible concern.

But adjudication in state courts also neglected choice-of-law issues. In particular, local rules on pleading, proof, and presumptions concerning the content of "foreign" laws (i.e., the legal regimes of other states) contributed to this development. While state courts always took judicial notice of forum law, the laws of other states were regarded as fact—these laws had to be pleaded.[249] Accordingly, unless established by a legal presumption, the content of foreign laws had to be proven.[250] In addition, any presumptions on foreign law were founded on an assumption of common law homogeneity. Hence, it was presumed that a foreign regime would accommodate the general principles of common law. Furthermore, if the forum's common law differed from other states' common law rules on a specific issue, and if the foreign common law was also unclear concerning its content, the "general rule [was] that that view of the common law taken by the courts of the forum will prevail in the absence of evidence of contrary rulings by the

is the language of Lord Justice Turner many years ago, accepted by the courts in this country, that no one has the right to represent his goods as the goods of somebody else.").

246 Act of February 20, 1905, U.S.C., title 15, sec. 81.

247 *See infra* p. 141 *et seq.*

248 *See* 148 A.L.R. 139 (1944), Introduction ("By far the greater number of cases involving an action for infringement of a trademark or for unfair competition are prosecuted in the Federal courts. Most of these cases present occurrences which go beyond the territory of one single state."); *see also* Sergei S. Zlinkoff, *Erie v. Tompkins: In Relation to the Law of Trade-Marks and Unfair Competition*, 42 Colum. L. Rev. 955, 956–957 (1942); Bartholomew Diggins, *Federal and State Regulation of Trade-Marks*, 14 Law & Contemp. Probs. 200, 202 (1949).

249 *See, e.g.*, Raleigh C. Minor, *Conflict of Laws; or, Private International Law* § 212, at 527 (1901) ("[T]he laws of other States are universally regarded as *facts* which, independently of statute, must be specially pleaded, wherever the lex fori requires other facts, under like circumstances, to be pleaded.").

250 *See id.* at § 213, at 528 ("Foreign laws are matters of fact, and like other facts should be proved, unless established by legal presumptions. A court will not take judicial notice of their existence or of their terms. And for this purpose the State of this Union are foreign to one another.").

courts of the foreign State whose law [was] in question."[251] In general, however, it was assumed that the common law was about the same everywhere.[252] At the turn of the century, Raleigh C. Minor expressed this in his treatise on *Conflict of Laws* with a simple but universal (and still modern) rationale:

The true basis of this presumption . . . is to be found in the unwillingness of the courts to deny relief to litigants coming before them, merely for want of a law to administer. Certainly the great weight of authority is in favor of the rule. Nor is it in most instances apt to work any material injustice, since a failure of both parties to present to the court any evidence of the proper foreign law may reasonably justify the court in presuming that neither party finds anything there which would place him in a position more advantageous than he occupies under the lex fori, or which would place his adversary in a less advantageous position. It is not unfair to presume therefore, whatever the real differences may be between the "proper law" and the lex fori, that for the purposes of the case in hand neither party can be injured by the presumption that the two laws are similar.[253]

As a consequence, trademark and unfair competition law at that time was governed by a hodgepodge of state and federal common law rules. There was no clear distinction between different states' laws. Consequently, courts rarely gave regard to questions of choice of law or to the fact that regulatory norms of different sovereigns might diverge. Necessarily, there was also no awareness of trademark territoriality.

[251] *Id.* at § 214, at 530–531. This presumption, however, did not necessarily exist with regard to states that had established codes and civil law systems—e.g., Louisiana, Texas, and Florida. *See* Charles E. Estabrook, *American Interstate Law* 45–46 (2nd edn., 1893); *but see also* Raleigh C. Minor, *Conflict of Laws; or, Private International Law* § 214, 531–532 (1901) ("If the foreign law in issue is the unwritten law of a State not originally subject to the common law, or in any event if it is a statute or written law, the above presumption does not apply .... To this strictly logical view some of the courts have subscribed .... But it must be conceded that the decided trend of the American decisions is towards the presumption, in the absence of contrary evidence, that the foreign law under which either party claims is identical with the lex fori.").

[252] *See supra* p. 132–134. *See also* Frank S. Moore, *Legal Protection of Goodwill* 10–11 (1936); Harry D. Nims, *The Law of Unfair Competition and Trade-Marks, with Chapters on Good-Will, Trade Secrets, Defamation of Competitors and Their Goods, Registration of Trade-Marks, Interference with Competitors' Business, etc., vol. I* § 218b, at 653 (4th edn., 1947) ("[T]rade-marks have not suffered from crossing the boundary lines of the States because the common law of trade-marks has not varied in any material respect in the different States."); Jack J. Rappeport, *Trade-Mark and Unfair Competition in International Conflict of Laws: An Analysis of the Choice of Law Problem*, 20 U. Pitt. L. Rev. 1, 1 and 3 (1958).

[253] Raleigh C. Minor, *Conflict of Laws; or, Private International Law* § 214, 533 (1901).

B The *Erie* Impact: The "Passive Figurehead" of State Sovereignty Reloaded

This situation would change fundamentally after the Supreme Court's 1938 decision in *Erie Railroad Co. v. Tompkins.*[254] As Justice Brandeis famously explained:

> Except in matters governed by the Federal Constitution or by acts of Congress, the law to be applied in any case is the law of the state. And whether the law of the state shall be declared by its Legislature in a statute or by its highest court in a decision is not a matter of federal concern. There is no federal general common law. Congress has no power to declare substantive rules of common law applicable in a state whether they be local in their nature or "general," be they commercial law or a part of the law of torts. And no clause in the Constitution purports to confer such a power upon the federal courts.[255]

Since the *Erie* doctrine applied to equitable suits and remedies based on legal rights,[256] all trademark and unfair competition cases fell within its scope.[257] Prima facie, therefore, *Erie* appeared to put an end to the existence of parallel state and federal regimes on trademark and unfair competition regulation. Some even predicted that the federal common law on trademarks, as a sophisticated body of case law, would disappear, leaving in its wake an underdeveloped common law of the states.[258] Indeed, the invalidation of existing federal common law was seen as a significant hindrance to the development of a comprehensive and sophisticated doctrine in unfair competition law.[259] This concern, however, was unjustified.

[254] *Erie R. Co. v. Tompkins*, 304 U.S. 64 (1938).
[255] *Id.* at 78.
[256] *Ruhlin v. New York Life Ins. Co.*, 304 U.S. 202, 205 (1938); *see also* Sergei S. Zlinkoff, *Erie v. Tompkins: In Relation to the Law of Trade-Marks and Unfair Competition*, 42 Colum. L. Rev. 955, 958–960 (1942).
[257] For the law/equity differentiation, *see supra* p. 78 *et seq.*
[258] *See* Sergei S. Zlinkoff, *Erie v. Tompkins: In Relation to the Law of Trade-Marks and Unfair Competition*, 42 Colum. L. Rev. 955, 960–961 (1942) ("It is true that the application of the Erie doctrine to this type of action may mean that an unusually large and important body of jurisprudence will perhaps be relegated to the scrap heap."); Edward S. Rogers, *Unfair Competition*, 35 Trademark Rep. 126, 130–131 (1945) ("Soon there was built up by decisions of the Federal courts a great body of Federal law dealing with trade-marks and unfair competition. . . . But then came Erie . . ., and there was chaos. There were 48 different sovereignties the decisions of whose courts were the law. The body of Federal decisions which had been 50 years evolving was not binding either on the state or Federal courts. No one knows what the law is. Theoretically, what the Federal courts are required to apply is the law of the State where they might sit. And it was frequently found that there were no applicable State decisions, or that the decisions of the States comprising the same circuit were not uniform. It may take fifty years to get a body of decisional law in the State of Illinois comparable to the one already developed in the Circuit Court of Appeals for the Seventh Circuit.").
[259] *See* Walter J. Derenberg, *The Influence of the French Code Civil on the Modern Law of Unfair Competition*, 4 Am. J. Comp. L. 1, 31 (1955).

Shortly after the *Erie* decision, its application to trademark and unfair competition cases appeared mandatory and comprehensive.[260] In the end, however, all attempts to establish a principle of state common law prevalence proved unsuccessful. The Supreme Court's first trademark case considered after *Erie* was decided in the same year. In *Kellogg Co. v. National Biscuit Co.*, Justice Brandeis included a footnote justifying the court's application of federal precedents:

> The federal jurisdiction rests on diversity of citizenship .... Most of the issues in the case involve questions of common law and hence are within the scope of Erie .... But no claim has been made that the local law is any different from the general law on the subject, and both parties have relied almost entirely on federal precedents.[261]

In other decisions, even lip service to *Erie* was amiss. One example is the US Supreme Court's 1938 case *Armstrong Paint & Varnish Works v. Nu-Enamel Corporation*,[262] in which the court did not refer to state law at all.[263] Similarly, circuit courts were ambiguous about applying *Erie* to trademark and unfair competition disputes. While, for example, in the 1939 case *Sinko v. Snow-Craggs Corp.*[264] the Court of Appeals for the Seventh Circuit founded its application of equitable principles on both pre-*Erie* federal court decisions and a Massachusetts state court decision, it adhered strictly to the *Erie* distinction in *Addressograph-Multigraph Corp. v. American Expansion Bolt & Mfg. Co.* two years later.[265]

260 *See, e.g.*, Edward S. Rogers, Statement, at 12–13, in United States House of Representatives, *Hearings Before the Committee on Patents, Subcommittee on Trade-Marks*, 75th Congress, 3rd Session on H.R. 9041 (15–18 March 1938) ("But you are obliged to consider the fact that there is no Federal common law. There is the common law of the various States and there are 48 States and, of course, the States can change the common law if they want to, and many of them have."); for the contrary position, *see, e.g.*, Zechariah Chafee, Jr., *Unfair Competition*, 53 Harv. L. Rev. 1289, 1300–1301 (1940) ("So far as Unfair Competition is concerned, the *Tompkins* case makes the United States a legal checkerboard. However, registered trademarks are probably immune. United States courts are likely to see the need for protecting such a device in the same way throughout the country. It may be objected that registration is often said not to create a new right but merely to recognize the preexisting common law right in the trademark; and hence, under the *Tompkins* doctrine, the extent of this common law right must be governed by state decisions. But these logical inferences from a vague theory are likely to break down before the desirability of nationwide uniformity.").

261 *Kellogg Co. v. National Biscuit Co.*, 305 U.S. 111, 113 n. 1 (1938).

262 *Armstrong Paint & Varnish Works v. Nu-Enamel Corporation*, 305 U.S. 315 (1938).

263 *See also* Bartholomew Diggins, *Federal and State Regulation of Trade-Marks*, 14 Law & Contemp. Probs. 200, 204 n. 36 (1949).

264 *Sinko v. Snow-Craggs Corp.*, 105 F.2d 450 (7th Cir. 1939).

265 *Addressograph-Multigraph Corp. v. American Expansion Bolt & Mfg. Co.*, 124 F.2d 706, 708 (7th Cir. 1941) ("It appears that the lower court decided the case upon general Federal law. ... We are therefore at the threshold of our consideration met with defendant's contention that under [Erie] the law of the state, as announced by its courts,

In addition, courts were insecure in their application of federal and state law to different issues of trademark and unfair competition infringement. Whenever a federally registered trademark was involved, federal law governed procedure and remedies.[266] In terms of parties' "substantive rights," however, the question was not clear. This issue was contested if, inter alia, the case concerned only intrastate commerce or if both the plaintiff's and the defendant's trademarks were unregistered under federal law.[267] As it seemed, the applicable law depended much more on the allegedly infringing activities than on the trademark rights at issue.[268]

Apart from insecurity concerning the reach of *Erie*, other factors contributed to the factual survival of federal common law. Many states' case law in the field of trademark and unfair competition law was far less developed than the federal law. The scarcity of state precedents provided federal courts with the discretion to continue adjudicating on the basis of old precedents and to further develop the body of federal common law that had technically been abolished. Furthermore, within the states, pre-*Erie* case law had often relied on federal precedents and doctrines. In this regard, the federal common law survived under the guise of "state precedents." Not surprisingly, many federal courts, searching for applicable state law, justified recourse to federal precedents by reference to an alleged identity of rules under both regimes. One example is the Seventh Circuit's decision in *American Photographic Pub. Co. v. Ziff-Davis Pub. Co.*:

> Although local law applies to unfair competition and common law trade-mark infringement where federal jurisdiction is based on diversity of citizenship, . . . the applicable local law does not differ from the general common law of trade-marks. Accordingly, decisions of federal courts and other jurisdictions are in point as illustrations of the common law.[269]

must be given effect, and that by such law, no cause of action was stated or proved. Plaintiff feebly responds to this argument by calling attention to the fact that neither of the parties relied upon the *Erie* case in their briefs . . ., and for this reason it should not be considered here. It further argues that the case, by its very nature, is and should be an exception to the rule therein announced. Neither contention is plausible. A study of the *Erie* case is convincing that it is of general application with the exception . . . 'Except in matters governed by the Federal Constitution or by acts of Congress, the law to be applied in any case is the law of the state.' . . . There is little room for argument but that the District Court, as well as this court, must give application to the Illinois law of unfair competition.").

266 *See, e.g.*, *Armstrong Paint & Varnish Works v. Nu-Enamel Corporation*, 305 U.S. 315, 333 (1938); Bartholomew Diggins, *Federal and State Regulation of Trade-Marks*, 14 Law & Contemp. Probs. 200, 209 (1949).

267 *See, e.g.*, *Philco Corp. v. Phillips Mfg. Co.*, 133 F.2d 663, 672 (7th Cir. 1943).

268 Bartholomew Diggins, *Federal and State Regulation of Trade-Marks*, 14 Law & Contemp. Probs. 200, 209 (1949).

269 *American Photographic Pub. Co. v. Ziff-Davis Pub. Co.*, 135 F.2d 569, 572 (7th Cir. 1943); *see also S.C. Johnson & Son v. Johnson*, 175 F.2d 176, 178 (2nd Cir. 1949)

In sum, fears that the United States would become a legal checkerboard of dozens of state regimes on unfair competition repression proved unwarranted.[270] Although *Erie* may have altered the concept of federal trademark law and ultimately spurred the promulgation of federal statutory trademark law,[271] the existing body of federal trademark case law was never truly invalidated.

Most importantly for this inquiry, with regard to common law uniformity, *Erie* did not significantly affect the universality of interstate trademark protection and unfair competition prevention. Hence, the inherent extraterritoriality of trademark rights survived.

III The 1946 Lanham Act: An Innovation of Almost Territorial Rights

Even though the 1946 Lanham Act stems from lawmakers' intent to give registered trademark rights a maximum extension throughout the territory of the United States, nationwide protection is still subject to a number of exceptions that can be traced back to the common law foundations of US trademark doctrine.[272] Modern domestic trademark doctrine is thus a system of "almost" territorial rights.

A The Common Law Foundation of Federal Statutory Rights

As described above, for a long time, the only source of rules for trademark protection had been judge-made common law. Beginning in the mid-nineteenth century, case law was gradually amended by states' statutory rules. Congress enacted the first trademark statute in 1870. Interestingly, the

(L. Hand, J.); *Coca-Cola Co. v. Busch*, 44 F.Supp. 405, 407 (E.D. Pa. 1942) ("Since jurisdiction here rests upon diversity of citizenship, and the issues involve questions of common law, the matter is within the scope of *Erie* .... This, however, is not of particular importance since the law as announced in the state courts is in no wise different from that laid down by the federal courts.").

270 *See* Zechariah Chafee, Jr., *Unfair Competition*, 53 Harv. L. Rev. 1289, 1300–1301 (1940) ("[N]asty questions of Conflict of Laws will arise under the *Tompkins* case. ... This particularism is out of place in Unfair Competition. Waltham Watches and Baker Chocolate and Yellow Cabs do not stop at state lines, and piratical imitators are equally ubiquitous. In an era of nationwide businesses, the Supreme Court has suddenly formulated an extreme doctrine of States' rights. So far as Unfair Competition is concerned, the *Tompkins* case makes the United States a legal checkerboard."). *See also* Sergei Zlinkoff's corresponding illustration of the risk that a place-of-the-wrong rule under these circumstances might be "apt to assume a Pandora-like character" (Sergei S. Zlinkoff, *Erie v. Tompkins: In Relation to the Law of Trade-Marks and Unfair Competition*, 42 Colum. L. Rev. 955, 965 (1942)).

271 *See, e.g.*, United States Senate Report No. 1333, 79th Congr., 2nd Sess. (14 May 1946), repr. in 1946 U.S. Code Cong. Service, 1274, 1275; *see also* Bartholomew Diggins, *Federal and State Regulation of Trade-Marks*, 14 Law & Contemp. Probs. 200, 204 (1949).

272 *See, e.g.*, 5 J. Thomas McCarthy, *McCarthy on Trademarks and Unfair Competition* § 26:31 (4th edn., 2016).

statute was described as part of "[a]n Act to revise, consolidate, and amend the statutes relating to patents and copyrights." Whether Congress was oblivious to the differences among intellectual property rights is not clear.[273] In 1879, the Supreme Court declared this first statute unconstitutional, thereby clarifying the difference between copyrights and patents on the one hand and trademarks on the other. The US Constitution,[274] the court argued, did not give Congress the authority to legislate in the area of trademark law; rather, the field was reserved for the states.[275] Correspondingly, the next attempt at federal legislation, in 1881, strictly adhered to the confines of Congress's authority granted under the Constitution's trade clause, concerning only the registration of marks that were "used in commerce with foreign nations, or with the Indian tribes."[276]

The first broadening of federal trademark protection prior to the Lanham Act occurred in 1905.[277] Notwithstanding a new option to federally register, the 1905 act did not alter the existing concept of use-based rights. But registration of a trademark under the act provided standing to sue in federal courts. In addition, the act enabled the plaintiff to enforce an injunction in any US court.[278] What was unclear under the 1905 act was whether federal registration would grant preemptive trademark protection beyond the actual area of use. *Tea Rose/Rectanus* had established a narrow rule of use-based trademark acquisition and protection. Against this backdrop, the reach of federal authority was critically important. Since federal power was limited to the regulation of interstate commerce, it was questionable whether a federal registration could protect against intrastate infringements that were remote from the area of actual use by the owner.

[273] For this interpretation, *see, e.g.*, Edward S. Rogers, *The Expensive Futility of the United States Trade-Mark Statute*, 12 Mich. L. Rev. 660, 661 (1913); *see also* Walter J. Derenberg, *Warenzeichen und Wettbewerb in den Vereinigten Staaten von Amerika* 11 (1931); Walter J. Derenberg, *Trade-Mark Protection and Unfair Trading* 2 (1936); Beverly W. Pattishall, *Two Hundred Years of American Trademark Law*, 68 Trademark Rep. 121, 129 (1978). Of course, the difference had already been explained before. *See, e.g.*, Francis H. Upton, *A Treatise on the Law of Trade Marks with a Digest and Review on the English and American Authorities* 14 (1860) ("The right of property in trade marks does not partake in any degree of the nature and character of a patent or copyright, to which it has sometimes been referred—nor is it safe to reason from any supposed analogies existing between them.").

[274] The US Constitution empowers Congress to "promote the Progress of Science and useful Arts, by securing for limited Times to Authors and Inventors the exclusive Right to their respective Writings and Discoveries." (U.S. Const. art. 1, § 8, cl. 8).

[275] *In re Trade-Mark Cases*, 100 U.S. 82, 93–94 (1879).

[276] Act of 3 March 1881, § 1, 21 Stat. 502, 502 (1881).

[277] Act of 20 February 1905, No. 16560, 33 Stat. 724, 724 (1905).

[278] *See, e.g.*, Walter J. Derenberg, *Warenzeichen und Wettbewerb in den Vereinigten Staaten von Amerika* 305–306 (1931); Wallace H. Martin, *Incentives to Register Given by the New Trade-Mark Act, Part I*, 36 Trademark Rep. 213, 214 (1946); Julius R. Lunsford, Jr., *Geographical Scope of Registered Rights—Then and Now*, 61 Trademark Rep. 411, 415 (1971).

In 1929, the Supreme Court decided on this issue in *U.S. Printing & Lithograph Co. v. Griggs, Cooper & Co.* In this case, the plaintiff had used the trademark "Home Brand" for food in several states and had registered the mark federally. The defendant had used the word "Home" on similar products and in combination with other words in states where the plaintiff had not done business before.[279] The Supreme Court of Ohio had decided that *Tea Rose/Rectanus* did not apply due to the plaintiff's federal registration and that the plaintiff's trademark rights would therefore be "project[ed] ... into all the states even in advance of the establishment of trade therein, and ... afford full protection to such registrant and owner."[280] The Supreme Court, however, did not see such a preemptive extension of rights beyond the common law basis. Justice Holmes declared:

> [N]either authority nor the plain words of the [1905] Act allow a remedy upon it for infringing a trade-mark registered under it, within the limits of a State and not affecting the commerce named. More obviously still it does not enlarge common-law rights within a State where the mark has not been used.[281]

But the *Home Brand* holding was of limited value for a comprehensive resolution. It concerned only intrastate competition.[282] For interstate competition, there was no Supreme Court precedent. Such competition had been an issue a few years earlier in the Second Circuit's 1916 *Bismarck* case. The plaintiff owned a federal registration, "Bismarck," that the defendant had allegedly infringed on by making use of the trademark in several states.[283] As the Court of Appeals for the Second Circuit explained, "The rights which a person obtains by registration of a trade-mark under those statutes are coterminous with the territory of the United States."[284] The Supreme Court had granted *certiorari*,[285] but the case was withdrawn before a decision could be rendered.[286] In the 1930s and after, the *Bismarck* holding was harshly contested in scholarly commentary, mostly by reference to the Supreme Court's rejection of federal rights extension in the *Home Brand* case.[287] Even though the two cases were not on all fours,

279 *U.S. Printing & Lithograph Co. v. Griggs, Cooper & Co.*, 279 U.S. 156 (1929).
280 *U.S. Printing & Lithograph Co. v. Griggs-Cooper & Co.*, 119 Ohio St. 151, 160, 162 N.E. 425, 428 (1928).
281 *U.S. Printing & Lithograph Co. v. Griggs, Cooper & Co.*, 279 U.S. 156, 158–159 (1929).
282 For this understanding, *see, e.g.*, Walter J. Derenberg, *Trade-Mark Protection and Unfair Trading* 464 (1936); Frank S. Moore, *Legal Protection of Goodwill* 75 (1936).
283 *Standard Brewery Co. of Baltimore City v. Interboro Brewing Co.*, 229 F. 543 (2nd Cir. 1916).
284 *Id.* at 544.
285 *Interboro Brewing Co. v. Standard Brewing Co. of Baltimore*, 246 U.S. 677 (1918).
286 Walter J. Derenberg, *Trade-Mark Protection and Unfair Trading* 465 (1936).
287 *See, e.g.*, Irvin H. Fathchild, *Territoriality of Registered Trade-Marks*, 3 Idaho L.J. 193, 197 (1933); Walter J. Derenberg, *Trade-Mark Protection and Unfair Trading* 465 (1936);

dominant opinion at the time seemed to agree that there was no extension of trademark rights *ab initio*. Hence, registration did not create new rights; instead, it merely recognized preexisting common law entitlements.[288] In sum, federal rights protection in the first half of the twentieth century was holey at best. Registration would not grant advance protection against infringements in intrastate commerce. With regard to interstate commerce, the situation was unclear but strongly tended toward the same result.[289]

It was therefore the Lanham Act of 1946 that created the first comprehensive system of nationwide registration and protection.[290] The act formally eliminated the effects of *Erie* and expanded the scope of trademark protection beyond the zones of protection that

Frank S. Moore, *Legal Protection of Goodwill* 155–157 (1936); *see also* Harry D. Nims, *The Law of Unfair Competition and Trade-Marks, with Chapters on Good-Will, Trade Secrets, Defamation of Competitors and Their Goods, Registration of Trade-Marks, Interference with Competitors' Business, etc., vol. I* § 218b, at 651 n. 12 (4th edn., 1947) ("In view of the decision of the Supreme Court [in the Homes Brand case], Standard Brewery . . ., no longer is authoritative on this question.").

288 *See, e.g., Estate of P.D. Beckwith v. Commissioner of Patents*, 252 U.S. 538, 543 (1920) (explaining that "[t]he Registration Act of 1905" had not "chang[ed] the substantive law of trade-marks"); *Dwinell-Wright Co. v. National Fruit Product Co.*, 129 F.2d 848, 851, 54 U.S.P.Q. 149 (1st Cir. 1942) ("Registration of a trade-mark under the Trade-Mark Act of 1905 neither enlarges nor abridges the registrant's substantive common-law rights in the mark."); *George W. Luft Co., Inc. v. Zande Cosmetic Co.*, 142 F.2d 536, 541 (2nd Cir. 1944) ("The Trade-Mark Act creates no new substantive rights in those who register their marks."); *see also* Milton Handler & Charles Pickett, *Trade-Marks and Trade Names—An Analysis and Synthesis: II*, 30 Colum. L. Rev. 759, 783 with n. 107 (1930) ("As has been said time and again, the advantages of registration are chiefly procedural; substantive rights are not enlarged."); William D. Shoemaker, *Trade-Marks—A Treatise on the subject of Trade-Marks with particular reference to the laws relating to registration thereof, vol. I* 578 (1931); Walter J. Derenberg, *Trade-Mark Protection and Unfair Trading* 13, 19 *et seq.*, and 460 *et seq.* (1936); Edward S. Rogers, *New Directions in the Law of Unfair Competition*, 74 N.Y. L. Rev. 317, 317 (1940); Harry D. Nims, *The Law of Unfair Competition and Trade-Marks, with Chapters on Good-Will, Trade Secrets, Defamation of Competitors and Their Goods, Registration of Trade-Marks, Interference with Competitors' Business, etc., vol. I* § 223a, at 732 *et seq.* (4th edn., 1947); Bartholomew Diggins, *Federal and State Regulation of Trade-Marks*, 14 Law & Contemp. Probs. 200, 202 (1949); Julius R. Lunsford, Jr., *Geographical Scope of Registered Rights—Then and Now*, 61 Trademark Rep. 411, 415 (1971); Roger E. Schechter, *The Case for Limited Extraterritorial Reach of the Lanham Act*, 37 Va. J. Int'l L. 619, 626 (1997).

289 For an illustrative critique of this situation, *see* Walter J. Derenberg, *Warenzeichen und Wettbewerb in den Vereinigten Staaten von Amerika* 1 (1931) ("Es will nur schwer einleuchten, daß die Vereinigten Staaten, die in der Außenpolitik und der Weltwirtschaft eine so entscheidende Rolle spielen, nach innen weder ihrem eigenen Bürger noch dem Ausländer gegenüber in der Lage sind, den Warenzeichen einen sich über das ganze Staatsgebiet erstreckenden Schutz zu verleihen.").

290 Julius R. Lunsford, Jr., *Geographical Scope of Registered Rights—Then and Now*, 61 Trademark Rep. 411, 415 (1971); Stephen L. Carter, *The Trouble with Trademark*, 99 Yale L.J. 759, 759 (1990); Roger E. Schechter, *The Case for Limited Extraterritorial Reach of the Lanham Act*, 37 Va. J. Int'l L. 619, 626 (1997).

had been acknowledged under the common law rules.[291] Under the act, trademark rights could be established throughout the entire national territory by simple registration, regardless of the registrant's zone of actual use.[292] In this regard, the provision on "constructive notice" in section 22 has been characterized as potentially the greatest advantage of registration.[293] By establishing constructive notice of the registrant's prior use, the *Tea Rose/Rectanus* doctrine was cut back. Once the mark was registered, a second-comer's use could no longer be excused by reference to her good faith and lack of knowledge about the senior trademark.[294] By the Trademark Law Revision Act of 1988, these effects were finally extended from registration to mere application.[295] For the first time, then, actual use was no longer a prerequisite for rights acquisition.[296]

Notwithstanding these modernizing amendments, the goodwill paradigm has remained the foundation of federal trademark protection.[297] And even though the Lanham Act has been characterized as placing federal trademark law "upon a new footing,"[298] trademarks under the act are not *aliud* to rights acquired under common law. The act has not changed the system's doctrinal foundation on use-based rights. Federal

[291] *See, e.g.*, Bartholomew Diggins, *Federal and State Regulation of Trade-Marks*, 14 Law & Contemp. Probs. 200, 213 (1949); William Jay Gross, *The Territorial Scope of Trademark Rights*, 44 U. Miami L. Rev. 1075, 1090 (1990).

[292] See *Application of Beatrice Foods Co.*, 429 F.2d 466, 474 (C.C.P.A. 1970); 5 J. Thomas McCarthy, *McCarthy on Trademarks and Unfair Competition* § 26:13 and § 26:32 (4th edn., 2016).

[293] 15 U.S.C. § 1072, i.e., § 22 Lanham Act. *See, e.g.*, Wallace H. Martin, *Incentives to Register Given by the New Trade-Mark Act, Part I*, 36 Trademark Rep. 213, 215 (1946); Julius R. Lunsford, Jr., *Geographical Scope of Registered Rights—Then and Now*, 61 Trademark Rep. 411, 415 (1971); Beverly W. Pattishall, *Two Hundred Years of American Trademark Law*, 68 Trademark Rep. 121, 139 (1978).

[294] *See, e.g., Dawn Donut Company v. Hart's Food Stores, Inc.*, 267 F.2d 358, 362 (2nd Cir. 1959); *Foxtrap, Inc. v. Foxtrap, Inc.*, 671 F.2d 636, 640 n. 5 (D.C. Cir. 1982); 5 J. Thomas McCarthy, *McCarthy on Trademarks and Unfair Competition* § 26:32 (4th edn., 2016).

[295] *See* Trademark Law Revision Act of 1988, Pub. L. No. 100–667, 102 Stat. 3935; 15 U.S.C. § 1057(c), i.e., § 7(c) Lanham Act.

[296] For an extensive criticism of the Trademark Law Revision Act, *see* Stephen L. Carter, *The Trouble with Trademark*, 99 Yale L.J. 759, 781 *et seq.*, 784 (1990).

[297] *See, e.g.*, United States Senate, Committee on Patents, Senate Report No. 1333, 79th Congr., 2nd Sess. (14 May 1946), repr. in 1946 U.S. Code Cong. Service, 1274, 1277 ("[T]he protection of trade-marks is merely protection to goodwill, to prevent diversion of trade through misrepresentation"); *see also* Stephen L. Carter, *The Trouble with Trademark*, 99 Yale L.J. 759, 767 (1990); Dan L. Burk, *Trademark Doctrines for Global Electronic Commerce*, 49 S. C. L. Rev. 695, 708 (1998); Sara Stadler Nelson, *The Wages of Ubiquity in Trademark Law*, 88 Iowa L. Rev. 731, 739 (2003).

[298] *See, e.g., S.C. Johnson & Son v. Johnson*, 175 F.2d 176, 178 (2nd Cir. 1949) (L. Hand, J.); *see also* Beverly W. Pattishall, *Two Hundred Years of American Trademark Law*, 68 Trademark Rep. 121, 139–141 (1978).

law as well is based on common law principles.[299] In fact, it has even been contended that the act changed nothing at all.[300] A look at some characteristic features of contemporary federal law can clarify this point.

As just mentioned, federal application and registration affords nationwide constructive notice of use or constructive use.[301] This largely prevents trademark right duplication within the United States. In most cases, therefore, a federal trademark owner is protected against other users' adoption of identical or similar marks in remote areas. Yet common-law-based exceptions still exist. First of all, neither application nor registration of a federal trademark can wipe out another's common law right acquired by use prior to the date of application.[302] In addition, even after a federal trademark application has been filed, a junior user may acquire common law trademark rights by use. In this case, the federal applicant may not be protected from a subsequent user's adoption of an identical or similar trademark prior to actual registration.[303] By this means, the statutory system restricts the effects of granting nationwide rights. If an independent common law right has been acquired prior to application or even prior to registration, the federal statutory right is ineffective throughout the local area of the preexisting use-based right. And the common law basis of the exception is also reflected in its inherent limitation: upon registration, the federal statutory right "freezes" the locally preexisting common law right in its current territorial expansion.[304]

[299] *See, e.g.*, *Inwood Laboratories, Inc. v. Ives Laboratories, Inc.*, 456 U.S. 844, 861 n. 2 (1982) (White, J., concurring) ("[T]he purpose of the Lanham Act was to codify and unify the common law of unfair competition and trademark protection."); *see also* Sara Stadler Nelson, *The Wages of Ubiquity in Trademark Law*, 88 Iowa L. Rev. 731, 738 n. 39 (2003); Robert C. Denicola, *Some Thoughts on the Dynamics of Federal Trademark Legislation and the Trademark Dilution Act of 1995*, 59 Law & Contemp. Probs. 75, 79 (1996); Kenneth L. Port, *The Illegitimacy of Trademark Incontestability*, 26 Ind. L. Rev. 519, 520 (1993).

[300] *See* Daphne Robert Leeds, *The Circular Trend in Trademarks*, 47 A.B.A. J. 256, 259 (1961) ("[T]he 1946 Act, as it is now interpreted, does not, in so far as registration is concerned, provide the realistic and rational approach to mid-twentieth century commercial practices as was envisaged by its proponents during the eight years of its pendency. The trend is back to the way we've always done it!"); *see also* Julius R. Lunsford, Jr., *Geographical Scope of Registered Rights—Then and Now*, 61 Trademark Rep. 411, 425 (1971).

[301] *See* 15 U.S.C. § 1072 and § 1057(c), i.e., §§ 22 and 7(c) Lanham Act.

[302] *See, e.g.*, *Johnny Blastoff, Inc. v. Los Angeles Rams Football Co.*, 188 F.3d 427, 435 (7th Cir. 1999); Restatement (Third) of Unfair Competition § 19 (1995), comment e; 5 J. Thomas McCarthy, *McCarthy on Trademarks and Unfair Competition* § 26:31, § 26:40, and § 26:53 (4th edn., 2016).

[303] *See* 15 U.S.C. § 1115(a) and (b), i.e., § 33(a) and (b) Lanham Act. For case law, *see, e.g.*, *Spartan Food Systems, Inc. v. HFS Corp.*, 813 F.2d 1279, 1282 (4th Cir. 1987); *Burger King of Fla., Inc. v. Hoots*, 403 F.2d 904, 907 (7th Cir. 1968).

[304] 5 J. Thomas McCarthy, *McCarthy on Trademarks and Unfair Competition* § 26:45 and § 26:53 (4th edn., 2016). A similar outcome results in cases of concurrent registration

The most intriguing example of common law pedigree is the so-called *Dawn Donut* doctrine. In *Dawn Donut Co. v. Hart's Food Stores, Inc.*,[305] the Court of Appeals for the Second Circuit established that a right owner is entitled to injunctive relief only if her mark has significance in the market—and such significance can exist only where the right owner actually serves her customers.[306] In *Dawn Donut*, the senior user had federally registered trademarks ("Dawn" and "Dawn Donut"). The junior user, a retail seller of donuts and baked goods, started to use the senior trademark in good faith, serving a geographic market different from that of the senior user. As the court concluded, even though a valid registration existed, there was no automatic protection; actual competition was required for relief. Even for registered rights, therefore, the marketplace focus has survived:

> We hold that because no likelihood of public confusion arises from the concurrent use of the mark in connection with retail sales of doughnuts and other baked goods in separate trading areas, and because there is no present likelihood that plaintiff will expand its retail use of the mark into defendant's market area, plaintiff is not now entitled to any relief under the Lanham Act.[307]

B Scholarly Distortions: A Mirage of "Territorial Extraterritoriality"

Comparing the Lanham Act's system of rights acquisition and extension with pre-1947 law, Roger E. Schechter has posited that trademark law was originally grounded on an "explicitly territorial foundation"[308] but that a different system has since been established due to the Lanham Act's

for two or more users in different parts of the federal territory under section 2(d) Lanham Act, 15 U.S.C. § 1052(d). *See* William Jay Gross, *The Territorial Scope of Trademark Rights*, 44 U. Miami L. Rev. 1075, 1097 *et seq.* (1990).

305 *Dawn Donut Company v. Hart's Food Stores, Inc.*, 267 F.2d 358, 362 (2nd Cir. 1959).

306 Stephen L. Carter, *The Trouble with Trademark*, 99 Yale L.J. 759, 790 (1990).

307 *Dawn Donut Company v. Hart's Food Stores, Inc.*, 267 F.2d 358, 360 (2nd Cir. 1959). Of course, the court went on to explain: "This is not to say that the defendant has acquired any permanent right to use the mark in its trading area. On the contrary, we hold that because of the effect of the constructive notice provision of the Lanham Act, should the plaintiff expand its retail activities into [defendant's trading area] the district court ... may enjoin defendant's use of the mark." *See also* Restatement (Third) of Unfair Competition § 19 (1995), comment e. For a similar argument in cases where a federally registered trademark has not yet achieved secondary meaning in a junior user's remote market area, *see, e.g.*, *Anheuser-Busch, Inc. v. Bavarian Brewing Company*, 264 F.2d 88, 92–93 (6th Cir. 1959) ("In areas where there has been no showing that plaintiff has achieved a secondary meaning for the term 'Bavarian' and so is not likely to cause confusion, it may be used fairly by others."). For a critique and further references, *see*, 5 J. Thomas McCarthy, *McCarthy on Trademarks and Unfair Competition* § 29:41 and § 29:42 (4th edn., 2016).

308 Roger E. Schechter, *The Case for Limited Extraterritorial Reach of the Lanham Act*, 37 Va. J. Int'l L. 619, 627 (1997).

peculiar features of registration, priority, and constructive notice. According to Schechter, the Lanham Act has created a situation of trademark rights' "domestic extraterritoriality."[309] The once territorial foundation has been enlarged beyond its initial scope to an area of nationwide protection. Because Lanham Act registration grants the owner a right to control others' uses outside her actual trading area, each area of non-use-based protection, Schechter argues, must be defined as "extraterritorial."[310] I will address his approach in more detail in the next chapter.[311] At this point, it suffices to take a closer look at Schechter's understanding of "territoriality" and "extraterritoriality." Even though his model may not be representative of scholarly commentary and practice, it is typical of the understanding of trademark rights extension in US doctrine. One aspect in particular is eye-catching: characterizing rights extension by the Lanham Act as extraterritorial illustrates the inseparability of rights and geography. Here as well, the common law model of use-based rights dominates legal thinking. *Tea Rose/Rectanus* made trademark acquisition inseparable from the geographic area of use. The implementation of a federal registration system with an option of immediate trademark acquisition upon application or registration has not altered this structure. An extension of rights beyond the area of actual use is therefore deemed extraordinary—in other words, extraterritorial.

A similar characteristic of legal doctrine is reflected in the hesitation to implement a federal law of unfair competition prevention. Suggestions were submitted even before *Erie*. None of these suggestions was implemented in practice, though: no uniform federal statute was enacted, and no common law solution was applied. Most prominently, based on its section 44(i), Edward S. Rogers suggested construing the Lanham Act as having laid out a federal action against unfair competition, covering all conduct that was condemned by either the revised 1883 Paris Convention or the 1929 Inter-American Convention.[312] The Ninth Circuit developed this idea into the *Stauffer* doctrine, named after its 1950 case *Stauffer v. Exley*.[313] Under this approach, any US citizen would receive the same

[309] *Id.*
[310] Correspondingly, he explains the difference between US copyright/patent law and trademark law: Unlike the enactment of trademark statutes, the enactment of copyright and patent statutes did not alter preexisting common law rights. Nor did those statutes alter the territorial scope of copyrights and patents; both common law copyrights and patents were nationwide in scope. *Id.*
[311] *See infra* p. 246–247.
[312] Edward S. Rogers, *The Lanham Act and the Social Function of Trade-Marks*, 14 Law & Contemp. Probs. 173, 183 (1949).
[313] *Stauffer v. Exley*, 184 F.2d 962 (9th Cir. 1950).

protective benefits that foreigners were entitled to under the United States' international obligations. A federal action against unfair competition would have eliminated the oft-enunciated detrimental effects of *Erie*.[314] Other circuits, however, did not follow *Stauffer*.[315] Nor did Congress adopt the suggestion of creating a federal cause of action. This cause of action could have been based on section 5 of the Federal Trade Commission Act.[316] In paragraph 1, this provision declares unlawful "unfair methods of competition in or affecting commerce, and unfair or deceptive acts or practices in or affecting commerce." In addition, it authorizes the Federal Trade Commission to prosecute unfair practices. With regard to the creation of a federal cause of action, it was suggested that the provision also be considered as a basis for private litigation among competitors.[317] But this was unsuccessful. In the end, unfair competition prevention protection remained largely an issue of common law and state law.[318] Until today, the concept of territorially uniform rules of unfair competition prevention has been only rudimentarily developed under the Lanham Act's provisions against unfair competition (e.g., section 43).[319]

IV Summary: Nonformalism and the Nonterritoriality of Trademarks

Political borders within the United States were practically irrelevant as far as the acquisition and protection of common law trademark rights was concerned. Early nineteenth-century trademark protection gave scant regard to state or even national boundaries. And even though the Supreme Court subsequently reduced the initial excess extension, the territoriality of rights remained a nonissue. Based on *Tea Rose/Rectanus*, courts found trademark and unfair competition law to constitute a uniform and comprehensive system of goodwill protection. As a result, the understanding of trademark protection as an instrument of market

[314] Walter J. Derenberg, *The Influence of the French Code Civil on the Modern Law of Unfair Competition*, 4 Am. J. Comp. L. 1, 32 (1955).

[315] *See, e.g.*, *American Auto. Ass'n v. Spiegel*, 205 F.2d 771, 774 (2nd Cir. 1953); *L'Aiglon Apparel v. Lana Lobell, Inc.*, 214 F.2d 649, 653 (3rd Cir. 1954). More recently, *see, e.g.*, *Mattel, Inc. v. MCA Records, Inc.*, 296 F.3d 894 (9th Cir. 2002).

[316] 15 U.S.C. § 45.

[317] *See* Charles Bunn, *The National Law of Unfair Competition*, 62 Harv. L. Rev. 987, 988 *et seq.* (1949); for the contrary position, *see* Walter J. Derenberg, *Trade-Mark Protection and Unfair Trading* 162 (1936).

[318] Some courts, however, have still read norms of the Paris Convention into the Lanham Act, creating a national regime of unfair competition prevention. *See, e.g.*, *General Motors Corp. v. Ignacio Lopez de Arriortua*, 948 F. Supp. 684, 689 (E.D. Mich. 1996); *Maison Lazard et Compagnie v. Manfra, Tordella & Brooks, Inc.*, 585 F. Supp. 1286, 1289 (S.D.N.Y. 1984).

[319] *See, e.g.*, Beverly W. Pattishall, *Two Hundred Years of American Trademark Law*, 68 Trademark Rep. 121, 139–140 (1978).

segmentation and allocation of market shares became the most fundamental characteristic of US trademark doctrine. In a sense, *Tea Rose/Rectanus* established a common law trademark model of immediate market/right correlations. And this distinctly apolitical common law pedigree of US trademark law also survived federalization beginning in the twentieth century. While *Erie* could have been deemed to have put an end to the casual cross-border adjudication in trademark and unfair competition cases, its impact was far less effective than expected. Courts rarely deal explicitly with rights territoriality or issues of state sovereignty. Finally, the Lanham Act, although implementing the first federal regime of acquisition and protection, did not jettison use-based rights as the doctrinal paradigm.

A final conclusion can be drawn in light of this genuine American trademark doctrine. It reflects a significant counterposition to the formalism of German and European law.[320] The acquisition and protection of rights, until today, has scarcely depended on formalities. In 1947, Nims summarized the history of US doctrine by comparing it with British trademark law (which had implemented a statutory registration system in the nineteenth century). He explained that in the United States, "trade-mark statutes, state as well as federal, play a less important part."[321] In the same year, Daphne Robert built on this understanding by arguing that "[a] trade-mark or service mark is not a Government grant."[322] Nims's and Robert's characterizations are representative of the understanding of trademark rights being founded, in large part, on use within the marketplace, not on state-granted privileges. In fact, state and federal registration were sometimes even explicitly deemed irrelevant and ineffective. A 1935 bulletin of the New York Bar Association put it clearly:

> Registration in the U.S. Patent Office is not at all essential for the protection of vested trade-mark rights. ... Vested trade-mark rights are recognized and protected by the courts in all the states irrespective of state or federal registration. ... State registration is helpful only in exceptional cases and the trade-mark owner should not be burdened with the large expense involved in securing such registration except in unusual cases.[323]

[320] *See supra* p. 74–75.

[321] Harry D. Nims, *The Law of Unfair Competition and Trade-Marks, with Chapters on Good-Will, Trade Secrets, Defamation of Competitors and Their Goods, Registration of Trade-Marks, Interference with Competitors' Business, etc., vol. II* § 222, at 730 (4th edn., 1947); *see also* Walter J. Derenberg, *Warenzeichen und Wettbewerb in den Vereinigten Staaten von Amerika* 16 (1931).

[322] Daphne Robert, *The New Trade-Mark Manual—A Handbook on Protection of Trade-Marks In Interstate Commerce* 10 (1947).

[323] Committee on Trade-Marks and Unfair Competition of the Association of the Bar of the City of New York, *Bulletin Regarding Circulars Recently Issued by Certain Self-Styled*

The association's praise for common law "vested rights" was issued in order to warn the public about alleged "Trade-Mark Specialists" trying to solicit business by overemphasizing the relevance of registration for rights acquisition, maintenance, and protection.[324] In explaining the current state of the law, the association unmistakably clarified the reluctance of traditional and contemporary trademark doctrine to adopt the formalities of registration.[325] In other words, a privilege theory never existed in American trademark law.

Section 3 International Trademark and Unfair Competition Law

The paradigm of market/rights correlation has not only survived the federal unification but also affected trademark and unfair competition conflicts law. As Dan Burk has suggested—aptly illustrating the common law approach—the grounding of likelihood-of-confusion testing on market analysis has made common law principles of trademark protection "quite capable of spanning national borders."[326] Accordingly, the question is not "whether an unauthorized use has occurred within a certain territory, but whether a particular use is likely to cause confusion."[327] In other words, it is an analysis not of territorial sovereignty but of market effects. Accordingly, the "*Bulova* test" established by the Supreme Court in 1952 for international trademark and unfair competition conflicts is founded on the "effects on United States commerce." This focus on commerce may have a basis in constitutional law; in essence, however, *Bulova* testing reflects a conventional common law analysis. Before I begin a more specific discussion on this aspect, it is necessary to point out a general characteristic: even though details of foreign rights'

"Trade-Mark Specialists," in *Committee Reports of the Section of Patent, Trade Mark and Copyright Law of the American Bar Association*, 17 J. Pat. Off. Soc'y 732, 740–741 (1935).

324 *Id.* at 736; *see also* Walter J. Derenberg, *Trade-Mark Protection and Unfair Trading* 469 *et seq.* (1936).

325 *See also* Roger's critique of the 1905 act, in which he pointed out that "[w]hat marks are being used is the important question to be answered because it is use alone that creates the right" (Edward S. Rogers, *The Expensive Futility of the United States Trade-Mark Statute*, 12 Mich. L. Rev. 660, 675 (1913)); *see also* Walter J. Derenberg, *Warenzeichen und Wettbewerb in den Vereinigten Staaten von Amerika* 17 (1931); William D. Shoemaker, *Trade-Marks—A Treatise on the subject of Trade-Marks with particular reference to the laws relating to registration thereof, vol. I* 112 (1931); Frank S. Moore, *Legal Protection of Goodwill* 73 and 161 (1936); Harry D. Nims, *The Law of Unfair Competition and Trade-Marks, with Chapters on Good-Will, Trade Secrets, Defamation of Competitors and Their Goods, Registration of Trade-Marks, Interference with Competitors' Business, etc., vol. I* § 214, at 626 (4th edn., 1947).

326 Dan L. Burk, *Trademark Doctrines for Global Electronic Commerce*, 49 S. C. L. Rev. 695, 720 (1998).

327 *Id.*

extension *into* US territory are still widely ambiguous, it is uncontested that market extensions do "carry" concurrent rights across national boundaries. National borders may be pierced by trademark rights—this happens not only from the outside into the United States but also the other way around.

I The Porosity of National Borders and International Goodwill Theory

Prima facie, questions of foreign rights' extension into the United States are not central to the field of conflicts law, or choice of law. After all, within the confines set by international agreements, nation-states are generally free to regulate trademark use and competition on their own soil; the issue, thus, seems to be primarily governed by domestic law. A look at the "well-known marks" doctrine, however, reveals a number of problematic aspects that are also important for this inquiry.[328] The doctrine implements US obligations under article 6*bis* of the Paris Convention.[329] Its aim is to avoid the registration and use of marks that might cause confusion with other marks that, albeit unregistered and unused, are already well known in the country of registration or use.[330] Even though foreign rights' extension into the United States presents the reverse scenario to domestic rights extraterritoriality, a look at how case law handles the protection of foreign trademarks is revealing for an understanding of *Bulova*.

A The Well-Known Marks Doctrine: Transnational Goodwill Misappropriation

Early illustrations of transnational goodwill protection can be found in the 1936 and 1959 New York Supreme Court cases *Maison Prunier v. Prunier's Rest. & Cafe*[331] and *Vaudable v. Montmartre, Inc.*, respectively.[332] In *Maison Prunier*, the plaintiff was operating a restaurant in France that had become famous under the name "Prunier" since the restaurant's founding in 1872. The restaurant had developed international repute, and the owners had opened a branch restaurant in London in 1935; they were also interested in extending their business to New York. Yet, in 1935, the defendants began implementing a business

328 For an overview on the doctrine *see, e.g.*, 5 J. Thomas McCarthy, *McCarthy on Trademarks and Unfair Competition* § 29:61 (4th edn., 2016).

329 *See also* art. 16(2) and 16(3) TRIPS Agreement.

330 G.H.C. Bodenhausen, *Guide to the Application of the Paris Convention for the Protection of Industrial Property* 90 (1968).

331 *Maison Prunier v. Prunier's Rest. & Cafe*, 159 Misc. 551, 552, 288 N.Y.S. 529, 530 (Sup. Ct. 1936).

332 *Vaudable v. Montmartre, Inc.*, 193 N.Y.S.2d 332 (Sup. Ct. 1959).

scheme for operating under the plaintiff's name in New York. In his decision, Justice Shientag began by lamenting the existing doctrine on rights acquisition and protection in geographically separated markets and the rules to be applied in zones of business expansion.[333] Closely following *Tea Rose/Rectanus*, he emphasized that both the reputation of the senior user and the good or bad faith of the second-comer would determine the outcome. As he acknowledged, "The protection may be extended to the market in which the meaning of the original mark has become known."[334] Moreover, he added that "[t]he deliberate appropriation of the name 'Prunier' is some evidence at least of plaintiff's wide repute."[335] And even though he refused to decide whether the defendants' activities were to be seen as "indefensible from an ethical viewpoint and [as] amounting to an aggravated form of commercial piracy,"[336] he enjoined them *pendente lite* from using the plaintiff's name in New York City.

In the second case, a restaurant operator had adopted the name "Maxim's" for his New York city dining place. The original world-famous "Maxim's," founded in Paris in 1893, had become famous for, among other things, having been a setting in Franz Lehár's operetta "The Merry Widow." The court found that there was "no doubt as to [the original restaurant's] unique and eminent position as a restaurant of international fame and prestige."[337] Accordingly, Justice Greenberg enjoined the New York restaurateur from using the name, even though the name owners had expressed no intention to expand their business activity to New York.[338] The court's reasoning, short as it was, displayed a distinct aspect of universality in misappropriation prevention and property protection:

> The trend of the law, both statutory and decisional, has been to extend the scope of the doctrine of unfair competition, whose basic principle is that commercial unfairness should be restrained whenever it appears that there has been a misappropriation, for the advantage of one person, of a property right belonging to another.[339]

Over time, however, this doctrine of an international zone of expansion has become increasingly problematic. Under modern socioeconomic

[333] *Maison Prunier v. Prunier's Rest. & Cafe*, 159 Misc. 551, 557, 288 N.Y.S. 529, 535 (Sup. Ct. 1936) ("The law on this subject, as Nims points out, 'is in a most unsatisfactory state.' ... To paraphrase a forceful judicial expression, it may be suggested whether in these days of rapid and constant intercommunication between states and nations any narrow lines of demarcation should be established on one side of which should stand moral wrong with legal liability, and upon the other moral wrong with legal immunity.").

[334] *Id.* [335] *Id.* at 559. [336] *Id.*

[337] *Vaudable v. Montmartre, Inc.*, 193 N.Y.S.2d 332, 334 (Sup. Ct. 1959).

[338] *Vaudable* is the "international version" of *Stork Restaurant, Inc. v. Sahati*, 166 F.2d 348 (9th Cir. 1948), where a San Francisco junior user was enjoined from using the famous New York nightclub name "The Stork Club."

[339] *Vaudable v. Montmartre, Inc.*, 193 N.Y.S.2d 332, 335 (Sup. Ct. 1959).

circumstances, two bedrock principles of American trademark law have come into sharp conflict. One is the requirement of territorial trademark "use" as a precondition for rights acquisition. The other is an understanding that trademark protection must be in conformity with market penetration. In their struggle to reconcile the two principles, courts have increasingly reverted to the paradigm of goodwill and its detachment from national-political territories. Three recent cases are telling.

In the 2003 *Int'l Bancorp LLC* case, a majority of the Fourth Circuit found the Monte-Carlo Casino's provision of services to American tourists in Monaco and its concurrent advertising for casino services in the United States sufficient to constitute "use in commerce" as a precondition for trademark protection under the Lanham Act.[340] In essence, the requirement of actual use "in the United States" was deemed dispensable. Against a vigorous dissent by Judge Motz,[341] the majority found it sufficient that modern American consumers would travel abroad to the place where services were rendered. Territoriality of use was substituted by customer-base mobility.

The issue of consumer mobility became even more pressing the following year. In the Ninth Circuit's 2004 *Grupo Gigante SA De CV v. Dallo & Co., Inc.* case, the dispute centered on a Mexican chain of grocery stores' use of the mark "Gigante" and an American party's use of the mark in Southern California. Even though the American party had priority of use in California, Judge Kleinfeld ruled in favor of the Mexican right owner:

> We hold … that there is a famous mark exception to the territoriality principle. While the territoriality principle is a long-standing and important doctrine within trademark law, it cannot be absolute. An absolute territoriality rule without a famous-mark exception would promote consumer confusion and fraud. Commerce crosses borders. In this nation of immigrants, so do people. Trademark is, at its core, about protecting against consumer confusion and "palming off." There can be no justification for using trademark law to fool immigrants into thinking that they are buying from the store they liked back home.[342]

340 *Int'l Bancorp, LLC v. Societe des Bains de Mer et du Cercle des Estrangers a Monaco*, 329 F.3d 359, 361 *et seq.* (4th Cir. 2003).

341 *Id.* at 383 (Motz J., dissenting) ("Under United States law, the holder of an unregistered mark must demonstrate 'use in commerce' of that mark in order to be eligible for trademark protection. … there are two essential elements that must be present to constitute 'use in commerce' for Lanham Act purposes: (1) advertising that employs the mark and (2) the rendering of services to which the mark attaches. Neither alone is sufficient. This two-pronged statutory meaning … is what I refer to when I say that [plaintiff] did not 'use' its mark in commerce because it did not 'use' the mark in the United States.").

342 *Grupo Gigante SA De CV v. Dallo & Co., Inc.*, 391 F.3d 1088, 1093–1094 (9th Cir. 2004).

In order for a mark to be characterized as "well known," the court required more than the mere existence of secondary meaning in the relevant market. The mark had to be familiar or known to a "substantial percentage" of consumers in the relevant market sector.[343]

This approach was rejected in 2007 by the Second Circuit in *ITC Ltd. v. Punchgini, Inc.*[344] The plaintiff, ITC, was an Indian corporation that owned and operated the world-famous restaurant "Bukhara" in New Delhi, India. In the 1980s, ITC had further licensed the name to numerous restaurants around the world, including in Chicago and New York. It had also acquired a US trademark registration for the name. Yet in the 1990s, ITC ceased its activities in the United States, and both restaurants were closed. The defendants opened their restaurant in 1999 in New York under the name "Bukhara Grill," with similar décor. Contrary to the Ninth Circuit's decision in *Grupo Gigante*, the Second Circuit denied an implementation of the well-known marks doctrine in federal trademark law.[345] Instead, Judge Raggi referred the case to the New York State high court and, inter alia, certified the question of whether the state's trademark and unfair competition law recognized such a doctrine. And even though the New York Court of Appeals responded that state law did not contain this doctrine, it acknowledged that unfair competition law provides for a claim against misappropriation in the tradition of *Prunier* and *Vaudable*. This is where the doctrine comes full circle:

> Under New York law, "[a]n unfair competition claim involving misappropriation usually concerns the taking and use of the plaintiff's property to compete against the plaintiff[']s own use of the same property" .... The term "commercial advantage" has been used interchangeably with "property" within the meaning of the misappropriation theory .... What *Prunier* and *Vaudable* stand for, then, is the proposition that for certain kinds of businesses (particularly cachet goods/services with highly mobile clienteles), goodwill can, and does, cross state and national boundary lines.[346]

What all decisions make clear is that the existence and extension of goodwill—and, in its wake, trademark rights protection—are largely independent of political borders. Goodwill has a rather organic

[343] *Id.* at 1098 ("[W]here the mark has not before been used in the American market, the court must be satisfied, by a preponderance of the evidence, that a *substantial* percentage of consumers in the relevant American market is familiar with the foreign mark. The relevant American market is the geographic area where the defendant uses the alleged infringing mark.").

[344] *ITC Ltd. v. Punchgini, Inc.*, 482 F.3d 135 (2nd Cir. 2007) certified question accepted, 8 N.Y.3d 994, 870 N.E.2d 151 (2007) and certified question answered, 9 N.Y.3d 467, 880 N.E.2d 852 (2007).

[345] *Id.* at 161 *et seq.*

[346] *ITC Ltd. v. Punchgini, Inc.*, 9 N.Y.3d 467, 478–479, 880 N.E.2d 852, 859 (2007).

structure: it grows and extends with its owner's marketing activities. Once goodwill has crossed a political boundary, the "new" market territory beyond this border becomes part of the uniform and homogeneous whole. This holistic understanding of goodwill has also influenced the reverse scenario: whenever owners of domestic trademarks seek protection against foreign-based conduct and invasion from abroad, the apolitical nature of goodwill tends toward an extension of domestic rights.

B Rudolf Callmann: A Theory of International Unitary Goodwill

While a porosity of national borders for goodwill and trademark rights seemed to be established from the beginning, the issue of where a particular business's goodwill should be situated troubled courts and legal scholars for some time. One famous and illustrative scholarly endeavor was Rudolf Callmann's suggestion that the *situs* of certain "worldmarks" be the place of manufacture and that there be no separate national goodwill or trademark rights in other jurisdictions.[347] Callmann's theory of unitary goodwill was based on two foundations. The first basis was the concept of trademark use in and across many different jurisdictions. According to Callmann, worldmarks identified a product that had been sold in so many countries and so successfully that the trademark had become known in a considerable part of the world—not only to the actual purchasers, but also to sectors of the public that would not consider a purchase. In the eyes of the public at large, he concluded, these trademarks enjoyed a worldwide status as the trademark of a certain business.[348] The second foundation was the idea that "a trademark has only one goodwill."[349] As Callmann

[347] Rudolf Callmann, *Thoughts on the Protection of World Marks*, 44 Trademark Rep. 1134, 1136 (1954); Rudolf Callmann, *Worldmarks and the Antitrust Law*, 11 Vand. L. Rev. 515, 518–519 (1958). Callmann's theory of worldmark protection is distinctly different from the idea of creating a genuine "world trademark." The latter idea concerned the implementation of an internationally valid registration comparable to the Madrid system—not the extension of use-based rights across international borders. It was raised by Edwin Katz in the 1920s (*see, e.g.*, Edwin Katz, *Weltmarkenrecht* (1926); for a critical commentary, *see, e.g.*, Ernst Heymann, *Zur Einführung der Weltmarke*, 1928 JW 2004, 2004; Eduard Reimer, *Warenzeichen-, Wettbewerbs- und Kartellrecht auf der Warschauer Konferenz der International Law Association*, 1928 GRUR 682, 683–684. For a modern version, *see, e.g.*, Graeme B. Dinwoodie, *Private International Aspects of the Protection of Trademarks, WIPO Forum on Private International Law and Intellectual Property*, WIPO/PIL/01/4 (19 January 2001), para. 25 n. 58.

[348] Rudolf Callmann, *Thoughts on the Protection of World Marks*, 44 Trademark Rep. 1134 (1954); Rudolf Callmann, *Worldmarks and the Antitrust Law*, 11 Vand. L. Rev. 515, 518 (1958).

[349] Rudolf Callmann, *Worldmarks and the Antitrust Law*, 11 Vand. L. Rev. 515, 519 (1958).

posited in language resembling nineteenth-century personality rights theory, a business's goodwill could not be "divorced from the source that supplies the market any more than the reputation of a person can be separated from the person."[350] Since a trademark's goodwill was held to be inseparable from the underlying business activity of the trademark owner, the business establishment and the trademark were interconnected with regard to both location and ownership.[351] As he concluded:

> [T]he situs of a worldmark's goodwill is the situs of the international business that produces the article, unless that business uses different national trademarks in the various countries where the article is made and/or sold. The public will, by and large, identify Ford and Coca-Cola with the United States, Coty, Chanel and Cointreau with France, Guiness [*sic*] and Jaguar with England, Fiat and Olivetti with Italy, 4711, Zeiss and Bayer with Germany, and Omega with Switzerland. In all these cases the situs of the goodwill of those marks is the situs of the main business in the United States, France, England, Italy, Germany and Switzerland, respectively. In the case of Unilever, however, its margarine is identified as "White Lune" in England, "Blauband" in Germany, "Start" in Holland, "Solo" in Belgium, "Astra" in France, and "Sava" in Turkey; the situs of the goodwill of each such mark would be in the country where the particular mark is used.[352]

This theory, which Callmann termed an "indivisible or unitary theory of goodwill," was also asserted by a handful of other voices.[353] One example was the decision by the US Commissioner of Patents in *Ex parte E. Leitz, Inc.*:

> It is true that as a result of the sale of German Leitz products in the United States by its American distributor, New York Leitz, a considerable amount of trade mark goodwill was generated in the United States, but such goodwill was not separated, indeed, it was inseparable, from the mark itself. In other words, the goodwill in the United States which was symbolized by the trade mark "Leitz" had its situs in Wetzlar, Germany, where the manufacturer was located. The American distributor acquired no rights in the trade mark or in the goodwill symbolized by it merely as a result of importation and sale in this country of the products of German Leitz.[354]

350 *Id.*

351 For case law on this issue, *see* Callmann's examples: *Ingenohl v. Walter E. Olsen & Co.*, 273 U.S. 541 (1927); *Baglin v. Cusenier Co.*, 221 U.S. 580 (1911); *Societe Vinicole de Champagne v. Mumm Champagne and Importation Co.*, 10 F.Supp. 289 (S.D.N.Y. 1935).

352 Rudolf Callmann, *Worldmarks and the Antitrust Law*, 11 Vand. L. Rev. 515, 518–519 (1958).

353 For a similar argument in Swiss theory, *see* Alois Troller, *Das internationale Privat- und Zivilprozeßrecht im gewerblichen Rechtsschutz und Urheberrecht* 202–203 (1952).

354 *Ex Parte E. Leitz, Inc.*, 105 U.S.P.Q. 481, 483 (Com'r Pat. & Trademarks 1955).

Yet the majority of courts[355] and legal scholars[356] rejected the concept of unitary goodwill. The idea that goodwill needed a *situs* was not contested. Critics did argue, however, that goodwill's extension was dependent on the scope of a business or trade. If the trade covered several national territories, each constituted a separate compartment of independent goodwill.[357] Most simply, for instance, a national market might be separated from neighboring states' markets by a modification of the product. This was Walter Derenberg's point of criticism. He argued that an international product may have different characteristics in different countries, reflecting local preferences. Each national product, due to these differences, would then constitute a separate market. Accordingly, different goodwill "portions" were to be distinguished.[358] Another reason for distinguishing markets was customer perception. On this basis, the District Court for the District of Columbia, in another *Leitz* case, rejected the concept of unitary goodwill: "if the public ever understood or now understands all products bearing the 'Leitz' mark as having originated with German Leitz, its understanding was and is erroneous."[359]

Notwithstanding the majority's rejection of goodwill transnationality and homogeneity, the core question remained unanswered: What would happen in cases where neither product differentiation nor customer perception provided a clear guideline for the geographical or territorial separation of markets? If goodwill really was a subject matter of organic growth, and if it was also apt to transcend national frontiers

[355] *See, e.g.*, Judge Rich's masterful summary of a goodwill-separation theory on the basis of different national laws' territorial validity and effectiveness, in *Roger & Gallet v. Janmarie, Inc.*, 245 F.2d 505, 509–510 (C.C.P.A. 1957): "We think it is a mistake to assume that all of the goodwill symbolized by a trademark in international use has its situs at the place where the goods bearing the mark are made . . .. We are concerned here with business and goodwill attached to United States trademarks, not French trademark rights existing under French law. We take it as axiomatic that neither the trademark law of France nor of the United States has any extraterritorial effect. Where, then, can *business* done under United States trademarks, registered in the United States Patent Office, and the goodwill symbolized by them have their situs except in the territory where United States law is enforceable? The location of the *owner* of such trademarks, the beneficiary of the goodwill attached to them, is an entirely different question."

[356] *See, e.g.*, Walter J. Derenberg, *Territorial Scope and Situs of Trademarks and Good Will*, 47 Va. L. Rev. 733, 736 (1961).

[357] *Id.* (citing to *Commissioners of Inland Revenue v. Muller & Co.'s Margarine, Ltd.* [1901] A. C. 217); for the modern version of this wisdom, *see* Christopher Wadlow, *The Law of Passing-Off—Unfair Competition by Misrepresentation* para. 3–079 (4th edn., 2011); Graeme B. Dinwoodie, *Private International Aspects of the Protection of Trademarks, WIPO Forum on Private International Law and Intellectual Property*, WIPO/PIL/01/4 (19 January 2001), para. 25.

[358] Walter J. Derenberg, *Territorial Scope and Situs of Trademarks and Good Will*, 47 Va. L. Rev. 733, 736 (1961).

[359] *E. Leitz, Inc. v. Watson*, 152 F.Supp. 631, 637 (D.D.C. 1957).

with the stream of commerce or even market communication, arguing in favor of a strictly political segmentation would be difficult. As we will see, the Supreme Court's 1952 *Steele* decision and its progeny have implemented a doctrine of unitary goodwill in the interest of national right owners.

II *Trademarks' Extraterritorial Scope:* Steele v. Bulova Watch Co. *and Its Progeny*

As seen earlier, the once-governing concept of trademark universality, a product of nineteenth-century property theory, was aptly illustrated by *Derringer* and *Kidd. Tea Rose/Rectanus* subsequently reduced these quasi unlimited rights.[360] The factual universality of rights, however, was never fully abolished. This is due to the fact that, unlike in Germany, in the United States this universality was not superseded by a political theory of rights. The disregard for state sovereignty and boundaries would prove determinative. Indeed, in 1952, the Supreme Court implemented the paradigm of an apolitical market relatedness in international trademark conflicts.

A The Epicenter of Extraterritoriality: *Steele v. Bulova Watch Co.*

The Supreme Court's 1952 decision in *Steele v. Bulova Watch Co.*[361] has been duly earmarked as the landmark or "seminal case" of US trademark and unfair competition conflicts law.[362] The majority's opinion was groundbreaking not only because it represented—and continues to do so—the sole Supreme Court decision on the issue. Far more influential than many of the court's precedents in other fields, the majority opinion in *Steele* linked different eras and sectors of US law. First, it connected the early common law precedents on unfair competition conflicts doctrine with a modern test for the then-new Lanham Act's subject-matter jurisdiction. Furthermore, the newly established analysis under the so-called *Bulova* test implemented a number of different strands of conflicts doctrine. Not only does the test require considering concepts of public international law, but it also connects the fields of tort choice of law, trademark conflicts, and international antitrust. In its combination of common law precedents, public international law doctrine, and

360 *See supra* p. 90–93 and p. 102–110.

361 *Steele v. Bulova Watch Co.*, 344 U.S. 280 (1952); *see also* the appellate decision *Bulova Watch Co. v. Steele*, 194 F.2d 567 (5th Cir. 1952).

362 *See, e.g.*, Pamela E. Kraver & Robert E. Purcell, *Application of the Lanham Act to Extraterritorial Activities: Trend Toward Universality or Imperialism?*, 77 Pat. & Trademark Off. Soc'y 115, 129 (1995); Dan L. Burk, *Trademark Doctrines for Global Electronic Commerce*, 49 S. C. L. Rev. 695, 726 (1997).

transnational regulatory litigation, *Steele* was as reactionary as it was innovative.[363]

"The issue," as Justice Clark started the majority's analysis in a rather circular fashion,

> is whether a United States District Court has jurisdiction to award relief to an American corporation against acts of trade-mark infringement and unfair competition consummated in a foreign country by a citizen and resident of the United States.[364]

As would soon become clear, this formulation invited a maximum scope of application for domestic trademark and unfair competition law.[365] As we have seen, traditional concepts of trademark territoriality dominating in contemporary German and European law would have rejected a similar formulation of the issue *ab initio*. Their starting point was strictly territorial: without inland conduct, no domestic rights could be found to be infringed on.[366] While the Supreme Court's dissent argued similarly, the majority disregarded old-fashioned territoriality.[367]

The case facts are as follows: Sidney Steele, the primary defendant in the case, was a US citizen residing in Texas. The plaintiff, Bulova Watch Co., was a watch manufacturer that had registered the "Bulova" trademark in the United States but not in Mexico. Upon learning about the company's lack of formal rights, Steele registered the mark in Mexico, bought watch parts in Switzerland and in the United States, and then had the parts assembled into watches, stamped with the mark "Bulova," and sold. All of this happened exclusively in Mexico. When Bulova learned of Steele's activities, it initiated litigation in the Texas district court. Meanwhile, upon parallel litigation started by Bulova in Mexico, the Mexican registration "Bulova" was eventually canceled. In the United States, the district court dismissed Bulova's complaint on the ground that the court lacked jurisdiction

363 For a highly informative illustration of the case's factual background, *see* Graeme W. Austin, *The Story of Steele v. Bulova: Trademarks on the Line*, 395, 395 *et seq.*, in *Intellectual Property Stories* (Jane C. Ginsburg & Rochelle Cooper Dreyfuss eds., 2006).

364 *Steele v. Bulova Watch Co.*, 344 U.S. 280, 281 (1952).

365 Robert Alpert, *The Export of Trademarked Goods from the United States: The Extraterritorial Reach of the Lanham Act*, 81 Trademark Rep. 125, 142–143 (1991).

366 *See supra* p. 64 *et seq.* and *infra* p. 193 *et seq.* (with numerous references).

367 As Graeme W. Austin has suggested, the court's decision was an "affront to orthodox principles of trademark territoriality," which is one of the reasons for its continued relevance and the ongoing controversy over its reasoning and outcome. *See* Graeme W. Austin, *The Story of Steele v. Bulova: Trademarks on the Line*, 395, 396, in *Intellectual Property Stories* (Jane C. Ginsburg & Rochelle Cooper Dreyfuss eds., 2006).

over the cause;[368] there was no illegal act committed within US territory. The case was then brought to the Court of Appeals, which reversed the decision. The Supreme Court affirmed.

B The *Steele* Progeny: A Motley Crew of Circuit Court Tests

Subsequent case law and scholarship have interpreted the Supreme Court's reasoning and holding as having established three test factors—known as the *Bulova* factors—for Lanham Act extraterritoriality: (1) "nationality or citizenship of defendant," (2) "effects on United States commerce," and (3) "conflicts or potential conflicts with foreign law."[369] Based on these factors, a variety of tests has developed among the circuits. Most prominent among these tests are the Second Circuit's *Vanity Fair* test, the Fifth Circuit's *American Rice* decision, and the Ninth Circuit's *Wells Fargo* or *Timberlane* rule of reason. In addition, the First Circuit has recently established a new test in *McBee v. Delica Co.* All of these tests consider the three *Bulova* factors. And even though the Ninth Circuit is somewhat the outlier, balancing "effects on United States commerce" in a rule of reason derived from antitrust extraterritoriality, the special comity factors integrated into the rule-of-reason test also contain "nationality" and "conflicts with foreign law," among others.

The Second Circuit's 1956 *Vanity Fair Mills, Inc. v. T. Eaton Co.*[370] decision marks the beginning of what has come to be called the *Vanity Fair* test, a modification of the *Bulova* test.[371] The plaintiff sued for trademark infringement stemming from the defendant's allegedly unauthorized use of the "Vanity Fair" name. The plaintiff was a Pennsylvania corporation that had sold women's underwear in the United States (since 1914) and Canada (since 1917). The defendant was a Canadian corporation that had been granted the Canadian trademark registration "Vanity Fair" for similar products, which it began selling in 1915. Due to the defendant's prior registration, the plaintiff was denied a trademark in Canada. When the defendant started selling both

[368] For an illustrative excerpt from the district court's record and the judge's doubts concerning the existence of "affirmative acts done in the United States," *see id.* at 400–401.

[369] *See e.g.*, 5 J. Thomas McCarthy, *McCarthy on Trademarks and Unfair Competition* § 29:58 (4th edn., 2016) (with further reference to case law in the circuits); for an early interpretation in scholarly commentary, *see* Jack J. Rappeport, *Trade-Mark and Unfair Competition in International Conflict of Laws: An Analysis of the Choice of Law Problem*, 20 U. Pitt. L. Rev. 1, 16 (1958).

[370] *Vanity Fair Mills, Inc. v. T. Eaton Co.*, 234 F.2d 633 (2nd Cir. 1956).

[371] For an overview of the Second Circuit's variation on the *Bulova* test, which was followed by other circuits, *see, e.g.*, Robert Butts, *Trademark Law: Interpreting the Congressional Intent of the Extraterritorial Application of the Lanham Trademark Act*, 8 Fla. J. Int'l L. 448 (1993).

the plaintiff's "Vanity Fair" products and its own merchandise under the brand, the plaintiff sought an injunction against the defendant's use in both Canada and the United States. The Second Circuit started by analyzing the Supreme Court's *Bulova* decision and then explained its own version of the three factors: First, the defendant's conduct had to have a "substantial" effect on US commerce. Second, the defendant had to be a US citizen. And finally, conflicts with foreign law were to be avoided. The *Vanity Fair* test was significantly relaxed in later decisions, due mainly to modifications in light of other circuits' interpretations of the *Bulova* test.[372]

In 1977, the Ninth Circuit adopted its own test version. In *Wells Fargo & Co. v. Wells Fargo Express Co.*,[373] it formulated a rule-of-reason approach for assessing the Lanham Act's international reach. In this case, the plaintiff had used the registered trademark "Wells Fargo" throughout the United States. The defendant, a foreign corporation, was using the same trademark in the United States and Europe. After the district court had rejected subject-matter jurisdiction based on *Vanity Fair*, the circuit court vacated the verdict and developed a circuit-specific test based on the jurisdictional rules of reason established in the Ninth Circuit's case law on antitrust extraterritoriality, particularly *Timberlane Lumber Co. v. Bank of America.*[374] This balancing test—a " 'jurisdictional rule of reason' of comity and fairness"— required only "some"[375] effects on US commerce and an additional analysis of several comity factors, notably:

> [1] the degree of conflict with foreign law or policy, [2] the nationality or allegiance of the parties and the locations or principal places of business of corporations, [3] the extent to which enforcement by either state can be expected to achieve compliance, [4] the relative significance of effects on the United States as compared with those elsewhere, [5] the extent to which there is explicit purpose to harm or affect American commerce, [6] the foreseeability of such effect, and [7] the relative importance to the violations charged of conduct within the United States as compared with conduct abroad.[376]

The Ninth Circuit's then-new balancing effort has been interpreted as a stark contrast to the Supreme Court's and the Second Circuit's allegedly

[372] *See, e.g.*, Anna R. Popov, *Watering Down Steele v. Bulova Watch Co. to Reach E-Commerce Overseas: Analyzing the Lanham Act's Extraterritorial Reach Under International Law*, 77 S. Cal. L. Rev. 705, 711 (2004); Brendan J. Witherell, *The Extraterritorial Application of the Lanham Act in an Expanding Global Economy*, 97 Trademark Rep. 1090, 1105 *et seq.* (2007) (for examples *within* the Second Circuit).

[373] *Wells Fargo & Co. v. Wells Fargo Exp. Co.*, 556 F.2d 406 (9th Cir. 1977).

[374] *Timberlane Lumber Co. v. Bank of America N.T. & S.A.*, 549 F.2d 597 (9th Cir. 1976).

[375] *Wells Fargo & Co. v. Wells Fargo Exp. Co.*, 556 F.2d 406, 428 (9th Cir. 1977).

[376] *Id.* at 428–429.

bright-line tests.[377] While the *Bulova* and *Vanity Fair* tests required taking into account only three test factors, the *Timberlane* formula seemed to establish a more sophisticated—and more problematic—analysis, allowing the Ninth Circuit's courts an allegedly wider range of interpretations.[378]

The last circuit to establish its own test was the First Circuit in *McBee v. Delica Co.*[379] In this case, the plaintiff, an American jazz musician, sued a Japanese clothing retailer that had adopted the trademark "Cecil McBee" (identical to the plaintiff's name) for its adolescent female clothing line. The defendant company held a Japanese trademark. Though it did not market its products outside of Japan, the company maintained a website where the trademark was displayed. After the plaintiff's unsuccessful attempt to have the trademark invalidated in the Japanese trademark registry, he filed a complaint asserting trademark dilution and unfair competition. The district court applied the *Vanity Fair* test and denied subject-matter jurisdiction. The circuit court formulated a new test, albeit producing an identical result. Under *McBee*, an inquiry into the defendant's nationality is the mandatory first step of any analysis. Only if the defendant is not a US national will "substantial effects" on US commerce become the determinative factor. As the court further explained, however, even if substantial effects on US commerce are found to exist, a separate comity analysis might still result in the nonapplication of US trademark law.[380]

This multitude of tests suggests that subject-matter jurisdiction under the Lanham Act is prone to various interpretations. The outcome depends on which version of the test is applied. Some courts (such as those in the Ninth Circuit) seem to be more deferential to international concerns and therefore tend to limit the reach of US law. The Second Circuit's *Vanity Fair* test, by contrast, is considered a bulwark for trademark owners against foreign-based infringing activities.[381] The most

[377] *See, e.g.*, Brendan J. Witherell, *The Extraterritorial Application of the Lanham Act in an Expanding Global Economy*, 97 Trademark Rep. 1090, 1108 (2007).

[378] For arguments that the Ninth Circuit's test would offer more options for manipulating the facts and, thus, ultimately result in legal uncertainty, *see, e.g.*, Thomas Berner, *Extraterritorial Application of the Lanham Act: Wells Fargo & Company v. Wells Fargo Express Company, 556 F.2d 406 (9th Cir. 1977)*, 18 Colum. J. Transnat'l L. 173, 192 (1979); Sarah Thomas-Gonzalez, *Extraterritorial Jurisdiction of the Lanham Act: American Rice, Inc. v. Arkansas Ricegrowers Cooperative Ass'n*, 11 Brook. J. Int'l L. 411, 431 (1985); Anna R. Popov, *Watering Down Steele v. Bulova Watch Co. to Reach E-Commerce Overseas: Analyzing the Lanham Act's Extraterritorial Reach Under International Law*, 77 S. Cal. L. Rev. 705, 716–717 (2004); Brendan J. Witherell, *The Extraterritorial Application of the Lanham Act in an Expanding Global Economy*, 97 Trademark Rep. 1090, 1108 (2007).

[379] *McBee v. Delica Co., Ltd.*, 417 F.3d 107 (1st Cir. 2005). [380] *Id.* at 121.

[381] For the idea that the Ninth Circuit test would grant more individual discretion and thereby result in "better" results in terms of justice, *see, e.g.*, Brendan J. Witherell, *The*

significant overextension of trademark protection, however, has probably occurred in the Fifth Circuit. In the 1983 *American Rice* case, both parties were US farmers' marketing cooperatives acting in the United States and abroad. The defendant was selling rice in Saudi Arabia under a trademark similar to the plaintiff's US registration.[382] Even though sales under the allegedly infringing trademark occurred solely in Saudi Arabia and "none of [the] products found their way back into the United States,"[383] the court saw an infringement of the plaintiff's US trademark. Effects on US commerce were seen in Saudi Arabian sales, particularly on the basis that the processing, packaging, transportation, and distribution of US-produced rice constituted activities "within commerce."[384]

III Doctrinal Analysis: Use-Based Rights and Commercial Effects

Before taking a closer look at the *Steele* progeny, I will examine the Supreme Court's majority's opinion from a historical-doctrinal perspective. While a number of attempts have been made to explain the reasoning and holding, there has yet to be a comprehensive analysis exploring how the majority connected pre-Lanham Act case law with the new act. Such an analysis reveals that the judges of the *Steele* majority extended common law tort and unfair competition conflicts law into their statutory interpretation of the Lanham Act's jurisdictional reach. As a result, the paradigm of market-based, organic, and apolitical goodwill extension seeped into modern trademark conflicts doctrine. In addition, in its reference to international antitrust precedents, the majority laid the foundation for a modern reliance on the effects-on-commerce test factor.

A The Common Law Roots of Lanham Act Subject-Matter Jurisdiction

As the *Steele* majority explained, prior to the Lanham Act's enactment, courts had already granted relief to US trademark owners "[u]nder similar factual circumstances."[385] Looking at these cases, they concluded that

Extraterritorial Application of the Lanham Act in an Expanding Global Economy, 97 Trademark Rep. 1090, 1108 (2007).

382 *American Rice, Inc. v. Arkansas Rice Growers Co-op. Ass'n*, 701 F.2d 408, 410 (5th Cir. 1983).

383 *Id.*

384 *Id.* at 414 ("[D]efendant's Saudi Arabian sales had more than an insignificant effect on United States commerce. Each of [the defendant's] activities, from the processing and packaging of the rice to the transportation and distribution of it, are activities within commerce."). For an approving commentary, *see, e.g.*, Sarah Thomas-Gonzalez, *Extraterritorial Jurisdiction of the Lanham Act: American Rice, Inc. v. Arkansas Ricegrowers Cooperative Ass'n*, 11 Brook. J. Int'l L. 411, 436 (1985).

385 *Steele v. Bulova Watch Co.*, 344 U.S. 280, 286 (1952).

the act's language of reaching "all commerce which may lawfully be regulated by Congress" could "not constrict prior law or deprive courts of jurisdiction previously exercised."[386] The Lanham Act's commerce provision thus became a conduit for incorporating common law doctrine into statutory trademark law. In its reference to pre-Lanham Act case law, the majority cited decisions by the New York and New Jersey circuit courts and the Supreme Court of New York.[387]

One of these decisions was the 1907 case *Vacuum Oil Co. v. Eagle Oil Co.*, in which the court had to decide on allegations of international trademark infringement. Both parties to the case were US companies engaged in oil exportation. The plaintiff was doing business in the United States and in Europe. The defendant, Eagle Oil, was purchasing barrels of oil in the United States and shipping them to Germany, among other places, for sale. Eagle Oil attached the plaintiff's trademark to these barrels, but not before their arrival in Germany. In addition to using the plaintiff's trademark, the defendant made false representations concerning the products' origin and production process.[388] The court held that Eagle Oil, its manager, and certain officers had committed fraud and unfair competition not only in Europe (notably Germany) but also in the United States:

> [T]he scheme was designed and intended to injure the defendant's business by the false and fraudulent use of its trade-names, while at the same time maintaining so far as possible an unassailable position. Sufficient evidence has been given to satisfy me that the scheme was conceived and partially, but to a material extent, carried out in this country. . . . It cannot be that the arm of the court is too short to reach and stop this fraudulent conduct, or so much of it, at least, as is carried on in this country. . . . The purchase and shipment of this oil for the purpose of selling it under false representations, and the sale of it under false representations and trade-names abroad in unfair competition with the complainant, was a single business, and each step in the transaction was part of a single fraudulent scheme . . . . This unfair competition has inflicted injury upon the complainant's business in this country by diminishing, or tending to diminish, its foreign trade.[389]

In addition to the domestic-injury-by-foreign-trade-impact paradigm, the court embraced an idea of internationally uniform standards of honesty in commerce. This, as explained in chapter 1, was a common perception at that time.[390] As the court wrote:

[386] *Id.* at 287.

[387] These cases were *George W. Luft Co. v. Zande Cosmetic Co.*, 142 F.2d 536 (2nd Cir. 1944); *Hecker H-O Co. v. Holland Food Corp.*, 36 F.2d 767 (2nd Cir. 1929); *Vacuum Oil Co. v. Eagle Oil Co. of New York*, 154 F. 867 (C.C. N.J. 1907); *Morris v. Altstedter*, 93 Misc. 329, 156 N.Y.S. 1103 (Sup. Ct. 1916).

[388] *Vacuum Oil Co. v. Eagle Oil Co. of New York*, 154 F. 867, 867 *et seq.* (C.C. N.J. 1907).

[389] *Id.* at 874. [390] *See supra* p. 60–63.

> The presumption is that the law in the foreign countries where any part of the fraudulent business was carried on is the same as our own, and that fraudulent acts are unlawful there as here. . . . It is apparent that an act that violates the law of fair dealing and good conscience must be of universal recognition. To assume the contrary is to suppose the foreign countries in question to be in a state of barbarism, and that is to assume a state of affairs that justify this court in applying the law of the forum. . . . But while the action is founded upon fraud, it is also of a transitory character, and the fact that some of the fraudulent acts were committed outside the jurisdiction of this court and outside of the United States will not avail the defendants.[391]

Another decision cited by the *Steele* majority was the 1916 New York Supreme Court's judgment in *Morris v. Altstedter*.[392] Both parties to the case were New York residents. The defendant had attempted to purchase the plaintiff's product for resale. Since an agreement with the plaintiff failed, however, he copied the plaintiff's artistic plaques and mottoes (known as woodenettes), which he then produced and sold solely in Canada. The proceeds, however, went to the defendant's US business. Holding for the plaintiff, and relying on *Vacuum Oil*, the court emphasized the fraudulent character of the defendant's conduct. Since fraud was frowned upon everywhere and an action was considered transitory, no question of territorial limitations came to the fore:

> It has been repeatedly held that an act that violates the law of fair dealing and good conscience must be of universal recognition. Unfair competition in trade is made cognizable by a court of equity, because of its essentially fraudulent character. . . . It has also been held that, while the action is founded upon fraud, it is also of a transitory character, and the fact that some of the fraudulent acts were committed outside of the jurisdiction of this state or the United States will not avail the defendant.[393]

The third decision referenced by the *Steele* majority was the 1944 Second Circuit decision *George W. Luft Co. v. Zande Cosmetic Co.* In this case, as in *Vacuum Oil*, the aspect of injury to the plaintiff's domestic business resulting from losses in foreign trade was present. The plaintiff and defendant, both New York corporations, were manufacturing and selling cosmetics. In a prior proceeding, the district court had found an infringement of the plaintiff's trademark. In its decree, the court had comprehensively enjoined the defendant from using the trademark. As the *Luft* court later explained, "Read literally this seem[ed] to preclude defendants from doing business under [their trademark] anywhere in the world."[394] The *Luft* court deemed this too sweeping, at least with regard to the foreign

[391] *Vacuum Oil Co. v. Eagle Oil Co. of New York*, 154 F. 867, 875 (C.C. N.J. 1907).
[392] *Morris v. Altstedter*, 93 Misc. 329, 332, 156 N.Y.S. 1103 (Sup. Ct. 1916). [393] *Id.*
[394] *George W. Luft Co. v. Zande Cosmetic Co.*, 142 F.2d 536, 540 (2nd Cir. 1944).

business activities of both parties. Hence, the court began its modification of the district court's decree by classifying the parties' business activities into three categories:

As to the foreign business, the evidence . . . bears upon a classification that we regard as relevant, as follows: (a) countries where both parties are doing business and the defendants have established their right by the local law to use the [trademark]; (b) countries where both parties are doing business and the defendants have not established such right; and (c) countries where the defendants are doing business and the plaintiff has not proved that it has ever done business or is likely to do it.[395]

Regarding the first category—countries where both parties had undertaken business activities—the court explained that the defendant's use of the allegedly infringing trademark could not constitute unfair competition or trademark infringement due to the existence of superior foreign rights. Granting a decree under such circumstances, the court felt, would give US trademark rights an extraterritorial effect, unduly interfering with foreign sovereign policies. The court also denied equitable relief against the defendant's activities within the United States that were exclusively concerned with the relevant foreign countries; there was no fraudulent scheme fulfilling the requirements of *Vacuum Oil.* Notwithstanding this liberal stance toward the defendant's foreign activities (founded on superior foreign rights), the concept of foreign-market protection surfaces with particular clarity in the two remaining categories. This is where the *Tea Rose/Rectanus* paradigm of market-based goodwill surfaces. The third category—that is, cases where the alleged infringer was doing business in a country where the domestic trademark owner was not active—is most revealing:

There remains for consideration class (c) countries where the defendants are doing business but the plaintiff has not proved that it ever has done business or is likely to do it. The Trade-Mark Act creates no new substantive rights in those who register their marks. . . . And it is well established that the right to a particular mark grows out of its use, not its mere adoption, and is not the subject of property except in connection with an existing business [inter alia reference to *Tea Rose/ Rectanus*]. Hence if the defendants are doing business in Turkey, for example, but the plaintiff has never extended its trade to that country and there is no evidence that it is likely to do so, the plaintiff has not been damaged by the defendants' Turkish business and is not entitled to restrain its continuance or to an accounting for damages and profits with respect to sales made there.[396]

Even though the *Luft* decision was later praised for avoiding sovereignty conflicts,[397] it actually displays a distinctly different stance. The court did

395 *Id.* 396 *Id.* at 541.

397 *See, e.g.*, Jack J. Rappeport, *Trade-Mark and Unfair Competition in International Conflict of Laws: An Analysis of the Choice of Law Problem*, 20 U. Pitt. L. Rev. 1, 25 (1958).

not double-check for territorial limitations. On the contrary, in its transnational projection of common law zones of protection, the court neglected the fact that US common law trademark rights, by definition, could never extend into foreign territories lacking a common law regime of trademark protection and unfair competition prevention—notably a civil law system like that of Turkey. The court's arguments reflect a focus on universality that also existed in the domestic context: protection follows the right owner's trade and business activities, and political boundaries are, at best, of secondary concern.[398]

The *Steele* majority, in its jurisdictional analysis, considered all these elements. First, it referred to an unlawful scheme on the part of the defendant. Since Sidney Steele had apparently acted with an intent to hide his improper activities in Mexico, it was easy for the majority to conclude that "[i]n sum, we do not think that petitioner by so simple a device can evade the thrust of the laws of the United States in a privileged sanctuary beyond our borders."[399] The defendant's evident bad faith made the analysis a simple task.[400] Less evident is the way the majority extended common law trademark principles. Nevertheless, as we will see below, this aspect has since become an important element of US trademark and unfair competition conflicts law. And it can also be traced to the *Steele* reasons: as the majority explained, the counterfeit watches, filtering into the United States from Mexico, "could well reflect adversely on Bulova Watch Company's trade reputation in markets cultivated by advertising here as well as abroad."[401] Protection of the US trademark "Bulova" against frivolous activities abroad was thus not only founded on the defendant's activities *inside* the United States. In addition, the cross-

[398] For the proposition that *Luft* is still good law and for a discussion of its practical results, *see* Gary D. Feldon, *The Antitrust Model of Extraterritorial Trademark Jurisdiction: Analysis and Predictions After F. Hoffmann-La Roche*, 20 Emory Int'l L. Rev. 651, 661 (2006) ("This rule [*Luft*] functionally gives U.S. companies the equivalent of a foreign trademark registration as soon as they are likely to do business in a foreign country unless their competitors get rights there first."). On *Luft, see also* Thomas Berner, *Extraterritorial Application of the Lanham Act: Wells Fargo & Company v. Wells Fargo Express Company, 556 F.2d 406 (9th Cir. 1977)*, 18 Colum. J. Transnat'l L. 173, 177 *et seq.* (1979).

[399] *Steele v. Bulova Watch Co.*, 344 U.S. 280, 287 (1952).

[400] For the impact of Sidney Steele's openly unfairly competitive business activities, *see* the appellate dissent: "We should not let our personal opinion of, and distaste for, unfair competition lead us into two fundamental errors, which, it seems to me, the majority opinion evidences." (*Bulova Watch Co. v. Steele*, 194 F.2d 567, 572 (5th Cir. 1952) (Russell, J., dissenting)). For a factual background of bad-faith analysis in the district court's proceedings, *see* Graeme W. Austin, *The Story of Steele v. Bulova: Trademarks on the Line*, 395, 402 *et seq.*, in *Intellectual Property Stories* (Jane C. Ginsburg & Rochelle Cooper Dreyfuss eds., 2006).

[401] *Steele v. Bulova Watch Co.*, 344 U.S. 280, 286 (1952).

border osmosis of common law rights—always closely tied to the extension of marketplaces—provided the basis for enjoining injurious activities abroad. In this regard, the court's summary of relevant facts from the record illustratively emphasized the plaintiff's extensive marketing "in the United States and foreign countries [in particular by] advertising [that] has penetrated Mexico."[402] Read in the context of the *Vacuum Oil* parameter of "diminishing ... foreign trade" and of the *Luft* common law rights extension, the Supreme Court formulated a theory of transnational goodwill protection.

Most interesting in this regard, finally, is the fact that neither the Supreme Court majority nor the dissent even mentioned the court's 1927 decision in *Ingenohl v. Walter E. Olsen & Co.*, where Justice Holmes had emphasized the political character of trademark rights.[403] While the concept that "a trade-mark started elsewhere depends for its protection in a foreign jurisdiction on the law prevailing therein, and confers no rights except by consent of that law," had still been highlighted as the guiding principle in Judge Russell's dissent in the Fifth Circuit a few months before,[404] the Supreme Court seemingly let these warnings of political-territorialist thought go unnoticed. In this regard, the American conception of transnational goodwill protection differs distinctly from the English doctrine of passing off in international infringement cases. Even though early case law pointed into the same direction,[405] modern doctrine contradicts an unrestrained extension of goodwill across national borders.[406]

In the end, the *Steele* majority established both domestic *and* foreign-based goodwill as protectable subject matter in multijurisdictional trademark and unfair competition cases. Its substance ever since has been characterized by organic growth across state and national borders—necessarily, therefore, marketplace extension trumps political territory. With *Steele*, an apolitical and nonterritorial interpretation of *Tea Rose/Rectanus* had gone global.

402 *Id.* at 284. For a discussion of the company's extensive advertising, *see also* Graeme W. Austin, *The Story of Steele v. Bulova: Trademarks on the Line*, 395, 398, in *Intellectual Property Stories* (Jane C. Ginsburg & Rochelle Cooper Dreyfuss eds., 2006).

403 *Ingenohl v. Walter E. Olsen & Co.*, 273 U.S. 541, 544 (1927). *See also supra* p. 132–134.

404 *Bulova Watch Co. v. Steele*, 194 F.2d 567, 573 (5th Cir. 1952) (Russell, J., dissenting).

405 *See, e.g., R. Johnston & Co. v. Archibald Orr Ewing & Co.* [1882] 7 App. Cas. 219 (case of exclusive export competition).

406 *See, e.g.*, Christopher Wadlow, *The Law of Passing-Off—Unfair Competition by Misrepresentation* para. 3–015 (4th edn., 2011); *see also* less critically Richard Plender & Michael Wilderspin, *The European Private International Law of Obligations* para. 18–095 (4th edn., 2015).

B An Element of Modernity: The Effects-on-Commerce Factor

Apart from the cross-border extension of use-based rights, *Steele* laid the foundation of effects testing in Lanham Act subject-matter-jurisdiction analysis. By this means, unlike civil law territoriality doctrine, *Steele* quite early incorporated a characteristic of economic regulation into US trademark conflicts law. Ever since, goodwill as a subject matter of protection and economic effects as an indicator for finding an infringement have been fused into a combined test for jurisdiction.

The majority's focus on the results of the defendant's activities starts with a reference to *American Banana.*[407] Initially, the court distinguished *Steele* from *American Banana* on the ground that Sidney Steele's alleged infringements were private and individual conduct, as opposed to the sovereign-state acts in *American Banana*. Nevertheless, international antitrust doctrine was found to be relevant in trademark law as well. As the majority explained, there was no

> blanket immunity on trade practices which radiate unlawful consequences here, merely because they were initiated or consummated outside the territorial limits of the United States. Unlawful effects in this country, absent in the posture of the Banana case before us, are often decisive.[408]

The concept of effects was still rejected by a strong dissent.[409] But this warning from old-school territorialists went unheard. On the contrary, over time it became the most influential factor of the *Bulova* test. One of the last circuit courts to explicitly decide on an issue of extraterritoriality was the First Circuit in 2005. In *McBee v. Delica Co.*,[410] the appellate court rejected the first instance's application of the *Vanity Fair* test and developed a new analysis in which it stated that the "sole touchstone to determine jurisdiction" over foreign defendants was whether the defendant's acts have a "substantial effect upon United States commerce." Interestingly, the First Circuit also referred to antitrust precedent, particularly the doctrine of *Hartford Fire.*[411] In this regard, *McBee* marks the end of a long series of decisions that have developed the analysis of Lanham Act subject-matter jurisdiction into a genuine effects test.

[407] *See Steele v. Bulova Watch Co.*, 344 U.S. 280, 288 (1952) (citing to *American Banana Co. v. United Fruit Co.*, 213 U.S. 347 (1909)).

[408] *Id.*

[409] *Id.* at 292 (Reed, J., dissenting) ("The Lanham Act . . . should be construed to apply only to acts done within the sovereignty of the United States.").

[410] *McBee v. Delica Co.*, 417 F.3d 107 (1st Cir. 2005).

[411] *Id.* at 118 *et seq.*

IV *A Bird's-Eye View: Taking Stock of Lanham Act Extraterritoriality*

The number of cases featuring opinions sufficiently detailed to allow for a closer analysis of the *Bulova* test or the circuit court variants is relatively small. Between 1952 and 2014, US federal courts have issued more than 140 opinions on the issue of Lanham Act subject-matter jurisdiction.[412] This relatively small number is quite surprising if we look at the prophesies anticipating an enormous rise in conflicts litigation in the field of international intellectual property.[413] On the other hand, under a more pragmatic perspective, this outcome is not too perplexing. If it is true that the king's writ reaches only as far as his sword, many, if not most, conflicts will remain unlitigated.[414] In a world where most foreign-based infringements cannot be prosecuted in domestic fora for lack of personal jurisdiction over the alleged infringer, it would be naïve to expect a large body of case law to have evolved. Despite this relative scarcity of cases, however, one may still attempt to examine case numbers and opinion content in order to verify two characteristics of US conflicts doctrine that have been highlighted thus far. One is the assumption of effects dominance in conflicts testing—that is, the idea that the existence and intensity of effects determine whether domestic rights will be protected and whether national policy will be enforced extraterritorially. The second aspect is the common law pedigree of modern trademark conflicts doctrine, particularly with regard to the traditional conception of market-related, organic, and thus necessarily nonterritorial rights under *Tea Rose*/*Rectanus*. While I will try to verify these two aspects by looking at the totality of opinions, I

412 For case selection and principles of the opinions' analysis, *see infra* appendix A and appendix B.

413 *See, e.g.*, Pamela E. Kraver & Robert E. Purcell, *Application of the Lanham Act to Extraterritorial Activities: Trend Toward Universality or Imperialism?*, 77 J. Pat. & Trademark Off. Soc'y 115, 115 (1995); Curtis A. Bradley, *Territorial Intellectual Property Rights in an Age of Globalism*, 37 Va. J. Int'l L. 505, 506 (1997); Dan L. Burk, *Trademark Doctrines for Global Electronic Commerce*, 49 S. C. L. Rev. 695, 728–731 (1997); Serge G. Avakian, *Global Unfair Competition in the Online Commerce Era*, 46 UCLA L. Rev. 905, 913 (1999); Roger E. Schechter & John R. Thomas, *Intellectual Property—The Law of Copyrights, Patents and Trademarks* 833 (2003); Xuan-Thao N. Nguyen, *The Digital Trademark Rights: A Troubling New Extraterritorial Reach of United States Law*, 81 N. C. L. Rev. 483, 483 (2003); Anna R. Popov, *Watering Down Steele v. Bulova Watch Co. to Reach E-Commerce Overseas: Analyzing the Lanham Act's Extraterritorial Reach Under International Law*, 77 S. Cal. L. Rev. 705, 706 (2004); Richard L. Garnett, *Trademarks and the Internet: Resolution of International IP-Disputes by Unilateral Application of U.S. Laws*, 30 Brook. J. Int'l L. 925, 926 (2005); Jason Webster, *Trademark Law—Extraterritorial Application of the Lanham Act—McBee v. Delica Co., Ltd., 417 F.3d 107 (1st Cir. 2005)*, 30 Suffolk Transnat'l L. Rev. 263, 269 (2006).

414 For this allegory in the context of internet regulation, *see, e.g.*, James Boyle, *Foucault in Cyberspace: Surveillance, Sovereignty, and Hardwired Censors*, 66 U. Cin. L. Rev. 177, 179 (1997).

am of course aware of the potential objections from an empirical standpoint.[415] This is why I will not call my inquiry an "empirical" study; instead, I will characterize it as a bird's-eye view of *Steele* and its progeny between 1952 and 2014.

A The Antitrust Gene: A Dominance of Effects

Looking at all of the opinions' test-factor analyses for the relevant period, we can divide the case population into two groups. The first group consists of opinions where the court's analysis of the three factors[416] found them all to point in the same direction—either in favor of or against extraterritoriality. Opinions in the second group decided the issue of Lanham Act application based on different test outcomes for the individual factors. The first group contains 48 opinions in which all three factors were found to either favor or disfavor application of the Lanham Act. The majority (40) of these opinions found the Lanham Act to apply, while the minority (8) rejected Lanham Act subject-matter jurisdiction. Since in all these opinions all three factors were found to point in the same direction, however, this group does not provide immediate insight into the relationship between factors.[417]

The picture is much more revealing for the second group, whose 92 opinions involved different factor results. Two subgroups can be distinguished within this second group. The first subgroup consists of 12 opinions that expressly and separately tested and decided on the result of the test for each of the three factors. The second subgroup consists of 80 opinions that—even though they also featured a discussion of at least one factor—applied the test only to the extent that the court found necessary. In other words, these opinions left at least one factor untested or undecided. Both subgroups provide information on the different factors' weight for the outcome.

My analysis of factor dominance begins with the smaller subgroup (12 in total) in which the courts expressly found different outcomes for each of the three test factors. Of the 10 opinions that found the Lanham Act not to apply, 7 denied the existence of "effects on United States commerce."[418] In 3 of these opinions, both test outcomes for defendant

415 *See again infra* in appendix A.

416 That is, either within a three-pronged test or within the *Timberlane* rule of reason (*see supra* p. 161–164).

417 One could assume, of course, that the outcome on a single factor's test (e.g., a finding of "effects on U.S. commerce") might influence the court's decision with respect to the other test factors. Yet, proof of such a hypothesis would require a more extended empirical approach than that followed here.

418 *Atlantic Richfield Co. v. Arco Globus Intern. Co.*, No. 95 CIV. 6361(JFK), 1997 WL 607488 (S.D.N.Y., 29 May 1997); *Atlantic Richfield Co. v. Arco Globus Intern. Co.*, 150

"nationality" and "conflicts with foreign law" would have favored application of the Lanham Act.[419] The other 3 opinions having found "effects" to exist but still not applying the Lanham Act found the defendant's foreign "nationality" and "conflicts with foreign law" to outweigh existing effects on US commerce. The first is a 1983 decision of the Western District of New York that still closely adhered to the circuit's 1956 precedent. The court found "substantial effects" but denied application of the Lanham Act in light of the *Vanity Fair* holding, the defendant's Canadian citizenship, and potential conflicts between the court's own ruling and a Canadian court ruling.[420] Another case was decided under the *Timberlane* rule of reason with the finding that the conflicts factor "weighs strongly against extraterritorial application of the Lanham Act."[421] Ultimately, the Court for the Central District of California balanced the comity subfactors with special regard to the fact that—although substantial ties to the United States (and, hence, sufficient "allegiance" under the *Timberlane* factor list) existed—some of the defendants were foreign citizens.[422] The third case, decided by the Easter District of New York under the Second Circuit's more recent *Sterling Drug* precedent,[423] featured a finding of both nationality and conflicts pointing toward nonapplication of the Lanham Act.[424] Of the 2 opinions

F.3d 189 (2nd Cir. 1998); *Groeneveld Transport Efficiency, Inc. v. Lubecore Intern., Inc.*, 730 F.3d 494 (6th Cir. 2013); *International Café, S.A.L. v. Hard Rock Café International (U.S.A.)*, 252 F.3d 1274 (11th Cir. 2001); *Southco, Inc. v. Fivetech Technology Inc.*, 982 F.Supp.2d 507 (E.D. Pa. 2013); *Tommy Hilfiger Licensing, Inc. v. Costco Companies, Inc.*, No. 99 Civ. 3894(LMM), 2001 WL 55735 (S.D.N.Y., 23 January 2001); *Trader Joe's Co. v. Hallatt*, 981 F.Supp.2d 972 (W.D. Wash. 2013).

419 *Atlantic Richfield Co. v. Arco Globus Intern. Co.*, No. 95 CIV. 6361(JFK), 1997 WL 607488 (S.D.N.Y., 29 May 1997); *Atlantic Richfield Co. v. Arco Globus Intern. Co.*, 150 F.3d 189 (2nd Cir. 1998); *Tommy Hilfiger Licensing, Inc. v. Costco Companies, Inc.*, No. 99 Civ. 3894(LMM), 2001 WL 55735 (S.D.N.Y., 23 January 2001).

420 *C-Cure Chemical Co., Inc. v. Secure Adhesives Corp.*, 571 F.Supp. 808, 821 (W.D.N.Y. 1983).

421 *Pinkberry, Inc. v. JEC Intern. Corp.*, No. CV 11-6540 PSG (PJWx), 2011 WL 6101828, at *5 (C.D. Cal., 7 December 2011).

422 *Id.* at *6 and *8 ("On balance, the factors weigh against extraterritorial application of the Lanham Act. This case is ultimately controlled by Star—Kist. Like Star—Kist, Plaintiffs seek adjudication of the right to use a foreign trademark in a foreign country where the parties include U.S. corporations who are contemporaneously litigating the validity and rights to the trademark in that foreign country. Indeed, Star—Kist concerned only U.S. parties. Here, Kawashima and Morioka are citizens of Japan and JEC has a place of business in Japan. Consequently, this situation presents an even greater concern for 'principles of international comity and fairness.' ").

423 For an extensive analysis of the Second Circuit's "modernized" *Vanity Fair* test under *Sterling Drug, Inc. v. Bayer AG*, 14 F.3d 733 (2nd Cir. 1994), *see infra* p. 507 *et seq.*

424 *United Air Lines, Inc. v. United Airways, Ltd.*, No. 09-CV-4743 (KAM)(JMA), 2013 WL 1290930, at *10–11 (E.D.N.Y., 4 March 2013).

that decided in favor of the Lanham Act's application, both featured a finding of sufficient "effects on United States commerce." One court found the defendant's US nationality—broadly understood under the *Timberlane* comity analysis—and effects on US commerce sufficient to outweigh conflicts with foreign law.[425] The other considered the defendant's foreign nationality negligible based on a simultaneous finding of effects and missing conflicts with foreign law.[426] In sum, therefore, it may appear as if "effects" alone or "nationality" and "conflicts with foreign law" together can make a difference.

This tentative finding is further strengthened by the results for the subgroup of opinions (80 in total) sparing a comprehensive discussion and application of *all* factors. Indeed, as a closer look unveils, these opinions reflect a significant pattern: they can be divided into a subpopulation where the court found "nationality" and "conflicts with foreign law" pointing toward nonapplication of the Lanham Act—then overcoming a positive finding of "effects" or making an "effects" analysis dispensable. In addition, a different segment of the population features opinions where the finding of "effects" or "no effects" was so significant that the other two factors were considered largely irrelevant. Excluding a few opinions that have featured extraordinary scenarios of the subject-matter jurisdiction test,[427] the group can be divided into 41 opinions applying the Lanham Act and 35 opinions denying its application.

A rough summary of factor testing and neglect shows that courts treated the three factors differently: The effects factor was disregarded, considered irrelevant, or considered neutral, or a decision on the effects test was left open in 20 of these 76 opinions (26.32%). The defendant's

[425] *Aristocrat Technologies, Inc. v. High Impact Design & Entertainment*, 642 F.Supp.2d 1228, 1237 (D. Nev. 2009) ("The second factor in the balancing test is the nationality or allegiance of the parties and the locations or principal places of business of the involved corporations. One of the plaintiffs ... is a Nevada corporation that is a subsidiary of ... an Australian corporation. ... Both of these parties have substantial contacts with the United States. As to the defendants, [one] is a Venezuela corporation whose principal place of business appears to be Venezuela, [the others are] allegedly a Nevada corporation, and ... Nevada residents. ... Because all but one of the parties have significant contacts to the United States, the second factor weighs in favor of extraterritorial application of the Lanham Act.") and *id.* at 1238 (for the balancing).

[426] *Libbey Glass, Inc. v. Oneida Ltd.*, 61 F.Supp.2d 720 (N.D. Ohio 1999).

[427] This notably concerns cases where the court ultimately did not balance all of the test factors with a clear result of application or nonapplication of the Lanham Act because it vacated a lower court's decision (*see, e.g.*, *Sterling Drug, Inc. v. Bayer AG*, 14 F.3d 733 (2nd Cir. 1994); *Nintendo of America, Inc. v. Aeropower Co., Ltd.*, 34 F.3d 246 (4th Cir. 1994)), or where the court's arguments concern different categories of defendants (*see, e.g.*, *RMS Titanic, Inc. v. Zaller*, 978 F.Supp.2d 1275 (N.D. Ga. 2013); *Aerogroup Intern., Inc. v. Marlboro Footworks, Ltd.*, 955 F.Supp. 220 (S.D.N.Y. 1997)).

nationality and potential conflicts with foreign law, by contrast, were ignored 49 times (64.47%) and 55 times (72.37%), respectively. In 33 of 76 opinions (43.42%), the courts decided the case solely upon finding effects to exist or be missing, and either did not address the nationality and conflicts factor at all or left a test decision open. Moreover, 31 of the 41 opinions (75.61%) finding the Lanham Act to apply also found sufficient effects on US commerce. In 17 of these opinions (54.84%), the courts left *both* "nationality" and "conflicts" undiscussed—in any case, undecided—and based their decisions solely on "effects."[428] In 6 opinions, the courts did not discuss nationality.[429] And in another 7 opinions, they did not perform a conflicts-with-foreign-law test.[430] Among the opinions that did not expressly find effects and nonetheless applied the Lanham Act are, notably, decisions

[428] *Citizens of Humanity, LLC v. Caitac Intern., Inc.*, No. B215232, 2010 WL 3007771 (Cal. Ct. App., 3 August 2010); *Dunkin' Donuts, Inc. v. Mercantile Ventures*, No. EP-91-CA-154-B, 1992 WL 156566 (W.D. Tex., 8 January 1992); *Dwyer Instruments, Inc. v. Sensocon, Inc.*, No. 3:09-CV-10 TLS, 2009 WL 8705579 (N.D. Indiana, 20 November 2009); *Gallup, Inc. v. Business Research Bureau (Pvt.) Ltd.*, No. C 08–01577 WHA, 2008 WL 4857027 (N.D. Cal., 10 November 2008); *General Motors Corp. v. Ignacio Lopez de Arriortua*, 948 F.Supp. 684 (E.D. Mich. 1996); *International Business Machines Corp. v. Comdisco, Inc.*, No. 91 C 6777, 1993 WL 155511 (N.D. Ill., 10 May 1993); *Jackson v. Grupo Industrial Hoteleros, S.A.*, No. 07–22046-CIV, 2008 WL 4648999 (S.D. Fla., 20 October 2008); *King v. Allied Vision, Ltd.*, 807 F.Supp. 300, 307 (S.D.N.Y. 1992); *Medimport, S.R.L. v. Cabreja*, No. 12–22255-CIV, 2012 WL 3632580 (S.D. Fla., 31 July 2012); *Mertik Maxitrol GmbH & Co. KG v. Honeywell Technologies SARL*, No. 10–12257, 2011 WL 2669370 (E.D. Mich., 7 July 2011); *Partners for Health and Home, L.P. v. Seung Wee Yang*, Nos. CV09-07849 RZ, CV10-04073 RZ, 2011 WL 6210452 (C.D. Cal., 14 December 2011); *Philip Morris, Inc. v. Midwest Tobacco, Inc.*, No. 88–1292-A., 1988 WL 150693 (E.D. Va., 4 November 1988); *Reebok Intern. Ltd. v. American Sales Corp.*, 11 U.S.P.Q.2d 1229 (C.D. Cal. 1989); *Scanvec Amiable Ltd. v. Chang*, 80 Fed.Appx. 171 (3rd Cir. 2003); *Three Degrees Enterprise, Inc. v. Three Degrees Worldwide, Inc.*, 22 U.S.P.Q.2d 1357 (3rd Cir. 1991); *Ubiquiti Networks, Inc. v. Kozumi USA Corp.*, No. C 12–2582 CW, 2012 WL 1901264 (N.D. Cal., 25 May 2012); *V'Soske, Inc. v. Vsoske.com*, No. 00 Civ. 6099(DV), 2003 WL 1747144 (S.D.N.Y., 1 April 2003).

[429] *Air Turbine Technology, Inc. v. Atlas Copco AB*, 295 F.Supp.2d 1334 (S.D. Fla. 2003); *Fun-Damental Too, Ltd. v. Gemmy Industries Corp.*, 111 F.3d 993 (2nd Cir. 1997); *Louis Vuitton Malletier, S.A. v. Akanoc Solutions, Inc.*, No. C 07–03952 JW, 2010 WL 5598337 (N.D. Cal., 19 March 2010); *Ramirez & Feraud Chili Co. v. Las Palmas Food Co.*, 146 F.Supp. 594 (S.D. Cal. 1956); *Scotch Whiskey Ass'n v. Barton Distilling Co.*, 489 F.2d 809 (7th Cir. 1973); *Star-Kist Foods, Inc. v. P.J. Rhodes & Co.*, 769 F.2d 1393 (9th Cir. 1985).

[430] *Babbit Electronics, Inc. v. Dynascan Corp.*, 38 F.3d 1161 (11th Cir. 1994); *Houbigant, Inc. v. Development Specialists, Inc.*, 229 F.Supp.2d 208 (S.D.N.Y. 2002); *Mattel, Inc. v. MCA Records, Inc.*, 296 F.3d 894 (9th Cir. 2002); *New Name, Inc. v. The Walt Disney Co.*, No. CV 07–5034 PA (RZx), 2008 WL 5587486 (C.D. Cal., 25 July 2008); *TNT USA, Inc. v. TrafiExpress, S.A. de C.V.*, 434 F.Supp.2d 1322 (S.D. Fla. 2006); *V'Soske, Inc. v. Vsoske.com*, No. 00 CIV 6099 DC, 2002 WL 230848 (S.D.N.Y., 15 February 2002); *Zenger-Miller, Inc. v. Training Team, GmbH*, 757 F.Supp. 1062 (N.D. Cal. 1991).

from the Fifth Circuit's cascade of *American Rice* opinions, where the subject-matter issue is handled particularly liberally with a virtually unrestricted scope of the Lanham Act.[431] Furthermore, in a number of opinions, the effects prong was subdued in the discussion, especially since the court applied an older, shortened, or exotic variant of subject-matter jurisdiction testing.[432] Disregarding this small group of outlier cases, it is evident that US law will rarely apply absent an express finding of "effects." In other words, the existence of "effects on US commerce" is a practical *conditio sine qua non* for Lanham Act subject-matter jurisdiction.

The effects prevalence is similarly evident with respect to opinions that ultimately denied subject-matter jurisdiction. Among the 35 that did not apply the Lanham Act, 23 expressly found "no effects" (65.71%). Among these, 16 opinions (69.57%) left out *both* nationality and conflicts testing or rejected a definite decision on both factors and based their finding that subject-matter jurisdiction is amiss on the lack of effects alone.[433] Yet as this bird's-eye view further unveils, despite its general prevalence, the

[431] See *American Rice, Inc. v. Arkansas Rice Growers Co-op. Ass'n*, 532 F.Supp. 1376, 1383 (D.C. Tex. 1982).

[432] *See, e.g., Euromarket Designs, Inc. v. Crate & Barrel Ltd.*, 96 F.Supp.2d 824 (N.D. Ill. 2000) (applying the court's own *Intermatic v. Toeppen* jurisdiction analysis (for cyber-squatting cases)); *see also* the gap of effects testing in *A.T. Cross Co. v. Sunil Trading Corp.*, 467 F.Supp. 47 (S.D.N.Y. 1979); *Blue Cross and Blue Shield Ass'n v. Group Hospitalization and Medical Services, Inc.*, 744 F.Supp. 700, 712–713 (E.D. Va. 1990); *John Walker and Sons, Ltd. v. DeMert & Dougherty, Inc.*, 821 F.2d 399 (7th Cir. 1987); *Menendez v. Faber, Coe & Gregg, Inc.*, 345 F.Supp. 527 (S.D.N.Y. 1972); and the short-capped analysis of internet-based infringements in *Stevo Design, Inc. v. SBR Marketing Ltd.*, 919 F.Supp.2d 1112, 1121 (D. Nev. 2013), and in *The Name LLC v. Arias*, No. 10 Civ. 3212(RMB), 2010 WL 4642456, at *5 (S.D.N.Y., 16 November 2010).

[433] *ACG Products, Ltd. v. Gu*, No. 10-cv-716-wmc, 2011 WL 7748354 (W.D. Wisc., 4 November 2011); *Baden Sports, Inc. v. Molten*, No. C06-210MJP, 2007 WL 2058673 (W.D. Wash., 16 July 2007); *Bernstein v. Medicis Pharmaceutical Corp.*, No. 03 C 5256, 2004 WL 2092001 (N.D. Ill., 15 September 2004); *Guantanamera Cigar Co. v. Corporacion Habanos, S.A.*, 672 F.Supp.2d 106 (D.C. 2009); *Gucci America, Inc. v. Guess?, Inc.*, 790 F.Supp.2d 136 (S.D.N.Y. 2011); *Hong Leong Finance Ltd. (Singapore) v. Pinnacle Performance Ltd.*, No. 12 Civ. 6010(JMF), 2013 WL 5746126 (S.D.N.Y., 23 October 2013); *International Academy of Business and Financial Management, Ltd. v. Mentz*, No. 12-cv-00463-CMA-BNB, 2013 WL 212640 (D. Colo., 18 January 2013); *Lithuanian Commerce Corporation, Ltd. v. Sara Lee Hosiery*, 47 F.Supp.2d 523 (D.N.J. 1999); *Love v. Associated Newspapers, Ltd.*, 611 F.3d 601 (9th Cir. 2010); *McBee v. Delica Co., Ltd.*, 417 F.3d 107 (1st Cir. 2005); *Mertik Maxitrol GmbH & Co. KG v. Honeywell Technologies Sarl*, No. 10–12257, 2011 WL 1454067 (E.D. Mich., 13 April 2011); *Omega S.A. v. Omega Engineering, Inc.*, 396 F.Supp.2d 166 (D. Conn. 2005); *Paul E. Hawkinson Co. v. Anderson Tire & Treads, Inc.*, No. 11–1168 ADM/JJG, 2011 WL 4590413 (D. Minn., 30 September 2011); *Tire Engineering and Distribution, LLC v. Shandong Linglong Rubber Co., Ltd.*, 682 F.3d 292 (4th Cir. 2012); *Totalplan Corp. of America v. Lure Camera Ltd.*, Nos. 82-CV-0698E(M) thru 82-CV-0701E(M), 1993 WL 117504 (W.D.N.Y., 12 April 1993); *World Book, Inc. v. IBM Corp.*, 354 F.Supp.2d 451 (S.D.N.Y. 2005).

effects factor is not completely unchallenged. Altogether, 6 opinions (including the 2 opinions in the *Vanity Fair* dispute[434])—even though effects had been alleged to exist—ultimately rejected jurisdiction on the basis of *both* nationality and conflicts, pointing against application of the Lanham Act. An ultimate and definite analysis of effects was then not undertaken.[435] Moreover, the Ninth Circuit's Court of Appeals decided that potential conflicts alone could hinder the Lanham Act's application even though sufficient effects on commerce were found to exist.[436] And district courts in the Second and the Ninth Circuit found, inter alia, the defendant's "nationality" (without an analysis of "conflicts") to be determinative—even though "effects" seemed to exist.[437]

This analysis helps us draw a conclusion: while the concept of effects was initially an element of antitrust doctrine, it has since become the most relevant test factor for Lanham Act application in cases of international trademark infringement and unfair competition violations. The "effects on US commerce" factor has been the one most often used by courts to decide on the issue of extraterritoriality, while the two other factors, at least taken individually, are less influential. The impact of the effects factor can go in either direction—either in favor of or against a finding of Lanham Act application. If effects are amiss, Lanham Act subject-matter jurisdiction is hard to establish; and if effects are found to exist, both nationality and the conflicts factors regularly lose impact—at least if not marching together in the opposite direction.

B Common Law Goodwill Protection: *Tea Rose/Rectanus* Goes Global

It was not just the antitrust pedigree of the *Steele* majority's arguments but also their common law foundation that has dominated trademark

434 *Vanity Fair Mills, Inc. v. T. Eaton Co.*, 133 F.Supp. 522 (S.D.N.Y. 1955); *Vanity Fair Mills, Inc. v. T. Eaton Co.*, 234 F.2d 633, 642–643 (2nd Cir. 1956). The *Steele* dissent as well as the dissent in the Fifth Circuit's *Bulova* opinion, actually, also rejected application of the Lanham Act on the basis of conflicts with foreign law. *See Bulova Watch Co. v. Steele*, 194 F.2d 567, 572–573 (5th Cir. 1952); *Steele v. Bulova Watch Co.*, 344 U.S. 280, 289–292 (1952).

435 *American White Cross Laboratories, Inc. v. H.M. Cote, Inc.*, 556 F.Supp. 753, 757–758 (S.D.N.Y. 1983); *Gelicity UK Ltd. v. Jell-E-Bath, Inc.*, No. 10 Civ. 5677(ILG)(RLM), 2013 WL 3315398, at *4 (E.D.N.Y., 1 July 2013); *Juicy Couture, Inc. v. Bella Intern. Ltd.*, 930 F.Supp.2d 489, 505–508 (S.D.N.Y. 2013); *Vespa of America Corp. v. Bajaj Auto Ltd.*, 550 F.Supp. 224 (N.D. Cal. 1982). The rigidity of *Vanity Fair* has been diluted by the Second Circuit Court of Appeals in *Sterling Drug, Inc. v. Bayer AG*, 14 F.3d 733 (2nd Cir. 1994). I will address this decision more closely *infra* in chapter 6.

436 *Star-Kist Foods, Inc. v. P.J. Rhodes & Co.*, 769 F.2d 1393, 1395–1396 (9th Cir. 1985).

437 *Playboy Enterprises, Inc. v. Chuckleberry Publishing, Inc.*, 511 F.Supp. 486 (S.D.N.Y. 1981); *Zenger-Miller, Inc. v. Training Team, GmbH*, 757 F.Supp. 1062 (N.D. Cal. 1991).

conflicts law ever since. While "effects on US commerce" have ultimately become the most relevant test factor in practice, the subject matter being protected was (and continues to be) the trademark owner's use-based goodwill. Lanham Act application in international conflicts—like the domestic doctrine of trademark protection—is based on the conception of preventing improper goodwill invasion, even on foreign territories if necessary.

Typically, when testing for "effects on US commerce," a court will start by defining the Lanham Act's substantive law policy, particularly regarding the prevention of consumer confusion and deception. In international trademark doctrine, an occurrence of consumer confusion usually equals the finding of effects.[438] In addition to consumer confusion, injury to the trademark owner may also indicate a relevant effect. In this regard, courts after *Steele* have developed and made use of a number of effects subfactors. This array of subfactors reflects the historical multitude of policies, primarily with respect to the development of legal doctrine in domestic trademark and unfair competition law. As we have seen, concepts of goodwill protection, along with diversion-of-sales and misappropriation prevention, have dominated the debate from the fields' nineteenth-century incipiencies forward.[439]

A bird's-eye view reveals that a substantial share of all opinions decided between 1952 and 2014 extended the effects test using a number of subfactor analyses. Overall, 119 opinions (85%) made use of different subfactors. The subfactors considered were the following:

- "consumer confusion" (tested in 51 opinions (36.43%))
- "diversion/loss of sales" (tested in 48 opinions (34.29%))
- domestic activities that provided "material support for foreign trademark use/business," that constituted "essential steps [within the United States] in the course of business consummated abroad," or that constituted the "orchestration of foreign activities" (tested in 46 opinions (32.86%))
- "damage to (ability to do) business and/or income" that affected the "value of plaintiff's holdings" or caused "monetary harm" or "losses to the right owner" in general (tested in 44 opinions (31.43%))
- "damage to/adverse reflection on reputation/goodwill" (tested in 43 opinions (30.71%))

[438] Recently, *see, e.g., McBee v. Delica Co.*, 417 F.3d 107, 121 (1st Cir. 2005) ("The 'substantial effects' test must be applied in light of the core purposes of the Lanham Act, which are both to protect the ability of American consumers to avoid confusion and to help assure a trademark's owner that it will reap the financial and reputational rewards associated with having a desirable name or product.").

[439] *See supra* p. 94 *et seq.*

- "sale/offering of goods abroad with subsequent entering into the U.S." (tested in 31 opinions (22.14%))
- "misrepresentation" without further specification (tested in 10 opinions (7.14%))
- "using/putting goods into the stream of U.S. commerce," making "physical use of the U.S. commerce stream," using "instrumentalities of U.S. commerce," or "availing oneself of business opportunities inside the U.S." (tested in 9 opinions (6.43%))
- "misappropriation/tarnishing of trademark rights/goodwill" (tested in 7 opinions (5%))
- a few more uncommon factors, such as "loaning funds in/transacting bank business in the U.S." (tested in 6 opinions (4.39%)); "financial gain of a U.S. entity [i.e., defendant] received from abroad" (tested in 5 opinions (3.57%)); and whether defendant had violated "fair competition rules" (tested in 1 opinion (0.71%)).

A number of these subfactors can be traced to the *Steele* majority's finding of an "unlawful scheme."[440] They aim primarily at the prevention of "unfairness," not at goodwill protection. They cover defendant activities that provide "material support for foreign trademark use/business," that undertake "essential steps [within the United States] in the course of business consummated abroad," or that involve the defendant's "orchestration of foreign activities." All of these subfactors are distinctly focused on the defendant's *territorial* activities. This means that they generally require conduct *within* the United States to be fulfilled.

In addition, one category of subfactors is only indirectly connected to the issue of goodwill protection; there is no connection to the right owner's market position. These subfactors reflect a concern for unfairness prevention and an aim to protect the right owner's financial assets or her business in general. Among this category are the subfactors "using/putting goods into the stream of U.S. commerce," making "physical use of the U.S. commerce stream," making "use of instrumentalities of U.S. commerce," and "availing oneself of business opportunities inside the U.S.," as well as a test for "damage to (ability to do) business and/or income" or for effects on the "value of plaintiff's holdings," "monetary harm," or "losses to the right owner" in general.[441]

Moreover, the subfactor "sale/offering of goods abroad with subsequent entering into the U.S." is a direct descendant of the Supreme

[440] *See supra* p. 164 *et seq.*

[441] With respect to the least common subfactors "loaning funds in/transacting bank business in the U.S.," "financial gain of a U.S. entity [i.e., defendant] received from abroad," and the test whether defendant has violated "fair competition rules," the lack of connex to the concept of goodwill protection is also evident.

Court's postsale confusion argument that the fake watches sold in Mexico might filter into the United States and injure the plaintiff's domestic goodwill.[442] Even though this subfactor is largely goodwill related, it concerns the plaintiff's *domestic* market and, accordingly, her *domestic* rights and goodwill position.

This is different for the remainder of the list:

- "consumer confusion,"
- "diversion/loss of sales,"
- "damage to/adverse reflection on reputation/goodwill,"
- "misrepresentation," and
- "misappropriation/tarnishing of trademark rights/goodwill."

A remarkable number of opinions in the group that used these subfactors followed what we can characterize as a "transnational goodwill" approach. This approach can be directly traced to the common law pedigree of the Supreme Court majority's decision in *Steele*. It represents the international projection of the traditional common law conception of trademark and goodwill acquisition and protection.[443] More concretely, in these opinions, the courts justified application of the Lanham Act based on the exclusive occurrence of one or more subfactors abroad, or on a simultaneous occurrence of one or more subfactors both abroad and within the United States. They thereby allowed for a transnationalization of the analysis—in other words, they permitted both domestic goodwill and foreign-based goodwill to be considered the subject matter of protection. Accordingly, under all these subfactors, both territorial and foreign-based conduct were qualified as "infringing upon" a plaintiff's trademark or goodwill.

Let us start the more detailed analysis with a look at some concrete examples of the courts' subfactor analyses. These opinions not only asked for a domestic occurrence of subfactor phenomena but also found sufficient effects to exist if these phenomena occurred on foreign territory. The *Steele* majority set the stage for this approach:

> In the light of the broad jurisdictional grant in the Lanham Act, we deem its scope to encompass petitioner's activities here. His operations and their effects were not confined within the territorial limits of a foreign nation. He bought component parts of his wares in the United States, and spurious "Bulovas" filtered through the Mexican border into this country; his competing goods could well reflect adversely on Bulova Watch Company's trade reputation in markets cultivated by advertising here as well as abroad.[444]

[442] *See supra* p. 168–169. [443] *See supra* p. 168 *et seq.*
[444] *Steele v. Bulova Watch Co.*, 344 U.S. 280, 286 (1952).

In other words, the majority found effects in potential damage to the plaintiff's goodwill that extended across the United States *and* Mexico.[445] By connecting the Lanham Act's jurisdictional grant with effects on commerce, and then connecting effects on commerce with a concept of rights that covers all geographic areas where the owner's goodwill exists, the majority established the basis on which later courts built domestic rights' extraterritoriality. Indeed, courts after *Steele* significantly extended this idea of goodwill protection on foreign territory. Of course, some courts distinguished between the national and international contexts, but many did not. The Second Circuit's *Atlantic Richfield* decision illustrates a cautious analysis:

> At best, [the plaintiff] has shown that [the defendant] has a geographic presence in the United States and ... that some decision-making regarding [the defendant's] foreign activities has taken place on American soil. We do not think that such a presence suffices to trigger an extraterritorial application of the Lanham Act. The ultimate purpose of the Lanham Act pertinent to this appeal is to encourage domestic sellers to develop trademarks to assist domestic buyers in their purchasing decisions. ... Where (i) an alleged infringer's foreign use of a mark does not mislead American consumers in their purchases or cause them to look less favorably upon the mark; (ii) the alleged infringer does not physically use the stream of American commerce to compete with the trademark owner by, for example, manufacturing, processing, or transporting the competing product in United States commerce; and (iii) none of the alleged infringer's American activities materially support the foreign use of the mark, the mere presence of the alleged infringer in the United States will not support extraterritorial application of the Lanham Act. The presence of a foreign infringer, without more, simply does not call into play any purpose of that Act.[446]

Yet the majority of courts have been less critical. In 2005, the First Circuit—visibly aware of the problem of policy and goodwill overextension—illustrated this approach in its creation of a new test variant in *McBee*:[447]

> McBee's second argument is that Delica's sales have confused Japanese consumers, hindering McBee's record sales and touring career in Japan. Evidence of economic harm to McBee in Japan due to confusion of Japanese consumers is less tightly tied to the interests that the Lanham Act intends to protect, since there is no United States interest in protecting Japanese consumers. American courts do, however, arguably have an interest in protecting American commerce by protecting McBee from lost income due to the tarnishing of his trademark in Japan. Courts have considered sales diverted from American companies in foreign

[445] *See also* Graeme W. Austin, *The Story of Steele v. Bulova: Trademarks on the Line*, 395, 413–414, in *Intellectual Property Stories* (Jane C. Ginsburg & Rochelle Cooper Dreyfuss eds., 2006).

[446] *Atlantic Richfield Co. v. Arco Globus Intern. Co., Inc.*, 150 F.3d 189, 193–194 (2nd Cir. 1998); *see also Tommy Hilfiger Licensing, Inc. v. Costco Companies, Inc.*, No. 99 Civ. 3894 (LMM), 2001 WL 55735 (S.D.N.Y., 23 January 2001).

[447] *McBee v. Delica Co., Ltd.*, 417 F.3d 107 (1st Cir. 2005).

countries in their analyses. ... Assuming arguendo that evidence of harm to an American plaintiff's economic interests abroad, due to the tarnishing of his reputation there, might sometimes meet the substantial effects test. ...[448]

Roughly speaking, three different aspects of the *Steele* common law extensions and its impact can be distinguished. The first is a general extension of legal policies underlying domestic trademark and unfair competition law; in particular, this concerns the subfactors of "consumer confusion" and "misrepresentation." As courts in the Ninth and the Fifth Circuit have assumed, the Lanham Act's policies extend beyond the domestic domain into international transacting. One example is the Southern District of California's 1989 *Van Doren Rubber Co., Inc. v. Marnatech Enterprises, Inc.*[449] decision, in which the court explained:

The Lanham Act imposes upon this Court "the duty to protect the entire gamut of purchasers, including non-English-speaking purchasers, in various countries throughout the world to which the defendants intend to export their [counterfeits]." ... Moreover, "Congress has the power to prevent unfair trade practices (even) in foreign commerce by citizens of the United States, although some of the acts are done outside the territorial limits of the United States."[450]

But *Van Doren Rubber Co.* not only reveals a view under which the Lanham Act's policies are considered universal. In addition, it illustrates a second instrument of overextension—the diversion-of-sales subfactor. As many courts have assumed, a diversion of sales, even on foreign territory, should be considered an invasion of foreign-based goodwill and should thus suffice to trigger application of the Lanham Act. In *Van Doren Rubber Co.*, the court also found a diversion of the plaintiff's foreign-based sales (in Mexico) and a resulting "decrease [in] the value of the American plaintiff's consolidated holdings," as well as direct damage to the "plaintiff's goodwill not only in Mexico but in the United States."[451] Further

[448] *Id.* at 125–126.

[449] *Van Doren Rubber Co., Inc. v. Marnatech Enterprises, Inc.*, CIV A. No. 89–1362 S BTM, 1989 WL 223017 (S.D. Cal., 17 October 1989).

[450] *Id.* at *3 (internal citations omitted). The court refers to another decision, *R.J. Reynolds Tobacco Co. v. Virginia International Export, Inc.*, 220 U.S.P.Q. 712 (E.D. Va. 1982). For the entire-gamut-of-purchasers argument, *see also Babbit Electronics, Inc. v. Dynascan Corp.*, 38 F.3d 1161, 1180 (11th Cir. 1994); *Reebok Intern. Ltd. v. American Sales Corp.*, 11 U.S.P.Q.2d 1229 (C.D. Cal. 1989). *See also Pearl Brewing Co. v. Trans-USA Corp.*, No. CIV.3:96-CV-3020-H, 1997 WL 340940, at *2 (N.D. Tex., 12 June 1997) ("The extraterritorial reach of the Lanham Act is intended to prevent foreign consumers from being confused and American producers from losing valuable goodwill in their marks abroad.").

[451] *Van Doren Rubber Co., Inc. v. Marnatech Enterprises, Inc.*, CIV A. No. 89–1362 S BTM, 1989 WL 223017, at *4–5 (S.D. Cal., 17 October 1989). For the diversion-of-sales subfactor in the Fifth Circuit, *see also American Rice, Inc. v. Arkansas Rice Growers Co-op. Ass'n*, 701 F.2d 408, 414–15 (5th Cir. 1983).

examples of the diversion-of-sales factor are the Ninth Circuit's *Reebok Intern. Ltd. v. Marnatech Enterprises, Inc.* decision and the Second Circuit's *Totalplan Corp. of America v. Colborne* ruling. In *Reebok*, the Ninth Circuit wrote:

> The district court found that, at the very least, Betech organized and directed the manufacture of counterfeit REEBOK shoes from the United States and knew that their counterfeit shoes went back to the United States with regular frequency. The district court further found that Betech's sales of counterfeit REEBOK shoes decreased the sale of genuine REEBOK shoes in Mexico and the United States and directly decreased the value of Reebok's consolidated holdings. . . . A review of the record indicates that those findings are in no way clearly erroneous. . . . Betech's activities thus affect American foreign commerce in a manner which causes an injury to Reebok cognizable under the Lanham Act.[452]

The Second Circuit used virtually the same language in *Totalplan*, explaining that

> the district judge did not err in finding that Totalplan failed to demonstrate that Lure's shipment of Love cameras abroad had a substantial effect on United States commerce. Unlike Bulova, there is no evidence that infringing goods have affected United States commerce by re-entering the country and causing confusion. Furthermore, although Totalplan relies on the Fifth Circuit's decision in [1983 American Rice] for the proposition that the packaging and shipment of goods from the United States constitutes a "substantial effect" on United States commerce, American Rice merely established that such activities, when combined with diversion of foreign sales from a plaintiff, constitute "more than an insignificant effect on United States commerce."[453]

More recently, finally, the Southern District of New York openly drew a direct line from the diversion-of-sales subfactor to the *Steele* conception of transnational goodwill:

> U.S. consumer confusion or harm to the plaintiff's goodwill in the U.S. certainly suffices. . . . Financial harm to an American trademark owner whether from the loss of foreign sales or the damage to the trademark owner's reputation abroad is at the very least, relevant to determining whether foreign infringement has a substantial effect on U.S. commerce. See Bulova Watch, 344 U.S. at 287 . . . (citing fact that defendant's "competing goods could well reflect adversely on Bulova Watch Company's trade reputation in markets cultivated by advertising

[452] *Reebok Intern. Ltd. v. Marnatech Enterprises, Inc.*, 970 F.2d 552, 554–555 (9th Cir. 1992). *See also, e.g., Best Western Intern., Inc. v. 1496815 Ontario, Inc.*, No. CV 04-1194-PHX-SMM, 2007 WL 779699, at *5 (D. Ariz., 13 March 2007).

[453] *Totalplan Corp. of America v. Colborne*, 14 F.3d 824, 830 (2nd Cir. 1994). *See also, e.g., Calvin Klein Industries, Inc. v. BFK Hong Kong, Ltd.*, 714 F.Supp. 78, 80 (S.D.N.Y. 1989); *Les Ballets Trockadero de Monte Carlo, Inc. v. Trevino*, 945 F.Supp. 563, 567 (S.D. N.Y. 1996).

here as well as abroad" as a factor weighing in favor of extraterritorial application of Lanham Act).[454]

Finally, a third aspect of transnational rights extension can be found in the *Luft* pedigree of *Steele*,[455] which is still alive. Until today, a number of courts have expressly described international trademark conflicts as an issue of foreign-market protection asking for the parties' positions in light of the traditional goodwill paradigm. In particular, this surfaces in the subfactors "damage to reputation" and "misappropriation of goodwill." One drastic example of this perspective is the Third Circuit's decision in the multijurisdictional trademark conflict *Three Degrees Enterprise, Inc. v. Three Degrees Worldwide, Inc.*,[456] which refers directly to the *Tea Rose/Rectanus* doctrine:

> [Plaintiff] Enterprise is unable to rely upon a registered mark. Accordingly, it is entitled to protection only in geographic areas where it has established a market for its goods.... The Court [in Hanover Star (1916)], held that the trademark of a prior user should be protected from infringement by a subsequent user of the same mark only in areas where the prior user has established a market for its goods: Since it is the trade, and not the mark, that is to be protected, a trademark acknowledges no territorial boundaries of municipalities or states or nations, but extends to every market where the trader's goods have become known and identified by his use of the mark. ... Thus, the senior user of a common law mark may not be able to obtain relief against the junior user in an area where it has no established trade, and hence, no reputation and no good will. ... It is in this context that the district court concluded that Enterprise had demonstrated "no presence" in locations other than the United States and Monte Carlo. The fact that Enterprise may have had isolated contracts in the past to perform using its service mark in England, Japan and Bahrain does not establish that it has accomplished the kind of market penetration that would warrant a worldwide injunction or even an injunction covering those countries.[457]

The paradigm of transnational goodwill protection in the sense of an organic and apolitical extension of rights across state and national borders can also be explained in numbers:

Altogether, 119 opinions (out of 140 (85%)) have made use of one or more subfactors. Among these, 59 opinions (49.58%) considered

[454] *Rodgers v. Wright*, 544 F.Supp.2d 302, 313 (S.D.N.Y. 2008).

[455] *See supra* p. 166 *et seq.*

[456] *Three Degrees Enterprise, Inc. v. Three Degrees Worldwide, Inc.*, 22 U.S.P.Q.2d 1357, 1360 (3rd Cir. 1991).

[457] *Id.* at 1360. For more approval of the *Luft* conception, *see Totalplan Corp. of America v. Colborne*, 14 F.3d 824, 831 (2nd Cir. 1994); *further also Leatherman Tool Group, Inc. v. Cooper Industries, Inc.*, 47 U.S.P.Q.2d 1045 (D. Or. 1997). A similar perspective surfaces in *Dunkin' Donuts Inc. v. Mercantile Ventures*, No. EP-91-CA-154-B, 1992 WL 156566, at *10 (W.D. Tex., 8 January 1992).

subfactors under the transnational-goodwill paradigm with respect to foreign-based scenarios. Among other things, they considered a loss of sales *abroad* or confusion of *foreign-based* consumers as potentially relevant to trigger a positive finding of the respective subfactor—and thus of a positive outcome for the "effects on US commerce" test. The extraterritoriality rate among these opinions (i.e., the percentage of opinions that actually applied the Lanham Act) is 72.88% (43 out of 59), compared to the overall rate of 59.29%.[458]

V Summary: An Era of International Trademark Propertization

Trademark and unfair competition conflicts law in the United States reflects a certain paradox. At the level of substantive trademark law, courts and scholars became increasingly cautious about extending protection into distant product markets starting in the 1930s. In addition, the issue of preventing anticompetitive extensions was hotly debated in domestic law, and concerns about trademark monopolies troubled decision makers until the 1960s.[459] And today, as we have seen, the extension of rights is still seen under a critical lens.[460] This consideration of the downsides of extensive protection, however, was never reflected in conflicts doctrine. On the contrary, as the *Steele* reasoning and progeny reveal, trademark conflicts law has been driven by an opposing trend, extending property rights and domestic interests further and further.

There are numerous possible reasons for this development. Trademark extraterritoriality may be due to an overly casual or unmindful application of precedent, or to the virtuous (albeit naïve) ambition to protect foreign consumers and foster the efficiency of foreign markets. Also, the assumption of the superiority of American trademark policies may have nourished (similarly naïve) ambitions to increase global welfare by extending domestic law. However, one aspect in particular stands out as influential: from the courts' point of view regarding private-party disputes, owners of national trademarks—the majority of whom consist of national entities—seem to be best protected against international trademark piracy and unfair competition by an extension of the Lanham Act. The idea that extraterritoriality is beneficial for domestic concerns continues to dominate the debate.[461] This also explains the difference with regard to the

[458] This rate correlates significantly with the finding of the transnational goodwill paradigm.

[459] See, e.g., *Smith v. Chanel, Inc.*, 402 F.2d 562, 567 (9th Cir. 1968); Joseph M. Livermore, *On Uses of a Competitor's Trademark*, 59 Trademark Rep. 30, 32–33 (1969); William S. Comanor & Thomas A. Wilson, *Advertising Market Structure and Performance*, 49 Rev. Econ. & Stat. 423, 437–438 (1967).

[460] *See supra* p. 126–127.

[461] For an extensive analysis, *see infra* p. 480 *et seq.*

debate concerning right extensions in the domestic arena: for domestic trademark conflicts, the benefits and detriments of the overextension of rights will have to be allocated and distributed within the national economy; a zero-sum game seems inescapable. The international extension of domestic rights, by contrast, appears to generate unidimensional rent transfers with domestic gains and foreign-based costs—in any event, it seems to prevent unjustified and illegitimate rent transfers from domestic right owners to foreign infringers. In this regard, the phenomenon of excess Lanham Act subject-matter jurisdiction is part of a bigger picture—notably a tendency in international economic law in which domestic concerns are prioritized over the interests of foreign constituencies.[462]

I will address these issues—particularly the question whether an approach based on the extraterritoriality of rights is effective or detrimental—in chapter 5. At this point, it suffices to conclude that *Steele* has not only perpetuated American courts' nineteenth-century tendency to protect exclusive rights against competition in favor of the prevailing mercantile and entrepreneurial elites[463] but also transnationalized the once domestic dogma of investment protection. With respect to the doctrinal and structural foundations, it was the common law goodwill paradigm, particularly the organic, market-based, and nonterritorial nature of trademark rights, that provided the foundation.

Conclusions

This comparative look at trademark and unfair competition conflicts doctrine has revealed a key divergence between the common law and the civil law. The central paradigm of civil law doctrine is the concept of state-granted privileges. The territoriality of trademark rights is one result of this German formalism. US common law, by contrast, has never been similarly attached to territoriality; protection has been and remains an issue of use-based rights. These rights are connected primarily to their owners' market activities. Nicholas de Belleville Katzenbach has lucidly explained this critical divergence in general terms with regard to English and continental law. His description also holds true for the comparison between US common law and German or European civil law:

[462] *See, e.g.*, Lea Brilmayer, *The Extraterritorial Application of American Law: A Methodological and Constitutional Appraisal*, 50 Law & Contemp. Probs. 11, 20–21 (1987).

[463] For the domestic development, *see* Morton J. Horwitz, *The Transformation of American Law, 1780–1860*, 253 *et seq.* (1977).

> Although it contained an element rooted in *jus gentium,* English private law was by and large a matter of remedies; historically its whole development had been in terms of expanding writs not rights. Statutes were few, loosely worded and drafted largely in terms of command to judges, hence in procedural language. Rights did not have their theoretical origin in the positive law, but rather in custom and morality—principles not formally tied down to political boundaries. The civilian, on the other hand, was greatly concerned with the other side of the coin. He, too, universalized his rights, but the limits of judicial authority were defined in terms of these rights (not writs) with their source in the written provisions of codes, statutes and ordinances.[464]

Seen in this light, the tale of German and US trademark conflicts doctrine is quite representative of the history of common law and civil law in general. For US common law, the fundament of trademark and unfair competition regulation has always been an issue of goodwill protection—which, by definition, is detached from political boundaries. For German civil law, the reign of the legal regime has always determined the scope of rights. Territoriality has therefore always been inherent to the system.

In addition, other commonalities and many more differences between German, European, and US doctrine have become visible in this historical comparison. First, the concept of trademark-as-property protection continues to be implemented in German and European law. Even though it appeared to fade in early twentieth-century German doctrine, the formalist trademark-as-property perspective has largely returned, particularly in the supranational rules of European trademark law instruments. In addition, the distinction between rights protection and conduct prevention has effectuated an internal separation. Early trademark law sought to protect the public from fraud. Over time, this impetus was lost—today, property protection is the main emphasis, while consumer protection is of secondary concern. Unfair competition law, by contrast, started on a foundation in tort law. Individual rights were paramount, and there was little regard for consumer protection. Yet contrary to trademark law, unfair competition doctrine has increasingly incorporated public policy concerns. It has become "politicized" and "socialized." In US law, of course, trademarks also epitomize private rights and individual property. But American nonformalism stands in stark contrast to European doctrine. In the United States, both trademark protection and unfair competition prevention are founded on a paradigm of goodwill protection, which is closely tied to the extension of marketplaces. This common foundation represents the homogeneity and uniformity of the two fields. In addition, consumer protection has remained a

[464] Nicholas de Belleville Katzenbach, *Conflicts on an Unruly Horse: Reciprocal Claims and Tolerances in Interstate and International Law*, 65 Yale L.J. 1087, 1114 (1956).

key concern throughout. But here as well, a trend toward propertization exists. The extension of trademark-as-goodwill protection into areas beyond consumer confusion prevention increasingly disconnects the two sectors.

These substantive law characteristics have also coined the evolution of conflicts doctrine. Modern German law still reflects a historical concept of state-granted privileges. Ever since it abandoned the nineteenth-century theory of personality rights protection, trademark conflicts law has adhered to a principle of strict territoriality. For a long time, therefore, a conduct-oriented rule of the *lex loci protectionis* has governed. Unfair competition choice of law, by contrast, is governed by a collision-of-interests, or marketplace, rule. Application of the law at the place where competition actually occurs is the new paradigm. By and large, this appears to be much better equipped to handle the challenges of globalized societies and economies. Not surprisingly, the *lex loci protectionis* rule in trademark conflicts law has recently been watered down in order to adapt to modern communication and marketplace conditions. The US system of international trademark and unfair competition law, by contrast, has always been based on an idea of goodwill protection and commercial effects. Prior to the Lanham Act, trademark conflicts were resolved under common law principles. Courts did not distinguish between intrastate or interstate conflicts. Domestically, this approach raised few concerns. But the general disregard for state sovereignty has also come to influence international trademark doctrine. The Supreme Court's *Steele* majority made *Tea Rose/Rectanus* virtually borderless.

In this light, it is evident that several dichotomies must be overcome in order to reconceptualize conflicts doctrine for the twenty-first century. For European doctrine, the hiatus between trademark protection and unfair competition prevention has become particularly questionable. The theory of state-granted privileges and an increasing propertization of trademark rights, accompanied by the concurrent socialization of modern unfair competition doctrine, have created a distinct bifurcation of the field. This not only distorts practical utility but fundamentally disregards the fact that trademark and unfair competition law has always been an area of market communication regulation. Current conflicts doctrine in Europe is accordingly distorted. While strict territoriality under the *lex loci protectionis* rule in trademark conflicts invites under-regulation, the marketplace principle in international unfair competition conflicts is far from clearly defined. Most problematic is the adherence to conduct as the most relevant connecting factor. Under modern trademark and unfair competition regulation, conduct has become obsolete. Therefore, much more emphasis should be put on information infrastructure and consumer decision making. In this regard, at least upon first sight, the American *Bulova* testing promises a more consistent approach. Yet the concrete implementation of this commercial-effects testing has not only resulted in an overextension of domestic trademark rights but also perpetuated another obsolete paradigm of trademark and unfair competition law's past. The protection of goodwill under a virtually apolitical, and therefore nonterritorial, common law approach has contributed to an overly extensive Lanham Act extraterritoriality. Here, the challenge is to formulate a more qualitatively governed effects test.

3 A Ragged Landscape of Theories

> It is difficult for people brought up under a different system of laws to unde[r]stand our situation. Under the Continental system, trade mark rights depend upon registration and "unfair competition" is a statutory wrong. The need of a better understanding becomes apparent the minute a group of men who are used to the different systems attempt to discuss the subjects of trade marks and unfair trading. They start at different points and diverge.
>
> Edward S. Rogers, *Protection of Industrial Property*, 27 Mich. L. Rev. 491, 492 (1929)

Introduction

As the previous chapters have shown, trademark and unfair competition law in Europe and the United States tells two tales of propertization—one of formal rights and another of informal value protection. Neither concept has ruined or ennobled doctrine at the domestic level. After all, substantive law in both jurisdictions provides a functioning system. Yet both versions of propertization and value protection have brought conflicts doctrine into an imbalance. And while attempts to explain this conundrum can be found on both sides of the Atlantic, a clear understanding is still absent. As an overview of the plethora of concepts and theories on trademark and unfair competition conflicts law unveils, it is still true that, as Friedrich K. Juenger clarified decades ago, only three approaches to conflicts law, or choice of law, appear to exist: substantive law, unilateralist, and multilateralist.[1] This chapter explores all of these. It starts with the conservative theories of European territoriality doctrines and moves on to the more recent applications of principles of international economic law under the marketplace effects principle as well as models developed in international soft-law instruments and by academic institutions. As we will see, all European doctrines in the field of trademark and unfair

[1] Friedrich K. Juenger, *Choice of Law and Multistate Justice* 45–46 (1993).

competition conflicts still adhere largely to Savignian multilateralism. This penchant toward civil law structures has also permeated attempts to promulgate uniform rules of soft law internationally (interestingly, on both sides of the Atlantic). Quite differently, American theories of international trademark law have traditionally been founded on a unilateralist concept. This widely replicates the approach in US practice, as analyzed in the previous chapter. Finally, in between the opposing camps of multilateralist and unilateralist approaches—and very likely as a consequence of growing discontent with their results—theories of substantive law promulgation have witnessed a heyday more recently, particularly following the rise of the internet and the advent of socioeconomic globalization.

In addition to these classic approaches on Juenger's shortlist, however, closer scrutiny reveals a still widely unexplained trend toward a convergence of methods and approaches. In fact, trademark and unfair competition conflicts law is particularly apt at illustrating this phenomenon. Ever since Ulrich Huber laid the foundation for conflicts law in the doctrine of international comity in the seventeenth century,[2] the fields of public international law and private international law have been drifting apart. Huber may still have understood comity and choice of law as an element of public international law and, accordingly, expected conflicts resolution to reconcile conflicting nation-state concerns.[3] The problem with this concept of comity, however, is that it has always been too nebulous to provide a practical guideline. Moreover, historical developments have invalidated the analytical and practical power that comity may have once had.[4] Therefore, the nationalization and diversification of both national substantive laws and choice-of-law regimes in the nineteenth and twentieth centuries ultimately made the act of reconciling conflicting national policies, as Franz Kahn stated, a "quadrature of the circle."[5] This particularly affected international trademark and unfair competition disputes where the growing politicization of substantive laws—that is, their increasingly regulatory character—made it ever more difficult to foster multilateral respect for foreign states' policies in choice of law.[6]

[2] *See infra* p. 398 *et seq.*

[3] *See* original text and translation in: Ernest G. Lorenzen, *Huber's De Conflictu Legum*, 136, 162 *et seq.*, in *Selected Articles on the Conflict of Laws* (Ernest G. Lorenzen ed., 1947).

[4] *See, e.g.*, Tim W. Dornis, *Comity*, in *Encyclopedia of Private International Law* (Jürgen Basedow et al. eds., forthcoming 2017). For an extensive discussion, *see infra* p. 408 *et seq.*

[5] Franz Kahn, *Über Inhalt, Natur und Methode des internationalen Privatrechts*, 255, 318, in *Abhandlungen zum internationalen Privatrecht, vol. I* (Otto Lenel & Hans Lewald eds., 1928). The challenge thus is to "reconcile the irreconcilable." *See* Friedrich K. Juenger, *Choice of Law and Multistate Justice* 21 (1993).

[6] *See supra* p. 53 *et seq.*

And the counter-concepts to old-Europe multilateralism have not fared much better. Per se, US unilateralism in conflicts resolution regularly downplays or neglects foreign regulatory concerns. The built-in preference for the *lex fori*, as my analysis of US case law has shown, surfaces with particular candor in the *Bulova* test and *Steele* progeny.[7] Scholarly analyses are also mostly prone to favor national policies at the expense of foreign states' regulatory concepts. Alternative theories of substantive law promulgation, finally, are prominently reflected in the cyberlaw movement and other concepts of modern theory on international intellectual property law. However, they hardly provide a better foundation of authority and legitimacy—not to speak of their impracticability. But that must not be the end of the inquiry. In fact, what makes international trademark and unfair competition law such an interesting object for analysis is a distinct convergence of functions and structures in both national substantive and conflicts law. In this regard, the field differs from many other areas of private law and private international law. First of all, it is densely predetermined by a framework of public international law underlying the national regimes, notably the Paris Convention and the Agreement on Trade-Related Aspects of Intellectual Property Rights (TRIPS). In addition, and most importantly, trademark protection and unfair competition prevention, at their core, aim to establish and uphold the free and unmanipulated flow of information within the marketplace. This shared structural foundation not only constitutes a thus far unexplored transnational architecture of market information infrastructure but also ultimately provides the blueprint for a uniform choice-of-law approach.

Before addressing issues of substantive law and public international law, as well as international comity, in more detail in the following chapters, however, I will lay the groundwork with an overview of the current scholarly debate. This is not an attempt to illustrate the entire panoply of positions in existence, for innumerable theoretical and practical suggestions have been made. Convincing arguments may be made for each of the models. Rather than furnishing a detailed microcritique of the status quo, this inquiry focuses on the way in which scholarship has dealt with the integration of economic concepts such as "competition" and "marketplace" into legal theory, the interplay between individual rights protection and public policy concerns, and the regulatory impact of choice-of-law norms. For this reason, my analysis excludes theories based on the country-of-origin principle, which, although falling within the wider context of the topic, are based on different considerations. While these approaches may be suitable for the European Union, which

[7] *See supra* p. 159 *et seq.*

covers a widely uniform marketplace and is structured by its member states' largely homogeneous concepts of regulation, they are not immediately relevant to an analysis of conflicts law and choice of law in a sphere where no such underlying and overarching elements of convergence exist.[8]

Section 1 Traditional Civil Law Trademark Conflicts

Prima facie, the territoriality of trademark rights is obsolete. In the context of socioeconomic globalization, particularly the circumstances surrounding online environments, limiting trademark protection to the prevention of infringement by territorial conduct will often leave domestic rights unprotected. Yet extending protection beyond national borders may be similarly detrimental. If any use of a mark on the internet, for instance, were an infringement of potentially innumerable national rights, online marketing activity would ultimately come to a halt due to exorbitant legal uncertainty. Not surprisingly, therefore, scholarly commentary has also come to question extraterritoriality in international intellectual property law. It appears as if a return to traditional models of territorial rights protection could provide a more adequate and consistent structure for rights protection in the global arena.[9]

I The Principle of Territoriality

International trademark law is part of international intellectual property (IP) law. The public international law regime of intellectual property protection, especially under the Paris Convention and other IP-related international agreements, however, does not expressly provide for a territorial restriction of the scope of national laws and rights; nor does

[8] The country-of-origin principle is an instrument of integration under the assumptions of both similar socioeconomic conditions and a preexisting level of substantive law harmonization. This particular focus, with its Europe-centric pedigree and the fact that it does not apply to non-European jurisdictions, makes the theory inapt to my analysis. For an extensive discussion of the country-of-origin principle in unfair competition choice of law, *see* Nina Dethloff, *Europäisierung des Wettbewerbsrechts—Einfluss des europäischen Rechts auf das Sach- und Kollisionsrecht des unlauteren Wettbewerbs* 282 *et seq.* (2001); more recently, *see also* Hamburg Group for Private International Law, *Comments on the European Commission's Draft Proposal for a Council Regulation on the Law Applicable to Non-Contractual Obligations*, 67 RabelsZ 1, 18–20 (2003); Oliver Baetzgen, *Internationales Wettbewerbs- und Immaterialgüterrecht im EG-Binnenmarkt* (2007). For an overview, *see also* Josef Drexl, in *Münchener Kommentar zum Bürgerlichen Gesetzbuch, vol. XI*, IntLautR para. 42 (Franz Jürgen Säcker et al. eds., 6th edn., 2015).

[9] *See, e.g.*, Curtis A. Bradley, *Territorial Intellectual Property Rights in an Age of Globalism*, 37 Va. J. Int'l L. 505, 584 (1997) (concluding that "globalism may actually increase the need for territorialism").

it set express choice-of-law rules for international conflicts.[10] Nonetheless, it is widely agreed on that intellectual property—including trademarks—is governed by the so-called territoriality principle.[11]

[10] *See, e.g.*, *Tod's and Tod's France*, C-28/04, para. 32 (30 June 2005), [2005] E.C.R. I-5781; BGE vol. 39 I 633, 635 (12 November 1913); Helmut Wirner, *Wettbewerbsrecht und internationales Privatrecht* 38 *et seq.* (1960); Alois Troller, *Unfair Competition (ch. 34)*, no. 34–1, in *International Encyclopedia of Comparative Law, vol. III, Private International Law* (Kurt Lipstein et al. eds., 1980); Frank Vischer, *Das Internationale Privatrecht des Immaterialgüterrechts nach dem schweizerischen IPR-Gesetzentwurf*, 1987 GRUR Int. 670, 676 *et seq.*; Kurt Siehr, *Das urheberrechtliche Folgerecht inländischer Künstler nach Versteigerung ihrer Werke im Ausland*, 1992 IPRax 29, 31; William Patry, *Choice of Law and International Copyright*, 48 Am. J. Comp. L. 383, 405 (2000); Richard Fentiman, *Choice of Law and Intellectual Property*, 129, 134, in *Intellectual Property and Private International Law—Heading for the Future* (Josef Drexl & Annette Kur eds., 2005); Nerina Boschiero, *Infringement of Intellectual Property Rights—A Commentary on Article 8 of the Rome II Regulation*, 9 Yearb. P.I.L. 87, 94 *et seq.* (2007); Andrew Dickinson, *The Rome II Regulation: The Law Applicable to Non-Contractual Obligations* para. 8.05 (2008); Graeme B. Dinwoodie, *Developing a Private International Intellectual Property Law: The Demise of Territoriality?*, 51 Wm. & Mary L. Rev. 711, 716 *et seq.* (2009); Karl-Heinz Fezer, *Markenrecht*, Einl H para. 24 (4th edn., 2009); James J. Fawcett & Paul Torremans, *Intellectual Property and Private International Law* para. 12.05 (2nd edn., 2011). The issue is contested for the protection of copyrights. *See, e.g.*, E. Bartin, *Localisation territoriale des monopoles intellectuels (Propriété littéraire et artistique propriété industrielle)*, 61 Clunet 781, 793 *et seq.* (1934); Paul Heinrich Neuhaus, *Freiheit und Gleichheit im internationalen Immaterialgüterrecht*, 40 RabelsZ 191, 193 (1976); Ulrich Drobnig, *Originärer Erwerb und Übertragung von Immaterialgüterrechten im Kollisionsrecht*, 40 RabelsZ 195, 196 *et seq.* (1976); Heimo Schack, *Urheberrechtsverletzung im internationalen Privatrecht aus der Sicht des Kollisionsrechts*, 1985 GRUR Int. 523; for US doctrine, *see, e.g.*, *Itar-Tass Russian News Agency v. Russian Kurier, Inc.*, 153 F.3d 82, 90 (2nd Cir. 1998); Jane C. Ginsburg, *Ownership of Electronic Rights and the Private International Law of Copyright*, 22 Colum.-VLA J. L. & Arts 165, 169–170 (1998); Graeme B. Dinwoodie, *Developing a Private International Intellectual Property Law: The Demise of Territoriality?*, 51 Wm. & Mary L. Rev. 711, 731 (2009). The dominant approach in modern commentary, however, contends a strict *lex loci protectionis* rule. *See, e.g.*, OLG Koblenz 1968 GRUR Int. 164—*Liebeshändel in Chioggia* (14 July 1967); Alois Troller, *Das internationale Privat- und Zivilprozeßrecht im gewerblichen Rechtsschutz und Urheberrecht* 20 (1952); Eugen Ulmer, *Die Immaterialgüterrechte im internationalen Privatrecht—Rechtsvergleichende Untersuchung mit Vorschlägen für die Vereinheitlichung in der Europäischen Wirtschaftsgemeinschaft* 10–11 (1975); Otto Sandrock, *Die kollisionsrechtliche Behandlung der Deliktshaftung bei der Verletzung von gewerblichen Schutzrechten und Urheberrechten*, 380, 404 *et seq.*, in *Vorschläge und Gutachten zur Reform des deutschen internationalen Privatrechts der außervertraglichen Schuldverhältnisse, vorgelegt im Auftrag der Zweiten Kommission des Deutschen Rates für Internationales Privatrecht* (Ernst von Caemmerer ed., 1983); Friedrich-Karl Beier, *Entwicklung und Grundprinzipien des internationalen Markenschutzes*, 85, 93, in *Festskrift till Stig Strömholm* (Ake Frändberg et al. eds., 1997); Curtis A. Bradley, *Territorial Intellectual Property Rights in an Age of Globalism*, 37 Va. J. Int'l L. 505, 547 *et seq.* (1997).

[11] Trademarks are treated under the same rules as copyrights and patent, design, and *sui generis* rights. *See* Karl Kreuzer, in *Münchener Kommentar zum Bürgerlichen Gesetzbuch, vol. X*, Nach Art. 38 EGBGB Anh. II para. 56 *et seq.* (Kurt Rebmann & Jürgen Säcker eds., 3rd edn., 1998). For Regulation (EC) No. 864/2007 of the European Parliament and of the Council of 11 July 2007 on the law applicable to non-contractual obligations (Rome II), O.J. EU (31 July 2007), L 199/40, *see* recital 26.

Although the principle, as such, is not a genuine conflicts rule, it does provide for a limitation of rights[12]—in other words, rights are deemed valid only within national borders. Accordingly, there is a limited territorial domain within which intellectual property rights can be utilized and protected.[13] Different national rights will be independent, and a rights owner may have several different national rights (known as a "bundle of rights"[14]). As a consequence of this territorial limitation and segmentation, it is widely acknowledged that rights' creation and scope of protection are governed by the *lex loci protectionis*—the law of the protecting country.[15] This is also the rule in article 8 of the Rome II Regulation.[16] The *lex loci protectionis* is a multilateral rule, at least with respect to its practical results. It authorizes the application of the laws of any country specified by the plaintiff.[17] Put another way, if a plaintiff claims that, in addition to her domestic right, foreign trademark rights are being

[12] *See* Leo Raape, *Internationales Privatrecht* § 60 (3rd edn., 1950); Karl Kreuzer, in *Münchener Kommentar zum Bürgerlichen Gesetzbuch, vol. X*, Nach Art. 38 EGBGB Anh. II para. 12 *et seq.* (Kurt Rebmann & Jürgen Säcker eds., 3rd edn., 1998); Jan Kropholler, *Internationales Privatrecht—einschließlich der Grundbegriffe des Internationalen Zivilverfahrensrechts* § 53 VI 2 (6th edn., 2006).

[13] Karl Kreuzer, in *Münchener Kommentar zum Bürgerlichen Gesetzbuch, vol. X*, Nach Art. 38 EGBGB Anh. II para. 13 (Kurt Rebmann & Jürgen Säcker eds., 3rd edn., 1998); Johannes Christian Wichard, *Europäisches Markenrecht zwischen Territorialität und Binnenmarkt*, 2002 ZEuP 23, 27.

[14] *See, e.g.*, Eugen Ulmer, *Die Immaterialgüterrechte im internationalen Privatrecht—Rechtsvergleichende Untersuchung mit Vorschlägen für die Vereinheitlichung in der Europäischen Wirtschaftsgemeinschaft* 7 *et seq.* (1975); Otto Sandrock, *Das Kollisionsrecht des unlauteren Wettbewerbs zwischen dem internationalen Immaterialgüterrecht und dem internationalen Kartellrecht*, 1985 GRUR Int. 507, 512–513 and 516; Josef Drexl, in *Münchener Kommentar zum Bürgerlichen Gesetzbuch, vol. XI*, IntImmGR para. 7 (Franz Jürgen Säcker et al. eds., 6th edn., 2015).

[15] *See also* Otto Sandrock, *Die kollisionsrechtliche Behandlung der Deliktshaftung bei der Verletzung von gewerblichen Schutzrechten und Urheberrechten*, 380, 381 *et seq.*, in *Vorschläge und Gutachten zur Reform des deutschen internationalen Privatrechts der außervertraglichen Schuldverhältnisse, vorgelegt im Auftrag der Zweiten Kommission des Deutschen Rates für Internationales Privatrecht* (Ernst von Caemmerer ed., 1983); Johannes Christian Wichard, *Europäisches Markenrecht zwischen Territorialität und Binnenmarkt*, 2002 ZEuP 23, 27; *see also IHT Internationale Heiztechnik v. Ideal-Standard*, C-9/93, para. 22 (22 June 1994), [1994] E.C.R. I-2789.

[16] Regulation (EC) No. 864/2007 of the European Parliament and of the Council of 11 July 2007 on the law applicable to non-contractual obligations (Rome II), O.J. EU (31 July 2007), L 199/40.

[17] The characteristic of multilateralism, however, is not uncontested. For the debate, *see, e.g.*, Karl-Heinz Fezer, *Markenrecht*, Einl H para. 54 (4th edn., 2009). For an understanding of the principle as a unilateralist rule, *see, e.g.*, Otto Sandrock, *Das Kollisionsrecht des unlauteren Wettbewerbs zwischen dem internationalen Immaterialgüterrecht und dem internationalen Kartellrecht*, 1985 GRUR Int. 507, 518; Frank Vischer, *Das Internationale Privatrecht des Immaterialgüterrechts nach dem schweizerischen IPR-Gesetzentwurf*, 1987 GRUR Int. 670, 678.

infringed, the court must treat the claim in different segments under all of the eligible regimes.

One aspect of rights territoriality is disturbing, though: infringement analysis is still often formalized insofar as a national right can be infringed on only by conduct *within* the national territory. Conduct outside the national territory will usually not lead to an infringement. Conversely, a foreign right may not be infringed on by conduct within the national territory.[18] This concept of trademark territoriality has increasingly come

[18] *See, e.g., IHT Internationale Heiztechnik v. Ideal-Standard*, C-9/93, para. 22 (22 June 1994), [1994] E.C. R. I-2789 ("[N]ational law can only provide relief in respect of acts performed on the national territory in question."); for Germany, RGZ vol. 118, 76, 83—*Springendes Pferd/Hengstenberg* (20 September 1927); BGHZ vol. 22, 1, 13—*Flava Erdgold* (2 October 1956); BGHZ vol. 41, 84, 91—*Maja* (22 January 1964); BGH 2005 GRUR 431, 432—*HOTEL MARITIME* (13 October 2004) ("Ein Unterlassungsanspruch [nach dem Markengesetz] setzt deshalb eine das Kennzeichenrecht verletzende Benutzungshandlung im Inland voraus."); BGH 2012 GRUR 1263, 1264—*Clinique happy* (25 April 2012); for Switzerland, *e.g.*, BG 2000 GRUR Int. 639, 640–641—*Kodak II* (7 December 1999); Handelsgericht Zürich 1985 GRUR Int. 411, 411 (9 January 1984); among scholarly commentary, *see, e.g.*, Arthur Nussbaum, *Deutsches internationales Privatrecht—Unter besonderer Berücksichtigung des österreichischen und schweizerischen Rechts* 338 (1932) ("Die im Inlande begangene Verletzung eines ausländischen Immaterialgüterrechts begründet ebensowenig einen Anspruch wie die im Auslande begangene Verletzung eines inländischen."); Erich Lichtenstein, *Der gewerbliche Rechtsschutz im internationalen Privatrecht*, 1964 NJW 1208, 1212; Friedrich-Karl Beier, *Territorialität des Markenrechts und internationaler Wirtschaftsverkehr*, 1968 GRUR Int. 8, 12 ("Die Wirkung des so vom Schutzlande gewährten Markenrechts ist auf das Gebiet dieses Landes beschränkt: Das inländische Markenrecht kann nicht durch Auslandshandlungen, das ausländische Markenrecht nicht durch Inlandshandlungen verletzt werden. Örtlicher Schutzbereich und Verletzungsort müssen übereinstimmen."); Lienhard Schikora, *Der Begehungsort im gewerblichen Rechtsschutz und Urheberrecht* 68–69 (1968); Tilman Weber, *Die Behandlung von Patent-, Warenzeichen- und Urheberrechtsverletzungen im internationalen Privat- und Zivilprozessrecht* 26 (1968); Eugen Ulmer, *Die Immaterialgüterrechte im internationalen Privatrecht—Rechtsvergleichende Untersuchung mit Vorschlägen für die Vereinheitlichung in der Europäischen Wirtschaftsgemeinschaft* 11 (1975) ("Grundsätzlich kann heute allgemein … davon ausgegangen werden, daß der Anwendungsbereich der nationalen Gesetze auf die im Inland erfolgten Eingriffshandlungen beschränkt bleibt."); Dieter Martiny, *Verletzung von Immaterialgüterrechten im Internationalen Privatrecht*, 40 RabelsZ 218, 220 (1976); Christian von Bar, *Territorialität des Warenzeichens und Erschöpfung des Verbreitungsrechts im Gemeinsamen Markt* 28, 29–30 (1977) ("Gewerbliche Schutzrechte können jedoch nur auf dem Gebiet des verleihenden Staates verletzt werden."); Alois Troller, *Immaterialgüterrecht, vol. I*, ch. 3, § 9 III (3rd edn., 1983); Max-Planck-Institut für ausländisches und internationales Patent-, Urheber- und Wettbewerbsrecht, *Stellungnahme zum Entwurf eines Gesetzes zur Ergänzung des internationalen Privatrechts (außervertragliche Schuldverhältnisse und Sachen)*, 1985 GRUR Int. 104, 106 ("Für die Verletzung von Immaterialgüterrechten … kann allein auf das Recht des Handlungsorts abgestellt werden, d.h. desjenigen Landes, in dessen Gebiet die beanstandete Verletzungshandlung jedenfalls teilweise begangen wurde. Dies folgt nicht nur aus dem Territorialitätsprinzip, sondern auch aus der Eigenart immaterialgüterrechtlicher Delikte. Die Verletzungstatbestände des gewerblichen Rechtsschutzes und Urheberrechts normieren Handlungsunrecht, sie knüpfen an die Vornahme bestimmter Verletzungshandlungen … im Inland an, ohne Rücksicht darauf,

under pressure with the globalization of communication and trade. Not surprisingly, therefore, a number of scholarly suggestions have been brought forward to modify the doctrine of strictly territorial rights. One of these concepts attempts to distinguish between registered rights and use-based rights. As Heimo Schack argues, for instance, a world of emerging and merging markets requires territoriality to be the exception rather than the rule. He therefore suggests that only rights based on the state's formal act of registration should be territorially confined. Use-based rights should be understood as territorially unrestricted.[19] I will address the registered/unregistered rights dichotomy in more detail below.[20] The principal defects of such a differentiation aside, it illustrates an important trend in modern scholarly theory—the conception of trademark policies being the component of an *overall* system of economic market regulation. Indeed, it is an understanding of converging policies in substantive law that has spurred modern theories to unify choice of law with respect to intellectual property, antitrust, and unfair competition. Alois Troller has been among the first to formulate such a theory for unfair competition and intellectual property

wo der schädigende Erfolg eingetreten ist."); Christian von Bar, *Kollisionsrecht, Fremdenrecht und Sachrecht für internationale Sachverhalte im Internationalen Urheberrecht*, 108 UFITA 27, 39 (1988); Rolf Sack, *Die kollisions- und wettbewerbsrechtliche Beurteilung grenzüberschreitender Werbe- und Absatztätigkeit nach deutschem Recht*, 1988 GRUR Int. 320, 332; Gerhard Schricker, in *Großkommentar—UWG: Gesetz gegen den unlauteren Wettbewerb, vol. I*, Einl para. F 5 (Rainer Jacobs et al. eds., 1994); Curtis A. Bradley, *Territorial Intellectual Property Rights in an Age of Globalism*, 37 Va. J. Int'l L. 505, 547–548 (1997) ("[T]he national treatment principle implies a territorial approach to choice of law, pursuant to which the applicable law is the law of the place where the conduct in question occurs."); Christopher Wadlow, *Enforcement of Intellectual Property in European and International Law—The New Private International Law of Intellectual Property in the United Kingdom and the European Community* 9 (1998); Frank Peter Regelin, *Das Kollisionsrecht der Immaterialgüterrechte an der Schwelle zum 21. Jahrhundert* 95 and n. 22, 220 (2000); Alexander Thünken, *Multi-state advertising over the Internet and the private international law of unfair competition*, 51 I.C.L.Q. 909, 917 (2002); Martin Ebner, *Markenschutz im internationalen Privat- und Zivilprozessrecht* 75 (2004); Rebekka Hye-Knudsen, *Marken-, Patent- und Urheberrechtsverletzungen im europäischen Internationalen Zivilprozessrecht* 7 (2005); Oliver Baetzgen, *Internationales Wettbewerbs- und Immaterialgüterrecht im EG-Binnenmarkt* para. 104 (2007) (*but see also id.* at para. 141); Karl-Heinz Fezer, *Markenrecht*, Einl H MarkenG para. 14 (4th edn., 2009); Richard Plender & Michael Wilderspin, *The European Private International Law of Obligations* para. 22–001 (4th edn., 2015).

[19] Heimo Schack, *Internationale Urheber-, Marken- und Wettbewerbsrechtsverletzungen im Internet—Internationales Privatrecht*, 2000 MMR 59, 62; Heimo Schack, *Das auf (formlose) Immaterialgüterrechte anwendbare Recht nach Rom II*, 651, 661 *et seq.*, in *Die richtige Ordnung—Festschrift für Jan Kropholler zum 70. Geburtstag* (Dietmar Baetge ed., 2008); Heimo Schack, *The Law Applicable to (Unregistered) IP Rights after Rome II*, 79, 90, in *Intellectual Property and Private International Law* (Stefan Leible & Ansgar Ohly eds., 2009); following Schack: Fabian Ropohl, *Zur Anknüpfung der formlosen Markenrechte im Internationalen Privatrecht* 55 *et seq.* (2003).

[20] *See infra* p. 200 *et seq.*

conflicts.[21] According to Troller, a uniform principle of territoriality would best correspond with the interests involved in international disputes on intellectual property rights and unfair competition. He concludes, however, that the law of the country where the relevant conduct (in unfair competition cases, "an act of competition") occurred would govern the dispute.[22] Working under the traditional assumption that unfair competition prevention is part of tort law, he explains that the "place of acting ... [is] to be distinguished from the place where the effect occurred" and that the applicable regime must be determined by the former.[23]

Under a similar lens, Otto Sandrock also changed directions with respect to the import of conduct and effects. He generally agrees with Troller on the overall idea that antitrust, intellectual property, and unfair competition conflicts should be treated uniformly.[24] But he embraces an ultimately antipodal technique for conflicts resolution. He rejects finding a uniform and universal concept for the place of violation or infringement. In particular, this place should no longer be determined by reference to an alleged infringer's conduct. Where an act of infringement or violation has occurred should instead be established under the *lex loci protectionis*.[25] Lately, this conception has been brought forward with respect to an extension of trademark protection in internet cases. One modern approach

[21] Alois Troller, *Das internationale Privat- und Zivilprozeßrecht im gewerblichen Rechtsschutz und Urheberrecht* 273 *et seq.* (1952); Alois Troller, *Unfair Competition (ch. 34)*, no. 34–14 and 34–16, in *International Encyclopedia of Comparative Law, vol. III, Private International Law* (Kurt Lipstein et al. eds., 1980).

[22] Alois Troller, *Unfair Competition (ch. 34)*, no. 34–14, in *International Encyclopedia of Comparative Law, vol. III, Private International Law* (Kurt Lipstein et al. eds., 1980).

[23] *Id.* at no. 34–4 and 34–16; *see also* Alois Troller, *Immaterialgüterrecht, vol. II*, ch. 19, § 60 V (3rd edn., 1985).

[24] Otto Sandrock, *Das Kollisionsrecht des unlauteren Wettbewerbs zwischen dem internationalen Immaterialgüterrecht und dem internationalen Kartellrecht*, 1985 GRUR Int. 507, 518 *et seq.; see also* Wolfgang F. Weber, *Die kollisionsrechtliche Behandlung von Wettbewerbsverletzungen mit Auslandsbezug—Eine Darstellung unter besonderer Berücksichtigung des österreichischen IPR-Gesetzes, des Schweizer Expertenentwurfs eines IPR-Gesetzes sowie der Möglichkeit von Harmonisierungsmaßnahmen im Kollisions- und Wettbewerbsrecht für die Europäische Gemeinschaft* 139 *et seq.* (1982); Wolfgang Weber, *Zum Anwendungsbereich des deutschen UWG beim Auslandswettbewerb zwischen Inländern*, 1983 GRUR Int. 26, 29–30.

[25] Otto Sandrock, *Das Kollisionsrecht des unlauteren Wettbewerbs zwischen dem internationalen Immaterialgüterrecht und dem internationalen Kartellrecht*, 1985 GRUR Int. 507, 515 ("Die Frage, an welchem Ort ein Immaterialgüterrecht verletzt worden ist, ist nach dem Recht des jeweiligen Schutzlandes zu beantworten. Es gibt also keinen einheitlichen Begriff des Deliktsortes, der etwa in einer allseitigen Kollisionsnorm der lex fori definiert werden könnte. Sondern der Deliktsort bestimmt sich—von Schutzland zu Schutzland unterschiedlich—nach der jeweiligen materiellrechtlichen ‚policy' der betreffenden Schutznorm.").

suggests the application of a modified tort choice-of-law rule: based on the idea of a potential ubiquity of places where an infringement could be found, the *locus delicti* in internet-based infringements can be both the place where infringing content is uploaded *and* the place from which a website can be accessed. Accordingly, both places qualify as a point of attachment or connecting factor in choice of law. Ultimately, there is no more absolute need for inland conduct.[26]

This shift from conduct to effects has also been implemented in practice. I have already introduced the German Bundesgerichtshof's *HOTEL MARITIME* decision.[27] Issued in the wake of the World Intellectual Property Organization's (WIPO) Joint Recommendation Concerning Provisions on the Protection of Marks, and Other Industrial Property Rights in Signs, on the Internet,[28] the court's decision was groundbreaking in its application of a rule of commercial effects to international trademark law. Applying this rule, it jettisoned the principle of strict trademark territoriality, instead establishing that domestic effects may suffice for finding an infringement of national rights, even absent domestic conduct.[29] In order to restrict the potential overreach of national law under this extension, the court, however, set a *de minimis* threshold of sufficient relevance of inland effects (*hinreichender wirtschaftlich relevanter Inlandsbezug*).[30] Scholarly commentary has proposed similar concepts for limiting the effects test's tendency to overconnect. These concepts comprise approaches that provide for sanctions in proportion to the impact of the allegedly infringing activities on the respective market, tests for the avoidability of the alleged infringements at issue, and techniques that prescribe

[26] *See, e.g.*, Rolf Sack, *Das internationale Wettbewerbs- und Immaterialgüterrecht nach der EGBGB-Novelle*, 2000 WRP 269, 277 *et seq.* Other commentary has extended the analysis to effects as such rather than individual conduct. *See, e.g.*, Karl-Heinz Fezer, *Markenrecht*, Einl H para. 28 *et seq.*, para. 49 (4th edn., 2009) and *infra* section 3 I.

[27] *See supra* p. 71–74.

[28] WIPO, *Joint Recommendation Concerning Provisions on the Protection of Marks, and Other Industrial Property Rights in Signs, on the Internet (with Explanatory Notes), adopted by the Assembly of the Paris Union for the Protection of Industrial Property and the General Assembly of the World Intellectual Property Organization (WIPO) at the Thirty-Sixth Series of Meetings of the Assemblies of the Member States of WIPO September 24 to October 3, 2001* (WIPO Pub. No. 845(E)). *See also infra* p. 225 *et seq.*

[29] BGH 2005 GRUR 431, 432–433—*HOTEL MARITIME* (13 October 2004).

[30] *See id.* at 432; for further case law, *see, e.g.*, LG Hamburg, 1999 MMR 612, 613—*Animal Planet* (5 May 1999); OLG Karlsruhe, 2002 MMR 814, 817—818—*Intel* (10 July 2002); OLG Hamm, 2004 MMR 177, 177—*nobia.se* (31 July 2003); OLG München, 2005 MMR 608, 609—*800-FLOWERS* (16 June 2005); OLG München, 2006 GRUR-RR 130, 131—*UltraMind* (12 January 2006).

a private-party interest balancing when looking for the reach of national trademark law and the extension of rights.[31]

II Analysis: The Curse of Formal Reasoning and Conduct Orientation

Evidently, strict territoriality will not fare well unless one is willing to acknowledge underregulation as an agreeable state of affairs.[32] Yet the extraterritoriality of domestic rights is no less problematic, for extending the protection beyond national borders may stifle international marketing activities through the implicit threat of potentially innumerable national laws to be applied.[33] Attempts to streamline unfair competition law with intellectual property conflicts law illustrate how the problem can be approached. Nevertheless, full accordance has yet to be established, and the historical formalism of trademark rights protection lingers. Efforts have been made, but none have so far managed to fully do away with the obsolete dichotomy between trademark and unfair competition conflicts law. A critical look at the examples of scholarly commentary illustrated above helps clarify the problems.

Let us return to the registered/unregistered rights distinction suggested by Heimo Schack. In his attempt to distinguish between different

[31] *See, e.g.*, Annette Kur, *Principles Governing Jurisdiction, Choice of Law and Judgments in Transnational Disputes: A European Perspective*, 2003 CRi 65, 72; Annette Kur, *Applicable Law: An Alternative Proposal for International Regulation—The Max-Planck Project on International Jurisdiction and Choice of Law*, 30 Brook. J. Int'l L. 951, 978 (2005); Ansgar Ohly, *Choice of Law in the Digital Environment—Problems and Possible Solutions*, 241, 254 *et seq.*, in *Intellectual Property and Private International Law—Heading for the Future* (Josef Drexl & Annette Kur eds., 2005); Stefan Koos, *Objektive Kriterien zur Feststellung des anwendbaren Rechts im Internationalen Wettbewerbs- und Immaterialgüterrecht*, 2007 IPRax 414, 416; Karl-Heinz Fezer, *Markenrecht*, Einl H para. 44 *et seq.* (4th edn., 2009); Karl-Heinz Fezer & Stefan Koos, in *Staudingers Kommentar zum Bürgerlichen Gesetzbuch: Internationales Wirtschaftsrecht*, Internationales Wettbewerbsprivatrecht para. 731, 918, and 943 (15th edn., 2010); Reinhard Ingerl & Christian Rohnke, *Kommentar zum Markengesetz: Gesetz über den Schutz von Marken und sonstigen Kennzeichen*, Einleitung para. 59–60 (3rd edn., 2010).

[32] *See* Leo Raape, *Internationales Privatrecht* § 61 II (3rd edn., 1950); more recently *see, e.g.*, Ludwig Baeumer, *Anmerkungen zum Territorialitätsprinzip im internationalen Patent- und Markenrecht*, 803, 804, in *Festschrift für Wolfgang Fikentscher zum 70. Geburtstag* (Bernhard Großfeld et al. eds., 1998); Karl-Heinz Fezer & Stefan Koos, in *Staudingers Kommentar zum Bürgerlichen Gesetzbuch: Internationales Wirtschaftsrecht*, Internationales Wettbewerbsprivatrecht para. 493 *et seq.* and *passim* (15th edn., 2010); Christoph Brömmelmeyer, *Internetwettbewerbsrecht, Das Recht der Ubiquität—Das Recht der Domain Names—Das Recht der kommerziellen Kommunikation* 177 (2007); Josef Drexl, in *Münchener Kommentar zum Bürgerlichen Gesetzbuch, vol. XI*, IntImmGR para. 251 *et seq.* (Franz Jürgen Säcker et al. eds., 6th edn., 2015).

[33] For the internet context, *see, e.g.*, BGH 2005 GRUR 432—*HOTEL MARITIME* (13 October 2004); Christoph Brömmelmeyer, *Internetwettbewerbsrecht, Das Recht der Ubiquität—Das Recht der Domain Names—Das Recht der kommerziellen Kommunikation* 177 (2007).

categories of rights, he posits that territoriality would be adequate for registered marks, for these rights are state-granted instruments. He questions, however, whether territoriality would make sense for unregistered and use-based rights.[34] This distinction—as we have seen in this book's historical analysis—trades on one particular aspect of traditional German and European trademark and unfair competition doctrine: use-based trademark rights do not seem to be granted by the state. Like tangible property, they must be acknowledged in their preexistence. Registered rights, by contrast, are understood as being genuinely created by the act of registration.[35] Of course, looking at use-based rights under a theory of market-based goodwill extension and protection of market information capital relies on the perception of a preexisting Something. This is not the case for registered rights, as Eugen Ulmer pointed out in the 1920s already.[36] Prima facie, therefore, a difference does exist. Yet the decision whether to acknowledge a preexisting stock of market information capital and to protect it under the guise of trademark rights is also an issue of legal policy. In essence, this is no different than rights registration. Protection for the preexisting and the newly created alike is a legal fiction. Ultimately, both registered and use-based rights are—as Jürgen Basedow has explained—"artifacts of positive law"[37] and are therefore necessarily state granted.[38] This means, however, that there can hardly be a difference regarding the territorial boundaries of registered and unregistered rights. Neither the validity of a state act nor the authority of a legal regime to prescribe protection for the preexisting Something will extend beyond a political boundary. In the end, this requires acknowledging that neither the formal right nor the entitlement granted *ex lege* by

[34] Heimo Schack, *Internationale Urheber-, Marken- und Wettbewerbsrechtsverletzungen im Internet—Internationales Privatrecht*, 2000 MMR 59, 62; *see also* Fabian Ropohl, *Zur Anknüpfung der formlosen Markenrechte im Internationalen Privatrecht* 55 *et seq.* (2003).

[35] Heimo Schack, *Internationale Urheber-, Marken- und Wettbewerbsrechtsverletzungen im Internet—Internationales Privatrecht*, 2000 MMR 59, 62; Fabian Ropohl, *Zur Anknüpfung der formlosen Markenrechte im Internationalen Privatrecht* 56–57 (2003). *See also* approvingly Karl-Heinz Fezer & Stefan Koos, in *Staudingers Kommentar zum Bürgerlichen Gesetzbuch: Internationales Wirtschaftsrecht*, Internationales Immaterialgüterprivatrecht para. 885 (15th edn., 2010). For the history of German doctrine, *see supra* p. 9 *et seq.* and p. 27 *et seq.*

[36] *See supra* p. 42–46.

[37] Jürgen Basedow, *Foundations of Private International Law in Intellectual Property*, 3, 8, in *Intellectual Property in the Global Arena—Jurisdiction, Applicable Law, and the Recognition of Judgments in Europe, Japan and the US* (Jürgen Basedow et al. eds., 2010).

[38] *See also* Frank Vischer, *Das IPR des Immaterialgüterrechts*, 363, 365–367, in *Kernprobleme des Patentrechts—Festschrift zum einhundertjährigen Bestehen des eidgenössischen Patentgesetzes* (Institut für gewerblichen Rechtsschutz (INGRES) ed., 1988); Alessandro L. Celli, *Internationales Kennzeichenrecht* 194 (2000); Josef Drexl, in *Münchener Kommentar zum Bürgerlichen Gesetzbuch, vol. XI*, IntImmGR para. 27 (Franz Jürgen Säcker et al. eds., 6th edn., 2015).

a certain regime will "follow the trade" into a different sovereign's territory, as was possible in the interstate and common law environment of *Tea Rose/Rectanus*.[39]

Apart from this principal flaw, Schack's theory of market-based extraterritoriality of nonregistered entitlements can be further criticized for an unjustified preference for use-based rights over registered rights.[40] If—as we have just seen—both registered and unregistered rights must be conceived of as being territorially limited, the question arises why the latter category (usually protected under rules of unfair competition prevention) should still be deemed largely nonterritorial. I will expand on this issue in the next chapter; here, a brief overview suffices to illustrate the paradox. The friction is the following: substantive rules of unfair competition prevention and intellectual property rights protection are usually closely interwoven. Indeed, the protection of rights in signs and symbols will often oscillate between both areas, depending on which legal regime one intends to apply.[41] Against this backdrop, unfair competition law and trademark law are barely distinguishable on the basis of categories of property rights or absolute and exclusive entitlements.[42] Accordingly, it is questionable why the former regime should have the capacity to cross national borders while the latter should not.

[39] *See supra* p. 129 *et seq.*

[40] *See, e.g.*, Christoph Brömmelmeyer, *Internetwettbewerbsrecht, Das Recht der Ubiquität—Das Recht der Domain Names—Das Recht der kommerziellen Kommunikation* 182 (2007).

[41] *See, e.g.*, Alois Troller, *Unfair Competition (ch. 34)*, no. 34–14, in *International Encyclopedia of Comparative Law, vol. III, Private International Law* (Kurt Lipstein et al. eds., 1980); Otto Sandrock, *Das Kollisionsrecht des unlauteren Wettbewerbs zwischen dem internationalen Immaterialgüterrecht und dem internationalen Kartellrecht*, 1985 GRUR Int. 507, 511–512; more recently, Rainer Hausmann & Inés Obergfell, in *Lauterkeitsrecht: Kommentar zum Gesetz gegen den unlauteren Wettbewerb (UWG), vol. I*, Einleitung I para. 33 *et seq.* (Karl-Heinz Fezer ed., 2nd edn., 2010) (with further references).

[42] *But see* Eugen Ulmer, *Die Immaterialgüterrechte im internationalen Privatrecht—Rechtsvergleichende Untersuchung mit Vorschlägen für die Vereinheitlichung in der Europäischen Wirtschaftsgemeinschaft* 22 and 25 (1975); Werner Riegl, *Streudelikte im Internationalen Privatrecht* 80 (1986); Gerhard Schricker, in *Großkommentar—UWG: Gesetz gegen den unlauteren Wettbewerb, vol. I*, Einl para. F 2 (Rainer Jacobs et al. eds., 1994); Rainer Hausmann & Inés Obergfell, in *Lauterkeitsrecht: Kommentar zum Gesetz gegen den unlauteren Wettbewerb (UWG), vol. I*, Einleitung I para. 223 (Karl-Heinz Fezer ed., 2nd edn., 2010) (suggesting a differentiation on the basis of absolute and exclusive rights in trademarks as opposed to the socialized function of unfair competition law); Peter Mankowski, in *Münchener Kommentar zum Lauterkeitsrecht, vol. I*, IntWettbR para. 8 (Peter W. Heermann et al. eds., 2nd edn., 2014); Josef Drexl, in *Münchener Kommentar zum Bürgerlichen Gesetzbuch, vol. XI*, IntImmGR para. 3 and 163 (Franz Jürgen Säcker et al. eds., 6th edn., 2015) (distinguishing between rights protection ("Rechtsgüterschutz") in trademark law and economic market regulation ("Schutz der Funktionsfähigkeit des Marktes") in unfair competition law) and also Katharina de la Durantaye, in *Rome Regulations*, Art. 8 para. 10 (Gralf-Peter Calliess ed., 2nd edn., 2015) as well as Nadine Klass, in *Großkommentar—UWG: Gesetz gegen den unlauteren Wettbewerb, vol. I*, Einl. para. 33 *et seq.* (Otto Teplitzky et al. eds., 2nd edn., 2014).

In sum, the major problem of trademark territoriality is the increasing number of infringements where conduct and injury are geographically and territorially detached. Further, the formal distinction between the protection of registered rights and unregistered rights not only has been problematic historically speaking but also distorts contemporary conflicts doctrine. In this regard, the unification of trademark and unfair competition choice of law, as suggested by Otto Sandrock, is welcome. With respect to the method and technique for conflicts resolution, he proposes that rather than strict territoriality, a modification of the *lex loci protectionis* rule toward a non-conduct-based approach provides a more promising foundation for a reconceptualization. A look at modern European unfair competition conflicts law sheds light on some of the important details.

Section 2 Modern Civil Law Unfair Competition Conflicts

One aspect has become evident in this book's historical overview: US doctrine does not strictly distinguish between the area of trademark protection and that of unfair competition prevention, whether in substance or with regard to conflicts resolution.[43] European and German laws, on the other hand, do. In fact, the formal dichotomy between the two sectors can be described as the most determinative characteristic of the field in European civil law.

I *The Marketplace Principle, Determination of Effects, and the* De Minimis *Rule*

A Collision-of-Interests and Substantive-Purpose Analysis

European courts and legal scholars have come to acknowledge conflicts determination under a collision-of-interests, or marketplace, principle. Broad consensus existed throughout the region prior to the unification of European choice of law.[44] And today, there is wide agreement that the

[43] *See supra* p. 84 *et seq.* and p. 159 *et seq.*

[44] *See supra* p. 64 *et seq.* and BGH 1962 GRUR 243, 245—*Kindersaugflaschen* (30 June 1961). For scholarly commentary, *see, e.g.*, Günther Beitzke, *Auslandswettbewerb unter Inländern—BGHZ 40, 391*, 1966 JuS 139, 143; Peter-Christian Müller-Graff, *Fakultatives Kollisionsrecht im Internationalen Wettbewerbsrecht?*, 48 RabelsZ 289, 307 (1984); Max-Planck-Institut für ausländisches und internationales Patent-, Urheber- und Wettbewerbsrecht, *Stellungnahme zum Entwurf eines Gesetzes zur Ergänzung des internationalen Privatrechts (außervertragliche Schuldverhältnisse und Sachen)*, 1985 GRUR Int. 104, 107; Adair Dyer, *Unfair Competition in Private International Law*, 211 Recueil des Cours 373, 431 *et seq.* (1988-IV); Rolf Sack, *Die kollisions- und wettbewerbsrechtliche Beurteilung grenzüberschreitender Werbe- und Absatztätigkeit nach deutschem Recht*, 1988 GRUR Int. 320, 322–323; Michael Kort, *Zur „multistate"-Problematik grenzüberschreitender Fernsehwerbung*, 1994 GRUR Int. 594, 598; Peter Mankowski,

marketplace principle has been incorporated into article 6(1) of the Rome II Regulation.[45] The theoretical debate started more than half a century ago.

Kamen Troller is often considered the first to have formulated the concept of interest collision, in 1962.[46] He rejected the traditional tort conflicts rule. Instead, he conceived of different categories of unfair competition and, inter alia, distinguished between conduct directed

Internet und Internationales Wettbewerbsrecht, 1999 GRUR Int. 909, 909 *et seq.*; Dieter Dubs, *Das Lauterkeitsstatut nach schweizerischem Kollisionsrecht—Zugleich ein Beitrag zur Materialisierung des Internationalprivatrechts* 57 *et seq.* (2000); Mirko Vianello, *Das internationale Privatrecht des unlauteren Wettbewerbs in Deutschland und Italien—Eine die europäischen und internationalen Harmonisierungsbestrebungen berücksichtigende Darstellung* 231 *et seq.* (2001); Hans R. Schibli, *Multistate-Werbung im internationalen Lauterkeitsrecht mit besonderer Berücksichtigung der Internet-Werbung* 108 (2004). For a general overview of European states' jurisdictions, *see* Peter Bernhard, *Das Internationale Privatrecht des unlauteren Wettbewerbs in den Mitgliedstaaten der EG* (1994).

45 Most recently for German case law, GemS-OGB 2013 GRUR 417 para. 15—*Medikamentenkauf im Versandhandel* (22 August 2012); in scholarly commentary, *see, e.g.*, Jan von Hein, *Die Kodifikation des europäischen Internationalen Deliktsrechts*, 102 ZVglRWiss 528, 555 (2003); Karl F. Kreuzer, *Die Vergemeinschaftung des Kollisionsrechts für außervertragliche Schuldverhältnisse (Rom II)*, 13, 36, in *Europäisches Kollisionsrecht* (Gerte Reichelt & Walter H. Rechberger eds., 2004); Michael Sonnentag, *Zur Europäisierung des Internationalen außervertraglichen Schuldrechts durch die geplante Rom II-Verordnung*, 105 ZVglRWiss 256, 285 (2006); Gerhard Wagner, *Internationales Deliktsrecht, die Arbeiten an der Rom II-Verordnung und der Europäische Deliktsgerichtsstand*, 2006 IPRax 372, 380; Francisco J. Garcimartín Alférez, *The Rome II Regulation: On the way towards a European Private International Law Code*, 7 EuLF-I 77, 86 (2007); Abbo Junker, *Die Rom II-Verordnung: Neues Internationales Deliktsrecht auf europäischer Grundlage*, 2007 NJW 3675, 3679; Gerhard Wagner, *Die neue Rom II-Verordnung*, 2008 IPRax 1, 8; Christian Handig, *Neues im Internationalen Wettbewerbsrecht—Auswirkungen der Rom II-Verordnung*, 2008 GRUR Int. 24, 27; Rolf Sack, *Internationales Lauterkeitsrecht nach der Rom II-VO*, 2008 WRP 845, 846; Pedro A. De Miguel Asensio, *The Private International Law of Intellectual Property and of Unfair Commercial Practices: Convergence or Divergence?*, 136, 151 *et seq.*, in *Intellectual Property and Private International Law* (Stefan Leible & Ansgar Ohly eds., 2009); Andreas Spickhoff, in *Beck'scher Online-Kommentar zum Bürgerlichen Gesetzbuch*, Art. 6 Rom II para. 4 (Heinz Georg Bamberger & Herbert Roth eds., 36th edn., 2013); Peter Mankowski, in *Münchener Kommentar zum Lauterkeitsrecht, vol. I*, IntWettbR para. 133 *et seq.* (Peter W. Heermann et al. eds., 2nd edn., 2014); Matthias Weller, in *Nomos-Kommentar-BGB, Rom-Verordnungen, vol. VI*, Art. 6 Rom II para. 1 and 16 (Rainer Hüßtege & Heinz-Peter Mansel eds., 2014); Wolfgang Wurmnest, in *juris-Praxiskommentar zum BGB*, Art. 6 Rom II para. 2 (Markus Würdinger ed., 7th edn., 2014); Nadine Klass, in *Großkommentar—UWG: Gesetz gegen den unlauteren Wettbewerb, vol. I*, Einl. para. 19 and 203 *et seq.* (Otto Teplitzky et al. eds., 2nd edn., 2014); Josef Drexl, in *Münchener Kommentar zum Bürgerlichen Gesetzbuch, vol. XI*, IntLautR para. 102 *et seq.* (Franz Jürgen Säcker et al. eds., 6th edn., 2015); Karsten Thorn, in *Palandt: Kommentar zum Bürgerlichen Gesetzbuch mit Nebengesetzen*, Art. 6 Rom II para. 9 (75th edn., 2016).

46 Kamen Troller, *Das internationale Privatrecht des unlauteren Wettbewerbs in vergleichender Darstellung der Rechte Deutschlands, Englands, Frankreichs, Italiens, der Schweiz und der USA* (1962); for an early, quite similar critique of the traditional tort doctrine of unfair competition conflicts law, *see* Andreas Froriep, *Der unlautere Wettbewerb im internationalen Privatrecht* 57 *et seq.* (1958).

toward a competitor's activity or organization and conduct actually affecting a competitor's market position or capacity.[47] He still considered unfair competition prevention as being primarily aimed at protecting competitors, not consumers.[48] Yet unfair competition was not infringement on a property right or a competitor's absolute entitlement—it was a violation of an objective rule of market conduct. Therefore, there was no actual place of damage.[49] Instead, the "marketplace" served as the point of attachment for determining the applicable law. Only in cases where the competitor's market activity was not directly concerned but where her production capacity or business organization was affected did the seat of her business serve as the point of attachment.[50]

Around the same time, and with results similar to Troller's collision-of-interests approach, Erwin Deutsch formulated a theory of unfair competition conflicts resolution that gave regard to substantive legal purposes.[51] His concept also placed ultimate emphasis on the interests involved in international unfair competition conflicts. In most cases, therefore, his results mirror the outcome under a marketplace rule. As Deutsch explained, if the legal norm at issue was to protect consumer interests, then the law of consumers' residence (usually the place of the sales market) would govern. Similarly, violations of competitor-protecting norms, if intended to protect a multitude of competitors, would be governed by the law of the marketplace.[52] Only in cases where competitive conduct was targeted toward a single competitor would, for instance, the parties' *lex domicilii communis* govern.[53]

[47] Kamen Troller, *Das internationale Privatrecht des unlauteren Wettbewerbs in vergleichender Darstellung der Rechte Deutschlands, Englands, Frankreichs, Italiens, der Schweiz und der USA* 127 *et seq.* (1962). For the Swiss Bundesgericht, *see, e.g.*, BGE vol. 91 II, 117, 123 *et seq.* (30 March 1965). For a similar categorization, *see* Helmut Wirner, *Wettbewerbsrecht und internationales Privatrecht* 110 *et seq.* (1960).

[48] Kamen Troller, *Das internationale Privatrecht des unlauteren Wettbewerbs in vergleichender Darstellung der Rechte Deutschlands, Englands, Frankreichs, Italiens, der Schweiz und der USA* 116–117 (1962).

[49] *Id.* at 127; *see also* Max Kummer, *Anwendungsbereich und Schutzgut der privatrechtlichen Rechtssätze gegen unlauteren und gegen freiheitsbeschränkenden Wettbewerb* 114–115 (1960); Verena Trutmann, *Das internationale Privatrecht der Deliktsobligationen—Ein Beitrag zur Auseinandersetzung mit den neueren amerikanischen kollisionsrechtlichen Theorien* 181 (1973).

[50] These cases comprised, inter alia, the enticing away of employees or a theft of trade secrets. *See* Kamen Troller, *Das internationale Privatrecht des unlauteren Wettbewerbs in vergleichender Darstellung der Rechte Deutschlands, Englands, Frankreichs, Italiens, der Schweiz und der USA* 139 *et seq.* (1962).

[51] Erwin Deutsch, *Wettbewerbstatbestände mit Auslandsbeziehung* 43 *et seq.* (1962).

[52] *Id.* at 47 *et seq.* and 59 *et seq.*; *see also* Stephan Briem, *Internationales und Europäisches Wettbewerbsrecht und Kennzeichenrecht* 33 *et seq.* (1995).

[53] Erwin Deutsch, *Wettbewerbstatbestände mit Auslandsbeziehung* 48 and 64 *et seq.* (1962). For modifications of this rule if no common domicile of the competing parties exists, *see*

Another contemporary approach, despite emanating from US scholarship, is conceptually similar to the early Swiss and German doctrines. In 1958, Jack J. Rappeport put forth what he called a "bull's-eye approach" to unfair competition conflicts. He maintained that multijurisdictional unfair competition should be seen as a composite and integrated tort, thereby rejecting the idea that cross-border unfair competition could create separate causes of action in different jurisdictions.[54] Instead, Rappeport argued that interstate or international unfair competition claims should constitute a single cause of action for all states or countries involved. He listed a number of considerations, all well known in traditional European conflicts doctrine, for selecting the applicable regime: inter alia, the "desire for a reasonable connection between the governing law and the place of injury," concerns for "ease and certainty of application," "predictability," and the "prevention of either party's ability to choose the applicable law."[55] While this "true singleness of liability"[56] is unique to Rappeport's theory, his technique of regime selection reflects a concern of substantive-policy analysis that can also be found in 1960s German and Swiss theories. Categorizing different causes of action, Rappeport classified cases according to the parties' domicile and the place of the harm, or according to whether the conduct at issue could be identified as exclusively or primarily harming either competitors or consumers. Accordingly, if the issue was the appropriation of business interests and there was "relatively little misleading of consumers,"[57] the law of the plaintiff's place of business would apply. By contrast, if an infringement constituted primarily consumer confusion or deception, the law of the respective marketplace would be preferable.[58]

This distinction between marketplace effects and individual-competitor injury also extends into modern doctrine. While early commentary still emphasized a rather unspecific "center of gravity" or "most significant part" of unfair competition as being determinative for choice-of-law attachment,[59] modern positions, even before the unification of choice of law under the Rome II Regulation, seemed to be more precise. They required identifying the place where the complementary side of the

id. at 49 and 66 (in these cases, the place where the parties actually compete should determine the applicable regime).

54 Jack J. Rappeport, *Trade-Mark and Unfair Competition in International Conflict of Laws: An Analysis of the Choice of Law Problem*, 20 U. Pitt. L. Rev. 1, 29 (1958).

55 *Id.* 56 *Id.* at 30. 57 *Id.* at 31.

58 *Id.* In addition, a common domicile of the parties was always a strong argument in favor of the *lex domicilii communis. See id.* at 31–32.

59 *See, e.g.*, Heinz Binder, *Zur Auflockerung des Deliktsstatuts*, 20 RabelsZ 401, 467, 494–495 (1955); Helmut Wirner, *Wettbewerbsrecht und internationales Privatrecht* 106 *et seq.* (1960); *see also* Eugen Ulmer, *Die Immaterialgüterrechte im internationalen Privatrecht—Rechtsvergleichende Untersuchung mit Vorschlägen für die Vereinheitlichung in der Europäischen Wirtschaftsgemeinschaft* 21 (1975).

market (consumers, purchasers, or suppliers) was approached and affected.[60] This usually made it necessary to consider the place of actual impact on the other side (*Einwirkungsort*).[61] Quite often, it was the *situs* of the customer that was determinative.[62] Yet if the conduct at issue was directed at a competitor's assets or other interests and was thus without direct effect on the marketplace, the general tort conflicts rule governed.[63]

I have already mentioned the Bundesgerichtshof's 1961 *Kindersaugflaschen* decision.[64] In essence, the court's reasoning in *Kindersaugflaschen* represents the governing version of the marketplace rule in unfair competition choice of law. As the court explained, unfair competition is deemed to occur at the place where competitors' interests collide; only at this place can a public policy of preventing unfair conduct be implemented.[65] This rule does not pose problems as long as advertising and transacting occur within the same jurisdiction. The issue, however,

[60] *See, e.g.*, Nina Dethloff, *Europäisierung des Wettbewerbsrechts—Einfluss des europäischen Rechts auf das Sach- und Kollisionsrecht des unlauteren Wettbewerbs* 65 (2001); in addition, *e.g.*, Helmut Köhler, in: Helmut Köhler & Joachim Bornkamm, *Gesetz gegen den unlauteren Wettbewerb*, Einl UWG para. 5.7 (33rd edn., 2015).

[61] *See, e.g.*, Karl F. Kreuzer, *Wettbewerbsverstöße und Beeinträchtigung geschäftlicher Interessen (einschl. der Verletzung kartellrechtlicher Vorschriften)*, 232, 272 and 277, in *Vorschläge und Gutachten zur Reform des deutschen internationalen Privatrechts der außervertraglichen Schuldverhältnisse, vorgelegt im Auftrag der Zweiten Kommission des Deutschen Rates für internationales Privatrecht* (Ernst von Caemmerer ed., 1983); Werner Riegl, *Streudelikte im Internationalen Privatrecht* 81 *et seq.* (1986); Rolf Sack, *Die kollisions- und wettbewerbsrechtliche Beurteilung grenzüberschreitender Werbe- und Absatztätigkeit nach deutschem Recht*, 1988 GRUR Int. 320, 324; Dieter Dubs, *Das Lauterkeitsstatut nach schweizerischem Kollisionsrecht—Zugleich ein Beitrag zur Materialisierung des Internationalprivatrechts* 58 (2000); Andreas Höder, *Die kollisionsrechtliche Behandlung unteilbarer Multistate-Verstöße—Das Internationale Wettbewerbsrecht im Spannungsfeld von Marktort-, Auswirkungs- und Herkunftslandprinzip* 35–36 and 116 (2002).

[62] Peter Mankowski, *Internet und Internationales Wettbewerbsrecht*, 1999 GRUR Int. 909, 909; Jost Kotthoff, *Werbung ausländischer Unternehmen im Inland—Die Beurteilung grenzüberschreitender Werbung nach dem internationalen Privatrecht, dem Wettbewerbsrecht und dem Recht der Europäischen Union* 18 *et seq.* (1995); Walter F. Lindacher, *Zum Internationalen Privatrecht des unlauteren Wettbewerbs*, 1996 WRP 645, 647; Wolfgang Drasch, *Das Herkunftslandprinzip im internationalen Privatrecht—Auswirkungen des europäischen Binnenmarktes auf Vertrags- und Wettbewerbsstatut* 327–328 (1997).

[63] Rolf Sack, *Die kollisions- und wettbewerbsrechtliche Beurteilung grenzüberschreitender Werbe- und Absatztätigkeit nach deutschem Recht*, 1988 GRUR Int. 320, 323 *et seq.*; Rolf Sack, *Marktortprinzip und allgemeine Ausweichklausel im internationalen Wettbewerbsrecht, am Beispiel der sog. Gran-Canaria-Fälle*, 1992 IPRax 24, 24 *et seq.*; Rolf Sack, *Das internationale Wettbewerbs- und Immaterialgüterrecht nach der EGBGB-Novelle*, 2000 WRP 269, 272; *see also* Walter F. Lindacher, *Zum Internationalen Privatrecht des unlauteren Wettbewerbs*, 1996 WRP 645, 649–650; Andreas Höder, *Die kollisionsrechtliche Behandlung unteilbarer Multistate-Verstöße—Das Internationale Wettbewerbsrecht im Spannungsfeld von Marktort-, Auswirkungs- und Herkunftslandprinzip* 116 *et passim* (2002).

[64] *See supra* p. 68–71.

[65] BGH 1962 GRUR 243, 245—*Kindersaugflaschen* (30 June 1961); more recently, *see* BGH 2010 GRUR 847, 848—*Ausschreibung in Bulgarien* (11 February 2010); GemS-

becomes complicated once the impact on the consumer (or purchaser or supplier) and the ensuing market effects diverge—notably if conduct and effects occur in different jurisdictions. The Bundesgerichtshof's 1990 *Kauf im Ausland* decision—also known as the *Gran Canaria* ruling—is paradigmatic of such a scenario. *Kauf im Ausland* concerned advertising by a German company targeting German tourists during their holidays in Spain. The advertising materials were written in German and did not target Spanish customers. The products (merino wool duvets and pillows) were delivered after the tourists' return in Germany. As the court explained, the final transaction (i.e., the actual delivery of the product) and potential damages to competitors on this market were indirect effects of the improper conduct and, therefore, had to be disregarded in the choice-of-law analysis. Similarly, the consumers' nationality, their place of residence, and the occurrence of preparatory activities were deemed irrelevant.[66] Accordingly, whenever the location of an alleged infringer's advertising conduct diverges from the place of the actual transaction, dominant opinion in practice and commentary acknowledges governance of the regime of the so-called advertising market.[67]

Ultimately, at the level of European unified choice of law, the marketplace principle has been integrated into article 6(1) of the Rome II Regulation.[68] This is mostly a consequence of the fact that the principle had already been established in many continental jurisdictions prior to the unification.[69] Yet the regulation's terminology and explanatory materials

OGB 2013 GRUR 417 para. 15—*Medikamentenkauf im Versandhandel* (22 August 2012).

66 BGH 1991 GRUR 463, 464—*Kauf im Ausland* (15 November 1990); BGH 1998 GRUR 419, 420—*Gewinnspiel im Ausland* (26 November 1997).

67 *See* BGH 1991 GRUR 463, 464—*Kauf im Ausland* (15 November 1990); BGH 1998 GRUR 419, 420—*Gewinnspiel im Ausland* (26 November 1997); BGH 2005 GRUR Int. 338, 339—*Rotpreis-Revolution* (13 May 2004); *see also* BGH 1972 GRUR 367, 369—*Besichtigungsreisen I* (3 December 1971); BGH 1976 GRUR 316, 317—*Besichtigungsreisen II* (7 November 1975); BGH 1977 GRUR 672, 673—*Weltweit-Club* (13 May 1977); OGH 1981 GRUR Int. 401—*Fremdenverkehrsverband* (8 July 1980). *See also* Rolf Sack, *Die kollisions- und wettbewerbsrechtliche Beurteilung grenzüberschreitender Werbe- und Absatztätigkeit nach deutschem Recht*, 1988 GRUR Int. 320, 323–324; Peter Mankowski, *Internet und Internationales Wettbewerbsrecht*, 1999 GRUR Int. 909, 911; Hans R. Schibli, *Multistate-Werbung im internationalen Lauterkeitsrecht mit besonderer Berücksichtigung der Internet-Werbung* 182 (2004); Martin Illmer, in *Rome II Regulation*, Art. 6 para. 46 (Peter Huber ed., 2011); Josef Drexl, in *Münchener Kommentar zum Bürgerlichen Gesetzbuch, vol. XI*, IntLautR para. 17 (Franz Jürgen Säcker et al. eds., 6th edn., 2015); Matthias Weller, in *Nomos-Kommentar-BGB, Rom-Verordnungen, vol. VI*, Art. 6 Rom II para. 18 (Rainer Hüßtege & Heinz-Peter Mansel eds., 2014).

68 *See supra* p. 203–204.

69 *See again supra* and further, *e.g.*, Commission of the European Communities, *Proposal for a Regulation of the European Parliament and the Council on the Law Applicable to Non-Contractual Obligations ("Rome II")*, Brussels, 22 July 2003, COM(2003) 427 final, 2003/0168 (COD), 16.

also reveal a distinctive attempt to further modernize the law by means of "translating" economic phenomena into legal concepts. Indeed, Rome II aims quite expressly at a regulation of marketplaces. The place of attachment in article 6(1) is defined as the country where "competitive relations or the collective interests of consumers are, or are likely to be, affected." Further, recital 21 makes clear that a triple purpose of protection must be considered:

> In matters of unfair competition, the conflict-of-law rule should protect competitors, consumers and the general public and ensure that the market economy functions properly. The connection to the law of the country where competitive relations or the collective interests of consumers are, or are likely to be, affected generally satisfies these objectives.[70]

As the European Commission has further explained, competitive relations and collective consumer interests will be affected where "competitors are seeking to gain the customer's favour." More concretely:

> This solution corresponds to the victims' expectations since the rule generally designates the law governing their economic environment. But it also secures equal treatment for all operators on the same market. The purpose of competition law is to protect a market; it pursues a macro-economic objective.[71]

Only "[w]here an act of unfair competition affects exclusively the interests of a specific competitor" does the general tort conflicts rule apply (article 6(2)). In particular, attempts to "economize" rules on unfair competition conflicts—notably by precisely defining market effects—and to strictly demarcate between market-related and bilateral acts pose both theoretical and practical problems. Before I address these issues, however, an illustration on the solutions presented for issues of multistate infringements shall complete the overview.

B Multistate Scenarios: Determination of Marketplace Effects and *De Minimis* Limitations

Toward the end of the last century, in the internet context, a potential extraterritorial overreach of national unfair competition regimes was identified as a pressing problem.[72] If minimal effects on a market would

[70] Recital 21 of Regulation (EC) No. 864/2007 of the European Parliament and of the Council of 11 July 2007 on the law applicable to non-contractual obligations (Rome II), O.J. EU (31 July 2007), L 199/40.

[71] Commission of the European Communities, *Proposal for a Regulation of the European Parliament and the Council on the Law Applicable to Non-Contractual Obligations ("Rome II")*, Brussels, 22 July 2003, COM(2003) 427 final, 2003/0168 (COD), 16.

[72] For some of the first extensive analyses with respect to internet conflicts, *see, e.g.*, Hermann-Josef Omsels, *Die Kennzeichenrechte im Internet*, 1997 GRUR 328, 336–337; Nina Dethloff, *Marketing im Internet und Internationales Wettbewerbsrecht*, 1998 NJW 1596, 1599 *et seq.*; Peter Mankowski, *Internet und Internationales Wettbewerbsrecht*, 1999

suffice to hold the corresponding national regime applicable, virtually all cross-border activities might be subject to a plethora of national norms. In the end, the most stringent law would govern. But this problem has never been limited to the online world.[73] In fact, all cross-border marketing and trade activity raises the question of where to locate unfair competition violations in order to find a point of attachment for conflicts analysis. Many offline cases may also require limiting the number of eligible regimes. In this regard, it has never been contested that marginal effects must not suffice for finding the corresponding state's regime applicable.[74] The methods and details of such limitation, however, are still far from clear.

The question first became apparent in the context of media spillover cases. In the pre-online environment, when print or radio media were distributed or broadcast to more than one national territory, the effects of such activities could be found in several "national markets." The issue at hand was what kind and intensity of effects should be required to find a certain national law applicable. For German doctrine, the Bundesgerichtshof set a rudimentary first standard in its 1970 *Tampax* decision.[75] The case concerned allegedly unfair advertising in a Swiss newspaper that was also sold in Germany. As the court explained, unfair competition could be found in both Switzerland and Germany since the newspaper was targeted to and sold in both jurisdictions. The spillover was part of a regular sale and distribution scheme for the newspaper at issue; effects on competition in Germany were foreseeable and thus sufficient to trigger the application of German law.[76]

GRUR Int. 909; Rolf Sack, *Das internationale Wettbewerbs- und Immaterialgüterrecht nach der EGBGB-Novelle*, 2000 WRP 269, 278.

[73] The internet only intensifies traditional problems of multistate advertising and marketing. *See* Jost Kotthoff, *Die Anwendbarkeit des deutschen Wettbewerbsrechts auf Werbemaßnahmen im Internet*, 1997 CR 676, 677.

[74] *See, e.g.*, Gerhard Schricker, *Die Durchsetzbarkeit deutscher Werberegelungen bei grenzüberschreitender Rundfunkwerbung*, 1982 GRUR Int. 720, 724; Max-Planck-Institut für ausländisches und internationales Patent-, Urheber- und Wettbewerbsrecht, *Stellungnahme zum Entwurf eines Gesetzes zur Ergänzung des internationalen Privatrechts (außervertragliche Schuldverhältnisse und Sachen)*, 1985 GRUR Int. 104, 108; Rolf Sack, *Die kollisions- und wettbewerbsrechtliche Beurteilung grenzüberschreitender Werbe- und Absatztätigkeit nach deutschem Recht*, 1988 GRUR Int. 320, 328–329; Jost Kotthoff, *Die Anwendbarkeit des deutschen Wettbewerbsrechts auf Werbemaßnahmen im Internet*, 1997 CR 676, 680; Jochen Glöckner, *Wettbewerbsverstöße im Internet—Grenzen einer kollisionsrechtlichen Problemlösung*, 99 ZVglRWiss 278, 293 *et seq.* (2000).

[75] BGH 1971 GRUR 153—*Tampax* (23 October 1970). For a critical commentary, *see* Erwin Deutsch, *Commentary to BGH, decision of 23 October 1971 (I ZR 86/69)—Tampax*, 1971 JZ 732, 732 *et seq.*

[76] BGH 1971 GRUR 153, 154—*Tampax* (23 October 1970). In order to determine so-called minimum perceptibility ("*Spürbarkeit*") in general, subsequent scholarship and

Today, the debate's major focus is on online advertising and trademark use. For these cases, the WIPO's Joint Recommendation[77] provides a succinct compilation of relevant aspects. Its list of factors to be considered in order to determine whether there are sufficient "effects" to trigger the application of a certain regime reflects the state of the debate in practice and scholarship.[78] As the WIPO recommendation states, in determining the commercial effects of using a sign on the internet, all relevant circumstances must be considered. Among the circumstances enumerated in a nonexhaustive list (art. 3(2)) are the intentions of the user of doing business within the jurisdiction at issue and the actual level and character of commercial activity. Further, the decision maker will have to consider whether customers have actually been served, whether postsale activities have occurred, and whether the product at issue may be lawfully delivered within the jurisdiction. In addition, disclaimers on a website (and actual adherence to these disclaimers), as well as information on the website concerning language, contact data, and currency of the available payment options, must be taken into account.[79]

What remains a contested issue is the question whether the minimum threshold should be determined by giving regard to the defendant's state of mind. It is little surprise that a tort-founded perspective requires "finality" of

practice have developed a number of tests and factors. *See, e.g.*, Jost Kotthoff, *Die Anwendbarkeit des deutschen Wettbewerbsrechts auf Werbemaßnahmen im Internet*, 1997 CR 676, 680; Peter Mankowski, *Internet und Internationales Wettbewerbsrecht*, 1999 GRUR Int. 909, 915 *et seq.*; for later analyses, *see, e.g.*, Andreas Höder, *Die kollisionsrechtliche Behandlung unteilbarer Multistate-Verstöße—Das Internationale Wettbewerbsrecht im Spannungsfeld von Marktort-, Auswirkungs- und Herkunftslandprinzip* 66 *et seq.* (2002); Christoph Brömmelmeyer, *Internetwettbewerbsrecht, Das Recht der Ubiquität—Das Recht der Domain Names—Das Recht der kommerziellen Kommunikation* 129 *et seq.* (2007); for a representative overview, *see, e.g.*, Helmut Köhler, in Helmut Köhler & Joachim Bornkamm, *Gesetz gegen den unlauteren Wettbewerb*, Einl UWG para. 5.8 (33rd edn., 2015).

[77] WIPO, *Joint Recommendation Concerning Provisions on the Protection of Marks, and Other Industrial Property Rights in Signs, on the Internet (with Explanatory Notes), adopted by the Assembly of the Paris Union for the Protection of Industrial Property and the General Assembly of the World Intellectual Property Organization (WIPO) at the Thirty-Sixth Series of Meetings of the Assemblies of the Member States of WIPO September 24 to October 3, 2001* (WIPO Pub. No. 845(E)). For a closer analysis, *see also infra* p. 226–228.

[78] For a representative overview on the relevant factors to be considered *see, e.g.*, Helmut Köhler, in Helmut Köhler & Joachim Bornkamm, *Gesetz gegen den unlauteren Wettbewerb*, Einl UWG para. 5.8 (33rd edn., 2015).

[79] For a similar factor analysis in German case law, *see, e.g.*, BGH 2005 GRUR 431, 432—*HOTEL MARITIME* (13 October 2004) (trademarks); BGH 2006 GRUR 513, 515—*Arzneimittelwerbung im Internet* (30 March 2006) (unfair competition); for the implementation of the WIPO guidelines to scholarly commentary, *see* Ansgar Ohly, in Ansgar Ohly & Olaf Sosnitza, *Gesetz gegen den unlauteren Wettbewerb mit Preisangabenverordnung (UWG)*, Einf B para. 24–26 (6th edn., 2014).

unfair competitive conduct.[80] As proponents of such an individualized perspective argue, neither turnover nor market-share numbers can provide testimony of the unfairness of competitive conduct. Instead, one must look at the conduct's underlying objective and aim—its targeting of a specific market. This necessarily requires considering the defendant's motivation.[81]

The contrary position suggests an objective perspective denying the relevance of the alleged infringer's intent. Proponents of this approach look only at the predictability or foreseeability of market effects. Such an approach has notably been put forward by the Institut de Droit International. During the institute's 1983 session, which resulted in the Cambridge Resolution on the Conflict-of-laws Rules on Unfair Competition, rapporteurs Willis Reese and Frank Vischer explained:

> Where injury is caused to a competitor's business in a particular market by conduct which could reasonably have been expected to have that effect, the internal law of the State in which that market is situated should apply.[82]

[80] *See, e.g.*, Erwin Deutsch, *Commentary to BGH, decision of 23 October 1971 (I ZR 86/69)—Tampax*, 1971 JZ 732, 733; Klaus-Georg Mook, *Internationale Rechtsunterschiede und nationaler Wettbewerb—Rechtliche Möglichkeiten zur Abwehr von Wettbewerbsstörungen und ihre Grenzen* 68–69 (1986); Rolf Sack, *Die kollisions- und wettbewerbsrechtliche Beurteilung grenzüberschreitender Werbe- und Absatztätigkeit nach deutschem Recht*, 1988 GRUR Int. 320, 328; Jürgen Möllering, *Das Recht des unlauteren Wettbewerbs in Europa: Eine neue Dimension*, 1990 WRP 1, 7; Jost Kotthoff, *Werbung ausländischer Unternehmen im Inland—Die Beurteilung grenzüberschreitender Werbung nach dem internationalen Privatrecht, dem Wettbewerbsrecht und dem Recht der Europäischen Union* 22–23 (1995); Jost Kotthoff, *Die Anwendbarkeit des deutschen Wettbewerbsrechts auf Werbemaßnahmen im Internet*, 1997 CR 676, 680; Peter Mankowski, *Internet und Internationales Wettbewerbsrecht*, 1999 GRUR Int. 909, 915 *et seq.*; Nina Dethloff, *Europäisierung des Wettbewerbsrechts—Einfluss des europäischen Rechts auf das Sach- und Kollisionsrecht des unlauteren Wettbewerbs* 58 *et seq.*, 92–93 (2001); Christoph Brömmelmeyer, *Internetwettbewerbsrecht, Das Recht der Ubiquität—Das Recht der Domain Names—Das Recht der kommerziellen Kommunikation* 129 (2007). For case law, *see, e.g.*, BGH 2006 GRUR 513, 515—*Arzneimittelwerbung im Internet* (30 March 2006); BGH 2007 GRUR 245, 245—*Schulden Hulp* (5 October 2006); OLG München, 2009 IPRax 256, 257 (6 December 2007); BGH 2010 GRUR 416, 463—*The New York Times* (2 March 2010).

[81] Interestingly, proponents of this theory (somewhat contradictorily) claim that their approach disregards "subjective factors" in favor of "objective finality." *See, e.g.*, Jost Kotthoff, *Die Anwendbarkeit des deutschen Wettbewerbsrechts auf Werbemaßnahmen im Internet*, 1997 CR 676, 680; representatively for this opinion in scholarly commentary, *see also* Helmut Köhler, in Helmut Köhler & Joachim Bornkamm, *Gesetz gegen den unlauteren Wettbewerb*, Einl UWG para. 5.8 (33rd edn., 2015). *See also* BGH 2006 GRUR 513, 515—*Arzneimittelwerbung im Internet* (30 March 2006); BGH 2007 GRUR 245, 245—*Schulden Hulp* (5 October 2006).

[82] Willis L. M. Reese & Frank Vischer (Rapporteurs of the twenty-first commission), *Institut de Droit International, Session of Cambridge—1983, The Conflict-of-laws Rules on Unfair Competition*, article II para. 1. *See also* Willis L. M. Reese & Frank Vischer, *The conflict-of-laws rules on unfair competition*, Annuaire de L'Institut de Droit International 60, I (1983), 159, 162–163; more recently on the objectivity of a finality rule, *see, e.g.*, Peter Mankowski, in *Münchener Kommentar zum Lauterkeitsrecht, vol. I,* IntWettbR para. 219–220 (Peter W. Heermann et al. eds., 2nd edn., 2014).

A similar threshold of predictability has been implemented for general tort choice of law in Switzerland, particularly under article 133(2) of the Swiss Private International Law Act (IPRG).[83] Analogous application of this rule to unfair competition conflicts, as has been suggested, would mean that if a specific instance of effects or interest collision is unforeseeable, it will not overcome the threshold.[84]

However, some voices have even rejected objective predictability or foreseeability for being an overly restrictive criterion. As Jochen Glöckner argues, internet activity necessarily implies the worldwide dissemination of communication and information. Accordingly, there should not be any requirement of foreseeability. Instead, a quantitative test of perceptibility should determine whether effects are sufficient to trigger the application of a particular national regime.[85] In effect, this replicates Gerhard Schricker's earlier suggestion based on a perceived paradigm shift: since unfair competition prevention has been transformed from a regime of competitor protection to a domain of market regulation, choice of law must give regard to effects alone.[86]

[83] Article 133(2) of the IPRG reads: "Haben Schädiger und Geschädigter ihren gewöhnlichen Aufenthalt nicht im gleichen Staat, so ist das Recht des Staates anzuwenden, in dem die unerlaubte Handlung begangen worden ist. Tritt der Erfolg nicht in dem Staat ein, in dem die unerlaubte Handlung begangen worden ist, so ist das Recht des Staates anzuwenden, in dem der Erfolg eintritt, wenn der Schädiger mit dem Eintritt des Erfolges in diesem Staat rechnen musste."

[84] Anne-Catherine Imhoff-Scheier, *La loi applicable à la publicité internationale en droit international privé suisse*, 41 SchwJbIntR 57, 80 (1985). For arguments opposing such an analogous application, however, *see, e.g.*, Rolf Bär, *Das Internationale Privatrecht (Kollisionsrecht) des Immaterialgüterrechts und des Wettbewerbsrechts*, 125, 166–167, in *Schweizerisches Immaterialgüter- und Wettbewerbsrecht, vol. I* (Roland von Büren & Lucas David eds., 2nd edn., 2002); Thomas Stäheli, *Kollisionsrecht auf dem Information Highway*, 597, 602, in *Information Highway—Beiträge zu rechtlichen und tatsächlichen Fragen* (Reto M. Hilty ed., 1996); Jochen Glöckner, *Wettbewerbsverstöße im Internet—Grenzen einer kollisionsrechtlichen Problemlösung*, 99 ZVglRWiss 278, 291 (2000); Hans R. Schibli, *Multistate-Werbung im internationalen Lauterkeitsrecht mit besonderer Berücksichtigung der Internet-Werbung* 202–203 (2004).

[85] Jochen Glöckner, *Wettbewerbsverstöße im Internet—Grenzen einer kollisionsrechtlichen Problemlösung*, 99 ZVglRWiss 278, 291 *et seq.* (2000); Jochen Glöckner, *Europäisches Lauterkeitsrecht* 298–299 (2006).

[86] Gerhard Schricker, *Die Durchsetzbarkeit deutscher Werberegelungen bei grenzüberschreitender Rundfunkwerbung*, 1982 GRUR Int. 720, 723–724; *see also* Karl F. Kreuzer, *Wettbewerbsverstöße und Beeinträchtigung geschäftlicher Interessen (einschl. der Verletzung kartellrechtlicher Vorschriften)*, 232, 276–277, in *Vorschläge und Gutachten zur Reform des deutschen internationalen Privatrechts der außervertraglichen Schuldverhältnisse, vorgelegt im Auftrag der Zweiten Kommission des Deutschen Rates für internationales Privatrecht* (Ernst von Caemmerer ed., 1983); Rolf Sack, *Die kollisions- und wettbewerbsrechtliche Beurteilung grenzüberschreitender Werbe- und Absatztätigkeit nach deutschem Recht*, 1988 GRUR Int. 320, 328–329; Rolf Sack, *Internationales Lauterkeitsrecht nach der Rom-II-VO*, 2008 WRP 845, 852; *see also* Michael Kort, *Zur „multistate"-Problematik grenzüberschreitender Fernsehwerbung*, 1994 GRUR Int. 594, 599.

An objectivized rule of minimum effects had also been initially suggested for the Rome II Regulation. The regulation's first draft indicated that the market would have to be "directly and substantially affected" in order to find the respective national regime applicable.[87] This provision, however, was removed from the final version. Nevertheless, according to dominant opinion, this noninclusion of a *de minimis* limitation must not be understood to mean that Rome II should be interpreted to cover even the slightest effects.[88] It may, however, be debated whether the limitation must be understood as a rule of choice of law or as an element of the respective substantive law regime.[89]

II Analysis: The Obsolescence of Tort Foundations

The marketplace rule in action reveals a number of doctrinal and economic inconsistencies. The most fundamental problem concerns an unanalyzed and almost naïve overestimation of substantive-policy convergence. Many approaches of this kind are oblivious to the fact that absent international unification or harmonization, the *lex fori* cannot provide a universally valid blueprint of unfair competition policies. Each country is largely free to choose its own system of market competition rules. Accordingly, it is often incorrectly assumed that the arsenal of the *lex fori*'s policies would provide for a sufficiently consolidated basis for characterization and conflicts determination.[90] This problem surfaces, for instance, with respect to the demarcation between "market-related" and "bilateral" acts under article 6 of the Rome II Regulation. Consensus

[87] *See* article 5 para. 1 draft Regulation (version of COM(2003) 427 final) and article 7 para. 1 draft Regulation (version of COM(2006) 83 final).

[88] *See, e.g.*, Stefan Leible & Matthias Lehmann, *Die neue EG-Verordnung über das auf außervertragliche Schuldverhältnisse anzuwendende Recht („Rom II")*, 2007 RIW 721, 729; Christian Handig, *Neues im Internationalen Wettbewerbsrecht—Auswirkungen der Rom II-Verordnung*, 2008 GRUR Int. 24, 28; Karl-Heinz Fezer & Stefan Koos, in *Staudingers Kommentar zum Bürgerlichen Gesetzbuch: Internationales Wirtschaftsrecht*, Internationales Wettbewerbsprivatrecht para. 643 and 652 (15th edn., 2010); Bert Keirsbilck, *The New European Law of Unfair Commercial Practices and Competition Law* 219 (2011).

[89] For the debate, *see infra* p. 499. *See also, e.g.*, Rolf Sack, *Internationales Lauterkeitsrecht nach der Rom II-VO*, 2008 WRP 845, 854; Ansgar Ohly, in Ansgar Ohly & Olaf Sosnitza, *Gesetz gegen den unlauteren Wettbewerb mit Preisangabenverordnung (UWG)*, Einf B para. 26 (6th edn., 2014).

[90] For a similar critique, *see* Wilhelm Wengler, *Die Gesetze über unlauteren Wettbewerb und das internationale Privatrecht*, 19 RabelsZ 401, 401 (1954); more recently, Peter Mankowski, in *Münchener Kommentar zum Lauterkeitsrecht, vol. I,* IntWettbR para. 137 (Peter W. Heermann et al. eds., 2nd edn., 2014); *see also* Tim W. Dornis, *Das Kollisionsrecht der auftragslosen Geschäftsführung—Ein Beispiel für Materialisierung und Typisierung im modernen europäischen IPR*, 80 RabelsZ 543, 557 *et seq.* (2016).

may exist that derogation from the general rule in article 6(1) must be interpreted narrowly.[91] Yet the determination of what should be characterized as a bilateral act under article 6(2) is still dominated by a tort-founded perspective on unfair competition policies. Not surprisingly, this invites nationally divergent results. One example is the European Commission's explanation of enticing away a competitor's employees as a bilateral act targeting a specific competitor:

> It is not entirely excluded that such conduct may also have a negative impact on a given market, but these are situations that have to be regarded as bilateral. There is consequently no reason why the victim should not enjoy the benefit of Article 3 [i.e., article 4 in the final version] relating to the common residence or the general exception clause.[92]

Scholarly commentary has followed in characterizing the scenarios explained by the commission—namely, the enticing away of a competitor's employees—as genuinely tortious.[93] Yet a more market-oriented perspective raises doubts: if there also exists a labor market where employers compete for employees, interference with the relations of a competitor's workforce will inevitably also be market related. Like improper solicitation of consumers, the enticing away of employees directly affects the market mechanism—the only difference is that it is a different market.[94] Why tort conflicts rules should then, however, prevail over the marketplace principle is hard to explain. The major

[91] *See, e.g.*, Costanza Honorati, *The Law Applicable to Unfair Competition*, 127, 157, in *The Unification of Choice of Law Rules on Torts and Other Non-Contractual Obligations in Europe—The "Rome II" Proposal* (Alberto Malatesta ed., 2006); Andrew Dickinson, *The Rome II Regulation: The Law Applicable to Non-Contractual Obligations* para. 6.28 (2008); Walter F. Lindacher, *Die internationale Dimension lauterkeitsrechtlicher Unterlassungsansprüche: Marktterritorialität versus Universalität*, 2008 GRUR Int. 453, 457; Martin Illmer, in *Rome II Regulation*, Art. 6 para. 3 (Peter Huber ed., 2011).

[92] Commission of the European Communities, *Proposal for a Regulation of the European Parliament and the Council on the Law Applicable to Non-Contractual Obligations ("Rome II")*, Brussels, 22 July 2003, COM(2003) 427 final, 2003/0168 (COD), 16.

[93] *See, e.g.*, Helmut Köhler, in Helmut Köhler & Joachim Bornkamm, *Gesetz gegen den unlauteren Wettbewerb*, Einl UWG para. 5.44 (33rd edn., 2015); Ansgar Ohly, in Ansgar Ohly & Olaf Sosnitza, *Gesetz gegen den unlauteren Wettbewerb mit Preisangabenverordnung (UWG)*, Einf B para. 21 (6th edn., 2014); Peter Mankowski, in *Münchener Kommentar zum Lauterkeitsrecht, vol. I*, IntWettbR para. 242–243 (Peter W. Heermann et al. eds., 2nd edn., 2014); *but see* Josef Drexl, in *Münchener Kommentar zum Bürgerlichen Gesetzbuch, vol. XI*, IntLautR para. 159 (Franz Jürgen Säcker et al. eds., 6th edn., 2015). For a more detailed analysis, *see infra* p. 566 *et seq.*

[94] The existence of competition on a "market for employees" becomes evident if looking at the historical origin of the cause of action in English law. The Black Plague in the fourteenth century made labor a scarce resource. Courts therefore soon began to sanction the enticing away of workforces. *See* Adair Dyer, *Unfair Competition in Private International Law*, 211 Recueil des Cours 373, 412 (1988-IV).

reason seems to be a desire to stick to traditional structures of tort/unfair competition demarcation.[95]

This problem reflects what my historical inquiry has brought to light: European unfair competition doctrine—notably in choice of law—still adheres to a paradigm of the past. The field is stuck between two divergent models. While choice of law under the marketplace principle determines the applicable regime through an analysis of competitive interests and marketplace conditions, its doctrinal foundation can still be found in international tort law.[96] Accordingly, the intentional and purposive—but, most importantly, tangible—impact on the consumer, supplier, or other market participant is what accounts for the place of the tort conduct (*Begehungs- and Einwirkungsort*).[97] This perspective remains rooted in a policy of regulating actual conduct and delimiting spatial spheres of market activity.[98] It thereby neglects, if not overlooks, the fact that

[95] *See* again Commission of the European Communities, *Proposal for a Regulation of the European Parliament and the Council on the Law Applicable to Non-Contractual Obligations ("Rome II")*, Brussels, 22 July 2003, COM(2003) 427 final, 2003/0168 (COD), 16.

[96] For traditional tort terminology and foundation, *see, e.g.*, BGH 1962 GRUR 243, 245—*Kindersaugflaschen* (30 June 1961); BG 1961 GRUR Int. 544 (9 May 1961); BG 1967 GRUR Int. 364, 365—*Sihl/Silbond* (15 November 1966); BGH 1991 GRUR 463, 464—*Kauf im Ausland* (15 November 1990); BGH 1977 GRUR 672, 673—*Weltweit-Club* (13 May 1977); *see also* Heinz Binder, *Zur Auflockerung des Deliktsstatuts*, 20 RabelsZ 401, 412 (1955); Lienhard Schikora, *Der Begehungsort im gewerblichen Rechtsschutz und Urheberrecht* 83–84 (1968); Alois Troller, *Unfair Competition (ch. 34)*, no. 34–3 and 34–4, in *International Encyclopedia of Comparative Law, vol. III, Private International Law* (Kurt Lipstein et al. eds., 1980); Gerhard Schricker, *Die Durchsetzbarkeit deutscher Werberegelungen bei grenzüberschreitender Rundfunkwerbung*, 1982 GRUR Int. 720, 722; Klaus-Georg Mook, *Internationale Rechtsunterschiede und nationaler Wettbewerb* 68 (1986); Christof Regelmann, *Die internationalprivatrechtliche Anknüpfung des Gesetzes gegen unlauteren Wettbewerb* 6–7 (1988); Walter F. Lindacher, *Zum Internationalen Privatrecht des unlauteren Wettbewerbs*, 1996 WRP 645, 646; Rolf Sack, *Das internationale Wettbewerbs- und Immaterialgüterrecht nach der EGBGB-Novelle*, 2000 WRP 269, 272; Andreas Höder, *Die kollisionsrechtliche Behandlung unteilbarer Multistate-Verstöße—Das Internationale Wettbewerbsrecht im Spannungsfeld von Marktort-, Auswirkungs- und Herkunftslandprinzip* 27 (2002); Josef Drexl, in *Münchener Kommentar zum Bürgerlichen Gesetzbuch, vol. XI*, IntLautR para. 1–10 (Franz Jürgen Säcker et al. eds., 6th edn., 2015); Peter Mankowski, in *Münchener Kommentar zum Lauterkeitsrecht, vol. I*, IntWettbR para. 9–10 (Peter W. Heermann et al. eds., 2nd edn., 2014).

[97] *See* BGH 1991 GRUR 463, 464—*Kauf im Ausland* (15 November 1990); more recently, BGH 2010 GRUR 847, 848—*Ausschreibung in Bulgarien* (11 February 2010); GemS-OGB 2013 GRUR 417 para. 15—*Medikamentenkauf im Versandhandel* (22 August 2012). *See also infra* p. 539 *et seq.*

[98] *See, e.g.*, Josef Drexl, in *Münchener Kommentar zum Bürgerlichen Gesetzbuch, vol. XI*, IntLautR para. 15 *et seq.* (Franz Jürgen Säcker et al. eds., 6th edn., 2015) ("Das Lauterkeitsrecht bestimmt die Zulässigkeit des Einwirkens von Unternehmen auf Märkte und grenzt dabei über die Definition von Verhaltensregeln die Verhaltensspielräume von Wettbewerbern gegeneinander ab. Abzustellen ist deshalb auf das unzulässige Einwirken auf einen Markt."); Peter Mankowski, in *Münchener Kommentar zum Lauterkeitsrecht, vol. I*, IntWettbR para. 142 (Peter W. Heermann et al.

unmanipulated consumer decision making and transacting is fundamental for the market mechanism to function properly. As I will discuss in more detail in the next chapter, the actual transaction (or its forbearance) is what constitutes the structural foundation of all marketplace activity. For choice of law, this means that the actual place of competitor conduct is no longer necessarily determinative.

In addition, further defects of tort foundation become obvious when looking at the issue of *de minimis* effects.[99] In terms of determining whether a sufficient quality and quantity of market effects has occurred, the understanding that "finality" should be determinative is questionable per se. Essentially, the alleged infringer's or violator's state of mind is beyond the range of modern policies in unfair competition doctrine.[100] The market mechanism seldom follows the individual's will. At best, the parties' intent can be an issue of proof. Courts' adherence to finality is thus due more to an adherence to traditional tort structures and to concerns of procedural efficiency than to doctrinal consistency and economic reason.

But initiatives to implement a more uncompromising modernization have not been very successful, either. Attempts to transfer or translate economic concepts into legal doctrine have actually led to more confusion than clarity. Definition and determination of the "market" as such is already complex and invites debate. Even more complicated, however, is elevating the concept of "markets"—with all its related issues, such as "competition" and "effects"—to the level of legal analysis.[101] Prima facie,

eds., 2nd edn., 2014); Martin Illmer, in *Rome II Regulation*, Art. 6 para. 38 (Peter Huber ed., 2011). For Swiss law, *see, e.g.*, Anton K. Schnyder, *Wirtschaftskollisionsrecht—Sonderanknüpfung und extraterritoriale Anwendung wirtschaftsrechtlicher Normen unter besonderer Berücksichtigung von Marktrecht* § 18 para. 498 (1990); Dieter Dubs, *Das Lauterkeitsstatut nach schweizerischem Kollisionsrecht—Zugleich ein Beitrag zur Materialisierung des Internationalprivatrechts* 64 (2000) ("Das Recht des unlauteren Wettbewerbs ist im weiteren marktordnendes Verhaltensrecht und insofern in erster Linie handlungsorientiert; mittels Verhaltensnormen soll das Regelungsziel eines lauteren und unverfälschten Wettbewerbs erreicht werden.").

99 *See supra* p. 209 *et seq.* For a deeper analysis, *see infra* p. 507 *et seq.*

100 *See* WIPO, *Protection Against Unfair Competition—Analysis of the Present World Situation*, Publ. no. 725(E), 24 (1994) ("[S]ubjective elements are therefore not essential to the notion of fairness in competition. Indeed, with certain exceptions, rather objective standards are applied for the purposes of establishing an act of unfair competition . . . ."); for the US, *see, e.g.*, Restatement of the Law—Unfair Competition (Third), § 1, comment c (1995); for Europe (Germany), e.g., Jochen Glöckner, in *Gesetz gegen den unlauteren Wettbewerb (UWG)*, UWG Einl C para. 102 (Henning Harte-Bavendamm & Frauke Henning-Bodewig eds., 3rd edn., 2013). *See also infra* p. 505–507 and p. 517–518.

101 For a representative critique, *see* Dieter Martiny, *Die Anknüpfung an den Markt*, 389, 390–391, and 407, in *Festschrift für Ulrich Drobnig zum siebzigsten Geburtstag* (Jürgen Basedow et al. eds., 1998) (*id.* at 407: "Von einer Anknüpfung an den 'Markt' zu sprechen, ist zu pauschal; es handelt sich um einen mehrdeutigen und vielschichtigen Begriff. Die Hoffnung, ein Geschehen einem Markt zuzurechnen und daraus die

therefore, relying instead on a "collision of interests" appears to provide a handy escape from the conundrum of defining marketplace effects or of determining where competition takes place. But the concept of interest collision is a deceptive proxy. A closer look at current commentary highlights the problem. As Costanza Honorati has explained, for instance, the marketplace can be defined as "the (legal) place where the bundle of all the individual and collective economic interests and relations meet and find their balance."[102] Yet the whole bundle of all potentially involved interests is hard to grasp. It may actually be impossible in some cases to locate all imaginable concerns within a single jurisdiction.[103] This problem is most illustratively reflected in the *Gran Canaria* scenario, in which the advertising market in Spain (*Werbemarkt*) served as the point of attachment. Effects on the sales market in Germany (*Absatzmarkt*) were deemed irrelevant.[104] Hence, all interests seemed to conflict or collide where the consumers were first affected—in this case, in Spain. But such a perspective hardly covers the full range of interests that are (or could be) involved and affected. Looking at the place of conduct in the advertising market alone will, for instance, disregard consumer interests that lie beyond it—interests that are usually located in the consumer's place of residence.[105] In addition, disregarding German law under the *Gran Canaria* rule neglects interests that may exist among the group of German-based competitors. A slight modification of the case facts highlights these defects: if the German tourists had bought more expensive

Entscheidung der Rechtsanwendungsfrage ablesen zu können, dürfte sich nicht erfüllen. Auf den Markt abzustellen, ist nämlich nur sinnvoll in Verbindung mit bestimmten Rechtsfragen und Aktivitäten. Der Ort der Marktaktivitäten läßt sich zwar einer Rechtsordnung zuordnen, allerdings nur, wenn er zuvor unter Zuhilfenahme weiterer Kriterien konkretisiert worden ist. Dies schränkt die Eignung des Marktes als Anknüpfungspunkt ein.").

102 Costanza Honorati, *The Law Applicable to Unfair Competition*, 127, 148, in *The Unification of Choice of Law Rules on Torts and Other Non-Contractual Obligations in Europe—The "Rome II" Proposal* (Alberto Malatesta ed., 2006). Equating "market" and "interests" similarly: Richard Plender & Michael Wilderspin, *The European Private International Law of Obligations* para. 20–050 (4th edn., 2015) ("The view that 'competitive relations or the collective interests of consumers' equates to 'the market' as connecting factors is, it is submitted, correct."); *see also* Andrew Dickinson, *The Rome II Regulation: The Law Applicable to Non-Contractual Obligations* para. 6.49 (2008).

103 Christopher Wadlow, *The new private international law of unfair competition and the "Rome II" Regulation*, 11 J. Intell. Prop. L. & Pract. 789, 793 (2009).

104 *See supra* p. 203 *et seq.*

105 *See, e.g.*, Harald Koch, *Commentary to BGH, decision of 15 November 1990—I ZR 22/89 (Kauf im Ausland)*, 1991 JZ 1039, 1041 (1991); Norbert Reich, *Rechtsprobleme grenzüberschreitender irreführender Werbung im Binnenmarkt*, 56 RabelsZ 444, 507–508 (1992); Karl-Heinz Fezer & Stefan Koos, in *Staudingers Kommentar zum Bürgerlichen Gesetzbuch: Internationales Wirtschaftsrecht*, Internationales Wettbewerbsprivatrecht para. 628 (15th edn., 2010).

goods (e.g., jewelry or automobiles) in Spain, their foreign-based transactions would have accommodated demand that would very likely have otherwise been taken care of by sellers at the place of the tourist-consumer's residence in Germany.[106]

In this respect, we can return to the issue of bilateral acts under article 6(2) Rome II Regulation. The deplorable state of scholarly commentary with respect to determining "markets" and defining "effects" is further illustrated by the variety of views on how to determine inter-competitor "exclusivity" required for finding a bilateral act. English commentary in particular has suggested a largely quantitative approach to determining the relevant effects for a demarcation. What is said to matter for the application of article 6(2) is whether the conduct at issue exerts significant effects primarily on a single competitor. Hence, if there is a preponderance of intercompetitor effects, the actual or potential concurrence of effects on the marketplace as a whole may be considered irrelevant.[107] Problems of such seemingly clear-cut quantification become evident, however, once the particular facts of a case do not allow for a simple "counting" of effects. The theft of trade secrets provides one example. Here, proponents of the quantitative analysis suggest that the theft, upon its completion, might tilt the scales for future competition, in turn immediately affecting the market. Accordingly, since the effect does not primarily play out in the inter-competitor relationship, article 6(1) should apply.[108] A contrary position tries to more qualitatively distinguish whether the theft is market related or competitor related. On this basis, looking at whether the impact on a competitor is "market mediated," some voices reject any finding of directness and recommend the application of article 6(2).[109] Others suggest further differentiation: with respect to the theft of a trade secret as such, they

[106] For a detailed analysis, *see infra* p. 539 *et seq.*

[107] *See, e.g.*, Andrew Dickinson, *The Rome II Regulation: The Law Applicable to Non-Contractual Obligations* para. 6.28–6.29 (2008); James J. Fawcett & Paul Torremans, *Intellectual Property and Private International Law* para. 16.08 (2nd edn., 2011); Dicey, Morris & Collins, *The Conflict of Laws, vol. II* para. 35–058 (Lord Collins of Mapesbury gen. ed., 15th edn., 2012); Richard Plender & Michael Wilderspin, *The European Private International Law of Obligations* para. 20–034–20–035 (4th edn., 2015).

[108] *See again* Andrew Dickinson, *The Rome II Regulation: The Law Applicable to Non-Contractual Obligations* para. 6.29 (2008); Richard Plender & Michael Wilderspin, *The European Private International Law of Obligations* para. 20–037 (4th edn., 2015).

[109] *See, e.g.*, Josef Drexl, in *Münchener Kommentar zum Bürgerlichen Gesetzbuch, vol. XI*, IntLautR para. 157 (Franz Jürgen Säcker et al. eds., 6th edn., 2015). *See also, e.g.*, Francisco J. Garcimartín Alférez, *The Rome II Regulation: On the way towards a European Private International Law Code*, 7 EuLF-I 77, 86 (2007); Walter F. Lindacher, *Die internationale Dimension lauterkeitsrechtlicher Unterlassungsansprüche: Marktterritorialität versus Universalität*, 2008 GRUR Int. 453, 457; Rolf Sack, *Art. 6 Abs. 2 Rom-II-VO und „bilaterales" unlauteres Wettbewerbsverhalten*, 2012 GRUR Int. 601, 604–605.

claim, no immediate impact on the market or the victim-competitor's position exists. Upon the thief's use of the secret information, however, competitive relations will be directly affected—then, article 6(1) should apply.[110] This status of the debate reflects what we have already seen: an analysis of "effects" or "interests" alone is far too imprecise. Effects may not only be hard to find; more often, they are ubiquitous. In the end, any instance of competitive conduct will have a certain effect on the market.[111] Any kind of quantitative analysis, as well as an effects-balancing or interest-balancing approach, will thus necessarily be flawed in principle. What is required is a consistent qualification of effects.

With respect to modern European choice of law, we can conclude that the substantive law doctrine of unfair competition prevention has begun to emancipate itself from traditional tort foundations; but this development is still to be completed. In addition, choice-of-law doctrine has started to implement insights from economic theory. Yet this also needs a more detailed analysis. In sum, choice of law must be unmoored from its tort foundations and must start to embrace a more precise understanding of economic concepts of market regulation.

Section 3 The New Paradigm—A Law of Market Regulation

As the foregoing discussion suggests, a more economic approach is needed in both substantive unfair competition law and choice of law. Such an approach has actually been brought forward as part of attempts to merge antitrust and unfair competition conflicts law. While this, at first sight, appears to accommodate the need to overcome the field's traditional tort foundation and to bring economic concepts into the focus, attempts to combine the two sectors into a uniform doctrine have ultimately remained unsuccessful.

I Antitrust Conflicts Reloaded: The Effects Principle

With regard to substantive law policies, antitrust and unfair competition laws have always been characterized as closely interrelated and complementary parts. Indeed, modern unfair competition law no longer provides protection for private rights and interests alone. Instead, it requires the

[110] *See, e.g.*, Peter Mankowski, in *Münchener Kommentar zum Lauterkeitsrecht, vol. I*, IntWettbR para. 333 (Peter W. Heermann et al. eds., 2nd edn., 2014). For the argument that impact should always be "unfair" (requiring improper consumer manipulation), *see* Helmut Köhler, *Wettbewerbsstatut oder Deliktsstatut? —Zur Auslegung des Art. 6 Rom-II-VO*, 501, 508, in *Festschrift für Dagmar Coester-Waltjen* (Katharina Hilbig-Lugani et al. eds., 2015).

[111] *See supra* p. 218.

extension of policies to protect the public's interest in undistorted competition. By this means, it seems, unfair competition law—together with antitrust doctrine—has become part of an overarching regime of market communication and regulation.[112] Not surprisingly, the unification of conflicts principles has also become an issue of debate. This appears to allow for an implementation of the basic antitrust conflicts rule under which virtually any effect can trigger the application of the legal regime governing an affected market.[113]

Suggestions of this kind are not new. In 1954, Wilhelm Wengler was the first to suggest that market effects should be the indicator and point of attachment not only in international antitrust law but also in international unfair competition conflicts.[114] Nonetheless, a broader debate did not commence until the end of the century. Gerhard Schricker again extended the concept by reference to substantive law's development from individual rights protection to market regulation.[115] More recently, doctrinal unification of the substance of antitrust, trademark, and unfair competition laws and conflicts has been suggested by Karl-Heinz Fezer and Stefan Koos.[116] And the issue has not been limited to scholarly commentary—Swiss statutory law has implemented an effects rule for unfair competition conflicts. While early Swiss practice still applied the *lex*

[112] For the substantive policies involved, *see infra* p. 325 *et seq.*

[113] The Rome II Regulation has, however, implemented a separate conflicts norm for antitrust violations that can be characterized as genuine effects rule. *See* art. 6 para. 3 ("The law applicable to a non-contractual obligation arising out of a restriction of competition shall be the law of the country where the market is, or is likely to be, affected.").

[114] *See* Wilhelm Wengler, *Die Gesetze über unlauteren Wettbewerb und das internationale Privatrecht*, 19 RabelsZ 401, 415 *et seq.* (1954); Wilhelm Wengler, *Laws Concerning Unfair Competition and the Conflict of Laws*, 4 Am. J. Comp. L. 167, 180–181 (1955). *See also* Rolf Bär, *Kartellrecht und Internationales Privatrecht* 366 *et seq.* (1965).

[115] Gerhard Schricker, *Die Durchsetzbarkeit deutscher Werberegelungen bei grenzüberschreitender Rundfunkwerbung*, 1982 GRUR Int. 720, 723; *see also* Max-Planck-Institut für ausländisches und internationales Patent-, Urheber- und Wettbewerbsrecht, *Stellungnahme zum Entwurf eines Gesetzes zur Ergänzung des internationalen Privatrechts (außervertragliche Schuldverhältnisse und Sachen)*, 1985 GRUR Int. 104, 107; Christof Regelmann, *Die internationalprivatrechtliche Anknüpfung des Gesetzes gegen unlauteren Wettbewerb* 129 and *passim* (1988); more recently also Stefanie Bünger, *Das Wettbewerbskollisionsrecht Deutschlands und Großbritanniens sowie seine europäische Harmonisierung* 105 *et seq.* (2006).

[116] Stefan Koos, *Grundsätze des Lauterkeitskollisionsrechts im Lichte der Schutzzwecke des UWG*, 2006 WRP 499, 504 *et seq.*; Stefan Koos, *Rom II und das Internationale Wirtschaftsrecht*, 6 EuLF 73 *et seq.* (2006); Karl-Heinz Fezer, *Markenrecht*, Einl H para. 1, 22, 38 and *passim* (4th edn., 2009); Karl-Heinz Fezer & Stefan Koos, in *Staudingers Kommentar zum Bürgerlichen Gesetzbuch: Internationales Wirtschaftsrecht*, Internationales Wettbewerbsprivatrecht para. 402 *et seq.*, 864 *et seq.*, 952 and *passim* (15th edn., 2010); Karl-Heinz Fezer & Stefan Koos, in *Staudingers Kommentar zum Bürgerlichen Gesetzbuch: Internationales Wirtschaftsrecht*, Internationales Kartellprivatrecht para. 61 (15th edn., 2010).

loci delicti commissi to cases of cross-border unfair competition, the Bundesgericht soon considered applying the market-effects principle.[117] With the enactment of article 136 of the IPRG, the effects approach appears to have become the statutory rule.[118] Finally, some voices even contend that a bare effects principle also invigorates the Rome II Regulation's rule on unfair competition in article 6(1). Proponents of this approach refer in particular to the integrated model of modern unfair competition law. The macroeconomic perspective in substantive law, they argue, indicates a corresponding interpretation of European choice-of-law norms.[119]

Not surprisingly, under a traditional tort-based perspective, a critique of the effects principle as a conflicts rule in unfair competition is still based primarily on its disregard for individual rights. Unfair competition prevention may serve common interests by maintaining free and unhindered competition; yet, as is further explained, it still needs to consider individual competitors' rights and positions.[120] In addition, the criterion of

[117] *See* Carl Baudenbacher, *Die wettbewerbsrechtliche Beurteilung grenzüberschreitender Werbe- und Absatztätigkeit nach schweizerischem Recht*, 1988 GRUR Int. 310, 316 *et seq.* (with references to case law); Hans R. Schibli, *Multistate-Werbung im internationalen Lauterkeitsrecht mit besonderer Berücksichtigung der Internet-Werbung* 108 *et seq.* (2004); BGE vol. 91 II, 117, 123 *et seq.* (30 March 1965).

[118] Article 136 of the IPRG provides: "Ansprüche aus unlauterem Wettbewerb unterstehen dem Recht des Staates, auf dessen Markt die unlautere Handlung ihre Wirkung entfaltet." *See, e.g.*, BG 1997 GRUR Int. 167—*item communication* (9 August 1995); Ivo Schwander, *Das UWG im grenzüberschreitenden Verkehr*, 161, 174 *et seq.*, in *Das UWG auf neuer Grundlage* (Carl Baudenbacher ed., 1989); Lorenza Ferrari, *Die Anknüpfung an die Marktauswirkung im Schweizerischen IPRG und ihre Konkretisierung* 52 *et seq.* (1993); Rolf Bär, *Das Internationale Privatrecht (Kollisionsrecht) des Immaterialgüterrechts und des Wettbewerbsrechts*, 125, 158, in *Schweizerisches Immaterialgüter- und Wettbewerbsrecht, vol. I* (Roland von Büren & Lucas David eds., 2nd edn., 2002); Rolf H. Weber, *Internationale Harmonisierungsansätze im Lauterkeitsrecht*, 1998 sic! 158, 171; Jochen Glöckner, *Wettbewerbsverstöße im Internet—Grenzen einer kollisionsrechtlichen Problemlösung*, 99 ZVglRWiss 278, 280, 283 (2000); Hans R. Schibli, *Multistate-Werbung im internationalen Lauterkeitsrecht mit besonderer Berücksichtigung der Internet-Werbung* 127 *et seq.* (2004).

[119] *See, e.g.*, Stefan Koos, *Rom II und das Internationale Wirtschaftsrecht*, 6 EuLF 73, 76–77 (2006); Christian Handig, *Neues im Internationalen Wettbewerbsrecht—Auswirkungen der Rom II-Verordnung*, 2008 GRUR Int. 24, 28 and 29; Jochen Glöckner, in *Gesetz gegen den unlauteren Wettbewerb (UWG)*, UWG Einl C para. 106 *et seq.* (Henning Harte-Bavendamm & Frauke Henning-Bodewig eds., 3rd edn., 2013); Karl-Heinz Fezer & Stefan Koos, in *Staudingers Kommentar zum Bürgerlichen Gesetzbuch: Internationales Wirtschaftsrecht*, Internationales Wettbewerbsprivatrecht para. 403 (15th edn., 2010); Hamburg Group for Private International Law, *Comments on the European Commission's Draft Proposal for a Council Regulation on the Law Applicable to Non-Contractual Obligations*, 67 RabelsZ 1, 19 (2003).

[120] *See, e.g.*, Helmut Wirner, *Wettbewerbsrecht und internationales Privatrecht* 101–102 (1960); Erwin Deutsch, *Wettbewerbstatbestände mit Auslandsbeziehung* 46–47 (1962); Kamen Troller, *Das internationale Privatrecht des unlauteren Wettbewerbs in vergleichender Darstellung der Rechte Deutschlands, Englands, Frankreichs, Italiens, der Schweiz und*

bare effects is denounced as being overly broad. Since effects can comprise almost any variation and alteration of market conditions or circumstances, domestic unfair competition law can apply virtually universally, and the number of potentially applicable regimes can rise to impracticability.[121] In light of this critique, proponents of the effects principle have suggested a limitation, primarily by excluding instances of minimal and economically negligible impact. In 1954 already, Wengler suggested giving regard only to effects on the *sales* market.[122] Since then, others have qualified the relevant effects by demanding that only direct or substantial effects be considered and that remote consequences of competitive conduct be neglected.[123]

II Analysis: The Unboundedness of Unqualified Effects

The idea of a uniform approach under an overarching effects test is tempting. I have explained the apparent advantages in my critique of the collision-of-interests and market-effects rule.[124] But we have also seen that, so far, a clear structure of effects testing has not been brought forward. The approach's consistency and practicality remain questionable. The most evident problem is a widely uncritical, and thus imprecise, policy foundation of the effects test. Of course, both areas have a common purpose: both antitrust and unfair competition laws prevent the improper

der USA 126–127 (1962); more recently, Dieter Dubs, *Das Lauterkeitsstatut nach schweizerischem Kollisionsrecht—Zugleich ein Beitrag zur Materialisierung des Internationalprivatrechts* 65 (2000).

[121] *See, e.g.*, Rolf Sack, *Marktortprinzip und allgemeine Ausweichklausel im internationalen Wettbewerbsrecht, am Beispiel der sog. Gran-Canaria-Fälle*, 1992 IPRax 24, 26; Andreas Höder, *Die kollisionsrechtliche Behandlung unteilbarer Multistate-Verstöße—Das Internationale Wettbewerbsrecht im Spannungsfeld von Marktort-, Auswirkungs- und Herkunftslandprinzip* 85 (2002); Josef Drexl, in *Münchener Kommentar zum Bürgerlichen Gesetzbuch, vol. XI*, IntLautR para. 16 (Franz Jürgen Säcker et al. eds., 6th edn., 2015).

[122] Wilhelm Wengler, *Die Gesetze über unlauteren Wettbewerb und das internationale Privatrecht*, 19 RabelsZ 401, 417 (1954).

[123] This namely is contended in Swiss antitrust conflicts doctrine. *See, e.g.*, Rolf Bär, *Kartellrecht und internationales Privatrecht* 377 *et seq.* (1965); Carl Baudenbacher, *Die wettbewerbsrechtliche Beurteilung grenzüberschreitender Werbe- und Absatztätigkeit nach schweizerischem Recht*, 1988 GRUR Int. 310, 318; Hans R. Schibli, *Multistate-Werbung im internationalen Lauterkeitsrecht mit besonderer Berücksichtigung der Internet-Werbung* 197 *et seq.* (2004): for the debate under Rome II, *see also, e.g.*, Karl-Heinz Fezer & Stefan Koos, in *Staudingers Kommentar zum Bürgerlichen Gesetzbuch: Internationales Wirtschaftsrecht*, Internationales Wettbewerbsprivatrecht para. 480 and para. 652 (15th edn., 2010); Martin Illmer, in *Rome II Regulation*, Art. 6 para. 97 *et seq.* (Peter Huber ed., 2011); Benedikt Buchner, in *Rome Regulations*, Art. 6 Rome II para. 37 and 38 (Gralf-Peter Calliess ed., 2011); Jochen Glöckner, in *Gesetz gegen den unlauteren Wettbewerb (UWG)*, UWG Einl C para. 49 *et seq.* (Henning Harte-Bavendamm & Frauke Henning-Bodewig eds., 3rd edn., 2013).

[124] *See supra* p. 203 *et seq.*

impingement of marketplace competition. Modern unfair competition doctrine (with its trinity of purposes) prescribes that protection of the market's functioning is inseparably linked to competitor and consumer protection.[125] Such an integrated model implies that it may be enough to protect fairness of competition as such in order to fulfill all three protection purposes under unfair competition law. A closer look, however, indicates a caveat: the field's core policy is not aimed at merely preventing market-distorting effects—rather, a more technical paradigm of "effects" governs.

This is where differences between antitrust law and unfair competition law become obvious. The former aims at preventing a wide array of conduct with anticompetitive market impact, and thus governs virtually *any* effect on free competition. Any change in market conditions and structure may be sufficient to trigger application of the respective regulatory regime.[126] In European antitrust conflicts law, therefore, the effects considered are conceived of broadly: territorial effect will be found upon almost any alteration of conditions in the domestic market or with regard to domestic competition.[127] Most generally, the demarcation between direct/indirect and substantial/insignificant effects is found by an analysis of market share alterations. In this regard, small changes in market share (<1%) may be deemed "effective" with regard to conflicts determination if an additional impact on the market can be found.[128] Alternatively, a change in market shares exceeding a threshold of 3% may suffice to constitute effects without further prerequisites.[129] And in the United States, the picture is not much different. While early practice still saw

[125] For an extensive analysis of unfair competition policies, *see infra* p. 295 *et seq.* and p. 348 *et seq.*

[126] *See, e.g.*, *T-Mobile Netherlands and Others*, C-8/08, para. 38 (4 June 2009), [2009] E.C.R. I-4529; for instructive critique, *see, e.g.*, Dieter Martiny, *Die Anknüpfung an den Markt*, 389, 390–391, and 399, in *Festschrift für Ulrich Drobnig zum siebzigsten Geburtstag* (Jürgen Basedow et al. eds., 1998).

[127] *See, e.g.*, Ulrich Immenga, in *Münchener Kommentar zum Bürgerlichen Gesetzbuch, vol. XI*, IntWettbR/IntKartellR para. 16 (Franz Jürgen Säcker et al. eds., 6th edn., 2015); Heinz Fezer & Stefan Koos, in *Staudingers Kommentar zum Bürgerlichen Gesetzbuch: Internationales Wirtschaftsrecht*, Internationales Kartellprivatrecht para. 180 *et seq.* (15th edn., 2010). For article 6(3) Rome II Regulation, *see, e.g.*, Peter Mankowski, *Das neue Internationale Kartellrecht des Art. 6 Abs. 3 der Rom-II-Verordnung*, 2008 RIW 177, 184 *et seq.*

[128] For instance, such an impact could be the defendant's access to know-how or additional production capacities. *See, e.g.*, BGH 1979 GRUR 790, 791–792–*Organische Pigmente* (29 May 1979).

[129] *See, e.g.*, Ulrich Immenga, in *Münchener Kommentar zum Bürgerlichen Gesetzbuch, vol. XI*, IntWettbR/IntKartellR para. 27 *et seq.* (Franz Jürgen Säcker et al. eds., 6th edn., 2015); Heinz Fezer & Stefan Koos, in *Staudingers Kommentar zum Bürgerlichen Gesetzbuch: Internationales Wirtschaftsrecht*, Internationales Kartellprivatrecht para. 220 *et seq.* (15th edn., 2010).

antitrust law as strictly territorial,[130] over time, the courts developed the proverbial paradigm of antitrust extraterritoriality.[131] In 1982, the Foreign Trade Antitrust Improvements Act established that the application of federal antitrust law requires a "direct, substantial and reasonably foreseeable effect" on US commerce (except for imports).[132] In its 1993 *Hartford Fire* decision, the Supreme Court explained that US courts would have jurisdiction when "foreign conduct ... was meant to produce and did in fact produce some substantial effect in the United States."[133] The issue was further clarified in 2004 in *F. Hoffmann-La Roche*.[134] Yet even though the court limited effects jurisdiction, the actual degree of effects required to trigger application of US law is still largely undecided—and, as in European doctrine, structurally unqualified.

Unfair competition law, by contrast, has a more specific focus. Thus far, this focus has usually been expressed in the context of conduct-regulation and intention-based theories. As we have seen, these suggestions are not on point with respect to doctrinal and economic structures of the field.[135] In the following chapters, I will demonstrate that the core focus of both trademark protection and unfair competition prevention is not free competition as such. Rather, it is the market information infrastructure and its relevance for individual transacting—more concretely, the consumer's decision making.[136] Accordingly, the analysis for choice of law must be more specific and precise, going beyond its obsolete tort foundations and staying behind the modern antitrust urge: it must not stop where the competitors' conduct has come to a halt, and it must not extend beyond the consumer's transaction by covering subsequent effects.

Section 4 Modern Soft Law—WIPO Recommendation, ALI Principles, and Others

In recent decades, a number of nongovernmental institutions and scholarly initiatives have brought forward alternative or supplementary norms for trademark and unfair competition conflicts resolution. I have already alluded to the Institut de Droit International and its 1983 Cambridge Resolution on the Conflict-of-laws Rules on Unfair

[130] *See, e.g.*, *American Banana Co. v. United Fruit Co.*, 213 U.S. 347 (1909).
[131] *See also infra* p. 445 *et seq.*
[132] Foreign Trade Antitrust Improvements Act of 1982, § 402, 15 U.S.C. § 6a.
[133] *Hartford Fire Ins. Co. v. California*, 509 U.S. 764, 796 (1993).
[134] *F. Hoffmann-La Roche Ltd. v. Empagran S.A.*, 542 U.S. 155, 164 (2004). *See also infra* p. 453 *et seq.*
[135] *See supra* p. 214 *et seq.* [136] *See infra* p. 275 *et seq.*

Competition. An exhaustive analysis of all attempts is not necessary. A look at the most influential instruments shall highlight the relevant aspects. Among the most important examples of alternative institutional suggestions are the Paris Union/WIPO Joint Recommendation on trademark use on the internet and the ALI and CLIP Principles on international intellectual property conflicts.

I Nonbinding Suggestions of Substantive Law and Conflicts Resolution

A The Joint Recommendation Concerning Provisions on the Protection of Marks, and Other Industrial Property Rights in Signs, on the Internet

In September 2001, the General Assembly of WIPO and the Assembly of the Paris Union for the Protection of Industrial Property adopted a set of recommendations[137] that seeks to "facilitate the application of existing laws relating to marks and other industrial property rights in signs"[138] to legal disputes arising from international conflicts on the internet. As the Joint Recommendation's preface explains, the instrument's provisions are not designed to determine the applicable law. Choice of law is instead "left to the private international laws of individual Member States."[139] Strictly speaking, therefore, the Joint Recommendation does not fit neatly into the line of instruments on choice of law or private international law.[140] Yet it has significantly contributed to and succinctly summarizes the debate, including arguments over how to determine the applicable law in international trademark and unfair competition conflicts. Regardless of theoretical differences between choice of law and a determination of sufficient effects at the level of substantive law, the arguments are practically identical.

The Joint Recommendation has two main components. The first spells out the intent to reduce internet trademark conflicts by defining what is required for the acquisition of rights and their infringement.[141] The second contains provisions concerning a flexible mediation of conflicts.[142] It establishes limited liability for trademark owners prior to receiving a notification of infringement. Absent bad faith, the infringing

[137] WIPO, *Joint Recommendation Concerning Provisions on the Protection of Marks, and Other Industrial Property Rights in Signs, on the Internet, adopted at the Thirty-Sixth Series of the Meeting of the Assemblies of the Member States of the WIPO, September 24 to October 2, 2001*, WIPO Publication no. 845(E).

[138] *Id.* at 2 and 5 (Preface and Preamble). [139] *Id.*

[140] For the distinction, *see, e.g.*, Annette Kur, *Applicable Law: An Alternative Proposal for International Regulation—The Max-Planck Project on International Jurisdiction and Choice of Law*, 30 Brook. J. Int'l L. 951, 968 (2005).

[141] Article 1 *et seq.* [142] Article 9 *et seq.*

user can avoid liability by expeditiously taking reasonable steps to "avoid a commercial effect" in the protecting country.[143] In addition, the Joint Recommendation suggests limitations on judicial remedies in accordance with the commercial effects at bar.[144] For this inquiry, the analysis of "commercial effects" in the recommendation's first part is most relevant.

Under article 2, "[u]se of a sign on the Internet shall constitute use in a Member State ... only if the use has a commercial effect in that Member State." The concept of "commercial effect" is defined in article 3(1), which includes a nonexhaustive list of factors, each of which may be taken into account to determine whether a "commercial effect" can be found.[145] Among the factors to be considered are "circumstances indicating that the user of a sign is doing, or has undertaken significant plans to do, business in the Member State" (art. 3(1)(a)) and the "level and character of commercial activity ... in relation to the Member State" (art. 3(1)(b)), including actual transactions with customers located in the state, the use of disclaimers regarding transactions with customers in a certain member state, whether the user "offers post-sale activities in the Member State," and whether she undertakes "further commercial activities in the Member State which are related to the use of the sign on the Internet but which are not carried out over the Internet" (art. 3(1)(b)(i)–(iv)). It must also be considered "whether the goods or services offered can be lawfully delivered in the Member State" (art. 3(1)(c)(i)), what data and information the internet communication contains (e.g., currency, language, and contact details) (arts. 3(1)(c)(ii) and 3(1)(d)(ii) and (iv)), and whether the internet communication is connected to a certain top-level domain (art. 3(1)(d)(iii)).

Article 3(2) of the Joint Recommendation explains that the factors listed in the first paragraph "are guidelines to assist the competent authority" in determining whether a commercial effect has been produced—

[143] Articles 9 and 10.

[144] Article 13 *et seq.* For an extensive discussion, *see, e.g.*, Torsten Bettinger, *Die WIPO-Vorschläge zum Schutz von Marken und anderen Zeichenrechten im Internet*, 2001 WRP 789, 793 *et seq.*; Graeme B. Dinwoodie, *Trademarks and Territory: Detaching Trademark Law from the Nation-State*, 41 Hous. L. Rev. 885, 932 *et seq.* (2004); Annette Kur, *Trademark Conflicts on the Internet: Territoriality Redefined?*, 175, 177 *et seq.*, in *Intellectual Property in the Conflict of Laws* (Jürgen Basedow et al. eds., 2005); Johannes Christian Wichard, *The Joint Recommendation Concerning Protection of Marks, and Other Industrial Property Rights in Signs, on the Internet*, 257, 262–263, in *Intellectual Property and Private International Law—Heading for the Future* (Josef Drexl & Annette Kur eds., 2005); Graeme B. Dinwoodie, *Developing a Private International Intellectual Property Law: The Demise of Territoriality?*, 51 Wm. & Mary L. Rev. 711, 777 *et seq.* (2009).

[145] Torsten Bettinger, *Die WIPO-Vorschläge zum Schutz von Marken und anderen Zeichenrechten im Internet*, 2001 WRP 789, 792; Graeme B. Dinwoodie, *Trademarks and Territory: Detaching Trademark Law from the Nation-State*, 41 Hous. L. Rev. 885, 908, 933 (2004).

they are "not pre-conditions for reaching that determination." Since the relevance of each factor may depend on the circumstances of the case, no binding method or guideline of application has been prescribed. The only technical predetermination (in the sense of finding a presumption for "commercial effect") has been explained in the context of bad-faith use (art. 4) and in article 3(1)(e).[146]

B ALI Principles, CLIP Principles, and the Japanese Transparency Proposal

In recent decades, alongside increasing debate on private international intellectual property law, scholarly institutions have also promulgated model codes and rules for applying and interpreting conflicts principles. The most prominent rules are the American Law Institute's Intellectual Property: Principles Governing Jurisdiction, Choice of Law, and Judgments in Transnational Disputes of 2007 (ALI Principles) and the Max Planck Institute's Principles on Conflict of Laws in Intellectual Property of 2011 (CLIP Principles). Inspired by these two model codes, the Japanese Transparency Project published its Transparency Proposal in 2009.[147] All three model codes contain compilations of rules that address topics ranging from determining court jurisdiction to establishing applicable law, as well as recognition and enforcement of judgments. Each compilation has specific rules on trademark and unfair competition conflicts.[148]

The ALI Principles, whose drafting began in 2001, represent the American Law Institute's first engagement with internet issues.[149] I will focus on part III of the principles, specifically those provisions that

[146] For the provision's ad hoc decision-making character and the relevance of bad faith (art. 4), *see* Torsten Bettinger, *Die WIPO-Vorschläge zum Schutz von Marken und anderen Zeichenrechten im Internet*, 2001 WRP 789, 793.

[147] Toshiyuki Kono et al., *Preface*, at V, in *Intellectual Property in the Global Arena—Jurisdiction, Applicable Law, and the Recognition of Judgments in Europe, Japan and the US* (Jürgen Basedow et al. eds., 2010).

[148] For an extensive analysis and debate of the ALI Principles, CLIP Principles, and Transparency Proposal, *see* Jürgen Basedow et al., in *Intellectual Property in the Global Arena—Jurisdiction, Applicable Law, and the Recognition of Judgments in Europe, Japan and the US* (Jürgen Basedow et al., 2010); for an overview of the development, *see, e.g.*, Graeme B. Dinwoodie, *Developing a Private International Intellectual Property Law: The Demise of Territoriality?*, 51 Wm. & Mary L. Rev. 711, 716 *et seq.* (2009).

[149] Lance Liebman, *Director's Foreword*, at IX, in *Intellectual Property—Principles Governing Jurisdiction, Choice of Law, and Judgments in Transnational Disputes* (American Law Institute ed., 2008). For an illustration of the drafting process and the debate, *see* Rochelle Cooper Dreyfuss, *The ALI Principles on Transnational Intellectual Property Disputes: Why Invite Conflicts?*, 30 Brook. J. Int'l L. 819 (2005); François Dessemontet, *A European Point of View on the ALI Principles—Intellectual Property: Principles Governing Jurisdiction, Choice of Law, and Judgments in Transnational Disputes*, 30 Brook. J. Int'l L. 849 (2005).

address the determination of the applicable law (secs. 301 et seq.). These rules are founded on the territoriality of intellectual property rights.[150] As the reporters explain, substantive intellectual property law may be more thoroughly harmonized in the future, or an international approach to choice of law may come into force. In the meantime, the ALI Principles are "intended to fill the gap and stimulate longer-term efforts in this vein."[151] Adherence to territoriality is described as the result of "powerful intuition." The legality of acts should thus be determined according to each jurisdiction without regard to the existence of global markets. In particular, territoriality should safeguard for "local cultural values and social policies."[152] Accordingly, section 301(1) states:

> The law applicable to determine the existence, validity, duration, attributes, and infringement of intellectual property rights and the remedies for their infringement is: (a) for registered rights, the law of each State of registration[,] (b) for other intellectual property rights, the law of each State for which protection is sought.

Furthermore, for unfair competition conflicts, section 301(2) provides:

> The law applicable to a noncontractual obligation arising out of an act of unfair competition is the law of each State in which direct and substantial damage results or is likely to result, irrespective of the State or States in which the act giving rise to the damage occurred.

As the comments to the ALI Principles explain, the "usual point of attachment for determining infringement" of unregistered rights, especially common law trademarks and commercial-name rights, is to be found in the "countries where the right owner's market for the work [or product] has been affected."[153] Attachment thus follows a so-called market-oriented approach in accordance with the markets that a right owner seeks to protect.[154] Market orientation is also upheld for unfair

[150] American Law Institute, *Introduction*, at 4, and *Introductory Note to Part III*, at 117, in *Intellectual Property—Principles Governing Jurisdiction, Choice of Law, and Judgments in Transnational Disputes* (American Law Institute ed., 2008). For an illustration, *see, e.g.*, François Dessemontet, *The ALI Principles: Intellectual Property in Transborder Litigation*, 31, 40 *et seq.*, in *Intellectual Property in the Global Arena—Jurisdiction, Applicable Law, and the Recognition of Judgments in Europe, Japan and the US* (Jürgen Basedow et al. eds., 2010). For exceptions to the territoriality approach, notably party autonomy, initial ownership of certain rights, and ubiquitous infringements, *see* §§ 302, 313, 321.

[151] American Law Institute, *Part III—Applicable Law*, at 117, in *Intellectual Property—Principles Governing Jurisdiction, Choice of Law, and Judgments in Transnational Disputes* (American Law Institute ed., 2008).

[152] *Id.* at 121 (Reporter's Note to Part III—Applicable Law).

[153] *Id.* at 122–123 (§ 301, comment c).

[154] *Id.* at 123 (§ 301, comment d). For a market impact rule, *see also* Annette Kur, *Applicable Law: An Alternative Proposal for International Regulation—The Max-Planck Project on International Jurisdiction and Choice of Law*, 30 Brook. J. Int'l L. 951, 966 *et seq.* (2005).

competition conflicts resolution. As the reporters explain, many jurisdictions provide for intellectual property and unfair competition claims to be entertained together, particularly in cases of trademark, trade name, and neighboring rights violations. Therefore, it is the law of the "place where competition is taking place" that should apply comprehensively to the entire dispute.[155]

The territoriality principle also governs with respect to the acquisition of title to intellectual property rights, with a slight differentiation between registered and unregistered rights. Rights that arise out of registration are governed by the law of the state of registration (sec. 311(1)). By contrast, initial title to unregistered trademark or trade-dress rights are governed by the law of the state where the trademark or trade dress "identifies and distinguishes the source of the goods or services"[156] (sec. 312(1)). In this regard, the principles' comments provide a precise definition of market rights under common law doctrine. Use-based and market-oriented rights acquisition is generally not limited by nation-state boundaries; rather, the goodwill paradigm mediates the market/rights correlation. Wherever consumers recognize a correlation between trade symbol and product, goodwill accounts for the acquisition and protection of individual entitlements. Under the principles' territorial concept, it is then the respective sovereign state that assigns the single and separate domestic right. Accordingly, a bundle of rights may come into existence (with different owners) in multinational markets.[157]

An important rule for online communication and commerce is found in section 321. This provision designates the applicable law in situations of "ubiquitous infringement." Whenever the law of more than one state is eligible for application, the court "may choose to apply to the issues of existence, validity, duration, attributes, and infringement of intellectual property rights and remedies" the law(s) of the state(s) with "close connections to the dispute." The close connection will be determined by

[155] American Law Institute, § 301, comment g, at 124, in *Intellectual Property—Principles Governing Jurisdiction, Choice of Law, and Judgments in Transnational Disputes* (American Law Institute ed., 2008).

[156] For both registered and unregistered rights, title may be governed by a different law if the right arises out of a contractual or other preexisting relationship among the parties (*see* §§ 311(2) and 312(2)).

[157] *Id.* at 136–137 (§ 312, comment a) ("Although trademark rights in some States do not arise out of registration . . ., they tend to be bounded. This is because trademarks symbolize the goodwill of the product or service to its consumers. The trademark exists where there is a market for the goods or services that the mark identifies. Unregistered trademark rights cannot arise without the connection between the mark and the goods or services. For some trademarks, market recognition may be worldwide; for others, it may be national or regional. Accordingly, the same mark may have different owners in different markets.").

analyzing relevant factors contained in a nonexhaustive list that includes but is not limited to the following: the place in which the parties reside; the place where the parties' relationship, if any, is centered; the extent of the activities; the investment of the parties; and the principal markets toward which the parties have directed their activities.[158] As the reporters explain, this rule is intended to "meet the territoriality and single-law approaches halfway."[159] I will address theories of "single law," or substantive law, resolution at the end of this chapter.[160] Here, suffice it to conclude that the rule for ubiquitous infringements structurally resembles a *de minimis* limitation in multijurisdictional conflicts in one respect: it is a rule of practicality, albeit one with significant implications for legal doctrine and policy.

The final version of the CLIP Principles, published in 2011, also distinguishes between jurisdiction, applicable law, and the recognition and enforcement of judgments. With regard to the law applicable to existence, validity, registration, scope and duration, initial ownership, and entitlement to rights arising out of registration, the *lex loci protectionis* governs. And the law applicable to an infringement is also "the law of each State for which protection is sought."[161] Similar to the ALI Principles, the CLIP Principles contain a rule for ubiquitous infringements. Where infringement is carried out through ubiquitous media (such as the internet), a court "may apply the law of the State having the closest connection with the infringement, if the infringement arguably takes place in every State in which the signals can be received."[162] In determining the closest connection, the court must consider a nonexhaustive list of several factors, including the infringer's habitual residence, her principal place of business, the place where substantial infringing activities took place, and the place where the most harm was caused by the infringing activities.[163]

[158] Section 321(1)(2) of the provision provides for an escape from the rule for cases where single regimes would yield a different outcome. For an earlier version of this rule, *see* Willis L. M. Reese & Frank Vischer, *The Conflict-of-laws Rules on Unfair Competition*, Annuaire de L'Institut de Droit International 60, I (1983), 159, 162.

[159] American Law Institute, § 321, comment 1, at 155, in *Intellectual Property—Principles Governing Jurisdiction, Choice of Law, and Judgments in Transnational Disputes* (American Law Institute ed., 2008).

[160] *See infra* p. 256 *et seq.*

[161] *See* articles 3:102, 3:201, and 3:601. For the transferability of rights and the *lex loci protectionis, see* article 3:301.

[162] Article 3:603.

[163] Article 3:603(2). For explanation of the interim version, *see* Axel Metzger, *Applicable Law under the CLIP Principles: A Pragmatic Revaluation of Territoriality*, 157, 173 *et seq.*, in *Intellectual Property in the Global Arena—Jurisdiction, Applicable Law, and the Recognition of Judgments in Europe, Japan and the US* (Jürgen Basedow et al. eds., 2010).

The CLIP Principles' *de minimis* rule in article 3:602(1) provides for another, more universal, limitation on the number of applicable laws in multistate cases. A state's legal regime will be applied only if "the defendant has acted to initiate or further the infringement in the State or the States for which protection is sought" or if "the activity by which the right is claimed to be infringed has substantial effect within, or is directed to the State or the States for which protection is sought." Paragraph 2 provides for an exception from this rule. This *de minimis* provision is not a rule of choice of law—it is founded on the application of a predetermined legal regime.[164]

Finally, the Japanese Transparency Proposal is worth mentioning because it provides an interesting extension of marketplace-oriented attachment in trademark and unfair competition conflicts. Under article 301(1), "[t]he law applicable to an intellectual property infringement shall be the law of the place where the results of the exploitation of intellectual property occur or are to occur."[165] Similarly, article 303's rule on unfair competition conflicts provides for application of the "law of the place where the results of unfair competition occur or are to occur." This proposal thereby seems to have adopted an across-the-board market-impact rule.[166] Correspondingly, the rule on ubiquitous infringements in article 302 provides for an application of the "law of the place where the results of the exploitation of intellectual property are or [are] to be maximized."

II Analysis: "Chips off the Old Block"

The following critique of the Joint Recommendation and related academic principles points out the key conceptual deficits that must be avoided when constructing a new and alternative approach to conflicts resolution. The Joint Recommendation's most striking flaw is its qualitatively imprecise use of the term "commercial effects," while the ALI and

[164] The provision is therefore, strictly speaking, systematically out of place. Yet it corresponds to the WIPO Joint Recommendation Concerning Provisions on the Protection of Marks, and Other Industrial Property Rights in Signs, on the Internet. *See also* Axel Metzger, *Applicable Law under the CLIP Principles: A Pragmatic Revaluation of Territoriality*, 157, 173, in *Intellectual Property in the Global Arena—Jurisdiction, Applicable Law, and the Recognition of Judgments in Europe, Japan and the US* (Jürgen Basedow et al. eds., 2010).

[165] Article 301(2) provides for an attachment to the law of the contract if the intellectual property infringement occurred in breach of an existing contractual obligation between the parties.

[166] Ryu Kojima, Ryo Shimanami & Mari Nagata, *Applicable Law to Exploitation of Intellectual Property Rights in the Transparency Proposal*, 179, 186–187, in *Intellectual Property in the Global Arena—Jurisdiction, Applicable Law, and the Recognition of Judgments in Europe, Japan and the US* (Jürgen Basedow et al. eds., 2010).

CLIP Principles contain a number of defects that replicate and perpetuate structural inconsistencies that I have already explored in my overview of traditional and current doctrine.

A The Joint Recommendation

Akin to tests for Lanham Act subject-matter jurisdiction,[167] the Joint Recommendation's list of factors to be considered for effects testing is not governed by strict qualitative or quantitative guidelines. The test for "commercial effects" requires ad hoc decision making, leaving ample space for the divergent treatment of national interests and individual concerns. Of course, this does not invalidate the recommendation's approach per se. After all, the drafters expected the relevant factors to be determined in close accordance with the unique circumstances of each case.[168] Nevertheless, the test is quite vague with regard to evaluation and balancing. Courts will likely develop a diversity of interpretations and applications, which will inhibit a consistent and uniform approach to resolving multijurisdictional conflicts.[169]

Most problematic, however, as we have seen with the *Bulova* test and its variants, is the lack of market relatedness in test structure and effects quality.[170] The "commercial context" that is supposed to be regulated requires a close connection to the market mechanism in order to prevent the overreach of single regimes. In fact, looking at all factors in article 3(1), it is striking that only some of the listed parameters are directly related to consumer decision making; a significant number of factors are non-market related. Beginning with the user's "significant plans to do ... business" within a jurisdiction, it is clear that the Joint Recommendation is not concerned with actual effects on the marketplace. It requires neither a specific focus on competition nor one on information economization, as could be expected for regulation in the field of trademark and unfair competition conflicts. Another example is the definition of customer "location" in subparagraph (b). The explanatory notes state that " 'location' is a purely factual concept, for which mere presence in the State should be sufficient."[171] This implies that the concept of customer

167 *See supra* p. 159 *et seq.*

168 *See* Explanatory Notes on Article 3 to the Joint Recommendation, WIPO Publication no. 845(E), 3.01 ("A competent authority is free to determine which factors are relevant in a given case.").

169 *See, e.g.*, Anna R. Popov, *Watering Down Steele v. Bulova Watch Co. to Reach E-Commerce Overseas: Analyzing the Lanham Act's Extraterritorial Reach Under International Law*, 77 S. Cal. L. Rev. 705, 737–738 (2004).

170 *See supra* p. 159 *et seq.*

171 *See* Explanatory Notes on Article 3 to the Joint Recommendation, WIPO Publication no. 845(E), 3.04.

location is a mere geographical guidepost, designed to facilitate the localization of effects. Since commercial effects, however, are what will be determined, one might expect that the actual or prospective transaction is what matters. Yet, as subparagraph (b)(iii) further illustrates, even postsale activity may be sufficient to establish effects. In the same vein, subparagraph (c)(i) provides that a court should give regard to whether "the goods or services offered can be lawfully delivered in the Member State." Both factors lack a direct relation to the market. As the explanatory notes further clarify with respect to the issue of lawful delivery, "[u]se of a sign on the Internet in conjunction with the offer of goods or services that do not comply with the product regulations of a particular Member State is less likely to produce a commercial effect."[172] Of course, some indicative value can be acknowledged with respect to a testing for commercial effects here: a finding of commercial effects is only less likely, not plainly excluded, if the goods or services cannot be lawfully delivered. Nevertheless, this standard is still misguided. The legality of goods or services is rarely directly connected to policies of trademark and unfair competition law. A trademark infringement or an unfair competition violation may be committed regardless of whether the right owner's or victim-competitor's product is or can be sold in compliance with legal requirements beyond the field of trademark and unfair competition regulation (e.g., regulation of medical products).[173]

In essence, therefore, the Joint Recommendation's list of factors is neither comprehensively market oriented nor oriented toward the protection of consumer decision making. The courts' balancing discretion under article 3(2) further allows for neglecting or suppressing certain factors in favor of others. Therefore, the balancing will not follow a strict concept of preventing impediments to competition and a free market.

B ALI Principles, CLIP Principles, and the Japanese Transparency Proposal

There is no doubt that all three models, in principle, provide for balanced solutions in most international intellectual property and unfair competition conflicts.[174] Yet adherence to territoriality bears the well-known

[172] *See id.* at 3.10.

[173] This has been plainly acknowledged under German unfair competition doctrine. *See, e.g.*, BGH 2005 GRUR 519, 520—*Vitamin-Zell-Komplex* (24 February 2005); *see also* RGZ vol. 117, 318, 321—*Kruschensalz* (24 June 1927).

[174] For the ALI Principles, *see, e.g.*, American Law Institute, *Introductory Note to Part III, Applicable law*, at 118, in *Intellectual Property—Principles Governing Jurisdiction, Choice of Law, and Judgments in Transnational Disputes* (American Law Institute ed., 2008) ("Any set of conflicts rules should be (and should be perceived to be) fair and neutral. The rules

problem of underregulation, and, conversely, efforts to promulgate more market-oriented rules for conflicts resolution may lead to overregulation. While a reinvention of the wheel is neither expected nor warranted, several aspects deserve closer scrutiny.

First, the key distinction between registered and unregistered rights, as implemented in the ALI Principles, is problematic because it advances the idea that differences should depend on formalities. I have analyzed this problem with respect to civil law doctrine in chapter 1.[175] The preliminary draft of the ALI Principles was criticized for this distinction. Under this former version, the law of the country of registration would have applied in cases of the infringement of registered rights. For unregistered rights, the applicable law would have been the "law of any country where the allegedly infringing act has or will significantly impact the market for the work or subject matter at issue."[176] As critics pointed out, this draft bore the risk of propagating a misunderstanding: the distinction could have been interpreted as a rejection of the market-impact rule for registered rights.[177] And even though the rule was altered in the final version, the explanatory comment has not corrected this potential for misconception since a detachment between registration and markets still exists. As the final version's comments explain, the infringement of "other rights" (particularly common law trademarks and commercial-name rights) will be attached to the "countries where the right owner's market ... has been affected."[178] This market-oriented approach, however, is still described only with respect to "other rights."

An additional aspect is perplexing. "Direct and substantial damage" is needed to find a specific national unfair competition regime applicable. As the ALI Principles' example illustrates,[179] the theft of trade secrets in one state may ultimately "affect competition" in other states by harming the commercial interests of and causing damage to the owner of the trade

should neither favor an intellectual property owner over an alleged infringer, nor should they privilege users over owners. Moreover, the rules should put domestic and foreign law on an equal footing ..., nor should they otherwise discriminate between local and foreign claimants."). For the cautious (and conservative) stance of the ALI and CLIP projects, *see* Annette Kur, *Applicable Law: An Alternative Proposal for International Regulation—The Max-Planck Project on International Jurisdiction and Choice of Law*, 30 Brook. J. Int'l L. 951, 953 (2005).

[175] *See supra* p. 27 *et seq.* and p. 64 *et seq.*

[176] For the former version and a critique, *see* Annette Kur, *Applicable Law: An Alternative Proposal for International Regulation—The Max-Planck Project on International Jurisdiction and Choice of Law*, 30 Brook. J. Int'l L. 951, 961 *et seq.* (2005).

[177] *Id.* at 969–970.

[178] American Law Institute, § 301, comment c and d, at 122–123, in *Intellectual Property—Principles Governing Jurisdiction, Choice of Law, and Judgments in Transnational Disputes* (American Law Institute ed., 2008).

[179] *See id.* at 124–125 (§ 301, comment g, illustration 3).

secret. Unfortunately, however, the principles do not specify what is required for a finding of "direct" and "substantial" damage. An unlimited extension of the applicable laws is thus possible. Even more delicate is the fact that the necessary degree and intensity of market effects for trademark rights protection is not even defined rudimentarily. The principles have limited themselves to specifying a "market-oriented approach" for other rights; for registered rights, however, the market relation is not even mentioned.[180] This leads to two problems. First, one can understand the ALI Principles as *not* requiring "direct and substantial damage" in trademark conflicts. Second, depending on the categorization of trademark/unfair competition claims, the reach of regulation may vary, and cause-of-action shopping may ensue, enabling the plaintiff to choose the more beneficial law by manipulating her pleadings with respect to the subject matter.

Finally, similarly problematic under both the ALI and CLIP Principles is the determination of a close or closest connection for ubiquitous infringements, with the result that only the "most interested" regime will be applied. Both instruments have an inherent penchant for applying the law of large markets. Whether it is the parties' investment, the main markets to which activities have been directed, or the infringer's substantial activities and corresponding harm to the right owner that are at play, large markets are usually the only markets with a sufficiently close connection to the infringement.[181] As a result, the dominance of US and European law looms.

Section 5 The American Scholarly Debate

Under the Supreme Court's *Bulova* test, application of the Lanham Act is an issue of subject-matter jurisdiction and depends on a three-pronged test that comprises nationality, effects on US commerce, and conflicts with foreign law. Although different tests among the federal circuits suggest a number of variations, on the whole the picture is homogeneous—a system of transnational goodwill protection that has been founded on and complemented by a distinct scholarly tradition of

[180] *See id.* at 123 (§ 301, comment d).

[181] Josef Drexl, *The Proposed Rome II Regulation: European Choice of Law in the Field of Intellectual Property*, 151, 171, in *Intellectual Property and Private International Law—Heading for the Future* (Josef Drexl & Annette Kur eds., 2005); Tim W. Dornis, *Commentary to Jürgen Basedow, Toshiyuki Kono & Axel Metzger, Intellectual Property in the Global Arena (Tübingen 2010)*, 76 RabelsZ 695, 698 (2012). The Japanese Transparency Proposal calls for the "maximization" of "results of exploitation" (art. 302(1)) and will similarly favor the application of large-market legal regimes.

"extraterritorial" intellectual property protection.[182] Several arguments have significantly affected this development. First, trademarks are often treated together with patents and copyrights under a common heading of intellectual "property." Second, in both scholarship and case law, the traditional paradigm of use-based rights still dominates the debate. International trademark conflicts are thus often conceived of in terms of global markets, not political territories. Finally, the idea that extraterritorial rights protection would be beneficial per se appears to have infused practically all scholarly analyses.

I *Common Law Tradition and Transnational Market Protection*

American scholarship has intensely analyzed the *Bulova* test and its effects on domestic and international commerce. Many critical arguments have been brought forward, targeted mostly at the test's overreach, its disregard for foreign jurisdictions' interests, and its violations of public international law.[183] A detailed review of all points of friction is neither possible nor necessary. Instead, I will focus on an outlier characteristic of trademarks among the group of intellectual property rights. The protection of trademarks differs from that of copyrights, patents, and other intellectual property insofar as the scope of trademark regulation appears to bear an inherent predisposition toward extraterritoriality. While this phenomenon of excess protection seems to be widely acknowledged in American scholarship, there is little consensus regarding the reasons behind such exceptionalism. Even though, ultimately, all roads lead to Rome, some are mysterious—quite often, as we will see, unorthodox arguments have guided the way. My inquiry will therefore dissect the most outstanding opinions, focusing on their peculiarities. First, I will discuss the major theories concerning the international "propertization" of intellectual property rights in patent and copyright doctrine; I will then undertake a more trademark-specific analysis that examines the ongoing importance of the act-of-state doctrine, its misconceived reinterpretation in terms of substantive policy, and Curtis A. Bradley's prominent pleading in favor of trademark territoriality. As we will see, one aspect has been

[182] *See supra* p. 164 *et seq.*

[183] For an extensive critique, *see, e.g.*, Pamela E. Kraver & Robert E. Purcell, *Application of the Lanham Act to Extraterritorial Activities: Trend Toward Universality or Imperialism?*, 77 Pat. & Trademark Off. Soc'y 115 (1995); Curtis A. Bradley, *Territorial Intellectual Property Rights in an Age of Globalism*, 37 Va. J. Int'l L. 505 (1997); Anna R. Popov, *Watering Down Steele v. Bulova Watch Co. to Reach E-Commerce Overseas: Analyzing the Lanham Act's Extraterritorial Reach Under International Law*, 77 S. Cal. L. Rev. 705 (2004); Xuan-Thao N. Nguyen, *The Digital Trademark Right: A Troubling New Extraterritorial Reach of United States Law*, 81 N.C. L. Rev. 483 (2003).

widely neglected: trademarks, especially under common law doctrine, are market founded by definition. This characteristic of common law doctrine has provided the most solid ground for a transnationalization of trademark rights. While copyright and patent law had to "invent" new structures in order to transnationalize rights protection, trademark law simply brought to heel the existing stock of common law doctrine.

A The General Tendency of Equitable Rights Limitlessness

Unlike international trademark practice, patents and copyrights are traditionally treated as strictly territorial.[184] They, too, however, have also seen their reach extended over time. It is the idea that intellectual property rights are transnational private entitlements that lies at the heart of this tendency toward extraterritoriality.

Since international patent and copyright doctrine is founded on the territoriality of rights,[185] US courts will generally not apply domestic patent or copyright law absent infringing conduct within the United States. However, judges have recognized a remarkable number of exceptions in which allegedly infringing conduct abroad is subject to domestic law. Two strands of such exceptions in international copyright protection are particularly illustrative for this development, both of which concern the gradual shift from a doctrine of conduct prevention to one of market regulation.[186] The so-called root-copy doctrine concerns the recovery of proceeds from alleged infringements in a foreign country. A root copy is a counterfeit or copy that has been made in the United States and has enabled foreign copying and distribution. Following this approach, courts have awarded damages not only for domestic copying but also for foreign infringements resulting from the domestic copying. Among the practical starting points of the doctrine was the 1939 decision by the Court of

[184] *See* Curtis A. Bradley, *Territorial Intellectual Property Rights in an Age of Globalism*, 37 Va. J. Int'l L. 505, 520 (1997).

[185] *See, e.g., Deepsouth Packing Co. v. Laitram Corp.*, 406 U.S. 518, 531 (1972) ("Our patent system makes no claim to extraterritorial effect."); *Subafilms, Ltd. v. MGM-Pathe Communications Co.*, 24 F.3d 1088, 1093 (9th Cir. 1994); *Quality King Distributors, Inc. v. L'anza Research Intern., Inc.*, 523 U.S. 135, 154 (1998) (Ginsburg, J., concurring: "Copyright protection is territorial. The rights granted by the United States Copyright Act extend no farther than the nation's borders."). For further examples, *see* Curtis A. Bradley, *Territorial Intellectual Property Rights in an Age of Globalism*, 37 Va. J. Int'l L. 505, 520 *et seq.* (1997); Graeme W. Austin, *Domestic Laws and Foreign Rights: Choice of Law in Transnational Copyright Infringement Litigation*, 23 Colum.-VLA J. L. & Arts 1, 14–15 (1999); Graeme W. Austin, *Private International Law and Intellectual Property Rights—A Common Law Overview, WIPO Forum on Private International Law and Intellectual Property*, WIPO/PIL/01/5 (15 January 2001), at 12.

[186] For the extension of patent law to extraterritorial conduct and proceeds, *see* Curtis A. Bradley, *Territorial Intellectual Property Rights in an Age of Globalism*, 37 Va. J. Int'l L. 505, 520–523 (1997).

Appeals for the Second Circuit in *Sheldon v. Metro-Goldwyn Pictures*.[187] In *Sheldon*, the defendants had made a motion picture that allegedly infringed on the plaintiff's copyrighted play. Manufacturing of the movie included the production of photographic negatives. These negatives were exported to Europe, where they were further proliferated. Even though use of the photographs in Europe was not an infringement within the United States, Learned Hand, writing for a unanimous court, found damages for foreign infringements recoverable under US copyright law. This finding was based on the principle of a "constructive trust":

> [The defendant] made the negatives in this country, or had them made here, and shipped them abroad, where the positives were produced and exhibited. The negatives were "records" from which the work could be "reproduced," and it was a tort to make them in this country. The plaintiffs acquired an equitable interest in them as soon as they were made, which attached to any profits from their exploitation, whether in the form of money remitted to the United States, or of increase in the value of shares of foreign companies held by the defendants. We need not decide whether the law of those countries where the negatives were exploited, recognized the plaintiffs' equitable interest; we can assume arguendo that it did not, for, as soon as any of the profits so realized took the form of property whose situs was in the United States, our law seized upon them and impressed them with a constructive trust, whatever their form.[188]

This principle was later upheld in the Second Circuit's 1988 decision in *Update Art, Inc. v. Modiin Publishing, Ltd.*[189] and found persuasive in the Ninth Circuit's 1998 decision in *Los Angeles News Service v. Reuters Television International*.[190] Both courts relied on "property" that was located and infringed on within the United States. They also interpreted the right owner's entitlement in equity as extending to profits derived from both domestic and foreign infringements.

Of course, under the root-copy doctrine, the concept of formal territorial rights protection never vanished completely. Therefore, absent a case of root copying, US courts have generally attempted to restrict the reach of domestic law.[191] After all, even Learned Hand's equity

[187] *Sheldon v. Metro-Goldwyn Pictures Corp.*, 106 F.2d 45, 52 (2nd Cir. 1939) (L. Hand, C.J.).

[188] *Id.*

[189] *Update Art, Inc. v. Modiin Pub., Ltd.*, 843 F.2d 67, 72 (2nd Cir. 1988); *see also* Graeme W. Austin, *Domestic Laws and Foreign Rights: Choice of Law in Transnational Copyright Infringement Litigation*, 23 Colum.-VLA J. L. & Arts 1, 8 n. 23 (1999) (with further reference to case law).

[190] *Los Angeles News Service v. Reuters Television Intern. Ltd.*, 149 F.3d 987. 990 *et seq.* (9th Cir. 1998).

[191] *See, e.g., Subafilms, Ltd. v. MGM-Pathe Communications Co.*, 24 F.3d 1088 (9th Cir. 1994). However, *Subafilms* has encountered strong criticism. *See, e.g., Curb v. MCA*

doctrine was founded on a territorially produced root copy as the basis of all claims. Yet the doctrine's underlying logic of equitable extraterritoriality reflects an idea of transnationally extended private entitlements. Indeed, this extension of protection invokes an assumption that the underlying policy should be without territorial limits. Ultimately, the rationale resembles natural law reasoning: the creator is entitled to all proceeds of her work, wherever they might occur—not just within the territory of creation.

Scholarship has criticized root-copy territoriality for its allegedly obsolete requirement of conduct.[192] Jane C. Ginsburg has suggested a "nerve center" approach, or source theory, for handling cases of global infringement: US law should always apply if a court is able to localize at least one point within the United States where an infringement has occurred or from where acts of foreign infringement have been planned or intellectually implemented. This point is the "nerve center," or source, of all resulting multinational infringements.[193] Ultimately, Ginsburg's approach extends economic reasoning further than the root-copy doctrine does, aiming toward an overarching system of market protection. In the nerve-center approach, the territorial foundation of rights protection has been fully attenuated. Whereas the root-copy approach targets foreign profits flowing from domestic acts of infringement, the nerve-center approach looks at the transnationally extended market (or potential market) for the rights infringed. The value of a copyright is its worldwide marketability; conduct localization has virtually become irrelevant.[194]

Records, Inc., 898 F.Supp. 586, 595 (M.D. Tenn. 1995); *Expediters Intern. of Washington, Inc. v. Direct Line Cargo Management Services, Inc.*, 995 F.Supp. 468, 477 (D.N.J. 1998); *see also* Graeme W. Austin, *Domestic Laws and Foreign Rights: Choice of Law in Transnational Copyright Infringement Litigation*, 23 Colum.-VLA J. L. & Arts 1, 10 (1999).

192 *See, e.g.*, Jane C. Ginsburg, *Comment, Extraterritoriality and Multiterritoriality in Copyright Infringement*, 37 Va. J. Int'l L. 587, 597 (1997); Jane C. Ginsburg, *Copyright Without Borders? Choice of Forum and Choice of Law for Copyright Infringement in Cyberspace*, 15 Cardozo Arts & Ent. L.J. 153, 171 (1997). *See also Richard Feiner & Co. v. Turner Entertainment Co.*, No. 96 Civ. 1472(RO), 1998 WL 78180, at *1–2 (S.D.N.Y., 24 February 1998).

193 Jane C. Ginsburg, *Comment, Extraterritoriality and Multiterritoriality in Copyright Infringement*, 37 Va. J. Int'l L. 587, 597–600 (1997); Jane C. Ginsburg, *Copyright without Borders? Choice of Forum and Choice of Law for Copyright Infringement in Cyberspace*, 15 Cardozo Arts & Ent. L.J. 153, 171 (1997).

194 For an interesting counterposition from within the Ginsburg family, *see Quality King Distributors, Inc. v. L'anza Research Intern., Inc.*, 523 U.S. 135, 154 (1998) (Ginsburg, J., concurring: "Copyright protection is territorial. The rights granted by the United States Copyright Act extend no farther than the nation's borders."). Similar to the nerve-center approach, English courts have also long acknowledged exceptions to the strict concepts of jurisdiction and choice of law in cases of fraudulent and piratical conduct. *See, e.g.*,

These concepts of rights extension illustrate a paradigmatic aspect common to all sectors of intellectual property. The territorial model of copyright protection started on a firm understanding of formal rights that could be infringed on only by conduct within the national territory. Yet, over time, a number of extensions have moved the field toward the protection of economic value and markets, particularly in the individual right owner's interest.[195] In this regard, international trademark protection is not too different—but rights extension, as we will now see, has been more subtle. Trademark rights are still generally considered to be territorial in principle;[196] yet a broad consensus exists that the Lanham Act must be interpreted widely when it comes to cross-border infringements.[197]

B The *Nintendo* Transformation: From Act-of-State-Doctrine to Substantive Dichotomy

The public policy aspect of intellectual property protection has regularly troubled scholars and decision makers in the international context. In fact, the issue has developed into a complex debate. It is universally acknowledged that intellectual property protection serves various purposes of socioeconomic regulation. However, the exact demarcations between the different policies and, accordingly, the different categories of intellectual property have long remained unclear.

John Walker & Sons Ltd. and Others v. Henry Ost & Co. Ltd. and Another [1970] 1 W.L.R. 917; *Mecklermedia Corporation and Another v. D.C. Congress GmbH* [1998] Ch. 40. A similar approach to trademark extraterritoriality is also applied when courts look at the orchestration of foreign activities (for instance, in the Ninth Circuit), or if they follow the *Steele* unlawful-scheme concept. *See supra* p. 164 *et seq.* and p. 171 *et seq.*

195 Graeme W. Austin, *Domestic Laws and Foreign Rights: Choice of Law in Transnational Copyright Infringement Litigation*, 23 Colum.-VLA J. L. & Arts 1, 21 (1999) ("[I]n the transnational context, the tort of copyright infringement becomes a civil wrong based on damage not to property rights, but to the plaintiff's pocket.").

196 *See, e.g., Person's Co. v. Christman*, 900 F.2d 1565, 1568–1569 (Fed. Cir. 1990) ("The concept of territoriality is basic to trademark law; trademark rights exist in each country solely according to that country's statutory scheme."); *Barcelona.com, Incorporated v. Excelentisimo Ayuntamiento De Barcelona*, 330 F.3d 617, 628 (4th Cir. 2003) ("[T]he fundamental doctrine of territoriality upon which our trademark law is presently based."); 5 J. Thomas McCarthy, *McCarthy on Trademarks and Unfair Competition*, § 29:25 (4th edn., 2016).

197 *See supra* p. 159 *et seq.* Further *see, e.g., Sterling Drug, Inc. v. Bayer AG*, 14 F.3d 733, 745 (2nd Cir. 1994) ("It is well-established that United States courts have jurisdiction to enforce the Lanham Act extraterritorially in order to prevent harm to United States commerce."); *McBee v. Delica Co.*, 417 F.3d 107, 110 (1st Cir. 2005) ("It has long been settled that the Lanham Act can, in appropriate cases, be applied extraterritorially."); 5 J. Thomas McCarthy, *McCarthy on Trademarks and Unfair Competition* § 29:57 (4th edn., 2016) ("extraterritorial sweep of American trademark law").

One troubling aspect of public policy in intellectual property conflicts law is the act-of-state doctrine. In its standard formulation, this doctrine provides that "the courts of one country will not sit in judgment on the acts of the government of another, done within its own territory."[198] The idea of administrative sovereignty has been picked up by legal scholars. As posited by David Nimmer, for instance, US courts should abstain from adjudicating foreign trademark and patent cases, for deciding on issues of international trademark and patent conflicts that involve foreign registrations would unduly "pass upon the validity of administrative acts undertaken by foreign officials."[199] By contrast, international copyright litigation involving foreign copyrights would not risk such an invasion of foreign sovereignty. Since copyrights are created by law—not by administrative action—the act-of-state doctrine is not an obstacle. Accordingly, copyright infringement constitutes a transitory cause of action that may be adjudicated in any forum, even outside the granting state's territory.[200] This concept of copyrights' transitoriness can also be found in practice, inter alia, in the oft-cited *London Film Productions Ltd. v. Intercontinental Communications, Inc.*[201] ruling. As the court explained, because trademarks require registration, a court adjudicating on issues of infringement of foreign trademarks would ultimately also sit in judgment on a foreign right's validity. This, it argued, must be avoided.[202]

Yet this distinction based on "administrative formality" has not escaped criticism. One influential critique is that brought forward in 1985 by David R. Toraya in a lengthy note on *London Film* and on an earlier edition of Nimmer's commentary.[203] Toraya's argument focuses on what he deems an arbitrary distinction between administrative formalities and substantive law policies.[204] As he explains, not only are states interested in having their administrative decisions remain untouched by foreign sovereigns, but there is also always a substantive law policy to be regarded in international conflicts: every state possesses a "sovereignty interest in preserving the socio-economic, cultural, and political benefits its copyright law intend[s] to advance."[205] Paradoxically, it was not this

[198] *Underhill v. Hernandez*, 168 U.S. 250, 252 (1897); *see also* Curtis A. Bradley, *Territorial Intellectual Property Rights in an Age of Globalism*, 37 Va. J. Int'l L. 505, 552 (1997).

[199] 3 Melville B. Nimmer & David Nimmer, *Nimmer on Copyright: A Treatise on the Law of Literary, Musical and Artistic Property, and the Protection of Ideas* § 17.03, 17–23 (2010).

[200] 3 Melville B. Nimmer & David Nimmer, *Nimmer on Copyright: A Treatise on the Law of Literary, Musical and Artistic Property, and the Protection of Ideas* § 17.03, 17–23/24 (2010).

[201] *London Film Productions Ltd. v. Intercontinental Communications, Inc.*, 580 F.Supp. 47 (S.D.N.Y. 1984).

[202] *Id.* at 49.

[203] David R. Toraya, *Note, Federal Jurisdiction over Foreign Copyright Infringement Actions—An Unsolicited Reply to Professor Nimmer*, 70 Cornell L. Rev. 1165 (1985).

[204] *Id.* at 1167–1168. [205] *Id.* at 1169.

fundamental argument of his article but a secondary aspect that was picked up by the Fourth Circuit in its 1994 decision in *Nintendo of America, Inc. v. Aeropower Co., Ltd.*[206] The defendants had sold video games to customers in the United States, Mexico, and Canada. Domestic copyright and trademark rights existed. The issue was whether extraterritorial application of the protecting statutes was possible. "Because the power is more extensive under the Lanham Act than under the Copyright Act, and because relief afforded under that Act probably would also protect any copyright interest,"[207] the court limited its analysis to the issue of trademark extraterritoriality. This focus was further explained in a footnote referencing Toraya's article, which seems to have convinced the court that the Lanham Act (even without regard to the act-of-state dichotomy) should still be treated differently from copyright and patent law and should thus have a broad extraterritorial reach.[208] In his article, Toraya argues that the differentiation between artistic and inventive products, on the one hand, and the symbol-protecting purposes of trademark law, on the other, demands that trademarks be treated differently with regard to the extraterritorial reach of domestic law.[209] The argument is intriguing: the extraterritorial application of copyright and patent law would deprive foreign marketplaces of something that the respective local law has made available. Toraya finds this effect to run counter to the foreign state's public interest in having innovative and creative information widely disseminated. Trademark law, he explains, does not prevent the free flow of information—it merely restricts the use of marketing symbols. Toraya thus concludes that the extraterritorial extension of trademark protection would result in only a minor deprivation—the use of a symbol—to the marketplace.[210] The *Nintendo* court, accordingly, concluded that trademark rights could be protected more extensively than copyrights and patents, particularly beyond national borders.

As we will see in the next section, this transformation of the act-of-state doctrine did not remain uncontested. Two suggestions have particularly influenced scholarly debate. One approach can be characterized as a quasi civil law approach to territoriality. The other, modeled on legal practice, builds rights protection on traditional common law foundations.

[206] *Nintendo of America, Inc. v. Aeropower Co., Ltd.*, 34 F.3d 246 (4th Cir. 1994).

[207] *Id.* at 249–250. [208] *Id.* at 250 n. 5.

[209] David R. Toraya, *Note, Federal Jurisdiction over Foreign Copyright Infringement Actions—An Unsolicited Reply to Professor Nimmer*, 70 Cornell L. Rev. 1165, 1171–1172 n. 41 (1985). A similar argument had already been made before. *See, e.g.*, Alan G. Kirios, *Territoriality and International Copyright Infringement Actions*, 22 Copyright L. Symp. (ASCAP) 53, 61–62 (1977).

[210] David R. Toraya, *Note, Federal Jurisdiction over Foreign Copyright Infringement Actions—An Unsolicited Reply to Professor Nimmer*, 70 Cornell L. Rev. 1165, 1171 n. 41 (1985).

C The Revival of Territoriality: A Quasi Continental Choice-of-Law Approach

The *Nintendo*/Toraya distinction between, on the one hand, copyrights and patents and, on the other, trademarks has been most prominently refuted by Curtis A. Bradley. In his appeal for stricter intellectual property territoriality, he does not focus on the act-of-state doctrine, instead analyzing the relevance of the presumption against extraterritoriality—that is, the presumption "that legislation of Congress, unless a contrary intent appears, is meant to apply only within the territorial jurisdiction of the United States."[211] As Bradley explains, the end of the twentieth century witnessed a trend toward extraterritoriality, which led to the theoretical foundations of the presumption against extraterritoriality being challenged. Admiralty, securities, and antitrust laws in particular came to regulate beyond US borders. Paradoxically, even though trademark law also seemed to fall within the category for which the presumption had begun to vanish, strict territoriality appeared to remain the standard for international copyright and patent law.[212] In his comparison of copyright, patent, and trademark conflicts, Bradley challenges this distinction. Two of his arguments are particularly relevant: one concerns the concept of intellectual property homogeneity, while the other concerns the correlation between trademark protection and competition.

Let us start with the first argument. Even though, as Bradley explains, patents and copyrights may differ from trademarks at the level of domestic law, there is ultimately no justification for a broader extraterritorial reach of the Lanham Act.[213] As he convincingly argues, the Lanham Act's "commerce" language is not enough to account for the act's extensive interpretation.[214] Nor is there any doctrinal or economic aspect that can account for the act's extraterritorial reach. In his comparison of substantive law policies of intellectual property protection, Bradley eventually deconstructs the Fourth Circuit's and Toraya's shared argument that extraterritorial patent and copyright protections would be more problematic than trademark extension in light of a potential deprivation to

[211] *E.E.O.C. v. Arabian American Oil Co.*, 499 U.S. 244, 248 (1991); *Foley Bros. v. Filardo*, 336 U.S. 281, 285 (1949); *see also* Curtis A. Bradley, *Territorial Intellectual Property Rights in an Age of Globalism*, 37 Va. J. Int'l L. 505, 510 *et seq.* (1997).

[212] Curtis A. Bradley, *Territorial Intellectual Property Rights in an Age of Globalism*, 37 Va. J. Int'l L. 505, 519 (1997).

[213] *Id.* at 536 *et seq.*

[214] *Id.* at 532. Even direct statutory reference to foreign commerce has not led to an extraterritorial extension of other instruments, such as the National Labor Relations Act and the Federal Employers Liability Act. Correspondingly, the Lanham Act's inclusion of "all commerce which may lawfully be regulated by Congress" hardly accounts for a tenable explanation of trademark extraterritoriality.

foreign markets: even under an assumption that the governmental interest in allowing the reproduction of foreign inventions and artistic creations is higher than in allowing the free use of trade symbols, the balancing of two governments' conflicting interests would also have to give regard to a higher interest in preventing reproduction on the side of the right-granting government.[215] Therefore, the argument referencing a potential cultural deprivation to foreign markets and an accordingly greater need for territoriality is circular. The granting state is no altruist, whether regarding copyrights, patents, or trademarks. In addition, as Bradley elaborates, the extended protection of patents and copyrights will rarely lead to a *complete* deprivation to foreign markets. At worst, such protection will result in higher prices for patented or copyrighted products in the foreign market. In this regard, however, trademarks are no different since the extraterritorial application of domestic trademark laws will also affect prices in the foreign market.[216]

Bradley's second argument concerns the distinction between the protection of private rights and that of the economy as a whole. In this regard, he distinguishes trademark law from antitrust, securities, and criminal law. As he explains, the latter areas of regulation are designed to protect the public interest and the national economy. Their design implies both internal and external regulation, and, accordingly, extraterritoriality is inherent. Quite differently, trademark and other intellectual property protection is explained to benefit society by "conferring particular property rights on individuals and companies."[217] In these cases, the reach of the domestic policies should remain within national boundaries. This distinction highlights an aspect of the debate in international intellectual property law that has more wide-reaching importance. In fact, Bradley's separation alludes to a long-existing divide between private and public law as well as private international and international economic law. Roughly speaking, private law and private international law are designed to micro-regulate private-party conflicts—nationally and internationally. This is a domain distinct from the state's concern for macro-regulation. The field of international economic law, by contrast, concerns international conflicts between the macro-regulatory laws (i.e., public laws) of different states. According to Bradley, trademarks are part of the former sector. Not surprisingly, he suggests a conflicts approach that is quasi Savignian: if different states' private law regimes primarily cater to private parties' concerns, they can more easily be substituted and exchanged in choice of law.[218] As Bradley concludes, therefore, US courts should

[215] *Id.* at 540. [216] *Id.* [217] *Id.* at 569.
[218] For an extensive discussion, *see infra* p. 383 *et seq.*

follow a multilateral approach and—if indicated—apply the respective foreign state's intellectual property law to conduct occurring abroad.[219] Even though Bradley rarely refers to civil law choice of law, his concept replicates the traditional multilateralism of European trademark territoriality.[220]

D The "Domestic Extraterritoriality" of Statutory Trademark Rights

In a harsh rejection of Bradley's concept, Roger E. Schechter has formulated what could be characterized as an abridged restatement of US common law trademark doctrine for the international arena. I have already introduced Schechter's theory of domestic trademark extraterritoriality.[221] In his critique of the territoriality approach, Schechter advances several arguments to illustrate the difference between patents and copyrights on the one hand and trademarks on the other. Two points are fundamental to his concept of trademark conflicts.

First, in explaining his idea of domestic extraterritoriality, Schechter, inter alia, distinguishes common law trademark rights from common law copyright and patent protection. When they were enacted, neither copyright nor patent statutes actually extended the scope of preexisting common law rights. This was different for the 1946 trademark statute: the Lanham Act modified the traditional use-based rights paradigm by extending the scope of rights beyond their actual trading areas. As Schechter adds, "[T]rademark law was originally grounded on an explicitly territorial foundation." And since use-based rights were territorial, the Lanham Act's extension of trademark rights to the nationwide area actually exceeded the territorial scope of rights.[222] This conclusion appears accurate: Congress extended rights from "territorial" to "nationwide" when it enacted the Lanham Act. Hence, it is only logical to infer

[219] Curtis A. Bradley, *Territorial Intellectual Property Rights in an Age of Globalism*, 37 Va. J. Int'l L. 505, 569 *et seq.* (1997). For an application of foreign law, *see also, e.g.*, Robert Alpert, *The Export of Trademarked Goods from the United States: The Extraterritorial Reach of the Lanham Act*, 81 Trademark Rep. 125, 148 n. 105 (1991); Pamela E. Kraver & Robert E. Purcell, *Application of the Lanham Act to Extraterritorial Activities: Trend Toward Universality or Imperialism?*, 77 Pat. & Trademark Off. Soc'y 115, 115–116 (1995); Richard L. Garnett, *Trademarks and the Internet: Resolution of International IP Disputes by Unilateral Application of U.S. Laws*, 30 Brook. J. Int'l L. 925, 947 *et seq.* (2005); Graeme W. Austin, *The Story of Steele v. Bulova: Trademarks on the Line*, 395, 421, in *Intellectual Property Stories* (Jane C. Ginsburg & Rochelle Cooper Dreyfuss eds., 2006); Graeme B. Dinwoodie, *Developing a Private International Intellectual Property Law: The Demise of Territoriality?*, 51 Wm. & Mary L. Rev. 711, 788 *et seq.* (2009).

[220] *See supra* p. 193 *et seq.* [221] *See supra* p. 147 *et seq.*

[222] Roger E. Schechter, *The Case for Limited Extraterritorial Reach of the Lanham Act*, 37 Va. J. Int'l L. 619, 627 (1997).

that "Congress would not be uncomfortable with the idea of extending the reach of the Lanham Act to conduct occurring abroad."[223] An inherent concept of extraterritoriality appears to underlie the statutory system of trademark rights.[224]

Second, Schechter adds a new argument in favor of distinguishing different categories of intellectual property and in favor of trademark exceptionalism. As he explains, a comparison of right owners' injuries reveals an additional detriment that will occur only in cases of trademark infringement. Whereas a copyright or patent infringement abroad will lead to the right owner's "loss" of foreign sales only, trademark infringement presents twofold damages. First, of course, the trademark owner will forego a foreign transaction that she would have otherwise concluded. In addition, she may also find damage to her domestic reputation and goodwill.[225] The trademark owner thereby suffers, as Schechter calls it, a "double whammy"—not only will the right owner suffer injury in foreign markets, but she will also run the risk of reputational harm and of damage from (potentially) declining domestic sales in the future.[226]

Overall, Schechter describes the extraterritorial protection of domestic trademark rights as a necessary instrument to fight international piracy. In summarizing the pros and cons of cross-border enforcement, he concludes that trademark extraterritoriality largely benefits US right owners in an international marketplace. I will address this issue in more detail later.[227] At this point, my focus is on common law trademark doctrine. The scholarly theory of what can be characterized as the factual globalization of *Tea Rose/Rectanus* helps rectify terminological and doctrinal confusion in the field.

E *Tea Rose/Rectanus* "Transnationalized": The Common Law Cross-Border Crusade

Trademark rights differ from copyrights and patents on the basis of their continuous dependence on what happens in the market. A trademark is predisposed to natural expansion; as the decisions in *Hanover Star* and *United Drug* made clear, use-based rights—following the trade—have the potential to grow like mushrooms in a forest. And like the organic growth of a natural substance, the evolution of trademark goodwill appears

[223] *Id.* at 628. [224] *Id.* [225] *Id.* at 628–629.

[226] *Id.* at 629; *see also* Gary D. Feldon, *The Antitrust Model of Extraterritorial Trademark Jurisdiction: Analysis and Predictions after F. Hoffmann-La Roche*, 20 Emory Int'l L. Rev. 651, 680 (2006). For an approval in practice, *see, e.g., McBee v. Delica Co., Ltd.*, 417 F.3d 107, 125 (1st Cir. 2005).

[227] *See infra* p. 480 *et seq.*

immune to the fictitious lines of political boundaries.[228] The expansion of communication and commerce has further detached economic markets from political boundaries, and the reality of globalization has brought the predisposition of extraterritoriality in the concept of goodwill protection to an extreme.

With this problem in mind, Graeme B. Dinwoodie has recently presented a redefinition. As he argues, the traditionally territorial model of trademark protection is in need of reconfiguration.[229] Dinwoodie describes two dimensions of territoriality in US trademark law. First, under the *United Drug* paradigm, common law rights are congruent with the trademark's area of actual use, reputation, and renown. These use-based rights are founded on the intrinsic purposes of trademark law, the most important of which is consumer protection. By contrast, rights acquired by registration reflect complementary trademark values, notably the expansion of rights and enforcement efficiency. Unlike use-based rights, registered rights are connected to political authority. Hence, as Dinwoodie concludes, two aspects of the territoriality of trademark rights and goodwill must be distinguished: "intrinsic territoriality" and "political territoriality."[230] It may be confusing to characterize both aspects as "territorial." After all, use-based rights rarely comply with state boundaries. In *Hanover Star*, the Supreme Court made this point clear when it explained that

> since it is the trade, and not the mark, that is to be protected, a trademark acknowledges no territorial boundaries of municipalities or states or nations, but extends to every market where the trader's goods have become known and identified by his use of the mark.[231]

Nonetheless, Dinwoodie's explanation of the dual territoriality is illuminating in its dissociation from Schechter's conception of domestic extraterritoriality. In this regard, he provides an important clarification in acknowledging that trademark registration is "decidedly territorial."[232]

[228] For the history of US practice, *see supra* p. 127 *et seq.* and p. 159 *et seq.*

[229] Graeme B. Dinwoodie, *Trademarks and Territory: Detaching Trademark Law from the Nation-State*, 41 Hous. L. Rev. 885, 908, 955–956 (2004). *See also* Graeme B. Dinwoodie, *Developing a Private International Intellectual Property Law: The Demise of Territoriality?*, 51 Wm. & Mary L. Rev. 711, 767–768 (2009).

[230] Graeme B. Dinwoodie, *Trademarks and Territory: Detaching Trademark Law from the Nation-State*, 41 Hous. L. Rev. 885, 899, 908, 958 and *passim* (2004). For a similar distinction founded on a trademark's "legal territoriality" and "collective 'consumer consciousness' " that would easily cross national borders, *see* Graeme W. Austin, *The Story of Steele v. Bulova: Trademarks on the Line*, 395, 420 *et seq.*, in *Intellectual Property Stories* (Jane C. Ginsburg & Rochelle Cooper Dreyfuss eds., 2006).

[231] *Hanover Star Milling Co. v. Metcalf*, 240 U.S. 403, 416 (1916).

[232] Graeme B. Dinwoodie, *Trademarks and Territory: Detaching Trademark Law from the Nation-State*, 41 Hous. L. Rev. 885, 898 (2004).

Common law rights may extend extraterritorially through the right owner's foreign-based trade and commerce. Hence, their "territoriality is rooted in social and commercial practices, which increasingly transcend national borders."[233] Registered rights, by contrast—albeit protectable against conduct occurring abroad under an effects test—will, strictly speaking, never "extend" beyond the national border. This makes them "decidedly" limited to the territory of the political entity.

This conceptualization of intrinsic territoriality is also important for this analysis. As revealed earlier, the *Tea Rose/Rectanus* doctrine provided the playground for the transnationalization of rights in the second half of the twentieth century.[234] Trademarks' market relatedness is what accounts for their differentiation from copyrights and patents. Structurally, trademarks' functions and their foundation in marketplace activities make them unbounded and apolitical rights. Copyrights and patents, on the other hand, are "politically territorial."

F The Shift to Effects Testing: An Idea of Transnational Market Regulation

The focus on individual rights and public policy with regard to competition and consumer protection is one relevant perspective. But a closer look reveals another important facet of US theory and practice: trademark conflicts law has increasingly become dominated by an idea of cross-border market regulation. This may be the most problematic aspect in US doctrine.

In fact, early on, market relatedness and competition regulation were understood as major concerns in international individual rights enforcement. In this regard, Jonathan Turley has analyzed the extraterritorial application of US law in a variety of sectors; the results show a distinction between "market" and "nonmarket" cases.[235] Market cases—for instance, those regarding international antitrust conflicts—are concerned primarily with protecting market interests and ensuring a level playing field at the international level. In nonmarket cases, other interests—mostly private rights—are at stake. Accordingly, as Turley explains, statutory law in both sectors has been interpreted either widely or narrowly in terms of its extraterritorial application. Both patent and copyright law are often still understood to constitute a sort of nonmarket protection.

[233] *Id.* at 900. [234] *See supra* p. 127 *et seq.* and p. 164 *et seq.*

[235] *See* Jonathan Turley, *"When in Rome": Multinational Misconduct and the Presumption Against Extraterritoriality*, 84 Nw. U. L. Rev. 598, 634 *et seq.* (1990). *See also* Curtis A. Bradley, *Territorial Intellectual Property Rights in an Age of Globalism*, 37 Va. J. Int'l L. 505, 519 (1997).

Hence, their scope is territorially limited.[236] International trademark and unfair competition disputes, by contrast, are classified as market cases—quite similar to international antitrust conflicts. And since antitrust and trademark law also appear to be conceptually similar, conflicts resolution in both fields has been suggested to correspond. Thus, the geographical reach of trademark protection has been extended to "transcend the invisible borders" of the country and to "protect the interest of the mark holder in relation to an economic market, not a political territory."[237]

This concept of regulation by trademark protection has been well received in practice. The First Circuit's decision in *McBee v. Delica Co.*,[238] an internet trademark conflict, is illustrative of the extension. Judge Lynch's reference to the academic debate on trademark characterization deserves citation at length:

> Some academics have criticized treating the Lanham Act differently from patent and copyright law, which generally are not applied extraterritorially [referring to Bradley and Schechter]. Nonetheless, the Supreme Court recently reaffirmed the Steele approach to extraterritorial jurisdiction. ... The question becomes one of articulating a test for Lanham Act jurisdiction over foreign infringing activities by foreign defendants. The decisions of the Supreme Court in the antitrust context seem useful to us as a guide. ...
>
> One can easily imagine a variety of harms to American commerce arising from wholly foreign activities by foreign defendants. There could be harm caused by ... passing off ... or confusion over sponsorship affecting American commerce and causing loss of American sales. Further, global piracy of American goods is a major problem for American companies: annual losses from unauthorized use of United States trademarks ... now amount to $200 billion annually [referring to Schechter]. In both the antitrust and the Lanham Act areas, there is a risk that absent a certain degree of extraterritorial enforcement, violators will either take advantage of international coordination problems or hide in countries without efficacious antitrust or trademark laws, thereby avoiding legal authority.[239]

The court's position is based on two important assumptions. First, trademark protection, like antitrust enforcement, contributes to overall national economic welfare. Second, and most importantly, trademark protection via the extraterritorial application of domestic law is efficient. Hence, granting national right owners extended protection is expected to

[236] Brendan J. Witherell, *The Extraterritorial Application of the Lanham Act in an Expanding Global Economy*, 97 Trademark Rep. 1090, 1119–1120 (2007). *See also supra* p. 244–246.

[237] Brendan J. Witherell, *The Extraterritorial Application of the Lanham Act in an Expanding Global Economy*, 97 Trademark Rep. 1090, 1120 (2007).

[238] *McBee v. Delica Co., Ltd.*, 417 F.3d 107 (1st Cir. 2005).

[239] *Id.* at 119. However, fairness requires mentioning that Judge Lynch ultimately did not apply the Lanham Act to alleged infringements in Japan and the United States. *See supra* p. 163.

ultimately provide for an economically optimal result. We will see later that the second assumption is erroneous.[240] At this point, it suffices to note that the assumption is widely acknowledged. Indeed, the idea of the efficiency of extraterritorial regulation is also deeply rooted in contemporary legal and economic thought.[241]

In sum, several characteristics can be found to dominate the debate in US scholarship. The most fundamental issue appears to be the distinction between the categories of intellectual property. The old conception of rights being acts of the state, at least if their existence depends on registration, still governs. This doctrine underlies the concept of subject-matter jurisdiction as a unilateral conflicts resolution rule. Foreign intellectual property, apart from copyrights, will thus seldom be protected in a US forum. In this regard, however, a strand of scholarly theory advocates a multilateral approach to conflicts law. Yet this still is a minority position. Contrary to such quasi continental proposals, key voices in US trademark scholarship still wish to resolve international trademark conflicts on the basis of the traditional concept of common law and use-based rights protection. In the tradition of *Tea Rose/Rectanus*, trademark rights have become transnationalized and unbounded economic entitlements. In addition, the extension of individual rights is accompanied by a strong impulse of market regulation by trademark protection. Ultimately, common law foundations and market-regulation policies have made extraterritoriality the governing paradigm in both US practice and scholarship.

II Analysis: Common Law Tradition Meets Extraterritorial Market Regulation

Three aspects are most relevant for a critical analysis. First, as we have seen, the distinction between different categories of intellectual property rights invites misconceptions at the conflicts level. Second, US theory still

240 *See infra* p. 480 *et seq.*

241 *See, e.g.*, Erika M. Brown, *The Extraterritorial Reach of United States Trademark Law: A Review of Recent Decisions Under the Lanham Act*, 9 Fordham Intell. Prop. Media & Ent. L.J. 863 (1999); Anna R. Popov, *Watering Down Steele v. Bulova Watch Co. to Reach E-Commerce Overseas: Analyzing the Lanham Act's Extraterritorial Reach Under International Law*, 77 S. Cal. L. Rev. 705, 733, 735 (2004); for an approving view of the *McBee* test, *see* Jason Webster, *Extraterritorial Application of the Lanham Act—McBee v. Delica Co., Ltd., 417 F.3d 107 (1st Cir. 2005)*, 30 Suffolk Transnat'l L. Rev. 263, 269 (2006). *See also* Brendan J. Witherell, *The Extraterritorial Application of the Lanham Act in an Expanding Global Economy*, 97 Trademark Rep. 1090, 1121 (2007); Gary D. Feldon, *The Antitrust Model of Extraterritorial Trademark Jurisdiction: Analysis and Predictions after F. Hoffmann-La Roche*, 20 Emory Int'l L. Rev. 651, 654, 680 *et seq.* (2006); James W. Dabney, *On the Territorial Reach of the Lanham Act*, 83 Trademark Rep. 465, 477 (1993).

adheres to the common law concept of rights acquisition and extension, which may result in an inaccurate understanding of territoriality. Third, the promotion of extraterritorial trademark protection as a means to also achieve international economic regulation is based on incorrect assumptions.

Concerning the first point of critique, what really matters with respect to the categorization of intellectual property rights is the direct market foundation of trademarks. This foundation is amiss in the field of patents and copyrights.[242] This divergence first plays out in the domestic arena. Unlike copyright and patent law, trademark and unfair competition law is not designed to protect creativity or invention—trademarks are protected largely for the identifying function they fulfill in the marketplace. They lower consumer search costs and allow for efficient competition.[243] In this way, trademark protection is not designed to incentivize trademark owners or competitors to create trademarks.[244] Instead, trademarks are part and parcel of the system of information transmission within the marketplace. This is what Roger Schechter's concept of a "double whammy" hints at with respect to international trademark protection, albeit without fully clarifying the foundation. An unlawfully branded product may exert effects in the marketplace not only in terms of lost sales but also in terms of disseminating incorrect information damaging the right owner's goodwill. This aspect is also reflected in *Steele*, where the majority enjoined the sale of counterfeits in order to prevent "spurious Bulovas filter[ing] through the Mexican border" and the subsequent negative effects to American customers' perception of the plaintiff's watches.[245] Accordingly, the different sectors of intellectual property are to be distinguished with regard to what may serve as a relevant factor in infringement analysis; the point of attachment will vary for each category. Patent and copyright violations are founded on the alleged

[242] I will address substantive law policy in the next chapter; here, a summary suffices for pointing out the critical shortfall.

[243] *See* William M. Landes & Richard A. Posner, *Trademark Law: An Economic Perspective*, 30 J. L. & Econ. 265 (1987); Stephen L. Carter, *Owning What Doesn't Exist*, 13 Harv. J. L. & Pub. Pol'y 99, 105 (1990).

[244] *See, e.g., Dastar Corp. v. Twentieth Century Fox Film Corp.*, 539 U.S. 23, 34 (2003) (" 'The Lanham Act,' we have said, 'does not exist to reward manufacturers for their innovation in creating a particular device; that is the purpose of the patent law and its period of exclusivity.' . . . Federal trademark law 'has no necessary relation to invention or discovery,' In re Trade-Mark Cases . . . but rather, by preventing competitors from copying 'a source-identifying mark,' 'reduce[s] the customer's costs of shopping and making purchasing decisions,' and 'helps assure a producer that it (and not an imitating competitor) will reap the financial, reputation-related rewards associated with a desirable product,' Qualitex Co. v. Jacobson Products Co.").

[245] *Steele v. Bulova Watch Co.*, 344 U.S. 280, 286 (1952).

infringer's conduct.[246] Trademark policy, by contrast, focuses on market information. Ultimately, it is the status of market information and effects on this status that must be given regard to. This structural difference is crucial: if conduct is what matters, foreign-based activities cannot be seen as an "infringement" unless an exception to the territoriality of rights has been established. The case is different, however, if the substantive law policies provide for effects to be qualified as an infringement. Here, the extraterritoriality of rights is a far more delicate issue. Current international intellectual property doctrine has yet to fully clarify these correlations.[247]

With respect to Toraya's and the *Nintendo* court's classification, another aspect is worth mentioning: in his attempt to differentiate the categories of intellectual property, Toraya overlooks the fact that these categories may—and actually often do—exist concurrently. The implications of international intellectual property protection will thus seldom be separable. Everything is a question of market prices: as with patented and copyrighted products, a premium will be paid for branded products. The more goodwill (in the sense of consumer recognition) is attached to a brand, the higher its price.[248] Hence, it does not matter whether an increase in market prices is caused by sanctions under patent, copyright, or trademark law. Since proliferation of a product is a function of its price, the cross-border extension of *any* category of intellectual property will limit the availability on foreign markets. And since copyrighted and patented products are usually also trademark protected, the "information depriving" effects can rarely be distinguished. This is illustrated lucidly by the *Nintendo* case, where the court

[246] *But cf.* Andreas P. Reindl, *Choosing Law in Cyberspace: Copyright Conflicts on Global Networks*, 19 Mich. J. Int'l L. 799, 836 *et seq.* (1998) (for the foundation of copyright conflicts on "effects on economic interests"). Similarly, an effects argument was brought forward by plaintiffs in *Subafilms, Ltd. v. MGM-Pathe Communications Co.*, 24 F.3d 1088, 1095 (9th Cir. 1994) ("Appellees additionally contend that, if liability for 'authorizing' acts of infringement depends on finding that the authorized acts themselves are cognizable under the Copyright Act, this court should find that the United States copyright laws do extend to extraterritorial acts of infringement when such acts 'result in adverse effects within the United States.' Appellees buttress this argument with the contention that failure to apply the copyright laws extraterritorially in this case will have a disastrous effect on the American film industry."). The court, however, ultimately rejected an effects approach to copyright conflicts. *See id.* at 1099. *See also* Graeme B. Dinwoodie, *Developing a Private International Intellectual Property Law: The Demise of Territoriality?*, 51 Wm. & Mary L. Rev. 711, 774 *et seq.* (2009).

[247] For a more detailed analysis of substantive law policies, *see infra* p. 295 *et seq.*

[248] Strong trademarks allow charging higher prices in exchange for savings in search costs on the side of the consumer. *See, e.g.*, William M. Landes & Richard A. Posner, *Trademark Law: An Economic Perspective*, 30 J. L. & Econ. 265, 275 *et seq.* (1987); Stephen L. Carter, *The Trouble with Trademark*, 99 Yale L.J. 759, 763 (1990).

focused on trademark protection, disregarding copyright concerns for reasons of procedural efficiency. Since the Lanham Act provided a more comprehensive system of protection, the jurisdictional analysis was limited accordingly.[249] This ultimately made trademark extraterritoriality—not the extension of copyright protection—the depriving instrument with regard to information markets in foreign territories. If one were follow Toraya's argument, strict territoriality would be as mandatory in trademark as in patent and copyright conflicts.

With regard to the common law foundations of US theory, a clarification of terminology is required to prevent confusion. We have already seen that a registration system does not become "extraterritorial" simply by a comparison with preexisting common law rights. Since common law, or use-based, rights acquisition in the United States is not territorial,[250] the parallel system of registered rights under the Lanham Act cannot be explained as having induced a shift toward extraterritoriality. On the contrary, the registration of rights is distinctly territorial.[251] In this regard, Dinwoodie is right with his characterization of Lanham Act registration as a system of "political territoriality." Yet Dinwoodie's second variant of goodwill classification—the "intrinsic territoriality"[252] of trademarks—is also problematic and requires clarification.

Generally defined, territoriality is "[t]he principle that a nation has the right of sovereignty within its borders."[253] The principle goes back to three maxims established in the seventeenth-century Netherlands. As Ulrich Huber explained at the time, (1) a state's laws have force only within the state's boundaries, (2) anyone found within the state's boundaries is subject to the state's authority, and (3) comity will discipline sovereign exercises of authority so that the territorial effect of each state's law is respected.[254] These principles have also been acknowledged as foundational for the modern concept of territoriality, particularly in intellectual property law.[255] But when applied to the specific

[249] *Nintendo of America, Inc. v. Aeropower Co., Ltd.*, 34 F.3d 246, 250 (4th Cir. 1994).

[250] *But cf.* Roger E. Schechter, *The Case for Limited Extraterritorial Reach of the Lanham Act*, 37 Va. J. Int'l L. 619, 627 (1997) ("[T]rademark law was originally grounded on an explicitly territorial foundation. One of the central goals of the Lanham Act was to enlarge the territorial scope of rights from local to nationwide.").

[251] *See also* the critique of Curtis A. Bradley in *Territorial Intellectual Property Rights in an Age of Globalism*, 37 Va. J. Int'l L. 505, 542 n. 189 (1997).

[252] *See* Graeme B. Dinwoodie, *Trademarks and Territory: Detaching Trademark Law from the Nation-State*, 41 Hous. L. Rev. 885, 898 and 908 (2004).

[253] Black's Law Dictionary, "territoriality" (9th edn., 2009).

[254] For an extensive discussion, *see infra* p. 398 *et seq.*

[255] *See, e.g.*, Paul Goldstein & P. Bernt Hugenholtz, *International Copyright: Principles, Law, and Practice* § 4.1, 95 (3rd edn., 2013). *See also supra* p. 193 *et seq.* and *infra* p. 483 *et seq.*

characteristics of common law trademark extraterritoriality, a friction surfaces: a registered trademark will be valid within the granting state's territory. The scope of rights will extend internally throughout the geographical area, confined by national borders. It will, however, not exceed those limitations for want of sovereign power beyond the nation-state's confines. Registered trademarks are thus emblematic of territoriality. Use-based rights are more vexing in character. A use-based right will extend over an area of product trade within (but not necessarily congruent with) the state's territory—but it still remains a "territorial" right since its scope cannot exceed state borders. As Justice Holmes made clear in his concurring opinion in *Hanover Star*, common law trademark rights are also founded on state sovereignty.[256] Use-based rights are not *aliud* to registered rights. On the contrary, any trademark right—even if not created by a formal state act—is a territorial right.

There is another facet in the *Hanover Star* case that may invite further misconception. I have already referred to the majority's explanation that

> since it is the trade, and not the mark, that is to be protected, a trademark acknowledges no territorial boundaries of municipalities or states or nations, but extends to every market where the trader's goods have become known and identified by his use of the mark.[257]

Under a common law perspective, this may not be overly troublesome: if the judge is to find the law, and if lawmakers have not established a statutory policy, territorial boundaries may be practically meaningless. This is true at least as long as the jurisdictions involved are of a common law origin and under the assumption that the common law is the same everywhere. However, this is no longer the state of affairs in modern trademark law, whether in the interstate or in the international context. Virtually everywhere, trademark policy has become an issue of lawmaking.

This brings us to the final characteristic of US conflicts doctrine that is important for this inquiry: although not uncontested, the idea that the extraterritorial protection of trademark rights is beneficial for right owners and the national economy alike continues to exist among courts and legal scholars. Some have even posited that extraterritoriality would enhance consumer protection and market conditions abroad.[258] I will address this issue in detail in chapter 5. Here, I will refer to what has been

[256] *Hanover Star Milling Co. v. Metcalf*, 240 U.S. 403, 425–426 (1916) (Holmes, J., concurring). *See also supra* p. 132–134.

[257] *Hanover Star Milling Co. v. Metcalf*, 240 U.S. 403, 416 (1916).

[258] For an example of such "trademark optimism," *see, e.g.*, Marshall A. Leaffer, *The New World of International Trademark*, 2 Marq. Intell. Prop. L. Rev. 1, 2 *et seq.* (1998).

discussed in chapters 1 and 2: the idea of domestic rights extraterritoriality neglects the potentially detrimental effects on domestic competitors in foreign markets. This problem, which was discussed in early twentieth-century German choice of law with respect to Arthur Nussbaum's rule of the *lex domicilii communis*,[259] remains the same: if domestic parties competing in a foreign market are subject to both their domestic law and the local regulations of the foreign state, they are at a disadvantage compared to their foreign-based competitors—at least as long as the domestic law's standards are stricter. In light of the Lanham Act's high substantive law protection level for trademark owners, the problem of extraterritoriality is particularly virulent.[260]

Section 6 Substantivism and Transnational Uniform Law

Another current of scholarly theory finds its foundation in the concept of rights-centered substantivism. Theories of this kind—propounded on both sides of the Atlantic—are called substantive law or single-governing-law approaches and are, in essence, not radically different from the current US approach. Like Lanham Act extraterritoriality, substantive law approaches tend toward deterritorialization in order to protect private rights. Ultimately, albeit usually disguised in a language of internationalist ideas, these concepts are not only flawed with respect to their doctrinal consistency but also unable to provide for a well-balanced limitation of private rights protection with respect to foreign-state third-party and public policy concerns.

I Overview

A Foundations

One of the concepts that has emerged from the American conflicts revolution is the substantive law approach. It has older foundations in Roman law and the *ius gentium*.[261] But its deeper theoretical analysis and foundation are mostly the result of the twentieth-century debate on choice-of-law methodologies. As many of the alternative conceptions, the substantive law approach mostly grew out of a general dissatisfaction with the traditional method, notably the rigidity and formality of classic multilateralism.[262] Friedrich Juenger, for instance, called for a system in which courts would do more than simply choose among the eligible legal

[259] *See supra* p. 64 *et seq.* [260] *See supra* p. 480 *et seq.*
[261] *See, e.g.*, Alex Mills, *The Private History of International Law*, 55 I.C.L.Q. 1, 5–6 (2006).
[262] *See* Peter Hay, Patrick J. Borchers & Symeon C. Symeonides, *Conflict of Laws* §§ 2.9–2.13 (5th edn., 2010).

regimes involved in a multistate dispute. In this regard, he did not stop with Robert Leflar's infamous recommendation to make a "better law" or "best law" selection. Rather, he suggested that judges prepare special substantive rules in interstate and international cases in order to reconcile all affected interests.[263] This concept was embraced and further developed during the latter decades of the century by Arthur Taylor von Mehren and Luther L. McDougal, among others.[264] It is part of today's common stock of modern conflicts methodologies.

Often overlooked is the fact that an almost identical suggestion had been made more than a decade prior to the start of the American academic debate. A general outlier to the dominant theory in German choice-of-law scholarship, particularly with reference to unfair competition conflicts law, is the work of Ernst Steindorff. His theory of internationally uniform substantive rules rejected the use of traditional conflicts theory for determining the applicable law.[265] According to Steindorff, international unfair competition conflicts would be inadequately resolved if they were submitted to a single national regime—a better method would be to look at all relevant and eligible regimes involved in a specific dispute.[266] In essence, his theory called for the ad hoc formulation of general rules in order to permit a genuinely international resolution of conflicts. Whenever a solution could be found that was reflected among the majority of eligible regimes, it would constitute the foundation for an international substantive rule.[267] Interestingly, Steindorff's conception of the formulation of substantive norms also made direct reference to the *Steele v. Bulova Watch Co.* and the New Jersey *Vacuum Oil* decisions, two cases already analyzed.[268] As Steindorff interpreted *Steele* and *Vacuum Oil*, the courts' application of forum law illustrated a preexistence of transnationally uniform law. Standards of the

[263] *See, e.g.*, Friedrich K. Juenger, *Choice of Law and Multistate Justice* 191 *et seq.* (1993); Friedrich K. Juenger, *The Need for a Comparative Approach to Choice-of-Law Problems*, 73 Tul. L. Rev. 1309, 1331–1332 (1999).

[264] *See, e.g.*, Luther L. McDougal III, *Toward Application of the Best Rule of Law in Choice of Law Cases*, 35 Mercer L. Rev. 483, 483–484 and *passim* (1984); Arthur Taylor von Mehren, *Special Substantive Rules for Multistate Problems: Their Role and Significance in Contemporary Choice of Law Methodology*, 88 Harv. L. Rev. 347 (1974); Arthur Taylor von Mehren, *Choice of Law and the Problem of Justice*, 41 Law & Contemp. Probs. 27 (1977).

[265] Ernst Steindorff, *Sachnormen im internationalen Privatrecht* 11 *et seq.* (1958). For an even earlier attempt to formulate a rule of uniform substantive law instead of choice of law (with regard to international sales law), *see* Rudolf Fränkel, *Der Irrgarten des internationalen Privatrechts*, 4 RabelsZ 239, 241–242 (1930).

[266] Ernst Steindorff, *Sachnormen im internationalen Privatrecht* 129 *et seq.*, 261 *et seq.* (1958).

[267] *Id.* at 184 *et seq.* [268] *See supra* p. 164 *et seq.*

domestic regime were deemed an appropriate substitute for the internationally uniform substantive law.[269]

Nonetheless, the substantive law approach has never been implemented in practice. Only one case in the United States has become famous for coming close to a consideration of "federal or national consensus common law" and for resembling a uniform-rule approach.[270] Moreover, the Restatement (Second) of Conflict of Laws alludes only faintly to the concept of "better law"—which is defined as one among the national laws involved, not a newly created norm for conflict cases. Similarly, European theory and practice have neglected the concept of substantive law formulation.[271]

B Modern Concepts of Substantivism in Intellectual Property Law

Despite having never been practically implemented, the idea of internationally uniform norm creation has recently gained ground again. As we have seen, Jane Ginsburg's nerve-center approach significantly extends protection by way of applying domestic law across national borders. As a result, domestic law has assumed the function of a universal intellectual property protection regime.[272] The major argument in favor of such transnationalism is that a single regime will achieve better global protection of right owners' economic interests than will the application of multiple laws based on the old-fashioned concept of territoriality.[273] The final step to be taken from here is not hard to imagine—namely,

[269] *Id.* at 186 ("Die amerikanische Entscheidung sieht in der lex fori den Ausdruck von Maßstäben eines überpositiven gerechten Rechts .... Die Grundsätze der lex fori fungieren hier als besondere Sachnormen für internationale Sachverhalte.").

[270] The case dealt not with trademark or unfair competition law but with product liability. *See In re Agent Orange Product Liability Litigation*, 580 F.Supp. 690, 712 (E.D.N.Y. 1984).

[271] The lack of internationally uniform standards of unfair competition protection has been listed as the primary argument against ad hoc creation of international unfair competition rules. *See, e.g.*, Helmut Wirner, *Wettbewerbsrecht und internationales Privatrecht* 104–105 (1960); Erwin Deutsch, *Wettbewerbstatbestände mit Auslandsbeziehung* 40–41 (1962); Christian Joerges, *Die klassische Konzeption des internationalen Privatrechts und das Recht des unlauteren Wettbewerbs*, 36 RabelsZ 421, 477–478 (1972); Adair Dyer, *Unfair Competition in Private International Law*, 211 Recueil des Cours 373, 409 (1988-IV).

[272] *See supra* p. 238–249. For international trademark protection and a similar domestic rights transnationalization, *see* Roger E. Schechter, *The Case for Limited Extraterritorial Reach of the Lanham Act*, 37 Va. J. Int'l L. 619, 629 (1997). For a similar characterization of international copyright protection, *see, e.g.*, Graeme W. Austin, *Domestic Laws and Foreign Rights: Choice of Law in Transnational Copyright Infringement Litigation*, 23 Colum.-VLA J. L. & Arts 1, 21 (1999).

[273] For an extensive analysis, *see* Jane C. Ginsburg, *The Private International Law of Copyright in an Era of Technological Change*, 273 Recueil des Cours 239, 322 *et seq.* (1998).

the creation and application of a truly transnational system, unified to guarantee an optimal level of protection and ultimately providing for the most efficient adjudication of international intellectual property conflicts.[274] It often goes unmentioned that the idea of an international code for intellectual property protection was originally contemplated over a century ago.[275] This idea was, conceptually, a parallel development to the drafting of the Berne Convention. But its proponents did not succeed in establishing a uniform world code. The modern system of international intellectual property law, including instruments such as the Paris and Berne Conventions, has made strides in achieving greater uniformity and harmonization over the last century. Nonetheless, even TRIPS has left a patchwork: beyond the binding minimum standards, members' local regimes differ significantly.[276]

Many versions of substantivism exist. Yet they all share a common characteristic: their proponents, mostly in the field of international copyright law, contend that choice of the applicable rules should be separated from territoriality[277] in order to determine the most protective regime.[278] In essence, this suggests abandoning traditional methodology. The discussion below will focus on two different variants. One proposes applying a single national law. Here, a certain "choice" of the

[274] Even though most single-governing-law approaches seem to be driven less by ideas of self-defense than by ideas of comprehensive rights exploitation, their proponents still rely heavily on the argument that protection levels need to be increased due to technological, social, and economic revolutions. *See, e.g.*, Graeme B. Dinwoodie, *A New Copyright Order: Why National Courts Should Create Global Norms*, 149 U. Pa. L. Rev. 469, 494 (2000). Another oft-enunciated argument in favor of unified international copyright enforcement rules is based on the assumption that divergent national laws and the resulting need for right owners to accommodate different national protection requirements would impose significant costs on the producers of protected works. These increased transaction costs would be charged to the consumer as "risk premium." *See id.* at 480.

[275] *See, e.g.*, William Briggs, *The Law of International Copyright* 162 (1906) ("The ideal universal law of copyright is a single code, binding throughout the world, and giving the fullest protection to the authors of every country, without distinction of nationality. Such a universal law would present the great advantage of simplicity as well as that of international equity.").

[276] Paul Edward Geller, *From Patchwork to Network: Strategies for International Intellectual Property in Flux*, 9 Duke J. Comp. & Int'l L. 69, 74 (1998).

[277] *See, e.g.*, Paul Edward Geller, *The Universal Electronic Archive: Issues in International Copyright*, 25 IIC 54, 55 (1994) (requiring a move "beyond territoriality").

[278] *See, e.g.*, Jane C. Ginsburg, *Private International Law Aspects of the Protection of Works and Objects of Related Rights Transmitted through Digital Networks*, WIPO Doc. No. GCPIC/2, November 30, 1998, at 35 *et seq.*; Paul Edward Geller, *Conflicts of Laws in Cyberspace: Rethinking International Copyright in a Digitally Networked World*, 20 Colum.-VLA J. L. & Arts 571, 602 (1996); for a similar view of "right-holder-friendly" conflicts rules, *see* Andreas P. Reindl, *Choosing Law in Cyberspace: Copyright Conflicts on Global Networks*, 19 Mich. J. Int'l L. 799, 830 *et seq.* (1998).

applicable law is still required. The other recommends applying newly formulated rules, which does not require a separate level of choosing the law.

The first variant is Paul E. Geller's proposal for a single-national-law approach for international copyright infringements. Geller suggests that copyright infringements in digital networks with multijurisdictional implications should, ideally, be governed by the most protective national regime. Conflicts should always be resolved in favor of applying the legal regime that grants the highest level of protection.[279] Jane Ginsburg has suggested a similar, albeit more pragmatic, theory: under the presumption that minimum protection levels under the Paris Convention, the Berne Convention, and the TRIPS Agreement have been implemented in all member states, courts should apply their forum law as the single governing regime to incidents of international infringements.[280] National law, by this means, becomes a kind of "supranational law."[281]

The second variant of substantive law approaches involves the formulation of new substantive rules. Graeme Dinwoodie in particular has suggested such a method for international copyright infringements. As he argues, international disputes implicate interests beyond those at stake in purely domestic cases. Courts should thus decide such disputes by creating new substantive norms and not by choosing a national law. As Dinwoodie contends, this substantive law method allows for a more detailed and flexible tailoring of applicable rules and available remedies. Accommodating relevant interests would be easier this way than through traditional choice of law.[282] His proposal essentially requires national courts to "develop" the applicable regime by considering international agreements and practices, national and regional laws, the "norms of developing post-national groupings," and "systemic conflicts

[279] Paul Edward Geller, *Conflicts of Laws in Cyberspace: Rethinking International Copyright*, 44 J. Copyright Soc'y U.S.A 103, 107 *et seq.* (1996).

[280] It would be for the defendant to prove that the laws of the countries involved have not assimilated the minimum protection standards of the Paris and Berne Conventions or the TRIPS Agreement. *See* Jane C. Ginsburg, *Private International Law Aspects of the Protection of Works and Objects of Related Rights Transmitted Through Digital Networks*, WIPO Doc. No. GCPIC/2, November 30, 1998, at 44; Jane C. Ginsburg, *The Cyberian Captivity of Copyright: Territoriality and Authors' Rights in a Networked World*, 15 Santa Clara Computer & High Tech. L.J. 347, 356 (1999).

[281] Jane C. Ginsburg, *The Cyberian Captivity of Copyright: Territoriality and Authors' Rights in a Networked World*, 15 Santa Clara Computer & High Tech. L.J. 347, 356 (1999). *See also* Graeme W. Austin, *Social Policy Choices and Choice of Law for Copyright Infringement in Cyberspace*, 79 Or. L. Rev. 575, 596 (2000).

[282] Graeme B. Dinwoodie, *A New Copyright Order: Why National Courts Should Create Global Norms*, 149 U. Pa. L. Rev. 469, 564 (2000).

values."[283] In its concrete application, courts would consider all interests and national laws involved, as well as the purposes that undergird these laws.[284] As Dinwoodie admits, however, analyzing foreign laws and their purposes can be complicated—though he argues that access to the relevant materials is continually improving.[285] Ultimately, Dinwoodie also recommends his method for international trademark conflicts.[286] Similar to the Uniform Domain-Name Dispute-Resolution Policy's function of regulating global domain-name disputes (e.g., cybersquatting cases), the development of an autonomous body of substantive law governing international trademark conflicts seems to offer a way out of choice-of-law dilemmas presented by multinational infringements.[287]

Substantivism of this last kind essentially replicates a concept of transnational common law that was present in the Romans' *ius commune*[288] and in the age-old idea of a *lex mercatoria*.[289] And, indeed, the transnational uniformity of rules seems to offer a number of advantages. First, giving the courts freedom to devise the legal rules themselves seems to foster adequate and quick reactions to new technological and socioeconomic developments. In contrast to traditional choice of law and public international lawmaking, substantive law appears to be a more dynamic approach.[290] It seems to accommodate concerns for flexibility and pluralism.[291] Second, since a pluralized perspective would be mandatory

283 *Id.* at 542–543, 552 *et seq.*; Graeme B. Dinwoodie, *International Intellectual Property Litigation: A Vehicle for Resurgent Comparativist Thought?*, 49 Am. J. Comp. L. 429, 444 (2001).

284 Graeme B. Dinwoodie, *A New Copyright Order: Why National Courts Should Create Global Norms*, 149 U. Pa. L. Rev. 469, 561 *et seq.* (2000).

285 *Id.* at 562.

286 *Id.* at 542–543 n. 226; Graeme B. Dinwoodie, *Trademarks and Territory: Detaching Trademark Law from the Nation-State*, 41 Hous. L. Rev. 885, 951–952 (2004); Graeme B. Dinwoodie, *Conflicts and International Copyright Litigation: The Role of International Norms*, 195, 206 *et seq.*, in *Intellectual Property in the Conflict of Laws* (Jürgen Basedow et al. eds., 2005).

287 *See, e.g.*, Graeme B. Dinwoodie, *Private International Aspects of the Protection of Trademarks, WIPO Forum on Private International Law and Intellectual Property*, WIPO/PIL/01/4 (19 January 2001), para. 115 and 126; Graeme B. Dinwoodie, *The Architecture of the International Intellectual Property System*, 77 Chi.-Kent L. Rev. 993, 1000 *et seq.* (2002); for similarities to the *lex mercatoria, see* Graeme B. Dinwoodie, *Conflicts and International Copyright Litigation: The Role of International Norms*, 195, 207–208, in *Intellectual Property in the Conflict of Laws* (Jürgen Basedow et al. eds., 2005).

288 *See, e.g.*, Friedrich K. Juenger, *Choice of Law and Multistate Justice* 193 (1993).

289 Paul Schiff Berman, *The Globalization of Jurisdiction*, 151 U. Pa. L. Rev. 311, 401 (2002).

290 Graeme B. Dinwoodie, *A New Copyright Order: Why National Courts Should Create Global Norms*, 149 U. Pa. L. Rev. 469, 569–570 (2000).

291 *Id.* at 476, 494, 569. *See also* more recently Graeme B. Dinwoodie, *Developing a Private International Intellectual Property Law: The Demise of Territoriality?*, 51 Wm. & Mary

for decision makers when addressing international conflicts, the individual substantive rule and the system of rules evolving over time may be ideal for accommodating a globalized world.[292] Finally, even though this may be a weakness in the beginning, the lack of uniformity and of a centralized superior court may ultimately prove advantageous. Prima facie, the substantive law approach provides little certainty. After all, national courts remain free to deviate from standards developed in other fora. It may thus be costly during an interim stage. In the long run, however, such an approach may be far more efficient than single-governing-law regimes or choice-of-law rules. Concordance would never be forced on the forum but would be due to the force of reason as a "more enduring basis for long-term convergence and acceptance of international standards."[293] Juenger has made a similar point:

> Instead of blinding judges to the quality of statutes and precedents, the quest for multistate justice directs attention to defects in the law and therefore yields a valuable by-product: reasoned judicial opinions on the merits of the competing rules of decision.[294]

C Nonterritorial Concepts: "Cyberlaw" and the "Collision of Rights"

Among modern substantive law approaches, two variants of international trademark theory deserve special attention. A closer look helps unveil the problems with substantive law theory in general. The first approach, cyberlaw theory, is the most radical and libertarian version. Its proponents envisage a new, apolitical, and deterritorialized system of internet regulation. Under cyberlaw theory, as far as internet activity is concerned, individual rights are no longer state granted—in fact, national laws are irrelevant. Among the prophets of this brave new

L. Rev. 711, 770 (2009) ("[T]he frequency of transborder disputes has made the cost of insisting on serial national litigation more substantial. The reality of international disputes about international markets makes partitioning of adjudication seem a costly and romantic hankering for the inefficiencies of a balkanized past."). For earlier arguments in this regard, *see* Friedrich K. Juenger, *Choice of Law and Multistate Justice* 192 (1993) ("Instead of confining the judiciary [in straitjackets], the substantive law approach imparts a welcome measure of creative freedom.").

292 Graeme B. Dinwoodie, *A New Copyright Order: Why National Courts Should Create Global Norms*, 149 U. Pa. L. Rev. 469, 550, and 570 (2000). *See also* Friedrich K. Juenger, *Choice of Law and Multistate Justice* 206 (1993).

293 Graeme B. Dinwoodie, *A New Copyright Order: Why National Courts Should Create Global Norms*, 149 U. Pa. L. Rev. 469, 570–571 (2000).

294 Friedrich K. Juenger, *Choice of Law and Multistate Justice* 193 (1993).

internet world—the "cyberenthusiasts"[295]—are David R. Johnson and David Post, who have conceived a new model of online jurisdiction.[296] Their cyberspace model is built on a principle of isolation: internet and real-world activity would remain distinctly separate. This separation, they contend, would not only create a need for rethinking traditional law and legal institutions but would "radically undermine[] the relationship between legally significant (online) phenomena and physical location" in a number of ways.[297] The liberation of online activity from real-world space restrictions would dissolve the link between geographical location and the power of national governments to control online conduct. Since cyberspace activities would create new phenomena that could not be governed by traditional offline law, they recommend "[t]reating Cyberspace as a separate 'space' to which distinct laws apply."[298] The internet would thus be seen as an independent jurisdictional entity with its own regime of rules.[299] With regard to trademarks, the authors not only suggest establishing a global registration system for domain names and "reputationally significant names and symbols used on the Net"[300] but are convinced that "[a] distinct set of rules applicable to trademarks in Cyberspace would greatly simplify matters by providing a basis to resist the inconsistent and conflicting assertions of geographically local prerogatives."[301]

Less radical—yet also founded on the idea of a widely depoliticized private rights regime in trademark regulation—is a theory that can best be characterized as a collision-of-rights approach. Its central aspect is the idea that a web-based collision of separate and independent national trademark rights, having been granted in different jurisdictions,

[295] For the term, *see, e.g.*, Graeme B. Dinwoodie, *International Intellectual Property Litigation: A Vehicle for Resurgent Comparativist Thought?*, 49 Am. J. Comp. L. 429, 444 (2001); *see also* James Boyle, *Foucault in Cyberspace: Surveillance, Sovereignty, and Hardwired Censors*, 66 U. Cin. L. Rev. 177, 178 (1997) ("Internet's enthusiasts").

[296] David R. Johnson & David Post, *Law and Borders—The Rise of Law in Cyberspace*, 48 Stan. L. Rev. 1367 (1996). For further references to Johnson and Post and their cyberlaw theory, *see* Paul Schiff Berman, *The Globalization of Jurisdiction*, 151 U. Pa. L. Rev. 311, 371 n. 231 (2002).

[297] David R. Johnson & David Post, *Law and Borders—The Rise of Law in Cyberspace*, 48 Stan. L. Rev. 1367, 1370 (1996).

[298] *Id.* at 1379.

[299] In addition, new lawmaking institutions within cyberspace would have to be developed. *See id.* at 1387.

[300] *Id.* at 1380. In addition, Johnson and Post suggested solutions for the collision between the "two worlds": "Such a Net-based regime could take account of the special claim of owners of strong global marks (as used on physical goods) and 'grandfather' these owners' rights to the use of their strong marks in the newly opened online territory." (*Id.*).

[301] *Id.*

constitutes a conflict not of legal systems but of private property rights.[302] This perspective also has a distinct libertarian flavor. Although it is seldom expressly admitted, under the proponents' rights-centered perspective, individual entitlements in trademark symbols exist *ex nihilo*, and the state was created to protect these rights. For choice of law, this focus has a fatally distortive effect. As under classic substantivist theory and the cyberlaw concept, choice-of-law determination has been structurally substituted in full. Instead of determining an applicable national law, proponents of collision-of-rights theories suggest that new substantive rules must be promulgated by ad hoc interest balancing. At first sight, the approach may appear as a panacea, for, on the internet, a system of universally applicable national trademark regimes may create a situation of mutually blocking rights.[303] Because each symbol could be registered as a different right in a different jurisdiction, using symbols on the internet could lead to innumerable conflicts, with each owner being able to block others based on the national priority of her right.[304] Ultimately, the new rules, as proponents suggest, should be implemented even in nation-states' trademark regimes. Identical or similar trademarks would then coexist internationally under a general unfair-use proviso.[305]

[302] *See, e.g.*, Torsten Bettinger & Dorothee Thum, *Territorial Trademark Rights in the Global Village—International Jurisdiction, Choice of Law and Substantive Law for Trademark Disputes on the Internet*, 31 IIC 285, 287 (2000); *see also* Graeme B. Dinwoodie, *Private International Aspects of the Protection of Trademarks, WIPO Forum on Private International Law and Intellectual Property*, WIPO/PIL/01/4 (19 January 2001), para. 58 ("This is not a conflict of legal rules regarding ownership of marks; rather it is a conflict in international markets between two persons with undisputed legitimate ownership of different national properties."); for the general conception of a "conflict of rights," *see* Ansgar Ohly, *Choice of Law in the Digital Environment—Problems and Possible Solutions*, 241, 245—246, in *Intellectual Property and Private International Law—Heading for the Future* (Josef Drexl & Annette Kur eds., 2005) ("Two territorially restricted rights conflict in a global medium."); Annette Kur, *Trademark Conflicts on the Internet: Territoriality Redefined?*, 175, 175, in *Intellectual Property in the Conflict of Laws* (Jürgen Basedow et al. eds., 2005); Josef Drexl, in *Münchener Kommentar zum Bürgerlichen Gesetzbuch, vol. XI*, IntLautR para. 175 n. 563 (Franz Jürgen Säcker et al. eds., 6th edn., 2015) ("Es ging [in der Hotel Maritime-Entscheidung] nicht um eine Kollision der Rechtsordnungen (conflict of laws), sondern um eine Kollision von Rechten in verschiedenen Staaten (conflict of rights).").

[303] For the online context *see, e.g.*, Torsten Bettinger & Dorothee Thum, *Territorial Trademark Rights in the Global Village—International Jurisdiction, Choice of Law and Substantive Law for Trademark Disputes on the Internet*, 31 IIC 285, 290 (2000).

[304] For the impasse of mutual blocking, *see* Graeme B. Dinwoodie, *Private International Aspects of the Protection of Trademarks, WIPO Forum on Private International Law and Intellectual Property*, WIPO/PIL/01/4 (19 January 2001), para. 55–56.

[305] Graeme B. Dinwoodie, *Private International Aspects of the Protection of Trademarks, WIPO Forum on Private International Law and Intellectual Property*, WIPO/PIL/01/4 (19 January 2001), para. 54–57; Torsten Bettinger & Dorothee Thum, *Territorial Trademark Rights in the Global Village—International Jurisdiction, Choice of Law and

II Analysis: The Fata Morgana of Universal Policy

The tendency toward globally uniform protection rules illustrates a somewhat paradoxical development. Whereas scholarship regarding the domestic context has sternly criticized the growing propertization of trademarks,[306] it is surprisingly silent when it comes to the same development on the international plane. A large part of the debate is founded on the argument of an alleged need to dissolve territorial boundaries—and since dissolution comes with more protection for domestic right owners, it is a theory of transnational propertization. Indeed, a look at some of the single-governing-law theories has revealed a thinking historically known as the universality doctrine.[307] A critique could go on at length, so I will focus on its major flaws.[308] The following discussion will explore deficits concerning consistency, as well as legitimacy and practicality issues regarding the ad hoc promulgation of substantive norms.

Let us start with the most significant deficit: the concept of "[t]reating Cyberspace as a separate 'space.'"[309] It actually is impossible to distinguish between online and offline worlds. To be fair, of course, we must acknowledge that during the initial stages of the internet, the new medium's actual real-world impetus was far from clear, and any prediction was necessarily based on assumptions. Today, however, the logical inconsistency of constructing parallel worlds of different applicable legal regimes is apparent, particularly in the field of trademark law. While there may be instances of online activities that do not have significant offline effects, the bulk of online communication and transacting exert a tangible influence on the offline world.[310] Even though domain names and other online uses of trademarks "exist operationally only on the

Substantive Law for Trademark Disputes on the Internet, 31 IIC 285, 287, 295 *et seq.*, 300–301 (2000).

306 For critical US theory on substantive trademark law, *see supra* p. 126–127.

307 *See supra* p. 21 *et seq.*

308 For an extended analysis, *see, e.g.*, Paul Schiff Berman, *The Globalization of Jurisdiction*, 151 U. Pa. L. Rev. 311, 370 *et seq.* (2002).

309 David R. Johnson & David Post, *Law and Borders—The Rise of Law in Cyberspace*, 48 Stan. L. Rev. 1367, 1379 (1996).

310 *See, e.g.*, Jack L. Goldsmith, *Against Cyberanarchy*, 65 U. Chi. L. Rev. 1199, 1250 (1998); Jack L. Goldsmith, *The Internet and the Abiding Significance of Territorial Sovereignty*, 5 Ind. J. Global Legal Stud. 475, 476 (1998); Andreas P. Reindl, *Choosing Law in Cyberspace: Copyright Conflicts on Global Networks*, 19 Mich. J. Int'l L. 799, 811 (1998); Dan L. Burk, *Trademark Doctrines for Global Electronic Commerce*, 49 S. C. L. Rev. 695, 717 (1998); Graeme B. Dinwoodie, *Private International Aspects of the Protection of Trademarks*, *WIPO Forum on Private International Law and Intellectual Property*, WIPO/PIL/01/4 (19 January 2001), para. 9. For a rejoinder to Goldsmith's attack, *see* David G. Post, *Against "Against Cyberanarchy,"* 17 Berkeley Tech. L.J. 1365 (2002) ("I remain an unrepentant Exceptionalist.").

Net,"[311] the online use of protected names and designations influences real-world market transactions and consumer perception. After all, this is trademarks' ultimate purpose. Trademarks are commercial communication, and commerce is a real-world phenomenon.

Furthermore, the concept of individual and self-contained "rights" in collision-of-rights theory smacks of circular reasoning. It implies a state-free, private, and unregulated area of trademark rights acquisition and use. But trademark rights, as well as entitlements granted under a regime of unfair competition law, are created neither apolitically nor by nonstate actors. Reliance on property rights always raises the question of who is the legal authority granting these rights. Accordingly, denying the relevance of national laws in creating individual entitlements inevitably risks eradicating the existence of such rights.[312] In this light, it is clear that the international coexistence of different rights must remain a question of different national laws. Each state is free to adopt, within the confines of its obligations under public international law, the intellectual property system it sees fit. There is no *telle quelle* acknowledgment of foreign rights beyond these minimum obligations.[313] Necessarily, however, this means that nation-state policies need to be given regard to in conflicts analysis.

Similarly problematic is the disregard for state sovereignty. Neither under public international law nor under common law theory will a nation-state have the authority to create norms for the regulation of conflicts in *foreign* territories. Graeme W. Austin has characterized this kind of extraterritoriality as a disregard for other states' "domestic self-determination."[314] Domestic self-determination, he explains, refers to sovereign nations' ability to establish and uphold their own intellectual property laws according to their local political, economic, and social

[311] David R. Johnson & David Post, *Law and Borders—The Rise of Law in Cyberspace*, 48 Stan. L. Rev. 1367, 1380 (1996).

[312] *See also* Andreas P. Reindl, *Choosing Law in Cyberspace: Copyright Conflicts on Global Networks*, 19 Mich. J. Int'l L. 799, 815 (1998) ("Efforts to localize infringing conduct on digital networks may be criticized for being too attached to conventional concepts of territorial laws and not sensitive enough for the non-territorial and extra-national nature of digital networks. This criticism, however, is not justified. Choice of law rules are merely the logical consequence of state-granted property rights.").

[313] *See* Carl Ludwig von Bar, *Theorie und Praxis des Internationalen Privatrechts, vol. II*, comment 358, at 278 (2nd edn., 1889). Further also Frank Vischer, *Das IPR des Immaterialgüterrechts*, 363, 367, in *Kernprobleme des Patentrechts—Festschrift zum einhundertjährigen Bestehen des eidgenössischen Patentgesetzes* (Institut für gewerblichen Rechtsschutz (INGRES) ed., 1988).

[314] *See, e.g.*, Graeme W. Austin, *Valuing "Domestic Self-Determination" in International Intellectual Property Jurisprudence*, 77 Chicago-Kent L. Rev. 1155, 1159–1160 (2002); *see also* Graeme W. Austin, *Social Policy Choices and Choice of Law for Copyright Infringement in Cyberspace*, 79 Or. L. Rev. 575, 597 *et seq.* (2000).

circumstances, as well as their relationships with other nations.[315] The international intellectual property system explicitly acknowledges the need to respect such a minimum of nation-state sovereignty.[316] Whereas this correlation seems to be better accepted in the context of copyright and patent protection, it has not been extensively analyzed in relation to trademark and unfair competition conflicts—an oversight due largely to the fact that trademark and unfair competition law is often explained as being more closely related to commerce than to cultural issues and information policy.[317] This perspective, however, overlooks the fact that social and cultural policies also underlie modern trademark regimes. Freedom of speech and parody with regard to trademark use are the most prominent examples.

In order to play down these technical-doctrinal defects, proponents of substantive law theory sometimes explain their approach as akin to the common law technique.[318] Yet this also cannot cover the lack of foundation. Indeed, Justice Holmes's oft-cited tenet on common law legitimacy powerfully contradicts such an unauthorized rule making by the courts: "The common law is not a brooding omnipresence in the sky, but the articulate voice of some sovereign or quasi sovereign that can be identified. . . . It always is the law of some state. . . ."[319] This requirement of source legitimacy also applies to the promulgation of an international common law. No national court has the authority to create substantive rules for international trademark conflicts.

Finally, at the practical level, international substantivism is unlikely to take over in the near future due to a number of more mundane obstacles. Most generally, the theory faces a language problem: as of today, there is no juridical *lingua franca* that allows courts to construct and efficiently utilize a body of transnational common law. While such an endeavor may work in the context of Anglo-American and Commonwealth jurisprudence, the non-English-speaking world would be largely excluded. Furthermore, we must consider courts' general tendency to follow a homing trend and apply the rules that most closely resemble their

[315] Graeme W. Austin, *Valuing "Domestic Self-Determination" in International Intellectual Property Jurisprudence*, 77 Chicago-Kent L. Rev. 1155, 1160 (2002).

[316] *See, e.g.*, the preamble to the TRIPS Agreement, which requires member states to provide "effective and appropriate means for the enforcement of trade-related intellectual property rights, taking into account differences in national legal systems."

[317] *See, e.g.*, Dan L. Burk, *Trademark Doctrines for Global Electronic Commerce*, 49 S. C. L. Rev. 695, 735 (1998).

[318] *See, e.g.*, Friedrich K. Juenger, *Choice of Law and Multistate Justice* 193 (1993); Graeme B. Dinwoodie, *A New Copyright Order: Why National Courts Should Create Global Norms*, 149 U. Pa. L. Rev. 469, 476 (2000).

[319] *Southern Pac. Co. v. Jensen*, 244 U.S. 205, 222 (1917).

domestic law.[320] In other words, given the option of promulgating substantive rules based on a collection of national laws and international conventions, judges will very likely tend to replicate their own domestic systems. Finally, there is no unified court system linking domestic judicial systems. Even if courts embraced the "greater comparative thought" of promulgating new and inventive substantive law,[321] there is no authoritative body to guide domestic systems toward a uniform interpretation and application of such norms.

Section 7 The Rediscovery of International Comity

This overview of scholarly theories will conclude by exploring an approach that is neither the most innovative nor the most prominent suggestion in the field of trademark and unfair competition conflicts law. Nonetheless, this concept is important for several reasons. It combines aspects of civil law, common law, and substantive law theories with the distinct aim of internationalism. In fact, as a closer look unveils, this approach can help guide the way toward a modern comity-based conflicts law.

I *The* Comitas *Approach*

Christian Joerges is one of the proponents of what can be called a "modern comity (*comitas*) approach." His suggestion, presented in 1972, resembles modern American interest analysis, though it is devoid of the preference for the *lex fori* that exists, for instance, in Currian and other neo-statutist theories on choice of law. With respect to unfair competition and trademark law, Joerges argued that the field can no longer be qualified as belonging entirely to either the private law or the public law domain.[322] While state and society seemed to have become somewhat separated in the mid-nineteenth century, the idea of an

320 For this problem, *see, e.g.*, Gary B. Born, *A Reappraisal of the Extraterritorial Reach of U.S. Law*, 24 Law & Pol'y Int'l Bus. 1, 95 (1992).

321 Graeme B. Dinwoodie, *International Intellectual Property Litigation: A Vehicle for Resurgent Comparativist Thought?*, 49 Am. J. Comp. L. 429, 445 (2001).

322 Christian Joerges, *Die klassische Konzeption des internationalen Privatrechts und das Recht des unlauteren Wettbewerbs*, 36 RabelsZ 421, 422, 439 *et seq.*, 450–451 (1972). He was not alone in making this conclusion. *See, e.g.*, Franz Kahn, *Die Lehre vom ordre public (Prohibitivgesetze)*, 161, 173, in *Abhandlungen zum internationalen Privatrecht, vol. I* (Otto Lenel & Hans Lewald eds., 1928) ("[E]in Gesetz wider den unlauteren Wettbewerb … [ist] gewiß im höchsten Maße zwingend, streng-positiv, sozial …."); Otto Mayer, *Die concurrence déloyale—Ein Beitrag aus dem französischen Rechte zur Lehre vom geistigen Eigenthum*, 26 Zeitschrift für das Gesammte Handelsrecht 363, 434, 437 (1881); and also Wilhelm Wengler, *Laws Concerning Unfair Competition and the Conflict of Laws*, 4 Am. J. Comp. L. 167, 184 (1955).

autonomous society and economy lost its justification toward the end of the century. Over time, state intervention led to an increasing entanglement of state, society, and economy—particularly in the field of trademark and unfair competition law.[323] As revealed in chapters 1 and 2, the field thereby developed from an area of interparty relations into a sector of state regulation and intervention—notably in the interest of third parties and the public. It is thus not much of a surprise that courts have usually had a preference for domestic policies in international trademark and unfair competition conflicts.[324] This also means that a true "choice" of law never came into play. Joerges even concluded that the traditional Savignian system of multilateral choice-of-law rules is virtually inept at accommodating international unfair competition conflicts.[325] Accordingly, he further reasoned, harmony of decision making should no longer be seen as the primary aim. Rather, international comity should determine the legitimacy of conflict resolution.[326] Technically, this means that the scope of application of a domestic regime will have to be defined on the basis of the policies of all national laws involved.[327]

II Analysis: A "Quadrature of the Circle"

As discussed earlier, the twentieth-century evolution of trademark and unfair competition law resulted in a distinct socialization and politicization of the field. In this regard, Joerges's starting point can be verified. What remains to be analyzed, however, is whether his suggested method for international conflicts resolution is adequate and workable. To this effect, a critical look at the comity (*comitas*) approach helps formulate the relevant questions for the remaining chapters.

Above all—the issue of impracticality aside[328]—Joerges's method of policy reconciliation and balancing in light of the *comitas* doctrine

[323] Christian Joerges, *Die klassische Konzeption des internationalen Privatrechts und das Recht des unlauteren Wettbewerbs*, 36 RabelsZ 421, 435–437 (1972); *see also* Christian Joerges, *Vorüberlegungen zu einer Theorie des internationalen Wirtschaftsrechts*, 43 RabelsZ 6, 35–36 (1979). *See also* Alois Troller, *Unfair Competition (ch. 34)*, no. 34–3, in *International Encyclopedia of Comparative Law, vol. III, Private International Law* (Kurt Lipstein et al. eds., 1980). For the general development, *see infra* p. 383 *et seq.*

[324] *See supra* p. 53 *et seq.* and p. 159 *et seq.*

[325] Christian Joerges, *Die klassische Konzeption des internationalen Privatrechts und das Recht des unlauteren Wettbewerbs*, 36 RabelsZ 421, 460–461 (1972).

[326] *Id.* at 470 ("Gerechtigkeit in internationalen Beziehungen bedeutet in jedem Falle, daß comitas geübt werden muß.").

[327] *Id.* at 467 *et seq.* Methodologically and terminologically, Joerges founded his approach on Currie's theory of interest analysis. Accordingly, he rejected a system of custom-made, preformulated, and uniform rules for conflicts resolution. *See id.* at 470 *et seq.*

[328] Joerges himself was probably not convinced of the practicality of the *comitas* approach. *See id.* at 478.

provides a solid foundation for the reconceptualization of trademark and unfair competition conflicts law. Several aspects are important. First, with his description of substantive trademark and unfair competition law as an increasingly publicized and politicized regime of economic regulation, Joerges has set the stage for the necessary rejection of traditional theories contending that trademark and unfair competition law concern individual and private property rights only. As I will explore in more detail later, the publicization of private law across all its sectors has resulted in a general de-Savignization of choice of law.[329] This particularly concerns trademark and unfair competition policies and therefore necessarily also affects choice of law. As I have illustrated in the preceding chapters and this one, conflicts law in the field is in a state of hybridity: at the center of the debate is the question whether international trademark protection and unfair competition prevention should be seen as a sector of international private law or as part of the domain of international economic law.

In addition, if Joerges is correct that Savigny's system has never been appropriate for trademark and unfair competition conflicts, the void must be filled. But the question is, by what? Joerges himself did not give a concrete answer. He did not provide much more than a general reference to the idea of *comitas*. In this respect, however, it is true that reconciling different nations' conflicting policies usually requires the proverbial "quadrature of the circle."[330] This is due to the fact that, from its beginning in seventeenth-century Dutch scholarship, the doctrine of international comity has been ambiguous and unreliable as a practical guide for decision making.[331] Inevitably, therefore, mere reference to the doctrine cannot suffice to reconceptualize conflicts law in the field. What is required instead is a structure of internationally uniform guidelines for policy-oriented conflicts rules, notably with respect to a determination of the necessary minimum degree and intensity of effects. The conception of such a system will be the challenge for the remaining chapters.

Conclusions

An overview of the panoply of scholarship on both sides of the Atlantic reveals a large number of divergent strands. The multitude of conceptions

[329] *See infra* p. 383 *et seq.*

[330] *See* Franz Kahn, *Über Inhalt, Natur und Methode des internationalen Privatrechts*, 255, 318, in *Abhandlungen zum internationalen Privatrecht, vol. I* (Otto Lenel & Hans Lewald eds., 1928).

[331] For an overview, *see, e.g.*, Tim W. Dornis, *Comity*, in *Encyclopedia of Private International Law* (Jürgen Basedow et al. eds., forthcoming 2017).

actually reflects many of the fundamental issues in modern choice of law and international economic law—not only in the sector of intellectual property but also in international antitrust and international torts conflicts doctrine.

Most generally, it has become evident that scholarly commentary on choice of law and conflicts law is regularly held captive by the theoretical constraints of substantive law doctrine. As demonstrated in chapters 1 and 2, the paradigm of trademark propertization has dominated substantive trademark and unfair competition law during the last two centuries in both Europe and the United States. Theoretical approaches to choice of law and conflicts resolution have accordingly been oriented along these lines. In European scholarship, the concept of strict trademark territoriality continues to be solidly implemented. While this concept's obsolescence has recently begun to be acknowledged, a comprehensive restructuring has yet to take place. Unfair competition conflicts, by contrast, have already been transformed into a more market-oriented approach. Despite this formal progress, however, the practical implementation of this new approach is still deficient. In particular, the approach is still predominantly based on obsolete concepts of a traditionally conduct-oriented tort doctrine. At the same time, the recent trend toward a universal doctrine of antitrust, trademark, and unfair competition conflicts resolution goes one step too far; this approach lacks a qualitative determination of relevant effects. A similarly large variety of contradictory approaches can be found in US law. In general, scholarly commentary and courts have always openly considered the issue of how domestic rights could be optimally protected in the international arena. This goal of extraterritorial protection has been coupled with the tendency to equate trademark and unfair competition law with the protection of other intellectual property. In this regard, the pendulum appears to have swung back. While Lanham Act subject-matter jurisdiction has evolved into an instrument of unilateral and extraterritorial domestic law application, scholarship has become increasingly aware of the problems of extraterritoriality. Notwithstanding these more cautious tendencies, the major current in American doctrine still focuses on the ideas of use-based trademark rights and the extension of domestic regulation in cross-border conflicts. A transnational *Tea Rose/Rectanus* doctrine, as established by *Steele v. Bulova*, is still present, not to say dominant. Despite this basis in common law doctrine, a modern effects test has been implemented, virtually equating international trademark cases with international antitrust conflicts. However, as with the German and European concepts, the quality and quantity aspects of effects testing have remained widely unresolved.

In sum, there is a need for key changes to conflicts law systems in Europe and the United States. Such modifications will not only allow for a consistent reconceptualization but also bring European and US doctrine into conformity with each other. Most fundamentally, we need to say farewell once and for all to traditional property rights and conduct-regulation paradigms of European trademark and unfair competition doctrine. Modern conflicts resolution must abandon the static concepts of "property" and "territorial conduct." In their stead, marketplace effects must be used as an indicator for the regulation of international commercial communication and transacting by means of conflicts law. Yet, over- and underregulation under an effects test can be avoided only by a clear delineation of different states' effects-triggered regulatory regimes. What must therefore also stand at the center of a new approach is a qualitative and quantitative determination of effects' relevance.

Against this backdrop, the roadmap for the rest of this book is set. Before I attempt to construct a consistent scheme for international trademark and unfair competition conflicts, I must undertake a deeper analysis of relevant policies—one that distinguishes between tort, intellectual property, antitrust, and trademark and unfair competition law. This will be the emphasis of the next chapter.

4 Substantive Policy

Convergent Foundations

Substantive law is both the origin and the terminus of private international law analysis. This is the natural cycle, not the all-too-often vicious circle. All conflicts norms have been developed—and will be developed anew every day—based on substantive law norms. Constructing a private international law regime without such a substantive law foundation would be akin to setting a spire into the vacuous air.

Author's translation from Franz Kahn, *Über Inhalt, Natur und Methode des internationalen Privatrechts*, 40 JherJB 1, 56 (1898)

Introduction

As seen in the preceding chapters, the fields of trademark and unfair competition conflicts law and choice of law suffer from a number of defects. Most of these deficiencies are due to misconceptions at the level of substantive law—specifically the interplay of substantive law and conflicts law, or choice of law.

One problem is the distortive positioning of substantive unfair competition law between the sectors of private law and economic, or regulatory, law. Theory and practice still primarily define unfair competition prevention as part of tort law and delicts protecting individual rights rather than as a sector of regulatory policies aimed at protecting market information infrastructure. This improper classification on the basis of an obsolete fundament necessarily also prevents a correct assessment of the relationship between policies of trademark protection and unfair competition prevention. Rather than explaining the two fields on the basis of their widely overlapping policies as part of a largely uniform and homogeneous sector of regulatory law, current doctrine differentiates between trademark "rights" protection and unfair competition "conduct" prevention. This misperceived trademark/unfair competition dichotomy accounts for a common sweeping explanation of trademark protection as a subdomain of intellectual property law in general rather than as a facet of economic regulation with a special focus on market information. Terminology is revealing: intellectual property—like *propriété intellectuelle* or *geistiges Eigentum*[1]—implies the existence of a comprehensive concept of unitary rights. This is where fallacy looms, particularly with respect to trademarks and trademark conflicts. While the law does protect many different products of human creativity, innovation, and labor, there is no uniform or comprehensive structure of immaterial rights. And since there is no uniformity of substantive law policies, no uniform choice-of-law doctrine exists. For trademark and unfair competition conflicts law and choice of law, this necessarily means that neither the traditional doctrine of international tort law nor the old-age formalism of intellectual property territoriality can provide for consistent rules of conflicts attachment.

Before I try to correct these issues related to conflicts resolution, however, I will take a closer look at substantive law doctrine in the fields of tort law, unfair competition and trademark law, the remainder of intellectual and industrial property law, and antitrust law. Although the debate has come a long way, the vast majority of arguments and explanations put forward have failed to adequately discuss the most distinctive feature: the fields' core policy aimed at protecting the market information infrastructure. Correct information transmission and processing within the marketplace is the most essential condition for an unmanipulated consumer decision making as the quintessence of market mechanics. The theoretical underpinnings of economic competition and the consumer's function as a referee in competition will thus be my starting point for the analysis (*see infra* p. 275 *et seq.*). As this will highlight, the concept of unmanipulated consumer decision making stands at the center of both trademark and unfair competition policies. Only in light of this tenet can a topography of substantive law policies succeed. In order to highlight the demarcations between different sectors of private law and economic regulatory law, I will start with a delineation of tort and unfair competition policies. In addition, I will take a closer look at the integral distinction between different "rights" in the field of intellectual property and will illustrate that antitrust law is a segment of economic regulatory law that must be distinguished from unfair competition and trademark law. On this basis, I will conclude by describing trademark and unfair competition law as a sector of widely overlapping policies aimed at the protection of market information infrastructure (*see infra* p. 295 *et seq.* and p. 348 *et seq.*).

[1] For the terminology (and the shift toward propertization), *see, e.g.*, Andreas Heinemann, *Immaterialgüterschutz in der Wettbewerbsordnung—Eine grundlagenorientierte Untersuchung zum Kartellrecht des geistigen Eigentums* 2 *et seq.* (2002).

Section 1 Foundations—The Market Mechanism

As we have seen so far, for both trademark and unfair competition law, the issue of marketplace determination is essential.[2] The question is inseparably connected with the notion of competition. My analysis will therefore start by exploring the economic and legal foundations of competition in a market economy.

I The Concept of "Economic Competition"

While, for instance, the nature and characteristics of "property" have been debated from the beginning of legal thinking, the notion of "competition" has become an object of legal analysis only relatively recently, in the late nineteenth century.[3] It is thus not too surprising that legal theories on competition are far from being fully developed. But it is not only the fact that ideas in the field still need more analysis and debate. The problem is more fundamental: economic concepts can seldom be comprehensively and convincingly explained in legal terms and with the traditional conceptions developed by lawyers. In most cases, their implementation needs a modification, if not alteration, of legal terminology and concepts. Looking for a solid reconceptualization therefore requires stepping outside the boundaries of traditional legal methodology. This is particularly important for an analysis of trademark and unfair competition law: at their core, both fields are concerned with decision making and transacting among consumers and other market participants. What matters are the microdynamics of market transacting—dynamics that are situated within an overall order of competition.

A The Legal Framework

Individual freedom is the centerpiece of a competitive order.[4] It thus also functions as the pacemaker of the market economy. Here, the law already comes into play: only if the legal backdrop of constitutional, public, and private law allows for economic activities to freely evolve will the market mechanism function unhinderedly.[5] Most basically, the degree of freedom and the corresponding characterization of the economy is an issue of

[2] *See supra* chapter 3 *passim*. [3] *See supra* chapters 1 and 2 *passim*.

[4] *See, e.g.*, Restatement of the Law—Unfair Competition (Third), § 1, comment a (1995) ("The freedom to engage in business and to compete for the patronage of prospective customers is a fundamental premise of the free enterprise system.").

[5] *See also* Ernst-Joachim Mestmäcker, *Der verwaltete Wettbewerb—Eine vergleichende Untersuchung über den Schutz von Freiheit und Lauterkeit im Wettbewerbsrecht* 78 *et seq.*, 83 (1984); Franz Böhm, *Wettbewerb und Monopolkampf—Eine Untersuchung zur Frage des wirtschaftlichen Kampfrechts und zur Frage der rechtlichen Struktur der geltenden Wirtschaftsordnung* 302 (1933).

constitutional law. An institutional order of competition results from the overall structure of civil rights protection and general regulatory legislation.[6] From such a macroperspective, we can identify different scenarios of the competitive order: market economies, social market economies, and socialist or communist state-directed economies.[7] In addition, a macroperspective may look at the structure of markets or, more concretely, the *status* of competition. It then provides a more specific snapshot of competitive relations. This is the primary domain of antitrust law. The allocation of power within a certain market may be characterized as a monopoly, oligopoly, polypoly, or any combination or variant thereof. With respect to trademark and unfair competition law, however, these macrostructures are only indirectly relevant. It is not the idea of competition as a constitutional or static order, but as a concrete description of market activity, that matters. The subject matter of protection, therefore, is a dynamic and individualized phenomenon—it is the evolution of competition within the macrostructures. Accordingly, any analysis of trademark and unfair competition policies requires a specific microperspective: it must focus on individual market participants and their transacting in the market.

B The Rediscovery of Chaos

There is consensus that competition is largely beneficial per se.[8] However, this is as far as the consensus goes. Despite innumerable

[6] *See also* Walter R. Schluep, *Was ist Wirtschaftsrecht?*, 25, 78, in *Festschrift für Walther Hug zum 70. Geburtstag* (Riccardo L. Jagmetti & Walter R. Schluep eds., 1968); Walter R. Schluep, *Allgemeines Wirtschaftsrecht und Schweizerisches Kartellgesetz*, 569, 574, in *Wirtschaftsordnung und Staatsverfassung—Festschrift für Franz Böhm zum 80. Geburtstag* (Heinz Saubermann & Ernst-Joachim Mestmäcker eds., 1975); *see also* BVerfGE vol. 4, 7, 17—*Investitionshilfe* (20 July 1954); BVerfG 1972 NJW 573, 573—*Grabsteinwerbung* (8 February 1972). For the 1986 Swiss Unfair Competition Act (UWG), this has been explicitly expressed by lawmakers: "Schutzobjekt ist . . . der freie und lautere Wettbewerb als eine der wesentlichsten Grundlagen unserer Wirtschaftsverfassung . . . ." (Botschaft zu einem Bundesgesetz gegen den unlauteren Wettbewerb (UWG), 18 May 1983, Bundesblatt (BBl.) 1983 II 1009, 1038).

[7] Walter Eucken was the first to promulgate a categorial foundation for Germany. *See, e.g.*, Walter Eucken, *Die Wettbewerbsordnung und ihre Verwirklichung*, 2 ORDO 1, 19 *et seq.* (1949).

[8] *See, e.g.*, Josef Kohler, *Der unlautere Wettbewerb—Darstellung des Wettbewerbsrechts* 18 (1914) ("Keiner hat im Verkehr ein Anrecht darauf, daß sein Geschäft gedeiht, und das individualistische System unserer Zeit beruht gerade darauf, daß jeder mit seinen wirtschaftlichen Kräften sich bestrebt, das Beste zu erreichen und dadurch das kaufende Publikum zu gewinnen. Dadurch soll die Kraft der Nation aufs höchste gesteigert, Produktion und Handel zur höchsten Blüte gebracht werden. Jeder soll seinen Egoismus anspannen, um zu leisten, was er leisten kann; er soll Tag und Nacht auf Verbesserung sinnen, um dadurch sein Geschäft empor zu bringen und den Gegner aus dem Felde zu schlagen."); for the United States, *see, e.g.*, Restatement of the Law—Unfair Competition (Third), § 1, comment a (1995).

attempts to define economic competition,[9] there is still no universally accepted definition. Neither economic nor legal theories have been able to comprehensively explain the functions of competition in a market economy or to address the complexity of the market mechanism.[10]

"Perfect competition" was the paradigm of early twentieth-century theory.[11] A market with perfect competition is the antithesis of a monopoly market. It requires a maximum number of participants on both the supply and the demand side, a homogeneity and substitutability of products, a uniformity of prices, and a lack of entry barriers to the market.[12] But it is questionable to assume that each market will and should consist of a plentitude of market participants (suppliers and consumers) and that all participants will always act rationally. Indeed, this model is unrealistic for a number of reasons[13] and, in the 1930s, began to lose its ground to new paradigms of competition policy. The most contrary and influential

[9] For legal theory in Germany, *see, e.g.*, Knut Borchardt & Wolfgang Fikentscher, *Wettbewerb, Wettbewerbsbeschränkung, Marktbeherrschung* (1957); Wolfgang Fikentscher, *Wettbewerb und gewerblicher Rechtsschutz—Die Stellung des Rechts der Wettbewerbsbeschränkungen in der Rechtsordnung* 39 (1958); Robert Knöpfle, *Der Rechtsbegriff „Wettbewerb" und die Realität des Wirtschaftslebens* (1966); Otto Sandrock, *Grundbegriffe des Gesetzes gegen Wettbewerbsbeschränkungen* (1968); Jürgen F. Baur, *Das Tatbestandsmerkmal „Wettbewerb,"* 134 ZHR 97 (1970); for an overview on recent doctrine, *see, e.g.*, Helmut Köhler, in Helmut Köhler & Joachim Bornkamm, *Gesetz gegen den unlauteren Wettbewerb*, Einl UWG para. 1.6 (33rd edn., 2015).

[10] Indeed, it has been suggested that a concise and comprehensive definition of the concept for legal theory may be impossible. *See, e.g.*, Jürgen F. Baur, *Das Tatbestandsmerkmal „Wettbewerb,"* 134 ZHR 97, 116, 150 (1970); Peter Ulmer, *Der Begriff „Leistungswettbewerb" und seine Bedeutung für die Anwendung von GWB und UWG-Tatbeständen*, 1977 GRUR 565, 567; Fritz Rittner, *Über das Verhältnis von Vertrag und Wettbewerb*, 188 AcP 101, 119 (1988); Stefan Koos, *Europäischer Lauterkeitsmaßstab und globale Integration—Beitrag zu einer weltmarktorientierten Sichtweise des nationalen und gemeinschaftlichen Wettbewerbsrechts* 7 (1996); Susy Frankel, *Unfair Competition Law—"Over Protection Stifles the Very Creative Force it is Supposed to Nurture,"* 267, 271, in *International Intellectual Property and the Common Law World* (Charles Rickett & Graeme Austin eds., 2000).

[11] For a first conception, *see* F.H. Knight, *Cost of Production and Price over Long and Short Periods*, 29 J. Pol. Econ. 304 (1921). Concepts of "perfect" and "pure" competition have differred in ways that are not relevant here. *See, e.g.*, Erich Hoppmann, *Workable Competition als wettbewerbspolitisches Konzept*, 145, 151–152, in *Theoretische und institutionelle Grundlagen der Wirtschaftspolitik: Theodor Wessels zum 65. Geburtstag* (Hans Albert et al. eds., 1967).

[12] Details vary and numerous definitions exist. For a concise summary, *see, e.g.*, Wolfgang Fikentscher, *Wirtschaftsrecht, vol. II: Deutsches Wirtschaftsrecht* § 22 III 3a (1983); Axel Beater, *Unlauterer Wettbewerb* § 2 para. 124 (2011).

[13] For an instructive debate on economics, law, and terminology in the legal context, *see, e.g.*, Knut Borchardt & Wolfgang Fikentscher, *Wettbewerb, Wettbewerbsbeschränkung, Marktbeherrschung* 1 *et seq.* (1957); Jürgen F. Baur, *Das Tatbestandsmerkmal „Wettbewerb,"* 134 ZHR 97, 100 *et seq.* (1970); more recently, *see, e.g.*, Otto-Friedrich Freiherr von Gamm, *Wettbewerbsrecht, vol. I*, ch. 1 para. 9 (5th edn., 1987); Inge Scherer, *Privatrechtliche Grenzen der Verbraucherwerbung* 24–25 (1996); Colin Scott & Julia Black, *Cranston's Consumers and the Law* 30 *et seq.* (3rd edn., 2000).

concept at the time was the model of "workable competition," conceived by John Maurice Clark.[14] Workable competition, he explained, is not a state of perfect competition. Nonetheless, it can still provide the foundation for a satisfactory and beneficial functioning of the market mechanism. Products may be heterogeneous, prices may vary, and market entry barriers may exist. And still, this kind of competition, "with all its defects—and these are serious—is better than the 'pure and perfect' norm, because it makes for progress."[15] Hence, workable competition, sometimes also called "monopolistic" or "effective" competition,[16] can contain elements of a monopoly market while still fostering economic progress.[17] The concept of workable competition, however, soon also came under attack for its rather static perspective. Clark had begun to stress the elements of progress and dynamics in his later works on the issue. Over time, it became questionable whether the *status* of competition in a specific marketplace was necessarily determinative for individual transacting and the overall development of competition. As suggested, for example, by Erich Hoppmann in the 1960s, the intensity of competition within a marketplace would not necessarily result from or be affected by the structures of market power or market shares: debates on static functions and on the quality of rivalry in competition are useless as long as the dynamics of competition are ignored.[18]

[14] A situation of workable competition in a certain market will not provide a perfectly competitive market. Certain inefficiencies must be accepted due to their beneficial effects for cost development and innovation. *See, e.g.*, J.M. Clark, *Toward a Concept of Workable Competition*, 30 Am. Econ. Rev. 241 (1940).

[15] In addition, as he described in his later modified concept, giving more regard to the dynamic aspect of competition, "Some departures from 'pure and perfect' competition are not only inseparable from progress, but necessary to it. The theory of effective competition is dynamic theory." J.M. Clark, *Competition As a Dynamic Process* ix (1961).

[16] *See* Edward Hastings Chamberlin, *The Theory of Monopolistic Competition—A Re-Orientation of the Theory of Value* (7th edn., 1956); J.M. Clark, *Toward a Concept of Workable Competition*, 30 Am. Econ. Rev. 241 (1940); J.M. Clark, *Imperfect Competition Theory and Basing-Point Problems*, 33 Am. Econ. Rev. 283 (1943); J.M. Clark, *Competition as a Dynamic Process* ix (1961) ("I am shifting the emphasis from 'workable' to 'effective competition' . . . ."); for Germany, *see* Wolfgang Fikentscher, *Wettbewerb und gewerblicher Rechtsschutz—Die Stellung des Rechts der Wettbewerbsbeschränkungen in der Rechtsordnung* 36–37 (1958); Jürgen F. Baur, *Das Tatbestandsmerkmal „Wettbewerb,"* 134 ZHR 97, 102 (1970).

[17] For the theory of workable competition in German scholarship, *see* Erhard Kantzenbach, *Die Funktionsfähigkeit des Wettbewerbs* 32 *et seq.* (2nd edn., 1967). More recent commentary can be found in Thomas C. Arthur, *The Costly Quest for Perfect Competition: Kodak and Nonstructural Market Power*, 69 N.Y.U. L. Rev. 1 (1994). For modern European unfair competition law and the paradigm of establishing workable competition in the marketplace, *see, e.g.*, Hans-W. Micklitz, in Norbert Reich & Hans-W. Micklitz, *Europäisches Verbraucherrecht* 438–439 (4th edn., 2003).

[18] *See, e.g.*, Erich Hoppmann, *Das Konzept der optimalen Wettbewerbsintensität—Rivalität oder Freiheit des Wettbewerbs: Zum Problem eines wettbewerbspolitisch adäquaten Ansatzes der Wettbewerbstheorie*, 179 JBNSt 286, 302 *et seq.*, 305 *et seq.* (1966); Erich Hoppmann,

Emphasizing these dynamics established an evolutionary concept of competition.

The gist of this concept has been captured most fittingly in Friedrich A. von Hayek's model of the market mechanism as a process of discovery. Under this model, markets are evolutionary chaos:[19] it is impossible to pay sufficient attention to all available information. Yet the transmission of information is at the core of competition. Individual decisions will therefore rarely ever be perfect in the sense of economic rationality. Nonetheless, the results of an ideally functioning market mechanism will be approximated if individual activity is allowed to develop spontaneously and on the basis of a principally unhindered flow of information. This free and dynamic process was already present in Adam Smith's understanding of the economy and his allegory of the invisible hand. Its conceptual parallel is the modern characterization of the market mechanism and competition as a self-regulating system.[20] For Smith, market participants' freedom to transact was vital.[21] Hayek extended and modified this concept of freedom into a general model of order for many different contexts. Accordingly, competition is a process of constant and repeated discovery in which individual participants promote progress

Workable Competition als wettbewerbspolitisches Konzept, 145, 180 and *passim*, in *Theoretische und institutionelle Grundlagen der Wirtschaftspolitik: Theodor Wessels zum 65. Geburtstag* (Hans Albert et al. eds., 1967). For process dynamics and a contemporary critique of the static perspective, *see* Rudolf Lukes, *Zum Verständnis des Wettbewerbs und des Marktes in der Denkkategorie des Rechts*, 199, 216 *et seq.*, in *Wirtschaftsordnung und Rechtsordnung: Festschrift zum 70. Geburtstag von Franz Böhm am 16. Febr. 1965* (Helmut Coing et al. eds., 1965).

19 This has of course also been a finding in Joseph Schumpeter's work. His concept of the market mechanism as a process of continuous innovation and creative destruction laid the foundation for the rediscovery of an evolutionary concept. *See, e.g.*, Joseph A. Schumpeter, *Theorie der wirtschaftlichen Entwicklung—Eine Untersuchung über Unternehmergewinn, Kapital, Kredit, Zins und den Konjunkturzyklus* 88 *et seq.*, 93 *et seq.* (2nd edn., 1926); Joseph A. Schumpeter, *Capitalism, Socialism, and Democracy* (2nd edn., 1947). For Clark's foundation on Schumpeter, *see* Erich Hoppmann, *Workable Competition als wettbewerbspolitisches Konzept*, 145, 153 n. 29, in *Theoretische und institutionelle Grundlagen der Wirtschaftspolitik: Theodor Wessels zum 65. Geburtstag* (Hans Albert et al. eds., 1967).

20 *See* Friedrich A. von Hayek, *Der Wettbewerb als Entdeckungsverfahren*, 3, 10, in *Kieler Vorträge gehalten am Institut für Weltwirtschaft an der Universität Kiel* (Erich Schneider ed., 1968); Friedrich A. von Hayek, *Bemerkungen über die Entwicklung von Systemen von Verhaltensregeln*, 144 *et seq.*, in *Freiburger Studien: Gesammelte Aufsätze* (Friedrich A. von Hayek, 1969) (on the evolutionary aspect of social behavior). *See also* Franz Böhm, *Freiheit und Ordnung in der Marktwirtschaft*, 22 ORDO 11, 18 (1971). With reference to Niklas Luhmann's 1986 work, *Ökologische Kommunikation*, and beyond, *see* Michael Lehmann, *Das Prinzip Wettbewerb*, 1990 JZ 61, 63.

21 *See, e.g.*, Adam Smith, *An Inquiry into the Nature and Causes of the Wealth of Nations, vol. I*, ch. 7 (1776).

and innovation through trial, error, and correction of their conduct on the basis of prior experience.[22]

C The Dynamics of Competition

The rediscovery of the chaotic nature of economic competition was the first crucial step toward modernization. The second step, particularly important for trademark and unfair competition law, was the description of competition as a process of two-tiered sequential transacting.

1 A Tradition of Competitor Protection

Early theoretical definitions of unfair competition referred only to the offer side of the market. Their focus, hence, was on the vulnerability of one competitor to the other.[23] This lopsidedness was also implemented in early court practice, which generally found competition to be an attempt to foster one's own enterprise at the expense of other enterprises.[24] Scholarly commentary throughout the first part of the twentieth century adopted the same perspective.[25] The Bundesgerichtshof's early

[22] *See, e.g.*, Friedrich A. von Hayek, *Der Wettbewerb als Entdeckungsverfahren*, 3, 3, 7 *et seq.*, 10, in *Kieler Vorträge gehalten am Institut für Weltwirtschaft an der Universität Kiel* (Erich Schneider ed., 1968). On the "fragmentation of knowledge," *see* Friedrich A. von Hayek, *Law, Legislation and Liberty, vol. I: Rules and Order* 11 *et seq.* (1973). For a detailed view of von Hayek's foundations, *see* Manfred E. Streit, *Wissen, Wettbewerb und Wirtschaftsordnung—Zum Gedenken an Friedrich August von Hayek*, 43 ORDO 1, 12 *et seq.* (1992); on the so-called Ordoliberal School in Germany, *see* Andreas Heinemann, *Die Freiburger Schule und ihre geistigen Wurzeln* 18 *et seq.* (1989).

[23] *See, e.g.*, Josef Kohler, *Der unlautere Wettbewerb—Darstellung des Wettbewerbsrechts* 17 (1914) ("Jeder soll seinen Egoismus anspannen, um zu leisten, was er leisten kann; er soll Tag und Nacht auf Verbesserung sinnen, um dadurch sein Geschäft empor zu bringen und den Gegner aus dem Felde zu schlagen. Ein jeder ist daher der vernichtenden Tätigkeit eines einsichtsvolleren und wirtschaftliche mächtigeren Wettbewerbers preisgegeben ....") and Adolf Lobe's famous explanation of competition in terms of sports in *Die Bekämpfung des unlauteren Wettbewerbs, vol. I: Der unlautere Wettbewerb als Rechtsverletzung* 8 (1907) ("Gesetzt, es findet ein Wettrudern statt. Wollte sich hierbei eine Partei ausserdem noch heimlich der treibenden Kraft eines versteckten Motors bedienen, so wäre das auf ihrer Seite zweifellos ein unlauteres Wettrudern."). *See also* Eugen Ulmer, *Sinnzusammenhänge im modernen Wettbewerbsrecht—Ein Beitrag zum Aufbau des Wettbewerbsrechts* 11 (1932).

[24] *See, e.g.*, RGSt vol. 58, 429, 430 (1 December 1924); RGZ vol. 134, 342, 351 *et seq.*—*Benrather Tankstelle* (18 December 1931).

[25] *See, e.g.*, Alfred Rosenthal, *Wettbewerbsgesetz nebst den materiellen Vorschriften des Warenzeichengesetzes systematisch erläutert, Kommentar, "Begriffsbestimmungen"* 2 (7th edn., 1928) ("Wettbewerb im wirtschaftlichen Sinne ist der Kampf mehrerer, mindestens zweier Personen (oder Personengruppen), von denen die eine vor der anderen einen Vorrang anstrebt."); Wolfgang Hefermehl, *Der Anwendungsbereich des Wettbewerbsrechts*, 283, 290, in *Festschrift für Hans Carl Nipperdey zum 60. Geburtstag* (Rolf Dietz et al. eds., 1955); Kamen Troller, *Das internationale Privatrecht des unlauteren Wettbewerbs in vergleichender Darstellung der Rechte Deutschlands, Englands, Frankreichs, Italiens, der Schweiz und der USA* 5 (1962); Robert Knöpfle, *Der Rechtsbegriff „Wettbewerb" und die Realität des Wirtschaftslebens* 81 *et seq.* (1966).

adjudication in the second half of the century also began with a restricted focus that saw competition as an invasion of customer relations and of a competitor's goodwill in order to divert business for the invader's own benefit.[26] But this perspective has changed over time. In modern scholarly commentary, Wolfgang Fikentscher's definition has remained an evergreen reference for the extended conception.[27] He described competition as the autonomous striving of competitors (whether supplying or demanding) to conclude transactions with third parties (customers) by advertising contractual terms and conditions in as beneficial a manner as possible. In addition, he stressed that competitors can and will affect one another through their market conduct.[28] This aspect is also key to this inquiry: over time, the perspective has changed from one focused on competitors alone to one that considers both sides of the market—in other words, one that gives regard to consumers and other market participants.

2 *The Advent of (Consumer) Decision Making*

Even though the perspective has been extended beyond mere intercompetitor relations, many definitions of competition still place little emphasis on the most determinative stage of the market mechanism: participants' decision making and transacting. Only if the actual transaction remains unmanipulated can individual decision making fulfill its function as the quantum part of the market economy. Accordingly, any legal conception of regulating competition must give regard not only to pretransactional conduct but also to the implementation of parties' decision making as the final stage of the competitive process.

As discussed earlier, European nineteenth-century doctrine of trademark protection largely excluded consumer interests from the field of

[26] *See* BGHZ vol. 19, 392, 396—*Freiburger Wochenbericht* (27 January 1956); BGHZ vol. 23, 365, 370—*SUWA* (22 February 1957); BGHZ vol. 51, 236, 242—*Stuttgarter Wochenblatt I* (18 December 1968).

[27] For a recent approval, *see, e.g.*, Matthias Leistner, in *Handbuch des Wettbewerbsrechts*, § 4 para. 20 (Michael Loschelder & Willi Erdmann eds., 4th edn., 2010).

[28] Wolfgang Fikentscher, *Wettbewerb und gewerblicher Rechtsschutz—Die Stellung des Rechts der Wettbewerbsbeschränkungen in der Rechtsordnung* 39 and 42 (1958) ("[W]ird daher der Wettbewerb ... definiert als das selbständige Streben sich objektiv gegenseitig im Wirtschaftserfolg beeinflussender Anbieter oder Nachfrager (Mitbewerber) nach Geschäftsverbindung mit Dritten (Kunden) durch Inaussichtstellen möglichst günstiger Geschäftsbedingungen." (*id.* at 39)); Wolfgang Fikentscher, *Neuere Entwicklungen der Theorie zum Tatbestandsmerkmal der Wettbewerbsbeschränkung* § 1 *GWB*, 1961 WuW 788, 798. For a modern reformulation, *see* Helmut Köhler, in Helmut Köhler & Joachim Bornkamm, *Gesetz gegen den unlauteren Wettbewerb*, Einl UWG para. 1.7 (33rd edn., 2015) ("Im Regelfall geht es um das Verhalten von Unternehmen, die auf einem bestimmten Markt unter Anwendung der verschiedensten Mittel (Aktionsparameter) zu Geschäftsabschlüssen mit Dritten (Kunden/Lieferanten) zu gelangen suchen.").

relevant considerations.[29] And the picture was not much different with respect to unfair competition prevention. Part of the debate surrounding the enactment of the 1896 and 1909 Unfair Competition Acts in Germany was whether unfair competition prevention would look only at competitors' concerns or whether it would also protect the concerns of consumers and the public. In the end, consumers' interests were deemed of secondary importance at best.[30] Even in the decades that followed, consumers and their functions within the marketplace only slowly became integrated into the conceptual framework of unfair competition policies. For most of the twentieth century, consumer protection was merely an instrument for determining the inadmissibility of competitive conduct vis-à-vis the competitor. Individual competitor protection was achieved by means of preventing consumer confusion; it was not an aim as such.[31]

Starting in the second half of the century, however, a genuine concern for consumer protection entered the stage in European unfair competition law.[32] The interest in free and fair competition sought to protect not only competitors but also—and above all—consumers. After all, the argument went, consumers were interested in optimal competition since it guarantees the best quality at the lowest prices.[33] At first, this interest led to a sweeping extension of consumer protection policies. More specifically, in 1975, the Council of the European Communities proclaimed

[29] *See supra* p. 24–27.

[30] *See, e.g.*, Otto von Gierke, *Der Rechtsgrund des Schutzes gegen unlauteren Wettbewerb*, 1895 GRUR (ZfGewRS) 109, 113; Gerhard Schricker, *Möglichkeiten zur Verbesserung des Schutzes der Verbraucher und des funktionsfähigen Wettbewerbs im Recht des unlauteren Wettbewerbs*, 139 ZHR 208, 213 (1975); Olaf Sosnitza, in *Münchener Kommentar zum Lauterkeitsrecht, vol. I*, § 1 UWG para. 3 *et seq.* (Peter W. Heermann et al. eds., 2nd edn., 2014) (with further references to the Reichsgericht's heterogeneous case law on the issue).

[31] *See, e.g.*, RGZ vol. 58, 281, 284–285—*Leinen garantiert vierfach* (17 June 1904); RG 1917 GRUR 125—*Unkosten* (30 March 1917); RGZ vol. 99, 23, 28—*Treuhänder* (23 April 1920); BGHZ vol. 13, 244, 253—*Cupresa-Seide* (11 March 1954); Hans Freiherr von Godin, *Wettbewerbsrecht, Kommentar zum Gesetz gegen den unlauteren Wettbewerb nebst Warenzeichenverletzungen, Zugabeverordnung und Rabattgesetz*, U § 1 para. 48 (2nd edn., 1974) ("Das Verbraucherinteresse zu wahren, war nicht die Aufgabe des Gesetzes, wie heute immer wieder fälschlich angenommen wird."); *see also* Axel Beater, *Verbraucherschutz und Schutzzweckdenken im Wettbewerbsrecht* 13 and 106–107 (2000) (with extensive illustration of the 1896 act's *travaux préparatoires*).

[32] *See, e.g.*, Colin Scott & Julia Black, *Cranston's Consumers and the Law* 292–293 (3rd edn., 2000) (for the United Kingdom); also Axel Beater, *Verbraucherschutz und Schutzzweckdenken im Wettbewerbsrecht* 14–15 (2000) (for Germany); for the effects of European law on German doctrine, *see* Hans-Wolfgang Micklitz, in *Münchener Kommentar zum Lauterkeitsrecht, vol. I*, EG D para. 5 *et seq.* (Peter W. Heermann et al. eds., 2nd edn., 2014).

[33] More recently, *see, e.g.*, BGH 2000 GRUR 521, 525—*Modulgerüst* (8 December 1999); Axel Beater, *Verbraucherschutz und Schutzzweckdenken im Wettbewerbsrecht* 122 *et seq.* (2000); Axel Beater, *Unlauterer Wettbewerb* § 14 para. 1084 (2011).

the paradigm of an "informed consumer."[34] And the Court of Justice implemented the idea through a "consumer information model" that was established in *Cassis-de-Dijon* and subsequent cases. Ever since, providing sufficient information to the consumer has become a means to facilitate the free movement of goods and services within the community market.[35] Protecting the consumer's informed decision making has thus gradually moved center stage.

At this point, an important caveat regarding the terms "consumer" and "consumer decision making" is in order. Any market transaction requires consideration of at least two sides of the market. Either side may consist of natural persons acting outside their trade or profession (usually termed "consumers") or professionals acting in an entrepreneurial or business function, including corporate entities. When looking at market transacting in general, however, the focus must be on the function, not the status, of the market participants involved. Yet for the sake of simplicity, I will use "consumer" and "consumer decision making" in order to illustrate that a market transaction concerns the "other side" of the market. This simplification does not, however, imply a limitation to transactions including natural persons.

3 *The Complementary Spheres of Transactional Freedom*

Against this backdrop, it is clear that two complementary spheres of participants' transacting exist. The starting point for competition is the entrepreneur's freedom to act and transact. Each competitor may autonomously decide on her activities. The freedom to conduct business is the most basic prerequisite for the formulation of a free market.[36] In addition,

[34] *See* Council of the European Communities, *Resolution of 14 April 1975 on a preliminary programme of the European Economic Community for a consumer protection and information policy*, O.J. EU (25 April 1975), No C 92/1; *further also* Council of the European Communities, *Resolution of 19 May 1981 on a second programme of the European Economic Community for a consumer protection and information policy*, O.J. EC (3 June 1981), No C 133/1; *see also* Holger Fleischer, *Vertragsschlußbezogene Informationspflichten im Gemeinschaftsprivatrecht*, 2000 ZEuP 772, 782; Wolfgang Schön, *Zwingendes Recht oder informierte Entscheidung—zu einer (neuen) Grundlage unserer Zivilrechtsordnung*, 1191, 1200, in *Festschrift für Claus-Wilhelm Canaris zum 70. Geburtstag* (Andreas Heldrich ed., 2007).

[35] *See Rewe v. Bundesmonopolverwaltung für Branntwein*, C-120/78 (20 February 1979), [1979] E.C.R. 649; *Pall v. Dahlhausen*, C-238/89 (13 December 1990), [1990] E.C.R. I-4827; *Verband Sozialer Wettbewerb v. Clinique Laboratoires and Estée Lauder*, C-315/92 (2 February 1994), [1994] E.C.R. I-317; *GB-INNO-BM v. Confédération du Commerce Luxembourgeois*, C-362/88 (7 March 1990), [1990] E.C.R. I-667; *Schutzverband gegen Unwesen i.d. Wirtschaft v. Rocher*, C-126/91 (18 May 1993), [1993] E.C.R. I-2361; *see also* Holger Fleischer, *Vertragsschlußbezogene Informationspflichten im Gemeinschaftsprivatrecht*, 2000 ZEuP 772, 782; Matthias Leistner, *Behavioural Economics und Lauterkeitsrecht*, 1 ZGE 3, 40–41 (2009).

[36] *See* Franz Böhm, *Wettbewerb und Monopolkampf—Eine Untersuchung zur Frage des wirtschaftlichen Kampfrechts und zur Frage der rechtlichen Struktur der geltenden*

on the consumer side of the market, the freedom of transacting complements the entrepreneur's freedom. This is the exact opposite of early twentieth-century theory explaining that "the public provides the ground upon which the competitors compete; the public is the instrument upon which the commercial actor plays."[37] Today, entrepreneurs' freedom and their activities provide the substrate for the consumer to effectuate her decision making. More drastically put, it is the consumer's decision that will both complement and complete the most essential element of the market mechanism. This is the gist of explanations of the consumer as the "referee" in competition and of consumer sovereignty as most fundamental.[38]

Seen in this light, it is clear that securing the consumer's freedom to transact has two basic prerequisites. Most generally, the consumer must be free to make the ultimate decision whether or not to transact. Prior to the decision, however, she must have access to optimal information. This is a more specific aspect of her freedom of decision making. Only if the consumer has complete and correct information on the relevant market parameters—particularly regarding quality, price, and available alternatives—can she execute a rational transaction. In this regard, the modern understanding of the market mechanisms is no longer based on the model of exchanging goods or services alone; rather, it is founded on a concept of information transmission.[39] It is these major phases of consumer decision making—the transmission and processing

Wirtschaftsordnung 302 (1933) ("Die möglichst vollkommene rechtstechnische Ausgestaltung und Ausstattung der Freiheits- und Herrschaftssphäre des Unternehmens ist eine der wichtigsten Vorbedingungen für das Funktionieren einer freien, kampfbeherrschten Verkehrswirtschaft."). More recently, *see, e.g.*, BGH 2009 GRUR 685, 689—*ahd.de* (19 February 2009); Peter Bülow, *Lauterkeitsrecht oder Unlauterkeitsrecht?*, 2012 GRUR 889, 890.

[37] *See* Rudolf Callmann, *Der unlautere Wettbewerb* 43 (2nd edn., 1932) ("Die Allgemeinheit gibt den Boden ab, auf dem sich die Mitbewerber begegnen; das Publikum ist das Instrument, auf dem der Gewerbetreibende spielt; . . . ." (author's translation)).

[38] For the concept of consumer-as-referee, *see, e.g.*, Colin Scott & Julia Black, *Cranston's Consumers and the Law* 8 *et seq.* (3rd edn., 2000); Hans W. Micklitz & Jürgen Keßler, *Europäisches Lauterkeitsrecht—Dogmatische und ökonomische Aspekte einer Harmonisierung des Wettbewerbsverhaltensrechts im europäischen Binnenmarkt*, 2002 GRUR Int. 885, 890. For an early explanation of the consumer's referee function, *see* Franz Böhm, *Wettbewerb und Monopolkampf—Eine Untersuchung zur Frage des wirtschaftlichen Kampfrechts und zur Frage der rechtlichen Struktur der geltenden Wirtschaftsordnung* 260 *et seq.* (1933) ("kampfrechtliche Schiedsrichterfunktion des freien Kunden").

[39] *See, e.g.*, Hans W. Micklitz & Jürgen Keßler, *Europäisches Lauterkeitsrecht—Dogmatische und ökonomische Aspekte einer Harmonisierung des Wettbewerbsverhaltensrechts im europäischen Binnenmarkt*, 2002 GRUR Int. 885, 889; Jürgen Keßler, *Vom Recht des unlauteren Wettbewerbs zum Recht der Marktkommunikation—Individualrechtliche und institutionelle Aspekte des deutschen und europäischen Lauterkeitsrechts*, 2005 WRP 1203, 1210 *et seq.*

of information, along with the subsequent transacting—that will guide my analysis.

II *The "Triangular" Structure of the Market Mechanism*

Looking at the two spheres of transactional freedom, it becomes obvious that different categories of regulatory policies can be at play when competition-related conduct is at issue. Figure 1 helps clarify this point. As mentioned above, my depiction of "consumers" does not imply that other market participants (e.g., commercial buyers or vendors) instead of consumers may not stand on the demand side of the market in a situation of competition between two or more market participants.

In the upper area of the figure—the horizontal level—a competitive relationship exists.[40] Freedom here requires that competitors be free from external restrictions resulting from state or private-party activities. A significant part of unfair competition doctrine concerns scenarios of restrictions of freedom among competitors.[41] This is the case, for

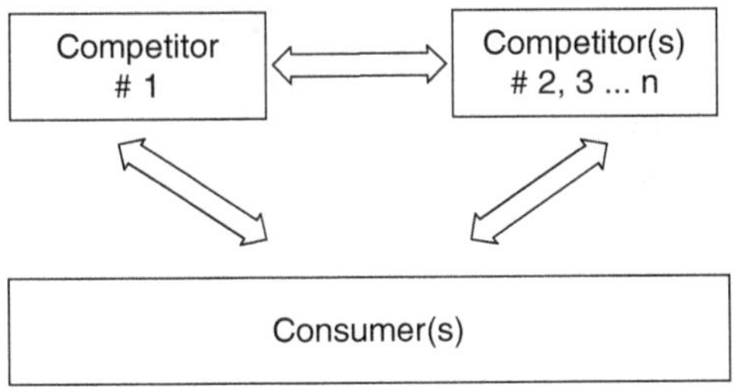

Figure 1 The "Triangular" Structure of the Market Mechanism

[40] For the distinction between horizontal and vertical relations, *see, e.g.*, Adair Dyer, *Unfair Competition in Private International Law*, 211 Recueil des Cours 373, 394 (1988-IV); Deutscher Bundestag, *Drucksache: Gesetzentwurf der Bundesregierung, Entwurf eines Ersten Gesetzes zur Änderung des Gesetzes gegen den unlauteren Wettbewerb*, 16. Wahlperiode, 16/10145 (20 August 2008), at 21; Axel Beater, *Unlauterer Wettbewerb* § 12 para. 901 (2011); *see also* Erich Hoppmann, *Zum Problem einer wirtschaftspolitisch praktikablen Definition des Wettbewerbs*, 9, 15 *et seq.*, in *Grundlagen der Wettbewerbspolitik, Schriften des Vereins für Socialpolitik, vol. 48* (Hans K. Schneider ed., 1968).

[41] WIPO has described these instances as a "direct attack on an individual competitor" (contrasting it with "surreptitious deception of the 'referee,' who in economic competition typically is the consumer"). *See* WIPO, *Protection against Unfair Competition—Analysis of the Present World Situation*, WIPO Publ. no. 725(E), 11 (1994). For deception of the "referee," *see infra* p. 287 *et seq.* Recitals 6 and 8 of the Unfair-Commercial Practices Directive provide a similar distinction. *See* Directive 2005/29/EC of the European Parliament and of the Council of 11 May 2005 concerning unfair business-to-consumer commercial practices in the internal market and amending Council Directive 84/450/EEC, Directives 97/7/EC, 98/27/EC and 2002/65/EC of the

instance, if a trade secret is stolen or if a competitor's business assets are destroyed. Strictly speaking, however, these instances of competition are not part of the core of process-oriented policies. They are devoid of an immediate influence on the market mechanism. Of course, many scenarios of direct hindrance to a competitor may completely cut off the market mechanism by isolating the victim-competitor from the competitive process. Such a situation thus necessarily comprises a factual reduction of the victim-competitor's sphere of activities. Yet there is no immediate effect on consumer decision making. This kind of anticompetitive effect is thus governed by the second category of unfair competition policies.

In the second category, limitation of competitor freedom ensues from conduct targeted primarily and directly toward the consumer. These limitations occur between the upper and the lower levels of the model, within the vertical relationship. There is no competition between competitors and consumers.[42] Nonetheless, their relationship is the pathway directly connected to the market mechanism. If a competitor addresses the consumer in order to execute a transaction, she will directly affect the consumer's freedom to transact, but at the same time, she will indirectly restrict her competitors' freedom to transact. This indirect relation among market participants on the upper level has also been laid out in the Unfair Commercial Practices (UCP) Directive.[43] While the directive's policy foundation ("purpose") in article 1 is centered on consumer protection,[44] its recitals explain that protecting consumer decision making also indirectly protects competitors' legitimate interests in competition.[45] Hence, what must remain untouched by external influences is consumer

European Parliament and of the Council and Regulation (EC) No 2006/2004 of the European Parliament and of the Council ("Unfair Commercial Practices Directive"), O.J. EU (11 June 2005), L 149/22.

[42] *See, e.g.*, Adair Dyer, *Unfair Competition in Private International Law*, 211 Recueil des Cours 373, 388 (1988-IV); Andrew Dickinson, *The Rome II Regulation: The Law Applicable to Non-Contractual Obligations* para. 6.05 (2008); Axel Beater, *Unlauterer Wettbewerb* § 12 para. 903 (2011).

[43] Directive 2005/29/EC of the European Parliament and of the Council of 11 May 2005 concerning unfair business-to-consumer commercial practices in the internal market and amending Council Directive 84/450/EEC, Directives 97/7/EC, 98/27/EC and 2002/65/EC of the European Parliament and of the Council and Regulation (EC) No 2006/2004 of the European Parliament and of the Council ("Unfair Commercial Practices Directive"), O.J. EU (11 June 2005), L 149/22.

[44] Article 1 reads: "The purpose of this Directive is to contribute to the proper functioning of the internal market and achieve a high level of consumer protection by approximating the laws, regulations and administrative provisions of the Member States on unfair commercial practices harming consumers' economic interests."

[45] *See* recital 6: "This Directive therefore approximates the laws of the Member States on unfair commercial practices, including unfair advertising, which directly harm consumers' economic interests and thereby indirectly harm the economic interests of legitimate competitors."

decision making. The consumer-as-referee must remain free to transact or not to transact, for consumer self-determination and sovereignty (*Konsumentensouveränität*) is the precondition of market efficiency.[46]

Before moving on, yet another clarification is necessary. As Figure 1 illustrates, the competitive process is actually not triangular but multi-angular. Each market transaction directly involves at least one party at the upper level and one at the lower level.[47] Of course, unless there is a monopoly on both sides of the market, there will be more parties involved. Almost always, the number of market participants on either side is much bigger. Yet in essence, the structure remains triangular: the consumer represents the decision maker choosing between two alternatives in the market.

III The Stages of Consumer Decision Making and Transacting

A casual look at the dichotomy between horizontal and vertical relations, particularly the emphasis accorded to the consumer's freedom of decision making, might imply that the distinction is merely an issue of consumer information—more specifically, the *transmission* of information. Such a perspective, however, would unduly restrict the analysis. Consumer transacting can be influenced and manipulated by more than misinformation. One example is the pressuring of a consumer. If a consumer is pressured, she may make a decision that she would not have made otherwise. Even though information may have been transmitted correctly, her transaction is the result of a restricted decision-making process. In such a case, the quality of pretransactional information and its transmission is not relevant. Therefore, in order to correctly assess the multiple possibilities of affecting the consumer's decision making, consumer behavior must be divided into stages.[48] First, the consumer collects information.

[46] *See also* Jürgen Keßler, *„Marktordnung, Wettbewerb und Meinungsfreiheit"—wettbewerbstheoretische und verfassungsrechtliche Aspekte des § 6e UWG*, 1987 WRP 75, 79; Jürgen Keßler, *Die umweltbezogene Aussage in der Produktwerbung—dogmatische und wettbewerbstheoretische Aspekte des Irreführungsverbots*, 1988 WRP 714, 716; Frauke Henning-Bodewig & Annette Kur, *Marke und Verbraucher—Funktionen der Marke in der Marktwirtschaft, vol. I: Grundlagen* 171 (1988). As to European unfair competition law, *see* Hans-W. Micklitz, in Norbert Reich & Hans-W. Micklitz, *Europäisches Verbraucherrecht* 439 (4th edn., 2003).

[47] Insofar, as I have explained *supra*, it does not make a difference whether the lower-level participant is a consumer or a commercially acting party.

[48] *See, e.g.*, Frauke Henning-Bodewig & Annette Kur, *Marke und Verbraucher—Funktionen der Marke in der Marktwirtschaft, vol. I: Grundlagen* 59 *et seq.* (1988); Michael Lehmann, Vertragsanbahnung durch Werbung—Eine juristische und ökonomische Analyse der bürgerlich-rechtlichen Haftung für Werbeangaben gegenüber dem Letztverbraucher 55 *et seq.* (1981); Inge Scherer, *Privatrechtliche Grenzen der Verbraucherwerbung* 69 *et seq.* (1996); Matthias Leistner, *Richtiger Vertrag und lauterer Wettbewerb—Eine grundlagenorientierte Studie unter besonderer Berücksichtigung der europäischen Perspektive* 133 *et seq.* (2007).

She then stores this information and processes it by comparing alternatives and eliminating unsuitable or less promising options. Ultimately, she implements the results of her information collecting and processing by concluding a transaction in the marketplace. The consumer's ultimate decision whether and how to transact—the principal subject matter of protection in trademark and unfair competition law—can be influenced during any stage of this process.

A Information Transmission

It is commonly understood that information transmission within the marketplace must be complete and undistorted. Yet even more fundamentally, a market-internal infrastructure of information transmission as such must exist. This problem has been well explored. George J. Stigler has addressed it as a central aspect of his theory of information economics.[49] As he explains, the market, in order to function, requires that its participants search for information. Stigler uses market prices as an example, but the principle applies universally: a market participant who wants to ascertain the most favorable conditions for her transaction must search for available options. While conditions of the ultimate transaction may improve with increased search efforts, the consumer will have to subtract her searching costs from the relative gains obtained from the transaction. This is the concept of search costs.[50] As Stigler goes on to explain, advertising is a method of providing information about market participants and market conditions; most optimistically, it is an "immensely powerful instrument for the elimination of ignorance—comparable in force to the use of the book instead of the oral discourse to communicate knowledge."[51] In essence, the effect of advertising is "equivalent to that of the introduction of a very large amount of search by a large portion of the potential buyers."[52] This theory has provided the foundation for today's understanding of market communication and the importance of information economization. A functioning system of information transmission—in other words, an infrastructure of market information—is essential for the marketplace to exist.

On a second level, the information transmitted through this infrastructure must be correct and truthful. This has been explained by George

[49] *See* George J. Stigler, *The Economics of Information*, 69 J. Pol. Econ. 213 (1961).

[50] *Id.* at 213. For further implications of information economics theory, *see, e.g.*, Kenneth J. Arrow, *Uncertainty and the Welfare Economics of Medical Care*, 53 Am. Econ. Rev. 941 (1963). For a general overview in the context of trademark and unfair competition doctrine, *see, e.g.*, Roger Van den Bergh & Michael Lehmann, *Informationsökonomie und Verbraucherschutz im Wettbewerbs- und Warenzeichenrecht*, 1992 GRUR Int. 588.

[51] George J. Stigler, *The Economics of Information*, 69 J. Pol. Econ. 213, 220 (1961).

[52] *Id.* at 224.

A. Akerlof, who illustrates the concept using the example of a used-car market, which features an asymmetry of information (a "market for lemons"). Usually, sellers have better and more knowledge than customers regarding the true value of a used car. But chances are high that sellers will not share this additional information with customers. This leads to bad deals for the buyers: because they cannot distinguish between cars on the basis of quality, they may therefore pay the same price for a good car as for a bad one (the latter being the proverbial "lemon"). Over time, then, if complete and correct information remains unavailable to consumers, the quality of products within a market will deteriorate. After all, sellers have no incentive to provide quality products if suboptimal quality guarantees the same return. Since buyers will increasingly avoid transacting in this market, it will ultimately vanish.[53] The ensuing costs of dishonesty have two components: the costs paid by cheated purchasers and the losses on behalf of the public resulting from the nonexistence of a market for quality products.[54] Protecting truthfulness in market information, therefore, has both individual and public aspects.

In order to overcome this informational asymmetry, the consumer has two resources. First, she can rely on existing information. This is the body of information developed by her own or other consumers' experiences. Existing information may also consist of information provided by intermediaries or authorities (e.g., product-testing information). In legal terms, this sort of information is transmitted through the product's or a competitor's market goodwill.[55] Second, the consumer can look to advertising as a source of newly created information.[56] This is information transmission beyond the goodwill mechanism; it need not rely on existing information within the marketplace. Together, both categories make up the "market language."[57] In general terms, therefore, market

[53] George A. Akerlof, *The Market for "Lemons": Quality Uncertainty and the Market Mechanism*, 84 Quarterly J. Econ. 488 *et seq.*, 495 (1970). For information asymmetries, *see also* Joseph E. Stiglitz, *Information and the Change in the Paradigm in Economics*, 92 Am. Econ. Rev. 460, 466 *et seq.*, 470 *et seq.* (2002).

[54] George A. Akerlof, *The Market for "Lemons": Quality Uncertainty and the Market Mechanism*, 84 Quarterly J. Econ. 488, 495 (1970).

[55] Howard Beales, Richard Craswell & Steven C. Salop, *The Efficient Regulation of Consumer Information*, 24 J. L. & Econ. 491, 493 and 501 *et seq.* (1981).

[56] Roger Van den Bergh & Michael Lehmann, *Informationsökonomie und Verbraucherschutz im Wettbewerbs- und Warenzeichenrecht*, 1992 GRUR Int. 588, 591–592.

[57] For the concept and terminology of market language, *see, e.g.*, Stephen L. Carter, *The Trouble with Trademark*, 99 Yale L.J. 759, 763 (1990); for an extended concept in trademark doctrine, *see* Rochelle Cooper Dreyfuss, *Expressive Genericity: Trademarks as Language in the Pepsi Generation*, 65 Notre Dame L. Rev. 397, 397 (1990).

language identifies sellers, buyers, prices, and product quality—parameters and conditions that are important for economically rational decision making. Market language—its existence and truthfulness—is the essence of every marketplace. It actually *is* the marketplace.[58]

B Information Processing

In addition to collecting market information, the consumer must also properly process the information in order to transact rationally. The outcome of decision making will depend both on the quality of information that has been transmitted and gathered, and on the decision-making process as such. In addition to manipulating market information, competitors can thus also try to exert an impact that is not based on incorrect information content but that affects the subsequent processing of information. This category of manipulation, although still within the reign of unfair competition prevention, is not necessarily governed by trademark law.[59]

Indeed, modern legal instruments for unfair competition also distinguish between an outright distortion of market information and other kinds of impact on consumer decision making. The UCP Directive,[60] for instance, separates "misleading" (arts. 6 and 7) and "aggressive" commercial practices (arts. 8 and 9). A commercial practice is regarded as misleading "if it contains false information and is therefore untruthful or in any way, including overall presentation, deceives or is likely to deceive the average consumer, even if the information is factually correct."[61] Quite differently, an aggressive commercial practice is not necessarily founded on information transmission. On the contrary, the focus is oriented toward the consumer's last stage of transacting. Article 8 explains a practice to be considered aggressive if,

[58] *See* Wolfgang Fikentscher, *Wirtschaftsrecht, vol. I: Weltwirtschaftsrecht, Europäisches Wirtschaftsrecht* § 1 I 11 (1983) ("Der Markt ist die Gesamtheit der Dialoge über wirtschaftliche Werte untereinander austauschbarer Güter. Für die Dialoge über wirtschaftliche Werte ist dabei die grundsätzliche Freiheit erforderlich, diese Dialoge zu führen. Das Ergebnis der Meinungsfreiheit, wirtschaftlich betrachtet, heißt Markt."). For a general explanation in the traditional terms of unfair competition doctrine, *see* WIPO, *Protection against Unfair Competition—Analysis of the Present World Situation*, WIPO Publ. no. 725(E), 37 (1994).

[59] *See* Mark P. McKenna, *A Consumer Decision-Making Theory of Trademark Law*, 98 Va. L. Rev. 67, 85 (2012). For the exact demarcations, *see infra* p. 359 *et seq.*

[60] Directive 2005/29/EC of the European Parliament and of the Council of 11 May 2005 concerning unfair business-to-consumer commercial practices in the internal market and amending Council Directive 84/450/EEC, Directives 97/7/EC, 98/27/EC and 2002/65/EC of the European Parliament and of the Council and Regulation (EC) No 2006/2004 of the European Parliament and of the Council ("Unfair Commercial Practices Directive"), O.J. EU (11 June 2005), L 149/22.

[61] *See* article 6 para. 1. "Misleading omissions" are defined in article 7.

in its factual context, taking account of all its features and circumstances, by harassment, coercion, including the use of physical force, or undue influence, it significantly impairs or is likely to significantly impair the average consumer's freedom of choice or conduct.

Examples of such manipulation can be found in annex I of the directive. According to number 30 of the so-called black list, for instance, a practice is considered unfair when a competitor "[e]xplicitly inform[s] a consumer that if he does not buy the product or service, the trader's job or livelihood will be in jeopardy." Information on the product or service may be correct; ultimately, however, this practice might affect the transaction by appealing to the addressee's feelings of sympathy. Since this kind of "ancillary information" is apt to pressure the consumer, it is considered an aggressive practice.[62] Of course, the directive's black-listed scenarios do not necessarily require an actual distortion of consumer behavior. Yet, as the example illustrates, some of these scenarios are apt to create a risk of undue impact beyond the actual content of essential product information. This is manipulation of the consumer's decision making on an intermediary level—between information transmission and final transacting. With regard to the importance of freedom of competition, both the protection of decision-making economization on the basis of correct information *and* the prevention of subsequent improper information processing have the same function.

C Implementation of the Consumer's Decision

Finally, there is a last stage of the decision-making process that is often neglected: the consumer's free implementation of her decision in the marketplace. Her decision-making process may be flawless and unmanipulated, and the outcome may be economically rational, but the market mechanism will still be distorted if her decision's final implementation is affected. Quite often, manipulation of this last stage cannot and need not be distinguished from improper impact on the processing. Take, for example, the case where consumers are physically prevented from entering a business's premises in order to divert them to another's business.[63] According to the definition in article 8 of the UCP Directive, this is an aggressive practice. There need not be an effect on information transmission or processing. Instead, the simple execution of the consumer's decision (i.e., its implementation in the market) is being frustrated. Like an improper impact on earlier stages,

[62] *See, e.g.*, Helmut Köhler, in Helmut Köhler & Joachim Bornkamm, *Gesetz gegen den unlauteren Wettbewerb*, Anh zu § 3 III UWG para. 30.1 (33rd edn., 2015).

[63] *See also* no. 24 and 25 in Annex I of the Unfair Commercial Practices Directive.

invasion of the final stage of the transaction process invalidates the entire mechanism.

Notwithstanding general acknowledgment of the consumer's referee function, the protection of her decision making is regularly limited to the mere preservation of information correctness and processing. The question of where a transaction is or would have been implemented is then simply overlooked. As a result, particularly in choice of law, the place of impact on information correctness or processing—and not the place where the consumer will actually effectuate or would have effectuated her decision through a market transaction—is deemed to matter as a point of attachment. One example is illustrative here: as the leading practitioners' legal commentary on the German Unfair Competition Act (UWG) explains, submitting an offer to the consumer (e.g., by e-mail) will be deemed to "affect" or "impact" the market at the place where the message is being received. Hence, ultimately, it is irrelevant how the consumer reacts after she has received the letter.[64] In particular, it will not matter in which jurisdiction the consumer will subsequently transact (or forbear to transact). This position is in line with the Bundesgerichtshof's decision in *Kauf im Ausland* and subsequent adjudication on cross-border unfair competition conduct.[65] Nevertheless, it does not duly accommodate the function of the consumer's transaction as the core element of a market economy. A slight modification of the facts suffices to take this simplified attachment rule ad absurdum: if the e-mail has been received during the consumer's holiday trip, where she is far away from her country of residence (and usual place of transacting), attaching choice of law to the temporary place of receipt would be incorrect. I will address this particular scenario in more detail in the last chapter.[66] Worth pointing out for now is that if consumer decision making is the most important factor for the functioning of the market mechanism, and if it is the consumer's referee function that can be described as the core element of free competition, then the ultimate outcome of decision making must not be disregarded—especially not in choice-of-law analysis.

In essence, therefore, the complete scope of the consumer's decision-making process must be protected against improper invasion. The protected domain starts with the transmission of information within the

[64] Helmut Köhler, in Helmut Köhler & Joachim Bornkamm, *Gesetz gegen den unlauteren Wettbewerb*, Einl UWG para. 5.34 and 5.35 (33rd edn., 2015).

[65] *See* BGH 1991 GRUR 463, 465—*Kauf im Ausland* (15 November 1990); *see also* BGH 1998 GRUR 419, 420—*Gewinnspiel im Ausland* (26 November 1997); BGH 2006 GRUR 513, 515—*Arzneimittelwerbung im Internet* (30 March 2006). *See supra* p. 207 *et seq.* and *infra* p. 539 *et seq.*

[66] *See infra* p. 539 *et seq.*

marketplace. It continues with the consumer's processing of information and then proceeds to cover the final result of the information processing—the consumer's transaction. Only if the consumer can carry out all of these stages without being externally manipulated can the outcome be considered to be economically rational.

D Caveat: Limitations of Consumer Decision Making

We have now seen that consumer sovereignty guarantees competitive efficiency and that it must be the subject matter of protection for regulation in terms of trademark protection and unfair competition prevention. But this is a mere theoretical ideal. In reality, human decision making is never perfect or completely rational. Indeed, many instances of consumer decision making will result in economically imperfect transactions. Not all consumers are *homines oeconomici.* Such imperfections were actually addressed quite early in economic theory. In the 1950s, Herbert A. Simon described a fundamental flaw in the concept of consumer autonomy—the phenomenon of bounded rationality.[67] His model illustrates that there will rarely ever exist a situation that allows for a perfectly rational *ex ante* processing of all relevant factors. While the individual may believe that she is making a rational decision, she seldom is. Furthermore, as critical theory went on to explain, maximum information will not bring out optimum competition, either. In fact, giving market participants a maximum of information may result in information overload, for consumers are limited in their cognitive capacities to collect and process market information.[68] In recent decades, many more doubts concerning consumer skills and capacities have been raised.[69]

[67] *See* Herbert A. Simon, *A Behavioral Model of Rational Choice*, 69 Quarterly J. Econ. 99 (1955) ("Traditional economic theory postulates an 'economic man,' who, in the course of being 'economic' is also 'rational.' This man is assumed to have knowledge of the relevant aspects of his environment which, if not absolutely complete, is at least impressively clear and voluminous. He is assumed also to have a well-organized and stable system of preferences, and a skill in computation that enables him to calculate, for the alternative courses of action that are available to him, which of these will permit him to reach the highest attainable point on his preference scale. ... [T]he concept of 'economic man' (and, I might add, of his brother 'administrative man') is in need of fairly drastic revision."); reprinted in Herbert A. Simon, *Models of Man, Social and Rational—Mathematical Essays on Rational Human Behavior in a Social Setting* 241 *et seq.* (1957).

[68] *See, e.g.*, Jürgen Keßler, *Wettbewerbstheoretische Aspekte des Irreführungsverbotes—eine ökonomische und dogmengeschichtliche Analyse*, 1990 WRP 73, 83.

[69] *See, e.g.*, Christine Jolls, Cass R. Sunstein & Richard H. Thaler, *A Behavioral Approach to Law and Economics*, 13 *et seq.*, 47, in *Behavioral Law and Economics* (Cass R. Sunstein ed., 2000); Richard H. Thaler, *Quasi Rational Economics* 3 *et seq.*, 77 *et seq.*, 137 *et seq.* and *passim* (2001); Mark Kelman, *Law and Behavioral Science: Conceptual Overviews*, 97 Nw. U. L. Rev. 1347 (2003); Faruk Gul & Wolfgang Pesendorfer, *Self-Control and the Theory of Consumption*, 72 Econometrica 119 (2004); Faruk Gul & Wolfgang Pesendorfer, *The Revealed Preference Theory of Changing Tastes*, 72 Rev. Econ. Stud. 429 (2005); *see*

An extended debate on behavioral economics is not necessary here, though one question is inevitable: If consumer decision making by its nature tends to result in irrational transacting, can it still serve as a factor for analysis in trademark and unfair competition law or choice of law? This is the point at which the characteristics of competition dynamics come into play again. As we have seen, the market economy is built on the sum of individual transactions.[70] By definition, these transactions are imperfect. Looking at competition from a perspective that embraces it as a dynamic and evolutionary process even requires a "natural" consumer, with all her decision-making deficits. Intrinsic limitations on rationality must then not only be accepted as a preexisting given—they may in fact be essential to the model.[71] Indeed, the steadfastly rational and profit-maximizing individual would be the death of discovery and innovation, and any regulation trying to substitute the consumer's decision with an artificially determined proxy that yields correct, just, and optimal results would disable the evolutionary mechanism of competition. Hence, there is no alternative to consumer decision making.

IV Summary

Economic competition requires freedom of transacting. The dynamic structure of competition reflects two different aspects of this freedom,

also Daniel Kahneman, *Thinking, Fast and Slow* (2011). For consumer protection policies in general, *see* Colin Scott & Julia Black, *Cranston's Consumers and the Law* ch. 1 and 9, in particular at 30 *et seq.* and 372 *et seq.* (3rd edn., 2000). For an extensive debate on consumer conduct, behavioral economics, and unfair competition law (in Germany, Switzerland, and Europe), *see* Axel Beater, *Verbraucherverhalten und Wettbewerbsrecht*, 87, 88 *et seq.*, in *Festschrift für Winfried Tilmann zum 65. Geburtstag* (Erhard Keller et al. eds., 2003).

[70] *See supra* p. 275 *et seq.*

[71] *See* Franz Böhm, *Wettbewerb und Monopolkampf—Eine Untersuchung zur Frage des wirtschaftlichen Kampfrechts und zur Frage der rechtlichen Struktur der geltenden Wirtschaftsordnung* 261–262 (1933) ("Eine Rechtsordnung, die der freien Willensentschließung derjenigen, die wirtschaftliche Leistungen nachfragen, eine so zentrale Gewalt über das Schicksal der Wirtschaft und der in ihr Tätigen einräumt, muß naturgemäß ein durchschnittlich hohes Maß von Urteilskraft bei der Masse der Nachfragenden voraussetzen. . . . Diese Fähigkeit setzt nun die Rechtsordnung voraus. . . . Ob diese Annahme nun aber zutrifft oder nicht, im rechtlichen System einer Wettbewerbsordnung wird sie jedenfalls als Fiktion unterstellt. Die Wahl, die der freie Kunde unter den konkurrierenden Angeboten trifft, kann nicht unter dem Gesichtspunkt rechtlich beanstandet werden, der Kunde verstehe sein eigenes Interesse nicht. Der Schaden, der für die Gesamtwirtschaft wie für den Einzelunternehmer daraus entstehen kann, daß die Fähigkeit zu verständiger Interessenwahrnehmung bei den Nachfragenden, sei es im ganzen, sei es in Einzelfällen, versagt, muß als ‚höhere Gewalt', als Schicksal, als Folge des Systems hingenommen werden. Es gibt keinen Rechtsanspruch darauf, daß der Kunde sein wirtschaftliches Selbstinteresse in intelligenter Weise wahrnimmt."). For a *sans alternatives* approach, *see* Mark P. McKenna, *A Consumer Decision-Making Theory of Trademark Law*, 98 Va. L. Rev. 67, 120 (2012) ("[D]ue regard for consumer autonomy requires us to live with these decisions even if they are bad.").

each concerning a separate relationship between market participants. First, freedom of transacting must exist between competitors (horizontal relationship). In addition, it must be preserved between competitors and the other side of the market, usually the consumers (vertical relationship). With respect to the mechanics of competition, the latter relationship is central, since it is the consumer's role as the "referee" in competition that is the most important factor for the functioning of the market mechanism. From a historical perspective, it becomes clear that legal doctrine initially focused on the horizontal level and only lately moved on to consider the vertical relationship. Initially, unfair competition law was aimed at protecting competitors—consumers were considered the substrate upon which competitors' battles were fought and decided. Under a modern understanding of competition, however, consumers' interests are considered determinative. The understanding of economic competition as a dynamic process of market communication and transacting provides the microstructure for our analysis. It is consumer decision making and transacting that serves as the core subject matter of protection under modern doctrines of trademark and unfair competition law. This subject matter necessarily also determines the reconceptualization of choice of law.

Section 2 Implementation—Substantive Law

The previous chapters have unveiled a number of defects in current doctrine. One major flaw is the alleged dichotomy between, on the one hand, subjective "rights" and "property" protected under tort and trademark law and, on the other, the system of objective rules of market "conduct" implemented under the regime of unfair competition law. Similarly problematic is unfair competition law's alleged socialization toward an often unqualified protection of "consumer interests." All of these defects require a reconceptualization—this also plays out with regard to choice of law. The key to the promulgation of a consistent conflicts doctrine lies in a precise definition of legal purposes in trademark and unfair competition law, as well as in a clear separation of the area from other fields of market regulation. Substantive law policies will thus provide my starting point. The following discussion will address the relevant questions of overlap and demarcation for the fields of torts and delicts, intellectual property, and antitrust law.

I Tort and Unfair Competition Law

As we have seen, legal doctrine has never managed to liberate unfair competition law from its tort heritage, whether in substantive law or choice of law. US law still treats intellectual property and unfair competition as a subspecies of business torts and tort law in general.[72] In Europe, the Rome II Regulation's treatment of both tort and unfair competition choice of law in a single instrument is a prominent example of their common heritage.[73] Nonetheless, notably in European law, it is also widely contended that the two areas pursue different purposes. Roughly speaking, tort law is deemed to protect absolute private rights. Unfair competition law is characterized as establishing a system of objective rules of market conduct.[74] While this characterization may often help support practically adequate results, it is not a doctrinally consistent explanation of the interrelation. Run-of-the-mill torts mostly concern noncompetitive activity, and they usually do not overlap with unfair competition law. With regard to commercial conduct, however, the picture is far more complex: legal policies of unfair competition prevention, especially at the horizontal level of intercompetitor relations, may be an issue of protecting "individual rights." Similarly, it is debated whether a "subjective right" can be found to exist in a competitor's position in the marketplace. In virtually all scenarios, therefore, both a tort concern for property or subjective right protection *and* an issue of fairness in competition may be at stake. This conundrum of overlapping policies reflects a general debate over how individual rights and freedom should be delimited in free markets. A close look at developments in US and European tort and unfair competition law highlights the most relevant aspects.

A The Mirage of Practical and Formal Differences

The debate on the interplay between tort and unfair competition policies and the question of how to differentiate the two sectors is mostly founded on practical and formalist arguments. Two aspects are regularly highlighted in order to explain the difference, though both are unconvincing. First, with regard to remedies, conventional wisdom usually refers to the practical realities that seem to illustrate that tort law is focused on compensation, while unfair competition law provides primarily for injunctive relief.[75] Some scholars have concluded therefrom that the system of

[72] For the early common law characterization, *see, e.g.*, John Henry Wigmore, *Select Cases on the Law of Torts—with Notes, and a Summary of Principles*, vol. I §§ 70 *et seq.* (1912); further also Restatement (First) of Torts §§ 711 *et seq.* (1938); more recently, *see, e.g.*, 1 J. Thomas McCarthy, *McCarthy on Trademarks and Unfair Competition* § 2:7 (4th edn., 2016) ("Since trademark infringement is a type of unfair competition and unfair competition is a tort, it follows that trademark infringement is a commercial tort.").

[73] *See supra* p. 64 *et seq.* and p. 203 *et seq.* [74] *See supra* p. 64 *et seq.* and p. 203 *et seq.*

[75] *See, e.g.*, Karl F. Kreuzer, *Wettbewerbsverstöße und Beeinträchtigung geschäftlicher Interessen (einschl. der Verletzung kartellrechtlicher Vorschriften)*, 232, 265–266, in *Vorschläge und*

unfair competition prevention is prohibitive yet noncompensatory. As they contend, prevention—not restitution—governs.[76] The divergent frequency of occurrence of different remedies in practice, however, hardly allows for a conclusion to be drawn. On the contrary, a look at the substantive law foundations of the field suggests a different outcome. First, history reveals that injunctive relief has only recently achieved its current importance in practice. Unfair competition prevention in early German doctrine, for instance, favored penal sanctions and compensatory relief at the expense of the victim's injunctive relief.[77] Furthermore, modern tort and unfair competition law largely provide for both injunctive relief and damages.[78] The difference in frequency is due to a mere practical necessity: in unfair competition disputes, an accounting of the plaintiff's actual damages is often difficult, sometimes even impossible. Injunctive relief, therefore, prevails as a practical matter in most proceedings.[79] In principle, however, unfair competitive conduct (if intentional or negligent) may of course also result in a finding of compensation—in addition to the remedy of injunctive relief.[80] Conversely,

Gutachten zur Reform des deutschen internationalen Privatrechts der außervertraglichen Schuldverhältnisse, vorgelegt im Auftrag der Zweiten Kommission des Deutschen Rates für internationales Privatrecht (Ernst von Caemmerer ed., 1983); Max-Planck-Institut für ausländisches und internationales Patent-, Urheber- und Wettbewerbsrecht, *Stellungnahme zum Entwurf eines Gesetzes zur Ergänzung des internationalen Privatrechts (außervertragliche Schuldverhältnisse und Sachen)*, 1985 GRUR Int. 104, 106 (for intellectual property rights protection); Karl-Heinz Fezer & Stefan Koos, in *Staudingers Kommentar zum Bürgerlichen Gesetzbuch: Internationales Wirtschaftsrecht,* Internationales Wettbewerbsprivatrecht para. 397 (15th edn., 2010); Helmut Köhler, *Die wettbewerbsrechtlichen Abwehransprüche (Unterlassung, Beseitigung, Widerruf)*, 1992 NJW 137, 137 (characterizing injunctive relief as a core area of unfair competition prevention).

[76] *See* Wilhelm Gloede, *Der deutsche Außenhandel und seine wettbewerbsrechtliche Beurteilung nach deutschem internationalem Privatrecht,* 1960 GRUR 464, 471; Karl F. Kreuzer, *Wettbewerbsverstöße und Beeinträchtigung geschäftlicher Interessen (einschl. der Verletzung kartellrechtlicher Vorschriften)*, 232, 265–266, in *Vorschläge und Gutachten zur Reform des deutschen internationalen Privatrechts der außervertraglichen Schuldverhältnisse, vorgelegt im Auftrag der Zweiten Kommission des Deutschen Rates für internationales Privatrecht* (Ernst von Caemmerer ed., 1983); Rainer Hausmann & Inés Obergfell, in *Lauterkeitsrecht: Kommentar zum Gesetz gegen den unlauteren Wettbewerb (UWG), vol. I,* Einleitung I para. 220 (Karl-Heinz Fezer ed., 2nd edn., 2010); *see also* Karl-Heinz Fezer & Stefan Koos, in *Staudingers Kommentar zum Bürgerlichen Gesetzbuch: Internationales Wirtschaftsrecht,* Einleitung para. 21 (15th edn., 2010).

[77] *See supra* p. 10–14.

[78] *See, e.g.*, Otto Teplitzky, *Wettbewerbsrechtliche Ansprüche und Verfahren*, ch. 29 (10th edn., 2011).

[79] *See id.* at ch. 53 para. 1. For the problem of calculating and proving damages, *see* Otto Teplitzky, *Die Durchsetzung des Schadensersatzzahlungsanspruchs im Wettbewerbsrecht,* 1987 GRUR 215; Gerd Leisse & Fritz Traub, *Schadensschätzung im unlauteren Wettbewerb,* 1980 GRUR 1; for case law on the issue, *see, e.g.*, BGH 2001 GRUR 329, 331—*Gemeinkostenanteil* (2 November 2000).

[80] Remarkably, the German Unfair Competition Act (sec. 9) even grants compensation for mere monetary or economic losses ("Vermögensschäden") in cases of simple negligence.

even though most tort suits center on the issue of compensation, injunctive relief is also available and (like in unfair competition law) does not require the defendant's fault.[81] In some areas of tort law, injunctions may even be the dominant practical remedy.[82] It is therefore true, as the Restatement of Unfair Competition Law (Third) explains, that "the judicial preference for injunctive relief in unfair competition cases is not an exception to ordinary remedial principles, but rather an application of those principles in a context in which injunctive relief is ordinarily the most appropriate remedy."[83]

Moreover, a formalist differentiation based on the alleged "absoluteness" of rights that are protected under tort law is no more helpful than a look at practical remedies. Historically, of course, unfair competition has been qualified as a tort or delict. Yet the discussion increasingly centers around the fact that the two sectors differ with respect to the relevant subject matter of protection. Unfair competition law, it is contended, aims to regulate market behavior through objective rules of conduct.[84] Quite differently, the subject matter in torts comprises absolute rights.[85]

This is more extensive than the general principles of tort law, where monetary losses without infringement of an absolute right (*see* section 823(1) of the German Civil Code (BGB)) will be compensated in cases of intentional delicts only.

[81] For the general doctrinal foundation of injunctive relief in German tort doctrine, *see* Hermann Reichold, *Lauterkeitsrecht als Sonderdeliktsrecht—Zur Rolle zivilistischen Denkens bei der Anwendung von* § 1 *UWG*, 193 AcP 204, 218 (1993) (with further references).

[82] Examples are defamation and personality rights protection.

[83] Restatement of the Law—Unfair Competition (Third), § 35, comment a (1995) (also explaining the usual "difficulty of proving the amount of loss and a causal connection with the defendant's wrongful conduct").

[84] It protects not individual entitlements but competitors, consumers, and the public alike. For case law, *see, e.g.*, RGZ vol. 108, 272, 274—*Merx* (27 May 1924); RGZ vol. 120, 47, 49—*Markenschutzverband* (24 January 1928); BGHZ vol. 81, 291, 295—*Bäckerfachzeitschrift* (3 July 1981). For scholarly commentary, *see* Kamen Troller, *Das internationale Privatrecht des unlauteren Wettbewerbs in vergleichender Darstellung der Rechte Deutschlands, Englands, Frankreichs, Italiens, der Schweiz und der USA* 33 (1962); Hans-Albrecht Sasse, *Grenzüberschreitende Werbung* 42–43 (1974); Karl F. Kreuzer, *Wettbewerbsverstöße und Beeinträchtigung geschäftlicher Interessen (einschl. der Verletzung kartellrechtlicher Vorschriften)*, 232, 265, in *Vorschläge und Gutachten zur Reform des deutschen internationalen Privatrechts der außervertraglichen Schuldverhältnisse, vorgelegt im Auftrag der Zweiten Kommission des Deutschen Rates für internationales Privatrecht* (Ernst von Caemmerer ed., 1983); Frauke Henning-Bodewig, *Was gehört zum Lauterkeitsrecht?*, 9, 18–19, in *Lauterkeitsrecht und Acquis Communautaire* (Reto M. Hilty & Frauke Henning-Bodewig eds., 2009); Reto M. Hilty, *The Law Against Unfair Competition and Its Interfaces*, 1 *et seq.*, in *Law Against Unfair Competition—Towards a New Paradigm in Europe?* (Reto M. Hilty & Frauke Henning-Bodewig eds., 2007).

[85] *See, e.g.*, Kamen Troller, *Das internationale Privatrecht des unlauteren Wettbewerbs in vergleichender Darstellung der Rechte Deutschlands, Englands, Frankreichs, Italiens, der Schweiz und der USA* 33, 111–112 (1962); Karl F. Kreuzer, *Wettbewerbsverstöße und Beeinträchtigung geschäftlicher Interessen (einschl. der Verletzung kartellrechtlicher Vorschriften)*, 232, 265, in *Vorschläge und Gutachten zur Reform des deutschen internationalen Privatrechts der außervertraglichen Schuldverhältnisse, vorgelegt im Auftrag der Zweiten*

But this also leads into the wrong direction. Rights and entitlements are always relative. Most illustratively, the relativity of rights can be shown to govern rules on tangible property. Owners of real property never enjoy unlimited power.[86] The statutory rule in the German Civil Code illustrates this point with clarity. As the code's provision on tangible property provides, "The owner of a thing may, as far as the law and the rights of others are not violated, deal with his property as he wishes and exclude others from interference."[87] Of course, this express relativity stands in stark contrast to William Blackstone's oft-enunciated definition of property as the "sole and despotic dominion which one man claims and exercises over the external things of the world, in total exclusion of the right of any other individual in the universe."[88] Yet this no longer represents a consensus on the nature of property rights and other entitlements. The German lawmakers' determination of limitations on tangible property, like all modern conceptions in the field, has been designed without the slightest remainder of such absolutist dominion.[89] And *a fortiori*, the relativity of rights also governs with regard to *intangible* subject matter.[90] The scope of personality rights and protection of personal reputation provides for an illustrative example. The protection of an individual's reputation against improper invasion by a competitor may be granted

Kommission des Deutschen Rates für internationales Privatrecht (Ernst von Caemmerer ed., 1983) ("Während Schutzgut des allgemeinen Deliktsrechts grundsätzlich ein (absolutes) subjektives Recht oder Rechtsgut eines individuellen Rechtsträgers bildet, das Ausdruck einer ausschließlichen Zuweisung des Gutes an den Inhaber ist, schützt das Wettbewerbsrecht die Interessen der Schutzadressaten (Mitbewerber, sonstige Marktbeteiligte, Allgemeinheit) an der Hintanhaltung unlauterer Wettbewerbshandlungen mit dem Instrument objektiver Verhaltensnormen; dies geschieht ohne Rücksicht auf Schadenseintritt oder auch nur (konkrete) Interessengefährdung."); more recently, *see, e.g.*, Frauke Henning-Bodewig, *Nationale Eigenständigkeit und europäische Vorgaben im Lauterkeitsrecht*, 2010 GRUR Int. 549, 552.

86 *See* Elinor Ostrom, *Governing the Commons—The Evolution of Institutions for Collective Action* (1990); on aspects of public property doctrine and sociability, *see* Carol Rose, *The Comedy of the Commons: Custom, Commerce, and Inherently Public Property*, 53 U. Chi. L. Rev. 711, 774 *et seq.* and *passim* (1986); *see also* Michael A. Carrier, *Cabining Intellectual Property Through A Property Paradigm*, 54 Duke L.J. 1, 52 *et seq.* (2004).

87 Section 903 German Civil Code (BGB) reads: "Der Eigentümer einer Sache kann, soweit nicht das Gesetz oder Rechte Dritter entgegenstehen, mit der Sache nach Belieben verfahren und andere von jeder Einwirkung ausschließen." The translation is borrowed from Jeremy Waldron, *What Is Private Property?*, 5 Ox. J. Leg. Stud. 313, 334 (1985).

88 William Blackstone, *Commentaries on the Laws of England in Four Books, vol. I, Second Book: Of the Rights of Things*, ch. 1, at 393 (1893). For Blackstonian absolutist theory and its gradual dephysicalization, *see* Kenneth J. Vandevelde, *The New Property of the Nineteenth Century: The Development of the Modern Concept of Property*, 29 Buff. L. Rev. 325, 331 *et seq.* (1980).

89 Jeremy Waldron, *What Is Private Property?*, 5 Ox. J. Leg. Stud. 313, 334 (1985).

90 *See* Anselm Kamperman Sanders, *Unfair Competition Law—The Protection of Intellectual and Industrial Creativity* 78 *et seq.* (1997).

concurrently under a general theory of tort law and under the system of unfair competition law.[91] But the right must always be balanced against other concerns—particularly freedom of speech.[92] In essence, therefore, the law creates an individual right only to the extent that this right fulfills a function and serves a common end or collective good. Truly absolute rights in intangibles do not exist. Accordingly, neither the actual state of affairs in courtroom practice nor the traditional formalist perspective on absolute personal entitlements helps provide a clear demarcation between the fields of torts and delicts on the one hand and unfair competition law on the other.

B The Relativity of Protection Levels

The determinative aspect must be sought elsewhere. All personal entitlements may be relative under modern private law doctrine. However, the metric for assessing the relativity of these rights varies. As we will now see, the relevant standard for a demarcation is based on the different regulatory policies that are designed to establish and maintain the state of free competition.

1 Early Starting Point: Claims "against the World at Large"

An early approach to the issue of rights relativity stems from Roscoe Pound. The definition of "property" in his 1922 *Introduction to the Philosophy of Law* illustrates the different options, notably with respect to the intensity of protection for different categories of individual entitlements. His explanation may not provide for a very practical guideline, but it lucidly illustrates the fundamental question: To what extent is a private entitlement to be considered "relative," and at what point does it become a "right against the world at large"?

In addition to rights in corporeal things, the freedom of industry and contract, and the guarantee of enforcement for promised performances, Pound explained a fourth category of claims that constitute "property":

> [T]here is a claim to be secured against interference by outsiders with economically advantageous relations with others, whether contractual, social, business, official or domestic. For not only do various relations which have an economic value involve claims against the other party to the relation, which one may demand that the law secure, but they also involve claims against the world at large that these advantageous relations, which form an important part of the

[91] *See, e.g.*, W. Page Keeton, *Prosser and Keeton on the Law of Torts* ch. 19 and ch. 24 (5th edn., 2004); further, *e.g.*, sections 823, 826 German Civil Code (BGB) and section 4 no. 1 and no. 2 Unfair Competition Act (UWG).

[92] For a comparative account, *see, e.g.*, Konrad Zweigert & Hein Kötz, *An Introduction to Comparative Law* § 43, 685 *et seq.*, 713 (3rd edn., 1998).

substance of the individual, shall not be interfered with. Legal recognition of these individual claims, legal delimitation and securing of individual interests of substance is at the foundation of our economic organization of society.[93]

This general understanding of claims "against the world at large" highlights what would soon become the central issue in twentieth-century unfair competition doctrine. My overview on the historical debate traced the contemporary struggle with trademark-as-property and goodwill protection, as well as other formalist constructs.[94] Pound's explanation did clarify that the determination of distinct categories and boundaries of such claims must be considered constitutive for socioeconomic transacting. After all, without protection, there was no incentive to explore, create, or maintain elements of the respective subject matter. Yet what he left unanswered was the question how to delimit the public domain from such claims "against the world at large." In terms of trademark and unfair competition doctrine, this question concretely asked whether individual competitors can claim an absolute and exclusive "right in competition," notably in the preservation of their customer base, their market share, or another kind of achievement in competition. A closer look at the development of legal thought in the United States and Germany will highlight the most crucial aspects of a journey from the initially sweeping if-value-then-right approach to the modern segmentation of market-regulation policies.

2 *United States: From Property to Policy and Back Again*

As we saw in chapters 1 and 2, throughout the nineteenth century, plaintiffs phrased their requests in terms of property, or subjective, rights. The propertization and protection of ever more interests accommodated a practical penchant to think in categories of absolute entitlements, especially in trademark and unfair competition disputes. This conceptual victory of individual property protection was an heir to Lockean theory: any position that could be related to someone's labor, effort, or investment was found to constitute an absolute, subjective, and exclusive right.[95] As we have also seen, this concept came under pressure in US legal thought at the beginning of the twentieth century.[96] Two aspects

[93] Roscoe Pound, *An Introduction to the Philosophy of Law* 192 (1922).

[94] *See supra* chapter 1 *passim* and chapter 2 *passim*.

[95] *See* once more Roscoe Pound, *An Introduction to the Philosophy of Law* 194–195 (1922). With particular regard to trademark doctrine and the paradigm of "if value, then right," *see* Rochelle Cooper Dreyfuss, *Expressive Genericity: Trademarks as Language in the Pepsi Generation*, 65 Notre Dame L. Rev. 397, 405 (1990); most famously, Felix S. Cohen, *Transcendental Nonsense and the Functional Approach*, 35 Colum. L. Rev. 809, 815 (1935). For a general historical account, *see* Morton J. Horwitz, *The Transformation of American Law, 1780–1860*, 258–259 (1977).

[96] *See supra* p. 110 *et seq.*

of the development are relevant here. First, the concept of property as such was redesigned soon after the turn of the century. Second, this also led to a change of paradigms in trademark and unfair competition doctrine, at least at the theoretical level.

The modern reconceptualization of property was influenced greatly by Wesley Newcomb Hohfeld. In 1913 and 1917, he presented a new scheme of property rights analysis, which consisted of eight fundamental legal relations as constituent elements of "property." This approach, he argued, was intended to establish "the lowest common denominators of the law."[97] Hohfeld attempted to explain all existing relations and facets of "property" as consisting of a basic toolbox of "rights," "privileges," "powers," and "immunities," as well as their jural opposites and correlatives.[98] Hohfeldian theory has been extensively analyzed and discussed, and while the debate's details go beyond the scope of this inquiry, two points are relevant. First, it appears that Hohfeld, even though a critic of legal formalism, ultimately perfected the formalist dephysicalization of property. This trend started much earlier, but Hohfeldian thought spurred the dissolution. Under his segmented system of differentiated property components, every individual entitlement or value could ultimately be classified as a property right. This malleability may have been convenient in terms of theory, but it had a fatal effect in practice: as reflected by case law at the time, the ubiquity and potential infinity of property rights resulted in the concept's ultimate demise.[99] Property had become arbitrary, and a new concept had to be found.

The second aspect concerns the structural foundations. Hohfeld, in clarifying the difference between legal "liberties" and legal "rights,"[100]

[97] Wesley Newcomb Hohfeld, *Some Fundamental Legal Conceptions as Applied in Judicial Reasoning*, 23 Yale L.J. 16, 30 *et seq.*, 58 (1913) ("If a homely metaphor be permitted, these eight conceptions,—rights and duties, privileges and no-rights, powers and liabilities, immunities and disabilities,—seem to be what may be called 'the lowest common denominators of the law.' "); *see also* Wesley Newcomb Hohfeld, *Fundamental Legal Conceptions as Applied in Judicial Reasoning*, 26 Yale L.J. 710 *et seq.* (1917).

[98] *E.g.*, the opposite of "right" was "no right," and its correlative was "duty."

[99] For an extensive discussion, *see* Kenneth J. Vandevelde, *The New Property of the Nineteenth Century: The Development of the Modern Concept of Property*, 29 Buff. L. Rev. 325, 362–363 (1980); Duncan Kennedy, *The Role of Law in Economic Thought: Essays on the Fetishism of Commodities*, 34 Am. U. L. Rev. 939, 954 (1985) ("[T]hey began by thinking of property in terms of objects, and ended by thinking of it, in very abstract terms, as ability to invoke state force to prevent interference with some position of advantage in the market system."). With particular regard to unfair competition and trademark law, *see* Daniel M. McClure, *Trademarks and Unfair Competition: A Critical History of Legal Thought*, 69 Trademark Rep. 305, 317–318 (1979).

[100] For an extensive discussion, *see* Joseph William Singer, *The Legal Rights Debate in Analytical Jurisprudence from Bentham to Hohfeld*, 1982 Wis. L. Rev. 975, 987 *et seq.* and *passim*.

actually set the stage for a remodeling of individual rights theory. The then-governing formalist reasoning had established a system of wide-ranging property and private rights protection. Hohfeld illustrated that injury alone would not imply a remedy. As he explained, an individual's liberty (or, in Hohfeld's terms, "privilege") to do something was not necessarily accompanied by a duty of others not to invade this sphere of freedom. Hence, liberty alone would not automatically signify a right.[101] By this means, he opened the debate for a new perspective on the metric used for delimiting individual rights from the public domain—one that was no longer a merely value-based rule of assumption. On this basis, realist critics suggested that value protection should be determined by reference to the policies of the community.[102] This open reorientation toward a new paradigm of policies was particularly influential for trademark and unfair competition theory.

One famous example—mentioned in chapter 2—is the realist critique in Oliver Wendell Holmes's writings and authored opinions. In the 1917 Supreme Court decision *E.I. Du Pont Nemours*, for instance, he explained the protection of trademarks and trade secrets under the rubric of property as a legally created construct: "The word 'property' as applied to trademarks and trade secrets is an unanalyzed expression of certain secondary consequences of the primary fact that the law makes some rudimentary requirements of good faith."[103] Good faith—as the expression of a general standard delimiting competitive conduct—was what determined whether something could be protected as a trademark, trade secret, or other intangible value. The following year, in his dissenting opinion in *International News Service*, Holmes further explained that "[p]roperty, a creation of law, does not arise from value, although exchangeable—a matter of fact."[104] Hence, policy, not value, should determine whether a position could be found protectable subject matter in unfair competition law.[105]

[101] *Id.* at 988.

[102] For an extensive discussion, *see, e.g.*, Duncan Kennedy, *The Role of Law in Economic Thought: Essays on the Fetishism of Commodities*, 34 Am. U. L. Rev. 939, 951 (1985).

[103] *E.I. Du Pont de Nemours Powder Co. v. Masland*, 244 U.S. 100, 102 (1917) (Holmes, J.).

[104] *International News Service v. Associated Press*, 248 U.S. 215, 246 (1918) (Holmes, J., dissenting).

[105] Justice Brandeis—also dissenting in *International News Service*—explained the concept of "property" in similarly policy-founded terms: "An essential element of individual property is the legal right to exclude others from enjoying it. If the property is private, the right of exclusion may be absolute; if the property is affected with a public interest, the right of exclusion is qualified. But the fact that a product of the mind has cost its producer money and labor, and has a value for which others are willing to pay, is not sufficient to ensure to it this legal attribute of property. The general rule of law is, that the noblest of human productions—knowledge, truths ascertained, conceptions, and

In 1935, no less famously than Holmes, Felix Cohen extended the attack on "property" in his seminal *Columbia Law Review* article.[106] I have already explained Cohen's criticism from a historical perspective.[107] Important here is that his article pointed to something else—a structure to be found below the surface of the skirmishes between formalists and realists:

> The prejudice that identifies the interests of the plaintiff in unfair competition cases with the interests of business and identifies the interests of business with the interests of society, will not be critically examined by courts and legal scholars until it is recognized and formulated. It will not be recognized or formulated so long as the hypostatization of "property rights" conceals the circularity of legal reasoning.[108]

In his critique of the distortion in contemporary interest analysis, Cohen anticipated the modern debate on the area's change from mere competitor protection to the protection of consumers and the public good. He did not elaborate further on the correlation of interests, though. Rather, the successor theory to legal realism built on this concept.

Cohen's "interests of society" (in modern terms, market efficiency and welfare) ultimately came center stage when the law and economics movement established what has become the dominant approach to many fields of modern US law ever since.[109] The law and economics approach seemed equipped to overcome traditional foundations. Its proponents substituted the background regime of formal property in trademarks and other entitlements with an objective efficiency calculus. After all, welfare economics in legal theory, as Duncan Kennedy has explained, helped purge legal theory of such concepts as "freedom," "justice," and "naturalness." In the end, efficiency would remain the eternal constant of legal purposes—a metric of absolute objectivity.[110] It is also true that modern

ideas—become, after voluntary communication to others, free as the air to common use. Upon these incorporeal productions the attribute of property is continued after such communication only in certain classes of cases where public policy has seemed to demand it" (*id.* at 250 (Brandeis, J., dissenting)). *See also* Oliver Wendell Holmes, Jr., *Privilege, Malice, and Intent*, 8 Harv. L. Rev. 1, 3 (1894) ("But whether, and how far, a privilege shall be allowed is a question of policy. Questions of policy are legislative questions, and judges are shy of reasoning from such grounds. Therefore, decisions for or against the privilege, which really can stand only upon such grounds, often are presented as hollow deductions from empty general propositions.").

[106] Felix S. Cohen, *Transcendental Nonsense and the Functional Approach*, 35 Colum. L. Rev. 809 (1935).

[107] *See supra* p. 112 *et seq.*

[108] Felix S. Cohen, *Transcendental Nonsense and the Functional Approach*, 35 Colum. L. Rev. 809, 817 (1935).

[109] *See supra* p. 121 *et seq.*

[110] Duncan Kennedy, *The Role of Law in Economic Thought: Essays on the Fetishism of Commodities*, 34 Am. U. L. Rev. 939, 949 (1985).

US trademark law has come to be dominated by the ideas of the Chicago school of law and economics. The concept is simple and comprehensive: "trademark law, like tort law in general ... can best be explained on the hypothesis that the law is trying to promote economic efficiency."[111] As a result, today's economists and lawyers view trademarks as essential aids for establishing and maintaining market efficiency.[112] As we have seen, the reduction of consumer search costs has become the most important trademark function. Even case law has integrated the concept.[113]

But a broader look reveals a different picture—one where the fortress of trademark-as-property protection still solidly stands. As we saw in my exploration of the post-Chicago development of US trademark law, despite the economization of policies, courts often pay only lip service to the change.[114] Indeed, ideas of property and goodwill protection and of the prevention of misappropriation and free riding, as well as a growing concern for trademark functions beyond the traditional concept of confusion prevention, have taken over. In the end, neither the realist attack nor the law and economics movement has initiated a groundbreaking change. In fact, trademark and unfair competition law has even become increasingly repropertized in recent decades.

3 Germany: The Eternal Dichotomy of Rights and Competition

Like in the United States, nineteenth-century formalist reasoning had developed an extended concept of individual rights protection in Germany and Europe.[115] In its attempt to construe the legal order as a consistent system of rights and duties, contemporary civil law thought introduced the concept of so-called subjective rights as subject matter or protection in tort and property law. The concept may seem strange and unfamiliar to common law jurists. Yet it mirrors the debate on common law property formalism. Theoretically, the subjective right was understood as an expression of personal autonomy and free will.[116] In practice,

[111] William M. Landes & Richard A. Posner, *Trademark Law: An Economic Perspective*, 30 J. L. & Econ. 265, 265–266 (1987); William M. Landes & Richard A. Posner, *The Economic Structure of Tort Law* (1987).

[112] Mark A. Lemley, *The Modern Lanham Act and the Death of Common Sense*, 108 Yale L.J. 1687 (1999).

[113] *See, e.g., Qualitex Co. v. Jacobson Prods. Co., Inc.*, 514 U.S. 159, 164 (1995); *New Kids on the Block v. News America Pub., Inc.*, 971 F.2d 302, 305 (9th Cir. 1992); *see also* Barton Beebe, *The Semiotic Analysis of Trademark Law*, 51 UCLA L. Rev. 621, 624 (2004). *See also supra* p. 123 *et seq.*

[114] *See supra* p. 126–127. [115] *See supra* p. 9 *et seq.*

[116] Andreas von Tuhr explained in 1910: "Der zentrale Begriff des Privatrechts und zugleich die letzte Abstraktion aus der Vielgestaltigkeit des Rechtslebens ist das Recht des Subjekts, das ‚subjektive Recht', wie man es im Gegensatz zum objektiven Recht

however, the issue was always whether a position could be seen as truly private and therefore not part of the public domain.[117] To use Pound's terminology, the question was whether there is a right "against the world at large."[118]

With regard to trademark rights, the situation should be clear—though it has been anything but. Following the concept of trademark-as-property protection, dominant case law and scholarly commentary have usually found trademarks to be subjective rights.[119] Remarkably, however, critical voices have forcefully rejected this view by arguing that trademarks are indications of product source only. As they contend, trademarks are not full-fledged assignments of intellectual property rights; they merely prevent unfair competition by prohibiting consumer confusion. Accordingly, the trademark owner is not entitled to (and thus has no subjective right in) the exclusive and comprehensive use of the symbol.[120] The situation has been even more contested with respect to the question whether subjective rights exist under a system of unfair competition prevention. While courts are still undecided on the issue, scholarly commentary largely rejects a subjective right of victim-competitors that could be found sufficiently absolute to warrant protection. Agreement exists only under a very narrow perspective: in cases of unfair product imitation and theft of trade secrets, a subjective right may be found.[121] Most other cases, however, are disputed. Some scholars, for instance, suggest finding a subjective right whenever the specific purpose of the norm at issue is to protect the

(der Rechtsnorm) zu nennen pflegt." (Andreas von Tuhr, *Der Allgemeine Teil des Deutschen Bürgerlichen Rechts, vol. I: Allgemeine Lehren und Personenrecht* 53 (1910)). For a concise overview of nineteenth-century legal thought, particularly the theories of von Savigny, Puchta, and Windscheid, *see* Ludwig Raiser, *Der Stand der Lehre vom subjektiven Recht im Deutschen Zivilrecht*, 1961 JZ 465; Walter R. Schluep, *Das Markenrecht als subjektives Recht* 265 *et seq.* (1964).

[117] *See* Philipp Heck, *Grundriß des Schuldrechts* 421 (1929). [118] *See supra* p. 300–301.

[119] *See, e.g.*, Wolfgang Fikentscher, *Wettbewerb und gewerblicher Rechtsschutz—Die Stellung des Rechts der Wettbewerbsbeschränkungen in der Rechtsordnung* 6 (1958); Walter R. Schluep, *Das Markenrecht als subjektives Recht* 328 *et seq.* (1964); Ernst von Caemmerer, *Bereicherung und unerlaubte Handlung*, 333, 398–399, in *Festschrift für Ernst Rabel—Rechtsvergleichung und internationales Privatrecht, vol. I* (Hans Dölle ed., 1954); for modern scholarly commentary, *see, e.g.*, Reinhard Ingerl & Christian Rohnke, *Kommentar zum Markengesetz: Gesetz über den Schutz von Marken und sonstigen Kennzeichen*, Vor §§ 14–19d para. 288 (3rd edn., 2010); for case law, *see, e.g.*, BGH 1987 GRUR 520, 523—*Chanel No. 5 (I)* (18 December 1986); BGH 2009 GRUR 515 para. 41—*Motorradreiniger* (18 December 2008).

[120] This is different for patents and copyrights. *See* Ernst-Joachim Mestmäcker, *Eingriffserwerb und Rechtsverletzung in der ungerechtfertigten Bereicherung*, 1958 JZ 521, 525; Ernst-Joachim Mestmäcker, *Recht und ökonomisches Gesetz* 534 *et seq.* (2nd edn., 1984). *See also* Ludwig Raiser, *Der Stand der Lehre vom subjektiven Recht im Deutschen Zivilrecht*, 1961 JZ 465, 468.

[121] *See* section 4 no. 3, and sections 17 and 18 Unfair Competition Act (UWG).

individual competitor only. They accordingly deny such rights if the norm is also aimed at protecting consumers or the public. Under a more tort-based foundation, again, subjective rights are denied unless a specific benefit has accrued on the side of the invader as a result of the violation.[122]

This doctrinal insecurity reflects historical developments. The subject matter of protection in unfair competition law was never satisfactorily defined—a void that, until today, accounts for many misperceptions. As we have seen, the idea of subjective rights protection under unfair competition law dates back to the paradigm of personality rights protection.[123] Participation in competition was deemed an emanation of the competitor's personality, which was characterized as a subjective right. And a subjective right was also seen in other elements of the business. In this regard, a look at Swiss law is particularly enlightening. As in Germany, practice had begun to identify competitor personality as the subject matter of protection.[124] Later on, however, protecting the competitor's business as such became determinative.[125] Article 48 of the 1911 Swiss Law of Obligations is characteristic: relations between a competitor and her customers were deemed a property-like entitlement. Accordingly, the improper invasion of customer relations (*Geschäftskundschaft*) was a tort.[126]

Ultimately, the debate in both Germany and Switzerland lost its focus on what the object of protection should be. Instead, like in the United States, scholarly attention was drawn toward the question of what policy

122 For the mainstream opinion, *see, e.g.*, Ernst von Caemmerer, *Bereicherung und unerlaubte Handlung*, 333, 356, 396 *et seq.*, in *Festschrift für Ernst Rabel—Rechtsvergleichung und internationales Privatrecht, vol. I* (Hans Dölle ed., 1954); Ulrich Loewenheim, *Bereicherungsansprüche im Wettbewerbsrecht*, 1997 WRP 913; Helmut Köhler, *Zur Bereicherungshaftung bei Wettbewerbsverstößen*, 167 *et seq.* in *Festschrift für Werner Lorenz zum 80. Geburtstag* (Thomas Rauscher & Heinz-Peter Mansel eds., 2001). For a view that does not take sides on the issue, *see* BGH 1990 GRUR 221, 221 *et seq.*—*Forschungskosten* (9 March 1989); BGH 1991 GRUR 914, 916–917—*Kastanienmuster* (23 May 1991).

123 *See supra* p. 21 *et seq.*

124 *See, e.g.*, BGE vol. 21 I 1181, 1188 (23 November 1895); BGE vol. 22 I 155, 161 (27 March 1896); BGE vol. 39 II 264, 267 (13 June 1913); BGE vol. 52 II 444, 445 (15 November 1926) ("Individualrecht des Gewerbetreibenden auf Anerkennung seiner Persönlichkeit"); Alois Troller, *Das Delikt des unlauteren Wettbewerbs nach dem Entwurf des Bundesrates vom 11. Juni 1934* 18 *et seq.* (1937); more recently, Dieter Dubs, *Das Lauterkeitsstatut nach schweizerischem Kollisionsrecht—Zugleich ein Beitrag zur Materialisierung des Internationalprivatrechts* 2 *et seq.* (2000).

125 For a similar approach in German theory *see, e.g.*, Rudolf Callmann, *Der unlautere Wettbewerb, Kommentar*, 28 *et seq.*, 43 *et seq.* (2nd edn., 1932); Eugen Ulmer, *Sinnzusammenhänge im modernen Wettbewerbsrecht—Ein Beitrag zum Aufbau des Wettbewerbsrechts* 7–8 (1932); Heinrich Tetzner, *Gesetz gegen den unlauteren Wettbewerb* Vorbem. para. 12 (2nd edn., 1957).

126 Carl Baudenbacher, in *Lauterkeitsrecht: Kommentar zum Gesetz gegen den unlauteren Wettbewerb (UWG)*, Art. 1 para. 3–4 (Carl Baudenbacher ed., 2001).

the law should pursue. As we saw earlier,[127] a trend toward socialization began in the first half of the twentieth century, and the concept of unfair competition law as an area of objective market regulation took over.[128] But there have always been attempts to reintroduce the concept of rights that are valid "against the world at large." Among the most prominent examples are Max Kummer's concept of the competitor's right to maintain her position in the marketplace (*Wettbewerbsstellung*)[129] and Wolfgang Fikentscher's suggestion that the individual's freedom to transact should be protected as such.[130] Both concepts are paradigmatic for the perseverance of subjective-right concepts in unfair competition law.[131] Kummer's concept proposing protection for the competitor's position in the marketplace was an attempt to create a right in intangibles directly under the regime of unfair competition law. As he explained, this right should be founded on an objective norm of market regulation, but it did not provide its own metric for delimiting the scope of protection.[132] Kummer saw subjective rights and regulatory policy as two sides of the same coin. This, however, was where his concept drifted

[127] *See supra* p. 50–52.

[128] *See, e.g.*, RGZ vol. 120, 47, 49 *et seq.*—*Markenschutzverband* (24 January 1928); Eugen Ulmer, *Wandlungen und Aufgaben im Wettbewerbsrecht*, 1937 GRUR 769, 771 ("Inhaltlich hat sich ... ein Wandel von einer individual- zu einer sozialethischen Beurteilung vollzogen."). For Swiss law, *see, e.g.*, E. Matter, *Zur Generalklausel im Bundesgesetz über den unlauteren Wettbewerb*, 87 ZBJV 449, 459 (1951); Mathis Berger, *Die funktionale Konkretisierung von Art. 2 UWG* 121 *et seq.* (1997); Dieter Dubs, *Das Lauterkeitsstatut nach schweizerischem Kollisionsrecht—Zugleich ein Beitrag zur Materialisierung des Internationalprivatrechts* 6 *et seq.* (2000).

[129] Max Kummer, *Anwendungsbereich und Schutzgut der privatrechtlichen Rechtssätze gegen unlauteren und gegen freiheitsbeschränkenden Wettbewerb* 77 *et seq.*, 87 *et seq.* (1960).

[130] *See infra* p. 309.

[131] *See* Max Kummer, *Anwendungsbereich und Schutzgut der privatrechtlichen Rechtssätze gegen unlauteren und gegen freiheitsbeschränkenden Wettbewerb* 89 (1960) ("Mit dem Persönlichkeitsrecht teilt es zunächst die Eigenschaft, absolutes Recht zu sein. Wie jenes richtet es sich virtuell gegen jedermann, allemal sofort zur Aktualität in Form eines Abwehranspruches gegen denjenigen aufspringend, der es unzulässigerweise stört—im Gegensatz zum obligatorischen Recht, das sich nur gegen einen bestimmten Schuldner richtet."); Wolfgang Fikentscher, *Wettbewerb und gewerblicher Rechtsschutz—Die Stellung des Rechts der Wettbewerbsbeschränkungen in der Rechtsordnung* 162, 226–227 and *passim* (1958).

[132] *See* Max Kummer, *Anwendungsbereich und Schutzgut der privatrechtlichen Rechtssätze gegen unlauteren und gegen freiheitsbeschränkenden Wettbewerb* 106 (1960) ("[T]rägt auch [das Recht an der Wettbewerbsstellung] dieses ausgesprochene Doppelgesicht von subjektiv- und objektivrechtlicher Prägung; subjektiv-rechtlich insoweit, als seine Verwirklichung im Einzelfall dem Berechtigten überlassen bleibt; objektivrechtlich in der Notwendigkeit, seinen Schutzumfang in jedem Einzelfall vermöge einer objektivrechtlichen Norm neu wertend auszumessen ...."). For a similar conception, *see* Wolfgang Portmann, *Wesen und System der subjektiven Privatrechte* para. 279 *et seq.* (1996). *See also* the critique of Florent Thouvenin, *Funktionale Systematisierung von Wettbewerbsrecht (UWG) und Immaterialgüterrechten* 120 (2007).

into circular reasoning: if the competitor's right is dependent on a case-by-case assessment—that is, if her subjective right exists only as far as rules of fair dealing and honesty prescribe[133]—then its substance is not independent and self-contained. Rather, rights are a reflex of public policy—not genuinely established or preexisting.

Wolfgang Fikentscher, by contrast, drew on an external position—the market participant's constitutional right to demand free and fair conduct in competition.[134] The position he conceived of was deemed largely independent of unfair competition policy. Taking individual freedom as a subjective right of the competitor (and the consumer) thus avoided the conceptual conundrum. But it could not escape the practical problem: individual rights do not come with a built-in metric for determining what is fair competition and what is not.[135] If we want to avoid falling back on the traditional view that standards of honesty and fairness should provide the demarcation,[136] we must address the fields' multitude of underlying substantive law policies.

C The Heterogeneity of Policies: Vertical and Horizontal Competition

The debate on the protectable subject matter in unfair competition law reflects a much deeper and older problem. Legal philosophy and private law theory still regularly inquire whether property is decreed by the sovereign or whether it is a prestate institution and thus a natural

[133] Max Kummer, *Anwendungsbereich und Schutzgut der privatrechtlichen Rechtssätze gegen unlauteren und gegen freiheitsbeschränkenden Wettbewerb* 104 (1960) ("[D]ie Wettbewerbsstellung ist nur im genannten Rahmen geschützt, nämlich gegen Treu und Glauben verletzende Angriffe, und nur insoweit zum subjektiven Recht erhoben . . . .").

[134] Wolfgang Fikentscher, *Wettbewerb und gewerblicher Rechtsschutz—Die Stellung des Rechts der Wettbewerbsbeschränkungen in der Rechtsordnung* 209 *et seq.*, 215–216, 226–227 and n. 40, and *passim* (1958).

[135] For this lack of structure in subjective rights models, *see* Niklas Luhmann, *Zur Funktion der subjektiven Rechte*, 322, 329, in *Die Funktion des Rechts in der modernen Gesellschaft, Jahrbuch für Rechtssoziologie und Rechtstheorie* (Rüdiger Lautmann et al. eds., 1970) ("[Die liberale Staats- und Gesellschaftslehre] belegt exemplarisch, wie leicht die Betonung des subjektiven Rechts als Recht zur Vernachlässigung von Strukturfragen führen kann.").

[136] *But see* Wolfgang Fikentscher's explanation of the contents of the subjective right in *Wettbewerb und gewerblicher Rechtsschutz—Die Stellung des Rechts der Wettbewerbsbeschränkungen in der Rechtsordnung* 229 (1958) ("Das Schutzgut des UWG . . . ist wiederum das Recht des einzelnen auf wirtschaftliche Betätigung, nun aber nicht in der Form der Wettbewerbsfreiheit . . ., sondern in der Form der Lauterkeit des Wettbewerbs. Hier liegt der Schwerpunkt des Rechts vom unlauteren Wettbewerb. . . . Vielmehr hat das subjektive Recht auf wirtschaftliche Betätigung den zweifachen Inhalt, daß man bei der Ausübung dieses Rechts sowohl von Eingriffen anderer in die Freiheit frei, als auch gegen unlautere Maßnahmen anderer geschützt wird.").

right.[137] The question is, does it come from the top down or from the bottom up? Does it ensue from lawmakers' institutionalization, or is it a preexisting Something?[138] These and similar questions have been long debated and still await a resolution. Full clarification cannot be provided in an analysis as specific as this one. My focus here—which will, however, provide clarity for the field of trademark and unfair competition regulation—is on the characteristic stratification of policies that helps explain why subjective rights and the process of competition are detached, and how they nevertheless remain interrelated.

1 *Two Types of Unfair Competition Cases and Regulatory Policies*

Any invasion of a competitor's marketplace position represents a redistribution of value. Courts have always, and often rather sweepingly, referred to this in terms of free riding, unjust enrichment, or misappropriation. What they have thereby neglected is the fact that the scenarios of such "misappropriation" differ. As we have seen, among the plethora of policies in tort and unfair competition law, different categories exist. Some aim to protect individual rights without giving immediate regard to the market mechanism. Others aim to regulate market dynamics with regard to consumer decision making. Revisiting two landmark cases—*International News Service* and *Apollinarisbrunnen*—analyzed in chapters 1 and 2 illustrates the key distinction within the institutional framework.

The majority in *International News Service* found misappropriation in the defendant's use of the plaintiff's "hot" news. The defendant directly usurped what the plaintiff had acquired through the investment of its own resources.[139] No consumer confusion was involved. Accordingly, the question the court found most relevant was "not so much the rights of either party as against the public but their rights as between themselves."[140] The scenario, therefore, can be explained as being situated at the horizontal

[137] *See, e.g.*, John Austin, *The Province of Jurisprudence Determined* (1832); with reference to Austin, *see also* H. L. A. Hart, *The Concept of Law* 26 *et seq.* (2nd edn., 1961); more recently, *e.g.*, N. Stephan Kinsella, *Against Intellectual Property*, 15 J. Libertarian Stud. 1 (2001).

[138] *See also, e.g.*, Richard A. Epstein, *International News Service v. Associated Press: Custom and Law as Sources of Property Rights in News*, 78 Va. L. Rev. 85, 85 (1992); for German and European doctrine, *see, e.g.*, Helmut Coing, *Zur Geschichte des Begriffs „subjektives Recht,"* 7 *et seq.*, in *Das subjektive Recht und der Rechtsschutz der Persönlichkeit* (Helmut Coing et al. eds., 1959); Ludwig Raiser, *Der Stand der Lehre vom subjektiven Recht im Deutschen Zivilrecht*, 1961 JZ 465, 465–466.

[139] *International News Service v. Associated Press*, 248 U.S. 215, 236 and 239–240 (1918) ("[T]he right to acquire property by honest labor or the conduct of a lawful business is as much entitled to protection as the right to guard property already acquired. ... [A]nd that defendant in appropriating it and selling it as its own is endeavoring to reap where it has not sown and ... is appropriating to itself the harvest of those who have sown.").

[140] *Id.* at 236.

level.[141] Seen in this light, the issue was actually whether a right "against the world at large" existed.[142] Quite differently, *Apollinarisbrunnen* featured a scenario at the vertical level.[143] The issue at hand was not limited to an analysis of subjective rights "as between" competitors. In fact, *Apollinarisbrunnen* was not a two-party scenario at all. Unlike *International News Service*, the *Apollinarisbrunnen* defendant had invaded the plaintiff's domain by means of deceiving the customer. Hence, the dispute concerned the multiangular structure of the market mechanism.[144]

Looking at this difference in light of the concept of economic competition explained above allows us to distinguish the policies involved. Above all, of course, unfair competition law regulates all kinds of market dynamics. Under the Hayekian concept of competition, the law serves as a necessary condition for the formation of a spontaneous order.[145] Any order delimits individual actors' spheres of sovereignty. The guarantee of protection against invasion by a fellow citizen or competitor establishes the groundwork for private individual planning. This is the most important function of the rules of just conduct—namely, to make clear which of the citizens' and competitors' expectations are justified. In other words, "Good fences make good neighbors."[146] This institutional framework, however, is further segmented internally. As von Hayek himself pointed out, a planned order, particularly by concrete legal regulation, is necessary whenever competition cannot work effectively. In this regard, as he explained by reference to patent protection, it will not suffice to recognize private property and freedom of contract alone to uphold a self-contained system of regulation by free competition.[147] Some areas of economic transacting cannot be adequately provided by private actors. In these sectors of the economy, legal regulation is indicated. In modern terms, the lawmakers' direct interference will be legitimate only whenever market failures must be corrected. Ultimately, this understanding of the legal order establishes a principle of subsidiarity. It is founded on the priority of self-regulation by the mechanics of competition.

Phrased in terms of unfair competition policy, two categories ensue. Even though both categories are designed to guarantee competition's

141 *See supra* p. 285–286. 142 *See supra* p. 300–301.

143 For the case and its analysis, *see supra* p. 27 *et seq.* 144 *See supra* p. 285–286.

145 *See supra* p. 276 *et seq.*

146 Friedrich A. von Hayek, *Law, Legislation and Liberty—A New Statement of the Liberal Principles of Justice and Political Economy, vol. I: Rules and Order* 102 and 107 (1973) (reference to Robert Frost's poem "Mending Wall"). *See also*, with further references, Hermann Reichold, *Lauterkeitsrecht als Sonderdeliktsrecht—Zur Rolle zivilistischen Denkens bei der Anwendung von* § 1 *UWG*, 193 AcP 204, 218 (1993).

147 Friedrich A. von Hayek, *The Road to Serfdom: Text and Documents* 87 (Bruce Caldwell ed., 2007 (original edn. 1944)).

unhindered evolution by the correction of market failure, their regulatory qualities differ—only one provides for claims "against the world at large." Protecting consumer decision making from improper information transmission and undue impact is the core policy. This is also the single specific paradigm of dishonesty reflected in the Paris Convention's norm on unfair competition in article 10*bis*(3).[148] By definition, subjective rights cannot exist under this policy of confusion prevention. The allocation of values in this category is not an issue for the legal order to establish. The process of consumer decision making, rather, is tasked with separating success from defeat and ultimately allocating and distributing values among competitors.[149]

The second category covers regulatory policies beyond competitor-consumer interactions. This is the horizontal level of intercompetitor relations. The Restatement of Unfair Competition (Third) clarifies the demarcation line quite lucidly. As the restatement's comments explain in general, the function of the law of unfair competition is "to delimit the circumstances in which a person may prohibit the appropriation by another of intangible business assets created through an investment of time, money, or effort."[150] Yet while one category of misappropriation concerns "appropriation of another's good will through misrepresentation" (especially with regard to trademark infringements), the category of "other appropriations can be more direct."[151] Within the latter category, patent and copyright laws provide for a delimitation at the level of federal

[148] Article 10*bis* Paris Convention states: "(1) The countries of the Union are bound to assure to nationals of such countries effective protection against unfair competition. (2) Any act of competition contrary to honest practices in industrial or commercial matters constitutes an act of unfair competition. (3) The following in particular shall be prohibited: 1. all acts of such a nature as to create confusion by any means whatever with the establishment, the goods, or the industrial or commercial activities, of a competitor; 2. false allegations in the course of trade of such a nature as to discredit the establishment, the goods, or the industrial or commercial activities, of a competitor; 3. indications or allegations the use of which in the course of trade is liable to mislead the public as to the nature, the manufacturing process, the characteristics, the suitability for their purpose, or the quantity, of the goods." For an analysis of the reflection of the principles in article 10*bis*(3) in numerous national regimes, *see* Anselm Kamperman Sanders, *Unfair Competition Law—The Protection of Intellectual and Industrial Creativity* 22 *et seq.* (1997).

[149] With regard to the lack of subjective rights in a system of free competition, *see* Ernst-Joachim Mestmäcker, *Eingriffserwerb und Rechtsverletzung in der ungerechtfertigten Bereicherung*, 1958 JZ 521, 526; Ludwig Raiser, *Der Stand der Lehre vom subjektiven Recht im Deutschen Zivilrecht*, 1961 JZ 465, 469; Erwin Deutsch, *Entwicklung und Entwicklungsfunktion der Deliktstatbestände*, 1963 JZ 385, 387; *see also* Franz Böhm, *Wettbewerb und Monopolkampf—Eine Untersuchung zur Frage des wirtschaftlichen Kampfrechts und zur Frage der rechtlichen Struktur der geltenden Wirtschaftsordnung* 290 (1933); Werner Flume, *Verbotene Preisabsprache und Einzelvertrag*, 1956 WuW 457, 465.

[150] Restatement of the Law—Unfair Competition (Third), § 1, comment f (1995).

[151] *Id.*

laws. Concerning unfair competition prevention, it is the law on protection of trade secrets, as well as on the "security against wrongful physical intrusions,"[152] that complements the horizontal level of protection policies. With respect to protection at this level, legislation must expressly decide how to delimit individual competitors' freedom of transacting and, ultimately, how to distribute resources and values. This second category of policies can thus truly be characterized as allocating and distributing subjective rights.

2 *Clarification: The Horizontality of* Neminem Laedere

In light of this segmentation, one last point requires clarification. Agreement exists that unfair competition law protects the *par conditio concurrentium.*[153] This seems to stand in contrast to tort doctrine, which exclusively protects the right owner. While tort law aims to prevent injury to private rights, unfair competition law upholds the state of a constant competitive struggle. Correspondingly, the tort principle of *neminem laedere* has been described as inapplicable under unfair competition doctrine. To the contrary, competition is said to require intentional harming of one's competitors.[154]

This imprecision invites misunderstanding. As we have discussed, tort law does not define absolute limitations on individual conduct; nor does unfair competition law. No absolute rights exist. The determination of individual spheres of activity and freedom is what defines the scope of private entitlements with regard to other individuals' respective domains.

[152] *Id. See also id.* at §§ 39 *et seq.* (on trade secrets).

[153] *See, e.g.*, Karl F. Kreuzer, *Wettbewerbsverstöße und Beeinträchtigung geschäftlicher Interessen (einschl. der Verletzung kartellrechtlicher Vorschriften)*, 232, 265, in *Vorschläge und Gutachten zur Reform des deutschen internationalen Privatrechts der außervertraglichen Schuldverhältnisse, vorgelegt im Auftrag der Zweiten Kommission des Deutschen Rates für internationales Privatrecht* (Ernst von Caemmerer ed., 1983) ("Ein wichtiges Ziel des Wettbewerbsrechts ist die Wahrung der Chancengleichheit aller Wettbewerber am Markt. . . . In diesem Sinne ist das Wettbewerbsrecht ein Komplex von Kampfregeln, eine Wett(bewerbs)kampfordnung."); more recently, *e.g.*, Peter Mankowski, in *Münchener Kommentar zum Lauterkeitsrecht, vol. I,* IntWettbR para. 138 (Peter W. Heermann et al. eds., 2nd edn., 2014).

[154] *See, e.g.*, Paul Gieseke, *Recht am Unternehmen und Schutz des Unternehmens—Alte und neue deutsche Rechtsprechung*, 1950 GRUR 298, 303; Erwin Deutsch, *Commentary to BGH, decision of 23 October 1971 (I ZR 86/69)—Tampax*, 1971 JZ 732, 733 ("Auszugehen ist ... von der Sonderstellung der Wettbewerbsverstöße im Gesamtgebiet des Haftungsrechts. Vom Wettbewerb wird nämlich der Grundsatz 'neminem laedere' auf den Kopf gestellt. Es ist geradezu erwünscht, den Mitbewerber zu treffen."); Kamen Troller, *Das internationale Privatrecht des unlauteren Wettbewerbs in vergleichender Darstellung der Rechte Deutschlands, Englands, Frankreichs, Italiens, der Schweiz und der USA* 27–28 (1962); more recently, Andreas Höder, *Die kollisionsrechtliche Behandlung unteilbarer Multistate-Verstöße—Das Internationale Wettbewerbsrecht im Spannungsfeld von Marktort-, Auswirkungs- und Herkunftslandprinzip* 105–106 (2002).

Per se, therefore, the principle of *neminem laedere* is a rule of relativity at best.[155] In addition, the principle's scope of application varies across the field. Again, a distinction between the horizontal and vertical levels is crucial. Horizontal relations (i.e., those among competitors) without a market relation are directly subjected to policy makers' decisions on how to calibrate the allocation of rights and duties. This is different for the sector of market-related transacting, where the main policy is to protect consumer decision making. At the horizontal level, it may thus actually be a background regime of *neminem laedere* that provides for a rule of non-invasion in legally determined rights. One example is the protection of trade secrets; another is the quasi intellectual property scenario of *International News Service*. In vertical relations, by contrast, individual rights are nonexistent by definition. Here, the principle of *neminem laedere* has no function.[156]

D Summary

Formal distinctions between tort and unfair competition law are not helpful, for they merely scratch the surface. In particular, the practical divergence between remedial relief and the terminological noise concerning absolute and subjective individual rights will not establish a workable distinction between the fields. From a deeper perspective, the contrary is true: the two fields widely overlap. The overall regime of background rules sets the stage for socioeconomic evolution. Tort and

[155] *See also* Friedrich A. von Hayek, *Law, Legislation and Liberty—A New Statement of the Liberal Principles of Justice and Political Economy, vol. I: Rules and Order* 103 (1973) ("The harm that one does to another which the law aims to prevent is thus not all harm but only the disappointment of such expectations as the law designates as legitimate. Only in this way can 'do not harm others' be made a rule with meaningful content for a group of men who are allowed to pursue their own aims on the basis of their own knowledge."); John Stuart Mill, *On Liberty* 79–80 (1859) ("In many cases, an individual, in pursuing a legitimate object, necessarily and therefore legitimately causes pain or loss to others, or intercepts a good which they had a reasonable hope of obtaining. . . . [I]t is, by common admission, better for the general interest of mankind, that persons should pursue their objects undeterred by this sort of consequences. In other words, society admits no right, either legal or moral, in the disappointed competitors, to immunity from this kind of suffering; and feels called on to interfere, only when means of success have been employed which it is contrary to the general interest to permit—namely, fraud or treachery, and force.").

[156] This is what Wolfgang Fikentscher has explained. It is the antinomy of freedom of transacting and individual rights protection that is to be found in protection of the competitor's personality right. *See* Wolfgang Fikentscher, *Wettbewerb und gewerblicher Rechtsschutz—Die Stellung des Rechts der Wettbewerbsbeschränkungen in der Rechtsordnung* 214 (1958) ("Der Grundsatz des ‚neminem laedere' bezieht sich nur auf die ‚Rechte anderer', also auf die geschützten Einzelrechte, nicht aber auf das Recht zur freien Entfaltung. Sonst wäre der Wettbewerb ein Unrecht. . . . [W]enn man ein allgemeines Persönlichkeitsrecht anerkennen will, man auch die ihm innewohnende Antinomie von Entfaltungsfreiheit und Güterschutz zugestehen muß . . . . ").

unfair competition law alike provide the institutional background for individuals' conduct to unfold. But depending on the specific situation of improper competitive conduct, these background rules will be drawn from different sources. Within the multiangular model of market-related conduct, protecting unmanipulated consumer decision making is one specific sector of the overall background regime. Consumer decision making is the blueprint for the construction of a liberal order of competition. Other cases of unfair competition, however—particularly those at the horizontal level of intercompetitor relations—must be decided under the rules of a different sector.

II Antitrust and Unfair Competition Law

In light of modern tendencies in both unfair competition and antitrust doctrine, the two fields' complementary policies are often unduly intermingled.[157] Yet a functional concept of market effects not only allows for a separation of tort and unfair competition law on the basis of the respective subject matter of regulation but also helps draw a clear line between the sectors of unfair competition and antitrust law.

For a long time, US theory and practice have seen unfair competition and antitrust governed by largely homogeneous policies. By contrast, in Europe, the approximation of policies in modern doctrine constitutes a more dramatic paradigm shift.[158] Previously, theory used to distinguish between antitrust and unfair competition law on the basis of a so-called specialty rule. Antitrust law was designed to preserve freedom of competition as a legal institution by preventing restraints on trade and abuses of economic power. Unfair competition prevention, on the other hand, was aimed at establishing and maintaining individual fairness in competition. It was deemed to protect only against minor wrongs below the threshold of antitrust violations.[159] But the picture has recently changed. Under a macroperspective, both areas are described as constituting a uniform

[157] *See supra* p. 220 *et seq.*

[158] Wilhelm Wengler, in his report to the Fourth International Congress of Comparative Law in Paris in 1954, summarized the difference between European and US doctrine as follows: "In the minds of European lawyers, there is still a gap between the rules against unfair competition and the rules against trusts and monopolies, whereas in the United States all these rules are generally regarded as a whole, the rules against unfair competition aiming primarily at certain means, the rules against monopolies at certain effects of competition." Wilhelm Wengler, *Laws Concerning Unfair Competition and the Conflict of Laws*, 4 Am. J. Comp. L. 167, 179 n. 38c (1955).

[159] For the doctrines of antitrust exclusivity ("Sperrwirkung"), specialty ("Vorfeldthese"), and separation ("Trennungstheorie"), *see, e.g.*, Hans Würdinger, *Freiheit der persönlichen Entfaltung, Kartell- und Wettbewerbsrecht*, 1953 WuW 721, 730 *et seq.*; Peter Ulmer, *Der Begriff „Leistungswettbewerb" und seine Bedeutung für die Anwendung von GWB und UWG-Tatbeständen*, 1977 GRUR 565, 577; Ernst-Joachim Mestmäcker, *Der verwaltete*

system of market regulation.[160] At the same time, antitrust law has gradually turned toward individual rights protection.[161] The Court of Justice, early on, began to spur the implementation of private remedies against antitrust violations.[162] Only recently have European lawmakers enacted a directive allowing for private damage actions with respect to antitrust violations.[163] As it appears, then, modern antitrust and unfair competition law (including trademarks) are part of a comprehensive framework of rules providing for free and unhindered competition.

The alleged homogeneity of substantive law policies also seems to have spurred uniformity in choice of law. As seen earlier, US law has never adhered to a clear-cut distinction.[164] Practice has actually made a great effort to align antitrust and trademark conflicts law. The Ninth and the First Circuit, in particular, have extrapolated the Supreme Court's antitrust-effects argument in *Steele*, literally applying antitrust conflicts principles to trademark conflicts.[165] In Europe, even though the merger of the fields has not come full circle, scholarly theory aims at a unification. Yet as the Rome II Regulation illustrates, the rules for conflicts resolution in article 6(1) and (3) are still—at least formally—supposed to differ.

Indeed, as a closer look at the fields' substantive law policies and their conflicts law structures explains, a genuine effects test must not be imported into trademark and unfair competition choice of law. While an unmodified effects test suits substantive law policies of regulating

Wettbewerb—Eine vergleichende Untersuchung über den Schutz von Freiheit und Lauterkeit im Wettbewerbsrecht 56 *et seq.*, 78 *et seq.*, and 143 *et seq.* (1984).

160 Among the plethora of scholarly theses on the issue, *see, e.g.*, Walter R. Schluep, *Vom lauteren zum freien Wettbewerb*, 1973 GRUR Int. 446, 447; Karsten Schmidt, *Kartellverfahrensrecht—Kartellverwaltungsrecht—Bürgerliches Recht* 409 (1977); Wolfgang Fikentscher, *Wirtschaftsrecht, vol. II: Deutsches Wirtschaftsrecht* § 22 I 6b cc (1983).

161 For this development, *see, e.g.*, Winfried Tilmann, *Über das Verhältnis von GWB und UWG*, 1979 GRUR 825, 829; for the modern development of antitrust and unfair competition uniformity, *see* Frauke Henning-Bodewig, *Was gehört zum Lauterkeitsrecht?*, 9, 20, in *Lauterkeitsrecht und Acquis Communautaire* (Reto M. Hilty & Frauke Henning-Bodewig eds., 2009).

162 *See Van Gend en Loos v. Administratie der Belastingen*, C-26/62 (5 February 1963), [1963] E.C.R. 1; *Courage and Crehan*, C-453/99, para. 25 *et seq.* (20 September 2001), [2001] E.C.R. I-6297; *Manfredi*, C-295/04 to 298/04, para. 58 *et seq.* (13 July 2006), [2006] E.C.R. I-6619.

163 Directive 2014/104/EU of the European Parliament and of the Council of 26 November 2014 on certain rules governing actions for damages under national law for infringements of the competition law provisions of the Member States and of the European Union, O.J. EU (5 December 2014), L 349/1.

164 *See supra* p. 164 *et seq.*

165 *See Wells Fargo & Co. v. Wells Fargo Exp. Co.*, 556 F.2d 406 (9th Cir. 1977); *McBee v. Delica Co., Ltd.*, 417 F.3d 107 (1st Cir. 2005); for an overview of the "antitrust transfer model" in the circuits' tests, *see* Gary D. Feldon, *The Antitrust Model of Extraterritorial Trademark Jurisdiction: Analysis and Predictions After F. Hoffmann-La Roche*, 20 Emory Int'l L. Rev. 651, 656 *et seq.* (2006).

marketplace activity under a macroperspective, it is problematic for choice of law in trademark and unfair competition conflicts. This is due to the fact that trademark and unfair competition policies are not designed to regulate the marketplace *in toto*. Their impetus is focused on the microdynamics of market activity, not on the static allocation of market power.[166] More concretely, antitrust regulation is not concerned with the market information infrastructure. It thus lacks a focus on consumer decision making as a qualitative determinant of both substantive law policy and conflicts structure. With respect to trademark and unfair competition conflicts, by contrast, an accordingly structured qualification of effects is indicated. This qualification must be oriented toward the triangular structure of marketplace transactions illustrated earlier.[167] Within this structure, the two levels of horizontal and vertical relations between market participants determine the choice of substantive law policies and the correlating choice-of-law principles.

In order to avoid misunderstanding, of course, we must acknowledge that this reconceptualization does not invalidate the model of two overlapping circles of unfair competition and antitrust prevention.[168] Policy makers may decide to characterize specific antitrust violations as also concurrently violating norms of unfair competition prevention, or vice versa. Nonetheless, at its core, trademark and unfair competition doctrine—characterized by a policy aimed at protecting consumer decision making—does not coincide with the field of antitrust law.[169]

III The Intellectual Property Dichotomy: Innovation vs. Competition

Now that we have explored the relationship between tort, antitrust, and unfair competition law, the next step is to analyze correlations and antinomies between trademark protection and unfair competition prevention. Before addressing this point, however, a closer look at the current model of formally uniform intellectual property rights is necessary. As we will see, several doctrinal frictions emerge from the perceived uniformity and functional homogeneity of rights. Trademark protection on the one side and copyright and patent protection on the other have separate foundations and characteristics. Identifying these demarcations will lay the groundwork for a reintegration of trademark and unfair competition law into the larger field of market communication regulation.

[166] *See supra* p. 275 *et seq.* and also *infra* p. 325 *et seq.* [167] *See supra* p. 285–286.

[168] For this common allegory in European doctrine, *see, e.g.*, Helmut Köhler, *Zur Konkurrenz lauterkeitsrechtlicher und kartellrechtlicher Normen*, 2005 WRP 645, 647.

[169] For choice of law in cases of unfair competition and antitrust concurrence, *see infra* p. 563–565.

A The Mistaken Concept of Intellectual Property Uniformity

As we have seen, the formal concept of "property" serves as an overarching paradigm between the different categories of intellectual property rights, especially copyrights, patents, and trademarks. Unfair competition prevention, by contrast, appears to be a separate field where no absolute rights exist and, consequently, a different system of protection governs. As a closer look reveals, however, the demarcation does not run between intellectual property and unfair competition law. The gap must be found between the fields of trademark and unfair competition law on the one hand and the rest of intellectual property on the other.

1 Historical Remnants: The "Immaterialization" of Trademarks

The meandering assessment of trademark rights and their ultimate propertization by inclusion in the category of intellectual property reflects a historical struggle. In the first chapter, I explored how Josef Kohler's theory of personality rights, combined with a paradigm of state-granted privileges, contributed to trademark-as-property protection and, eventually, to the reign of strict territoriality in trademark choice of law.[170] With regard to the distinction between trademarks, patents, and copyrights, another look at history illustrates yet another facet of doctrinal misconceptions.

Kohler's conception of intellectual property distinguished between two categories of individual entitlements. The first category, personality rights, comprised the prevention of unfair competition and the protection of trademark rights.[171] The second category concerned absolute rights in so-called immaterial goods (*Immaterialgüter*). This was where he located copyrights and patents.[172] However, his categorization was

[170] *See supra* p. 21 *et seq.* and p. 53 *et seq.*

[171] *See, e.g.*, Josef Kohler, *Das Recht des Markenschutzes mit Berücksichtigung ausländischer Gesetzgebungen und mit besonderer Rücksicht auf die englische, anglo-amerikanische, französische, belgische und italienische Jurisprudenz* 5 (1884) ("Zu den Individualrechten eines jeden subjectiven Rechtswesens gehört aber vor Allem das Recht zu verlangen, dass das Individuum als solches in seiner Besonderheit und Individualität anerkannt und jede Vermischung mit andern Individuen ferngehalten wird."); further also Josef Kohler, *Warenzeichenrecht—Zugleich zweite Auflage des Rechts des Markenschutzes mit Berücksichtigung ausländischer Gesetzgebungen (1884)* 67 (2nd edn., 1910).

[172] *See, e.g.*, Josef Kohler, *Das Autorrecht, eine zivilistische Abhandlung* (1880); Josef Kohler, *Lehrbuch des Patentrechts* 13 *et seq.* (1908); Josef Kohler, *Das Recht des Markenschutzes mit Berücksichtigung ausländischer Gesetzgebungen und mit besonderer Rücksicht auf die englische, anglo-amerikanische, französische, belgische und italienische Jurisprudenz* (1884); Josef Kohler, *Die Idee des geistigen Eigentums*, 82 AcP 141 (1894); *see also* Albert Osterrieth, *Lehrbuch des gewerblichen Rechtsschutzes* 13 (1908) ("Indessen darf man sich nicht verleiten lassen, den Namen, die Firma oder die Warenzeichen den Erfindungen oder Mustern, oder allgemein, den immateriellen Gütern gleichzusetzen.

never universally acknowledged. In particular, the characterization of trademarks as personality rights provoked criticism. Critics contended that trademarks were more akin to tangible business assets than to their owners' personality.[173] In the end, they won but did not reject Kohler's categorization per se—instead, they simply transferred trademarks from the category of personality rights to the class of immaterial goods.[174] From then on, trademarks were deemed to be immaterial rights alongside patents and copyrights. This would ultimately prove problematic since trademarks seemed to have become somewhat isolated from the issue of marketplace competition.

2 *Current Doctrine: Intellectual Property Homogeneity*

The historical immaterialization of trademark rights can still be found in modern law. As we have seen, US intellectual property law sometimes tends to neglect differences between trademarks, patents, and copyrights.[175] In addition, trademark propertization has increasingly diluted the traditional idea of market information protection as the central policy. The trend is to categorize broadly; patents, copyrights, and trademarks are often seen as just another species of property.[176] The same problem exists in Europe. Overall, intellectual property law provides for the right owner's effective protection under a concept of

Denn sie tragen ihren Wert nicht in sich selbst, sie gewinnen ihn erst aus der Beziehung zum Inhaber und zu dessen Betätigung.").

173 For a representative critique, *see, e.g.*, Richard Alexander-Katz, *Die rechtliche Natur des Markenrechts sowie des Rechts an Waarenausstattungen*, 1901 GRUR 102, 103 *et seq.*; Adolf Lobe, *Die Bekämpfung des unlauteren Wettbewerbs, vol. I: Der unlautere Wettbewerb als Rechtsverletzung nach dem Bürgerlichen Gesetzbuch und den Nebengesetzen* 163 (1907) ("Endlich sind auch Name, Marke und Zeichen keine Persönlichkeitsrechte, weil keine Teile der Persönlichkeit. Sie sind lediglich Mittel, um die Persönlichkeit in ihrer Individualität zu bezeichnen, Individualisierungsmittel und als solche immaterielle Güter."); *see also* Wolfgang Fikentscher, *Wettbewerb und gewerblicher Rechtsschutz—Die Stellung des Rechts der Wettbewerbsbeschränkungen in der Rechtsordnung* 146–147 (1958) (illustrating the Reichsgericht's meandering position).

174 *See, e.g.*, Julius Magnus, *Warenzeichenrecht*, 1923 GRUR 162, 163; Kurt Bußmann, *Verfolgung ausländischer Zeichenverletzungen in Deutschland*, 1929 MuW 419; *see also* Eugen Ulmer, *Warenzeichen und unlauterer Wettbewerb in ihrer Fortbildung durch die Rechtsprechung* 9 (1929); for a summary, *see* Wolfgang Fikentscher, *Wettbewerb und gewerblicher Rechtsschutz—Die Stellung des Rechts der Wettbewerbsbeschränkungen in der Rechtsordnung* 146–147 (1958); Walter R. Schluep, *Das Markenrecht als subjektives Recht* 333–335 (1964); Adriano Vanzetti, *Funktion und Rechtsnatur der Marke (2. Teil)*, 1965 GRUR Ausl. 185, 189.

175 *See supra* p. 236 *et seq.*

176 Mark A. Lemley, *The Modern Lanham Act and the Death of Common Sense*, 108 Yale L.J. 1687, 1688 (1999); Michael A. Carrier, *Cabining Intellectual Property Through A Property Paradigm*, 54 Duke L.J. 1, 8 *et seq.* and *passim* (2004); Mark A. Lemley, *Property, Intellectual Property, and Free Riding*, 83 Tex. L. Rev. 1031, 1033 *et seq.* (2005).

absolute and exclusive property rights.[177] Trademarks are deemed a foundational pillar of this system, equivalent to other categories of intellectual property, particularly copyrights and patents.[178]

Of course, ideas on the functions of trademarks have varied. But ultimately, as the Court of Justice's case law illustrates, the concept of homogeneity prevailed. The court's 1971 *Sirena* decision was still influenced by a certain disdain—and thus an idea of trademark rights being different from other kinds of intellectual property rights:

> The exercise of a trade-mark right is particularly apt to lead to a partitioning of markets, and thus to impair the free movement of goods between States which is essential to the Common Market. Moreover, a trade-mark right is distinguishable in this context from other rights of industrial and commercial property, inasmuch as the interests protected by the latter are usually more important, and merit a higher degree of protection, than the interests protected by an ordinary trade-mark.[179]

This cavalier attitude toward trademarks, however, changed twenty years later, in the *HAG II* decision.[180] The public's interest in trademark protection was expressly acknowledged in Advocate General Jacobs's opinion:

> The truth is that, at least in economic terms, and perhaps also "from the human point of view", trade marks are no less important, and no less deserving of protection, than any other form of intellectual property. They are, in the words

[177] *See, e.g.*, Norbert Reich, in Norbert Reich & Hans-W. Micklitz, *Europäisches Verbraucherrecht* 225–226 (4th edn., 2003); Pedro A. De Miguel Asensio, *The Private International Law of Intellectual Property and of Unfair Commercial Practices: Convergence or Divergence?*, 137, 141, in *Intellectual Property and Private International Law* (Stefan Leible & Ansgar Ohly eds., 2009).

[178] *See, e.g.*, article 2 Council Regulation (EC) No 1383/2003 of 22 July 2003 concerning customs action against goods suspected of infringing certain intellectual property rights and the measures to be taken against goods found to have infringed such rights, O.J. EU (2 August 2003), L 196/7; Recital 26 of Regulation (EC) No. 864/2007 of the European Parliament and of the Council of 11 July 2007 on the law applicable to non-contractual obligations (Rome II), O.J. EU (31 July 2007), L 199/40; *see also* Eugen Ulmer, *Die Immaterialgüterrechte im internationalen Privatrecht—Rechtsvergleichende Untersuchung mit Vorschlägen für die Vereinheitlichung in der Europäischen Wirtschaftsgemeinschaft* 4–5 (1975); WIPO, *Protection Against Unfair Competition—Analysis of the Present World Situation*, WIPO Publ. no. 725(E), 10 (1994); Andrew Dickinson, *The Rome II Regulation: The Law Applicable to Non-Contractual Obligations* para. 8.13 (2008).

[179] *Sirena v. Eda*, C-40/70, para. 7 (11 February 1971), [1971] E.C.R. 69. Advocate General *Dutheillet de Lamothe* had paved the way toward this finding by extended reference to a "human point of view": "Both from the economic and from the human point of view the interests protected by patent legislation merit greater respect than those protected by trade-marks. … From the human point of view, the debt which society owes to the 'inventor' of the name 'Prep Good Morning' [a brand of shaving cream] is certainly not of the same nature, to say the least, as that which humanity owes to the discoverer of penicillin" (opinion to case 40/70 *Sirena* [1971] E.C.R. 69, at 87).

[180] *CNL-SUCAL v. HAG* ("HAG II"), C-10/89 (17 October 1990), [1990] E.C.R. I-3711.

of one author, "nothing more nor less than the fundament of most market-place competition".... Like patents, trade marks find their justification in a harmonious dovetailing between public and private interests. Whereas patents reward the creativity of the inventor and thus stimulate scientific progress, trade marks reward the manufacturer who consistently produces high-quality goods and they thus stimulate economic progress. Without trade mark protection there would be little incentive for manufacturers to develop new products or to maintain the quality of existing ones.[181]

Even though *HAG II* appeared to introduce a policy-oriented perspective and emphasized marketplace competition as the foundation of trademark protection, it maintained the immaterialization of trademarks. As the advocate general had explained, intellectual property rights were generally conceived of as "dovetailing" public and private interests. Yet whether trademarks and other categories of intellectual property should be further distinguished remained untouched.

B Rectification: A Grounded Intangibility of Trademarks

While historical doctrine may have been justified in rejecting trademarks' character as personality rights, its lumping together of trademarks, copyrights, and patents under the umbrella of intellectual property is questionable. Trademarks are different from copyrights, patents, and other categories of intellectual property insofar as rights acquisition, protection, and maintenance are inextricably connected to their owner's ongoing marketplace activity.

1 The Difference in Intellectual Property Incentive Structures

Much ink has been spilled on the economic foundations and doctrinal structures of intellectual property rights, especially with respect to the characteristics of different rights.[182] What we need to look at closely are the incentives that are provided for under the categories.

Quite early, the internal dichotomy within intellectual property was succinctly and fittingly expressed in the US Constitution, which gives Congress the power "[t]o promote the Progress of Science and useful

[181] Opinion of Advocate General Jacobs, para. 17–18 (13 March 1990), [1990] E.C.R. I-3725. Jacobs started this explanation with explicit reference to Dutheillet de Lamothe in the *Sirena* case (*see* fn. 179 *supra*) and the depreciation of trademark functions and values founded on the comparison between penicillin and day-to-day trademarks: "It is noteworthy that this conception of the relative merits of trade marks and other forms of intellectual property was based on an invidious comparison between a rather trivial trade mark and one of the most important discoveries in the history of medicine. Different comparisons might have produced different results, more favourable to trade marks."

[182] For an instructive and comprehensive analysis, *see, e.g.*, Andreas Heinemann, *Immaterialgüterschutz in der Wettbewerbsordnung—Eine grundlagenorientierte Untersuchung zum Kartellrecht des geistigen Eigentums* 11 *et seq.* (2002).

Arts, by securing for limited Times to Authors and Inventors the exclusive Right to their respective Writings and Discoveries."[183] At times, this clause may have caused confusion,[184] but it unequivocally illustrates two things: First, the protection of copyrights and patents concerns the promotion of creativity and innovation. Second, trademarks fall outside this category.[185] Under the patent regime, the invention itself is the relevant subject matter. If the invention has been reduced to practice, then it is eligible for protection. Application for the patent, its disclosure, and its registration constitute formal prerequisites. In this regard, details may vary among national systems, but the fundamentals correspond.[186] A similar concept governs in copyright law. The author's expression of an idea is protected from the moment of promulgation and creation.[187] Patents and copyrights are granted protection once patentable or copyrightable subject matter has been developed; there are no further requirements.[188] In this regard, patents and copyrights are true "intangibles." Their only subject matter of protection is the product of the human mind.[189]

Trademarks are another story. While the public has an interest in encouraging innovation and creativity in general, it does not have an interest in the mere creation of symbols or marketing concepts. As a result, there is no protection for a trademark symbol's creation or

[183] U.S. Const. art. 1, § 8, cl. 8.

[184] Apparently, early lawmakers were not overly precise about how to characterize and distinguish different sectors of intellectual property. As least with regard to terminology, a clear distinction did not exist. *See* Justice Miller's explanation in *In re Trade-Mark Cases* (100 U.S. 82, 92 (1879)): "The entire legislation of Congress in regard to trade-marks is of very recent origin. It is first seen in . . . the act of July 8, 1870, entitled 'An Act to revise, consolidate, and amend the statutes relating to patents and copyrights.' . . . The part of this act relating to trade-marks is embodied in chap. 2, tit. 60, sects. 4937 to 4947, of the Revised Statutes."

[185] Stephen L. Carter, *Owning What Doesn't Exist*, 13 Harv. J. L. & Pub. Pol'y 99, 102 (1990); Lionel Bently & Brad Sherman, *Intellectual Property Law* 814–815 (4th edn., 2014).

[186] *See* article 27 para. 1 of the TRIPS Agreement: "[P]atents shall be available for any inventions, whether products or processes, in all fields of technology, provided that they are new, involve an inventive step and are capable of industrial application."

[187] For more details, *see, e.g.*, William Cornish, David Llewelyn & Tanya Aplin, *Intellectual Property: Patents, Copyright, Trade Marks and Allied Rights* para. 11.32 *et seq.* (8th edn., 2013); for continental regimes, *see, e.g.*, Florent Thouvenin, *Funktionale Systematisierung von Wettbewerbsrecht (UWG) und Immaterialgüterrechten* 308–309 (2007).

[188] *See* Stephen L. Carter, *The Trouble with Trademark*, 99 Yale L.J. 759, 767 (1990). For European patent law and the instantaneous assignment of rights, *see, e.g.*, *Centrafarm BV and Others v. Sterling Drug*, C-15/74, para. 9 (31 October 1974), [1974] E.C.R. 1147.

[189] For an iconic liberal perspective, *see* Ayn Rand, *Patents and Copyrights (The Objectivist Newsletter, May 1964)*, reprinted in *Capitalism: The Unknown Ideal*, 141, 141 (1967) ("Patents and copyrights are the legal implementation of the base of all property rights: a man's right to the product of his mind.").

invention as such. In principle, the owner is not selling the trademark—she is marketing a branded product.[190] In other words, the subject matter of protection is the "trade," not the "mark." Consequently, the incentive provided for by the system of trademark protection is different. The use of trademarks in commerce results in an accumulation of goodwill for the branded product and the creation and maintenance of its owner's reputation. A trademark's use in commerce builds up a stock of information on product and producer properties. Only upon the accumulation of market information will the owner receive a corresponding share of protection. Trademark protection is thus the quid pro quo for competitive commitment and investment in the marketplace.

Viewed in this way, it becomes clear that trademark protection (unlike patent and copyright protection) does not insulate the right owner from competition. In fact, it encourages—even requires—constant competitive commitment and investment.[191] Strictly speaking, competition ends with the invention or creation of patentable or copyrightable subject matter; it starts, however, with the acquisition of a trademark.[192]

2 *An Apparent Exception: The Trademark Register*

Though registered trademarks appear to be more closely aligned with patents and copyrights, in that such rights can be acquired immediately upon registration, the similarities end there. Registration only temporally suspends the correlation between rights and competition. Trademarks remain market related, whether acquired by use or by registration. As we have seen, Eugen Ulmer was the first to point out that registration promotes the development of trademark rights for a registrant's nascent trade.[193]

[190] *See Bonito Boats, Inc. v. Thunder Craft Boats, Inc.*, 489 U.S. 141, 157 (1989) ("[The law of unfair competition's] general concern is with protecting consumers from confusion as to source. While that concern may result in the creation of 'quasi-property rights' in communicative symbols, the focus is on the protection of consumers, not the protection of producers as an incentive to product innovation."); *Dastar Corp. v. Twentieth Century Fox Film Corp.*, 539 U.S. 23, 24 (2003) (" 'The Lanham Act,' we have said, 'does not exist to reward manufacturers for their innovation in creating a particular device; that is the purpose of the patent law and its period of exclusivity.'"). *See also* Edwin Katz, *Weltmarkenrecht* 2–3 (1926); Stephen L. Carter, *The Trouble with Trademark*, 99 Yale L.J. 759, 767 (1990).

[191] Stacey L. Dogan & Mark A. Lemley, *The Merchandising Right: Fragile Theory or Fait Accompli?*, 54 Emory L.J. 461, 467 (2005); Mark A. Lemley & Mark P. McKenna, *Owning Mark(et)s*, 109 Mich. L. Rev. 137, 173–174 (2010).

[192] For a similar description, *see* Alois Troller, *Das internationale Privat- und Zivilprozeßrecht im gewerblichen Rechtsschutz und Urheberrecht* 41 (1952); Alois Troller, *Die territoriale Unabhängigkeit der Markenrechte im Warenverkehr*, 1960 GRUR Ausl. 244, 246; Frank Peter Regelin, *Das Kollisionsrecht der Immaterialgüterrechte an der Schwelle zum 21. Jahrhundert* 76 (2000).

[193] *See supra* p. 42–46.

In addition, the register informs the public about the stock of existing rights,[194] thereby providing legal certainty for later-comers and junior users in their choice of new brands and helping avoid the social costs of wasted resources resulting from a duplication of trademarks.[195] Later on, in the case of trademark collisions, the registration system offers a convenient and practical way to decide on priority disputes.[196] These functions of the register, however, may run counter to the core trademark policy. Indeed, seen in light of the market information paradigm, the early stage of trademark protection gives the registrant more than she deserves.[197] Such an assignment goes beyond the markets in which she has done or is doing business. The register-provided benefits exceed the actual investment in market activity. In other words, without prior use of a symbol in the marketplace, the benefits that consumers expect from the trademark cannot come into existence.[198] Accordingly, rights acquisition upon registration (or application) distorts the natural *do ut des* of the market-based goodwill mechanism. Registration, therefore, provides an advance performance to the registrant without demanding the counterperformance of goodwill creation and maintenance that the public is interested in. It is just for the early stages of the trademark's life cycle that the correlation between right protection, market investment, and competition is suspended. Only in this regard will the actual and potential detriments of advance performance to the registrant be outweighed by concurrent benefits of the register.

In the same vein, the ultimate dependence of registered rights on goodwill is also illustrated by the fact that under most trademark regimes there exists only a limited grace period for nonuse after a trademark's application or registration.[199] If the trademark is not animated through actual use in the marketplace within a certain period, then it will be

[194] *See, e.g.*, BGH 2005 GRUR 1044, 1046—*Dentale Abformmasse* (22 September 2005); Karl-Heinz Fezer, *Markenschutzfähigkeit der Kommunikationszeichen (§§ 3 und 8 MarkenG) und Kommunikationsschutz der Marken (§§ 14 und 23 MarkenG)*, 2010 WRP 165, 172.

[195] William M. Landes & Richard A. Posner, *Trademark Law: An Economic Perspective*, 30 J.L. & Econ. 265, 282 (1987); William P. Kratzke, *Normative Economic Analysis of Trademark Law*, 21 Mem. St. U. L. Rev. 199, 231 (1991).

[196] *See, e.g.*, Eugen Ulmer, *Warenzeichen und unlauterer Wettbewerb in ihrer Fortbildung durch die Rechtsprechung* 70 (1929).

[197] Stephen L. Carter, *The Trouble with Trademark*, 99 Yale L.J. 759, 786 (1990).

[198] William P. Kratzke, *Normative Economic Analysis of Trademark Law*, 21 Mem. St. U. L. Rev. 199, 231 (1991).

[199] *See also, e.g.*, article 5(C) Paris Convention and article 19 TRIPS. For a comparative overview, *see, e.g.*, Gerhard Schricker, *Der Benutzungszwang im Markenrecht—Rechtsvergleichende Betrachtungen zur Einführung des Benutzungszwangs in das deutsche Warenzeichengesetz*, 1969 GRUR Int. 14.

subject to cancellation. The same happens in cases of abandonment. The trademark must be used to distinguish products in the market. Registered or not, the trademark is not a property right in gross.[200] Seen in this light, registration is just a shell. The formal right will be invigorated only as far as equity can resort to a stock of information capital in the marketplace.[201]

C Summary

The field of intellectual property is far from homogeneous. Trademark rights are directly connected to and based on marketplace activities. Market goodwill and information capital are critically important for the acquisition and existence of rights. Although the possibilities of rights acquisition by registration have sometimes clouded these characteristics, the dominance of registration systems in modern trademark regimes around the world has not altered the fundamental conception. Conversely, patent and copyright protection is granted immediately, exclusively, and absolutely, without regard to the owner's subsequent marketplace or competitive activities. While the unification of intellectual property under a common umbrella of formal rights may not cause many problems in substantive law, this is not the case for choice of law. Here, we must take a close look at the parallel layers of "rights" that exist whenever a trademark is both registered and actually used in commerce. The shell and its substance need to be kept separate. The following section will thus address the relation between legal rights and substantive equity.

IV Trademark and Unfair Competition Law: Framing the Information Infrastructure

European law separates the areas of trademark protection and unfair competition prevention: in principle, one area exists to protect individual property, while the other takes care of the public interest.[202] This propertization/socialization dichotomy has also been projected into choice of law, particularly articles 6 and 8 of the Rome II Regulation. As we will now see, this distinction is particularly questionable with regard to the

[200] *See, e.g., United Drug Co. v. Theodore Rectanus Co.*, 248 U.S. 90, 101 (1918).

[201] For a similar explanation contrasting "trademark right" and "possessory position," *see* Eugen Ulmer, *Warenzeichen und unlauterer Wettbewerb in ihrer Fortbildung durch die Rechtsprechung* 15 (1929) ("Berufener Träger der Werte, die wir im Registersystem sehen, ist das Warenzeichenrecht; der Schutz derjenigen, die im Besitzstand begründet liegen, kommt dem Wettbewerbsrecht zu."). For the general property/possession dichotomy, *see supra* p. 42 *et seq.*

[202] *See supra* p. 9 *et seq.* and p. 193 *et seq.*, p. 203 *et seq.*

two sectors' common policy foundation. Since both trademark protection and unfair competition prevention, at their core, are aimed at regulating market participants' use of information infrastructure, a uniform approach to conflicts law is required.

A The Illusion of a Formal Divergence

In European doctrine, the double-tracked system of property rights and conduct regulation has become so deeply implemented that it can be aptly characterized as conventional wisdom.[203] Here, it is not necessary to fully deconstruct the dichotomy. Instead, I will highlight the most crucial aspects that shed doubt. With respect to choice of law in cross-border and multijurisdictional cases of trademark infringement and unfair competition, we must see the fields as largely homogeneous. The common policy of regulating market communication is what makes this so.

1 Recapitulation: Trademark Property vs. Consumer Protection

As we have seen, European doctrine has never managed to shed the conceptual straightjacket calling for a dichotomy between the fields of trademark and unfair competition law. German law in particular is still caught in this straightjacket. Starting with a doctrine of preemption in *Apollinarisbrunnen*, the Reichsgericht slowly reversed its approach, moving from a strict prioritization of trademark law to one of unfair competition law. Even Ulmer's formidable attempt to reconcile the two areas did not manage to establish uniformity or homogeneity. To the contrary, subsequent scholarship and practice have rather deepened the breach than help overcome the formal trademark/unfair competition divide.[204] Such a bright line has never existed in US doctrine. In the United States, the two areas have generally been treated as homogeneous fields under the common umbrella of passing off.[205] Section 1 of the current Restatement of Unfair Competition Law (Third) prominently represents this homogeneity, providing for an equation of "deceptive marketing" conduct in general with the "infringement of trademarks and other indicia of identification."[206] With respect to the correlation between competitor and consumer protection, US doctrine is also based on interwoven policies. First under traditional common law doctrine and then under the Lanham Act, US trademark law has been seen as promoting a dual policy

[203] For John Kenneth Galbraith's definition of "conventional wisdom," *see The Affluent Society* 6 *et seq.* (1958). For the "march of events" as a deconstructing factor, *see id.* at 11.
[204] *See supra* p. 50 *et seq.* [205] *See supra* p. 84 *et seq.*
[206] Restatement of the Law—Unfair Competition (Third), § 1(a)(1) and (2) (1995).

of protecting both consumers and trademark owners.[207] Consumer protection and right-owner protection are often described as opposite sides of the same coin and as mutually reinforcing benefits of the regime of trademark protection.[208] Consumer and right-owner interests thus appear to be in harmony, and consumer protection is seen as the core of trademark purposes.[209] In European trademark law, such a deep foundation of consumer protection has never been laid out.[210] Here, neither an individual right of the consumer nor a public policy of consumer protection seems to exist. Theory and practice have acknowledged only reflex protection for the consumer, and the public interest is fostered only by granting the right owner specific individual entitlements.[211]

[207] *See, e.g.*, United States Senate, Committee on Patents, Senate Report No. 1333, 79th Congr., 2nd Sess. (14 May 1946), repr. in 1946 U.S. Code Cong. Service, 1274, 1275 ("There is no essential difference between trade-mark infringement and what is loosely called unfair competition. Unfair competition is the genus of which trade-mark infringement is one of the species; 'the law of trade-marks is but a part of the broader law of unfair competition' [United Drug]. All trade-mark cases are cases of unfair competition and involve the same legal wrong."); *see also, e.g.*, Harry D. Nims, *The Law of Unfair Competition and Trade-Marks, vol. I* § 1, 10, 36 *et seq.* (4th edn., 1947); Stephen L. Carter, *The Trouble with Trademark*, 99 Yale L.J. 759, 764 (1990); Robert N. Klieger, *Trademark Dilution: The Whittling Away of the Rational Basis for Trademark Protection*, 58 U. Pitt. L. Rev. 790, 795 (1997); more recently, Michael Grynberg, *Trademark Litigation as Consumer Conflict*, 83 N.Y.U. L. Rev. 60, 64–65 (2008); Deborah R. Gerhardt, *Consumer Investment in Trademark*, 88 N.C. L. Rev. 427, 430 (2010).

[208] *See, e.g., James Burrough Ltd. v. Sign of Beefeater, Inc.*, 540 F.2d 266, 274 (7th Cir. 1976) (what is infringed on is "the right of the public to be free of confusion and the synonymous right of the trademark owner to control his product's reputation"); *Sundor Brands, Inc. v. Borden, Inc.*, 653 F.Supp. 86, 93 (M.D. Fla. 1986); Robert P. Merges, Peter S. Menell & Mark A. Lemley, *Intellectual Property in the New Technological Age* 534 (3rd edn., 2003) ("In general, then, the 'consumer protection' and 'producer incentive' theories of trademark law often seem to be flip sides of the same coin.").

[209] *See, e.g., Bonito Boats, Inc. v. Thunder Craft Boats, Inc.*, 489 U.S. 141, 157 (1989) ("[The law of unfair competition's] general concern is with protecting consumers from confusion as to source. While that concern may result in the creation of 'quasi-property rights' in communicative symbols, the focus is on the protection of consumers, not the protection of producers as an incentive to product innovation."); *see also* Rudolf Rayle, *The Trend Towards Enhancing Trademark Owner's Rights—A Comparative Study of U.S. and German Trademark Law*, 7 J. Intell. Prop. L. 227, 240 and *passim* (2000); Mark P. McKenna, *The Normative Foundations of Trademark Law*, 82 Notre Dame L. Rev. 1839, 1843 (2007); Michael Grynberg, *Trademark Litigation as Consumer Conflict*, 83 N.Y.U. L. Rev. 60, 65 (2008); Mark P. McKenna, *A Consumer Decision-Making Theory of Trademark Law*, 98 Va. L. Rev. 67, 77 (2012).

[210] By contrast, a consumer protection function has often been categorically rejected. For Germany, *see, e.g.*, Winfried Tilmann, *Frage 80: Marke und Verbraucherschutz, Bericht im Namen der deutschen Landesgruppe*, 1983 GRUR 103, 104–105; for Switzerland, *see, e.g.*, Lucas David, in *Markenschutzgesetz, Muster- und Modellgesetz*, Einleitung para. 13 (Heinrich Honsell et al. eds., 2nd edn., 1999).

[211] *See, e.g.*, Frauke Henning-Bodewig & Annette Kur, *Marke und Verbraucher—Funktionen der Marke in der Marktwirtschaft, vol. I: Grundlagen* 210, 225 (1988); Josef Drexl, *Die wirtschaftliche Selbstbestimmung des Verbrauchers—Eine Studie zum Privat- und*

2 *Cracks in the Foundation: A Remerger of the Fields*

Upon closer scrutiny, however, this seemingly iron-clad separation between the fields in European doctrine dissolves. If we consider the question of how to define "consumer protection" and the "public interest," the two fields no longer seem that far apart. In fact, giving close regard to the consumer's position within the marketplace helps reconcile the seemingly divergent concepts of rights enforcement, conduct regulation, and consumer protection. Seen in this light, the transatlantic dichotomy also shrinks—US and European doctrines then actually no longer differ so fundamentally.

a *The Statutory Framework: Unfair Commercial Practices Directive*

In fact, recent developments in European trademark and unfair competition law have spurred a remerger. This has also led to alterations in national doctrine. Until the end of the twentieth century, in light of the longstanding tendency of separating the fields, German case law and commentary had agreed that trademark law was the *lex specialis* to rules of unfair competition prevention. Trademark protection was thus deemed to take strict and formal priority over unfair competition claims (*Vorrangthese*). As the Bundesgerichtshof explained, issues of unauthorized trademark use were governed by norms of trademark law alone. Remedies under unfair competition and tort law would not be admitted per se.[212] But this approach has been drawn into question by the 2005 UCP Directive.[213] Within the directive's scope of application (B2C), it explicitly provides for the prevention of confusion as a situation of "unfair competition" in cases of unauthorized and confusing trademark use.[214] It further provides that competitors and consumer

Wirtschaftsrecht unter Berücksichtigung gemeinschaftsrechtlicher Bezüge 595 (1998); Horst-Peter Götting, *Gewerblicher Rechtsschutz—Patent-, Gebrauchsmuster-, Design- und Markenrecht* § 5 para. 30 (10th edn., 2014). For a common law/civil law comparative angle, *see* Kenneth L. Port, *The Congressional Expansion of American Trademark Law: A Civil Law System in the Making*, 35 Wake Forest L. Rev. 827, 833 (2000).

212 *See, e.g.*, BGH 1999 GRUR 161—*MAC Dog* (30 April 1998); BGH 1999 GRUR 252—*Warsteiner II* (2 July 1998); BGH 2001 GRUR 73—*Stich den Buben* (10 August 2000). For scholarly commentary, *see, e.g.*, Joachim Bornkamm, *Markenrecht und wettbewerbsrechtlicher Kennzeichenschutz—Zur Vorrangthese der Rechtsprechung*, 2005 GRUR 97, 98 *et seq.*

213 Directive 2005/29/EC of the European Parliament and of the Council of 11 May 2005 concerning unfair business-to-consumer commercial practices in the internal market and amending Council Directive 84/450/EEC, Directives 97/7/EC, 98/27/EC and 2002/65/EC of the European Parliament and of the Council and Regulation (EC) No 2006/2004 of the European Parliament and of the Council ("Unfair Commercial Practices Directive"), O.J. EU (11 June 2005), L 149/22.

214 *See* articles 3 and 6(2) lit. a as well as no. 13 of the Directive's so-called black list (in annex I).

associations—not just trademark owners—are generally entitled to apply for relief against confusing trademark use.[215] As a result, case law and scholarly commentary of late contend a relationship of equivalence (*Gleichrang*) between the fields.[216] Even though this *Gleichrang* also bears the mark of separation—after all, trademark protection and unfair competition prevention are still depicted as autonomous systems of regulation with different policies and different legal consequences[217]—it cannot be denied that unfair competition doctrine has reconquered a large area. Be it a single theory or two concurrent instruments of protection for information truthfulness, what matters is that, under the 2005 UCP Directive, unfair competition doctrine has been significantly extended into the reign of trademark protection. And even though the extension may be limited to B2C relations, it signals a trend of unification. This surfaces especially in single national regimes, such as Germany, where the directive's implementation has been more wide-reaching, as it also covers B2B relations.[218] Important for this analysis is that European lawmakers have increasingly come to prioritize the protection of consumer decision making, which results in a growing overlap between the once deemed separate fields. Hence, the dichotomy's *raison d'être* has visibly come under pressure.

b The Consolidation of Interests: Depropertization and Desocialization

The UCP Directive's consolidation actually represents a more slow and subtle trend. Individual rights protection has not always been the genuine purpose of trademark law. As we have seen, during the nineteenth century, trademark law was explicitly and sometimes almost exclusively

[215] *See* article 11. *See also* Jochen Glöckner, *Der Schutz vor Verwechslungsgefahr im Spannungsfeld von Kennzeichenrecht und verbraucherschützendem Lauterkeitsrecht*, 145, 165 *et seq.*, in *Geistiges Eigentum und Gemeinfreiheit* (Ansgar Ohly & Diethelm Klippel eds., 2007); Helmut Köhler, *Das Verhältnis des Wettbewerbsrechts zum Recht des geistigen Eigentums—Zur Notwendigkeit einer Neubestimmung auf Grund der Richtlinie über unlautere Geschäftspraktiken*, 2007 GRUR 548, 550–551.

[216] *See* BGH 2013 GRUR 1161, 1165—*Hard Rock Cafe* (15 August 2013); Reinhard Ingerl & Christian Rohnke, *Kommentar zum Markengesetz: Gesetz über den Schutz von Marken und sonstigen Kennzeichen*, § 2 para. 2 (3rd edn., 2010); Christian Alexander, *Der Verwechslungsschutz gem. § 5 Abs. 2 UWG*, 23, 26–27, in *Festschrift für Helmut Köhler zum 70. Geburtstag* (Christian Alexander et al. eds., 2014). For the Swiss doctrine of equivalence and concurrent application, *see* BGE vol. 129 III 353, 358—*Puls-Tip* (17 March 2003).

[217] *See, e.g.*, Helmut Köhler, *Das Verhältnis des Wettbewerbsrechts zum Recht des geistigen Eigentums—Zur Notwendigkeit einer Neubestimmung auf Grund der Richtlinie über unlautere Geschäftspraktiken*, 2007 GRUR 548, 550; Karl-Heinz Fezer, in *Lauterkeitsrecht: Kommentar zum Gesetz gegen den unlauteren Wettbewerb (UWG), vol. I*, Einleitung E para 336 *et seq.* (Karl-Heinz Fezer ed., 2nd edn., 2010).

[218] *See, e.g.*, Christian Alexander, *Der Verwechslungsschutz gem. § 5 Abs. 2 UWG*, 23, 25, in *Festschrift für Helmut Köhler zum 70. Geburtstag* (Christian Alexander et al. eds., 2014).

concerned with protection of public interests, notably through fraud prevention policies.[219] And this once "social" impetus was never expressly ousted by a clear change of policies. Rather, it was the formalistic paradigm of trademark-as-property protection that, throughout the nineteenth and twentieth centuries, barred a more visible entry and osmosis of consumer protection concerns. Indeed, even though giving regard to consumer interests is still widely described as a mere reflex of trademark protection, the consumer has never been locked out completely. The trademark owner alone is tasked with enforcing her rights—prima facie, therefore, she is not the avenger of the consumer.[220] But a part of what she does in her function as right owner mirrors concurrent interests of the public and, thus, necessarily of the consumer. The fading out of consumer protection concerns only a certain kind of consumer interests. If and to the extent that "consumer protection" is understood as protection of the consumer beyond her function as a referee in competition—that is, as a private individual and citizen with civil rights—there is no congruence of interests. With respect to the consumer's function as a referee, however, trademark protection with an aim of confusion prevention necessarily also caters to the concerns of the consuming public. As my exploration of the market mechanism has illustrated,[221] the consumer's decision making is the focal point where both her private and the public interest in free competition coincide.

The picture is similar in unfair competition doctrine, where an excessive protection of consumer interests would also exceed the regulatory scheme. It may have been the foreclosure of consumer interests in trademark law that led to a concurrent socialization of unfair competition law. Ultimately, unfair competition doctrine had to serve as a reservoir for public policies of all kinds.[222] Most notably, it became an area of consumer protection in terms of civil rights. But this has changed in recent years. In fact, unfair competition doctrine has recently witnessed its own era of desocialization. I will address the integrated model of unfair competition law in more detail soon.[223] Worth mentioning for now is the fact

[219] *See supra* p. 9 *et seq.*

[220] For the term, *see Ely-Norris Safe Co. v. Mosler Safe Co.*, 7 F.2d 603, 604 (2nd Cir. 1925) (Hand, J.) (the plaintiff is not the "vicarious avenger" of the defendant's customers). For German doctrine, *see* Frauke Henning-Bodewig & Annette Kur, *Marke und Verbraucher—Funktionen der Marke in der Marktwirtschaft, vol. I: Grundlagen* 210 (1988).

[221] *See supra* p. 275 *et seq.*, p. 287 *et seq.*

[222] For an overview, *see, e.g.*, Wolfgang B. Schünemann, *Ökonomische Analyse der europäischen und deutschen Regelung*, 41 *et seq.*, in *Lauterkeitsrecht im Umbruch—Europa, Deutschland, Österreich* (Heinz Krejci et al. eds., 2005).

[223] *See infra* p. 359 *et seq.*

that modern policies of unfair competition prevention—as trademark protection—are concerned primarily with the unhindered functioning of the market mechanism and with the autonomy of consumer decision making.[224]

In light of this modern depropertization of trademark policies and the concurrent desocialization of unfair competition doctrine, we can identify a common territory of both fields. At the vertical level of the model of marketplace competition, the core policies of both trademark-as-property protection and consumer protection through unfair competition prevention have come to largely coincide.[225] This common core of both areas is what determines the analysis: trademark protection and unfair competition prevention must give regard to the consumer and to the purpose of protecting her domain as a referee in competition against improper invasion. Accordingly, the trademark owner no longer has exclusive control over a dispute with respect to deciding whether to enjoin infringing uses of her trademark or to not police the violation at all. Since trademark and unfair competition causes of action will coexist without a hierarchical relationship, there is no more priority of absolute rights.[226]

c *The Practical Picture: A Subtle Recapture* Court practice further illustrates that the merger is in full swing. In fact, many issues that are today classified as questions of trademark protection started as judge-made doctrines of unfair competition prevention. Antidilution and post-sale confusion scenarios are lucid examples.[227] The homogeneity of policies is therefore not a recent invention of European lawmakers. The UCP Directive has merely institutionalized a practical symbiosis. In addition, in recent courtroom practice, the fields seem to have moved even closer. First, the Court of Justice has increasingly macerated old-age formalisms of traditional trademark doctrine throughout the last decade.

[224] *See, e.g.*, Hans-Wolfgang Micklitz, in *Münchener Kommentar zum Lauterkeitsrecht, vol. I*, EG D para. 94 (Peter W. Heermann et al. eds., 2006) ("[Die] Dominanz des Verbraucherschutzgedankens ... findet jedoch ihre innere Rechtfertigung nicht in einem ‚sozialrechtlichen Kontext', sondern in der Notwendigkeit, den Verbraucher erst für den Gemeinsamen Markt und dann für den Binnenmarkt zu instrumentalisieren.").

[225] For the multiangular structure of the market mechanism in consumer decision making, *see supra* p. 285–286.

[226] *See, e.g.*, Joachim Bornkamm, *Die Schnittstellen zwischen gewerblichem Rechtsschutz und UWG—Grenzen des lauterkeitsrechtlichen Verwechslungsschutzes*, 2011 GRUR 1, 4; Karl-Nikolaus Peifer, in *Lauterkeitsrecht: Kommentar zum Gesetz gegen den unlauteren Wettbewerb (UWG), vol. II*, § 5 para. 41 (Karl-Heinz Fezer ed., 2nd edn., 2010) ("Die Abgrenzung zum individualrechtlichen Kennzeichenschutz wird stark verwischt, so dass jedenfalls im Verbraucherschutz die lautere Markenführung ein Stück weit wieder kollektiviert wird."). For the same concept, *see* Walter R. Schluep, *Das Markenrecht als subjektives Recht* 112 (1964).

[227] *See infra* p. 349 *et seq.*

While the court still pays lip service to trademark-as-property and exclusive rights protection, its actual implementation of protection structures has widely abandoned formalism. Indeed, under the court's theory of trademark functions, the paradigm of trademark-as-property protection may dissolve far more quickly than expected. The "functionalization" of trademark rights can be lucidly seen in the list provided in *L'Oréal* and *Google France*, enumerating "not only the essential function of the trade mark, which is to assure to consumers the origin of the goods or services ('the function of indicating origin'), but also its other functions, in particular that of guaranteeing the quality of the goods or services in question and those of communication, investment or advertising."[228] Of course, such literal extensions of the scope of protection seem to imply an over-extension of rights.[229] Yet a function-based approach also provides possibilities for rights limitation. One example can be found in cases on "keyword advertising." The court has started to backpaddle significantly here: the advertising function has been described to no longer be affected, and the question of relevant impact on the function to indicate origin has been referred to a specifically fact-based analysis.[230] Unlike formal rights protection, functionalism is far more flexible and, as such, receptive to a significant relativization of rights. On this basis, the absoluteness or exclusivity of rights can no longer be explained as a leitmotif. In essence, a trademark's functions reflect different policies of protection. None of these policies, however, provide for an isolated domain of trademark rights. Consequently, the trademark owner no longer holds a position of "absolute" individual property—instead, her entitlement reflects a bundle of policies of conditional protection.

The last aspect of a fact-based infringement analysis further illustrates that the tests for finding consumer confusion in trademark law and in unfair competition law have become increasingly similar. For a long time, doctrine treated the concepts of consumer confusion in trademark law and of consumer confusion in unfair competition law as distinct. Whereas confusion testing in trademark law was seen as focusing on the abstract comparison between conflicting symbols, confusion testing in unfair

[228] *Google France and Google*, C-236/08, 237/08, and 238/08, para. 77 (23 March 2010), [2010] E.C.R. I-2417; *L'Oréal and Others*, C 487/07, para. 58 (18 June 2009), [2009] E.C.R. I-5185.

[229] For a critique, *see, e.g.*, Martin Senftleben, *Trade Mark Protection—A Black Hole in the Intellectual Property Galaxy*, 42 IIC 383, 384 *et seq.* (2011).

[230] *See, e.g., Google France and Google*, C-236/08, 237/08, and 238/08, para. 82 *et seq.* (23 March 2010), [2010] E.C.R. I-2417; *BergSpechte*, C-278/08, para. 33 *et seq.* (25 March 2010), [2010] E.C.R. I-2517; *Portakabin*, C-558/08, para. 32 *et seq.* (8 July 2010), [2010] E.C.R. I-6963; *see also* Lionel Bently & Brad Sherman, *Intellectual Property Law* 1051 *et seq.* (4th edn., 2014).

competition law was seen as requiring concrete consideration of the factual circumstances of each individual case. The latter was a narrower test and less protective.[231] Under the Court of Justice's recent application of trademark law, however, the consumer-confusion standard has begun to resemble its unfair competition counterpart. In its 2008 decision in *O2 Holdings and O2 (UK)*, the court expressly established that consumer-confusion standards should be the same for both trademark and unfair competition doctrines.[232] This approach was reinforced three years later in the court's *Interflora* decision, which set a heretofore almost unknown requirement of market information transparency for trademark-infringement testing. As the court explained, a finding of adverse effects on the trademark's function of indicating origin will depend "in particular on the manner in which that advertisement is presented."[233] Hence, for issues of trademark infringement as well, the trier of facts will actually have to inquire whether an advertisement's use of a foreign trademark "is sufficient to enable a reasonably well-informed and reasonably observant internet user" to distinguish the sources of the competing parties' products.[234] Ultimately, both standards for confusion prevention have come to coincide.[235]

d The Relicts of Antiquity: Pockets of Resistance Notwithstanding these wide-reaching tectonic shifts, some specific areas of trademark protection still seem to be distinctly isolated and therefore resistant to a merger of the fields. Yet here, too, the perceived obstacles are not as decisive as one might think. Several of the scenarios that have been identified as allegedly uniquely trademark related are founded on

[231] *See, e.g.*, BGH 2004 GRUR 860, 863—*Internet-Versteigerung I* (11 March 2004); Annette Kur, *Markenrecht, Verbraucherschutz und Wettbewerbsrecht*, 190, 196, in *Die Neuordnung des Markenrechts in Europa—10. Ringberg-Symposium des Max-Planck-Instituts für ausländisches und internationales Patent-, Urheber- und Wettbewerbsrecht* (Gerhard Schricker & Friedrich-Karl Beier eds., 1996).

[232] *O2 Holdings and O2 (UK)*, C-533/06, para. 49 (12 June 2008), [2008] E.C.R. I-4231 ("In the light of recitals 13 to 15 of Directive 97/55, the same interpretation must be given to the term 'confusion' used in both Article 5(1)(b) of Directive 89/104 and Article 3a(1)(d) of Directive 84/450."). For Swiss law, *see* BGE vol. 116 II 365, 370—*Nivea* (12 July 1990) (identical standard of confusion testing).

[233] *Interflora and Interflora British Unit*, C-323/09, para. 44 *et seq.* (22 September 2011), [2012] E.T.M.R. 1.

[234] *Id.* at para. 53.

[235] *See also* Reinhard Ingerl & Christian Rohnke, *Kommentar zum Markengesetz: Gesetz über den Schutz von Marken und sonstigen Kennzeichen*, § 2 para. 3 (3rd edn., 2010); Christian Alexander, *Der Verwechslungsschutz gem. § 5 Abs. 2 UWG*, 23, 28, in *Festschrift für Helmut Köhler zum 70. Geburtstag* (Christian Alexander et al. eds., 2014); more critically, however, *e.g.*, Franz Hacker, in *Kommentar zum Markengesetz*, § 2 para. 28 *et seq.* (Paul Ströbele & Franz Hacker eds., 11th edn., 2015).

a policy that is distinctly separate from the traditional concepts of passing off, confusion prevention, and information economization. They thus fall outside the common domain of consumer decision-making regulation, meaning that their separate treatment under a doctrine of "trademarks only" does not present a challenge to the hypothesis of a trademark/unfair competition merger. In addition, upon closer scrutiny, the remainder of allegedly resistant scenarios can actually be explained as specific instances of a policy merger.

To start with the former category, one oft-enunciated example of the separation of policies is the protection of newly registered and still unknown trademarks. These trademarks tend to be protected only under trademark law.[236] Protection under unfair competition and like doctrines will begin only upon the accumulation of goodwill—and only with respect to those markets where information capital has actually been accumulated. With respect to the first stage of a registered trademark's protection, however, the policy at play is of a different kind. It does not directly aim at information economization. On the contrary, protection of newly registered trademarks, as authoritatively outlined by Ulmer, only temporarily overextends core trademark policy in the interest of promoting the development of rights. Over time, however, upon the acquisition of goodwill, the aim of developing nascent trademarks would yield to the principles of preventing confusion.[237]

What seems to be more challenging for the consolidation hypothesis are scenarios where pragmatic cost balancing—not doctrinal reasons—lead to a prioritization of trademark protection rules in practice. One example is a case where competitors with the same name, trade name, or trademark have established separate goodwill in different marketplaces, and where their indications' geographical reaches suddenly collide (usually due to a growth of markets). These are *Tea Rose/Rectanus* scenarios.[238] As contended by case law and scholarly commentary in Germany, a certain degree of consumer confusion may have to be tolerated in order to allow for both parties' continued use. The only requirement is that confusion must be reduced as far as is possible and reasonable.[239] Since consumer confusion will never be fully eliminated, one could argue that it is individual rights protection—and hence trademark policy—that

[236] *See, e.g.*, Joachim Bornkamm, in Helmut Köhler & Joachim Bornkamm, *Gesetz gegen den unlauteren Wettbewerb*, § 5 UWG para. 4.238 (33rd edn., 2015); Franz Hacker, in *Kommentar zum Markengesetz*, § 2 para. 33 (Paul Ströbele & Franz Hacker eds., 11th edn., 2015).

[237] *See supra* p. 42–46.

[238] For the *Tea Rose/Rectanus* doctrine, *see supra* p. 102 *et seq.* and p. 129 *et seq.*

[239] *See, e.g.*, BGH 2010 GRUR 738—*Peek & Cloppenburg* (31 March 2010); BGH 2013 GRUR 397, 398 *et seq.*—*Peek & Cloppenburg III* (24 January 2013).

prevails.[240] This, however, is not the full picture. The gist of this doctrine is unveiled only when looking at alternative solutions: coexistence, even though causing a certain degree of consumer confusion, is the result of optimum cost balancing for all constituencies involved in the dispute. Easily overlooked is the fact that completely enjoining one party from using the name or trademark at issue—as the strict enforcement of unfair competition rules might suggest—would not avoid consumer confusion, either. Granting one side the right to use the trademark for the whole market, thereby fully excluding the other party, would invalidate the latter's goodwill. Not only would this destroy the individual right owner's investment, but it would also force her customers to renew and rearrange their information capital with respect to the products and brands at issue. Actual consumer "confusion" under such a black-and-white solution would thus be more severe than under coexistence.[241] What matters here is that an optimal economization of marketplace information can be achieved only by cost balancing. The situation therefore verifies the growing homogeneity of the two fields on the basis of a common core policy.

Similarly, licensing and coexistence agreements, as well as a court's granting to a trademark-infringing defendant a conversion period during which sale for counterfeits is still admissible, can be explained under a theory of cost balancing.[242] As in cases where the alleged trademark infringer has raised the defense of unclean hands, laches or acquiescence, or limitation or prescription, it is possible that the degree of consumer confusion is so strong that unfair competition prevention must ultimately kick in.[243] In all these cases, there is another way to look at it: especially in the latter case, it is difficult to contend that if the trademark owner has lingered so long that her claim for injunctive relief is barred under a trademark-related provision on limitation or prescription, third parties

[240] BGH 2013 GRUR 397, 398 *et seq.*—*Peek & Cloppenburg III* (24 January 2013); critically, however, Franz Hacker, in *Kommentar zum Markengesetz*, § 2 para. 38 (Paul Ströbele & Franz Hacker eds., 11th edn., 2015).

[241] For increased costs for "junior consumers" in cases where a senior trademark trumps, *see* Michael Grynberg, *Trademark Litigation as Consumer Conflict*, 83 N.Y.U. L. Rev. 60, 93 (2008). For similar reasoning in early German case law concerning the admissibility of a certain level of confusion, *see, e.g.*, BGH 1958 GRUR 444, 447—*Emaillelack* (28 February 1958); BGH 1963 GRUR 36, 39—*Fichtennadelextrakt* (13 July 1962).

[242] For owner consent, in particular with regard to licensing and coexistence agreements, *see* Restatement of the Law—Unfair Competition (Third), § 29, comment b and c (1995) ("[I]f the use permitted under a consent agreement is likely to cause substantial confusion that threatens significant harm to consumers, the agreement may be unenforceable as a matter of public policy."); for licensing and the requirement of "reasonable control" by the owner, *see id.* at § 33, comment c.

[243] For current German (and European) doctrine on the fields' correlation in these cases, *see, e.g.*, Joachim Bornkamm, *Die Schnittstellen zwischen gewerblichem Rechtsschutz und UWG—Grenzen des lauterkeitsrechtlichen Verwechslungsschutzes*, 2011 GRUR 1, 4–5.

should not have access to claims under the rules on unfair competition prevention.[244] After all, the public is still interested in preventing confusion and deception. Accordingly, competitors (aside from the lingering trademark owner) and consumer associations should be allowed to litigate unfair competition claims.[245] Necessarily, interparty relations between a right owner and an alleged infringer are irrelevant with regard to the public.[246]

In sum, none of the "exceptional" cases of alleged trademark priority prevent us from concluding that the fields are doctrinally interrelated—more concretely, that they overlap with respect to the regulation of information infrastructure. In addition, the merger of the fields remains unaffected by the different types of remedial options. While trademark law may grant more far-reaching remedies, particularly concerning the scope and computation of damages,[247] this does not allow an inference with respect to the unifying capacity of market information policies. The different character of remedies is mostly a result of practical necessities, not of policy differences. Furthermore, injunctive relief dominates both fields in practice and therefore ultimately accounts for the actual effectuation of policies. In this regard, the fields have been in wide conformity for a long time.[248]

[244] For US doctrine, *see* Restatement of the Law—Unfair Competition (Third), § 31, comment a, and § 32, comment a (1995) ("Because of the public interest in protecting consumers from confusion as to the source or sponsorship of goods and services, unreasonable delay by the trademark owner does not necessarily constitute a complete defense to liability."). For the debate in German and European law, *see, e.g.*, Annette Kur, *Verwechslungsgefahr und Irreführung—zum Verhältnis von Markenrecht und § 3 UWG*, 1989 GRUR 240, 242; *but see* BGH 2013 GRUR 1161, 1166—*Hard Rock Cafe* (15 August 2013); critically with convincing arguments, however, Christian Alexander, *Der Verwechslungsschutz gem. § 5 Abs. 2 UWG*, 23, 27–28, in *Festschrift für Helmut Köhler zum 70. Geburtstag* (Christian Alexander et al. eds., 2014).

[245] Jochen Glöckner, *Der Schutz vor Verwechslungsgefahr im Spannungsfeld von Kennzeichenrecht und verbraucherschützendem Lauterkeitsrecht*, 145, 173, in *Geistiges Eigentum und Gemeinfreiheit* (Ansgar Ohly & Diethelm Klippel eds., 2007); Joachim Bornkamm, *Die Schnittstellen zwischen gewerblichem Rechtsschutz und UWG—Grenzen des lauterkeitsrechtlichen Verwechslungsschutzes*, 2011 GRUR 1, 6–7.

[246] *See* Annette Kur, *Verwechslungsgefahr und Irreführung—zum Verhältnis von Markenrecht und § 3 UWG*, 1989 GRUR 240, 249; Christian Alexander, *Der Verwechslungsschutz gem. § 5 Abs. 2 UWG*, 23, 27–28, in *Festschrift für Helmut Köhler zum 70. Geburtstag* (Christian Alexander et al. eds., 2014).

[247] *See, e.g.*, Joachim Bornkamm, in Helmut Köhler & Joachim Bornkamm, *Gesetz gegen den unlauteren Wettbewerb*, § 5 UWG para. 4.253 (33rd edn., 2015); Christian Alexander, *Der Verwechslungsschutz gem. § 5 Abs. 2 UWG*, 23, 25–26, in *Festschrift für Helmut Köhler zum 70. Geburtstag* (Christian Alexander et al. eds., 2014); for English doctrine, *see, e.g.*, Lionel Bently & Brad Sherman, *Intellectual Property Law* 1238 *et seq.* (4th edn., 2014).

[248] For the practical prevalence of injunctive relief, *see supra* p. 296 *et seq*. For the historical development in trademark and unfair competition doctrine, *see* the discussion of law and equity in US doctrine *supra* p. 78 *et seq.*

e *The Myth of the Public Samaritan* Finally, another oft-enunciated argument can be shown to be irrelevant for the fields' underlying structural homogeneity: despite what is often contended, plaintiffs in both trademark *and* unfair competition cases act as private attorneys general—no matter whether they sue on the basis of a private right or claim the violation of a rule of fair conduct. Of course, a rational right owner will seldom care about consumer protection when enforcing her right in a trademark. This, however, does not invalidate her function as the proverbial private attorney general of the public interest. She may neither formally nor intentionally play the role of a vicarious avenger of the consumer,[249] but she does serve the public function of establishing and upholding an environment of truthful market communication.[250] The enforcement of private rights thereby establishes and maintains the overall order of information economization as part of the information infrastructure within the marketplace. This specific order—not a general, extended, and unspecific concern for public policy—is the institution to be protected under trademark law. In this regard, and under an accordingly delimited scope of consumer protection concerns, the trademark owner's formal right is the mirror image of public policy. Or, as Ralph S. Brown, Jr. explained in 1948:

> [W]hat appear to be private disputes among hucksters almost invariably touch the public welfare. We shall therefore be concerned to ask, when courts protect trade symbols, whether their decisions further public as well as private goals.[251]

Furthermore, a closer look at the incentives at play when private rights are enforced suggests the validity of skepticism toward the idea that consumer concerns would be protected only under a system of unfair competition law. As is commonly argued, unfair competition law—unlike trademark protection—specifically protects the public interest by extending personal standing and enforcement options for competitors in general and for consumer associations in particular. In these cases, competitors are supposed to act as deputies tasked with protecting the public interest.[252] Upon a second look, however, this idea proves

[249] *See again Ely-Norris Safe Co. v. Mosler Safe Co.*, 7 F.2d 603, 604 (2nd Cir. 1925) (Hand, J.).

[250] For the trademark owner's role, *see* Michael Grynberg, *Trademark Litigation as Consumer Conflict*, 83 N.Y.U. L. Rev. 60, 90 (2008); William P. Kratzke, *Normative Economic Analysis of Trademark Law*, 21 Mem. St. U. L. Rev. 199, 268 (1991); Carl Baudenbacher, *Zur funktionalen Anwendung von § 1 des deutschen und Art. 1 des schweizerischen UWG*, 144 ZHR 145, 152 (1980).

[251] Ralph S. Brown, Jr., *Advertising and the Public Interest: Legal Protection of Trade Symbols*, 57 Yale L.J. 1165, 1167 (1948).

[252] *See, e.g.*, Alfons Kraft, *Verbraucherschutz und Markenrecht*, 1980 GRUR 416, 419; Wolfgang Fikentscher, *Wirtschaftsrecht, vol. II: Deutsches Wirtschaftsrecht* § 22 XI 10

illusory. The incentive to police violations of both unfair competition and trademark norms will be strong whenever investment in goodwill or private interests in general is concerned. Whenever a market participant suffers an individual detriment that is substantial, she will have an incentive to instigate judicial or administrative enforcement. Litigation, however, is not dependent on whether a competitor considers herself as acting on behalf of the public.[253] Nor does it depend on the existence or nonexistence of formal subjective rights. If no individual investment is at stake, there will be no incentive to privately police a violation. This is not a rare case. Quite often, violations of unfair competition norms will not affect a specific competitor directly, nor will they be detrimental at all. Another example of the disinterested plaintiff can be seen in situations where certain unfair practices are common or have become tolerated within the trade.[254] In these cases, it is unlikely that competition or intercompetitor litigation will bring about the best result for the public—as there is honor among thieves, there also is honor among unfair competitors.

In any case, finally, one should not overestimate the litigiousness of consumer associations. In light of their usually scarce financial resources, a more practical doubt exists: quite often, associations that have standing to sue are acting undercover on behalf of a single competitor. If litigation is initiated and financed by an individual competitor, however, it no longer fulfills an allegedly exclusively "public" function.[255]

3 Summary

The fields of trademark and unfair competition law have witnessed a tectonic shift away from traditional tort law paradigms toward a modern regime of market information regulation. Whether the paradigm of "property" or "subjective rights" in trademarks should be maintained is not the main concern here. More important is the classification of trademark and unfair competition scenarios according to the underlying

(1983); Frauke Henning-Bodewig & Annette Kur, *Marke und Verbraucher—Funktionen der Marke in der Marktwirtschaft, vol. I: Grundlagen* 210–211 (1988).

[253] *See* Wolfgang Hefermehl, *Der Anwendungsbereich des Wettbewerbsrechts*, 283, 288, in *Festschrift für Hans Carl Nipperdey zum 60. Geburtstag* (Rolf Dietz et al. eds., 1955) ("Der aus UWG klagende selbstverletzte oder bedrohte Wettbewerber will seine Interessen, sein Unternehmen, schützen, nicht aber im öffentlichen Interesse Grundsätze lauteren Wettbewerbs durchsetzen.").

[254] For these scenarios, *see* Elias Wolf, *Kritische Betrachtungen zum Entwurf für ein Bundesgesetz über den „unerlaubten" Wettbewerb*, 31 SJZ 145, 146 (1934); *see also* Gerhard Schricker, *Möglichkeiten zur Verbesserung des Schutzes der Verbraucher und des funktionsfähigen Wettbewerbs im Recht des unlauteren Wettbewerbs*, 139 ZHR 208, 233 (1975).

[255] For this situation, *see* Gerhard Schricker, *Hundert Jahre Gesetz gegen den unlauteren Wettbewerb—Licht und Schatten*, 1996 GRUR Int. 473, 478.

policies. The oft-enunciated argument that trademark law provides protection to the consumer only as a reflex of private rights enforcement is unconvincing, both with respect to the private rights/public policy dichotomy and with regard to enforcement efficiency. Protection of the consumer's role as referee in competition is central to both trademark and unfair competition law. It is the connecting link between both areas. Subsequently, regulating market communication—more concretely, protecting the information infrastructure within the marketplace—is the common core policy. As I will argue in the following, a corresponding separation of policies is necessary to promulgate a guideline for choice-of-law determination.

B The Structural Congruency of Trademark and Unfair Competition Law

Trademark and unfair competition law have increasingly evolved toward the regulation of market communication. In addition to this common denominator, additional policies can be found in close vicinity. These policies include, namely, trademark-as-property protection (e.g., antidilution theory) and consumer protection beyond the referee function (e.g., privacy protection). Before I address each of these policies, I will take a concluding look at the common core: the overarching aim of providing an order for the information infrastructure of the marketplace.

1 The Common Core: Information Economization

I have already analyzed the economic concept of market language.[256] With respect to trademark and unfair competition law—notably with regard to the common core of policies—the communication function is particularly important. Information truthfulness and correctness are paramount for the functioning of the market mechanism based on consumer decision making. In terms of trademark doctrine, the correlation between market information and efficiency has been described on the basis of the functions of goodwill. A trademark's goodwill is shorthand for search-cost reduction. It performs the economizing function of facilitating information transmission.[257] Trademark protection encourages investment in product quality. Once reputations within the market have been established, repeat purchases and referrals will generate higher

[256] *See supra* p. 288–289.

[257] *See* William M. Landes & Richard A. Posner, *Trademark Law: An Economic Perspective*, 30 J.L. & Econ. 265, 269 (1987); *see also*, more recently, Stacey L. Dogan & Mark A. Lemley, *Trademark and Consumer Search Costs on the Internet*, 41 Hous. L. Rev. 777, 778, 786 *et seq.* (2004) (with numerous references).

transaction numbers.[258] At the same time, the branded product can command a premium price, reflecting the search-cost savings by consumers.[259] This is a self-reinforcing cycle of reputation creation, maintenance, and sometimes decay and destruction. In addition, trademarks can be used more generally to transfer information, not only by the right owner herself, but also by other market participants. Examples of such transmission are comparative advertising and the descriptive use of trademarks. In essence, the trademark is the most efficient and universal purveyor of market information.[260]

Trademarks are but one segment of the market's vocabulary, for the marketplace trades on nonbranded information as well. As search terms and information shortcuts, trademarks constitute part of the stock of nouns in the lexicon, leaving ample space for other elements of market language. This is the area of general advertising. It covers all types of communication concerning products and market participants, whether related to trademarks and goodwill or whether consisting of the transmission of non-goodwill-related information. In this respect, as well, information economization is essential. It is evident that if information is unreliable, consumer decision making will remain in the dark. For trademark-based and nonbranded market information alike, it is true that without an "informal unwritten guarantee"[261] of information truthfulness, the market will not function. Information economization therefore constitutes the common core of policies in both trademark and unfair

[258] William M. Landes & Richard A. Posner, *Trademark Law: An Economic Perspective*, 30 J.L. & Econ. 265, 270 (1987); Robert N. Klieger, *Trademark Dilution: The Whittling Away of the Rational Basis for Trademark Protection*, 58 U. Pitt. L. Rev. 790, 855 (1997); Stacey L. Dogan & Mark A. Lemley, *Trademark and Consumer Search Costs on the Internet*, 41 Hous. L. Rev. 777, 813 (2004); Robert G. Bone, *Hunting Goodwill: A History of the Concept of Goodwill in Trademark Law*, 86 B. U. L. Rev. 547, 556 (2006). For prominent case law, *see, e.g., Park 'N Fly, Inc. v. Dollar Park and Fly, Inc.*, 469 U.S. 189, 198 (1985) ("[T]rademarks foster competition and the maintenance of quality by securing to the producer the benefits of a good reputation.").

[259] *See* George J. Stigler, *The Economics of Information*, 69 J. Pol. Econ. 213, 224 (1961) ("'Reputation' is a word which denotes the persistence of quality, and reputation commands a price (or exacts a penalty) because it economizes on search."). *See also* Stephen L. Carter, *The Trouble with Trademark*, 99 Yale L.J. 759, 763 (1990); Roger Van den Bergh & Michael Lehmann, *Informationsökonomie und Verbraucherschutz im Wettbewerbs- und Warenzeichenrecht*, 1992 GRUR Int. 588, 592.

[260] William P. Kratzke, *Normative Economic Analysis of Trademark Law*, 21 Mem. St. U. L. Rev. 199, 216 (1991); *see also* Karl-Heinz Fezer, *Markenrecht*, Einl D para. 1 *et seq.* (4th edn., 2009); Sypros Maniatis & Dimitris Botis, *Trade Marks in Europe: A Practical Jurisprudence* para. 6–157 (2nd edn., 2010).

[261] *See again* George A. Akerlof, *The Market for "Lemons": Quality Uncertainty and the Market Mechanism*, 84 Quarterly J. Econ. 488, 500 (1970). More extensively also *supra* p. 287 *et seq.*

competition law. Most abstractly, we can say that both sectors, together, establish and uphold the market's information infrastructure.

2 *Beyond Confusion: Alternative Theories of Trademark Protection*

But additional policies exist in both trademark and unfair competition law. These policies, especially with respect to trademark protection, are also relevant for the construction of the marketplace's information infrastructure. As we have seen,[262] trademark doctrine in particular has recently undergone a process of propertization. Among the most heavily criticized aspects of this development is the emergence of non-confusion-based infringement theories. Antidilution theory, as well as initial-interest and postsale confusion theories, may cover instances where consumers are deceived or confused. Under all theories, however, an infringement can also be found *without* actual consumer confusion at the point of sale. By this means, theory and practice in the United States and Europe have come to integrate ever more aspects of protection that are disconnected from the fields' common core policy.

Of course, it is possible to see antidilution doctrine as also preventing a specific aspect of consumer confusion.[263] One can argue that by preventing distinctive trademarks from being watered down, enjoining dilutive uses also protects the public's and the consumer's interest in efficient transacting.[264] Yet even if one acknowledges this explanation, it is not the direct impact on consumer decision making that will qualify dilution as a violation of market information norms. After all, there is no transmission of genuinely *incorrect* information, and the consumer's immediate transaction generally remains presumptively rational. Detriments will materialize only in the long run, if at all. In principle, this is also the case in situations of initial-interest and postsale confusion.[265] As it appears, the consumer makes a transactional decision without having been misled by incorrect information.

[262] *See supra* chapter 1 *passim* and chapter 2 *passim*.

[263] Landes and Posner have explained the potential for confusion in situations of dilutive trademark use. The consumer, when seeing the dilutive mark, will think both of the owner and the diluter. This will "water down" the connotations of the famous original. Mere blurring, however, is not the kind of confusion that confusion prevention policy aims at. *See* William M. Landes & Richard A. Posner, *Trademark Law: An Economic Perspective*, 30 J. L. & Econ. 265, 307 (1987). *See also Ty Inc. v. Perryman*, 306 F.3d 509, 510 and 511 (7th Cir. 2002) (Posner, J.).

[264] *See, e.g.*, Mark A. Lemley, *The Modern Lanham Act and the Death of Common Sense*, 108 Yale L.J. 1687, 1704 and n. 90 (1999); Stacey L. Dogan & Mark A. Lemley, *What the Right of Publicity Can Learn from Trademark Law*, 58 Stan. L. Rev. 1161, 1197–1198 (2006).

[265] For more details, *see infra* p. 350 *et seq.*

Indeed, it is this detachment from traditional unfair competition doctrine that brings alternative theories of trademark protection closer to other scenarios of intellectual property protection. As is often explained, the protection of intellectual property rights is designed to create scarcity in a certain public good in which it is ordinarily absent. In patent and copyright doctrine, this theory is commonplace.[266] For trademarks, the idea of scarcity is more complex. In general, the creation of scarcity is intended to release innovative and creative power on the side of prospective right owners and to spur production. However, there is no public interest per se in creating more trademark symbols. Rather, restrictions on trademark use under a theory of preventing consumer confusion create scarcity for a single reason: to establish and maintain transparency in the marketplace.[267] Yet alternative theories of trademark-as-property protection have changed this picture to gray. For non-confusion-related instances of trademark protection, scarcity is, in fact, also artificially created. But this is intended to promote the creation of value beyond informational transparency. The goodwill protected does not serve as a navigation instrument to aid the consumer's marketplace search. It is an additional value—a "surplus," so to speak, that the trademark provides. Protecting famous and well-known trademarks against appropriation by a competitor (absent consumer confusion) provides an incentive for the owner to create or add to the symbol's prestige by constantly shaping its image and exclusivity.[268] Let us recall Brown's famous illustration:

> The buyer of an advertised good buys more than a parcel of food or fabric; he buys the pause that refreshes, the hand that has never lost its skill, the priceless ingredient that is the reputation of its maker. All these may be illusions, but they cost money to create, and if the creators can recoup their outlay, who is the poorer?[269]

[266] *See, e.g.*, Boudewijn Bouckaert, "*What is Property?*," 13 Harv. J.L. & Pub. Pol'y 775, 797 *et seq.* (1990) (with further references).

[267] *See, e.g.*, William P. Kratzke, *Normative Economic Analysis of Trademark Law*, 21 Mem. St. U. L. Rev. 199, 204 (1991).

[268] William M. Landes & Richard A. Posner, *Trademark Law: An Economic Perspective*, 30 J. L. & Econ. 265, 307–308 (1987); Mark A. Lemley, *Property, Intellectual Property, and Free Riding*, 83 Tex. L. Rev. 1031, 1057 (2005); Jeremy N. Sheff, *Veblen Brands*, 96 Minn. L. Rev. 769, 822 (2012). For the terminology of "surplus value," *see* Rochelle Cooper Dreyfuss, *Expressive Genericity: Trademarks as Language in the Pepsi Generation*, 65 Notre Dame L. Rev. 397, 402–403 (1990).

[269] Ralph S. Brown, Jr., *Advertising and the Public Interest: Legal Protection of Trade Symbols*, 57 Yale L.J. 1165, 1181 (1948); *see also* Eugen Ulmer, *Warenzeichen und unlauterer Wettbewerb in ihrer Fortbildung durch die Rechtsprechung* 29 (1929); Walter R. Schluep, *Das Markenrecht als subjektives Recht* 345 *et seq.* (1964). Finally also, in the hearty language of a US federal judge, Alex Kozinski, *Trademarks Unplugged*, 68 N.Y.U. L. Rev. 960, 970 (1993).

The creation of such surplus goodwill and the corresponding premium that the consumer must pay is not directly compensated by a concurrent savings in search costs. Rather, it is a true excess payment—in economic terms, it is the creation of deadweight losses. More concretely, the consumer pays for exclusivity, scarcity, prestige, or other aspects that are not directly related to the product's qualities. This is actually a paradigmatic characteristic of other kinds of intellectual property, particularly copyrights and patents.[270] Hence, what we can term the surplus goodwill of a trademark is a subject matter different from the information capital required to navigate the marketplace. Accordingly, it is protected under an alternative policy more akin to those underlying copyright and patent laws.

To avoid misunderstanding, of course, we must keep in mind that the parallels to copyright and patent protection are not absolute. Antidilution doctrine provides a good example of the aim to prevent, as Barton Beebe explains, the exhaustion of trademark utility by copying: if branded products are copied dilutively, the trademark will ultimately lose its distinctive character and value.[271] In this respect, alternative trademark policy differs crucially from the general ideology underlying other sectors of intellectual property law. While it is commonly acknowledged that use of patented inventions and copyrighted works is inexhaustible and nonrivalrous, the quality and quantity of rivalrous trademark uses do affect rights in and use of the original symbol.[272]

Against this backdrop, it is also evident that despite a certain detachment from information economization, the ensuing "property rights" in trademarks and goodwill remain competition related. The umbilical cord between the trademark right and its creating mechanism—marketplace competition—cannot be cut. The value protected under theories other than information economization is still connected to market information.

[270] Mark A. Lemley, *Property, Intellectual Property, and Free Riding*, 83 Tex. L. Rev. 1031, 1059 (2005); Mark A. Lemley & Mark P. McKenna, *Owning Mark(et)s*, 109 Mich. L. Rev. 137, 179 (2010).

[271] Barton Beebe, *Intellectual Property Law and the Sumptuary Code*, 123 Harv. L. Rev. 809, 847 (2010).

[272] Thomas Jefferson famously expressed the idea that intellectual creations are inexhaustible and nonrivalrous in a letter to Isaac McPherson. *See* Thomas Jefferson, *Letter to Isaac McPherson (Monticello, 13 August 1813)*, 326, 334, in 13 *The Writings of Thomas Jefferson* (Albert Ellery Bergh ed., 1905) ("He who receives an idea from me, receives instruction himself without lessening mine; as he who lights his taper at mine, receives light without darkening me."). For the difference regarding the traditional trademark doctrine of confusion prevention, *see* William M. Landes & Richard A. Posner, *The Economic Structure of Intellectual Property Law* 172–173 (2003); Florent Thouvenin, *Funktionale Systematisierung von Wettbewerbsrecht (UWG) und Immaterialgüterrechten* 267–268, 355 *et seq.*, 525 *et seq.* (2007).

In other words, generating goodwill under the theories of dilution prevention and of initial-interest and postsale confusion requires establishing and upholding a brand image in the marketplace that is strong enough to warrant protection. Here, too, the consumer's mind determines the extent of trademark protection. The trademark's "psychological hold upon the public" is what qualifies as protectable subject matter.[273]

3 Two Sides of the Coin: Law and Equity in Market Communication

Seeing trademark protection as based on the overarching concept of market communication implies an inseparability of private rights and public policy. This was demonstrated by Ulmer's reconciliation model. He may not have done away with the dominant individual rights perspective in trademark law.[274] However, his concept did contain an important qualification of the value that was to be protected under trademark and unfair competition law. He actually replicated the common law dichotomy between law and equity, whereby the trademark owner is assigned a legal title from the time of registration—but, in the end, equity is what determines her scope of rights. A closer look at the policies at stake helps formulate a more exact metric.

Confusion prevention theory provides for a simple equation. The trademark owner is protected as far as the relevant consumer group is at risk of being confused by a third party's use of the trademark. The scope of protection is not a static measure; rather, it depends on different parameters. The domain of the right owner may vary according to the target group and to the owner's investment, especially her past activities in the marketplace. The goodwill may have a different value depending on the psychological connection that exists between a trademark's or a market participant's reputation and the relevant group of consumers.[275] Such a two-sides-of-the-coin perspective is common in US doctrine,[276] where the right owner's equitable position has traditionally been protected under a system of use-based—and thus, ultimately, also market-related—rights.[277] And civil law doctrine is no longer much different.

[273] Frank I. Schechter, *The Rational Basis of Trademark Protection*, 40 Harv. L. Rev. 813, 818 (1927). Similarly, in Brown's words, the owner of the "persuasive symbol . . . has stored up in a number of persons' brain cells some degree of desire to buy goods bearing the symbol." Ralph S. Brown, Jr., *Advertising and the Public Interest: Legal Protection of Trade Symbols*, 57 Yale L.J. 1165, 1191 (1948); Walter R. Schluep, *Das Markenrecht als subjektives Recht* 345 *et seq.* (1964); more recently, Mark A. Lemley & Mark P. McKenna, *Owning Mark(et)s*, 109 Mich. L. Rev. 137, 153–154 (2010).

[274] *See supra* p. 42–46.

[275] This aspect is also reflected in its most extreme variation: if a trademark evolves into a generic term, its goodwill vanishes. It is then, once again, the perception of the relevant consumer group that determines the (non)existence of rights.

[276] *See supra* p. 326–327. [277] *See supra* p. 94 *et seq.*

A similar interrelation between scope of rights and substantive law policy was lucidly explained in the Court of Justice's 1993 decision in *Deutsche Renault v. AUDI*:

> A trade-mark right as an exclusive right and protection against marks giving rise to risk of confusion are in reality . . . two sides of the same coin: reducing or extending the scope of protection against the risk of confusion simply reduces or extends the scope of the right itself.[278]

The nonexistence of a goodwill paradigm and a different policy foundation of the registered-rights model have led to an initial neglect of the equitable nature of rights in European civil law doctrine. A slightly modified perspective, however, allows us to also understand the trademark owner's right as a legal title: the applicant or registrant may be the formal proprietor from the time of application or registration. Nonetheless, it is market information capital that ultimately determines the scope of her right.

Prima facie, this issue appears more complicated with regard to theories of non-confusion-based infringement. These theories implement different policies of rights acquisition and protection. Yet even though information economization may not be their primary focus, these alternative theories also contribute to the protection of market information capital. The trademark owner's right in the brand symbol and its use will ultimately also depend on goodwill—albeit goodwill of a different quality. Any impact on this capital, be it through dilutive use, a bait-and-switch scheme, or invasion of trademark scarcity and exclusivity, will be effectuated by direct communication with the consumer.

This correlation, however, is not yet fully clarified. Initially, European trademark law focused on a trademark's guarantee of the identity of origin as its essential function.[279] Yet an analysis in light of non-confusion-based theories also considers other trademark functions.[280] As explained earlier,

[278] *Deutsche Renault AG v AUDI AG*, C-317/91, para. 31 (30 November 1993), [1993] E.C.R. I-6227.

[279] For the essential function of indicating origin, *see, e.g., O2 Holdings and O2 (UK)*, C-533/06, para. 57 (12 June 2008), [2008] E.C.R. I-4231; *Philips*, C-299/99, para. 30 (18 June 2002), [2002] E.C.R. I-5475; *CNL-SUCAL v. HAG* ("HAG II"), C-10/89, para. 13–14 (17 October 1990), [1990] E.C.R. I-3711.

[280] *See, e.g.*, Rupert Schreiner, *Die Dienstleistungsmarke—Typus, Rechtsschutz und Funktion* 451 *et seq.* (1983); Michael Lehmann, *Die wettbewerbswidrige Ausnutzung und Beeinträchtigung des guten Rufs bekannter Marken, Namen und Herkunftsangaben—Die Rechtslage in der Bundesrepublik Deutschland*, 1986 GRUR Int. 6, 17; Frauke Henning-Bodewig & Annette Kur, *Marke und Verbraucher—Funktionen der Marke in der Marktwirtschaft, vol. I: Grundlagen* 8–9, 278 and *passim* (1988); Thomas Schönfeld, *Die Gemeinschaftsmarke als selbständiger Vermögensgegenstand eines Unternehmens—Eine rechtsdogmatische und ökonomische Analyse zur Property-Rights-Theory* 170 *et seq.* (1994).

the Court of Justice further specified and amended the list in *L'Oréal* and *Google France*:

> [Trademark] functions include not only the essential function of the trade mark, which is to guarantee to consumers the origin of the goods or services ("the function of indicating origin"), but also its other functions, in particular that of guaranteeing the quality of the goods or services in question and those of communication, investment or advertising.[281]

It is particularly the advertising and investment function that requires qualification. In this regard, as the Court of Justice elaborated in *Interflora*, the "advertising" function of a trademark is the owner's "opportunity of using [her] mark effectively to inform and win over consumers."[282] In addition, the investment function—though possibly overlapping with the advertising function—empowers "its proprietor to acquire or preserve a reputation capable of attracting consumers and retaining their loyalty."[283] Reading this literally, one might expect the trademark owner to be allowed to skim all profits ensuing from investment in the trademark.[284] But this would neglect the trademark's roots in market communication. *Interflora* highlights this point: as the court explained, the investment function of a trademark will be invaded only if its reputation is affected and maintenance of the reputation is jeopardized.[285] No detrimental effect can be found if use of the trademark occurs "in conditions of fair competition that respect the trade mark's function as an indication of origin" and if "the only consequence of that use is to oblige the proprietor of that trade mark to adapt its efforts to acquire or preserve a reputation capable of attracting consumers and retaining their loyalty."[286] This understanding of the investment function implies that the right embodies its owners' goodwill as the active and

[281] *Google France and Google*, C-236/08, 237/08, and 238/08, para. 77 (23 March 2010), [2010] E.C.R. I-2417; *L'Oréal and Others*, C 487/07, para. 58 (18 June 2009), [2009] E.C.R. I-5185.

[282] *Interflora and Interflora British Unit*, C-323/09, para. 59 (22 September 2011), [2012] E.T.M.R. 1.

[283] *Id.* at para. 60.

[284] This has been brought forward, for example, in situations of keyword advertising where trademark owners have no choice but to "buy" their own trademarks as keywords from search-engine providers. The ensuing reduction of trademark earnings might be seen as contravening the owner's interest in trademark investment and the corresponding trademark function. *See, e.g.*, Ansgar Ohly, *Keyword Advertising auf dem Weg zurück von Luxemburg nach Paris, Wien, Karlsruhe und Den Haag*, 2010 GRUR 776, 781; for the dangerous openness of the concept, however, *see* Jonathan Cornthwaite, *Say It with Flowers: The Judgment of the Court of Justice of the European Union in Interflora v. Marks & Spencer*, 34(2) EIPR 127, 132 (2012).

[285] *Interflora and Interflora British Unit*, C-323/09, para. 63 (22 September 2011), [2012] E.T.M.R. 1.

[286] *Id.* at para. 64.

effective information capital in the marketplace only. Accordingly, investment in a trademark is protectable only within the confines of the trademark's capacity as a search term and instrument of market communication.[287] What determines the scope of rights is the trademark's being part and parcel of marketplace information infrastructure—ultimately, only directly communication-related investment matters.[288]

Seen in this light, the European understanding of trademark rights resembles Brown's allegory of the trademark as a bridge for advertising.[289] A trademark establishes communicative relationships between market participants and serves as an information-transmission instrument. The value protected is the information capital as a keystone of the information infrastructure within the marketplace. Formal rights, as ironclad as they may have been described to be under statutory or judge-made rules, will never be absolute. It is the relativity of market conditions and the equities of goodwill that determine their boundaries.

C Summary

The illustration in Figure 2 (on the next page) summarizes the policies at stake in the fields of trademark and unfair competition law.

The common core of protective purposes in trademark and unfair competition law is information economization. This is competitor-consumer relations at the vertical level of the competitive process. In this respect, trademark rights are legal entitlements and are just a formal shell. The equitable substance is provided for by trademark and unfair competition law's core policy of confusion prevention. I have characterized the information capital at stake in these cases as navigation goodwill.[290] Beyond this core area, the two fields harbor additional policies. Theories of non-confusion-based trademark infringement have been developed in order to protect surplus goodwill. Here, information economization has fallen out of the picture. Nevertheless, non-confusion-based theories are still founded on market information and its transmission to the consumer. As we will see, therefore, all communication-based theories of trademark

[287] For the search-term characterization, *see id.* at para. 44.

[288] *See also Smith v. Chanel, Inc.*, 402 F.2d 562, 568 (9th Cir. 1968) ("A large expenditure of money does not in itself create legally protectable rights.").

[289] Ralph S. Brown, Jr., *Advertising and the Public Interest: Legal Protection of Trade Symbols*, 57 Yale L.J. 1165, 1187 (1948) ("The symbol itself then becomes a vital link. It is a narrow bridge over which all the traffic powered by the advertising must pass. If an imitator can seize the bridge, he can collect the rich toll."). *See also* Wolfgang Fikentscher, *Wettbewerb und gewerblicher Rechtsschutz—Die Stellung des Rechts der Wettbewerbsbeschränkungen in der Rechtsordnung* 140 (1958) ("Brücke zum Kunden").

[290] The trademark register reflects a slightly divergent doctrine. *See supra* p. 42–46.

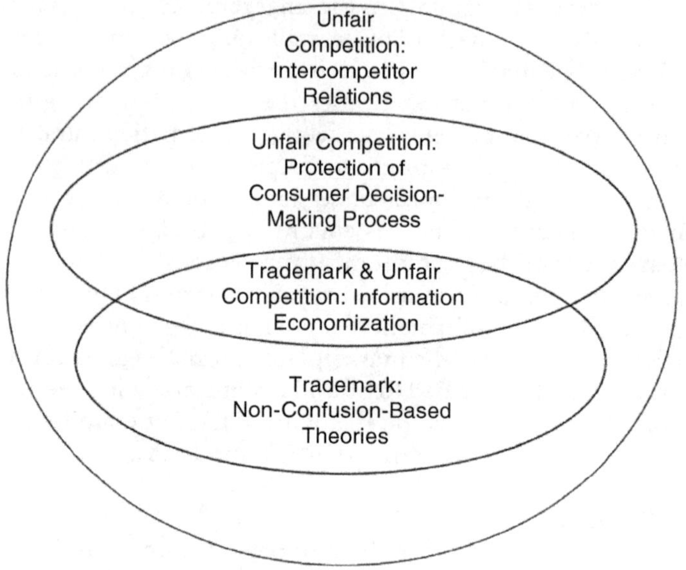

Figure 2 The Interrelation of Trademark and Unfair Competition Policies

and unfair competition law are subject to a similar structure of choice-of-law and conflicts rules. The outer rim of policies in unfair competition law, finally, is the protection of fairness in intercompetitor relations. This is the domain of non-information-based regulation of competitive activities—the horizontal level of the competition process. Since scenarios of this kind are situated beyond the market mechanism of consumer decision making, they are usually governed under genuine tort conflicts rules.

Section 3 Application—Functional Structures in Trademark and Unfair Competition Doctrine

The following dissection of trademark and unfair competition policies will lay the groundwork for the resolution of choice-of-law questions in the last chapter. It will take a closer look at different scenarios of trademark infringement and unfair competition violations, pointing out the respective functional structures of the policies involved. Independent of national law peculiarities and differences in substantive law doctrine, a functional perspective of international trademark and unfair competition disputes provides a consistent and comprehensive guideline for choice-of-law and conflicts analysis.

I Trademark Protection

By looking at information infrastructure and its function in the marketplace, we can identify two different kinds of information capital or goodwill. The traditional passing off and confusion prevention policy protects "navigation goodwill," which is utilized by the consumer to navigate the market. The subject matter of protection under alternative theories of trademark law, by contrast, concerns "surplus goodwill," which comprises all other instances of protection under modern theory that are not founded primarily on the idea of preventing consumer confusion.

A Navigation Goodwill: Confusion-Based Infringement Theory

At their core, the fields of trademark and unfair competition law serve the same purpose: protecting free and unhindered consumer decision making, which is the quintessence of competition. This protection determines trademark right extensions and competition fairness standards. US doctrine in both areas remains founded on a practical concept of trade diversion by confusion. While search-cost analysis has taken over in legal theory, the notion of goodwill has come to capture the common functions of trademark protection and unfair competition prevention in practice. The proprietary goodwill of the owner and the psychological goodwill in the public's mind is the object of protection. Even though the debate over propertization and the misgivings of extending trademark rights is far from resolved, the concept of goodwill has remained the ultimate connection between individual rights, markets, and competition.[291] In Europe, by contrast, trademark and unfair competition doctrines have never been comparably linked by a common denominator. Although there have been attempts to overcome the separation, the dichotomy has, to date, remained almost insurmountable. One major reason may be the lack of a technical concept functionally similar to goodwill. Indeed, a comparison of the systems suggests that the interrelatedness of confusion prevention and rights protection could far more easily be constructed and explained under the concept of trademark goodwill than under the civil law doctrine of state-granted privileges and conduct regulation.[292] Notwithstanding these differences in doctrinal instruments, US and European regimes have both moved toward a common core policy of protecting consumer decision making. Indeed, looking at the systems in total, the idea of protecting the market mechanism by establishing conditions for optimal consumer transacting can be explained as a transnationally uniform paradigm. With respect to

[291] *See supra* p. 121 *et seq.* [292] *See supra* p. 27 *et seq.*, p. 64 *et seq.*, and *passim.*

trademarks, information capital provides for consumer navigation within the marketplace. Since the consumer is the one who determines the individual market transaction, impact on information capital will occur at the place of consumer decision making—or, more precisely, at the place where the consumer turns her decision into a market transaction. This, as we will see in chapter 6, is determinative for attachment in choice of law.

B Surplus Goodwill: Non-Confusion-Based and Time-Shifted Infringement Theories

The consumer's decision-making process is similarly central for conflicts resolution on issues arising under alternative theories of trademark protection. Yet the doctrinal and structural foundations are different. For a clear determination of the point of attachment in choice of law, we must dissect the relevant subject matter of protection. As discussed earlier, trademark rights have been extended beyond the concept of confusion prevention. Examples include the practical recognition of actionable confusion prior to and after the point of sale, as well as antidilution theory. Regardless of whether these theories adequately fit into a balanced system of trademark protection, none of the alternative concepts will diverge from the confusion prevention doctrine insofar as the consumer always stands at the center of infringement analysis. Alternative theories of trademark protection, therefore, are accordingly founded on policies designed to protect the market information infrastructure. This is what ultimately also matters for choice of law and conflicts resolution.

1 Antidilution Doctrine

As discussed earlier, US and European trademark and unfair competition laws have extended infringement theories beyond the idea of confusion at the point of sale. The development of antidilution doctrine in particular has pushed the protection of trademark goodwill beyond the strict limitations of consumer confusion. Different types of dilution have been acknowledged ever since Frank I. Schechter laid the doctrinal foundation in 1927 with his explanation of trademark uniqueness and singularity as a protectable value.[293] The determinative issue for all types is whether the dilutive use of a famous trademark results in a deterioration of distinctiveness. Under US doctrine, a trademark's distinctiveness (i.e., its ability to clearly distinguish the source of a product) can be reduced through blurring or

[293] *See* Frank I. Schechter, *The Rational Basis of Trademark Protection*, 40 Harv. L. Rev. 813, 831 (1927). *See also supra* p. 117–121.

tarnishment.[294] Both variants require probable harm or injury to the mark.[295] Dilution by blurring further requires that the mark's ability to denote only one source of the product be diminished by third parties' use in a nonconfusing way.[296] Here, the harm involved is not due to what traditional doctrine describes as consumer confusion.[297] Rather, it is due to the actual or potential erosion of trademark strength—the weakening of consumers' mental association between mark and product.[298] Dilution by tarnishment occurs where the unauthorized use of a trademark has the potential to degrade positive consumer associations of the mark, thereby harming its reputation.[299] Sometimes, in addition to blurring and tarnishment, a third variant of dilution has been suggested: free riding on a famous trademark's reputation may also be found to improperly appropriate the owner's goodwill.[300] As in the United States, blurring and tarnishment are two recognized forms of dilution in European law. In addition, the Court of Justice has expressly acknowledged a doctrine of free riding and misappropriation prevention wherever a defendant takes "unfair advantage of the distinctive character of the repute of [a] trade mark."[301] Under European

[294] *See, e.g.*, Restatement of the Law—Unfair Competition (Third), § 25 and comment c (1995); *further also, e.g.*, 4 J. Thomas McCarthy, *McCarthy on Trademarks and Unfair Competition*, § 24:67 (4th edn., 2016); Stacey L. Dogan & Mark A. Lemley, *Trademark and Consumer Search Costs on the Internet*, 41 Hous. L. Rev. 777, 790 *et seq.* (2004).

[295] 4 J. Thomas McCarthy, *McCarthy on Trademarks and Unfair Competition*, § 24:67 (4th edn., 2016).

[296] Restatement of the Law—Unfair Competition (Third), § 25, comment c (1995); 4 J. Thomas McCarthy, *McCarthy on Trademarks and Unfair Competition*, § 24:69 (4th edn., 2016).

[297] This issue is not uncontested, however. Some courts have identified dilution and confusion as different aspects of the same phenomenon. *See, e.g.*, *Nabisco, Inc. v. PF Brands, Inc.*, 191 F.3d 208, 219 (2nd Cir. 1999). For Europe, a similar doctrine has been described. *See, e.g.*, *Davidoff*, C-292/00, para. 30 (9 January 2003), [2003] E.C.R. I-389; Reinhard Ingerl & Christian Rohnke, *Kommentar zum Markengesetz: Gesetz über den Schutz von Marken und sonstigen Kennzeichen*, § 14 para. 1282 (3rd edn., 2010).

[298] *See, e.g.*, *Mead Data Cent., Inc. v. Toyota Motor Sales, U.S.A., Inc.*, 875 F.2d 1026, 1031 (2nd Cir. 1989). For the argument that dilution increases consumer search costs, *see* Richard A. Posner, *When Is Parody Fair Use?*, 21 J. Legal Stud. 67, 75 (1992); Mark A. Lemley, *The Modern Lanham Act and the Death of Common Sense*, 108 Yale L.J. 1687, 1704 (1999).

[299] *See, e.g.*, *Hormel Foods Corp. v. Jim Henson Productions, Inc.*, 73 F.3d 497, 507 *et seq.* (2nd Cir. 1996); *see also* 4 J. Thomas McCarthy, *McCarthy on Trademarks and Unfair Competition*, § 24:89 (4th edn., 2016).

[300] *See, e.g.*, *Ty Inc. v. Perryman*, 306 F.3d 509, 512 (7th Cir. 2002) (Posner, J.); *see also* William M. Landes & Richard A. Posner, *The Economic Structure of Intellectual Property Law* 206 *et seq.* (2003).

[301] *See, e.g.*, *Intel Corporation*, C-252/07, para. 27–28 (27 November 2008), [2008] E.C.R. I-8823; *L'Oréal and Others*, C 487/07, para. 38 *et seq.* (18 June 2009), [2009] E.C.R. I-5185; *Interflora and Interflora British Unit*, C-323/09, para. 74 (22 September 2011), [2012] E.T.M.R. 1. For German law, *see, e.g.*, BGH 2010 GRUR 726—*Opel-Blitz II* (14 January 2010).

law, therefore, "exploitation on the coat-tails of a mark with a reputation" may suffice for an infringement; actual injury to the famous mark is not required.[302]

This typology reflects a principal distinction between two markets that can be affected by dilutive trademark use.[303] In the first market, where the famous mark functions as a product signifier, dilutive use will only indirectly affect consumer decision making. The idea is not to prevent consumer confusion in the direct sense—it is to prevent the long-term loss in efficiency of market information. When the consumer sees, for instance, a "Tiffany" fast-food restaurant or a "Chanel" used-car dealer, she will think both about the original trademark owner and the restaurant or car dealer. Even though she will not be confused, connotations of the name might blur and the trademark's communicative value for its owner could diminish. Detrimental effects to the consumer's perception will develop only after illegitimate use of a trademark has been made. Over time, the trademark may lose its function as an extraordinary signifier of quality and source.[304] With respect to antidilution doctrine in the second market—that is, the market for the diluter's product—a different rationale governs. Here, under both European doctrine and parts of US theory, a policy of preventing misappropriation, free riding, and parasitism plays the most significant role. The primary legal purpose is not to reduce search costs but to prevent unjust enrichment and misappropriation of another's investment.[305]

Conflicts law does not need to clarify whether the protection of surplus goodwill is sound. What must be done instead is the spelling out of the exact structural foundation of protecting information capital.

[302] *L'Oréal and Others*, C 487/07, para. 43 (18 June 2009), [2009] E.C.R. I-5185; *Interflora and Interflora British Unit*, C-323/09, para. 74 (22 September 2011), [2012] E.T.M.R. 1. For an extensive critique, *see, e.g.*, Seán Mc Guinness, *Observations on free riding after L'Oréal v. Bellure*, 7 J. Intell. Prop. L. & Pract. 890, 892 *et seq.* (2012).

[303] It is important to note, however, that cases of trademark dilution can also occur within a single market. *See supra* fn. 297.

[304] *See* Robert N. Klieger, *Trademark Dilution: The Whittling Away of the Rational Basis for Trademark Protection*, 58 U. Pitt. L. Rev. 789, 823–828 (1997); Stacey L. Dogan & Mark A. Lemley, *The Merchandising Right: Fragile Theory or Fait Accompli?*, 54 Emory L.J. 461, 493–494 (2005); *but cf.* Chris Brown, *A Dilution Delusion: The Unjustifiable Protection of Similar Marks*, 72 U. Cin. L. Rev. 1023, 1038–1039 (2004) (citing psychology evidence that a mental processing of related uses may strengthen rather than blur the brand-association power); *see also* Graeme W. Austin, *Trademarks and the Burdened Imagination*, 69 Brook. L. Rev. 827, 904–905 (2004) (questioning traditional perceptions of limited consumer thoughtfulness).

[305] *See, e.g.*, David S. Welkowitz, *Reexamining Trademark Dilution*, 44 Vand. L. Rev. 531, 545–546, 560 *et seq.* (1991); Anselm Kamperman Sanders, Unfair Competition Law—The Protection of Intellectual and Industrial Creativity 94 (1997); David J. Franklyn, *Debunking Dilution Doctrine: Toward a Coherent Theory of the Anti-Free-Rider Principle in American Trademark Law*, 56 Hastings L.J. 117, 118 (2004).

If surplus goodwill is captured through the dilutive (ab)use of a trademark, depending on the perspective, the infringement may be found in two different ways. It could be based on either the potential diminution of information capital (in other words, the trademark's distinctiveness) in the original brand's market or the misappropriation of information capital for the purpose of transacting in a different market (the marketplace where the second-comer's product is marketed). As my conflicts typology for dilution scenarios in chapter 6 will reveal, it is the *situs* of the respective goodwill substance that matters for determining the applicable law.

2 Temporal Extensions of Goodwill Protection

In addition to antidilution doctrine, trademark-as-property protection has been extended under at least two more theories: initial-interest confusion and postsale confusion. Typical cases of confusion affect the consumer's mind and decision making at the point of sale. With initial-interest and postsale confusion, however, confusion occurs before and after the point of sale, respectively. To accommodate these scenarios, US case law has extended trademark infringement theory accordingly. For its part, European trademark practice has been more cautious in considering such incidents for the issue of trademark infringement.[306] The bulk of initial-interest and postsale confusion cases, particularly in German doctrine, tends to be covered by norms of unfair competition prevention.[307]

a Postsale Confusion Succinctly defined, postsale confusion is confusion experienced by the consumer upon viewing the trademarked product after purchase. In principle, postsale confusion theory—similar to point-of-sale confusion—is founded on the idea of information truthfulness. One variation is bystander confusion, which comprises sales to nonconfused consumers who use the product in the company of potential

[306] A modest beginning of postsale confusion analysis seems to be found in the Court of Justice's *Arsenal* judgment, in which the judges explained that the alleged infringer's notice to his customers that his goods "are not official Arsenal FC products" would not suffice to avoid confusion since "there [was] a clear possibility . . . that some consumers, in particular if they come across the goods after they have been sold . . ., may interpret the sign [on the goods] as designating Arsenal FC as the undertaking of origin of the goods" (*Arsenal Football Club plc v. Matthew Reed*, C-206/01, para. 56–57 (12 November 2002), [2002] E.C.R. I-10273). But this judgment remained virtually the only attempt to give regard to postsale confusion aspects. For an overview on the Court of Justice's judgments and European national laws, *see* Olaf Sosnitza, *Nach dem Spiel ist vor dem Spiel—Das Konzept der „Post-Sale Confusion" im Common Law, im europäischen und im deutschen Markenrecht*, 1 ZGE 457 (2009).

[307] I will address these scenarios in the typology *infra* p. 556–560. Thus far, a structural analysis will suffice.

purchasers who are or might be confused regarding the source of the product. If these potential purchasers, by viewing the product, do or could acquire a negative impression of its qualities and thus refrain from a transaction, the injury to the trademark owner is clear.[308] A similar problem exists with downstream confusion, in which the nonconfused purchaser resells the product in a secondary market, where the sale results in consumer confusion.[309] Even though the impairment occurs during and through the postsale spreading of incorrect information,[310] the scenario of potential damage to the trademark's goodwill is still founded on a genuine concept of consumer misinformation.

Practice, however, has extended the doctrine to situations where the risk of confusion is doubtable or even nonexistent.[311] In this regard, as with antidilution doctrine, a different category of goodwill is affected. The decision of the US Court of Appeals for the Sixth Circuit in *Ferrari S.P.A. v. Roberts*[312] provides a telling example. The defendant had been selling construction kits for full-scale Ferrari replicas. Once assembled, the kits were to be attached to the chassis of other cars. In this case, however, none of the purchasers were confused about the product's originality at the point of sale. Further, it seemed obvious that the kits, even once combined with the car chassis, could be reasonably distinguished from an original Ferrari. But the court majority nevertheless ruled that the likelihood-of-confusion test for trademark infringement was not limited to a finding of purchaser confusion. As the court explained, confusion of "members of the public" would suffice for finding an infringement.[313] It particularly emphasized the detrimental effects that a cheap imitation's poor appearance could have on the original's reputation for prestige and quality:

[308] A similar argument was made in the Supreme Court majority's *Steele* opinion. *See supra* p. 159 *et seq.*

[309] For bystander and downstream confusion, *see* Jeremy N. Sheff, *Veblen Brands*, 96 Minn. L. Rev. 769, 779 *et seq.*, 785 *et seq.* (2012).

[310] Robert G. Bone, *Hunting Goodwill: A History of the Concept of Goodwill in Trademark Law*, 86 B. U. L. Rev. 547, 608 (2006). For the German doctrine of improper product imitation (section 4 no. 3 Unfair Competition Act (UWG)) and actual or potential damages, *see* BGH 1993 GRUR 55, 57 *et seq.*—*Tchibo/Rolex II* (17 June 1992).

[311] Prominent examples of cases where genuine consumer confusion is debatable include, *e.g.*, *Mastercrafters Clock & Radio Co. v. Vacheron & Constantin-Le Coultre Watches, Inc.*, 221 F.2d 464 (2nd Cir. 1955), *Lois Sportswear, U.S.A., Inc. v. Levi Strauss & Co.*, 799 F.2d 867 (2nd Cir. 1986), and *Ferrari S.P.A. v. Roberts*, 944 F.2d 1235 (6th Cir. 1991). *See also Nabisco, Inc. v. PF Brands, Inc.*, 191 F.3d 208, 218 (2nd Cir. 1999). For further analysis and critique, *see* Barton Beebe, *Intellectual Property Law and the Sumptuary Code*, 123 Harv. L. Rev. 809, 851 *et seq.* (2010); Jeremy N. Sheff, *Veblen Brands*, 96 Minn. L. Rev. 769 *passim* (2012).

[312] *Ferrari S.P.A. v. Roberts*, 944 F.2d 1235 (6th Cir. 1991).

[313] *Id.* at 1245.

> Since Congress intended to protect the reputation of the manufacturer as well as to protect purchasers, the [Lanham] Act's protection is not limited to confusion at the point of sale. Because Ferrari's reputation in the field could be damaged by the marketing of [the] replicas, the district court did not err in permitting recovery despite the absence of point of sale confusion.[314]

The court continued, sharing the district court's conception of scarcity and exclusivity protection:

> If the country is populated with hundreds, if not thousands, of replicas of rare, distinct, and unique vintage cars, obviously they are no longer unique. Even if a person seeing one of these replicas driving down the road is not confused, Ferrari's exclusive association with this design has been diluted and eroded. If the replica Daytona looks cheap or in disrepair, Ferrari's reputation for rarity and quality could be damaged.[315]

In his dissenting opinion, Judge Kennedy pointed out the central issue of postsale confusion doctrine. He acknowledged that cases of actual postsale confusion could ultimately transmit detrimental misinformation to the presale and point-of-sale levels. He had no doubt that if potential purchasers saw a cheap imitation or replica of the original, the original manufacturer's reputation might be damaged.[316] Yet, as he continued, the transfer of confusion among and over different stages of the consumer's decision-making process must find a limit in the fact that, under traditional doctrine, it is confusion with regard to a *purchase* that is required for finding an infringement. At the time of the court's decision, statutory causes of action under the Lanham Act were still limited to confusion prevention; there was no cause of action for dilution. The majority, as Kennedy concluded, had thus transformed traditional confusion theory into an *extra legem* version of antidilution protection and protection of product exclusivity and scarcity.[317]

Looking at the different scenarios of postsale confusion infringement, it is clear that the theory bears a distinct element of information-economization policy: bystanders may acquire incorrect impressions of the original's qualities when observing an imitation after the point of sale. Sales in downstream markets may ultimately also reflect negatively on consumers' perception of the original product. In both cases, incorrect

[314] *Id.* For the 1967 Lanham Act amendment removing language that limited liability to conduct confusing "purchasers," *see* Jeremy N. Sheff, *Veblen Brands*, 96 Minn. L. Rev. 769, 777 (2012).

[315] *Ferrari S.P.A. v. Roberts*, 944 F.2d 1235, 1245 (6th Cir. 1991).

[316] *Id.* at 1249–1250.

[317] *Id.* at 1250; *see also* Robert G. Bone, *Hunting Goodwill: A History of the Concept of Goodwill in Trademark Law*, 86 B. U. L. Rev. 547, 611 (2006); Barton Beebe, *Intellectual Property Law and the Sumptuary Code*, 123 Harv. L. Rev. 809, 845 *et seq.* (2010).

information is transmitted and the consumer's decision making could, at least in the long run, be distorted by the deterioration of trademark information value. Quite often, however, consumers do not bear the slightest risk of either point-of-sale or postsale confusion—the market will then not be subject to misinformation. In these cases, the competing products are qualitatively equivalent or clearly distinguishable at the point of sale and in their postsale environments.[318] Nonetheless, courts have increasingly come to grant protection to prestigious and reputed trademarks in such cases. In these cases of so-called status confusion, it is not the information value of trademark communication but the social signaling function of the trademark that is protected. Here, the rationale differs, for it is based on the preservation of distinctiveness and reputation.[319] Ultimately, the brand is substituted for the product.[320] The trademark owner is selling the luxury and prestige of the product, not the product as such.[321] Trademark scarcity, exclusivity, and prestige ultimately constitute the surplus goodwill that is protected under an extended theory of postsale confusion.

In Germany and other European jurisdictions, similar cases of product imitation have been found actionable, albeit under a doctrine of unfair competition prevention.[322] I will address both postsale confusion and unfair imitation cases in more detail in an instant.[323]

[318] *See, e.g., Mastercrafters Clock & Radio Co. v. Vacheron & Constantin-Le Coultre Watches, Inc.*, 221 F.2d 464 (2nd Cir. 1955); *Mastercrafters Clock & Radio Co. v. Vacheron & Constantin-Le Coultre Watches, Inc.*, 119 F.Supp. 209, 213 *et seq.* (S.D.N.Y. 1954) (finding that no confusion existed at the point of purchase). For a concise overview, *see* Robert G. Bone, *Hunting Goodwill: A History of the Concept of Goodwill in Trademark Law*, 86 B. U. L. Rev. 547, 607 *et seq.* (2006); for German law and a comparative analysis, *see* Olaf Sosnitza, *Nach dem Spiel ist vor dem Spiel—Das Konzept der „Post-Sale Confusion" im Common Law, im europäischen und im deutschen Markenrecht*, 1 ZGE 457–480 (2009).

[319] *See, e.g., Rolex Watch U.S.A., Inc. v. Canner*, 645 F.Supp. 484, 495 (S.D. Fla. 1986).

[320] Jeremy N. Sheff, *Veblen Brands*, 96 Minn. L. Rev. 769, 802 (2012). This is what Beebe has termed "fiat property": trademarks here have "no significant characteristic other than that they are property, that they are forms of exclusivity, of rarity, of difference." Barton Beebe, *Intellectual Property Law and the Sumptuary Code*, 123 Harv. L. Rev. 809, 888 (2010).

[321] *See also* most fittingly for French doctrine Paul Roubier, *Le Droit de la Propriété Industrielle, vol. II: Partie Spéciale* 515 (1954) ("Alors la marque n'apparaît plus seulement comme l'accessoire d'une marchandise, elle apparaît comme un bien principal, ayant une valeur propre par elle-même.").

[322] For the German *Rolex* case, *see infra* p. 370–373. As in *Mastercrafters Clock & Radio Co. v. Vacheron & Constantin-Le Coultre Watches, Inc.*, 221 F.2d 464 (2nd Cir. 1955), and *Rolex Watch U.S.A., Inc. v. Canner*, 645 F.Supp. 484 (S.D. Fla. 1986), the case concerned an imitation of famous watches. *See* BGH 1985 GRUR 876—*Tchibo/Rolex* (8 November 1984); BGH 1993 GRUR 55—*Tchibo/Rolex II* (17 June 1992); *see also* BGH 2001 GRUR 443, 445—*Viennetta* (19 October 2000); BGH 2005 GRUR 349, 352—*Klemmbausteine III* (2 December 2004); BGH 2007 GRUR 795, 799—*Handtaschen* (11 January 2007). For Austria, *see, e.g.*, OGH 2001 GRUR Int. 793, 795–796—*Lego-Klemmbausteine* (24 October 2000).

[323] *See infra* p. 370–373.

b *Initial-Interest Confusion* Similar to the prohibition of initial-interest confusion under US trademark law, civil law unfair competition doctrine has established a prohibition on bait-and-switch schemes.[324] Both initial-interest confusion and bait-and-switch schemes are characterized by a common element of consumer diversion by improper information. The element of "misinformation," however, will usually dissolve before the consumer reaches the ultimate stage of decision making.[325] The inherent unfairness stops short of actual point-of-purchase confusion insofar as the consumer usually realizes her initial error, corrects a potential misperception, and ultimately transacts on the basis of correct and complete information. It appears as if no harm is done. Yet the trademark owner may still be injured: First, she may lose on sales if the consumer is actually diverted to a competitor. Second, she may suffer the loss of a sale if the consumer fails to complete a transaction with both the competitor and—as initially intended—the owner based on the assumption that the competitor's product (with inferior characteristics) was the original.[326]

Here as well, different scenarios must be distinguished. In the first, the consumer's confusion dissipates quickly and there is no cost attached to the reshifting of her attention to the original product, so she reorients herself. In the second, she stays with the violator, despite being aware of the difference in products. In both cases, initial-interest confusion may add an economically rational element to the process of decision making.[327] If the confusion dissipates early enough and at low enough costs, the initial disorientation will present just another alternative for transacting. Market information has not deteriorated. A typical example is internet advertising: even if the consumer has been improperly directed away from the original brand, she usually easily reorients herself and

[324] Bait-and-switch schemes are usually categorized as instances of unfair competitor hindrance; they are seldom debated under a rubric of trademark protection. *See, e.g.*, Olaf Sosnitza, *Nach dem Spiel ist vor dem Spiel—Das Konzept der „Post-Sale Confusion" im Common Law, im europäischen und im deutschen Markenrecht*, 1 ZGE 457, 483 (2009). For an equation of initial-interest confusion with bait-and-switch competition, *see, e.g.*, *Dorr-Oliver, Inc. v. Fluid-Quip., Inc.*, 94 F.3d 376, 382 (7th Cir. 1996). For so-called switch selling in English doctrine, *see, e.g.*, Christopher Wadlow, *The Law of Passing-Off—Unfair Competition by Misrepresentation* para. 7–058 *et seq.* (4th edn., 2011).

[325] *See, e.g.*, *Eli Lilly & Co. v. Natural Answers, Inc.*, 233 F.3d 456, 464 (7th Cir. 2000); *Grotrian, Helfferich, Schulz, Th. Steinweg Nachf. v. Steinway & Sons*, 365 F.Supp. 707, 717 (S.D.N.Y. 1973).

[326] *See, e.g.*, *Ferrari S.P.A. v. Roberts*, 944 F.2d 1235, 1249–1250 (6th Cir. 1991) (Kennedy, J., dissenting).

[327] Michael Grynberg, *Trademark Litigation as Consumer Conflict*, 83 N.Y.U. L. Rev. 60, 103 *et seq.* (2008).

completes the initially intended transaction.[328] The situation is different, however, in cases where the "switching costs" are so high that they keep the customer with the alleged violator. Whenever the inconvenience of initiating a new search for the genuine product is so substantial that the consumer will literally not "go out again" to search for the original, instead consummating her transaction with the violator, consumer decision making in the relevant market has been negatively affected.[329] An example of this situation is a billboard advertising a brand-name fast-food chain on the highway but actually directing the consumer to a far-away no-name establishment. Once there, the misguided consumer may stay with the fake.[330]

3 The Common Denominator

All theories of antidilution, postsale, and initial-interest confusion share a structural element: consumer perception determines whether an infringement has occurred. This reflects the fact that trademark rights remain grounded to the marketplace. In terms of information infrastructure, the trademark as a communication channel will begin its transmission as soon as—often even before—the branded product enters the market, and it will not stop transmission at the point of sale.

Two different scenarios can thus be distinguished. The first consists of cases where the consumer is actually or potentially confused. In these situations, the consumer's referee function is impeded; damage will occur as a result of distorted decision making and transacting. What is affected in these cases is navigation goodwill. The second scenario, by contrast, comprises cases where the consumer's market transaction remains unmanipulated in terms of information correctness and the freedom of decision making. These cases may be characterized as protecting a different category of trademark goodwill—concretely, surplus goodwill. Protection then especially focuses on a trademark's prestige, association-creating capacity, or scarcity-signaling properties.

What is important to note, however, is that despite the two categories' doctrinal differences, the relevant (mis)appropriation always takes a

[328] Stacey L. Dogan & Mark A. Lemley, *Trademark and Consumer Search Costs on the Internet*, 41 Hous. L. Rev. 777, 815 (2004); Robert G. Bone, *Hunting Goodwill: A History of the Concept of Goodwill in Trademark Law*, 86 B. U. L. Rev. 547, 613 (2006). For such a constellation of internet advertising—yet, with the court holding in favor of claimants on the basis of passing off—*see Phones 4u Ltd. v. Phone4u.co.uk. Internet Ltd.* [2006] EWCA Civ 244, [2007] R.P.C. 5.

[329] *See* Stacey L. Dogan & Mark A. Lemley, *Trademark and Consumer Search Costs on the Internet*, 41 Hous. L. Rev. 777, 814 (2004).

[330] For choice of law in these scenarios, *see infra* p. 558–560.

detour through the consumer's mind. No matter which kind of goodwill is affected, dilutive uses and initial-interest and postsale confusion cases always constitute an appropriation of market information capital. There may be no direct loss to the right owner. Instead, the usurpation of her trademark's reputation suffices as an infringement. Hence, regardless of whether one wants to subscribe to the numerous rationales of alternative protection theories, they share a common characteristic: market information infrastructure is usurped.

In terms of choice of law as well, two categories must be distinguished. Some of the alternative categories still directly relate to the consumer's decision making. This is the case for initial-interest confusion if it prevents or impedes an unmanipulated decision. If the "confused" consumer is affected in her transacting by excessively high reorientation costs, the infringement at issue has ultimately diverted a transaction away from the market where it would have been consummated without manipulation. Hence, like in genuine confusion-based infringement theory, the market is affected at the place of alternative transactions. This is the place of attachment for conflicts determination. In the second category of alternative theories, substantive law policy is not necessarily focused on regulating a competitive relationship. This is the case for antidilution theory under a paradigm of preventing the watering-down of a famous trademark or for postsale status confusion. These categories are usually founded on the deterioration of information capital in a different market or at a later point. Regarding choice of law, it must accordingly connect to the place of damage to trademark distinctiveness, reputation, or scarcity. In principle, this place must be distinguished from the place where the concrete transaction occurs or where alternative transactions were supposed to occur. Even though, in practice, these places may often coincide, choice-of-law analysis must take note of the difference.[331]

II *Unfair Competition Prevention*

With regard to the information infrastructure of the marketplace, both trademark protection and unfair competition policies widely overlap. Beyond the common area of protecting the consumer's decision making on the basis of unmanipulated market information, however, a number of additional policies can be found in traditional unfair competition doctrine. I have already identified cases that concern intercompetitor relations at the horizontal level—this is related to the issue of what can be characterized a bilateral tort.[332] The following analysis of information

[331] *See infra* p. 556 *et seq.* [332] *See supra* p. 285–287.

infrastructure policies will allow us to further differentiate cases within the categories situated at the vertical level of the competition model.

A Recapitulation: Stages of Decision Making and Policy Differences

In practice, the bulk of scenarios covered by unfair competition doctrine concerns information transmission and collection. This is a part of the common domain of trademark and unfair competition law. The most common cases of misinformation beyond trademark infringement are those regarding otherwise confusing or deceptive advertising. In all these cases, information economization is at stake—in other words, protection of the first stage of the decision-making process.[333] Moreover, unfair competition law includes unfair practices that do not directly influence information transmission but that may still affect consumer decision making in subsequent stages. Examples include unsolicited home visits or phone calls, undue psychological pressure, and aggressive advertising.[334] In principle, none of these examples concern the transmission of incorrect information. What policy makers argue when cases of this kind are classified as unfair competition is that certain marketing methods may cut short the consumer's second thoughts or search for alternatives, causing her ensuing transaction to then be irrational. The distinction between what is acceptable and what exceeds the boundaries of due influence is part of an age-old debate on the benefits and detriments of advertising. In a sense, in many cases the issue is still, as Justice Holmes said almost a century ago, "a question of how strong an infusion of fraud is necessary to turn a flavor into a poison."[335] In addition, legal thought in some of these scenarios is influenced by concurrent concerns that relate only marginally to consumer decision making. The most often-referenced question may relate to the right to privacy: the prohibition of unsolicited phone calls is one example where a court

[333] For the stages of consumer decision making, *see supra* p. 287 *et seq.*

[334] For an illustration, *see, e.g.*, WIPO, *Protection Against Unfair Competition—Analysis of the Present World Situation*, WIPO Publ. no. 725(E), 65 *et seq.* (1994). *See also* recital 16 and annex 1 ("black list") of Directive 2005/29/EC of the European Parliament and of the Council of 11 May 2005 concerning unfair business-to-consumer commercial practices in the internal market and amending Council Directive 84/450/EEC, Directives 97/7/EC, 98/27/EC and 2002/65/EC of the European Parliament and of the Council and Regulation (EC) No 2006/2004 of the European Parliament and of the Council ("Unfair Commercial Practices Directive"), O.J. EU (11 June 2005), L 149/22 ("[P]ractices which significantly impair the consumer's freedom of choice . . . are practices using harassment, coercion, including the use of physical force, and undue influence.").

[335] *See International News Service v. Associated Press*, 248 U.S. 215, 247 (1918) (Holmes, J., dissenting).

decision may appear to be based on unfair competition, but where the substance is actually trespass to privacy. An exact demarcation of the different policies is difficult. Of course, an overly censorious perspective is arguably no longer adequate. After all, the modern consumer is seldom manipulated by officiousness, extra benefits, or giveaways to such an extent that her capacity to make rational decisions is obstructed. Yet the determination where admissible influence turns into undue manipulation may still vary depending on the national culture or other peculiarities.[336]

For choice of law, one thing is paramount: although we need not resolve all contested issues in substantive law, we must separate the policies actually or allegedly involved in the different categories of "unfairness." This is the necessary foundation for consistent conflicts attachment. The model of the competition process (with its triangular structure), as well as the market-mechanistic structure of relations at the vertical level, will guide the way. Accordingly, the remainder of the discussion will highlight substantive law policies and their impact on conflict law for the most common unfair competition scenarios.

B An Integrated Model of Unfair Competition Law (Including Passing Off)

As a consequence of the strong socialization tendencies during the twentieth century, European unfair competition law used to aim at protecting the "public interest" in many different respects. In order to explain conduct as "unfair," courts regularly referred to concerns such as public health, morality, and general decency. Quite often, the purpose of unfair competition prevention was seen as preventing undue deviations in competition in general (*Auswüchse des Wettbewerbs*).[337] Over time, however, a more focused perspective has come to dominate. Public interest, though still accepted as a concern of unfair competition law in principle, is limited

[336] *See, e.g.*, recital no. 7 Directive 2005/29/EC where the European lawmakers have explained that the Directive does not address "legal requirements related to taste and decency which vary widely among the Member States." Hence, "[c]ommercial practices such as, for example, commercial solicitation in the streets, may be undesirable in Member States for cultural reasons. Member States should accordingly be able to continue to ban commercial practices in their territory, in conformity with Community law, for reasons of taste and decency even where such practices do not limit consumers' freedom of choice."

[337] *See, e.g.*, BGH 1955 GRUR 541, 542—*Bestattungswerbung* (8 July 1955); BGH 1959 GRUR 285, 287—*Bienenhonig* (23 January 1959); BGH 1965 GRUR 315, 316—*Werbewagen* (4 December 1964); BGH 1970 GRUR 523—*Telefonwerbung I* (19 June 1970); *see also* Eugen Ulmer, *Das Recht des unlauteren Wettbewerbs in den Mitgliedsstaaten der Europäischen Gemeinschaft, vol. I: Vergleichende Darstellung mit Vorschlägen zur Rechtsangleichung (unter Mitwirkung von Friedrich-Karl Beier)* 49–50 (1965).

to the free and unhindered functioning of the market mechanism.[338] But even on the basis of this more economized doctrine, a problem persists. Particularly in European law, the fields of consumer protection and unfair competition have become increasingly intermingled.[339] Until today, the relation between freedom of competition and consumer protection appears almost inseparable. One example of this intermingling can be found in the 2005 UCP Directive's recitals:

> This Directive directly protects consumer economic interests from unfair business-to-consumer commercial practices. Thereby, it also indirectly protects legitimate businesses from their competitors who do not play by the rules in this Directive and thus guarantees fair competition in fields coordinated by it.[340]

Prima facie, the text prioritizes consumer concerns. It thereby appears to allow for—even require—an extension of consumer protection policies beyond the domain of mere decision-making autonomy.[341] Correspondingly, scholarly commentary has found a priority of consumer protection in both primary community law and secondary law unfair competition doctrine.[342] Proponents of this theory reject the

338 *See, e.g.*, Wolfgang B. Schünemann, *Ökonomische Analyse der europäischen und deutschen Regelung*, 41 *et seq.*, in *Lauterkeitsrecht im Umbruch—Europa, Deutschland, Österreich* (Heinz Krejci et al. eds., 2005); Reto M. Hilty, Hans Caspar von der Crone & Rolf H. Weber, *Stellungnahme zur Anpassung des UWG: Ambush Marketing*, 2006 sic! 702, 704; Wolfgang B. Schünemann, in *Gesetz gegen den unlauteren Wettbewerb (UWG)*, UWG § 1 para. 61 *et seq.* (Henning Harte-Bavendamm & Frauke Henning-Bodewig eds., 3rd edn., 2013).

339 For an overview, *see, e.g.*, Marlene Schmidt, *Zur Annäherung von Lauterkeitsrecht und Verbraucherprivatrecht*, 2007 JZ 78; *see also* Tobias Lettl, *Der lauterkeitsrechtliche Schutz vor irreführender Werbung in Europa* 63 (2004).

340 Recital 8 of Directive 2005/29/EC of the European Parliament and of the Council of 11 May 2005 concerning unfair business-to-consumer commercial practices in the internal market and amending Council Directive 84/450/EEC, Directives 97/7/EC, 98/27/EC and 2002/65/EC of the European Parliament and of the Council and Regulation (EC) No 2006/2004 of the European Parliament and of the Council ("Unfair Commercial Practices Directive"), O.J. EU (11 June 2005), L 149/22. *See also* Josef Drexl, in *Münchener Kommentar zum Bürgerlichen Gesetzbuch, vol. XI*, IntLautR para. 7 (Franz Jürgen Säcker et al. eds., 6th edn., 2015) ("Der Richtlinie geht es insgesamt um den ‚unmittelbaren' Schutz der Verbraucher und nur um einen ‚mittelbaren' Schutz der lauter handelnden Wettbewerber.").

341 Christoph Brömmelmeyer, *Der Binnenmarkt als Leitstern der Richtlinie über unlautere Geschäftspraktiken*, 2007 GRUR 295, 296; Frauke Henning-Bodewig, *Der Schutzzweck des UWG und die Richtlinie über unlautere Geschäftspraktiken*, 2013 GRUR 238, 240.

342 *See, e.g.*, Karl-Heinz Fezer, *Modernisierung des deutschen Rechts gegen den unlauteren Wettbewerb auf der Grundlage einer Europäisierung de Wettbewerbsrechts*, 2001 WRP 989, 993; Karl-Heinz Fezer, *Plädoyer für eine offensive Umsetzung der Richtlinie über unlautere Geschäftspraktiken in das deutsche UWG—Originärer Verbraucherschutz durch Lauterkeitsrecht als Paradigma der europäischen Rechtsharmonisierung*, 2006 WRP 781, 785–786; Rogier W. de Vrey, *Towards a European Unfair Competition Law, A Clash*

idea that the UCP Directive is founded mainly on the freedom of competition. Instead, they posit, consumer protection is supposed to be an independent and equivalent aim among unfair competition policies. In this regard, they point out that the directive's "black list" of unfair commercial practices emphasizes an overarching concern for consumer protection.[343] In addition, they refer to other European regulations—particularly in the fields of tobacco, alcohol, and health-related advertising—as examples of universal consumer protection policies.[344]

But the directive does not go this far. The instrument's prioritization of consumer interests is expressly qualified: it focuses on the consumer's *economic* interests,[345] not her civil rights or any other concern. At its core, therefore, the directive does not demand across-the-board protection. Rather, it is founded on a two-sides-of-the-coin conception of consumer and competitor protection as constituent elements of an institutional guarantee of undistorted competition. Hence, protection of the consumer's position as a referee—not as a citizen—is what stands at the center. In essence, therefore, the instrument is aimed at a functional regulation of competition.[346] Of course, exceptions to this implementation exist, for

Between Legal Families—A comparative study of English, German and Dutch law in light of existing European and international legal instruments 45 *et seq.*, 48, 59 *et seq.* (2006); Alexander Peukert, *Der Wandel der europäischen Wirtschaftsverfassung im Spiegel des Sekundärrechts—Erläutert am Beispiel des Rechts gegen unlauteren Wettbewerb*, 173 ZHR 536 *passim* (2009).

343 Alexander Peukert, *Die Ziele des Primärrechts und ihre Bedeutung für das Europäische Lauterkeitsrecht: Auflösungserscheinungen eines Rechtsgebiets?*, 27, 46, in *Lauterkeitsrecht und Acquis Communautaire* (Reto M. Hilty & Frauke Henning-Bodewig eds., 2009); *see also* Matthias Leistner, *Bestand und Entwicklungsperspektiven des Europäischen Lauterkeitsrechts*, 2009 ZEuP 56, 72.

344 *See, e.g.*, Hans W. Micklitz & Jürgen Keßler, *Europäisches Lauterkeitsrecht—Dogmatische und ökonomische Aspekte einer Harmonisierung des Wettbewerbsverhaltensrechts im europäischen Binnenmarkt*, 2002 GRUR Int. 885, 890; with reference to Directive 2003/33/EC (tobacco advertising) and Regulation 1924/2006/EC (nutrition and health claims made on foods): Alexander Peukert, *Die Ziele des Primärrechts und ihre Bedeutung für das Europäische Lauterkeitsrecht: Auflösungserscheinungen eines Rechtsgebiets?*, 27, 47–49, in *Lauterkeitsrecht und Acquis Communautaire* (Reto M. Hilty & Frauke Henning-Bodewig eds., 2009).

345 *See* again recital 6 and recital 8.

346 *See, e.g.*, Jochen Glöckner & Frauke Henning-Bodewig, *EG-Richtlinie über unlautere Geschäftspraktiken: Was wird aus dem „neuen" UWG?*, 2005 WRP 1311, 1314; Jochen Glöckner, Europäisches Lauterkeitsrecht 509, 512 *et seq.* (2006); Christopher Wadlow, *The Case for Reclaiming European Unfair Competition Law from Europe's Consumer Lawyers*, 175, 177 *et seq.*, in *The Regulation of Unfair Commercial Practices under EC Directive 2005/29—New Rules and Techniques* (Stephen Weatherill & Ulf Bernitz eds., 2007); Christoph Brömmelmeyer, *Der Binnenmarkt als Leitstern der Richtlinie über unlautere Geschäftspraktiken*, 2007 GRUR 295, 296 *et seq.*; Matthias Leistner, *Bestand und Entwicklungsperspektiven des Europäischen Lauterkeitsrechts*, 2009 ZEuP 56, 59. For the general prevalence of market integration concerns—inter alia, unhindered competition—over other policies (particularly consumer protection) in

European unfair competition law has yet to be comprehensively harmonized. Since the UCP Directive concerns B2C relations only, the field of B2B relations remains widely an issue of member states' laws. In addition, the directive has implemented escape provisions for national lawmakers in several fields, notably with regard to health-related regulation and "legal requirements related to taste and decency."[347] Yet these examples do not require a fundamental reconceptualization. On the contrary, unfair competition doctrine in Europe—more than ever—seeks primarily to rationalize consumer decision making; other policies will prevail in exceptional situations only.

The situation appears different with regard to the English doctrine of passing off. A law of unfair competition, as is often explained, is unknown in the UK. Courts are said to shy away from drawing clear lines between what is "fair" and "unfair" competition.[348] Only in cases of consumer deception is court-moderated regulation considered acceptable and legitimate.[349] Such scenarios are traditionally treated under the doctrine of passing off.[350] However, a closer look at the "classical trinity" of passing off—goodwill, damage, and misrepresentation—unveils that the doctrine is also founded on a conception of consumer decision making.[351] While the subject matter of protection, at least formally, seems to be goodwill (as private property), the basis of the action has always been misrepresentation, most commonly with regard to the source or the qualities of a product.[352] And even though, over

European law, *see, e.g.*, Jürgen Basedow, *Zielkonflikte und Zielhierarchien im Vertrag über die Europäische Gemeinschaft*, 49, 68, in *Festschrift für Ulrich Everling, vol. I* (Ole Due et al. eds., 1995).

347 *See* art. 3(3) and recital 7.

348 *See, e.g.*, *The Mogul Steamship Company, Ltd. v. McGregor, Gow, & Co., and Others* [1889] 23 Q.B.D. 598, 625–626 (per Fry, L.J.) ("To draw a line between fair and unfair competition, between what is reasonable and unreasonable, passes the power of the Courts.").

349 *See, e.g.*, *Hodgkinson Corby Ltd. and Another v. Wards Mobility Services Ltd.* [1995] F.S.R. 169, 175 (per Jacob, J.) ("At the heart of passing off lies deception or its likelihood, deception of the ultimate consumer in particular. … Never has the tort shown even a slight tendency to stray beyond cases of deception. Were it to do so it would enter the field of honest competition, declared unlawful for some reason other than deceptiveness. Why there should be any such reason I cannot imagine. It would serve only to stifle competition.").

350 A doctrine which is then, quite paradoxically, sometimes explained as synonymous with "unfair competition." *See, e.g.*, *Arsenal Football Club Plc. v. Reed* [2003] EWCA Civ 696, 715 (per Aldous, L.J.).

351 For an illustration of the trinity (and its variations), *see* Christopher Wadlow, *The Law of Passing-Off—Unfair Competition by Misrepresentation* para. 1–014 *et seq.* (4th edn., 2011).

352 *See, e.g.*, Christopher Wadlow, *The Law of Passing-Off—Unfair Competition by Misrepresentation* para. 5–001 *et seq.* (4th edn., 2011); Lionel Bently & Brad Sherman, *Intellectual Property Law* 826 *et seq.*, 848 *et seq.* (4th edn., 2014).

time, the field has become increasingly complex, the gravamen of a claim is still misinformation in the marketplace: in order to succeed, the plaintiff must show that the conduct at issue is deceptive.[353]

Indeed, seen in light of these foundations, the divergence between passing off and the UCP Directive or the bases of unfair competition prevention in civil law doctrine no longer seems very large. Of course, liability for passing off exists only between competitors; consumers and consumer associations have no claim and no standing to sue. One might thus conclude that passing off should simply coexist with the directive for lack of overlap between B2B and B2C relations.[354] But such a formal perspective is too narrow. Looking at the policies involved actually highlights the congruency. Preventing deception under a doctrine of passing off requires, among other things, that the misrepresentation at issue be "material"—hence, apt to actually influence the prospective consumer.[355] In this regard, passing off corresponds with the modern approach of protecting consumer decision making from "material distortion" under articles 5 et seq. of the UCP Directive.[356] Consequently, most scenarios decided under the traditional doctrine of passing off will also qualify as unfair under the directive's focus on the market mechanism.[357]

For choice of law, this implies a simple rule: in cases that directly concern consumer decision making, it is the place of transacting—more concretely, of transaction alternatives—that determines the applicable regime. However, in cases where the concrete policy at stake is not primarily aimed at the protection of consumer decision making, a different rule may govern. This distinction can be explained by taking a closer look at the heterogeneous nature of harassment prevention policies in unfair competition doctrine.

[353] *See, e.g., Phones 4u Ltd. v. Phone4u.co.uk. Internet Ltd.* [2006] EWCA Civ 244, [2007] R.P.C. 5; *Hodgkinson Corby Ltd. and Another v. Wards Mobility Services Ltd.* [1995] F.S.R. 169, 175 (per Jacob, J.); *Barnsley Brewery Company Ltd. v. RBNB* [1997] F.S.R. 462, 467 (per Robert Walker, J.); further also Lionel Bently & Brad Sherman, *Intellectual Property Law* 859 (4th edn., 2014).

[354] Christopher Wadlow, *The Law of Passing-Off—Unfair Competition by Misrepresentation* para. 2–075 to 2–076 (4th edn., 2011).

[355] *See id.* at para. 5–019, para. 5–124 *et seq.*

[356] *Id.* at para. 2–077 *et seq.* For the defendant's purpose to "change the market behaviour of potential customers" in passing-off cases, *see also* Richard Plender & Michael Wilderspin, *The European Private International Law of Obligations* para. 20–034 (4th edn., 2015); and also James J. Fawcett & Paul Torremans, *Intellectual Property and Private International Law* para. 16.21 to 16.22 (2nd edn., 2011).

[357] These arguments can also be brought forward with regard to the doctrine of injurious falsehood. There as well, misrepresentation is the gravamen of the action. *See* Christopher Wadlow, *The Law of Passing-Off—Unfair Competition by Misrepresentation* para. 6–001 *et seq.* (4th edn., 2011).

C An Amalgam of Policies: Harassment, Privacy, and Decision Making

Undue harassment and coercion have traditionally been deemed improper under many national unfair competition regimes.[358] Modern examples of undue consumer harassment through unsolicited contact include cold calling and e-mail spamming. Under the UCP Directive, harassment is generally analyzed in light of the prohibition on aggressive practices. For a commercial practice to be regarded as aggressive, it must have the potential to significantly impair the average consumer's freedom of choice or conduct in a manner that will lead to a transactional decision that she would not have otherwise made.[359] Seen in this light, the prevention of undue harassment may be an issue of protecting consumer decision making.[360] But harassment may also be characterized as infringement of the consumer's right to privacy. A prohibition will then have to be founded on a quite different policy.[361] Indeed, the UCP Directive implies that there may be even more relevant policies beyond the scope of protecting consumer decision making. Notably, undue harassment can also be found "for reasons of taste and decency,"[362] even if no actual or potential impact on the decision-making process is to be feared.[363]

358 For Germany, *see, e.g.*, Axel Beater, *Allgemeininteressen und UWG*, 2012 WRP 1, 9 *et seq.* For a particularly gross case of molestation, *see, e.g.*, RGZ vol. 145, 396, 402—*Bestattungsunternehmen I* (9 November 1934); *see also* BGH 1955 GRUR 541, 542—*Bestattungswerbung* (8 July 1955).

359 *See* articles 8 and 9 Unfair Commercial Practices Directive.

360 *See, e.g.*, Helmut Köhler, *Zur Umsetzung der Richtlinie über unlautere Geschäftspraktiken*, 2005 GRUR 793, 800; Jochen Glöckner & Frauke Henning-Bodewig, *EG-Richtlinie über unlautere Geschäftspraktiken: Was wird aus dem „neuen" UWG?*, 2005 WRP 1311, 1334; Peter Mankowski, in *Lauterkeitsrecht: Kommentar zum Gesetz gegen den unlauteren Wettbewerb (UWG), vol. II*, § 7 para. 26 (Karl-Heinz Fezer ed., 2nd edn., 2010).

361 *See, e.g.*, Julian Burmeister, *Belästigung als Wettbewerbsverstoß* 57 *et seq.* (2006); Axel Beater, *Unlauterer Wettbewerb* § 28 para. 2376 *et seq.*, 2380 (2011). Indeed, courts and the lawmakers in Germany have always focused on the issue of privacy invasion. *See, e.g.*, BGH 2005 GRUR 443, 444–445—*Ansprechen in der Öffentlichkeit II* (9 September 2004); BGH 2004 GRUR 699, 700—*Ansprechen in der Öffentlichkeit* (1 April 2004); Deutscher Bundestag, *Drucksache: Gesetzentwurf der Bundesregierung, Entwurf eines Gesetzes gegen den unlauteren Wettbewerb (UWG)*, 15. Wahlperiode, 15/1487 (22 August 2003), at 21.

362 *See* recital 7: "This Directive . . . does not address legal requirements related to taste and decency which vary widely among the Member States. Commercial practices such as, for example, commercial solicitation in the streets, may be undesirable in Member States for cultural reasons. Member States should accordingly be able to continue to ban commercial practices in their territory, in conformity with Community law, for reasons of taste and decency even where such practices do not limit consumers' freedom of choice. Full account should be taken of the context of the individual case concerned in applying this Directive, in particular the general clauses thereof."

363 *See also* Jochen Glöckner & Frauke Henning-Bodewig, *EG-Richtlinie über unlautere Geschäftspraktiken: Was wird aus dem „neuen" UWG?*, 2005 WRP 1311, 1334;

At this point, again, the heterogeneity of policies—and its importance for choice of law—surfaces. The consumer may be protected either as a person or in her function as a referee in competition; sometimes, both policies may work together. This complexity illustrates the segmentation that will govern the following analysis on choice of law. The prohibition on harassment is not homogeneous in terms of the protectable subject matter at stake, which could be consumer decision making, individual privacy, or a more general concern for decency in competition. Accordingly, the point of conflicts law attachment may vary.

D Beware of the Consumer's "Economic Personality Right"

The heterogeneity of policies in harassment prevention illustrates the manner in which the consumer's position has been transformed in recent decades. Her status has evolved from being a mere parameter in inter-competitor dispute resolution to being the center of unfair competition doctrine. However, as we have seen, this development has been partially reversed in recent years. Today, all-encompassing consumer protection has become outdated. Desocialization entails at least a certain degree of depersonalization.[364]

As we have seen, under historical German doctrine, a competitor's rights in the field of trademark and unfair competition protection were genuinely founded on her personality. This theory was perpetuated under the guise of unfair competition individualism: the analysis of economic rights and interests was focused on the competitor side alone. As a result, the understanding of personality rights doctrine was lopsided. While the competitor could claim violations of fairness standards and an intrusion of personality rights, the consumer's personality was—if at all—regarded with a view to its noneconomic dimension. Individual rights protection within the marketplace was not available for consumers, at least not on the basis of personality rights.[365] This changed with the advent of consumer protection policies in the second half of the twentieth century. Examples of the early acknowledgment of a sacrosanct sphere include the protection of privacy and the rights to be left alone and to be free from undue harassment.[366] This protection was initially limited to

Helmut Köhler, *Zur Umsetzung der Richtlinie über unlautere Geschäftspraktiken*, 2005 GRUR 793, 794.

[364] *See supra* p. 328 *et seq.*

[365] Wolfgang Fikentscher, *Wirtschaftsrecht, vol. II: Deutsches Wirtschaftsrecht* § 21 III 3e (1983).

[366] The most common examples are the prohibition of cold calling, of the unsolicited delivery of goods, and of undue psychological or subliminal pressure. *See, e.g.*, BGH 1970 GRUR 523—*Telefonwerbung I* (19 June 1970); BGH 1959 GRUR 277—*Künstlerpostkarten* (11 November 1958); BGH 1973 GRUR 81—*Gewinnübermittlung* (22 September 1972); BGH 1959 GRUR 143—*Blindenseife* (14 November 1958).

noneconomic aspects; the consumer had no domain of an "economic personality right." But the final decades of the century brought change.[367] Against the backdrop of the former myopia concerning consumer rights, this extension was revolutionary. The economic personality right comprised not only the consumer's right to be left alone but also a right to engage in autonomous transactional decision making. Hence, consumer personality and freedom were to be protected both generally with respect to noneconomic activities and more specifically within the marketplace.[368]

Over time, many cases came to be described as invasions of personality rights. These invasions were most commonly attributed to subliminal advertising and psychological pressure.[369] Overall, however, the scope of protection was unclear. One example was deceptive advertising. As some proponents of economic personality rights theory contended, deception alone—unlike, for example, physical or psychological manipulation—would not directly infringe on the freedom of decision making as such and hence would not invade the consumer's personality right.[370] Yet such a differentiation was duly criticized as inconsistent: after all, both physical/

[367] *See* Wolfgang Fikentscher, *Wirtschaftsrecht, vol. II: Deutsches Wirtschaftsrecht* § 21 III 3e, § 22 I 1 and 2 (1983); for an earlier suggestion, *see* Wolfgang Fikentscher, *Wettbewerb und gewerblicher Rechtsschutz—Die Stellung des Rechts der Wettbewerbsbeschränkungen in der Rechtsordnung* 227 and 238 (1958); *see also* Michael Lehmann, *Vertragsanbahnung durch Werbung—Eine juristische und ökonomische Analyse der bürgerlich-rechtlichen Haftung für Werbeangaben gegenüber dem Letztverbraucher* (1981); Stefan Freund, *Das Persönlichkeitsrecht des Umworbenen—Ein bürgerlich-rechtlicher Beitrag zum Verbraucherschutz unter Berücksichtigung des Wettbewerbsrechts* (1983); Wolfram Ehlers, *Der persönlichkeitsrechtliche Schutz des Verbrauchers vor Werbung*, 1983 WRP 187 *et seq.*

[368] Wolfgang Fikentscher, *Wirtschaftsrecht, vol. II: Deutsches Wirtschaftsrecht* § 22 I 2b (1983); *see also* Michael Lehmann, *Vertragsanbahnung durch Werbung—Eine juristische und ökonomische Analyse der bürgerlich-rechtlichen Haftung für Werbeangaben gegenüber dem Letztverbraucher* (1981); Wolfram Ehlers, *Der persönlichkeitsrechtliche Schutz des Verbrauchers vor Werbung*, 1983 WRP 187, 194; Michael Lehmann, *Das wirtschaftliche Persönlichkeitsrecht von Anbieter und Nachfrager*, 255, 266, in *Beiträge zum Schutz der Persönlichkeit und ihrer schöpferischen Leistungen—Festschrift für Heinrich Hubmann zum 70. Geburtstag* (Hans Forkel & Alfons Kraft eds., 1985).

[369] *See, e.g.*, Michael Lehmann, Vertragsanbahnung durch Werbung—Eine juristische und ökonomische Analyse der bürgerlich-rechtlichen Haftung für Werbeangaben gegenüber dem Letztverbraucher 265 *et seq.*, 270, 273 (1981); Stefan Freund, *Das Persönlichkeitsrecht des Umworbenen—Ein bürgerlich-rechtlicher Beitrag zum Verbraucherschutz unter Berücksichtigung des Wettbewerbsrechts* 141 *et seq.*, 215 (1983); Wolfram Ehlers, *Der persönlichkeitsrechtliche Schutz des Verbrauchers vor Werbung*, 1983 WRP 187, 193–194; Michael Lehmann, *Das wirtschaftliche Persönlichkeitsrecht von Anbieter und Nachfrager*, 255, 267, in *Beiträge zum Schutz der Persönlichkeit und ihrer schöpferischen Leistungen—Festschrift für Heinrich Hubmann zum 70. Geburtstag* (Hans Forkel & Alfons Kraft eds., 1985).

[370] *See, e.g.*, Michael Lehmann, *Vertragsanbahnung durch Werbung—Eine juristische und ökonomische Analyse der bürgerlich-rechtlichen Haftung für Werbeangaben gegenüber dem Letztverbraucher* 275 (1981).

psychological pressure and deception appeared similarly apt to degrade the consumer to an "object" of market competition.[371] Some scholars went even further, describing emotionally loaded advertising as a violation of personality rights.[372] In essence, the problem with economic personality rights doctrine was its tendency to dilute the demarcation between the consumer's civil rights and her freedom of transaction. Ultimately, almost any impact on the consumer, regardless of its effect on the decision-making mechanism, would qualify as a violation as long as the practice could be found harassing, compelling, or otherwise manipulative.

Quite differently, under the integrated model's functional approach to competition regulation, the referee function—not the consumer's status as an individual and as a citizen—is to be protected. Two examples illustrate this difference. Proponents of consumer personality rights protection have contended that consumer rights will be violated by hidden data collection concerning consumption habits.[373] This is correct in terms of privacy protection. Conduct deemed improper under such a civil rights perspective, however, need not necessarily result in a manipulation of the market mechanism or a distortion of competition. On the contrary, offering the consumer exactly what she desires can be rather efficient from a perspective of information economization. After all, there is no undue impact on the decision-making process as such. Another example of "unfair" competition within this category is "shock advertising" (or shockvertising). The use of shocking communication vis-à-vis the consumer is a problem primarily with regard to her personality rights. After all, drastic communication may be offensive and unwanted. It may sometimes affect the decision-making process, but this need not necessarily be the case. The fact that the content of commercial communication is outrageous will not necessarily lead to an irrational transaction. Both examples illustrate that at least two spheres of normative concern exist. One is the market mechanism, which has become the genuine domain of modern unfair competition policy. The other comprises policies beyond this core domain. This sphere, which involves protecting the consumer as an individual and as a citizen, is determined by many different policies (e.g., privacy, property, and so on). Not all of these

[371] *See, e.g.*, Stefan Freund, *Das Persönlichkeitsrecht des Umworbenen—Ein bürgerlichrechtlicher Beitrag zum Verbraucherschutz unter Berücksichtigung des Wettbewerbsrechts* 144 (1983).

[372] *See id.* at 221 *et seq.*

[373] *See, e.g.*, Michael Lehmann, *Das wirtschaftliche Persönlichkeitsrecht von Anbieter und Nachfrager*, 255, 266 n. 76, in *Beiträge zum Schutz der Persönlichkeit und ihrer schöpferischen Leistungen—Festschrift für Heinrich Hubmann zum 70. Geburtstag* (Hans Forkel & Alfons Kraft eds., 1985).

individual civil or constitutional positions will coincide with the interest in free competition.[374]

What is important for this inquiry is that in a triangular model of the market mechanism, the field of individual and civil rights protection must be located beyond the categories of horizontal and vertical market relations. To the extent that consumer protection does not cover referee decision making, its specific policy will be neither an issue of intercompetitor relations nor one of the integrated model of unfair competition doctrine. Therefore, choice-of-law doctrine needs to inquire about a different aspect—this implies choice of a different point of attachment.

E Quasi IP Rights: The Gray Zone of Product Imitation

Like US trademark doctrine, German unfair competition law has implemented a specific aspect of quasi IP protection under the concept of preventing misappropriation and free riding on a competitor's achievements. The problem is usually debated in the context of allegedly improper product imitation. This category overlaps significantly with the theory of postsale confusion.[375] The analytical challenge here is to clearly distinguish relevant policies with respect to the consumer's referee function and concerns beyond the protection of the market mechanism.

The category of product imitation relates to activities that attempt to appropriate a competitor's market share by imitating her product. By reproducing, for example, a specific shape or other property of the product, the competitor may (without infringing on copyrights, trademark, design, or patent rights) acquire value that may be deemed to belong to the market participant who established the market position of the original product. The mere exploitation of another's achievement is not, in itself, inconsistent with a system of free-market competition. As is regularly explained, imitation is a genuine form of competition.[376] Nevertheless, excessive imitation must be prevented in order to assure that the incentives to innovate remain sufficient.[377] The question, however, is how to

[374] *See, e.g.*, Christian Alexander, *Die Sanktions- und Verfahrensvorschriften der Richtlinie 2005/29/EG über unlautere Geschäftspraktiken im Binnenmarkt—Umsetzungsbedarf in Deutschland*, 2005 GRUR Int. 809, 813; Susanne Augenhofer, *Individualrechtliche Ansprüche des Verbrauchers bei unlauterem Wettbewerbsverhalten des Unternehmers*, 2006 WRP 169, 172–173; Olaf Sosnitza, in *Münchener Kommentar zum Lauterkeitsrecht, vol. I*, § 1 UWG para. 28 (Peter W. Heermann et al. eds., 2nd edn., 2014).

[375] *See supra* p. 353–356.

[376] *See, e.g., Bonito Boats, Inc. v. Thunder Craft Boats, Inc.*, 489 U.S. 141 (1989); for early German doctrine, *see, e.g.*, RGZ vol. 135, 385, 394—*Künstliche Blumen* (19 March 1932); *see also* WIPO, *Protection Against Unfair Competition—Analysis of the Present World Situation*, WIPO Publ. no. 725(E), 55 (1994).

[377] *See, e.g.*, Axel Beater, *Unlauterer Wettbewerb* § 22 para. 1912 *et seq.* (2011); Volker Emmerich, *Unlauterer Wettbewerb* § 11 para. 6 (9th edn., 2012).

demarcate admissible from excessive imitation. A basic tenet seems uncontested: imitation of a product alone will usually not suffice to characterize it as a case of unfair misappropriation.[378] A finding of improper imitation always requires additional elements of "unfairness." Several categories of misappropriation cases can be distinguished; the relevant aspect of unfairness varies across these categories.

One category of product imitation involves consumer deception. For example, the statutory provision in section 4 no. 3(a) of the German Unfair Competition Act (UWG) provides for a case of unfairness if a competitor "offers goods or services that are replicas of goods or services of a competitor [and] if he ... causes avoidable deception of the purchaser regarding their commercial origin." Here, the necessary prerequisite qualifying an imitation as improper is purchaser deception. This standard resembles the test for confusion in trademark infringement analysis.[379] Yet the debate over the underlying policies has never been resolved. And the issue has become even more complicated under the UCP Directive.[380] Again, choice-of-law analysis does not require a comprehensive solution of the problems at the level of substantive law. Regardless of whether avoiding consumer confusion is a relevant policy, any case of product imitation entails instrumentalization of the consumer's mind. It is the consumer's transaction that ultimately leads to an invasion of the competitor's right. Accordingly, conflicts attachment will have to give regard to the localization of this last stage of the consumer's decision-making process.

A second category of product imitation centers on the exploitation or impairment of the original product's reputation or goodwill (*Rufausbeutung* and *Rufbeeinträchtigung*).[381] While such cases may include an element of

[378] This has become commonplace in unfair competition doctrine. *See* (under a comparative perspective) Walter J. Derenberg, *The Influence of the French Code Civil on the Modern Law of Unfair Competition*, 4 Am. J. Comp. L. 1, 22 *et seq.* (1955).

[379] *See, e.g.*, Volker Emmerich, *Unlauterer Wettbewerb* § 11 para. 20 (9th edn., 2012).

[380] As established by case law and legal commentary, the primary aim of preventing deceptive imitations is to protect the individual competitor's performance—not to protect the consumer from confusion. *See, e.g.*, Deutscher Bundestag, *Drucksache: Gesetzentwurf der Bundesregierung, Entwurf eines Ersten Gesetzes zur Änderung des Gesetzes gegen den unlauteren Wettbewerb*, 16. Wahlperiode, 16/10145 (20 August 2008), 17 *et seq.*; BGH 2010 GRUR 80, 81—*LIKEaBIKE* (28 May 2009); BGH 2007 GRUR 984 para. 23—*Gartenliege* (24 May 2007); *but see* Helmut Köhler, *Das Verhältnis des Wettbewerbsrechts zum Recht des geistigen Eigentums—Zur Notwendigkeit einer Neubestimmung auf Grund der Richtlinie über unlautere Geschäftspraktiken*, 2007 GRUR 548, 552; Axel Beater, *Unlauterer Wettbewerb* § 22 para. 2051 (2011).

[381] Section 4 no. 3(b) German Unfair Competition Act (UWG) provides for unfairness if a competitor "offers goods or services that are replicas of goods or services of a competitor if he ... unreasonably exploits or impairs the assessment of the replicated goods or services."

consumer confusion, this is not a prerequisite. What is required and sufficient is the exploitation or deterioration of the genuine product's reputation. Parallels to the US postsale confusion theory, notably the *Ferrari* doctrine,[382] are manifest. An oft-cited case in German doctrine, the *Tchibo/Rolex* decision, illustrates the structure. In this case, a producer of cheap wristwatches had imitated the specific design of the Rolex originals and was selling the copies for approximately 1% of the original price. The Bundesgerichtshof deemed the original's appearance sufficient to constitute a distinctive indication of commercial origin and, accordingly, found in favor of the plaintiff who claimed that the defendant's product was an improper imitation. Remarkably, however, the court did not require confusion about product origin to exist among *consumers*. Instead, it was enough that the *bystanding public*—that is, the social environment of the imitation's buyers—may have been confused. On this basis, the imitation was deemed a misappropriation of the original product's reputation for quality and prestige.[383] Here as well, a structural analysis points to the consumer's mind as most relevant for choice of law. As the court acknowledged, the Rolex imitations may not have created a risk of consumer confusion at the point of sale, and consumer decision making may not have been unduly manipulated with respect to its economic rationality. Further, the court left undecided the issue of whether the plaintiff's (and her product's) reputation or goodwill was actually injured by the defendant's free riding.[384] Hence, at least prima facie, no problem of information (mis)economization existed.[385] Nevertheless, consumer perception was what made invasion of the first-comer's position improper. The information-related capital accumulated by the producer of the original Rolex was utilized for a different product market. It is the *situs* of this surplus goodwill that determines the point of attachment in choice of law.

A third category of product imitation is the direct or immediate appropriation of a product's design or properties (*unmittelbare Leistungsübernahme*). Under German law, this category appears to have been jettisoned in large part.[386] In some jurisdictions, however, direct

[382] *See supra* p. 353–356.

[383] BGH 1985 GRUR 876, 878—*Tchibo/Rolex* (8 November 1984); *see also* BGH 1993 GRUR 55—*Tchibo/Rolex II* (17 June 1992). The decision has been harshly criticized. *See, e.g.*, Axel Beater, *Unlauterer Wettbewerb* § 22 para. 1908 (2011).

[384] BGH 1985 GRUR 876, 878—*Tchibo/Rolex* (8 November 1984).

[385] For potential postsale consumer confusion in similar scenarios, however, notably concerning US postsale confusion theory, *see supra* p. 353–356.

[386] *See, e.g.*, BGH 1968 GRUR 591, 592—*Pulverbehälter* (3 May 1968); BGHZ vol. 141, 329, 341–342—*Tele-Info-CD* (6 May 1999); Axel Beater, *Unlauterer Wettbewerb* § 22 para. 1944 (2011).

appropriation may still be deemed unfair per se. The lack of an alleged infringer's own efforts in creativity or investment then qualifies the scenario as unfair. Sometimes even the *modus operandi*—for example, the ordering of samples from a victim-competitor in order to imitate the product—may suffice.[387] Accordingly, these cases will often imply neither consumer confusion nor goodwill misappropriation.[388]

Against this backdrop, it is clear that widely differing policies may apply in cases of product imitation. The relevant policy might be information economization, goodwill protection, or genuine misappropriation prevention. Moreover, the different policies may be at work concurrently. In many cases, of course, the consumer's mind is the link that connects conduct and effects. This might lead one to conclude that the customer side of the market is affected in all cases of product imitation.[389] This perspective is duly rooted in the market connectivity of the conduct at issue. However, it risks disregarding the relevance of consumer decision making as a more specific element of the market mechanism. If consumer decision making per se is not being influenced, there is no element of unfairness with respect to the vertical relationship. Notably, the policy involved in the prohibition of direct appropriation or improper use of know-how will seldom affect the consumer's referee function. This also makes a difference with regard to conflicts resolution. As we will see in more detail in the last chapter, the points of attachment depend on whether the substantive law policy at issue is aimed at protecting consumer decision making or at something else.[390]

387 *See* WIPO, *Protection against Unfair Competition—Analysis of the Present World Situation*, WIPO Publ. no. 725(E), 58 *et seq.* (1994); for a general analysis in economic terms, *see* Frank H. Easterbrook, *Intellectual Property Is Still Property*, 13 Harv. J. L. & Pub. Pol'y 108, 114–115 (1990); *see also* Matthias Leistner, *Unfair Competition Law Protection Against Imitations: A Hybrid under the Future Art. 5 Rome II Regulation?*, 129, 131, in *Intellectual Property in the Conflict of Laws* (Jürgen Basedow et al. eds., 2005).

388 For an extensive discussion of French, Swiss, German, and British law, *see* Florent Thouvenin, *Funktionale Systematisierung von Wettbewerbsrecht (UWG) und Immaterialgüterrechten* 208 *et seq.* (2007). This last category of improper imitation also encompasses downstream protection against the theft of trade secrets; for instance, section 4 no. 3(c) of the German Unfair Competition Act (UWG) provides for a finding of "unfairness" if the defendant "offers goods or services that are replicas of goods or services of a competitor if he ... (c) dishonestly obtained the knowledge or documents needed for the replicas."

389 *See, e.g.*, Matthias Leistner, *Unfair Competition Law Protection against Imitations: A Hybrid under the Future Art. 5 Rome II Regulation?*, 129, 145 *et seq.*, in *Intellectual Property in the Conflict of Laws* (Jürgen Basedow et al. eds., 2005); Matthias Leistner, *Comments: The Rome II Regulation Proposal and its Relation to the European Country-of-Origin Principle*, 177, 184, in *Intellectual Property and Private International Law—Heading for the Future* (Josef Drexl & Annette Kur eds., 2005).

390 *See infra* p. 560–563.

F The Continental Dark Horse: Breach of Statutory Duties as Unfair Competition

Finally, it is necessary to explore a concept of "unfairness" that exists primarily in civil law systems. Under this model, unfairness may be found if a competitor breaches a statutory duty and (as result of the violation) attains an advantage or head start in competition. As its proponents argue, the breach of a statutory duty or provision may distort the overall equality of competitors under the *par conditio concurrentium.*[391] Yet the issue of "unfair statutory breach" has received little attention in common law doctrine. In English law, for instance, the breach of a statutory duty is acknowledged as giving a right of action in tort if the claimant has suffered a loss as a result of the breach of an administrative or criminal norm.[392] A court may also grant injunctive relief.[393] Such relief, however, will be granted under general tort law, not as a device to prevent unfair competition.[394] Besides, the category has not been included in the UCP Directive. Accordingly, it may no longer be comprehensively evoked in member states' national doctrine.[395] In Germany, for instance, only the breach of a norm that is intended to regulate market conduct can qualify for the category.[396] Hence, violation of a statutory provision as such—for example, speeding or tax evasion—is not sufficient to establish a case of unfairness.[397] This was not always the case, though. During the twentieth century, the scope of norms found eligible to establish an anticompetitive

[391] *See, e.g.*, for Germany: Helmut Köhler, in Helmut Köhler & Joachim Bornkamm, *Gesetz gegen den unlauteren Wettbewerb*, § 4 UWG para. 11.6 (33rd edn., 2015); for Switzerland, Carl Baudenbacher, in *Lauterkeitsrecht: Kommentar zum Gesetz gegen den unlauteren Wettbewerb (UWG)*, *Art.* 2 para. 315, Art. 7 para. 10 (Carl Baudenbacher ed., 2001).

[392] *See, e.g., Lonrho Ltd v Shell Petroleum Co Ltd* (No.2) [1982] A.C. 173, 183; *Cutler v Wandsworth Stadium Ltd* [1949] A.C. 398, 407; with further examples Hazel Carty, *An Analysis of the Economic Torts* 88 *et seq.* (2nd edn., 2010).

[393] *See, e.g., McCall v. Abelesz and Another* [1976] Q.B. 585; with further references also Simon Deakin, Angus Johnston & Basil Markesinis, *Tort Law* 377 *et seq.* (6th edn., 2008).

[394] *See, e.g.*, Ansgar Ohly, *Richterrecht und Generalklausel im Recht des unlauteren Wettbewerbs—Ein Methodenvergleich des englischen und des deutschen Rechts* 46 (1997); Florent Thouvenin, *Funktionale Systematisierung von Wettbewerbsrecht (UWG) und Immaterialgüterrechten* 246–247 (2007).

[395] *See, e.g.*, Volker Emmerich, *Unlauterer Wettbewerb* § 20 para. 13 (9th edn., 2012).

[396] Section 3a Unfair Competition Act (UWG) provides for unfairness if a competitor "infringes a statutory provision that is also intended to regulate market behaviour in the interest of market participants, and if the breach is suitable to tangible impairment of the interests of consumers, other market participants, or competitors."

[397] In other European jurisdictions—for instance, France, Belgium, the Netherlands, and Switzerland—a mere violation may already suffice. *See, e.g.*, Gerhard Schricker, *Gesetzesverletzung und Sittenverstoss—Rechtsvergleichende Untersuchung zur wettbewerbsrechtlichen Haftung bei Verletzung außerwettbewerbsrechtlicher Normen* (1970); Volker Emmerich, *Unlauterer Wettbewerb* § 20 para. 2 (9th edn., 2012).

breach was still quite extensive.[398] Courts and legal scholars, however, increasingly adopted a policy-oriented selection of norms that could qualify.[399] In particular, the prerequisite that the norm at issue must be in the "interest of market participants" has proven complex. After all, almost any norm that regulates market conduct will also affect the public interest in one way or another. More recently, the debate centers on the question whether only norms protecting the consumer's referee function should qualify or whether norms more generally protecting "the public" could also be eligible.[400]

Here again, a closer look at substantive law policies is relevant for choice of law. One aspect is paramount: the finding of unfairness depends on the breach of a norm as such. Such a breach will, however, not necessarily affect consumer decision making. One example is professional regulations (e.g., rules on admission to the bar for lawyers). If admission to the profession is achieved without the fulfillment of formal requirements (and thus in breach of the regulation), an instance of unfair competition will be found even without actual activity in the "professional market."[401] In essence, therefore, the category of statutory breach is to be distinguished from other scenarios of unfair competition where the consumer's decision making or competitor-related concerns are the direct beneficiaries of protection. Choice-of-law determination will be accordingly detached.[402]

III A Hybrid Category: Geographical Indications

Finally, it is important to address the law on designations of origin and geographical indications as a field at the crossroads of trademark protection and unfair competition prevention. A number of international agreements exist, and the European Union has introduced regulations dealing with designations of origin and geographical indications for food and

[398] For an overview of the wide array of so-called non-competition-related norms ("außerwettbewerbliche Gesetze"), *see* Otto-Friedrich Freiherr von Gamm, *Wettbewerbsrecht, vol. I*, ch. 4 para. 4 and ch. 31 (5th edn., 1987).

[399] *See, e.g.*, BGH 1999 GRUR 1128—*Hormonpräparate* (3 December 1998); BGH 2000 GRUR 237—*Giftnotruf-Box* (6 October 1999); BGH 2000 GRUR 1076—*Abgasemissionen* (11 May 2000).

[400] Case law and commentary still include public-interest protection policies in general, for example, product safety and the protection of public health and the young. *See, e.g.*, BGH 2010 GRUR 754, 755–756—*Golly Telly* (10 December 2009); Gregor Elskamp, *Gesetzesverstoß und Wettbewerbsrecht—zur wettbewerbsrechtlichen Unzulässigkeit von Verstößen gegen außerwettbewerbsrechtliche Gesetze* 149–150 (2008).

[401] *See, e.g.*, BGH 2005 GRUR 353, 354 (2005)—*Testamentsvollstreckung durch Banken* (11 November 2004).

[402] *See infra* p. 565–566.

agricultural products.[403] Although national laws are still not uniform, the underlying policies are well reflected in a cursory categorization of geographical designations: the most general subject matter of protection is found in designations indicating a certain product's geographical origin.[404] Such a designation will be protected against use that is misinforming with respect to the product's geographical origin.[405] In addition, an incorrect designation may further infringe on a geographical designation if it also signals certain properties or qualities and if the product offered does not, in fact, fulfill these standards.[406] Finally, national laws may provide for the protection of famous geographical designations against nonconfusing uses if their special reputation could be injured or misappropriated.[407]

Beyond this categorization, a more formalistic debate is going on with respect to the legal nature of geographical designations. Some describe geographical designations as subjective rights, comparable to intellectual property.[408] Others view them as distinct from trademarks and trade names and hence from the category of intellectual property. Under this perspective, the subject matter of protection is the collective goodwill of a designation's beneficiaries; yet no absolute and exclusive rights exist.[409]

[403] For an overview, *see, e.g.*, Lionel Bently & Brad Sherman, *Intellectual Property Law* 1110 *et seq.* (4th edn., 2014); Stefan Jonas Schröter, *Der Schutz geographischer Herkunftsangaben nach Marken-, Wettbewerbs- und Registerrecht in Deutschland und der Schweiz* (2011).

[404] The legal terminology regarding geographical designations and indications of source is complex. For an overview, *see, e.g.*, Lionel Bently & Brad Sherman, *Intellectual Property Law* 1112 *et seq.* (4th edn., 2014).

[405] *See, e.g.*, section 127(1) of the Trademark Act in Germany. For French and Swiss law, *see, e.g.*, Florent Thouvenin, *Funktionale Systematisierung von Wettbewerbsrecht (UWG) und Immaterialgüterrechten* 411 *et seq.* (2007). For English law and the action under a doctrine of so-called extended passing off (protecting inter alia against misrepresentation with respect to geographical origin), *see* Lionel Bently & Brad Sherman, *Intellectual Property Law* 878 *et seq.* (4th edn., 2014).

[406] This notably concerns so-called appellations of origin (*appellations d'origine*) that designate product qualities or characteristics that are due exclusively or essentially to the geographical environment, including natural and human factors. *See, e.g.*, Art. 5 Regulation (EU) No 1151/2012 of the European Parliament and of the Council of 21 November 2012 on quality schemes for agricultural products and foodstuffs, O.J. EU (14 December 2012), L 343/1.

[407] This is the case in Germany, for instance, under section 127(3) of the Trademark Act (MarkenG).

[408] *See, e.g.*, Roland Knaak, *Der Schutz geographischer Herkunftsangaben im neuen Markengesetz*, 1995 GRUR 103, 105; Karl-Heinz Fezer, *Markenrecht*, § 126 para. 4 (4th edn., 2009); Lionel Bently & Brad Sherman, Intellectual Property Law 1111 (4th edn., 2014).

[409] *See, e.g.*, BGH 1999 GRUR 252, 253–254—*Warsteiner II* (2 July 1998); BGH 2001 GRUR 73, 76–77—*Stich den Buben* (10 August 2000); BGH 2007 GRUR 884—*Cambridge Institute*, para. 38 (28 June 2007); *see also* Karl Matthiolius, *Der Rechtsschutz geographischer Herkunftsangaben* 2, 5, and 6 (1928).

Admittedly, with regard to terminology, the Court of Justice and the European Commission appear to classify geographical designation as "intellectual property."[410] Terminology, however, hardly determines doctrinal characterization. By contrast, a closer look at the underlying policies indicates that geographical designations are largely part of the sector of unfair competition prevention. Several aspects are determinative: by definition, geographical designations cannot grant exclusive rights since they do not establish a single "owner" or a definite group of "owners." The number of beneficiaries is potentially infinite, for the nearly unlimited group of producers situated within the given geographical area may make use of the indication.[411] The number of "owners" may grow or shrink at any time, depending only on the amount of producers moving in or out of the geographical area. In addition, depending on the respective national law, an "infringer" may be enjoined by both the beneficiaries of the designation and, for instance, a consumer association.[412] This latter fact points toward a characterization as unfair competition prevention.[413] An exception may be found in the protection of geographical designations with a special reputation—for instance, Champagne.[414] Protection of such reputed indications establishes a non-confusion-based theory of infringement that protects additional value. Here, too, therefore, two different kinds of goodwill—navigation and surplus—can be distinguished.[415]

[410] *See, e.g., Exportur v. LOR and Confiserie du Tech*, C-3/91, para. 23 *et seq.* (10 November 1992), [1992] E.C.R. I-5529; *Ravil* ("Grana Padano"), C-469/00, para. 49 (20 May 2003), [2003] E.C.R. I-5053; *Consorzio del Prosciutto di Parma and Salumificio S. Rita*, C-108/01, para. 62 *et seq.* (20 May 2003), [2003] E.C.R. I-5121; *see also* Statement by the Commission concerning Article 2 of Directive 2004/48/EC of the European Parliament and of the Council on the enforcement of intellectual property rights (2005/295/EC), O.J. EU (13 April 2005), L 94/37.

[411] Stephen Stern, *Are GIs IP?*, 29(2) EIPR 39, 41–42 (2007); Florent Thouvenin, *Funktionale Systematisierung von Wettbewerbsrecht (UWG) und Immaterialgüterrechten* 415 (2007).

[412] *See, e.g.*, section 128(1) of the German Trademark Act (MarkenG) and section 8(3) of the Unfair Competition Act (UWG).

[413] *See also* Karl Matthiolius, *Der Rechtsschutz geographischer Herkunftsangaben* 5 (1928) ("Der Mißbrauch geographischer Herkunftsangaben ist demnach wirtschaftlich gekennzeichnet als sowohl in der Form wie in der Wirkung besonders schwerer unlauterer Wettbewerb."), and *id.* at 32 ("Die Benutzung einer geographischen Herkunftsangabe entfließt also nicht einem dem Warenzeichenrecht ähnlichen subjektiven Recht, sondern geschieht in Ausübung natürlicher freier Betätigung. Dieser Betätigung sind Grenzen dort gezogen, wo in einer gegen die guten Sitten verstoßenden Weise die Freiheit der gewerblichen Betätigung des Mitbewerbers verletzt wird.").

[414] For these scenarios, *see, e.g.*, BGH 1988 GRUR 453, 455—*Ein Champagner unter den Mineralwässern* (4 June 1987); BGH 2002 GRUR 426, 427—*Champagner bekommen, Sekt bezahlen* (17 January 2002).

[415] *See supra* p. 349 *et seq.*

Thus, with respect to choice of law, the specific character of geographical designations—notably the difference in underlying policies—requires a treatment either in accordance with the marketplace-effects rule or with close regard to the locus of the collective goodwill. While the former is an expression of a policy protecting consumer navigation, the latter concerns the surplus goodwill provided by a geographical designation.[416]

Conclusions

Two dimensions of competitive activities exist—horizontal and vertical. While the horizontal level concerns cases of intercompetitor wrongs, the vertical level is where the cynosure of competition can be found; this is where market transactions occur. This vertical/horizontal demarcation highlights many contested issues concerning the interrelations between tort, unfair competition, trademark, and antitrust law.

Looking at consumer decision making and transacting as the most determinative element of the market mechanism will resolve these issues in both substantive law and choice of law. Let us start with the seemingly inseparable nexus between tort and unfair competition law: it is only through a close look at the consumer's decision making and transacting that a disentanglement can be undertaken. A large part of civil law unfair competition doctrine still covers tortious conduct that does not have an immediate impact on consumer decision making. These areas must be distinguished from the core area of unfair competition policy. They can be found at the horizontal level of the market mechanism. Policies on the vertical track, by contrast, regulate conduct that immediately affects consumer decision making and transacting. This is the actual domain of "competition" with a direct connection to the market.

These micromechanics of market transacting also explain the segmentation of the field of intellectual property rights. In light of their common core policy, we can say that trademark and unfair competition law protect the information infrastructure of the marketplace. Looking at the fields under this lens reveals that both areas are complementary sectors of a regulatory regime governing the currents of communication between market participants.

Several important points arise. First, with regard to the separation between trademarks and other intellectual property, it is important to acknowledge that there is no uniform category of "intellectual property." The granting of trademark rights is driven by a concern that is fundamentally different from general intellectual property theory. Rights creation

[416] *See infra* p. 549 *et seq.* and p. 556 *et seq.*

and protection under trademark doctrine is intended to provide an incentive to invest in marketplace competition. Unlike patents and copyrights, the system of trademark protection is not a time-limited *perpetuum mobile* of individual entitlements in creative or innovative intangibles. Rather, trademark protection is founded on a *continuum* of goodwill creation and maintenance.

Such a market-mechanistic perspective also helps clarify inconsistencies in unfair competition doctrine. While consumers' interests generally coincide with the public's interest in unhindered competition and free markets, the policy of "consumer protection" is not homogeneous. It is founded on different conceptions of the "consumer." One aspect concerns the protection of the private citizen—notably, the protection of personality and privacy. Another facet involves the protection of the consumer as a referee in competition. Protective policies beyond this narrow focus are detached from the market mechanism and from the integrated concept of modern unfair competition law. In addition to distinguishing between citizen and referee, we can identify further policies that are not concerned primarily with protecting consumer decision making. Both trademark and unfair competition doctrines host such additional policies of goodwill protection. This is the field of surplus goodwill, often characterized as brand reputation, prestige, scarcity, or exclusivity. Examples include antidilution, postsale confusion, and product-imitation doctrines. Policies concerned with protecting such surplus goodwill are not immediately aimed at protecting consumer decision making. Yet they are nevertheless bound to information.

Choice of law must closely follow these demarcations in substantive law policy. Competitive conduct can consist of competitor-related activity that bypasses the market mechanism of consumer decision making. This is the category of bilateral torts that makes up competition at the horizontal level of the market-mechanism model. Under choice-of-law doctrine, tort conflicts rules will accordingly take precedence (see article 6(2) of the Rome II Regulation). At the vertical level, impact on the decision-making process, including the final stage of transacting, can affect the market mechanism at its core. This is the cynosure of competition and, as we will see, the epicenter of choice-of-law analysis for all policies that are designed to establish and protect the information infrastructure of the marketplace (see article 6(1) of the Rome II Regulation). In addition, however, beyond this common core of trademark protection and unfair competition prevention, a wide array of additional policies exists. Among them are regulatory restrictions on matters related to the public interest in general—for example, the prevention of consumer harassment in order to protect civil rights concerns of privacy. Another example is the prohibition of competitive conduct deemed offensive, immoral, or otherwise indecent. Further categories comprise elements of postsale confusion and antidilution doctrine, as well as quasi IP rights protection against product imitation. Undue manipulation of consumer decision making will be unlikely in many of these cases. For choice-of-law analysis, the underlying policies must be kept separate and will, accordingly, lead to an attachment that is—at least in principle—different from the choice of law in market-oriented unfair competition.

5 International Comity

A Doctrine of Self-Restraint

Different nations entertain different doctrines and different usages in regard to them. The jurists of different countries hold opinions opposite to each other, as to some of the fundamental principles, which ought to have a universal operation; and the jurists of the same nation are sometimes as ill agreed among themselves. Still, however, with all these deductions, it is manifest, that many approximations have been already made towards the establishment of a general system of international jurisprudence, which shall elevate the policy, subserve the interests, and promote the common convenience of all nations. We may thus indulge the hope, that, at no distant period, the comity of nations will be but another name for the justice of nations.

Joseph Story, Commentaries on the Conflict of Laws, § 645 (1834)

Introduction

As demonstrated in chapter 3, the most fundamental question in trademark and unfair competition conflicts law pertains to the exact demarcation of spatial boundaries for individual rights protection and marketplace regulation. The solutions that have been suggested are manifold. Apart from substantivist theories jettisoning the nation-state paradigm *in toto*, all models are founded on a common denominator; the protection of rights and the enforcement of policies are inseparably tied to the concept of nation-state sovereignty. Although not always clearly expressed, the existence of a universally accepted principle is implied: in the international sphere, the scope of individual rights and nation-state policies must be limited. In other words, some form of conflict resolution is needed to provide for an avoidance—or at least a reconciliation—of conflicting sovereign interests.

Seen in this light, international trademark and unfair competition conflicts fall squarely into the sector of international economic and regulatory law. After all, the debate on the territoriality of regulation and its demarcations has been taking place much longer there. And it is well accepted that many gray areas exist where once genuinely "private" law has become "loaded" by concerns of regulatory public policy. Trademark and unfair competition law can be found in this gray area. The multiplication of trade and commerce and its increasing internationalization in the twentieth century have not only publicized and politicized the field but also infused its conflicts law with the potential of causing inter-nation discord when conflicting regulatory interests are disregarded. Yet this is rarely explained with clarity, nor are the correct conclusions drawn. Most illustrative of this lack of clarity, as we have seen, is the traditional neglect of public policy concerns in European unfair competition choice of law, which is still characterized by obsolete paradigms of international tort doctrine and a focus on market participants' territorial conduct as the object of regulation. In US doctrine, by contrast, the pendulum has swung in the other direction. Here, the aspect of public policy is overemphasized in a genuinely unqualified commercial effects test. This is combined with an almost naïve trust that the extraterritorial extension of trademark rights and unfair competition policies guarantees effective cross-border market regulation.

In order to provide the basis for a reconceptualization, I will begin by explaining how public and private law have come closer to one another and how this has been extrapolated to the international sphere through an increasing interconnectedness between public international law and private international law. This can be described as the fragment of a larger evolution of conflicts law and choice of law. Indeed, it highlights the subtle transformation of the Savignian conception of a genuinely "private" conflicts law into a public law instrument of cross-border regulation in a world of globalized societies and economies (*see infra* p. 383 *et seq.*). This development is closely tied to the history of the doctrine of international comity. Starting with the doctrine's incipiencies in seventeenth-century Netherlands, I will illustrate its degradation in twentieth-century doctrine and its more recent (though widely unrecognized) resurrection. Two sectors are particularly apt for the illustration: the field of international antitrust law as a core area of international regulatory law and the field of international human rights litigation as part of a private rights enforcement regime (*see infra* p. 432 *et seq.*). Drawing on the results of these analyses, I will highlight the intricacies of international trademark and unfair competition conflicts. Here, too, we can see the doctrine of international comity at work. European jurists, of course, may be far more hesitant than their American counterparts to acknowledge the doctrine as an instrument of legal analysis, not to speak of its practical implementation.[1] But

[1] For this traditional civil law/common law divergence (and the potential of an increasing convergence in the future), *see* Tim W. Dornis, *Comity*, in *Encyclopedia of Private International Law* (Jürgen Basedow et al. eds., forthcoming 2017).

terminology and tradition must not impede the analysis at its core: what is uncontested is the fact that matters of internationally conflicting regulatory interests require moderation and reconciliation in systematic structures. The doctrine of international comity is the traditional vehicle for this function, as we will see in both US conflicts doctrine and early nineteenth-century European choice of law. It may thus also serve as a modern instrument of "civilization." As closer analysis will show, the doctrine is multifaceted. In addition to its historic role of avoiding discord among countries, it maintains convenience in international transacting and commerce (*see infra* p. 480 *et seq.*).

Section 1 From *Comitas Gentium* to Transnational Law

Legitimacy of jurisdiction is a recurring theme in international economic law. The international scope of domestic regulation is usually determined by looking closely at the principles of public international law and comity.[2] While comity is, strictly speaking, not understood as a principle of public international law,[3] it is usually credited with fulfilling the same function.[4] Until today, the exact character and meaning of the doctrine have remained unclear.[5] A detailed analysis would go beyond the scope of this chapter, and, in any case, a wealth of excellent scholarship already exists. What I will focus on is a specific facet of the doctrine of international comity that, albeit often overlooked, is of special importance for this inquiry: the issue of jurisdictional self-restraint and abstention.

[2] Also termed, for example, *comitas, courtoisie internationale*, and *Völkercourtoisie*.

[3] *See* Michael Akehurst, *Jurisdiction in International Law*, 46 Brit. Y.B. Int'l L. 145, 215–216 (1972/73); Joel R. Paul, *Comity in International Law*, 32 Harv. Int'l L.J. 1, 44 (1991); Peter Macalister-Smith, *Comity*, 671, 671–672, in *Encyclopedia of Public International Law, vol. I* (Rudolf Bernhardt ed., 1992).

[4] Harold G. Maier, *Extraterritorial Jurisdiction at a Crossroads: An Intersection between Public and Private International Law*, 76 Am. J. Int'l L. 280, 281 (1982). Comity thus appears to be a crucible for conflicts resolution norms and their legitimacy under international law. As Sir Ian Brownlie explained, beyond "[n]eighbourliness, mutual respect, and the friendly waiver of technicalities," the concept of comity is used in at least four ways: "(1) as a synonym for international law; (2) as equivalent to private international law (conflict of laws); (3) as a policy basis for, and source of, particular rules of conflict of laws; and (4) as the reason for and source of a rule of international law." *See* Ian Brownlie, *Principles of Public International Law* 28–29 (7th edn., 2008); *see also* Peter Macalister-Smith, *Comity*, 671, 672, in *Encyclopedia of Public International Law, vol. I* (Rudolf Bernhardt ed., 1992); Harold Hongju Koh, *Is International Law Really State Law?*, 111 Harv. L. Rev. 1824, 1856 (1998).

[5] For a summary of definitions and explanations regarding international comity doctrine, *see* Joel R. Paul, *Comity in International Law*, 32 Harv. Int'l L.J. 1, 3 *et seq.* with fn. 4 to 18 (1991). For an overview of civil law (and other) jurisdictions' rudimentary treatment of comity doctrine, *see* Tim W. Dornis, *Comity*, in *Encyclopedia of Private International Law* (Jürgen Basedow et al. eds., forthcoming 2017).

This element of comity has become somewhat defunct throughout the last century. Today, it is widely assumed that the more there exists an international or transnational consensus on substantive norms and policies, the less need there is for the single nation-state's jurisdictional abstention. One could say that theory and practice of transnationalization have established an apotheosis of substantive-norm and substantive-policy universality. Without a divergence on the level of substantive norms and policies, no more conflict exists. Hence, choice of law and conflicts law—it would seem—are obsolete and outdated. International human rights litigation is a prime example of such normativity "beyond the state." In fact, an increasing number of legal sectors are infiltrated by a transnational law subtext. In all these areas, the domain of choice of law and conflicts law seems to have vanished. The main problem with such transnationalization, however, is its disregard for pitfalls in the functioning of the international community, especially with respect to socioeconomic communication and transacting. So far, this has not been explored with clarity. It is overlooked particularly with respect to international trademark and unfair competition law.

Interestingly, early theorists in the field were more cautious in this regard. Ulrich Huber and his contemporaries' seventeenth-century understanding of the *comitas gentium* expressly provided for a basic guarantee of international harmony as a core element of the doctrine. This was extended by Joseph Story and Friedrich Carl von Savigny. During the nineteenth century, the purpose of conflicts law and choice of law was to secure the utility and convenience of international transacting and commerce. It is this traditional function that still must be fulfilled. The world's legal orders may find themselves in full swing toward approximation, convergence, and even unification. Yet a mere blending of substantive norms and policies will not overcome the real-world obstacles that stand in the way of a truly globalized jurisdictional system. Without a concordant universality of international enforcement structures, transnationalization remains incomplete. Accordingly, the need for traditional instruments of conflicts law and choice of law still exists—notably for a doctrine of jurisdictional self-restraint and abstention.

I *The Status Quo: A Publicization of Private International Law*

The fields of private international law (also known as conflicts law or choice of law) and public international law (formerly often called the law of nations) have traditionally been treated as two distinct systems. Harold G. Maier's description of public international law as seeking to "regulate[] activity among human beings operating in groups called nation-states" fittingly expresses this traditional view. Private international law, by contrast, "regulates the activities of smaller subgroups or individuals as they interact with eachother."[6] Upon a closer look, however, the dichotomy is no longer so black and white—if it ever was.

A The (Non)Historical Dichotomy: Private and Public International Law

In nineteenth-century Europe, public and private international law were seen as complementary parts of a universal discipline. The modern nation-state was yet to be formed. Conflicts law, which was not codified, consisted of court decisions and scholarly commentary. Eminent scholars such as von Savigny, Johann Caspar Bluntschli, and Pasquale Stanislao Mancini were internationalist authorities. Their conceptions of conflicts law and choice of law, similar in nature, incorporated elements of public international law doctrine.[7] The idea that private international law had its roots in the law of nations remained dominant in European doctrine until the early twentieth century.[8] This understanding began to change with the advent of private law codifications throughout the continent. In the course of codifying their nation-states' substantive private laws, lawmakers also came across the field of private international law.[9] In addition, public international law and national laws began to be separated along the lines of the individual's status—while she was a potent actor in the domestic sphere, she was virtually nonexistent in the international arena. Hence, the regulation of private relationships—even if they were of an international nature—was beyond the scope of public international law.[10] Absent international agreements obliging nation-states to provide

[6] Harold G. Maier, *Extraterritorial Jurisdiction at a Crossroads: An Intersection between Public and Private International Law*, 76 Am. J. Int'l L. 280, 280 (1982).

[7] For an overview of contemporary public international law and its protagonists, *see* Martti Koskenniemi, *The Gentle Civilizer of Nations: The Rise and Fall of International Law 1870–1960*, 11 *et seq.* (2001). For nineteenth-century internationalists, *see* Otto Kahn-Freund, *The Growth of Internationalism in English Private International Law (Lionel Cohen Lectures)* 6–7 (1960); more recently, *see* Heinz-Peter Mansel, *Staatlichkeit des Internationalen Privatrechts und Völkerrecht*, 89, 95–96, in *Völkerrecht und IPR* (Stefan Leible & Matthias Ruffert eds., 2006). For an enlightening (and biting) contemporary critique, *see* Franz Kahn, *Über Inhalt, Natur und Methode des internationalen Privatrechts*, 255, 280–281, in *Abhandlungen zum internationalen Privatrecht, vol. I* (Otto Lenel & Hans Lewald eds., 1928).

[8] Arthur Nussbaum, *Rise and Decline of the Law-of-Nations Doctrine in the Conflict of Laws*, 42 Colum. L. Rev. 189, 194 (1942).

[9] Karl-Heinz Ziegler, *Völkerrechtliche Verpflichtung zur Anwendung oder nur „freundliche Beachtung" fremden Rechts? Die comitas-Lehre heute (Betrachtungen eines Rechtshistorikers)*, 43, 50 in *Völkerrecht und IPR* (Stefan Leible & Matthias Ruffert eds., 2006).

[10] For the contemporary approach among public international law scholars in Germany, *see, e.g.*, Heinrich Triepel, *Völkerrecht und Landesrecht*, 20 (1899) ("[Die Stellung des

for a certain regulation of private relations, the authority to determine the application of forum and foreign laws in conflicts cases was understood as falling within the exclusive domain of the domestic regime.[11]

Of course, time and again, scholarly theory attempted to reestablish the unity of public and private international laws. In German doctrine, Ernst Zitelmann became famous for his turn-of-the-century approach, the "law-of-nations doctrine."[12] But his effort was futile. Franz Kahn's disdainful rejection has become well known:

> For what is the public-international-law choice of law of this school? A law of nations that has never been practiced or acknowledged anywhere, that has always and anywhere been disobeyed and trespassed, and that—all this notwithstanding—still has to exist since it seems to be the Right and the naturally Necessary to theorists according to their general principles.[13]

Individuums] kann nicht die eines Rechtssubjekts sein. Der Einzelne ist vom Standpunkte einer die Staaten als solche verbindenden Rechtsgemeinschaft unfähig, Träger eigener, von der Rechtsordnung dieser Gemeinschaft ausgehenden Rechte und Pflichten zu sein. Es ist gleichgültig, dass es in grossem Umfange seine Interessen sind, deren Wahrung völkerrechtliche Sätze im Auge haben.").

[11] *See, e.g.*, Kurt Lipstein, *The General Principles of Private International Law*, 135 Recueil des Cours 97, 167 *et seq.* (1972-I); Karl-Heinz Ziegler, *Völkerrechtliche Verpflichtung zur Anwendung oder nur „freundliche Beachtung" fremden Rechts? Die comitas-Lehre heute (Betrachtungen eines Rechtshistorikers)*, 43, 50–51, in *Völkerrecht und IPR* (Stefan Leible & Matthias Ruffert eds., 2006).

[12] *See, e.g.*, Ernst Zitelmann, *Internationales Privatrecht, vol. I* 71 *et seq.*, 122 *et seq.* (1897) (*e.g.*, *id.* at 71–72: "Aus der allgemeinen völkerrechtlichen Herrschaftsabgrenzung zwischen den Staaten können wir nun auf dem Wege besonderer Schlußfolgerung die Abgrenzung der Gesetzgebungsgewalt der verschiedenen Staaten in privatrechtlichen Dingen ermitteln; wir können danach feststellen, wie weit jeder einzelne Staat subjektive Privatrechte verleihen und entziehen kann."); Ernst Zitelmann, *Geltungsbereich und Andwendungsbereich der Gesetze*, 207 *et seq.*, in *Festgabe der Bonner Juristischen Fakultät für Karl Bergbohm zum 70. Geburtstag* (1919). For a system akin to Zitelmann's conception, though not directly founded on public international law, *see* Ernst Frankenstein, *Internationales Privatrecht (Grenzrecht), vol. I* 1 *et seq.* (1926). For continental scholarship at the turn of the century and other attempts to reestablish (or maintain) the unity, *see* Arthur Nussbaum, *Rise and Decline of the Law-of-Nations Doctrine in the Conflict of Laws*, 42 Colum. L. Rev. 189, 194–195 (1942). For Zitelmann's theory, *see* Max Gutzwiller, *Zitelmanns völkerrechtliche Theorie des Internationalprivatrechts*, 16 Archiv für Rechts- und Wirtschaftsphilosophie 468 (1922); more recently, *see* Erik Jayme, *Völkerrecht und Internationales Privatrecht—eine entwicklungsgeschichtliche Betrachtung*, 23, 34–35, in *Völkerrecht und IPR* (Stefan Leible & Matthias Ruffert eds., 2006).

[13] Franz Kahn, *Über Inhalt, Natur und Methode des internationalen Privatrechts*, 255, 274, in *Abhandlungen zum internationalen Privatrecht, vol. I* (Otto Lenel & Hans Lewald eds., 1928) ("Denn was ist das völkerrechtliche internationale Privatrecht jener Schule? Ein Völkerrecht, das nie und nirgends geübt oder anerkannt, das immer und überall mißachtet und übertreten worden ist, und das alledem zum Trotz doch bestehen muß, weil es den Theoretikern nach allgemeinen Grundsätzen als das Richtige, als das Naturnotwendige erscheint." (author's translation)). For the Reichsgericht's rejection, *see* RGZ vol. 95, 164, 165 (11 March 1919) ("Am wenigsten vermag die Berufung auf Zitelmann eine selbständige Begründung der gegenteiligen Meinung zu ersetzen. Der Verfasser erhebt gar nicht den Anspruch, das internationale Privatrecht so darzustellen,

While there have been modern attempts to revive Zitelmann's approach,[14] overall, the idea that choice of law can be controlled by principles of public international law has not gained ground.

Thus, it is conventional wisdom today that public international law seldom has a direct impact on private law conflicts resolution. Only a few tenets of public international law may actually be considered binding. For instance, a nation-state must not reject the application of foreign law per se. In addition, each state should provide for, at the very least, a rudimentary conflicts regime.[15] By and large, however, the content of choice of law is undetermined and unaffected by international law.[16]

The picture in the United States is similar. Story, commonly referred to as the founding father of American conflicts theory, considered private and public international law as homogeneously overlapping systems.[17] But this conceptual unity of regimes was never implemented in legal practice, and the law-of-nations doctrine, as Arthur Nussbaum

wie es tatsächlich in Geltung ist. Er will zu wissenschaftlich unanfechtbaren Rechtssätzen dadurch gelangen, daß er, von unmittelbar einleuchtenden Postulaten ausgehend, auf deduktivem Wege das System aufbaut. Dabei geht er von Voraussetzungen aus, die, wie er selbst nicht verkennt, mit dem tatsächlich herrschenden Zustande nicht gegeben sind. Er unterstellt eine völkerrechtlich sichere Abgrenzung des Machtbereichs der Staaten in der vielfachen Verschlungenheit von Personal- und Gebietshoheit gegeneinander, von der das heutige Völkerrecht noch weit entfernt ist.").

[14] For example, those of Georges Scelle, Hans Wiebringhaus, Frederick A. Mann, and Albert Bleckmann. *See* Georges Scelle, *Manuel élémentaire de droit international public* (1943); Georges Scelle, *Préface à l'ouvrage de Charles Carabiber, Les jurisdictions internationales de droit privé* 7 *et seq.* (1947); Hans Wiebringhaus, *Beitrag zur Frage des Verhältnisses von Internationalprivat- und Völkerrecht*, 1952 JR 383; Hans Wiebringhaus, *Das Gesetz der funktionellen Verdoppelung—Beitrag zu einer universalistischen Theorie des Internationalprivat- und Völkerrechts* (2nd edn., 1955); F. A. Mann, *The Doctrine of Jurisdiction in International Law*, 111 Recueil des Cours 1 (1964-I); Albert Bleckmann, *Die völkerrechtlichen Grundlagen des internationalen Kollisionsrechts* 59 *et seq.*, 166, *et passim* (1992).

[15] For the axiom of recognizing foreign states' legal regimes and the general openness to the application of foreign laws under a concept of comity, *see* Franz Kahn, *Über Inhalt, Natur und Methode des internationalen Privatrechts*, 255, 286–287, in *Abhandlungen zum internationalen Privatrecht, vol. I* (Otto Lenel & Hans Lewald eds., 1928); *see also* Klaus Schurig, *Völkerrecht und IPR: Methodische Verschleifung oder strukturierte Interaktion?*, 55, 60–61, in *Völkerrecht und IPR* (Stefan Leible & Matthias Ruffert eds., 2006).

[16] *See, e.g.*, Ernst Rabel, *Rechtsvergleichung und internationale Rechtsprechung*, 1 RabelsZ 5, 5–6 (1927); Ernst Rabel, *The Conflict of Laws—A Comparative Study, vol. I* 6 *et seq.* (2nd edn., 1958); Kurt Lipstein, *The General Principles of Private International Law*, 135 Recueil des Cours 97, 167 *et seq.* (1972-I); Egon Lorenz, *Zur Struktur des Internationalen Privatrechts* 56 *et seq.*, 87–88 (1977); Paul Heinrich Neuhaus, *Der Beitrag des Völkerrechts zum Internationalen Privatrecht*, 21 German Y.B. Int'l L. 60, 64 *et seq.* (1978); Christian von Bar & Peter Mankowski, *Internationales Privatrecht—vol. I: Allgemeine Lehren* § 3 para. 1 *et seq.* (2nd edn., 2003).

[17] *See infra* p. 400 *et seq.*

summarized in 1942, "never won a real foothold."[18] And even though the vested rights approach so powerfully brought forward by Joseph Beale and ultimately also integrated into the Restatement (First) of Conflict of Laws may have been interpreted as having implemented a theory quite analogous to the uniformity of private and public international law,[19] this fragile structure was soon destroyed by the realists' attack. Around mid-century, American legal thought, particularly regarding choice of law, began to reject an overly cosmopolitan perspective. Instead, it began to narrow its focus to domestic law and the interstate arena. Legal realism virtually turned conflicts theory inward.[20] For conflicts law, this meant that public international law would not be a binding authority. Nor would it limit national lawmaking.[21]

B The Duality of Methods

This systematic isolation of national regimes from the law of nations, or international law, is reflected in the structure and technique of European choice of law. In the Savignian tradition, the field covers collisions between private law norms only. The interchangeability of national norms is founded on the assumption that private law is apolitical and an issue of interparty concerns. Accordingly, choice of law, at its core, should not inquire about a foreign law's content but instead simply ensure "conflicts justice" by choosing the spatially most adequate legal order.[22]

[18] Arthur Nussbaum, *Rise and Decline of the Law-of-Nations Doctrine in the Conflict of Laws*, 42 Colum. L. Rev. 189, 197 (1942). *See also* John R. Stevenson, *The Relationship of Private International Law to Public International Law*, 52 Colum. L. Rev. 561, 565 (1952).

[19] Beale himself did not consider his conflicts law approach to be founded on public international law or comity. *See, e.g.*, Joseph H. Beale, *A Treatise on the Conflict of Laws, vol. I: Jurisdiction* § 1.10 (1935); *see also* John R. Stevenson, *The Relationship of Private International Law to Public International Law*, 52 Colum. L. Rev. 561, 566 (1952). *But see* Arthur Nussbaum, *Rise and Decline of the Law-of-Nations Doctrine in the Conflict of Laws*, 42 Colum. L. Rev. 189, 198 (1942).

[20] Matthias Reimann, *A New Restatement—For the International Age*, 75 Ind. L.J. 575, 577 and n. 17 (2000); for a similar point, *see* Kurt Lipstein, *The General Principles of Private International Law*, 135 Recueil des Cours 97, 140–141 (1972-I); more recently, Harold Hongju Koh, *Transnational Legal Process*, 75 Neb. L. Rev. 181, 182 (1996); for the mid-nineteenth-century isolationism of US conflicts scholarship, *see* Gerhard Kegel, *Wandel auf dünnem Eis*, 35, 41, in *Zum Wandel des internationalen Privatrechts* (Friedrich K. Juenger ed., 1974).

[21] For an illustrative summary, *see* Walter Wheeler Cook, *The Logical and Legal Bases of the Conflict of Laws* 13–14 (1949).

[22] *See, e.g.*, Paul Heinrich Neuhaus, *Die Grundbegriffe des internationalen Privatrechts* 2, 33 *et seq.* (1962); Klaus Vogel, *Der räumliche Anwendungsbereich der Verwaltungsrechtsnorm* 215 *et seq.* (1965); Christian Joerges, *Zum Funktionswandel des Kollisionsrechts—Die "Governmental Interest Analysis" und die "Krise des Internationalen Privatrechts"* 151 *et seq.* (1971); Eckard Rehbinder, *Zur Politisierung des Internationalen Privatrechts*, 1973 JZ 151, 151.

There are just a few categories of norms that are not deemed interchangeable. For example, the area of regulatory norms—often referred to as mandatory laws, *lois d'application immédiate*, or simply public law[23]—will generally not be subjected to the classic jurisdiction-selecting technique. Savigny himself categorized these norms as "laws [] whose peculiar nature does not admit of so free an application of the community of law obtaining between different states."[24] The two kinds of norms he distinguished within this class were "laws of a strictly positive, imperative nature" and "legal institutions of a foreign state, of which the existence is not at all recognized in ours, and which, therefore, have no claim to the protection of our courts." The latter category makes up the modern public policy exception. The former, important for this inquiry, is the sector of what, today, is commonly termed "international economic or international commercial law."[25] Unlike choice of law for genuine private law norms, a conflict between different nations' regulatory norms cannot be an issue for multilateralism. The assumption of interchangeable norms—and, accordingly, the paradigm of the seat of the parties' relationship—is inapplicable.[26] In essence, this approach remains founded on the statutists' conception, which was essentially a method of introspection: the scope of application of a certain law must be determined on the basis of the specific norm at issue. Inevitably, without the assumption of content neutrality and interchangeability, issues of public international law legitimacy (re)arise.[27]

[23] For an extensive discussion of international terminology, *see* Kurt Siehr, *Ausländische Eingriffsnormen im inländischen Wirtschaftskollisionsrecht*, 52 RabelsZ 41, 42–43 (1988).

[24] *See* Friedrich Carl von Savigny, *Private International Law and the Retrospective Operation of Statutes—A Treatise on the Conflict of Laws and the Limits of Their Operation in Respect of Place and Time* § 349, at 76 (William Guthrie transl., 2nd edn., 1880); *see also* the German original text in Friedrich Carl von Savigny, *System des heutigen römischen Rechts, vol. VIII* § 349, at 32 (1849).

[25] In civil law terminology, this is the area of international economic (conflicts) law ("Wirtschaftskollisionsrecht"). One example is antitrust conflicts. *See* Jürgen Basedow, *Entwicklungslinien des internationalen Kartellrechts—Ausbau und Differenzierung des Auswirkungsprinzips*, 1989 NJW 627, 628; Klaus Schurig, *Zwingendes Recht, "Eingriffsnormen" und neues IPR*, 54 RabelsZ 217, 227 (1990); *see also* Anton K. Schnyder, *Wirtschaftskollisionsrecht—Sonderanknüpfung und extraterritoriale Anwendung wirtschaftsrechtlicher Normen unter besonderer Berücksichtigung von Marktrecht* (1990).

[26] *See, e.g.*, Rudolf Wiethölter, *Zur Frage des internationalen ordre public*, 133, 157 *et seq.*, in *Berichte der Deutschen Gesellschaft für Völkerrecht, vol. 7* (1967); Kurt Lipstein, *The General Principles of Private International Law*, 135 Recueil des Cours 97, 165 (1972-I); Jürgen Basedow, *Wirtschaftskollisionsrecht—Theoretischer Versuch über die ordnungspolitischen Normen des Forumstaates*, 52 RabelsZ 8, 8–9 and 20 (1988); Anton K. Schnyder, *Wirtschaftskollisionsrecht—Sonderanknüpfung und extraterritoriale Anwendung wirtschaftsrechtlicher Normen unter besonderer Berücksichtigung von Marktrecht* § 2 para. 29 *et seq.* (1990).

[27] Jürgen Basedow, *Wirtschaftskollisionsrecht—Theoretischer Versuch über die ordnungspolitischen Normen des Forumstaates*, 52 RabelsZ 8, 12–13 (1988); for a general overview

In US law, while choice of law and international economic, or regulatory, law are also distinguished, the technical dichotomy is less incisive. Formally, of course, choice of law and international economic law are even subject to two different restatements. Simply put, the Restatement (Second) of Conflict of Laws addresses conflicts resolution on private law issues, while the Restatement (Third) of Foreign Relations Law concerns collisions between federal regulatory and foreign states' policies and interests.[28] Upon a closer look, however, the techniques of conflicts resolution are less divergent. For one, the Restatement (Third) of Foreign Relations Law is founded on the Restatement (Second) of Conflict of Laws.[29] Further, scholars of international economic law not only have found the field infused with principles of public international law and comity but have also recommended the application of choice-of-law principles.[30] And legal practice is replete with cases where the issues have been intermingled. An oft-cited example is Judge Learned Hand's reasoning in the *Alcoa* decision, where he explained that limitations to the extraterritorial application of US antitrust law "generally correspond to those fixed by the 'Conflict of Laws'."[31] Similarly, and more recently, Justice Scalia's dissenting opinion in *Hartford Fire* implemented choice-of-law principles in the analysis of jurisdictional sovereignty.[32] As he explained, courts should look at the law of nations or customary international law to determine the reach of domestic norms. A statute should never be construed to "regulate foreign persons or conduct if that regulation would conflict with principles of international law." As he went on,

and critique, *see* Eckard Rehbinder, *Zur Politisierung des Internationalen Privatrechts*, 1973 JZ 151, 156 *et seq.*

28 For the (often implicit) distinction, *see, e.g.*, Harold G. Maier, *Extraterritorial Jurisdiction at a Crossroads: An Intersection between Public and Private International Law*, 76 Am. J. Int'l L. 280, 289 (1982) (distinguishing "transnational regulatory cases" from "nonregulatory choice-of-law cases"); for the distinction between "traditional choice-of-law scholarship" and "international regulatory issues," *see* Andrew T. Guzman, *Choice of Law: New Foundations*, 90 Geo. L.J. 883, 889 (2002).

29 *See* one of the rapporteurs' explanations in Andreas F. Lowenfeld, *Public Law in the International Arena: Conflict of Laws, International Law, and Some Suggestions for Their Interaction*, 163 Recueil des Cours 311, 329 (1979-II).

30 *See id.* at 328; Jean-Gabriel Castel, *The Extraterritorial Effects of Antitrust Laws*, 179 Recueil des Cours 9, 53, 110, 114 *et seq.* (1983-I); Lea Brilmayer, *The Extraterritorial Application of American Law: A Methodological and Constitutional Appraisal*, 50 Law & Contemp. Probs. 11, 11 *et seq.* (1987); Gary B. Born, *A Reappraisal of the Extraterritorial Reach of U.S. Law*, 24 Law & Pol'y Int'l Bus. 1, 84 *et seq.* (1992); *but see* Friedrich Juenger, *Constitutional Control of Extraterritoriality?: A Comment on Professor Brilmayer's Appraisal*, 50 L. & Contemp. Probs. 39, 41 (1987) (denying relations).

31 *U.S. v. Aluminum Co. of America*, 148 F.2d 416, 443 (2nd Cir. 1945).

32 For Scalia's "distinctly 'private' view of antitrust enforcement" and a critique, *see* Herbert Hovenkamp, *Federal Antitrust Policy—The Law of Competition and Its Practice* § 21.2b (3rd edn., 2005).

" 'The controlling considerations' in this choice-of-law analysis were 'the interacting interests of the United States and of foreign countries'."[33]

C A Blurring of Boundaries

Indeed, principles of public international law and international comity are increasingly regaining access to national conflicts law. This is due to the field's growing politicization and publicization—that is, an increasingly policy-oriented resolution of once genuinely private law conflicts. Several phenomena are illustrative.

First, at the doctrinal level, European choice of law—as US conflicts doctrine—is no longer (if it ever was) as disinterested in norm content and substantive law policies as has often been explained. In principle, of course, the divergence between Europe and the United States may still be emblematized by the theories once put forth by two key scholars: Gerhard Kegel and David Cavers. In defense of the European tradition, Kegel advocated a distinct disregard for the content of the relevant laws when determining the applicable regime. Choice of law, he explained, aims to find not the "objectively best law" but the "spatially best law"; accordingly, "conflicts justice takes functional precedence over substantive justice."[34] US doctrine, on the other hand, is still characterized by Cavers's conclusion that, in conflicts law, "[t]he court is not idly choosing a law; it is determining a controversy. How can it choose wisely without considering how that choice will affect that controversy?"[35] This preference for policy analysis implies a rejection of mechanical conflicts rules.[36] And although the scholarly field is diverse, the majority of American choice-of-law theories are content-selecting, not jurisdiction-selecting, models.[37] Early on, key voices called for a similar politicization of German and European doctrine.[38] And even

[33] *Hartford Fire Ins. Co. v. California*, 509 U.S. 764, 814–816 (1993) (Scalia, J., dissenting).

[34] Author's translation of Gerhard Kegel & Klaus Schurig, *Internationales Privatrecht* § 2, at 131 (9th edn., 2004) ("Deswegen ist die internationalprivatrechtliche Gerechtigkeit der materiell-privatrechtlichen funktionell vorgeordnet."); *see also* Gerhard Kegel, *Begriffs- und Interessenjurisprudenz im internationalen Privatrecht*, 259, 270, in *Festschrift Hans Lewald* (Max Gerwig et al. eds., 1978).

[35] David F. Cavers, *A Critique of the Choice-of-Law Problem*, 47 Harv. L. Rev. 173, 189 (1933).

[36] *See, e.g.*, Brainerd Currie, *The Disinterested Third State*, 28 Law & Contemp. Probs. 754, 778 (1963); Brainerd Currie, *Selected Essays on the Conflict of Laws*, ch. 13: *Justice Traynor and the Conflict of Laws*, 629, 637–638 (1963).

[37] For an overview, *see, e.g.*, Anton K. Schnyder, *Interessenabwägung im Kollisionsrecht—Zu Brainerd Curries „governmental-interest analysis,"* 105 ZfSchwR 101, 108–109 (1986); Christian von Bar & Peter Mankowski, *Internationales Privatrecht—vol. I: Allgemeine Lehren* § 6 para. 81 *et seq.* (2nd edn., 2003); on the general lack of consensus *see* Larry Kramer, *Rethinking Choice of Law*, 90 Colum. L. Rev. 277, 279 (1990).

[38] *See, e.g.*, Christian Joerges, *Zum Funktionswandel des Kollisionsrechts—Die "Governmental Interest Analysis" und die "Krise des Internationalen Privatrechts"* (1971); Eckard Rehbinder, *Zur Politisierung des Internationalen Privatrechts*, 1973 JZ 151.

though in the 1970s these ideas were still strongly rejected, over time, the hiatus has grown smaller. Indeed, modern communitarian choice of law in Europe has, at least in part, forsworn the once strictly followed concept of content-neutral jurisdiction selection.[39] Tort conflicts are emblematic: a number of provisions of the Rome II Regulation actually give express regard to substance, as can be seen in the instrument's consumer protection impetus in product-liability conflicts, the multiple policies accommodated under the rules for international unfair competition conflicts, the express aim of international environmental protection, and the rigid regulation of choice-of-law clauses.[40]

This last aspect reflects a second facet of publicization that can be found in the changes in many countries' domestic private law regimes. Since the twentieth century, the immemorial dichotomy between private and public law has been widely dissolved. Private and public law have never been as strictly separated under US legal thought as under the civil law tradition. In any event, the realist attack has further blurred distinctions that may have once existed in American law.[41] And even though the private/public law distinction has traditionally been very concise in Germany, there, too, the legal system has witnessed a growing publicization of private law. Indeed, as far as the substantive private/public law dichotomy is concerned, it has become increasingly questionable whether the formal means of norm enforcement and a qualification of norms as pertaining either to "public law" or to "private law" should still matter. Of course, public law will directly "regulate" issues with which it is concerned; and this regulation is for state agencies to enforce. Private law, by contrast, establishes a system of order among individuals. The state will not directly intervene; it will merely provide for institutions to adjudicate and enforce.[42] But the picture is no longer so simple. The nineteenth-century model of the liberal state as being distinct from a self-contained private law community has lost its formative function for legal structure and order.[43] Today, many areas of private law

[39] For an extensive account, *see* Tim W. Dornis, *"Local Data" in European Choice of Law: A Trojan Horse from Across the Atlantic?*, 44 Ga. J. Int'l & Comp. L. 2015 (forthcoming) (with numerous references).

[40] *See* art. 5, 6, 7 & 14 Rome II, as well as recitals 20, 21, 25 & 31.

[41] *See, e.g.*, Robert Post, *The Challenge of Globalization to American Public Law Scholarship*, 2 Theoretical Inq. L. 323, 324 (2001); *see also* John Henry Merryman, *The Public Law—Private Law Distinction in European and American Law*, 17 J. Publ. L. 3, 8–9 (1968); Morton J. Horwitz, *The History of the Public/Private Distinction*, 130 U. Pa. L. Rev. 1423, 1425–1426 (1982).

[42] John Henry Merryman, *The Public Law—Private Law Distinction in European and American Law*, 17 J. Publ. L. 3, 11–12 (1968).

[43] John Henry Merryman, *The Public Law—Private Law Distinction in European and American Law*, 17 J. Publ. L. 3, 15 (1968); *see also id.* at 15 n. 44 (referring to Jennings's allegory that the "public lawyer is ousting the private lawyer"); in addition

have been enriched by public policy concerns. Private individuals may still act as citizens. But their conduct and activities implement public and regulatory policies. Private law of this kind no longer provides a neutral framework for transactions among private individuals. It has mutated by becoming "socialized" and "publicized."[44] Contract law's and tort law's increasing concern for consumer protection are primary examples. The field of trademark protection and unfair competition prevention is another. As we have seen, the public policy of unfair competition prevention has evolved from an instrument of competitor protection into the integrated model of concurrent protection for competitors, consumers, and the public.[45] And since disputes are no longer purely private or interindividual, conflicts resolution has also become an issue of colliding regulatory policies. By this means, the socialization of private law has effectuated a progressive decrease in interchangeability. If private law norms are public policy loaded, it will be harder to fit them into a system of multilateral conflicts resolution.[46]

Finally, a third reason accounts for the increasing enrichment of choice-of-law doctrine by governmental interests. This aspect is seldom pointed out with clarity. Even if a private law norm is not intended to "regulate," it may still be found to exert significant impact under a perspective of international trade and commerce. In these cases, the state can no longer limit its role to acting as an umpire between individual parties alone. Such a perspective would neglect correlations between private-party conflicts and the international regulatory effects that may be exerted, for instance, by a discriminatory application of market-relevant norms of private law. Heinrich Kronstein alluded to this phenomenon in a 1949 article entitled "Crisis of 'Conflict of Laws' ":

> Before the rapid development of standardization and concentration in economic life ... reached its present phase, courts dealt with very many independent

see, e.g., Klaus Schurig, *Kollisionsnorm und Sachrecht* 18–19 (1981); Jürgen Basedow, *Wirtschaftskollisionsrecht—Theoretischer Versuch über die ordnungspolitischen Normen des Forumstaates*, 52 RabelsZ 8, 16 *et seq.* (1988).

[44] John Henry Merryman, *The Public Law—Private Law Distinction in European and American Law*, 17 J. Publ. L. 3, 15–16 (1968); Eckard Rehbinder, *Zur Politisierung des Internationalen Privatrechts*, 1973 JZ 151, 154; for German private law, *see* Franz Wieacker, *Privatrechtsgeschichte der Neuzeit unter besonderer Berücksichtigung der deutschen Entwicklung* 514 *et seq.* (1967). For a law and economics perspective, *see, e.g.*, Joel P. Trachtman, *Conflict of Laws and Accuracy in the Allocation of Government Responsibility*, 26 Vand. J. Transnat'l L. 975, 1009–1010 (1994).

[45] *See supra* p. 275 *et seq.*

[46] *See* Larry Kramer, *Vestiges of Beale: Extraterritorial Application of American Law*, 1991 Sup. Ct. Rev. 179, 188; Christian Joerges, *Vorüberlegungen zu einer Theorie des internationalen Wirtschaftsrechts*, 43 RabelsZ 6, 36 (1979); Gunther Kühne, *Die Entsavignysierung des Internationalen Privatrechts insbesondere durch sog. Eingriffsnormen*, 815, 817, in *Festschrift für Andreas Heldrich zum 70. Geburtstag* (Stephan Lorenz et al. eds., 2005).

> transactions between many independent persons of different countries. Each of these cases was unique, to be evaluated on its own merits and on nothing else.... There, in fact, the private interests in each of these hundreds of transactions prevailed over the possible public interest and no one had to worry about a systematic shift of the law in an entire field of life. ... When the present principles on conflict of laws were prepared, investment in foreign fields was the principal aim. Today the principal function of participation or technological and marketing agreements (patents, trademarks) is regulation of power and markets. Can we use, there, the same rules in conflict as before? ... [U]nder present conditions the "legal concept" is a characterization test which does not deal with individual unrelated contracts or participations, but with an entire type of transaction. If a certain law applies to one of those transactions, it applies to all of the same type. It applies rather to an institution than to a transaction. The public interest in cases of these types is obvious.[47]

Private law norms no longer represent individual interests alone. A clear separation between private and governmental interests no longer exists, and it is doubtful whether the state may still be seen as not caring about private individual concerns.[48] The actual or potential multitude of individual interests as a whole constitutes the combined public interest. Private rights have become institutionalized. In sum, the multiplication of international transacting has made the extension and limitation of individual entitlements an issue of international competition, trade wars, and economic hegemony. Accordingly, the state no longer has an altruistic interest in private law.[49]

In sum, many areas formerly deemed private law and private international law have had their character altered in a way that no longer allows them to be neatly categorized. The merger of private and public law at the level of national regimes has dissolved clear structures. And this dissolution has resulted in a publicization and politization of conflicts law and choice-of-law methods. The field has thus become subsumed by a debate

[47] Heinrich Kronstein, *Crisis of "Conflict of Laws,"* 37 Geo. L.J. 483, 486–487 (1949). *See also* Rudolf Wiethölter, *Zur Frage des internationalen ordre public*, 133, 135–136, in *Berichte der Deutschen Gesellschaft für Völkerrecht, vol. 7* (1967); Eckard Rehbinder, *Zur Politisierung des Internationalen Privatrechts*, 1973 JZ 151, 154.

[48] For more illustration, *see* Tim W. Dornis, *Die Erbensuche im Kollisionsrecht—von grenzüberschreitender "Menschenhülfe" zu internationaler Marktregulierung*, 2015 ZfPW 376–384.

[49] *But see* Gerhard Kegel, *The Crisis of Conflict of Laws*, 112 Recueil des Cours 91, 183 (1964-II) ("The state has an altruistic rather than egoistic interest in private law, concerning itself primarily with a *just* ordering of private life. In this respect even its domestic private law is not 'its own' private law; it rather strives to seek the best and fairest solution for *all* men."). For Currie's general critique of the traditional approach, *see, e.g.*, Brainerd Currie, *Selected Essays on the Conflict of Laws*, ch. 5: *The Constitution and the Choice of Law: Governmental Interests and the Judicial Function*, 188, 191 (1963) ("The rational pursuit of self-interest is preferable to such irrational altruism.").

on underlying public international law structures and on limitations to jurisdiction under the doctrine of international comity. As a result, this has created a number of gray areas of public international, private international, and international economic law.

II In the Shadows: The Creeping Deformation of Comity

The coalescence of private and public international law spheres is an important feature of the so-called transnationalization of the law. In essence, this phenomenon involves a constant mutation of public international law into something that is both more "private" and more "national." At the same time, domestic laws are increasingly becoming enriched by norms and policies of public international law; hence, they are less "private" and less "national." A prominent cause for this evolution was the change in the private individual's status in the international arena. While private actors were virtually nonexistent under the classical system, modern international law accords them extensive rights and duties. Private relations are no longer isolated from public international law—as seen most evidently in the case of human rights protection.[50] The individual's emancipation opened the door to the implementation of public international law in domestic private law regimes and, vice versa, a growing privatization of public international law.[51] This mind-set has been further bolstered by the idea that concepts of nation-state sovereignty and territoriality are increasingly outdated. Since the world is becoming more and more "borderless," traditional structures of lawmaking and policy making no longer seem to provide for a functioning order and regulation.

This development ultimately came along with the claim that a new paradigm of conflicts law and choice of law is needed. Like public international law, which was famously characterized as a "gentle civilizer of nations" by Martti Koskenniemi,[52] the doctrine of international comity

[50] *See, e.g.*, Hermann Mosler, *Völkerrecht als Rechtsordnung*, 36 ZaöRV 6, 30–31 (1976); Alfred Verdross & Bruno Simma, *Universelles Völkerrecht*, § 47 *et seq.* (3rd edn., 1984); Heinz-Peter Mansel, *Staatlichkeit des Internationalen Privatrechts und Völkerrecht*, 89, 94, in *Völkerrecht und IPR* (Stefan Leible & Matthias Ruffert eds., 2006). For a famous historical characterization of international law as non-individualist law *inter nationes, see*, however, Franz Kahn, *Über Inhalt, Natur und Methode des internationalen Privatrechts*, 255, 275 and 277, in *Abhandlungen zum internationalen Privatrecht, vol. I* (Otto Lenel & Hans Lewald eds., 1928).

[51] *See, e.g.*, Anne-Marie Slaughter & William Burke-White, *The Future of International Law Is Domestic (or, the European Way of Law)*, 47 Harv. Int'l L.J. 327, 350 (2006); Ralf Michaels, *Public and Private International Law: German Views on Global Issues*, 4 J. Priv. Int'l L. 121, 122–123 (2008); Paul B. Stephan, *Privatizing International Law*, 97 Va. L. Rev. 1573 (2011).

[52] Martti Koskenniemi, *The Gentle Civilizer of Nations: The Rise and Fall of International Law 1870–1960* (2001).

used to be understood as an instrument to facilitate and moderate international transacting and commerce. But the doctrine virtually evaporates as the dichotomies between public and private, international and national, "there" and "here" dissolve. In other words, the more a transnational consensus on norms and policies can be found, the less need there seems to be for a "civilization" of international transacting and commerce. Succinctly put, there appears to be a substitution: what used to be a quest for nation-state consensus in the interest of convenient and utile international transacting in the seventeenth-century Dutch Republic has become a search for globally uniform and universal norms and policies in modern legal thought.

In the following, I will explore how transnationalization has come to herald the decline of nation-state conflicts law and choice of law. Before beginning my analysis on this topic, however, one final clarification is in order: of course, the concept of transnationalization encompasses more than the domestication of international legal norms or policies. Orders of transnational quality may implement norms of public international law origin, as well as private law norms unrelated to the law of nations or nation-state regimes. The latter category is usually discussed under the labels of the medieval *lex mercatoria* and its modern counterparts of the new law merchant. Mainly created by private parties, these regimes seek to govern interindividual relations.[53] They do not, however, encompass regulatory or policy-oriented subject matter beyond what is required for international commerce.[54] Third-party and public interests are seldom part of the contracting parties' focus. Since these concerns are central to trademark and unfair competition law, both in substance and with respect to choice of law, however, the *lex mercatoria* is not important for this inquiry. Hence, I will focus on the debate's "regulatory" side.

A Transnationalization: A Resurrection of the *Ius Cosmopoliticum*

As mentioned earlier, US conflicts theory witnessed an era of introspection. The mid-century conflicts revolution was described as a product of parochialism—reflecting a "time when interest in foreign law and transnational issues was at an all-time low among American conflicts thinkers."[55]

[53] Leon E. Trakman, *The Law Merchant: The Evolution of Commercial Law* 7 *et seq.* (1983); Gregory Shaffer, *Transnational Legal Process and State Change*, 37 Law & Soc. Inquiry 229, 232–233 (2012).

[54] Ralf Michaels, *The True Lex Mercatoria: Law beyond the State*, 14 Ind. J. Glob. Leg. Stud. 447, 457 (2007).

[55] Matthias Reimann, *A New Restatement—For the International Age*, 75 Ind. L.J. 575, 578 (2000).

But the 1950s were not an era of complete seclusion. On the contrary, the second half of the century saw a sketch of internationalism formulated by Philip C. Jessup in 1956. His ideas would come to dominate modern conflicts law theory in the late twentieth and early twenty-first centuries.[56] Jessup's idea of transnational law relied heavily on traditional categories of international legal orders, particularly in the field of maritime law.[57] But he also opened the door for a new and heretofore largely unanalyzed concept of a *Weltrecht*, or of a global *droit idéal*. As Jessup expected, national law and public international law would merge and bring out a new substance. This hybrid was what he explained as transnational law, comprising "all law which regulates actions or events that transcend national frontiers. Both public and private international law are included, as are other rules which do not wholly fit into such standard categories."[58] Almost necessarily, this hybridity implied a universality (or near universality) of content. And inevitably, it seemed to dissolve conflicts law—when there is no longer a divergence on the substance of norms, the need for conflicts resolution disappears. In a sense, therefore, Jessup's theory of transnational law paved the way for modern concepts of the *ius cosmopoliticum*.

Of course, none of these ideas were new in 1956. In fact, the *ius cosmopoliticum*, understood as the legal order governing within an international community of private individuals, was already the basis of Savigny's system.[59] The expectation that conflicts law would become obsolete with the progress of substantive-norm harmonization had also already been expressed.[60] What Jessup's twentieth-century formulation of transnational law and the *ius cosmopoliticum* brought to the fore, however, was an exclusivity of normative substance. Early conceptions of international comity, of the community of nation-states, and of an international consensus on conflicts law, all had a technical corrective in common. They were built on the idea that conflicts resolution would

[56] For an early comparative analysis of transnational legal norms and substantive law theory, *see* Rudolf Fränkel, *Der Irrgarten des internationalen Privatrechts*, 4 RabelsZ 239, 241–242 (1930). For later scholarship in Germany, *see, e.g.*, Rudolf Wiethölter, *Zur Frage des internationalen ordre public*, 133, 158, in *Berichte der Deutschen Gesellschaft für Völkerrecht, vol. 7* (1967); Eugen Langen, *Vom Internationalen Privatrecht zum Transnationalen Handelsrecht*, 1969 NJW 358; Eugen Langen, *Transnationales Handelrecht*, 1969 NJW 2229; Eugen Langen, *Transnationales Recht* (1981).

[57] *See* Philip C. Jessup, *Transnational Law (Storrs Lectures on Jurisprudence)* 108 *et seq.* (1956).

[58] *Id.* at 2.

[59] *See, e.g.*, Klaus Vogel, *Der räumliche Anwendungsbereich der Verwaltungsrechtsnorm* 220 (1965); Christian Joerges, *Die klassische Konzeption des internationalen Privatrechts und das Recht des unlauteren Wettbewerbs*, 36 RabelsZ 421, 434 (1972); Ernst-Joachim Mestmäcker, *Staatliche Souveränität und offene Märkte—Konflikte bei der extraterritorialen Anwendung von Wirtschaftsrecht*, 52 RabelsZ 205, 213 *et seq.* (1988).

[60] *See infra* p. 398 *et seq.*

always have to give regard to a fundamental interest: upholding the utility and convenience of international transactions and commercial exchanges. This aspect was dropped in the course of the twentieth-century transnationalization of the private and public international legal orders.

B The Historical Leitmotif: Convenience of International Transacting

The doctrine of international comity is inseparably connected with seventeenth-century scholar Huber.[61] According to Huber, three axioms of interstate cooperation followed from the territorial sovereignty of the nation-state. In order to establish and maintain a functioning system of international law, the following had to be guaranteed:

(1) the laws of sovereign nation-states have force within, but not beyond, states' boundaries;
(2) only those individuals found within a nation-state's boundaries—regardless of whether they are there permanently or temporarily—are subject to the nation-state's authority; and
(3) sovereign authority must be exercised by way of comity, and the laws of every nation-state should retain their effect everywhere as long as they do not prejudice the powers or rights of another state or its subjects.[62]

In essence, a clear division exists between the sovereign state's internal affairs and the external domain of public international law. For the internal sphere, international comity is supposed to provide for rules of recognition and effectuation of another sovereign's acts or laws. This concerns, for instance, the recognition and enforcement of foreign courts' verdicts. In the external arena, the doctrine of comity prevents a state from extending its power to the territory governed by another sovereign.[63] This latter aspect is of interest for my analysis. Comity was usually understood as

[61] For the Dutch school and its theorists' contributions, *see, e.g.*, Kurt Lipstein, *The General Principles of Private International Law*, 135 Recueil des Cours 97, 121 *et seq.* (1972-I); Alex Mills, *The Private History of International Law*, 55 I.C.L.Q. 1, 24 *et seq.* (2006).

[62] Translated in D. J. Llewelyn Davies, *The Influence of Huber's de Conflictu Legum on English Private International Law*, 18 Brit. Y.B. Int'l L. 49, 56–67 (1937). *See also* Ernest G. Lorenzen, *Huber's De Conflictu Legum*, 136, 162 *et seq.*, in *Selected Articles on the Conflict of Laws* (Ernest G. Lorenzen ed., 1947).

[63] Huber's theses were incorporated into both civil law and common law theory and practice. *See* Joseph Story, *Commentaries on the Conflict of Laws* § 38, at 37 (1834) (with numerous references in n. 3). More recently, *see, e.g.*, Kurt H. Nadelmann, *Introduction to Yntema, The Comity Doctrine*, 65 Mich. L. Rev. 1, 2 *et seq.* (1966); Joel R. Paul, *Comity in International Law*, 32 Harv. Int'l L.J. 1, 17 *et seq.* (1991). For an extensive discussion of the doctrine's history and development, *see* Ernest G. Lorenzen, *Huber's De Conflictu Legum*, 136 *et seq.*, in *Selected Articles on the Conflict of Laws* (Ernest G. Lorenzen, 1947); D. J. Llewelyn Davies, *The Influence of Huber's de Conflictu Legum on English Private International Law*, 18 Brit. Y.B. Int'l L. 49, 52 (1937); Hessel E. Yntema, *The Comity*

offering a guideline for political decision making in the sense of providing a standard for a state's external conduct.[64] The doctrine was not seen as possessing a normative quality; it merely defined—not prescribed—a system of the international legal order.[65] This characteristic of unenforceable voluntariness, combined with a lack of clear structures, has been the major obstacle to the doctrine's practical implementation. As Harold Maier has sarcastically, yet fittingly, explained, comity doctrine has never overcome the stage of describing "an amorphous never-never land whose borders are marked by fuzzy lines of politics, courtesy, and good faith."[66]

In the debate over whether comity is a doctrine of mere political content, however, one important aspect has often been neglected: Huber not only contended that comity was a corollary of nation-state sovereignty but also described compliance with the doctrine's requirements as a precondition for the unhindered functioning of international transacting and commerce. This understanding also surfaces in Story's and Savigny's later works on the conflict of laws. Even though their

Doctrine, 65 Mich. L. Rev. 9 (1966); more recently William S. Dodge, *International Comity in American Law*, 115 Colum. L. Rev. 2071 (2015).

64 For the *Charming Betsy* doctrine and its function of avoiding conflicts with (stronger) foreign nations, *see Talbot v. Seeman*, 5 U.S. 1 (1801); Frederick C. Leiner, *The Charming Betsy and the Marshall Court*, 45 Am. J. Leg. Hist. 1, 18 (2001).

65 *See Hilton v. Guyot*, 159 U.S. 113, 163–164 (1895) (" 'Comity,' in the legal sense, is neither a matter of absolute obligation, on the one hand, nor of mere courtesy and good will, upon the other."). *See also* Joseph H. Beale, *A Treatise on the Conflict of Laws, vol. III: Administration and Procedure* § 71 (1935) ("The doctrine [of comity] seems really to mean only that in certain cases the sovereign is not prevented by any principle of international law, but only by his own choice, from establishing any rule he pleases for the conflict of laws. In other words, it is an enabling principle rather than one which in any particular case would determine the actual rule of law."); Otto Kahn-Freund, *The Growth of Internationalism in English Private International Law (Lionel Cohen Lectures)* 8 (1960) ("[C]omity supplies a legislative motive rather than a legislative content. In this respect it is comparable to the 'maxims of equity' rather than to a particular legal norm."); Michael Akehurst, *Jurisdiction in International Law*, 46 Brit. Y.B. Int'l L. 145, 215 *et seq.* (1972/73).

66 Harold G. Maier, *Extraterritorial Jurisdiction at a Crossroads: An Intersection between Public and Private International Law*, 76 Am. J. Int'l L. 280, 281 (1982); *see also* Samuel Livermore, *Dissertations on the Questions which arise from the Contrariety of the Positive Laws of Different States and Nations* 27 (1828) ("Comity implies a right to reject; and the consequence of such rejection would probably be a judgment ordering a party to do that, which he had never obligated himself to do. This phrase has not always been harmless in its effects, for I have not unfrequently seen it inspire judges with so great confidence in their own authority, that arrogating to themselves sovereign power, they have disregarded the foreign law, which ought to have governed their decision, because of some fancied inconvenience, which might result to the citizens of their state."); *Loucks v. Standard Oil Co.*, 120 N.E. 198, 201–202, 224 N.Y. 99, 111 (N.Y. 1918) (Cardozo, J.) ("The misleading word 'comity' has been responsible for much of the trouble. It has been fertile in suggesting a discretion unregulated by general principles.").

teachings have often been explained as founded on different conceptions of comity and of the relationship between private and public international law, they share common ground regarding the fact that the international consensus on jurisdiction is not a deontological concept based on axioms of territoriality and sovereignty alone. The doctrine of comity is also the means to an end insofar as it is supposed to guarantee useful and convenient international transacting and commerce.

1 Joseph Story: The Consensual Administration of Conflicts

Story's 1834 *Commentaries on the Conflict of Laws* was founded on the concept of private international law as a branch of both public law and public international law.[67] This was a consequence of his understanding that the central principle of the field was the "equality and independence of nations."[68] At the same time, it reflects a concern that private law conflicts avoidance was necessary to guarantee and maintain political order at the interstate level of the young American union. As is well explored, Story's understanding of comity was influenced by a conflict smoldering in the 1800s in the United States: frictions between free states and slave states within the union were commonplace.[69] The conflict between a slaveholder's assertion of property rights in slaves and a freed slave's right to personal liberty could not be resolved without leaving one side frustrated.[70] Under Story's concept, comity was conflicts resolution's lowest common denominator. It virtually guaranteed reconciling the irreconcilable by localizing slaveholder rights within their respective fora. Comity would neither require a free state to acknowledge property rights in slaves nor require a slave state to accept the liberty of recaptured slaves.[71] In other words, there was no "absolute paramount obligation, superseding all discretion on the subject." Accordingly, the doctrine was

[67] Joseph Story, *Commentaries on the Conflict of Laws* § 9, at 9 (1834). For Story's understanding of public and private international law as part of the same field of law, *see, e.g.*, F. A. Mann, *The Doctrine of Jurisdiction in International Law*, 111 Recueil des Cours 1, 33 (1964-I); Joel R. Paul, *Comity in International Law*, 32 Harv. Int'l L.J. 1, 25 and 78 (1991).

[68] Joseph Story, *Commentaries on the Conflict of Laws* § 8, at 8 (1834).

[69] For the historical background on Story's commentaries, *see* Paul Finkelman, *An Imperfect Union: Slavery, Federalism, and Comity* (1981); more recently, Paul Finkelman, *When International Law Was a Domestic Problem*, 44 Val. U. L. Rev. 779, 802 *et seq.* (2010); Joel R. Paul, *Comity in International Law*, 32 Harv. Int'l L.J. 1, 19 *et seq.* (1991); Joel R. Paul, *The Transformation of International Comity*, 71 Law & Contemp. Probs. 19, 24 (2008). For a critical assessment of this historical explanation, *see*, however, Alan Watson, *Joseph Story and the Comity of Errors—A Case Study in the Conflict of Laws* (1992).

[70] For Story's emphatic rejection of slavery while sitting as a justice in Massachusetts, *see U.S. v. the La Jeune Eugenie*, 26 F. Cas. 832, 845 (C.C.D. Mass. 1822).

[71] Joel R. Paul, *Comity in International Law*, 32 Harv. Int'l L.J. 1, 24 (1991).

to be considered "not the comity of the courts, but the comity of the nation."[72]

Nevertheless, as Story also explained, comity had to be "administered, and ascertained in the same way, and guided by the same reasoning, by which all other principles of the municipal law are ascertained and guided."[73] Comity, hence, did have a normative character. Even though there was no absolute legal obligation to afford foreign laws a priority of application, deciding which law to apply and how far to extend a national regime was an issue of legal analysis. One aspect is important here. Story's formulation of the function of the comity doctrine deeply embraced Huber's conception. Avoiding the distortion of interstate transacting was paramount; anything else would be "inconvenient to commerce and to international usage."[74] As Story put it:

> The true foundation, on which the administration of international law must rest, is, that the rules, which are to govern, are those, which arise from mutual interest and utility, from a sense of the inconveniences, which would result from a contrary doctrine, and from a sort of moral necessity to do justice, in order that justice may be done to us in return.[75]

Under this perspective, the patchwork of national regimes was held together by a system of self-restraint.[76] The doctrine of comity was a

[72] Joseph Story, *Commentaries on the Conflict of Laws* § 33, at 33, and § 36, at 36 (1834). For the same interpretation and reference to Story in modern case law, *see, e.g.*, *Laker Airways Ltd. v. Sabena, Belgian World Airlines*, 731 F.2d 909, 937 (D.C.C., 1984) (with further case-law references).

[73] Joseph Story, *Commentaries on the Conflict of Laws* § 38, at 37 (1834).

[74] *See* Ulrich Huber, *De Conflictu Legum* (translation in Ernest G. Lorenzen, *Selected Articles on the Conflict of Laws* 164–165 (1947) ("[T]he solution to the [choice-of-law] problem must be derived not exclusively from the civil law, but from convenience and the tacit consent of nations. Although the laws of one nation can have no force directly with another, yet nothing could be more inconvenient to commerce and to international usage than that transactions valid by the law of one place should be rendered of no effect elsewhere on account of a difference in the law.").

[75] Joseph Story, *Commentaries on the Conflict of Laws* § 35, at 34 (1834) with reference to Samuel Livermore, among others. More than five years earlier, in similar words, Livermore had formulated this concern in his *Dissertations on the Questions which arise from the Contrariety of the Positive Laws of Different States and Nations* 27–28 (1828) ("Even with sovereigns it is not so clear, that the recognition of foreign laws is merely a matter of comity. . . . if a desire to promote their own interest induces them to cultivate an intercourse with other people, they must necessarily adopt such principles, as a sense of common utility and of justice will inspire. . . . It has not been from comity, but from a sense of mutual utility, that nations have admitted the extension of personal statutes. It has arisen from a sort of necessity, and from a sense of the inconveniences which would result from a contrary doctrine, by which the state and condition of a man, his capacity or incapacity, would change with every change of abode, for however short a time or transitory purpose.").

[76] Ernest G. Lorenzen, *Story's Commentaries on the Conflict of Laws—One Hundred Years After*, 48 Harv. L. Rev. 15, 35 (1934); *see also* Donald Earl Childress III, *Comity as*

true civilizer of international transacting. And Story qualified the system in one more respect: mutuality under the command of common utility further required that "the interest of all nations [be] consulted, and not that of only one."[77] This interpretation of Huberian maxims made the consideration of genuinely internationalist concerns the paradigm of conflicts resolution. In addition, it implemented a dynamic method of interest reconciliation. The aim was not to achieve international fairness or to promulgate a one-size-fits-all rule[78]—it was to establish a process-based model of interest balancing, which would guarantee the smooth functioning of international transacting.

2 *Friedrich Carl von Savigny: A Legal Community* In Statu Nascendi
Prima facie, Savigny's understanding of the international legal order and its impact on national choice of law was fundamentally different. As has often been explained, Savigny formally replaced comity and public international law with abstract and apolitical choice-of-law mechanics.[79] In his system of transmissive private law regimes, the equivalence and substitutability of domestic and foreign private law became the governing paradigm. Indeed, it almost seems as if he thereby emancipated choice-of-law theory from the need to consider comity and from the need to give regard to nation-state sovereignty. In essence, as is commonly contended, Savigny privatized the system of choice of law.[80]

In this light, Savigny's system appears to be anything but founded on public international law or comity.[81] This is correct as far as his technique

Conflict: Resituating International Comity as Conflict of Laws, 44 U.C. Davis L. Rev. 11, 27 *et seq.* (2010).

77 Joseph Story, *Commentaries on the Conflict of Laws* § 36, at 36 (1834).

78 Against this idea, *see id.* at § 28, at 29.

79 Paul Heinrich Neuhaus, *Savigny und die Rechtsfindung aus der Natur der Sache*, 15 RabelsZ 364, 372–373 (1949/50); Ulrike Seif, *Savigny und das Internationale Privatrecht des 19. Jahrhunderts*, 65 RabelsZ 492, 508 (2001).

80 *See, e.g.*, Christian Joerges, *Zum Funktionswandel des Kollisionsrechts—Die "Governmental Interest Analysis" und die "Krise des Internationalen Privatrechts"* 7 *et seq.* (1971); Fritz Sturm, *Savigny und das internationale Privatrecht seiner Zeit*, 92, 106, in *Ius Commune VIII (Vorträge zum 200. Geburtstag von F.C. von Savigny)* (Helmut Coing ed., 1979); Ralf Michaels, *Globalizing Savigny? The State in Savigny's Private International Law and the Challenge from Europeanization and Globalization*, 119, 132, in *Aktuelle Fragen zu politischer und rechtlicher Steuerung im Kontext der Globalisierung* (Michael Stolleis & Wolfgang Streeck eds., 2007); Ralf Michaels, *The New European Choice-of-Law Revolution*, 82 Tul. L. Rev. 1607, 1613 (2008).

81 At least, this appears to be common ground among modern European scholars. *See, e.g.*, Christian Joerges, *Zum Funktionswandel des Kollisionsrechts—Die "Governmental Interest Analysis" und die "Krise des Internationalen Privatrechts"* 7 *et seq.* (1971); Egon Lorenz, *Zur Struktur des Internationalen Privatrechts* 49–50 (1977); Paul Heinrich Neuhaus, *Der Beitrag des Völkerrechts zum internationalen Privatrecht*, 21 German Y.B. of Int'l L. 60, 62 (1978); Christian Joerges, *Vorüberlegungen zu einer Theorie des internationalen*

for conflicts resolution is concerned. Yet his conception, like Story's model of mutuality and utility, was still based on the idea of a legal community of nations. As he explained, what was to be achieved was a "*völkerrechtliche Gemeinschaft der miteinander verkehrenden Nationen.*"[82] Literally, this translates to a "public international law community of transacting nations."[83] In 1869, William Guthrie changed this into a slightly awkward sounding "international common law of nations having intercourse with one another."[84] But these ambiguities aside, the gist of what Savigny wanted to express remains untouched: he deemed the legal community

Wirtschaftsrechts, 43 RabelsZ 6, 11 *et seq.* (1979); Fritz Sturm, *Savigny und das internationale Privatrecht seiner Zeit*, 92, 106, in *Ius Commune VIII (Vorträge zum 200. Geburtstag von F.C. von Savigny)* (Helmut Coing ed., 1979); Gerhard Kegel, *Story and Savigny*, 37 Am. J. Comp. L. 39, 58–59 (1989); Ulrike Seif, *Savigny und das Internationale Privatrecht des 19. Jahrhunderts*, 65 RabelsZ 492, 508–509 (2001); Ralf Michaels, *The New European Choice-of-Law Revolution*, 82 Tul. L. Rev. 1607, 1614 (2008); *but see, e.g.*, Arthur Nussbaum, *Rise and Decline of the Law-of-Nations Doctrine in the Conflict of Laws*, 42 Colum. L. Rev. 189, 192 (1942) ("Savigny clearly agrees with the Dutch jurists in that, as a matter of principle, he puts the conflicts doctrine upon an international basis. He differs, however, from them in that he deems the independent nations bound by international law (rather than by comity) to apply in the appropriate cases the laws of other members of that international community."); John R. Stevenson, *The Relationship of Private International Law to Public International Law*, 52 Colum. L. Rev. 561, 565 (1952) (explaining that the law-of-nations theory "received its initial impetus" from Savigny's writings); Max Gutzwiller, *Der Einfluß Savignys auf die Entwicklung des Internationalprivatrechts* 43–44 (1923) (*cf. id.* at 43: "Für Savigny ist die völkerrechtliche Gemeinschaft 'Grundlage und letztes Ziel unserer ganzen Lehre'; sie, und sie allein ermöglicht den selbständigen, eben internationalen Kern seiner Theorie ..." with *id.* at 44: "Diese Rechtsgemeinschaft ist die nicht wegzudenkende Grundbedingung für die Möglichkeit einer allgemeingiltigen Theorie; Savigny zufolge soll sie die Basis sein, und er behauptet für diese Basis Positivität. Hier aber liegen die Grenzen seiner Lehre. In Wirklichkeit stehen seine völkerrechtliche Behauptung und die Ableitung seines Hauptsatzes vom 'Sitze' nebeneinander und sind durch keine juristische Konstruktion in Beziehung gesetzt. Savigny zieht aus seiner völkerrechtlichen Grundlage keine einzige der vielen denkbaren Folgerungen ...."); Franz Kahn, *Gesetzeskollisionen—Ein Beitrag zur Lehre des internationalen Privatrechts*, 1, 3, in *Abhandlungen zum internationalen Privatrecht, vol. I* (Otto Lenel & Hans Lewald eds., 1928) ("[D]ie andere [Auffassung], welche man auf *Savigny* zurückführen kann, ... erkennt darin ein internationales Recht im eigentlichsten Sinn, dessen Quelle außerhalb der einzelnen Territorialgesetzgebungen zu suchen ist, ein 'werdendes Weltrecht'." (with numerous contemporary references)).

[82] Friedrich Carl von Savigny, *System des heutigen römischen Rechts, vol. VIII* § 348, at 27 (1849).

[83] For illustration of the so-called *Rechtsgemeinschaft der Völker, see* Friedrich K. Juenger, *Choice of Law and Multistate Justice* 36 (1993). For further reference to the legal community of nations ("*völkerrechtliche* Gemeinschaft") in volume VIII of Savigny's system, *see* Friedrich Carl von Savigny, *System des heutigen römischen Rechts, vol. VIII* § 348 (at 27, 29, 30, 31), § 349 (at 35), § 360 (at 117), § 361 (at 128), § 365 (at 160), and § 374 (at 288 and 292–293) (1849).

[84] Friedrich Carl von Savigny, *Private International Law and the Retrospective Operation of Statutes—A Treatise on the Conflict of Laws and the Limits of Their Operation in Respect of Place and Time* § 348, at 70 (William Guthrie transl., 2nd edn., 1880).

or the international common law of nations not only the foundation but the ultimate goal ("highest aim") of all conflicts and choice-of-law theory.[85] Indeed, this approach was distinctly internationalist: since the community of nations was governed by a paradigm of amenable relations among equal sovereigns, any member was encouraged to construct its conflicts regime accordingly.[86] This ultimately contradicts the conclusion that Savigny intended to jettison public international law and international comity as the basis of his system. Savigny's idea of private law may have been apolitical,[87] but it did not require isolating choice of law from the influence of the sphere that constituted relations among sovereign nations.

Moreover, like Story, Savigny conceived of this community as being founded not only on common values and Christianity but also on a quest for mutual benefit and utility.[88] As he explained, in the absence of binding choice-of-law norms (and such an absence was regularly the case in his time), judges would not be free to ignore foreign law and revert to the *lex fori*.[89] On the contrary:

> The more multifarious and active the intercourse between different nations, the more will … reciprocity in dealing with cases which is so desirable, and the consequent equality in judging between natives and foreigners, which, on the

[85] Friedrich Carl von Savigny, *Private International Law and the Retrospective Operation of Statutes—A Treatise on the Conflict of Laws and the Limits of Their Operation in Respect of Place and Time* § 360, at 138 (William Guthrie transl., 2nd edn., 1880). For the original text, *see* Friedrich Carl von Savigny, *System des heutigen römischen Rechts, vol. VIII* § 360, at 117 (1849) ("[D]ie angenommene Gegenseitigkeit, die sich, allgemeiner aufgefaßt, in eine völkerrechtliche Gemeinschaft, als Grundlage und letztes Ziel unsrer ganzen Lehre auflöst (§ 348).").

[86] Alexander N. Makarov, "Internationales Privatrecht und Völkerrecht," 129, 129, in *Wörterbuch des Völkerrechts, vol. II* (Hans-Jürgen Schlochauer ed., 2nd edn., 1961); *see also* Ulrich Drobnig, *Private International Law*, 1115, 1115, in *Encyclopedia of Public International Law, vol. III* (R. Bernhardt ed., 1997).

[87] *See, e.g.*, Friedrich Carl von Savigny, *System des heutigen Römischen Rechts, vol. I* § 9, at 22–23 (1840) ("[Das Privatrecht hat zum Gegenstand] die Gesammtheit der Rechtsverhältnisse, welche den einzelnen Menschen umgeben, damit er in ihnen sein inneres Leben führe und zu einer bestimmten Gestalt bilde … daß in dem Privatrecht der einzelne Mensch für sich Zweck ist, und jedes Rechtsverhältnis sich nur als Mittel auf sein Daseyn oder seine besonderen Zustände bezieht.").

[88] *See also* Gerhard Kegel, *Story and Savigny*, 37 Am. J. Comp. L. 39, 57 n. 125 (1989) (on the wide contemporary agreement (with references) on the subject of mutual utility and convenience). Similar to Savigny, though prior to Story, *see* Samuel Livermore, *Dissertations on the Questions which arise from the Contrariety of the Positive Laws of Different States and Nations* 30 (1828).

[89] Savigny found the judge to be bound by domestic statutory law on the issue of conflicts. Yet, as he also explained, this obligation was not overly broad for want of a sophisticated contemporary doctrine on the issue. *See* Friedrich Carl von Savigny, *Private International Law and the Retrospective Operation of Statutes—A Treatise on the Conflict of Laws and the Limits of Their Operation in Respect of Place and Time* § 361, at 146 (William Guthrie transl., 2nd edn., 1880). For the original text, *see* Friedrich Carl von Savigny, *System des heutigen römischen Rechts, vol. VIII* § 361, at 130 (1849).

whole, is dictated by the common interest of nations and of individuals ... [effectuate] that, in cases of conflict of laws, the same legal relations (cases) have to expect the same decision, whether the judgment be pronounced in this state or in that.

The standpoint to which this consideration leads us, is that of an international common law [i.e. a public international law community] of nations having intercourse with one another; and this view has in the course of time always obtained wider recognition, under the influence of a common Christian morality, and of the real advantage which results from it to all concerned.[90]

The interest in a seamless functioning of the international system, understood in terms of socioeconomic transacting, was expressed in the concept of respecting foreign states' laws and of a harmony of decision making.

Finally, Savigny emphasized one aspect as being the most determinative: the evolution of legal doctrine on choice of law was expected to mirror nation-state consensus. As he explained, within the community, a constant evolution of choice-of-law norms toward a uniform system had already set in. The final stage of international uniformity should be established either by scholarly theory and its practical implementation or by means of international agreements and treaties. With respect to normative content, both ways would ultimately have to follow the same guideline. Each rule of choice of law would have to pass a test to determine whether it could be transformed into an international agreement:

If the development of the law thus begun is not disturbed by unforeseen external circumstances, it may be expected that it will at length lead to a complete accord in the treatment of questions of collision in all states. Such an accord might be brought about by means of juridical science, and the practice of the tribunals guided by it. It could also be effected by a positive law, agreed to and enacted by all states, with respect to the collision of territorial laws. I do not say that this is likely, or even that it would be more convenient and salutary than mere scientific agreement; but the notion of such a law may serve as a standard to test every rule that we shall lay down as to collision. We have always to ask ourselves whether such a rule would be well adapted for reception into that common statute law of all nations.[91]

[90] Friedrich Carl von Savigny, *Private International Law and the Retrospective Operation of Statutes—A Treatise on the Conflict of Laws and the Limits of Their Operation in Respect of Place and Time* § 348, at 69–70 (William Guthrie transl., 2nd edn., 1880). For the original text, *see* Friedrich Carl von Savigny, *System des heutigen römischen Rechts, vol. VIII* § 348, at 26–27 (1849).

[91] Friedrich Carl von Savigny, *Private International Law and the Retrospective Operation of Statutes—A Treatise on the Conflict of Laws and the Limits of Their Operation in Respect of Place and Time* § 360, at 137 (William Guthrie transl., 2nd edn., 1880). For the original text, *see* Friedrich Carl von Savigny, *System des heutigen römischen Rechts, vol. VIII* § 360, at 114–115 (1849). *See also id.* at § 348, at 28 and 30–31. For an understanding of Savigny's reasoning as seeking a "pure law" and as an ontological concept (limited to analysis of § 348), *see* Joachim Rückert, *The Unrecognized Legacy: Savigny's Influence on German Jurisprudence after 1900*, 37 Am. J. Comp. L. 121, 136 (1989).

On this evolutionary basis, Savigny saw the complete disappearance of conflicts as a mere matter of time. He expected the number of conflicts between political and absolute norms outside the system of apolitical and interchangeable private law norms to shrink continuously:

> These two cla[s]ses of absolute laws, however they may differ in other respects, agree in this: that they are withdrawn from that community of law between all states of which we have asserted the existence in regard to collisions; and they are therefore, in this respect, anomalous. It is to be expected, however, that these exceptional cases will gradually be diminished with the natural legal development of nations.[92]

Gerhard Kegel later explained that "[t]he 'völkerrechtliche Gemeinschaft' thus has the double task of privatizing private international law and of driving it towards universal uniformity (so that it will be judged according to the same law everywhere)."[93] This understanding of an ultimate uniformity was further extended at the end of the nineteenth century.

3 Ernst Zitelmann: The Weltrecht *of Uniform Policy*

But the extension had a slightly different angle that would prove significant for the development of internationalist legal thought throughout the twentieth century. One example of the early conceptions of a transnational law—which lucidly illustrates the roots of modern legal thought on transnationalization and its deviation from earlier conflicts-based approaches—is Ernst Zitelmann's 1888 proposal for a *Weltrecht*.

Zitelmann's *Weltrecht* concerned more than a system of conflicts resolution and choice of law—it proposed the far more ambitious concept of *substantive* uniformity of norms and policies. At the same time, his suggestion stayed behind these earlier conceptions insofar as he did not describe uniformity as being founded on public international legal standards or the doctrine of comity; instead, he substituted the idea of interstate consensus and compromise with a new paradigm. The *Weltrecht*, Zitelmann explained, would be a uniform substantive law governing all nations, at least those with a Christian culture.[94] Focusing on private law, he called for distinguishing several aspects of uniformity and universality. His starting point was the assumption that the rules of logic and reason were universal in nature. Accordingly, any legal system would have to be

[92] Friedrich Carl von Savigny, *Private International Law and the Retrospective Operation of Statutes—A Treatise on the Conflict of Laws and the Limits of Their Operation in Respect of Place and Time* § 349, at 80 (William Guthrie transl., 2nd edn., 1880). For the original text, *see* Friedrich Carl von Savigny, *System des heutigen römischen Rechts, vol. VIII* § 349, at 38 (1849).

[93] Gerhard Kegel, *Story and Savigny*, 37 Am. J. Comp. L. 39, 59 (1989).

[94] Ernst Zitelmann, *Die Möglichkeit eines Weltrechts* 5 (1888).

founded on an identical structure of legal reasoning.[95] In an allegory, he compared the legal order to human language, describing the structure of a legal system as analogous to grammar. While the content of each system may vary, the overall structures of human expression (language/law) are the same.[96] Further, he identified several factors as determinative for unification toward a *Weltrecht*: ethics, religion, utility, and consistency.[97] Among these factors, Zitelmann found utility to be the most important with respect to the trend toward a global private law. He argued that whenever real-world circumstances in different states were identical or similar, these different states' legal norms would automatically find the one utile and consistent—hence, socioeconomically reasonable—legal solution.[98]

In this respect, Zitelmann's *praesumptio similitudinis* anticipated the quintessence of modern transnational law theory. He provided the ground for a streamlining along the lines of globally uniform standards and metrics. The identity of real-world circumstances and structures was what accounted for the transnationalization of norms. Uniformity was no longer an issue of conflicts law or choice of law but a question of substantive law policy. Furthermore, unlike Storyan and Savignian concepts, Zitelmann's *Weltrecht* was detached from the law-of-nations paradigm and international comity.[99]

4 Summary

A common theme among theorists since Huber was the idea that it was paramount for conflicts law and choice of law to guarantee frictionless

95 *Id.* at 13 ("Damit ist die überall gleiche logische Form des Rechtssatzes gegeben: auch sie ist weltrechtlicher Natur.").

96 *Id.* at 9–10 ("Wir wollen ein neues Buch kennen lernen, wir ahnen nicht, welchen Gedankeninhalt es birgt—aber eines wissen wir sicher: die logische Gliederung der Satzteile wird die uns bekannte sein, Subjekte, Prädikate usw. werden auch hier unterschieden sein müssen. Das ganze Verstehenkönnen fremder Rede beruht darauf; es wäre unmöglich, wenn wir nicht von vornherein absolut sicher wären, dasselbe logische Gefüge, in dem wir selbst denken, auch in der fremden Gedankenmitteilung wiederzufinden. In diesem Sinne gibt es eine einheitliche Sprachlehre, in gleichem Sinne auch eine einheitliche Rechtslehre."). For Zitelmann's rejection of natural law theory, *see id.* at 8–9.

97 *Id.* at 14 *et seq.*, particularly *id.* at 17 ("Zu entscheiden haben die ethischen und religiösen Ideen, welche wir als wahr anerkennen, die Zweckmäßigkeitserwägungen, welche objektiv für die gegebenen Verhältnisse richtig sind, d.h. das wirklich Zweckmäßige treffen, und die Konsequenzziehungen, welche logisch gerechtfertigt sind.").

98 *Id.* at 19 ("Man wird vielmehr finden, daß einmal ein sehr großer Teil der grundlegenden Sätze unseres Privatrechts in seiner Wirkung, also in seiner Zweckmäßigkeit von Verhältnissen abhängt, die überall völlig einander konform sind: er bezieht sich auf wirtschaftliche Grundtatsachen, welche mit Notwendigkeit bei jedem Volke dieselben sind. Weil aber diese einfachsten Faktoren, mit denen der Rechtssatz zu rechnen hat, die gleichen sind, so kann auch der Rechtssatz der gleiche sein.").

99 *Id.* at 35 *et seq.; see also* Peter Klein, *Die Möglichkeit eines Weltprivatrechts*, 3, 6 *et seq.*, in *Festschrift für Ernst Zitelmann* (Fritz Stier-Somlo ed., 1913).

and convenient transacting in the international arena. Story was the first to convincingly explain this idea for conflicts law on the basis of nation-state consensus. Building on Story, Savigny further projected it into the concept of a legal community of sovereign nations. His ideal was to have nation-states agree on universal norms of choice of law. Most characteristic of this theory is its proponents' understanding of "consensus." As Huber, Story, and Savigny agreed, it was not actual consensus among nation-states or within the international community as such that was required; the aim was to simulate such a consensus in order to establish and maintain the utility and convenience of international transacting. Seen in this light, two aspects can be explained as characteristic of traditional doctrine. One is the function of nation-state sovereignty. Since nation-states constitute the international community, any model of conflicts law or choice of law must be founded on the principles of public international law and on the doctrine of international comity. The other aspect concerns the supra-positivistic side of conflicts law that aims to secure the utility and convenience of international transacting and commerce.

Comparing these traditional authorities with the modern debate on transnationalism highlights a phenomenon that has been largely overlooked: the quite practical concerns of facilitating and civilizing international transacting and commerce explained by Huber, Story, and Savigny seem to have virtually sunk into oblivion throughout the last century. This is most illustratively reflected in Zitelmann's *Weltrecht*. His concept of a global coalescence of private law norms is a theory of substantive uniformity. It was in his model where the most characteristic feature of transnationalization made its first appearance, which can actually be explained as an early parting of the ways: Zitelmann no longer required a context of public international law, nor did he conceive of conflicts law or choice of law as a functional element of international transacting and commerce. Modern theory has carried these ideas further.

C The Modernity of Transnational Law: An Apotheosis of Substantive Uniformity

The idea that national laws would converge over time always inspired theorists to search for a global uniformity of values and policies. In this regard, Jessup provided the theoretical foundation for the modern process of transnationalization. His concept of transnational law hybridity and uniformity implied an evolution toward a *droit idéal* of universal substantive norms. While early twentieth-century theory and practice had still been founded on the nation-state paradigm, Jessup's conceptual framework changed the scenery. From then on, transnationalists no longer had to look through the magnifying glass of nation-state politics; state interests were no longer imperative. Instead, norms and policies created beyond the state and its institutions became the product of a new and increasingly homogeneous world society.

1 *Philip C. Jessup: The Hybridity and Universality of Transnational Law*

According to Jessup, international consensus on regulatory standards and individual rights protection would grow continually over time. One example he used was the evolution of maritime law.[100] But he extended the perspective. Since the categorical confines (e.g., public/private and foreign/domestic) had been blurred, he suggested that the selection and promulgation of norms in conflicts cases follow a standard of convenience:

> Transnational law . . . includes both civil and criminal aspects, it includes what we know as public and private international law, and it includes national law, both public and private. There is no inherent reason why a judicial tribunal, whether national or international, should not be authorized to choose from all of these bodies of law the rule considered to be most in conformity with reason and justice for the solution of any particular controversy.[101]

He prophesized that traditional categories of decision making in conflicts law would vanish.[102] The new standard of decision making was "conformity with reason and justice."[103] In a sense, this idea of conformity adopted and extended Savigny's view of a shrinking domain of true conflicts. As Savigny had anticipated with respect to the doctrine of public policy (*ordre public*), the domain of absolute laws resisting classification under a multilateral system would ultimately be reduced in the course of the expansion of international transacting, the approximation of policies, and the repeated adjudication of international conflicts.[104] Under modern transnational law theory, it is not just the public policy exception that is supposed to disappear over time; the norms to be applied in transnationality will ultimately become universal. In the words of Anne-Marie Slaughter:

> This . . . marks a move from comity among the "world's legal systems," in which judges view one another as operating in equal but distinct legal spheres, to the presumption of an integrated system. This presumption, in turn, rests on a

[100] Philip C. Jessup, *Transnational Law (Storrs Lectures on Jurisprudence)* 108 *et seq.* (1956).
[101] *Id.* at 106.
[102] *Id.* at 106–107 ("The choice need not be determined by territoriality, personality, nationality, domicile, jurisdiction, sovereignty, or any other rubric save as these labels are reasonable reflections of human experience with the absolute and relative convenience of the law and of the forum.").
[103] *Id.* at 106. [104] *See supra* p. 402 *et seq.*

conception of a single global economy, in which borders are increasingly irrelevant, and an accompanying legal system, in which litigants can choose from among multiple fora to resolve a dispute ... Whereas a presumption of a world of separate sovereigns mandates transjudicial relations marked by courtesy and periodic deference, the presumption of an integrated system takes mutual respect for granted and focuses instead on how well the system works.[105]

Here again, Zitelmann's *Weltrecht* comes to mind. The concept of an integrated system of global norms no longer follows the primary aim of securing the utility and convenience of international transacting. It has become an aim in itself. The universality of norms and policies is the ultimate goal.

2 *Twentieth Century: Conflicts Doctrine Internationalized*

As we have seen, traditional European choice of law in the Savignian tradition is structurally indifferent to substantive law policy. It also rarely gives regard to public international law or international comity. Similarly, US theory, notably the American revolutionists, rejected a consideration of public international law.[106] Brainerd Currie may have adopted Story's comity-founded concept insofar as he described sovereign "governmental" interests as determinative. But this was more a technical aspect than a matter of the international legal order. Giving regard to the interests of the community of nation-states or to international comity, as Currie understood, was too vague and speculative to allow for a jettisoning of more concrete domestic concerns.[107] Nevertheless, time and again, public international law and international comity have made inroads into national choice-of-law doctrine. I will focus on the most important examples of these inroads that share a distinct element of internationalism—their ultimate goal is the promulgation of universal norms of conflicts resolution. In a sense, all these approaches have attempted to materialize the contents of international comity. Yet during the twentieth century, this doctrine lost much of its initial gloss when the concept of a truly universal legal order, widely detached from the sphere of nation-state politics and from enforcement issues, made its first appearance in practice.

105 Anne-Marie Slaughter, *A Global Community of Courts*, 44 Harv. Int'l L.J. 191, 204–205 (2003).

106 *See supra* p. 384 *et seq.*

107 For Currie's parallels to *comitas* theory, *see, e.g.*, Albert A. Ehrenzweig, *A Treatise on the Conflict of Laws* § 122, at 348–349 (1962); *see also* Christian Joerges, *Zum Funktionswandel des Kollisionsrechts—Die "Governmental Interest Analysis" und die "Krise des Internationalen Privatrechts"* 61, 83, and 154 *et seq.* (1971); Donald Earl Childress III, *Comity as Conflict: Resituating International Comity as Conflict of Laws*, 44 U.C. Davis L. Rev. 11, 42 *et seq.* (2010).

a *Maritime Internationalism: The* Lauritzen *Doctrine* The American conflicts revolution broke up traditional structures concerning the private/ public law distinction, private rights adjudication, and territoriality. Even though interest analysis acknowledged multistate policies and, accordingly, did not exclude the application of foreign law *ab initio*,[108] *lex fori* prevalence in true-conflict and unprovided-for cases made the consideration of multistate policies just one among several concerns. Around the same time, at the peak of American conflicts parochialism, Jessup coined the concept of transnationalization. He described maritime conflicts cases as a prime example of what had been "predominantly transnational" since antiquity.[109] And, indeed, the US Supreme Court followed a truly internationalist approach in a number of maritime cases beginning in the 1950s. A concern for the functioning of international commerce and transacting was the basic purpose behind this practical internationalism.

In the 1953 case *Lauritzen v. Larsen*,[110] the Supreme Court was tasked with deciding on the application of the Jones Act, a maritime workers' compensation statute. The case centered on a Danish seaman's claim against the Danish owner of a vessel on which he had been employed. The seaman had suffered injuries in the course of this employment. The court deemed the Jones Act inapplicable. Instead, the law of the ship's flag (Danish law) was to be applied. Although the act literally applied to "every seaman," Justice Jackson pointed out that Congress had used such broad language with the understanding that courts would read it to accommodate US interests with those of other countries in light of international legal principles. International maritime law was a universally acknowledged system of regulating international maritime activities:

> It has the force of law, not from extraterritorial reach of national laws, nor from abdication of its sovereign powers by any nation, but from acceptance by common consent of civilized communities of rules designed to foster amicable and workable commercial relations.[111]

The decision formally entailed choice-of-law determination,[112] yet defied both contemporary vested-rights theory and interest analysis. Repeating

[108] *See, e.g.*, Brainerd Currie, *The Disinterested Third State*, 28 Law & Contemp. Probs. 754, 757 *et seq.* (1963); David F. Cavers, *The Choice-of-Law Process* 120–121 (1965); Luther L. McDougal III, *Comprehensive Interest Analysis versus Reformulated Governmental Interest Analysis: An Appraisal in the Context of Choice-of-Law Problems Concerning Contributory and Comparative Negligence*, 26 UCLA L. Rev. 439, 448–449 (1979); Joseph William Singer, *Real Conflicts*, 69 B.U. L. Rev. 1, 47 *et seq.* (1989).

[109] Philip C. Jessup, *Transnational Law (Storrs Lectures on Jurisprudence)* 109–110 (1956).

[110] *Lauritzen v. Larsen*, 345 U.S. 571 (1953). [111] *Id.* at 582.

[112] Maier, however, characterizes *Lauritzen* and *Romero* (*see infra* p. 412–413) as transnational regulatory cases. *See* Harold G. Maier, *Extraterritorial Jurisdiction at a Crossroads: An*

the oft-enunciated dichotomy of public and private international law, the court rejected a narrowly nationalistic and territorial approach in favor of a systemic analysis. "[C]onsiderations of comity, reciprocity and long-range interests"[113] dominated the court's argument.

Similar regard to the "legitimate concern of the international community" was paid a few years later in *Romero v. International Terminal Operating Co.*[114] Again, the court refused to apply the Jones Act, this time to a claim brought by a Spanish seaman on a Spanish-flagged ship owned by a Spanish corporation (even though the injury had occurred in a US port). The *Romero* reasoning made it clear that the court would not undertake a comparative weighing of nation-state interests—instead, the aim was to uphold a reciprocally fair system of international regulation:

> [W]e must apply those principles of choice of law that are consonant with the needs of a general federal maritime law and with due recognition of our self-regarding respect for the relevant interests of foreign nations in the regulation of maritime commerce as part of the legitimate concern of the international community. These principles do not depend upon a mechanical application of a doctrine like that of *lex loci delicti commissi*. The controlling considerations are the interacting interests of the United States and of foreign countries, and in assessing them we must move with the circumspection appropriate when this Court is adjudicating issues inevitably entangled in the conduct of our international relations.[115]

Again, the court's reasons were devoid of what the contemporary approach of interest analysis demanded.[116] Instead, the court established a conflicts resolution paradigm focused on an entirety of international interests.[117] Nevertheless it is important to note (since that would soon

Intersection between Public and Private International Law, 76 Am. J. Int'l L. 280, 303–304 (1982). Applying Maier's own definition and distinction between choice of law and regulatory law, however, leads to a different conclusion: both disputes were about private parties' rights and obligations (i.e., interests) in tort suits. Correspondingly, the Supreme Court used choice-of-law language. *See Lauritzen v. Larsen*, 345 U.S. 571, 583 (1953) ("We therefore review the several factors which, alone or in combination, are generally conceded to influence choice of law to govern a tort claim."). *See also* Larry Kramer, *Vestiges of Beale: Extraterritorial Application of American Law*, 1991 Sup. Ct. Rev. 179, 195–196 and 207 (interpreting the issue as a choice-of-law problem).

113 *Lauritzen v. Larsen*, 345 U.S. 571, 582 (1953).

114 *Romero v. International Terminal Operating Co.*, 358 U.S. 354 (1959).

115 *Id.* at 382–383.

116 *Cf. also* Brainerd Currie, *Selected Essays on the Conflict of Laws*, ch. 7: *The Silver Oar and All That: A Study of the Romero Case*, 361, 364, 366–367 and *passim* (1963) (describing both cases as textbook illustrations of how to analyze choice-of-law problems after having discarded traditional theory); Larry Kramer, *Vestiges of Beale: Extraterritorial Application of American Law*, 1991 Sup. Ct. Rev. 179, 196.

117 This point was also explained in *M/S Bremen v. Zapata Off-Shore Co.* The majority emphasized the aim of supporting an efficient international system of transacting. An oft-cited passage of the decision reads: "The expansion of American business and

change) that the court's concerns were still founded on the idea of state-promulgated policies and interests. In other words, the court maintained the model of a community of nation-states and a resolution of conflicts with regard to what different national policy makers considered important.

b *Savigny Diluted: A Theory of Separate Attachment* Around the same time, a similar approach evolved in Europe. As we have seen, civil law conflicts doctrine does not subject issues of public, economic, or regulatory law to choice-of-law mechanics. Usually, forum law applies. But the dissolution of the private/public law dichotomy called this practice into question.[118]

An early strand of theory challenging this inconsistency was enunciated by Konrad Zweigert, Karl Neumayer, and Wilhelm Wengler. It became known as the theory of separate attachment or special connection theory (*Sonderanknüpfung* or *lois d'application immédiate*).[119] While many variants of this theory exist,[120] they all share the technique of implementing universal policies in national law. The theory of separate attachment largely rejects the presumption that foreign public law must not be applied in a domestic forum.[121] Nonetheless, the application of foreign

industry will hardly be encouraged if, notwithstanding solemn contracts, we insist on a parochial concept that all disputes must be resolved under our laws and in our courts.... We cannot have trade and commerce in world markets and international waters exclusively on our terms, governed by our laws, and resolved in our courts." *See M/S Bremen v. Zapata Off-Shore Co.*, 407 U.S. 1, 9 (1972). For similar language, *see Scherk v. Alberto-Culver Co.*, 417 U.S. 506, 516–517 (1974).

118 *See supra* p. 384 *et seq.*

119 *See, e.g.*, Wilhelm Wengler, *Die Anknüpfung des zwingenden Schuldrechts im internationalen Privatrecht*, 54 ZVglRWiss 168 (1941); Konrad Zweigert, *Nichterfüllung auf Grund ausländischer Leistungsverbote*, 14 RabelsZ 283 (1942); Karl H. Neumayer, *Die Notgesetzgebung des Wirtschaftsrechts im internationalen Privatrecht*, 35, 44 *et seq.*, in *Berichte der Deutschen Gesellschaft für Völkerrecht, vol. 2* (1958); Konrad Zweigert, *Internationales Privatrecht und öffentliches Recht*, 124, in *Fünfzig Jahre Institut für Internationales Recht an der Universität Kiel* (Max Sörensen et al. eds., 1965). For the terminology of "special connection," *see also* Jürgen Basedow, *The Law of Open Societies—Private Ordering and Public Regulation of International Relations*, Recueil des Cours 360 (2012), 1, 330 *et seq.*

120 For an overview of scholarly theory and practice, *see* Walter J. Habscheid, *Territoriale Grenzen der staatlichen Rechtsetzung*, 47, 49 *et seq.*, in *Berichte der Deutschen Gesellschaft für Völkerrecht, vol. 11* (1973); Ivo Schwander, *Lois d'application immédiate, Sonderanknüpfung, IPR-Sachnormen und andere Ausnahmen von der gewöhnlichen Anknüpfung im internationalen Privatrecht* (1975); Karl Kreuzer, *Ausländisches Wirtschaftsrecht vor deutschen Gerichten* 55 *et seq.* (1986).

121 *See, e.g.*, Walter Rudolf, *Territoriale Grenzen der staatlichen Rechtsetzung*, 7, 37, in *Berichte der Deutschen Gesellschaft für Völkerrecht, vol. 11* (1973); Kurt Lipstein, *Conflict of Public Laws—Visions and Realities*, 357, 357, in *Festschrift für Imre Zajtay* (Ronald H. Graveson et al. eds., 1982); Kurt Siehr, *Ausländische Eingriffsnormen im inländischen Wirtschaftskollisionsrecht*, 52 RabelsZ 41, 73 (1988). Most prominently, the Institut de Droit International voted on a corresponding resolution in 1975 (17 ArchVölkR 130,

public or mandatory norms—in modern European Union terms, overriding mandatory provisions—must not contradict the forum state's interests or its *ordre public*.[122] In order to avoid such a conflict, Zweigert suggested a distinction: looking at conflicts on a mere case-by-case basis, he explained, would yield a nationalist and possibly parochial approach. While this may be justified in areas where national interests have traditionally prevailed (e.g., family law), it unduly restricts the harmony and uniformity of decision making where no such prevalence exists. In these cases, he instead considered it necessary to identify an internationally acknowledged interest (*international-typisches Interesse*). Depending on the identification of such a global or universal interest conformity, one would decide in favor or against the application of foreign regulatory law. By this means, the handling of such "political" norms would resemble the standard treatment of pure private law collisions in the Savignian system.[123]

In essence, subjecting both private and public norms to the same model of conflicts mechanics dilutes Savignian mechanics. It also replicates and verifies his prophecy: as Savigny explained, the field of public law constitutes an exception to multilateralism. Hence, "laws of a strictly positive, imperative nature" should be treated differently from private legal norms.[124] The reason is evident: public law norms were emanations of lawmakers' regulatory will and were thus to be understood as a class of rules beyond the apolitical regime of private law norms.[125] At the same time, Savigny expected the category of such norms to shrink and

135 (1976)). For an extensive critique, *see* F. A. Mann, *Conflict of Laws and Public Law*, 132 Recueil des Cours 107 (1971-I).

[122] Frank Vischer, *Zwingendes Recht und Eingriffsgesetze nach dem schweizerischen IPR-Gesetz*, 53 RabelsZ 438, 451–452 (1989); Christian von Bar & Peter Mankowski, *Internationales Privatrecht—vol. I: Allgemeine Lehren* § 4 para. 105 (2nd edn., 2003).

[123] Konrad Zweigert, *Nichterfüllung auf Grund ausländischer Leistungsverbote*, 14 RabelsZ 283, 291 (1942) ("Dieser Widerspruch [i.e., durch Anwendung des fremden Rechts] kann vermieden werden, weil der international verbreiteten ablehnenden Reaktion auf ausländische Verbotsgesetze eines bestimmten Typs offenbar nicht eigenwillig nationale Interessen zugrunde liegen, sondern international-typische Interessen aller Staaten, in denen die Frage der Anwendung ausländischer Verbotsgesetze zur Sprache kommt. Gelingt es, diese international-typische Interessenlage zu ermitteln, kraft deren irgendein Staat bei der Würdigung eines ausländischen Verbotsgesetzes den Grundsatz der Entscheidungsharmonie zurückstellen, das ausländische Verbotsgesetz als Rechtssatz also nicht berücksichtigen wird, so ist damit die gesuchte Kollisionsnorm für die Anwendung ausländischer Verbotsgesetze gefunden.").

[124] *See supra* p. 384 *et seq.*

[125] Friedrich Carl von Savigny, *Private International Law and the Retrospective Operation of Statutes—A Treatise on the Conflict of Laws and the Limits of Their Operation in Respect of Place and Time* § 349, at 78 (William Guthrie transl., 2nd edn., 1880). For the original text, *see* Friedrich Carl von Savigny, *System des heutigen römischen Rechts, vol. VIII* § 349, at 35–36 (1849).

disappear over time. The constant evolution of the international community would eventually dissolve the dichotomy. Members states' legal regimes would grow increasingly similar during the course of international transacting and commerce, and, in the end, a transnational *ordre public* would set a uniform standard of regulation.[126]

As in the US Supreme Court's concept of maritime law, however, despite the universality that was expected to evolve, norm and policy promulgation in separate-attachment theory remained an issue of nation-state politics. The theory's underlying model was still state-community founded. Attachment in accordance with a classification of foreign states as either congenial or alien divides national regimes along the lines of shared socioeconomic and political values.[127] However, at this point, one may nonetheless be inclined to find the beginning of a dissolution. The perspective no longer seems solely state-centered and political—it is increasingly drawn toward an informal group consensus. Indeed, a more destatized perspective was to take over in judicial practice.

c Public International Law Osmosis: The Ordre Public International

Internalization of a then new and innovative kind concerned the implementation of public international law in the form of an *ordre public international* in conflicts law.[128] In principle, the doctrine of *ordre public* is limited to two understandings. It has a negative side, correcting the result of multilateral conflicts rules. Foreign norms found to be incompatible with the national regime's fundamental values will then not be applied. And it has a positive side, embracing foundational rules of the forum that must be applied regardless of what choice of law would actually require.[129] In addition, however, the doctrine of *ordre public* has tacitly been turned into another rule of the internalization of internationally common policies.

[126] *See supra* p. 402 *et seq.*

[127] *See* Konrad Zweigert, *Internationales Privatrecht und öffentliches Recht*, 124, 131, in *Fünfzig Jahre Institut für Internationales Recht an der Universität Kiel* (Max Sörensen et al. 1965). This segmentation had already been described by Franz Kahn in his 1900 report for the Congrès international de droit comparé as a phenomenon of partial internationality ("partielle Internationalität") of the *ordre public*. *See* Franz Kahn, *Bedeutung der Rechtsvergleichung mit Bezug auf das internationale Privatrecht*, 491, 501, in *Abhandlungen zum internationalen Privatrecht, vol. I* (Otto Lenel & Hans Lewald eds., 1928).

[128] Kahn had already explained that the law of nations might sometimes exert an impact on national regimes by requiring minimum consistency with standards of the international community. *See* Franz Kahn, *Über Inhalt, Natur und Methode des internationalen Privatrechts*, 255, 288 *et seq.*, in *Abhandlungen zum internationalen Privatrecht, vol. I* (Otto Lenel & Hans Lewald eds., 1928) (*id.* at 290: "Dieser wirklich internationale *ordre public* ist überhaupt keine Materie des internationalen Privatrechts, sondern ausschließlich des Völkerrechts.").

[129] *See, e.g.*, Paul Lagarde, *Public Policy*, in *International Encyclopedia of Comparative Law, vol. III*, ch.11, sect. 2 (Kurt Lipstein et al. eds., 1994).

A splendid example is the Bundesgerichtshof's 1972 *Nigerian Masks* case, in which the court decided on the validity of a transportation insurance contract for African art. Since the export had violated Nigerian law, the court found the insurance contract invalid. While the decision was based on the German Civil Code's provision on public policy,[130] the court's interpretation was sensitive to international concerns. It referred to the UNESCO Convention on the Means of Prohibiting and Preventing the Illicit Import, Export and Transfer of Ownership of Cultural Property,[131] despite the fact that Germany had not yet acceded to the treaty at the time of the court's decision. According to the court, the convention illustrated that

> the circumvention of such a protective [Nigerian] statute must be regarded as reprehensible; it contradicts the interests of all people in the preservation of their cultural heritage in its original environment, an interest that according to modern standards must be generally respected. Certain basic convictions exist within the community of nations concerning the right of each country to protect its cultural heritage and regarding as reprehensible practices which interfere with this heritage; accordingly these practices must be prevented.[132]

The court did not directly implement public international law. Rather, it applied forum law as the *lex causae*.[133] The court's motivation, however,

[130] Section 138 German Civil Code (BGB).

[131] United Nations, Convention on the Means of Prohibiting and Preventing the Illicit Import, Export and Transfer of Ownership of Cultural Property, 14 November 1971, in force 24 April 1972, 823 U.N.T.S. 231, 10 ILM (1971), 289. Article 2 of the Convention reads: "1. The States Parties to this Convention recognize that the illicit import, export and transfer of ownership of cultural property is one of the main causes of the impoverishment of the cultural heritage of the countries of origin of such property and that international co-operation constitutes one of the most efficient means of protecting each country's cultural property against all the dangers resulting therefrom. 2. To this end, the States Parties undertake to oppose such practices with the means at their disposal, and particularly by removing their causes, putting a stop to current practices, and by helping to make the necessary reparations." Under article 3 of the Convention, "[t]he import, export or transfer of ownership of cultural property effected contrary to the provisions adopted under this Convention by the States Parties thereto" is defined to "be illicit." Specific obligations of member states to prevent exportation and importation can be found in art. 6 *et seq.* For an extended illustration, *see, e.g.*, Albert Bleckmann, *Sittenwidrigkeit wegen Verstoßes gegen den ordre public international*, 34 ZaöRV 112, 120 *et seq.* (1974).

[132] BGHZ vol. 59, 82, 85–86 (22 June 1972) (the translation is borrowed from Bernhard Großfeld & C. Paul Rogers, *A Shared Values Approach to Jurisdictional Conflicts in International Economic Law*, 32 I.C.L.Q. 931, 938 (1983)). For further case law, *see, e.g.*, RGZ vol. 108, 241, 243–244 (3 October 1923); RGZ vol. 161, 296, 299–300 (17 June 1939); BGHZ vol. 34, 169, 178 (21 December 1960). For later cases, *see, e.g.*, BGHZ vol. 64, 183—*August Vierzehn* (16 April 1975); BGHZ vol. 69, 295, 298 (29 September 1977); BGHZ vol. 94, 268 (8 May 1985).

[133] Kurt Siehr, *Ausländische Eingriffsnormen im inländischen Wirtschaftskollisionsrecht*, 52 RabelsZ 41, 79 (1988).

was not to prevent a breach of national law.[134] Nor was it to protect a specifically domestic interest.[135] Instead, the court took an internationalist perspective, allowing public international law to enter the national regime and thus acknowledging an international *ordre public*.[136] Courts in other jurisdictions have similarly adjudicated in light of the comity of nations.[137] In this regard, *Nigerian Masks* represents another step toward the truly universal normativity of transnational law. The sovereign nation-state and its internal political process may still form the foundation of "internationalism." After all, it is the "community of nations" that determines what is part of the *ordre public international*. Yet reference to the "interests of all people" is all too evident. This is an aspect of the global legal order that lies beyond the nation-state paradigm. And this destatization took over only a few years later in scholarly attempts to conceive of a non-state-founded model of transnationalization.

3 Turn of the Century: The Unearthly Detachment of Transnationalization

Recent decades have witnessed a large array of innovative attempts to reconceptualize conflicts theory and choice of law. However, none of these attempts have proved ideal, for breaking the chains of established theory and practice generally leaves a void that cannot be filled swiftly, easily, and with guidelines that guarantee clarity and workability. Many deficits of recent approaches are well known and need not be explored here. One aspect in particular calls our attention: with the modern-day dissolution of the Westphalian state, as transnationalists argue, global and community-centered norms, rights, and policies have replaced or are about to replace state-founded political processes. In what can be seen as a reinterpretation of the Savignian world view on a *ius cosmopoliticum*, liberal regimes of private law and individual rights have become detached from their former foundations on state sovereignty and governance. With

134 For a different opinion, *see, e.g.*, Kirsten Anderegg, *Ausländische Eingriffsnormen im internationalen Vertragsrecht* 169 *et seq.* (1989); Christian von Bar & Peter Mankowski, *Internationales Privatrecht—vol. I: Allgemeine Lehren* § 4 para. 129 (2nd edn., 2003).

135 Daniel Busse, *Die Berücksichtigung ausländischer „Eingriffsnormen" durch die deutsche Rechtsprechung*, 95 ZVglRWiss 386, 406 (1996).

136 Albert Bleckmann, *Sittenwidrigkeit wegen Verstoßes gegen den ordre public international*, 34 ZaöRV 112, 113, 124 *et seq.* (1974). For an extensive discussion of the international *ordre public, see* Günther Jaenicke, *Zur Frage des internationalen ordre public*, 77, in *Berichte der Deutschen Gesellschaft für Völkerrecht, vol. 7* (1967); Rudolf Wiethölter, *Zur Frage des internationalen ordre public*, 133, in *Berichte der Deutschen Gesellschaft für Völkerrecht, vol. 7* (1967) (conflict of laws *in statu nascendi*).

137 *See, e.g., Regazzoni v. KC Sethia (1944) Ltd.* [1958] A.C. 301, 318–319; *Foster v. Driscoll and Others* [1929] 1 K.B. 470; *De Wut v. Hendricks* [1824] 2 Bing. 314, 315 *et seq.*, 130 E.R. 326.

this new paradigm, a quest for super-values has begun. These super-values are supposed to substitute traditional mechanisms of civilizing international conflicts by giving regard to principles of international law. In other words, these values—as protagonists of the new transnational legal order suggest—provide the metric and standard to resolve international norm conflicts. From the plethora of scholarly voices, a few are particularly illustrative for the challenges that exist. Next, I will examine three examples, starting with a more traditional model of nation-state policy analysis and its extension into law and economics, and ending with a look at the large strand of scholarship in global legal pluralist theory.

a The Odyssey of Interest Analysis: Currie's Game-Theoretical Return to Savigny The basic difference between the Savignian system of choice of law and Currie's interest analysis is the treatment of state policies. Interest analysis is politicized—it accords ultimate regard to the policies involved, notably those of the forum state. Yet there are voices in post-Currian scholarship that, while still adhering to policy analysis, have again depoliticized conflicts law through the back door. William Baxter's approach and its advancement by Larry Kramer are one example of a more rule-based, almost neo-formalistic approach. Their suggestions illustrate the conundrum presented by the quest for an alternative to the Savignian system.[138]

Baxter's analysis of US conflicts law in the 1960s and his suggestion for a modified interest analysis became known as the comparative-impairment approach.[139] He largely followed Currie's interest analysis by looking at governmental interests and classifying their conflicts as either "true" or "false." Since in false conflicts, only one state actually had an interest in the application of its law, there were no conflicting policies to be reconciled, and the interested state's law could be applied. The situation was different for true conflicts and "unprovided for" cases. Currie had suggested applying forum law in such cases, for whenever the forum state had an actual interest in a case's outcome, application of forum law would avoid super-value judgments that domestic judges were neither qualified nor authorized to make.[140] This is where Baxter's criticism started. He

[138] One must be aware of the fact that, as Friedrich Juenger explained, "[t]here are almost as many approaches as there are legal writers" (*see* Friedrich K. Juenger, *General Course on Private International Law*, 193 Recueil des Cours 119, 219 (1985-IV)). I will thus focus on the most illustrative examples.

[139] William F. Baxter, *Choice of Law and the Federal System*, 16 Stan. L. Rev. 1 (1963).

[140] In cases where none of the states involved have an actual stake in the outcome, forum law should also apply, mainly for reasons of practicability. *See, e.g.*, Brainerd Currie, *Selected Essays on the Conflict of Laws*, ch. 2: *Married Women's Contracts: A Study in Conflict-of-Laws Method*, 76 *et seq.*, ch. 4: *Notes on Methods and Objectives in the Conflict of Laws*, 177,

rejected a simple interest analysis, considering its results to be arbitrary.[141] Baxter instead suggested maximizing utility on the basis of simulated negotiations between the jurisdictions involved. Essentially, this meant applying the law of the state whose policy would be most seriously impaired by nonapplication. Unlike Currie, therefore, Baxter ultimately accepted the challenge of *weighing* the conflicting policies at stake.[142] And this was what made finding a substitute for Currie's super-value rule of *lex fori* preference necessary. He found it in a process-oriented model: if states could negotiate each case, they would forfeit less important domestic concerns for the sake of more important interests. This "policy trading," as Baxter posited, would result in an optimal compromise on the enforcement of different legal purposes.[143]

This last aspect highlights the game-theoretical nature of Baxter's approach. Parallels to the traditional doctrine of international comity are obvious. Just as game theory in choice of law deals with optimization (whether of individual interests or of state policies), the doctrine of comity was initially designed to foster the utility and convenience of international transacting and commerce.[144] In addition, this illustrates that Baxter's exploration of nation-state policies and their hierarchy aimed for a long-term equilibrium of maximum utility for all actors. In this regard, his model actually provided for a conceptual framework necessary for an international order to evolve.[145] The idea of a common law of nations, as conceived of by Savigny, loomed again.[146]

181 *et seq.*, and ch. 5: *The Constitution and the Choice of Law: Governmental Interests and the Judicial Function*, 188, 188 *et seq.* (1963).

141 William F. Baxter, *Choice of Law and the Federal System*, 16 Stan. L. Rev. 1, 9, 19 (1963).

142 Albeit only in the form of comparing the loss ensuing from their hypothetical impairment. *See* Peter Hay, Patrick J. Borchers & Symeon C. Symeonides, *Conflict of Laws* § 2.9, 33–34 (5th edn., 2010).

143 *See* William F. Baxter, *Choice of Law and the Federal System*, 16 Stan. L. Rev. 1, 10 *et seq.*, 18 (1963); *see also* Larry Kramer, *Rethinking Choice of Law*, 90 Colum. L. Rev. 277, 315 *et seq.* (1990).

144 *See also* Lea Brilmayer, *Conflict of Laws: Foundations and Future Directions* 157–158 (1991) ("What makes the game theory literature so helpful is that it illustrates the possibility of developing rational strategies that achieve better results through cooperation than through short-run pursuit of selfish gains. Even in a situation where there is no authoritative enforcer of choice of law rules, states may in some circumstances be able to do significantly better in achieving their own goals if they act with awareness of the goals they share with others. In older choice of law cases, this point was intuitively described in terms of comity and reciprocity.").

145 Quite differently, Currie expressly rejected inclusion of multistate interests—in his words, policies of "deliberate altruism"—into his equation. *See, e.g.*, Brainerd Currie, *Selected Essays on the Conflict of Laws* 616–617 (1963).

146 For the process orientation of international comity, *see* Tim W. Dornis, *Comity*, in *Encyclopedia of Private International Law* (Jürgen Basedow et al. eds., forthcoming 2017).

This neo-traditional model has been further developed in recent decades, as extensions of game theory in choice of law have eliminated the state and its political process from the ledger. Kramer has undertaken such a modification of Baxter's model, with the primary aim of achieving more practicability. In essence, he agrees with Baxter that there is no general theory of the "better law" that could be employed to resolve conflicts.[147] Since states are equal sovereigns, true conflicts will always constitute situations where at least two equally legitimate solutions can be found.[148] To escape this conundrum, Kramer suggests adjudicating on the basis of a hypothetical multistate agreement. He formulates canons of construction reflecting the kind of compromises that equal sovereign states negotiating multistate conflicts would be likely to make.[149] As he explains, the ideal solution to conflicts problems is always a negotiated compromise. Courts confronted with choice-of-law issues should thus ask what lawmakers would likely have achieved from a multistate agreement.[150]

Both Baxter's theory and Kramer's extension still formally reject genuine super-value judgments.[151] Yet Kramer goes one step further, bringing interest analysis almost back to where it started. He describes conflicts as encompassing the prisoner's dilemma: if a state decides to yield to another state's interests or to a multistate concern, reciprocity is not guaranteed. Indeed, a state might actually be more successful in advancing its own policies if it unilaterally applies forum law.[152] In order to break this vicious circle of nonreciprocity, Kramer counsels states to apply a common canon of interpretation rules. Mutual application of

[147] Larry Kramer, *Rethinking Choice of Law*, 90 Colum. L. Rev. 277, 339 (1990) ("[T]here is no theory of 'conflicts justice' against which courts can measure the conflicting laws of different states."). *See also* Larry Kramer, *Return of the Renvoi*, 66 N.Y.U. L. Rev. 979, 1015 *et seq.* (1991); Larry Kramer, *Vestiges of Beale: Extraterritorial Application of American Law*, 1991 Sup. Ct. Rev. 179, 221 *et seq.*

[148] *See, e.g.*, Larry Kramer, *Rethinking Choice of Law*, 90 Colum. L. Rev. 277, 280 (1990); Larry Kramer, *On the Need for a Uniform Choice of Law Code*, 89 Mich. L. Rev. 2134, 2140 (1991).

[149] Larry Kramer, *Rethinking Choice of Law*, 90 Colum. L. Rev. 277, 318 *et seq.* (1990); Larry Kramer, *On the Need for a Uniform Choice of Law Code*, 89 Mich. L. Rev. 2134, 2140–2141 (1991).

[150] Larry Kramer, *Rethinking Choice of Law*, 90 Colum. L. Rev. 277, 315–316 (1990); Larry Kramer, *Vestiges of Beale: Extraterritorial Application of American Law*, 1991 Sup. Ct. Rev. 179, 218.

[151] Both theories are largely founded on the concept of states within a federation. But the assumption of states being equal sovereigns with equivalent policies is not unlike scenarios of international conflicts. As Kramer submits, a general condition of anarchy exists among both federal states and nation-states. There is no source of principles to resolve the regulatory conflict. Even the US Constitution, as Kramer explains, is devoid of a conflicts resolution mechanism. *See* Larry Kramer, *Rethinking Choice of Law*, 90 Colum. L. Rev. 277, 339 n. 223 (1990).

[152] For an extensive discussion, *see id.* at 339 *et seq.*, 342.

the canon would help avoid the dilemma. Since all states must repeatedly decide under identical conflicts rules, they would, over time, discover the benefits of cooperation. A uniform canon would secure the advancement of multistate policies, reduce forum shopping, and provide greater assurance that a state's law will be applied in those cases that the state cares most about.[153] Among the canon rules he suggests are, inter alia, rules of party choice for contract conflicts, of the *favor negotii*,[154] and of applying the law upon which the parties to a transaction have actually relied.[155]

Ultimately, and perhaps unintendedly, Kramer's approach comes full circle in terms of doctrinal history. He starts on the basis of interest analysis by accepting the relevance of governmental interests. This can be duly called a revolutionist starting point. In the end, however, he arrives at a concept that essentially mirrors Savigny's system of an international common law of nations. This common law of the international community of nation-states, as we have seen, not only sought to replicate international agreement among sovereign entities but also aimed at a harmony of decision making by providing for the same international conflicts rules everywhere.[156] Like the Savignian system, conflicts resolution under Kramer's canons of construction eventually invalidates regard for public policy and state interests through reference to more technical and content-neutral rules. By this means, Kramer makes legal certainty, predictability, and harmony of decision making on the interstate and international level the basis for a reconceptualized choice-of-law theory.[157] Savigny would surely have concurred.

b Law and Economics: The Super-Value of Welfare Maximization

The destatization of choice of law did not end with Kramer. In fact, the technique of state-policy substitution has evolved from simulated negotiations and canons of interpretation to the computation and maximization of agglomerated individual economic welfare. The most prominent strand of conflicts theory in this regard was suggested by Andrew Guzman

[153] *Id.* at 314 *et seq.* and 341 *et seq.*; *see also* Larry Kramer, *On the Need for a Uniform Choice of Law Code*, 89 Mich. L. Rev. 2134, 2146 *et seq.* (1991) (suggesting a choice-of-law code by a decentralized decision-making body); Larry Kramer, *Vestiges of Beale: Extraterritorial Application of American Law*, 1991 Sup. Ct. Rev. 179, 222.

[154] *See* Larry Kramer, *Rethinking Choice of Law*, 90 Colum. L. Rev. 277, 329 *et seq.* (1990).

[155] *See id.* at 336 *et seq.*

[156] Friedrich Carl von Savigny, *Private International Law and the Retrospective Operation of Statutes—A Treatise on the Conflict of Laws and the Limits of Their Operation in Respect of Place and Time* § 360, at 137 (William Guthrie transl., 2nd edn. 1880). For the original text, *see* Friedrich Carl von Savigny, *System des heutigen römischen Rechts, vol. VIII* § 360, at 114–115 (1849). *See also id.* at § 348, at 28 and 30–31.

[157] Larry Kramer, *Rethinking Choice of Law*, 90 Colum. L. Rev. 277, 320, 322, and 330 (1990).

in 2002.[158] At its core, Baxter's model was an early formulation of law and economics theory.[159] Guzman has brought these modest beginnings to an interim peak.

Above all, Guzman's model aims to maximize global welfare.[160] As he explains, choice of law determines the applicable substantive law and therefore also "regulates" at the international level.[161] Choice of law must not be understood as a system of content-neutral and outcome-indifferent mechanics. On the contrary, the meta-regulatory character of conflicts law requires that particular regard be given to the economic interests involved. And even though, in this regard, Guzman's theory actually resembles traditional interest analysis, it departs significantly from Currie's approach. First, Guzman bases his concept on the welfare of private individuals, not on the interests of states.[162] In addition, he concretely connects private individuals' welfare with the notion of effects. When a certain conduct has no effect on individuals within a certain state, there is no reason to regulate this conduct. Conversely, any effect on residents within a jurisdiction generally provides an interest of the respective state in regulating the conduct at issue.[163] As Guzman assumes, however, any state will usually pursue its own self-interest. This means that it will rationally aim at a maximum benefit for its residents. Its choice-

[158] Andrew T. Guzman, *Choice of Law: New Foundations*, 90 Geo. L.J. 883 (2002).

[159] Joel P. Trachtman, *Conflict of Laws and Accuracy in the Allocation of Government Responsibility*, 26 Vand. J. Transnat'l L. 975, 1017 (1994); William H. Allen & Erin A. O'Hara, *Second Generation Law and Economics of Conflict of Laws: Baxter's Comparative Impairment and Beyond*, 51 Stan. L. Rev. 1011, 1014 (1999).

[160] Similar approaches have been suggested. Luther L. McDougal III is one example that goes beyond contemporary substantive law approaches of searching for the "better law." McDougal liberates courts from the duty to promulgate new rules from among the legal regimes involved in a conflict. Instead, he describes the optimum rule as the "one that best promotes net aggregate long-term common interests." *See* Luther McDougal III, *Toward the Application of the Best Rule of Law in Choice of Law Cases*, 35 Mercer L. Rev. 483, 483–484 (1984). Regarding the interests a court should take into account, he explains that it should be "the interests asserted by the decisionmakers of all significantly affected states, any interests decisionmakers of the various states have asserted concerning the resolution of transstate cases, interests of the significantly affected states reflected in applicable community policies, and multistate interests of the collective community of states." *See id.* at 484. Moreover, McDougal's approach also contains an element of transnationalization: even though a single conflicts decision may not significantly influence collective community interests, the "whole flow of decisions over time does have substantial effects on collective community value processes." *See id.* at 496–497. For the maximization of global welfare, *see also* Joel P. Trachtman, *Conflict of Laws and Accuracy in the Allocation of Government Responsibility*, 26 Vand. J. Transnat'l L. 975, 1032 *et seq.* (1994).

[161] Andrew T. Guzman, *Choice of Law: New Foundations*, 90 Geo. L.J. 883, 885 (2002).

[162] Notions such as national interest and comity are regarded only if and to the extent that they affect the overall assessment of welfare. *Id.* at 894.

[163] *Id.* at 894–895.

of-law rules will thus be chosen with an eye toward an internalization of benefits and an externalization of costs. In other words, a rational lawmaker, when determining the applicable law, will take into account only the effects on its own residents and will ignore effects on nonresidents.[164]

This potential conflict of interests on behalf of national lawmakers makes conflicts law and choice of law an unruly horse. The challenge in constructing an efficient and welfare-maximizing system of conflicts law is thus to "align national interests with those of the global community."[165] Since the global-welfare effect must consider all individual effects resulting worldwide, national governments must be encouraged—against their rational self-interest—to internalize costs instead of externalizing negative effects to foreigners.[166] Ultimately, this implies that an ideal rule of conflicts determination permits transactions only when their impact on global welfare is positive. Vice versa, it will prevent a transaction when its net effect on global welfare is negative.

In essence, this concept of welfare-enhancement sits on well-known foundations. Huber, Story, and Savigny believed that international welfare was founded on nation-states' unimpeded and consensual transacting. Ever since Adam Smith, liberalist theory has suggested that the market and its mechanism should serve as the ultimate and determinative institution for legitimizing the allocation and distribution of wealth.[167] With Guzman's efficiency-based approach, belief in the superiority of an unhindered market mechanism is projected into conflicts resolution. The individual's freedom of transacting provides the starting point and analytical tool for liberalizing international relations.[168] For conflicts resolution theory, this means that nation-state policies, rules of public international law, and the doctrine of international comity have been substituted by economics. And indeed, Guzman's approach comes closer to a universal theory than those of many of his predecessors. Looking at global welfare directs the decision maker's perspective away from potential national or even parochial biases and other imprecisions in interest balancing or comparative impairment analysis. Yet making efficiency the guideline imports defects of its own kind. A theory of welfare maximization through choice of law reflects general deficits of law and economics

[164] *Id.* at 899. [165] *Id.* at 886. [166] *Id.* at 885 n. 5.

[167] For European and German legal thought, *see* Christian Joerges, *Die klassische Konzeption des internationalen Privatrechts und das Recht des unlauteren Wettbewerbs*, 36 RabelsZ 421, 432 *et seq.* (1972); for the United States, *see* Morton J. Horwitz, *The History of the Public/Private Distinction*, 130 U. Pa. L. Rev. 1423, 1424 (1982).

[168] *See* Christian Joerges, *Die klassische Konzeption des internationalen Privatrechts und das Recht des unlauteren Wettbewerbs*, 36 RabelsZ 421, 437 (1972); Christian Joerges, *Vorüberlegungen zu einer Theorie des internationalen Wirtschaftsrechts*, 43 RabelsZ 6, 11 *et seq.* (1979).

theory.[169] Although my focus here is not on the utility of efficiency as an analytical tool *in toto*,[170] one aspect is important: what is most problematic for Guzman's model is the unfeasibility of comparing utility and welfare at the interindividual level across different jurisdictions. Even if we are willing to acknowledge economic effects and efficiency as a general metric, a cross-border or global utility comparison is still—and may remain for many more decades—unfeasible. Computing costs across countries and their populations must take national socioeconomic differences into account. But there is no appropriate index or metric for comparing or measuring different nations' welfare.[171] One problematic consequence is inevitable: since different states' (and their residents') welfare differs, a simple nominal comparison of the respective welfare status will favor wealthy states over poorer ones.[172] As long as there is no universally acknowledged metric, disparities cannot be resolved.[173]

Not surprisingly, therefore, Guzman must conjure a hypothetical "single benevolent and well-informed global policymaker"[174] to resolve international conflicts. Under his model, individual interests are still "administered" in national systems. The reallocation of gains and losses requires a corresponding political solution. Like his predecessors, therefore, he must acknowledge that nation-states function as the definitive policy makers. Ultimately, Guzman must even recur to international cooperation as a method of conflicts resolution when he explains that only state-to-state negotiations will yield balanced results under a

[169] The question "Why efficiency?" has been extensively debated elsewhere. *See, e.g.*, Ronald M. Dworkin, *Why Efficiency?*, 8 Hofstra L. Rev. 563 (1980); Horst Eidenmüller, *Effizienz als Rechtsprinzip—Möglichkeiten und Grenzen der ökonomischen Analyse des Rechts* 169 *et seq.* (3rd edn., 2005) (with further references).

[170] For an extensive analysis, *see* Gisela Rühl, *Statut und Effizienz—Ökonomische Grundlagen des Internationalen Privatrechts* 146 *et seq.*, and *passim* (2011).

[171] Guzman concedes this only in passing. *See* Andrew T. Guzman, *Choice of Law: New Foundations*, 90 Geo. L.J. 883, 898 n. 60 (2002); for an instructive analysis, *see* Jack L. Goldsmith & Alan O. Sykes, *Lex Loci Delictus and Global Economic Welfare: Spinozzi v. ITT Sheraton Corp.*, 120 Harv. L. Rev. 1137, 1139 *et seq.* (2007).

[172] Law and economics theory has explained problems of diminishing marginal utility in the context of comparing different individuals' private utility. The same problem arises in the international context. Similarly, an assessment of welfare that considers the situation only at the time of decision making will neglect effects that occur over time.

[173] This has been pointed out most clearly in the context of internationally uniform antitrust policies. *See* Eleanor M. Fox, *Trade, Competition, and Intellectual Property—TRIPS and its Antitrust Counterparts*, 29 Vand. J. Transnat'l L. 481, 499 (1996) ("Most [less developed countries] have no interest in following a muse of increased aggregate wealth in the world when their own people lag at the low end of wealth and opportunity."); *see also* Kazuaki Kagami, *The Systematic Choice of Legal Rules for Private International Law: An Economic Approach*, 15, 23, in *An Economic Analysis of Private International Law* (Jürgen Basedow & Toshiyuki Kono eds., 2006).

[174] Andrew T. Guzman, *Choice of Law: New Foundations*, 90 Geo. L.J. 883, 898 (2002).

do-ut-des mechanism.[175] Hence, even though Guzman starts with the express assumption that an efficiency-based choice of law would "abandon" the "traditional and almost universal reliance on notions of sovereignty,"[176] his welfare analysis does not do away with the paradigm. On the contrary, aligning national interests with those of the global community stands at the heart of global-welfare theory. Accordingly, nation-state policy making is still front and center.

c *Global Legal Pluralism: Fragmentation, Functionality, and Universality*

This last stand of the nation-state's sovereign powers has also eroded. Since the 1990s, attempts to retheorize the nation-state paradigm and to reinvent the concept of jurisdiction in an era of globalization have blossomed.[177] Common to all approaches is the alteration of normativity in conflicts resolution. Concepts of nation-state sovereignty and of a world that consists of a segmented checkerboard of regulatory units have given way to a theory of transnational legal orders. As we have just seen, all critics of traditional choice of law have ultimately returned to the idea that interstate agreements and their simulation are determinative. More recent concepts, however, have taken the destatization of conflicts law and choice of law, as well as the absolutization of universality, to an extreme. One variant of these theories in the tradition of socio-legal studies is "global legal pluralism" as suggested most prominently by Paul Schiff Berman.[178] His model seeks to change the system of

[175] *Id.* at 932 *et seq.; see also* Joel P. Trachtman, *Economic Analysis of Prescriptive Jurisdiction*, 42 Va. J. Int'l L. 1, 57 *et seq.*, 66 *et seq.* (2002); Eleanor M. Fox, *Modernization of Effects Jurisdiction: From Hands-Off to Hands-Linked*, 42 N.Y.U. J. Int'l L. & Pol. 159, 169 and *passim* (2009); Edward T. Swaine, *Cooperation, Comity, and Competition Policy: United States*, 1, 18 *et seq.*, in *Cooperation, Comity, and Competition Policy* (Andrew T. Guzman ed., 2010).

[176] Andrew T. Guzman, *Choice of Law: New Foundations*, 90 Geo. L.J. 883, 884 (2002).

[177] *See, e.g.*, Richard T. Ford, *Law's Territory (A History of Jurisdiction)*, 97 Mich. L. Rev. 843 (1999); Saskia Sassen, *Territory and Territoriality in the Global Economy*, 15 Int'l Soc. 372 (2000); Paul Schiff Berman, *The Globalization of Jurisdiction*, 151 U. Pa. L. Rev. 311 (2002); Kal Raustiala, *The Geography of Justice*, 73 Fordham L. Rev. 2501, 2548 and 2555 (2005); for an overview, *see, e.g.*, Peer Zumbansen, *Defining the Space of Transnational Law: Legal Theory, Global Governance, and Legal Pluralism*, 21 Transnat'l L. & Contemp. Probs. 305 (2012). For an early and prominent analysis on the issue of "law beyond the state," *see* Gunther Teubner (ed.), *Global Law without a State* (1997).

[178] *See* his comprehensive monograph on the issue: Paul Schiff Berman, *Global Legal Pluralism—A Jurisprudence of Law beyond Borders* (2012). For the earliest description of legal pluralism—albeit not yet much "globalized"—*see* the German jurist Eugen Ehrlich and his foundations on socio-legal theory in Eugen Ehrlich, *Grundlegung der Soziologie des Rechts* (1913), and also Eugen Ehrlich, *Das lebende Recht der Völker der Bukowina*, in *Recht und Wirtschaft* 1 (1912), 273 *et seq.* and 322 *et seq.* (reprinted in *Eugen Ehrlich—Recht und Leben, Gesammelte Schriften zur Rechtstatsachenforschung und zur Freirechtslehre* (Manfred Rehbinder ed., 1967)).

geographically segmented territories as basic constituents of traditional conflicts resolution into a dynamic model of relationships between different communities (local, national, transnational, international, and cosmopolitan). By this means, Berman disregards the territorial characteristics of disputes. He instead "conceptualize[s] legal jurisdiction in terms of social interactions that are fluid processes, not motionless demarcations frozen in time and space."[179] He argues that the courts must no longer look at territory or nationality to establish the relevant legal ties for an assertion of jurisdictional authority over transnational processes. The outcome of cross-border conflicts should be determined not by an objectivized "counting of contacts" but by the "normative desirability of conceptualizing the parties before a court as members of the same legal jurisdiction."[180] Of course, even under Berman's conception, a "choice" of laws or of relevant norms is still the *a priori* issue in conflicts resolution. But community affiliation—and not the state-centered paradigm of a Westphalian world—now governs the analysis.[181]

And it is not just with respect to the normative sources that destatization has been advanced. The process of norm promulgation has also been subjected to a new paradigm: not only is the state dissolved as an institution, but norm creation is further detached from the political—and also democratic—processes within national boundaries. This idea has been brought forward, among others, by Gunther Teubner and Andreas Fischer-Lescano.[182] Like Berman, they call for disconnecting conflicts resolution from the political process and establishing a new system of normativity and community affiliation.[183] Building on Niklas Luhmann's 1970s theorization of a world society and its sectorial fragmentation, they

[179] Paul Schiff Berman, *The Globalization of Jurisdiction*, 151 U. Pa. L. Rev. 311, 322, 472 *et seq.* (2002).

[180] *Id.* at 322–323; Paul Schiff Berman, *Towards a Cosmopolitan Vision of Conflict of Laws: Redefining Governmental Interests in a Global Era*, 153 U. Pa. L. Rev. 1819, 1822 (2005). For the significance of jurisdictional architecture in creating group statuses, *see* Richard T. Ford, *Law's Territory (A History of Jurisdiction)*, 97 Mich. L. Rev. 843, 922 *et seq.* (1999).

[181] Paul Schiff Berman, *Towards a Cosmopolitan Vision of Conflict of Laws: Redefining Governmental Interests in a Global Era*, 153 U. Pa. L. Rev. 1819, 1845, 1857 *et seq.*, 1863 *et seq.* (2005); Paul Schiff Berman, *Global Legal Pluralism*, 80 S. Cal. L. Rev. 1155, 1169 *et seq.* (2007); Paul Schiff Berman, *Towards a Jurisprudence of Hybridity*, 2010 Utah L. Rev. 11.

[182] Andreas Fischer-Lescano & Gunther Teubner, *Regime-Collisions: The Vain Search for Legal Unity in the Fragmentation of Global Law*, 25 Mich. J. Int'l L. 999, 1012, 1039 and *passim* (2004). For the foundation of Teubner's conception, *see* Gunther Teubner, *"Global Bukowina": Legal Pluralism in the World Society*, 3 *et seq.*, in *Global Law Without a State* (Gunther Teubner ed., 1997).

[183] *See, e.g.*, Andreas Fischer-Lescano & Gunther Teubner, *Regime-Collisions: The Vain Search for Legal Unity in the Fragmentation of Global Law*, 25 Mich. J. Int'l L. 999, 1012 and *passim* (2004).

propose developing an intersystemic conflicts approach.[184] The only way to overcome the fragmentation of legal structures, they explain, is through a process of networking between the fragments and their separated substantive private law regimes.[185] Of course, with a decentering of politics, there is no single authority that can provide for a hierarchy among legal norms and systems. Norm creation and promulgation will thus become an issue of re-relating the splintered sectorial regimes.

Teubner and Fischer-Lescano exemplify their model with an example from international copyright conflicts. Similar to Graeme B. Dinwoodie and Berman, they suggest that conflicts resolution should choose among functional regimes, not national laws.[186] Ultimately, this will result in the development of "substantive rules through the law of inter-regime-conflicts itself."[187] As a result, ad hoc norm promulgation will create a transnational body of law beyond "territorial, organizational and institutional legal spheres."[188] One section of their explanation in particular warrants quotation:

> [T]he goal would be a strange legal Esperanto of regimes within which national, international and trans-national legal acts clamor for attention. Concerned courts—national courts and transnational instances of conflict resolution—would be required to meet the challenges of creating transnational substantive norms out of this chaos.[189]

I have already addressed the practical obstacles to such a "legal Esperanto,"[190] which, at its core, is not even a new idea. Instead, let us recall Jessup's discussion of transnational norm hybridity:

> There is no inherent reason why a judicial tribunal, whether national or international, should not be authorized to choose from all of these bodies of law the rule considered to be most in conformity with reason and justice for the solution of any particular controversy.[191]

[184] *Id.* at 1000. For Luhmann's world society, *see* Niklas Luhmann, *Die Weltgesellschaft*, 57 Archiv für Rechts- und Sozialphilosophie 1 (1971).

[185] Andreas Fischer-Lescano & Gunther Teubner, *Regime-Collisions: The Vain Search for Legal Unity in the Fragmentation of Global Law*, 25 Mich. J. Int'l L. 999, 1017 (2004). For the fundamentals of a networked world order, *see* Anne-Marie Slaughter, *A New World Order* 15 *et seq.*, and *passim* (2004).

[186] Andreas Fischer-Lescano & Gunther Teubner, *Regime-Collisions: The Vain Search for Legal Unity in the Fragmentation of Global Law*, 25 Mich. J. Int'l L. 999, 1021 (2004). For Dinwoodie's substantive law theory, *see supra* p. 258 *et seq.*

[187] Andreas Fischer-Lescano & Gunther Teubner, *Regime-Collisions: The Vain Search for Legal Unity in the Fragmentation of Global Law*, 25 Mich. J. Int'l L. 999, 1022 (2004).

[188] *Id.* at 1022–1023. [189] *Id.* [190] *See supra* p. 265–268.

[191] Philip C. Jessup, *Transnational Law (Storrs Lectures on Jurisprudence)* 2–3 and 106 (1956).

The concept is not too different from Zitelmann's 1888 prophesy, which drew a similar allegoric comparison between law and language.[192] As Zitelmann argued, whenever socioeconomic circumstances are similar, legal norms should and will comply.[193] In the same vein, just to illustrate that these ideas are far from new, John Henry Merryman described the homogenization of culture and growing international exchanges as providing an impetus for the natural convergence of legal systems.[194] In sum, under all theories of global legal pluralism, both classic and modern, functionality is paramount: socioeconomic context determines norm structure and content.[195]

But the extension of concepts for normative sources and their creation is not the only alteration of traditional conflicts and choice-of-law theory that has been suggested. While Berman, Teubner, and Fischer-Lescano are still critical of the idea of a completely universal and uniform global legal order,[196] others are not. One such approach suggesting the evolution of a truly uniform order has been put forth by Anne-Marie Slaughter in the larger context of a "new world order."[197] Like Berman, she argues that judicial comity is what the global community of courts exercises in its dialogue on transnational conflicts resolution. She expects that judges will increasingly feel as "participants in the same dispute resolution system."[198] This cooperation is founded on "common principles and an awareness of a common enterprise that will help make simple participation in transnational litigation into an engine of common identity and

[192] He explained that content may vary in both language and law but that overall structures of human expression would always be the same. *See* Ernst Zitelmann, *Die Möglichkeit eines Weltrechts* 9–10 (1888). For another allegory of language and (transnational) law, *see* Lawrence M. Friedman, *Borders: On the Emerging Sociology of Transnational Law*, 32 Stan. J. Int'l L. 65, 67 and 76 (1996).

[193] Ernst Zitelmann, *Die Möglichkeit eines Weltrechts* 19 (1888).

[194] *See* John Henry Merryman, *On the Convergence (and Divergence) of the Civil Law and the Common Law*, 17 Stan. J. Int'l L. 357, 365 *et seq.* (1981).

[195] For a lucid illustration of a new global legal order in terms of culture (production, consumption, entertainment, and so on), *see* Lawrence M. Friedman, *Erewhon: The Coming Global Legal Order*, 37 Stan. J. Int'l L. 347 (2001).

[196] *See, e.g.*, Paul Schiff Berman, *Towards a Cosmopolitan Vision of Conflict of Laws: Redefining Governmental Interests in a Global Era*, 153 U. Pa. L. Rev. 1819, 1860 *et seq.* (2005); Paul Schiff Berman, *Global Legal Pluralism*, 80 S. Cal. L. Rev. 1155, 1180 *et seq.*, 1192 (2007); Andreas Fischer-Lescano & Gunther Teubner, *Regime-Collisions: The Vain Search for Legal Unity in the Fragmentation of Global Law*, 25 Mich. J. Int'l L. 999, 1004, 1007–1008 (2004).

[197] *See* Anne-Marie Slaughter, *A New World Order* (2004).

[198] Anne-Marie Slaughter, *A Global Community of Courts*, 44 Harv. Int'l L.J. 191, 193–194 (2003); *see also* chapter 2 ("Judges: Constructing a Global Legal System") in Anne-Marie Slaughter, *A New World Order* 65 *et seq.* (2004). For procedural aspects of the emerging international judicial system, *see, e.g.*, Jenny S. Martinez, *Towards an International Judicial System*, 56 Stan. L. Rev. 429 (2003).

community."[199] In the tradition of universalist theories, Slaughter focuses on transnational uniformity and consensus. The emergence of judicial comity and the creation of a "global legal system,"[200] she explains, should result from the repetitive process of norm promulgation, approximation, and transnationalization. Ultimately, she expects this process to "meld[ ] the once distinct planes of national and international law."[201] In this regard, her concept corresponds to what Harold Hongju Koh has characterized as the transnational legal process:

> Transnational legal process describes the theory and practice of how public and private actors—nation-states, international organizations, multinational enterprises, non-governmental organizations, and private individuals—interact in a variety of public and private, domestic and international fora to make, interpret, enforce, and ultimately, internalize rules of transnational law.[202]

More concretely, Koh expects transnational legal norms to materialize "through repeated cycles of 'interaction-interpretation-internalization.' " By this means, he prophesizes, "interpretations of applicable global norms are eventually internalized into states' domestic regimes."[203] His exemplification using computer imagery is particularly illustrative: the repetitive "downloading" of international norms to the national level, along with the "uploading" of national norms to the international sphere, will ultimately generate wide-ranging homogeneity among formerly autonomous and heterogeneous domestic laws.[204]

Both Koh and Slaughter represent a strand of theory that extends the idea of hybrid norms to incorporate fluidity and norm blending—with an ultimate creation of global uniformity. The constant evolution of norms, as demonstrated by the international human rights framework, is expected to result in "public law concepts . . ., rooted in shared national norms and emerging international norms, that have similar or identical

[199] Anne-Marie Slaughter, *A Global Community of Courts*, 44 Harv. Int'l L.J. 191, 196 (2003). For a critical assessment of the "global judicial dialogue" on empirical grounds, *see* David S. Law & Wen-Chen Chang, *The Limits of Global Judicial Dialogue*, 86 Wash. L. Rev. 523 (2011).

[200] Anne-Marie Slaughter, *A Global Community of Courts*, 44 Harv. Int'l L.J. 191, 218 (2003).

[201] *Id.* at 196.

[202] Harold Hongju Koh, *Transnational Legal Process*, 75 Neb. L. Rev. 181, 183–184 (1996); *see also* Harold Hongju Koh, *Why Transnational Law Matters*, 24 Penn. St. Int'l L. Rev. 745, 746 (2006).

[203] Harold Hongju Koh, *Why Transnational Law Matters*, 24 Penn. St. Int'l L. Rev. 745, 747 (2006).

[204] For the computer imagery, *see id.* at 745–746. *See also* Mayo Moran, *An Uncivil Action: The Tort of Torture and Cosmopolitan Private Law*, 661, 680, in *Torture as Tort* (C. Scott ed., 2001).

meaning in every national system."[205] Mayo Moran has described this development as a shifting of normativity from the domestic to the supranational sphere. While domestic law still provides the machinery for enforcement, normativity becomes an issue of international law.[206] The hybridity, interpenetration, and convergence of different legal orders will then automatically suggest jettisoning the traditional method of choosing among different and mutually exclusive regimes of law. Choice of law will disappear, giving way to a cosmopolitan and integrative blend of substantive norms.[207] The universality of norms and policies—a true transnational *droit idéal*—is the final stage in a constant game of norm generation and optimization.

While many questions have been left unanswered, a full-fledged critique of cosmopolitanism and pluralist theory is not necessary here.[208] The big picture projected by transnational common law is hard to reject for being illogical or inconsistent. Rather, it is the microperspective where problems are manifest. The problem of practicality is particularly important for this inquiry. Applicability is a general problem. How is the domestic judge supposed to contribute to a global legal order if she must cope with the scarcity of time, information, knowledge, and authority?[209] Furthermore, more specifically, the problem of a dichotomy

[205] Harold Hongju Koh, *The Globalization of Freedom*, 26 Yale J. Int'l L. 305, 306 (2001).

[206] Mayo Moran, *An Uncivil Action: The Tort of Torture and Cosmopolitan Private Law*, 661, 668–669, in *Torture as Tort* (C. Scott ed., 2001).

[207] *Id.* at 683.

[208] One must not be as sarcastic as Kegel when he formulated his 1964 critique of the then-still-young Currian analysis. With regard to the trouble of rejecting innovative theories, however, the situation has not changed much. *See* Gerhard Kegel, *The Crisis of Conflict of Laws*, 112 Recueil des Cours 91, 206 (1964-II) ("[C]onflicts law is complicated and sensitive. Bold theories are easy to conceive and difficult to reject."). For a biting modern critique of transnational law and alternative approaches, *see* Christian von Bar & Peter Mankowski, *Internationales Privatrecht—vol. I: Allgemeine Lehren* § 2 para. 94 (2nd edn., 2003).

[209] *See supra* p. 265 *et seq. See also* Paul Schiff Berman, *Global Legal Pluralism*, 80 S. Cal. L. Rev. 1155, 1196 *et seq.* (2007) (particularly *id.* at 1195: "[A] pluralist framework must always be understood as a middle ground between strict territorialism on the one hand and universalism on the other. The key, therefore, is to try to articulate and maintain a balance between these two poles. As such, successful mechanisms, institutions, or practices will be those that simultaneously celebrate both local variation and international order, and recognize the importance of preserving both multiple sites for contestation and an interlocking system of reciprocity and exchange. Of course, actually doing that in difficult cases is a Herculean and perhaps impossible task." And also *id.* at 1197: "[E]ach of the mechanisms described ... encounter excruciatingly difficult and probably impossible to resolve problems as to how best to determine when norms of one community should give way to norms of another and when, in contrast, pluralism can be maintained. This sort of line-drawing question can never be resolved definitively or satisfactorily because there is at root level no way to 'solve' problems of hybridity; the debates are ongoing.").

between substance and procedure looms. This has seldom been explained with clarity. But the ultimate step toward a true *Weltrecht* has not yet been taken: the foundations for the legitimacy and authority of transnational norms and policies may have moved beyond the state. But the nation-state continues to serve as the primary repository of processes for litigation and often as the only purveyor of enforcement services. Since national courts still decide the bulk of international conflicts cases, there is hardly a comprehensive system of conflicts resolution covering both substantive norms and policies as well as procedural norms and enforcement structures. This, as the rest of this chapter will show, is a crucial aspect, notably with regard to the extension of a state's regulatory laws to transactions beyond national borders.

III Summary

The nineteenth-century nationalization and codification of national private law and choice of law temporarily isolated nation-states' internal systems of choice of law from the external structures of conflicts resolution—particularly from the law of nations. But this was not the final word. International economic law always cultivated an inherent doctrine of jurisdictional limitations under principles of public international law and comity. Further, the twentieth-century publicization of private international law and the privatization of public international law have brought the quest for universality back to the fore. The paradigm of a transnational common law of conflicts resolution, and—ultimately—the quest for a *Weltrecht* of universal norms and policies are examples of such "new" old ideas. Yet, although widely unnoticed, the modern debate has suppressed an important characteristic of the Huberian, Storyan, and Savignian models. In particular, US theory has undergone a shift toward nation-state dissolution and normative universalism. As is commonly assumed, international consensus and the ensuing universality of norms and policies are the panacea to all jurisdictional issues. In other words, if content is universally agreed on, there will be no more conflicts. But this perspective overlooks one important aspect. It is not just the universality of substantive law that accounts for the functioning of the transnational legal order. The mirror image to substantive law doctrine is its procedural enforcement. This was considered in the works of early theorists. Even though they may not have analyzed issues of enforcement efficiency at length, the requirement that conflicts law and choice of law had to provide for convenience in international transacting and commerce provided for a safeguard mechanism. With the twentieth-century destatization of conflicts law and choice of law, this element of "civilization by comity" got lost. This defect of modern theory will be the focus of the following sections. As a look at international antitrust conflicts and human rights litigation illustrates, the optimism of universalist transnationalism has given way to a sobering interpretation of international comity that adopts a more balanced rule of jurisdictional self-restraint.

Section 2 Transnationalization Exhausted

For quite some time, courts around the world seemed to follow suit in the apotheosis of substantive law universality. Only recently, however, has the pluralist and transnationalist Camelot begun to disappear—at least to a certain extent. This development is due to a number of reasons. In the United States, it has been explained as a success of isolationist or anti-internationalist tendencies, particularly as an expression of the general discontent with the US judiciary's being the battleground for foreign disputes.[210] But this is not the only explanation. The phenomenon can—indeed, *must*—also be characterized under a less provocative and politicized lens. Such a more neutral view on the mechanics of international conflicts resolution leads us back to the beginnings of choice of law and conflicts law, when the law of nations, especially the doctrine of international comity, was still used as a civilizing element of international transacting and commerce. There are a number of areas where a tendency of retraction can be found. Two are particularly illustrative and shall therefore serve as *pars pro toto* for the resurrection of moderating instruments in conflicts law. The first is international antitrust law, with its reliance on effects testing and a significant overlap with trademark and unfair competition conflicts doctrine. As a closer analysis highlights, international antitrust law has evolved from an initial concept of almost nonexistent limitations on regulatory jurisdiction all the way to a practice of jurisdictional self-restraint. The second field is international human rights litigation under the rubric of the Alien Tort Statute (ATS). As a sector of international tort doctrine, human rights protection appears to be an issue of individual rights protection and thus nonregulatory. A closer look, however, reveals that this impression is incorrect. Here, too, it is no surprise that recent developments illustrate a trend toward more comity-based self-restraint. Seen in combination, both international antitrust and international tort law thus illustrate a resurrection of the doctrine of

[210] *See, e.g.*, Vivian Grosswald Curran, *Extraterritoriality, Universal Jurisdiction, and the Challenge of Kiobel v. Royal Dutch Petroleum Co.*, 28 Md. J. Int'l L. 76, 81 (2013); Austen L. Parrish, *Kiobel, Unilateralism, and the Retreat from Extraterritoriality*, 28 Md. J. Int'l L. 208, 226 *et seq.* (2013).

international comity, notably its instrumental function of civilizing international transacting and commerce.[211]

I International Antitrust: A History of Effects, Public International Law, and Comity

Disputes in international economic law are often characterized as transnational regulatory conflicts or transnational regulatory litigation.[212] This terminology implies that the conflict is of public or regulatory nature (rather than a dispute between private parties). In addition, more recently, it has begun to convey something more. As a result of the increasing approximation of national regimes and the growing harmonization of substantive law policies around the world, the resolution of conflicts between different regimes is deemed an issue of globally uniform regulation.[213] Courts adjudicating cases of transnational regulatory litigation seem to act in the interest of an international community, even though their decisions refer to the application of domestic law. This interest, it is contended, is reflected in a global consensus on norms and policies.[214] Accordingly, as the argument goes, the consolidation of litigation in fora with efficient civil procedure systems fosters the enforcement of universally acknowledged standards.[215] A rigid adherence to territoriality will only inhibit the benefits of extended domestic jurisdiction.[216]

In this light, the international convergence of policies appears to have led to a new stage of transnationalization—a global system of regulation in the common interest. But the picture is not that simple. Indeed, many sectors of international economic law may be on a path toward convergence. This

[211] In addition, of course, other areas of conflicts law and international regulatory law can be seen as representative for this development. One example is international securities regulation. *See, e.g., Morrison v. Nat'l Australia Bank Ltd.*, 561 U.S. 247 (2010). For a comprehensive overview on the Supreme Court's more recent handling of these areas, *see* Stephen Breyer, *The Court and the World—American Law and the New Global Realities* 89–164 (2015).

[212] *See, e.g.*, Harold G. Maier, *Extraterritorial Jurisdiction at a Crossroads: An Intersection between Public and Private International Law*, 76 Am. J. Int'l L. 280, 283 and 289 (1982).

[213] Hannah L. Buxbaum, *Transnational Regulatory Litigation*, 46 Va. J. Int'l L. 251, 255 (2006).

[214] This was the plaintiffs' argument in *Empagran* when they pointed out that pricing cartels are condemned under virtually all antitrust regimes around the world. *See Brief for Respondents, F. Hoffmann-La Roche Ltd. v. Empagran S.A.*, 542 U.S. 155 (2004) (No. 03-724), 2004 WL 533935 (U.S.), at *47. For a detailed analysis, *see infra* p. 453 *et seq.*

[215] For a closer analysis of efficient "deterrence" in international antitrust enforcement, *see Brief of Amici Curiae* (by Joseph E. Stiglitz & Peter R. Orszag), *F. Hoffmann-La Roche Ltd. v. Empagran S.A.*, 542 U.S. 155 (2004) (No. 03-724), 2004 WL 533934, at *8.

[216] Hannah L. Buxbaum, *Transnational Regulatory Litigation*, 46 Va. J. Int'l L. 251, 283 (2006).

does not guarantee, however, that the enforcement of universal policies will always maximize global welfare. Nor does it guarantee that national welfare will be enhanced. An overview of the development of antitrust conflicts doctrine illustrates this problem.

A *Lotus* Isolationism: A Lacuna of Nation-State Sovereignty

The Permanent Court of International Justice's *S.S. Lotus*[217] decision is central to a theory of limitations regarding state sovereignty under public international law. The case was the starting point for effects testing under public international law. It centered on a French steamer that had collided with a Turkish ship on high seas. The Turkish ship sank, and eight crew members lost their lives. Upon entering the port of Constantinople, one of the French officers was arrested, prosecuted, and convicted of manslaughter under Turkish criminal law. The court had to decide whether the exertion of jurisdiction by Turkish authorities was in accordance with public international law. The judges held in favor of Turkey, finding the country's exercise of jurisdictional powers to fall within the jurisdictional limitations set by international law. Regardless of the debate over the holding,[218] the court's reasoning has become famous for the theory of international jurisdiction. The decision has been understood as having pronounced a principle of presumptive freedom of state action. Under this principle, there exists no limitation to a state's jurisdictional power; in particular, a state can regulate conduct occurring outside its territory that causes harmful results within.[219] One passage of the court's decision is well-known:

> It does not, however, follow that international law prohibits a State from exercising jurisdiction in its own territory, in respect of any case which relates to acts which have taken place abroad, and in which it cannot rely on some permissive rule of international law. Such a view would only be tenable if international law contained a general prohibition to States to extend the application of their laws and the jurisdiction of their courts to persons, property and acts outside their territory, and if, as an exception to this general prohibition, it allowed States to do so in certain specific cases. But this is certainly not the case under international law as it stands at present. Far from laying down a general prohibition to the effect that States may not extend the application of their laws and the jurisdiction of

[217] P.C.I.J. Series A.—No. 10 (7 September 1927), *The Case of the S.S. "Lotus"*.

[218] For a summary critique, *see, e.g.*, Viktor Bruns, *Völkerrecht als Rechtsordnung I.*, 1 ZaöRV 1, 50 *et seq.* (1929); F. A. Mann, *The Doctrine of Jurisdiction in International Law*, 111 Recueil des Cours 1, 35 (1964-I).

[219] *See, e.g.*, R. Y. Jennings, *Extraterritorial Jurisdiction and the United States Antitrust Laws*, 33 Brit. Y.B. Int'l L. 146, 149 (1957); Walter Rudolf, *Territoriale Grenzen der staatlichen Rechtsetzung*, 7, 18, in *Berichte der Deutschen Gesellschaft für Völkerrecht, vol. 11* (1973); *Laker Airways Ltd. v. Sabena, Belgian World Airlines*, 731 F.2d 909, 922 (D.C.C. 1984).

their courts to persons, property and acts outside their territory, it leaves them in this respect a wide measure of discretion which is only limited in certain cases by prohibitive rules; as regards other cases, every State remains free to adopt the principles which it regards as best and most suitable.

This discretion left to States by international law explains the great variety of rules which they have been able to adopt without objections or complaints on the part of other States; ... In these circumstances all that can be required of a State is that it should not overstep the limits which international law places upon its jurisdiction; within these limits, its title to exercise jurisdiction rests in its sovereignty.[220]

The practical implications of *Lotus* have been debated ever since. While an overriding consensus still appears to favor the concept of absolute state sovereignty,[221] critical voices have challenged unrestricted jurisdictional authority. In general, these critics call such authority into question by referring to public international law's role as the provider of peace and legal certainty. If the international legal order assigns sovereignty rights to its members, as the critics argue, these members can exert their powers only within the confines set by the granting regime.[222] Consensual conflicts resolution and self-restraint are therefore inherent to a system of public international law that is built on the concept of nation-state sovereignty.[223] But even though critics acknowledge that jurisdictional self-restraint is required, for a long while they could not agree on how to define restrictions.

B General Principles: The *Droit Idéal* of Public International Law

It is broadly acknowledged that, in principle, national choice of law is not limited by any rule of public international law.[224] International economic law, however, is different. There, the scope of nation-state jurisdiction is limited according to certain principles of public international law and international comity. In general terms, a "genuine link" must be found

220 P.C.I.J. Series A.—No. 10 (7 September 1927), *The Case of the S.S. "Lotus,"* at 19.

221 *See, e.g.*, Harold G. Maier, *Resolving Extraterritorial Conflicts, or "There and Back Again,"* 25 Va. J. Int'l L. 7, 12 (1984).

222 *See* Viktor Bruns, *Völkerrecht als Rechtsordnung I.*, 1 ZaöRV 1, 35 (1929) ("Die freie Selbstbestimmung steht dem Staat, der Mitglied dieser Rechtsgemeinschaft ist, nicht zu; seine Mitgliedschaft bedeutet ein Unterworfensein unter die Völkerrechtsordnung. ... Der Völkerrechtsjurist hat also nicht nach Beschränkungen der ursprünglichen Unabhängigkeit des Staates zu fragen. Er muß vielmehr die von der Völkerrechtsordnung geschaffenen Rechte und Pflichten feststellen.").

223 *See, e.g.*, Hermann Mosler, *Völkerrecht als Rechtsordnung*, 36 ZaöRV 6, 40–41 (1976); Sir Gerald Fitzmaurice, *The Future of Public International Law and of the International Legal System in the Circumstances of Today*, 196, 216–217, in *Institut de Droit International, Livre du Centenaire 1873–1973* (1973); Luzius Wildhaber, *Jurisdiktionsgrundsätze und Jurisdiktionsgrenzen im Völkerrecht*, 41 SchwJbIntR 99, 104 (1985).

224 *See supra* p. 385 *et seq.*

between the regulating state and the facts of the case in order for an exertion of jurisdiction to be considered legitimate.[225] The genuine-link requirement is said to be based on two International Court of Justice cases, *Nottebohm* and *Barcelona Traction*.

In *Nottebohm*, the court explained that a genuine connection was required in order for a state to effectively confer nationality and grant consular protection.[226] Sir Gerald Fitzmaurice applied the same reasoning in his individual opinion in *Barcelona Traction*:

> [I]nternational law does not impose hard and fast rules on States delimiting spheres of national jurisdiction in such matters . . ., but leaves to States a wide discretion in the matter. It does however (a) postulate the *existence* of limits—though in any given case it may be for the tribunal to indicate what these are for the purposes of that case; and (b) involve for every State an obligation to exercise moderation and restraint as to the extent of the jurisdiction assumed by its courts in cases having a foreign element, and to avoid undue encroachment on a jurisdiction more properly appertaining to, or more appropriately exercisable by, another State.[227]

On this basis, legal scholars have construed different bases for jurisdictional self-restraint, notably with respect to principles against *abus de droit*, cooperation, and noninterference. The literature is extensive.[228] Frederick A. Mann's 1964 description succinctly summarizes the various suggestions brought forward:

> It must be possible to point to a reasonable relation, that is to say, to the absence of abuse of rights or of arbitrariness. In the final analysis, however, the question will be whether international law, as embodied in the sources enumerated by Art. 38 [of the International Court of Justice Statute], sanctions the exercise of jurisdiction, special regard being had to the practice of States and the general principles of law recognised by civilised nations. There will thus be definite barriers beyond which

[225] *See, e.g.*, Alfred Verdross & Bruno Simma, *Universelles Völkerrecht*, § 1183 (3rd edn., 1984); Werner Meng, *Extraterritoriale Jurisdiktion im öffentlichen Wirtschaftsrecht* 541 *et seq.* (1994); Ian Brownlie, *Principles of Public International Law* 311–312 (7th edn., 2008).

[226] *See* I.C.J., *Nottebohm Case (Liechtenstein v. Guatemala)*, second phase, 6 April 1955, I.C.J. Reports 1955, at 4, 24.

[227] I.C.J., *Barcelona Traction, Light and Power Company, Limited (Belgium v. Spain)*, second phase, 5 February 1970, Separate Opinion of Judge Sir Gerald Fitzmaurice, I.C.J. Reports 1970, at 64, 105.

[228] *See, e.g.*, Eckard Rehbinder, *Extraterritoriale Wirkungen des deutschen Kartellrechts* 55 *et seq.* (1965); Rolf Bär, *Kartellrecht und Internationales Privatrecht* 327 *et seq.* (1965); Otto Sandrock, *Neuere Entwicklungen im Internationalen Verwaltungs-, insbesondere im Internationalen Kartellrecht*, 69 ZVglRWiss 1, 10–11 (1968); Michael Akehurst, *Jurisdiction in International Law*, 46 Brit. Y.B. Int'l L. 145, 189 (1972/73); Rainer Deville, *Die Konkretisierung des Abwägungsgebotes im internationalen Kartellrecht* 9–10 (1990); Werner Meng, *Extraterritoriale Jurisdiktion im öffentlichen Wirtschaftsrecht* 569 *et seq.* (1994); Ian Brownlie, *Principles of Public International Law* 311–312 (7th edn., 2008).

the exercise of jurisdiction is unlawful ... The reference to the paramountcy of international law implies what one may call the requirement of non-interference in the affairs of foreign States.... In the last resort it is good faith and reasonableness in international relations that will be the rule of decision. A further significant element in the process of assessing the closeness of connection will be ... the universality or mutuality of the character of jurisdiction. ... International lawyers know that the remedy again lies in a policy of tolerance, reasonableness and good faith.[229]

The principle of good faith has received particular attention. It is commonly considered part of the reserve of general principles of international law and national regimes.[230] The principle does not create rights or obligations—it only restricts their scope. The main problem with the good-faith principle, however, is that it is designed as a standard of wide discretion; it seldom works as a concrete guideline. Similarly problematic is the theory that attempts to restrict national jurisdiction on the basis of a principle preventing the abuse of rights.[231] Most fundamentally, it is questionable whether the principle preventing the abuse of rights is part of public international law at all.[232] By and large, therefore, recourse to general principles of public international law has only sporadically, if at all, proven fruitful for formulating clear and workable rules of conflicts resolution. General principles will usually provide a solution only for extreme and exceptional cases of overreach. In sum, however, the principles of public international law provide neither a consistent nor a comprehensive system of rules limiting national jurisdiction.

C The Practical Proxy: Interest Balancing

In order to overcome the normative vacuum, courts and scholars have developed more concrete methods of conflicts resolution. One mostly

229 F. A. Mann, *The Doctrine of Jurisdiction of International Law*, 111 Recueil des Cours 1, 46–48 (1964-I).

230 *See* Hermann Mosler, *Völkerrecht als Rechtsordnung*, 36 ZaöRV 6, 44–45 (1976); Alfred Verdross & Bruno Simma, *Universelles Völkerrecht*, §§ 459–462 (3rd edn., 1984); Werner Meng, *Extraterritoriale Jurisdiktion im öffentlichen Wirtschaftsrecht* 587–588 (1994).

231 For an early discussion, *see, e.g.*, Nicolas-Socrate Politis, *Le problème des limitations de la souveraineté et la théorie de l'abus des droits dans les rapports internationaux*, 6 Recueil des Cours 5 (1925-I); Gerhard Leibholz, *Das Verbot der Willkür und des Ermessensmißbrauches im völkerrechtlichen Verkehr der Staaten*, 1 ZaöRV 77 (1929); with regard to antitrust extraterritoriality, *see* R. Y. Jennings, *Extraterritorial Jurisdiction and the United States Antitrust Laws*, 33 Brit. Y.B. Int'l L. 146, 152 *et seq.* (1957).

232 Scholarly commentary has refused to find an established rule against an abuse of rights in international law. *See, e.g.*, Walter Rudolf, *Territoriale Grenzen der staatlichen Rechtsetzung*, 7, 21, in *Berichte der Deutschen Gesellschaft für Völkerrecht, vol. 11* (1973); Winfried Veelken, *Interessenabwägung im Wirtschaftskollisionsrecht* 147 (1988); *but see* Michael Akehurst, *Jurisdiction in International Law*, 46 Brit. Y.B. Int'l L. 145, 189 (1972/73); Alfred Verdross & Bruno Simma, *Universelles Völkerrecht* § 60 *et seq.* (3rd edn, 1984).

practical approach is that of interest balancing. Per se, interest balancing is not a rule of international law[233] but a practical tool to help determine the limitations of nation-state jurisdiction. Even though the technique of balancing has been described as requiring a judge "to take all relevant considerations into account and tailor them to the particular case,"[234] balancing is inherently noninternationalist. This means that it is often characterized by a domestic view. In addition, it is designed to resolve concrete conflicts, not to establish a universal jurisdictional conflicts resolution system. Three major variants of interest balancing can be distinguished.[235] The first variant addresses just nation-state concerns, whether at the domestic or international level, and is based entirely on public international law. The second approach addresses both state and private-party concerns. This approach was famously applied in *Timberlane*. Finally, the third approach represents a symbiosis of public international law, choice of law, and substantive law policy balancing; this variant can be found in Andreas F. Lowenfeld's interpretation of the Restatement of Foreign Relations Law.

1 Theoretical Approaches

Karl M. Meessen has suggested a method of interest balancing in antitrust conflicts on the basis of the rule of noninterference, or nonintervention.[236] As he posits, public international law requires considering the principle of sovereign equality. Each state thus must have an equal opportunity to regulate what it deems relevant for its economy.[237] In cases of conflicting regulatory interests, Meessen explains, "a state is prohibited from taking measures of antitrust law if the regulatory interests it is pursuing are outweighed by the interests of one or more foreign states likely to be seriously

[233] *See, e.g.*, *Laker Airways Ltd. v. Sabena, Belgian World Airlines*, 731 F.2d 909, 937 (D.C.C., 1984) ("[T]here is no evidence that interest balancing represents a rule of international law."); Karl Matthias Meessen, *Antitrust Jurisdiction under Customary International Law*, 78 Am. J. Int'l L. 783, 786, 801–802 (1984); Hannah L. Buxbaum, *Territory, Territoriality, and the Resolution of Jurisdictional Conflict*, 57 Am. J. Comp. L. 631, 649 (2009); *but see* Restatement (Third) of Foreign Relations Law, § 403 comment a (balancing under the rule of reason "has emerged as a principle of international law").

[234] *See* Larry Kramer, *Vestiges of Beale: Extraterritorial Application of American Law*, 1991 Sup. Ct. Rev. 179, 207–221.

[235] Ernst-Joachim Mestmäcker, *Staatliche Souveränität und offene Märkte—Konflikte bei der extraterritorialen Anwendung von Wirtschaftsrecht*, 52 RabelsZ 205, 241–242 (1988).

[236] *See, e.g.*, Karl M. Meessen, *Völkerrechtliche Grundsätze des internationalen Kartellrechts* 202–203, 231–232 *et passim* (1975); Karl M. Meessen, *Antitrust Jurisdiction under Customary International Law*, 78 Am. J. Int'l L. 783, 804 *et seq.* (1984); Karl M. Meessen, *Kollisionsrecht der Zusammenschlußkontrolle* 26 *et seq.* (1984).

[237] Karl M. Meessen, *Antitrust Jurisdiction under Customary International Law*, 78 Am. J. Int'l L. 783, 804 (1984).

injured by those measures."[238] Repeated decision making under this rule of interest balancing will, over time, establish a general principle of public international law.[239] Meessen openly admits the fundamental problem of balancing: "There is indeed no universal standard and usually no standard common to the states party to the particular dispute that would allow interests to be measured and compared in a satisfactory manner."[240] As an escape, he suggests that states involved enter into direct negotiations. Domestic jurisdiction should be upheld only if actual negotiations are unsuccessful.[241]

Another approach for overcoming the subjectivity of interest evaluation has been suggested by Bernhard Großfeld and C. Paul Rogers. Under their variant, reference to foreign mandatory law may have some merit if it is based on values that are shared among the states involved in the conflict.[242] Whenever the values match, the manner of expressing these values is irrelevant.[243] This approach strongly replicates the internationalist structures shown in US maritime law and under the theory of separate attachment.[244] While searching for common values appears to be a more systematic and structured approach than interest balancing, this approach nevertheless has to revert to ad hoc discretion in cases where values and policies differ. Even though common values may sometimes exist, complete consensus on detailed policies and on the means necessary to achieve common goals will be an exception.[245]

In the end, these vagaries are a problem inherent in all balancing approaches. Not only is it difficult to evaluate foreign interests and policies under a domestic perspective, but it also requires a certain trade-off

[238] *Id.*

[239] Karl M. Meessen, *Völkerrechtliche Grundsätze des internationalen Kartellrechts* 232 (1975); *see also* R. Y. Jennings, *Extraterritorial Jurisdiction and the United States Antitrust Laws*, 33 Brit. Y.B. Int'l L. 146, 153 (1957).

[240] Karl M. Meessen, *Antitrust Jurisdiction under Customary International Law*, 78 Am. J. Int'l L. 783, 808 (1984).

[241] *Id.*

[242] Bernhard Großfeld & C. Paul Rogers, *A Shared Values Approach to Jurisdictional Conflicts in International Economic Law*, 32 I.C.L.Q. 931, 939 (1983).

[243] One prime example that Großfeld and Rogers provide for the practicality of their theory is the application of foreign bank secrecy laws by forum courts. These laws should be recognized as directly applicable when they correspond to similar provisions in forum law. Since the similarity reflects shared values among legal systems, minor deviations should not stand in the way of an application of the foreign legal norm. *Id.* at 941–942; *see also* Franz Gamillscheg, *Gedanken zu einem System des internationalen Arbeitsrechts*, 23 RabelsZ 819, 837 (1958).

[244] *See supra* p. 410 *et seq.*

[245] Jean-Gabriel Castel, *The Extraterritorial Effects of Antitrust Laws*, 179 Recueil des Cours 9, 21 (1983-I).

between foreign and domestic concerns.[246] Interest balancing may thus sometimes provide more clarity and predictability than the general principles of public international law. Nevertheless, the methodology of balancing will not (and in fact, cannot) implement an all-encompassing conflicts resolution approach. Apart from the few situations where shared values exist, interest balancing remains an issue of ad hoc decision making that neglects the development of systemic structures. This is actually the major flaw of all balancing techniques, and it has been particularly visible in their practical application.

2 *The Practice:* Timberlane *and* Mannington Mills

By the 1970s, the extraterritorial extension of US antitrust law, which had begun after the Second World War, had started to lead to political frictions.[247] In reaction, other nations enacted "blocking statutes" to cut short US discovery rules, refused to recognize or enforce US treble-damage awards, and allowed defendants to "claw back" judgments that had been rendered against them.[248] This international discord spurred attempts in the United States to curb extraterritoriality.[249] In two famous cases from the 1970s—*Timberlane Lumber Co. v. Bank of America, N.T. and S.A.*[250] and *Mannington Mills, Inc. v. Congoleum Corp.*[251]—the courts undertook a balancing of nation-state interests in order to establish a reasonable self-limitation of judicial powers.

[246] *See, e.g.*, Harold G. Maier, *Extraterritorial Jurisdiction at a Crossroads: An Intersection between Public and Private International Law*, 76 Am. J. Int'l L. 280, 317 (1982); *see also* Herbert Hovenkamp, *Federal Antitrust Policy—The Law of Competition and Its Practice* § 21.2b (3rd edn., 2005) ("The degree of conflict with foreign law cannot be measured in pounds, and the relevant weight to be given to conduct in the United States cannot be measured in inches. Even if they could be, we could still not balance pounds against inches.").

[247] *See Timberlane Lumber Co. v. Bank of America N.T. & S.A.*, 549 F.2d 597, 609 (9th Cir. 1976). Apparently, according to a list promulgated by the then chief of the Foreign Commerce Section of the Antitrust Division, none of the more than 200 institutions and dispositions of foreign trade cases brought by the US Department of Justice before 1973 were dismissed for lack of jurisdiction. *See* Wilbur Lindsay Fugate, *Foreign Commerce and the Antitrust Laws*, Appendix B, 498 *et seq.* (2nd edn., 1973); for a general overview, *see* Gary B. Born & Peter B. Rutledge, *International Civil Litigation in United States Courts* 680 *et seq.* (5th edn., 2011).

[248] For an extensive discussion of the European perspective, *see* Anton K. Schnyder, *„Gegenmassnahmen" im Internationalen Privat- und Zivilverfahrensrecht*, 73, in *Berichte der Deutschen Gesellschaft für Völkerrecht, vol. 37* (1998); *see also* Edward T. Swaine, *Cooperation, Comity, and Competition Policy: United States*, 1, 10, in *Cooperation, Comity, and Competition Policy* (Andrew T. Guzman ed., 2011); Gary B. Born & Peter B. Rutledge, *International Civil Litigation in United States Courts* 682 (5th edn., 2011).

[249] Edward T. Swaine, *Cooperation, Comity, and Competition Policy: United States*, 1, 10, in *Cooperation, Comity, and Competition Policy* (Andrew T. Guzman ed., 2011).

[250] *Timberlane Lumber Co. v. Bank of America N.T. & S.A.*, 549 F.2d 597 (9th Cir. 1976).

[251] *Mannington Mills, Inc. v. Congoleum Corp.*, 595 F.2d 1287 (3rd Cir. 1979).

In *Timberlane*, the plaintiffs alleged a number of conspiratorial acts that had resulted in impediments to Timberlane's export of lumber from Honduras.[252] In its analysis, the Ninth Circuit clarified that mere testing of "direct and substantial effect[s]" would never suffice to determine the reach of US antitrust law.[253] Instead, the court recommended a tripartite analysis for deciding whether to apply US antitrust regulation. The first two parts determine whether an effect exists and whether such an effect is sufficiently large to present a cognizable injury. The third part determines

> whether the interests of, and links to, the United States—including the magnitude of the effect on American foreign commerce—are sufficiently strong, vis-[à]-vis those of other nations, to justify an assertion of extraterritorial authority.[254]

The evaluation and balancing required under this test included the consideration of seven factors:

> the degree of conflict with foreign law or policy, the nationality or allegiance of the parties and the locations or principal places of business of corporations, the extent to which enforcement by either state can be expected to achieve compliance, the relative significance of effects on the United States as compared with those elsewhere, the extent to which there is explicit purpose to harm or affect American commerce, the foreseeability of such effect, and the relative importance to the violations charged of conduct within the United States as compared with conduct abroad.[255]

The court described its approach as taking account of "international comity and fairness"; it argued that the United States should not be allowed to exercise jurisdictional powers beyond the "point [where] the interests of the United States are too weak and the foreign harmony incentive for restraint too strong to justify an extraterritorial assertion of jurisdiction."[256] A few years after this decision, the Third Circuit adopted the *Timberlane* analysis in *Mannington Mills*. As the court explained, it would be "unwise to ignore the fact that foreign policy, reciprocity, comity, and limitations of judicial power are considerations that should have a bearing on the decision to exercise or decline jurisdiction."[257] Interestingly, even though both courts explicitly based their analyses on the concept of international comity, neither mentioned an interest of the international community as a separate factor to be regarded and weighed. Neither in *Timberlane* nor in *Mannington Mills* did the court search for a transnational or universal policy. This changed with the restatement's rule-of-reason approach.

[252] *Timberlane Lumber Co. v. Bank of America N.T. & S.A.*, 549 F.2d 597, 604–605 (9th Cir. 1976).

[253] *Id.* at 610 and 611–612. [254] *Id.* at 613. [255] *Id.* at 614. [256] *Id.* at 613 and 609.

[257] *Mannington Mills, Inc. v. Congoleum Corp.*, 595 F.2d 1287, 1296 (3rd Cir. 1979).

3 The Rule of Reason

In 1958, Kingman Brewster, credited as the first to propose a jurisdictional rule of reason,[258] brought forward a resolution scheme for international antitrust conflicts. As he posited, "Ad hoc weighing of conflicting interests at both the level of administration and judicial determination seems better suited to antitrust than would any hard-and-fast jurisdictional rule based on territoriality or nationality."[259] He further specified that officials, enforcement officers, and judges weigh a number of different constituent variables. Some of the factors he conceived subsequently found their way into court practice—namely, the *Timberlane* standard.[260] Brewster's analysis, however, was still limited. It was the interests of the United States and the interests of states involved in the conflict that had to be submitted to the balancing. There was no express regard for an international community or the functioning of international commerce and transacting.

Nor did this change in 1965, when the American Law Institute published the Restatement (Second) of Foreign Relations Law. Acknowledging that the principles of territoriality, personality, and effects testing are fundamental to the scope of legislative jurisdiction, section 40 of the restatement limited the exertion of jurisdiction:

> Where two states have jurisdiction to prescribe and enforce rules of law and the rules they may prescribe require inconsistent conduct upon the part of a person, each state is required by international law to consider, in good faith, moderating the exercise of its enforcement jurisdiction, in the light of such factors as
> (a) vital national interests of each of the states,
> (b) the extent and the nature of the hardship that inconsistent enforcement actions would impose upon the person,
> (c) the extent to which the required conduct is to take place in the territory of the other state,
> (d) the nationality of the person, and
> (e) the extent to which enforcement by action of either state can reasonably be expected to achieve compliance with the rule prescribed by that state.[261]

258 *Timberlane Lumber Co. v. Bank of America N.T. & S.A.*, 549 F.2d 597, 613 (9th Cir. 1976).

259 Kingman Brewster, Jr., *Antitrust and American Business Abroad* 445 (1958).

260 *See id.* at 446 (his list of factors includes "(a) the relative significance to the violations charged of conduct within the United States as compared with conduct abroad; (b) the extent to which there is explicit purpose to harm or affect American consumers or Americans' business opportunity; (c) the relative seriousness of effects on the United States as compared with those abroad; (d) the nationalitiy or allegiance of the parties or in the case of business associations, their corporate location, and the fairness of applying our law to them; (e) the degree of conflict with foreign laws and policies; and (f) the extent to which conflict can be avoided without serious impairment of the interests of the United States or the foreign country.").

261 Restatement (Second) of Foreign Relations Law of the United States (1965), § 40.

Like Brewster's compilation, the list did not include a concern for systemic values of the international order or a community of nation-states. Only when Andreas F. Lowenfeld analyzed the restatement in 1979 did a different element enter the stage.[262] Lowenfeld introduced a truly innovative perspective into the rule-of-reason approach when he suggested that the exercise of legislative jurisdiction required a finding of internationalist reasonableness.[263] As Brewster had done before, he also proposed a list of factors to be regarded but amended it in one critical aspect (see item (iv)):

> (i) the character of the activity to be regulated; (ii) the basic policies underlying the regulation; (iii) the link between the State under whose authority the regulation is to be carried out and the person or persons principally responsible for the activity to be regulated; (iv) the needs and traditions of the international political, legal and economic system; (v) the protection of justified expectations; (vi) the conflicts, if any, between the regulation in question and the exercise of legislative jurisdiction pursuant to the authority of another State; (vii) the conflicts, if any, between the regulation in question and the potential exercise of legislative jurisdiction pursuant to the authority of another State; (viii) the territory in which the activity is principally carried on; (ix) the direct and foreseeable effect of the activity; (x) in the case of exercise of delegated authority, the intention of the person or body that has delegated the authority.[264]

The "needs and traditions of the international political, legal and economic system" may not have been very important for Lowenfeld. In fact, in an analysis of case law and legal thought on the issue, he barely made reference to international aspects of the argument.[265] As a result, his internationalist amendment to the list of factors passed largely unnoticed.

Even the reasonableness analysis implemented in the current restatement is still somewhat ambiguous. Yet it still features prominently. Section 402 of the restatement provides for different bases of jurisdiction to prescribe. Under the territoriality principle, for instance, a state has jurisdiction with respect to conduct, persons, and things within its territory. Under the effects principle, conduct outside the state's territory will be subject to the state's jurisdiction if the conduct has or is intended to have effects within the national territory. Under the nationality principle, a citizen's

[262] *See* Andreas F. Lowenfeld, *Public Law in the International Arena: Conflict of Laws, International Law, and Some Suggestions for Their Interaction*, 163 Recueil des Cours 313, 400 *et seq.* (1979-II).

[263] *Id.* at 329, 401–402. [264] *Id.* at 328–329.

[265] *See id.* at 383 (in his analysis of the *Alcoa* case, Lowenfeld addressed the international system as one factor to be regarded, but downplayed its relevance: "As for the traditions of the international system, one could have different views: my own would be that trade in non-ferrous metals ... does not come within the category of special concern of the international system.").

activities, interests, status, and relations outside and inside the territory are subject to the state's jurisdiction.[266] Even when one of these grounds for jurisdiction is present, however, a state may not exercise jurisdiction over a person or conduct connected with another state when the exercise of such jurisdiction would be unreasonable (section 403(1)). The restatement provides for a definition of reasonableness in section 403(2). The list of factors to be considered is extensive. Yet similar to Lowenfeld's formulation, "the importance of the regulation to the international political, legal, or economic system" (lit. e) and "the extent to which the regulation is consistent with the traditions of the international system" (lit. f) must be considered.

This reference to reasonableness factors involving an "international political, legal, or economic system" and "traditions of the international system" forms the crucial difference vis-à-vis earlier versions of balancing tests and the rule of reason.[267] Granted, there may still be ample factors favoring a traditional conflicts resolution scheme of balancing only those national interests that are concretely involved. Furthermore, the factors are not listed in any order of priority, and not all factors may have the same weight. Balancing still depends on the circumstances.[268] But the section's language expressly recognizes an internationalist approach. As Harold Maier has correctly pointed out, the restatement can be interpreted as requiring courts to fashion decisions in a way that contributes incrementally to the construction of an internationalist norm of jurisdictional authority and allocation.[269]

Nevertheless, one aspect remains to be noted: neither Lowenfeld's suggestion of internationalism nor the restatement's factors favoring a more comprehensive analysis have been prominently featured in practice.

[266] Finally, the protective principle subjects certain conduct directed against a limited class of state interests (e.g., security) to domestic jurisdiction.

[267] A similar concept reflecting a comparably benevolent stance toward the international system can be found in the Restatement (Second) of Conflict of Laws. Comment (d) to its section 6 states, under the heading "Needs of the interstate and international systems": "Probably the most important function of choice-of-law rules is to make the interstate and international systems work well. Choice-of-law rules, among other things, should seek to further harmonious relations between states and to facilitate commercial intercourse between them. In formulating rules of choice of law, a state should have regard for the needs and policies of other states and of the community of states. Rules of choice of law formulated with regard for such needs and policies are likely to commend themselves to other states and to be adopted by these states. Adoption of the same choice-of-law rules by many states will further the needs of the interstate and international systems and likewise the values of certainty, predictability and uniformity of result." (Restatement (Second) of Conflict of Laws § 6 (1971)).

[268] *See* Restatement (Third) of Foreign Relations Law, Part IV, Chapter 1, Sub-Chapter A, § 403 comment b.

[269] Harold G. Maier, *Extraterritorial Jurisdiction at a Crossroads: An Intersection between Public and Private International Law*, 76 Am. J. Int'l L. 280, 301 (1982).

On the contrary, all variants of interest balancing, as well as the rule-of-reason approach in action, suffer from the same deficit. Practical interest balancing and reasonableness analysis show a distinct disregard for internationalist and communitarian concerns. For want of an actual substantive guideline for decision making, courts faced with balancing interests or applying a rule of reason have tended to adopt a case-by-case approach.[270] As long as the internationalist concern is just one of many factors, the overall picture of an international community will be neglected.[271] Hence, it is of little surprise that none of the approaches explored above have established a universal and universalist system of allocating jurisdictional authority.

D The Effects Principle: From Unboundedness to Self-Restraint

The 1987 Restatement (Third) of Foreign Relations Law did more than implement an elaborate reasonableness approach. It also expressly endorsed territorial effects as a legitimate basis of prescriptive jurisdiction.[272] This approval reflects a change in twentieth-century international economic law. With the growing globalization of communication and socioeconomic transacting, commercial effects had to become the dominant element of jurisdictional analyses. Of course, effects had never been blindly acknowledged as a legitimate basis of jurisdiction under public international law. For a long time, it was contested whether effects should qualify as a factor at all.[273] Today, however, the assertion of jurisdiction based on effects is no longer seen as illegitimate.[274] International antitrust law is the field where the issue has been most extensively debated.

[270] *See* Frank Vischer, *Das neue Restatement "Conflict of Laws,"* 38 RabelsZ 128, 149 (1974); Harold G. Maier, *Resolving Extraterritorial Conflicts, or "There and Back Again,"* 25 Va. J. Int'l L. 7, 10 (1984).

[271] For a critique of the Restatement (Second) of Foreign Relations Law in this regard, *see, e.g.*, Harold G. Maier, *Extraterritorial Jurisdiction at a Crossroads: An Intersection between Public and Private International Law*, 76 Am. J. Int'l L. 280, 295 (1982). For similar restrictions of the Restatement (Second) of Conflict of Laws, *see, e.g.*, Arthur Taylor von Mehren, *Choice-of-Law Theories and the Comparative-Law-Problem*, 23 Am. J. Comp. L. 751, 755 (1975).

[272] Restatement (Third) of Foreign Relations Law § 402 (1987), comment d.

[273] For a critique, *see, e.g.*, Luzius Wildhaber, *Jurisdiktionsgrundsätze und Jurisdiktionsgrenzen im Völkerrecht*, 41 SchwJbIntR 99, 105–106 (1985); Ernst-Joachim Mestmäcker, *Staatliche Souveränität und offene Märkte—Konflikte bei der extraterritorialen Anwendung von Wirtschaftsrecht*, 52 RabelsZ 205, 220 (1988).

[274] *See, e.g.*, Gary B. Born, *A Reappraisal of the Extraterritorial Reach of U.S. Law*, 24 Law & Pol'y Int'l Bus. 1, 69 *et seq.* (1992); Jürgen Basedow, Weltkartellrecht 19 *et seq.* (1998); Eleanor M. Fox, *Modernization of Effects Jurisdiction: From Hands-Off to Hands-Linked*, 42 N.Y.U. J. Int'l L. & Pol. 159, 167 (2009); Ralf Michaels, *Empagran's Empire: International Law and Statutory Interpretation in the U.S. Supreme Court of the Twenty-*

1 *Europe: A Theory of Public International Law Limitations*

Antitrust effects testing has a longer and arguably richer practical and scholarly history in US doctrine. Nevertheless, a look at European antitrust is warranted. Several characteristics are fundamental. Public international law limitations and substantive antitrust policy have been determinants from the beginning. Antitrust law has traditionally been conceived of as belonging to public law enforcement. Since private litigation has only recently become a part of European antitrust doctrines,[275] the primary emphasis has historically been on limitations to the reach of administrative and regulatory state actions.[276] Particularly in Germany, lawmakers implemented the effects principle quite early on as a key instrument for the allocation of prescriptive jurisdiction. The 1957 German Act against Restraints on Competition provides for the application of German law based on inland effects but has not laid out an explicit limitation to the quality or quantity of such effects necessary to trigger its application.[277] These limitations were left to be developed by scholarly commentary and courts. One voice on the issue was Eckard Rehbinder, who explained in 1965 that the scope of German antitrust law could never be an issue of self-determined jurisdictional authority alone. As he contended, constitutional law stipulated a prevalence of public international law, so any excess of jurisdictional limitations under public international law would also void the statutory provision or administrative act at issue.[278] I have already mentioned similar theories in the field.[279] The idea that public international law limited jurisdictional authority had several consequences. In general, it was clear that insignificant effects alone could not trigger the application of domestic law.[280] More

First Century, 533, 537, in *International Law in the U.S. Supreme Court—Continuity and Change* (David L. Sloss et al. eds., 2011).

275 *See supra* p. 315–317. *See also* Andreas Heinemann, *The Rise of a Private Competition Law Culture: Experience and Visions*, 218 *et seq.*, in *Private Enforcement of Competition Law* (Jürgen Basedow et al. eds., 2011).

276 David J. Gerber, *The Extraterritorial Application of the German Antitrust Laws*, 77 Am. J. Int'l L. 756, 758 (1983); Hannah L. Buxbaum, *Territory, Territoriality, and the Resolution of Jurisdictional Conflict*, 57 Am. J. Comp. L. 631, 661–662 (2009).

277 Now section 130 para. 2 GWB. The code was enacted on 27 July 1957 (BGBl. I 1957, 1081). The act has actually been interpreted as establishing a genuine effects principle. *See* David J. Gerber, *The Extraterritorial Application of the German Antitrust Laws*, 77 Am. J. Int'l L. 756, 761 (1983).

278 Eckard Rehbinder, *Extraterritoriale Wirkungen des deutschen Kartellrechts* 30–31, 47–48 and *passim* (1965); Ivo E. Schwartz, *Deutsches Internationales Kartellrecht* 29 *et seq.*, and *passim* (2nd edn., 1968); for an extensive discussion, *see* Ivo E. Schwartz & Jürgen Basedow, *Restrictions on Competition (ch. 35)*, in *International Encyclopedia of Comparative Law, vol. III: Private International Law* (Kurt Lipstein ed., 2011).

279 With regard to nonintervention, *see* Meessen's approach *supra* p. 438–440.

280 *See* Eckard Rehbinder, *Extraterritoriale Wirkungen des deutschen Kartellrechts* 155 *et seq.* and *passim* (1965).

specifically, Rehbinder and, shortly after, Ivo E. Schwartz proposed distinct policy-oriented restrictions. Thus, the quality and quantity of effects were to be determined according to the particular kind of violation and policy at issue.[281] This approach was also adopted in practice.[282] Ultimately, a detailed system of different minimum thresholds evolved in case law and commentary. What is required for the application of German antitrust law are—with some simplification—direct, actual, considerable, and foreseeable effects within German territory.[283]

Modern European antitrust doctrine does not differ much. Articles 101 and 102 of the Treaty on the Functioning of the European Union fail to expressly indicate when to regulate extraterritorially. Nonetheless, several doctrines allow for an extension beyond European borders.[284] Since the 1960s, the European Commission has embraced a broad conception of effects.[285] In 1988, the Court of Justice followed suit—if not literally, then at least with respect to the practical results. In *Wood Pulp*, the court was concerned with price-fixing agreements among wood-pulp producers. Non–European Union entities sued by the European Commission were accused of having restrained trade within the European Union. The Court of Justice rejected the defendants' argument that jurisdiction was amiss since they were located outside the territory of the European Union. Although the court did not refer to effects, it found the "implementation" of anticompetitive agreements within European territory sufficient to trigger the application of European antitrust principles. Selling to purchasers within the European Union

[281] *See* Eckard Rehbinder, *Extraterritoriale Wirkungen des deutschen Kartellrechts* 30–31, 47–48 and *passim* (1965); Ivo E. Schwartz, *Deutsches Internationales Kartellrecht* 29 *et seq.*, and *passim* (2nd edn., 1968); for modern commentary *see, e.g.*, Florian Wagner-von Papp & Wolfgang Wurmnest, in *Münchener Kommentar—Europäisches und Deutsches Wettbewerbsrecht, vol. I: Europäisches Wettbewerbsrecht*, Einl. para. 1543 and 1631 (Günter Hirsch ed., 2nd edn., 2015).

[282] *See, e.g.*, BGH 1973 WM 1070, 1071—*Ölfeldrohre* (12 July 1973). For further illustration, *see, e.g.*, David J. Gerber, *The Extraterritorial Application of the German Antitrust Laws*, 77 Am. J. Int'l L. 756, 764–765 (1983) (including a partial translation of the *Ölfeldrohre* decision); Jürgen Basedow, *Entwicklungslinien des internationalen Kartellrechts—Ausbau und Ausdifferenzierung des Auswirkungsprinzips*, 1989 NJW 627, 628 *et seq.*; Anton K. Schnyder, *Wirtschaftskollisionsrecht—Sonderanknüpfung und extraterritoriale Anwendung wirtschaftsrechtlicher Normen unter besonderer Berücksichtigung von Marktrecht* § 6 para. 162 *et seq.* (1990); Dietmar Baetge, *Globalisierung des Wettbewerbsrechts* 272–273 (2009).

[283] For modern commentary, *see, e.g.*, Eckard Rehbinder, in *Kommentar zum Europäischen Kartellrecht (Wettbewerbsrecht, vol. I: EU/part 1)*, IntWbR para. 13 *et seq.* (Ulrich Immenga & Ernst-Joachim Mestmäcker eds., 5th ed., 2012).

[284] For an extensive discussion, *see* Damien Geradin, Marc Reysen & David Henry, *Extraterritoriality, Comity, and Cooperation in EU Competition Law*, 21, 21 *et seq.*, in *Cooperation, Comity, and Competition Policy* (Andrew T. Guzman ed., 2011).

[285] *See, e.g.*, Joseph P. Griffin, *Extraterritoriality in U.S. and EU Antitrust Enforcement*, 67 Antitrust L.J. 159, 173 (1999) (with further references).

would thus suffice.[286] Notwithstanding this apparent hesitation to base extraterritorial regulation expressly on effects,[287] *Wood Pulp* has been widely interpreted as having established an effects-based principle of jurisdiction.[288]

2 Alcoa *to* Hartford Fire*: From Unlimited to Substantial Effects*

The practical history of effects testing in US antitrust doctrine was longer and arguably more troubled than in Europe. For this reason, along with some determinative differences, it is particularly illustrative for my analysis. One aspect that has had a significant impact on legal doctrine—and that may account for the major differences between Europe and the United States—is the paradigm of a private attorney general. Antitrust in the United States has traditionally been enforced not only by public authorities but also through civil actions by private litigants injured by anticompetitive conduct.[289] Another aspect is the doctrine of international comity, which still prevails in the analysis of jurisdictional self-restraint. In the United States, unlike in Europe, antitrust regulation and its territorial scope of application have only rarely been found directly limited by principles of public international law. Instead, the doctrine of

[286] *See Ahlström Osakeyhtiö et al. v. Commission*, C-89/85, para. 16 (27 September 1988), [1988] E.C.R. 5193. The Court of First Instance went even further toward acknowledging a genuine effects doctrine in a merger-control case, holding that the European Commission had jurisdiction in a case where activities outside the common market had an "immediate and substantial effect in the Community," significantly impeding effective competition within the common market (*Gencor v. Commission*, T-102/96, para. 89 *et seq.* (25 March 1999), [1999] E.C.R. II-753).

[287] *See* Andreas F. Lowenfeld, *Conflict, Balancing of Interests, and the Exercise of Jurisdiction to Prescribe: Reflections on the Insurance Antitrust Case*, 89 Am. J. Int'l L. 42, 47 (1995) ("In contrast to the European Court of Justice, which is still reluctant to pronounce the E word, the U.S. Supreme Court takes the effects doctrine for granted.").

[288] *See, e.g.*, Eleanor M. Fox, *Modernization of Effects Jurisdiction: From Hands-Off to Hands-Linked*, 42 N.Y.U. J. Int'l L. & Pol. 159, 165 (2009); Hannah L. Buxbaum, *Territory, Territoriality, and the Resolution of Jurisdictional Conflict*, 57 Am. J. Comp. L. 631, 642 (2009); less convinced, *e.g.*, Joseph P. Griffin, *Extraterritoriality in U.S. and EU Antitrust Enforcement*, 67 Antitrust L.J. 159, 186 *et seq.* (1999); for a critique, *see* Anton K. Schnyder, *Gemeinschaftsrechtliches Kollisionsrecht?—Zur Anwendbarkeit des EG-Wettbewerbsrechts bei Sachverhalten mit Beziehungen zu Drittstaaten*, 3, 6 *et seq.*, in *Europäisches Gemeinschaftsrecht und Internationales Privatrecht* (Christian von Bar ed., 1991); *see also* Damien Geradin, Marc Reysen & David Henry, *Extraterritoriality, Comity, and Cooperation in EU Competition Law*, 21, 26 *et seq.*, in *Cooperation, Comity, and Competition Policy* (Andrew T. Guzman ed., 2011).

[289] The Clayton Act is the statutory foundation of private litigation. For the private attorney general in domestic antitrust law, *see, e.g.*, David J. Gerber, *Private Enforcement of Competition Law: A Comparative Perspective*, 431 *et seq.*, in *The Enforcement of Competition Law in Europe* (Thomas M. J. Möllers & Andreas Heinemann eds., 2007); for international antitrust, *see* Hannah L. Buxbaum, *The Private Attorney General in a Global Age: Public Interests in Private International Antitrust Litigation*, 26 Yale J. Int'l L. 219 (2001).

international comity has been at the center of the debate. Both the private attorney general and the doctrine of international comity have led to a different understanding of limitations to jurisdictional authority and of the relevance of substantive law policy on the scope of legislative jurisdiction.

The first milestone for the doctrine of US antitrust conflicts was set by the Supreme Court in 1909. In *American Banana*, Justice Holmes explained that "construction of any statute as intended to be confined in its operation and effect to the territorial limits over which the lawmaker has general and legitimate power. 'All legislation is *prima facie* territorial.' "[290] Since the defendant had not acted within US territory (but rather in Panama and Costa Rica), Holmes denied jurisdiction and rejected the application of the Sherman Act. Of course, this limited understanding of regulatory power did not endure the socioeconomic developments of the twentieth century. During the first decades of the century, US antitrust law began to witness a number of cases that eroded the strict *American Banana* territoriality.[291] The about-face occurred in 1945. In *U.S. v. Aluminum Co. of America*[292] (*Alcoa*), the Second Circuit had to decide on a typical phenomenon of the antitrust detachment between conduct and effects. Judge Learned Hand, speaking for the Second Circuit as the court of final appeal, essentially reversed Justice Holmes's approach to conduct-related territoriality.[293] Ever since, the effects test has dominated the analysis in antitrust conflicts.

The *Alcoa* facts are complex. In a nutshell, European and Canadian aluminum companies had agreed on quotas for aluminum production. If a party exceeded its allocated quota, it had to pay royalties, which were distributed among the others. Although the agreement did not expressly cover imports into the United States, it was clear that such imports should be included. The intended result was to discourage the production of aluminum. In what has become one of the most frequently cited passages from the case, Judge Learned Hand explained that neither effects absent intent nor intent absent effects would trigger jurisdiction.[294] This result was based on a general explanation of limitations on extraterritoriality. Learned Hand started with the question whether Congress (within limitations set by the constitution) had intended for a statutory provision to

290 *American Banana Co. v. United Fruit Co.*, 213 U.S. 347, 357 (1909).

291 *See, e.g., U.S. v. Pacific & Arctic Railway & Navigation Co.*, 228 U.S. 87 (1913); *Thomsen v. Cayser*, 243 U.S. 66 (1917); *U.S. v. Sisal Sales Corp.*, 274 U.S. 268 (1927).

292 *United States v. Aluminum Co. of America*, 148 F.2d 416 (2nd Cir. 1945) (L. Hand, J.).

293 For an extensive discussion, *see* Edward T. Swaine, *Cooperation, Comity, and Competition Policy: United States*, 1, 5, in *Cooperation, Comity, and Competition Policy* (Andrew T. Guzman ed., 2011). Since the Supreme Court lacked a quorum to decide the *Alcoa* case, the Second Circuit acted as the court of last instance.

294 *U.S. v. Aluminum Co. of America*, 148 F.2d 416, 443–444 (2nd Cir. 1945) (L. Hand, J.).

reach beyond national borders. He considered himself bound by the constitutional standard, but went on to explain that

> we are not to read general words, such as those in this Act, without regard to the limitations customarily observed by nations upon the exercise of their powers; limitations which generally correspond to those fixed by the "Conflict of Laws." We should not impute to Congress an intent to punish all whom its courts can catch, for conduct which has no consequences within the United States.[295]

Ultimately, it may have been the particular case and its specific outcome that has made *Alcoa* a paradigm of unbounded effects testing. The scope of Learned Hand's effects test, however, was not without a limit. After all, it required giving regard to the principles of the "conflict of laws." In addition, Learned Hand's approach was intended to stay within the confines of an internationally acknowledged standard:

> [I]t is settled law . . . that any state may impose liabilities, even upon persons not within its allegiance, for conduct outside its borders that has consequences within its borders which the state reprehends; and these liabilities other states will ordinarily recognize.[296]

What he did not spell out was an express definition of the necessary quantity and quality of effects.[297] This eventually became the test's major flaw. Later courts and lawmakers had to refine the standard.[298] We have already seen how the interest-balancing approach under *Timberlane* and *Mannington Mills* developed in response to the overextension of antitrust effects.[299] But the balancing of interests soon stopped dominating. One famous example that illustrates the practical failure and rejection of the balancing approach can be found in the District Court for the District of Columbia's 1984 decision in *Laker Airways, Ltd. v. Sabena, Belgian World Airlines.*[300] The problem of how far US antitrust laws would extend was debated in the context of a dispute over adjudicatory jurisdiction.[301] Laker Airways claimed that several competitors, both American and foreign based, were violating antitrust regulations. It further contended that the

[295] *Id.* at 443. [296] *Id.*

[297] Yet he described an implicit limitation: "Almost any limitation of the supply of goods in Europe, for example, or in South America, may have repercussions in the United States if there is trade between the two. Yet when one considers the international complications likely to arise from an effort in this country to treat such agreements as unlawful, it is safe to assume that Congress certainly did not intend the Act to cover them." (*Id.*).

[298] For the development, *see, e.g.*, Herbert Hovenkamp, *Federal Antitrust Policy—The Law of Competition and Its Practice* § 21.2a *et seq.* (3rd edn., 2005).

[299] *See supra* p. 440–441.

[300] *Laker Airways Ltd. v. Sabena, Belgian World Airlines*, 731 F.2d 909 (D.C.C., 1984).

[301] *Id.* at 917 *et seq.*; for a succinct litigation history and case review, *see* Hannah L. Buxbaum, *The Private Attorney General in a Global Age: Public Interests in Private International Antitrust Litigation*, 26 Yale J. Int'l L. 219, 232 *et seq.* (2001).

defendants had driven it out of the transatlantic air travel market and, ultimately, out of business.[302] The parties' concrete conflict before the district court arose from the defendants' attempt to block US proceedings via a UK antisuit injunction. The district court had to decide whether it could properly issue an injunction to protect domestic jurisdiction on the issue against interference by a UK injunction. On the merits, the court rejected interest balancing and the reasonableness test. As Judge Wilkey elaborated, not only were courts ill-equipped to neutrally balance conflicting state interests, but balancing as such was inadequate to promote international comity.[303] In his extensive critique of contemporary interest-balancing theory and practice, he pointed out that courts were unqualified and lacked the necessary time and resources to undertake a full-fledged evaluation and balancing of political issues. In addition, and as a result of this judicial inability to handle political issues, he found a *favor legis fori* to govern in almost all cases: "When push comes to shove, the domestic forum is rarely unseated."[304]

In addition to *Laker Airways*, contemporary federal case law contributed to the practical elimination of interest-balancing approaches.[305] And statutory law, too, has circumscribed attempts to balance conflicting interests. The 1982 Foreign Trade Antitrust Improvements Act is one example of the shift toward "unbalanced" effects testing. The act provides that US antitrust laws "shall not apply to conduct involving trade or commerce ... with foreign nations."[306] Hence, the act should not apply to export trade from the United States. However, an exception to this limited scope exists where the export trade at issue also harms imports, domestic commerce, or American exporters.[307] Such effects on US commerce, however, must overcome a threshold. They must be "direct, substantial, and reasonably foreseeable."[308] At least formally, no more balancing is required.

This was also the result when the Supreme Court had to decide on the issue of international antitrust jurisdiction in *Hartford Fire* in 1993. The case involved claims by several US states and private parties that a group of domestic and foreign insurers, reinsurers, and brokers had violated the

302 *Laker Airways Ltd. v. Sabena, Belgian World Airlines*, 731 F.2d 909, 916 *et seq.* (D.C.C., 1984).
303 *Id.* at 948. 304 *Id.* at 948 *et seq.*, 951.
305 For further examples, *see, e.g.*, Hannah L. Buxbaum, *The Private Attorney General in a Global Age: Public Interests in Private International Antitrust Litigation*, 26 Yale J. Int'l L. 219, 233 *et seq.* (2001).
306 15 U.S.C. § 6a.
307 *F. Hoffmann-La Roche Ltd. v. Empagran S.A.*, 542 U.S. 155, 158 (2004).
308 15 U.S.C. § 6a. *See also F. Hoffmann-La Roche Ltd. v. Empagran S.A.*, 542 U.S. 155, 162 (2004).

Sherman Act by engaging in conspiracies designed to force other insurers to change the terms of their insurance policies.[309] Justice Souter's opinion for the majority held that it is "well established by now that the Sherman Act applies to foreign conduct that was meant to produce and did in fact produce some substantial effect in the United States."[310] After finding sufficient effect in the United States, he left it open whether Congress had intended for courts to decline to exercise jurisdiction on the grounds of international comity. He reduced this analysis to a question of foreign sovereign compulsion (i.e., testing whether the defendant's allegedly violative conduct was *required* by foreign law). As Souter concluded, in accordance with the then current restatement, "no conflict exists … 'where a person subject to regulation by two states can comply with the laws of both.' "[311] In the end, denying that a true conflict existed allowed for a detour around international comity analysis.[312]

Not so for Justice Scalia's dissenting opinion. He took a different approach, emphasizing international comity. Scalia recognized Congress's broad legislative jurisdiction over acts on foreign territories under the Sherman Act; indeed, congressional intent to apply US antitrust law extraterritorially was not to be doubted.[313] But he established a second level of analysis: in statutory construction, a court would first have to give regard to the presumption of territoriality. Only if the presumption is rebutted (as he deemed to be the case in *Hartford Fire*) would a "second canon of statutory construction" become relevant.[314] Here, he referred to the *Charming Betsy* standard that the Supreme Court had set in 1804: "[A]n act of congress ought never to be construed to violate the law of nations if any other possible construction remains."[315] In other words, this meant that public international law, including "customary international law," provides limitations to the exercise of prescriptive jurisdiction. In principle, Congress has the

309 *Hartford Fire Ins. Co. v. California*, 509 U.S. 764, 764 (1993). 310 *Id.* at 796.

311 *Id.* at 799.

312 For a critique, *see, e.g.*, Andreas F. Lowenfeld, *Conflict, Balancing of Interests, and the Exercise of Jurisdiction to Prescribe: Reflections on the Insurance Antitrust Case*, 89 Am. J. Int'l L. 42, 46 (1995); Joel R. Paul, *The Transformation of International Comity*, 71 Law & Contemp. Probs. 19, 35 *et seq.* (2008); Hannah L. Buxbaum, *Territory, Territoriality, and the Resolution of Jurisdictional Conflict*, 57 Am. J. Comp. L. 631, 651 (2009).

313 *Hartford Fire Ins. Co. v. California*, 509 U.S. 764, 813 (1993) (Scalia, J., dissenting).

314 *Id.* at 814–815.

315 *Id.* For the *Charming Betsy* decision, *see Murray v. Schooner Charming Betsy*, 2 Cranch 64, 118, 2 L.Ed. 208 (1804) (Marshall, C.J.) ("It has also been observed that an act of Congress ought never to be construed to violate the law of nations if any other possible construction remains, and consequently can never be construed to violate neutral rights, or to affect neutral commerce, further than is warranted by the law of nations as understood in this country.").

authority to overstep these limitations. But it should never be presumed to intend such a violation.

Scalia's references are revealing. His solution was based not only on Story's conception of the "comity of nations"[316] but also on Learned Hand's (often overlooked) explanation that limitations to antitrust effects testing existed under the principles of "conflict of laws."[317] He also drew heavily on Supreme Court precedents in maritime law cases, particularly *Lauritzen* and *Romero*. On this basis of international comity, Scalia harshly rejected the majority's conclusion that no "true conflict" existed:

> That breathtakingly broad proposition [that a conflict exists only if compliance with US law constitutes a violation of foreign law] . . . will bring the Sherman Act and other laws into sharp and unnecessary conflict with the legitimate interests of other countries—particularly our closest trading partners.[318]

But this remained the dissenting opinion only. And courts after *Hartford Fire* failed to develop a consistent approach to issues of antitrust effects and international comity. Indeed, as it appeared at the end of the century, comity was considered to have little impact on the future of antitrust effects testing. But that only seemed to be.

3 Empagran*: The About-Face toward Comity*

In the 2004 case *Hoffmann-La Roche Ltd. v. Empagran S.A.*,[319] the Supreme Court reestablished the doctrine of international comity, similar to Justice Scalia's approach in *Hartford Fire*.[320] In the case, the plaintiffs brought a class-action suit alleging that the defendants—foreign and domestic vitamin manufacturers and distributors—had conspired to fix prices in the global vitamin market. They sought, among other things, compensation for damages resulting from purchases outside the United States. Even though the cartelization had also affected the American market, the court denied jurisdiction over the foreign plaintiffs' claims, arguing that effects in the United States caused by the defendants' cartelization were independent of any effects occurring abroad. Thus, under the Foreign Antitrust Improvements Act of 1982, a Sherman Act claim would not arise on the basis of effects of a foreign price-fixing scheme if this scheme did not have immediate domestic effects. Mere effects in the

[316] *Hartford Fire Ins. Co. v. California*, 509 U.S. 764, 817 (1993) (Scalia, J., dissenting).
[317] *Id.* [318] *Id.* at 820.
[319] *F. Hoffmann-La Roche Ltd. v. Empagran S.A.*, 542 U.S. 155 (2004).
[320] The *Empagran* majority cited to Scalia's dissent in *Hartford Fire. See F. Hoffmann-La Roche Ltd. v. Empagran S.A.*, 542 U.S. 155, 164 (2004). For the change in directions, *see* Herbert Hovenkamp, *Federal Antitrust Policy—The Law of Competition and Its Practice* § 21.2b (3rd edn., 2005); Hannah L. Buxbaum, *Territory, Territoriality, and the Resolution of Jurisdictional Conflict*, 57 Am. J. Comp. L. 631, 652 (2009).

United States would not suffice to trigger jurisdiction of the US antitrust regime.[321] Apart from this civil lawsuit, other types of law enforcement had taken place on the issue. One of these was a class-action suit initiated in the United States by American purchasers, which ended with a billion-dollar settlement. In addition, in other countries, private litigation had resulted in further (albeit smaller) payments by the violators. Finally, antitrust agencies in the United States, Europe, and other jurisdictions had imposed administrative fines.[322]

Writing for a unanimous court, and contrary to the *Hartford Fire* majority, Justice Breyer put forth what can be characterized as a public international law framework for antitrust conflicts. Analyzing the Supreme Court's *Charming Betsy* standard, he explained that ambiguous statutes must always be construed in order to "avoid unreasonable interference with the sovereign authority of other nations."[323] As he continued, this "rule of construction reflects principles of customary international law—law that … Congress ordinarily seeks to follow."[324] By this means, the majority's theoretical foundation has come full circle with regard to implementing the limitations of public international law in the analysis of jurisdictional powers. With *Empagran*, the Supreme Court appears to have abandoned extraterritorial overregulation and returned to the Storyan virtues of intersovereign respect and equality. In fact, Justice Breyer's explanation echoes traditional conflicts and comity doctrine and its consideration of the utility and convenience of international transacting and commerce:

> This rule of statutory construction cautions courts to assume that legislators take account of the legitimate sovereign interests of other nations when they write American laws. It thereby helps the potentially conflicting laws of different nations work together in harmony—a harmony particularly needed in today's highly interdependent commercial world.[325]

[321] *F. Hoffmann-La Roche Ltd. v. Empagran S.A.*, 542 U.S. 155, 175 (2004). For more details and a critique, *see, e.g.*, Hannah L. Buxbaum, *Transnational Regulatory Litigation*, 46 Va. J. Int'l L. 251, 273 *et seq.* (2006).

[322] Ralf Michaels, *Empagran's Empire: International Law and Statutory Interpretation in the U.S. Supreme Court of the Twenty-First Century*, 533, 533, in *International Law in the U.S. Supreme Court—Continuity and Change* (David L. Sloss et al. eds., 2011).

[323] *F. Hoffmann-La Roche Ltd. v. Empagran S.A.*, 542 U.S. 155, 164 (2004). For the *Charming Betsy* standard, *see Murray v. Schooner Charming Betsy*, 2 Cranch 64, 118, 2 L.Ed. 208 (1804) (Marshall, C.J.) ("It has also been observed that an act of Congress ought never to be construed to violate the law of nations if any other possible construction remains, and consequently can never be construed to violate neutral rights, or to affect neutral commerce, further than is warranted by the law of nations as understood in this country.")

[324] *F. Hoffmann-La Roche Ltd. v. Empagran S.A.*, 542 U.S. 155, 164 (2004).

[325] *Id.* at 164–165.

But the impression of an overarching *comitas* is fleeting. A closer look at the decision reveals that the court did not develop its analysis into a coherent system of conflicts resolution. While there is some reference to what could be characterized as a concept of a global trading of regulatory orders,[326] nothing implies that the court intended to create a universal system for allocating jurisdictional authority. As Justice Breyer explained, national antitrust laws may be converging across the globe, with the potential for policy conflicts shrinking. Nevertheless, crucial differences still exist. Not only do national regimes disagree on appropriate remedies, but also the system of civil litigation in American courts creates the risk of interference with other countries' administrative and criminal law enforcement procedures.

This last aspect is important. As the US government argued as amicus curiae in *Empagran*, the threat of private enforcement could detrimentally interfere with the executive's proceedings of investigation and enforcement: if a defendant fears having to pay massive private compensation and damages as the result of a future civil lawsuit in the United States, cooperation with other states' government agencies in prior proceedings will no longer be attractive.[327] In the end, the court rejected a detailed analysis comparing foreign and domestic antitrust policies:

> [T]his approach is too complex to prove workable. The Sherman Act covers many different kinds of anticompetitive agreements. Courts would have to examine how foreign law, compared with American law, treats not only price fixing but also, say, information-sharing agreements . . ., in respect to both primary conduct and remedy. The legally and economically technical nature of the enterprise means lengthier proceedings, appeals, and more proceedings—to the point where procedural costs and delays could themselves threaten interference with a foreign nation's ability to maintain the integrity of its own antitrust enforcement system.[328]

[326] *Id.* at 167 ("Congress might have hoped that America's antitrust laws, so fundamental a component of our own economic system, would commend themselves to other nations as well. But, if America's antitrust policies could not win their own way in the international marketplace for such ideas, Congress, we must assume, would not have tried to impose them, in an act of legal imperialism, through legislative fiat.").

[327] *Id.* at 167–168; *see also Brief of the United States as Amicus Curiae, F. Hoffmann-La Roche Ltd. v. Empagran S.A.*, 542 U.S. 155 (2004) (No. 03–724), 2004 WL 234125, at *19–25 (*id.* at 20: "The court of appeals' interpretation of Section 6a would undermine the effectiveness of the government's amnesty program. Even those conspirators who come forward and receive amnesty from criminal prosecution still face exposure to private treble damage actions under 15 U.S.C. 15(a).").

[328] *F. Hoffmann-La Roche Ltd. v. Empagran S.A.*, 542 U.S. 155, 168–169 (2004). *See also* Wolfgang Wurmnest, *Foreign Private Plaintiffs, Global Conspiracies, and the Extraterritorial Application of U.S. Antitrust Law*, 28 Hastings Int'l & Comp. L. Rev. 205, 220 *et seq.* (2005).

4 *The* Empagran *Critique: Capitulation, Isolationism, and Imperialism*

Conceiving of a universal jurisdictional order was not the aim in *Empagran*. The doctrine of comity was used, at best, as an escape technique, not as a constructive concept.[329] This preference for caution over activity has been harshly criticized. One example is Joel R. Paul's rejection of *Empagran*'s regard for a "highly interdependent commercial world." Such deference to the requirements of a global market, he explains, risks sacrificing important domestic policies.[330] As he concludes, limiting jurisdiction on account of globalized markets and international transactions reflects the decline of domestic autonomy: "In this globalized economy, courts serve a higher master and the sovereign's will must yield to the will of the market."[331] Indeed, Paul's critique of *Empagran* and of the court's apparently new formulation of comity is striking, at least at first glance. The plaintiffs in the case had argued, quite similarly, that antitrust deterrence may be massively impaired by a strictly territorial understanding of domestic jurisdiction. If developed countries' antitrust enforcers turn their back to violations in developing countries, where no real threat of prosecution and enforcement exists, perpetrators can offset their liability for violations imposed in, for example, the United States, by undiminished gains in those other jurisdictions. In the end, therefore, protecting consumers in foreign markets may also protect American interests.[332] Consequently, deference to anything other than genuine state interests and policies (particularly to the intricacies of what Justice Breyer called an "interdependent commercial world") appears to unduly subvert national interests.

A similar argument has been put forth from a different angle, one with a more internationalist flavor. Hannah L. Buxbaum and Ralf Michaels have characterized the Supreme Court's new comity approach as isolationist. As Buxbaum explains, *Empagran* presented a situation of transnational regulatory litigation where the rules to be applied would have been, in principle, largely agreed on by the international community. In fact, the case did not present a "true" conflict between nation-state policies but

[329] *But cf.* Justice Breyer's slightly different explanation in *The Court and the World—American Law and the New Global Realities* 133 (2015) ("The Court's changing approach tracks a similar change in its conception of comity—from one emphasizing the more formal objective of simple conflict avoidance to the more practical objective of maintaining cooperative working arrangements with corresponding enforcement authorities of different nations.").

[330] Joel R. Paul, *The Transformation of International Comity*, 71 Law & Contemp. Probs. 19, 36 (2008).

[331] *Id.* at 37 and 38.

[332] For a similar argument, *see Pfizer, Inc. v. Gov't of India*, 434 U.S. 308, 314–315 (1978); *Kruman v. Christie's Int'l PLC*, 284 F.3d 384, 403 (2nd Cir. 2002).

rather offered an opportunity to enhance global procedural efficiency and deterrence on the basis of a universally acknowledged rule prohibiting hard-core pricing cartels. Had the Supreme Court applied domestic antitrust law to the global cartel, consumer protection worldwide—and, ultimately, global welfare—would have improved.[333] The court's abstention, therefore, was a missed opportunity. Michaels has further extended this point. What the court actually did, he argues, was interpret comity in the sense that each country must regulate its own market and nothing else; each state must "act in isolation for itself."[334] Even though the court turned comity into a doctrine of international policy and thereby assumed the role of a global governor, it nonetheless rejected taking responsibility by retreating to an approach of strict territoriality.[335] In the end, Michaels concludes, isolationism turns into hegemonialism by restricting foreign private plaintiffs' access to US law. Even though there exists a universal consensus on substantive law policies such as price fixing, the court's denial of access to efficient enforcement ultimately leaves many countries unprotected against the power of transnational antitrust perpetrators—often US corporate actors.[336] In the end, a retreat to nineteenth-century territoriality amounts to an imperialistic denial of justice to developing countries' consumers, even though these countries may be interested in the enforcement of US antitrust policies.[337]

5 *The Comity of Self-Defense: Ostracizing the Private Attorney General*

This critique is not to be rejected per se. Of course, the prohibition of pricing cartels is a virtually universally acknowledged standard, and the efficient enforcement of US antitrust law would have been largely in compliance with other nations' policies and, arguably, public international law. But the internationalist critics overlook an important aspect: the universality of substantive law policies should not be used as an

[333] Hannah L. Buxbaum, *Transnational Regulatory Litigation*, 46 Va. J. Int'l L. 251, 260–261, 270 *et seq.*, 283 and *passim* (2006).

[334] Ralf Michaels, *Empagran's Empire: International Law and Statutory Interpretation in the U.S. Supreme Court of the Twenty-First Century*, 533, 538, in *International Law in the U.S. Supreme Court—Continuity and Change* (David L. Sloss et al. eds., 2011).

[335] *Id.* at 539.

[336] For a similar conclusion, *see* Wolfgang Wurmnest, *Foreign Private Plaintiffs, Global Conspiracies, and the Extraterritorial Application of U.S. Antitrust Law*, 28 Hastings Int'l & Comp. L. Rev. 205, 216 (2005).

[337] As Michaels explains, today's imperialism is not like the old-fashioned imperialism that sought to impose US law on the rest of the world. It is the rejection of the access to justice necessary to protect the world against "Western corporate actors." *See* Ralf Michaels, *Empagran's Empire: International Law and Statutory Interpretation in the U.S. Supreme Court of the Twenty-First Century*, 533, 541 *et seq.*, in *International Law in the U.S. Supreme Court—Continuity and Change* (David L. Sloss et al. eds., 2011).

argument for overriding the limitations of international comity, especially in its traditional Huberian and Storyan shape. One consequence of a more traditional perspective is that comity analysis—beyond giving regard to substantive norms and policies—must also give regard to potential distortions resulting from an international divergence of procedural and enforcement structures. This means that even if a domestic policy at issue is in compliance with internationally acknowledged standards, its stringent extraterritorial enforcement may backfire. In international antitrust cases, the problem has several facets.

One facet of the argument has been put forth by Paul B. Stephan under a national-welfare perspective. As Stephan explains, the environment in American courts is highly favorable to civil-litigation plaintiffs. The right to a jury trial, the "American rule" on attorney fees, pretrial discovery, the class-action device, and overcompensatory recoveries are characteristics that contribute to what Stephan describes as a "gap between the U.S. mechanisms of civil justice and those of the rest of the world."[338] One consequence of this gap is the increased "settlement value" of claims brought before US courts compared with litigation in a foreign forum.[339] Granting forum jurisdiction too generously, he concludes, will ultimately run the risk of overdeterrence on the domestic market. This risk is aggravated by the fact that the determination of whether certain practices constitute an antitrust violation is difficult due to the general ambiguity of the substantive law policies at play. This is the well-known phenomenon of overinclusive law enforcement. If enforced to the letter, most rules may be found to encompass more fact patterns than intended by policy makers.[340] The policy implemented will then be overextended, with all its negative effects attached. Hence, had *Empagran* found sufficient effects to exist, many potentially beneficial activities could have been challenged before the courts. As Stephan argues, therefore, allowing broad jurisdictional interference can result in a "tax on potentially

[338] Paul B. Stephan, *Empagran: Empire Building or Judicial Modesty*, 553, 554, in *International Law in the U.S. Supreme Court—Continuity and Change* (David L. Sloss et al. eds., 2011). *See also* Jean-Gabriel Castel, *The Extraterritorial Effects of Antitrust Laws*, 179 Recueil des Cours 9, 39 (1983-I); P. M. Roth, *Reasonable Extraterritoriality: Correcting the "Balance of Interests,"* 41 I.C.L.Q. 245, 249 (1992).

[339] Justice Scalia made a similar point with his Shangri-La allegory in *Morrison*. *See Morrison v. Nat'l Australia Bank Ltd.*, 561 U.S. 247, 270 (2010) ("While there is no reason to believe that the United States has become the Barbary Coast for those perpetrating frauds on foreign securities markets, some fear that it has become the Shangri-La of class-action litigation for lawyers representing those allegedly cheated in foreign securities markets.").

[340] William M. Landes & Richard A. Posner, *The Private Enforcement of Law*, 4 J. Legal Stud. 1, 38 (1975).

desirable economic behavior."[341] Conversely, narrowing jurisdiction contributes to deregulation and ultimately protects the domestic economy.[342]

Yet the *Empagran* impetus to limit access to the courthouse can also be seen in a more comprehensive light than that suggested by simple reference to an aim of protecting domestic competitiveness. There is also a global-welfare concern—and this brings international comity to the fore. The issue must be explained in light of procedural rules: in order to come to a verdict in an international antitrust case, a forum court must first establish personal jurisdiction over an alleged violator.[343] One might thus assume that the bulk of defendants in US courts consist of domestic entities. But this is not the case. Modern antitrust litigation regularly also features multinational entities and foreign corporate actors. Particularly in countries where the number of foreign companies doing business is high, as in the United States, establishing personal jurisdiction is not an insurmountable obstacle. Often, sufficient contacts or assets within the domestic territory exist.[344] Notably, the doctrine of minimum contacts allows for an exercise of personal jurisdiction if a foreign defendant transacts business in the forum or is the parent corporation of a domestic subsidiary.[345] Hence, in international antitrust cases, domestic defendants are not the only actors who must bear a tax on potentially desirable operations. A national-welfare perspective may thus be too narrow, for the problem of overinclusive law enforcement and the ensuing risk of stifling beneficial competition are global in scope.

Furthermore, a look at the divergence of enforcement structures in different jurisdictions highlights another potential drawback of the

[341] Paul B. Stephan, *Empagran: Empire Building or Judicial Modesty*, 553, 556, in *International Law in the U.S. Supreme Court—Continuity and Change* (David L. Sloss et al. eds., 2011). For the chilling effect of overdeterrence in antitrust enforcement, *see* Max Huffman, *A Standing Framework for Private Extraterritorial Antitrust Enforcement*, 60 SMU L. Rev. 103, 114 *et seq.* (2007).

[342] Paul B. Stephan, *Empagran: Empire Building or Judicial Modesty*, 553, 557–558, in *International Law in the U.S. Supreme Court—Continuity and Change* (David L. Sloss et al. eds., 2011).

[343] Also, an enforcement of the forum court's judgment will be possible only if there is sufficient international cooperation or if the defendant has assets in the forum state that can be seized. *See* William S. Dodge, *Antitrust and the Draft Hague Judgments Convention*, 32 Law & Pol'y Int'l Bus. 363, 366 (2001).

[344] *See* Rolf Bär, *Kartellrecht und Internationales Privatrecht* 24 (1965). More recently, *see, e. g.*, William S. Dodge, *Breaking the Public Law Taboo*, 43 Harv. Int'l L.J. 161, 223–224 (2002); William S. Dodge, *Antitrust and the Draft Hague Judgments Convention*, 32 Law & Pol'y Int'l Bus. 363, 364 *et seq.* (2001).

[345] For an extensive overview of the doctrine of personal jurisdiction in international antitrust cases and references to case law, *see* Herbert Hovenkamp, *Federal Antitrust Policy—The Law of Competition and Its Practice* § 21.3 (3rd edn., 2005).

transnational enforcement paradigm. Antitrust regulation in Europe is still largely within the hands of public authorities. Private litigation has long been the exception rather than the rule.[346] This is different in the United States, where public and private enforcement structures coexist and where the magnitude of private actions even exceeds the government's enforcement efforts.[347] It is this privatization of regulation that leads to problems on the international plane. In fact, it is mainly the private attorney general who enforces antitrust policies in the United States. The idea is that personal interest in seeking redress provides a sufficiently strong incentive for private parties to vindicate their rights. Governmental enforcement is then no longer needed (or can be reduced) since the litigant concurrently asserts a cause of action in her own interest *and* vindicates an interest of the public.[348] Yet the private attorney general has no obligation to sue.[349] And in contrast to a public prosecutor or state official, she will give primary or even exclusive regard to her private interests—in other words, profit maximization.[350] This is where the problem looms. While the nonexistence of a cooperating or controlling instance for the private-attorney-general mechanism is a key part of the concept in the domestic sphere, the lack of effective control is a major drawback in the international arena. In economic terms, again, in a system of private enforcement, all laws will be enforced as long as their enforcement provides a positive expected net return. In contrast to public officials, private attorney generals will rarely undertake "discretionary nonenforcement" for reasons beyond the economic

[346] *See supra* p. 315–317.

[347] *See, e.g.*, Clifford A. Jones, *Exporting Antitrust Courtrooms to the World: Private Enforcement in a Global Market*, 16 Loy. Consumer L. Rev. 409, 411 (2004).

[348] For an early and famous description of the technique, *see Associated Indus. of New York State v. Ickes*, 134 F.2d 694, 704 (2nd Cir. 1943) ("Instead of designating the Attorney General, or some other public officer . . ., Congress can constitutionally enact a statute conferring on any non-official person, or on a designated group of non-official persons, authority to bring a suit . . ., and there is nothing constitutionally prohibiting Congress from empowering any person, official or not, to institute a proceeding involving such a controversy, even if the sole purpose is to vindicate the public interest. Such persons, so authorized, are, so to speak, private Attorney Generals."). *See also* John C. Coffee, Jr., *Rescuing the Private Attorney General: Why the Model of the Lawyer as Bounty Hunter Is Not Working*, 42 Md. L. Rev. 215 (1983); Evan Caminker, *The Constitutionality of Qui Tam Actions*, 99 Yale L.J. 341, 342–343 and 345 (1989); Hannah L. Buxbaum, *The Private Attorney General in a Global Age: Public Interests in Private International Antitrust Litigation*, 26 Yale J. Int'l L. 219, 222 *et seq.* (2001).

[349] *See Mitsubishi Motors Corp. v. Soler Chrysler-Plymouth, Inc.*, 473 U.S. 614, 636 (1985).

[350] *See* William M. Landes & Richard A. Posner, *The Private Enforcement of Law*, 4 J. Legal Stud. 1, 15 (1975); David J. Gerber, *Private Enforcement of Competition Law: A Comparative Perspective*, 431, 440, in *The Enforcement of Competition Law in Europe* (Thomas M.J. Möllers & Andreas Heinemann eds., 2007).

rationale.[351] Hence, they will not abstain from a lawsuit as long as it seems profitable—regardless of whether it is in the interest of third parties or the public. Judicial self-restraint and the consideration of foreign policies or governmental interests are the last things the private attorney general cares about in international litigation.[352]

Of course, courts should be and often are a "controlling" instance in private-attorney-general litigation with regard to concepts of public policy, equity, and comity. But their effectiveness must be doubted—particularly in the international arena. In my historical account, I analyzed problems of propertization in US trademark law. During the twentieth century, domestic law concepts of equity and goodwill protection were not suitable to prevent the growing extension of trademark rights.[353] Extraterritoriality in international economic law is no different. On the contrary, the problem is even more virulent here. The courts' perspective is too narrow: they are generally at risk of overlooking political and economic concerns since their focus is usually on the parties' individual rights, not on the larger political and economic context.[354] Distortions beyond the setting of the lawsuit and the individual parties' interests will thus often remain invisible until after a decision is made. In addition, long-term drawbacks of extensive jurisdiction are regularly more difficult to evaluate than short-term benefits.[355] Hence, it is the lack of a coordinating and controlling instance among the group of private attorneys general or within the judiciary that accounts for the risk of extraterritorial overextension of regulatory policies. Seen in this light, a traditional reading of the principle of international comity counsels jurisdictional self-restraint and abstention—just as the Supreme Court did in *Empagran*.

Such a concept of international comity is also in line with other recent developments in international antitrust law. The general trend here as well is toward cooperative self-discipline. One aspect is the shift from judicial conflicts resolution to affirmative administrative and regulatory

351 William M. Landes & Richard A. Posner, *The Private Enforcement of Law*, 4 J. Legal Stud. 1, 38 *et seq.* (1975).

352 *See also* Joseph P. Griffin, *Extraterritoriality in U.S. and EU Antitrust Enforcement*, 67 Antitrust L.J. 159, 194 (1999); Hannah L. Buxbaum, *The Private Attorney General in a Global Age: Public Interests in Private International Antitrust Litigation*, 26 Yale J. Int'l L. 219, 236–237, 253 (2001); Max Huffman, *A Standing Framework for Private Extraterritorial Antitrust Enforcement*, 60 SMU L. Rev. 103, 114 (2007).

353 *See supra* p. 110 *et seq.*

354 Curtis A. Bradley, *The Costs of International Human Rights Litigation*, 2 Chi. J. Int'l L. 457, 459 (2001).

355 Lea Brilmayer, *The Extraterritorial Application of American Law: A Methodological and Constitutional Appraisal*, 50 Law & Contemp. Probs. 11, 20 (1987).

cooperation, sometimes also termed "positive comity."[356] Under a positive-comity approach, antitrust regulation in the international arena has become a question of administrative and political consultation and collaboration.[357] This is particularly important since antitrust enforcement in many jurisdictions has been increasingly transformed from civil litigation into criminal prosecution.[358] As mentioned earlier, in *Empagran*, the German, Canadian, and US governments contended that the interference of extended civil litigation in criminal law enforcement mechanisms would distort their regulatory systems.[359] This phenomenon is known as inverse deterrence: excessive civil liability may decrease a violator's incentive to participate in leniency programs in an effort to avoid criminal sanctions. In the end, overregulation will result in underdeterrence.[360] In fact, the civil-to-criminal shift has led to an increase in public enforcement and a concurrent relocation of antitrust conflicts resolution to the executive and administrative levels.[361]

Against this backdrop, one further point of the *Empagran* criticism can be clarified. As Ralf Michaels has explained, the Supreme Court missed a dutiful exercise of its self-assigned role as a "global governor."[362] As he

[356] For international antitrust law, *see, e.g.*, Jean-Gabriel Castel, *The Extraterritorial Effects of Antitrust Laws*, 179 Recueil des Cours 9, 93 *et seq.* (1983-I). More recently, *e.g.*, Anne-Marie Slaughter, *A New World Order* 30 (2004).

[357] *See, e.g.*, Joseph P. Griffin, *Extraterritoriality in U.S. and EU Antitrust Enforcement*, 67 Antitrust L.J. 159, 180 *et seq.* (1999); Eleanor M. Fox, *Modernization of Effects Jurisdiction: From Hands-Off to Hands-Linked*, 42 N.Y.U. J. Int'l L. & Pol. 159, 169 *et seq.* (2009); Dietmar Baetge, *Globalisierung des Wettbewerbsrechts* 301 *et seq.* (2009); *Developments in the Law—Extraterritoriality, Comity and Extraterritoriality in Antitrust Enforcement*, 124 Harv. L. Rev. 1269, 1276–1277 (2011).

[358] *Developments in the Law—Extraterritoriality, Comity and Extraterritoriality in Antitrust Enforcement*, 124 Harv. L. Rev. 1269, 1271 and 1274 *et seq.* (2011).

[359] *F. Hoffmann-La Roche Ltd. v. Empagran S.A.*, 542 U.S. 155, 168 (2004).

[360] *See* Max Huffman, *A Standing Framework for Private Extraterritorial Antitrust Enforcement*, 60 SMU L. Rev. 103, 115–116 (2007); for an overview, *see* Wolfgang Wurmnest, *Foreign Private Plaintiffs, Global Conspiracies, and the Extraterritorial Application of U.S. Antitrust Law*, 28 Hastings Int'l & Comp. L. Rev. 205, 212 *et seq.* (2005).

[361] Even though enforcement might be less efficient in administrative proceedings compared to plaintiffs' extended options in civil litigation (*see* Jürgen Basedow, *Weltkartellrecht* 31–33 (1998) (illustrating the difference between public/criminal law enforcement and enforcement through private litigation in the United States)), scholarly commentary appears to agree that the shift was successful. As has been contended, the shift has actually led to an optimization of international deterrence. *See, e.g.*, Max Huffman, *A Standing Framework for Private Extraterritorial Antitrust Enforcement*, 60 SMU L. Rev. 103, 116 (2007); *Developments in the Law—Extraterritoriality, Comity and Extraterritoriality in Antitrust Enforcement*, 124 Harv. L. Rev. 1269, 1279 (2011); *but see also* Hannah L. Buxbaum, *Transnational Regulatory Litigation*, 46 Va. J. Int'l L. 251, 295–296 (2006).

[362] Ralf Michaels, *Empagran's Empire: International Law and Statutory Interpretation in the U.S. Supreme Court of the Twenty-First Century*, 533, 536, and 541 *et seq.*, in *International Law in the U.S. Supreme Court—Continuity and Change* (David L. Sloss et al. eds., 2011).

concludes, the *Empagran* outcome thus resulted in an imperialistic denial of justice to Third World countries and their consumers. But the court did not necessarily trifle with this issue. First of all, US courts have no mandate or duty to heal the world. This is a concern particularly if such altruism comes at the cost of entertaining an expensive federal judiciary as a forum for foreign parties' claims. This perspective may be debatable with regard to human rights violations.[363] Yet there is no compelling reason to risk causing more damage than benefits when confronted with the far more mundane issues of international economic law. This is all the more true in light of existing alternatives. The US federal judiciary may well fill the role of a global enforcer. But the question remains whether the courtroom is the right stage in which to act. As we have just seen, the drawbacks of international private-attorney-general litigation are significant. A better alternative—particularly with regard to its political controllability—could thus be to extend public authorities' capacity to consider transactions and improper gains outside the domestic sphere when determining the remedies required to establish a sufficiently strong deterrent.[364] Far less exposed to the risks of private-attorney-general usurpation, this variant can guarantee efficient enforcement by developed countries' antitrust authorities and protect markets and consumers in developing countries. The danger of distortion in other jurisdictions' enforcement systems—and with respect to the utility and convenience of international transacting—is accordingly reduced.

E Summary

The effects test, as illustrated by my exploration of international antitrust doctrine, has become the preeminent determinant of legislative, or prescriptive, jurisdiction in regulatory conflicts. The scope of jurisdiction, if tested on the basis of economic, commercial, or marketplace effects, has always been restricted by principles of public international law and comity. Yet the idea of transnational regulation and of a universality of policies has increasingly gained hold. If consensus on policies exists, as some have suggested, there is no further risk of jurisdictional conflict. Accordingly, domestic courts should be authorized to enforce such "global" policies both territorially and extraterritorially. However, a more fundamental and traditional aspect of limitations to legislative jurisdiction has recently emerged. With the Supreme Court's 2004 *Empagran* decision, antitrust conflicts doctrine in the United States has returned to a

363 *See infra* p. 464 *et seq.*

364 For a similar approach in Europe, *see* Michaels, Buxbaum, and Muir Watt in their *Brief of Amici Curiae, F. Hoffmann-La Roche Ltd. v. Empagran S.A.*, 542 U.S. 155 (2004) (No. 03-724), 2004 WL 542780, at *16–17.

more cogent understanding of international comity, quite similar to what Huber, Story, and Savigny had conceived of as necessary for the utility and convenience of international transacting and commerce. As *Empagran* illustrates, the problem of finding adequate limitations to jurisdiction cannot be resolved by mere reference to a global uniformity of substantive law policies. As long as nation-states' enforcement systems diverge, even universal policies cannot be extended extraterritorially without causing a distortion of international competition.

II The Zenith of Transnationalization: A Story of Alien Tort Statute Contraction

For decades, international human rights litigation has been transnationalists' favorite plaything. Private-party litigation in this field somewhat reflects the growing dissolution and fragmentation of the nation-state. In particular, the American variant of international human rights litigation, under the rubric of the ATS, has been described as transforming national courts into fora of interconnected decision makers who are creating a transnational common law. But not only have human rights become a universal currency in many national regimes; more generally, normativity has become independent of nation-state politics and has therefore become a truly universalist matter. In this light, the end of choice of law seems to have arrived. Transcendental norms are internalized *eo instanti* and without modification. Yet a closer look at the landscape of ATS litigation implies that the pendulum is about to swing back—or has already done so.

A The "Legal Lohengrin": From Comity to Settled International Law

The US Judiciary Act of 1789 provides for federal courts' jurisdiction over "any civil action by an alien for a tort only, committed in violation of the Law of Nations or a Treaty of the United States."[365] Today, this provision is known as the Alien Tort Statute. The statute was regarded as largely obsolete and remained unapplied for almost two centuries before the Second Circuit Court of Appeals decided on its resurrection—one could say "Lohengrin style"[366]—in 1980.[367]

[365] Judiciary Act of 1789, § 9, 1 Stat. 73, 76–77 (28 U.S.C. § 1350).

[366] *IIT v. Vencap, Ltd.*, 519 F.2d 1001, 1015 (2nd Cir. 1975) ("This old but little used section is a kind of legal Lohengrin; although it has been with us since the first Judiciary Act . . . no one seems to know whence it came." (Friendly, J.)).

[367] For the statute's history, *see, e.g.*, Kenneth C. Randall, *Federal Jurisdiction over International Law Claims: Inquiries into the Alien Tort Statute*, 18 N.Y.U. J. Int'l L. & Pol. 1, 4 n. 15 (1985); Beth Stephens, *Translating Filártiga: A Comparative and*

In *Filártiga v. Peña-Irala*,[368] the plaintiffs, citizens of Paraguay, inter alia alleged that the defendant, a former Paraguayan police officer, had kidnapped their son and tortured him to death in 1976. The defendant had come to the United States in 1978 and was living in New York at the time of the case's filing. The key issue confronting the court was how to determine the requirements for a tort in violation of the law of nations. The District Court for the Eastern District of New York in the first instance had held that a foreign government's treatment of its own citizens did not constitute such a violation. The Second Circuit reversed the decision, finding jurisdiction under the ATS since "official torture is ... prohibited by the law of nations."[369] Chief Judge Kaufman, writing for the court, explained that "the general assent of civilized nations" could turn a "standard that began as one of comity only" and transform it "into 'a settled rule of international law.' "[370] Any norm not founded on such a consensus, he pointed out, would run the risk of imposing idiosyncratic legal rules in the name of applying international law. Hence, it was important to determine a clear framework for categorizing public international law norms. In this regard, Kaufman referred to the 1964 Supreme Court decision in *Banco Nacional de Cuba v. Sabbatino*,[371] where a court majority had declined to rule on the validity of the Cuban government's expropriation of a foreign-owned corporation's assets. The issue had been whether the act-of-state doctrine would preclude a determination that the expropriation had violated international law. *Sabbatino* repeated a frequently occurring theme in transnational litigation:

> It should be apparent that the greater the degree of codification or consensus concerning a particular area of international law, the more appropriate it is for the judiciary to render decisions regarding it, since the courts can then focus on the application of an agreed principle to circumstances of fact rather than on the sensitive task of establishing a principle not inconsistent with the national interest or with international justice. It is also evident that some aspects of international law touch much more sharply on national nerves than do others; the less important the implications of an issue are for our foreign relations, the weaker the justification for exclusivity in the political branches.[372]

Taking this *Sabbatino* continuum of international consensus as his starting point, Kaufman found the case scenario in *Filártiga* to reflect a

International Law Analysis of Domestic Remedies for International Human Rights Violations, 27 Yale J. Int'l L. 1, 7 (2002); William R. Casto, *The New Federal Common Law of Tort Remedies for Violations of International Law*, 37 Rutgers L.J. 635, 635 (2006); for a general overview, *see also* Gary B. Born & Peter B. Rutledge, *International Civil Litigation in United States Courts* 33 *et seq.* (5th edn., 2011).

[368] *Filártiga v. Peña-Irala*, 630 F.2d 876 (2nd Cir. 1980). [369] *Id.* at 884.

[370] *Id.* at 880–881; *The Paquete Habana*, 175 U.S. 677, 700 (1900).

[371] *Banco Nacional de Cuba v. Sabbatino*, 376 U.S. 398 (1964). [372] *Id.* at 428.

sufficiently developed international agreement. As he elaborated, "there are few, if any, issues in international law today on which opinion seems to be so united as the limitations on a state's power to torture persons held in its custody."[373] Interestingly, the *Sabbatino* majority had actually refused to decide on the legitimacy of the Cuban expropriation at issue, making an express reference to the aim of preserving international and political stability. Abstention was said to be in the interests of the United States *and* the international community.[374] As would soon become apparent, *Filártiga* established the contrary approach using the same argument.

Since *Filártiga*, as has often been said, US federal courts have been "flooded" with civil human rights litigation.[375] While this is an exaggeration considering the actual case numbers,[376] the scope of ATS lawsuits has indeed increased. Courts have assumed jurisdiction over, inter alia, cases of alleged genocide, summary execution, disappearance, and arbitrary detention, as well as slave labor, apartheid war crimes, and torture. The categories of defendants subject to the act's reach have been understood to include officers and officials of the United States, representatives of foreign and de facto governments, and—particularly important in more recent case law—corporate entities. In this respect, the issue is usually the corporate defendants' alleged aiding and abetting of foreign governments' human rights violations.[377] Among this plethora of issues, one aspect is important here: the hybridity and universality of norms that have been acknowledged for internalization under the ATS illustrates a facet of transnationalism that works at the expense of comity. The Supreme Court provided an insight in 2004.

B The *Sosa* Transnationalization: Hybridity, Universality, and Specificity

The line of events that resulted in *Sosa v. Alvarez-Machain*[378] began in 1985 when a US drug enforcement agent was tortured and murdered in Mexico. A Mexican physician, Humberto Álvarez-Machaín, was suspected

[373] *Filártiga v. Peña-Irala*, 630 F.2d 876, 881 (2nd Cir. 1980).

[374] *Banco Nacional de Cuba v. Sabbatino*, 376 U.S. 398, 436–437 (1964).

[375] Tara Elliott, *Risky Business: The Alien Tort Claims Act and the Foreign Corrupt Practices Act Expand the Reach of U.S. Courts in a Global Economy*, 62 Rutgers L. Rev. 211, 225 (2009); *Developments in the Law—Extraterritoriality, Comity and Extraterritoriality in Antitrust Enforcement*, 124 Harv. L. Rev. 1226, 1234 *et seq.* (2011).

[376] Beth Stephens, *The Curious History of the Alien Tort Statute*, 89 Notre Dame L. Rev. 1467, 1487 (2014).

[377] Tara Elliott, *Risky Business: The Alien Tort Claims Act and the Foreign Corrupt Practices Act Expand the Reach of U.S. Courts in a Global Economy*, 62 Rutgers L. Rev. 211, 224–225 (2009); Ingrid Wuerth, *Kiobel v. Royal Dutch Petroleum Co.: The Supreme Court and the Alien Tort Statute*, 107 Am. J. Int'l L. 601, 604 (2013) (both with references to case law).

[378] *Sosa v. Alvarez-Machain*, 542 U.S. 692 (2004).

as having assisted in the crime. The US Drug Enforcement Administration hired a group of Mexican nationals, including the later defendant José Francisco Sosa, to kidnap Álvarez-Machaín in Mexico and bring him to the United States. However, the government failed to present sufficient evidence for a conviction, and, after his acquittal, Álvarez-Machaín sued the United States and Sosa under the ATS. Even though the Supreme Court ultimately rejected the claim, finding that the kidnapping had not violated a norm of international law,[379] the majority's analysis represents the concept of transnational law. Hybridity and universality are the governing paradigms.

At the time of the ATS's enactment in the late eighteenth century, the majority explained, American legal thought held the law of nations to comprise not only norms governing relations among nation-state sovereigns but also judge-made rules for international individual transacting—so to speak, a law merchant for international commerce.[380] In addition to these intercountry and interindividual norms, however, was a third category. These "hybrid international norms" were found in an area of overlap that concurrently governed both state relationships and individual rights and duties.[381] On this basis, as the *Sosa* majority concluded, the ATS was not only a jurisdictional grant but also

> best read as having been enacted on the understanding that the common law would provide a cause of action for the modest number of international law violations with a potential for personal liability at the time.[382]

In his concurring opinion, Justice Scalia rejected this concept of "internalization" of customary international law. The court's internal dispute on this issue evolved primarily around questions of judicial powers and constitutional limitations—however, it also reveals the ideas of transnationalization that had captured the US judiciary at the turn of the century. Indeed, the hybridity of national and international law was a key point of contention.

Scalia rejected the majority's concept of norm hybridization by focusing on the post-*Erie* paradigm of internalization. The conception of law as preexisting—and hence potentially universal—rather than a product of the national legislature, he explained, had been jettisoned in 1938. Ever since the Supreme Court's *Erie* decision, "the law is not so much found or

[379] *Id.* at 725.
[380] *Id.* at 714–715. *See also* Louis Henkin, *International Law as Law in the United States*, 82 Mich. L. Rev. 1555, 1557–1558 (1984); Harold Hongju Koh, *Is International Law Really State Law?*, 111 Harv. L. Rev. 1824, 1830 (1998).
[381] *Sosa v. Alvarez-Machain*, 542 U.S. 692, 715 (2004).
[382] *Id.* at 724.

discovered as it is either made or created."[383] In this regard, Scalia also made reference to Justice Holmes's oft-enunciated dissent in *Black and White Taxicab & Transfer Co.*, critically depicting the traditional view of the common law as a "transcendental body of law outside of any particular State but obligatory within it unless and until changed by statute."[384] After the death of this old conception of the general common law in *Erie*, as Scalia then went on to explain, the federal judiciary would need a new "federal-common-law-making authority"—without such a constitutional foundation, it could not materialize norms of the international legal order into national law. Accordingly, the mere existence of external rules of customary international law would never suffice to implement it in American law.[385] In sum, this meant that national law was isolated from a transnationalist osmosis—legal norms, according to Justice Scalia, are the product of national politics rather than an obscure world community consensus.

In response to this critique, the majority noted that judicial power was not completely barred by *Erie*. On the contrary, as they understood, it still allowed for the recognition of new substantive federal common law rules, since that was what the court had done for two centuries and was what Congress had always tolerated. With respect to norm internalization, the majority concluded that "the door is still ajar subject to vigilant

[383] *Erie R. Co. v. Tompkins*, 304 U.S. 64, 79 (1938) ("The fallacy underlying the rule declared in Swift v. Tyson is made clear by Mr. Justice Holmes. The doctrine rests upon the assumption that there is 'a transcendental body of law outside of any particular State but obligatory within it unless and until changed by statute,' ... 'But law in the sense in which courts speak of it today does not exist without some definite authority behind it. The common law so far as it is enforced in a State, whether called common law or not, is not the common law generally but the law of that State existing by the authority of that State without regard to what it may have been in England or anywhere else.[']"); for the Holmesian perspective, *see* Oliver Wendell Holmes, Jr., *The Common Law* 35–36 (1881)).

[384] *Sosa v. Alvarez-Machain*, 542 U.S. 692, 725 (2004); *Black & White Taxicab & Transfer Co. v. Brown & Yellow Taxicab & Transfer Co.*, 276 U.S. 518, 532–534 (1928) (Holmes, J., dissenting).

[385] *Sosa v. Alvarez-Machain*, 542 U.S. 692, 742 *et seq.* (2004) (Scalia, J., concurring). For an extensive account of constitutional arguments against incorporation of international law as federal common law, *see*, Curtis A. Bradley & Jack L. Goldsmith, *Customary International Law as Federal Common Law: A Critique of the Modern Position*, 110 Harv. L. Rev. 815 (1997); Curtis A. Bradley, Jack L. Goldsmith & David H. Moore, *Sosa, Customary International Law, and the Continuing Relevance of Erie*, 120 Harv. L. Rev. 869 (2007). For the contrary position, *see*, Louis Henkin, *International Law as Law in the United States*, 82 Mich. L. Rev. 1555, 1560 *et seq.* (1984); more recently, Harold Hongju Koh, *Is International Law Really State Law?*, 111 Harv. L. Rev. 1824 (1998); Gerald L. Neuman, *Sense and Nonsense about Customary International Law: A Response to Professors Bradley and Goldsmith*, 66 Fordham L. Rev. 371 (1997); William S. Dodge, *Customary International Law and the Question of Legitimacy*, 120 Harv. L. Rev. F. 19, 20 *et seq.* (2007).

doorkeeping, and thus open to a narrow class of international norms today."[386] Of course, in defining this narrow class of norms eligible for implementation, the majority cautioned against accepting norms with "less definite content and acceptance among civilized nations than the historical paradigms familiar when [the ATS] was enacted."[387] Hence, both international consensus and the specificity of content would be necessary in order to qualify a norm of international law as actionable. Analyzing the plaintiff's claim under this standard, the majority ultimately rejected application of the ATS for want of specificity. Álvarez-Machaín's detention may have been illegal, but it did not violate a "norm of customary international law so well defined as to support the creation of a federal remedy."[388]

Evidently, *Sosa* did not provide for an unmistakable definition of what was necessary for a norm to qualify as universally acknowledged and sufficiently specific.[389] But this was not the only problem, since transnationalization was understood to carry further implications. Justice Scalia's critique made clear that the consolidation of international and national law bears the risk not only of national policies being usurped by private parties but of foreign states' retaliation in general.[390] In addition, economic and commercial distortion was identified as a major drawback of transnational human rights protection by the federal judiciary.

C Pandora's Box: Politics and Economics

Like international antitrust, internalization under the ATS seems to implement and enforce globally acknowledged standards. There do not appear to be any drawbacks in such a brave new world of transnational law. Yet several aspects indicate that the osmosis of norms and policies

[386] *Sosa v. Alvarez-Machain*, 542 U.S. 692, 729 (2004). As the court went on to explain, "[I]t would be unreasonable to assume that the First Congress would have expected federal courts to lose all capacity to recognize enforceable international norms simply because the common law might lose some metaphysical cachet on the road to modern realism" (*id.* at 731).

[387] *Sosa v. Alvarez-Machain*, 542 U.S. 692, 732 (2004). [388] *Id.* at 738.

[389] Beth Stephens, *The Curious History of the Alien Tort Statute*, 89 Notre Dame L. Rev. 1467, 1511 (2014).

[390] The first part of his critique highlights an aspect mentioned earlier: the disempowerment of the state allows private parties to usurp domestic courtrooms. In Scalia's critical voice: "The notion that a law of nations, redefined to mean the consensus of states on *any* subject, can be used by a private citizen to control a sovereign's treatment of its own citizens within its own territory is a 20th-century invention of internationalist law professors and human rights advocates. ... The Framers would, I am confident, be appalled by the proposition that, for example, the American peoples' democratic adoption of the death penalty ... could be judicially nullified because of the disapproving views of foreigners." (*Sosa v. Alvarez-Machain*, 542 U.S. 692, 749–750 (2004) (Scalia, J., concurring)).

may be less optimal than often portrayed. The first concern is that human rights adjudication in US courts may lead to political repercussions in both the short term and long term.[391] Judge Kleinfeld's dissenting opinion to the Ninth Circuit's 2011 *Sarei v. Rio Tinto, PLC* decision, echoing Justice Scalia's critique in *Sosa*, vividly highlighted this concern:

> [O]nce we release the genie of universal jurisdiction from the bottle, we cannot control for whom the genie works its magic. Other countries with different values are likely to use universal jurisdiction against us. There could be a class action, perhaps in Papua New Guinea, brought by a Cherokee against descendants of those who obtained Cherokee land when President Jackson's administration forced their ancestors to leave their homes for the West. A foreign court could entertain a class action on behalf of African-Americans against American banks whose corporate ancestors profited from interest on loans for the purchase of American slaves. The law of nations provides no statute of limitations for universal offenses, so these class actions might well be cognizable in foreign courts. Why should descendants of those who have suffered great wrongs in America limit themselves to largely unavailable American remedies when foreign courts may be more advantageous?[392]

Even though there is scant empirical proof for the retaliation of foreign states,[393] this idea seems to have also influenced the Supreme Court's *Kiobel* majority in 2013, which I will address in more detail in an instant. As the majority there argued, restricting the reach of ATS litigation through the presumption against extraterritoriality would contribute to leaving foreign policy decisions to the political branches and avoid "that other nations ... could hale [US] citizens into their courts for alleged violations of the law of nations."[394]

The second aspect—more complex than the first—concerns potential economic repercussions of ATS litigation. Two facets must be distinguished: a direct drawback for international trade and direct investment and an indirect effect on competition in international commerce.

As Gary Hufbauer and Nicholas Mitrokostas contended with some grain of exaggeration in the pre-*Sosa* era, ATS litigation may ultimately

391 For an early and extensive description of international political frictions, *see* the opinions in *Tel-Oren v. Libyan Arab Republic*, 726 F.2d 774, 798 *et seq.* (Bork, J., concurring), and 823 *et seq.* (Robb, J., concurring) (D.C. Cir. 1984).

392 *Sarei v. Rio Tinto, PLC*, 671 F.3d 736, 816–17 (9th Cir. 2011) (Kleinfeld, J., dissenting). For the costs of retaliation, *see* Curtis A. Bradley, *The Costs of International Human Rights Litigation*, 2 Chi. J. Int'l L. 457, 461 *et seq.* (2001); *see also* Austen L. Parrish, *Reclaiming International Law from Extraterritoriality*, 93 Minn. L. Rev. 815, 857 *et seq.* (2009).

393 *See, e.g.*, William R. Casto, *The ATS Cause of Action Is Sui Generis*, 89 Notre Dame L. Rev. 1545, 1559 n. 89 (2014).

394 *Kiobel v. Royal Dutch Petroleum Co.*, 133 S.Ct. 1659, 1669, 185 L.Ed.2d 671 (2013).

have the potential to "devastate global trade and investment."[395] International trade and investment, they claimed, could suffer from the risk of high damage awards against American or foreign-based multinational companies. In particular, foreign direct investment might decline.[396] As the authors further predicted, these chilling effects, if left unchecked, might eventually offset the liberalization progress achieved under the recent World Trade Organization agenda.[397] But their numbers game has never been bolstered empirically and has hence remained speculative, particularly in light of the comparatively small number of ATS lawsuits.[398] Yet transnationalization undoubtedly has an economic underpinning. In this regard, a different aspect is less obvious, though far more convincing.

There is a more fundamental problem of enforcement inefficiency in the international arena. As Justice Breyer, referring to *Empagran*, explained in his concurring opinion in *Sosa*, it is important to "ensure that 'the potentially conflicting laws of different nations' will 'work together in harmony,' a matter of increasing importance in an ever more interdependent world."[399] He further elaborated:

> Since different courts in different nations will not necessarily apply even similar substantive laws similarly, workable harmony, in practice, depends upon more than substantive uniformity among the laws of those nations. That is to say, substantive uniformity does not *automatically* mean that universal jurisdiction is appropriate.[400]

In other words, if normative uniformity is not accompanied by an internationally uniform level of enforcement, the transnationalization of

[395] Gary Clyde Hufbauer & Nicholas K. Mitrokostas, *Awakening the Monster: The Alien Tort Statute of 1789* 1–2 (2003); Gary Clyde Hufbauer & Nicholas K. Mitrokostas, *International Implications of the Alien Tort Statute*, 16 St. Thomas L. Rev. 607, 607 (2004).

[396] Gary Clyde Hufbauer & Nicholas K. Mitrokostas, *Awakening the Monster: The Alien Tort Statute of 1789* 37 *et seq.* (2003); Gary Clyde Hufbauer & Nicholas K. Mitrokostas, *International Implications of the Alien Tort Statute*, 16 St. Thomas L. Rev. 607, 607–608 (2004). For a more recent debate and concrete example, *see, e.g.*, Alan O. Sykes, *Corporate Liability for Extraterritorial Torts under the Alien Tort Statute and Beyond: An Economic Analysis*, 100 Geo. L.J. 2161, 2195–2196 (2012).

[397] For a prediction of damages, *see* Gary Clyde Hufbauer & Nicholas K. Mitrokostas, *Awakening the Monster: The Alien Tort Statute of 1789* 37 *et seq.* (2003); Gary Clyde Hufbauer & Nicholas K. Mitrokostas, *International Implications of the Alien Tort Statute*, 16 St. Thomas L. Rev. 607, 614 *et seq.* (2004).

[398] For a biting critique of the authors' "doomsday scenario of economic loss and devastation," *see, e.g.*, Harold Hongju Koh, *Separating Myth from Reality about Corporate Responsibility Litigation*, 7 J. Int'l Econ. L. 263, 269 (2004).

[399] *Sosa v. Alvarez-Machain*, 542 U.S. 692, 761 (2004) (Breyer, J., concurring). For *Empagran*, *see supra* p. 453 *et seq.*

[400] *Id.* at 761–762.

substantive norms and policies is problematic. This alludes to what I have already discussed in the context of international antitrust litigation.[401] In addition, a cost-based argument must be brought forward. The economics of comity starts with procedural law here: a court considers a dispute when it has authority over both the parties and the action. In US terminology, this is personal and subject-matter jurisdiction.[402] The first obstacle for the plaintiff to overcome, therefore, is the establishment of personal jurisdiction. Often, constitutional law requires that a defendant have a minimum level of contact with the forum. For corporate entities, this usually equals incorporation in, having the primary place of business in, or conducting commerce within the forum state. If a case is brought against a national or corporate entity of the forum state, establishing personal jurisdiction is usually no problem. Foreign defendants, however, often may not be subjected to the court's jurisdiction under these standards; in addition, service of process may be impossible or difficult.[403] This means that unless the lawsuit specifically comprises subject matter in which domestic and foreign defendants are evenly or almost evenly subject to a certain forum's jurisdiction, it is generally easier to sue a domestic party than a foreigner. As we have seen, international antitrust is a field where this difference between domestic and foreign parties does not play out dramatically.[404] Yet a number of other areas present a different scenario—one of them is international torts.

As Alan O. Sykes has explained, so-called discriminatory domestic law application can be a key economic factor in international torts, notably with respect to ATS litigation.[405] If a party acts in more than one jurisdiction, including the forum state where she is domiciled or incorporated, she will always be—regardless of what happens abroad—subject to the forum courts' jurisdiction. If this forum's law provides for stricter

[401] *See supra* p. 456 *et seq.*

[402] *See* Gary B. Born & Peter B. Rutledge, *International Civil Litigation in United States Courts* ch. 1 and ch. 2 (5th edn., 2011).

[403] *Id.* at ch. 10. For an instructive analysis of US (and other) rules on personal jurisdiction, *see* Axel Halfmeier, *Menschenrechte und Internationales Privatrecht im Kontext der Globalisierung*, 68 RabelsZ 653, 655 *et seq.* (2004).

[404] For international antitrust litigation, *see supra* p. 457 *et seq.*

[405] Alan O. Sykes, *Transnational Tort Litigation as a Trade and Investment Issue, John M. Olin Program in Law and Economics Stanford Law School, Working Paper No. 331* (January 2007), at 11 *et seq.*; Jack L. Goldsmith & Alan O. Sykes, *Lex Loci Delictus and Global Economic Welfare: Spinozzi v. ITT Sheraton Corp.*, 120 Harv. L. Rev. 1137, 1144 (2007); Alan O. Sykes, *Corporate Liability for Extraterritorial Torts under the Alien Tort Statute and Beyond: An Economic Analysis*, 100 Geo. L.J. 2161, 2194 (2012). For a quite similar argument, *see* Lea Brilmayer, *Rights, Fairness, and Choice of Law*, 98 Yale L.J. 1277, 1311 (1989).

standards of liability than the other jurisdictions' laws and if it extends to the party's conduct at issue, the domestic party will be at a disadvantage in competition. This becomes clear upon a comparison with actors that are not domiciled or incorporated in the forum and are hence far less at risk of being subjected to its courts' jurisdiction. First, according to Sykes, the discriminatory application of domestic tort law conflicts with a national-welfare perspective. This is a perspective that focuses on the welfare maximization of a state's own citizens only and disregards effects on the welfare of foreign states' citizens. To put it simply, a foreign plaintiff suing in the United States will ultimately ask for a transfer of wealth (usually monetary funds for, for example, damages and reparation) from domestic defendants.[406] This suggests a detriment to the national economy. But the application of stricter standards of the forum's law is also undesirable under a global-welfare perspective. Even if it is superior in terms of economic efficiency, the expectation that applying forum law will always enhance global welfare is mistaken.[407] If we distinguish between the short-term and long-term effects of discriminatory forum law application, we see that the effects on welfare differ over time. Let us presume that a particular sector of a foreign market's industry is in a competitive equilibrium. In this case, an increase in liability for one type of actor in the market[408] may improve welfare in the short run. This is true, at least, if the forum's rules are economically superior to the rules that would otherwise apply under the foreign regime. One example where this effect might exist is the prescription of higher safety standards on hotel premises in foreign-based holiday locations. The increase in safety in hotels run by forum-based actors will (as we assume) benefit the consumer in the short term.[409] But this changes over time if the stricter standards are not comprehensively enforced throughout the market—hence if not *all* actors are subject to the enhanced standards. In the long run, then, the discriminatory increase of liability will raise the overall costs for those actors subject to the forum courts' jurisdiction. Since, in sum, the industry's total output in the foreign market stays the same, however, the market participants ultimately left will be those *not* subject to stricter liability rules. The other type of actors will ultimately leave the market and will be

[406] *See* Alan O. Sykes, *Transnational Tort Litigation as a Trade and Investment Issue, John M. Olin Program in Law and Economics Stanford Law School, Working Paper No. 331* (January 2007), at 8.

[407] *Id.* at 11; Jack L. Goldsmith & Alan O. Sykes, *Lex Loci Delictus and Global Economic Welfare: Spinozzi v. ITT Sheraton Corp.*, 120 Harv. L. Rev. 1137, 1146 (2007).

[408] These actors are drawn from the category of defendants subject to forum courts' jurisdiction and, therefore, to stricter liability standards.

[409] *See, e.g.*, *Spinozzi v. ITT Sheraton Corp.*, 174 F.3d 842 (7th Cir. 1999) (Posner, C.J.).

replaced by those that are isolated from the reach of the higher-standards jurisdiction.[410]

Of course, it is questionable whether the ATS could ever become so wide-reaching in its discriminatory enforcement that it could exert a significant impact on international competition.[411] Finding an answer to this question is not important here. Instead, what matters is the general conclusion that is seldom contested: the discriminatory submission of a certain class of defendants to higher standards of compliance is a problem for all private law and regulatory regimes when it comes to extraterritorial enforcement. Regardless of whether the substantive norms and policies at issue are universal, the divergence of procedural standards and efficiency can create anticompetitive distortions. The only way to avoid such distortions is a retraction of litigation and enforcement options in jurisdictions with more efficient systems—notably a cutting back of extraterritorial and universal application of substantive laws and policies. This aspect is important in trademark and unfair competition conflicts. Before I address this issue, however, I will conclude the overview on transnationalism with a final look at the US Supreme Court.

D *Kiobel v. Royal Dutch Petroleum Co.*: The Swan Song of Transnationalization?

In September 2002, the *Kiobel* petitioners, a group of Nigerian nationals who had formerly resided in Ogoniland, Nigeria, filed a suit that alleged a violation of the law of nations by the respondents. Two of the respondents were holding companies incorporated in the Netherlands and England. Another respondent company was incorporated in Nigeria, where it was engaged in oil exploration and production. As the complaint specified, the respondents had enlisted the Nigerian government in the 1990s to suppress demonstrations by Ogoniland residents against the environmental effects of the respondents' oil exploration and production activities. In the course of the suppression, the Nigerian military and police forces attacked residents of Ogoni villages—including the petitioners—and

[410] Alan O. Sykes, *Transnational Tort Litigation as a Trade and Investment Issue, John M. Olin Program in Law and Economics Stanford Law School, Working Paper No. 331* (January 2007), at 18–19; *see also* Jack L. Goldsmith & Alan O. Sykes, *Lex Loci Delictus and Global Economic Welfare: Spinozzi v. ITT Sheraton Corp.*, 120 Harv. L. Rev. 1137, 1146 (2007).

[411] *See, e.g.*, Chimène I. Keitner, *Response, Optimizing Liability for Extraterritorial Torts: A Response to Professor Sykes*, 100 Geo. L.J. 2211, 2215 *et seq.* (2012). Alan Sykes has cited concrete examples of economic and competitive distortion. *See* Alan O. Sykes, *Corporate Liability for Extraterritorial Torts under the Alien Tort Statute and Beyond: An Economic Analysis*, 100 Geo. L.J. 2161, 2195–2196 (2012). Overall, however, the situation does not seem too troubling. *See* Harold Hongju Koh, *Separating Myth from Reality about Corporate Responsibility Litigation*, 7 J. Int'l Econ. L. 263, 269–270 (2004).

committed a number of crimes and atrocities. According to the complaint, the respondents aided and abetted these atrocities by, inter alia, providing the Nigerian forces with food, transportation, and compensation.[412] The petitioners filed suit alleging jurisdiction under the ATS in the Southern District of New York. While the district court was less decided on the petitioners' claims, the Second Circuit dismissed the entire complaint, explaining that the law of nations does not recognize corporate liability for human rights violations.[413]

The Supreme Court majority, in an opinion delivered by Chief Justice John G. Roberts, phrased the issue quite differently. The question, Roberts explained, "is not whether petitioners have stated a proper claim under the ATS, but whether a claim may reach conduct occurring in the territory of a foreign sovereign."[414] This brought the presumption against extraterritoriality into focus. The ATS may be a strictly jurisdictional rather than regulatory statute. Nonetheless, adjudication on conduct within the territory of other sovereign states still bears "the danger of unwarranted judicial interference in the conduct of foreign policy."[415] In light of these foreign policy implications, application of the ATS must be subject to the presumption against extraterritoriality. As the opinion further explained, the ATS lacks a clear textual indication of intended extraterritoriality, and the historical background suggests that the presumption cannot be overcome if the conduct at issue occurred in the territory of another sovereign.[416] And even if the claims "touch and concern the territory of the United States," as the majority concluded, "they must do so with sufficient force" in order to overcome the presumption.[417] Since conduct in the case had taken place outside the United States, the ATS could not be applied.[418]

It may be an overinterpretation to conclude that the Supreme Court, with only its second decision on the ATS, has put an end to international

[412] *Kiobel v. Royal Dutch Petroleum Co.*, 133 S.Ct. 1659, 1662–1663, 185 L.Ed.2d 671 (2013).

[413] *Kiobel v. Royal Dutch Petroleum Co.*, 621 F.3d 111, 124 (2nd Cir. 2010), aff'd on other grounds, 133 S.Ct. 1659 (2013).

[414] *Kiobel v. Royal Dutch Petroleum Co.*, 133 S.Ct. 1659, 1664, 185 L.Ed.2d 671 (2013).

[415] *Id.* [416] *Id.* at 1665–1666. [417] *Id.* at 1669.

[418] The majority opinion is accompanied by three concurring opinions, one of which substantially differs from the majority's reasoning and arguments. Unlike the majority, Justice Breyer did not apply the presumption against territoriality; rather, he used the principles and practices of foreign relations law (inter alia, the restatement) as a guideline for applying the ATS. The statute would then apply where the allegedly violative conduct occurs on US territory, where the defendant is an American national, or where the defendant's conduct "substantially and adversely affects an important American national interest," including an "interest in preventing the United States from becoming a safe harbor (free of civil as well as criminal liability) for a torturer or other common enemy of mankind." *See id.* at 1670–1678 (Breyer, J., concurring).

human rights litigation. Of course, according to the majority in *Kiobel*, the presumption against extraterritoriality constrains the federal courts' power under the ATS. Prima facie, at least, this holding limits options to sue—particularly since the bulk of ATS litigation so far has concerned conduct outside the United States. Yet this need not necessarily be a full bar to litigation under the statute.[419] The majority's holding is actually narrow in the sense that the exclusion may not cover all instances of international human rights violations, especially not conduct that "touches and concerns" the territory of the United States. Scenarios that may still go forward might therefore cover claims against US citizens, including corporate entities, or against foreign citizens living in the United States.[420] And, indeed, the continuing current of litigation in lower federal courts somewhat defies the prediction that ATS transnationalization at the federal level has come to a halt.[421] In addition, ATS litigation may continue in state courts.[422] Accordingly, it would be far-fetched to conclude that it is about to disappear soon the way it arrived—Lohengrin style.[423]

Overall, however, it comes as no surprise that the court would ultimately restrict the scope and degree of transnationalization—at least in its practical explosiveness and with respect to the looming detriments. Whether the majority "misunderstood" (and hence misapplied) the presumption against extraterritoriality—since *international* human rights are

[419] For the suggestion that the Supreme Court (perhaps) has "crafted a middle ground," *see* Stephen Breyer, *The Court and the World—American Law and the New Global Realities* 160–161 (2015).

[420] Austen L. Parrish, *Kiobel, Unilateralism, and the Retreat from Extraterritoriality*, 28 Md. J. Int'l L. 208, 239 (2013); Ralph G. Steinhardt, *Determining Which Human Rights Claims "Touch and Concern" the United States: Justice Kennedy's Filartiga*, 89 Notre Dame L. Rev. 1695, 1703 (2014).

[421] For examples *see, e.g.*, Doug Cassel, *Suing Americans for Human Rights Torts Overseas: The Supreme Court Leaves the Door Open*, 89 Notre Dame L. Rev. 1773, 1784 *et seq.* (2014).

[422] William S. Dodge, *Alien Tort Litigation: The Road Not Taken*, 89 Notre Dame L. Rev. 1577, 1607 (2014).

[423] For the romantic figure of Lohengrin, the mystery of his name, and his forced return after revelation of the name, *see* Richard Wagner, Lohengrin, 3rd act, 2nd scene (Elsa): "Laß dein Geheimnis mich erschauen, daß, wer du bist, ich offen seh'! ... Meiner Treue enthülle deines Adels Wert! Woher du kamst, sag ohne Reue—durch mich sei Schweigens Kraft bewährt! ... Den Namen sag mir an! .... " And in the final scene, with Lohengrin ultimately riding back on the swan, 3rd act, 3rd scene (Lohengrin): "Ihr hörtet alle, wie sie mir versprochen, daß nie sie wollt' erfragen, wer ich bin? Nun hat sie ihren teuren Schwur gebrochen, treulosem Rat gab sie ihr Herz dahin! ... So hehrer Art doch ist des Grales Segen, enthüllt—muß er des Laien Auge fliehn; des Ritters drum sollt Zweifel ihr nicht hegen, erkennt ihr ihn—dann muß er von euch ziehn. ... Vom Gral ward ich zu euch daher gesandt: Mein Vater Parzival trägt seine Krone, sein Ritter ich—bin Lohengrin genannt. ... Mein lieber Schwan! Ach, diese letzte, traur'ge Fahrt, wie gern hätt' ich sie dir erspart!"

beyond the domain of *domestic* law and thus cannot raise an issue of extraterritoriality[424]—is not relevant for this inquiry. What is relevant is that the court laid, or at least attempted to lay, the foundation for a rule of self-restraint with respect to universal jurisdiction. Let us remember that transnationalist theory and practice seemed to agree that internalization is unproblematic as long as the norm or policy at issue is universal. In short, a globally uniform norm or policy is deemed to also be globally enforceable without the risk of invading another state's sovereignty.[425] The majority opinion in *Sarei v. Rio Tinto, PLC*, illustrated this point with candor:

> The norms being applied under the ATS are international, not domestic, ones, derived from international law. As a result, the primary considerations underlying the presumption against extraterritoriality—the foreign relations difficulties and intrusions into the sovereignty of other nations likely to arise if we claim the authority to require persons in other countries to obey our laws—do not come into play. This is because ... we are not asserting an entitlement to "make law" for the "entire planet." ... Instead, and especially in light of *Sosa*, the ATS provides a domestic forum for claims based on conduct that is illegal everywhere, including the place where that conduct took place. It is no infringement on the sovereign authority of other nations, therefore, to adjudicate claims cognizable under the ATS, so long as the requirements for personal jurisdiction are met.[426]

This perspective, as we have seen throughout this chapter, illustrates a worrisome myopia with respect to the overall and long-term consequences of universal jurisdiction. One aspect is foreign policy friction. This was emphasized by the *Kiobel* majority.[427] No less important is the

424 *See, e.g.*, David L. Sloss, *Kiobel and Extraterritoriality: A Rule without a Rationale*, 28 Md. J. Int'l L. 241, 243 (2013); Anthony J. Colangelo, *Kiobel: Muddling the Distinction between Prescriptive and Adjudicative Jurisdiction*, 28 Md. J. Int'l L. 65 (2013).

425 For human rights in general, *see, e.g.*, Sara L. Seck, *Home State Responsibility and Local Communities: The Case of Global Mining*, 11 Yale Hum. Rts. & Dev. L.J. 177, 177 (2008). For antitrust conflicts, this was expressed by Ralf Michaels, Hannah Buxbaum, and Horatia Muir Watt in their *Brief of Amici Curiae, F. Hoffmann-La Roche Ltd. v. Empagran S.A.*, 542 U.S. 155 (2004) (No. 03-724), 2004 WL 542780, at *20–21 ("When no conflict exists, a jurisdictional restraint analysis is unnecessary." (with reference to *Steele v. Bulova Watch Co.*)). *See also Developments in the Law—Extraterritoriality, Comity and Extraterritoriality in Antitrust Enforcement*, 124 Harv. L. Rev. 1226, 1230 (2011) ("[I]nternational law's powerful norm against extraterritoriality sometimes yields to consensual political objectives.").

426 *Sarei v. Rio Tinto, PLC*, 671 F.3d 736, 746 (9th Cir. 2011). For similar formulations in scholarly commentary, *see, e.g.*, Anthony J. Colangelo, *Kiobel: Muddling the Distinction between Prescriptive and Adjudicative Jurisdiction*, 28 Md. J. Int'l L. 65, 71–72 (2013); Roger P. Alford, *The Future of Human Rights Litigation after Kiobel*, 89 Notre Dame L. Rev. 1749, 1771 (2014). The argument has also been brought forward in, for instance, German doctrine. *See, e.g.*, Andreas Spickhoff, *Der völkerrechtsbezogene ordre public*, 275, 280–281, in *Völkerrecht und IPR* (Stefan Leible & Matthias Ruffert eds., 2006) (with further references).

427 *Kiobel v. Royal Dutch Petroleum Co.*, 133 S.Ct. 1659, 1664, 185 L.Ed.2d 671 (2013).

international imbalance of enforcement structures and efficiency: even if a case at bar does not raise a question of conflicting policies, the long-term perspective may still demand jurisdictional self-restraint. The universality of rights and policies aside, there is no panacea to the inherent defect of the system of transnational litigation. As long as enforcement structures and efficiency diverge, transnational consensus is ineffective. No state can act as a decentralized enforcer without facing a risk of such global transaction costs.[428]

Coming back to the expectable consequences, the *Kiobel* decision in its entirety—including majority and concurrent opinions—indicates an at least rudimentary resurrection of the traditional doctrinal structures that got lost in the course of the late twentieth-century transnationalist movement. With respect to litigation in federal courts, the scope of the ATS is now subjected to yet another limiting element of scrutiny. Whether this is the presumption against extraterritoriality or—as Justice Breyer suggested—"further limiting principles such as exhaustion, *forum non conveniens*, and comity" that "would do the same"[429] does not matter. Ultimately, the once seemingly unlimited reach of transnational norms has been cut back. And if it should prove to be true that ATS claims may increasingly be brought in state courts, the doctrine of international human rights litigation has actually come full circle. If international human rights violations are brought as transitory tort cases, states' rules on choice of law will be key.[430] Then, however, one way or the other, the system of comity-based conflicts rules—either technical as conceived of by Savigny or expressly political as suggested by Currie—has taken over again. The die may not be cast yet with respect to the ultimate status of ATS litigation *in toto*. But it is cast insofar as the Supreme Court—without slamming the door shut[431]—has left it ajar for a much more limited number of cases. The comity of abstention, again, has pointed the way.

III Summary

The effects test dominates conflicts resolution in international economic law—namely, international antitrust. It evolved from a reflection of

[428] For terminology of the "decentralized enforcer," *see* Anthony J. Colangelo, *The Alien Tort Statute and the Law of Nations in Kiobel and Beyond*, 44 Geo. J. Int'l L. 1329, 1334 (2013).

[429] *Kiobel v. Royal Dutch Petroleum Co.*, 133 S.Ct. 1659, 1674, 185 L.Ed.2d 671 (2013) (Breyer, J., concurring).

[430] Roger P. Alford, *The Future of Human Rights Litigation after Kiobel*, 89 Notre Dame L. Rev. 1749, 1761 *et seq.* (2014).

[431] Stephen Breyer, *The Court and the World—American Law and the New Global Realities* 161 (2015).

unbounded nation-state sovereignty under the Permanent Court of International Justice's *Lotus* enigma into a less unruly horse, domesticated by techniques of interest balancing and international comity. The meandering illustrates the crossroads at which theory and practice have arrived. While transnationalist theory contends that the global consensus on policies has shrunk, the need for a practical corrective—in other words, a doctrine of jurisdictional self-restraint—suggests otherwise. The question is whether the enforcement of universal policies will ultimately enhance global and national welfare. The answer is difficult to provide, particularly without empirical data. International regulatory litigation appears beneficial both nationally and globally if the policies enforced are "transnational"—and, notably, if the procedural setting provides for efficient handling. The counterposition advocates a consideration of the risks of a practical extension of litigation and the concurrent burdening of potential defendants' international commercial activities. Without globally uniform enforcement procedures, the internalization of universal policies will distort international competition and commerce. In this regard, no international level playing field exists, and the situation will likely not change in the near future.

Even though it concerns a field that appears unchallenged by economic considerations and is hence nonregulatory, international human rights protection reveals similar problems. The perception that transnational consensus on human rights had grown seemed to imply the disappearance of conflicts and a corresponding extension of jurisdictional capacities. As thorough analyses suggest, however, more caution is indicated. Liberating the courts from the traditional confines of jurisdiction will—as in international antitrust—ultimately risk surrendering the judiciary to the dynamics of private litigants' decision making. Without a controlling mechanism, a spontaneous order of public international law privatization may be in the making. And of course, at the end of this process, a true *ius cosmopoliticum* may ensue. Still, however, a reckless and unchecked expanding of jurisdictional capacities deactivates the instruments designed to "civilize" international transacting and commerce.

No matter how venerable the underlying policies and goals, the economic backlash of such "decivilization" can be significant. Of course, human rights protection and enforcement is a field where the cost-benefit ratio must not and cannot be determined by a focus on pecuniary arguments. In this regard, the field is exceptional. But this is not the case for areas of economic regulation, especially trademark and unfair competition law. If the focus is on commerce and competition, there is hardly a reason to risk distortion caused by an overextension of regulatory policies to foreign markets. In any event, the issue of drawbacks resulting from extraterritoriality or universality is far more important. Accordingly, the doctrine of international trademark and unfair competition law must offer a limiting instrument to cut back the outgrowth of extraterritoriality or universality. In this regard, as I will now address, jurisdictional abstention can also be a question of self-interest instead of altruism—therefore, the doctrine of international comity is about to reveal one more facet of what is required for a civilizing of international transacting and commerce.

Section 3 The Shadowy Existence of Trademark and Unfair Competition Conflicts

Based on our findings in the preceding sections, we can now complete our analysis of international trademark and unfair competition law by taking a concluding look at the most fundamental defect in contemporary doctrine. International trademark and unfair competition law is one of the areas given short shrift when compared to the mass of analyses in other sectors. Reasons for the field's low attractiveness are numerous. As it seems, trademark and unfair competition conflicts present a far more mundane, and thus scholarly less attractive, field than do human rights. Trademark protection is no life-saver. Another reason is trademark and unfair competition law's focus on private rights and its apparent lack of domestic or global regulatory importance. In contrast to antitrust violations, trademark and unfair competition conflicts rarely constitute a "clash of giants"—the overall socioeconomic importance of the concrete dispute at bar appears small and negligible.[432] It is especially this latter perspective that invites fallacy. A party-centered angle may be typical for civil judges confronted with "private hucksters" fighting over trademark use and fairness in competition. But limiting the analysis to the concrete case at bar comes with a disregard for overall and long-term consequences.[433] This ultimately distorts the analysis in current theory and practice on both sides of the Atlantic.

[432] *See, e.g.*, William M. Landes & Richard A. Posner, *Trademark Law: An Economic Perspective*, 30 J. L. & Econ. 265, 289 (1987) ("Since the allocative effects of individual trademark abuses are pretty much limited to raising consumer search costs, the potential misallocations are much smaller than in most antitrust cases.").

[433] *See* Ralph S. Brown, Jr., *Advertising and the Public Interest: Legal Protection of Trade Symbols*, 57 Yale L.J. 1165, 1167 (1948) ("One thing the examination will reveal is that what appear to be private disputes among hucksters almost invariably touch the public welfare.").

I The Mirage of Extraterritorial Enforcement Efficiency

A common perception still governing international trademark theory and practice is the idea that transnational enforcement of trademark rights is effective. Not surprisingly, the fear, rather, is that the extraterritorial overextension of domestic laws might be contrary to the limitations of national jurisdiction set by rules of public international law. Indeed, particularly in American economic law, some voices even adhere to the assumption that extending the reach of domestic law is preferred over international treaty making and strict territoriality.[434] In international trademark and unfair competition conflicts, this understanding is founded on a particularly vicious fallacy: the extraterritoriality of domestic law is thought to ameliorate protection levels globally and, in doing so, enhance national and global welfare. Of course, in European unfair competition conflicts doctrine, the drawbacks of "extraterritoriality" have been debated ever since Nussbaum had suggested that the *lex domicilii communis* should apply to all domestic competitors' activities in foreign markets. The argument that trade diversion might ensue from overextending domestic law was brought forward beginning in the 1930s.[435] In US commentary as well, the anticompetitive effects of extraterritoriality have been alluded to.[436] Nonetheless, dominant opinion still counsels in favor of domestic law extension. In particular, US theory regarding international economic law tends to approve extraterritorial regulation.[437] The explanation seems plausible: since legal instruments of economic regulation are concerned with market-related interests and aim at establishing and maintaining an international level playing field, their extension reflects the fact that the object of regulation is an international market, not a political territory. As has been suggested, therefore, a reasonable way to enforce market statutes is to extend their reach to the entire relevant market—if necessary, across national borders. The tacit assumption is that enforcement capacities in the international arena are virtually unlimited. According to this approach, the extraterritoriality of domestic law may even serve as a placeholder in cases where an

[434] *See, e.g.*, Austen L. Parrish, *Reclaiming International Law from Extraterritoriality*, 93 Minn. L. Rev. 815, 846 *et seq.* (2009).

[435] *See supra* p. 64 *et seq.* Internationally, Wilhelm Wengler first alluded to similar detriments in the 1950s. *See* Wilhelm Wengler, *Laws Concerning Unfair Competition and the Conflict of Laws*, 4 Am. J. Comp. L. 167, 182 (1955).

[436] Robert Alpert, *The Export of Trademarked Goods for the United States: The Extraterritorial Reach of the Lanham Act*, 81 Trademark Rep. 125, 145 (1991); Gary B. Born, *A Reappraisal of the Extraterritorial Reach of U.S. Law*, 24 Law & Pol'y Int'l Bus. 1, 90–91 (1992).

[437] *See supra* p. 246 *et seq.*

international agreement on the unification of regulation has not been achieved.[438] Lanham Act extraterritoriality in particular has thus also been criticized for putting foreign defendants at a disadvantage. Since foreign-based alleged infringers may have intentionally and legitimately chosen a foreign jurisdiction as their zone of activity owing to lower regulatory standards, the application of US law to exactly this activity seems to unfairly extend the Lanham Act's stricter rules.[439]

This assumption also dominates in practice. An early example is the Seventh Circuit's 1944 decision in *Branch v. Federal Trade Commission*,[440] where the court found jurisdiction under the Federal Trade Commission Act to exist over a domestic correspondence school offering courses in Latin America. Looking at US competitors in the foreign market, the court found that jurisdiction existed on the basis that the Federal Trade Commission's injunction "aimed at compelling the petitioner to use fair methods in competing with his fellow countrymen."[441] Domestic law "does not assume to protect the petitioner's customers in Latin America. It seeks to protect the petitioner's competitors from his unfair practices."[442] The same philosophy, adopted in the *Nussbaum/Stahlexport* doctrine, has guided German practice and scholarship.[443] The general assumption is that extraterritoriality is beneficial for domestic right owners and, accordingly, for national economic interests.[444]

In a more recent case, it was the First Circuit Court of Appeals in *McBee v. Delica Co., Ltd.*[445] that made reference to a calculation of the overall piracy-related losses to American companies. Chapter 2 analyzed

[438] *See, e.g.*, Tonya L. Putnam, *Courts without Borders: Domestic Sources of U.S. Extraterritoriality in the Regulatory Sphere*, 63 International Organization 459, 469 *et seq.* and 485–486 (2009); *see also* Kal Raustiala, *Empire and Extraterritoriality in Twentieth Century America*, 40 Sw. L. Rev. 605, 614 (2011); Austen L. Parrish, *Evading Legislative Jurisdiction*, 87 Notre Dame L. Rev. 1673, 1707 (2012); for an elaborate analysis of international antitrust regulation, *see* William S. Dodge, *Extraterritoriality and Conflict-of-Laws Theory: An Argument for Judicial Unilateralism*, 39 Harv. Int'l L.J. 101, 152 *et seq.* (1998).

[439] Anna R. Popov, *Watering Down Steele v. Bulova Watch Co. to Reach E-Commerce Overseas: Analyzing the Lanham Act's Extraterritorial Reach under International Law*, 77 S. Cal. L. Rev. 705, 727 (2004); Pamela E. Kraver & Robert E. Purcell, *Application of the Lanham Act to Extraterritorial Activities: Trend toward Universality or Imperialism?*, 77 J. Pat. & Trademark Off. Soc'y 115, 115 (1995).

[440] *Branch v. Federal Trade Commission*, 141 F.2d 31 (7th Cir. 1944). [441] *Id.* at 34.

[442] *Id.* [443] *See supra* p. 64 *et seq.*

[444] *See, e.g.*, Roger E. Schechter, *The Case for Limited Extraterritorial Reach of the Lanham Act*, 37 Va. J. Int'l L. 619, 634–635 (1997) ("[E]xtraterritoriality gives U.S. trademark owners an additional weapon in the fight against commercial piracy around the globe. . . . [I]f we can design an approach that minimizes conflict with foreign states while maximizing protection for U.S. companies against acts that poach on their goodwill, that approach would seem highly desirable.").

[445] *McBee v. Delica Co., Ltd.*, 417 F.3d 107 (1st Cir. 2005).

the *McBee* test.[446] The plaintiff, an American jazz musician, sued a Japanese clothing retailer that had adopted the trademark "Cecil McBee" (identical to the plaintiff's name) for its adolescent female clothing line. The defendant company held a Japanese trademark; and although it did not market its products outside of Japan, it maintained a website where the trademark was extensively displayed. Even though the court ultimately denied subject-matter jurisdiction and application of the Lanham Act for lack of a "substantial effect on United States commerce," the reasoning reveals a presumption that the extraterritorial extension of US law to infringements on foreign territory are beneficial for American commerce, particularly domestic trademark holders:

> One can easily imagine a variety of harms to American commerce arising from wholly foreign activities by foreign defendants. There could be harm caused by false endorsements, passing off, or product disparagement, or confusion over sponsorship affecting American commerce and causing loss of American sales. Further, global piracy of American goods is a major problem for American companies: annual losses from unauthorized use of United States trademarks, according to one commentator, now amount to $200 billion annually. . . . In both the antitrust and the Lanham Act areas, there is a risk that absent a certain degree of extraterritorial enforcement, violators will either take advantage of international coordination problems or hide in countries without efficacious antitrust or trademark laws, thereby avoiding legal authority.[447]

Judge Lynch's argument that extraterritorial enforcement is necessary and efficient has been met with approval.[448] Yet even though conventional wisdom still seems to suggest that extraterritorial rights protection is an ultimately welfare-maximizing approach, a closer look unveils the fallacy.

II The Reality of International Trademark Rights Protection

Enforcement efficiency is a key component of an economic perspective on international trademark and unfair competition law. In essence, this efficiency depends on the actors involved and on their interrelation. If parties to a dispute are members of a community—notably if they are all subject to the same state courts' jurisdiction—enforcement is largely unproblematic. This is the case in many co-resident disputes, as well as

446 *See supra* p. 161–164.
447 *McBee v. Delica Co., Ltd.*, 417 F.3d 107, 119 (1st Cir. 2005).
448 *See, e.g.*, Jason Webster, *Trademark Law—Extraterritorial Application of the Lanham Act—McBee v. Delica Co., Ltd., 417 F.3d 107 (1st Cir. 2005)*, 30 Suffolk Transnat'l L. Rev. 263, 269 (2006); Brendan J. Witherell, *The Extraterritorial Application of the Lanham Act in an Expanding Global Economy*, 97 Trademark Rep. 1090, 1105 *et seq.* (2007).

antitrust suits against transnational entities that are unable to evade the reach of extraterritorial regulatory systems, particularly the cross-border extension of national or supranational antitrust regimes.[449] International trademark and unfair competition violations, however, provide for a more complex and complicated scenario.

A International Intellectual Property Rights Segmentation

A universal and comprehensive definition of the concept of "territoriality" in intellectual property law does not exist.[450] But there is agreement on two key aspects. First, the scope of a national right is generally limited to the granting state's territory; in other words, the right owner may exercise her right only within the state's boundaries.[451] Second, it is uncontested that this geographical-political confinement results in an international segmentation of independent rights. Since each national right is geographically and politically limited, and since all rights are independent, no single solid "global right" exists. If a party has collected

[449] *See also supra* p. 457 *et seq.*

[450] *See, e.g.*, Franz Kahn, *Die Lehre vom ordre public (Prohibitivgesetze)*, 161, 240, in *Abhandlungen zum internationalen Privatrecht, vol. I* (Otto Lenel & Hans Lewald eds., 1928). ("[A]lle möglichen und denkbaren Anknüpfungen verbergen sich ja in dem Proteus der ‚Territorialität', alle schillern sie gleichzeitig bunt nebeneinander; welche sollen wir ins Auge fassen, auf welche kommt es gerade an?"). For the modern landscape, *see, e.g.*, Arnulf Weigel, *Gerichtsbarkeit, internationale Zuständigkeit und Territorialitäts-Prinzip im deutschen gewerblichen Rechtsschutz* 77–78 (1973); Christian von Bar, *Kollisionsrecht, Fremdenrecht und Sachrecht für internationale Sachverhalte im Internationalen Urheberrecht*, 108 UFITA 27, 48 (1988); Kurt Siehr, *Das urheberrechtliche Folgerecht inländischer Künstler nach Versteigerung ihrer Werke im Ausland*, 1992 IPRax 29, 31 ("Das Territorialitätsprinzip ist ein hoffnungslos mehrdeutiger Begriff, der nichts darüber aussagt, durch welches Anknüpfungsmerkmal örtlich angeknüpft wird."); Christopher Wadlow, *Enforcement of Intellectual Property in European and International Law—The New Private International Law of Intellectual Property in the United Kingdom and the European Community* para. 1–22 (1998) ("Territoriality has such a wide range of meanings that it may fairly be criticised for being a term without a concept, and in some of its ramifications without much justification."); Frank Peter Regelin, *Das Kollisionsrecht der Immaterialgüterrechte an der Schwelle zum 21. Jahrhundert* 46 (2000); Christian von Bar & Peter Mankowski, *Internationales Privatrecht—vol. I: Allgemeine Lehren* § 4 para. 64 (2nd edn., 2003); Graeme B. Dinwoodie, *Developing a Private International Intellectual Property Law: The Demise of Territoriality?*, 51 Wm. & Mary L. Rev. 711, 725 (2009) ("That principle is somewhat more chameleon-like than most scholars assume. Its protean nature serves only to obscure the real grounds for decisions in this area and to forestall the development of a genuine private international law reflecting the complexity demanded by contemporary exploitation of intellectual property.").

[451] *See, e.g.*, Erwin Deutsch, *Wettbewerbstatbestände mit Auslandsbeziehung* 20 *et seq.* (1962); Arnulf Weigel, *Gerichtsbarkeit, internationale Zuständigkeit und Territorialitäts-Prinzip im deutschen gewerblichen Rechtsschutz* 99 (1973); Karl-Heinz Fezer, *Markenrecht*, Einl H MarkenG para. 7 (4th ed., 2009).

protection in different states, she holds a "bundle of rights."[452] Thus, rather than being concerned with a uniform body of transnational goodwill, international trademark protection deals with a checkerboard of individual entitlements.[453]

This segmentation is commonly explained on a number of legal grounds. Most conventionally, intellectual property rights are still seen as state-granted licenses. Such an act of the state can extend only within its political boundaries.[454] Another approach describes the territorial segmentation of rights as a consequence of national lawmakers' voluntary self-restraint.[455] Accordingly, it is the inherent limitation of the right that determines its restricted scope.[456] But territoriality can also be seen in light of natural limitations to nation-state capacities. It must then be understood as a mirror image of actual state power.[457] Under such a realist lens, territoriality is a factual rather than a legal concept.[458]

[452] *IHT Internationale Heiztechnik v. Ideal-Standard*, C-9/93, para. 24–25 (22 June 1994), [1994] E.C.R. I-2789; BGHZ vol. 41, 84, 91—*Maja* (22 January 1964); BGHZ vol. 22, 1, 13—*Flava Erdgold* (2 October 1956); Gerhard Kegel, in *Soergel: Kommentar zum Bürgerlichen Gesetzbuch, Einführungsgesetz, vol. X*, Anh. Art. 12 para. 16 (W. Siebert ed., 12th edn., 1996) (so-called Kegel'sche Bündeltheorie); Graeme B. Dinwoodie, *Developing a Private International Intellectual Property Law: The Demise of Territoriality?*, 51 Wm. & Mary L. Rev. 711, 766 (2009); Michael Grünberger, in *Nomos-Kommentar-BGB, Rom-Verordnungen, vol. VI*, Art. 8 Rom II para. 3 (Rainer Hüßtege & Heinz-Peter Mansel eds., 2014).

[453] The European Community's trademark is a supranational right with the same segmented character as national rights, but extended within the geographical-political boundaries of the community. For the idea of a *Weltrecht* of trademarks under substantive law theories, *see supra* p. 258 *et seq.*

[454] This is the so-called *Verwaltungsaktlehre*. *See, e.g.*, RGZ vol. 118, 76 (20 September 1927); Arthur Nussbaum, *Deutsches internationales Privatrecht—Unter besonderer Berücksichtigung des österreichischen und schweizerischen Rechts* 337–338 (1932) ("Das Territorialitätsprinzip besagt mithin, daß das Immaterialgüterrecht nur innerhalb des ‚Verleihungsstaates' wirkt."); Erwin Deutsch, *Wettbewerbstatbestände mit Auslandsbeziehung* 21 *et seq.* (1962); Christian von Bar, *Territorialität des Warenzeichens und Erschöpfung des Verbreitungsrechts im Gemeinsamen Markt* 30 (1977).

[455] *See, e.g.*, RGZ vol. 149, 102, 105 (19 October 1935); Lienhard Schikora, *Der Begehungsort im gewerblichen Rechtsschutz und Urheberrecht* 55 (1968); Arnulf Weigel, *Gerichtsbarkeit, internationale Zuständigkeit und Territorialitäts-Prinzip im deutschen gewerblichen Rechtsschutz* 109 *et seq.* (1973).

[456] Arthur Nussbaum, *Deutsches internationales Privatrecht—Unter besonderer Berücksichtigung des österreichischen und schweizerischen Rechts* 337–338 (1932); *see also* Dieter Pfaff, *Das Internationale Privatrecht des Ausstattungsschutzes*, 1109, 1123, in *Handbuch des Ausstattungsrechts—Der Schutz der nichteingetragenen Marke und Ausstattung im In- und Ausland, Festgabe für Friedrich-Karl Beier zum 60. Geburtstag* (Gerhard Schricker & Dieter Stauder eds., 1986).

[457] *See, e.g.*, Jürgen Basedow, *Entwicklungslinien des internationalen Kartellrechts—Ausbau und Differenzierung des Auswirkungsprinzips*, 1989 NJW 627, 638; Larry Kramer, *Vestiges of Beale: Extraterritorial Application of American Law*, 1991 Sup. Ct. Rev. 179, 207–208.

[458] *See* Justice Holmes in *American Banana* (213 U.S. 347, 356–357 (1909)): "Law is a statement of the circumstances, in which the public force will be brought to bear upon men through the courts. . . . The foregoing considerations would lead, in case of doubt,

Indeed, the public international law of intellectual property protection does not expressly provide for the principle of territoriality.[459] Nor do national laws appear to have ever expressly implemented the idea of a nation-state's self-limitation.[460] Segmentation in the international arena, therefore, primarily reflects the realities of limited capacities. The equation is simple: in the domestic arena, states are endowed with the power of enforcement; rights creation and protection is their exclusive and absolute domain. At the international level, however, the state's power to enforce is limited by definition.

B The International Vacuum of Nation-State Capacities

This last aspect of limited factual powers highlights the most relevant characteristic of international intellectual property protection. Since there is no world state to create property rights, protection in the international sphere is deficient. Indeed, a quasi-Hobbesian state of nature exists.[461] States have always been largely "powerless" vis-à-vis their sovereign counterparts and particularly vis-à-vis private individuals outside their borders. International agreements on judicial cooperation, recognition, and enforcement may have improved the situation. But the vacuum of capacities still exists. And this impotency is further intensified by the increasing detachment of conduct and effects. Globalization has accelerated and dephysicalized communication and transacting. Examining trademark and unfair competition law in this light illustrates the key differences between domestic and international conflicts. In the domestic sphere, efficient enforcement is—at least in principle—guaranteed by the territorial sovereign. At the international level, two scenarios must be distinguished. The extraterritorial enforcement of national rights and policies can be efficient. This is usually the case in international antitrust conflicts: as we have seen, both domestic and foreign-based violators are regularly equally subject to the regulating states' jurisdiction. If, however, right protection and policy enforcement are inefficient, anticompetitive distortion looms. As we have seen, this is the problem

to a construction of any statute as intended to be confined in its operation and effect to the territorial limits over which the lawmaker has general and legitimate power."

459 *See supra* p. 193 *et seq.*

460 My comparative-historical overview has presented many examples to the contrary. *See supra* chapters 1 and 2 *passim.*

461 *See* Hans-Jörg Schmidt-Trenz & Dieter Schmidtchen, *Private International Trade in the Shadow of the Territoriality of Law: Why Does It Work?*, 58 Southern Economic Journal 329, 331 (1991); for terminology and the concept in general, *see* Anthony T. Kronman, *Contract Law and the State of Nature*, 1 J. L., Econ. & Org. 5, 6 (1985); for choice of law, *see* Hessel E. Yntema, *The Historic Bases of Private International Law*, 2 Am. J. Comp. L. 297, 297 (1953).

underlying international human rights protection. Trademark and unfair competition conflicts is another example in this category.

C Trademark Extraterritoriality: Individual Propertization and Overall Taxation

Parallels between international tort law and trademark and unfair competition choice of law are manifest. As in international human rights litigation, notably personal jurisdiction rules can account for a nominal prevalence of domestic defendants in cross-border disputes. If forum law applies and provides for higher protection levels, this results in a discriminatory application of stricter standards and—ultimately—in anticompetitive distortions on foreign-based markets. Especially under US trademark doctrine, this phenomenon—which we might call an eye-of-the-needle effect—is further ratcheted by the first *Bulova* test factor.

The *Steele* progeny provides illustration:[462] by requiring "nationality" as one factor in the analysis of subject-matter jurisdiction, the *Bulova* test complicates suits against non-US nationals and entities. A cursory look at post-*Steele* case law on international trademark conflicts through 2014 reveals that defendants in 34 out of 140 opinions (24.29%) were American individuals or corporate entities. In 61 out of 140 opinions (43.57%), both national and foreign individuals and/or corporate entities were on the defendant side. Hence, overall, 95 out of 140 opinions featured at least one defendant party that was either an American individual or entity (67.86%). Courts have favored the application of domestic law in 26 out of 34 opinions where defendants were solely US nationals and entities (76.47%). In scenarios where the defendants consisted of both US and foreign nationals and/or entities, courts decided in favor of Lanham Act application in 35 out of 61 opinions (57.38%). If there were only foreign nationals or entities on the defendant side, the Lanham Act applied in only 9 out of 31 opinions (29.03%).[463]

Taking further into account that substantive law and procedural law in the United States are favorable to right owners, they will usually prefer to litigate foreign infringements in US federal courts, not in courts abroad. Since the extraterritorial application of domestic law will not be efficient enough to establish perfectly economized market information structures

[462] For a bird's-eye view on the *Steele* progeny *see* p. 171 *et seq.* and appendix A.

[463] For a comparison, the overall extraterritoriality rate (i.e., the Lanham Act application rate) across all opinions in the *Steele* progeny was 59.29%. It is important to note, however, that under a Chi-square test of independence, there is a statistically significant relationship between the defendant's nationality and the Lanham Act application rate only for cases where the defendants were foreign nationals or entities only.

in a foreign territory,[464] the primary effect that will ensue is the "taxation" of domestic actors.[465]

Under this perspective, the drawbacks of extraterritoriality can also be described as a specific facet of propertization. The extension of trademark rights' substantive scope of application may somewhat increase domestic owners' rights, but it creates transaction costs for all other market participants. As Mark Lemley explains in general terms, "The more we propertize, the more transaction costs we impose on everyone."[466] In the transnational sphere, domestic parties competing in foreign markets are the first to bear these costs. In the end, however, it is consumers in these foreign markets who suffer. While rights extension across national borders may lead to an immediate and short-term trademark propertization for the individual right owner, over time, it suffocates competition *in toto*.

III Summary

A general misperception exists in trademark and unfair competition conflicts doctrine. Often, courts and scholars assume that domestic actors can be efficiently protected both inside and outside national borders. Reality, however, is different. Unlike international antitrust violations, extraterritorial trademark infringements and unfair competition violations are usually hard to police comprehensively through forum courts. One consequence is that from among the group of

464 The fact that the domestic regime's extension to other jurisdictions may be more efficient per se must not lead to the conclusion that competition in the foreign market would move toward an optimal stage. In the short run, the application of stricter (and presumably more efficient) standards of trademark and unfair competition law might enhance market information quality. The prosecution of unfair competitive conduct will then "clean" the market from incorrect information. The actual impact, however, is negligible. Even the agglomeration of numerous instances of extraterritorial regulation will not suffice to establish a comprehensively efficient market information climate in the foreign market. The bulk of foreign-based competitors (not subject to extraterritorial jurisdiction) are at a competitive advantage. This corresponds to the situation in international tort litigation (*see supra* p. 469 *et seq.*).

465 *See, e.g.*, Jack L. Goldsmith & Alan O. Sykes, *Lex Loci Delictus and Global Economic Welfare: Spinozzi v. ITT Sheraton Corp.*, 120 Harv. L. Rev. 1137, 1146 (2007). This result may seem paradoxical to the conventional theory of antiextraterritorialism, which contends that extraterritorial regulation is an undemocratic extension of domestic laws to foreigner-competitors as outsiders without a voice in or the ability to influence domestic politics. *See, e.g.*, Mark D. Rosen, *The Surprisingly Strong Case for Tailoring Constitutional Principles*, 153 U. Pa. L. Rev. 1513, 1616 (2005) ("[I]t is violative of basic democratic principles for outsiders of the political community to dictate laws to the community. Such regulations may be thought of as extraterritorial in nature, and are just a step away from the 'taxation without representation' that so vexed our country's forefathers.").

466 Mark A. Lemley, *The Modern Lanham Act and the Death of Common Sense*, 108 Yale L.J. 1687, 1696 (1999).

competing actors in foreign markets, it is mostly domestic parties that are drawn as defendants into forum courts, resulting in a distortion of competition. Counterintuitively, therefore, we must conclude that extraterritoriality is detrimental for domestic parties and foreign consumers alike. Accordingly, jurisdictional self-restraint and abstention should be practiced not so much in the interest of other sovereign states but in the regulator's own interest in protecting its domestic constituencies.

Conclusions

The twentieth-century merger of private and public law as well as the concurrent fusion of public and private international law used to be seen as the starting point for a new era of transnational law uniformity. The dissolution of legal categories also seemed to deconstruct nation-state boundaries. Yet, more recent practical realities tell a different story. The fields of international antitrust and human rights litigation are exemplary for the disenchantment that has replaced the interim transnationalist euphoria. Today, in many sectors, it seems as if jurisdictional self-restraint is the order of the day. Indeed, it seems as if a doctrine of international comity as a principle of jurisdictional self-restraint and abstention has re-materialized. Regardless of whether one is willing to acknowledge international comity as a legal instrument, it is hardly contestable that the doctrine's subject matter of "civilizing" international private and regulatory law affairs is *the* requirement of a functioning order of transnational communication and socioeconomic transacting. As a closer look at trademark protection and unfair competition prevention in the international arena reveals, such a civilizing doctrine must be understood to have at least two different sides. First, it is conceived of in the traditional sense as a rule of co-sovereign respect. In this regard, it particularly demands self-restraint in international regulatory matters. By this means, the illegitimate invasion of foreign sovereigns' spheres of statal power is avoided in the interest of international harmony and concord. This aspect has always been acknowledged when the territoriality of rights was explained as a consequence of the international segmentation of regulatory state capacities. In addition however—and this is still widely overlooked—the doctrine can also be understood as a rule of genuinely self-interested abstention. In this sense, it is intended to prevent a regulator's extraterritorial overreach, resulting in a discriminatory application of the domestic (presumably stricter) regime of rights protection and economic regulation to its own constituencies. Like in international antitrust and human-rights litigation, in the long run, it may be particularly domestic parties that will be damaged. In order to guarantee what Story termed the "mutual interest and utility" and what Savigny, quite similarly, explained as "the real advantage" of a civilized system of conflicts resolution, a dual limitation is indicated: both over- and under-extension of national laws must be avoided. This is the challenge when conflicts law and choice of law for international trademark protection and unfair competition prevention is at stake. In the next and final chapter, we will formulate concrete rules of application in order to implement this insight into legal practice.

6 Reconceptualization, Reinterpretation, and Typology

> Our aim to establish harmony of laws can be seen as attainable if the colliding substantive laws are in a closer relationship, if their material fundaments consonantly point in the same direction. It will then be possible to identify a conflicts norm with a simple rule of attachment which, in all of the different legal orders, . . . can (not must!) be accepted, since none of these regimes must thereby sacrifice material substantive law interests in favor of certainty in choice of law. If this uniform conflicts norm is of a plausible expedience, of a convincing power, it will achieve regular international practice; over time, then, it may develop into a public international law standard.
>
> Author's translation from Franz Kahn, Über Inhalt, Natur und Methode des internationalen Privatrechts, 40 JherJB 1, 76 (1898)

Introduction

As Franz Kahn explained in 1898—and this still holds true for modern choice of law and conflicts law—the "material fundaments" of substantive laws must point in the same direction in order to make the promulgation of uniform conflicts rules a theoretically imaginable option.[1] Only if the underlying substantive law policies concordantly allow for and indicate a certain structure of conflicts resolution will a uniform system be acceptable and ultimately be successful as a rule of the "harmonious" choice of law that had been prophesized by Friedrich Carl von Savigny fifty years earlier. Indeed, both icons' wisdom is fundamentally reflected in modern choice-of-law theory and its so-called functional method. Functionality actually lies at the crossroads of two disciplines—it is the ultimate connex between choice of law, or conflicts law, and comparative law.[2] My analysis in the foregoing chapters laid the foundation for such a

[1] *See* citation *supra*.

[2] *See, e.g.*, Jan Kropholler, *Internationales Privatrecht—einschließlich der Grundbegriffe des Internationalen Zivilverfahrensrechts* § 17 (6th edn., 2006) for choice of law; further also for comparative law, *see* Konrad Zweigert & Hein Kötz, *An Introduction to Comparative Law* § 3 II (3rd edn., 1998) ("The basic methodological principle of all comparative law is that of functionality.").

functional approach. The earlier chapters revealed the history and status quo of doctrine in the United States and Europe: ever since *Steele*, US law has adhered to commercial effects as the indicator of Lanham Act subject-matter analysis. The German Bundesgerichtshof, by contrast, has only recently begun to refer to a similar paradigm of commercial effects, as demonstrated in *HOTEL MARITIME*. Finally, in European unfair competition choice of law, the marketplace effects rule has found its way into the Rome II Regulation. With respect to choice-of-law and conflicts law structure, therefore, the issue no longer seems to be whether a test of "commercial effects" or "marketplace effects" can be accepted as such. On the contrary, the instrument is virtually universally acknowledged. Yet a number of questions still await answers—these answers must be based on a functional analysis of the fields in both substantive law and choice of law. The comparative inquiry in the preceding two chapters provided the necessary groundwork. Comparing the different common law and civil law phenotypes of substantive law doctrine and of different variants of trademark protection and unfair competition prevention unveils a fundamental convergence of policies. At least with respect to the core policies in both trademark and unfair competition law, it can be said that—so to speak—a common genotype of trademark and unfair competition policies exists. Virtually everywhere, consumer decision making is acknowledged as the most essential element of the market mechanism. Protection of the information infrastructure thereby provides the architecture of a functioning system of free competition. This is the quintessence of a free and unmanipulated evolution of competition as a dynamic process of marketplace transacting. On the basis of these structural similarities across different jurisdictions' systems, I will use this chapter to reconceptualize choice of law and conflicts law and present a practical guideline for implementing the results of my historical-comparative, theoretical, and doctrinal inquiry. I will begin by outlining the essential structure of choice of law in international trademark and unfair competition disputes (*see infra* p. 492 *et seq.*). On this basis, I will attempt to suggest some modest correctives and an according reformulation of the current rules in US and European law (*see infra* p. 521 *et seq.*). Finally, I will promulgate a typology of typical cross-border conflicts scenarios and thereby illustrate the reconceptualized conflicts resolution structure "in action" (*see infra* p. 548 *et seq.*).

Section 1 The New Conflicts Resolution Structure

The first issue of reconstruction, as we have seen, concerns the traditional dichotomy between trademark conflicts and unfair competition choice of law. In light of the two fields' common core of policies aimed at protecting market information infrastructure, a jettisoning of the formal distinction is needed. Extending the view to this virtually universal functional architecture unveiled in chapter 4 further suggests the need to overcome the traditional fixation on conduct that still governs in European civil law doctrine in particular. But the pendulum must not swing too far into the domain of effects testing—notably not toward the US doctrine of an over-extensively vague understanding of "commercial effects." Therefore, the effects test must be transformed into a uniform system of protecting consumer decision making—this implies a new qualitative standard for determining effects relevance. In addition, we also need a metric for determining minimum effects quantity. Civil law doctrine calls it a *de minimis* limitation, while US law deals with the issue in light of the *Bulova* test, mostly with respect to the aim of avoiding "conflicts with foreign law." This aspect requires drawing on what we have learned with respect to the doctrine of international comity.

I Trademark/Unfair Competition Uniformity: Core Policies

The previous chapters' findings on substantive law policy indicate that the existing divergence between the two approaches to trademark and unfair competition conflicts must be overcome. Above all, both sectors' core policies are homogeneous. Trademark protection and unfair competition prevention are the normative backbone of market information infrastructure.[3] This implies that the uniform basis of conflicts attachment is marketplace effects—more concretely, effects on market information that are relevant for the consumer's decision making.

Of course, black letter law in Europe has formally consolidated a dichotomy via articles 6 and 8 of the Rome II Regulation. But this does not preclude a uniform and homogeneous approach. Given the common core of trademark and unfair competition policies, conflicts resolution techniques will be structurally identical and yield consistent results if founded on a consolidated marketplace effects approach. In US trademark law, although the effects test seems to govern both trademark and unfair competition conflicts doctrine, a reconceptualization must be reconciled with the actual practice of subject-matter jurisdiction. The *Steele* doctrine constitutes a unilateral and quasi statutist rule. US courts, when confronted with an international dispute, will determine whether federal trademark law applies and, in doing so, will conflate subject-matter jurisdiction and choice of law

[3] *See supra* p. 325 *et seq.*

into one test.[4] Here, too, a consolidated marketplace or effects test can and should be integrated into existing structures.[5]

Such an implementation of the effects test into trademark and unfair competition conflicts law requires a foundation on a uniform effects-based *lex loci protectionis* rule. This rule still allows for a multilateral determination of the applicable law or laws. It is actually a choice-of-law technique in the sense initially proposed by Friedrich Carl von Savigny. In practice, a plaintiff must plead and specify the regime for resolution of the conflict at issue.[6] She will thus reasonably tailor her pleading to the jurisdiction(s) where a right exists or where a violation of unfair competition rules has occurred or is about to occur; this concerns all locations where marketplace effects have already occurred or may occur in the future.

II Quality of Effects: A Rule of Alternatives

My analysis of substantive law has revealed that the protection of trademark rights, like the prevention of unfair competition at its core, is a question of market information regulation. Consumers' minds determine the extension of rights and the issue of competitive fairness. The analysis, therefore, must take into account effects on the transmission of information, on the consumer's decision-making process, and on her transacting.[7] Under such a functionally qualified effects test, the point of attachment—that is, the locale of relevant effects' occurrence—must be found in the last stage of the consumer's decision making. This last stage of transacting is the focal point of the decision-making process.

In many cases, the point of attachment under such a perspective can be determined according to the consumer's actual point of transacting. Quite often, this is the point of sale. Yet the multiangular structure of

[4] For the similar approach in international antitrust cases, *see* Hannah L. Buxbaum & Ralf Michaels, *Jurisdiction and Choice of Law in International Antitrust Law—A US Perspective*, 225, 227, in *International Antitrust Litigation: Conflict of Laws and Coordination* (Jürgen Basedow et al. eds., 2012); *see also* Friedrich K. Juenger, *Constitutional Control of Extraterritoriality?: A Comment on Professor Brilmayer's Appraisal*, 50 Law & Contemp. Probs. 39, 45 (1987).

[5] *See infra* p. 521 *et seq.*

[6] For a similar technique, *see, e.g.*, BGH 2007 GRUR Int. 928, 931—*Wagenfeld-Leuchte* (15 February 2007); BGH 2007 GRUR 691, 691—*Staatsgeschenk* (24 May 2007); Stephan Briem, *Internationales und Europäisches Wettbewerbsrecht und Kennzeichenrecht* 113 (1995); Rolf Bär, *Das Internationale Privatrecht (Kollisionsrecht) des Immaterialgüterrechts und des Wettbewerbsrechts*, 125, 147, in *Schweizerisches Immaterialgüter- und Wettbewerbsrecht, vol. I* (Roland von Büren & Lucas David eds., 2nd edn., 2002); Andrew Dickinson, *The Rome II Regulation: The Law Applicable to Non-Contractual Obligations* para. 8.26 (2008); Michael Grünberger, in *Nomos-Kommentar-BGB, Rom-Verordnungen, vol. VI*, Art. 8 Rom II para. 30–31 (Rainer Hüßtege & Heinz-Peter Mansel eds., 2014); Christian Heinze, in *juris-Praxiskommentar zum BGB*, Art. 8 para. 12 and 14 (Markus Würdinger ed., 7th edn., 2014).

[7] *See supra* p. 287 *et seq.*

market competition requires more precision. This is due to the fact that trademark infringement, as unfairly competitive conduct, not only causes an actually or potentially improper transaction (between consumer and trademark infringer or competitor-violator) but also always causes the consumer to forego an alternative transaction—with the trademark owner or one of the competitors that was striving toward the transaction.[8] It is the locale of these alternative transactions that represents the extension of the respective market and the place(s) where actual or potential competition existed.[9] The point of sale can only then serve as a (but need not necessarily be the only) point of attachment if the consumer had at least one alternative to transact there. More generally, however, the localization of relevant effects requires considering more than one locale of unimplemented alternative transactions. The question is, Where did the alternatives to the actual transaction exist, or—if the consumer actually forwent a transaction—where could a transaction have been made absent the infringer's or competitor-violator's interference? In this way, it is also clear that the point of attachment is not necessarily the alleged infringer's place of conduct (*Werbemarkt*) or the place of impact (*Einwirkungsort*). Nor is it the place where potentially ubiquitous "commercial effects" may occur (*Auswirkungsort*). My typology of conflicts attachment presented in the last section of this chapter will clarify many practical questions in this regard.[10] For the moment, an example from Austria shall serve as an illustration of the basic principle.

In 1986, the Circuit Court of Innsbruck decided on a case in which a German airline company had advertised its services (flights from the United States to Austria) to US customers by offering free ski rental in Austria for each flight ticket purchased.[11] The court applied Austrian law, arguing that the Austrian market for ski rentals had been affected by the defendant's US marketing. It thereby did not apply the rule of the advertising market, instead undertaking a result-oriented analysis. The collision of interests, the court explained, was to be found in the Austrian

[8] *See supra* p. 285 *et seq.*

[9] For a similar market determination in international antitrust law, *see, e.g.*, Michael Hellner, *Unfair Competition and Acts Restricting Free Competition—A Commentary on Article 6 of the Rome II Regulation*, 9 Yearb. P.I.L. 49, 59 (2007), and Andrew Dickinson, *The Rome II Regulation: The Law Applicable to Non-Contractual Obligations* para. 6.63 (2008) (with further references).

[10] *See infra* p. 548 *et seq.*

[11] *See* OLG Innsbruck, 1986 HWR 34 *et seq.*—*Skizugaben* (24 March 1986); *see also* Lothar Wiltschek, *Die Beurteilung grenzüberschreitender Werbe- und Absatztätigkeit nach österreichischem Wettbewerbsrecht*, 1988 GRUR Int. 299, 306–307, and Stephan Briem, *Internationales und Europäisches Wettbewerbsrecht und Kennzeichenrecht* 55 *et seq.* (1995).

market for ski equipment and rentals.[12] This approach would arguably be questionable under current European choice of law. After all, "interests" existed in both the United States (i.e., consumers and competitor airlines) and Austria (i.e., consumers, competitor airlines, and ski-rental providers). Under the marketplace effects rule in unfair competition conflicts, notably under the *Gran Canaria* doctrine relying on the advertising market, US law rather than Austrian law should have been applied.[13] And a transfer of the antitrust conflicts rule to unfair competition choice of law, considering largely unqualified effects in both markets, might have even called for an application of both American and Austrian law.[14]

Quite differently, avoiding the vagaries of interest analysis and unqualified effects testing, looking for the consumer's decision making and the alternatives to her actual transaction allows the inquiry to be reduced to the core aspect of a market economy: the consumer must be able to freely decide how, when, and where to transact. Under a functional perspective, depending on the product at issue, the outcome may differ. If flights to Europe (or Austria) are at issue, alternative transactions existed only in the United States. Looking at ski-rental services provided for alternatives in Austria alone.[15] Yet even though the ultimate detriment may have occurred in the Austrian market for ski-rental services, these effects were irrelevant with respect to consumers' decision making. What was at issue in the defendant's advertising campaign was the sale of *flights* to Europe. In this regard, the search for alternative transactions should have led to an application of American law. At best, therefore, the case could have been understood as a scenario of unfair competition by breach of a statutory norm in Austrian law. This, however, as we will see in more detail later, is not a question of "marketplace" effects.[16] The court's decision to apply Austrian law may have been ultimately correct with regard to the breach of a statutory duty in Austria—but its analysis was beside the point when based on "effects" on the Austrian market for ski-rental services.

Finally, with respect to cross-border trademark infringements, further clarification is indicated: it is important to notice that giving regard to territorial effects under a rule of alternative transactions does not

[12] *See also* Karl-Heinz Fezer & Stefan Koos, in *Staudingers Kommentar zum Bürgerlichen Gesetzbuch: Internationales Wirtschaftsrecht*, Internationales Wettbewerbsprivatrecht para. 499 (15th edn., 2010).

[13] *See supra* p. 203 *et seq.* and *infra* p. 539 *et seq.*

[14] *See supra* p. 220 *et seq.*

[15] This requires assuming that American tourists would not rent their ski equipment in the United States. Considering the cost of transportation, it is quite safe to say that competition did not exist in the United States.

[16] *See infra* p. 565–566.

"extend" domestic trademark rights.[17] To correct this misunderstanding, we must distinguish between the protection of domestic (or territorial) goodwill and the protection of foreign-based (or extraterritorial) goodwill. The former concerns effects that occur within the national territory, no matter whether they have been caused by conduct inside or outside. One example is confusion of the forum's consumers. Even if the conduct occurs abroad (e.g., through the upload of confusing information to a foreign website), the effect still materializes territorially. Conduct may have occurred abroad, but regulation and rights protection are domestic. Foreign-based goodwill, by contrast, will be protected if the effects that are regulated occur beyond the national territory. In this case, one could actually speak of an extraterritorial "extension" of rights. This is the case if foreign-based consumers' confusion is prevented by the application of domestic law. The national regime will then address the impact on foreign markets in the sense of protecting goodwill and rights abroad.[18]

III Quantity of Effects: *Jurisdictional Self-Restraint*

Virtually all suggestions for choice of law in both trademark and unfair competition disputes that have been brought forward in the form of an effects test or a marketplace principle require a limitation: *de minimis* effects must be found within a state's territory (or its market) in order to apply the respective state's law.[19] The precise demarcations of such a *de minimis* test, however, are far from clear. This is due to the fact that the unqualified reference to minimum effects unduly intermingles several factors that must be kept apart. First, many suggestions still rely on nominal or intent-based standards to determine minimum effects. But we have already seen that actual numbers, as well as an alleged infringer's state of mind, must be disregarded in a system of market information regulation determined by modern trademark and unfair competition laws.[20] In addition (and this has yet to be subjected to a structured analysis), a well-balanced marketplace effects test requires an additional

[17] For the concept of "extended rights," *see, e.g.*, Anna R. Popov, *Watering Down Steele v. Bulova Watch Co. to Reach E-Commerce Overseas: Analyzing the Lanham Act's Extraterritorial Reach under International Law*, 77 S. Cal. L. Rev. 705, 728 (2004); Martin Ebner, *Markenschutz im internationalen Privat- und Zivilprozessrecht* 68 (2004); Karl-Heinz Fezer, *Markenrecht*, Einl H MarkenG para. 37 (4th edn., 2009). For the English doctrine of passing off—notably its protection of foreign-based goodwill—*see, e.g.*, Richard Plender & Michael Wilderspin, *The European Private International Law of Obligations* para. 18–095 (4th edn., 2015); *but see* Christopher Wadlow, *The Law of Passing-Off—Unfair Competition by Misrepresentation* para. 3–015 (4th edn., 2011).

[18] As illustrated in the historical-comparative analysis, US courts have and still do adhere to such a paradigm. *See supra* p. 164 *et seq.*

[19] *See supra* p. 209 *et seq.* [20] *See supra* p. 214 *et seq.*

threshold below which effects—even if qualified and foreseeable—will not be deemed sufficient to trigger the application of the territorial regime. Unlike current theory and practice, the description of such a threshold requires a comity-based *de minimis* analysis in the interest of avoiding both over- and underregulation.

A A Word in Advance: Practical Relativity

Multistate infringements and the application of potentially innumerable national regimes to cross-border marketing activity appear to be a serious practical concern. The situation does not require extensive explanation: a website may be accessed from virtually anywhere on the planet—accordingly, an infringement of trademark rights or a violation of unfair competition laws may occur everywhere. Prior to the internet, similar problems existed with newspaper, radio, and television marketing activities. In all of these cases, the collision-of-interests approach could lead to a cumulative application of different national laws. In general, injunctive relief and damages will then be territorially segmented. Each jurisdiction will govern only those claims related to its national territory.[21] The issue is less critical with regard to damages and compensation claims, where determining the relevant jurisdiction is largely a practical problem of computation and proof. But injunctive relief can be problematic. The concurrent application of numerous legal regimes, as is usually warned, could create serious problems if the marketing activity or method at issue is indivisible. In such cases, it will ultimately be the strictest law that governs the whole case, usually leading to a complete prohibition of the activities at issue.[22] Suggestions for remedying this problem are legion.[23] And, of course, there are strong arguments in favor of setting limitations to the judicial overreach of regulatory laws.[24] In particular, concerns of procedural and court efficiency must not be undervalued. Nevertheless, a

[21] For the so-called mosaic approach, *see, e.g.*, OGH 2012 GRUR Int. 468, 474—*Rohrprodukte* (20 September 2011); *see also* Michael Kort, *Zur „multistate"-Problematik grenzüberschreitender Fernsehwerbung*, 1994 GRUR Int. 594, 599–600; Nina Dethloff, *Europäisierung des Wettbewerbsrechts—Einfluss des europäischen Rechts auf das Sach- und Kollisionsrecht des unlauteren Wettbewerbs* 122 *et seq.* (2001); Rainer Hausmann & Eva Inés Obergfell, in *Lauterkeitsrecht: Kommentar zum Gesetz gegen den unlauteren Wettbewerb (UWG), vol. I*, Einleitung I para. 286 *et seq.* (Karl-Heinz Fezer ed., 2nd edn., 2010).

[22] *See, e.g.*, OGH 2012 GRUR Int. 468, 474—*Rohrprodukte* (20 September 2011); *see also* Christoph Brömmelmeyer, *Internetwettbewerbsrecht, Das Recht der Ubiquität—Das Recht der Domain Names—Das Recht der kommerziellen Kommunikation* 108 *et seq.* (2007); Rainer Hausmann & Eva Inés Obergfell, in *Lauterkeitsrecht: Kommentar zum Gesetz gegen den unlauteren Wettbewerb (UWG), vol. I*, Einleitung I para. 300 (Karl-Heinz Fezer ed., 2nd edn., 2010); Jochen Glöckner, in *Gesetz gegen den unlauteren Wettbewerb (UWG)*, UWG Einl C para. 154 (Henning Harte-Bavendamm & Frauke Henning-Bodewig eds., 3rd edn., 2013).

[23] *See supra* p. 209 *et seq.* [24] *See supra* p. 480 *et seq.*

number of clarifications are necessary. First, it must be noted that any judicial self-limitation with respect to the applicable law is an issue of substantive law doctrine rather than a rule of choice of law. The question is inseparably connected to local lawmakers' interest in regulating market communication.[25] Moreover, before developing a rule for judicial self-restraint, we must take a closer look at the circumstances of transnational and cross-border competition. This reveals that the situation is far less dramatic than is sometimes explained. Most fundamentally, as Jack L. Goldsmith points out in his provocative critique of cyberenthusiast suggestions on internet self-regulation, it is questionable whether the right to economic activity should be granted "without borders." Many proponents of practicality approaches assume that right owners' activities in foreign markets should always be supported by beneficial regulatory circumstances. Under this rather parochial perspective, foreign policies seem only to stand in the way of unlimited international transacting. Looking beyond the false front of free-market demands, however, reveals that foreign regulation is a logical obstacle. If cross-border activity extends marketplaces, the application of foreign laws' limitations is attached to these new domains, just as are all other market parameters that determine the costs of a commercial venture. There is no reason to expect cross-border activities to receive special treatment with regard to regulatory circumstances.[26]

[25] *See, e.g.*, article 3:602 CLIP Principles and Preamble, WIPO, *Standing Committee on the Law of Trademarks, Industrial Designs and Geographical Indications, SCT/5/2 (21 June 2000)*, 5 and *id.* at 8 (notes on section 2) ("The provision is only intended to deal with the question of whether use of a sign on the Internet can be deemed to have taken place in a particular Member State. The legal effects of such use in that Member State would have to be determined under the applicable law."). Correspondlingly, *HOTEL MARITIME* has been interpreted as having established a substantive rule of *de minimis* effects. *See supra* p. 71 *et seq.*, and *also, e.g.*, Severin Löffler, *Werbung im Cyberspace—Eine kollisionsrechtliche Betrachtung*, 2001 WRP 379, 383; Annette Kur, *Trademark Conflicts on the Internet: Territoriality Redefined?*, 175, 182–183, in *Intellectual Property in the Conflict of Laws* (Jürgen Basedow et al. eds., 2005); Axel Metzger, *Applicable Law under the CLIP Principles: A Pragmatic Revaluation of Territoriality*, 157, 173, in *Intellectual Property in the Global Arena—Jurisdiction, Applicable Law, and the Recognition of Judgments in Europe, Japan and the US* (Jürgen Basedow et al. eds., 2010); Ansgar Ohly, in Ansgar Ohly & Olaf Sosnitza, *Gesetz gegen den unlauteren Wettbewerb mit Preisangabenverordnung (UWG)* Einf B para. 26 (6th edn., 2014); *but see* James J. Fawcett & Paul Torremans, *Intellectual Property and Private International Law* para. 15.49 (2nd edn., 2011); Andreas Höder, *Die kollisionsrechtliche Behandlung unteilbarer Multistate-Verstöße—Das Internationale Wettbewerbsrecht im Spannungsfeld von Marktort-, Auswirkungs- und Herkunftslandprinzip* 46–49 (2002); Peter Mankowski, in *Münchener Kommentar zum Lauterkeitsrecht, vol. I*, IntWettbR para. 212 (Peter W. Heermann et al. eds., 2nd edn., 2014).

[26] Jack L. Goldsmith, *Against Cyberanarchy*, 65 U. Chi. L. Rev. 1199, 1220 *et seq.*, 1244 (1998); Jack L. Goldsmith, *The Internet and the Abiding Significance of Territorial Sovereignty*, 5 Ind. J. Global Legal Stud. 475, 485 (1998); *see also* (on unfair competition

In addition, warnings about legal uncertainty concerning the applicable law(s) and the risks for domestic entities involved in international economic activities are often exaggerated. We have already seen why and how enforcement capacities are limited in the international arena.[27] If individuals or entities have no local presence or assets within a certain jurisdiction, that state's regime is seldom enforceable.[28] An individual's expectation of conflict with foreign law is thus often more an issue of assessing the risk of being successfully haled into court (which is unlikely) than a question of whether the foreign law will actually prohibit the conduct at issue (which does not matter absent a realistic threat of litigation). A risk of litigation exists only where ties to the jurisdiction are sufficient. In other words, the more an activity is focused on a certain market, the less we should balk if the relevant legal regime is found applicable to the individual's conduct.

In this regard, one more aspect is important: with respect to the oft-enunciated risk of having the strictest law applied to instances of "indivisible" marketing activity, the conundrum has evolved into a pseudo problem for many relevant scenarios, particularly in the online environment. The issue is usually debated with an eye on cases of internet advertising. Yet the technical possibilities for segmenting and stratifying online activities have been significantly enhanced since the creation of the internet. As Jack Goldsmith explained in 1998 already, cyberspace is anything but "borderless," and territorial segmentation is possible.[29] Apart from geolocation techniques, which have significantly enhanced over time,[30] content providers have the option of conditioning access to their websites on the users' presentation of information. Considering the progress made in the technical control of information flow, it is no longer impossible to reterritorialize online activity on a geographical basis.

conflicts): Jost Kotthoff, *Werbung ausländischer Unternehmen im Inland* 28 (1995); Andreas Spickhoff, in *Beck'scher Online-Kommentar zum Bürgerlichen Gesetzbuch*, Art. 6 Rom II para. 5 (Heinz Georg Bamberger & Herbert Roth eds., 36th edn., 2015).

[27] *See supra* p. 480 *et seq.*

[28] *See, e.g.*, James Boyle, *Foucault in Cyberspace: Surveillance, Sovereignty, and Hardwired Censors*, 66 U. Cin. L. Rev. 177, 179 (1997) ("If the king's writ reaches only as far as the king's sword, then much of the content on the Internet might be presumed to be free from the regulation of any particular sovereign.").

[29] *See* Jack L. Goldsmith, *Against Cyberanarchy*, 65 U. Chi. L. Rev. 1199, 1212–1213, 1226, 1228 and *passim* (1998); Jack L. Goldsmith, *The Internet and the Abiding Significance of Territorial Sovereignty*, 5 Ind. J. Global Legal Stud. 475, 484–485 (1998).

[30] Already by 2009, geolocation accuracy at the national level was over 99%, and on track to become even better. *See* Kevin F. King, *Geolocation and Federalism on the Internet: Cutting Internet Gambling's Gordian Knot*, 11 Colum. Sci. & Tech. L. Rev. 42, 58–59 (2010); Dan Jerker B. Svantesson, *Time for the Law to Take Internet Geolocation Technologies Seriously*, 8 J. Priv. Int'l L. 473 (2012) (both with further references); *see also* Joel R. Reidenberg, *Technology and Internet Jurisdiction*, 153 U. Pa. L. Rev. 1951 (2005).

Effects within foreign territories can be avoided much more than used to be the case.[31]

In this light, we no longer face the tremendous problem of spillover effects (if we ever did). With regard to the volume of litigation, contrary to what has been prophesied, the number of international and multistate conflicts has not exploded during recent decades. In any case, a less hurried look at the costs and opportunities of international marketing reveals that a certain degree of concurrent regulation and regime overlap is not a phenomenon that must be avoided at any cost. Indeed, many scenarios cannot and need not be withdrawn from the reach of multiple concurrent laws. Rather than completely avoiding conflicts, therefore, the challenge for a modern conception of choice of law is to provide for rules of minimum conflict.

B Objective Foreseeability

One early example of a *de minimis* principle is the Institut de Droit International's suggestion in its 1983 Conflict-of-laws Rules on Unfair Competition, which require applying the law of the state where effects occurred that "could reasonably have been expected."[32] The institute did not elaborate further on the structural foundations of this factor. It described foreseeability by reference to the "injury to the competitor's business." This was still rather individual-competitor focused than truly policy oriented.[33] Notwithstanding this narrow perspective, its choice of terminology illustrates a central aspect of quantitative analysis: *de minimis* limitation is a question of reasonable party expectations—more concretely—of foreseeable effects.

1 Party Expectations and the International Private Law Order

A requirement of foreseeability reflects the limitations of human cognition. In legal analysis, this mostly concerns the facts of a case. We may, for

[31] With respect to the alleged risk of a circumvention of geolocation technique, the question is whether a content provider should be held responsible for individual users' activities. Unless the content provider actively solicits or expects such circumvention, this is highly questionable. *See also* Karl-Heinz Fezer & Stefan Koos, in *Staudingers Kommentar zum Bürgerlichen Gesetzbuch: Internationales Wirtschaftsrecht*, Internationales Immaterialgüterprivatrecht para. 945, 1155–1156 (15th edn., 2010); Thomas Nägele & Sven Jacobs, *Rechtsfragen des Cloud Computing*, 2010 ZUM 281, 285 n. 54.

[32] *See* Willis L. M. Reese & Frank Vischer (rapps.), *The Conflict-of-laws Rules on Unfair Competition*, article II para. 1 (Institut de Droit International, Session of Cambridge, 1983) ("Where injury is caused to a competitor's business in a particular market by conduct which could reasonably have been expected to have that effect, the internal law of the State in which that market is situated should apply to determine the rights and liabilities of the parties, whether such conduct occurs in that State or in some other State or States.").

[33] For this approach, *see supra* p. 64 *et seq.*, and p. 203 *et seq.*

instance, ask, Could the defendant have foreseen or expected the plaintiff's injuries? Yet foreseeability is about more than the factual realities. The background regime of legal norms also plays an important part of the reference frame for expectations to materialize. In fact, the direct correlation between our normative environment and our expectations ultimately underlies any conception of conduct-regulating legal policies. The order of private law forms the basis on which the individual can conduct her activities, guided by reasonable expectations of the rules that apply to this conduct.[34] Conversely, this means that commercial activity in particular cannot be conceived of as being devoid of at least rudimentary expectations that norms of just conduct must be complied with.[35] Expectations are no less important when it comes to activities touching on the international sphere. In fact, territoriality must generally be taken as axiomatic for conflicts law purposes.[36] This axiom particularly concerns choice of law with respect to regulatory norms. There, it is the individual parties' territorial connex to the regulating state that determines the actual choice of law. Such a connection—in other words, submission of private individuals to the application of a certain regime—can be found in either the individual's consent to submission or in her receiving of benefits upon contact with a state. Both aspects are reflected in the factors "presence within" or "doing business in" a territory.[37] They are necessarily founded on the knowledge and acknowledgment of the possibility that the state's legal regime might apply. This aspect actually reflects a larger shift in modern private international law: from an initial focus on single jurisdictions and laws, private international law has turned into the internal private law of socioeconomic transacting in a multijurisdictional world.[38] More concretely, this means that with the growth of transnational activity, in addition to domestic law, legal norms of foreign origin may also constitute a part of the framework that shapes private individuals' activities. Necessarily, therefore, with respect to conduct that may touch on interests beyond the national border, individual expectations will

[34] Friedrich A. von Hayek, *Legislation and Liberty—A New Statement of the Liberal Principles of Justice and Political Economy, vol. I: Rules and Order*, 102 *et seq.*, 106 *et seq.* (1973).

[35] With particular reference to competition, *see id.* at 102.

[36] Lea Brilmayer, *Rights, Fairness, and Choice of Law*, 98 Yale L.J. 1277, 1303 *et seq.* (1989).

[37] *Id.* at 1303 *et seq.*, 1308. *See also* David F. Cavers, *The Choice-of-Law Process* 139 *et seq.* (1965).

[38] Jürgen Basedow, *The Law of Open Societies—Private Ordering and Public Regulation of International Relations*, 360 Recueil des Cours 1, 35, 473 (2012). *See also supra* p. 384 *et seq.*

comprise not just domestic law but also limitations under possibly many foreign legal regimes.[39]

In this regard, one more aspect is important, though often neglected: parties' expectations must be assessed objectively. Foreseeability in choice-of-law doctrine is often still understood as depending on subjective perspectives. Legal certainty also appears to be founded on a consideration of individual expectations.[40] This may be a remnant of the Savignian era, where private law and choice of law were conceived of as systems of apolitical norms for national and international community members' self-determination.[41] The picture changes, however, if norm conflicts are seen in light of the underlying regulatory purposes and if one acknowledges that international private law has increasingly come to serve as an order for international socioeconomic transacting.[42] Of course, an individual will act in accordance with her subjective expectations. The overall order, as a system of limiting all private individuals' freedom, however, will not ask for the single individual's state of mind. Rules of conduct are objectivized by definition. With regard to competition-related activities covered by trademark and unfair competition law, this concept of objectivity reflects an essential economic logic: the extension of a market not only provides opportunities to increase profits but also implies costs. One facet of these costs is compliance with foreign laws. Hence, whatever can be foreseen as an opportunity abroad should also be foreseen as being attached to a corresponding set of limitations. Accordingly, it is the foreseeability of foreign-based effects that implies the application of foreign law regulating these effects.[43]

[39] *See also Spinozzi v. ITT Sheraton Corp.*, 174 F.3d 842, 846 (7th Cir. 1999) (Posner, C.J.). For further analysis of the correlation *see* Tim W. Dornis, *"Local Data" in European Choice of Law: A Trojan Horse from Across the Atlantic?*, 44 Ga. J. Int'l & Comp. L. 2015 (forthcoming); Tim W. Dornis, *Das Kollisionsrecht der auftragslosen Geschäftsführung—Ein Beispiel für Materialisierung und Typisierung im modernen europäischen IPR*, 80 RabelsZ 543, 563 *et seq.* (2016).

[40] *See, e.g.*, Jan Kropholler, *Internationales Privatrecht—einschließlich der Grundbegriffe des Internationalen Zivilverfahrensrechts* § 4 IV, § 14 II, and § 21 II (6th edn., 2006).

[41] *See supra* p. 402 *et seq.*

[42] *See supra* p. 383 *et seq.* *See also* Anton K. Schnyder, *Wirtschaftskollisionsrecht—Sonderanknüpfung und extraterritoriale Anwendung wirtschaftsrechtlicher Normen unter besonderer Berücksichtigung von Marktrecht* § 8 para. 255 (1990) ("Je relevanter nämlich die Verwirklichung bestimmter Ordnungsvorstellungen für die Gesamtordnung ist, desto weniger kann auf allfällige Parteierwartungen—selbst wenn sie nicht einem 'bad faith' entspringen—Rücksicht genommen werden. Insofern sind hier Einzelinteressen dem staatlichen Gesamtinteresse untergeordnet.").

[43] Foreseeability is also to be regarded in personal jurisdiction analysis. *See, e.g., Zippo Mfg. Co. v. Zippo Dot Com, Inc.*, 952 F.Supp 1119, 1123 (W.D. Pa. 1997); *World-Wide Volkswagen Corp. v. Woodson*, 444 U.S. 286, 297 (1980); for Europe, *e.g., Wintersteiger*, C-523/10, para. 23 *et seq.* (19 April 2012), [2012] E.T.M.R. 31 (for trademark infringements); *eDate Advertising and Others,* C-509/09 and C-161/10, para. 37 *et seq.* (25

2 *Technique and Factors of Market Analysis*

Regarding the subject matter of protection, as we have seen, the analysis must be founded on a policy of protecting consumer decision making. The ultimate stage of the consumer's decision should be protected from manipulation. The point(s) of attachment will thus be determined according to where alternatives to the transaction (or nontransaction) exist.[44] The analysis to be undertaken must be conducted from a dual perspective. First, it has to determine the relevant product market. Second, it must consider the specific instance of marketing.

With respect to a market's geographical scope, the globalization of commerce and trade has dissolved former boundaries between "national" marketplaces. Looking at a product market requires giving regard to the bulk of factors discussed in my summary of scholarship on the issue.[45] Even though a marketing medium may be unlimited in its reach, the product at issue can still be geographically (and, at the same time, territorially) limited in its availability. One example is restaurant or movie-theater advertising that (even if online) usually solicits local customers only. Another example is a physician's, dentist's, or lawyer's advertising that commonly focuses on potential customers within a local or regional reach.[46] The situation might differ, however, for advertising by an upscale gourmet restaurant, the New York Metropolitan Opera, an international law firm, or a renowned plastic surgeon's clinic. In essence, the central issue for assessing market extension is the ratio between the costs of transporting a good or performing a service (or transporting the consumer to the provider's place) and the value of the product. In addition, it may be relevant whether the goods or services at issue are prestigious or without an adequate local substitute.[47]

Furthermore, the concrete presentation of the marketing activity at issue may lead to a geographical and territorial confinement of relevant product alternatives. I have already mentioned the advertising language

October 2011), [2011] E.C.R. I-10269; for German law, *see* BGH 2010 GRUR 416, 463 *et seq.*—*The New York Times* (2 March 2010).

[44] *See supra* p. 494–497. [45] *See supra* p. 203 *et seq.*

[46] For examples, *see, e.g.*, Peter Mankowski, *Internet und Internationales Wettbewerbsrecht*, 1999 GRUR Int. 909, 918 (1999); Nina Dethloff, *Europäisierung des Wettbewerbsrechts—Einfluss des europäischen Rechts auf das Sach- und Kollisionsrecht des unlauteren Wettbewerbs* 117 (2001); Jochen Glöckner, in *Gesetz gegen den unlauteren Wettbewerb (UWG)*, UWG Einl C para. 164 (Henning Harte-Bavendamm & Frauke Henning-Bodewig eds., 3rd edn., 2013); Nadine Klass, in *Großkommentar—UWG: Gesetz gegen den unlauteren Wettbewerb, vol. I*, Einl. para. 223–224 (Otto Teplitzky et al. eds., 2nd edn., 2014).

[47] A similar ratio is reflected in the doctrine on the territorial scope of goodwill in passing-off cases. Notably in cases where foreign plaintiffs claim domestic goodwill, the outcome will depend on the value of the goods or services at issue and the distance to the domestic forum. *See, e.g.*, Christopher Wadlow, *The Law of Passing-Off—Unfair Competition by Misrepresentation* para. 3–089 to 3–091 (4th edn., 2011).

and methods of payment or delivery options.[48] The context of an advertisement may also matter, particularly whether the advertisement is published in a local or an international context.[49] In this regard, it is important to remember that trademark and unfair competition laws are intended to regulate market information. If a specific instance of market communication cannot reach the consumer or if it lacks the capacity to influence her decision making, then it will not be relevant. The most evident example is internet advertising in a language that is practically unknown to the population in a certain jurisdiction.[50] Finally, of course, the capacity of market communication to reach the consumer or customer will always also depend on the target group. Commercial customers may be more versatile and willing to overcome language barriers or pay transportation costs than private consumers.[51]

3 Clarification: Defendant's Intent and Actual Effects

Against this backdrop, two clarifying remarks are in order. The first one concerns the suggestion that so-called finality or the intentional targeting of marketing activities should determine the applicable law. As discussed earlier, this must be rejected: if we accept the idea that trademark and unfair competition law aims to protect consumer decision making, we must also avoid elements of subjectivity for conflicts law and choice of law. The field has evolved into a regime of market information regulation. The traditional tort paradigms, notably intent and other subjective elements, are thus largely irrelevant.[52] There is one aspect, however, that requires further analysis. Of course, the burden of proof is an issue that each national regime is free to establish under its own substantive or procedural law. Sensibly, however, it should be common understanding that the plaintiff, as part of her claim, must assert (and prove) that the effects at issue were foreseeable. Once this has been established, mere assertions by the alleged violator that she did not intend to target a certain

[48] *See supra* p. 209 *et seq.*

[49] For an extensive discussion, *see* Peter Mankowski, *Internet und Internationales Wettbewerbsrecht,* 1999 GRUR Int. 909, 919; Peter Mankowski, in *Münchener Kommentar zum Lauterkeitsrecht, vol. I,* IntWettbR para. 164 *et seq.* (Peter W. Heermann et al. eds., 2nd edn., 2014); Jochen Glöckner, in *Gesetz gegen den unlauteren Wettbewerb (UWG)*, UWG Einl C para. 165 *et seq.* (Henning Harte-Bavendamm & Frauke Henning-Bodewig eds., 3rd edn., 2013).

[50] This was why the defendant's website in Japanese was deemed not to have resulted in "any real confusion of American consumers, or diminishing of [plaintiff's] reputation" in *McBee v. Delica Co., Ltd.*, 417 F.3d 107, 123 *et seq.* (1st Cir. 2005). For the *McBee* case, *see supra* p. 159–164.

[51] Jochen Glöckner, *Der grenzüberschreitende Lauterkeitsprozess nach BGH v. 11.2.2010—Ausschreibung in Bulgarien,* 2011 WRP 137, 145.

[52] *See supra* p. 214 *et seq.*

market must generally be disregarded; otherwise, this would provide bad-faith defendants with escape options.[53] With regard to the defendant's assertions, therefore, intent is irrelevant. But the reverse scenario is different. If proven, the defendant's intent may be a proxy for the foreseeability of marketplace effects. This is a rule of procedural efficiency: most of the time, the judge is a nonexpert in the sector of the litigant parties' industry and trade. It is hence often difficult, if not impossible, for her to correctly assess and evaluate the conflict at bar with respect to the underlying short- and long-term economics. Quite differently, however, the parties must be presumed to have the necessary skills and to act rationally. They will thus undertake only those activities that promise favorable outcomes—in other words, their cost–benefit analysis has a higher probability of being correct than the judge's evaluation.[54] Consequently, if intent on the side of the defendant has been established, effects on the relevant market should be deemed foreseeable.[55]

In addition, a second clarification concerns the issue of seemingly insignificant *actual* effects. As we have seen, the German Bundesgerichtshof found sufficient effects in its 1970 decision in *Tampax* on the basis of a spillover of Swiss newspaper advertising into Germany.[56] The case illustrates that the problem is not instances of actual impact. Trademark protection, like unfair competition prevention, does not look at actual

[53] *See, e.g.*, Peter Mankowski, *Internet und Internationales Wettbewerbsrecht*, 1999 GRUR Int. 909, 919; Eva-Maria Kieninger, *Die Lokalisierung von Wettbewerbsverstößen im Internet—Ist das Marktortprinzip zukunftsfähig?*, 121, 128, in *Die Bedeutung des Internationalen Privatrechts im Zeitalter der neuen Medien* (Stefan Leible ed., 2003); Stefan Koos, *Objektive Kriterien zur Feststellung des anwendbaren Rechts im Internationalen Wettbewerbs- und Immaterialgüterrecht*, 2007 IPRax 414, 415.

[54] This is a practical variant of John Stuart Mill's noninterference principle and should be a common-sense argument in courtrooms around the world. *See* John Stuart Mill, *Principles of Political Economy with some of their Applications to Social Philosophy, book V*, ch. XI, V.11.29 (William J. Ashley ed., 7th edn., 1909) ("The ground of the practical principle of non-interference must here be, that most persons take a juster and more intelligent view of their own interest, and of the means of promoting it, than can either be prescribed to them by a general enactment of the legislature, or pointed out in the particular case by a public functionary.").

[55] This aspect was also considered for international antitrust in *Alcoa. See U.S. v. Aluminum Co. of America*, 148 F.2d 416, 444–445 (2nd Cir. 1945). *But see* (apparently differently for trademark and unfair competition conflicts) BGH 2012 GRUR 621, 624—*OSCAR* (8 March 2012). *See also* Stefan Koos, *Rom II und das Internationale Wirtschaftsrecht*, 6 EuLF 73, 77 (2006); Karl-Heinz Fezer & Stefan Koos, in *Staudingers Kommentar zum Bürgerlichen Gesetzbuch: Internationales Wirtschaftsrecht*, Internationales Wettbewerbsprivatrecht para. 517 (15th edn., 2010); Peter Mankowski, in *Münchener Kommentar zum Lauterkeitsrecht, vol. I*, IntWettbR para. 219 (Peter W. Heermann et al. eds., 2nd edn., 2014).

[56] BGH 1971 GRUR 153, 154—*Tampax* (23 October 1970). The 1966 Bundesgericht's *Sihl/Silbond* case centered on the reverse spillover of a German newspaper into Swiss territory. *See* BG 1967 GRUR Int. 364, 365—*Sihl/Silbond* (15 November 1966).

injury. *Potential* effects are what matter.[57] The *Tampax* reasons, read more closely, also highlight this point: the spillover may have had anywhere from no effect (if the newspaper had remained unread) to a significant effect (if the newspaper's marketing message had been circulated and proliferated repeatedly). The court, however, saw no need for further inquiry. It did not care about actual numbers but correctly based its finding on the fact alone that the newspaper's distribution had occurred in the course of usual business activity providing for the possibility of sufficient effects.[58] Another case illustrates how this point can be brought to an extreme: the Oberlandesgericht Hamburg, in a scenario concerning advertising for printing equipment in a French trade magazine, found a sufficient basis for German law to be applied even though the magazine had only two regular German subscribers.[59] The court's correct finding highlights that market structures matter. If the market is small enough with regard to the buyer side, even a nominally minuscule impact will suffice to exert sufficient effects. There is no blanket *de minimis* rule to be applied.

C International Comity

But foreseeability analysis as such does not constitute a comprehensive rule. There is one more aspect that must be given regard to—the requirement of jurisdictional self-restraint *beyond* the framework of public international law limitations. This is given short shrift in current theory and

[57] *See also* Peter Mankowski, *Internet und Internationales Wettbewerbsrecht*, 1999 GRUR Int. 909, 916 ("Umsätze und Marktanteile der beteiligten Unternehmen spielen im Wettbewerbsrecht jedoch anders als im Kartellrecht keine Rolle. Wettbewerbsrecht hat es mit Potentialitäten zu tun."). A similar argument can be made in the context of personal jurisdiction analysis, particularly the exercise of specific jurisdiction by US courts. *See Zippo Mfg. Co. v. Zippo Dot Com, Inc.*, 952 F.Supp 1119, 1127 (W.D. Pa. 1997) ("[The defendant] argues that its forum-related activities are not numerous or significant enough to create a 'substantial connection' with Pennsylvania. Defendant points to the fact that only two percent of its subscribers are Pennsylvania residents. However, the Supreme Court has made clear that even a single contact can be sufficient. ... The test has always focused on the 'nature and quality' of the contacts with the forum and not the quantity of those contacts."); *see also* Paul Torremans, *Jurisdiction and Choice of Law Issues in United States Intellectual Property Cases: From Dodging the Bullet to Biting It*, 1999 I.P.Q. 372, 374. For the contrary understanding—denying relevant effects even for purposeful activities on the basis of a mere counting of single newspaper copies—*see* OLG Stuttgart, 1987 GRUR 925—*expo data* (22 August 1986).

[58] This argument was also made by the Reichsgericht in *Primeros*. *See* RG 1936 GRUR 670, 676—*Primeros* (10 January 1936) ("Von einem 'Verbreiten' könnte allerdings nicht gesprochen werden, wenn nur da u. dort einmal durch Dritte ein Stück oder eine Mehrzahl von Stücken der ausländischen Druckerzeugnisse über die Grenze gelangt. Anders steht es aber mit einer im regelmäßigen Geschäftsbetrieb vor sich gehenden Versendung durch den Zeitungsverlag ...."); *see also* Hans-Albrecht Sasse, *Grenzüberschreitende Werbung—Die Anwendbarkeit und die Anwendung deutschen Rechts vor deutschen Gerichten auf inländische Auswirkungen von Werbeaussagen in ausländischen Werbemedien* 86 (1974).

[59] OLG Hamburg 1987 GRUR Int. 105, 107—*IR/UV-Kombinationstrockner* (15 May 1986).

practice both in the United States and in Europe. Most approaches thus share a defect: they conflate fundamentally different aspects of *de minimis* analysis and lack a precise structural guideline regarding when and how to limit the territorial scope of national laws.

1 Current De Minimis *Standards*

I have already explored the *HOTEL MARITIME* case.[60] An interesting counterpart in US practice can be found in the Second Circuit's 1994 *Sterling Drug v. Bayer AG* opinion.[61] The court had to decide on an American right owner's claim of trademark infringement by a European drug company that was using the same trademark as the plaintiff—not only in Europe, but also in the United States. While the plaintiff had rights in the United States, the defendant relied on trademark rights in Germany. Even though the Second Circuit and the Bundesgerichtshof began with a different understanding of their respective law's scope,[62] both decisions are representative of a widely convergent technique of *de minimis* limitation.

a The Paradigm of "Shields" and "Swords" Under the law as it stood in 1994, the plaintiff's situation in *Sterling Drug* was precarious. The Second Circuit's governing precedent at the time (*Vanity Fair*) was unfortunate for US trademark owners trying to fend off a foreign right owner's use of a validly registered foreign trademark abroad.[63] As the Second Circuit explained:

> [I]f we applied the Vanity Fair test mechanically to the instant case, we would forbid the application of the Lanham Act abroad against a foreign corporation that holds superior rights to the mark under foreign law. But such an unrefined application of that case might mean that we fail to preserve the Lanham Act's goals of protecting American consumers against confusion, and protecting holders of American trademarks against misappropriation of their marks.[64]

[60] *See supra* p. 71 *et seq.*
[61] *Sterling Drug, Inc. v. Bayer AG*, 14 F.3d 733 (2nd Cir. 1994).
[62] The Second Circuit highlighted, "It is well-established that United States courts have jurisdiction to enforce the Lanham Act extraterritorially in order to prevent harm to United States commerce" (*Sterling Drug, Inc. v. Bayer AG*, 14 F.3d 733, 745 (2nd Cir. 1994)). The Bundesgerichtshof, by contrast, emphasized the long-established theory of territoriality by pointing out that an injunction may generally be issued only if infringing trademark use can be found within the domestic territory ("[E]in Unterlassungsanspruch . . . setzt deshalb eine das Kennzeichenrecht verletzende Benutzungshandlung im Inland voraus. Diese ist regelmäßig gegeben, wenn im Inland unter dem Zeichen Waren oder Dienstleistungen angeboten werden." (BGH 2005 GRUR 431, 432—*HOTEL MARITIME* (13 October 2004)).
[63] For *Vanity Fair* and the Second Circuit's *Bulova* test variant, *see supra* p. 161–164.
[64] *Sterling Drug, Inc. v. Bayer AG*, 14 F.3d 733, 746 (2nd Cir. 1994).

Even though Chief Judge Newman ultimately distinguished the case from *Vanity Fair*,[65] it was clear that a rigid adherence to a binary system of conflicts resolution—in other words, an all-or-nothing approach—had become obsolete. On the one hand, nonapplication of the Lanham Act would neglect the protection of US customers against confusion initiated by uses of foreign trademarks abroad. On the other, applying the Lanham Act indiscriminately would also be unreasonable. Required instead was a concretized and fact-specific tailoring of remedies in accordance with the instances of the trademark use at issue. As Newman further pointed out—and this is critical—a certain degree of consumer confusion within the national territory may have to be tolerated in order to prevent a breakdown of international commercial communication and advertising activities:

> In today's global economy, where a foreign TV advertisement might be available by satellite to U.S. households, not every activity of a foreign corporation with any tendency to create some confusion among American consumers can be prohibited by the extraterritorial reach of a District Court's injunction.[66]

A decade later, in Germany, the Bundesgerichtshof expressed the same concern in the context of the online dispute at the center of the *HOTEL MARITIME* case. As the court warned, if each instance of internet use were found to constitute a legally relevant effect in the protecting country, it would result in a problematic return to the nineteenth-century paradigm of trademark universality. Such an overextension of domestic rights would ultimately stifle international communication and transacting:

> Not any use of a mark on the internet is subject to the national legal order's protection of marks against confusion. Otherwise, protection of national rights would be extended shorelessly and would—contrary to the European freedom to provide services . . . —inadequately restrict self-expression of foreign enterprises. This would involve a significant limitation of opportunities to make use of rights on the internet since owners of confusingly similar marks, protected in different countries, could—irrespective of the priority of the conflicting marks—reciprocally demand forbearance of use from the other side.[67]

[65] *Id.* [66] *Id.* at 747.

[67] BGH 2005 GRUR 431, 432—*HOTEL MARITIME* (13 October 2004), author's translation (for the original German text *see supra* chapter 1 fn. 235). For an earlier expression of the same concern (albeit in an "offline" world), *see* RGZ vol. 118, 76, 83—*Springendes Pferd/Hengstenberg* (20 September 1927) ("Dem deutschen Verkäufer, der von den ihm . . . verliehenen Rechten Gebrauch macht, kann nicht schlechthin angesonnen werden, zu vermeiden, daß durch eine ihm erlaubte Inlandsbetätigung die Verletzung eines fremden Zeichenrechts in irgendeinem fremden Lande ermöglicht oder dem Inhaber dieses Rechts Konkurrenz gemacht werde.").

Indeed, both opinions can be seen as expressions of an internationalist understanding in trademark conflicts law. Judicial self-restraint is a must. Newman's allegoric reference to "swords" and "shields" is fitting:

> Though Congress did not intend the Lanham Act to be used as a sword to eviscerate completely a foreign corporation's foreign trademark, it did intend the Act to be used as a shield against foreign uses that have significant trademark-impairing effects upon American commerce.[68]

While fending off an invasion or impairment of national policies is acceptable, there exists a certain threshold of minimum effects below which domestic rights protection becomes an offense rather than a mere defense. It is the appropriate balancing of offensive and defensive measures that enables a functioning environment for international transacting and commerce.

b Analysis: An Ad Hoc Rule of "International-Individual Equity"

What becomes evident from looking at both decisions in light of my findings on policy and comity is that both courts' reasons are based on an underdeveloped structural concept of self-restraint. Both courts applied a similar technique of effects testing. The Second Circuit tested for *significant* trademark-impairing effects on US commerce.[69] The Bundesgerichtshof explained that the risk of mutually blocking trademarks in the international arena could be avoided only by requiring *sufficient* economic effects within the German territory.[70] Both courts' tests, however, neglect two specific aspects: they suggest a widely unqualified effects analysis and they do not distinguish between private-party and public interests.

The Bundesgerichtshof's arguments are particularly illustrative: even though starting from the World Intellectual Property Organization's (WIPO) Joint Recommendation and its criterion of "commercial effects," the court ultimately did not apply the recommendation's factor list to its analysis of commercial effects.[71] Instead, the judges roughly and without further qualification compared the parties' interests, concluding that the plaintiff's interest in receiving the requested injunction was less significant than the defendant's interest in advertising for its hotel.[72] Had the

[68] *Sterling Drug, Inc. v. Bayer AG*, 14 F.3d 733, 746 (2nd Cir. 1994). [69] *Id.* at 747.

[70] BGH 2005 GRUR 431, 433—*HOTEL MARITIME* (13 October 2004); *see also* BGH 2012 GRUR 621, 624—*OSCAR* (8 March 2012).

[71] For the Joint Recommendation's list of factors, *see* article 3. *See also supra* p. 225 *et seq.*

[72] BGH 2005 GRUR 431, 433—*HOTEL MARITIME* (13 October 2004) ("Ist die Beeinträchtigung der Klägerin auf Grund des Angebots der ausländischen Dienstleistungen der Beklagten im Inland aber nur unwesentlich und ist deshalb von einem Fehlen wirtschaftlicher Auswirkungen auf den Schutz der Kennzeichenrechte der

court considered the defendant's conduct in more detail, however, the outcome might have been quite different. After all, the list of factors in the recommendation would have allowed for several of the case's facts to be actually interpreted to predetermine a finding of "commercial effect": the defendant not only served German customers in its hotel but also solicited online reservations on its website, which was fully available in German. In addition, the defendant had sent German-language advertising brochures to prospective customers in Germany.[73]

The court's direct reference to the WIPO Joint Recommendation may explain why it did not attempt to formulate a guideline for the qualitative determination of what should be given regard to when analyzing and evaluating effects. The Senate did not undertake a policy-oriented analysis. This left its interest-balancing approach in a rather ambiguous and imprecise stage. Under a rule of alternatives,[74] the ultimate outcome could have actually been more consistently explained: since the defendant's hotel services were offered in Copenhagen, alternatives to a stay at the defendant's hotel were to be found in Copenhagen and the vicinity. The marketplace at issue was coterminous with the city. Application of German law, thus, would have been an issue of non-confusion-based goodwill invasion only.[75]

What is further remarkable in the court's arguments is that only private-party concerns and interests were deemed essential. This also was the analysis in *Sterling Drug.*[76] Since the economic or commercial effects of the defendant's advertising on the plaintiff's business in Germany were deemed insignificant (*unwesentlich*), the balancing of interests could not provide for a prevalence of the plaintiff's concerns.[77] Similar to the collision-of-rights theories in legal scholarship, the solution of international trademark conflicts seems to lie in a doctrine of international-individual equity.[78] Another facet of this perspective actually comes to the fore in a

Klägerin auszugehen, haben ihre Interessen im Rahmen einer Gesamtabwägung zurückzutreten.").

[73] These elements, at least under article 3 of the WIPO Joint Recommendation, could have justified the application of German trademark law with more rigor—enjoining at least some parts of the defendant's trademark use. In addition, even though the plaintiff had started using the trademark more than twenty years before the defendant and had more than forty hotels in Germany, there was no discussion of bad faith on side of the defendant.

[74] *See supra* p. 494–497.

[75] For the non-confusion-based policies in trademark law, *see supra* p. 350 *et seq.* and *infra* p. 556 *et seq.*

[76] *Sterling Drug, Inc. v. Bayer AG*, 14 F.3d 733, 747 (2nd Cir. 1994) ("Where ... both parties have legitimate interests, consideration of those interests must receive especially sensitive accomodation in the international context.").

[77] BGH 2005 GRUR 431, 433—*HOTEL MARITIME* (13 October 2004).

[78] *See supra* p. 256 *et seq.*

more recent opinion by the Bundesgerichtshof. In a cross-border dispute over the use of the trademark "Oscar," the owner of a German trademark registration (and organizer of the annual Academy Awards ceremony) asserted infringement through the defendant's use of the word "Oscar" in the titles of several Italian television broadcasts. The defendant (an Italian television company) had broadcast its programs via satellite to Germany and a number of other countries. As the court explained:

> What is required is . . . a comprehensive balancing of the parties' interests that, in addition to considering the weight of effects of the symbol's use at issue on the trademark owner's domestic economic interests, must also give regard to the question of how far it was possible and reasonable for the defendant to avoid an inland infringement.[79]

Since satellite transmission cannot be precisely separated along national boundaries, the court assumed, it will inevitably find receivers in several countries. An overly strict enforcement of trademark rights might hence make European satellite transmission impossible. Necessarily, therefore, the court concluded, the spillover of trademark-infringing effects—if and to the extent that these effects are unavoidable—must be acknowledged and cannot be infringed by a domestic right owner.[80]

In this light, the status quo of *de minimis* analysis can be summarized by a few basic rules: confronted with cross-border trademark infringement, courts will not limit their consideration of interests to those of the plaintiff; equally important are the other side's concerns. In addition, as long as effects within a certain jurisdiction cannot be reasonably "avoided," application of the respective regime is problematic. In particular, if economic or commercial activity (e.g., satellite or internet communication) would be hindered by an overly strict enforcement of trademark rights, the tendency is to abstain from judicial intervention. However, there is no structured and precise qualitative standard for determining the significance or sufficiency of effects. Instead, courts apply an ad hoc rule of international-individual equity.

2 *Reconceptualization*

Of course, the current practice of *de minimis* testing provides for acceptable results in many cases. As I have already alluded to, there often is no "costless" solution for international trademark and unfair competition

[79] BGH 2012 GRUR 621, 624—*OSCAR* (8 March 2012) ("Erforderlich ist . . . eine Gesamtabwägung der Interessen der Parteien, in die neben dem Gewicht der Auswirkungen der Kennzeichenbenutzung auf die inländischen wirtschaftlichen Interessen des Zeicheninhabers auch einfließen muss, inwieweit es den Bekl[agten] möglich und zumutbar war, Rechtsverletzungen im Inland zu vermeiden." (author's translation)).

[80] *Id.*

disputes—many cases will not allow for a complete avoidance of right and policy conflicts. Hence, a balancing of individual interests seems to be most pragmatic and reasonable. After all, from the court's perspective, the litigant parties' concrete dispute is the only thing that must be resolved. In addition, these are the interests that a judge can practically ascertain with acceptable effort. Yet distortion looms beyond the picture of interparty relations. If courts limit their analysis accordingly—especially by neglecting long-term effects with respect to the policies involved—they lose sight of the structure of conflicts resolution and choice of law "under the surface."[81]

a *Structural Underpinning and Relevant Interests* First, it is necessary to challenge the governing technique of ad hoc decision making, which claims to focus on rather vague concepts of interest balancing and proportionality in general. Even though "interests" are indeed what must be evaluated and balanced, the conceptual self-limitation of current doctrine overlooks a critical aspect: the evaluation and balancing of interests in international trademark and unfair competition conflicts is not an issue of general "fairness" or "equity," nor is the judge left to her own devices. The area of trademark and unfair competition conflicts is founded on dense structures of international agreements—in particular, however, on a transnational convergence of substantive law policies. My analysis of substantive trademark and unfair competition law has illustrated this infrastructural underpinning, which also predetermines choice of law. Any interest, in order to be eligible for consideration, must thus be founded on or be correlated with the regulation of market information. The lack of a qualitative functional analysis aside, at this point, it is questionable whether the *HOTEL MARITIME* court actually used the correct numbers—that is, the costs ensuing from the defendant's impact on market information, not the actual turnover numbers or other costs—for its calculation and balancing. Unfortunately, the court's reasons do not explain the metric that was used to compute the "insignificance" of commercial effects.[82]

Second, following from this qualification, it is important to distinguish private-party concerns from state interests. Under current doctrine, interest balancing is based on the private parties' "legitimate interests"[83] or

[81] *See supra* p. 480 *et seq.*
[82] *See* BGH 2005 GRUR 431, 433—*HOTEL MARITIME* (13 October 2004).
[83] *See, e.g.*, Annette Kur, *Principles Governing Jurisdiction, Choice of Law and Judgments in Transnational Disputes: A European Perspective*, 2003 CRi 65, 72; Ansgar Ohly, *Choice of Law in the Digital Environment—Problems and Possible Solutions*, 241, 255, in *Intellectual Property and Private International Law—Heading for the Future* (Josef Drexl & Annette Kur eds., 2005).

"equities."[84] While this may seem fair to the parties, it neglects the overall impact of conflicts resolution in the field. This defect stems from the field's doctrinal history of private rights protection. And it is somewhat reflective of the courts' limited focus on private-individual parties and their interests—not on the overall consequences of legal doctrine in the field.[85] Yet the analysis must not be limited to individual or private-party interests; it always requires reconciling the state interests involved.[86] All issues in the core area of trademark and unfair competition law are oriented toward market information infrastructure and its protection.[87] For conflicts law and choice of law, the conclusion is inevitable: the conflict is between legal regimes, not private rights.[88] It is thus not a rule of international "equity" but one of international "comity" that must be applied.

In this light, international trademark and unfair competition conflicts usually entail at least two states' divergent interests[89]—namely, divergent interests regarding the freedom or the limitations that are necessary to establish or maintain the optimum status of market information. We must be aware of the fact that what fosters one state's interest often undermines the other's. Accordingly, conflicts resolution will seldom be costless in the sense of allowing for a comprehensive avoidance or reconciliation of all concerns involved. Let us return to the *HOTEL MARITIME* scenario for illustration, with slightly modified facts: if a market actor uses a certain trademark in online advertising targeted at her seat jurisdiction, but if this advertising can also be accessed abroad where the identical symbol is already in use as a trademark by a competitor (for identical products), the conflict is not limited to the individual parties. While the first actor's seat jurisdiction has an interest in the trademark's domestic functions (notably search cost reduction among local customers), accessibility of the advertising in the other competitor's jurisdiction may cause consumer confusion there—and, accordingly, higher search costs among the other jurisdiction's consumers. If a binary technique of conflicts law requires an all-or-nothing approach under one single chosen law, it is either the defendant's domestic customer base that is divested of valuable market

[84] *See Sterling Drug, Inc. v. Bayer AG*, 14 F.3d 733, 747 (2nd Cir. 1994).
[85] *See supra* p. 480 *et seq.*
[86] In this regard, I define "interest" in the Currian sense as "the product of (a) a governmental policy and (b) the concurrent existence of an appropriate relationship between the state having the policy and the transaction, the parties, or the lititgation." *See* Brainerd Currie, *Selected Essays on the Conflict of Laws* 621 (1963).
[87] *See supra* p. 325 *et seq.* [88] *See supra* p. 265 *et seq.*
[89] In multistate conflicts, it is consequences in multiple states that must be taken into account.

information or the foreign-based consumers who are being confused.[90] At an abstract level, both jurisdictions involved may follow widely corresponding policies fostering an optimal level of market information within their respective territories. But the policies in action—and each jurisdiction's concrete interest in the outcome of the case—are in open conflict.

But the analysis is not complete with a look at the immediate costs and benefits alone. In addition, the long-term consequences of the court's decision must be taken into account. This brings us back to my analysis of international economic law and the doctrine of international comity: extending domestic law beyond national borders, as is commonly argued, risks invading foreign jurisdictions' sovereignty with respect to regulating their internal information infrastructure. But this is not the only problem. Although US practice under the *McBee* fallacy still contends otherwise,[91] it is usually impossible to regulate foreign markets through the cross-border extension of national law. What may then ensue is an anticompetitive discriminatory application of different regulatory standards—mostly to the detriment of domestic parties.[92] And even if extraterritorial regulation should be effective, an ultimate distortion of international transacting may yet result from retaliation. In other words, the risk that other jurisdictions could apply the same overextensive rules would ultimately paralyze many sectors of communication.[93]

b *Practical Rules and Presumptions* Against this backdrop, a more detailed practical guideline of *de minimis* analysis can be suggested. Even though the reconceptualization of jurisdictional self-restraint cannot provide for a one-size-fits-all rule or an exact demarcation between admissible and inadmissible extension of national rights and policies, it does provide for a more solid and comprehensive test.

(i) Starting Point: Fact-Based Crafting of Remedies In essence, the decision maker is referred to a multistep analysis. Since there is no one-size-fits-all solution if the defendant's conduct covers more than one kind of marketing activity, the court must undertake a separate analysis for all single instances of alleged infringement.[94] For each single instance,

[90] I have already discussed this conflict with respect to *Hanover Star* scenarios and under the civil law doctrine of same-name conflicts in trademark law. *See supra* p. 333–336.

[91] *See supra* p. 481 *et seq.* [92] *See supra* p. 483 *et seq.*

[93] This was drastically explained *supra* for internet and satellite communication in *HOTEL MARITIME* and *OSCAR*.

[94] In *HOTEL MARITIME*, for instance, this would have required separating website communication and advertising by mail. In *Sterling Drug*, the court correctly

then, she must determine the overall consequences of *both* the alleged infringer's or violator's activity *and* a court-crafted remedy (usually an injunction). This fact-based analysis provides the fundament for a flexible tailoring of redress.

In detail, what is to be considered with respect to market information requires comparing all market parameters, particularly the parties' sales numbers, the geographical span of their markets, sales channels, and consumer sophistication. *Sterling Drug* provides for an illustration of such a salient fact-based analysis. Under the rubric of "Background,"[95] both the district and circuit court summed up the factual background and extensively analyzed the economic setting of the conflict. On this basis, then, with respect to the actual redress, a court should compare all available options of court-crafted remedies. Quite often, the judge has a continuum of measures of corrective court invasion in her hands. An example of such a comparison can be found, at least rudimentarily, in Judge Newman's instructions to the district court: inter alia, he required the lower instance to consider adequate restrictions to the defendant's international marketing activity by means of a categorization of the relevant print media.[96] In this regard, he explained, the "placing [of] a full-page 'Bayer' advertisement in the U.S. edition of a foreign magazine or newspaper" should not be considered admissible.[97] An injunction in Sterling Drug's favor would, accordingly, cover a prohibition on this kind of marketing activity. However, he went on to explain that "it might be inappropriate [for the district court] to leave the injunction so broad as to ban the announcement of new medical research in *Lancet*, or an employment notice in *Handelsblatt* [a leading German business newspaper]."[98] This differentiation reflects the fact that the dispute primarily concerned a consumer product (pharmaceuticals) and its marketing vis-à-vis consumers. Necessarily, therefore, the instruments of market communication would cover popular national media but not scientific journals or foreign newspapers. In essence, the court undertook an individualized and probability-based infringement analysis: the higher the probability of infringing by a certain communication instrument's circulation in the United States, the more stringent the court's remedy.

distinguished between television and print advertising. *See Sterling Drug, Inc. v. Bayer AG*, 14 F.3d 733, 747 (2nd Cir. 1994).

[95] For the district court's analysis of the market parameters, *see Sterling Drug, Inc. v. Bayer AG*, 792 F.Supp. 1357, 1359 *et seq.* (S.D.N.Y. 1992). For the circuit court, *see Sterling Drug, Inc. v. Bayer AG*, 14 F.3d 733, 736 *et seq.* (2nd Cir. 1994).

[96] *Sterling Drug, Inc. v. Bayer AG*, 14 F.3d 733, 747 *et seq.* (2nd Cir. 1994).

[97] *Id.* at 747. [98] *Id.*

One aspect is important under a methodological perspective: this approach can provide for only a reasonable approximation of the cost-benefit ratio of cross-border regulation and extraterritoriality of rights. Yet by spelling out the factual basis of its verdict, the court helps avoid a defect in future decision making. An expressly fact-based finding makes clear that the court's holding is founded on the concrete and individual case. It thereby prevents a mis- and overinterpretation of the holding in the sense of an all-encompassing and generally valid rule of law.[99] In other words, the more detailed a court's factual analysis, the clearer the instruction to later courts to question their cases' factual basis and, if necessary, distinguish their case from the precedent. The message should be clear: each case requires its own fact-specific analysis.

In this regard, apart from the lack of qualification of effects, the *HOTEL MARITIME* holding can be shown as imprecise, if not incorrectly decided, in at least one more respect. The court's analysis suffered from the traditional individual-party focus. By looking just at the litigants, the court found that the defendant's use of the mark caused only negligible and insignificant injury. After all, the small competitor-defendant did not seem to pose a real threat to the trademark owner's large hotel chain. The issue would have become more complex, however, had the court also taken into account potential later-comers' use of the plaintiff's trademark—hence, if it had also considered the long-term effects of their holding. In essence, under the court's doctrine, hardly any kind of use of a competitor's trademark—if only the alleged infringer is small enough—can be characterized as exerting sufficient effects abroad. By this means, the court created a risk that the number of small competitors' use of an identical or similar trademark may multiply. In the end, large-company trademark owners have been factually outlawed with respect to attacks by small foreign-based competitors.

(ii) Prima Facie "Effects Sufficiency": Defendant's Intent We have already seen that if intent on the side of the defendant can be proven, the foreseeability of effects should be acknowledged: an attempt to reach across the border will be undertaken only if economic success looms.[100] A similar rule can be formulated when a limitation in light of international comity is at issue. Here as well, the parties' cost-benefit analysis has a higher probability of being correct than the judge's evaluation. If that is true, however, a long-term perspective suggests that the expectation of a

[99] For the contrary assumption and an approach of universal substantive law promulgation, *see supra* p. 256 *et seq.*
[100] *See supra* p. 505–507.

positive output will invite imitation by others. It is then no longer the individual and concrete interparty cost-benefit analysis that matters. Over time, the sum of effects must be expected to increase. In light of the long-run perspective, therefore, effects are not negligible and must be presumed to be above the *de minimis* threshold. Here again, we must be aware that a presumption can provide only for a rule of approximation. Of course, the defendant's intent is a test factor that focuses primarily on the concrete case and the individual parties. In the long run, however, it provides a guideline for private-party marketplace activity in general and thereby functions as a regulatory corrective. It will ultimately bring out the next-best result to a precise cost-benefit calculation.

Once more, we can explain the *HOTEL MARITIME* holding as partly imprecise. As already mentioned, with respect to the choice-of-law question, the court failed to account for the defendant's active targeting of a German customer base.[101] In the case, both the defendant's website and its mail advertising were directed at a German public. They offered extensive information in German, and it was even possible to make online reservations in German. There was no explanation for the use of the German language or for the soliciting of German consumers other than that it was a lucrative kind of marketing from the defendant's point of view. Accordingly, the court should not have neglected this kind of marketing as having only insignificant commercial effects. Quite differently, for the sake of illustration, the English case *Euromarket Designs Inc. v. Peters and Crate & Barrel Ltd.*[102] presented a case of apparently *de minimis* effects in a similar scenario: the defendants ran a single retail store for household goods and furniture in Dublin, Ireland, and operated a website on which the plaintiff's UK and European Community trademark "Crate & Barrel" was used. Judge Jacob, denying an infringement, emphasized two facts. First, the mere accessibility of the website was not enough. As he put it, "[T]he website owner should [not] be regarded as putting a tentacle onto the user's screen." Second, the defendants had not actively gone out to solicit customers in the UK.[103]

(iii) Caveat: "Effects Unavoidability" Finally, case law and commentary have discussed cases where effects within a jurisdiction are

[101] Interestingly, the judges did acknowledge the defendant's active solicitation of customers in Germany with respect to the issue of personal jurisdiction. *See* BGH 2005 GRUR 431, 432—*HOTEL MARITIME* (13 October 2004).

[102] *Euromarket Designs Inc. v. Peters and Crate & Barrel Ltd.* [2001] F.S.R. 20.

[103] *Id.* at 24; *see also* James J. Fawcett & Paul Torremans, *Intellectual Property and Private International Law* para. 10.29–30 (2nd edn., 2011).

deemed *de minimis* if a defendant's actions include a reasonable effort to avoid or minimize an infringement. A common-sense approach seems to be that infringing use of a trademark (or unfair competition) should not be deemed to occur if the defendant takes reasonable steps to avoid interference with the domestic market to the best possible degree.[104] While analysis in these cases has often been unduly curtailed, asking for the avoidability of effects makes sense as a practical proxy for determining the sufficiency of effects.

Of course, if effects within a jurisdiction are truly avoidable, there does not exist any conflict of policies or interests. This is the case, for instance, where confusion can effectively be excluded by a disclaimer.[105] In many disputes, however, the alleged infringer or violator cannot prevent her conduct from having effects in more than one jurisdiction—no matter what she does. One example is the use of a word mark that is not well known in the defendant's seat jurisdiction as part of a domain name under this jurisdiction's top-level domain. If the website can be accessed in other jurisdictions where the symbol is well known for a competitor's products, the conflict—in the sense of effects on the trademark's reputation and prestige—can hardly be avoided (at least not by a disclaimer).[106] Asking for the avoidability of effects in such a case implies that the defendant's conduct—and, accordingly, this conduct's effect—is legitimate. Otherwise, a genuine rule of avoidability would actually require *completely* ceasing the activity at issue. This assumption of legitimacy can best be explained by reference to the collision-of-rights perspective.

As we have seen, under a lens centered on individual parties and rights, it seems as if the conflicts panacea can be found in a rule of international-individual equity.[107] Looking at the same dispute in light of the policies and state interests involved, however, indicates the need for a balancing

[104] *See, e.g.*, BGH 2012 GRUR 621, 624—*OSCAR* (8 March 2012) and *supra* p. 507 *et seq.* For the internet context, *see, e.g.*, Annette Kur, *Territorialität versus Globalität—Kennzeichenkonflikte im Internet*, 2000 WRP 935, 940, and Annette Kur, *Trademark Conflicts on the Internet: Territoriality Redefined?*, 175, 181, in *Intellectual Property in the Conflict of Laws* (Jürgen Basedow et al. eds., 2005). *See also* Carl Baudenbacher, *Die wettbewerbsrechtliche Beurteilung grenzüberschreitender Werbe-und Absatztätigkeit nach schweizerischem Recht*, 1988 GRUR Int. 310, 319.

[105] The WIPO Joint Recommendation's rules on notice and avoidance of conflicts reflect this idea, providing for isolation from liability if a defendant takes "reasonable measures which are effective to avoid a commercial effect" (art. 10 (iii)), particularly by using a disclaimer (art. 12). For the WIPO Recommendation, *see also supra* p. 225 *et seq.*

[106] For a similar factual constellation, *see, e.g.*, OGH 2012 GRUR Int. 464—*alcom-international at* (9 August 2011). For the substantive law policy in these cases, *see supra* p. 350 *et seq.*

[107] For this approach, *see supra* p. 256 *et seq.*, and *supra* in this chapter p. 510 *et seq.*

rule beyond the individual parties' concerns. In certain cases, the result of the interest balancing may actually differ from the individual parties' avoidability scheme. Back to our example: even if the defendant's online use of a symbol that is a famous trademark abroad should be limited to a "reasonable minimum" or to the "best possible degree," she may still not be ordered to cease using the disputed domain name. Hence, one might have to find the injury resulting from its ongoing use to be "unavoidable." Yet the overall perspective on all short-term and long-term interests in regulating market information may indicate that completely enjoining the defendant's use would be less costly in terms of the public interests involved in all jurisdictions. A probability-based infringement analysis and cost balancing may bring out different results than the individual equity balancing. Particularly if the plaintiff's market information capital is large, even an absolute minimum use of the symbol—the defendant's bad faith aside—may so significantly distort the market information infrastructure (e.g., through misguided online searches) that it will ultimately result in an overall negative cost-benefit account in both jurisdictions.

Nonetheless, the rule of avoidability has practical value. Often, the analysis of conflicting interests and the cost-benefit computation is difficult. A court will then shy away from making harsh all-or-nothing decisions and will tend to find the equitable "compromise." And this need not be unreasonable in terms of procedural efficiency. As long as it is unclear whether an alternative structuring of the transnational information infrastructure—by means of a court-crafted remedy for the dispute at bar—is less costly and more beneficial under an overall and long-term perspective, the court should follow a rule of avoidability. As a rule of practical approximation, it brings substantive-policy analysis and procedural efficiency to conformity.

IV Summary

Looking at trademark and unfair competition conflicts in light of the underlying policies indicates a uniform approach. Whenever a conflict involves conduct that has an effect on consumer decision making and transacting, the point of attachment must be found at the place (or places) where alternative transactions exist. As this convergence implies, there is no difference between the fields with respect to the quality of effects required for conflicts determination. In light of this qualitative assessment of effects, the necessary quantity or intensity of actual or potential effects will be determined by testing for objective foreseeability. What judges must undertake is a market analysis concerning the product and marketing communication at issue. Finally, conflicts resolution calls for a separate testing of international comity aspects in addition to the analysis of effects foreseeability. In essence, courts must undertake a fact-based analysis and craft their remedies accordingly. Both defendant intent and effects avoidability may serve as a practical proxy.

Section 2 The Reinterpretation of *Steele* and Rome II

This consolidated conflicts resolution structure calls for a new interpretation of existing trademark conflicts and unfair competition choice-of-law rules. Both US conflicts law and European choice of law can be reconceptualized through moderate modifications to the *Bulova* test and its variants, as well as by reinterpreting the Rome II Regulation.

I US Lanham Act Subject-Matter Jurisdiction

As discussed earlier, some have suggested extending the unilateral *Bulova* test in order to establish a multilateral rule of trademark conflicts law.[108] This would result in the application of foreign laws in US federal fora. Indeed, this option is not too exotic. For example, international copyright infringements are deemed to bring into existence a so-called transitory cause of action when foreign copyright laws are applied by US courts.[109] Also, international tort conflicts may require that foreign laws be applied.[110] And finally, the Judicial Improvements Act of 1990 allows district courts in civil actions, if they have original jurisdiction over the action, to exercise supplemental jurisdiction "over all other claims that are so related to claims in the action within such original jurisdiction that they form part of the same case or controversy."[111] At least in cases where the effects at issue trigger the application of the Lanham Act and, concurrently, of other countries' trademark and unfair competition laws, a multilateral conflicts resolution would not be anathema to procedural doctrine.[112] Indeed, the concurrent application of different trademark or unfair competition regimes may provide for a reasonable resolution of conflicts, particularly with regard to economic and regulatory concerns.

Nonetheless, it is questionable whether conceptions of such a groundbreaking reformulation of US conflicts doctrine have much prospect of success. A more realistic suggestion should focus on the most oft-

[108] For US scholarship and arguments, *see supra* p. 244 *et seq.*
[109] *See supra* p. 241 *et seq.* [110] *See, e.g., supra* p. 383 *et seq.* [111] 28 U.S.C. § 1367 (a).
[112] For limitations on federal courts' supplemental jurisdiction under 28 U.S.C. § 1367 (particularly (c)) in international copyright conflicts, *see, e.g., Torah Soft Ltd. v. Drosnin*, 136 F.Supp.2d 276, 292 (S.D.N.Y. 2001); with regard to international antitrust, *see* Hannah L. Buxbaum & Ralf Michaels, *Jurisdiction and Choice of Law in International Antitrust Law—A US Perspective*, 225, 235 *et seq.*, in *International Antitrust Litigation: Conflict of Laws and Coordination* (Jürgen Basedow et al. eds., 2012).

debated factor in both multilateral and unilateral conflicts resolution—the restriction of the domestic regime's scope of application. My focus will thus be on current doctrine. As I will demonstrate, shifting the focus of the *Bulova* effects prong toward a more functional analysis can be consistently adapted to and implemented in the analysis of Lanham Act subject-matter jurisdiction. This means that it will not be "some," "substantial," or "significant" effects that determine the finding of a relevant impact on US commerce but a modified test factor of foreseeable minimum effects—on consumer decision making. In addition, modification of the "nationality" and "conflicts with foreign law" factors will bring US doctrine into conformity with a comity-based requirement of jurisdictional self-restraint.

A Modification: A Qualitative Reformulation of "Effects on US Commerce"

The chapter on international comity explored the detrimental effects of trademark extraterritoriality on international competition.[113] In fact, this is the most crucial problem with Lanham Act subject-matter jurisdiction, albeit one that is widely ignored. It is due, among other things, to the indeterminate terminology and application of the *Bulova* effects prong in different circuits.[114]

The divergence can be illustrated, for instance, by a comparison between the Fifth Circuit's *American Rice* "some effects" factor and the Second Circuit's "substantial effects" requirement. Interestingly, neither the Supreme Court majority in *Steele* nor the dissenting justices gave an express definition of effects as "substantial," "significant," or otherwise.[115] This was different for the appellate decision at the lower level. The Fifth Circuit majority opinion in *Bulova Watch Co. v. Steele*[116] was the first to make use of the term "substantial economic effects."[117] Although the opinion has not received significant attention in case law or scholarship, it apparently had some genuinely "terminological" influence on the Second Circuit in *Vanity Fair*. There, Judge Waterman, making reference to the Fifth Circuit's decision, adopted a requirement of "substantial effects" without

[113] *See supra* p. 480 *et seq.* [114] *See supra* p. 159 *et seq.*

[115] Serge G. Avakian, *Global Unfair Competition in the Online Commerce Era*, 46 UCLA L. Rev. 905, 924 (1999); Thomas Berner, *Extraterritorial Application of the Lanham Act: Wells Fargo & Company v. Wells Fargo Express Company, 556 F.2d 406 (9th Cir. 1977)*, 18 Colum. J. Transnat'l L. 173, 181 (1979); Robert Butts, *Trademark Law: Interpreting the Congressional Intent of the Extraterritorial Application of the Lanham Trademark Act*, 8 Fla. J. Int'l L. 447, 452 (1993); Anna R. Popov, *Watering Down Steele v. Bulova Watch Co. to Reach E-Commerce Overseas: Analyzing the Lanham Act's Extraterritorial Reach Under International Law*, 77 S. Cal. L. Rev. 705, 711 (2004).

[116] *Bulova Watch Co. v. Steele*, 194 F.2d 567 (5th Cir. 1952). [117] *Id.* at 570.

further elaboration.[118] In the end, *Vanity Fair* was not based on a finding of effects. Nonetheless, it has proven to be remarkably successful. Even today, this requirement remains an element of the Second Circuit's test, and it has influenced the tests used by a majority of federal circuits.[119] Outside New York, the Nevada district court in *Wells Fargo* was the first court to pick up the *Vanity Fair* standard of "substantial effects."[120] The Ninth Circuit appellate court, however, corrected the district court's holding in 1977, stating that *Steele* contains no substantiality requirement.[121] Shortly after, the Fifth Circuit in *American Rice* adopted the Ninth Circuit's standard and held that "some effects" would be sufficient.[122] Over time, these different standards have spread throughout the circuits. The Eleventh Circuit, for example, still interprets *Steele* as requiring "substantial effects."[123] Other circuits either follow one specific circuit's approach or apply a combined test.[124] The Fourth Circuit, for instance, has established a "significant effects" standard derived from the three-pronged *Vanity Fair* test.[125]

As illustrated by the variety of tests, particularly the terminological noise and confusion in the debate on effects determination, there is no truly authoritative standard of qualification. Ultimately, therefore, as a

[118] *Vanity Fair Mills, Inc. v. T. Eaton Co.*, 234 F.2d 633, 642 (2nd Cir. 1956).

[119] *See, e.g., McBee v. Delica Co., Ltd.*, 417 F.3d 107, 121 (1st Cir. 2005).

[120] Even though the District Court for the Southern District of California—in the only reported pre-*Wells Fargo* decision—referred to *Vanity Fair* in 1956 (*see Ramirez & Feraud Chili Co. v. Las Palmas Food Co.*, 146 F.Supp. 594, 602 (S.D. Cal. 1956)), its requirement of "substantial effects" stems from a comparison of international trademark infringements with the interstate concept of separating state and federal powers, not from an adoption of the Second Circuit's approach.

[121] In addition, it qualified the effects necessary for Lanham Act extraterritoriality by referring to the distinction between intrastate and interstate commerce: "Next, although foreign activities must of course have some effect on United States foreign commerce before they can be reached, we disagree with the district court's requirement that that effect must be 'substantial.' Bulova contains no such requirement. And, as we noted in Timberlane, since the origins of the 'substantiality' test apparently lie in the effort to distinguish between intrastate commerce, which Congress may not regulate as such, and interstate commerce, which it can control, it may be unwise blindly to apply the factor in the area of foreign commerce over which Congress has exclusive authority. *See* Timberlane . . . ." *See Wells Fargo & Co. v. Wells Fargo Exp. Co.*, 556 F.2d 406, 428 (9th Cir. 1977).

[122] *American Rice, Inc. v. Arkansas Rice Growers Co-op. Ass'n*, 701 F.2d 408, 414 (5th Cir. 1983).

[123] *See, e.g., Air Turbine Technology, Inc. v. Atlas Copco AB*, 295 F.Supp.2d 1334, 1343 (S. D. Fla. 2003); *International Café, S.A.L. v. Hard Rock Café International (U.S.A.), Inc.*, 252 F.3d 1274, 1278 (11th Cir. 2001).

[124] For the Third Circuit *see, e.g., Lithuanian Commerce Corporation, Ltd. v. Sara Lee Hosiery*, 47 F.Supp.2d 523, 536 (D.N.J. 1999) (leaving open the decision to require "some" or "substantial" effects); *Scanvec Amiable Ltd. v. Chang*, 80 Fed.Appx. 171, 181 (3rd Cir. 2003) (leaving the decision open, instead speaking of "commercial nexus requirement of Steele"). For the Seventh Circuit, *see, e.g., Thomas & Betts Corp. v. Panduit Corp.*, 71 F.Supp.2d 838, 842 (N.D. Ill. 1999) (combining the Second, Fifth, and Ninth Circuits' tests and requiring at least "some effects").

[125] *Nintendo of America, Inc. v. Aeropower Co., Ltd.*, 34 F.3d 246, 250–251 (4th Cir. 1994).

practical consequence, almost any effect might be sufficient to trigger the application of the Lanham Act. This brings out the specter of overextension by effects indeterminacy. One case in the wake of *Steele* lucidly illustrates this problem. In the 1983 *American Rice* case, both parties were American agricultural cooperatives acting in the United States and abroad. Their dispute arose out of a trademark resembling the plaintiff's US registration, which the defendant used for selling rice in Saudi Arabia.[126] Even though the defendant's sales occurred solely in Saudi Arabia and "none of [the] products found their way back into the United States,"[127] the Fifth Circuit held that the plaintiff's US trademark had been infringed on. Sufficient effects were found on the basis that processing, packaging, transporting, and distributing US-produced rice constituted activities "within commerce."[128] It was not reported whether other competitors in the Saudi Arabian market made use of allegedly infringing symbols. Very likely, however, most of them could not be haled into a US court for want of personal jurisdiction, and the prospects of successfully litigating before Saudi Arabian courts were likely also dismal (at least if compared with litigation in US federal courts). Consequently, deciding on the dispute between domestic competitors, the *American Rice* court—even though formally extending protection for the owner of a domestic right—factually burdened a national competitor. Ultimately, the discriminatory application of US law resulted in an uneven burden to other domestic parties competing with the right owner abroad.[129]

What is most striking in *American Rice* is that virtually completely unqualified effects—fully detached from the actual marketplace—sufficed to trigger the application of the Lanham Act, a statute that is specifically designed to regulate market communication and information.[130] More generally, this tendency of rights extension can actually be seen in a large portion of the *Steele* progeny between 1952 and 2014. As my bird's-eye view in chapter 2 has brought up, both the idiosyncrasies of an unqualified effects test *and* the common law pedigree of transnational goodwill and trademark rights acquisition and protection have contributed to a wide extension of national rights into foreign-based marketplaces.[131] A first corrective is thus necessary: the void of qualitative guidance must be filled

[126] *American Rice, Inc. v. Arkansas Rice Growers Co-op. Ass'n*, 701 F.2d 408, 410 (5th Cir. 1983).

[127] *Id.*

[128] *Id.* at 414 ("[The] defendant's Saudi Arabian sales had more than an insignificant effect on United States commerce. Each of [the defendant's] activities, from the processing and packaging of the rice to the transportation and distribution of it, are activities within commerce.").

[129] For the theoretical background, *see supra* p. 480 *et seq.*

[130] *See supra* p. 325 *et seq.*

[131] *See supra* p. 171 *et seq.*

by looking at the core policy of trademark protection and unfair competition prevention.[132] In essence, this requires saying farewell to the debate on merely terminological nuances; it does not matter whether effects are "substantial" or "significant," or whether "some" effects will do. Instead, the basis of effects testing must be a policy-oriented analysis of the impact that defendant activities have on market information infrastructure. Only if the infrastructure is affected, will relevant "effects on US commerce" be found. On this basis, for the *American Rice* scenario, the correct outcome is then easy to find: selling rice under an allegedly infringing trademark in Saudi Arabia did not affect the market infrastructure—nor consumer decision making—in the United States. There were no relevant *domestic* effects for the regulatory policies at issue. Accordingly, there should have also been none for the triggering of the *Bulova* effects prong.

B Reinterpretation: Dusting Off "Nationality" and "Conflicts with Foreign Law"

The picture is no less complicated regarding the other two *Bulova* test factors: "nationality" and "conflicts with foreign law." A constant corrosion has been going on behind the scenes, in which both of these factors have been increasingly invalidated. In this regard as well, however, a few modifications help correct existing aberrations.

1 Nationality, Citizenship, and What Else—or Nothing at All?

Testing the nationality or citizenship of a defendant in an international trademark or unfair competition dispute seems a simple task. In fact, the nationality principle has always been acknowledged as a legitimate instrument of choice of law.[133] Practically, it is a convenient test factor. The preconditions set by *Steele*, *Vanity Fair*, and subsequent case law are straightforward. In the same vein, the First Circuit's *McBee* test recently established the defendant's nationality as the primary test factor by setting different standards for US and foreign infringers. For US citizens, the court explained, jurisdiction is a matter of domestic law "that raises no serious international concerns, even when the citizen is located abroad."[134] By contrast, for foreign defendants, a court's subject-matter jurisdiction would have to be based on the conduct's effects on US commerce and, therefore, on a different constitutional power.[135] Even though virtually all courts adhere to this seemingly easy and unbiased

[132] *See supra* p. 494 *et seq.*
[133] *See, e.g.*, Joseph Story, *Commentaries on the Conflict of Laws* § 21, at 22 (1834).
[134] *McBee v. Delica Co., Ltd.*, 417 F.3d 107, 118 (1st Cir. 2005). [135] *Id.* at 118–119.

test, the results can differ significantly. In fact, as a closer look reveals, the nationality factor has developed into an empty shell.

Steele already treated the nationality factor casually. The majority phrased it simply:

> The issue is whether a US District Court has jurisdiction to award relief to an American corporation against acts of trade-mark infringement and unfair competition consummated in a foreign country by a citizen and resident of the United States.[136]

In a footnote, the court stated, "Joined as parties defendant were S. Steele y Cia, S.A., a Mexican corporation to whose rights Steele had succeeded, and Steele's wife Sofia who possessed a community interest under Texas law."[137] In spite of this actually quite heterogeneous "citizenship" status, the court continued to refer to Sidney Steele as the sole petitioner. Accordingly, the majority based its constitutional analysis of jurisdiction on Steele's US citizenship.[138] Certainly, the existence of a Mexican corporation would not (and should not) have been enough to alter the outcome. But the majority's treatment of the issue may be understood as having set the stage for the lower courts' ultimately broad construction.

In fact, opinions after *Steele* have gone far beyond that of the Supreme Court. As demonstrated in my bird's-eye view on the *Steele* progeny between 1952 and 2014, the nationality prong has been a weak corrective for the effects factor's dominance. At best, a defendant's foreign nationality may present an obstacle to subject-matter jurisdiction when *both* nationality and conflicts with foreign law point toward nonapplication of the Lanham Act.[139] And the nationality prong also has an enforcing impact when it bends in the other direction. Among 58 opinions where the defendant's nationality (or allegiance) was found to point toward application of the Lanham Act, the courts applied US law 50 times (86.21%).[140]

In addition, another aspect becomes visible upon a closer look at the microstructure of nationality testing: among the opinions that substantially discussed the defendant's nationality, citizenship, or allegiance, the definition of "US nationality" has significantly varied and has ultimately been extended. First, after 1977, in the Ninth Circuit, the *Timberlane* comity test expressly allowed for a substitution of citizenship by a finding on "the nationality or allegiance of the parties and the locations or principal places of business of corporations," which may include a party's

[136] *Steele v. Bulova Watch Co.*, 344 U.S. 280, 281 (1952). [137] *Id.* at 281 n. 1.
[138] *Id.* at 285–286. [139] *See supra* p. 172 *et seq.*
[140] Under a Chi-square test of independence, there is a statistically significant relationship between nationality and application of the Lanham Act.

residence.[141] This gave courts wide discretion to neglect their defendants' foreign nationalities. In other circuits, nationality neglect may have evolved under a surface of formalities, but it was nonetheless drastic: quite often, where a judge had to find that the defendant was not a US national or entity, or that the group of defendants contained at least one foreign national or entity, many courts extended their definition of "US citizenship" to include foreign nationals with US residence and corporate responsibility for a US entity, or some other responsibility for the alleged infringements.[142] Typically, this was expressed by finding a foreign defendant to be the "controlling force"[143] behind a US company. In addition, many opinions relied on more unspecified findings of close corporate relationships between American and foreign defendants, the commission of allegedly infringing acts by corporate subsidiaries in the United States, or the nationality prong already being satisfied through at least one defendant's US citizenship.[144] Two opinions even based their finding of the defendant's American "citizenship" on a prior agreement between the parties that submitted certain issues to US law and jurisdiction.[145] Courts in the Second Circuit in particular have coined this extensive understanding of nationality as "constructive citizenship."[146] In terms of numbers, among all 140 opinions in the *Steele* progeny, a total of 28 (20%) regarded foreign defendant parties as US nationals for reasons of "constructive citizenship" or for a similar connex to the United States, notably based on their corporate function, their residence in the United States, or other significant contacts (e.g., choice-of-law or choice-of-court agreements). The

[141] *See, e.g., Wells Fargo & Co. v. Wells Fargo Exp. Co.*, 556 F.2d 406, 428 (9th Cir. 1977).

[142] *See, e.g., A.T. Cross Co. v. Sunil Trading Corp.*, 467 F.Supp. 47, 50 (S.D.N.Y. 1979); *GAP, Inc. v. Stone International Trading, Inc.*, 169 F.R.D. 584, 592 (S.D.N.Y. 1997); for the Ninth Circuit, *see, e.g., Reebok International, Ltd. v. Marnatech Enterprises, Inc.*, 970 F.2d 552, 556–557 (9th Cir. 1992).

[143] *See, e.g., Calvin Klein Industries, Inc. v. BFK Hong Kong, Ltd.*, 714 F.Supp. 78, 80 (S.D. N.Y. 1989).

[144] *See, e.g., Houbigant, Inc. v. Development Specialists, Inc.*, 229 F.Supp.2d 208, 227 (S.D. N.Y. 2002); *Mattel, Inc. v. MCA Records, Inc.*, 28 F.Supp.2d 1120, 1130 (C.D. Cal. 1998); *Levi Strauss & Co. v. Sunrise Intern. Trading, Inc.*, 51 F.3d 982, 985 (11th Cir. 1995); *Reebok Intern., Ltd. v. Marnatech Enterprises, Inc.*, 737 F.Supp. 1515, 1520 (S.D. Cal. 1989); *Van Doren Rubber Co., Inc. v. Marnatech Enterprises, Inc.*, No. 89–1362 S BTM, 1989 WL 223017, at *6 (S.D. Cal., 17 October 1989); *Software AG, Inc. v. Consist Software Solutions, Inc.*, No. 08 Civ. 389(CM)(FM), 2008 WL 563449, at *14 (S.D.N.Y., 21 February 2008); *TNT USA, Inc. v. TrafiExpress, S.A. de C.V.*, 434 F.Supp.2d 1322, 1328 (S.D. Fla. 2006).

[145] *See Amway v. Dyson*, No. 1:97-CV-295, 1997 U.S. Dist. LEXIS 15735, at *15 (W.D. Mich., 24 September 1997); *Warnaco Inc. v. VF Corp.*, 844 F.Supp. 940, 952 (S.D.N.Y. 1994).

[146] *See, e.g., Calvin Klein Industries, Inc. v. BFK Hong Kong, Ltd.*, 714 F.Supp. 78, 80 (S.D. N.Y. 1989); *A.V. by Versace, Inc. v. Gianni Versace, S.p.A.*, 126 F.Supp.2d 328, 337–338 (S.D.N.Y. 2001).

extraterritoriality rate among these opinions (i.e., the rate of Lanham Act application) was 26 out of 28 (92.86%, compared to 59.29% overall).[147] It seems that whenever necessary, the nationality prong has been handled with remarkable discretion—usually in favor of applying US law.

2 *Conflicts with Foreign Law: Another Shell of Formalities*

The nationality test is not the only one to have been twisted and turned. The conflicts test—that is, courts' determination of whether a "conflict which might afford [the defendant] a pretext that . . . relief would impugn foreign law"[148] exists—also paints a complicated picture.

I will refer once again to decisions issued between 1952 and 2014. Apart from considering whether the defendant actually owned a foreign trademark or had applied for registration in a foreign jurisdiction (32 opinions, or 22.86%),[149] some courts looked at the overall legality of a defendant's activities abroad, including by comparing the plaintiff's claims with the defendant's defense under foreign laws (15 opinions, or 10.71%).[150] In this regard, some courts even expressly found a conflict to exist if a foreign jurisdiction's interest in freedom of competition afforded the defendant immunity against the extension of US law.[151] These cases account for a relatively internationalist approach, acknowledging both foreign rights and policies to warrant consideration. This also applied to another group of decisions that defined conflicts more formally, based on the stage of actual or potential litigation. Courts there asked, inter alia, whether litigation outcomes in the United States and abroad might be inconsistent (8 opinions, or 5.71%).[152]

[147] Under a Chi-square test of independence, there is a statistically significant relationship between a finding of constructive citizenship and application of the Lanham Act.

[148] *Steele v. Bulova Watch Co.*, 344 U.S. 280, 288 (1952).

[149] *See id. See also, e.g., Aerogroup International, Inc. v. Marlboro Footworks, Ltd.*, 955 F. Supp. 220, 230 (S.D.N.Y. 1997); *Groeneveld Transport Efficiency, Inc. v. Lubecore Intern., Inc.*, 730 F.3d 494 (6th Cir. 2013); *Libbey Glass, Inc. v. Oneida Ltd.*, 61 F. Supp.2d 720 (N.D. Ohio 1999); *Rodgers v. Wright*, 544 F.Supp.2d 302 (S.D.N.Y. 2008); *Southco, Inc. v. Fivetech Technology Inc.*, 982 F.Supp.2d 507 (E.D. Pa. 2013); *Warnaco Inc. v. VF Corp.*, 844 F.Supp. 940, 952 (S.D.N.Y. 1994).

[150] *See, e.g., Calvin Klein Industries, Inc. v. BFK Hong Kong, Ltd.*, 714 F.Supp. 78 (S.D.N.Y. 1989); *GAP, Inc. v. Stone International Trading, Inc.*, 169 F.R.D. 584 (S.D.N.Y. 1997); *Les Ballets Trockadero de Monte Carlo, Inc. v. Trevino*, 945 F.Supp. 563, 567–568 (S.D. N.Y. 1996); *Scotch Whiskey Ass'n v. Barton Distilling Co.*, 489 F.2d 809 (7th Cir. 1973).

[151] *See, e.g., Vespa of America Corp. v. Bajaj Auto Ltd.*, 550 F.Supp. 224, 229 (N.D. Ca. 1982); *Procter & Gamble Co. v. Colgate-Palmolive Co.*, No. 96 Civ. 9123(RPP), 1998 WL 788802, at *67 (S.D.N.Y., 9 November 1998).

[152] *See, e.g., Best Western International, Inc. v. 1496815 Ontario, Inc.*, No. CV 04–1194-PHX-SMM, 2007 WL 779699, at *6 (D. Ariz., 13 March 2007); *C-Cure Chemical Co., Inc. v. Secure Adhesives Corp.*, 571 F.Supp. 808, 821 (W.D.N.Y. 1983); *International Café, S.A.L. v. Hard Rock Café International (U.S.A.)*, 252 F.3d 1274, 1279 (11th Cir. 2001); *Mattel, Inc. v. MCA Records, Inc.*, 28 F.Supp.2d 1120, 1130 (C.D. Cal. 1998); *Star-Kist Foods, Inc. v. P.J. Rhodes & Co.*, 769 F.2d 1393, 1396 (9th Cir. 1985).

A large group of opinions, however, established a less egalitarian perspective on foreign laws. Courts within this group refused to find a conflict to exist as long as no foreign court had *actually* ruled that the defendant had a legal right to use a trademark (6 opinions, or 4.29%). This approach governs especially in the Fifth and Ninth Circuits.[153] In the same vein, some courts found the burden to be on the defendant "to show that [she] has a superior right in a foreign country to prevent the imposition of an injunction."[154] Evidently, therefore, both substantive law doctrine and procedural law can prevent a court from placing too much emphasis on the existence of conflicts with foreign law.[155] Like the nationality test, the conflicts test thus—even though formally tailored to give regard to international consensus and convenience of transacting—tends to neglect comity.

3 *A New Paradigm*

Against this backdrop, it is clear that modernization of the *Bulova* test factors for "nationality" and "conflicts with foreign law" requires a dual reorientation. The test for a defendant's nationality is not only obsolete but economically misconceived; parties' nationalities should be disregarded. And the test for conflicts with foreign law—though not as problematic as the nationality test—requires at least some restructuring.

a *The Neutralization of Nationality and Citizenship* As seen earlier, the nationality factor's application has resulted in circumvention and invalidation, suggesting that the test factor is outdated. In addition to

[153] *See, e.g., American Rice, Inc. v. Arkansas Rice Growers Co-op. Ass'n*, 701 F.2d 408, 415–416 (5th Cir. 1983); *Global Healing Center LP v. Nutritional Brands Inc.*, No. 4:14-CV-269, 2014 WL 897817, at *11 (S.D. Tex., 6 March 2014); *Louis Vuitton Malletier, S.A. v. Akanoc Solutions, Inc.*, No. C 07–03952 JW, 2010 WL 5598337, at *8 (N.D. Ca., 19 March 2010); *Rhino Membranes and Coatings, Inc. v. Rhino Seamless Membrane System, Inc.*, No. H-06–2112, 2006 WL 1984606, at *4 (S.D. Tex., 14 July 2006); *Seed Services, Inc. v. Winsor Grain, Inc.*, 868 F.Supp.2d 998, 1006 (E.D. Ca. 2012).

[154] *See, e.g., Leatherman Tool Group, Inc. v. Cooper Industries, Inc.*, 47 U.S.P.Q.2d 1045, 1047 (D. Or. 1997); *Star-Kist Foods, Inc. v. P.J. Rhodes & Co.*, 769 F.2d 1393, 1394–1395 (9th Cir. 1985); *see also, e.g.*, Robert Alpert, *The Export of Trademarked Goods from the United States: The Extraterritorial Reach of the Lanham Act*, 81 Trademark Rep. 125, 139 (1991).

[155] Finally, the argument that prior party agreements form the basis for a finding of "nationality" or equivalent ties to the United States has also been used to overcome potential conflicts with foreign laws. *See, e.g., Amway v. Dyson*, No. 1:97-CV-295, 1997 U.S. Dist. LEXIS 15735, at *15–16 (W.D. Mich., 24 September 1997) ("The third factor set out in Vanity Fair is whether there is a conflict with trade-mark rights established under the law of Great Britain. In Vanity Fair, the court explained that 'the Lanham Act … should not be given extraterritorial application against foreign citizens acting under presumably valid trade-marks in a foreign country.' … In the present case the settlement agreement … stated that the Agreement, and consequently any disputes that might arise under it, would be interpreted under the laws of Michigan. Consequently, there is no issue as to whether there are differences between the Lanham Act and the laws of Great Britain.").

practical failure, aspects of conflicts theory and economic reason counsel jettisoning nationality as one of the pillars of Lanham Act subject-matter jurisdiction.

Let us start with a deontological argument: I have already alluded to Lea Brilmayer's political rights theory requiring that conflicts determination and application of a certain national law must have a rights-based justification. As Brilmayer explains, in conflicts scenarios, a party's nationality or citizenship is one of the relevant aspects that may justify a state's coercion exerted through choice of this state's law and its application.[156] But this is only one factor. In addition, she also specifies more flexible connections that can justify choice and application of a state's law. One example is individual consent, notably in the form of a party's residence or traveling in a state's territory; another example is the benefit that a party receives upon initiating purposeful contact with a state.[157] The rise of transnational communication and transacting requires acknowledging a shift in the relative importance of the different connecting factors. In the old days, of course, nationality and citizenship constituted a rather precise presumption for a connex between the sedentary actors' activities, these activities' consequences, and the local regulator. Since individual mobility was low, and the effects of most activities were local, nationality was a valid basis for the application of a state's law in most cases. But modernity no longer allows for such an automatic conclusion. First of all, in today's world, the connection between conduct and the local law's regulatory purpose is no longer guaranteed. Before the rise of international transactions and communication, conduct and effects were often conflated within a single place. Effects occurred in the vicinity of conduct and thus served as a handy proxy for effects.[158] Today, however, this connection is no longer guaranteed. This does not necessarily mean, as is sometimes contended, that the traditional "link between law and land" has been broken.[159] There is actually no change in the subject matter of what is regulated: effects have been and will be the ultimate determinant. Accordingly, particularly in the area of economic regulation, it has become more and more acknowledged that "territorial" jurisdiction may be based either on local conduct or on the local occurrence of effects.[160] In the same vein, the national affiliation of individuals

[156] Lea Brilmayer, *Rights, Fairness, and Choice of Law*, 98 Yale L.J. 1277, 1297 *et seq.* (1989).

[157] *Id.* at 1303 *et seq.*

[158] For the proxy function of conduct, *see* Andrew T. Guzman, *Choice of Law: New Foundations*, 90 Geo. L.J. 883, 922 *et seq.* (2002); Joel P. Trachtman, *Economic Analysis of Prescriptive Jurisdiction*, 42 Va. J. Int'l L. 1, 34–35 (2002).

[159] Kal Raustiala, *The Geography of Justice*, 73 Fordham L. Rev. 2501, 2548 (2005).

[160] *See, e.g.*, Restatement (Third) of Foreign Relations Law § 402 (1987), comment d ("Jurisdiction with respect to activity outside the state, but having or intended to have

and corporate entities has increasingly lost its relevance for where they act or where effects of their activities will ultimately occur. In a world of highly mobile individuals and corporate actors, where everybody can virtually cause effects everywhere, national affiliation and citizenship no longer provide for a significant connex.

Finally, a closely related economic aspect must be considered. As we saw in chapter 5, giving regard to the parties' nationality in trademark and unfair competition conflicts law may result in an anticompetitive burden for domestic competitors in foreign markets.[161] By the 1930s, Arthur Nussbaum's explanation of the *lex domicilii communis* in unfair competition choice of law had been criticized for this structural deficit.[162] The same problem exists with the nationality prong in *Steele*: domestic competitors in foreign markets are the primary actors subjected to US courts' personal jurisdiction; in addition, with respect to subject-matter jurisdiction, a nationality-based *Bulova* test further extends the risk of constraining competition. After all, as my bird's-eye view has shown, it will multiply chances that stricter rules of US trademark protection apply if the defendant is a US national or corporate entity—but not if a foreign actor is on the defendant's bench.

b The Deformalization and Depropertization of "Conflicts with Foreign Law" With respect to the third test factor, the Second Circuit's decision in *Sterling Drug* is again remarkable. While the court's analysis of effects and its flexible tailoring of remedies were certainly innovative, its testing of "conflicts with foreign law" was anything but. Chief Judge Newman's analysis of the foreign-compulsion doctrine in *Hartford Fire* is revealing:

> In the context of [Hartford Fire], the Court found no "conflict" warranting a declination of jurisdiction because there was no claim that conformity with the requirements of United States law required the defendants to do any act in violation of British law. . . . [W]e think [this approach to the comity issue] is not automatically transferable to the trademark context, especially where the contending parties both hold rights in the same mark under the respective laws of their countries. It is one thing for the British reinsurers in Hartford Fire to be barred under United States law from boycotting activity that they might be free to engage in without violating British law. But it is quite a different thing for the holder of rights in a mark under German law to be ordered by a United States court to refrain from uses of that mark protected by German law.[163]

substantial effect within the state's territory, is an aspect of jurisdiction based on territoriality, although it is sometimes viewed as a distinct category.").

[161] *See supra* p. 480 *et seq.* [162] *See supra* p. 64 *et seq.*

[163] *Sterling Drug, Inc. v. Bayer AG*, 14 F.3d 733, 746–747 (2nd Cir. 1994).

Both parties, Sterling Drug and Bayer, owned trademarks in their respective home jurisdictions. Consequently, the court expected to be on solid ground when it distinguished *Hartford Fire* on the basis that the defendant could refer to a valid right in Germany. Yet, by this means, the existing policy conflict and its resolution were hidden behind a veil of formal rights. This is due to, inter alia, the fact that the reasoning in *Sterling Drug*, like US doctrine in general, was founded on a remainder of the act-of-state doctrine:[164] the validity of foreign trademark rights is generally not questioned since these rights are conceived of as foreign political acts. This deceptively clear-cut situation changes, however, if the conflict involves not two private "rights" but one formal entitlement and a nonformal nation-state policy, or two divergent nonformal nation-state policies. While one jurisdiction may favor the trademark owner's interest in protecting her right, the other jurisdiction may foster freedom of competition by granting a more liberal domain of market communication. From a court's perspective, it is already virtually impossible to determine which of the conflicting policies involved—the domestic one or the foreign one—should prevail.[165] How much more should it then be feasible to determine the "weight" of domestic and foreign policies on the basis of their formal implementation? In other words and more concretely, are common law use-based rights "weaker" or "less valid" than civil law registered trademarks?

To further illustrate this point, let us modify the *Sterling Drug* facts: if the parties' dispute had not been on the use of both parties' trademark "Bayer" but on an allegedly improper claim of advertising, the outcome would not have been different—even though in this variation of the facts, there was no conflict of "rights." Let us assume that Sterling Drug (this time as the defendant) had expressly advertised its products as "imitations" of the European Bayer company's drugs and that there had been significant spillover of the advertising to Europe. Then, a similar issue of potential "conflict with foreign law" would have existed. This is due to the fact that in cases of "imitation" or "replication" claims, European doctrine, under the Misleading and Comparative Advertising Directive,[166] not only finds both trademark and unfair competition law affected but also disallows comparative advertising stating (whether explicitly or implicitly) that the product at issue is an imitation or replica of a product

[164] *See supra* p. 241 *et seq.*
[165] For this problem, *see* the debate in interest-analysis conflicts scholarship *supra* p. 417 *et seq.*
[166] *See* article 4 lit. g. Directive 2006/114/EC of the European Parliament and of the Council of 12 December 2006 concerning misleading and comparative advertising, O.J. EU (27 December 2006), L 376/21.

bearing a well-known trademark.[167] US doctrine, by contrast, is grounded on the conviction that if a seller has a legal right to copy a product, she must also have the right to inform the public accordingly.[168] Imitation and replication claims are thus not improper per se. In an international conflict like in the modified *Sterling Drug* scenario, the issue—if phrased individually—would be to resolve a dispute between one party's "right" (i.e., trademark) and the other party's economic freedom (i.e., liberty to correctly describe her product). In essence, however, as under the unmodified facts, the dispute requires a reconciliation of divergent levels of economic freedom. The existence or nonexistence of formal entitlements does not make a difference. It therefore cannot determine the conflicts issue.

II European Trademark and Unfair Competition Choice of Law

As with US doctrine, European trademark and unfair competition choice of law can be reformulated without much turbulence by several modest but effective modifications of the existing rules. This requires acknowledging that the common core of trademark and unfair competition policies implies a unified approach at the conflicts level. In addition, a qualitative effects test helps reconceptualize the regulatory function of choice of law in the field. Finally, effects testing must be accompanied by a comity-based rule of self-restraint.

A Clarification: Characterization of Trademark and Unfair Competition Conflicts

While terminology varies, characterization is widely understood as the classification, qualification, or interpretation of laws that may apply to an international dispute. The judge, therefore, before addressing the actual *choice* of law must first determine the nature and character of the dispute before her. She will thereby have to find out which conflicts norm(s) to use to identify the applicable substantive law.[169] The public international law system of trademark protection and unfair competition prevention does not provide a detailed guideline for characterization. There are no common normative standards that universally define

[167] *See, e.g., L'Oréal and Others*, C 487/07, para. 80 (18 June 2009), [2009] E.C.R. I-5185.

[168] *See, e.g., Saxlehner v. Wagner*, 216 U.S. 375, 379 *et seq.* (1910) (Holmes, J.); *Smith v. Chanel, Inc.*, 402 F.2d 562 (9th Cir. 1968).

[169] *See, e.g.*, Jan Kropholler, *Internationales Privatrecht—einschließlich der Grundbegriffe des Internationalen Zivilverfahrensrechts* § 15 I 1 (6th edn., 2006). For the terminological confusion in the field, *see* Friedrich K. Juenger, *Choice of Law and Multistate Justice* 4–5 (1993).

"unfairness" or "dishonesty" in competition.[170] Nor are there express rules on the differentiation between trademark protection and unfair competition prevention. The question whether a litigated claim is to be qualified as a cause of "trademark infringement," "unfair competition," or "torts" is therefore still an issue of forum law.[171]

Accordingly, the unified European choice of law under the Rome II Regulation is based on the idea of autonomous characterization.[172] This requires the application of a single supranational standard, notably in light of recital 21 of the Rome II Regulation, which provides for a triple purpose of protection:

> In matters of unfair competition, the conflict-of-law rule should protect competitors, consumers and the general public and ensure that the market economy functions properly. The connection to the law of the country where competitive relations or the collective interests of consumers are, or are likely to be, affected generally satisfies these objectives.

In light of member states' diverging substantive laws, however, such a uniform approach used to be difficult to conceive.[173] For a long time, the supranational stage of substantive law harmonization was not much more advanced than the international level; at least with respect to a larger sector of unfair competition prevention, though, this seems to have changed more recently in the course of an increasing harmonization through European secondary legislation. As Peter Mankowski explains, a modest convergence concerning the definition of what constitutes

[170] James J. Fawcett & Paul Torremans, *Intellectual Property and Private International Law* para. 16.05–16.08 (2nd edn., 2011); Jochen Glöckner, in *Gesetz gegen den unlauteren Wettbewerb (UWG)*, UWG Einl C para. 86 *et seq.* (Henning Harte-Bavendamm & Frauke Henning-Bodewig eds., 3rd edn., 2013); *but see* Richard Plender & Michael Wilderspin, *The European Private International Law of Obligations* para. 20–007 to 20–033 (4th edn., 2015); Dicey, Morris & Collins, *The Conflict of Laws, vol. II* para. 35–054 (Lord Collins of Mapesbury gen. ed., 15th edn., 2012) (with respect to Art. 10*bis* Paris Convention).

[171] *See, e.g.*, Jan Kropholler, *Internationales Privatrecht—einschließlich der Grundbegriffe des Internationalen Zivilverfahrensrechts* § 16 I, II 2 (6th edn., 2006); Karl-Heinz Fezer & Stefan Koos, in *Staudingers Kommentar zum Bürgerlichen Gesetzbuch: Internationales Wirtschaftsrecht*, Internationales Wettbewerbsprivatrecht para. 390 (15th edn., 2010); Josef Drexl, in *Münchener Kommentar zum Bürgerlichen Gesetzbuch, vol. XI*, IntLautR para. 109 (Franz Jürgen Säcker et al. eds., 6th edn., 2015).

[172] *See* recital 11 Regulation (EC) No. 864/2007 of the European Parliament and of the Council of 11 July 2007 on the law applicable to non-contractual obligations (Rome II), O.J. EU (31 July 2007), L 199/40; *further, e.g.*, Christopher Wadlow, *The new private international law of unfair competition and the "Rome II" Regulation*, 11 J. Intell. Prop. L. & Pract. 789, 790 (2009); Dicey, Morris & Collins, *The Conflict of Laws, vol. II* para. 35–054 (Lord Collins of Mapesbury gen. ed., 15th edn., London 2012); Martin Illmer, in *Rome II Regulation*, Art. 6 para. 4 (Peter Huber ed., 2011).

[173] Richard Plender & Michael Wilderspin, *The European Private International Law of Obligations* para. 20–011 *et seq.* (4th edn., 2015).

unfair competitive conduct can be found in European substantive law, particularly in the Unfair Commercial Practices Directive's[174] definition of "commercial practices" in article 2(d), which provides that

> "business-to-consumer commercial practices" … means any act, omission, course of conduct or representation, commercial communication including advertising and marketing, by a trader, directly connected with the promotion, sale or supply of a product to consumers.[175]

As Mankowski concludes, within this core area of substantive law convergence, a common and uniform characterization of "unfair competition" is both possible and required.[176] One could also refer to the Directive on Misleading and Comparative Advertising as an additional part of the relevant European *acquis*.[177] Yet despite the incipiencies of substantive law consolidation, these directives provide for a rudiment at best. Both instruments have a limited scope.[178] Notably, the Unfair Commercial Practices Directive provides for "unfair business-to-consumer commercial practices" but "neither covers nor affects the national laws on unfair commercial practices which harm only competitors' economic interests or which relate to a transaction between traders."[179] Not surprisingly, therefore, scholarly suggestions try to amend the arsenal of references and sources by including not only article 10*bis* of the 1883 Paris Convention and the TRIPS Agreement but also, for instance, soft-law standards like the 1983 Conflict-of-Laws Rules on Unfair Competition by the Institut de Droit International[180] and the WIPO Model Provisions

[174] Directive 2005/29/EC of the European Parliament and of the Council of 11 May 2005 concerning unfair business-to-consumer commercial practices in the internal market and amending Council Directive 84/450/EEC, Directives 97/7/EC, 98/27/EC and 2002/65/EC of the European Parliament and of the Council and Regulation (EC) No 2006/2004 of the European Parliament and of the Council ("Unfair Commercial Practices Directive"), O.J. EU (11 June 2005), L 149/22.

[175] *See also* Peter Mankowski, *Was soll der Anknüpfungsgegenstand des (europäischen) Internationalen Wettbewerbsrechts sein?*, 2005 GRUR Int. 634, 635 et seq.

[176] *Id.* at 636; *see also* Susanne Augenhofer, in *Rome Regulations*, Art. 6 para. 13–14 (Gralf-Peter Calliess ed., 2nd edn., 2015); Nadine Klass, in *Großkommentar—UWG: Gesetz gegen den unlauteren Wettbewerb, vol. I*, Einl. para. 20 *et seq.* (Otto Teplitzky et al. eds., 2nd edn., 2014).

[177] Directive 2006/114/EC of the European Parliament and of the Council of 12 December 2006 concerning misleading and comparative advertising, O.J. EU (27 December 2006), L 376/21. *See, e.g.*, Martin Illmer, in *Rome II Regulation*, Art. 6 para. 5 (Peter Huber ed., 2011).

[178] *See, e.g.*, Josef Drexl, in *Münchener Kommentar zum Bürgerlichen Gesetzbuch, vol. XI*, IntLautR para. 111 (Franz Jürgen Säcker et al. eds., 6th edn., 2015).

[179] *See* art. 3(1), art. 5(1), and recital 6. *See also, e.g.*, Martin Illmer, in *Rome II Regulation*, Art. 6 para. 21 (Peter Huber ed., 2011); Richard Plender & Michael Wilderspin, *The European Private International Law of Obligations* para. 20–027 (4th edn., 2015).

[180] *See supra* p. 501.

on Protection against Unfair Competition.[181] In addition, agreement exists that the European member states' national law concepts must be given regard to in the promulgation of an autonomous concept of "unfair competition."[182]

Contrast this with US conflicts law. If a scenario does not concern federal law issues, notably in cases where common law or state statutory unfair competition claims are litigated (e.g., trade secret misappropriation), courts treat unfair competition claims as genuine torts. They then apply the forum state's choice-of-law rules, regularly referring to an interstate consensus expressed in common law rules on when and how to characterize a tortious act as unfair competition.[183] The technique is different with respect to federal law trademark and unfair competition claims. Under the Lanham Act, international trademark infringements and violations of federal unfair competition law are a question of the federal courts' subject-matter jurisdiction. The scope of Lanham Act subject-matter jurisdiction is determined under *Steele* and the circuits' different test variants.[184] Moreover, absent concurrent causes of action under US law, courts tend to dismiss claims based on foreign law under the doctrine of *forum non conveniens.*[185] Hence, if the case at bar does not contain a sufficient connection to the United States, it will be dismissed. Foreign law is not applied. Factually, this is a unilateral conflicts rule. Even though characterization appears redundant, this analysis implicitly still determines whether the case at bar falls within the domain of "trademarks" or "unfair competition." Hence, it contains at least a rudiment of characterization on the basis of the Lanham Act's substantive law

[181] *See* art. 1 *et seq.* in WIPO, *Model Provisions on Protection against Unfair Competition—Articles and Notes, presented by the International Bureau of WIPO, Geneva 1996*, WIPO Publication No. 832(E). Critically, however, Peter Mankowski, in *Münchener Kommentar zum Lauterkeitsrecht, vol. I*, IntWettbR para. 14a (Peter W. Heermann et al. eds., 2nd edn., 2014).

[182] For the collection of different sources and references, *see, e.g.*, Michael Hellner, *Unfair Competition and Acts Restricting Free Competition—A Commentary on Article 6 of the Rome II Regulation*, 9 Yearb. P.I.L. 49, 67 *et seq.* (2007); Martin Illmer, in *Rome II Regulation*, Art. 6 para. 8 *et seq.* (Peter Huber ed., 2011); Richard Plender & Michael Wilderspin, *The European Private International Law of Obligations* para. 20–007 *et seq.* (4th edn., 2015); Peter Mankowski, in *Münchener Kommentar zum Lauterkeitsrecht, vol. I*, IntWettbR para. 11 (Peter W. Heermann et al. eds., 2nd edn., 2014). Critically with respect to the reference to national legislation, however, *see* Andrew Dickinson, *The Rome II Regulation: The Law Applicable to Non-Contractual Obligations* para. 6.17 (2008).

[183] *See, e.g., BP Chemicals Ltd. v. Formosa Chemical & Fibre Corp.*, 229 F.3d 254, 264 *et seq.* (3rd Cir. 2000). *See also* § 145 Restatement (Second) of Conflict of Laws, comment f.

[184] *See supra* p. 159 *et seq.*

[185] *See, e.g., Wells Fargo & Co. v. Wells Fargo Exp. Co.*, 556 F.2d 406, 431 (9th Cir. 1977); *American White Cross Laboratories, Inc. v. H.M. Cote, Inc.*, 556 F.Supp. 753, 758 (S.D. N.Y. 1983).

policies. Essentially, however, the analysis of jurisdiction includes and replaces an actual choice-of-law decision.[186]

But characterization need not be an issue of public international law conventions, supranational legal instruments, and national or state law alone. These approaches may be useful for producing adequate results in inter-US or intra-European conflicts. But they cannot provide for uniformity beyond the respective federal or supranational entity. What is required instead is a transnational standard. This must be founded on a broader consensus, which brings us back to the analysis of a functional core of policies in trademark and unfair competition law.[187] While a genuinely comparative characterization, as suggested by Ernst Rabel,[188] may still lack a solid foundation with regard to practical feasibility, characterization based on universal structures of substantive law policy provides for a different situation. As my analysis has revealed, the core function of both trademark and unfair competition law is the protection of consumer decision making—this is the "whole Law and the Prophets on the subject."[189] Protection of market information infrastructure and unmanipulated consumer decision making are the pillars of a transnational architecture of competition fairness. This foundation guarantees universality on the basis of economic theory. And since such a functionally structured approach provides a uniform basis for characterization in the core areas of both trademark and unfair competition law, a rule of *lex specialis* differentiation between the two sectors is not required.[190]

Beyond this functional core of policies, of course, there is still no harmonized concept. We have seen that the area extends much wider, particularly with respect to the prevention of unfairly competitive torts at the horizontal level. Another area beyond the core sector is international antitrust conflicts.[191] In these cases, whether a specific instance of competitive conduct falls into the formal category of "unfair competition" is not an issue of its immediate impact on consumer decision making. For

[186] For the conflation of conflicts and jurisdiction testing in US doctrine, *see supra* p. 521.

[187] *See supra* p. 325 *et seq.*

[188] *See* Ernst Rabel, *Das Problem der Qualifikation*, 5 RabelsZ 241, 257 (1931).

[189] For Judge Learned Hand's dictum—that actually explained customer diversion by misrepresentation as root of all evil to be prevented by unfair competition and trademark law—*see Yale Elec. Corp. v. Robertson*, 26 F.2d 972, 973 (2nd Cir. 1928).

[190] For the debate in European choice of law on the relationship between art. 6 and art. 8 Rome II and the suggestion that the latter conflicts rule should take precedence as *lex specialis, see, e.g.*, Susanne Augenhofer, in *Rome Regulations*, Art. 6 para. 32 *et seq.* (Gralf-Peter Calliess ed., 2nd edn., 2015).

[191] *See supra* p. 315–317.

want of a uniform functional basis, characterization will then remain an issue of the forum's (supra)national law.[192]

B Foundation: Marketplace Effects Rule and the *Lex Loci Protectionis*

Putting consumer decision making at the center of conflicts analysis does not require a reformulation of statutory choice-of-law rules. For Rome II, the specification of the place "where competitive relations or the collective interests of consumers are, or are likely to be, affected" in article 6(1) can be reinterpreted. The regulation's recitals explain that the collision-of-interests approach or the marketplace rule is "not an exception to the general rule in Article 4(1) but rather a clarification of it."[193] Formally, therefore, the country where competitive relations or the collective interests of consumers are affected is the place "in which the damage occurs irrespective of the [place] in which the event giving rise to the damage occurred and irrespective of the [places] in which the indirect consequences of that event occur" (art. 4(1)).[194] While this clarification has overcome conduct- and damage-centrism, it needs further specification regarding the element of "competition" or "marketplace" that must be affected in order to establish "damage." In this regard, as we have seen, reference to concepts of economic theory, notably the "marketplace" or the place of "competition," as well as the proxy of collective consumer interests, can be problematic.[195] Problems can be avoided, though, by looking at the model of the market mechanism in more detail. Such a perspective clarifies the issue of what kind of marketplace effects should be seen as relevant damage. It is not, as we have seen, effects on a competitor's position or her market share; rather, it is effects on consumer decision making and transacting that determine the place where the damage occurs and where competitive relations or consumer interests are affected.

[192] For more details, *see*, *e.g.*, Bert Keirsbilck, *The New European Law of Unfair Commercial Practices and Competition Law* 217 (2011); Susanne Augenhofer, in *Rome Regulations*, Art. 6 para. 8 *et seq.* (Gralf-Peter Calliess ed., 2nd edn., 2015).

[193] Recital 21.

[194] *See also* Michael Hellner, *Unfair Competition and Acts Restricting Free Competition—A Commentary on Article 6 of the Rome II Regulation*, 9 Yearb. P.I.L. 49, 54 (2007). The commission's reference to *Marinari v. Lloyd's Bank* (C-364/93 (19 September 1995), [1995] E.C.R. I-2719) illustrates how the place-of-injury rule has been limited to direct and immediate effects. *See* Commission of the European Communities, *Proposal for a Regulation of the European Parliament and the Council on the Law Applicable to Non-Contractual Obligations ("Rome II")*, Brussels, 22 July 2003, COM(2003) 427 final, 2003/0168 (COD), 11.

[195] *See supra* p. 214 *et seq.*

While this makes clear that no structural reinterpretation of the marketplace rule in article 6 of Rome II is required, reconstruction—at least upon first sight—appears more complicated for the *lex loci protectionis* rule in article 8 of Rome II. The law applicable to a trademark infringement is "the law of the country for which protection is claimed." Prima facie, no effects rule is implemented. The *lex loci protectionis*, however, is a multilateral and a quasi statutist rule of conflicts determination.[196] This means that each regime determines its own scope of application. The substantive law provides for the relevant aspects required to find an infringement of domestic rights. On this basis, no national law is obliged to implement a strictly conduct-based concept of territoriality. On the contrary, applying domestic law to effects within the state's territory—particularly to effects on consumer decision making—will not extend national trademark rights illegitimately.[197] In sum, therefore, under the Rome II Regulation, both for trademark and unfair competition conflicts, a qualified effects approach can be implemented by reinterpretation of the *lex lata*.

C Application: Marketplace Effects and the *Gran Canaria* Conundrum

Before we develop a concluding typology of trademark and unfair competition conflicts,[198] let us test this concept on one of the most contested scenarios in European doctrine: the German Bundesgerichtshof's 1990 *Kauf im Ausland* decision, also known as the *Gran Canaria* case. This case is a result of what can be characterized as a merger of once separate national markets into a single multijurisdictional marketplace. I have already explained how globalization has perforated national borders. And we have seen that in order for regulation to keep up with this development, adherence to a paradigm of conduct-based choice-of-law theory must be overcome. The place of conduct or impact no longer provides for a sound attachment.[199] This perspective also requires a change of directions in cases of the *Gran Canaria* kind.

1 *Recapitulation: The* Gran Canaria *Scenario*

For many marketing activities, the place of conduct and the place of transacting still coincide. Transactions occur at the point of (or in close proximity to) the competitor's preceding marketing conduct. The place of conduct, then, is also the place of interest collision or marketplace

[196] *See supra* p. 193 *et seq.* and p. 493 *et seq.* [197] *See also supra* p. 480 *et seq.*
[198] *See infra* p. 548 *et seq.* [199] *See supra* p. 193 *et seq.* and p. 203 *et seq.*

effects. This is where the consumer has an interest in true and honest information, where competitors' interest in fair competition arises, and where the public is interested in the free and unhindered functioning of competition and the market mechanism.[200] Conduct in, impact on, and effects within the marketplace coincide.[201] This is not the case, however, if the place of competitor conduct and the place of consumer transacting are different—for example, when advertising takes place in one state's territory for a product that is available only in another's,[202] or when advertising takes place abroad but targets domestic consumers in order to lead to an inland transaction. These cases, though most common in an online environment, can also occur in the offline world. The Bundesgerichtshof's decision in the *Kauf im Ausland* case addressed such a scenario.[203]

The facts are well known:[204] German tourists in Gran Canaria, Spain, were solicited through German advertising materials. The contract was in German, and delivery of the products (merino wool duvets and pillows) was to occur in Germany upon the tourists' return. According to its terms, Spanish law was to apply to the contract. Even though the core issue may have appeared to be whether the choice of Spanish contract law was valid, the case was initiated on claims that the contract, in fact, violated German

[200] *See, e.g.*, BGH 1972 GRUR 367, 368—*Besichtigungsreisen* (3 December 1971); BGH 1998 GRUR 419, 420—*Gewinnspiel im Ausland* (26 November 1997); BGH 1991 GRUR 463, 465—Kauf im Ausland (15 November 1990); Erwin Deutsch, *Wettbewerbstatbestände mit Auslandsbeziehung* 59 *et seq.* (1962); Rolf Sack, *Die kollisions- und wettbewerbsrechtliche Beurteilung grenzüberschreitender Werbe- und Absatztätigkeit nach deutschem Recht*, 1988 GRUR Int. 320, 322 *et seq.*; Peter Bernhard, *Insel-Recht auf Gran Canaria—Zum internationalen Privatrecht des unlauteren Wettbewerbs*, 1992 GRUR Int. 366, 370; Gerhard Schricker, in *Großkommentar—UWG: Gesetz gegen den unlauteren Wettbewerb, vol. I*, Einl para. F 204 (Rainer Jacobs et al. eds., 1994); Ignace Van Meenen, *Lauterkeitsrecht und Verbraucherschutz im IPR—Eine Untersuchung des vertrags- und delikts-kollisionsrechtlichen Schutzes gegen verbraucherfeindliche Rechtswahlvereinbarungen* 148 *et seq.* (1995); Andreas Höder, *Die kollisionsrechtliche Behandlung unteilbarer Multistate-Verstöße—Das Internationale Wettbewerbsrecht im Spannungsfeld von Marktort-, Auswirkungs- und Herkunftslandprinzip passim* (2002).

[201] Under dominant collision-of-interests theory, the indirect effects of improper market conduct will not qualify for conflicts relevance. Mere preparatory activity will not affect the analysis, either. Similarly, consumer nationality or residence and actual damages to the affected competitor will be deemed irrelevant. *See, e.g.*, BGHZ vol. 40, 391, 395 *et seq.*—*Stahlexport* (20 December 1963); BGH 1991 GRUR 463, 465—*Kauf im Ausland* (15 November 1990); Rolf Sack, *Die kollisions- und wettbewerbsrechtliche Beurteilung grenzüberschreitender Werbe- und Absatztätigkeit nach deutschem Recht*, 1988 GRUR Int. 320, 323; Rolf Sack, *Das internationale Wettbewerbs- und Immaterialgüterrecht nach der EGBGB-Novelle*, 2000 WRP 269, 273 *et seq.*; Josef Drexl, in *Münchener Kommentar zum Bürgerlichen Gesetzbuch, vol. XI*, IntLautR para. 116–117 (Franz Jürgen Säcker et al. eds., 6th edn., 2015).

[202] *See, e.g.*, BGH 1972 GRUR 367—*Besichtigungsreisen* (3 December 1971).

[203] BGH 1991 GRUR 463—*Kauf im Ausland* (15 November 1990).

[204] *See supra* p. 208.

unfair competition law. The plaintiff, a German consumer association, contended that the defendant's Spanish sales associate had not properly informed buyers of their right to rescind the contract under German consumer protection law. The information requirement in German law was due to European secondary law[205] and was considered an issue of both consumer protection and unfair competition law. Accordingly, the consumer association as plaintiff claimed that actual noninformation constituted a case of statutory breach under German unfair competition law.[206] As the Bundesgerichtshof explained in its decision—which has been widely approved by courts and scholars—the place of the advertising market (*Werbemarkt*) generally serves as the point of attachment if advertising conduct and effects occur in different territories.[207] Critics are in the minority when they contend that the advertising market need not necessarily be the place where effects materialize, and that consumer and competitor interests may also exist in the sales market (*Absatzmarkt*), constituting the relevant effects for conflicts determination.[208]

2 *Problem: Economic Concepts and Legal Terminology*

The case and its doctrinal handling reveal a general deficit of conflicts theory and practice. As alluded to earlier, this deficit is due to, among other things, the incongruity between economic concepts and legal terminology.[209] Lawyers tend to directly "translate" economic concepts

205 At the time of the *Gran Canaria* case, Spain (unlike Germany) had not yet implemented Council Directive of 20 December 1985 to protect the consumer in respect of contracts negotiated away from business premises (85/577/EEC). Hence, under Spanish contract law, no duty to provide notice of the right to cancel a contract existed.

206 The rule is now implemented in § 3a German Unfair Competition Act (UWG).

207 *See, e.g.*, BGH 1991 GRUR 463, 465—*Kauf im Ausland* (15 November 1990); *see also* BGH 1977 GRUR 672, 673—*Weltweit-Club* (13 May 1977); BGH 1998 GRUR 419, 420—*Gewinnspiel im Ausland* (26 November 1997); for scholarly commentary, *see* Rolf Sack, *Marktortprinzip und allgemeine Ausweichklausel im internationalen Wettbewerbsrecht, am Beispiel der sog. Gran-Canaria-Fälle*, 1992 IPRax 24, 25–26; Gerhard Schricker, in *Großkommentar—UWG: Gesetz gegen den unlauteren Wettbewerb, vol. I*, Einl para. F 204 (Rainer Jacobs et al. eds., 1994); Jost Kotthoff, *Die Anwendbarkeit des deutschen Wettbewerbsrechts auf Werbemaßnahmen im Internet*, 1997 CR 676, 677; Peter Mankowski, *Internet und Internationales Wettbewerbsrecht*, 1999 GRUR Int. 909, 911; Rolf Sack, *Internationales Lauterkeitsrecht nach der Rom-II-VO*, 2008 WRP 845, 848; Rainer Hausmann & Eva Inés Obergfell, in *Lauterkeitsrecht: Kommentar zum Gesetz gegen den unlauteren Wettbewerb (UWG), vol. I*, Einleitung I para. 281–282 (Karl-Heinz Fezer ed., 2nd edn., 2010); Josef Drexl, in *Münchener Kommentar zum Bürgerlichen Gesetzbuch, vol. XI*, IntLautR para. 17 and 136 (Franz Jürgen Säcker et al. eds., 6th edn., 2015).

208 *See, e.g.*, Ignace Van Meenen, *Lauterkeitsrecht und Verbraucherschutz im IPR—Eine Untersuchung des vertrags- und deliktskollisionsrechtlichen Schutzes gegen verbraucherfeindliche Rechtswahlvereinbarungen* 144 *et seq.* (1995); Karl-Heinz Fezer & Stefan Koos, in *Staudingers Kommentar zum Bürgerlichen Gesetzbuch: Internationales Wirtschaftsrecht*, Internationales Wettbewerbsprivatrecht para. 497 *et seq.*, 645 *et seq.* (15th edn., 2010).

209 *See supra* p. 214 *et seq.*

into legal terms. However, in doing so, they neglect to integrate these concepts into proper doctrinal structures. Legal arguments are often founded on the localization of a "market" without proper guidance as to how this market's geographical scope should be determined. As we have also seen, modern statutory language has further replicated this unfortunate tendency in unfair competition conflicts. Under article 6(1) of Rome II, effects on the "competitive relations" or the "collective interests of consumers" are supposed to help determine the relevant point of attachment. But this proxy is a poor substitute. It is of particularly low utility in a transnational market setting, where consumer and competitor interests are nearly ubiquitous and highly elusive.[210]

In order to avoid this untested and sweeping translation of economic concepts, a more detailed perspective is required. We have seen that consumer decision making is central to market functioning; and it is market information that provides the basis for the consumer's decision making.[211] If trademark and unfair competition law are considered to regulate the market's information infrastructure, it is this infrastructure that must determine choice of the applicable law. This change of perspective brings a new understanding that the geographical extension of the market must be determined by the consumer's transaction alternatives.[212] As long as two options present themselves to the consumer as true alternatives, they are part of the same market.[213] In this light, the *Gran Canaria* scenario featured only one *single* marketplace—albeit multijurisdictionally extended. Formerly separate markets had "merged" in the course of increasing consumer mobility.

3 Analysis: The Chronology of Consumer Decision Making

The *Kauf im Ausland* decision and scholarly commentary in its wake have established a dichotomous understanding of what constitutes the "marketplace." Only two relevant stages of market transacting appear to exist—accordingly, two separate market segments must be distinguished. One stage of transacting is the competitor's "conduct." This is deemed to determine the place where the consumers are affected—in other words, the locale of the advertising market (*Werbemarkt*). The other stage of transacting is performance or delivery. This is described

[210] *See supra* p. 214 *et seq.* [211] *See supra* p. 275 *et seq.* [212] *See supra* p. 494–497.

[213] *See also* Dieter Martiny, *Die Anknüpfung an den Markt*, 389, 392, in *Festschrift für Ulrich Drobnig zum siebzigsten Geburtstag* (Jürgen Basedow et al. eds., 1998) ("Die Breite des Marktes wird von den Ausweichmöglichkeiten der Marktgegenseite bestimmt. Solange die Austauschbarkeit angenommen werden kann, kann man noch von einem Markt sprechen.").

as the sales or performance market (*Absatzmarkt*). But this model of market transacting is unduly curtailed. The sequence of marketing activities and transacting conduct is more complex. Different stages must be distinguished.

The *Kauf im Ausland* reasons start with a reference to the tort foundation of unfair competition law and traditional conflicts determination under the *locus delicti* rule.[214] On the basis of the *Kindersaugflaschen* doctrine,[215] the court explained that the place where the competitors' interests collided would serve as the point of attachment.[216] For advertising activity, this place would have to be located within the marketplace in which an impact on the customers' decision was intended.[217] Other factors, such as the customers' nationality or place of residence, were deemed irrelevant. The court also explained that places where preparatory activities are undertaken or where damage to the victim-competitor occurs should be irrelevant.[218] Therefore, the applicable law would be based on the place where the specific activity at issue was intended to affect the customer, regardless of where a later transaction might occur.[219] Scholarly commentary has widely followed, looking at the impact on the consumer or on the other side of the market (*Einwirkungsprinzip*).[220] Leading scholars have expressly described the "place of conduct" as determinative.[221] Even the most sophisticated analyses, looking at the

[214] *See* BGH 1991 GRUR 463, 464—*Kauf im Ausland* (15 November 1990) ("Sittenwidrige Wettbewerbshandlungen gehören zu den unerlaubten Handlungen; das anzuwendende Recht ergibt sich bei ihnen grundsätzlich aus dem Begehungsort.").

[215] *See supra* p. 68 *et seq.* and p. 207–209.

[216] BGH 1991 GRUR 463, 464—*Kauf im Ausland* (15 November 1990).

[217] *Id.* ("Im Streitfall geht es um die wettbewerbsrechtliche Beurteilung eines Verhaltens bei der Gewinnung von Kunden. In einem solchen Fall ist als Ort der wettbewerblichen Interessenkollision grundsätzlich der Marktort anzusehen, an dem durch dieses Verhalten im Wettbewerb mit anderen Unternehmen auf die Entschließung des Kunden eingewirkt werden soll.").

[218] *Id.* at 465.

[219] *Id.* ("Wenn es um die Beurteilung von Maßnahmen bei der Gewinnung von Kunden geht, ist der Marktort, an dem diese Maßnahmen auf den Kunden einwirken sollen, auch dann der für die Bestimmung des anwendbaren Rechts maßgebliche Ort der wettbewerblichen Interessenkollision, wenn der spätere Absatz auf einem anderen Markt stattfinden soll. In einem solchen Fall ist zwar auch das Absatzinteresse anderer Wettbewerber auf diesem Markt berührt, es handelt sich aber insoweit nur um Auswirkungen des zu beurteilenden Wettbewerbsverhaltens, die nicht zur Anwendbarkeit des Rechts des Absatzmarktes führen ....").

[220] *See supra* p. 206 *et seq.*

[221] *See, e.g.*, Rolf Sack, *Marktortprinzip und allgemeine Ausweichklausel im internationalen Wettbewerbsrecht, am Beispiel der sog. Gran-Canaria-Fälle*, 1992 IPRax 24, 25 ("Es ist der Ort der beanstandeten Wettbewerbshandlung."); *also* Peter Bernhard, *Insel-Recht auf Gran Canaria—Zum internationalen Privatrecht des unlauteren Wettbewerbs*, 1992 GRUR Int. 366, 370.

consumer's referee function, have limited the scope to the place where the *conduct* at issue actually affects the consumer.[222]

This understanding risks unnecessarily limiting the perspective on *Kauf im Ausland* scenarios, and it also partly misconceives the structure of unfair competition conflicts. First, it is important to note that the Bundesgerichtshof did not require the defendant's *conduct* to serve as the point of attachment. Rather, the place where marketing or advertising activity was *intended to affect* the customer—and not the place where the defendant would actually act—was defined as the place where interests collided and, accordingly, served as the point of attachment.[223] Actual conduct in marketing activity is thus only the starting point. As we have seen, it precedes the first stage of consumer decision making.[224] Therefore, the place of "impact" on consumer decision making may well differ from the place of "conduct." Internet advertising provides an evident example of such a divergence: there is uploading on one side ("conduct") and accessing or downloading on the other ("impact"). Another example where this correlation is apparent can be found in cases where the consumer relocates after having contact with the marketing conduct at issue—but prior to transacting. This can be found, for instance, in advertising vis-à-vis commuters crossing a state border on their way to work and back home. The consumer-commuter is "impacted" at her workplace abroad but "transacts" at home.

And one more aspect is important. The *Kauf im Ausland* court seemed unperturbed when declaring that the sales market (*Absatzmarkt*) should be deemed irrelevant as a point of attachment if it is understood only as a place where the results of improper conduct come into existence.[225] Here as well, more precision is required. Of course, the sales market is commonly understood as the place where the contract is performed through the delivery of goods or the performance of services. In laymen's terms, this is usually the successful final stage of the contract. But the consumer's decision to transact and the localization of its implementation into the

[222] *See, e.g.*, Axel Beater, *Unlauterer Wettbewerb* § 9 para. 733 (2011); Peter Mankowski, in *Münchener Kommentar zum Lauterkeitsrecht, vol. I,* IntWettbR para. 161–162 (Peter W. Heermann et al. eds., 2nd edn., 2014); Josef Drexl, in *Münchener Kommentar zum Bürgerlichen Gesetzbuch, vol. XI,* IntLautR para. 134 (Franz Jürgen Säcker et al. eds., 6th edn., 2015).

[223] *See supra* fn. 217. [224] *See supra* p. 287 *et seq.*

[225] BGH 1991 GRUR 463, 465—*Kauf im Ausland* (15 November 1990). *See also* Rolf Sack, *Marktortprinzip und allgemeine Ausweichklausel im internationalen Wettbewerbsrecht, am Beispiel der sog. Gran-Canaria-Fälle,* 1992 IPRax 24, 25–26; Walter F. Lindacher, *Zum Internationalen Privatrecht des unlauteren Wettbewerbs,* 1996 WRP 645, 648; Peter Mankowski, *Internet und Internationales Wettbewerbsrecht,* 1999 GRUR Int. 909, 916.

marketplace must be distinguished;[226] neither product delivery nor performance of services constitutes the completion of the transaction in economic terms. Those acts may complete the performance scheme under the parties' contract. Yet with respect to the market mechanism, it is generally the conclusion of the contract that determines the final act in the consumer's decision-making process. When and where performance will later actually take place is of secondary relevance at best.

4 *Implementation: Alternative Transactions and the Merger of Markets*

Of course, resolving cross-border unfair competition conflicts in light of the consumer decision-making model does not necessarily mean that the place of competitor conduct is irrelevant. The place of acting will provide for at least one possible point of attachment if the transaction is also concluded there. In *Kauf im Ausland*, therefore, under the assumption that actual or potential competition existed in Spain—in other words, that the German tourists could have also transacted with the defendant's competitors in *Gran Canaria*—application of Spanish law would be part of a consistent solution.[227] But the issue is not resolved with this conclusion.

Dominant scholarly commentary still widely agrees with the Bundesgerichtshof's exclusive choice of the Spanish unfair competition regime. Josef Drexl, for instance, has defended the *Kauf im Ausland* holding under a perspective of regulatory sovereignty and with respect to the aim of upholding a level playing field of international competition.[228] As he posits, the Spanish state's regulatory interest is attached to the specific conduct within its national territory; neither consumer nationality nor residence will matter. In addition, he explains, unfair competition law aims to establish a *par conditio concurrentium* in the marketplace. Any extraterritorial extension of other states' laws (in this case, German law) would therefore not only affect the Spanish state's interest in an autonomous regulation of its own markets but also distort competition. In other words, if German law had been applied, German competitors would have

[226] *See also* Karl-Heinz Fezer & Stefan Koos, in *Staudingers Kommentar zum Bürgerlichen Gesetzbuch: Internationales Wirtschaftsrecht*, Internationales Wettbewerbsprivatrecht para. 509 (15th edn., 2010).

[227] For this assumption, *see, e.g.*, Jochen Glöckner, in *Gesetz gegen den unlauteren Wettbewerb (UWG)*, Einl C para. 143 (Henning Harte-Bavendamm & Frauke Henning-Bodewig eds., 3rd edn., 2013); for a convincing critique, *see* Karl-Heinz Fezer & Stefan Koos, in *Staudingers Kommentar zum Bürgerlichen Gesetzbuch: Internationales Wirtschaftsrecht*, Internationales Wettbewerbsprivatrecht para. 512 (15th edn., 2010).

[228] Josef Drexl, in *Münchener Kommentar zum Bürgerlichen Gesetzbuch, vol. XI*, IntLautR para. 17 (Franz Jürgen Säcker et al. eds., 6th edn., 2015); Josef Drexl, *Zum Verhältnis von lauterkeits- und kartellrechtlicher Anknüpfung nach der Rom-II-VO*, 2713 *et seq.*, in *Festschrift für Klaus J. Hopt zum 70. Geburtstag: Unternehmen, Markt und Verantwortung* (Stefan Grundmann ed., 2010).

been disadvantaged, for they would have had to comply with their stricter home regime. Spanish enterprises, by contrast, could act under the more liberal conditions of Spanish law, thereby bearing lower costs.[229]

I have already analyzed the underlying economics of a discriminatory application of stricter forum laws.[230] Yet there is an additional aspect that must not be overlooked. The *Kauf im Ausland* case presented a truly multijurisdictional conflict. Of course, all lawmakers are interested in their local order of market communication—this necessarily requires a certain degree of regulation of local conduct. But this does not mean that any other state's interest must be rejected *ab initio*. Even if we assume that there was competition in Spain, this does not invalidate German lawmakers' concurrent interest in regulating their own local order of market communication and transacting. Exclusive application of Spanish law cannot be argued on the grounds that the tourists were targeted in Spanish territory only and that they had no option of transacting with competitors in Germany.[231] This perspective loses sight of the correlation between market extension and product properties.[232] It thus necessarily overlooks the fact that actual effects on consumer decision making and on the process of market transacting also existed in Germany. Among scholarly commentary, Jochen Glöckner provides one example of this approach. As he argues, it would be far-fetched to imply that the German tourists would have waited until their return to Germany to buy the products.[233] This argument may be convincing for products that have a short consumption period (e.g., restaurant or entertainment services). A Gran Canarian bar will thus generally not compete with a Spanish restaurant in Munich. The situation changes, however, if the product at issue is not to be used or consumed within a short time. Duvets and pillows, as textiles in general, have a far longer life and consumption span. Potential buyers thus might well consider deferring

[229] Josef Drexl, in *Münchener Kommentar zum Bürgerlichen Gesetzbuch, vol. XI*, IntLautR para. 17 (Franz Jürgen Säcker et al. eds., 6th edn., 2015); Josef Drexl, *Zum Verhältnis von lauterkeits- und kartellrechtlicher Anknüpfung nach der Rom-II-VO*, 2713, 2730, in *Festschrift für Klaus J. Hopt zum 70. Geburtstag: Unternehmen, Markt und Verantwortung* (Stefan Grundmann ed., 2010).

[230] *See supra* p. 480 *et seq.*

[231] *But see* Jochen Glöckner, in *Gesetz gegen den unlauteren Wettbewerb (UWG)*, UWG Einl C para. 142–143 (Henning Harte-Bavendamm & Frauke Henning-Bodewig eds., 3rd edn., 2013).

[232] *See supra* p. 218–219.

[233] Jochen Glöckner, in *Gesetz gegen den unlauteren Wettbewerb (UWG)*, UWG Einl C para. 143 n. 346 (Henning Harte-Bavendamm & Frauke Henning-Bodewig eds., 3rd edn., 2013); *but see* Karl-Heinz Fezer & Stefan Koos, in *Staudingers Kommentar zum Bürgerlichen Gesetzbuch: Internationales Wirtschaftsrecht*, Internationales Wettbewerbsprivatrecht para. 512 (15th edn., 2010).

a purchase for more than a few days and ultimately buying the product back home. And products of the kind offered by the defendant were actually also available in Germany. Hence, the tourists did have "German alternatives" to their purchase in Gran Canaria. Technically, the tourists as peripatetic consumers had extended the scope of their activities geographically, thereby bringing the market with them—literally in their luggage.

Moreover, it is also not a valid argument that competition in the "Spanish market" could be distorted by the application of German law to the defendant's conduct. Of course, as we have seen, extraterritoriality of stricter national policies bears a risk of anticompetitive overregulation.[234] But this problem must not lead to an *ab initio* rejection of the application of laws other than the local regime. On the contrary, if qualified and sufficiently intensive effects exist within another lawmaker's territory, application of the respective regime is principally justified. As we have also seen, effects, not conduct, are what trigger the interest in regulating market communication and transacting. Per se, the mere occurrence of conduct in one territory does not provide for a prevalence of the local regulatory interest vis-à-vis other regimes' concerns—even though it may be territorial *effects* only that can be found there.[235] In sum, it is determinative that the marketplace in *Kauf im Ausland* extended across both jurisdictions. Accordingly, both Spanish and German unfair competition law should have been applied concurrently.[236]

A different question is whether the application of a certain regime—here, German law—should yield to a comity-based rule of jurisdictional self-restraint. As illustrated earlier, this is the last prong in choice-of-law analysis.[237] In this regard, Drexl's proposal to avoid anticompetitive distortion bears some value. Nonetheless, this argument does not require excluding the application of German law. On the contrary, the *Kauf im Ausland* facts called for an application of German law. Even though actual transaction numbers may have been small, the defendant found it worthwhile to conceive of a scheme of "market relocation." In other words, it decided to selectively affect German consumers during their holidays in Spain. The aim was to circumvent stricter German laws on consumer protection. In this light, no legitimate interest on the side of Spanish

[234] *See supra* p. 480 *et seq.*

[235] For the obsolescence of conduct and the validity of effects testing, *see supra* p. 494 *et seq.*

[236] Apparently in favor of the same result (albeit on the basis of a different concept that looks at the place of consumer demand) are Karl-Heinz Fezer & Stefan Koos, in *Staudingers Kommentar zum Bürgerlichen Gesetzbuch: Internationales Wirtschaftsrecht*, Internationales Wettbewerbsprivatrecht para. 511 (15th edn., 2010); *but see id.* at para. 707 *et seq.*

[237] *See supra* p. 507 *et seq.*

lawmakers could be found to provide for "more leeway of commercial transacting" on their territory.[238] Unlike Germany, Spain at that time was in default with its implementation of the European directive that provided for the relevant provision on consumer information and protection. Under the intent-based proxy rule of *de minimis* effects explained above,[239] this suffices to overcome the threshold that is required in the interest of jurisdictional self-restraint.

5 Conclusion

The consumer's decision making and the implementation of her decision by transacting constitute the cynosure of the market mechanism. The core of trademark and unfair competition policies aims at the regulation of market information infrastructure as the basis of the consumer's decision-making process. Accordingly, the process of the consumer's decision making must determine the place of conflicts attachment. Looking at the consumer's alternatives to her transaction (or nontransaction) helps clarify and interpret concepts of the "marketplace" and the place of "interest collision" that are often too casually referred to in statutory provisions, case law, and commentary. At the same time, the concept of transaction alternatives also helps explain that there is no reasonable differentiation between an "advertising market" and a "sales market." In *Gran Canaria* scenarios, the consumer has left her place of residence, but she has not transacted in a truly "foreign" market. She has extended the market's geographical scope by her own mobility. Accordingly, more than one national regime applies.

Section 3 The Typology of Trademark and Unfair Competition Conflicts

I now have arrived at the final part of my inquiry—the presentation of a practical typology of trademark and unfair competition choice of law. Autonomy in consumer decision making and transacting is the ultimate subject matter of protection in trademark and unfair competition law. Choice of law requires an accordant conceptualization. This shifts the perspective away from traditional conduct-based and formality-founded methods, thus yielding, in many cases, results contrary to those proclaimed by conventional wisdom.

[238] *But see* Josef Drexl, *Zum Verhältnis von lauterkeits- und kartellrechtlicher Anknüpfung nach der Rom-II-VO*, 2713, 2730, in *Festschrift für Klaus J. Hopt zum 70. Geburtstag: Unternehmen, Markt und Verantwortung* (Stefan Grundmann ed., 2010).

[239] For the rule in scenarios of intentional market invasion, *see supra* p. 517–518.

I Consumer Decision Making: Protecting the Market Information Infrastructure

Both in trademark conflicts and in unfair competition choice of law, the analysis will require giving regard to the effects on the market mechanism. With respect to the core policy of protecting consumer decision making and transacting, a "rule of alternatives" must be used to determine the applicable law.[240]

A The Common Core of Trademark and Unfair Competition Policies

1 Advertising Communication: A General "Rule of Alternatives"

Example (similar scenario to the Court of Justice's *L'Oréal v. Bellure* case[241]): Acme GmbH, incorporated in Germany, manufactures "smell alike" perfumes for sale on the British market. Acme GmbH's products replicate the fragrances of numerous brand-name perfumes, including those of Blammo Perfumes SARL, a company incorporated in France that sells its "original" fragrances worldwide. Acme GmbH's products are packaged in a way to avoid confusion with Blammo Perfumes SARL's trademarks. Yet Acme GmbH advertises its products as "imitations" and "replicas" of the original brands.

The category of unfair competitive conduct that concerns market information and its transmission comprises, inter alia, deceptive and confusing advertising, including comparative advertising and hidden advertising. In terms of current US doctrine, section 1 of the Restatement of Unfair Competition (Third) explains these scenarios as practices relating to "deceptive marketing" and "infringement of trademarks and other indicia of identification."[242] As shown in the analysis of the *Gran Canaria* scenario, an alleged violator-competitor's conduct in the advertising market (*Werbemarkt*) does not necessarily serve as the point of attachment.[243] What matters is the place of alternatives to the consumer's transaction or nontransaction.[244] These alternatives may be

240 *See supra* p. 494–497.
241 *L'Oréal and Others*, C-487/07 (18 June 2009), [2009] E.C.R. I-5185.
242 Restatement of the Law—Unfair Competition (Third), § 1(a)(1) and (2) (1995). Deceptive Marketing notably covers actions brought under § 43(a) of the Lanham Act, 15 U.S.C.A. § 1125(a), or under the states' statutory law against deceptive trade practices. *See id.* at introductory note to chapter 2.
243 For dominant opinion to the contrary, *see supra* p. 203 *et seq.* and p. 539 *et seq.*
244 A "nontransaction" is considered if the unfair competition conduct at issue causes the consumer to forgo a transaction with the plaintiff.

located in a territory other than the place of the violator-competitor's conduct and the place of impact on the consumer.

Solution: In the example, the places of conduct (advertising), impact (perception of the advertising by consumers), and transacting (point of sale) are situated in the UK. The UK also seems to be the only place where alternatives to consumers' transactions with Acme GmbH exist. Thus, British law applies.

At this point, it is important to note that this rule of alternatives under article 6(1) of Rome II will also apply to most scenarios within the specific categories of common law torts of passing off, as well as malicious falsehood and defamation in a business context.[245] English scholarly commentary partly contends otherwise; yet the bulk of cases regarding passing off concern issues of actual or potential manipulation of consumer decision making ("misrepresentation").[246] Accordingly, in passing-off scenarios, the market mechanism is usually directly affected and there is no bilaterality under article 6(2) of Rome II.[247]

Finally, the category of unfair advertising communication may also include communication vis-à-vis the customer *after* concluding a contract whenever such communication is intended to affect decision making with respect to the existing contract and the consumer's potential alternatives. Contrary to dominant scholarly commentary, it is also a rule of alternatives—not an attachment to the place of the consumer's residence (where she sees, reads, or otherwise perceives the communication at issue)[248]—that must govern.

[245] So that they are not excluded by article 1(g) Rome II Regulation. For nonexclusion, *see, e.g.*, James J. Fawcett & Paul Torremans, *Intellectual Property and Private International Law* para. 16.21–16.24, para. 16.68–16.71, and para. 16.89 (2nd edn., 2011); Cheshire, North & Fawcett, *Private International Law* 809 (Sir Peter North consult. ed., 14th edn., 2008); Dicey, Morris & Collins, *The Conflict of Laws, vol. II* para. 35–054 (Lord Collins of Mapesbury gen. ed., 15th edn., 2012).

[246] *See supra* p. 361 *et seq.*

[247] *But see, e.g.*, Christopher Wadlow, *The Law of Passing-Off—Unfair Competition by Misrepresentation* para. 10–079 (4th edn., 2011). In favor of applying art. 6(1) Rome II, however, *see, e.g.*, Andrew Dickinson, *The Rome II Regulation: The Law Applicable to Non-Contractual Obligations* para. 6.25 and 6.29 (2008); James J. Fawcett & Paul Torremans, *Intellectual Property and Private International Law* para. 16.22 (passing off), and 16.70 (malicious falsehood) (2nd edn., 2011); apparently undecided, *e.g.*, Richard Plender & Michael Wilderspin, *The European Private International Law of Obligations* para. 20–034 (4th edn., 2015).

[248] *But see, e.g.*, Helmut Köhler, in Helmut Köhler & Joachim Bornkamm, *Gesetz gegen den unlauteren Wettbewerb*, Einl UWG para. 5.36 (33rd edn., 2015); Ansgar Ohly, in Ansgar Ohly & Olaf Sosnitza, *Gesetz gegen den unlauteren Wettbewerb mit Preisangabenverordnung (UWG)* Einf B para. 17 (6th edn., 2014).

2 No Exceptions: Trademarks, Trade Names, Geographical Indications, and Designations of Origin

Example (modified scenario of *Grupo Gigante SA De CV v. Dallo & Co., Inc.*[249]): Acme GmbH, incorporated in Germany, is a grocery chain that intends to open an online shop under the name Titan Marché. The website (which uses, among others, the address "titan-marche.fr") will offer online grocery sales and delivery services in many German cities, including those in the German-French border region. The brand name Titan Marché is well known for grocery services in Algeria. Blammo Groceries SARL owns rights to the service mark for Algeria but not for the European Union, Germany, or France, where, so far, no registration exists. A significant number of French citizens, however, are familiar with the Algerian grocery chain.

Existing doctrine on trademark conflicts and the rule of the *lex loci protectionis* need not be changed with respect to its territorial foundation. However, it should be amended by jettisoning the conduct/formality dichotomy. Under a reconceptualized effects principle for trademark conflicts, a plaintiff (i.e., right owner) will have to specify the applicable regime under which she believes her rights are infringed on.[250] The court will then determine the existence and foreseeability of effects and will undertake a comity-based analysis of jurisdictional self-restraint in order to establish the admissible territorial scope of the relevant regime.

Solution: In order for Blammo Groceries SARL to enjoin Acme GmbH from using the service mark Titan Marché, it must find a cause of action under either German or French trademark or unfair competition law. Grocery services are local; hence, alternatives to consumers' transactions with Acme GmbH—notably the potential use of the service mark by Blammo Groceries SARL—must be found in either Germany or France. Since the mark is not registered in either of these places, it is essential for Blammo Groceries SARL to prove the existence of an unregistered service mark, or—if no such right exists—to resort to enjoining Acme GmbH by means of an unfair competition claim. Considering that the potential customer base is located in France, the case will have to be decided under French law.

If a state's lawmakers have implemented additional policies to prevent, for instance, preparatory activities, the approach may vary. One example of such concurrent policies is article 9(2) of the European Community's trademark regulation, which prohibits conduct at the premarket level (e.g., affixing trademarks to goods or packaging).[251] In these scenarios,

[249] *Grupo Gigante SA De CV v. Dallo & Co., Inc.*, 391 F.3d 1088 (9th Cir. 2004).
[250] *See supra* p. 493–494.
[251] Article 9 Council Regulation (EC) No. 207/2009 (of 26 February 2009 on the Community Trade Mark, O.J. EU (24 March 2009), L 78/1) provides: "The following, inter alia, may be prohibited under paragraph 1: (a) affixing the sign to the goods or to the packaging thereof."

lawmakers have expressly detached infringing conduct from effects on consumer decision making. Accordingly, the place of the alleged infringer's activity—regardless of its ultimate effects on the market mechanism—determines the applicable law.

Beyond the core of trademark rights protection, finally, there is some dispute concerning the treatment of trade names, geographical indications, and designations of origin. While the protection of trade names and work titles in Germany, for instance, has traditionally been an issue of unfair competition doctrine,[252] modern statutory law has implemented protection into express provisions of the Trademark Act.[253] Not surprisingly, therefore, despite wide agreement that trade-name protection will not amount to full "rights" status, conflicts resolution has been based on the *lex loci protectionis.*[254] Under Rome II, this requires application of the conflicts provision for intellectual property rights in article 8.[255] Similarly, application of article 8 of Rome II has been suggested for the infringement of geographical indications.[256] This approach has been supported by a number of arguments, among them the assertion that geographical indications are akin to intellectual property rights.[257] As we have seen,

[252] *See, e.g.*, BGHZ vol. 11, 214, 215—*KfA* (8 December 1953); Gerhard Schricker, in *Großkommentar—UWG: Gesetz gegen den unlauteren Wettbewerb, vol. I*, Einl para. F 198 (Rainer Jacobs et al. eds., 1994).

[253] *See* sections 5, 15, and 126 *et seq.* Trademark Act.

[254] *See, e.g.*, BGH 2002 GRUR 972, 973–974—*FROMMIA* (2 May 2002); BGH 2007 GRUR 884, 886—*Cambridge Institute* (28 June 2007); *see also* OGH 1986 GRUR Int. 735, 737—*Hotel Sacher* (14 January 1986); Jürgen F. Baur, *Zum Namensschutz im deutschen internationalen Privatrecht unter besonderer Berücksichtigung des Schutzes der Handelsnamen*, 167 AcP 535, 541 (1967); Gerhard Schricker, in *Großkommentar—UWG: Gesetz gegen den unlauteren Wettbewerb, vol. I*, Einl para. F 198–199 (Rainer Jacobs et al. eds., 1994).

[255] *See more recently, e.g.*, OGH 2012 GRUR Int. 464, 465—*alcom-international.at* (9 August 2011); for scholarly commentary, *see, e.g.*, Josef Drexl, in *Münchener Kommentar zum Bürgerlichen Gesetzbuch, vol. XI*, IntImmGR para. 164 (Franz Jürgen Säcker et al. eds., 6th edn., 2015); Katharina de la Durantaye, in *Rome Regulations*, Art. 8 para. 10 (Gralf-Peter Calliess ed., 2nd edn., 2015).

[256] *See, e.g.*, Rainer Hausmann & Eva Inés Obergfell, in *Lauterkeitsrecht: Kommentar zum Gesetz gegen den unlauteren Wettbewerb (UWG), vol. I*, Einleitung I para. 285 (Karl-Heinz Fezer ed., 2nd edn., 2010); Josef Drexl, in *Münchener Kommentar zum Bürgerlichen Gesetzbuch, vol. XI*, IntLautR para. 124 *et seq.* (Franz Jürgen Säcker et al. eds., 6th edn., 2015); Michael Grünberger, in *Nomos-Kommentar-BGB, Rom-Verordnungen, vol. VI*, Art. 8 Rom II para. 28 (Rainer Hüßtege & Heinz-Peter Mansel eds., 2014); Nadine Klass, in *Großkommentar—UWG: Gesetz gegen den unlauteren Wettbewerb, vol. I*, Einl. para. 36 (Otto Teplitzky et al. eds., 2nd edn., 2014); for a differentiation between unauthorized use of (then art. 8) and misrepresentation in relation to geographical indications (then art. 6): Martin Illmer, in *Rome II Regulation*, Art. 6 para. 21 (Peter Huber ed., 2011). German case law is heterogeneous. *See, e.g.*, BGH 2007 GRUR 884, 886—*Cambridge Institute* (28 June 2007); BGH 2007 GRUR 67, 68—*Pietra di Soln* (5 October 2006).

[257] *See supra* p. 376.

however, these arguments are based on a misguided concept of the formality of rights.[258] The trademark-as-property (or geographical-indication-as-property) paradigm must be rejected. Accordingly, with respect to conflicts resolution, a homogeneous treatment under the modernized marketplace effects principle is indicated. Categories of "conduct" and "property" are irrelevant. Instead, effects on consumer decision making and transacting are what determine the applicable law. Only if, however, the policy at issue goes beyond the protection of navigation goodwill (e.g., for famous geographical indications) will the conflicts rule have to accommodate different requirements for the protection of surplus goodwill. I will address this exception in more detail in an instant.[259]

B Implementation of Decision-Making Results: Transacting

1 The Core Policy

As my look at trademark and unfair competition policies has shown, the domain of unfair competition prevention goes beyond the rationale of trademark protection.[260] In contrast to the two fields' common core policy, the prevention of other acts of unfair competition protects the consumer's decision-making process subsequent to the transmission of information. This notably concerns cases of unfair conduct that force the consumer into a transaction that she would not have made if she had been free to decide. The goal there, too, however, is to prevent unfree and presumptively unreasonable transacting. Among the numerous scenarios of such impact on stages following the transmission of marketplace information, undue psychological pressure may be the most common example.[261]

Example (compare with no. 30 of annex I of the Unfair Commercial Practices Directive[262]): Acme Books, an English bookseller, sells postcards to German

[258] *See supra* p. 377–378. For a different stance in English scholarly commentary, *see, e.g.*, Christopher Wadlow, *The new private international law of unfair competition and the "Rome II" Regulation*, 11 J. Intell. Prop. L. & Pract. 789, 792 (2009); Richard Plender & Michael Wilderspin, *The European Private International Law of Obligations* para. 20–043 and 22–014 *et seq.* (4th edn., 2015).

[259] *See infra* p. 556 *et seq.*

[260] *See supra* p. 325 *et seq.* and p. 359 *et seq.*

[261] *See, e.g., supra* p. 366 *et seq.*

[262] Directive 2005/29/EC of the European Parliament and of the Council of 11 May 2005, concerning unfair business-to-consumer commercial practices in the internal market and amending Council Directive 84/450/EEC, Directives 97/7/EC, 98/27/EC and 2002/65/EC of the European Parliament and of the Council and Regulation (EC) No 2006/2004 of the European Parliament and of the Council ("Unfair Commercial Practices Directive"), O.J. EU (11 June 2005), L 149/22.

customers. These postcards are marketed as "handpainted" by the handicapped. In its advertising materials, Acme Books accentuates that if these cards are not sold successfully within the weeks to come, the painters' livelihoods will be in jeopardy.

With regard to conflicts attachment, this case is no different from those where the transmission of market information is affected. The information transmitted here need not be incorrect; there may be no element of confusion involved. Ultimately, however, both scenarios concern improper impacts on consumer transacting. Unless the specific policy is combined with a concern for protecting the consumer as an individual—notably with respect to her individual rights—the place of alternatives will constitute the point of attachment. In the example case, therefore, German law will apply.

Finally, this rule also governs fact patterns where other policies intended to regulate commercial communication are at issue. One example (implying neither an improper transmission of information nor an undue influence on the decision-making process) is the prohibition against the bundling of commercial offers with a lottery. Such marketing methods are popular, notably in the form of sales that include an option to participate in a lottery by means of returning a part of the product packaging (e.g., the label). Not long ago, some European civil law regimes used to qualify such kind of advertising as improper manipulation of the consumer's decision making.[263] The underlying policies of such a prohibition may be deemed obsolete in light of the modern European consumer paradigm. Nonetheless, such a rule against bundling is intended to prevent "irrational" consumer decision making. Accordingly, choice-of-law determination will—contrary to what dominant commentary argues—be based on the place where the consumer's alternatives to the underlying transaction exist.[264] The place where potential or actual lottery prizes will be granted and transferred is also irrelevant for conflicts determination.

[263] *See, e.g., Plus Warenhandelsgesellschaft*, C-304/08 (14 January 2010), [2010] E.C.R. I-217; BGH 2011 GRUR Int. 537—*Millionen-Chance II* (5 October 2010).

[264] *But see* Rainer Hausmann & Eva Inés Obergfell, in *Lauterkeitsrecht: Kommentar zum Gesetz gegen den unlauteren Wettbewerb (UWG), vol. I*, Einleitung I para. 313–314 (Karl-Heinz Fezer ed., 2nd edn., 2010); Peter Mankowski, in *Münchener Kommentar zum Lauterkeitsrecht, vol. I*, IntWettbR para. 298 (Peter W. Heermann et al. eds., 2nd edn., 2014); Nadine Klass, in *Großkommentar—UWG: Gesetz gegen den unlauteren Wettbewerb, vol. I*, Einl. para. 249 *et seq.* (Otto Teplitzky et al. eds., 2nd edn., 2014) (all contending the application of the advertising market's law or the law at the place where addressee-consumers reside); *but see* Karl-Heinz Fezer & Stefan Koos, in *Staudingers Kommentar zum Bürgerlichen Gesetzbuch: Internationales Wirtschaftsrecht*, Internationales Wettbewerbsprivatrecht para. 740 *et seq.* (15th edn., 2010).

2 *Policies Beyond*

Under a strict separation of protection policies, the point of attachment will vary if a marketing method is deemed to constitute an additional wrong beyond the mere manipulation of consumer decision making. The subject matter of protection, then, is different: it is not the consumer-as-referee but the consumer-as-citizen.

Example: Acme Co., incorporated in England, is a marketing company that employs telephone operators and offers "advertising and marketing services" for special opportunities. For instance, one can hire Acme Co.'s personnel to call potential customers almost anywhere in Europe, including Germany.[265]

If a legislature prohibits cold calling or spamming for the sake of protecting consumers beyond their capacity as referees in competition, conflicts determination will differ from the alternative-transaction model. If marketing conduct is prohibited only to protect consumer privacy, traditional tort choice-of-law rules will govern. This would then be a case not of article 6 of Rome II but of the national regime's autonomous choice of law.[266] The practical problem is determining which policy ultimately prevails. Usually, a joint concern for protecting the consumer's privacy *and* her role as referee in competition will drive the implementation of the relevant unfair competition norm. Two (or even more) different jurisdictions' laws may then be eligible for choice of law: the one (or more) where the market mechanism is affected and the one where the consumer's privacy is invaded. Choice-of-law attachment will have to function accordingly—that is, with a potential multitude of applicable regimes.

Solution: Depending on what the plaintiff asserts, a European court will either apply article 6 of the Rome II Regulation or resort to the national choice-of-law regime. If the claim is invasion of privacy in violation of article 13 of the ePrivacy Directive[267] only, and there is no claim of effects on consumer decision making,

[265] Another example similar to this scenario of so-called cold calling is e-mail spamming.

[266] *See also* Ansgar Ohly, in Ansgar Ohly & Olaf Sosnitza, *Gesetz gegen den unlauteren Wettbewerb mit Preisangabenverordnung (UWG)* Einf B para. 16a (6th edn., 2014); Helmut Köhler, *Wettbewerbsstatut oder Deliktsstatut?—Zur Auslegung des Art. 6 Rom-II-VO*, 501, 503–504, in *Festschrift für Dagmar Coester-Waltjen* (Katharina Hilbig-Lugani et al. eds., 2015); *but see* Peter Mankowski, in *Münchener Kommentar zum Lauterkeitsrecht, vol. I,* IntWettbR para. 278 (Peter W. Heermann et al. eds., 2nd edn., 2014); Karl-Heinz Fezer & Stefan Koos, in *Staudingers Kommentar zum Bürgerlichen Gesetzbuch: Internationales Wirtschaftsrecht*, Internationales Wettbewerbsprivatrecht para. 732–733 (15th edn., 2010) (applying article 6(1) of Rome II by reference to the impact on "collective interests of consumers"); LG Stuttgart 2007 MMR 668, 669—*Marktortprinzip bei E-Mail-Werbung* (15 May 2007).

[267] Directive 2002/58/EC of the European Parliament and of the Council of 12 July 2002, concerning the processing of personal data and the protection of privacy in the electronic communications sector (Directive on privacy and electronic communications), O.J. EU (31 July 2002), L 201/37.

the national forum's choice of law will determine the applicable tort regime. If, however, the plaintiff also asserts a manipulation of the consumer's decision-making process through cold calling, the court will also have to consider the regime where alternative transactions can be found.

II Theories of Misappropriation and Other Impact on Competition

Apart from their aim to ensure unmanipulated consumer decision making, trademark and unfair competition law are sometimes also founded on an alternative concept of preventing the misappropriation of a competitor's position in the market. The thrust of such protection is quite different from the functional core of trademark and unfair competition policies. Rather than fostering information correctness and unhindered consumer decision making, misappropriation doctrine is aimed at preventing a moral wrong.[268] I have already discussed the scholarly criticism. In the United States, antidilution, initial-interest, and postsale confusion theories, as well as the recognition of merchandising rights, have been cited as examples of such aberrations.[269] Similarly, civil law concepts of unfair competition law preventing the misappropriation of a competitor's goodwill (often discussed in the context of product imitation) have been characterized as improper outgrowths and overprotection. Finally, beyond both these domains of anticonfusion and antimisappropriation theories, additional policies of unfair competition prevention exist. Some are unique to European civil law. Most prominently debated are cases of antitrust and unfair competition concurrence and the so-called breach of statutory duties. As a closer look at these fact patterns reveals, conflicts resolution must be categorized in accordance with whether the substantive law policy at issue is one of protection of consumer decision making or whether it has a broader aim.

A Modern Extensions of Trademark-Infringement Theory

Modern extensions of trademark protection and the traditional theory of point-of-sale confusion prevention have one thing in common: they are founded on a general policy aimed at preventing improper consumer instrumentalization. Unlike in cases of confusion prevention, however, the instrumentalization at issue in extended protection theories is not necessarily achieved through the transmission of *incorrect* information. It is a different form of usurping the consumer's mind.[270] Accordingly, choice of law must be conceived of differently.

[268] The US Supreme Court famously described its core as "reap[ing] where [one] has not sown." *See International News Service v. Associated Press*, 248 U.S. 215, 239 (1918).
[269] *See supra* p. 126–127 and p. 341 *et seq.* [270] *See supra* p. 350 *et seq.*

Example (variation of the *Gran Canaria* case):[271] Acme SL, incorporated in Spain, runs a supermarket chain on the Canary Islands. The symbol that it utilizes as a product designation for its own food products is similar to a well-known trademark registered and used in Germany by Best Decoration GmbH. Best Decoration GmbH, however, has registered the trademark, which it uses exclusively for jewelry; it has no registration in Spain or the European Union. Acme SARL makes intentional use of the designation in its advertising vis-à-vis German tourists on holiday in Gran Canaria.

Under the rule of the *lex loci protectionis*, the law of the protecting country decides on its own scope of protection and the extension of domestic trademark rights. While the traditional rule provided for a requirement of conduct within the country of protection,[272] modifications are indicated on the basis of marketplace effects comparable to the rule in unfair competition choice of law. However, the subject matter of protection varies. This particularly concerns the area of non-confusion-based infringement theories in trademark law. In a number of fact patterns governed by theories beyond confusion prevention, no competition exists. Use of the trademark by a second-comer will then not immediately affect the market mechanism with regard to the original brand's product. Cases of trademark dilution provide one example where relevant effects will generally be found not in a collision of competitive interests but in the actual or potential deterioration of market information capital (goodwill).[273] Accordingly, the point of attachment must be the place where the senior trademark owner's market capitalization is in danger of being diminished. In most cases, this is the place of residence of the relevant consumer group for the original brand's product.[274] But it will not necessarily coincide with the place of the alleged infringer's conduct.

[271] For a similar scenario, *see* OGH 2002 GRUR Int. 344—*BOSS-Zigaretten* (29 May 2001).

[272] For the traditional rule and its critique, *see supra* p. 193 *et seq.*

[273] The fact that the consumer's mind still is what determines conflicts attachment in these cases somewhat verifies but ultimately invalidates Walter Wheeler Cook's famous critique of the idea that goodwill has a "situs." *See* Walter Wheeler Cook, *The Logical and Legal Bases of the Conflict of Laws* 299–300 (2nd edn., 1949) ("To sum up: the Restatement's 'intangible things which exist in fact apart from law' have no more real existence than unicorns or griffins; what is involved in the examples given (goodwill of a business; trade name) is the 'transfer' of a group of legal relations which have no reference to a definite physical object. It follows that to state the rules of the conflict of laws for the choice of law as if we were actually dealing with the transfer of an interest in an existing 'thing' which has a location in space is inconsistent with clarity of thought in at least two ways: (1) it tends to obscure the actual basis for our choice of law; and (2) it tends to lead us to mistake the results of our decision for the reasons therefor. . . . [I]n the case of the so-called 'intangible thing,' the statement that it has a 'situs,' or that it 'exists in fact in' a certain state is at best a misleading way of stating our result, namely, that we have decided (of course for other reasons) to apply the law of the specified state.").

[274] For a lucid definition of the relevant public in trademark dilution, *see Intel Corporation*, C-252/07, para. 33 *et seq.* (27 November 2008), [2008] E.C.R. I-8823.

Solution: In the example, conduct on Spanish territory can be found. However, the case must be seen primarily as a scenario of trademark-impairing effects to be found with regard to the right owner's goodwill in Germany. The target group—as in the *Gran Canaria* case—is German consumers. Accordingly, at issue is the concern that tourist-consumers' minds could be affected and that (in the long run) a deterioration of trademark distinctiveness with regard to the German public could take place. In principle, therefore, German trademark law is to be applied to the foreign-based dilutive conduct.[275]

Similarly, theories of preventing initial-interest confusion or bait-and-switch schemes require a differentiated perspective. Two variants must be distinguished.[276] If lawmakers have established a concept of preventing initial-interest confusion that provides for protection without regard to the impact on the consumer's decision making, a theory of genuine misappropriation prevention governs. We then apply the conflicts rule described above for antidilution prevention.

Example (modification of *Brookfield Communications, Inc. v. West Coast Entertainment Corp.*[277]): Plaintiff Brookfield Communications is an entertainment-industry information provider incorporated in the United States. It owns the US trademark registration MOVIEBUFF. Defendant West Coast GmbH is a German-based company and provides internet services, including downloads and streaming of movies and music. West Coast has included "moviebuff" and similar terms in the metatags of its movie-search websites, which are offered in both English and German.

Solution: Use of the MOVIEBUFF trademark in metatags may not create *actual* confusion among the visitors of West Coast's websites, as long as these sites prominently display West Coast's own trademarks.[278] Under German law, however, unauthorized use of a competitor's trademark in metatags may constitute an infringement without regard to actual confusion. Even such hidden use of the trademark may suffice if it is used to improperly redirect internet searches to the company's own website.[279] Yet if the plaintiff has no trademark rights in Germany, no claim exists. Under the rule of the *lex loci protectionis*, however, the decision maker must also look at other jurisdictions that could be affected (at least if indicated by the plaintiff). Following the rules on initial-interest confusion in US doctrine, use of the term "moviebuff" in metatags will divert potential customers to West Coast's website. West Coast thereby "improperly benefits from the goodwill that Brookfield developed in its

[275] In addition, of course, the decisionmaker will have to analyze issues of *de minimis* limitation. *See supra* p. 507 *et seq.*

[276] For the substantive law policies, *see supra* p. 353 *et seq.*

[277] *Brookfield Communications, Inc. v. West Coast Entertainment Corp.*, 174 F.3d 1036 (9th Cir. 1999).

[278] *See id.* at 1062.

[279] *See, e.g.*, BGH 2007 GRUR 65 para. 17—*Impuls* (18 May 2006); BGH 2010 GRUR 835 para. 25—*POWER BALL* (4 February 2010).

mark."[280] Considering this specific goodwill-centered policy in American trademark law—and disregarding the lack of actual confusion[281]—relevant effects may be found in the United States. Accordingly, at least with respect to the requirement of "effects on US commerce," Lanham Act subject-matter jurisdiction exists.[282]

On the contrary, if it is impact on the consumer's decision-making process that is conceived of as the only element of impropriety (notably in terms of increasing search costs), a structurally different conflicts rule applies. This is usually the case when so-called reorientation or switching costs for the consumer are large.[283] These scenarios must be treated under the general conflicts rule for the manipulation of market information.[284]

Example[285]: Acme GmbH, incorporated in Germany, runs food restaurants A-Burgers along the German and French highways. Along the French side of a highway, it erects a billboard that reads, "A-Burgers—next exit, 10 kilometers (across the French border)—everything 50% off." When automobilists leave the highway and drive into the German countryside, however, they learn that the discount period is over. "The billboard," as they are told by an employee, "has been outdated since last year—but it still boosts our sales. Isn't that great!" Most of the misdirected customers, although frustrated by the sham, shy away from a new search for a burger place and ultimately eat at A-Burgers (and pay full prices).

In these cases, choice of law must take into account that the consumers' decision making has been immediately affected with the initial confusion. The manipulation—that is, misinformation—may not have endured until the point of actual transaction. Yet the decision-making process has still been distorted by means of raising the costs of alternative transacting (i.e., the additional effort of searching anew). In this light, it is clear that the applicable law will have to be determined in accordance with the place(s) where alternative transactions existed.

280 *See Brookfield Communications, Inc. v. West Coast Entertainment Corp.*, 174 F.3d 1036, 1062 (9th Cir. 1999).

281 *See, e.g., Bihari v. Gross*, 119 F.Supp.2d 309, 319–320 (including fn. 15) (S.D.N.Y. 2000). For an extensive critique, *see* Stacey L. Dogan & Mark A. Lemley, *Trademarks and Consumer Search Costs on the Internet*, 41 Hous. L. Rev. 777, 815 *et seq.* (2004).

282 Whether the scope of US law should then be limited with respect to a possible *de minimis* quantity of effects under a comity-based rule is a different issue. *See supra* p. 507 *et seq.*

283 For the substantive law policies, *see supra* p. 353 *et seq.*

284 *See supra* p. 494 *et seq.*

285 Compare nos. 5 and 6 of annex I of Directive 2005/29/EC of the European Parliament and of the Council of 11 May 2005, concerning unfair business-to-consumer commercial practices in the internal market and amending Council Directive 84/450/EEC, Directives 97/7/EC, 98/27/EC and 2002/65/EC of the European Parliament and of the Council and Regulation (EC) No 2006/2004 of the European Parliament and of the Council ("Unfair Commercial Practices Directive"), O.J. EU (11 June 2005), L 149/22.

Solution: The detour forced upon the consumer can lead to a transaction that is different from what the consumer would have decided without manipulation. The consumer may have been aware of the scam at the time of transacting, but reorientation or switching costs were too large to make it reasonable to start a new search. Depending on where the misdirected consumers had alternatives, German and/or French law applies.

Finally, for the category of postsale confusion, choice of law also requires a differentiation. In all subcategories of postsale confusion, the trademark owner's goodwill as market information capital must be protected against deterioration.[286] The place where a trademark owner's market information capital exists and will (or may) be damaged determines the applicable law. Again, the place of conduct and the place of relevant effects can diverge. Even though the sale of an improperly branded product may occur abroad, its trademark-impairing effects can still occur, after the point of sale, in domestic territory.

Example (*Steele v. Bulova Watch Co.*[287]): The defendant manufactures and sells wristwatches in Mexico, where he also stamps the watches with the plaintiff's trademark, Bulova. These watches are mostly purchased by American tourists and ultimately "filter" into Texas and other US states. There, the plaintiff's contract dealers are confronted with customers' complaints of low quality.

Solution: The defendant's conduct—even though carried out exclusively on Mexican territory—creates the risk of deteriorating the plaintiff's US-based goodwill. Hence, effects on trademark goodwill occur mainly in the United States. Accordingly, US trademark law applies.[288]

B Product Imitation

As we have seen, the consumer's referee function does not necessarily stand at the center of protection with regard to the prevention of improper product imitation.[289] Before I address the implications of substantive law policies, however, I must clarify one aspect. The scholarly debate sometimes centers on the question whether to apply an unfair competition conflicts rule or to follow the *lex loci protectionis* principle. While the practical results are largely the same, a difference exists at the doctrinal level. The prevention of unfair product imitation may be related to intellectual property rights protection, particularly to the protection of trademarks and design rights. Accordingly, despite the

286 *See supra* p. 353 *et seq.* 287 *Steele v. Bulova Watch Co.*, 344 U.S. 280 (1952).

288 For the *Bulova* test and the US trademark conflicts doctrine in practice, *see supra* p. 159 *et seq.*

289 *See supra* p. 370 *et seq.*

fact that no formally state-granted rights exist, it may not be too far-fetched to suggest that the *lex loci protectionis* should apply.[290] The contrary position follows a characterization as unfair competition and accordingly contends that the law at the place of the sales market should govern.[291] This is the place where the original product and its imitation can be found to be in competition.[292] An effects-based approach helps avoid both approaches' inherent defect of conduct foundation. The analysis differs with respect to the substantive law policy at issue. Two cases must be distinguished.

Example (variation of BGH *Rillenkoffer* case[293]): R-Bag GmbH manufactures exquisite luggage and travel accessories. Among its products is a pilot case made from aluminum. This case is well known for its outer appearance, notably the characteristic striation pattern. R-Bag GmbH sells the case in countries across Europe, through a network of exclusive dealers. It does not sell in Switzerland, though. I-Bag GmbH, a start-up incorporated in Switzerland, manufactures

[290] *See, e.g.*, Alois Troller, *Unfair Competition (ch. 34)*, no. 34–14, in *International Encyclopedia of Comparative Law, vol. III, Private International Law* (Kurt Lipstein et al. eds., 1980); Rolf Sack, *Die kollisions- und wettbewerbsrechtliche Beurteilung grenzüberschreitender Werbe- und Absatztätigkeit nach deutschem Recht*, 1988 GRUR Int. 320, 334–335; Gerhard Schricker, in *Großkommentar—UWG: Gesetz gegen den unlauteren Wettbewerb, vol. I*, Einl. para. F 200 (Rainer Jacobs et al. eds., 1994); Rainer Hausmann & Eva Inés Obergfell, in *Lauterkeitsrecht: Kommentar zum Gesetz gegen den unlauteren Wettbewerb (UWG), vol. I*, Einleitung I para. 339 (Karl-Heinz Fezer ed., 2nd edn., 2010).

[291] *See, e.g.*, Matthias Leistner, *Unfair Competition Law Protection Against Imitations: A Hybrid under the Future Art. 5 Rome II Regulation?*, 129, 145, 153, in *Intellectual Property in the Conflict of Laws* (Jürgen Basedow et al. eds., 2005); Rolf Sack, *Internationales Lauterkeitsrecht nach der Rom-II-VO*, 2008 WRP 845, 859; Karl-Heinz Fezer & Stefan Koos, in *Staudingers Kommentar zum Bürgerlichen Gesetzbuch: Internationales Wirtschaftsrecht*, Internationales Wettbewerbsprivatrecht para. 407 and 780 (15th edn., 2010); Josef Drexl, in *Münchener Kommentar zum Bürgerlichen Gesetzbuch, vol. XI*, IntLautR para. 123 and 165 (Franz Jürgen Säcker et al. eds., 6th edn., 2015); Peter Mankowski, in *Münchener Kommentar zum Lauterkeitsrecht, vol. I*, IntWettbR para. 270 (Peter W. Heermann et al. eds., 2nd edn., 2014); for the English tort of passing off *see, e.g.*, Christopher Wadlow, *The new private international law of unfair competition and the "Rome II" Regulation*, 11 J. Intell. Prop. L. & Pract. 789, 792 (2009). As proponents of the *lex loci protectionis* admit, however, the practical results will not differ much since the sales market usually serves as the point of attachment. *See, e.g.*, Rainer Hausmann & Eva Inés Obergfell, in *Lauterkeitsrecht: Kommentar zum Gesetz gegen den unlauteren Wettbewerb (UWG), vol. I*, Einleitung I para. 341 (Karl-Heinz Fezer ed., 2nd edn., 2010); Martin Illmer, in *Rome II Regulation*, Art. 6 para. 18 (Peter Huber ed., 2011).

[292] On the sales market, all relevant interests are deemed to be affected. *See, e.g.*, BGH 1962 GRUR 243 *et seq.*—*Kindersaugflaschen* (30 June 1961); *see also* Rolf Sack, *Internationales Lauterkeitsrecht nach der Rom-II-VO*, 2008 WRP 845, 859; Peter Mankowski, in *Münchener Kommentar zum Lauterkeitsrecht, vol. I*, IntWettbR para. 270 (Peter W. Heermann et al. eds., 2nd edn., 2014).

[293] BGH 2008 GRUR 793—*Rillenkoffer* (30 April 2008).

medium-priced luggage, which it sells in its only store, at the Zurich airport. For customers who cannot take the purchase with them, the store offers delivery abroad. When I-Bag GmbH starts to sell an almost identical replica of the original aluminum striation case, R-Bag GmbH sues in Germany.

With respect to cases of consumer deception and confusion, regardless of whether protecting consumer decision making is to be seen as the primary subject matter of protection, the plaintiff's quasi IP right will be invaded by manipulation of the consumer's mind. Here as well, in terms of the English passing-off doctrine, misrepresentation is the most significant element.[294] Despite what is argued by dominant opinion, however, it is not the sales market of the *imitation* that matters.[295] Instead, the place of alternatives—in other words, where the *original* has been or is being offered—will serve as the point of attachment. In the example case, even though the imitation is marketed in Switzerland, the court should also consider applying German or other European countries' unfair competition laws since the sale of the imitation to travelers from abroad also affects the original's European consumer base.

The issue appears similarly straightforward for cases of improper exploitation and impairment of a product's reputation or goodwill.[296] Scholarly commentary sweepingly characterizes cases of exploitation as an invasion of the competitor's interests and, accordingly, calls for the law of the sales market of the imitation (*Absatzmarkt*) to be applied. This is deemed to be the place of confusion, reputational exploitation, and impact on the original producer's sales.[297] Even though, in practice, the

[294] *See supra* p. 549–550.

[295] *But see, e.g.*, BGH 1962 GRUR 243 *et seq.—Kindersaugflaschen* (30 June 1961); OLG Koblenz 1993 GRUR 763, 764—*Kfz-Reinigungsmittel* (25 February 1993); Alexander Thünken, *Multi-state advertising over the Internet and the private international law of unfair competition*, 51 I.C.L.Q. 909, 919 (2002); Matthias Leistner, *Unfair Competition Law Protection against Imitations: A Hybrid under the Future Art. 5 Rome II Regulation?*, 129, 145, 153, in *Intellectual Property in the Conflict of Laws* (Jürgen Basedow et al. eds., 2005); James J. Fawcett & Paul Torremans, *Intellectual Property and Private International Law* para. 16.22 (2nd edn., 2011); Richard Plender & Michael Wilderspin, *The European Private International Law of Obligations* para. 20–034 (4th edn., 2015); Josef Drexl, in *Münchener Kommentar zum Bürgerlichen Gesetzbuch, vol. XI*, IntLautR para. 164 (Franz Jürgen Säcker et al. eds., 6th edn., 2015).

[296] *See, e.g.*, Section 4 no. 3 lit. b German Unfair Competition Act (UWG).

[297] *See, e.g.*, Karl Kreuzer, in *Münchener Kommentar zum Bürgerlichen Gesetzbuch, vol. X*, Art. 38 EGBGB para. 245 (Kurt Rebmann & Jürgen Säcker eds., 3rd edn., 1998); Rainer Hausmann & Eva Inés Obergfell, in *Lauterkeitsrecht: Kommentar zum Gesetz gegen den unlauteren Wettbewerb (UWG), vol. I*, Einleitung I para. 341 (Karl-Heinz Fezer ed., 2nd edn., 2010); Peter Mankowski, in *Münchener Kommentar zum Lauterkeitsrecht, vol. I*, IntWettbR para. 274 (Peter W. Heermann et al. eds., 2nd edn., 2014) ("Eine Rufausbeutung wird ebenfalls auf dem Markt relevant, auf welchem die Waren abgesetzt werden sollen, bei deren Vermarktung beabsichtigt ist, sich an den guten Ruf oder den guten Namen eines Konkurrenten anzulehnen. Dort materialisieren sich die

"sales market" may often be where choice of law has to be attached, doctrinal intricacies of what is being protected make a more precise determination necessary. Most importantly, this scenario will often *not* entail an element of "competition" among the parties. As illustrated by, for instance, the German *Rolex* case and the US *Ferrari* doctrine, a junior party may be trying to benefit from utilizing the senior party's brand or other indication of source. The junior party's products, however, will not be seen as an alternative for the consumer.

Example (variation of BGH *Rolex* case[298]): A German supermarket chain sells wristwatches that imitate the design of a famous Swiss timepiece. The sales price of the "imitation" is only 1% of the Swiss original's price. Since Swiss customers are increasingly frequenting the chain's German supermarkets in the South of Germany, the original's manufacturer is concerned about the potential spill of cheap imitations into Switzerland and the deterioration of its timepieces' air of exclusivity and prestige.

For want of actual competition, this scenario implies a different determination of the connecting factor. The issue is not consumer confusion or deception; accordingly, there is no attachment to the place of alternative transactions. Instead, it is the *situs* of the plaintiff's goodwill that matters for choice-of-law determination. This is the place where the original product is marketed—and while this can be the place where the imitation is offered, it not need be. As *Rolex* (similar to *Ferrari* in the United States) implies, the factor that prevails in cases where the original's reputation and scarcity are to be protected is not transacting or transaction-related confusion; it is damage to market information capital in the sense of surplus goodwill. In the example case, therefore, Swiss law will apply.[299]

C The Antitrust Concurrence

Example (variation of BGH *20 Minuten Köln* case[300]): Acme SARL, a large French publisher, offers a free weekly German-language magazine at all kiosks, petrol stations, and other sales locations in the border region with Germany. B-News GmbH, a local newspaper publisher in the city of Freiburg (near the French border), complains that the free offer by Acme SARL will eventually deteriorate its sales and ultimately push its newspaper "out of the market."

Irreführungsmomente, dort entsteht die Täuschungsgefahr, dort werden die Absatz- und Umsatzchancen desjenigen betroffen, dessen Ruf ausgebeutet wird.").

298 BGH 1985 GRUR 876—*Tchibo/Rolex* (8 November 1984).

299 Again, this does not imply that there is no restriction under a comity-based *de minimis* rule. *See supra* p. 507 *et seq.*

300 BGH 2004 GRUR 602—*20 Minuten Köln* (20 November 2003).

For certain situations of competitive conduct, a concurrent application of unfair competition and antitrust law is debated. Examples include boycotting a competitor, selling below the cost of production, and market disruption and disturbance (*Marktbehinderung* and *Marktstörung*).[301] All of these scenarios bear a general risk of distorting competition.[302] While cases of boycotting may be understood to also target an individual competitor, in the other cases, no obvious individualized focus on competitive unfairness exists.[303] In this light, application of a multilateral antitrust effects principle—as implemented in article 6(3) of Rome II—seems to suggest itself. According to scholarly commentary, under such a rule, national law should apply to effects within the national market, while foreign law should apply if a foreign market has been affected.[304] Yet Peter Mankowski has criticized this approach. As he posits, a genuine marketplace effects rule will provide the same results. The specific policy of protecting fair competition as an institution (as implemented in antitrust law) should not disguise the fact that market disruption and distortion—when effectuated through unfair competitive conduct—would also (and in particular) affect competitors' interests, notably through an intentional attack on their market positions.[305] While the practical results under both approaches may not differ too much, structural differences exist. Again, looking at the core of unfair competition policies helps resolve the issue. What matters is the impact on the consumer's decision-making process.

[301] *See, e.g.*, Michael Hellner, *Unfair Competition and Acts Restricting Free Competition—A Commentary on Article 6 of the Rome II Regulation*, 9 Yearb. P.I.L. 49, 69 (2007); Josef Drexl, in *Münchener Kommentar zum Bürgerlichen Gesetzbuch, vol. XI*, IntLautR para. 132 (Franz Jürgen Säcker et al. eds., 6th edn., 2015). *But cf.* Stéphanie Francq & Wolfgang Wurmnest, *International Antitrust Claims under the Rome II Regulation*, 91, 104 *et seq.*, in *International Antitrust Litigation—Conflicts of Laws and Coordination* (Jürgen Basedow et al. eds., 2012) (looking at the "main focus" if claims are based on rules that serve both fields' policies).

[302] *See* BGH 2004 GRUR 602, 603—*20 Minuten Köln* (20 November 2003).

[303] Karl-Heinz Fezer & Stefan Koos, in *Staudingers Kommentar zum Bürgerlichen Gesetzbuch: Internationales Wirtschaftsrecht*, Internationales Wettbewerbsprivatrecht para. 747–748 (15th edn., 2010).

[304] *See, e.g.*, Gerhard Schricker, in *Großkommentar—UWG: Gesetz gegen den unlauteren Wettbewerb, vol. I*, Einl para. F 209–210 (Rainer Jacobs et al. eds., 1994); Rolf Sack, *Internationales Lauterkeitsrecht nach der Rom-II-VO*, 2008 WRP 845, 850; Karl-Heinz Fezer & Stefan Koos, in *Staudingers Kommentar zum Bürgerlichen Gesetzbuch: Internationales Wirtschaftsrecht*, Internationales Wettbewerbsprivatrecht para. 749 (15th edn., 2010); for a distinction between sale-below-cost cases and boycott cases, *see* Rainer Hausmann & Eva Inés Obergfell, in *Lauterkeitsrecht: Kommentar zum Gesetz gegen den unlauteren Wettbewerb (UWG), vol. I*, Einleitung I para. 317 *et seq.* (Karl-Heinz Fezer ed., 2nd edn., 2010).

[305] Peter Mankowski, in *Münchener Kommentar zum Lauterkeitsrecht, vol. I*, IntWettbR para. 275–276 (Peter W. Heermann et al. eds., 2nd edn., 2014).

Solution: As the example of selling below production costs (or giving away for free) illustrates, such conduct will not lead to an unduly influenced consumer decision. After all, the consumer will execute an economically rational transaction, buying the cheapest or accepting a costless product. It is the subsequent effect on market conditions that lawmakers may intend to prevent. This, however, is a genuine antitrust concern. As such, it must also be treated under a genuine antitrust conflicts rule.

D Breach of Statutory Duties as Unfair Competition

Example (taken from BGH *Rotpreis-Revolution*[306]): Acme GmbH runs a retail store in Luxembourg, near the border with Germany. It advertises a "special sales deal" in the daily newspaper of Trier, a nearby German city where many of its customers come from. This sales deal will take place on a Sunday. Unlike in Luxembourg, in Germany stores are generally prohibited from opening on Sundays and public holidays. A breach of such shopping-hours regulations is qualified as unfair competition under section 3a of the German Unfair Competition Act.

As explained in my analysis of substantive law policies, the category of statutory breach is structurally foreign to the field of trademark and unfair competition law. It does not directly concern the market information infrastructure.[307] Nonetheless, a market-oriented conflicts approach has been suggested. In scholarly literature, for instance, it is contended that cases of breach should be characterized in accordance with the respective interests affected. Hence, the market effects rule would apply whenever the interests of consumers or the public have been affected by a breach of a statutory duty.[308] Similarly, the market where a competitor attains a competitive advantage (by the breach) has been deemed the relevant point of attachment.[309]

On the basis of a reconceptualized approach, a different focus is indicated. As demonstrated earlier, the prerequisite for unfair competition within this category is that a statutory norm be breached.[310] The breach per se, however, neither implies nor requires an impact on market information and consumer decision making; take, for instance,

[306] BGH 2005 GRUR Int. 338, 339—*Rotpreis-Revolution* (13 May 2004).

[307] *See supra* p. 374–375.

[308] *See, e.g.*, Ansgar Ohly, in Ansgar Ohly & Olaf Sosnitza, *Gesetz gegen den unlauteren Wettbewerb mit Preisangabenverordnung (UWG)*, Einf B para. 15 (5th edn., 2010); *but* different in 6th edn. (2014) at Einf B para. 17.

[309] *See, e.g.*, Jochen Glöckner, in *Gesetz gegen den unlauteren Wettbewerb (UWG)*, UWG Einl C para. 183 (Henning Harte-Bavendamm & Frauke Henning-Bodewig eds., 3rd edn., 2013); Rainer Hausmann & Eva Inés Obergfell, in *Lauterkeitsrecht: Kommentar zum Gesetz gegen den unlauteren Wettbewerb (UWG), vol. I*, Einleitung I para. 331 *et seq.* (Karl-Heinz Fezer ed., 2nd edn., 2010).

[310] *See supra* p. 375.

the bribery of a competitor's employees. It is not effects on the market mechanism that determine whether a breach is found to be unfair; it is the breach as such that constitutes the requirement for unfairness. Consequently, the applicable regime will have to be determined by the plaintiff's indication. She must plead that a cause of action exists under a certain law. Within this framework, the judge must first inquire whether the applicable law acknowledges a claim for breach of statutory duties at all, and—if this is the case—resolve the issue of an actual statutory breach.[311] Depending on the norm that is claimed to have been breached, this may or may not require territorial conduct on behalf of the defendant.

Solution: The breach of a shopping-hours regulation may constitute the basis for an unfair competition claim under German law. A German-based competitor may thus claim unfair competitive conduct and indicate the application of German law. Yet Acme GmbH's conduct *in Luxembourg* cannot breach the local regulation *in Germany*. Nor can the nonexistent breach trigger the application of an unfair competition cause of action under the German Unfair Competition Act.

III Competitor-Related and Bilateral Commercial Torts

If unfair competitive conduct directly targets a specific competitor, conflicts determination may be more complicated. In this case, individual rights—in addition to or instead of third-party consumer interests or the public—will be affected. This special category of unfair competition has been defined (and the European Commission has acknowledged its categorization for Rome II) as including defamation, bribery and corruption, theft and use of competitors' trade secrets (industrial espionage), the improper approaching or enticing away of foreign staff, and the inducing of a breach of contract.[312] Since conduct in these

[311] This was the court's implicit choice-of-law technique in the *Kauf im Ausland* decision (*see supra* p. 539–541). Since it denied the application of German unfair competition law, the issue of whether a statutory norm had been breached was obsolete. *See also* BGH 1980 GRUR 858, 860—*Asbestimporte* (9 May 1980); BGH 1987 GRUR 172, 174—*Unternehmensberatungsgesellschaft I* (9 October 1986) ("[K]ann jedoch die klagende Partei ihre Ansprüche aus der Rechtsordnung herleiten, die sie dafür am geeignetsten hält .... Insoweit hat sich die Kl., wie ihr Klagevortrag ergibt, im Streitfall für die Anwendung deutschen Rechts entschieden."); BGH 2005 GRUR Int. 338, 339—*Rotpreis-Revolution* (13 May 2004); *see also* Peter Mankowski, in *Münchener Kommentar zum Lauterkeitsrecht, vol. I,* IntWettbR para. 279 (Peter W. Heermann et al. eds., 2nd edn., 2014).

[312] *See, e.g.*, Karl F. Kreuzer, *Wettbewerbsverstöße und Beeinträchtigung geschäftlicher Interessen (einschl. der Verletzung kartellrechtlicher Vorschriften)*, 232, 281–282, in *Vorschläge und Gutachten zur Reform des deutschen internationalen Privatrechts der außervertraglichen Schuldverhältnisse, vorgelegt im Auftrag der Zweiten Kommission des*

cases is targeted toward a specific competitor, the purpose of individual rights protection seems to suggest the application of the *lex loci delicti commissi*. Both the place of conduct and the seat of the victim-competitor have accordingly been identified as possible points of attachment.[313] Recourse to tort conflicts principles is also what the Rome II Regulation has implemented in its article 6(2): "Where an act of unfair competition affects exclusively the interests of a specific competitor, Article 4 shall apply." As we have seen, however, practical problems exist with the terminology and the concept of bilateral situations in competition in general.[314] While some instances of competitive conduct may be easily categorized as either market related or primarily competitor related, certain cases require more extensive debate. To summarize: at the center of all problems is the fact that almost all conduct classified as "bilateral" can be said to concurrently also affect consumer interests and the public's interest in unhindered competition. There is seldom such a thing as competitive conduct that has no effects on the market at all. Indeed, the notion of "competitive conduct" implies that there must be at least some contact with the market, as well as some effect—at least sooner or later. Concepts of competitor relatedness, market impact, or effects directness, therefore, are not helpful. What is required, again, is a look at the triangular structure of the market mechanism. Competition unravels between individuals on the basis of consumer decision making and transacting (or nontransacting). This is the domain of the marketplace effects rule. Bilateral torts, by contrast, do not target the consumer directly; there is no attempt to influence decision making or its implementation. A different sphere is thus being invaded—the victim-competitor's assets. Of course, such an impact may also immediately affect the victim-competitor's market activities—for example, by impinging on her capacity to compete (especially in cases of

Deutschen Rates für internationales Privatrecht (Ernst von Caemmerer ed., 1983); Gerhard Schricker, in *Großkommentar—UWG: Gesetz gegen den unlauteren Wettbewerb, vol. I*, Einl para. F 212–214 (Rainer Jacobs et al. eds., 1994); Commission of the European Communities, *Proposal for a Regulation of the European Parliament and the Council on the Law Applicable to Non-Contractual Obligations ("Rome II")*, Brussels, 22 July 2003, COM(2003) 427 final, 2003/0168 (COD), 16.

313 *See, e.g.*, Helmut Wirner, *Wettbewerbsrecht und internationales Privatrecht* 116 (1960); Wilhelm Gloede, *Der deutsche Außenhandel und seine wettbewerbsrechtliche Beurteilung nach deutschem internationalem Privatrecht*, 1960 GRUR 464, 471; Erwin Deutsch, *Wettbewerbstatbestände mit Auslandsbeziehung* 65–66 (1962); Gerhard Schricker, in *Großkommentar—UWG: Gesetz gegen den unlauteren Wettbewerb, vol. I*, Einl para. F 213 (Rainer Jacobs et al. eds., 1994); Stephan Briem, *Internationales und Europäisches Wettbewerbsrecht und Kennzeichenrecht* 64 *et seq.* (1995); Rolf Sack, *Das internationale Wettbewerbs- und Immaterialgüterrecht nach der EGBGB-Novelle*, 2000 WRP 269, 274.

314 *See supra* p. 214 *et seq.*

actual hindrance). The invasion, however, will not be undertaken by means of the market mechanism. Thus, the justification for a different attachment for bilateral situations is not the closer proximity to general torts or delicts, or the stronger focus on individual rights protection. What is amiss in these situations is an involvement of the market mechanism by means of a direct targeting of consumer decision making.

In this light, the examples cited in the European Commission's explanation reveal a number of scenarios that require clarification:

Example: While on a business trip in India, Alice, an English producer of technical equipment, writes a letter to one of her customers in Germany. The letter is concerned primarily with a sales offer to the customer. However, it also contains a paragraph on Alice's strongest competitor, the French producer Claire. Alice "discloses" to her customer that Claire is close to being declared bankrupt (which is actually not true).

Defamation, the spreading of malicious falsehoods, and calls for boycotting a market participant will usually directly affect market information transmission.[315] It is not only the defamed competitor's or boycotted participant's individual interest at stake but also the public's interest in unhindered competition by availability of unmanipulated information.[316]

[315] The exclusion of article 1 (g) Rome II Regulation will not apply if acts are undertaken in a commercial and business context. *See, e.g.*, James J. Fawcett & Paul Torremans, *Intellectual Property and Private International Law* para. 16.69 and 16.89 (2nd edn., 2011); Jochen Glöckner, in *Gesetz gegen den unlauteren Wettbewerb (UWG)*, UWG Einl C para. 85 (Henning Harte-Bavendamm & Frauke Henning-Bodewig eds., 3rd edn., 2013).

[316] *See, e.g.*, BGH 2010 GRUR 847, 849—*Ausschreibung in Bulgarien* (11 February 2010). For scholarly commentary, *see, e.g.*, Nina Dethloff, *Europäisierung des Wettbewerbsrechts—Einfluss des europäischen Rechts auf das Sach- und Kollisionsrecht des unlauteren Wettbewerbs* 76 (2001); Rolf Sack, *Internationales Lauterkeitsrecht nach der Rom-II-VO*, 2008 WRP 845, 850; Josef Drexl, in *Münchener Kommentar zum Bürgerlichen Gesetzbuch, vol. XI*, IntLautR para. 148 and 156 (Franz Jürgen Säcker et al. eds., 6th edn., 2015); Peter Mankowski, in *Münchener Kommentar zum Lauterkeitsrecht, vol. I*, IntWettbR para. 290 (Peter W. Heermann et al. eds., 2nd edn., 2014); Matthias Weller, in *Nomos-Kommentar-BGB, Rom-Verordnungen, vol. VI*, Art. 6 Rom II para. 13 (Rainer Hüßtege & Heinz-Peter Mansel eds., 2014); Martin Illmer, in *Rome II Regulation*, Art. 6 para. 3 (Peter Huber ed., 2011); Susanne Augenhofer, in *Rome Regulations*, Art. 6 para. 27 (Gralf-Peter Calliess ed., 2nd edn., 2015); for the contrary opinion, *see* Cheshire, North & Fawcett, *Private International Law* 810 (Sir Peter North consult. ed., 14th edn., 2008); James J. Fawcett & Paul Torremans, *Intellectual Property and Private International Law* para. 16.71 (2nd edn., 2011); Jochen Glöckner, in *Gesetz gegen den unlauteren Wettbewerb (UWG)*, UWG Einl C para. 177 (Henning Harte-Bavendamm & Frauke Henning-Bodewig eds., 3rd edn., 2013); Wolfgang Wurmnest, in *juris-Praxiskommentar zum BGB*, Art. 6 Rom II para. 19 and 26 (Markus Würdinger ed., 7th edn., 2014); Karsten Thorn, in *Palandt: Kommentar zum Bürgerlichen Gesetzbuch mit Nebengesetzen*, Art. 6 Rom II para. 9 (75th edn., 2016).

These torts, therefore, are not isolated from the consumer's decision making. Consequently, at the conflicts level, the marketplace principle governs.[317] Under a rule of alternatives, however, this must not correspond to the consumer's residence or (more generally) the location of the other side of the market (*Marktgegenseite*).[318]

Similarly, the enticing away of a competitor's personnel or agents will immediately affect the market—at least with respect to the market for employees and employers. This is the only direct effect, but it suffices to preclude application of article 6(2) of Rome II.[319]

Example (continued): On the same business trip, Alice visits a job fair at Bangalore University, where she has several job talks with local graduates. She learns that they have all signed contracts with her English competitor Best Ltd. to work in its Indian branch in Mumbai. Alice successfully offers several of these employees a "financial incentive" to breach their contract and start working for her Indian subsidiary instead.

Of course, the improper poaching of foreign employees will seldom directly affect markets at the next level of production.[320] There may be

[317] *See also* BGH 2014 GRUR 601, 640—*Englischsprachige Pressemitteilung* (12 December 2013).

[318] *See supra* p. 494–497. *But see, e.g.*, Rolf Sack, *Die kollisions- und wettbewerbsrechtliche Beurteilung grenzüberschreitender Werbe- und Absatztätigkeit nach deutschem Recht*, 1988 GRUR Int. 320, 330; Peter Mankowski, in *Münchener Kommentar zum Lauterkeitsrecht, vol. I*, IntWettbR para. 343 (Peter W. Heermann et al. eds., 2nd edn., 2014).

[319] For a critique, *see supra* p. 214 *et seq*. *But cf.* Commission of the European Communities, *Proposal for a Regulation of the European Parliament and the Council on the Law Applicable to Non-Contractual Obligations ("Rome II")*, Brussels, 22 July 2003, COM(2003) 427 final, 2003/0168 (COD), 16 (for application of tort conflicts law, art. 6(2) Rome II); *further also, e.g.*, Stephan Briem, *Internationales und Europäisches Wettbewerbsrecht und Kennzeichenrecht* 70–71 (1995); Nina Dethloff, *Europäisierung des Wettbewerbsrechts—Einfluss des europäischen Rechts auf das Sach- und Kollisionsrecht des unlauteren Wettbewerbs* 75 (2001); Matthias Leistner, *Unfair Competition Law Protection Against Imitations: A Hybrid under the Future Art. 5 Rome II Regulation?*, 129, 145, in *Intellectual Property in the Conflict of Laws* (Jürgen Basedow et al. eds., 2005); Peter Mankowski, in *Münchener Kommentar zum Lauterkeitsrecht, vol. I*, IntWettbR para. 334–336 (Peter W. Heermann et al. eds., 2nd edn., 2014); Cheshire, North & Fawcett, *Private International Law* 810 (Sir Peter North consult. ed., 14th edn., 2008); Timo Rosenkranz & Eva Rohde, *The Law Applicable to Non-contractual Obligations Arising out of Acts of Unfair Competition and Acts Restricting Free Competition under Article 6 Rome II Regulation*, 26 NIPR 435, 438 (2008); Thomas Kadner Graziano, *Das auf außervertragliche Schuldverhältnisse anzuwendende Recht nach Inkrafttreten der Rom II-Verordnung*, 73 RabelsZ 1, 56 (2009); Rolf Sack, *Art. 6 Abs. 2 Rom-II-VO und „bilaterales" unlauteres Wettbewerbsverhalten*, 2012 GRUR Int. 601, 606.

[320] *But cf.* Michael Hellner, *Unfair Competition and Acts Restricting Free Competition—A Commentary on Article 6 of the Rome II Regulation*, 9 Yearb. P.I.L. 49, 57 (2007) (finding effects in the state where the enticing away has occurred, as well as effects on competitive relations in a *different* market in which both tortfeasor and victim-competitor operate).

reverberations on the product market over time, due to the improper enticing. Yet these are indirect effects. Effects on the labor market, by contrast, are direct. Whether poaching is accompanied by deception, bribery, or other forms of undue influence does not matter. In each case, the triangular structure of competitor-employee relations parallels the competitor-consumer relationship. In the example case, therefore, Indian unfair competition law, not the law of the victim-competitor's seat, will apply. On the same basis, enticing a competitor's customers to breach their contracts will affect the market.[321] It is thus the marketplace rule modified as a rule of alternatives that applies.

Example (continued): On the same business trip, Alice learns that a Chinese competitor is close to filing for patent protection with respect to a certain apparatus. Alice has tried to gain patent protection for the same mechanism for some time but has been unsuccessful. By accident, she gets to know a former employee of the Chinese competitor, who discloses the relevant technical information. Back in England, Alice immediately adjusts her production methods to the more cost-efficient innovation. She is thereby able to lower her prices.

The analysis differs with respect to theft of trade secrets. The theft as such may provide a competitive advantage to the thief since competitive superiority usually depends on innovation and know-how.[322] Over time, this advantage will affect the market: cheaper production due to savings in research and development may ultimately increase the thief's market

[321] *See, e.g.*, Nina Dethloff, *Europäisierung des Wettbewerbsrechts—Einfluss des europäischen Rechts auf das Sach- und Kollisionsrecht des unlauteren Wettbewerbs* 75 (2001); Matthias Leistner, *Unfair Competition Law Protection Against Imitations: A Hybrid under the Future Art. 5 Rome II Regulation?*, 129, 145, in *Intellectual Property in the Conflict of Laws* (Jürgen Basedow et al. eds., 2005); Karl-Heinz Fezer & Stefan Koos, in *Staudingers Kommentar zum Bürgerlichen Gesetzbuch: Internationales Wirtschaftsrecht*, Internationales Wettbewerbsprivatrecht para. 656 (15th edn., 2010); Josef Drexl, in *Münchener Kommentar zum Bürgerlichen Gesetzbuch, vol. XI*, IntLautR para. 159 (Franz Jürgen Säcker et al. eds., 6th edn., 2015); *but see* Commission of the European Communities, *Proposal for a Regulation of the European Parliament and the Council on the Law Applicable to Non-Contractual Obligations ("Rome II")*, Brussels, 22 July 2003, COM(2003) 427 final, 2003/0168 (COD), 16; Cheshire, North & Fawcett, *Private International Law* 810 (Sir Peter North consult. ed., 14th edn., 2008); Walter F. Lindacher, *Die internationale Dimension lauterkeitsrechtlicher Unterlassungsansprüche: Marktterritorialität versus Universalität*, 2008 GRUR Int. 453, 457; Thomas Kadner Graziano, *Das auf außervertragliche Schuldverhältnisse anzuwendende Recht nach Inkrafttreten der Rom II-Verordnung*, 73 RabelsZ 1, 56 (2009); Jochen Glöckner, *Der grenzüberschreitende Lauterkeitsprozess nach BGH v. 11.2.2010—Ausschreibung in Bulgarien*, 2011 WRP 137, 142; Rolf Sack, *Art. 6 Abs. 2 Rom-II-VO und „bilaterales" unlauteres Wettbewerbsverhalten*, 2012 GRUR Int. 601, 607.

[322] *See supra* p. 219–220. *See also* WIPO, *Protection against Unfair Competition—Analysis of the Present World Situation*, WIPO Publ. no. 725(E), 49 (1994).

shares. However, this effect is not immediate—in particular, it does not affect consumer decision making.[323] It is a tort on the premarket stage. None of the protective purposes related to market information and consumer decision making are affected. Consequently, traditional tort choice of law rules will determine the applicable regime.[324]

[323] Josef Drexl, in *Münchener Kommentar zum Bürgerlichen Gesetzbuch, vol. XI*, IntLautR para. 157 (Franz Jürgen Säcker et al. eds., 6th edn., 2015); *see also* Christopher Wadlow, *Trade Secrets and the Rome II Regulation on the Law Applicable to Non-Contractual Obligations*, 30 EIPR 309, 310, 312 (2008). *But see, e.g.*, Andrew Dickinson, *The Rome II Regulation: The Law Applicable to Non-Contractual Obligations* para. 6.29 (2008); Richard Plender & Michael Wilderspin, *The European Private International Law of Obligations* para. 20–037 (4th edn., 2015); Rainer Hausmann & Eva Inés Obergfell, in *Lauterkeitsrecht: Kommentar zum Gesetz gegen den unlauteren Wettbewerb (UWG), vol. I*, Einleitung I para. 327 (Karl-Heinz Fezer ed., 2nd edn., 2010); Peter Mankowski, in *Münchener Kommentar zum Lauterkeitsrecht, vol. I*, IntWettbR para. 333 (Peter W. Heermann et al. eds., 2nd edn., 2014).

[324] The same principle applies to the issuance of so-called cease-and-desist letters (founded on an incorrect claim of intellectual property infringement or unfair competition), which is a competitive tort under civil law doctrine. Issuance of the letter will detrimentally affect the competitor-addressee. In this case, there is no impact on consumer decision making. The situation differs, however, if the issuance is effectuated vis-à-vis other market participants, notably the competitor's customers. *See* Nina Dethloff, *Europäisierung des Wettbewerbsrechts—Einfluss des europäischen Rechts auf das Sach- und Kollisionsrecht des unlauteren Wettbewerbs* 75 (2001); Rolf Sack, *Internationales Lauterkeitsrecht nach der Rom-II-VO*, 2008 WRP 845, 851; Rolf Sack, *Art. 6 Abs. 2 Rom-II-VO und „bilaterales" unlauteres Wettbewerbsverhalten*, 2012 GRUR Int. 601, 607; Karl-Heinz Fezer & Stefan Koos, in *Staudingers Kommentar zum Bürgerlichen Gesetzbuch: Internationales Wirtschaftsrecht*, Internationales Wettbewerbsprivatrecht para. 656 (15th edn., 2010); Rainer Hausmann & Eva Inés Obergfell, in *Lauterkeitsrecht: Kommentar zum Gesetz gegen den unlauteren Wettbewerb (UWG), vol. I*, Einleitung I para. 328 (Karl-Heinz Fezer ed., 2nd edn., 2010); Peter Mankowski, in *Münchener Kommentar zum Lauterkeitsrecht, vol. I*, IntWettbR para. 337 *et seq.* (Peter W. Heermann et al. eds., 2nd edn., 2014); Karsten Thorn, in *Palandt: Kommentar zum Bürgerlichen Gesetzbuch mit Nebengesetzen*, Art. 6 Rom II para. 9 (75th edn., 2016); *but see* Josef Drexl, in *Münchener Kommentar zum Bürgerlichen Gesetzbuch, vol. XI*, IntLautR para. 162 (Franz Jürgen Säcker et al. eds., 6th edn., 2015); without differentiation for an application of art. 6(2): Wolfgang Wurmnest, in *juris-Praxiskommentar zum BGB*, Art. 6 Rom II para. 25 (Markus Würdinger ed., 7th edn., 2014).

Appendix A Case Selection and Coding

This appendix describes the data collection process undertaken for the bird's-eye view of US law in chapter 2 and the additional analysis in chapters 5 and 6. It provides details on the case population that I term the *Steele* progeny—that is, US court opinions between 1952 and 2014.

1 Case Selection

The initial group of opinions was retrieved by searches in the Westlaw and LEXIS databases. Searching legal databases does not always uncover all of the disputes or court decisions on a given topic. Most problematic is the fact that not all decisions are published and thus may not be included in the databases. In addition, many disputes are settled prior to the stage of actual decision making. Limitations of this kind are not easily overcome.[1] Yet this should not make an inquiry into the empirical realities futile. On the contrary, as long as one is aware of the limitations, a closer look at "existing" case law can yield results that help critically analyze and challenge a purely doctrinally or economically founded theory of the law. In addition, a more subtle but no less pressing problem is that of the database search query itself. First, there may have been cases where neither the court nor the parties expounded on the problem of extraterritoriality despite the existence of such an issue.[2] A second challenge that must be overcome is the courts' use of terminology. A court may discuss

[1] For a discussion of the inherent defects and biases in database searches, *see, e.g.*, Kimberly D. Krawiec & Kathryn Zeller, *Common-Law Disclosure Duties and the Sin of Omission: Testing the Meta-Theories*, 91 Va. L. Rev. 1795, 1884 *et seq.* (2005); Ahmed E. Taha, *Data and Selection Bias: A Case Study*, 75 UMKC L. Rev. 171 (2006).

[2] Concerning the courts' "blind eye" in respect of extraterritoriality, the final research population actually contains Circuit Court decisions where the lower court did not discuss the issue. *See, e.g.*, *Fun-Damental Too, Ltd. v. Gemmy Industries Corp.*, 111 F.3d 993, 1006 (2nd Cir. 1997). *See also, e.g.*, *Sterling Drug, Inc. v. Bayer AG*, 792 F.Supp. 1357 (S.D.N.Y. 1992); *Scotch Whiskey Ass'n v. Barton Distilling Co.*, 338 F.Supp. 595 (N.D. Ill. 1971); *Scanvec Amiable Limited v. Chang*, No. Civ.A. 02–6950, 2002 WL 32341772 (E.D. Pa., 1 November 2002).

the issue of extraterritoriality without using the word "extraterritorial" or related vocabulary. Even though such a dispute may fit squarely into the research population, a database search that is limited to "extraterritorial" or other iterations would miss it.

As to the first problem, if a court overlooked the issue, or if it was only implicitly handled, the corresponding decision would not appear in the database search results. This deficit, however, is not detrimental to the research results. Again, since my study is intended to analyze how courts have actually handled the issue of Lanham Act subject-matter jurisdiction when confronted with it, my primary interest is in cases where the court has expressly dealt with the problem. With respect to the second problem, I used search methods and terms designed to capture all decisions included in the two databases that made any reference to Lanham Act subject-matter jurisdiction. A search in the Westlaw ALLCASES database with the connectors (trademark! trade-mark! "unfair competition" "lanham act") and (extraterritorial! extra-territorial! bulova) yielded a total of 1,312 decisions. A search in the LEXIS Federal & State Cases, Combined, database (with identical search terms) yielded a total of 1,328 decisions. To produce the relevant population, I combined both lists. Each court opinion—in other words, majority, concurring, or dissenting—contained in this combined list was then reviewed in order to determine its eligibility for the final research population.

As to the time frame occupied by the research population, I excluded cases that were decided prior to the Fifth Circuit's and the Supreme Court's decisions in *Steele v. Bulova*.[3] This limits the population of opinions to those made between January 1952 and November 2014 (the latter date being when I conducted the database research). With respect to the subject matter, I further reduced the number of cases. Not unexpectedly, the search brought up a number of cases where the courts dealt with extraterritoriality in a context different from or unrelated to trademark or unfair competition law. These cases were excluded.[4] Also in this category are decisions not directly dealing with the issue of subject-matter

[3] The District Court's decision in the dispute was not available.

[4] This notably concerned cases on international copyright, patent, securities, or bankruptcy law. *See, e.g., Litecubes, LLC v. Northern Light Products, Inc.*, 523 F.3d 1353 (Fed. Cir. 2008) (copyright); *In re Maxwell Communication Corp. plc*, 186 B.R. 807, 821 (S.D.N.Y. 1995) (bankruptcy); *Oceanic Exploration Co. v. ConocoPhillips, Inc.*, No. 04–332 (EGS), 2006 WL 2711527 (D.D.C., 21 September 2006) (RICO); *U.S. v. International Broth. of Teamsters*, 945 F.Supp. 609 (S.D.N.Y. 1996) (labor law); *Consolidated Gold Fields PLC v. Minorco, S.A.*, 871 F.2d 252 (2nd Cir. 1989) (securities regulation); *Williams & Humbert, Ltd. v. Ruiz-Mateos*, 18 U.S.P.Q.2d (BNA) 2041 (D.D.C. 1991) (expropriation of trademark rights by foreign government).

jurisdiction, but with *forum non conveniens* or personal jurisdiction.[5] A different line of cases in this group concerns the issue of holding a party in contempt for violating court orders—for example, a temporary restraining order or an injunction issued in a preceding trademark dispute.[6] Likewise excluded were scenarios presenting the "reverse, or perhaps the mirror image"[7] of the *Steele* and *Vanity Fair* constellations. In these cases, the court was concerned not with the extraterritorial scope of US laws but with the ability to gain protection for trademarks *within* the United States.[8] In addition, the final population does not include cases brought under the Anticybersquatting Consumer Protection Act (ACPA) concerning domain names and websites registered with a US registrar. Even though these cases sometimes smack of extraterritoriality, they are subject to the special rules of the 1999 ACPA and accordingly irrelevant for my inquiry.[9] Finally, I excluded all cases where the court did not make *substantial* use of the *Bulova*, *Vanity Fair*, or other test factors. I defined "substantial" as including an analysis beyond the mere mention of the issue of subject-matter jurisdiction, the mere citation to the issue, or the mere restatement of another court's finding on the issue.[10]

[5] *See, e.g., Del Monte Fresh Produce Co. v. Dole Food Co., Inc.*, 136 F.Supp.2d 1271, 1278 (S.D. Fla. 2001); *Royal Gist-Brocades N.V. v. Sierra Prods., Ltd.*, No. CIV. A. 97–1147, 1997 WL 792905 (E.D. Pa., 22 December 1999).

[6] *See, e.g., Reebok Intern. Ltd. v. McLaughlin*, 49 F.3d 1387 (9th Cir. 1995); *A.V. by Versace, Inc. v. Gianni Versace, S.p.A.*, 87 F.Supp.2d 281 (S.D.N.Y. 2000). Similarly, decisions affirming a preceding court order or adhering to an original decision with mere repetition of the prior court's reasoning have been excluded. *See, e.g., Tommy Hilfiger Licensing, Inc. v. Costco Companies, Inc.*, No. 99 Civ. 3894(LMM), 2001 WL 262590 (S.D.N.Y., 14 March 2001).

[7] *Buti v. Perosa, S.R.L.*, 139 F.3d 98, 102 (2nd Cir. 1998).

[8] One line of cases where this problem comes up is where a court must decide whether certain activities abroad are sufficient to constitute use in commerce and thereby receive US trademark protection. *See, e.g., Buti v. Perosa, S.R.L.*, 139 F.3d 98, 102 (2nd Cir. 1998); *International Bancorp, LLC v. Societe des Bains de Mer et du Cercle des Etrangers a Monaco*, 329 F.3d 359 (4th Cir. 2003); *General Healthcare Ltd. v. Qashat*, 364 F.3d 332 (1st Cir. 2004).

[9] *See, e.g., Barcelona.com, Inc. v. Excelentisimo Ayuntamiento de Barcelona*, 330 F.3d 617 (4th Cir. 2003); *Harrods Ltd. v. Sixty Internet Domain Names*, 302 F.3d 214 (4th Cir. 2002); *Cable News Network, LP, LLLP v. CNNews.com*, 56 Fed.Appx. 599 (4th Cir. 2003); *America Online, Inc. v. Aol.Org*, 259 F.Supp.2d 449 (E.D. Va. 2003).

[10] *See, e.g., Commodore Import Corp. v. Hiraoka & Co., Ltd.*, 422 F.Supp. 628, 632 (S.D.N.Y. 1976) ("Having found that no violation of [the Lanham Act] exists, I need not reach the jurisdictional defense raised by defendant ... that the extraterritorial application of the Lanham Act is inappropriate as to it [citation to *Vanity Fair*]"). For further examples of insubstantial analysis *see, e.g., Toys "R" Us, Inc. v. Abir*, No. 97 Civ. 8673 (JGK), 1997 WL 857229 (S.D.N.Y., 19 December 1997); *Liberty Toy Co. v. Fred Silber Co.*, 149 F.3d 1183 (6th Cir. 1998); *Kashlan v. TCBY Systems, LLC*, No. 4:06-CV-00497 GTE, 2006 WL 2460616 (E.D. Ark., 23 August 2006); *Kolbe v. Trudel*, 945 F. Supp. 1268 (D. Ariz. 1996); *Internet Billions Domains, Inc. v. Venetian Casino Resort, LLC*, No. 01CV5417, 2002 WL 1610032 (E.D. Pa., 31 May 2002).

2 Coding

After the database search and the manual screening and selection, a list of 140 opinions remained to be analyzed. I started by coding all opinions into an Excel spreadsheet. Once the initial case coding (consisting of three rounds) was complete, all of the coding was double-checked by research assistants who had not been involved in my earlier coding.[11] The coding instrument's categories—as far as the bird's-eye view undertaken here is concerned—were designed to include (1) general information about each opinion, such as its caption, date, and court level, and (2) specific data regarding both the relations between the *Bulova* factors and the courts' adherence to the common law goodwill paradigm. In this regard, the coding categories include, among other things, the result of the court's analysis with respect to the application or nonapplication of the Lanham Act, the parties' nationalities, and the courts' definition and determination of the three *Bulova* (or *Vanity Fair*) factors. In addition, I coded the definition and finding of certain peculiarities, such as "constructive citizenship." With respect to the analysis of the common law goodwill paradigm—notably in the form of the effects factor's subfactors—I coded the different categories of subfactors and whether the courts found the respective subfactors (e.g., consumer confusion) to exist within or outside the United States. The final statistical processing was conducted using Stata 14.1. The coding instrument, Excel spreadsheet, and Stata file are available upon request.

[11] For problems of data collection and bias in general and with respect to the fact that the data were primarily coded by the author, *see, e.g.*, Robert M. Lawless, Jennifer K. Robbenolt & Thomas S. Ulen, *Empirical Methods in Law* ch. 7 and *passim* (2010); Lee Epstein & Gary King, *The Rules of Inference*, 69 U. Chi. L. Rev. 1 (2002).

Appendix B Case list (*Steele* progeny)

A.T. Cross Co. v. Sunil Trading Corp., 467 F.Supp. 47 (S.D.N.Y. 1979).

A.V. by Versace, Inc. v. Gianni Versace, S.p.A., No. 96 Civ. 9721PKLTHK, 98 Civ. 0123PKLTHK, 01 Civ. 9645PKLTHK, 2006 WL 90062 (S.D.N.Y., 12 January 2006).

A.V. by Versace, Inc. v. Gianni Versace, S.p.A., 126 F.Supp.2d 328 (S.D.N.Y. 2001).

ACG Products, Ltd. v. Gu, No. 10-cv-716-wmc, 2011 WL 7748354 (W.D. Wisc., 4 November 2011).

Aerogroup Intern., Inc. v. Marlboro Footworks, Ltd., 152 F.3d 948 (Fed. Cir. 1998).

Aerogroup Intern., Inc. v. Marlboro Footworks, Ltd., No. 97–1125, 97–1281, 97–1282, 1998 U.S. App. LEXIS 7733 (Fed. Cir., 13 April 1998) (Gajarsa, J., dissenting).

Aerogroup Intern., Inc. v. Marlboro Footworks, Ltd., 955 F.Supp. 220 (S.D.N.Y. 1997).

Aerogroup Intern., Inc. v. Marlboro Footworks, Ltd., 956 F.Supp. 427 (S.D.N.Y. 1996).

Air Turbine Technology, Inc. v. Atlas Copco AB, 295 F.Supp.2d 1334 (S.D. Fla. 2003).

Airwair International Ltd. v. Vans, Inc., No. 5:12-CV-05060-EJD, 2013 WL 3786309 (N.D. Cal., 17 July 2013).

Alcar Group, Inc. v. Corporate Performance Systems, Ltd., 109 F.Supp.2d 948 (N.D. Ill. 2000).

American Rice, Inc. v. Arkansas Rice Growers Co-op. Ass'n, 532 F.Supp. 1376 (S.D. Tex. 1982).

American Rice, Inc. v. Arkansas Rice Growers Co-op. Ass'n, 701 F.2d 408 (5th Cir. 1983).

American Rice, Inc. v. Producers Rice Mill, Inc., No. H-05-3227, 2006 WL 1984592 (S.D. Tex., 14 July 2006).

American Rice, Inc. v. Producers Rice Mill, Inc., 518 F.3d 321 (5th Cir. 2008).

American White Cross Laboratories, Inc. v. H.M. Cote, Inc., 556 F.Supp. 753 (S.D.N.Y. 1983).

Amway v. Dyson, No. 1:97-CV-295, 1997 U.S. Dist. LEXIS 15735 (W.D. Mich., 24 September 1997).

Aristocrat Technologies, Inc. v. High Impact Design & Entertainment, 642 F.Supp.2d 1228 (D. Nev. 2009).

Atlantic Richfield Co. v. Arco Globus Intern. Co., Inc., 150 F.3d 189 (2nd Cir. 1998).

Atlantic Richfield Co. v. Arco Globus Intern. Co., No. 95 CIV.6361(JFK), 1997 WL 607488 (S.D.N.Y., 29 May 1997).

Aurora World, Inc. v. Ty, Inc., 719 F.Supp.2d 1115 (C.D. Cal. 2009).

Babbit Electronics, Inc. v. Dynascan Corp., 38 F.3d 1161 (11th Cir. 1994).

Baden Sports, Inc. v. Molten, No. C06-210MJP, 2007 WL 2058673 (W.D. Wash., 16 July 2007).

Basis Intern. Ltd. v. Research in Motion Ltd., 827 F.Supp.2d 1302 (D.N.M. 2011).

Bernstein v. Medicis Pharmaceutical Corp., No. 03 C 5256, 2004 WL 2092001 (N.D. Ill., 15 September 2004).

Best Western Intern., Inc. v. 1496815 Ontario, Inc., No. CV 04-1194-PHX-SMM, 2007 WL 779699 (D.Ariz., 13 March 2007).

Blue Cross and Blue Shield Ass'n v. Group Hospitalization and Medical Services, Inc., 744 F.Supp. 700 (E.D. Va. 1990).

Bulova Watch Co. v. Steele, 194 F.2d 567 (5th Cir. 1952).

Bulova Watch Co. v. Steele, 194 F.2d 567 (5th Cir. 1952) (Russell J., dissenting).

C-Cure Chemical Co., Inc. v. Secure Adhesives Corp., 571 F.Supp. 808 (W.D.N.Y. 1983).

Calvin Klein Industries, Inc. v. BFK Hong Kong, Ltd., 714 F.Supp. 78 (S.D.N.Y. 1989).

Citizens of Humanity, LLC v. Caitac Intern., Inc., No. B215232, 2010 WL 3007771 (Cal. Ct. App., 3 August 2010).

Dunkin' Donuts, Inc. v. Mercantile Ventures, No. EP-91-CA-154-B, 1992 WL 156566 (W.D. Tex., 8 January 1992).

Dwyer Instruments, Inc. v. Sensocon, Inc., No. 3:09-CV-10 TLS, 2009 WL 8705579 (N.D. Indiana, 20 November 2009).

Euromarket Designs, Inc. v. Crate & Barrel Ltd., 96 F.Supp.2d 824 (N.D. Ill. 2000).

Fun-Damental Too, Ltd. v. Gemmy Industries Corp., 111 F.3d 993 (2nd Cir. 1997).

Gallup, Inc. v. Business Research Bureau (Pvt.) Ltd., No. C 08-01577 WHA, 2008 WL 4857027 (N.D. Ca., 10 November 2008).

Gallup, Inc. v. Business Research Bureau (Pvt.) Ltd., 688 F.Supp.2d 915 (N.D. Cal. 2010).

GAP, Inc. v. Stone International Trading, Inc., 169 F.R.D. 584 (S.D.N.Y. 1997).

Gelicity UK Ltd. v. Jell-E-Bath, Inc., No. 10 Civ. 5677(ILG)(RLM), 2013 WL 3315398 (E.D.N.Y., 1 July 2013).

General Motors Corporation v. Ignacio Lopez de Arriortua, 948 F.Supp. 684 (E.D. Mich. 1996).

Gibson Brands Inc. v. Viacom Intern. Inc., No. CV 12-10870 DDP (AJWx), 2013 WL 5940826 (C.D. Cal., 5 November 2013).

Global Healing Center LP v. Nutritional Brands Inc., No. 4:14-CV-269, 2014 WL 897817 (S.D. Tex., 6 March 2014).

Gordon and Breach Science Publishers S.A. v. American Institute of Physics, 905 F.Supp. 169 (S.D.N.Y. 1995).

Groeneveld Transport Efficiency, Inc. v. Lubecore Intern., Inc., 730 F.3d 494 (6th Cir. 2013).

Guantanamera Cigar Co. v. Corporacion Habanos, S.A., 672 F.Supp.2d 106 (D.D.C. 2009).

Gucci America, Inc. v. Guess?, Inc., 790 F.Supp.2d 136 (S.D.N.Y. 2011).

Herb Reed Enterprises, Inc. v. Monroe Powell's Platters LLC, No. 2:11-CV-02010-PMP-RJJ, 2014 WL 2727094 (D. Nev., 17 June 2014).

Hong Leong Finance Ltd. (Singapore) v. Pinnacle Performance Ltd., No. 12 Civ. 6010(JMF), 2013 WL 5746126 (S.D.N.Y., 23 October 2013).

Houbigant, Inc. v. Development Specialists, Inc., 229 F.Supp.2d 208 (S.D.N.Y. 2002).

International Academy of Business and Financial Management, Ltd. v. Mentz, No. 12-cv-00463-CMA-BNB, 2013 WL 212640 (D. Colo., 18 January 2013).

International Business Machines Corp. v. Comdisco, Inc., No. 91 C 6777, 1993 WL 155511 (N.D. Ill., 10 May 1993).

International Café, S.A.L. v. Hard Rock Café International (U.S.A.), Inc., 252 F.3d 1274 (11th Cir. 2001).

Jackson v. Grupo Industrial Hoteleros, S.A., No. 07-22046-CIV, 2008 WL 4648999 (S.D. Fla., 20 October 2008).

John Walker and Sons, Ltd. v. DeMert & Dougherty, Inc., No. 84 C 7928, 1986 WL 4455 (N.D. Ill., 9 April 1986).

John Walker and Sons, Ltd. v. DeMert & Dougherty, Inc., 821 F.2d 399 (7th Cir. 1987).

Juicy Couture, Inc. v. Bella Intern. Ltd., 930 F.Supp.2d 489 (S.D.N.Y. 2013).

King v. Allied Vision, Ltd., 807 F.Supp. 300 (S.D.N.Y. 1992).

Leatherman Tool Group, Inc. v. Cooper Industries, Inc., 47 U.S.P.Q.2d 1045 (D. Or. 1997).

Les Ballets Trockadero de Monte Carlo, Inc. v. Trevino, 945 F.Supp. 563 (S.D.N.Y. 1996).

Levi Strauss & Co. v. Sunrise Intern. Trading Inc., 51 F.3d 982 (11th Cir. 1995).

Libbey Glass, Inc. v. Oneida Ltd., 61 F.Supp.2d 720 (N.D. Ohio 1999).
Lithuanian Commerce Corp., Ltd. v. Sara Lee Hosiery, 47 F.Supp.2d 523 (D.N.J. 1999).
Louis Vuitton Malletier, S.A. v. Akanoc Solutions, Inc., No. C 07-03952 JW, 2010 WL 5598337 (N.D. Ca., 19 March 2010).
Love v. Associated Newspapers, Ltd., 611 F.3d 601 (9th Cir. 2010).
Love v. The Mail on Sunday, 473 F.Supp.2d 1052 (C.D. Cal. 2007).
Mattel, Inc. v. MCA Records, Inc., 28 F.Supp.2d 1120 (C.D. Cal. 1998).
Mattel, Inc. v. MCA Records, Inc., 296 F.3d 894 (9th Cir. 2002).
Maurer Rides USA, Inc. v. Beijing Shibaolai Amusement Equipment Co., Ltd., No. 6:10-cv-1718-Orl-37KRS, 2014 WL 3687098 (M.D. Fla., 24 July 2014).
McBee v. Delica Co., Ltd., No. 02-198-P-C, 2004 WL 2634465 (D. Me., 19 August 2004).
McBee v. Delica Co., Ltd., No. Civ. 02-198-P-C, 2004 WL 2674360 (D. Me., 19 November 2004).
McBee v. Delica Co., Ltd., 417 F.3d 107 (1st Cir. 2005).
Medimport, S.R.L. v. Cabreja, No. 12-22255-CIV, 2012 WL 3632580 (S.D. Fla., 31 July 2012).
Menendez v. Faber, Coe & Gregg, Inc., 345 F.Supp. 527 (S.D.N.Y. 1972).
Mertik Maxitrol GmbH & Co. KG v. Honeywell Technologies SARL, No. 10-12257, 2011 WL 1454067 (E.D. Mich., 13 April 2011).
Mertik Maxitrol GmbH & Co. KG v. Honeywell Technologies SARL, No. 10-12257, 2011 WL 2669370 (E.D. Mich., 7 July 2011).
New Name, Inc. v. The Walt Disney Co., No. CV 07-5034 PA (RZx), 2008 WL 5587486 (C.D. Ca., 25 July 2008).
NewMarkets Partners LLC v. Oppenheim, 638 F.Supp.2d 394 (S.D.N.Y. 2009).
Nintendo of America, Inc. v. Aeropower Co., Ltd., 34 F.3d 246 (4th Cir. 1994).
Ocean Garden, Inc. v. Marktrade Co., Inc., 953 F.2d 500 (9th Cir. 1991).
Omega S.A. v. Omega Engineering, Inc., 396 F.Supp.2d 166 (D. Conn. 2005).
Partners for Health and Home, L.P. v. Seung Wee Yang, Nos. CV09-07849 RZ, CV10-04073 RZ, 2011 WL 6210452 (C.D. Ca., 14 December 2011).
Paul E. Hawkinson Co. v. Anderson Tire & Treads, Inc., No. 11-1168 ADM/JJG, 2011 WL 4590413 (D. Minn., 30 September 2011).
Paulsson Geophysical Services, Inc. v. Sigmar, 529 F.3d 303 (5th Cir. 2008).
Pearl Brewing Co. v. Trans-USA Corp., No. CIV.3:96-CV-3020-H, 1997 WL 340940 (N.D. Tex., 12 June 1997).

Philip Morris, Inc. v. Midwest Tobacco, Inc., No. 88-1292-A., 1988 WL 150693 (E.D. Va., 4 November 1988).

Piccoli A/S v. Calvin Klein Jeanswear Co., 19 F.Supp.2d 157 (S.D.N.Y. 1998).

Pinkberry, Inc. v. JEC Intern. Corp., No. CV 11-6540 PSG (PJWx), 2011 WL 6101828 (C.D. Ca., 7 December 2011).

Playboy Enterprises, Inc. v. Chuckleberry Pub., Inc., 511 F.Supp. 486 (S.D.N.Y. 1981).

Procter & Gamble Co. v. Colgate-Palmolive Co., No. 96 Civ. 9123(RPP), 1998 WL 788802 (S.D.N.Y., 9 November 1998).

Ramirez & Feraud Chili Co. v. Las Palmas Food Co., 146 F.Supp. 594 (S.D. Cal. 1956).

Reebok Intern. Ltd. v. American Sales Corp., 11 U.S.P.Q.2d 1229 (C.D. Cal. 1989).

Reebok Intern. Ltd. v. Marnachtech Enterprises, Inc., 737 F.Supp. 1515 (S.D. Cal. 1989).

Reebok Intern. Ltd. v. Marnachtech Enterprises, Inc., 970 F.Supp. 552 (9th Cir. 1992).

Reebok Intern. Ltd. v. Sebelen, 930 F.Supp. 720 (D. Puerto Rico 1996).

Rhino Membranes and Coatings, Inc. v. Rhino Seamless Membrane System, Inc., No. H-06-2112, 2006 WL 1984606 (S.D. Tex., 14 July 2006).

RMS Titanic, Inc. v. Zaller, 978 F.Supp.2d 1275 (N.D. Ga. 2013).

Rodgers v. Wright, 544 F.Supp.2d 302 (S.D.N.Y. 2008).

Roquette America, Inc. v. Alymum N.V., No. 03 Civ. 0434(DC), 2004 WL 1488384 (S.D.N.Y., 1 July 2004).

Scanvec Amiable Ltd. v. Chang, 80 Fed.Appx. 171 (3rd Cir. 2003).

Schreiber v. Dunabin, 938 F.Supp.2d 587 (E.D. Va. 2013).

Scotch Whiskey Ass'n v. Barton Distilling Co., 489 F.2d 809 (7th Cir. 1973).

Seed Services, Inc. v. Winsor Grain, Inc., 868 F.Supp.2d 998 (E.D. Cal. 2012).

Software AG, Inc. v. Consist Software Solutions, Inc., No. 08 Civ. 389 (CM)(FM), 2008 WL 563449 (S.D.N.Y., 21 February 2008).

Southco, Inc. v. Fivetech Technology Inc., 982 F.Supp.2d 507 (E.D. Pa. 2013).

Space Imaging Europe, Ltd. v. Space Imaging L.P., No. 98 Civ. 2291(DC), 1999 WL 511759 (S.D.N.Y., 19 July 1999).

Spartan Chemical Co., Inc. v. ATM Enterprises of America, No. 83 C 2444, 1986 WL 2616 (N.D. Ill., 20 February 1986).

Square D Co. v. Pioneer Breaker & Supply Co., No. A-07-CA-810-SS, 2009 WL 5170211 (W.D. Tex., 18 December 2009).

Star-Kist Foods, Inc. v. P.J. Rhodes & Co., 769 F.2d 1393 (9th Cir. 1985).

Steele v. Bulova Watch Co., 73 S.Ct. 252, 344 U.S. 280, 97 L.Ed. 319 (1952).
Steele v. Bulova Watch Co., 73 S.Ct. 252, 344 U.S. 280, 97 L.Ed. 319 (1952) (Reed J., dissenting).
Sterling Drug, Inc. v. Bayer AG, 14 F.3d 733 (2nd Cir. 1994).
Stevo Design, Inc. v. SBR Marketing Ltd., 919 F.Supp.2d 1112 (D. Nev. 2013).
The Name LLC v. Arias, No. 10 Civ. 3212(RMB), 2010 WL 4642456 (S.D.N.Y., 16 November 2010).
Thomas & Betts Corp. v. Panduit Corp., 71 F.Supp.2d 838 (N.D. Ill. 1999).
Three Degrees Enterprises, Inc. v. Three Degrees Worldwide, Inc., No. 89-5131, 1990 WL 121506 (E.D. Pa., 17 August 1990).
Three Degrees Enterprise, Inc. v. Three Degrees Worldwide, Inc., 22 U.S.P.Q. 2d 1357 (3rd Cir. 1991).
Tire Engineering and Distribution, LLC v. Shandong Linglong Rubber Co., Ltd., 682 F.3d 292 (4th Cir. 2012).
TNT USA, Inc. v. TrafiExpress, S.A. de C.V., 434 F.Supp.2d 1322 (S.D. Fla. 2006).
Tommy Hilfiger Licensing, Inc. v. Costco Companies, Inc., No. 99 Civ. 3894(LMM), 2001 WL 55735 (S.D.N.Y., 23 January 2001).
Totalplan Corp. of America v. Colborne, 14 F.3d 824 (2nd Cir. 1994).
Totalplan Corp. of America v. Lure Camera Ltd., Nos. 82-CV-0698E(M) thru 82-CV-0701E(M), 1993 WL 117504 (W.D.N.Y., 12 April 1993).
Trader Joe's Co. v. Hallatt, 981 F.Supp.2d 972 (W.D. Wash. 2013).
Ubiquiti Networks, Inc. v. Kozumi USA Corp., No. C 12-2582 CW, 2012 WL 1901264 (N.D. Ca., 25 May 2012).
Ubiquiti Networks, Inc. v. Kozumi USA Corp., 2012 WL 2343670 (N.D. Cal. 2012).
United Air Lines, Inc. v. United Airways, Ltd., No. 09-CV-4743 (KAM) (JMA), 2013 WL 1290930 (E.D.N.Y., 4 March 2013).
V'Soske, Inc. v. Vsoske.com, No. 00 CIV 6099 DC, 2002 WL 230848 (S.D.N.Y., 15 February 2002).
V'Soske, Inc. v. Vsoske.com, No. 00 Civ. 6099(DV), 2003 WL 1747144 (S.D.N.Y., 1 April 2003).
Van Doren Rubber Co., Inc. v. Marnatech Enterprises, Inc., No. 89-1362 S BTM, 1989 WL 223017 (S.D. Cal., 17 October 1989).
Vanity Fair Mills, Inc. v. T. Eaton Co., 133 F.Supp. 522 (S.D.N.Y. 1955).
Vanity Fair Mills, Inc. v. T. Eaton Co., 234 F.2d 633 (2nd Cir. 1956).
Versace v. Versace, 213 Fed.Appx. 34 (2nd Cir. 2007).
Vespa of America Corp. v. Bajaj Auto Ltd., 550 F.Supp. 224 (N.D. Cal. 1982).

Warnaco, Inc. v. VF Corp., 844 F.Supp. 940 (S.D.N.Y. 1994).

Wells Fargo & Co. v. Wells Fargo Exp. Co., 358 F.Supp. 1065 (D. Nev. 1973).

Wells Fargo & Co. v. Wells Fargo Exp. Co., 556 F.2d 406 (9th Cir. 1977).

Winterland Concessions Co. v. Fenton, 835 F.Supp. 529 (N.D. Cal. 1993).

World Book, Inc. v. International Business Machines Corp., 354 F.Supp.2d 451 (S.D.N.Y. 2005).

Zenger-Miller, Inc. v. Training Team, GmbH, 757 F.Supp. 1062 (N.D. Cal. 1991).

Zosma Ventures, Inc. v. Nazari, No. CV 12-1404 RSWL (FFMx), 2013 WL 2372231 (C.D. Cal., 30 May 2013).

Bibliography

Akehurst, Michael, Jurisdiction in International Law, 46 *Brit. Y.B. Int'l L.* 145 (1972/1973).

Akerlof, George A., The Market for "Lemons": Quality Uncertainty and the Market Mechanism, 84 *Quarterly J. Econ.* 488 (1970).

Alexander, Christian, Der Verwechslungsschutz gem. § 5 Abs. 2 UWG, 23–50, in *Festschrift für Helmut Köhler zum 70. Geburtstag* (Christian Alexander et al. eds.), Munich: C.H. Beck Verlag, 2014.

Alexander, Christian, Die Sanktions- und Verfahrensvorschriften der Richtlinie 2005/29/EG über unlautere Geschäftspraktiken im Binnenmarkt—Umsetzungsbedarf in Deutschland, 2005 *GRUR Int.* 809.

Alexander, Miles J. & Coil, James H., Geographic Rights in Trademarks and Service Marks, 68 *Trademark Rep.* 101 (1978).

Alexander-Katz, Richard, Die rechtliche Natur des Markenrechts sowie des Rechts an Waarenausstattungen, 1901 *GRUR* 102.

Alford, Roger P., The Future of Human Rights Litigation After Kiobel, 89 *Notre Dame L. Rev.* 1749 (2014).

Allen, William H. & O'Hara, Erin A., Second Generation Law and Economics of Conflict of Laws: Baxter's Comparative Impairment and Beyond, 51 *Stan. L. Rev.* 1011 (1999).

Allfeld, Philipp, *Gesetz zum Schutz der Warenbezeichnungen vom 12. Mai 1894, Erläutert unter Berücksichtigung insbesondere der Motive, der Reichstagsverhandlungen, der Literatur und Rechtsprechung über Markenschutz*, Munich: C.H. Beck'sche Verlagsbuchhandlung, 1894.

Allfeld, Philipp, *Grundriss des gewerblichen Rechtsschutzes*, Leipzig: Verlag von G.A. Gloeckner, 1910.

Allfeld, Philipp, *Kommentar zu den Reichsgesetzen über das Gewerbliche Urheberrecht, Patentgesetz, Gesetz, betr. das Urheberrecht an Mustern und Modellen, Gesetz, betr. den Schutz von Gebrauchsmustern, Gesetz zum Schutz der Warenbezeichnungen sowie zu den internationalen Verträgen zum Schutze des gewerblichen Urheberrechts*, Munich: C.H. Beck'sche Verlagsbuchhandlung, 1904.

Alpert, Robert, The Export of Trademarked Goods from the United States: The Extraterritorial Reach of the Lanham Act, 81 *Trademark Rep.* 125 (1991).

American Law Institute, *Intellectual Property—Principles Governing Jurisdiction, Choice of Law, and Judgments in Transnational Disputes, as Adopted and Promulgated by the American Law Institute at San Francisco, California, May 14, 2007*, St. Paul/MN: American Law Institute Publishers, 2008.

American Law Institute, *Restatement of the Law (First) of Torts, vol. III (div. 3–9)*, St. Paul/MN: American Law Institute Publishers, 1938.

American Law Institute, *Restatement of the Law (Second), Conflict of Laws, as Adopted and Promulgated by the American Law Institute at Washington, D.C.*, St. Paul/MN: American Law Institute Publishers, 1971 (and later).

American Law Institute, *Restatement of the Law (Second), Foreign Relations Law of the United States, May 26, 1962, as Adopted and Promulgated by the American Law Institute at Washington, D.C.*, St. Paul/MN: American Law Institute Publishers, 1965.

American Law Institute, *Restatement of the Law (Third), Foreign Relations Law of the United States, as Adopted and Promulgated by the American Law Institute at Washington, D.C.*, St. Paul/MN: American Law Institute Publishers, 1987 (and later).

American Law Institute, *Restatement of the Law, Unfair Competition (Third), as Adopted and Promulgated by the American Law Institute at Washington, D.C., May 11, 1993*, St. Paul/MN: American Law Institute Publishers, 1995.

American Law Reports, 148 *A.L.R. 139, Conflict of Laws, with Respect to Trademark Infringement or Unfair Competition, Including the Area of Conflict between Federal and State Law* (originally published in 1944, E.H. Schopflocher).

Anderegg, Kirsten, *Ausländische Eingriffsnormen im internationalen Vertragsrecht*, Tübingen: J.C.B. Mohr (Paul Siebeck) Verlag, 1989.

Arrow, Kenneth J., Uncertainty and the Welfare Economics of Medical Care, 53 *Am. Econ. Rev.* 941 (1963).

Arthur, Thomas C., The Costly Quest for Perfect Competition: Kodak and Nonstructural Market Power, 69 *N.Y.U. L. Rev.* 1 (1994).

Augenhofer, Susanne, Individualrechtliche Ansprüche des Verbrauchers bei unlauterem Wettbewerbsverhalten des Unternehmers, 2006 *WRP* 169.

Austin, Graeme W., Domestic Laws and Foreign Rights: Choice of Law in Transnational Copyright Infringement Litigation, 23 *Colum.-VLA J. L. & Arts* 1 (1999).

Austin, Graeme W., Private International Law and Intellectual Property Rights—A Common Law Overview, *WIPO Forum on Private International Law and Intellectual Property, WIPO/PIL/01/5* (15 January 2001) (online resource: available under www.wipo.int/meetings/en/details.jsp?meeting_id=4243 (12 February 2016)).

Austin, Graeme W., Social Policy Choices and Choice of Law for Copyright Infringement in Cyberspace, 79 *Or. L. Rev.* 575 (2000).

Austin, Graeme W., The Story of Steele v. Bulova: Trademarks on the Line, 395–425, in *Intellectual Property Stories* (Jane C. Ginsburg & Rochelle Cooper Dreyfuss eds.), New York: Foundation Press, 2006.

Austin, Graeme W., Trademarks and the Burdened Imagination, 69 *Brook. L. Rev.* 827 (2004).

Austin, Graeme W., Valuing "Domestic Self-Determination" in International Intellectual Property Jurisprudence, 77 *Chi.-Kent L. Rev.* 1155 (2002).

Austin, John, *The Province of Jurisprudence Determined*, London: John Murray, 1832.

Avakian, Serge G., Global Unfair Competition in the Online Commerce Era, 46 *UCLA L. Rev.* 905 (1999).

Baehr, Sonja Martina, *Die historische Entwicklung des Markenrechts in Deutschland*, Munich: Verlag Dr. Hut, 2008.

Baetge, Dietmar, *Globalisierung des Wettbewerbsrechts—Eine internationale Wettbewerbsordnung zwischen Kartell- und Welthandelsrecht*, Tübingen: Verlag Mohr Siebeck, 2009.

Baetzgen, Oliver, *Internationales Wettbewerbs- und Immaterialgüterrecht im EG-Binnenmarkt*, Cologne et al.: Carl Heymanns Verlag, 2007.

Baeumer, Ludwig, Anmerkungen zum Territorialitätsprinzip im internationalen Patent- und Markenrecht, 803–821, in *Festschrift für Wolfgang Fikentscher zum 70. Geburtstag* (Bernhard Großfeld et al. eds.), Tübingen: Verlag Mohr Siebeck, 1998.

Balz, Manfred, Paradigmenwechsel im Warenzeichenrecht?—Zu einigen Grundsatzproblemen der Europamarke, 45 *RabelsZ* 317 (1981).

Bamberger, Heinz Georg & Roth, Herbert, eds., *Beck'scher Online-Kommentar zum Bürgerlichen Gesetzbuch*, Munich: Verlag C.H. Beck, 36th edn., 2015 (online resource: database).

Bar, Carl Ludwig von, *Theorie und Praxis des Internationalen Privatrechts, vol. II*, Hannover: Hahnsche Buchhandlung, 2nd edn., 1889.

Bar, Christian von, Kollisionsrecht, Fremdenrecht und Sachrecht für internationale Sachverhalte im Internationalen Urheberrecht, 108 *UFITA* 27 (1988).

Bar, Christian von, *Territorialität des Warenzeichens und Erschöpfung des Verbreitungsrechts im Gemeinsamen Markt*, Frankfurt am Main: Alfred Metzner Verlag, 1977.

Bar, Christian von & Mankowski, Peter, *Internationales Privatrecht—vol. I: Allgemeine Lehren*, Munich: Verlag C.H. Beck, 2nd edn., 2003.

Bär, Rolf, Das Internationale Privatrecht (Kollisionsrecht) des Immaterialgüterrechts und des Wettbewerbsrechts, 125–177, in *Schweizerisches Immaterialgüter- und Wettbewerbsrecht, vol. I* (Roland von Büren & Lucas David eds.), Basel et al.: Helbing & Lichtenhahn, 2nd edn., 2002.

Bär, Rolf, *Kartellrecht und Internationales Privatrecht—Die kollisionsrechtliche Behandlung wirtschaftsrechtlicher Eingriffe, dargestellt am Beispiel der Gesetze gegen Wettbewerbsbeschränkungen*, Karlsruhe: Verlag Versicherungswirtschaft e.V., 1965.

Bartin, E., Localisation territoriale des monopoles intellectuels (Propriété littéraire et artistique propriété industrielle), 61 *Clunet* 781 (1934).

Basedow, Jürgen, Entwicklungslinien des internationalen Kartellrechts—Ausbau und Differenzierung des Auswirkungsprinzips, 1989 *NJW* 627.

Basedow, Jürgen, Foundations of Private International Law in Intellectual Property, 3–29, in *Intellectual Property in the Global Arena—Jurisdiction, Applicable Law, and the Recognition of Judgments in Europe, Japan and the US* (Jürgen Basedow et al. eds.), Tübingen: Verlag Mohr Siebeck, 2010.

Basedow, Jürgen, The Law of Open Societies—Private Ordering and Public Regulation of International Relations, 360 *Recueil des Cours* 1 (2012).

Basedow, Jürgen, *Weltkartellrecht—Ausgangslage und Ziele, Methoden und Grenzen der internationalen Vereinheitlichung des Rechts der Wettbewerbsbeschränkungen*, Tübingen: Verlag Mohr Siebeck, 1998.

Basedow, Jürgen, Wirtschaftskollisionsrecht—Theoretischer Versuch über die ordnungspolitischen Normen des Forumstaates, 52 *RabelsZ* 8 (1988).

Basedow, Jürgen, Zielkonflikte und Zielhierarchien im Vertrag über die Europäische Gemeinschaft, 49–68, in *Festschrift für Ulrich Everling, vol. I* (Ole Due et al. eds.), Baden-Baden: Nomos Verlagsgesellschaft, 1995.

Baudenbacher, Carl, Die wettbewerbsrechtliche Beurteilung grenzüberschreitender Werbe- und Absatztätigkeit nach schweizerischem Recht, 1988 *GRUR Int.* 310.

Baudenbacher, Carl, ed., *Lauterkeitsrecht: Kommentar zum Gesetz gegen den unlauteren Wettbewerb (UWG)*, Basel et al.: Helbing & Lichtenhahn Verlag, 2001.

Baudenbacher, Carl, Zur funktionalen Anwendung von § 1 des deutschen und Art. 1 des schweizerischen UWG, 144 *ZHR* 145 (1980).

Baur, Jürgen F., Das Tatbestandsmerkmal „Wettbewerb," 134 *ZHR* 97 (1970).

Baur, Jürgen F., Zum Namensschutz im deutschen internationalen Privatrecht unter besonderer Berücksichtigung des Schutzes der Handelsnamen, 167 *AcP* 535 (1967).

Baxter, William F., Choice of Law and the Federal System, 16 *Stan. L. Rev.* 1 (1963).

Beale, Joseph H., *A Treatise on the Conflict of Laws, vol. I: Jurisdiction & vol. III: Administration and Procedure*, New York: Baker, Voorhis & Co., 1935.

Beales, Howard, Craswell, Richard & Salop, Steven C., The Efficient Regulation of Consumer Information, 24 *J. L. & Econ.* 491 (1981).

Beater, Axel, Allgemeininteressen und UWG, 2012 *WRP* 6.

Beater, Axel, *Unlauterer Wettbewerb*, Tübingen: Verlag Mohr Siebeck, 2011.

Beater, Axel, *Verbraucherschutz und Schutzzweckdenken im Wettbewerbsrecht*, Tübingen: Mohr Siebeck, 2000.

Beater, Axel, Verbraucherverhalten und Wettbewerbsrecht, 87–104, in *Festschrift für Winfried Tilmann zum 65. Geburtstag* (Erhard Keller et al. eds.), Cologne et al.: Carl Heymanns Verlag, 2003.

Becher, Carl, *Warenzeichengesetz und Internationale Registrierung*, Berlin: Carl Heymanns Verlag, 1931.

Bechtel, Heinrich, *Wirtschaftsgeschichte Deutschlands—Vom Beginn des 16. bis zum Ende des 18. Jahrhunderts, vol. II*, Munich: Verlag Georg D.W. Callwey, 1952.

Beebe, Barton, Intellectual Property Law and the Sumptuary Code, 123 *Harv. L. Rev.* 809 (2010).

Beebe, Barton, The Semiotic Analysis of Trademark Law, 51 *UCLA L. Rev.* 621 (2004).

Beier, Friedrich-Karl, Die Funktionen der Marke, 225–236, in *Markenrechtliche Abhandlungen: Beiträge zur neueren Entwicklung des Warenzeichen-, Ausstattungs- und Herkunftsschutzes, 1956–1986* (Friedrich-Karl Beier ed.), Cologne et al.: Heymann Verlag, 1986.

Beier, Friedrich-Karl, Entwicklung und Grundprinzipien des internationalen Markenschutzes, 85–108, in *Festskrift till Stig Strömholm, vol. I* (Ake Frändberg et al. eds.), Uppsala: Iustus Förlag, 1997.

Beier, Friedrich-Karl, Gedanken zum Verhältnis von Warenzeichen- und Ausstattungsschutz im künftigen deutschen Markenrecht, 1967 *GRUR* 628.

Beier, Friedrich-Karl, *Grundfragen des französischen Markenrechts*, Munich et al.: Carl Heymanns Verlag, 1962.

Beier, Friedrich-Karl, Territorialität des Markenrechts und internationaler Wirtschaftsverkehr, 1968 *GRUR Int.* 8.

Beier, Friedrich-Karl, Warenzeichenrecht—Rückkehr zum Eintragungsprinzip? Überlegungen zur Reform des Markenrechts, 1973 *GRUR Int.* 407.

Beier, Friedrich-Karl & Krieger, Ulrich, Wirtschaftliche Bedeutung, Funktionen und Zweck der Marke (68), Bericht erstattet im Namen der Landesgruppe der Bundesrepublik Deutschland, 1976 *GRUR Int.* 125.

Beier, Friedrich-Karl & Kur, Annette, Das Verhältnis von Markenrecht und Recht des unlauteren Wettbewerbs im Wandel der Zeiten, 477–493, in *Festschrift für Wolfgang Fikentscher zum 70. Geburtstag* (Bernhard Großfeld et al. eds.), Tübingen: Verlag Mohr Siebeck, 1998.

Beitzke, Günther, Auslandswettbewerb unter Inländern—BGHZ 40, 391, 1966 *JuS* 139.

Bently, Lionel & Sherman, Brad, *Intellectual Property Law*, Oxford: Oxford University Press, 4th edn., 2014.

Berger, Mathis, *Die funktionale Konkretisierung von Art. 2 UWG*, Zurich: Schulthess Polygraphischer Verlag, 1997.

Berman, Paul Schiff, *Global Legal Pluralism—A Jurisprudence of Law Beyond Borders*, Cambridge: Cambridge University Press, 2012.

Berman, Paul Schiff, Global Legal Pluralism, 80 *S. Cal. L. Rev.* 1155 (2007).

Berman, Paul Schiff, The Globalization of Jurisdiction, 151 *U. Pa. L. Rev.* 311 (2002).

Berman, Paul Schiff, Towards a Cosmopolitan Vision of Conflict of Laws: Redefining Governmental Interests in a Global Era, 153 *U. Pa. L. Rev.* 1819 (2005).

Berman, Paul Schiff, Towards a Jurisprudence of Hybridity, 2010 *Utah L. Rev.* 11.

Berner, Thomas, Extraterritorial Application of the Lanham Act: Wells Fargo & Company v. Wells Fargo Express Company, 556 F.2d 406 (9th Cir. 1977), 18 *Colum. J. Transnat'l L.* 173 (1979).

Bernhard, Peter, *Das Internationale Privatrecht des unlauteren Wettbewerbs in den Mitgliedstaaten der EG*, Baden-Baden: Nomos Verlagsgesellschaft, 1994.

Bernhard, Peter, Insel-Recht auf Gran Canaria—Zum internationalen Privatrecht des unlauteren Wettbewerbs, 1992 *GRUR Int.* 366.

Beseler, Georg, *Kommentar über das Strafgesetzbuch für die Preußischen Staaten und das Einführungsgesetz vom 14. April 1851*, Leipzig: Verlag Weidmann, 1851.

Bettinger, Torsten, Die WIPO-Vorschläge zum Schutz von Marken und anderen Zeichenrechten im Internet, 2001 *WRP* 789.

Bettinger, Torsten & Thum, Dorothee, Territorial Trademark Rights in the Global Village—International Jurisdiction, Choice of Law and Substantive Law for Trademark Disputes on the Internet, 31 *IIC* 162 et seq. (part I) and 285 et seq. (part II) (2000).

Biddle, A. S., Good-Will (Part 1), 23 *Am. L. Reg.* 1 (1875).

Bigelow, Melville Madison, *The Law of Torts*, Boston: Little, Brown, and Company, 7th edn., 1901.

Binder, Heinz, Zur Auflockerung des Deliktsstatuts, 20 *RabelsZ* 401 (1955).

Blackstone, William, *Commentaries on the Laws of England in Four Books. In Two Volumes* (ed. George Sharswood), vol. I, books I & II, Philadelphia: J.B. Lippincott Co., 1893.

Blackstone, William & Cooley, Thomas M., *Commentaries on the Laws of England in Four Books*, Chicago: Callaghan and Company, 3rd edn., 1884.

Blanc, Étienne, *Traité de la contrefaçon et de sa poursuite en justice*, Paris: Raymond, 1838.

Bleckmann, Albert, *Die völkerrechtlichen Grundlagen des internationalen Kollisionsrechts*, Cologne et al.: Carl Heymanns Verlag, 1992.

Bleckmann, Albert, Sittenwidrigkeit wegen Verstoßes gegen den ordre public international, 34 *ZaöRV* 112 (1974).

Bluntschli, J. K., *Deutsches Privatrecht*, Munich: Literarisch-artistische Anstalt der J.G. Cotta'schen Buchhandlung, 3rd edn., 1864.

Bodenhausen, G. H. C., *Guide to the Application of the Paris Convention for the Protection of Industrial Property*, Geneva: United International Bureaux for the Protection of Intellectual Property (BIRPI), 1968.

Böhm, Franz, Freiheit und Ordnung in der Marktwirtschaft, 22 *ORDO* 11 (1971).

Böhm, Franz, *Wettbewerb und Monopolkampf—Eine Untersuchung zur Frage des wirtschaftlichen Kampfrechts und zur Frage der rechtlichen Struktur der geltenden Wirtschaftsordnung*, Baden-Baden: Nomos Verlagsgesellschaft, reprint of 1933 edn., 2010.

Bolle, Johannes Andreas, *Entwicklungslinien und systematische Stellung der Regeln über den unlauteren Wettbewerb im deutschen und englischen Recht*, Borna-Leipzig: Universitätsverlag von Robert Noske, 1928.

Bone, Robert G., Hunting Goodwill: A History of the Concept of Goodwill in Trademark Law, 86 *B. U. L. Rev.* 547 (2006).

Bone, Robert G., Schechter's Ideas in Historical Context and Dilution's Rocky Road, 24 *Santa Clara Computer & High Tech. L.J.* 469 (2008).

Borchardt, Kurt, Are Trademarks an Antitrust Problem? Part I, 33 *Trademark Rep.* 49 (1943).

Borchardt, Knut & Fikentscher, Wolfgang, *Wettbewerb, Wettbewerbsbeschränkung, Marktbeherrschung*, Stuttgart: Ferdinand Enke Verlag, 1957.

Born, Gary B., A Reappraisal of the Extraterritorial Reach of U.S. Law, 24 *Law & Pol'y Int'l Bus.* 1 (1992).

Born, Gary B. & Rutledge, Peter B., *International Civil Litigation in United States Courts*, New York: Wolters Kluwer Law & Business, 5th edn., 2011.

Bornkamm, Joachim, Die Schnittstellen zwischen gewerblichem Rechtsschutz und UWG—Grenzen des lauterkeitsrechtlichen Verwechslungsschutzes, 2011 *GRUR* 1.

Bornkamm, Joachim, Markenrecht und wettbewerbsrechtlicher Kennzeichenschutz—Zur Vorrangthese der Rechtsprechung, 2005 *GRUR* 97.

Boschiero, Nerina, Infringement of Intellectual Property Rights—A Commentary on Article 8 of the Rome II Regulation, 9 *Yearb. P.I.L.* 87 (2007).

Bouckaert, Boudewijn, What is Property?, 13 *Harv. J.L. & Pub. Pol'y* 775 (1990).

Boyle, James, Foucault in Cyberspace: Surveillance, Sovereignty, and Hardwired Censors, 66 *U. Cin. L. Rev.* 177 (1997).

Bradley, Curtis A., The Costs of International Human Rights Litigation, 2 *Chi. J. Int'l L.* 457 (2001).

Bradley, Curtis A., Territorial Intellectual Property Rights in an Age of Globalism, 37 *Va. J. Int'l L.* 505 (1997).

Bradley, Curtis A. & Goldsmith, Jack L., Customary International Law as Federal Common Law: A Critique of the Modern Position, 110 *Harv. L. Rev.* 815 (1997).

Bradley, Curtis A., Goldsmith, Jack L. & Moore, David H., Sosa, Customary International Law, and the Continuing Relevance of Erie, 120 *Harv. L. Rev.* 869 (2007).

Brewster, Kingman, Jr., *Antitrust and American Business Abroad*, New York: McGraw-Hill Book Company, Inc., 1958.

Breyer, Stephen, *The Court and the World—American Law and the New Global Realities*, New York: Alfred A. Knopf, 2015.

Briem, Stephan, *Internationales und Europäisches Wettbewerbsrecht und Kennzeichenrecht*, Vienna: Verlag Orac, 1995.

Briggs, William, *The Law of International Copyright—with Special Sections on the Colonies and the United States of America*, London: Stevens & Haynes, 1906.

Brilmayer, Lea, *Conflict of Laws: Foundation and Future Directions*, Boston: Little, Brown and Company, 1991.

Brilmayer, Lea, Rights, Fairness, and Choice of Law, 98 *Yale L.J.* 1277 (1989).

Brilmayer, Lea, The Extraterritorial Application of American Law: A Methodological and Constitutional Appraisal, 50 *Law & Contemp. Probs.* 11 (1987).

Brömmelmeyer, Christoph, Der Binnenmarkt als Leitstern der Richtlinie über unlautere Geschäftspraktiken, 2007 *GRUR* 295.

Brömmelmeyer, Christoph, *Internetwettbewerbsrecht, Das Recht der Ubiquität—Das Recht der Domain Names—Das Recht der kommerziellen Kommunikation*, Tübingen: Verlag Mohr Siebeck, 2007.

Brown, Chris, A Dilution Delusion: The Unjustifiable Protection of Similar Marks, 72 *U. Cin. L. Rev.* 1023 (2004).

Brown, Erika M., The Extraterritorial Reach of United States Trademark Law: A Review of Recent Decisions Under the Lanham Act, 9 *Fordham Intell. Prop. Media & Ent. L.J.* 863 (1999).

Brown, Ralph S., Jr., Advertising and the Public Interest: Legal Protection of Trade Symbols, 57 *Yale L.J.* 1165 (1948).

Brownlie, Ian, *Principles of Public International Law*, Oxford: Oxford University Press, 7th edn., 2008.

Bruns, Viktor, Völkerrecht als Rechtsordnung I., 1 *ZaöRV* 1 (1929).

Brunstein, Joseph Ludwig, *Studien im österreichischen Markenrecht—Ausschliessliches Gebrauchsrecht, Markendelict, Processhindernde Vorfragen*, Vienna: Manz'sche K.u.K. Hof-Verlags- und Universitätsbuchhandlung, 1895.

Bühler, Walter, *Die zivilrechtliche Bekämpfung des unlauteren Wettbewerbs in der Praxis des schweizerischen Bundesgerichts—Eine rechtsvergleichende Studie über ihre Entwicklung und ihren heutigen Stand*, Zurich: Druckerei A.-G. Gebr. Leemann & Co., 1930.

Bullington, John P., Trade-Names and Trade-Marks—Territorial Extent of the Right Acquired, 3 *Tex. L. Rev.* 300 (1924).

Bülow, Peter, Lauterkeitsrecht oder Unlauterkeitsrecht?, 2012 *GRUR* 889.

Bünger, Stefanie, *Das Wettbewerbskollisionsrecht Deutschlands und Großbritanniens sowie seine europäische Harmonisierung*, Munich: Martin Meidenbauer Verlagsbuchhandlung, 2006.

Bunn, Charles, The National Law of Unfair Competition, 62 *Harv. L. Rev.* 987 (1949).

Burk, Dan L., Trademark Doctrines for Global Electronic Commerce, 49 *S. C. L. Rev.* 695 (1998).

Burmeister, Julian, *Belästigung als Wettbewerbsverstoß*, Munich: Verlag C.H. Beck, 2006.

Busse, Daniel, Die Berücksichtigung ausländischer „Eingriffsnormen" durch die deutsche Rechtsprechung, 95 *ZVglRWiss* 386 (1996).

Bußmann, Kurt, Verfolgung ausländischer Zeichenverletzungen in Deutschland, 1929 *MuW* 419.

Butts, Robert, Trademark Law: Interpreting the Congressional Intent of the Extraterritorial Application of the Lanham Trademark Act, 8 *Fla. J. Int'l L.* 447 (1993).

Buxbaum, Hannah L., Territory, Territoriality, and the Resolution of Jurisdictional Conflict, 57 *Am. J. Comp. L.* 631 (2009).

Buxbaum, Hannah L., The Private Attorney General in a Global Age: Public Interests in Private International Antitrust Litigation, 26 *Yale J. Int'l L.* 219 (2001).

Buxbaum, Hannah L., Transnational Regulatory Litigation, 46 *Va. J. Int'l L.* 251 (2006).

Buxbaum, Hannah L. & Michaels, Ralf, Jurisdiction and Choice of Law in International Antitrust Law—A US Perspective, 225–244, in *International Antitrust Litigation: Conflict of Laws and Coordination* (Jürgen Basedow et al. eds.), Oxford: Hart Publishing, 2012.

Caemmerer, Ernst von, Bereicherung und unerlaubte Handlung, 333–401, in *Festschrift für Ernst Rabel—Rechtsvergleichung und internationales Privatrecht, vol. I* (Hans Dölle ed.), Tübingen: Verlag Mohr Siebeck, 1954.

Calliess, Gralf-Peter, ed., *Rome Regulations (commentary)*, 2nd edn., Alphen aan den Rijn: Kluwer Law International, 2015.

Calliess, Gralf-Peter, ed., *Rome Regulations (commentary)*, Alphen aan den Rijn: Kluwer Law International, 2011.

Callmann, Rudolf, *Der unlautere Wettbewerb, Kommentar zum Gesetz gegen den unlauteren Wettbewerb mit Notverordnung vom 9. März 1932 zu den materiellen Vorschriften des Gesetzes zum Schutz der Warenbezeichnungen*, Mannheim et al.: J. Bensheimer Verlag, 2nd edn., 1932.

Callmann, Rudolf, Thoughts on the Protection of World Marks, 44 *Trademark Rep.* 1134 (1954).

Callmann, Rudolf, Unfair Competition Without Competition?—The Importance of the Property Concept in the Law of Trade-Marks, 95 *U. Pa. L. Rev.* 443 (1947).

Callmann, Rudolf, Vorschläge für eine EWG-Marke unter Berücksichtigung der Markenprobleme in USA, 1960 *GRUR* 514.

Callmann, Rudolf, What Is Unfair Competition?, 28 *Geo. L.J.* 585 (1940).

Callmann, Rudolf, Worldmarks and the Antitrust Law, 11 *Vand. L. Rev.* 515 (1958).

Caminker, Evan, The Constitutionality of Qui Tam Actions, 99 *Yale L.J.* 341 (1989).

Carrier, Michael A., Cabining Intellectual Property Through a Property Paradigm, 54 *Duke L.J.* 1 (2004).

Carter, Stephen L., Does It Matter Whether Intellectual Property Is Property?, 68 *Chi.-Kent L. Rev.* 715 (1993).
Carter, Stephen L., Owning What Doesn't Exist, 13 *Harv. J. L. & Pub. Pol'y* 99 (1990).
Carter, Stephen L., The Trouble with Trademark, 99 *Yale L.J.* 759 (1990).
Carty, Hazel, *An Analysis of the Economic Torts*, Oxford: Oxford University Press, 2nd edn., 2010.
Cassel, Doug, Suing Americans for Human Rights Torts Overseas: The Supreme Court Leaves the Door Open, 89 *Notre Dame L. Rev.* 1773 (2014).
Castel, Jean-Gabriel, The Extraterritorial Effects of Antitrust Laws, 179 *Recueil des Cours* 9 (1983–I).
Casto, William R., The ATS Cause of Action Is Sui Generis, 89 *Notre Dame L. Rev.* 1545 (2014).
Casto, William R., The New Federal Common Law of Tort Remedies for Violations of International Law, 37 *Rutgers L.J.* 635 (2006).
Cavers, David F., A Critique of the Choice-of-Law Problem, 47 *Harv. L. Rev.* 173 (1933).
Cavers, David F., *The Choice-of-Law Process*, Ann Arbor/MI: University of Michigan Press, 1965.
Celli, Alessandro L., *Internationales Kennzeichenrecht*, Basel & Munich: Helbing & Lichtenhahn & Verlag C.H. Beck, 2000.
Chafee, Zechariah, Jr., Unfair Competition, 53 *Harv. L. Rev.* 1289 (1940).
Chamberlin, Edward Hastings, *The Theory of Monopolistic Competition—A Re-Orientation of the Theory of Value*, Cambridge/MA: Harvard University Press, 5th edn., 1947.
Chandler, Alfred D., Jr., *Scale and Scope—The Dynamics of Industrial Capitalism*, Cambridge/MA: Harvard University Press, 1990.
Cheshire, North & Fawcett, *Private International Law* (J.J. Fawcett & J.M. Carruthers eds.), Oxford: Oxford University Press, 14th edn., 2008.
Childress, Donald Earl III, Comity as Conflict: Resituating International Comity as Conflict of Laws, 44 *U.C. Davis L. Rev.* 11 (2010).
Christie, J. Roberton, Goodwill in Business, 8 *Jurid. Rev.* 71 (1896).
Clark, J. M., *Competition as a Dynamic Process*, Washington/ DC: The Brookings Institution, 1961.
Clark, J. M., Imperfect Competition Theory and Basing-Point Problems, 33 *Am. Econ. Rev.* 283 (1943).
Clark, J. M., Toward a Concept of Workable Competition, 30 *Am. Econ. Rev.* 241 (1940).
Coffee, John C., Jr., Rescuing the Private Attorney General: Why the Model of the Lawyer as Bounty Hunter Is Not Working, 42 *Md. L. Rev.* 215 (1983).
Coffin, E. R., Fraud as an Element of Unfair Competition, 16 *Harv. L. Rev.* 272 (1903).
Cohen, Felix S., Transcendental Nonsense and the Functional Approach, 35 *Colum. L. Rev.* 809 (1935).
Cohen, Jehoram Tobias, van Nispen, Constant & Huydecoper, Tony, *European Trademark Law—Community Trademark Law and Harmonized National Trademark Law*, Austin: Kluwer Law International BV, 2010.

Coing, Helmut, Zur Geschichte des Begriffs „subjektives Recht," 7–23, in *Das subjektive Recht und der Rechtsschutz der Persönlichkeit* (Helmut Coing et al. eds.), Frankfurt am Main und Berlin: Alfred Metzner Verlag, 1959.

Colangelo, Anthony J., The Alien Tort Statute and the Law of Nations in Kiobel and Beyond, 44 *Geo. J. Int'l L.* 1329 (2013).

Colangelo, Anthony J., Kiobel: Muddling the Distinction Between Prescriptive and Adjudicative Jurisdiction, 28 *Md. J. Int'l L.* 65 (2013).

Comanor, William S. & Wilson, Thomas A., Advertising Market Structure and Performance, 49 *Rev. Econ. & Stat.* 423 (1967).

Comment, The Nature of Business Goodwill, 16 *Harv. L. Rev.* 135 (1902).

Comment, The Scope of Territorial Protection of Trademarks, 65 *Nw. U. L. Rev.* 781 (1970).

Commission of the European Communities, *Proposal for a Regulation of the European Parliament and the Council on the Law Applicable to Non-Contractual Obligations ("Rome II")*, Brussels, 22 July 2003, COM(2003) 427 final, 2003/0168 (COD).

Committee on Trade-Marks and Unfair Competition of the Association of the Bar of the City of New York, Bulletin Regarding Circulars Recently Issued by Certain Self-Styled "Trade-Mark Specialists," in Committee Reports of the Section of Patent, Trade Mark and Copyright Law of the American Bar Association, 17 *J. Pat. Off. Soc'y* 732 (1935).

Commons, John R., *Industrial Goodwill*, New York: McGraw-Hill Book Company, Inc., 1919.

Cook, Walter Wheeler, *The Logical and Legal Bases of the Conflict of Laws*, Cambridge/MA: Harvard University Press, 2nd print of 1942 edn., 1949.

Cooley, Thomas M. (Commentator: John Lewis), *A Treatise on the Law of Torts or the Wrongs which Arise Independently of Contract, vol. II*, Chicago: Callaghan & Company, 3rd edn., 1906.

Cooter, Robert B., Jr. & Ulen, Thomas, *Law and Economics*, Essex: Pearson Education Ltd., 6th edn., 2014.

Cornish, William, Llewelyn, David & Aplin, Tanya, *Intellectual Property: Patents, Copyright, Trade Marks and Allied Rights*, London: Sweet & Maxwell, 8th edn., 2013.

Cornthwaite, Jonathan, Say It with Flowers: The Judgment of the Court of Justice of the European Union in Interflora v. Marks & Spencer, 34(2) *EIPR* 127 (2012).

Council of the European Communities, *Resolution of 14 April 1975 on a preliminary programme of the European Economic Community for a consumer protection and information policy*, O.J. EU (25 April 1975), No C 92/1.

Council of the European Communities, *Resolution of 19 May 1981 on a second programme of the European Economic Community for a consumer protection and information policy*, O.J. EC (3 June 1981), No C 133/1.

Curran, Vivian Grosswald, Extraterritoriality, Universal Jurisdiction, and the Challenge of Kiobel v. Royal Dutch Petroleum Co., 28 *Md. J. Int'l L.* 76 (2013).

Currie, Brainerd, The Disinterested Third State, 28 *Law & Contemp. Probs.* 755 (1963).

Currie, Brainerd, *Selected Essays on the Conflict of Laws*, Durham/NC: Duke University Press, 1963.

Cushing, Grafton Dulany, On Certain Cases Analogous to Trade-Marks, 4 *Harv. L. Rev.* 321 (1890).

Czempiel, Benedict, *Das bestimmbare Deliktsstatut—Zur Zurechnung im internationalen Deliktsrecht*, Berlin: Duncker & Humblot, 1991.

Dabney, James W., On the Territorial Reach of the Lanham Act, 83 *Trademark Rep.* 465 (1993).

Danielcik, Ist unlauterer Wettbewerb im Ausland vor deutschen Gerichten und nach deutschem Recht verfolgbar?, 1936 *JW* 2613.

Davies, D. J. Llewelyn, The Influence of Huber's de Conflictu Legum on English Private International Law, 18 *Brit. Y.B. Int'l L.* 49 (1937).

De Miguel Asensio, Pedro A., The Private International Law of Intellectual Property and of Unfair Commercial Practices: Convergence or Divergence?, 137–190, in *Intellectual Property and Private International Law* (Stefan Leible & Ansgar Ohly eds.), Tübingen: Mohr Siebeck Verlag, 2009.

Déak, Francis, Contracts and Combinations in Restraint of Trade in French Law—A Comparative Study, 21 *Iowa L. Rev.* 397 (1936).

Deakin, Simon, Johnston, Angus & Markesinis, Basil, *Markesinis and Deakin's Tort Law*, Oxford: Oxford University Press, 6th edn., 2008.

Denicola, Robert C., Some Thoughts on the Dynamics of Federal Trademark Legislation and the Trademark Dilution Act of 1995, 59 *Law & Contemp. Probs.* 75 (1996).

Derenberg, Walter J., The Influence of the French Code Civil on the Modern Law of Unfair Competition, 4 *Am. J. Comp. L.* 1 (1955).

Derenberg, Walter J., Territorial Scope and Situs of Trademarks and Good Will, 47 *Va. L. Rev.* 733 (1961).

Derenberg, Walter J., *Trade-Mark Protection and Unfair Trading*, Albany: Matthew Bender & Company, Inc., 1936.

Derenberg, Walter J., *Warenzeichen und Wettbewerb in den Vereinigten Staaten von Amerika*, Berlin: Carl Heymanns Verlag, 1931.

Dessemontet, François, The ALI Principles: Intellectual Property in Transborder Litigation, 31–48, in *Intellectual Property in the Global Arena—Jurisdiction, Applicable Law, and the Recognition of Judgments in Europe, Japan and the US* (Jürgen Basedow et al. eds.), Tübingen: Verlag Mohr Siebeck, 2010.

Dessemontet, François, A European Point of View on the ALI Principles—Intellectual Property: Principles Governing Jurisdiction, Choice of Law, and Judgments in Transnational Disputes, 30 *Brook. J. Int'l L.* 849 (2005).

Dethloff, Nina, *Europäisierung des Wettbewerbsrechts—Einfluss des europäischen Rechts auf das Sach- und Kollisionsrecht des unlauteren Wettbewerbs*, Tübingen: Verlag Mohr Siebeck, 2001.

Dethloff, Nina, Marketing im Internet und Internationales Wettbewerbsrecht, 1998 *NJW* 1596.

Deutsch, Erwin, Commentary to BGH, decision of 23 October 1971 (I ZR 86/69)—Tampax, 1971 *JZ* 732.

Deutsch, Erwin, Entwicklung und Entwicklungsfunktion der Deliktstatbestände, 1963 *JZ* 385.

Deutsch, Erwin, *Wettbewerbstatbestände mit Auslandsbeziehung*, Stuttgart: Ferdinand Enke Verlag, 1962.

Deutscher Bundestag, *Drucksache: Gesetzentwurf der Bundesregierung, Entwurf eines Gesetzes gegen den unlauteren Wettbewerb (UWG),* 15. Wahlperiode, 15/1487 (22 August 2003) (online resource: available under www.bundestag.de/drs (12 February 2016)).

Deutscher Bundestag, *Drucksache: Gesetzentwurf der Bundesregierung, Entwurf eines Ersten Gesetzes zur Änderung des Gesetzes gegen den unlauteren Wettbewerb,* 16. Wahlperiode, 16/10145 (20 August 2008) (online resource: available under www.bundestag.de/drs (12 February 2016)).

Deutscher Reichstag, *Stenographische Berichte der Verhandlungen des Deutschen Reichstages (stenographic reports), 1867–1942 with protocols and additional documents* (online resource: available under www.reichstagsprotokolle.de/index.html (12 February 2016)).

Developments in the Law—Extraterritoriality, Comity and Extraterritoriality in Antitrust Enforcement, 124 *Harv. L. Rev.* 1269 (2011).

Deville, Rainer, *Die Konkretisierung des Abwägungsgebotes im internationalen Kartellrecht,* Baden-Baden: Nomos Verlagsgesellschaft, 1990.

Diamond, Sidney A., The Historical Development of Trademarks, 65 *Trademark Rep.* 265 (1975).

Dicey, Morris & Collins, *The Conflict of Laws, vol. I & II* (Lord Collins of Mapesbury gen. ed.), London: Sweet & Maxwell, 15th edn., 2012.

Dichtl, Erwin, Grundidee, Entwicklungsepochen und heutige wirtschaftliche Bedeutung des Markenartikels, 17–33, in *Markenartikel heute: Marke, Markt und Marketing* (Clemens-August Andreae et al.), Wiesbaden: Gabler, 1978.

Dickinson, Andrew, *The Rome II Regulation: The Law Applicable to Non-Contractual Obligations,* Oxford: Oxford University Press, 2008.

Diggins, Bartholomew, Federal and State Regulation of Trade-Marks, 14 *Law & Contemp. Probs.* 200 (1949).

Dinwoodie, Graeme B., The Architecture of the International Intellectual Property System, 77 *Chi.-Kent L. Rev.* 993 (2002).

Dinwoodie, Graeme B., A New Copyright Order: Why National Courts Should Create Global Norms, 149 *U. Pa. L. Rev.* 469 (2000).

Dinwoodie, Graeme B., Conflicts and International Copyright Litigation: The Role of International Norms, 195–210, in *Intellectual Property in the Conflict of Laws* (Jürgen Basedow et al. eds.), Tübingen: Mohr Siebeck Verlag, 2005.

Dinwoodie, Graeme B., Developing a Private International Intellectual Property Law: The Demise of Territoriality?, 51 *Wm. & Mary L. Rev.* 711 (2009).

Dinwoodie, Graeme B., International Intellectual Property Litigation: A Vehicle for Resurgent Comparativist Thought?, 49 *Am. J. Comp. L.* 429 (2001).

Dinwoodie, Graeme B., *Private International Aspects of the Protection of Trademarks, WIPO Forum on Private International Law and Intellectual Property,* WIPO/PIL/01/4 (19 January 2001) (online resource: available under www.wipo.int/meetings/en/details.jsp?meeting_id=4243 (12 February 2016)).

Dinwoodie, Graeme B., Trademarks and Territory: Detaching Trademark Law from the Nation-State, 41 *Hous. L. Rev.* 885 (2004).

Dodge, William S., Alien Tort Litigation: The Road Not Taken, 89 *Notre Dame L. Rev.* 1577 (2014).

Dodge, William S., Antitrust and the Draft Hague Judgments Convention, 32 *Law & Pol'y Int'l Bus.* 363 (2001).

Dodge, William S., Breaking the Public Law Taboo, 43 *Harv. Int'l L.J.* 161 (2002).

Dodge, William S., Customary International Law and the Question of Legitimacy, 120 *Harv. L. Rev. F.* 19 (2007).

Dodge, William S., Extraterritoriality and Conflict-of-Laws Theory: An Argument for Judicial Unilateralism, 39 *Harv. Int'l L.J.* 101 (1998).

Dodge, William S., International Comity in American Law, 115 *Colum. L. Rev.* 2071 (2015).

Dodge, William S., Loose Canons: International Law and Statutory Interpretation in the Twenty-First Century, 547–552, in *International Law in the U.S. Supreme Court—Continuity and Change* (David L. Sloss et al. eds.), Cambridge: Cambridge University Press, 2011.

Dogan, Stacey L. & Lemley, Mark A., The Merchandising Right: Fragile Theory or Fait Accompli?, 54 *Emory L.J.* 461 (2005).

Dogan, Stacey L. & Lemley, Mark A., Trademark and Consumer Search Costs on the Internet, 41 *Hous. L. Rev.* 777 (2004).

Dogan, Stacey L. & Lemley, Mark A., What the Right of Publicity Can Learn from Trademark Law, 58 *Stan. L. Rev.* 1161 (2006).

Dölle, Hans, Rechtsdogmatik und Rechtsvergleichung, 34 *RabelsZ* 403 (1970).

Dornis, Tim W., Comity, in *Encyclopedia of Private International Law* (Jürgen Basedow et al. eds.), Cheltenham: Edward Elgar, forthcoming 2017.

Dornis, Tim W., Commentary to Jürgen Basedow, Toshiyuki Kono & Axel Metzger, Intellectual Property in the Global Arena (Tübingen 2010), 76 *RabelsZ* 695 (2012).

Dornis, Tim W., Das Kollisionsrecht der auftragslosen Geschäftsführung—Ein Beispiel für Materialisierung und Typisierung im modernen europäischen IPR, 80 *RabelsZ* 543 (2016).

Dornis, Tim W., Die Erbensuche im Kollisionsrecht—von grenzüberschreitender "Menschenhülfe" zu internationaler Marktregulierung, 2015 *ZfPW* 376.

Dornis, Tim W., "Local Data" in European Choice of Law: A Trojan Horse from Across the Atlantic?, 44 *Ga. J. Int'l & Comp. L.* 2015 (forthcoming).

Drasch, Wolfgang, *Das Herkunftslandprinzip im internationalen Privatrecht—Auswirkungen des europäischen Binnenmarktes auf Vertrags- und Wettbewerbsstatut*, Baden-Baden: Nomos-Verlagsgesellschaft, 1997.

Drescher, Thomas D., The Transformation and Evolution of Trademarks—From Signals to Symbols to Myth, 82 *Trademark Rep.* 301 (1992).

Drexl, Josef, *Die wirtschaftliche Selbstbestimmung des Verbrauchers—Eine Studie zum Privat- und Wirtschaftsrecht unter Berücksichtigung gemeinschaftsrechtlicher Bezüge*, Tübingen: Verlag Mohr Siebeck, 1998.

Drexl, Josef, The Proposed Rome II Regulation: European Choice of Law in the Field of Intellectual Property, 151–176, in *Intellectual Property and Private International Law—Heading for the Future* (Josef Drexl & Annette Kur eds.), Oxford and Portland/OR: Hart Publishing, 2005.

Drexl, Josef, Zum Verhältnis von lauterkeits- und kartellrechtlicher Anknüpfung nach der Rom-II-VO, 2713–2732, in *Festschrift für Klaus J. Hopt zum 70. Geburtstag: Unternehmen, Markt und Verantwortung* (Stefan Grundmann ed.), Berlin: Verlag DeGruyter, 2010.

Dreyfuss, Rochelle Cooper, Expressive Genericity: Trademarks as Language in the Pepsi Generation, 65 *Notre Dame L. Rev.* 397 (1990).

Dreyfuss, Rochelle Cooper, The ALI Principles on Transnational Intellectual Property Disputes: Why Invite Conflicts?, 30 *Brook. J. Int'l L.* 819 (2005).

Drobnig, Ulrich, Originärer Erwerb und Übertragung von Immaterialgüterrechten im Kollisionsrecht, 40 *RabelsZ* 195 (1976).

Drobnig, Ulrich, Private International Law, 1115–1120, in *Encyclopedia of Public International Law, vol. III* (Rudolf Bernhardt ed.), Amsterdam et al.: North-Holland, 1997.

Dubs, Dieter, *Das Lauterkeitsstatut nach schweizerischem Kollisionsrecht—Zugleich ein Beitrag zur Materialisierung des Internationalprivatrechts*, Buttikon: Prisma Druck, 2000.

Dutheillet de Lamothe, Alain, Advocate General, opinion to European Court of Justice case *Sirena,* 40/70, 1971 E.C.R. 85.

Dworkin, Ronald M., Why Efficiency?, 8 *Hofstra L. Rev.* 563 (1980).

Dyer, Adair, Unfair Competition in Private International Law, 211 *Recueil des Cours* 373 (1988–IV).

Easterbrook, Frank H., Intellectual Property Is Still Property, 13 *Harv. J. L. & Pub. Pol'y* 108 (1990).

Ebner, Martin, *Markenschutz im internationalen Privat- und Zivilprozessrecht*, Cologne et al.: Carl Heymanns Verlag, 2004.

Ehlers, Wolfram, Der persönlichkeitsrechtliche Schutz des Verbrauchers vor Werbung, 1983 *WRP* 187.

Ehrenzweig, Albert A., *A Treatise on the Conflict of Laws*, St. Paul/MN: West Publishing Co., 1962.

Ehrlich, Eugen, *Das lebende Recht der Völker der Bukowina*, in Recht und Wirtschaft 1 (1912), 273 (reprinted in *Eugen Ehrlich—Recht und Leben, Gesammelte Schriften zur Rechtstatsachenforschung und zur Freirechtslehre* (Manfred Rehbinder ed.), Berlin: Duncker & Humblot, 1967).

Ehrlich, Eugen, *Grundlegung der Soziologie des Rechts*, Berlin: Duncker & Humblot, 4th reprint of 1913 edn., 1989.

Eidenmüller, Horst, *Effizienz als Rechtsprinzip—Möglichkeiten und Grenzen der ökonomischen Analyse des Rechts*, Tübingen: Mohr-Siebeck, 3rd edn., 2005.

Eisenführ, Günter & Schennen, Detlef, *Kommentar zur Gemeinschaftsmarkenverordnung*, Cologne: Carl Heymanns Verlag, 4th edn., 2014.

Elliott, Tara, Risky Business: The Alien Tort Claims Act and the Foreign Corrupt Practices Act Expand the Reach of U.S. Courts in a Global Economy, 62 *Rutgers L. Rev.* 211 (2009).

Elskamp, Gregor, *Gesetzesverstoß und Wettbewerbsrecht—zur wettbewerbsrechtlichen Unzulässigkeit von Verstößen gegen außerwettbewerbsrechtliche Gesetze*, Baden-Baden: Nomos-Verlagsgesellschaft, 2008.

Elster, Alexander, *Gewerblicher Rechtsschutz umfassend Urheber- und Verlagsrecht, Patent- und Musterschutzrecht, Warenzeichenrecht und Wettbewerbsrecht*, Berlin and Leipzig: Verlag Walter de Gruyter & Co., 1921.

Emmerich, Volker, *Unlauterer Wettbewerb*, Munich: Verlag C.H. Beck, 9th edn., 2012.

Endemann, Wilhelm, Der Markenschutz nach dem Reichsgesetz vom 30. November 1874, 32 *Archiv für Theorie und Praxis des Allgemeinen Deutschen Handels- und Wechselrechts* 1 (1875).

Epstein, Lee & King, Gary, The Rules of Inference, 69 *U. Chi. L. Rev.* 1 (2002).

Epstein, Richard A., International News Service v. Associated Press: Custom and Law as Sources of Property Rights in News, 78 *Va. L. Rev.* 85 (1992).

Estabrook, Charles E., *American Interstate Law*, Chicago: Callaghan and Company, 2nd edn., 1893.

Eucken, Walter, Die Wettbewerbsordnung und ihre Verwirklichung, 2 *ORDO* 1 (1949).

Fathchild, Irvin H., Statutory Unfair Competition, 1 *Mo. L. Rev.* 20 (1936).

Fathchild, Irvin H., Territoriality of Registered Trade-Marks, 3 *Idaho L.J.* 193 (1933).

Fawcett, James J. & Torremans, Paul, *Intellectual Property and Private International Law*, Oxford: Oxford University Press, 2nd edn., 2011.

Feldon, Gary D., The Antitrust Model of Extraterritorial Trademark Jurisdiction: Analysis and Predictions After F. Hoffmann-La Roche, 20 *Emory Int'l L. Rev.* 651 (2006).

Fentiman, Richard, Choice of Law and Intellectual Property, 129–148, in *Intellectual Property and Private International Law—Heading for the Future* (Josef Drexl & Annette Kur eds.), Oxford and Portland/OR: Hart Publishing, 2005.

Ferrari, Lorenza, *Die Anknüpfung an die Marktauswirkung im Schweizerischen IPRG und ihre Konkretisierung*, Basel: Dissertation Thesis, 1993.

Fezer, Karl-Heinz, ed., *Lauterkeitsrecht: Kommentar zum Gesetz gegen den unlauteren Wettbewerb (UWG), vol. I & II*, Munich: Verlag C. H. Beck, 2nd edn., 2010.

Fezer, Karl-Heinz, *Markenrecht*, Munich: Verlag C.H. Beck, 4th edn., 2009.

Fezer, Karl-Heinz, Markenschutzfähigkeit der Kommunikationszeichen (§§ 3 und 8 MarkenG) und Kommunikationsschutz der Marken (§§ 14 und 23 MarkenG), 2010 *WRP* 165.

Fezer, Karl-Heinz, Modernisierung des deutschen Rechts gegen den unlauteren Wettbewerb auf der Grundlage einer Europäisierung des Wettbewerbsrechts, 2001 *WRP* 989.

Fezer, Karl-Heinz, Plädoyer für eine offensive Umsetzung der Richtlinie über unlautere Geschäftspraktiken in das deutsche UWG—Originärer Verbraucherschutz durch Lauterkeitsrecht als Paradigma der europäischen Rechtsharmonisierung, 2006 *WRP* 781.

Fezer, Karl-Heinz & Koos, Stefan, *Staudingers Kommentar zum Bürgerlichen Gesetzbuch mit Einführungsgesetz und Nebengesetzen, Einführungsgesetz zum Bürgerlichen Gesetzbuche/IPR, Internationales Wirtschaftsrecht (IPR des KartellR, LauterkeitsR, MarkenR, PatentR und UrheberR)*, Berlin: Verlag Sellier-de Gruyter, 15th edn., 2010.

Fikentscher, Wolfgang, Neuere Entwicklungen der Theorie zum Tatbestandsmerkmal der Wettbewerbsbeschränkung § 1 GWB, 1961 *WuW* 788.

Fikentscher, Wolfgang, *Wettbewerb und gewerblicher Rechtsschutz—Die Stellung des Rechts der Wettbewerbsbeschränkungen in der Rechtsordnung*, Munich and Berlin: C.H. Beck'sche Verlagsbuchhandlung, 1958.

Fikentscher, Wolfgang, *Wirtschaftsrecht, vol. I: Weltwirtschaftsrecht, Europäisches Wirtschaftsrecht*, Munich: C.H. Beck'sche Verlagsbuchhandlung, 1983.

Fikentscher, Wolfgang, *Wirtschaftsrecht, vol. II: Deutsches Wirtschaftsrecht*, Munich: C.H. Beck'sche Verlagsbuchhandlung, 1983.

Finger, Christian, *Das Reichsgesetz zum Schutz der Warenbezeichnungen vom 12. Mai 1894 nebst den Ausführungsbestimmungen und dem internationalen Warenbezeichnungsrecht*, Berlin: Verlag von Franz Vahlen, 2nd edn., 1906.

Finkelman, Paul, *An Imperfect Union: Slavery, Federalism, and Comity*, Chapel Hill: University of North Carolina Press, 1981.

Finkelman, Paul, When International Law Was a Domestic Problem, 44 *Val. U. L. Rev.* 779 (2010).

Fischer-Lescano, Andreas & Teubner, Gunther, Regime-Collisions: The Vain Search for Legal Unity in the Fragmentation of Global Law, 25 *Mich. J. Int'l L.* 999 (2004).

Fisher, William W. III, et al. (eds.), *American Legal Realism*, Oxford and New York: Oxford University Press, 1993.

Fitzmaurice, Gerald, The Future of Public International Law and of the International Legal System in the Circumstances of Today, 196–402, in *Institut de Droit International, Livre du Centenaire 1873–1973*, Basel: S. Karger, 1973.

Fleischer, Holger, Vertragsschlußbezogene Informationspflichten im Gemeinschaftsprivatrecht, 2000 *ZEuP* 772.

Flume, Werner, Verbotene Preisabsprache und Einzelvertrag, 1956 *WuW* 457.

Ford, Richard T., Law's Territory (A History of Jurisdiction), 97 *Mich. L. Rev.* 843 (1999).

Foreman, C. J., Conflicting Theories of Good Will, 22 *Colum. L. Rev.* 638 (1922).

Fox, Eleanor M., Modernization of Effects Jurisdiction: From Hands-Off to Hands-Linked, 42 *N.Y.U. J. Int'l L. & Pol.* 159 (2009).

Fox, Eleanor M., Trade, Competition, and Intellectual Property—TRIPS and its Antitrust Counterparts, 29 *Vand. J. Transnat'l L.* 481 (1996).

Francq, Stéphanie & Wurmnest, Wolfgang, International Antitrust Claims under the Rome II Regulation, 91–129, in *International Antitrust Litigation—Conflicts of Laws and Coordination* (Jürgen Basedow et al. eds.), Oxford and Portland/OR: Hart Publishing, 2012.

Fränkel, Rudolf, Der Irrgarten des internationalen Privatrechts, 4 *RabelsZ* 239 (1930).

Frankel, Susy, Unfair Competition Law—"Over Protection Stifles the Very Creative Force it is Supposed to Nurture," 267–284, in *International Intellectual Property and the Common Law World* (Charles Rickett & Graeme Austin eds.), Oxford and Portland/OR: Hart Publishing, 2000.

Frankenstein, Ernst, *Internationales Privatrecht (Grenzrecht), vol. I*, Berlin-Grunewald: Dr. Walther Rothschild, 1926.

Franklyn, David J., Debunking Dilution Doctrine: Toward a Coherent Theory of the Anti-Free-Rider Principle in American Trademark Law, 56 *Hastings L.J.* 117 (2004).

Freund, Stefan, *Das Persönlichkeitsrecht des Umworbenen—Ein bürgerlich-rechtlicher Beitrag zum Verbraucherschutz unter Berücksichtigung des Wettbewerbsrechts*, Munich: Verlag V. Florentz, 1983.

Friedman, Lawrence M., *A History of American Law*, New York et al.: Simon & Schuster, 3rd edn., 2005.

Friedman, Lawrence M., Borders: On the Emerging Sociology of Transnational Law, 32 *Stan. J. Int'l L.* 65 (1996).
Friedman, Lawrence M., Erewhon: The Coming Global Legal Order, 37 *Stan. J. Int'l L.* 347 (2001).
Froriep, Andreas, *Der unlautere Wettbewerb im internationalen Privatrecht*, Winterthur: Verlag Keller, 1958.
Fugate, Wilbur Lindsay, *Foreign Commerce and the Antitrust Laws*, Little, Boston: Brown & Company, 2nd edn., 1973.
Galbraith, John Kenneth, *The Affluent Society*, Boston: Houghton Mifflin Company, 40th Anniversary Edition, 1998 (original edn., 1958).
Gamillscheg, Franz, Gedanken zu einem System des internationalen Arbeitsrechts, 23 *RabelsZ* 819 (1958).
Gamm, Otto-Friedrich Freiherr von, *Wettbewerbsrecht, vol. I*, Cologne et al.: Carl Heymanns Verlag, 5th edn., 1987.
Garcimartín Alférez, Francisco J., The Rome II Regulation: On the way towards a European Private International Law Code, 7 *EuLF-I* 77 (2007).
Gareis, Carl, Das juristische Wesen der Autorrechte, sowie des Firmen- und Markenschutzes, 35 *Archiv für Theorie und Praxis des Allgemeinen Deutschen Handels- und Wechselrechts* 185 (1877).
Garnett, Richard L., Trademarks and the Internet: Resolution of International IP Disputes by Unilateral Application of U.S. Laws, 30 *Brook. J. Int'l L.* 925 (2005).
Gastambide, Adrien, *Traité théorique et pratique des contrefaçons en tous genres, ou de la propriété en matière de littérature, théatre, musique, peinture, dessin, gravure, dessins de manufactures, sculpture, sculptures industrielles, marques, noms, raisons commerciales, enseignes, etc.*, Paris: Legrand et Descauriet, 1837.
Geller, Leo, *Österreichisches Markenschutzgesetz*, Vienna: Verlag von Moritz Perles, 4th edn., 1906.
Geller, Paul Edward, Conflicts of Laws in Cyberspace: Rethinking International Copyright, 44 *J. Copyright Soc'y U.S.A.* 103 (1996).
Geller, Paul Edward, Conflicts of Laws in Cyberspace: Rethinking International Copyright in a Digitally Networked World, 20 *Colum.-VLA J. L. & Arts* 571 (1996).
Geller, Paul Edward, From Patchwork to Network: Strategies for International Intellectual Property in Flux, 9 *Duke J. Comp. & Int'l L.* 69 (1998).
Geller, Paul Edward, The Universal Electronic Archive: Issues in International Copyright, 25 *IIC* 54 (1994).
Geradin, Damien, Reysen, Marc & Henry, David, Extraterritoriality, Comity, and Cooperation in EU Competition Law, 21–44, in *Cooperation, Comity, and Competition Policy* (Andrew T. Guzman ed.), New York et al.: Oxford University Press, 2011.
Gerber, David J., The Extraterritorial Application of the German Antitrust Laws, 77 *Am. J. Int'l L.* 756 (1983).
Gerber, David J., Private Enforcement of Competition Law: A Comparative Perspective, 431–451, in *The Enforcement of Competition Law in Europe* (Thomas M.J. Möllers & Andreas Heinemann eds.), Cambridge: Cambridge University Press, 2007.
Gerhardt, Deborah R., Consumer Investment in Trademark, 88 *N.C. L. Rev.* 427 (2010).

Gierke, Otto von, Der Rechtsgrund des Schutzes gegen unlauteren Wettbewerb, 1895 *GRUR (ZfGewRS)* 109.

Gierke, Otto von, *Deutsches Privatrecht, vol. I: Allgemeiner Teil und Personenrecht*, Berlin: Verlag Duncker & Humblot, reprint of 1895 edn., 2010.

Gieseke, Paul, Recht am Unternehmen und Schutz des Unternehmens—Alte und neue deutsche Rechtsprechung, 1950 *GRUR* 298.

Ginsburg, Jane C., Comment, Extraterritoriality and Multiterritoriality in Copyright Infringement, 37 *Va. J. Int'l L.* 587 (1997).

Ginsburg, Jane C., Copyright Without Borders? Choice of Forum and Choice of Law for Copyright Infringement in Cyberspace, 15 *Cardozo Arts & Ent. L.J.* 153 (1997).

Ginsburg, Jane C., The Cyberian Captivity of Copyright: Territoriality and Authors' Rights in a Networked World, 15 *Santa Clara Computer & High Tech. L.J.* 347 (1999).

Ginsburg, Jane C., Ownership of Electronic Rights and the Private International Law of Copyright, 22 *Colum.-VLA J.L. & Arts* 165 (1998).

Ginsburg, Jane C., *Private International Law Aspects of the Protection of Works and Objects of Related Rights Transmitted through Global Networks*, WIPO document GCPIC/2 (30 November 1998) (online resource: available under www.wipo.int/meetings/en/doc_details.jsp?doc_id=926 (12 February 2016)).

Ginsburg, Jane C., The Private International Law of Copyright in an Era of Technological Change, 273 *Recueil des Cours* 239 (1998).

Glöckner, Jochen, Der grenzüberschreitende Lauterkeitsprozess nach BGH v. 11.2.2010—Ausschreibung in Bulgarien, 2011 *WRP* 137.

Glöckner, Jochen, Der Schutz vor Verwechslungsgefahr im Spannungsfeld von Kennzeichenrecht und verbraucherschützendem Lauterkeitsrecht, 145–179, in *Geistiges Eigentum und Gemeinfreiheit* (Ansgar Ohly & Diethelm Klippel eds.), Tübingen: Mohr Siebeck Verlag, 2007.

Glöckner, Jochen, *Europäisches Lauterkeitsrecht*, Munich: Verlag C.H. Beck, 2006.

Glöckner, Jochen, Wettbewerbsverstöße im Internet—Grenzen einer kollisionsrechtlichen Problemlösung, 99 *ZVglRWiss* 278 (2000).

Glöckner, Jochen & Henning-Bodewig, Frauke, EG-Richtlinie über unlautere Geschäftspraktiken: Was wird aus dem „neuen" UWG?, 2005 *WRP* 1311.

Gloede, Wilhelm, Der deutsche Außenhandel und seine wettbewerbsrechtliche Beurteilung nach deutschem internationalem Privatrecht, 1964 *GRUR* 464.

Gloy, Wolfgang, Die Entwicklung des Wettbewerbsrechts und seiner Nebengebiete, 855–896, in *Gewerblicher Rechtsschutz und Urheberrecht in Deutschland, Festschrift zum hundertjährigen Bestehen der Deutschen Vereinigung für gewerblichen Rechtsschutz und Urheberrecht und ihrer Zeitschrift, vol. II* (Friedrich-Karl Beier et al. eds.), Weinheim: VCH Verlagsgesellschaft mbH, 1991.

Godin, Hans Freiherr von, *Wettbewerbsrecht, Kommentar zum Gesetz gegen den unlauteren Wettbewerb nebst Warenzeichenverletzungen, Zugabeverordnung und Rabattgesetz*, Berlin and New York: Walter de Gruyter, 2nd edn., 1974.

Goldsmith, Jack L., Against Cyberanarchy, 65 *U. Chi. L. Rev.* 1199 (1998).

Goldsmith, Jack L., The Internet and the Abiding Significance of Territorial Sovereignty, 5 *Ind. J. Global Legal Stud.* 475 (1998).

Goldsmith, Jack L. & Sykes, Alan O., Lex Loci Delictus and Global Economic Welfare: Spinozzi v. ITT Sheraton Corp., 120 *Harv. L. Rev.* 1137 (2007).

Goldstein, Paul & Hugenholtz, P. Bernt, *International Copyright: Principles, Law, and Practice*, Oxford and New York: Oxford University Press, 3rd edn., 2013.

Gordon, Wendy J., A Property Right in Self-Expression: Equality and Individualism in the Natural Law of Intellectual Property, 102 *Yale L.J.* 1533 (1993).

Götting, Horst-Peter, *Gewerblicher Rechtsschutz—Patent-, Gebrauchsmuster-, Design- und Markenrecht*, Munich: Verlag C.H. Beck, 10th edn., 2014.

Götting, Horst-Peter et al., Länderteil Deutschland, 199–339, in *Handbuch des Ausstattungsrechts—Der Schutz der nichteingetragenen Marke und Ausstattung im In- und Ausland, Festgabe für Friedrich-Karl Beier zum 60. Geburtstag* (Gerhard Schricker & Dieter Stauder eds.), Weinheim: VCH Verlagsgesellschaft mbH, 1986.

Griffin, Joseph P., Extraterritoriality in U.S. and EU Antitrust Enforcement, 67 *Antitrust L.J.* 159 (1999).

Großfeld, Bernhard & Rogers, C. Paul, A Shared Values Approach to Jurisdictional Conflicts in International Economic Law, 32 *I.C.L.Q.* 931 (1983).

Gross, William Jay, The Territorial Scope of Trademark Rights, 44 *U. Miami L. Rev.* 1075 (1990).

Grynberg, Michael, Trademark Litigation as Consumer Conflict, 83 *N.Y.U. L. Rev.* 60 (2008).

Gul, Faruk & Pesendorfer, Wolfgang, The Revealed Preference Theory of Changing Tastes, 72 *Rev. Econ. Stud.* 429 (2005).

Gul, Faruk & Pesendorfer, Wolfgang, Self-Control and the Theory of Consumption, 72 *Econometrica* 119 (2004).

Gutzwiller, Max, *Der Einfluß Savignys auf die Entwicklung des Internationalprivatrechts*, Fribourg/CH: Universitäts-Buchhandlung (Gschwend, Tschopp & Co.), 1923.

Gutzwiller, Max, Zitelmanns völkerrechtliche Theorie des Internationalprivatrechts, 16 *Archiv für Rechts- und Wirtschaftsphilosophie* 468 (1922).

Guzman, Andrew T., Choice of Law: New Foundations, 90 *Geo. L.J.* 883 (2002).

Habscheid, Walther J., Territoriale Grenzen der staatlichen Rechtsetzung, 47–76, in *Berichte der Deutschen Gesellschaft für Völkerrecht (vol. 11)*, Karlsruhe: Verlag C.F. Müller 1973.

Hack, Friedrich, Die Aufgabe des Staats in Beziehung auf das gewerbliche Leben mit Rücksichtnahme auf die bestehenden Staats-Einrichtungen, 23 *Zeitschrift für die gesammte Staatswissenschaft* 39 (1867).

Hagens, Alfred, *Warenzeichenrecht*, Berlin and Leipzig: Verlag Walter de Gruyter & Co., 1927.

Hahn, Otto, *Das deutsche Markenschutzgesetz sowie Vorschläge zur Aenderung desselben auf Grund der bisherigen Erfahrungen*, Stuttgart: W. Kohlhammer Verlag, 1887.

Haines, Charles Grove, Efforts to Define Unfair Competition, 29 *Yale L.J.* 1 (1919).

Halfmeier, Axel, Menschenrechte und Internationales Privatrecht im Kontext der Globalisierung, 68 *RabelsZ* 653 (2004).

Hamburg Group for Private International Law, Comments on the European Commission's Draft Proposal for a Council Regulation on the Law Applicable to Non-Contractual Obligations, 67 *RabelsZ* 1 (2003).

Hamilton, Adelbert, Note, Good-Will, 15 *Fed. Rep.* 315 (1883).

Handig, Christian, Neues im Internationalen Wettbewerbsrecht—Auswirkungen der Rom II-Verordnung, 2008 *GRUR Int.* 24.

Handler, Milton & Pickett, Charles, Trade-Marks and Trade Names—An Analysis and Synthesis: I, 30 *Colum. L. Rev.* 168 (1930).

Handler, Milton & Pickett, Charles, Trade-Marks and Trade Names—An Analysis and Synthesis: II, 30 *Colum. L. Rev.* 759 (1930).

Harris, E. P., Random Thoughts on Trade and Advertising, 8 *Inland Printer* 202 (December 1890).

Hart, H. L. A., *The Concept of Law*, Oxford: Clarendon Press, 2nd edn., 1961.

Harte-Bavendamm, Henning & Henning-Bodewig, Frauke, eds., *Gesetz gegen den unlauteren Wettbewerb (UWG)*, Munich: Verlag C.H. Beck, 3rd edn., 2013.

Hauser, Marco, *Die Inzidenz der Publikumsinteressen auf Wesen und Umfang des Markenrechts*, Chur: Buch- und Offsetdruckerei Bündner Tagblatt, 1966.

Hay, Peter, Borchers, Patrick J. & Symeonides, Symeon C., *Conflict of Laws*, St. Paul/MN: Thomson Reuters, 5th edn., 2010.

Hayek, Friedrich August von, Bemerkungen über die Entwicklung von Systemen von Verhaltensregeln, 144–160, in *Freiburger Studien: Gesammelte Aufsätze*, Tübingen: Mohr Siebeck, 1969.

Hayek, Friedrich August von, Der Wettbewerb als Entdeckungsverfahren, 3–20, in *Kieler Vorträge gehalten am Institut für Weltwirtschaft an der Universität Kiel* (Erich Schneider ed.), Kiel: Universität, Institut für Wirtschaftsrecht, 1968.

Hayek, Friedrich August von, *Law, Legislation and Liberty—A New Statement of the Liberal Principles of Justice and Political Economy, vol. I: Rules and Order*, Chicago: University of Chicago Press, 1973.

Hayek, Friedrich August von, *The Road to Serfdom: Text and Documents*, Bruce Caldwell ed., Chicago: University of Chicago Press, 2007 (original edn., 1944).

Heck, Philipp, *Grundriß des Schuldrechts*, Aalen: Scientia Verlag, 3rd reprint of 1929 edn., 1994.

Heermann, Peter W., et al., eds., *Münchener Kommentar zum Lauterkeitsrecht, vol. I & II*, Munich: Beck-Verlag, 2nd edn., 2014.

Heermann, Peter W., et al., eds., *Münchener Kommentar zum Lauterkeitsrecht, vol. I & II*, Munich: Beck-Verlag, 2006.

Hefermehl, Wolfgang, Der Anwendungsbereich des Wettbewerbsrechts, 283–301, in *Festschrift für Hans Carl Nipperdey zum 60. Geburtstag* (Rolf Dietz et al. eds.), Munich and Berlin: C.H. Beck'sche Verlagsbuchhandlung, 1955.

Hefermehl, Wolfgang & Baumbach, Adolf, *Wettbewerbsrecht—Gesetz gegen den unlauteren Wettbewerb, Zugabeverordnung, Rabattgesetz und Nebengesetze*, Munich: Beck-Verlag, 18th edn., 1995.

Hein, Jan von, Die Kodifikation des europäischen Internationalen Deliktsrechts—Zur geplanten EU-Verordnung über das auf außervertragliche Schuldverhältnisse anzuwendende Recht, 102 *ZVglRWiss* 528 (2003).

Heinemann, Andreas, *Die Freiburger Schule und ihre geistigen Wurzeln*, Munich: Verlag V. Florentz, 1989.

Heinemann, Andreas, *Immaterialgüterschutz in der Wettbewerbsordnung—Eine grundlagenorientierte Untersuchung zum Kartellrecht des geistigen Eigentums*, Tübingen: Verlag Mohr Siebeck, 2002.

Heinemann, Andreas, The Rise of a Private Competition Law Culture: Experience and Visions, 218–229, in *Private Enforcement of Competition Law* (Jürgen Basedow et al. eds.), Baden-Baden: Nomos-Verlagsgesellschaft, 2011.

Hellner, Michael, Unfair Competition and Acts Restricting Free Competition—A Commentary on Article 6 of the Rome II Regulation, 9 *Yearb. P.I.L.* 49 (2007).

Henkin, Louis, International Law as Law in the United States, 82 *Mich. L. Rev.* 1555 (1984).

Henning-Bodewig, Frauke, Der Schutzzweck des UWG und die Richtlinie über unlautere Geschäftspraktiken, 2013 *GRUR* 238.

Henning-Bodewig, Frauke, Marke und Verbraucher, 176–189, in *Die Neuordnung des Markenrechts in Europa—10. Ringberg-Symposium des Max-Planck-Instituts für ausländisches und internationales Patent-, Urheber- und Wettbewerbsrecht* (Gerhard Schricker & Friedrich-Karl Beier eds.), Baden-Baden: Nomos-Verlagsgesellschaft, 1996.

Henning-Bodewig, Frauke, Nationale Eigenständigkeit und europäische Vorgaben im Lauterkeitsrecht, 2010 *GRUR Int.* 549.

Henning-Bodewig, Frauke, Was gehört zum Lauterkeitsrecht?, 9–24, in *Lauterkeitsrecht und Acquis Communautaire* (Reto M. Hilty & Frauke Henning-Bodewig eds.), Berlin: Springer Verlag, 2009.

Henning-Bodewig, Frauke & Kur, Annette, *Marke und Verbraucher—Funktionen der Marke in der Marktwirtschaft, vol. I: Grundlagen*, Weinheim: VCH Verlagsgesellschaft mbH, 1988.

Hesseltine, Norman F., *A Digest of the Law of Trade-Marks and Unfair Trade*, Boston: Little, Brown & Co., 1906.

Heydt, Ludwig, Wege zur Vereinheitlichung des europäischen Markenrechts, 1960 *GRUR Ausl.* 348.

Heydt, Ludwig, Zum Begriff der Weltmarke, 1952 *GRUR* 321.

Heymann, Ernst, Zur Einführung der Weltmarke, 1928 *JW* 2004.

Hiebert, Timothy H., *Parallel Importation in U.S. Trademark Law*, Westport/CT: Greenwood Press, 1994.

Hilty, Reto M., The Law Against Unfair Competition and Its Interfaces, 1–52, in *Law Against Unfair Competition—Towards a New Paradigm in Europe?* (Reto M. Hilty & Frauke Henning-Bodewig eds.), Berlin: Springer Verlag, 2007.

Hilty, Reto M., von der Crone, Hans Caspar & Weber, Rolf H., Stellungnahme zur Anpassung des UWG: Ambush Marketing, 2006 *sic!* 702.

Hirsch, Günter, ed., *Münchener Kommentar: Europäisches und Deutsches Wettbewerbsrecht, vol. I: Europäisches Wettbewerbsrecht*, Munich: Beck-Verlag, 2nd edn., 2015.

Hobson, John A., *The Evolution of Modern Capitalism—A Study of Machine Production*, London: George Allen & Unwin Ltd., 1913.

Höder, Andreas, *Die kollisionsrechtliche Behandlung unteilbarer Multistate-Verstöße—Das Internationale Wettbewerbsrecht im Spannungsfeld von Marktort-, Auswirkungs- und Herkunftslandprinzip*, Munich: Verlag C.H. Beck, 2002.

Hoffmann, J. G., *Die Befugniss zum Gewerbebetriebe. Zur Berichtigung der Urtheile über Gewerbefreiheit und Gewerbezwang, mit besonderer Rücksicht auf den Preussischen Staat dargestellt*, Berlin: Verlag der Nicolaischen Buchhandlung, 1841.

Hohfeld, Wesley Newcomb, Fundamental Legal Conceptions as Applied in Judicial Reasoning, 26 *Yale L.J.* 710 (1917).

Hohfeld, Wesley Newcomb, Some Fundamental Legal Conceptions as Applied in Judicial Reasoning, 23 *Yale L.J.* 16 (1913).

Holmes, Oliver Wendell, Jr., Privilege, Malice, and Intent, 8 *Harv. L. Rev.* 1 (1894).

Holmes, Oliver Wendell, Jr., *The Common Law*, New York: Dover Publications, Inc., reprint of 1881 edn., 1991.

Honorati, Costanza, The Law Applicable to Unfair Competition, 127–158, in *The Unification of Choice of Law Rules on Torts and Other Non-Contractual Obligations in Europe—The "Rome II" Proposal* (Alberto Malatesta ed.), Padova: CEDAM, 2006.

Honsell, Heinrich, et al., eds., *Markenschutzgesetz, Muster- und Modellgesetz*, Basel et al.: Helbing & Lichtenhahn, 2nd edn., 1999.

Hopkins, James Love, *The Law of Trademarks, Tradenames, and Unfair Competition*, Chicago: Callaghan & Co., 2nd edn., 1905.

Hoppmann, Erich, Das Konzept der optimalen Wettbewerbsintensität—Rivalität oder Freiheit des Wettbewerbs: Zum Problem eines wettbewerbspolitisch adäquaten Ansatzes der Wettbewerbstheorie, 179 *JBNSt* 286 (1966).

Hoppmann, Erich, Workable Competition als wettbewerbspolitisches Konzept, 145–197, in *Theoretische und institutionelle Grundlagen der Wirtschaftspolitik: Theodor Wessels zum 65. Geburtstag* (Hans Albert et al. eds.), Berlin: Duncker & Humblot Verlag, 1967.

Hoppmann, Erich, Zum Problem einer wirtschaftspolitisch praktikablen Definition des Wettbewerbs, 9–49, in *Grundlagen der Wettbewerbspolitik, Schriften des Vereins für Socialpolitik, vol. 48* (Hans K. Schneider ed.), Berlin: Verlag Duncker und Humblot, 1968.

Horwitz, Morton J., The History of the Public/Private Distinction, 130 *U. Pa. L. Rev.* 1423 (1982).

Horwitz, Morton J., *The Transformation of American Law, 1780–1860*, Cambridge/MA: Harvard University Press, 1977.

Hoth, Jürgen, Territoriale Grenzen des Schutzbereichs von Warenbezeichnungen, 1968 *GRUR* 64.

Hovenkamp, Herbert, *Federal Antitrust Policy—The Law of Competition and Its Practice*, St. Paul/MN: Thomson West, 3rd edn., 2005.

Huber, Peter, ed., *Rome II Regulation (commentary)*, Munich: Sellier European Law Publishers, 2011.

Hufbauer, Gary Clyde & Mitrokostas, Nicholas K., *Awakening the Monster: The Alien Tort Statute of 1789*, Washington/DC: Institute for International Economics, 2003.

Hufbauer, Gary Clyde & Mitrokostas, Nicholas K., International Implications of the Alien Tort Statute, 16 *St. Thomas L. Rev.* 607 (2004).

Huffman, Max, A Standing Framework for Private Extraterritorial Antitrust Enforcement, 60 *SMU L. Rev.* 103 (2007).

Hüßtege, Rainer & Mansel, Heinz-Peter, eds., *Nomos-Kommentar-BGB, Rom-Verordnungen, vol. VI*, Baden-Baden: Nomos-Verlag, 2014.

Hye-Knudsen, Rebekka, *Marken-, Patent- und Urheberrechtsverletzungen im europäischen Internationalen Zivilprozessrecht*, Tübingen: Verlag Mohr Siebeck, 2005.

Imhoff-Scheier, Anne-Catherine, La loi applicable à la publicité internationale en droit international privé suisse, 41 *SchwJbIntR* 57 (1985).

Immenga, Ulrich & Mestmäcker, Ernst-Joachim, eds., *Kommentar zum Europäischen Kartellrecht (Wettbewerbsrecht, vol. I: EU/part 1)*, Munich: Verlag C.H. Beck, 5th edn., 2012.

Ingerl, Reinhard & Rohnke, Christian, *Kommentar zum Markengesetz: Gesetz über den Schutz von Marken und sonstigen Kennzeichen*, Munich: Beck-Verlag, 3rd edn., 2010.

Institut de Droit International, Resolution, in 17 *ArchVölkR* 130 (1976).

Isay, Hermann, Die Gefährdung des gewerblichen Rechtsschutzes durch die Anwendung des § 1 UWG, 1928 *GRUR* 71.

Isay, Hermann, Die Selbständigkeit des Rechts an der Marke, 1929 *GRUR* 23.

Jacobs, Advocate General, opinion to Court of Justice case *CNL-SUCAL v. HAG* ("HAG II"), C-10/89, 1990 E.C.R. I—3725.

Jacobs, Rainer, et al., eds., *Großkommentar—UWG: Gesetz gegen den unlauteren Wettbewerb, vol. I*, Berlin et al.: De Gruyter Verlag, 1991 (and later).

Jaenicke, Günther, Zur Frage des internationalen ordre public, 77–132, in *Berichte der Deutschen Gesellschaft für Völkerrecht (vol. 7)*, Karlsruhe: C.F. Müller Verlag, 1967.

Jayme, Erik, Völkerrecht und Internationales Privatrecht—eine entwicklungsgeschichtliche Betrachtung, 23–41, in *Völkerrecht und IPR* (Stefan Leible & Matthias Ruffert eds.), Jena: Jenaer Wissenschaftliche Verlagsgesellschaft, 2006.

Jefferson, Thomas, Letter to Isaac McPherson (Monticello, 13 August 1813), 326–337, in *The Writings of Thomas Jefferson* (Andrew A. Lipscomb & Albert Ellery Bergh eds.), part 13, Washington/ DC: Issued under the auspices of the Thomas Jefferson Memorial Association of the United States, 1905.

Jennings, R. Y., Extraterritorial Jurisdiction and the United States Antitrust Laws, 33 *Brit. Y.B. Int'l L.* 146 (1957).

Jessup, Philip C., *Transnational Law (Storrs Lectures on Jurisprudence)*, New Haven: Yale University Press, 1956.

Joerges, Christian, Die klassische Konzeption des internationalen Privatrechts und das Recht des unlauteren Wettbewerbs, 36 *RabelsZ* 421 (1972).

Joerges, Christian, Vorüberlegungen zu einer Theorie des internationalen Wirtschaftsrechts, 43 *RabelsZ* 6 (1979).

Joerges, Christian, *Zum Funktionswandel des Kollisionsrechts—Die „Governmental Interest Analysis" und die „Krise des Internationalen Privatrechts,"* Tübingen: J.C.B. Mohr (Paul Siebeck), 1971.

Johnson, David R. & Post, David, Law and Borders—The Rise of Law in Cyberspace, 48 *Stan. L. Rev.* 1367 (1996).

Jolls, Christine, Sunstein, Cass R. & Thaler, Richard H., A Behavioral Approach to Law and Economics, 13–58, in *Behavioral Law and Economics* (Cass R. Sunstein ed.), Cambridge: Cambridge University Press, 2000.

Jones, Clifford A., Exporting Antitrust Courtrooms to the World: Private Enforcement in a Global Market, 16 *Loy. Consumer L. Rev.* 409 (2004).

Juenger, Friedrich K., *Choice of Law and Multistate Justice*, Dordrecht et al.: Martinus Nijhoff Publishers, 1993.

Juenger, Friedrich K., Constitutional Control of Extraterritoriality?: A Comment on Professor Brilmayer's Appraisal, 50 *Law & Contemp. Probs.* 39 (1987).

Juenger, Friedrich K., General Course on Private International Law, 193 *Recueil des Cours* 119 (1985–IV).

Juenger, Friedrich K., The Need for a Comparative Approach to Choice-of-Law Problems, 73 *Tul. L. Rev.* 1309 (1999).

Jüngel, Friedrich & Magnus, Julius, *Das deutsche Warenzeichenrecht*, Berlin und Leipzig: Verlag Walter de Gruyter & Co., 6th edn., 1933.

Junker, Abbo, Die Rom II-Verordnung: Neues Internationales Deliktsrecht auf europäischer Grundlage, 2007 *NJW* 3675.

Kadner Graziano, Thomas, Das auf außervertragliche Schuldverhältnisse anzuwendende Recht nach Inkrafttreten der Rom II-Verordnung, 73 *RabelsZ* 1 (2009).

Kagami, Kazuaki, The Systematic Choice of Legal Rules for Private International Law: An Economic Approach, 15–31, in *An Economic Analysis of Private International Law* (Jürgen Basedow & Toshiyuki Kono eds.), Tübingen: Mohr Siebeck, 2006.

Kahn, Franz, Bedeutung der Rechtsvergleichung mit Bezug auf das internationale Privatrecht, 491–503, in *Abhandlungen zum internationalen Privatrecht, vol. I* (Otto Lenel & Hans Lewald eds.), Munich: Verlag Duncker & Humblot, 1928.

Kahn, Franz, *Die Lehre vom ordre public (Prohibitivgesetze)*, 161–254, in *Abhandlungen zum internationalen Privatrecht, vol. I* (Otto Lenel & Hans Lewald eds.), Munich: Verlag Duncker & Humblot, 1928.

Kahn, Franz, Gesetzeskollisionen—Ein Beitrag zur Lehre des internationalen Privatrechts, 1–160, in *Abhandlungen zum internationalen Privatrecht, vol. I* (Otto Lenel & Hans Lewald eds.), Munich: Verlag Duncker & Humblot, 1928.

Kahn, Franz, Über Inhalt, Natur und Methode des internationalen Privatrechts, 255–326, in *Abhandlungen zum internationalen Privatrecht, vol. I* (Otto Lenel & Hans Lewald eds.), Munich: Verlag Duncker & Humblot, 1928 (reprint of *Über Inhalt, Natur und Methode des internationalen Privatrechts*, 40 JherJB 1 (1898)).

Kahn-Freund, Otto, *The Growth of Internationalism in English Private International Law (Lionel Cohen Lectures)*, Jerusalem: Magnes Press, Hebrew University, 1960.

Kahneman, Daniel, *Thinking, Fast and Slow*, London: Penguin Books, Ltd., 2011.

Kamperman Sanders, Anselm, *Unfair Competition Law—The Protection of Intellectual and Industrial Creativity*, Oxford: Clarendon Press, 1997.

Kantzenbach, Erhard, *Die Funktionsfähigkeit des Wettbewerbs*, Göttingen: Verlag Vandenhoeck & Ruprecht, 2nd edn., 1967.

Katz, Edwin, *Gesetz zum Schutz der Waarenbezeichnungen und unlauterer Wettbewerb, Vortrag gehalten vor der Juristischen Gesellschaft von Berlin und im Berliner Anwaltsverein, Veröffentlichungen des Berliner Anwalt-Vereins*, Heft 4, Berlin: Verlag Siemenroth & Worms, 1894.

Katz, Edwin, *Weltmarkenrecht*, Berlin: Carl Heymanns Verlag, 1926.

Katzenbach, Nicholas de Belleville, Conflicts on an Unruly Horse: Reciprocal Claims and Tolerances in Interstate and International Law, 65 *Yale L.J.* 1087 (1956).

Katzenberger, Paul, Kollisionsrecht des unlauteren Wettbewerbs, 218–230, in *Neuordnung des Wettbewerbsrechts, 11. Ringberg-Symposium des Max-Planck-*

Instituts für ausländisches und internationales Patent-, Urheber- und Wettbewerbsrecht (Gerhard Schricker & Frauke Henning-Bodewig eds.), Baden-Baden: Nomos Verlagsgesellschaft, 1998.

Keeton, W. Page, *Prosser and Keeton on the Law of Torts*, St. Paul/MN: West Publ., 5th edn., 2004.

Kegel, Gerhard, Begriffs- und Interessenjurisprudenz im internationalen Privatrecht, 259–288, in *Festschrift Hans Lewald* (Max Gerwig et al. eds.), Vaduz/Liechtenstein: Topos Verlag, reprint of 1953 edn., 1978.

Kegel, Gerhard, The Crisis of Conflict of Laws, 112 *Recueil des Cours* 91 (1964–II).

Kegel, Gerhard, Story and Savigny, 37 *Am. J. Comp. L.* 39 (1989).

Kegel, Gerhard, Wandel auf dünnem Eis, 35–44, in *Zum Wandel des internationalen Privatrechts* (Friedrich K. Juenger ed.), Karlsruhe: Müller Verlag, 1974.

Kegel, Gerhard & Schurig, Klaus, *Internationales Privatrecht*, Munich: Beck-Verlag, 9th edn., 2004.

Keirsbilck, Bert, *The New European Law of Unfair Commercial Practices and Competition Law*, Oxford and Portland/OR: Hart Publishing, 2011.

Keitner, Chimène I., Response, Optimizing Liability for Extraterritorial Torts: A Response to Professor Sykes, 100 *Geo. L.J.* 2211 (2012).

Kelman, Mark, Law and Behavioral Science: Conceptual Overviews, 97 *Nw. U. L. Rev.* 1347 (2003).

Kennedy, Duncan, Form and Substance in Private Law Adjudication, 89 *Harv. L. Rev.* 1685 (1976).

Kennedy, Duncan, The Role of Law in Economic Thought: Essays on the Fetishism of Commodities, 34 *Am. U. L. Rev.* 939 (1985).

Kent, Paul, *Das Reichsgesetz zum Schutz der Waarenbezeichnungen vom 12. Mai 1894—Unter Berücksichtigung in- und ausländischer Literatur und Rechtsprechung sowie der Praxis des Patentamts*, Berlin: Carl Heymanns Verlag, 1897.

Keßler, Jürgen, Die umweltbezogene Aussage in der Produktwerbung—dogmatische und wettbewerbstheoretische Aspekte des Irreführungsverbots, 1988 *WRP* 714.

Keßler, Jürgen, „Marktordnung, Wettbewerb und Meinungsfreiheit"—wettbewerbstheoretische und verfassungsrechtliche Aspekte des § 6e UWG, 1987 *WRP* 75.

Keßler, Jürgen, Vom Recht des unlauteren Wettbewerbs zum Recht der Marktkommunikation—Individualrechtliche und institutionelle Aspekte des deutschen und europäischen Lauterkeitsrechts, 2005 *WRP* 1203.

Keßler, Jürgen, Wettbewerbstheoretische Aspekte des Irreführungsverbotes—eine ökonomische und dogmengeschichtliche Analyse, 1990 *WRP* 73.

Kieninger, Eva-Maria, Die Lokalisierung von Wettbewerbsverstößen im Internet—Ist das Marktortprinzip zukunftsfähig?, 121–133, in *Die Bedeutung des Internationalen Privatrechts im Zeitalter der neuen Medien* (Stefan Leible ed.), Stuttgart et al.: Richard Boorberg Verlag, 2003.

King, Kevin F., Geolocation and Federalism on the Internet: Cutting Internet Gambling's Gordian Knot, 11 *Colum. Sci. & Tech. L. Rev.* 42 (2010).

Kinsella, N. Stephan, Against Intellectual Property, 15 *J. Libertarian Stud.* 1 (2001).

Kirios, Alan G., Territoriality and International Copyright Infringement Actions, 22 *Copyright L. Symp. (ASCAP)* 53 (1977).

Klein, Peter, Die Möglichkeit eines Weltprivatrechts, 3–23, in *Festschrift für Ernst Zitelmann* (Fritz Stier-Somlo ed.), Munich and Leipzig: Verlag Duncker & Humblot, 1913.

Kleinschrod, C. Th., *Beiträge zu einer deutschen Gewerbeordnung mit Rücksicht auf die bayerische Gewerbsgesetzgebung*, Augsburg: Verlag der K. Kollmann'schen Buchhandlung, 1840.

Klieger, Robert N., Trademark Dilution: The Whittling Away of the Rational Basis for Trademark Protection, 58 *U. Pitt. L. Rev.* 789 (1997).

Klippel, Diethelm, Die Bedeutung des Rheinischen Rechts für die Entwicklung des Namens- und Firmenschutzes in Deutschland, 123–156, in *Revolution, Reform, Restauration: Formen der Veränderung von Recht und Gesellschaft* (Heinz Mohnhaupt ed.), Frankfurt am Main: Vittorio Klostermann, 1988.

Klostermann, R., *Das geistige Eigenthum an Schriften, Kunstwerken und Erfindungen, nach Preussischem und internationalem Rechte, vol. I (Allgemeiner Theil—Verlagsrecht und Nachdruck)*, Berlin: Verlag von I. Guttentag, 1867.

Klostermann, R., *Das geistige Eigenthum an Schriften, Kunstwerken und Erfindungen, nach Preussischem und internationalem Rechte, vol. II (Patentgesetzgebung—Musterschutz—Waarenbezeichnungen)*, Berlin: Verlag von I. Guttentag, 1869.

Knaak, Roland, Der Schutz geographischer Herkunftsangaben im neuen Markengesetz, 1995 *GRUR* 103.

Knight, F. H., Cost of Production and Price over Long and Short Periods, 29 *J. Pol. Econ* 304 (1921).

Knöpfle, Robert, *Der Rechtsbegriff "Wettbewerb" und die Realität des Wirtschaftslebens*, Cologne et al.: Carl Heymanns Verlag, 1966.

Koch, Harald, Commentary to BGH, decision of 15 November 1990—I ZR 22/89 (Kauf im Ausland), 1991 *JZ* 1039.

Koh, Harold Hongju, Is International Law Really State Law?, 111 *Harv. L. Rev.* 1824 (1998).

Koh, Harold Hongju, Separating Myth from Reality About Corporate Responsibility Litigation, 7 *J. Int'l Econ. L.* 263 (2004).

Koh, Harold Hongju, The Globalization of Freedom, 26 *Yale J. Int'l L.* 305 (2001).

Koh, Harold Hongju, Transnational Legal Process, 75 *Nebr. L. Rev.* 181 (1996).

Koh, Harold Hongju, Why Transnational Law Matters, 24 *Penn. St. Int'l L. Rev.* 745 (2006).

Köhler, Helmut, Das Verhältnis des Wettbewerbsrechts zum Recht des geistigen Eigentums—Zur Notwendigkeit einer Neubestimmung auf Grund der Richtlinie über unlautere Geschäftspraktiken, 2007 *GRUR* 548.

Köhler, Helmut, Die wettbewerbsrechtlichen Abwehransprüche (Unterlassung, Beseitigung, Widerruf), 1992 *NJW* 137.

Köhler, Helmut, Wettbewerbsstatut oder Deliktsstatut?—Zur Auslegung des Art. 6 Rom-II-VO, 501–510, in *Festschrift für Dagmar Coester-Waltjen* (Katharina Hilbig-Lugani et al. eds.), Bielefeld: Verlag Ernst und Werner Gieseking, 2015.

Köhler, Helmut, Zur Bereicherungshaftung bei Wettbewerbsverstößen, 167–182, in *Festschrift für Werner Lorenz zum 80. Geburtstag* (Thomas Rauscher & Heinz-Peter Mansel eds.), Munich: Sellier, European Law Publishers, 2001.

Köhler, Helmut, Zur Konkurrenz lauterkeitsrechtlicher und kartellrechtlicher Normen, 2005 *WRP* 645.

Köhler, Helmut, Zur Umsetzung der Richtlinie über unlautere Geschäftspraktiken, 2005 *GRUR* 793.

Köhler, Helmut & Bornkamm, Joachim, *Gesetz gegen den unlauteren Wettbewerb: UWG (mit PAngV, UKlaG, DL-InfoV)*, Munich: Verlag C.H. Beck, 33rd edn., 2015.

Kohler, Josef, *Das Autorrecht, eine zivilistische Abhandlung—Zugleich ein Beitrag zur Lehre vom Eigenthum, vom Miteigenthum, vom Rechtsgeschäft und vom Individualrecht*, Jena: Verlag von Gustav Fischer, 1880.

Kohler, Josef, *Das Recht des Markenschutzes mit Berücksichtigung ausländischer Gesetzgebungen und mit besonderer Rücksicht auf die englische, anglo-amerikanische, französische, belgische und italienische Jurisprudenz*, Würzburg: Stahel'sche Universitätsbuchhandlung, 1884.

Kohler, Josef, *Der unlautere Wettbewerb—Darstellung des Wettbewerbsrechts*, Berlin und Leipzig: Verlag Dr. Walther Rothschild, 1914.

Kohler, Josef, Die Idee des geistigen Eigentums, 82 *AcP* 141 (1894).

Kohler, Josef, *Lehrbuch des Patentrechts*, Mannheim und Leipzig: Verlag von J. Bensheimer, 1908.

Kohler, Josef, *Warenzeichenrecht—Zugleich zweite Auflage des Rechts des Markenschutzes mit Berücksichtigung ausländischer Gesetzgebungen (1884)*, Mannheim und Leipzig: Verlag J. Bensheimer, 2nd edn., 1910.

Köhler, Walter, Verwechselungsgefahr im Ausland, 1933 *MuW* 332.

Kojima, Ryu, Shimanami, Ryo & Nagata, Mari, Applicable Law to Exploitation of Intellectual Property Rights in the Transparency Proposal, 179–228, in *Intellectual Property in the Global Arena—Jurisdiction, Applicable Law, and the Recognition of Judgments in Europe, Japan and the US* (Jürgen Basedow et al. eds.), Tübingen: Verlag Mohr Siebeck, 2010.

Kono, Toshiyuki et al., Preface, V-VI, in *Intellectual Property in the Global Arena—Jurisdiction, Applicable Law, and the Recognition of Judgments in Europe, Japan and the US* (Jürgen Basedow et al. eds.), Tübingen: Mohr Siebeck, 2010.

Koos, Stefan, *Europäischer Lauterkeitsmaßstab und globale Integration—Beitrag zu einer weltmarktorientierten Sichtweise des nationalen und gemeinschaftlichen Wettbewerbsrechts*, Munich: Verlag C.H. Beck, 1996.

Koos, Stefan, Grundsätze des Lauterkeitskollisionsrechts im Lichte der Schutzzwecke des UWG, 2006 *WRP* 499.

Koos, Stefan, Objektive Kriterien zur Feststellung des anwendbaren Rechts im Internationalen Wettbewerbs- und Immaterialgüterrecht, 2007 *IPRax* 414.

Koos, Stefan, Rom II und das Internationale Wirtschaftsrecht, 6 *EuLF* 73 (2006).

Kort, Michael, Zur „multistate"-Problematik grenzüberschreitender Fernsehwerbung, 1994 *GRUR Int.* 594.

Koskenniemi, Martti, *The Gentle Civilizer of Nations: The Rise and Fall of International Law 1870–1960*, Cambridge: Cambridge University Press, 2001.

Kotthoff, Jost, Die Anwendbarkeit des deutschen Wettbewerbsrechts auf Werbemaßnahmen im Internet, 1997 *CR* 676.

Kotthoff, Jost, *Werbung ausländischer Unternehmen im Inland—Die Beurteilung grenzüberschreitender Werbung nach dem internationalen Privatrecht, dem Wettbewerbsrecht und dem Recht der Europäischen Union*, Baden-Baden: Nomos Verlagsgesellschaft, 1995.

Kozinski, Alex, Trademarks Unplugged, 68 *N.Y.U. L. Rev.* 960 (1993).

Kraft, Alfons, Die Entwicklung des Warenzeichenrechts als Teil des allgemeinen Wettbewerbsrechts, 729–763, in *Gewerblicher Rechtsschutz und Urheberrecht in Deutschland, Festschrift zum hundertjährigen Bestehen der Deutschen Vereinigung für gewerblichen Rechtsschutz und Urheberrecht und ihrer Zeitschrift, vol. II* (Friedrich-Karl Beier et al. eds.), Weinheim: VCH Verlagsgesellschaft mbH, 1991.

Kraft, Alfons, Verbraucherschutz und Markenrecht, 1980 *GRUR* 416.

Kramer, Larry, On the Need for a Uniform Choice of Law Code, 89 *Mich. L. Rev.* 2134 (1991).

Kramer, Larry, Rethinking Choice of Law, 90 *Colum. L. Rev.* 277 (1990).

Kramer, Larry, Return of the Renvoi, 66 *N.Y.U. L. Rev.* 979 (1991).

Kramer, Larry, Vestiges of Beale: Extraterritorial Application of American Law, 1991 *Sup. Ct. Rev.* 179.

Krasser, Rudolf, Die Entwicklung der Ordnung des Wettbewerbsrechts in der französischen und deutschen Rechtsprechung des 19. Jahrhunderts, 145–162, in *Wissenschaft und Kodifikation des Privatrechts im 19. Jahrhundert, vol. IV* (Helmut Coing & Walter Wilhelm eds.), Frankfurt am Main: Klostermann, 1979.

Kratzke, William P., Normative Economic Analysis of Trademark Law, 21 *Mem. St. U. L. Rev.* 199 (1991).

Kraver, Pamela E. & Purcell, Robert E., Application of the Lanham Act to Extraterritorial Activities: Trend Toward Universality or Imperialism?, 77 *Pat. & Trademark Off. Soc'y* 115 (1995).

Krawiec, Kimberly D. & Zeller, Kathryn, Common-Law Disclosure Duties and the Sin of Omission: Testing the Meta-Theories, 91 *Va. L. Rev.* 1795 (2005).

Kreuzer, Karl F., *Ausländisches Wirtschaftsrecht vor deutschen Gerichten—Zum Einfluß fremdstaatlicher Eingriffsnormen auf private Rechtsgeschäfte*, Heidelberg: C.F. Müller Juristischer Verlag, 1986.

Kreuzer, Karl F., Die Vergemeinschaftung des Kollisionsrechts für außervertragliche Schuldverhältnisse (Rom II), 13–62, in *Europäisches Kollisionsrecht* (Gerte Reichelt & Walter H. Rechberger eds.), Vienna: Manzsche Verlags- und Universitätsbuchhandlung, 2004.

Kreuzer, Karl F., Wettbewerbsverstöße und Beeinträchtigung geschäftlicher Interessen (einschl. der Verletzung kartellrechtlicher Vorschriften), 232–297, in *Vorschläge und Gutachten zur Reform des deutschen internationalen Privatrechts der außervertraglichen Schuldverhältnisse, vorgelegt im Auftrag der Zweiten Kommission des Deutschen Rates für internationales Privatrecht* (Ernst von Caemmerer ed.), Tübingen: J.C.B. Mohr (Paul Siebeck), 1983.

Krieger, Albrecht, Das Warenzeichen als Eigentumsrecht im Sinne des Artikels 14 des Grundgesetzes, 1980 *GRUR* 335.

Kronman, Anthony T., Contract Law and the State of Nature, 1 *J. L., Econ. & Org.* 5 (1985).

Kronstein, Heinrich, Crisis of "Conflict of Laws," 37 *Geo. L.J.* 483 (1949).

Kropholler, Jan, *Internationales Privatrecht—einschließlich der Grundbegriffe des Internationalen Zivilverfahrensrechts*, Tübingen: Verlag Mohr Siebeck, 6th edn., 2006.

Krug, G., *Ueber den Schutz der Fabrik- und Waarenzeichen nebst den einschlagenden Gesetzen sämmtlicher deutscher Staaten*, Darmstadt and Leipzig: Verlag Eduard Zernin, 1866.

Kühne, Gunther, Die Entsavignysierung des Internationalen Privatrechts insbesondere durch sog. Eingriffsnormen, 815–830, in *Festschrift für Andreas Heldrich zum 70. Geburtstag* (Stephan Lorenz et al. eds.), Munich: Beck-Verlag, 2005.

Kummer, Max, *Anwendungsbereich und Schutzgut der privatrechtlichen Rechtssätze gegen unlauteren und gegen freiheitsbeschränkenden Wettbewerb*, Bern: Verlag Stämpfli & Cie., 1960.

Kur, Annette, Applicable Law: An Alternative Proposal for International Regulation—The Max-Planck Project on International Jurisdiction and Choice of Law, 30 *Brook. J. Int'l L.* 951 (2005).

Kur, Annette, Markenrecht, Verbraucherschutz und Wettbewerbsrecht, 190–206, in *Die Neuordnung des Markenrechts in Europa—10. Ringberg-Symposium des Max-Planck-Instituts für ausländisches und internationales Patent-, Urheber- und Wettbewerbsrecht* (Gerhard Schricker & Friedrich-Karl Beier eds.), Baden-Baden: Nomos-Verlagsgesellschaft, 1996.

Kur, Annette, Principles Governing Jurisdiction, Choice of Law and Judgments in Transnational Disputes: A European Perspective, 2003 *CRi* 65.

Kur, Annette, Territorialität versus Globalität—Kennzeichenkonflikte im Internet, 2000 *WRP* 935.

Kur, Annette, Trademark Conflicts on the Internet: Territoriality Redefined?, 175–193, in *Intellectual Property in the Conflict of Laws* (Jürgen Basedow et al. eds.), Tübingen: Verlag Mohr Siebeck, 2005.

Kur, Annette, Verwechslungsgefahr und Irreführung—zum Verhältnis von Markenrecht und § 3 UWG, 1989 *GRUR* 240.

Lagarde, Paul, Public Policy, in *International Encyclopedia of Comparative Law, vol. III* (Kurt Lipstein et al. eds.), Tübingen: Mohr, 1994.

Laird, Pamela Walker, *Advertising Progress: American Business and the Rise of Consumer Marketing*, Baltimore and London: Johns Hopkins University Press, 1998.

Lammel, Siegbert, Recht zur Ordnung des Wettbewerbs: Deutschland, 3806–3821, and Österreich, 3821–3830, in *Handbuch der Quellen und Literatur der neueren europäischen Privatrechtsgeschichte, vol. III: Das 19. Jahrhundert, 3rd part: Gesetzgebung zu den privatrechtlichen Sondergebieten* (Helmut Coing ed.), Munich: C.H. Beck'sche Verlagsbuchhandlung, 1986.

Landenberger, Anmerkungen auf der Versammlung des Deutschen Vereins für den Schutz des gewerblichen Eigentums vom 19. Januar 1928, 1928 *GRUR* 206.

Landes, William M. & Posner, Richard A., *The Economic Structure of Intellectual Property Law*, Cambridge/MA: Belknap Press, 2003.

Landes, William M. & Posner, Richard A., *The Economic Structure of Tort Law*, Cambridge/MA: Harvard University Press, 1987.

Landes, William M. & Posner, Richard A., The Private Enforcement of Law, 4 *J. Legal Stud.* 1 (1975).

Landes, William M. & Posner, Richard A., Trademark Law: An Economic Perspective, 30 *J. L. & Econ.* 265 (1987).

Lane, Wallace R., Development of Secondary Rights in Trade Mark Cases, 18 *Yale L.J.* 571 (1909).

Lane, Wallace R., The Transfer of Trademarks and Trade Names, 6 *Ill. L. Rev.* 46 (1911).

Langen, Eugen, Transnationales Handelsrecht, 1969 *NJW* 2229.

Langen, Eugen, *Transnationales Recht*, Heidelberg: Verlagsgesellschaft Recht und Wirtschaft, 1981.

Langen, Eugen, Vom Internationalen Privatrecht zum Transnationalen Handelsrecht, 1969 *NJW* 358.

Law, David S. & Chang, Wen-Chen, The Limits of Global Judicial Dialogue, 86 *Wash. L. Rev.* 523 (2011).

Lawless, Robert M., Robbenolt, Jennifer K. & Ulen, Thomas S., *Empirical Methods in Law*, New York: Aspen Publishers, 2010.

Leaffer, Marshall A., The New World of International Trademark Law, 2 *Marq. Intell. Prop. L. Rev.* 1 (1998).

Leeds, Daphne Robert, The Circular Trend in Trademarks, 47 *A.B.A. J.* 256 (1961).

Lehmann, Michael, Das Prinzip Wettbewerb, 1990 *JZ* 61.

Lehmann, Michael, Das wirtschaftliche Persönlichkeitsrecht von Anbieter und Nachfrager, 255–269, in *Beiträge zum Schutz der Persönlichkeit und ihrer schöpferischen Leistungen—Festschrift für Heinrich Hubmann zum 70. Geburtstag* (Hans Forkel & Alfons Kraft eds.), Frankfurt am Main: Alfred Metzner Verlag, 1985.

Lehmann, Michael, Die wettbewerbswidrige Ausnutzung und Beeinträchtigung des guten Rufs bekannter Marken, Namen und Herkunftsangaben—Die Rechtslage in der Bundesrepublik Deutschland, 1986 *GRUR Int.* 6.

Lehmann, Michael, *Vertragsanbahnung durch Werbung—Eine juristische und ökonomische Analyse der bürgerlich-rechtlichen Haftung für Werbeangaben gegenüber dem Letztverbraucher*, Munich: C.H. Beck'sche Verlagsbuchhandlung, 1981.

Leibholz, Gerhard, Das Verbot der Willkür und des Ermessensmißbrauches im völkerrechtlichen Verkehr der Staaten, 1 *ZaöRV* 77 (1929).

Leible, Stefan & Lehmann, Matthias, Die neue EG-Verordnung über das auf außervertragliche Schuldverhältnisse anzuwendende Recht („Rom II"), 2007 *RIW* 721.

Leiner, Frederick C., The Charming Betsy and the Marshall Court, 45 *Am. J. Leg. Hist.* 1 (2001).

Leisse, Gerd & Traub, Fritz, Schadensschätzung im unlauteren Wettbewerb, 1980 *GRUR* 1.

Leistner, Matthias, Behavioural Economics und Lauterkeitsrecht, 1 *ZGE* 3 (2009).

Leistner, Matthias, Bestand und Entwicklungsperspektiven des Europäischen Lauterkeitsrechts, 2009 *ZEuP* 56.

Leistner, Matthias, Comments: The Rome II Regulation Proposal and its Relation to the European Country-of-Origin Principle, 177–199, in *Intellectual Property and Private International Law—Heading for the Future* (Josef Drexl & Annette Kur eds.), Oxford and Portland/OR.: Hart Publishing, 2005.

Leistner, Matthias, *Richtiger Vertrag und lauterer Wettbewerb—Eine grundlagenorientierte Studie unter besonderer Berücksichtigung der europäischen Perspektive*, Tübingen: Verlag Mohr Siebeck, 2007.

Leistner, Matthias, Unfair Competition Law Protection Against Imitations: A Hybrid under the Future Art. 5 Rome II Regulation?, 129–157, in *Intellectual Property in the Conflict of Laws* (Jürgen Basedow et al. eds.), Tübingen: Verlag Mohr Siebeck, 2005.

Lemley, Mark A., Property, Intellectual Property, and Free Riding, 83 *Tex. L. Rev.* 1031 (2005).

Lemley, Mark A., Romantic Authorship and the Rhetoric of Property, 75 *Tex. L. Rev.* 873 (1997).

Lemley, Mark A., The Modern Lanham Act and the Death of Common Sense, 108 *Yale L.J.* 1687 (1999).

Lemley, Mark A. & McKenna, Mark P., Irrelevant Confusion, 62 *Stan. L. Rev.* 413 (2010).

Lemley, Mark A. & McKenna, Mark P., Owning Mark(et)s, 109 *Mich. L. Rev.* 137 (2010).

Lettl, Tobias, *Der lauterkeitsrechtliche Schutz vor irreführender Werbung in Europa*, Munich: C.H. Beck-Verlag, 2004.

Leuchs, Johann Carl, *Gewerb- und Handelsfreiheit; oder über die Mittel das Glük der Völker, den Reichthum und die Macht der Staaten zu begründen*, Nuremberg: Verlag Contor der Handlungs-Zeitung, 1827.

Lichtenstein, Erich, Der gewerbliche Rechtsschutz im internationalen Privatrecht, 1964 *NJW* 1208.

Lindacher, Walter F., Die internationale Dimension lauterkeitsrechtlicher Unterlassungsansprüche: Marktterritorialität versus Universalität, 2008 *GRUR Int.* 453.

Lindacher, Walter F., Zum Internationalen Privatrecht des unlauteren Wettbewerbs, 1996 *WRP* 645.

Lipstein, Kurt, Conflict of Public Laws—Visions and Realities, 357–378, in *Festschrift für Imre Zajtay* (Ronald H. Graveson et al. eds.), Tübingen: J.C.B. Mohr (Paul Siebeck) Verlag, 1982.

Lipstein, Kurt, The General Principles of Private International Law, 135 *Recueil des Cours* 97 (1972–I).

Livermore, Joseph M., On Uses of a Competitor's Trademark, 59 *Trademark Rep.* 30 (1969).

Livermore, Samuel, *Dissertations on the Questions which arise from the Contrariety of the Positive Laws of Different States and Nations*, New Orleans: printed by B. Levy, 1828 (e-source: Sabin Americana, Gale, Cengage Leaning, 2011).

Lobe, Adolf, *Die Bekämpfung des unlauteren Wettbewerbs, vol. I: Der unlautere Wettbewerb als Rechtsverletzung nach dem Bürgerlichen Gesetzbuch und den Nebengesetzen*, Leipzig: Dieterichsche Verlagsbuchhandlung Theodor Weicher, 1907.

Locke, John, *Two Treatises of Government—In the Former, The False Principles and Foundation of Sir Robert Filmer, and His Followers, Are Detected and Overthrown: The Latter, Is an Essay Concerning the Original, Extent, and End, of Civil Government, vol. V*, London: Thomas Tegg et al., 1823 (McMaster University, Archive of the History of Economic Thought (eDoc 2000)).

Loewenheim, Ulrich, Bereicherungsansprüche im Wettbewerbsrecht, 1997 *WRP* 913.

Loewenheim, Ulrich, Warenzeichen, freier Warenverkehr, Kartellrecht, 1051–1091, in *Gewerblicher Rechtsschutz und Urheberrecht in Deutschland, Festschrift zum hundertjährigen Bestehen der Deutschen Vereinigung für gewerblichen Rechtsschutz und Urheberrecht und ihrer Zeitschrift, vol. II* (Friedrich-Karl Beier et al. eds.), Weinheim: VCH Verlagsgesellschaft mbH, 1991.

Löffler, Severin, Werbung im Cyberspace—Eine kollisionsrechtliche Betrachtung, 2001 *WRP* 379.

Long, Clarisa, Dilution, 106 *Colum. L. Rev.* 1029 (2006).

Long, Doris E., *Unfair Competition and the Lanham Act*, Washington/DC: The Bureau of National Affairs, Inc., 1993.

Lorenz, Egon, *Zur Struktur des Internationalen Privatrechts—Ein Beitrag zur Reformdiskussion*, Berlin: Duncker & Humblot, 1977.

Lorenzen, Ernest G., Huber's De Conflictu Legum, 136–180, in *Selected Articles on the Conflict of Laws*, New Haven: Yale University Press, 1947.

Lorenzen, Ernest G., Story's Commentaries on the Conflict of Laws—One Hundred Years After, 48 *Harv. L. Rev.* 15 (1934).

Loschelder, Michael & Erdmann, Willi, eds., *Handbuch des Wettbewerbsrechts*, Munich: Verlag C.H. Beck, 4th edn., 2010.

Lowenfeld, Andreas F., Conflict, Balancing of Interests, and the Exercise of Jurisdiction to Prescribe: Reflections on the Insurance Antitrust Case, 89 *Am. J. Int'l L.* 42 (1995).

Lowenfeld, Andreas F., Public Law in the International Arena: Conflict of Laws, International Law, and Some Suggestions for Their Interaction, 163 *Recueil des Cours* 311 (1979–II).

Luhmann, Niklas, Die Weltgesellschaft, 57 *Archiv für Rechts- und Sozialphilosophie* 1 (1971).

Luhmann, Niklas, *Ökologische Kommunikation: Kann die moderne Gesellschaft sich auf ökologische Gefährdungen einstellen?*, Opladen: Westdt. Verlag, 1986.

Luhmann, Niklas, Zur Funktion der subjektiven Rechte, 322–330, in *Die Funktion des Rechts in der modernen Gesellschaft, Jahrbuch für Rechtssoziologie und Rechtstheorie* (Rüdiger Lautmann et al. eds.), Bielefeld: Bertelsmann-Universitätsverlag, 1970.

Lukes, Rudolf, Zum Verständnis des Wettbewerbs und des Marktes in der Denkkategorie des Rechts, 199–226, in *Wirtschaftsordnung und Rechtsordnung: Festschrift zum 70. Geburtstag von Franz Böhm am 16. Febr. 1965* (Helmut Coing et al. eds.), Karlsruhe: C.F. Müller Verlag, 1965.

Lunney, Glynn S., Jr., Trademark Monopolies, 48 *Emory L.J.* 367 (1999).

Lunsford, Julius R., Jr., Geographical Scope of Registered Rights—Then and Now, 61 *Trademark Rep.* 411 (1971).

Macalister-Smith, Peter, Comity, 671–674, in *Encyclopedia of Public International Law, vol. I* (Rudolf Bernhardt ed.), Amsterdam: Elsevier Science Publishers B.V., 1992.

Magnus, Julius, Warenzeichenrecht (Bericht), 1923 *GRUR* 162.

Maier, Harold G., Extraterritorial Jurisdiction at a Crossroads: An Intersection between Public and Private International Law, 76 *Am. J. Int'l L.* 280 (1982).

Maier, Harold G., Resolving Extraterritorial Conflicts, or "There and Back Again," 25 *Va. J. Int'l L.* 7 (1984).

Makarov, Alexander N., Internationales Privatrecht und Völkerrecht, in *Wörterbuch des Völkerrechts, vol. II* (Hans-Jürgen Schlochauer ed.), Berlin: Verlag Walter de Gruyter & Co., 2nd edn., 1961.

Mangini, Vito, Die Marke: Niedergang der Herkunftsfunktion?, 1996 *GRUR Int.* 462.

Maniatis, Spyros & Botis, Dimitris, *Trade Marks in Europe: A Practical Jurisprudence*, London: Thomson Reuters, 2nd edn., 2010.

Mankowski, Peter, Das neue Internationale Kartellrecht des Art. 6 Abs. 3 der Rom-II-Verordnung, 2008 *RIW* 177.

Mankowski, Peter, Internet und Internationales Wettbewerbsrecht, 1999 *GRUR Int.* 909.

Mankowski, Peter, Was soll der Anknüpfungsgegenstand des (europäischen) Internationalen Wettbewerbsrechts sein?, 2005 *GRUR Int.* 634.

Mann, F. A., Conflict of Laws and Public Law, 132 *Recueil des Cours* 107 (1971–I).

Mann, F. A., The Doctrine of Jurisdiction in International Law, 111 *Recueil des Cours* 1 (1964–I).

Mansel, Heinz-Peter, Staatlichkeit des Internationalen Privatrechts und Völkerrecht, 89–130, in *Völkerrecht und IPR* (Stefan Leible & Matthias Ruffert eds.), Jena: Jenaer Wissenschaftliche Verlagsgesellschaft, 2006.

Marcus, Ist die Unterlassungsklage nach dem Wettbewerbsgesetz noch statthaft, wenn die Handlung vor Klageerhebung seitens des Täters rückgängig gemacht war?, 1903 *JZ* 172.

Martin, Wallace H., Incentives to Register Given by the New Trade-Mark Act, Part I, 36 *Trademark Rep.* 213 (1946).

Martinez, Jenny S., Towards an International Judicial System, 56 *Stan. L. Rev.* 429 (2003).

Martiny, Dieter, Die Anknüpfung an den Markt, 389–408, in *Festschrift für Ulrich Drobnig zum siebzigsten Geburtstag* (Jürgen Basedow et al. eds.), Tübingen: Verlag Mohr Siebeck, 1998.

Martiny, Dieter, Verletzung von Immaterialgüterrechten im Internationalen Privatrecht, 40 *RabelsZ* 218 (1976).

Marx, Claudius, *Deutsches, europäisches und internationales Markenrecht*, Cologne: Luchterhand, 2nd edn., 2007.

Matter, E., Zur Generalklausel im Bundesgesetz über den unlauteren Wettbewerb, 87 *ZBJV* 449 (1951).

Matthiolius, Karl, *Der Rechtsschutz geographischer Herkunftsangaben*, Bonn: dissertation thesis, 1928.

Max-Planck-Institut für ausländisches und internationales Patent-, Urheber- und Wettbewerbsrecht, Stellungnahme zum Entwurf eines Gesetzes zur Ergänzung des internationalen Privatrechts (außervertragliche Schuldverhältnisse und Sachen), 1985 *GRUR Int.* 104.

Mayer, Otto, Die concurrence déloyale—Ein Beitrag aus dem französischen Rechte zur Lehre vom geistigen Eigenthum, 26 *Zeitschrift für das Gesammte Handelsrecht* 363 (1881).

McCarthy, J. Thomas, *McCarthy on Trademarks and Unfair Competition*, Clark Boardman Callaghan/Westlaw, 4th edn., 2016 (Online Resource: Database).

McClure, Daniel M., Trademarks and Competition: The Recent History, 59 *Law & Contemp. Probs.* 13 (1996).

McClure, Daniel M., Trademarks and Unfair Competition: A Critical History of Legal Thought, 69 *Trademark Rep.* 305 (1979).

McDougal, Luther L. III, Comprehensive Interest Analysis Versus Reformulated Governmental Interest Analysis: An Appraisal in the Context of Choice-of-Law Problems Concerning Contributory and Comparative Negligence, 26 *UCLA L. Rev.* 439 (1979).

McDougal, Luther L. III, Toward the Application of the Best Rule of Law in Choice of Law Cases, 35 *Mercer L. Rev.* 483 (1984).

McGuinness, Seán, Observations on free riding after L'Oréal v. Bellure, 7 *J. Intell. Prop. L. & Pract.* 890 (2012).

McKenna, Mark P., A Consumer Decision-Making Theory of Trademark Law, 98 *Va. L. Rev.* 67 (2012).

McKenna, Mark P., The Normative Foundations of Trademark Law, 82 *Notre Dame L. Rev.* 1839 (2007).

Meessen, Karl M., Antitrust Jurisdiction under Customary International Law, 78 *Am. J. Int'l L.* 783 (1984).

Meessen, Karl M., *Kollisionsrecht der Zusammenschlußkontrolle*, Baden-Baden: Nomos-Verlag, 1984.

Meessen, Karl M., *Völkerrechtliche Grundsätze des internationalen Kartellrechts*, Baden-Baden: Nomos-Verlag, 1975.

Mehren, Arthur Taylor von, Choice of Law and the Problem of Justice, 41 *Law & Contemp. Probs.* 27 (1977).

Mehren, Arthur Taylor von, Choice-of-Law Theories and the Comparative-Law Problem, 23 *Am. J. Comp. L.* 751 (1975).

Mehren, Arthur Taylor von, Special Substantive Rules for Multistate Problems: Their Role and Significance in Contemporary Choice of Law Methodology, 88 *Harv. L. Rev.* 347 (1974).

Meili, F., *Das Markenstrafrecht auf Grund des eidgenössischen Markenschutzgesetzes sowie der von der Schweiz abgeschlossenen Staatsverträge und der internationalen Konvention von 1883*, Bern: Commissionsverlag Rud. Jenni's Buchhandlung, 1888.

Meissner, Heinrich August, *Die Fabrikgerichte in Frankreich*, Leipzig: Brockhaus, 1846.

Meng, Werner, *Extraterritoriale Jurisdiktion im öffentlichen Wirtschaftsrecht*, Berlin: Springer-Verlag, 1994.

Merges, Robert P., One Hundred Years of Solicitude: Intellectual Property Law, 1900–2000, 88 *Cal. L. Rev.* 2187 (2000).

Merges, Robert P., Menell, Peter S. & Lemley, Mark A., *Intellectual Property in the New Technological Age*, New York: Aspen Publishers, 3rd edn., 2003.

Merryman, John Henry, On the Convergence (and Divergence) of the Civil Law and the Common Law, 17 *Stan. J. Int'l L.* 357 (1981).

Merryman, John Henry, The Public Law-Private Law Distinction in European and American Law, 17 *J. Publ. L.* 3 (1968).

Mertzlufft, Hans, *Markenschutz und unlauterer Wettbewerb*, Zurich: Diss.-Druckerei A.-G. Gebr. Leemann & Co., 1936.

Mestmäcker, Ernst-Joachim, *Der verwaltete Wettbewerb—Eine vergleichende Untersuchung über den Schutz von Freiheit und Lauterkeit im Wettbewerbsrecht*, Tübingen: J.C.B. Mohr (Paul Siebeck), 1984.

Mestmäcker, Ernst-Joachim, Eingriffserwerb und Rechtsverletzung in der ungerechtfertigten Bereicherung, 1958 *JZ* 521.

Mestmäcker, Ernst-Joachim, *Recht und ökonomisches Gesetz—Über die Grenzen von Staat, Gesellschaft und Privatautonomie*, Baden-Baden: Nomos Verlagsgesellschaft, 2nd edn., 1984.

Mestmäcker, Ernst-Joachim, Staatliche Souveränität und offene Märkte—Konflikte bei der extraterritorialen Anwendung von Wirtschaftsrecht, 52 *RabelsZ* 205 (1988).

Metzger, Axel, Applicable Law under the CLIP Principles: A Pragmatic Revaluation of Territoriality, 157–178, in *Intellectual Property in the Global Arena—Jurisdiction, Applicable Law, and the Recognition of Judgments in Europe, Japan and the US* (Jürgen Basedow et al. eds.), Tübingen: Verlag Mohr Siebeck, 2010.

Michaels, Ralf, Empagran's Empire: International Law and Statutory Interpretation in the U.S. Supreme Court of the Twenty-First Century, 533–546, in *International Law in the U.S. Supreme Court—Continuity and Change* (David L. Sloss et al. eds.), Cambridge: Cambridge University Press, 2011.

Michaels, Ralf, Globalizing Savigny? The State in Savigny's Private International Law and the Challenge from Europeanization and Globalization, 119–146, in *Aktuelle Fragen zu politischer und rechtlicher Steuerung im Kontext der Globalisierung* (Michael Stolleis & Wolfgang Streeck eds.), Baden-Baden: Nomos-Verlagsgesellschaft, 2007.

Michaels, Ralf, Public and Private International Law: German Views on Global Issues, 4 *J. Priv. Int'l L.* 121 (2008).

Michaels, Ralf, The New European Choice-of-Law Revolution, 82 *Tul. L. Rev.* 1607 (2008).

Michaels, Ralf, The True Lex Mercatoria: Law Beyond the State, 14 *Ind. J. Glob. Leg. Stud.* 447 (2007).

Micklitz, Hans-W. & Keßler, Jürgen, Europäisches Lauterkeitsrecht—Dogmatische und ökonomische Aspekte einer Harmonisierung des Wettbewerbsverhaltensrechts im europäischen Binnenmarkt, 2002 *GRUR Int.* 885.

Mill, John Stuart, *On Liberty*, Mineola/NY: Dover Publ., reprint of 1859 edn., 2002.

Mill, John Stuart, *Principles of Political Economy with some of their Applications to Social Philosophy*, William J. Ashley, ed. 1909 (Online Resource: Library of Economics and Liberty (24 November 2015)).

Mills, Alex, The Private History of International Law, 55 *I.C.L.Q.* 1 (2006).

Minor, Raleigh C., *Conflict of Laws; or, Private International Law*, Boston: Little, Brown, and Company, 1901.

Mitchell, Oliver R., Unfair Competition, 10 *Harv. L. Rev.* 275 (1896).

Mittermaier, C. J. A., *Grundsätze des gemeinen deutschen Privatrechts mit Einschluß des Handels-, Wechsel- und Seerechts, In zwei Abtheilungen: Erste Abtheilung*, Landshut: Verlag Philipp Krüll, 4th edn., 1830.

Mohl, Robert von, *Die Polizei-Wissenschaft nach den Grundsätzen des Rechtsstaates, vol. III*, Tübingen: Verlag der H. Laupp'schen Buchhandlung, 2nd edn., 1845.

Möllering, Jürgen, Das Recht des unlauteren Wettbewerbs in Europa: Eine neue Dimension, 1990 *WRP* 1.

Möllers, Thomas M.J. & Heinemann, Andreas, eds., *The Enforcement of Competition Law in Europe*, Cambridge: Cambridge University Press, 2007.

Mook, Klaus-Georg, *Internationale Rechtsunterschiede und nationaler Wettbewerb—Rechtliche Möglichkeiten zur Abwehr von Wettbewerbsstörungen und ihre Grenzen*, Berlin: Duncker & Humblot, 1986.

Moore, Frank S., *Legal Protection of Goodwill—Trade-Marks, Trade Emblems, Advertising, Unfair Competition*, New York: Ronald Press Company, 1936.

Moran, Mayo, An Uncivil Action: The Tort of Torture and Cosmopolitan Private Law, 661–685, in *Torture as Tort* (C. Scott ed.), Oxford: Hart Publishing, 2001.

Mosler, Hermann, Völkerrecht als Rechtsordnung, 36 *ZaöRV* 6 (1976).

Mostert, Frederick W., Well-Known and Famous Marks: Is Harmony Possible in the Global Village?, 86 *Trademark Rep.* 103 (1996).

Mueller, Charles E., Sources of Monopoly Power: A Phenomenon Called "Product Differentiation," 18 *Am. U. L. Rev.* 1 (1968).

Müller-Graff, Peter-Christian, Fakultatives Kollisionsrecht im Internationalen Wettbewerbsrecht?, 48 *RabelsZ* 289 (1984).

Nadelmann, Kurt H., Introduction to Yntema, The Comity Doctrine, 65 *Mich. L. Rev.* 1 (1966).

Nägele, Thomas & Jacobs, Sven, Rechtsfragen des Cloud Computing, 2010 *ZUM* 281.

Nelson, Sara Stadler, The Wages of Ubiquity in Trademark Law, 88 *Iowa L. Rev.* 731 (2003).

Neuhaus, Paul Heinrich, Der Beitrag des Völkerrechts zum Internationalen Privatrecht, 21 *German Y.B. Int'l L.* 60 (1978).

Neuhaus, Paul Heinrich, *Die Grundbegriffe des internationalen Privatrechts*, Berlin and Tübingen: Walter De Gruyter & Co. and J.C.B. Mohr (Paul Siebeck), 1962.

Neuhaus, Paul Heinrich, Freiheit und Gleichheit im internationalen Immaterialgüterrecht, 40 *RabelsZ* 191 (1976).

Neuhaus, Paul Heinrich, Savigny und die Rechtsfindung aus der Natur der Sache, 15 *RabelsZ* 364 (1949/1950).

Neuman, Gerald L., Sense and Nonsense about Customary International Law: A Response to Professors Bradley and Goldsmith, 66 *Fordham L. Rev.* 371 (1997).

Neumayer, Karl H., Die Notgesetzgebung des Wirtschaftsrechts im internationalen Privatrecht, 35–72, in *Berichte der Deutschen Gesellschaft für Völkerrecht (vol. 2)*, Karlsruhe, 1958.

Nguyen, Xuan-Thao N., The Digital Trademark Right: A Troubling New Extraterritorial Reach of United States Law, 81 *N.C. L. Rev.* 483 (2003).

Nimmer, Melville B. & Nimmer, David, *Nimmer on Copyright: A Treatise on the Law of Literary, Musical and Artistic Property, and the Protection of Ideas*, New York: Matthew Bender, 1978 (and later).

Nims, Harry D., *The Law of Unfair Competition and Trade-Marks, with Chapters on Good-Will, Trade Secrets, Defamation of Competitors and Their Goods, Registration of Trade-Marks, Interference with Competitors' Business, etc., vol. I & vol. II*, New York: Baker, Voorhis & Co., Inc., 4th edn., 1947.

Nussbaum, Arthur, *Deutsches internationales Privatrecht—Unter besonderer Berücksichtigung des österreichischen und schweizerischen Rechts*, Tübingen: Verlag von J.C.B. Mohr, 1932.

Nussbaum, Arthur, Rise and Decline of the Law-of-Nations Doctrine in the Conflict of Laws, 42 *Colum. L. Rev.* 189 (1942).

Ohly, Ansgar, Choice of Law in the Digital Environment—Problems and Possible Solutions, 241–256, in *Intellectual Property and Private International Law—Heading for the Future* (Josef Drexl & Annette Kur eds.), Oxford and Portland/OR: Hart Publishing, 2005.

Ohly, Ansgar, Keyword Advertising auf dem Weg zurück von Luxemburg nach Paris, Wien, Karlsruhe und Den Haag, 2010 *GRUR* 776.

Ohly, Ansgar, *Richterrecht und Generalklausel im Recht des unlauteren Wettbewerbs—Ein Methodenvergleich des englischen und des deutschen Rechts*, Cologne et al.: Carl Heymanns Verlag, 1997.

Ohly, Ansgar & Sosnitza, Olaf, *Gesetz gegen den unlauteren Wettbewerb mit Preisangabenverordnung (UWG)*, Munich: Verlag C.H. Beck, 5th edn., 2010.

Ohly, Ansgar & Sosnitza, Olaf, *Gesetz gegen den unlauteren Wettbewerb mit Preisangabenverordnung (UWG)*, Munich: Verlag C.H. Beck, 6th edn., 2014.

Omsels, Hermann-Josef, Die Kennzeichenrechte im Internet, 1997 *GRUR* 328.

Oppenheim, Walther, *Die Verwirkung im gewerblichen Rechtsschutz*, Berlin: Heymann, 1932.

Ossenbühl, Fritz, Anmerkung zu Bundesverwaltungsgericht, 1. Senat, 09.08.1983, 1 C 142/80 - Esslinger Neckarhalde, 1984 *GRUR* 351.

Osterrieth, Albert, *Lehrbuch des gewerblichen Rechtsschutzes*, Leipzig: A. Deichert'sche Verlagsbuchhandlung Nachf. (Georg Böhme), 1908.

Ostertag, Fritz, Territorialität oder Universalität im Markenrecht, 212–223, in *Festgabe zum siebzigsten Geburtstag von Fritz Goetzinger* (Juristische Fakultät der Universität Basel und Appellationsgericht des Kantons Basel-Stadt eds.), Basel: Verlag Helbing & Lichtenhahn, 1935.

Ostrom, Elinor, *Governing the Commons—The Evolution of Institutions for Collective Action*, Cambridge: Cambridge University Press, 1990.

Pahlow, Louis, Das Recht an der Marke als Benutzungsrecht des Markeninhabers, 2006 *MarkenR* 97.

Palandt, *Kommentar zum Bürgerlichen Gesetzbuch mit Nebengesetzen*, Munich: C.H. Beck Verlag, 75th edn., 2016.

Papandreou, A. G., The Economic Effect of Trademarks, 44 *Cal. L. Rev.* 503 (1956).

Parrish, Austen L., Evading Legislative Jurisdiction, 87 *Notre Dame L. Rev.* 1673 (2012).

Parrish, Austen L., Kiobel, Unilateralism, and the Retreat from Extraterritoriality, 28 *Md. J. Int'l L.* 208 (2013).

Parrish, Austen L., Reclaiming International Law from Extraterritoriality, 93 *Minn. L. Rev.* 815 (2009).

Paster, Benjamin G., Trademarks—Their Early History, 59 *Trademark Rep.* 551 (1969).

Patry, William, Choice of Law and International Copyright, 48 *Am. J. Comp. L.* 383 (2000).

Pattishall, Beverly W., Trade-Marks and the Monopoly Phobia, 50 *Mich. L. Rev.* 967 (1952).

Pattishall, Beverly W., Two Hundred Years of American Trademark Law, 68 *Trademark Rep.* 121 (1978).

Paul, Amasa C., *The Law of Trade-Marks, Including Trade-Names and Unfair Competition*, St. Paul/MN: Keefe-Davidson, 1903.

Paul, Joel R., Comity in International Law, 32 *Harv. Int'l L.J.* 1 (1991).

Paul, Joel R., The Transformation of International Comity, 71 *Law & Contemp. Probs.* 19 (2008).

Peukert, Alexander, Der Wandel der europäischen Wirtschaftsverfassung im Spiegel des Sekundärrechts—Erläutert am Beispiel des Rechts gegen unlauteren Wettbewerb, 173 *ZHR* 536 (2009).

Peukert, Alexander, Die Ziele des Primärrechts und ihre Bedeutung für das Europäische Lauterkeitsrecht: Auflösungserscheinungen eines Rechtsgebiets?, 27–59, in *Lauterkeitsrecht und Acquis Communautaire* (Reto M. Hilty & Frauke Henning-Bodewig eds.), Berlin and Heidelberg: Springer-Verlag, 2009.

Pfaff, Dieter, Das Internationale Privatrecht des Ausstattungsschutzes, 1109–1165, in *Handbuch des Ausstattungsrechts—Der Schutz der nichteingetragenen Marke und Ausstattung im In- und Ausland, Festgabe für Friedrich-Karl Beier zum 60. Geburtstag* (Gerhard Schricker & Dieter Stauder eds.), Weinheim: VCH Verlagsgesellschaft mbH, 1986.

Pfister, Rudolf, *Untersuchungen über das Verhältnis der Grundsätze über den unlauteren Wettbewerb zu den Bestimmungen der gewerblichen Spezialgesetze*, Bern and Leipzig: Verlag Paul Haupt, 1936.

Pinzger, Werner & Heinemann, Felix, *Das deutsche Warenzeichenrecht—Kommentar des Reichsgesetzes zum Schutz der Warenbezeichnungen nebst den internationalen Verträgen*, Berlin: Verlag von Otto Liebmann, 1926.

Plender, Richard & Wilderspin, Michael, *The European Private International Law of Obligations*, London: Sweet & Maxwell, 4th edn., 2015.

Politis, Nicolas-Socrate, Le problème des limitations de la souveraineté et la théorie de l'abus des droits dans les rapports internationaux, 6 *Recueil des Cours* 1 (1925–I).

Popov, Anna R., Watering Down Steele v. Bulova Watch Co. to Reach E-Commerce Overseas: Analyzing the Lanham Act's Extraterritorial Reach Under International Law, 77 *S. Cal. L. Rev.* 705 (2004).

Port, Kenneth L., The Congressional Expansion of American Trademark Law: A Civil Law System in the Making, 35 *Wake Forest L. Rev.* 827 (2000).

Port, Kenneth L., The Illegitimacy of Trademark Incontestability, 26 *Ind. L. Rev.* 519 (1993).

Portmann, Wolfgang, *Wesen und System der subjektiven Privatrechte*, Zurich: Schulthess Polygraphischer Verlag, 1996.

Posner, Richard A., When Is Parody Fair Use?, 21 *J. Legal Stud.* 67 (1992).

Post, David G., Against "Against Cyberanarchy," 17 *Berkeley Tech. L.J.* 1365 (2002).

Post, Robert, The Challenge of Globalization to American Public Law Scholarship, 2 *Theoretical Inq. L.* 323 (2001).

Pouillet, Eugène, *Traité des marques de fabrique et de la concurrence déloyale en tous genres*, Paris: Marchal et Billard, 5th edn., 1906.

Pound, Roscoe, *An Introduction to the Philosophy of Law*, New Haven: Yale University Press, 1922.

Putnam, Tonya L., Courts Without Borders: Domestic Sources of U.S. Extraterritoriality in the Regulatory Sphere, 63 *International Organization* 459 (2009).

Raape, Leo, *Internationales Privatrecht*, Berlin and Frankfurt am Main: Verlag für Rechtswissenschaft, vormals Franz Vahlen, 3rd edn., 1950.

Rabel, Ernst, Aufgabe und Notwendigkeit der Rechtsvergleichung, 1924 *Rheinische Zeitschrift für Zivil- und Prozessrecht*, 279–301, reprinted in *Gesammelte Aufsätze: Arbeiten zur Rechtsvergleichung und zur Rechtsvereinheitlichung, 1919–1954, vol. III* (Hans G. Leser ed.), Tübingen: Mohr Siebeck, 1967.

Rabel, Ernst, Das Problem der Qualifikation, 5 *RabelsZ* 241 (1931).

Rabel, Ernst, Rechtsvergleichung und internationale Rechtsprechung, 1 *RabelsZ* 5 (1927).

Rabel, Ernst, *The Conflict of Laws—A Comparative Study, vol. I, Introduction: Family Law*, Ann Arbor: University of Michigan Law School, 2nd edn., 1958.

Raiser, Ludwig, Der Stand der Lehre vom subjektiven Recht im Deutschen Zivilrecht, 1961 *JZ* 465.

Rand, Ayn, Patents and Copyrights (The Objectivist Newsletter, May 1964), reprinted in *Capitalism: The Unknown Ideal*, 141–145, New York: Signet, reprint of 1967 edn., 1987.

Randall, Kenneth C., Federal Jurisdiction Over International Law Claims: Inquiries into the Alien Tort Statute, 18 *N.Y.U. J. Int'l L. & Pol.* 1 (1985).

Rappeport, Jack J., Trade-Mark and Unfair Competition in International Conflict of Laws: An Analysis of the Choice of Law Problem, 20 *U. Pitt. L. Rev.* 1 (1958).

Rau, Karl Heinrich, *Lehrbuch der politischen Oekonomie, vol. II—Grundsätze der Volkswirthschaftspolitik*, Heidelberg: Acad. Verlagsbuchhandlung von C.F. Winter, 2nd edn., 1839.

Raustiala, Kal, Empire and Extraterritoriality in Twentieth Century America, 40 *Sw. L. Rev.* 605 (2011).

Raustiala, Kal, The Geography of Justice, 73 *Fordham L. Rev.* 2501 (2005).

Rayle, Rudolf, The Trend Towards Enhancing Trademark Owner's Rights—A Comparative Study of U.S. and German Trademark Law, 7 *J. Intell. Prop. L.* 227 (2000).

Rebmann, Kurt & Säcker, Jürgen, eds., *Münchener Kommentar zum Bürgerlichen Gesetzbuch, vol. X: EGBGB, Internationales Privatrecht*, Munich: C.H. Beck'sche Verlagsbuchhandlung, 3rd edn., 1998.

Reese, Willis L. M. & Vischer, Frank, The Conflict-of-Laws Rules on Unfair Competition, *Annuaire de L'Institut de Droit International* 60, I (1983), 159.

Reese, Willis L. M. & Vischer, Frank (rapporteurs of the twenty-first commission), *The Conflict-of-laws Rules on Unfair Competition*, Institut de Droit International, Session of Cambridge, 1983 (online resource: available under www.justitiaetpace.org/resolutions_chrono.php?start=1977&end=1983 (12 February 2016)).

Regelin, Frank Peter, *Das Kollisionsrecht der Immaterialgüterrechte an der Schwelle zum 21. Jahrhundert*, Frankfurt am Main et al.: Peter Lang Verlag, 2000.

Regelmann, Christof, *Die internationalprivatrechtliche Anknüpfung des Gesetzes gegen unlauteren Wettbewerb—Eine Darstellung unter Berücksichtigung der Rechtslage in Österreich und der Schweiz*, Konstanz: Hartung-Gorre Verlag, 1988.

Rehbinder, Eckard, *Extraterritoriale Wirkungen des deutschen Kartellrechts*, Baden-Baden: Nomos Verlagsgesellschaft, 1965.

Rehbinder, Eckard, Zur Politisierung des Internationalen Privatrechts, 1973 *JZ* 151.

Reich, Norbert, Rechtsprobleme grenzüberschreitender irreführender Werbung im Binnenmarkt, 56 *RabelsZ* 444 (1992).

Reich, Norbert & Micklitz, Hans-W., *Europäisches Verbraucherrecht*, Baden-Baden: Nomos Verlagsgesellschaft, 4th edn., 2003.

Reichold, Hermann, Lauterkeitsrecht als Sonderdeliktsrecht—Zur Rolle zivilistischen Denkens bei der Anwendung von § 1 UWG, 193 *AcP* 204 (1993).

Reidenberg, Joel R., Technology and Internet Jurisdiction, 153 *U. Pa. L. Rev. 1951* (2005).

Reimann, Matthias, A New Restatement—For the International Age, 75 *Ind. L.J.* 575 (2000).

Reimer, Eduard, Warenzeichen-, Wettbewerbs- und Kartellrecht auf der Warschauer Konferenz der International Law Association, 1928 *GRUR* 682.

Reimer, Eduard, *Wettbewerbs- und Warenzeichenrecht, vol. II: Kommentar zum Gesetz gegen den unlauteren Wettbewerb, zum Zugabe- und Rabattrecht und zu den einschlägigen Bestimmungen des Gesetzes über Wirtschaftswerbung*, Berlin: Carl Heymanns Verlag, 1935.

Reindl, Andreas P., Choosing Law in Cyberspace: Copyright Conflicts on Global Networks, 19 *Mich. J. Int'l L.* 799 (1998).

Rhenius, W., *Gesetz zum Schutz der Waarenbezeichnungen vom 12. Mai 1894 (Für die Praxis erläutert)*, Berlin: Carl Heymanns Verlag, 1897.

Richter, Reinhold, Studie über die Lehre vom akzessorischen Charakter des dem Ausländer gewährten Markenrechts, 1926 *GRUR* 100.

Riegl, Werner, *Streudelikte im Internationalen Privatrecht*, Augsburg: dissertation thesis, 1986.

Rittner, Fritz, Über das Verhältnis von Vertrag und Wettbewerb, 188 *AcP* 101 (1988).

Robert, Daphne, *The New Trade-Mark Manual—A Handbook on Protection Of Trade-Marks In Interstate Commerce*, Washington/DC: The Bureau of National Affairs, Inc., 1947.

Rogers, Edward S., Comments on the Modern Law of Unfair Trade, 3 *Ill. L. Rev.* 551 (1909).

Rogers, Edward S., New Concepts of Unfair Competition Under the Lanham Act, 38 *Trademark Rep.* 259 (1948).

Rogers, Edward S., New Directions in the Law of Unfair Competition, 74 *N.Y. L. Rev.* 317 (1940).

Rogers, Edward S., Protection of Industrial Property, 27 *Mich. L. Rev.* 491 (1929).

Rogers, Edward S., Some Historical Matter Concerning Trade-Marks, 9 *Mich. L. Rev.* 29 (1910).

Rogers, Edward S., *Statement, in Hearings Held Before the Committee on Patents*, House of Representatives, 72nd Congress, 1st Session (8 and 9 February 1932).

Rogers, Edward S., *Statement, in Hearings Before the Committee on Patents, Subcommittee on Trade-Marks*, House of Representatives, 75th Congress, 3rd Session on H.R. 9041 (15–18 March 1938).

Rogers, Edward S., The Expensive Futility of the United States Trade-Mark Statute, 12 *Mich. L. Rev.* 660 (1913).

Rogers, Edward S., The Lanham Act and the Social Function of Trade-Marks, 14 *Law & Contemp. Probs.* 173 (1949).

Rogers, Edward S., Unfair Competition, 35 *Trademark Rep.* 126 (1945).

Ropohl, Fabian, *Zur Anknüpfung der formlosen Markenrechte im Internationalen Privatrecht*, Göttingen: V&R unipress, 2003.

Rose, Carol, The Comedy of the Commons: Custom, Commerce, and Inherently Public Property, 53 *U. Chi. L. Rev.* 711 (1986).

Rosen, Mark D., The Surprisingly Strong Case for Tailoring Constitutional Principles, 153 *U. Pa. L. Rev.* 1513 (2005).

Rosenkranz, Timo & Rohde, Eva, The Law Applicable to Non-contractual Obligations Arising out of Acts of Unfair Competition and Acts Restricting Free Competition under Article 6 Rome II Regulation, 26 *NIPR* 435 (2008).

Rosenthal, Alfred, Die geistige Einstellung des Richters zu Prozessen betr. Nachahmung von Firmen- und Warenbezeichnungen, 1923 *MuW* 145.

Rosenthal, Alfred, *Wettbewerbsgesetz nebst den materiellen Vorschriften des Warenzeichengesetzes systematisch erläutert, Kommentar*, Berlin: Verlag von Franz Vahlen, 7th edn., 1928.

Roth, P. M., Reasonable Extraterritoriality: Correcting the "Balance of Interests," 41 *I.C.L.Q.* 245 (1992).

Röttger, Martin, Gedanken zur Schaffung einer EWG-Marke, 1959 *GRUR Ausl.* 329.

Roubier, Paul, *Le Droit de la Propriété Industrielle, vol. II: Partie Spéciale*, Paris: Éditions du Recueil Sirey S.A., 1954.

Rückert, Joachim, The Unrecognized Legacy: Savigny's Influence on German Jurisprudence after 1900, 37 *Am. J. Comp. L.* 121 (1989).

Rudolf, Walter, Territoriale Grenzen der staatlichen Rechtsetzung, 7–46, in *Berichte der Deutschen Gesellschaft für Völkerrecht (vol. 11)*, Karlsruhe: Verlag C.F. Müller, 1973.

Rühl, Giesela, *Statut und Effizienz—Ökonomische Grundlagen des Internationalen Privatrechts*, Tübingen: Mohr Siebeck, 2011.

Sack, Rolf, Art. 6 Abs. 2 Rom-II-VO und „bilaterales" unlauteres Wettbewerbsverhalten, 2012 *GRUR Int.* 601.

Sack, Rolf, Das internationale Wettbewerbs- und Immaterialgüterrecht nach der EGBGB-Novelle, 2000 *WRP* 269.

Sack, Rolf, Die kollisions- und wettbewerbsrechtliche Beurteilung grenzüberschreitender Werbe- und Absatztätigkeit nach deutschem Recht, 1988 *GRUR Int.* 320.

Sack, Rolf, Internationales Lauterkeitsrecht nach der Rom-II-VO, 2008 *WRP* 845.

Sack, Rolf, Marktortprinzip und allgemeine Ausweichklausel im internationalen Wettbewerbsrecht, am Beispiel der sog. Gran-Canaria-Fälle, 1992 *IPRax* 24.

Säcker, Franz Jürgen, et al., eds., *Münchener Kommentar zum Bürgerlichen Gesetzbuch, vol. XI: Internationales Privatrecht II, Internationales Wirtschaftsrecht,*

Einführungsgesetz zum Bürgerlichen Gesetzbuche (Art. 25–248), Munich: Verlag C.H. Beck, 6th edn., 2015.

Sandreuter, Karl Martin, *Rechtliche Natur, Entstehung und Endigung des Markenrechts*, Basel: Verlag Helbing & Lichtenhahn, 1932.

Sandrock, Otto, Das Kollisionsrecht des unlauteren Wettbewerbs zwischen dem internationalen Immaterialgüterrecht und dem internationalen Kartellrecht, 1985 *GRUR Int.* 507.

Sandrock, Otto, Die kollisionsrechtliche Behandlung der Deliktshaftung bei der Verletzung von gewerblichen Schutzrechten und Urheberrechten, 380–439, in *Vorschläge und Gutachten zur Reform des deutschen internationalen Privatrechts der außervertraglichen Schuldverhältnisse, vorgelegt im Auftrag der Zweiten Kommission des Deutschen Rates für internationales Privatrecht* (Ernst von Caemmerer ed.), Tübingen: J.C.B. Mohr (Paul Siebeck), 1983.

Sandrock, Otto, *Grundbegriffe des Gesetzes gegen Wettbewerbsbeschränkungen*, Munich: C.H. Beck'sche Verlagsbuchhandlung, 1968.

Sandrock, Otto, Neuere Entwicklungen im Internationalen Verwaltungs-, insbesondere im Internationalen Kartellrecht, 69 *ZVglRWiss* 1 (1968).

Sasse, Hans-Albrecht, *Grenzüberschreitende Werbung—Die Anwendbarkeit und die Anwendung deutschen Rechts vor deutschen Gerichten auf inländische Auswirkungen von Werbeaussagen in ausländischen Werbemedien*, Kiel: dissertation thesis, 1974.

Sassen, Saskia, Territory and Territoriality in the Global Economy, 15 *Int'l Soc.* 372 (2000).

Sattler, Andreas, *Emanzipation und Expansion des Markenrechts—Die Entstehungsgeschichte des Markengesetzes von 1995*, Tübingen: Mohr Siebeck Verlag, 2015.

Savigny, Friedrich Carl von, *System des heutigen Römischen Rechts, vol. I*, Berlin: Veit und Camp, 1840.

Savigny, Friedrich Carl von, *System des heutigen römischen Rechts, vol. VIII*, Aalen: Scientia Verlag, 2nd reprint of 1849 edn., 1981.

Savigny, Friedrich Carl von, *Private International Law and the Retrospective Operation of Statutes—A Treatise on the Conflict of Laws and the Limits of Their Operation in Respect of Place and Time*, William Guthrie transl., Edinburgh: T.&T. Clark, 2nd edn., 1880.

Scelle, Georges, *Manuel élémentaire de droit international public (avec les textes essentiels)*, Paris: Éditions Domat-Montchrestien, 1943.

Scelle, Georges, Préface à l'ouvrage de Charles Carabiber, 7–31, in *Les juridictions internationales de droit privé*, Neuchatel: Éditions de la Baconnière, 1947.

Schack, Heimo, Das auf (formlose) Immaterialgüterrechte anwendbare Recht nach Rom II, 651–669, in *Die richtige Ordnung—Festschrift für Jan Kropholler zum 70. Geburtstag* (Dietmar Baetge ed.), Tübingen: Mohr Siebeck Verlag, 2008.

Schack, Heimo, Internationale Urheber-, Marken- und Wettbewerbsrechtsverletzungen im Internet – Internationales Privatrecht, 2000 *MMR* 59.

Schack, Heimo, The Law Applicable to (Unregistered) IP Rights After Rome II, 79–96, in *Intellectual Property and Private International Law* (Stefan Leible & Ansgar Ohly eds.), Tübingen: Verlag Mohr Siebeck, 2009.

Schack, Heimo, Urheberrechtsverletzung im internationalen Privatrecht aus der Sicht des Kollisionsrechts, 1985 *GRUR Int.* 523.

Schechter, Frank I., Fog and Fiction in Trade-Mark Protection, 36 *Colum. L. Rev.* 60 (1936).

Schechter, Frank I., *The Historical Foundations of the Law Relating to Trade-Marks*, New York: Columbia University Press, 1925.

Schechter, Frank I., The Rational Basis of Trademark Protection, 40 *Harv. L. Rev.* 813 (1927).

Schechter, Roger E., The Case for Limited Extraterritorial Reach of the Lanham Act, 37 *Va. J. Int'l L.* 619 (1997).

Schechter, Roger E. & Thomas, John R., *Intellectual Property—The Law of Copyrights, Patents and Trademarks*, St. Paul/MN: Thomson West, 2003.

Scherer, Inge, *Privatrechtliche Grenzen der Verbraucherwerbung*, Berlin: Duncker & Humblot, 1996.

Schibli, Hans R., *Multistate-Werbung im internationalen Lauterkeitsrecht mit besonderer Berücksichtigung der Internet-Werbung*, Zurich et al.: Schulthess Juristische Medien, 2004.

Schikora, Lienhard, *Der Begehungsort im gewerblichen Rechtsschutz und Urheberrecht*, Munich: Dissertationsdruck Schön, 1968.

Schluep, Walter R., Allgemeines Wirtschaftsrecht und Schweizerisches Kartellgesetz, 569–602, in *Wirtschaftsordnung und Staatsverfassung—Festschrift für Franz Böhm zum 80. Geburtstag* (Heinz Saubermann & Ernst-Joachim Mestmäcker eds.), Tübingen: Mohr Siebeck, 1975.

Schluep, Walter R., *Das Markenrecht als subjektives Recht*, Basel: Verlag für Recht und Gesellschaft, 1964.

Schluep, Walter R., Vom lauteren zum freien Wettbewerb, 1973 *GRUR Int.* 446.

Schluep, Walter R., Was ist Wirtschaftsrecht?, 25–95, in *Festschrift für Walther Hug zum 70. Geburtstag* (Riccardo L. Jagmetti & Walter R. Schluep eds.), Bern: Stämpfli Verlag, 1968.

Schmidt, Karsten, *Kartellverfahrensrecht—Kartellverwaltungsrecht—Bürgerliches Recht. Kartellrechtspflege nach deutschem Recht gegen Wettbewerbsbeschränkungen*, Cologne et al.: Carl Heymanns Verlag, 1977.

Schmidt, Marlene, Zur Annäherung von Lauterkeitsrecht und Verbraucherprivatrecht, 2007 *JZ* 78.

Schmidt-Trenz, Hans-Jörg & Schmidtchen, Dieter, Private International Trade in the Shadow of the Territoriality of Law: Why Does It Work?, 58 *Southern Economic Journal* 329 (1991).

Schmoller, Gustav, *Zur Geschichte der deutschen Kleingewerbe im 19. Jahrhundert—Statistische und nationalökonomische Untersuchungen*, Halle: Verlag der Buchhandlung des Waisenhauses, 1870.

Schnyder, Anton K., „Gegenmassnahmen" im Internationalen Privat- und Zivilverfahrensrecht, 73–107, in *Berichte der Deutschen Gesellschaft für Völkerrecht (vol. 37), Gegenmaßnahmen; Referate und Thesen*, Heidelberg: C.F. Müller Verlag, 1998.

Schnyder, Anton K., Gemeinschaftsrechtliches Kollisionsrecht?—Zur Anwendbarkeit des EG-Wettbewerbsrechts bei Sachverhalten mit Beziehungen zu Drittstaaten, 3–15, in *Europäisches Gemeinschaftsrecht und Internationales Privatrecht* (Christian von Bar ed.), Cologne et al.: Carl Heymanns Verlag, 1991.

Schnyder, Anton K., Interessenabwägung im Kollisionsrecht—Zu Brainerd Curries "governmental-interest analysis," 105 *ZfSchwR* 101 (1986).

Schnyder, Anton K., *Wirtschaftskollisionsrecht—Sonderanknüpfung und extraterritoriale Anwendung wirtschaftsrechtlicher Normen unter besonderer Berücksichtigung von Marktrecht*, Zurich: Schulthess Polygraphischer Verlag, 1990.

Schön, Wolfgang, Zwingendes Recht oder informierte Entscheidung—zu einer (neuen) Grundlage unserer Zivilrechtsordnung, 1191–1211, in *Festschrift für Claus-Wilhelm Canaris zum 70. Geburtstag* (Andreas Heldrich ed.), Munich: C.H. Beck Verlag, 2007.

Schönfeld, Thomas, *Die Gemeinschaftsmarke als selbständiger Vermögensgegenstand eines Unternehmens—Eine rechtsdogmatische und ökonomische Analyse zur Property-Rights-Theory*, Baden-Baden: Nomos Verlagsgesellschaft, 1994.

Schreiner, Rupert, *Die Dienstleistungsmarke—Typus, Rechtsschutz und Funktion. Eine rechtstatsächliche und rechtsvergleichende Untersuchung aus Anlaß der Einführung des Formalschutzes der Dienstleistungszeichen im deutschen Recht*, Cologne et al.: Carl Heymanns Verlag, 1983.

Schricker, Gerhard, Der Benutzungszwang im Markenrecht—Rechtsvergleichende Betrachtungen zur Einführung des Benutzungszwangs in das deutsche Warenzeichengesetz, 1969 *GRUR Int.* 14.

Schricker, Gerhard, Die Durchsetzbarkeit deutscher Werberegelungen bei grenzüberschreitender Rundfunkwerbung, 1982 *GRUR Int.* 720.

Schricker, Gerhard, *Gesetzesverletzung und Sittenverstoss—Rechtsvergleichende Untersuchung zur wettbewerbsrechtlichen Haftung bei Verletzung außerwettbewerbsrechtlicher Normen*, Munich: C.H. Beck'sche Verlagsbuchhandlung, 1970.

Schricker, Gerhard, Hundert Jahre Gesetz gegen den unlauteren Wettbewerb—Licht und Schatten, 1996 *GRUR Int.* 473.

Schricker, Gerhard, Möglichkeiten zur Verbesserung des Schutzes der Verbraucher und des funktionsfähigen Wettbewerbs im Recht des unlauteren Wettbewerbs, 139 *ZHR* 208 (1975).

Schricker, Gerhard, Territoriale Probleme und Klagerecht bei unlauterem Wettbewerb, 1973 *GRUR Int.* 453.

Schröter, Stefan Jonas, *Der Schutz geographischer Herkunftsangaben nach Marken-, Wettbewerbs- und Registerrecht in Deutschland und der Schweiz*, Jena: JWV Jenaer Wissenschaftliche Verlagsgesellschaft mbH, 2011.

Schuhmacher, Wolfgang, *Verbraucher und Recht in historischer Sicht*, Vienna: Verlag der Österreichischen Staatsdruckerei, 1981.

Schuler, Hans, *Die Concurrence déloyale und ihre Beziehungen zu Name, Firma, Marke, Fabrik- und Geschäftsgeheimnis im französischen, schweizerischen und deutschen Recht*, Zurich: Albert Raustein, vormals Meyer & Zeller's Verlag, 1895.

Schumpeter, Joseph A., *Capitalism, Socialism, and Democracy*, New York and London: Harper & Brothers Publishers, 2nd edn., 1947.

Schumpeter, Joseph A., *Theorie der wirtschaftlichen Entwicklung—Eine Untersuchung über Unternehmergewinn, Kapital, Kredit, Zins und den Konjunkturzyklus*, Munich and Berlin: Verlag von Duncker und Humblot, 2nd edn., 1926.

Schünemann, Wolfgang B., Ökonomische Analyse der europäischen und deutschen Regelung, 41–80, in *Lauterkeitsrecht im Umbruch—Europa,*

Deutschland, Österreich (Heinz Krejci et al. eds.), Vienna: Manz'sche Verlags- und Universitätsbuchhandlung, 2005.

Schurig, Klaus, *Kollisionsnorm und Sachrecht—Zu Struktur, Standort und Methode des internationalen Privatrechts*, Berlin: Duncker & Humblot, 1981.

Schurig, Klaus, Völkerrecht und IPR: Methodische Verschleifung oder strukturierte Interaktion?, 55–70, in *Völkerrecht und IPR* (Stefan Leible & Matthias Ruffert eds.), Jena: Jenaer Wissenschaftliche Verlagsgesellschaft, 2006.

Schurig, Klaus, Zwingendes Recht, »Eingriffsnormen« und neues IPR, 54 *RabelsZ* 217 (1990).

Schwander, Ivo, Das UWG im grenzüberschreitenden Verkehr, 161–186, in *Das UWG auf neuer Grundlage* (Carl Baudenbacher ed.), Bern and Stuttgart: Verlag Paul Haupt, 1989.

Schwander, Ivo, *Lois d'application immédiate, Sonderanknüpfung, IPR-Sachnormen und andere Ausnahmen von der gewöhnlichen Anknüpfung im internationalen Privatrecht*, Zurich: Schulthess Polygraphischer Verlag, 1975.

Schwartz, Ivo E., *Deutsches Internationales Kartellrecht*, Cologne et al.: Carl Heymanns Verlag, 2nd edn., 1968.

Schwartz, Ivo E. & Basedow, Jürgen, Restrictions on Competition (ch. 35), in *International Encyclopedia of Comparative Law, vol. III: Private International Law, part 2* (Kurt Lipstein ed.), Tübingen: Verlag Mohr Siebeck, 2011.

Scott, Colin & Black, Julia, *Cranston's Consumers and the Law*, London et al.: Butterworths, 3rd edn., 2000.

Seck, Sara L., Home State Responsibility and Local Communities: The Case of Global Mining, 11 *Yale Hum. Rts. & Dev. L.J.* 177 (2008).

Seif, Ulrike, Savigny und das Internationale Privatrecht des 19. Jahrhunderts, 65 *RabelsZ* 492 (2001).

Seligsohn, Arnold, *Gesetz zum Schutz der Warenbezeichnungen (bearbeitet in Gemeinschaft mit Martin Seligsohn)*, Berlin: Verlag J. Guttentag, Verlagsbuchhandlung, 2nd edn., 1905.

Seligsohn, Martin, Die örtlichen Grenzen des Zeichenrechts, 193–208, in *Abhandlungen zum Arbeitsgebiet des Reichspatentamts—Festgabe zur Feier des 50jährigen Bestehens des Reichspatentamts* (Hermann Isay ed.), Berlin: Carl Heymann Verlag, 1927.

Senftleben, Martin, Trade Mark Protection—A Black Hole in the Intellectual Property Galaxy, 42 *IIC* 383 (2011).

Seville, Catherine, *EU Intellectual Property Law and Policy*, Cheltenham/UK: Edward Elgar, 2009.

Shaffer, Gregory, Transnational Legal Process and State Change, 37 *Law & Soc. Inquiry* 229 (2012).

Sheff, Jeremy N., Veblen Brands, 96 *Minn. L. Rev.* 769 (2012).

Shoemaker, William D., *Trade-Marks—A Treatise on the subject of Trade-Marks with particular reference to the laws relating to registration thereof, vol. I*, Washington/DC: H.D. Williams Company, 1931.

Siebert, W., ed., *Soergel: Kommentar zum Bürgerlichen Gesetzbuch, Einführungsgesetz, vol. X*, Stuttgart et al.: Kohlhammer Verlag, 12th edn., 1996.

Siehr, Kurt, Ausländische Eingriffsnormen im inländischen Wirtschaftskollisionsrecht, 52 *RabelsZ* 41 (1988).

Siehr, Kurt, Das urheberrechtliche Folgerecht inländischer Künstler nach Versteigerung ihrer Werke im Ausland, 1992 *IPRax* 29.

Simon, Herbert A., A Behavioral Model of Rational Choice, 69 *Quarterly J. Econ.* 99 (1955).

Simon, Herbert A., *Models of Man, Social and Rational—Mathematical Essays on Rational Human Behavior in a Social Setting*, New York: John Wilkey & Sons, Inc., 1957.

Simon, Jürgen, *Das allgemeine Persönlichkeitsrecht und seine gewerblichen Erscheinungsformen—Ein Entwicklungsprozess*, Berlin: Duncker & Humblot, 1981.

Singer, Joseph William, Real Conflicts, 69 *B. U. L. Rev.* 1 (1989).

Singer, Joseph William, The Legal Rights Debate in Analytical Jurisprudence from Bentham to Hohfeld, 1982 *Wis. L. Rev.* 975.

Slaughter, Anne-Marie, A Global Community of Courts, 44 *Harv. Int'l L.J.* 191 (2003).

Slaughter, Anne-Marie, *A New World Order*, Princeton and Oxford: Princeton University Press, 2004.

Slaughter, Anne-Marie & Burke-White, William, The Future of International Law is Domestic (or, the European Way of Law), 47 *Harv. Int'l L.J.* 327 (2006).

Sloss, David L., Kiobel and Extraterritoriality: A Rule Without a Rationale, 28 *Md. J. Int'l L.* 241 (2013).

Smith, Adam, *An Inquiry into the Nature and Causes of the Wealth of Nations, vol. I*, London: W. Strahan and T. Cadell, 1776.

Sonnentag, Michael, Zur Europäisierung des Internationalen außervertraglichen Schuldrechts durch die geplante Rom II-Verordnung, 105 *ZVglRWiss* 256 (2006).

Sosnitza, Olaf, Nach dem Spiel ist vor dem Spiel—Das Konzept der "Post-Sale Confusion" im Common Law, im europäischen und im deutschen Markenrecht, 1 *ZGE* 457 (2009).

Spickhoff, Andreas, Der völkerrechtsbezogene ordre public, 275–310, in *Völkerrecht und IPR* (Stefan Leible & Matthias Ruffert eds.), Jena: Jenaer Wiss. Verlags-Gesellschaft, 2006.

Stäheli, Thomas, Kollisionsrecht auf dem Information Highway, 597–623, in *Information Highway—Beiträge zu rechtlichen und tatsächlichen Fragen* (Reto M. Hilty ed.), Bern and Munich: Stämpfli and C.H. Beck, 1996.

Starck, Joachim, Die Auswirkungen des Markengesetzes auf das Gesetz gegen unlauteren Wettbewerb, 1996 *DZWir* 313.

Stechow, Henning von, *Das Gesetz zur Bekämpfung des unlauteren Wettbewerbs vom 27. Mai 1896—Entstehungsgeschichte und Wirkung*, Berlin: Duncker & Humblot Verlag, 2002.

Steindorff, Ernst, *Sachnormen im internationalen Privatrecht*, Frankfurt am Main: Vittorio Klostermann Verlag, 1958.

Steinhardt, Ralph G., Determining Which Human Rights Claims "Touch and Concern" the United States: Justice Kennedy's Filartiga, 89 *Notre Dame L. Rev.* 1695 (2014).

Stephan, Paul B., Empagran: Empire Building or Judicial Modesty, 553–558, in *International Law in the U.S. Supreme Court—Continuity and Change* (David L. Sloss et al. eds.), Cambridge: Cambridge University Press, 2011.

Stephan, Paul B., Privatizing International Law, 97 *Va. L. Rev.* 1573 (2011).
Stephens, Beth, The Curious History of the Alien Tort Statute, 89 *Notre Dame L. Rev.* 1467 (2014).
Stephens, Beth, Translating Filártiga: A Comparative and International Law Analysis of Domestic Remedies for International Human Rights Violations, 27 *Yale J. Int'l L.* 1 (2002).
Stern, Stephen, Are GIs IP?, 29(2) *EIPR* 39 (2007).
Stevenson, John R., The Relationship of Private International Law to Public International Law, 52 *Colum. L. Rev.* 561 (1952).
Stigler, George J., The Economics of Information, 69 *J. Pol. Econ.* 213 (1961).
Stiglitz, Joseph E., Information and the Change in the Paradigm in Economics, 92 *Am. Econ. Rev.* 460 (2002).
Stolte, Keith M., How Early Did Anglo-American Trademark Law Begin? An Answer to Schechter's Conundrum, 88 *Trademark Rep.* 564 (1998), reprint of 8 *Fordham Intell. Prop. Media & Ent. L.J.* 505 (1998).
Story, Joseph, *Commentaries on the Conflict of Laws, Foreign and Domestic, in Regard to Contracts, Rights, and Remedies, and Especially in Regard to Marriages, Divorces, Wills, Successions, and Judgments*, Boston: Hilliard, Gray & Co., 1834.
Story, Joseph, *Commentaries on the Law of Partnership, as a Branch of Commercial and Maritime Jurisprudence, With Occasional Illustrations from the Civil and Foreign Law*, Boston: Little, Brown and Company, 4th edn., 1855.
Streit, Manfred E., Wissen, Wettbewerb und Wirtschaftsordnung—Zum Gedenken an Friedrich August von Hayek, 43 *ORDO* 1 (1992).
Ströbele, Paul & Hacker, Franz, eds., *Kommentar zum Markengesetz*, Cologne: Carl Heymanns Verlag, 11th edn., 2015.
Stubenrauch, Moriz von, *Das österreichische Marken- und Musterschutzgesetz mit Rücksicht auf die Bedürfnisse des Handels- und Gewerbestandes*, Vienna: Verlag von Friedrich Manz, 1859.
Sturm, Fritz, Savigny und das internationale Privatrecht seiner Zeit, 92–109, in *Ius Commune VIII—Vorträge zum 200. Geburtstag von F.C. von Savigny* (Helmut Coing ed.), Frankfurt am Main: Vittorio Klostermann Verlag, 1979.
Stuve, *Das industrielle Eigenthum und die Nachbildung*, Elberfeld: Verlag Carl Joseph Becker, 1843.
Svantesson, Dan Jerker B., Time for the Law to Take Internet Geolocation Technologies Seriously, 8 *J. Priv. Int'l L.* 473 (2012).
Swaine, Edward T., Cooperation, Comity, and Competition Policy: United States, 1–20, in *Cooperation, Comity, and Competition Policy* (Andrew T. Guzman ed.), Oxford: Oxford University Press, 2010.
Swayze, Francis J., The Growing Law, 25 *Yale L.J.* 1 (1915).
Sykes, Alan O., Corporate Liability for Extraterritorial Torts Under the Alien Tort Statute and Beyond: An Economic Analysis, 100 *Geo. L.J.* 2161 (2012).
Sykes, Alan O., *Transnational Tort Litigation as a Trade and Investment Issue, John M. Olin Program in Law and Economics Stanford Law School, Working Paper No. 331* (January 2007) (online resource: available under http://papers.ssrn.com/sol3/papers.cfm?abstract_id=956668##).
Taha, Ahmed E., Data and Selection Bias: A Case Study, 75 *UMKC L. Rev.* 171 (2006).

Teplitzky, Otto, Die Durchsetzung des Schadensersatzzahlungsanspruchs im Wettbewerbsrecht, 1987 *GRUR* 215.

Teplitzky, Otto, et al., eds., *Großkommentar—UWG: Gesetz gegen den unlauteren Wettbewerb, vol. I*, Berlin et al.: De Gruyter Verlag, 2nd edn., 2014.

Teplitzky, Otto, *Wettbewerbsrechtliche Ansprüche und Verfahren, Unterlassung—Beseitigung, Auskunft—Schadensersatz, Anspruchsdurchsetzung und Anspruchsabwehr*, Cologne et al.: Carl Heymanns Verlag, 10th edn., 2011.

Tetzner, Heinrich, *Gesetz gegen den unlauteren Wettbewerb*, Cologne: Verlag Dr. Otto Schmidt, 2nd edn., 1957.

Teubner, Gunther, "Global Bukowina": Legal Pluralism in the World Society, 3–28, in: *Global Law Without a State* (Gunther Teubner ed.), Aldershot/UK: Dartmouth Publishing Company Limited, 1997.

Thaler, Richard H., *Quasi Rational Economics*, New York: Russell Sage Foundation, 2001.

Thomas-Gonzalez, Sarah, Extraterritorial Jurisdiction of the Lanham Act: American Rice, Inc. v. Arkansas Ricegrowers Cooperative Ass'n, 11 *Brook. J. Int'l L.* 411 (1985).

Thouvenin, Florent, *Funktionale Systematisierung von Wettbewerbsrecht (UWG) und Immaterialgüterrechten*, Cologne et al.: Carl Heymanns Verlag, 2007.

Thünken, Alexander, Multi-state advertising over the Internet and the private international law of unfair competition, 51 *I.C.L.Q.* 909 (2002).

Tilmann, Winfried, Frage 80: Marke und Verbraucherschutz, Bericht im Namen der deutschen Landesgruppe, 1983 *GRUR* 103.

Tilmann, Winfried, Über das Verhältnis von GWB und UWG, 1979 *GRUR* 825.

Timberg, Sigmund, Trade-Marks, Monopoly, and the Restraint of Competition, 14 *Law & Contemp. Probs.* 323 (1949).

Toraya, David R., Note, Federal Jurisdiction over Foreign Copyright Infringement Actions—An Unsolicited Reply to Professor Nimmer, 70 *Cornell L. Rev.* 1165 (1985).

Torremans, Paul, Jurisdiction and Choice of Law Issues in United States Intellectual Property Cases: From Dodging the Bullet to Biting It, 1999 *I.P.Q.* 372.

Trachtman, Joel P., Conflict of Laws and Accuracy in the Allocation of Government Responsibility, 26 *Vand. J. Transnat'l L.* 975 (1994).

Trachtman, Joel P., Economic Analysis of Prescriptive Jurisdiction, 42 *Va. J. Int'l L.* 1 (2002).

Trakman, Leon E., *The Law Merchant: The Evolution of Commercial Law*, Littleton/CO: Fred B. Rothman & Co., 1983.

Treece, James M., Security for Federally Registered Mark Owners Against Subsequent Users, 39 *Geo. Wash. L. Rev.* 1008 (1971).

Triepel, Heinrich, *Völkerrecht und Landesrecht*, Leipzig: Verlag von C.L. Hirschfeld, 1899.

Troller, Alois, *Das Delikt des unlauteren Wettbewerbs nach dem Entwurf des Bundesrates vom 11. Juni 1934*, Lungern/CH: Buchdruckerei Burch & Cie, 1937.

Troller, Alois, *Das internationale Privat- und Zivilprozeßrecht im gewerblichen Rechtsschutz und Urheberrecht*, Basel: Verlag für Recht und Gesellschaft, 1952.

Troller, Alois, Die territoriale Unabhängigkeit der Markenrechte im Warenverkehr, 1960 *GRUR Ausl.* 244.

Troller, Alois, *Immaterialgüterrecht, vol. I*, Basel and Frankfurt am Main: Verlag Helbing & Lichtenhahn, 3rd edn., 1983.

Troller, Alois, *Immaterialgüterrecht, vol. II*, Basel and Frankfurt am Main: Verlag Helbing & Lichtenhahn, 3rd edn., 1985.

Troller, Alois, Unfair Competition (ch. 34), in *International Encyclopedia of Comparative Law, vol. III, Private International Law* (Kurt Lipstein et al. eds.), Tübingen: J.C.B. Mohr, 1980.

Troller, Kamen, *Das internationale Privatrecht des unlauteren Wettbewerbs in vergleichender Darstellung der Rechte Deutschlands, Englands, Frankreichs, Italiens, der Schweiz und der USA*, Fribourg/CH: Universitätsverlag Freiburg, 1962.

Trüeb, Hans, Markenschutz beim Import von Konzernware—Bemerkungen zur Rechtsprechung des Schweizerischen Bundesgerichts, 1962 *GRUR Ausl.* 10.

Trutmann, Verena, *Das internationale Privatrecht der Deliktsobligationen—Ein Beitrag zur Auseinandersetzung mit den neueren amerikanischen kollisionsrechtlichen Theorien*, Basel and Stuttgart: Verlag Helbing & Lichtenhahn, 1973.

Tuhr, Andreas von, *Der Allgemeine Teil des Deutschen Bürgerlichen Rechts, vol. I: Allgemeine Lehren und Personenrecht*, Leipzig: Verlag von Duncker & Humblot, 1910.

Turley, Jonathan, "When in Rome": Multinational Misconduct and the Presumption Against Extraterritoriality, 84 *Nw. U. L. Rev.* 598 (1990).

Tushnet, Rebecca, Gone in Sixty Milliseconds: Trademark Law and Cognitive Science, 86 *Tex. L. Rev.* 507 (2008).

Ulmer, Eugen, Commentary to Reichsgericht, decision of 14 April 1931 (421/30 II)—Supra, 1931 *JW* 1906.

Ulmer, Eugen, *Das Recht des unlauteren Wettbewerbs in den Mitgliedsstaaten der Europäischen Gemeinschaft, vol. I: Vergleichende Darstellung mit Vorschlägen zur Rechtsangleichung (unter Mitwirkung von Friedrich-Karl Beier)*, Munich and Cologne: C.H. Beck'sche Verlagsbuchhandlung and Carl Heymanns Verlag, 1965.

Ulmer, Eugen, *Die Immaterialgüterrechte im internationalen Privatrecht—Rechtsvergleichende Untersuchung mit Vorschlägen für die Vereinheitlichung in der Europäischen Wirtschaftsgemeinschaft*, Cologne et al.: Carl Heymanns Verlag, 1975.

Ulmer, Eugen, *Sinnzusammenhänge im modernen Wettbewerbsrecht—Ein Beitrag zum Aufbau des Wettbewerbsrechts*, Berlin: Verlag von Julius Springer, 1932.

Ulmer, Eugen, Wandlungen und Aufgaben im Wettbewerbsrecht, 1937 *GRUR* 769.

Ulmer, Eugen, *Warenzeichen und unlauterer Wettbewerb in ihrer Fortbildung durch die Rechtsprechung*, Berlin: Verlag von Julius Springer, 1929.

Ulmer, Peter, Der Begriff „Leistungswettbewerb" und seine Bedeutung für die Anwendung von GWB und UWG-Tatbeständen, 1977 *GRUR* 565.

United States House of Representatives, *Hearings Before the Committee on Patents, Subcommittee on Trade-Marks*, 75th Congress, 3rd Session on H.R. 9041 (15–18 March 1938).

United States House of Representatives, *Hearings Before the Committee on Patents, Trade-Marks*, 72nd Congress, 1st Session (8 and 9 February 1932).

United States Senate, *Committee on Patents*, Senate Report No. 1333, 79th Congress, 2nd Session (14 May 1946), repr. in 1946 U.S. Code Cong. Service, 1274 et seq.

Upton, Francis H., *A Treatise on the Law of Trade Marks with a Digest and Review on the English and American Authorities*, Albany: Weare C. Little, 1860.

Van den Bergh, Roger & Lehmann, Michael, Informationsökonomie und Verbraucherschutz im Wettbewerbs- und Warenzeichenrecht, 1992 *GRUR Int.* 588.

Van Meenen, Ignace, *Lauterkeitsrecht und Verbraucherschutz im IPR—Eine Untersuchung des vertrags- und deliktskollisionsrechtlichen Schutzes gegen verbraucherfeindliche Rechtswahlvereinbarungen*, Frankfurt am Main et al.: Peter Lang Verlag, 1995.

Vandevelde, Kenneth J., The New Property of the Nineteenth Century: The Development of the Modern Concept of Property, 29 *Buff. L. Rev.* 325 (1980).

Vanzetti, Adriano, Die Funktion der Marke in einem System der freien Übertragbarkeit, 1999 *GRUR Int.* 205.

Vanzetti, Adriano, Funktion und Rechtsnatur der Marke (2. Teil), 1965 *GRUR Ausl.* 185.

Veblen, Thorstein, *The Theory of Business Enterprise*, New Brunswick/NJ: Transaction Books, 1904.

Veelken, Winfried, *Interessenabwägung im Wirtschaftskollisionsrecht*, Baden-Baden: Nomos-Verlag, 1988.

Verdross, Alfred & Simma, Bruno, *Universelles Völkerrecht—Theorie und Praxis*, Berlin: Duncker & Humblot, 3rd edn., 1984.

Vianello, Mirko, *Das internationale Privatrecht des unlauteren Wettbewerbs in Deutschland und Italien—Eine die europäischen und internationalen Harmonisierungsbestrebungen berücksichtigende Darstellung*, Frankfurt am Main et al.: Verlag Peter Lang, 2001.

Vischer, Frank, Das Internationale Privatrecht des Immaterialgüterrechts nach dem schweizerischen IPR-Gesetzentwurf, 1987 *GRUR Int.* 670.

Vischer, Frank, Das IPR des Immaterialgüterrechts, 363–385, in *Kernprobleme des Patentrechts—Festschrift zum einhundertjährigen Bestehen eines eidgenössischen Patentgesetzes* (Institut für gewerblichen Rechtsschutz (INGRES), ed.), Bern: Verlag Stämpfli & Cie, 1988.

Vischer, Frank, Das neue Restatement "Conflict of Laws," 38 *RabelsZ* 128 (1974).

Vischer, Frank, Zwingendes Recht und Eingriffsgesetze nach dem schweizerischen IPR-Gesetz, 53 *RabelsZ* 438 (1989).

Vogel, Klaus, *Der räumliche Anwendungsbereich der Verwaltungsrechtsnorm—Eine Untersuchung über die Grundfragen des sog. Internationalen Verwaltungs- und Steuerrechts*, Frankfurt am Main and Berlin: Alfred Metzner Verlag, 1965.

Vrey, Rogier W. de, *Towards a European Unfair Competition Law, A Clash Between Legal Families—A comparative study of English, German and Dutch law in light of existing European and international legal instruments*, Leiden and Boston: Martinus Nijhoff Publishers, 2006.

Wadle, Elmar, Das rheinisch-französische Deliktsrecht und die Judikatur des Reichsgerichts zum unlauteren Wettbewerb, 365–380, in *Geistiges Eigentum—Bausteine zur Rechtsgeschichte, vol. II* (Elmar Wadle ed.), Munich: C.H. Beck, 2003.

Wadle, Elmar, Der Weg zum gesetzlichen Schutz des geistigen und gewerblichen Schaffens—Die deutsche Entwicklung im 19. Jahrhundert, 93–183, in *Gewerblicher Rechtsschutz und Urheberrecht in Deutschland, Festschrift zum hundertjährigen Bestehen der Deutschen Vereinigung für gewerblichen Rechtsschutz und Urheberrecht und ihrer Zeitschrift, vol. I* (Friedrich-Karl Beier et al. eds.), Weinheim: VCH Verlagsgesellschaft mbH, 1991.

Wadle, Elmar, Entwicklungslinien des deutschen Markenschutzes im 19. Jahrhundert, 1979 *GRUR* 383.

Wadle, Elmar, *Fabrikzeichenschutz und Markenrecht—Geschichte und Gestalt des deutschen Markenschutzes im 19. Jahrhundert, Erster Teil: Entfaltung*, Berlin: Verlag Duncker & Humblot, 1977.

Wadle, Elmar, *Fabrikzeichenschutz und Markenrecht—Geschichte und Gestalt des deutschen Markenschutzes im 19. Jahrhundert, Zweiter Teil: Historisch-dogmatische Grundlinien*, Berlin: Verlag Duncker & Humblot, 1983.

Wadle, Elmar, Werden und Wandel des deutschen Markenrechts, 337–363, in *Geistiges Eigentum—Bausteine zur Rechtsgeschichte, vol. II* (Elmar Wadle ed.), Munich: C.H. Beck, 2003.

Wadlow, Christopher, *Enforcement of Intellectual Property in European and International Law—The New Private International Law of Intellectual Property in the United Kingdom and the European Community*, London: Sweet & Maxwell, 1998.

Wadlow, Christopher, The Case for Reclaiming European Unfair Competition Law from Europe's Consumer Lawyers, 175–189, in *The Regulation of Unfair Commercial Practices under EC Directive 2005/29—New Rules and Techniques* (Stephen Weatherill & Ulf Bernitz eds.), Oxford and Portland/OR: Hart Publishing, 2007.

Wadlow, Christopher, *The Law of Passing-Off—Unfair Competition by Misrepresentation*, London: Sweet & Maxwell, 4th edn., 2011.

Wadlow, Christopher, The new private international law of unfair competition and the "Rome II" Regulation, 11 *J. Intell. Prop. L. & Pract.* 789 (2009).

Wadlow, Christopher, Trade Secrets and the Rome II Regulation on the Law Applicable to Non-Contractual Obligations, 30 *EIPR* 309 (2008).

Wagner, Gerhard, Die neue Rom II-Verordnung, 2008 *IPRax* 1.

Wagner, Gerhard, Internationales Deliktsrecht, die Arbeiten an der Rom II-Verordnung und der Europäische Deliktsgerichtsstand, 2006 *IPRax* 372.

Waldkirch, Ed. v., Der Gebrauch der Marke nach schweizerischem Recht, 50 *ZfSchwR* 127 (1931).

Waldron, Jeremy, What Is Private Property?, 5 *Ox. J. Leg. Stud.* 313 (1985).

Warnecke, Ernst Adolf Friedrich, *Warenzeichenschutz und unlauterer Wettbewerb unter besonderer Berücksichtigung des Verhältnisses der §§ 12 und 14 WZG und 1 und 16 UWG untereinander und zu anderen Gesetzen*, Erlangen: dissertation thesis, 1928.

Watson, Alan, *Joseph Story and the Comity of Errors—A Case Study in the Conflict of Laws*, Athens/GA: The University of Georgia Press, 1992.

Weber, Rolf H., Internationale Harmonisierungsansätze im Lauterkeitsrecht, 1998 *sic!* 158.

Weber, Tilman, *Die Behandlung von Patent-, Warenzeichen- und Urheberrechtsverletzungen im internationalen Privat- und Zivilprozessrecht*, Munich: dissertation thesis, 1968.

Weber, Wolfgang F., *Die kollisionsrechtliche Behandlung von Wettbewerbsverletzungen mit Auslandsbezug—Eine Darstellung unter besonderer Berücksichtigung des österreichischen IPR-Gesetzes, des Schweizer Expertenentwurfs eines IPR-Gesetzes sowie der Möglichkeit von Harmonisierungsmaßnahmen im Kollisions- und Wettbewerbsrecht für die Europäische Gemeinschaft*, Frankfurt am Main: Haag und Herchen Verlag, 1982.

Webster, Jason, Trademark Law—Extraterritorial Application of the Lanham Act—McBee v. Delica Co., Ltd., 417 F.3d 107 (1st Cir. 2005), 30 *Suffolk Transnat'l L. Rev.* 263 (2006).

Weigel, Arnulf, *Gerichtsbarkeit, internationale Zuständigkeit und Territorialitäts-Prinzip im deutschen gewerblichen Rechtsschutz—Zur Abgrenzung der Begriffe*, Bielefeld: Verlag Ernst und Werner Gieseking, 1973.

Welkowitz, David S., Reexamining Trademark Dilution, 44 *Vand. L. Rev.* 531 (1991).

Wengler, Wilhelm, Die Anknüpfung des zwingenden Schuldrechts im internationalen Privatrecht, 54 *ZVglRWiss* 168 (1941).

Wengler, Wilhelm, Die Gesetze über unlauteren Wettbewerb und das internationale Privatrecht, 19 *RabelsZ* 401 (1954).

Wengler, Wilhelm, Laws Concerning Unfair Competition and the Conflict of Laws, 4 *Am. J. Comp. L.* 167 (1955).

Wichard, Johannes Christian, Europäisches Markenrecht zwischen Territorialität und Binnenmarkt, 2002 *ZEuP* 23.

Wichard, Johannes Christian, The Joint Recommendation Concerning Protection of Marks, and Other Industrial Property Rights in Signs, on the Internet, 257–264, in *Intellectual Property and Private International Law—Heading for the Future* (Josef Drexl & Annette Kur eds.), Oxford and Portland/OR: Hart Publishing, 2005.

Wieacker, Franz, *Privatrechtsgeschichte der Neuzeit unter besonderer Berücksichtigung der deutschen Entwicklung*, Göttingen: Verlag Vandenhoeck & Ruprecht, 1967.

Wiebringhaus, Hans, Beitrag zur Frage des Verhältnisses von Internationalprivat- und Völkerrecht, 1952 *JR* 383.

Wiebringhaus, Hans, *Das Gesetz der funktionellen Verdoppelung—Beitrag zu einer universalistischen Theorie des Internationalprivat- und Völkerrechts*, Saarbrücken: West-Ost-Verlag, 2nd edn., 1955.

Wiethölter, Rudolf, Zur Frage des internationalen ordre public, 133–185, in *Berichte der Deutschen Gesellschaft für Völkerrecht (vol. 7)*, Karlsruhe: C.F. Müller Verlag, 1967.

Wigmore, John Henry, *Select Cases on the Law of Torts—with Notes, and a Summary of Principles, vol. I*, Boston: Little, Brown, and Company, 1912.

Wildhaber, Luzius, Jurisdiktionsgrundsätze und Jurisdiktionsgrenzen im Völkerrecht, 41 *SchwJbIntR* 99 (1985).

Wilf, Steven, The Making of the Post-War Paradigm in American Intellectual Property Law, 31 *Colum. J.L. & Arts* 139 (2008).

Wilkins, Mira, The Neglected Intangible Asset: The Influence of the Trade Mark on the Rise of the Modern Corporation, 34 *Bus. Hist.* 66 (1992).

Wiltschek, Lothar, Die Beurteilung grenzüberschreitender Werbe- und Absatztätigkeit nach österreichischem Wettbewerbsrecht, 1988 *GRUR Int.* 299.

WIPO, *Joint Recommendation Concerning Provisions on the Protection of Marks, and Other Industrial Property Rights in Signs, on the Internet, adopted at the Thirty-Sixth Series of the Meeting of the Assemblies of the Member States of the WIPO, September 24 to October 2, 2001*, WIPO Publication no. 845(E) (online resource: available under www.wipo.int/portal/en/index.html (12 February 2016)).

WIPO, *Model Provisions on Protection against Unfair Competition—Articles and Notes, presented by the International Bureau of WIPO*, WIPO Publication No. 832(E), 1996 (online resource: available under www.wipo.int/portal/en/index.html (12 February 2016)).

WIPO, *Protection Against Unfair Competition—Analysis of the Present World Situation*, WIPO Publication no. 725(E), Geneva: International Bureau of WIPO, 1994.

WIPO, *Standing Committee on the Law of Trademarks, Industrial Designs and Geographical Indications, Fifth Session, Geneva, September 11 to 15, 2000, Protection of Industrial Property Rights in Relation to the Use of Signs on the Internet*, SCT/5/2 (21 June 2000) (online resource: available under www.wipo.int/portal/en/index.html (12 February 2016)).

Wirner, Helmut, *Wettbewerbsrecht und internationales Privatrecht*, Munich et al.: Carl Heymanns Verlag, 1960.

Witherell, Brendan J., The Extraterritorial Application of the Lanham Act: The First Circuit Cuts the Fat from the Vanity Fair Test, 29 *W. New Eng. L. Rev.* 193 (2006); reprinted as The Extraterritorial Application of the Lanham Act in an Expanding Global Economy, 97 *Trademark Rep.* 1090 (2007).

Wolf, Elias, Kritische Betrachtungen zum Entwurf für ein Bundesgesetz über den "unerlaubten" Wettbewerb, 31 *SJZ* 145 (1934).

Wolff, John, Non-Competing Goods in Trademark Law, 37 *Colum. L. Rev.* 582 (1937).

Wolff, Martin, *Das Internationale Privatrecht Deutschlands*, Berlin et al.: Springer-Verlag, 2nd edn., 1949.

Wolff, Martin, *Private International Law*, Oxford: Clarendon Press, 2nd edn., 1950.

Wuerth, Ingrid, Kiobel v. Royal Dutch Petroleum Co.: The Supreme Court and the Alien Tort Statute, 107 *Am. J. Int'l L.* 601 (2013).

Würdinger, Hans, Freiheit der persönlichen Entfaltung, Kartell- und Wettbewerbsrecht, 1953 *WuW* 721.

Würdinger, Markus ed., *juris-Praxiskommentar zum BGB*, Saarbrücken: juris-GmbH, 7th edn., 2014 (online resource: database).

Wurmnest, Wolfgang, Foreign Private Plaintiffs, Global Conspiracies, and the Extraterritorial Application of U.S. Antitrust Law, 28 *Hastings Int'l & Comp. L. Rev.* 205 (2005).

Yntema, Hessel E., The Comity Doctrine, 65 *Mich. L. Rev.* 9 (1966).

Yntema, Hessel E., The Historic Bases of Private International Law, 2 *Am. J. Comp. L.* 297 (1953).

Ziegler, Karl-Heinz, Völkerrechtliche Verpflichtung zur Anwendung oder nur „freundliche Betrachtung" fremden Rechts? Die comitas-Lehre heute (Betrachtungen eines Rechtshistorikers), 43–54, in *Völkerrecht und IPR* (Stefan Leible & Matthias Ruffert eds.), Jena: Jenaer Wissenschaftliche Verlagsgesellschaft, 2006.

Zitelmann, Ernst, *Die Möglichkeit eines Weltrechts*, Munich and Leipzig: Verlag von Duncker & Humblot, reprint of 1888 edn., 1916.

Zitelmann, Ernst, Geltungsbereich und Anwendungsbereich der Gesetze, 207–241, in *Festgabe der Bonner Juristischen Fakultät für Karl Bergbohm zum 70. Geburtstag*, Bonn: A. Marcus & E. Webers Verlag, 1919.

Zitelmann, Ernst, *Internationales Privatrecht, vol. I*, Leizpig: Verlag von Duncker & Humblot, 1897.

Zlinkoff, Sergei S., Erie v. Tompkins: In Relation to the Law of Trade-Marks and Unfair Competition, 42 *Colum. L. Rev.* 955 (1942).

Zumbansen, Peer, Defining the Space of Transnational Law: Legal Theory, Global Governance, and Legal Pluralism, 21 *Transnat'l L. & Contemp. Probs.* 305 (2012).

Zweigert, Konrad, Internationales Privatrecht und öffentliches Recht, 124–140, in *Fünfzig Jahre Institut für Internationales Recht an der Universität Kiel* (Max Sörensen et al. eds.), Kiel 1965.

Zweigert, Konrad, Nichterfüllung auf Grund ausländischer Leistungsverbote, 14 *RabelsZ* 283 (1942).

Zweigert, Konrad & Kötz, Hein, *An Introduction to Comparative Law*, Oxford: Clarendon Press, 3rd edn., 1998.

Index

Cambridge Intellectual Property and Information Law

Titles in the series (formerly known as *Cambridge Studies in Intellectual Property Rights)*

Brad Sherman and Lionel Bently
The Making of Modern Intellectual Property Law

Irini A. Stamatoudi
Copyright and Multimedia Products: A Comparative Analysis

Pascal Kamina
Film Copyright in the European Union

Huw Beverly-Smith
The Commercial Appropriation of Personality

Mark J. Davison
The Legal Protection of Databases

Robert Burrell and Allison Coleman
Copyright Exceptions: The Digital Impact

Huw Beverly-Smith, Ansgar Ohly and Agnès Lucas-Schloetter
Privacy, Property and Personality: Civil Law Perspectives on Commercial Appropriation

Catherine Seville
The Internationalisation of Copyright Law: Books, Buccaneers and the Black Flag in the Nineteenth Century

Philip Leith
Software and Patents in Europe

Geertrui Van Overwalle
Gene Patents and Clearing Models

Lionel Bently, Jennifer Davis and Jane C. Ginsburg
Trade Marks and Brands: An Interdisciplinary Critique

Jonathan Curci
The Protection of Biodiversity and Traditional Knowledge in International Law of Intellectual Property

Lionel Bently, Jennifer Davis and Jane C. Ginsburg
Copyright and Piracy: An Interdisciplinary Critique

Megan Richardson and Julian Thomas
Framing Intellectual Property: Legal Constructions of Creativity and Appropriation 1840–1940

Dev Gangjee
Relocating the Law of Geographical Indications

Andrew Kenyon, Megan Richardson and Ng-Loy Wee-Loon
The Law of Reputation and Brands in the Asia Pacific Region

Annabelle Lever
New Frontiers in the Philosophy of Intellectual Property

Sigrid Sterckx and Julian Cockbain
Exclusions from Patentability: How the European Patent Office is Eroding Boundaries

Sebastian Haunss
Conflicts in the Knowledge Society: The Contentious Politics of Intellectual Property

Helena R. Howe and Jonathan Griffiths
Concepts of Property in Intellectual Property Law

Rochelle Cooper Dreyfuss and Jane C. Ginsburg
Intellectual Property at the Edge: The Contested Contours of IP

Normann Witzleb, David Lindsay, Moira Paterson and Sharon Rodrick
Emerging Challenges in Privacy Law: Comparative Perspectives

Paul Bernal
Internet Privacy Rights: Rights to Protect Autonomy

Peter Drahos
Intellectual Property, Indigenous People and their Knowledge

Susy Frankel and Daniel Gervais
The Evolution and Equilibrium of Copyright in the Digital Age

Edited by Kathy Bowrey and Michael Handler
Law and Creativity in the Age of the Entertainment Franchise

Sean Bottomley
The British Patent System and the Industrial Revolution 1700-1852: From Privileges to Property

Susy Frankel
Test Tubes for Global Intellectual Property Issues: Small Market Economies

Jan Oster
Media Freedom as a Fundamental Right

Sara Bannerman
International Copyright and Access to Knowledge

Andrew T. Kenyon
Comparative Defamation and Privacy Law

Pascal Kamina
Film Copyright in the European Union, Second Edition

CPSIA information can be obtained
at www.ICGtesting.com
Printed in the USA
LVHW03*2043170718
584093LV00010B/218/P

9 781107 155060